Guide to World Maps

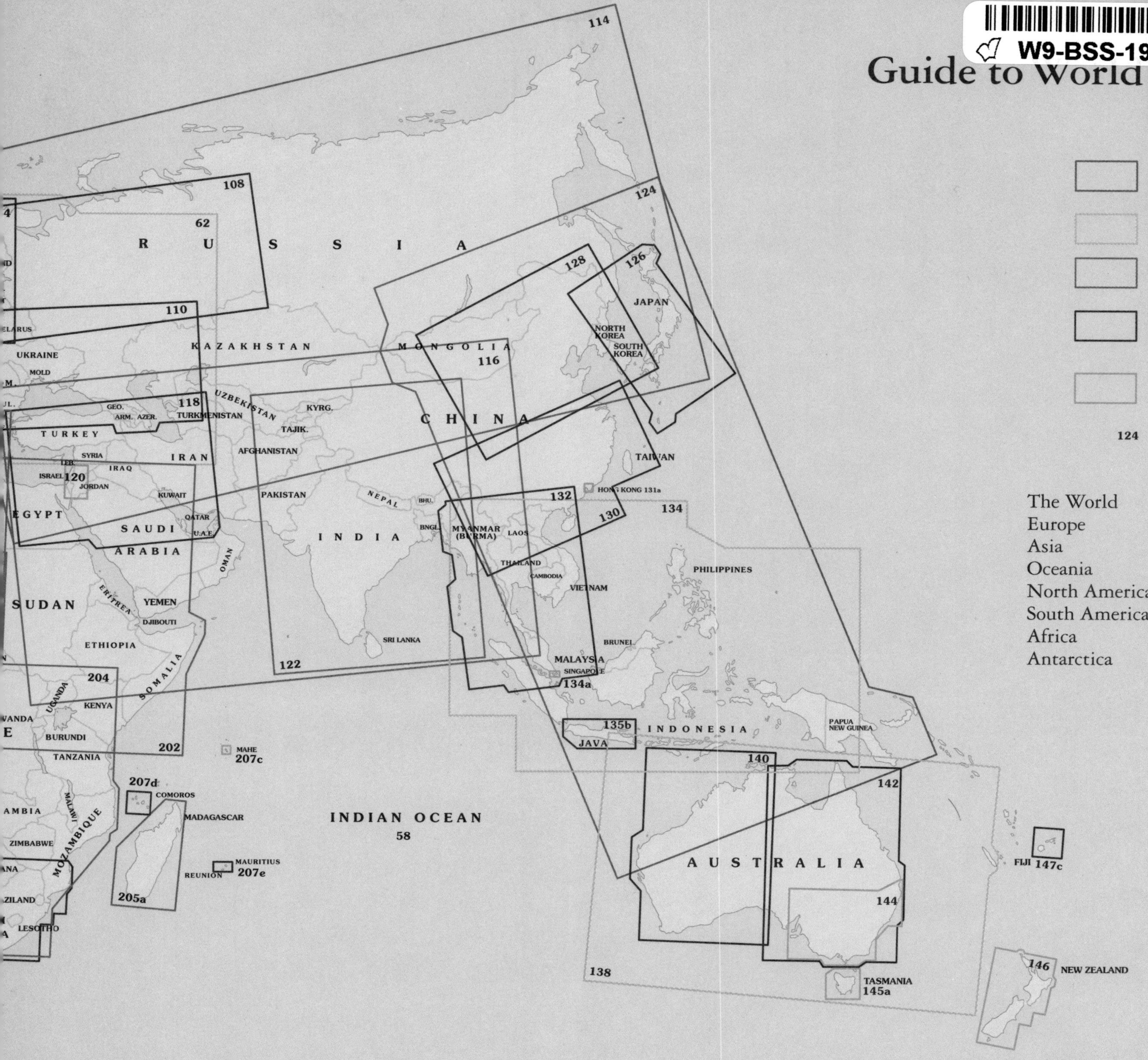

map scale

1:18,000,000
1:16,000,000
1:15,000,000

1:12,000,000

1:9,000,000
1:8,000,000

1:6,000,000
1:4,500,000

1:3,500,000
and larger

124 page reference

INDIAN OCEAN 58

map scale

1:3,000,000

1:1,750,000

1:1,500,000

104 page reference

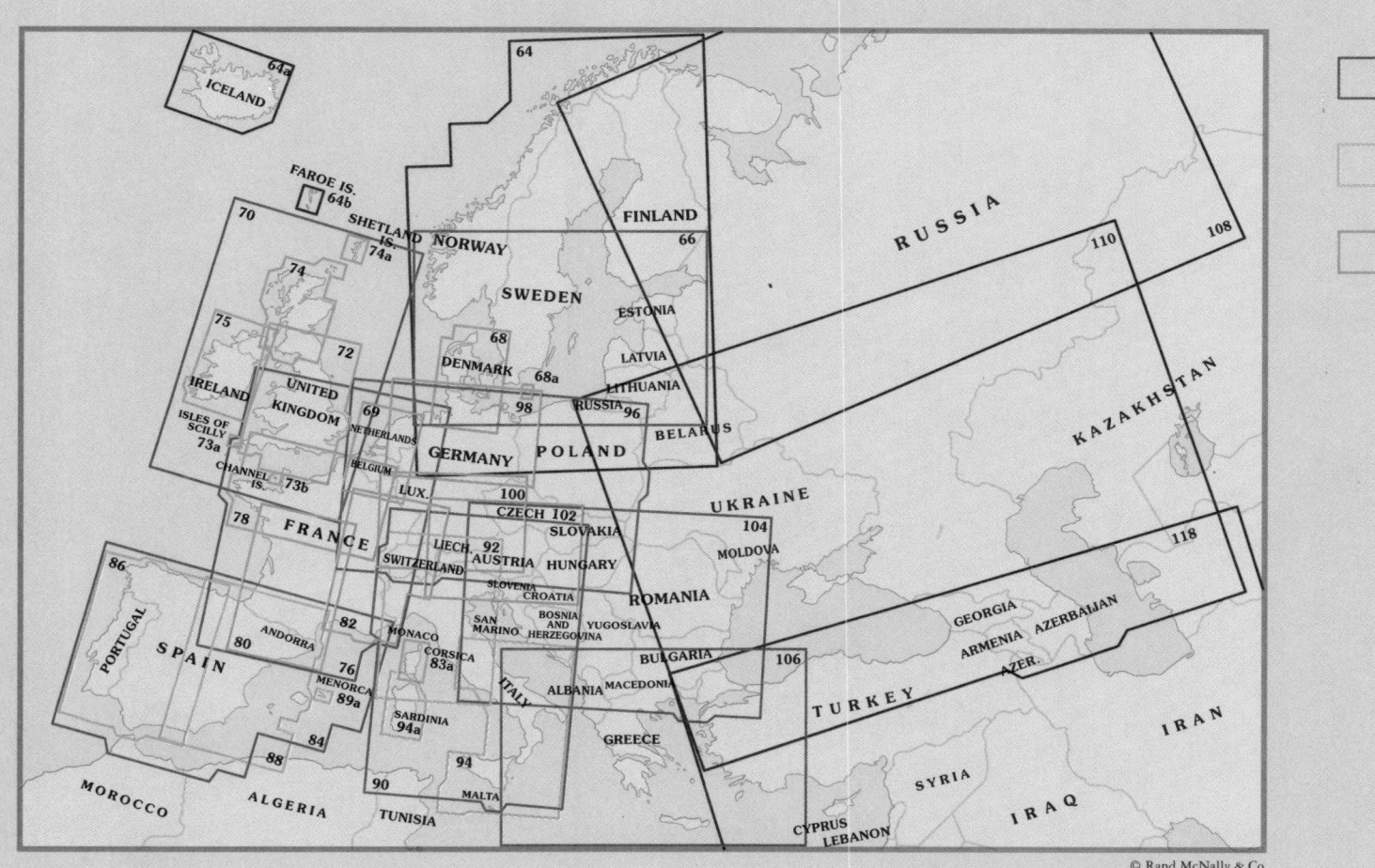

© Rand McNally & Co.

READER'S DIGEST
ILLUSTRATED
GREAT WORLD ATLAS

Reader's Digest

THE READER'S DIGEST ASSOCIATION, INC.
Pleasantville, New York/Montreal

The Reader's Digest *Illustrated Great World Atlas*
was adapted from the British edition, published by
The Reader's Digest Association Limited, London.

STAFF
PROJECT EDITOR Thomas A. Ranieri
PROJECT ART EDITOR Sandra Berinstein
PROJECT RESEARCH EDITOR Mary Hart
EDITOR Bryce S. Walker
ASSOCIATE EDITOR Richard M. Mazurek
SENIOR RESEARCH EDITOR Maymay Quey Lin
RESEARCH EDITORS Kathleen Derzipilski, Deirdre van Dyk
CARTOGRAPHIC EDITOR Alison Ewington (U.K.)
ASSISTANT CARTOGRAPHIC EDITOR David Irvine (U.K.)
EDITORIAL ASSISTANT Vita Gardner

CONTRIBUTORS
WRITERS Justin Cronin, Tod Olson, Richard Scheffel,
William G. Scheller, Christina Wilsdon
COPY EDITOR Mel Minter
CONSULTANT Robert E. Budliger, Director of Education,
New York State Dept. of Environmental Conservation (Ret.)

Maps of the World
The maps on pages 56 to 208 and the endsheets, and the
index to maps were specially created for this atlas by Rand
McNally & Company. © 1997 Rand McNally & Company.

The Story of the Earth and Nations of the World
Designed for Reader's Digest by
Duncan Baird Publishers Limited, London
MANAGING EDITOR Catherine Bradley
ART DIRECTOR Tony Cobb
CONTRIBUTORS Michael Chisholm (Emeritus Professor of
Geography, University of Cambridge, England), Laura Ivill,
Chris Madsen, Rebecca Renner, Dr. Brian Turner
CONSULTANTS Michael Allaby, Neil Curtis, David Gould,
Gareth Wyn Jones, Robert MacDonald, Sally Morgan, Dr.
Douglas Palmer, Giles Sparrow, Martin Walters

Statistical information from *The Europa World Year Book,*
supplied courtesy of Europa Publications Limited, London.

Reader's Digest General Books
EDITOR-IN-CHIEF, BOOKS AND HOME ENTERTAINMENT
Barbara J. Morgan
EDITOR, U.S. GENERAL BOOKS David Palmer
EXECUTIVE EDITOR Gayla Visalli
MANAGING EDITOR Christopher Cavanaugh

The credits and acknowledgments that appear on page
288 are hereby made a part of this copyright page.

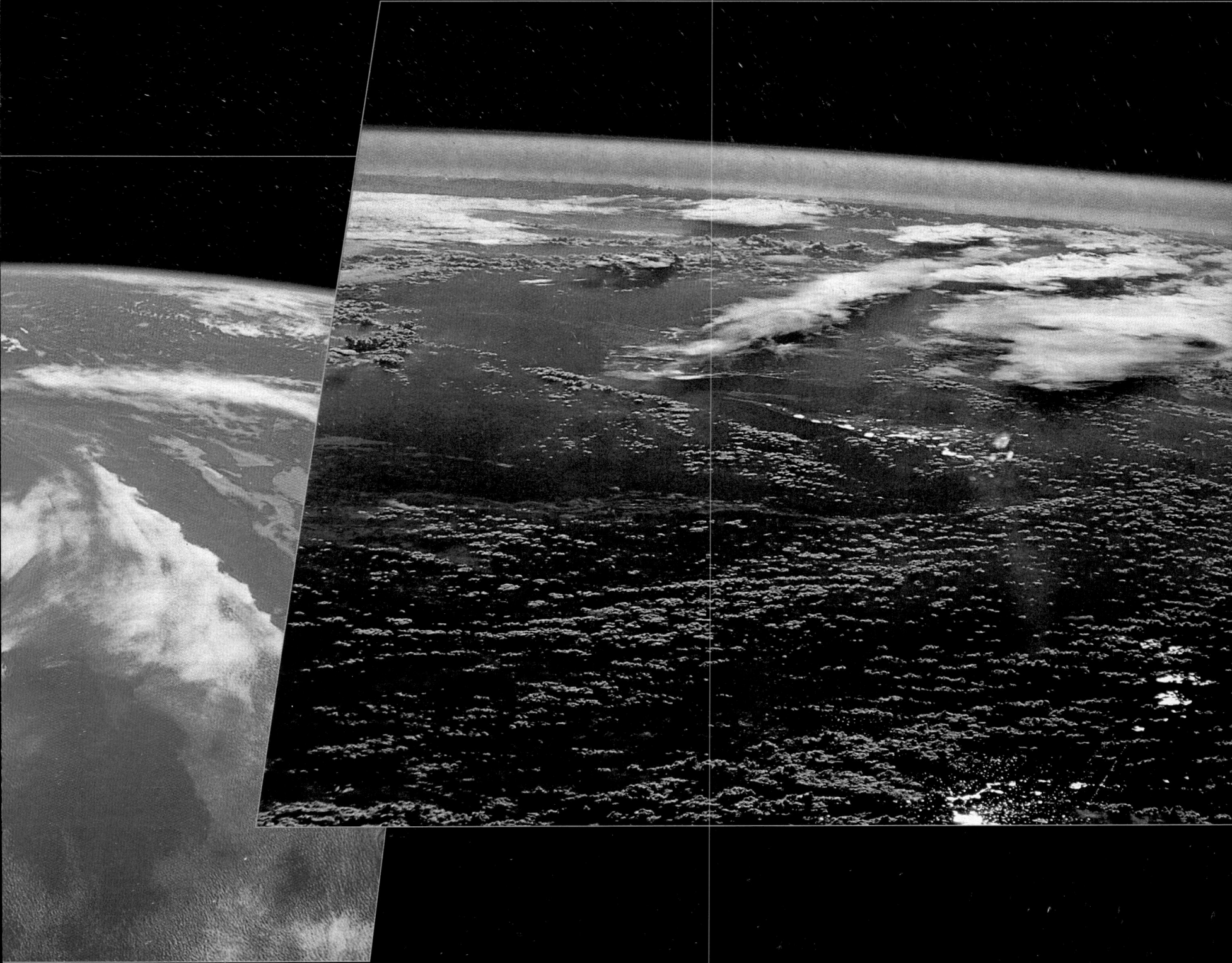

CONTENTS

Front and rear endpapers: Guide to World Maps

OUR PLACE IN THE UNIVERSE

Everything in the universe is thought to have been created between 8 and 15 billion years ago in an unimaginably huge explosion – a cataclysmic event that scientists have dubbed the "big bang." In a mere fraction of a second, goes the theory, incredibly dense, hot matter expanded at the speed of light into a swirling ball of elementary particles. As the fiery ball of particles cooled, some of them combined to form protons and neutrons, which themselves formed atoms of the gases hydrogen and helium. These gases make up most of the universe as we know it today. Astronomers believe that the universe may still be expanding outward, although this expansion may one day slow to a halt before contracting once again in a final, fatal implosion – a so-called "big crunch."

The big bang, as depicted by an artist

Giant in space

The Andromeda galaxy (background) is the closest large group of stars to our own Milky Way galaxy, yet light from it still takes 2.2 million years to reach earth. Andromeda is spiral shaped, like our own galaxy, but it contains almost twice as many stars.

The scale of the universe

Looking out from our planet (far right), we can see that the universe is made up of successively larger structures. Earth is just one of nine planets orbiting the Sun, and the Sun is one among 200 billion stars in the Milky Way galaxy. This galaxy is a large member of a cluster known as the Local Group, which is itself a member of our Local Supercluster – one of around 50 such clusters that collectively make up the largest known structure in the universe.

The universe

The big bang's cosmic afterglow and the remains of the structure it formed are captured in this image from COBE, the Cosmic Background Explorer satellite.

Supercluster

Between the vast superclusters of galaxies, the universe contains voids – areas where almost no matter is detectable. The Local Supercluster to which our Local Group belongs is so big that it takes light 100 million years to cross it.

Local Group

Our home galaxy, the Milky Way, is one of a cluster of galaxies in nearby space called the Local Group. This cluster is roughly 2.5 million light-years across, and contains the Andromeda galaxy (background) as well as about 30 smaller, elliptical galaxies.

Milky Way

The Sun is just one of 200 billion stars within the spiral disc of our Milky Way galaxy. Our solar system lies in one of the Milky Way's spiral "arms." This explains why most stars viewed from Earth – looking along the disc – appear in a white band across the sky.

Solar system

Nine known planets, together with smaller objects such as comets and asteroids, form the solar system in orbit around our Sun. The outer curve of Pluto's orbit stretches as far as 4 billion mi. (6 billion km.) from the Sun. Planets orbit stars other than the Sun; bodies as large as Jupiter orbit several nearby stars.

The life and death of a star

A star like our Sun is a ball of hydrogen gas, pulled together by gravitational forces so powerful that, at its core, atoms of hydrogen fuse together. This fusion creates helium gas and causes energy to be released. The hydrogen is used up over billions of years, until the star becomes unstable, swells into a "red giant," then dwindles into a tiny burned-out star – a "white dwarf." Stars larger than the Sun can destroy themselves in vast explosions, called supernovas.

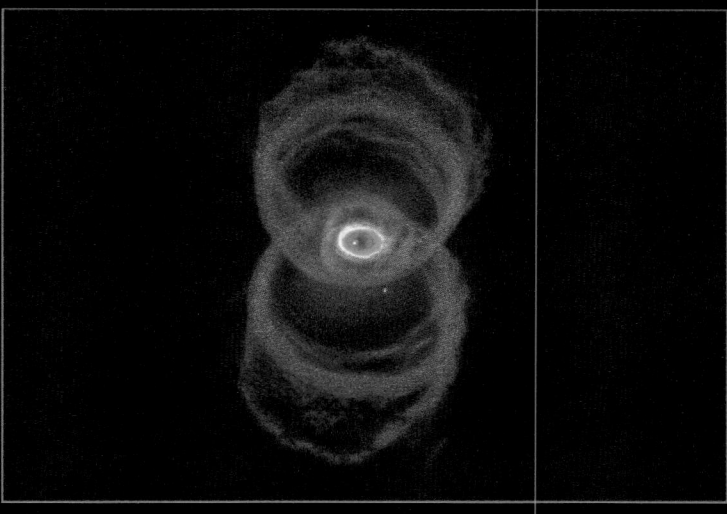

Deathly glow

When a star similar in size to the Sun has nearly run out of fuel for its internal nuclear reactions, it undergoes a series of violent convulsions. These throw off the star's outer layers of gas, which form a glowing nebula like the one shown at left. The nebula often appears as circles of bright gas around the dull dot of the dying star. Its hourglass shape may result from a ring of matter that circles the star's equator, absorbing some of the ejected material and forcing the gas to expand in two lobes, above and below the star. Cooler, outer gas layers are dark red, while younger layers, closer to the central star, glow white hot.

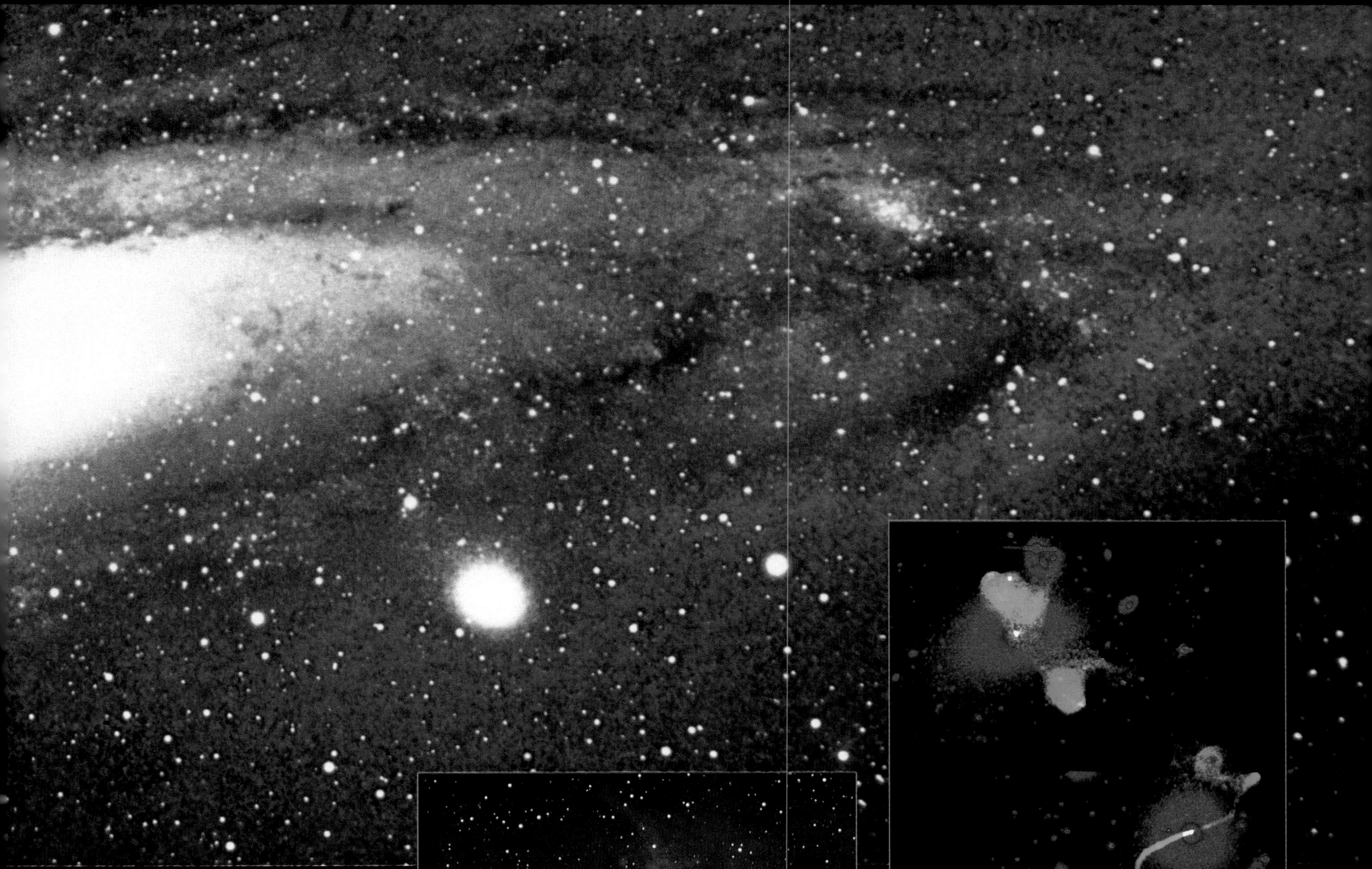

Nurseries of the stars

A star is born when a pressure wave passes through a huge interstellar gas cloud. The galaxy generates these waves as it rotates, or they can result from distant supernova explosions of huge stars. The wave compresses gas in the cloud, so that molecules begin to come together under gravity, pulling in more matter from around themselves to form spinning balls of gas. At the core of these balls, atoms are packed so closely together that their tiny nuclei collide, triggering a chain of nuclear reactions. The energy released by these becomes the first light emitted by the new star.

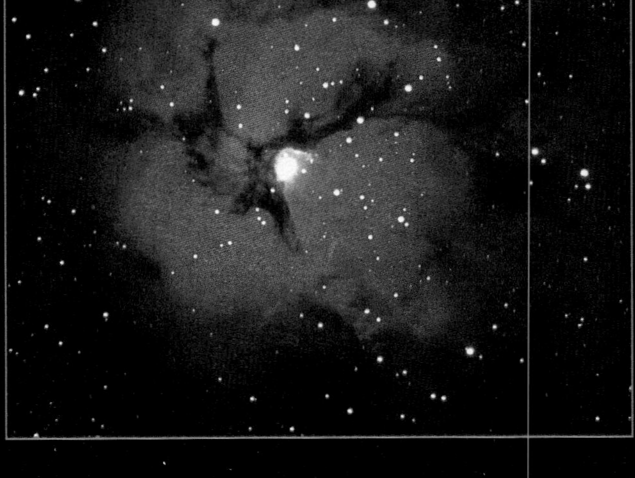

Trifid Nebula

The Trifid Nebula (left) is a cloud of dust and gas. The cloud has no light of its own but shines only by reflection. The region glowing red is made up of hydrogen gas, lit by the young stars forming within it. Above it is an area of dust reflecting blue light from an older star within the nebula.

Black holes

The centers of many galaxies may contain black holes – collapsed stars with gravity so powerful that even light is sucked into them. In active galaxies (above) gas is trapped in a black hole's magnetic field and ejected at the poles, forming gas jets (shown above as pale blue and green areas).

THE SOLAR SYSTEM

Five billion years ago, the solar system existed only as a cloud of dust and gas floating in space. A supernova explosion in our Milky Way galaxy is believed to have created an immense pressure wave that swept through this conglomeration. A small part of the cloud was compressed to the point at which it collapsed under its own gravity, pulling in gas and heating up until nuclear reactions ignited in its core. Around this newborn star – the Sun – orbited a huge disc of gas and dust. The inner planets (Mercury, Venus, Earth, and Mars) were formed close to the Sun in a belt swept free of gas; the outer planets (Jupiter, Saturn, Uranus, and Neptune) were created in a part that was still rich in gas. The disc's outer regions were the birthplace of the planet Pluto and a stream of asteroids and comets.

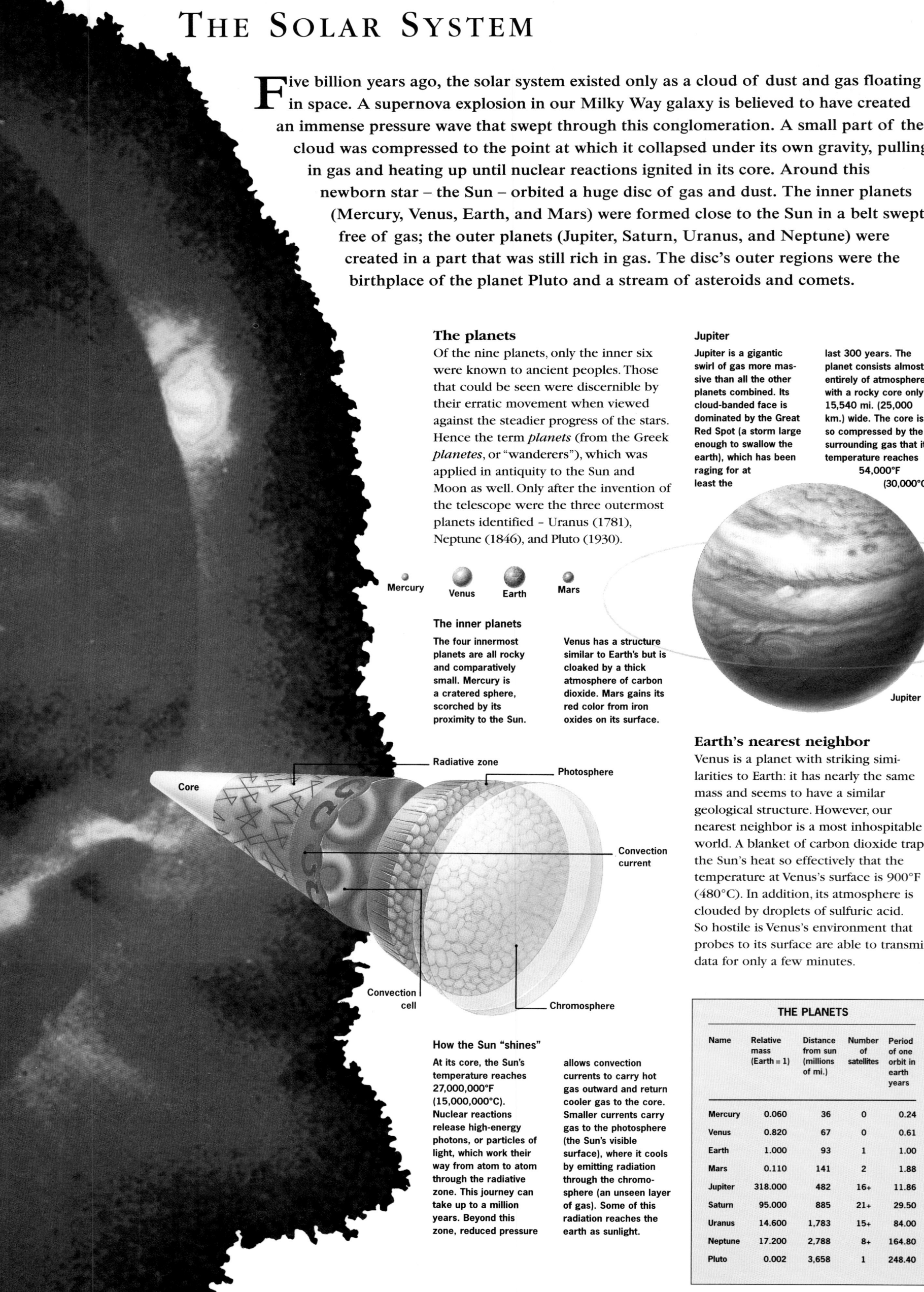

The planets

Of the nine planets, only the inner six were known to ancient peoples. Those that could be seen were discernible by their erratic movement when viewed against the steadier progress of the stars. Hence the term *planets* (from the Greek *planetes*, or "wanderers"), which was applied in antiquity to the Sun and Moon as well. Only after the invention of the telescope were the three outermost planets identified – Uranus (1781), Neptune (1846), and Pluto (1930).

Mercury Venus Earth Mars

The inner planets

The four innermost planets are all rocky and comparatively small. Mercury is a cratered sphere, scorched by its proximity to the Sun.

Venus has a structure similar to Earth's but is cloaked by a thick atmosphere of carbon dioxide. Mars gains its red color from iron oxides on its surface.

Jupiter

Jupiter is a gigantic swirl of gas more massive than all the other planets combined. Its cloud-banded face is dominated by the Great Red Spot (a storm large enough to swallow the earth), which has been raging for at least the last 300 years. The planet consists almost entirely of atmosphere, with a rocky core only 15,540 mi. (25,000 km.) wide. The core is so compressed by the surrounding gas that its temperature reaches 54,000°F (30,000°C).

Jupiter

Earth's nearest neighbor

Venus is a planet with striking similarities to Earth: it has nearly the same mass and seems to have a similar geological structure. However, our nearest neighbor is a most inhospitable world. A blanket of carbon dioxide traps the Sun's heat so effectively that the temperature at Venus's surface is 900°F (480°C). In addition, its atmosphere is clouded by droplets of sulfuric acid. So hostile is Venus's environment that probes to its surface are able to transmit data for only a few minutes.

Core — Radiative zone — Photosphere — Convection current — Chromosphere — Convection cell

How the Sun "shines"

At its core, the Sun's temperature reaches 27,000,000°F (15,000,000°C). Nuclear reactions release high-energy photons, or particles of light, which work their way from atom to atom through the radiative zone. This journey can take up to a million years. Beyond this zone, reduced pressure allows convection currents to carry hot gas outward and return cooler gas to the core. Smaller currents carry gas to the photosphere (the Sun's visible surface), where it cools by emitting radiation through the chromosphere (an unseen layer of gas). Some of this radiation reaches the earth as sunlight.

THE PLANETS				
Name	Relative mass (Earth = 1)	Distance from sun (millions of mi.)	Number of satellites	Period of one orbit in earth years
Mercury	0.060	36	0	0.24
Venus	0.820	67	0	0.61
Earth	1.000	93	1	1.00
Mars	0.110	141	2	1.88
Jupiter	318.000	482	16+	11.86
Saturn	95.000	885	21+	29.50
Uranus	14.600	1,783	15+	84.00
Neptune	17.200	2,788	8+	164.80
Pluto	0.002	3,658	1	248.40

How planets move

The planets move in elliptical orbits. All except Pluto orbit very nearly on the same plane. Pluto's path is a more pronounced ellipse, inclined so that the planet sometimes approaches closer to the Sun than Neptune. The planets are not the only bodies orbiting the Sun. Between Jupiter and Mars is the asteroid belt, made up of rocky debris from the solar system's formation. On the system's outskirts are comets. The best-known, Halley's comet, reappears every 76 years.

Planetary paths

The farther away a planet is from Earth, the more slowly it appears to move in relation to the stars. Lying between Earth and the Sun, Mercury and Venus are the "inferior planets"; the other six are "superior." Owing to differences in relative speeds, planets can sometimes seem to move backward when viewed from earth.

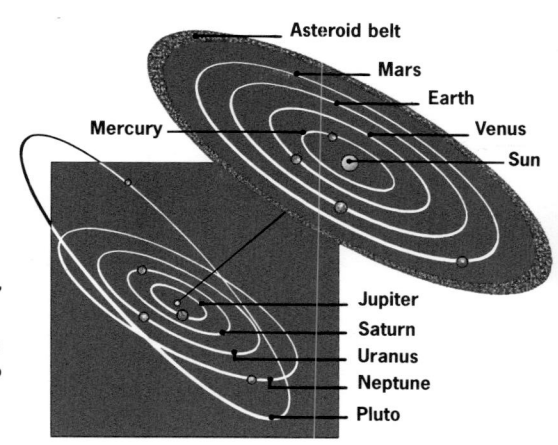

Asteroid belt
Mars
Earth
Venus
Sun
Mercury
Jupiter
Saturn
Uranus
Neptune
Pluto

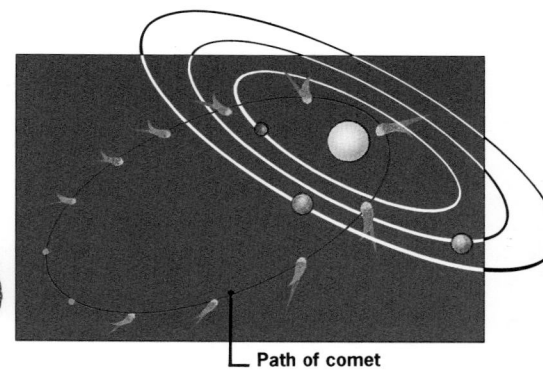

Path of comet

Celestial streamers

Most comets voyage unseen at the outer limits of the solar system. The ones that we do see follow paths that take them close to the Sun. As a comet nears the inner planets (above), its forward surface is vaporized by solar radiation. Two tails form, pointing away from the sun (not always away from the direction of the comet's motion). One tail is glowing gas; the other, slower-moving dust.

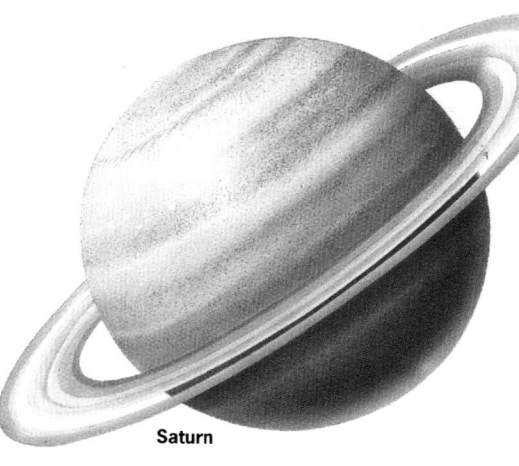

Saturn

Saturn

The second-largest planet is a faintly banded globe encircled by a series of rings. The bands are caused by traces of water and ammonia compounds in the atmosphere of the planet. The rings are made up of dust and ice particles. Saturn's composition is thought to be very similar to that of Jupiter – mostly consisting of the gases hydrogen and helium.

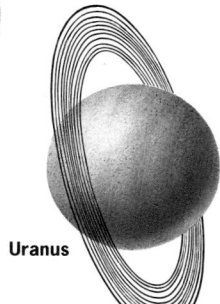

Uranus

Uranus

This planet's green-blue hue derives from methane clouds in its atmosphere. Uranus is encircled by at least nine rings. Its largest moon is named Titania.

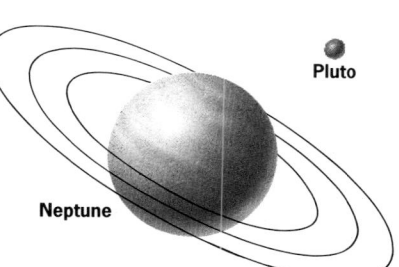

Neptune

Pluto

Neptune and Pluto

Neptune, the "blue planet," has faint rings of methane ice crystals. Pluto is a tiny, icy body, with a moon, Charon, about half its own size.

Venusian vista

The extinct volcano of Sapas Mons (left) on Venus is surrounded by bright solidified lava flows. Similar areas lie around Gula Mons (above). In all these *Magellan* images, the vertical scale has been exaggerated.

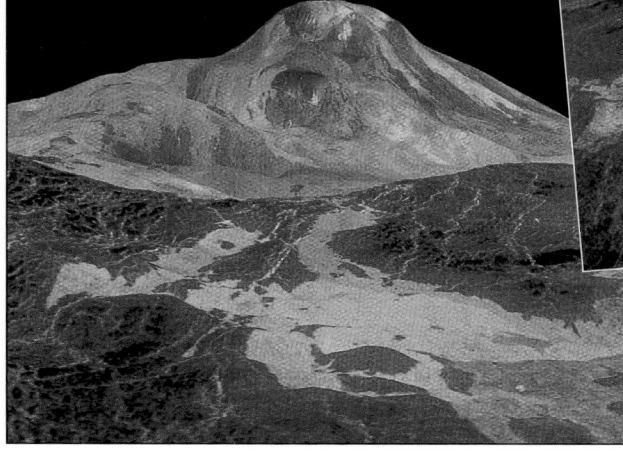

Volcano on Venus

In 1993 the *Magellan* probe used radar to penetrate Venus's thick clouds. Maat Mons (left) was one of the extinct volcanoes revealed.

Stormy weather

The banded appearance of Jupiter is caused by its own particular "weather" – low-pressure belts where dark-colored chemicals collect in the upper atmosphere, and high-pressure zones that reveal paler material below. At the boundaries between these areas, huge, turbulent storms rage, the most powerful of which, the so-called "Great Red Spot," is visible from Earth. The *Galileo* probe, which entered Jupiter's atmosphere in 1995, found violent winds below the visible surface of the spot, with speeds up to 400 m.p.h. (640 km.p.h.).

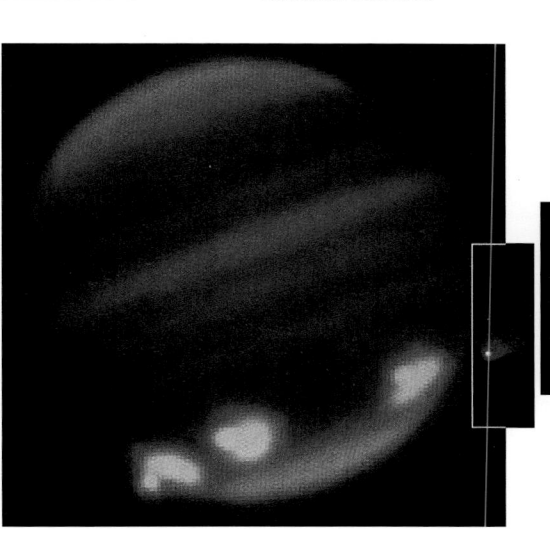

Cosmic collision

In July 1994 comet Shoemaker-Levy was drawn by Jupiter's gravity into a collision with the planet (left). The immense forces exerted on the comet at first broke it up into smaller fragments, each with its own tail (above). The fragments entered the far side of the planet's atmosphere and became visible from Earth only as the planet turned to reveal its "scars." Three of them are clearly visible in this infrared image.

9

THE EVER CHANGING WORLD

The apparent solidity of the earth belies an inner turmoil that dates back to its origin some 4.5 billion years ago. Our planet is thought to have formed from swirling clouds of dust, which gravity fused together into a sphere. The pressure and heat became more and more intense until the interior of the sphere partially melted, forming an ocean of molten magma 125 to 250 mi. (200 to 400 km.) below the surface. Gradually, this swirling mass separated into distinct layers, with the least-dense rock forming a crust on the exterior and the most-dense materials – namely, iron and nickel – trapped inside the core. Signs of the tremendous energy contained within the earth's structure can still be seen today in the violent, dynamic processes of volcanoes and earthquakes. Both phenomena are related to plate tectonics, the division of the earth's crust into constantly moving slabs that carry both continents and oceans with them.

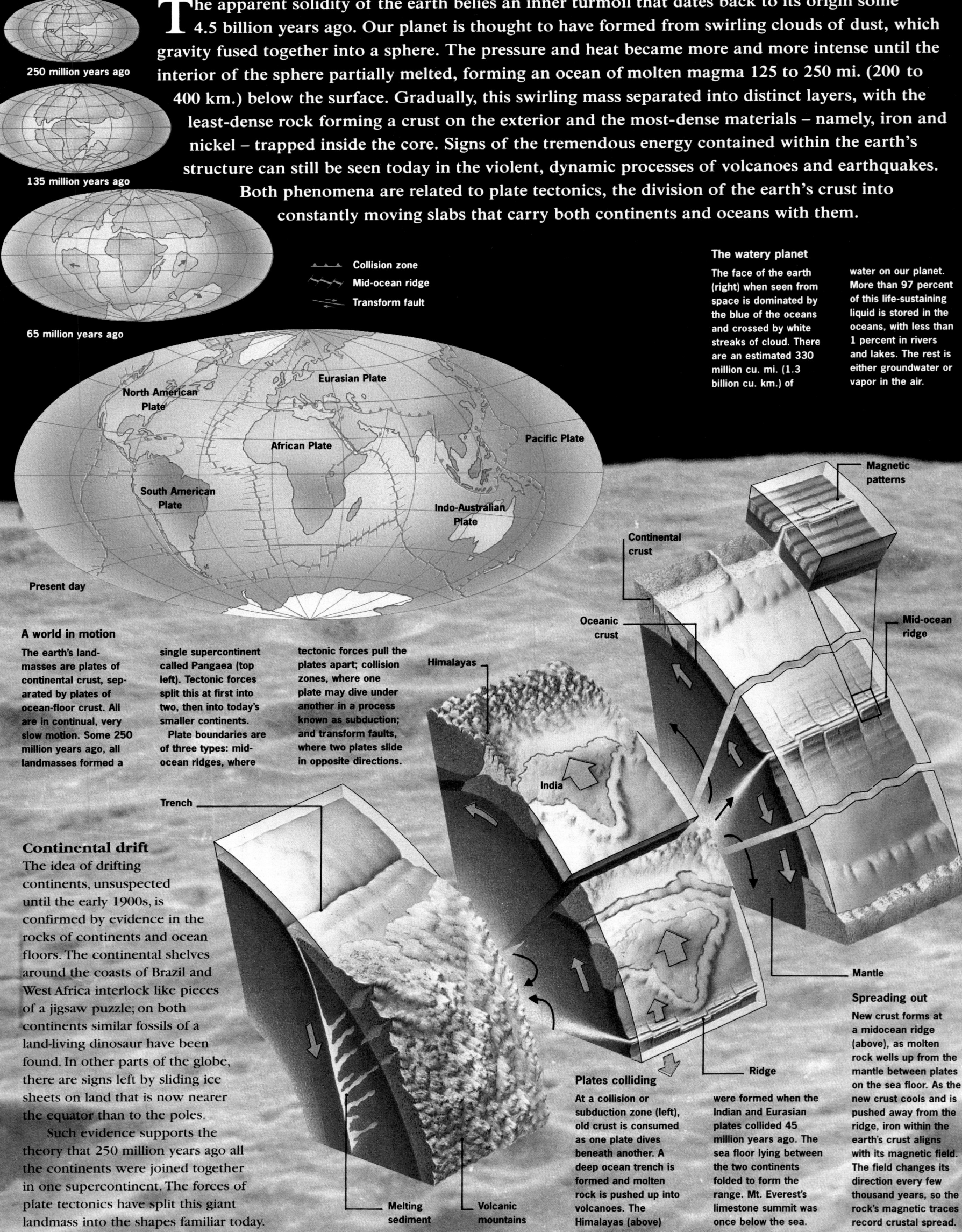

250 million years ago

135 million years ago

65 million years ago

Collision zone
Mid-ocean ridge
Transform fault

Eurasian Plate

North American Plate

African Plate

South American Plate

Pacific Plate

Indo-Australian Plate

Present day

The watery planet

The face of the earth (right) when seen from space is dominated by the blue of the oceans and crossed by white streaks of cloud. There are an estimated 330 million cu. mi. (1.3 billion cu. km.) of water on our planet. More than 97 percent of this life-sustaining liquid is stored in the oceans, with less than 1 percent in rivers and lakes. The rest is either groundwater or vapor in the air.

Magnetic patterns

Continental crust

Oceanic crust

Mid-ocean ridge

Himalayas

India

Mantle

Trench

Ridge

Melting sediment

Volcanic mountains

A world in motion

The earth's land-masses are plates of continental crust, separated by plates of ocean-floor crust. All are in continual, very slow motion. Some 250 million years ago, all landmasses formed a single supercontinent called Pangaea (top left). Tectonic forces split this at first into two, then into today's smaller continents.

Plate boundaries are of three types: mid-ocean ridges, where tectonic forces pull the plates apart; collision zones, where one plate may dive under another in a process known as subduction; and transform faults, where two plates slide in opposite directions.

Continental drift

The idea of drifting continents, unsuspected until the early 1900s, is confirmed by evidence in the rocks of continents and ocean floors. The continental shelves around the coasts of Brazil and West Africa interlock like pieces of a jigsaw puzzle; on both continents similar fossils of a land-living dinosaur have been found. In other parts of the globe, there are signs left by sliding ice sheets on land that is now nearer the equator than to the poles.

Such evidence supports the theory that 250 million years ago all the continents were joined together in one supercontinent. The forces of plate tectonics have split this giant landmass into the shapes familiar today.

Plates colliding

At a collision or subduction zone (left), old crust is consumed as one plate dives beneath another. A deep ocean trench is formed and molten rock is pushed up into volcanoes. The Himalayas (above) were formed when the Indian and Eurasian plates collided 45 million years ago. The sea floor lying between the two continents folded to form the range. Mt. Everest's limestone summit was once below the sea.

Spreading out

New crust forms at a midocean ridge (above), as molten rock wells up from the mantle between plates on the sea floor. As the new crust cools and is pushed away from the ridge, iron within the earth's crust aligns with its magnetic field. The field changes its direction every few thousand years, so the rock's magnetic traces record crustal spread.

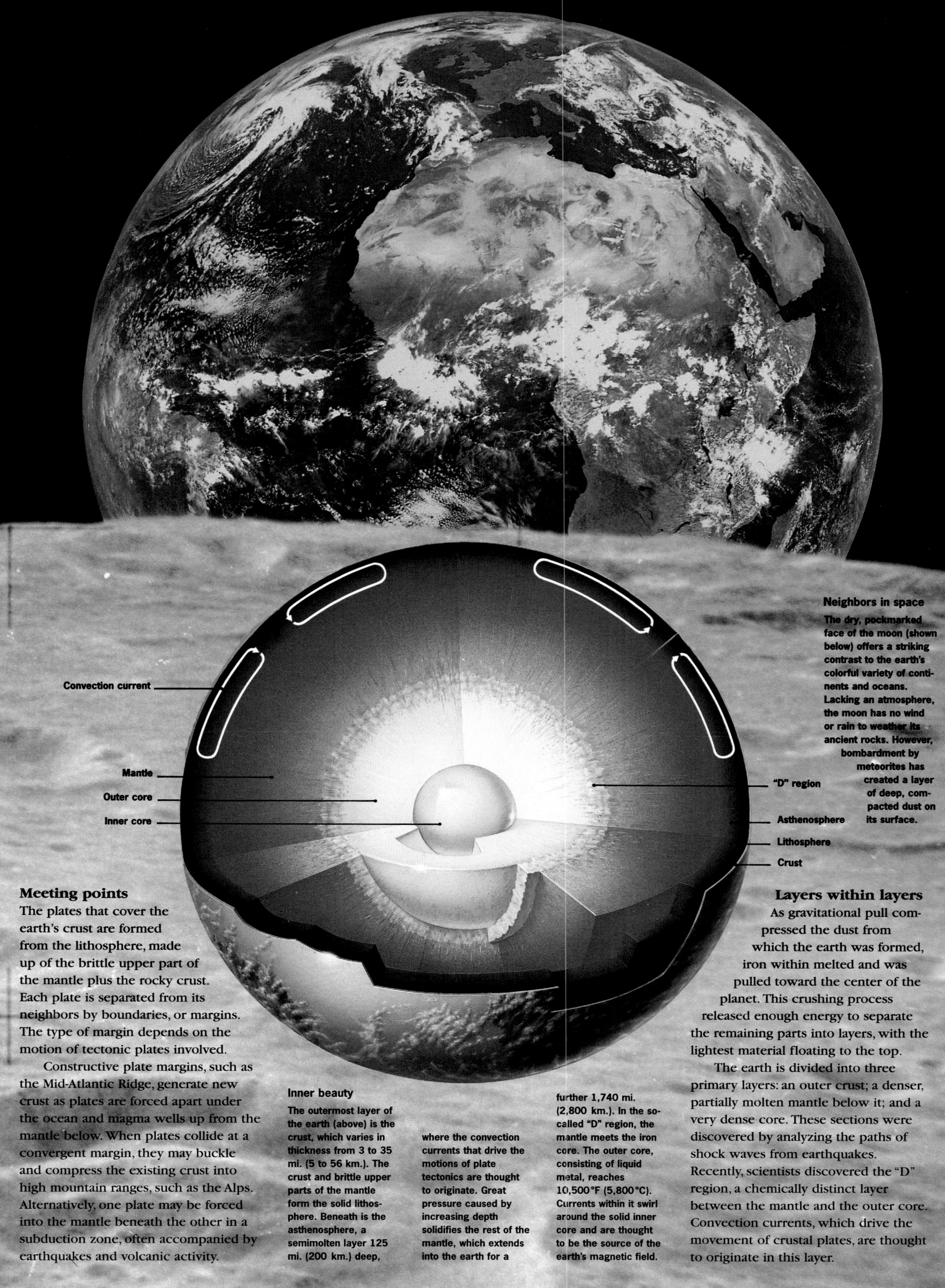

Convection current

Convection current

Mantle

Outer core

Inner core

Neighbors in space

The dry, pockmarked face of the moon (shown below) offers a striking contrast to the earth's colorful variety of continents and oceans. Lacking an atmosphere, the moon has no wind or rain to weather its ancient rocks. However, bombardment by meteorites has created a layer of deep, compacted dust on its surface.

"D" region

Asthenosphere

Lithosphere

Crust

Meeting points

The plates that cover the earth's crust are formed from the lithosphere, made up of the brittle upper part of the mantle plus the rocky crust. Each plate is separated from its neighbors by boundaries, or margins. The type of margin depends on the motion of tectonic plates involved.

Constructive plate margins, such as the Mid-Atlantic Ridge, generate new crust as plates are forced apart under the ocean and magma wells up from the mantle below. When plates collide at a convergent margin, they may buckle and compress the existing crust into high mountain ranges, such as the Alps. Alternatively, one plate may be forced into the mantle beneath the other in a subduction zone, often accompanied by earthquakes and volcanic activity.

Inner beauty

The outermost layer of the earth (above) is the crust, which varies in thickness from 3 to 35 mi. (5 to 56 km.). The crust and brittle upper parts of the mantle form the solid lithosphere. Beneath is the asthenosphere, a semimolten layer 125 mi. (200 km.) deep,

where the convection currents that drive the motions of plate tectonics are thought to originate. Great pressure caused by increasing depth solidifies the rest of the mantle, which extends into the earth for a

further 1,740 mi. (2,800 km.). In the so-called "D" region, the mantle meets the iron core. The outer core, consisting of liquid metal, reaches 10,500°F (5,800°C). Currents within it swirl around the solid inner core and are thought to be the source of the earth's magnetic field.

Layers within layers

As gravitational pull compressed the dust from which the earth was formed, iron within melted and was pulled toward the center of the planet. This crushing process released enough energy to separate the remaining parts into layers, with the lightest material floating to the top.

The earth is divided into three primary layers: an outer crust; a denser, partially molten mantle below it; and a very dense core. These sections were discovered by analyzing the paths of shock waves from earthquakes. Recently, scientists discovered the "D" region, a chemically distinct layer between the mantle and the outer core. Convection currents, which drive the movement of crustal plates, are thought to originate in this layer.

THE SCULPTING OF THE EARTH

The earth's amazing array of rocks and their endlessly varied formations are the products of 4.5 billion years of change. Upwellings of the planet's slowly churning mantle alter the visible face of the outer crust, while at the same time old lands are worn down by weathering and erosion. First, the rocks are disintegrated by forces such as frost, heating and cooling, abrasion, chemical reaction, and the impact of animals and plants. Then the debris is eroded and carried away by water, wind, or ice, to be deposited elsewhere. The magnificent Grand Canyon in Arizona is a dramatic reminder of the erosive power of running water, for the Colorado River has maintained its level as the walls of the chasm have risen on either bank, creating a "scar" in the earth's crust measuring 6,250 ft. (1,910 m.) deep. Moving glaciers also cause erosion. During the long, cold glacials, or ice ages, the effect of glaciers upon the landscape was profound, leaving a lasting topographical legacy.

Ice in retreat
During the last cold phase of the Ice Age 20,000 years ago, ice caps covered 11 million sq. mi. (28.5 million sq. km.) of land that today is free of ice.

20,000 years ago

Present day

Cycles of ice
The term *ice age* refers to any period of glaciation, but specifically the last one (the Ice Age), in the Pleistocene epoch, at the close of prehistoric times. Over the last 2.5 million years, the earth has passed through about 20 ice ages (glacials), separated by warmer "interglacials." A major factor in their creation is thought to be the periodic variation of the earth's solar orbit. During each glacial, falling temperatures have promoted the growth of polar ice caps and of mountain glaciers on the world's highest peaks. Though such glacials could have lasted tens of thousands of years, they often ended fairly abruptly, with the glaciers and ice caps shrinking back to their present size. Major glacial advances "locked up" such great quantities of water that the sea level dropped significantly, exposing large areas of continental shelf.

An icy end
When a glacier is in retreat, meltwater is channeled through tunnels below the ice and runs out from the glacier's snout (below). Subglacier tunnels can be huge (inset).

Eventually these tunnels become choked with rocky debris. The glacier finally melts, leaving behind ribbons of sediment (eskers) marking the old melt-water channels.

Rivers of ice
Glaciers such as this one in Alaska (above) form atop high mountains. When layers of snow build up in hollows, the bottom layers are compressed into ice. Where the ice touches rock, pressure melts its base, reducing friction so that a river of ice (a glacier) begins to slide down the mountainside. As it moves, it incorporates broken rock in its base layer, grinding away the underlying rock. Debris from the valley walls falls onto the glacier's edge and is carried along as a lateral moraine. Where two glaciers meet, their lateral moraines form a medial moraine, as in this example from Alaska (above right). As the glacier descends, the ice begins to melt and streams bearing sediment issue from its snout. If the glacier stays still for a number of years, a terminal moraine may build up in front of it.

Formed by ice
Glaciated landscapes are characterized by erosion in mountains and by deposition on surrounding lowlands. U-shaped valleys, such as Glen Coe in Scotland's Grampian Highlands (above), were formed when an original V-shaped river valley was deeply excavated by an Ice Age glacier. Striated rocks, indicative of ice scarring, are here as high as 3,280 ft. (1,000 m.). They show that the ice flow may have overtopped the mountains on its way toward the Atlantic.

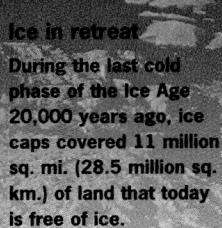

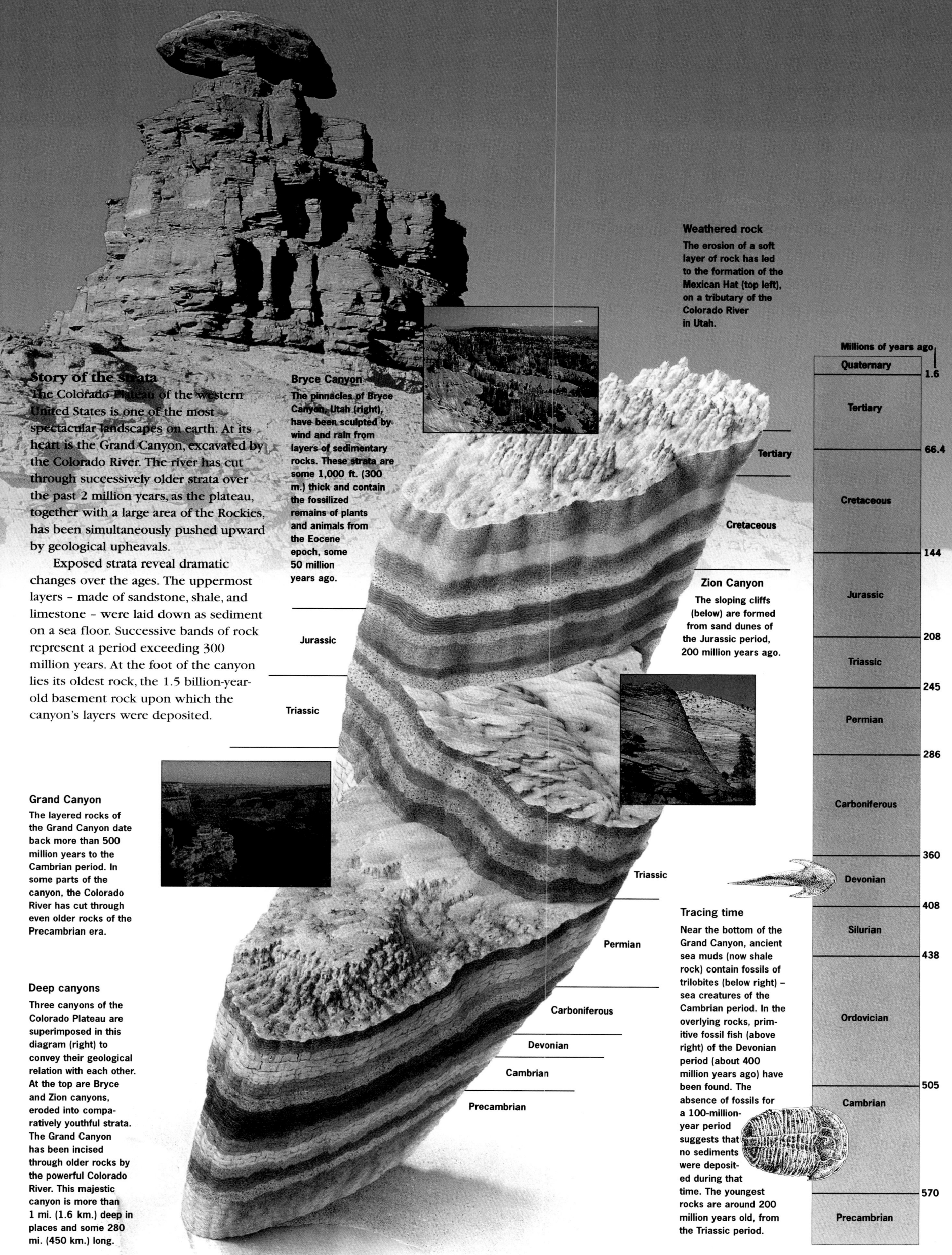

Weathered rock

The erosion of a soft layer of rock has led to the formation of the Mexican Hat (top left), on a tributary of the Colorado River in Utah.

Story of the strata

The Colorado Plateau of the western United States is one of the most spectacular landscapes on earth. At its heart is the Grand Canyon, excavated by the Colorado River. The river has cut through successively older strata over the past 2 million years, as the plateau, together with a large area of the Rockies, has been simultaneously pushed upward by geological upheavals.

Exposed strata reveal dramatic changes over the ages. The uppermost layers – made of sandstone, shale, and limestone – were laid down as sediment on a sea floor. Successive bands of rock represent a period exceeding 300 million years. At the foot of the canyon lies its oldest rock, the 1.5 billion-year-old basement rock upon which the canyon's layers were deposited.

Bryce Canyon

The pinnacles of Bryce Canyon, Utah (right), have been sculpted by wind and rain from layers of sedimentary rocks. These strata are some 1,000 ft. (300 m.) thick and contain the fossilized remains of plants and animals from the Eocene epoch, some 50 million years ago.

Zion Canyon

The sloping cliffs (below) are formed from sand dunes of the Jurassic period, 200 million years ago.

Grand Canyon

The layered rocks of the Grand Canyon date back more than 500 million years to the Cambrian period. In some parts of the canyon, the Colorado River has cut through even older rocks of the Precambrian era.

Deep canyons

Three canyons of the Colorado Plateau are superimposed in this diagram (right) to convey their geological relation with each other. At the top are Bryce and Zion canyons, eroded into comparatively youthful strata. The Grand Canyon has been incised through older rocks by the powerful Colorado River. This majestic canyon is more than 1 mi. (1.6 km.) deep in places and some 280 mi. (450 km.) long.

Tracing time

Near the bottom of the Grand Canyon, ancient sea muds (now shale rock) contain fossils of trilobites (below right) – sea creatures of the Cambrian period. In the overlying rocks, primitive fossil fish (above right) of the Devonian period (about 400 million years ago) have been found. The absence of fossils for a 100-million-year period suggests that no sediments were deposited during that time. The youngest rocks are around 200 million years old, from the Triassic period.

Strata labels (center diagram)
- Tertiary
- Cretaceous
- Jurassic
- Triassic
- Triassic
- Permian
- Carboniferous
- Devonian
- Cambrian
- Precambrian

Geological time scale (right)

Period	Millions of years ago
Quaternary	1.6
Tertiary	66.4
Cretaceous	144
Jurassic	208
Triassic	245
Permian	286
Carboniferous	360
Devonian	408
Silurian	438
Ordovician	505
Cambrian	570
Precambrian	

13

THE FURY WITHIN

Volcanoes and earthquakes are the most obvious – and most dramatic – evidence of the mighty forces of plate tectonics. Both are capable of enormous devastation. The first documented major volcanic event took place in the year AD 79 with the eruption of Mount Vesuvius and the destruction of the Roman towns of Pompeii and Herculaneum by clouds of ash and toxic gas. In recent times the 1993 earthquake in the Maharashtra state of India leveled 50 towns in a matter of just a few seconds, killing tens of thousands of people. The effects of such disasters may be felt worldwide. In 1991 the largest eruption of this century blasted more than 2 cu. mi. (8 cu. km.) of ash and 22 million tons (20 million metric tons) of sulfur dioxide from Mount Pinatubo in the Philippines 12 to 15 mi. (19 to 24 km.) into the stratosphere. This created a haze that shrouded the planet, reflecting sunlight back into space and lowering average temperatures worldwide by 0.9°F (0.5°C).

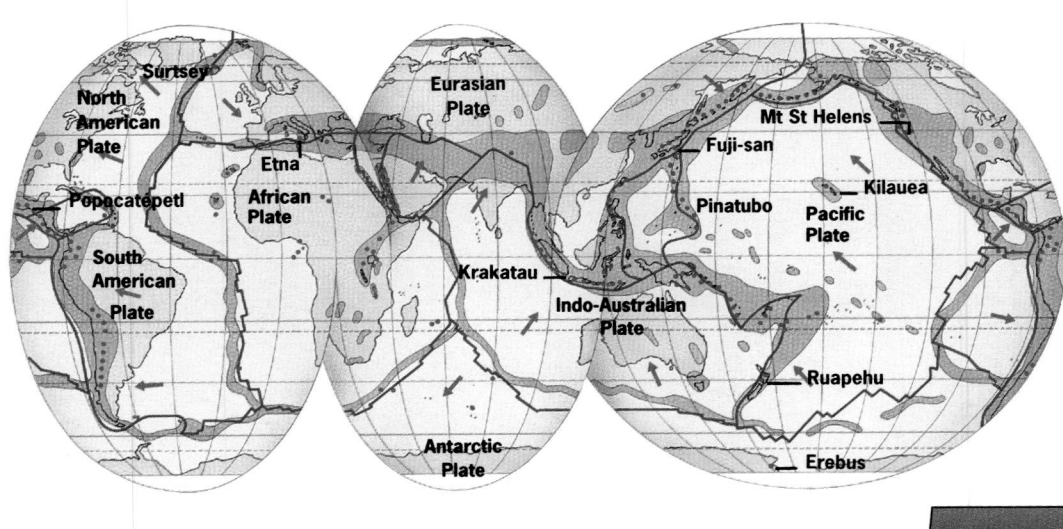

 Earthquake zones    Volcanoes   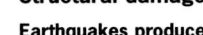 Plate margins

Interactive plates

The motion of one crustal plate against another produces earthquakes and allows magma from the earth's core to reach the surface and form volcanoes. Of the 600 or so active land volcanoes, the majority form where two plates collide, as they do under the Pacific Ocean. This collision results in major faults in New Zealand and Japan and the so-called "ring of fire," which comprises volcanoes from Mount Erebus in Antarctica to those around the Pacific rim and down through the Andes. Other seismic events occur where plates pull apart to form new rocks on the ocean floor.

Plates under stress

Earthquakes can be terrifying natural phenomena. They are concentrated along fracture zones in the earth's crust, where two plates move against one another. The huge pressures that build up are eventually released by faulting and by a violent quaking motion.

Danger zones are monitored by satellite, but signs of impending disaster can also come from less scientific sources. In 1975 a tremor at Haicheng in China was heralded by animals that became agitated and wells that bubbled. However, 18 months later no such signs were detected before another earthquake in China, which killed more than a quarter of a million people.

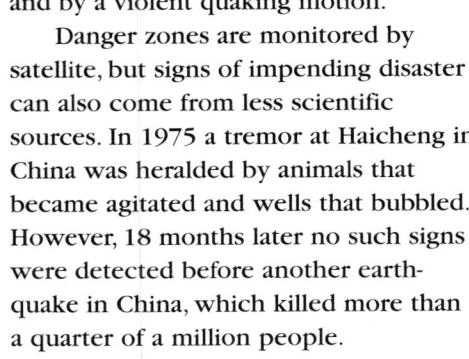

Structural damage

Earthquakes produce immense forces that oscillate several times per second, pulling apart even the strongest structures, such as this highway, destroyed in the 1994 quake in Los Angeles.

Dividing line

This fracture (left) is part of the San Andreas Fault in California. It occurs where the Pacific Plate and the North American Plate grind past each other at a rate of 1 in. (2.5 cm.) per year.

Earthquake zone

The San Andreas Fault runs out into the Pacific Ocean just south of San Francisco. It is shown as a red line on this satellite image (left). The arrows show the relative movements of the North American Plate and the Pacific Plate. Millions of years in the future, southwest California will become detached from the mainland and be carried north until it is an island off the coast of present-day Canada.

Fiery outpouring

Kilauea is not only the youngest of the Hawaiian volcanoes but also the most active one on earth. During the 20th century it has been erupting molten rock at a rate of 177 cu. ft. (5 cu. m.) per second to build up the vast, gently sloping flanks typical of a shield volcano. Lava has been pouring effusively from one of the craters on the eastern flank of Kilauea (top right) since 1983.

Rivers of rock

At more than 2,066°F (1,130°C), basalt lava flows readily, even on gentle slopes (middle row). As the upper surface begins to cool, it forms a hard crust, beneath which molten lava continues to run (top left).

Solidifying rock

Hawaiian basalt lava has two main forms, both of which have local names: rubbly-surfaced *aa* and smooth *pahoehoe*. The former results from fast flows; the latter (bottom left and bottom right) flows more slowly, at the rate of 3 ft. (1 m.) per minute. Its surface can cool to form a thin shell that later cracks and bursts to release more oddly shaped bulges and coils of rope-like lava. In some places the pahoehoe flows directly into the sea, where it solidifies fast in clouds of steam (bottom center).

Types of volcanoes

The shape of a volcano is determined mostly by the nature of the lava it produces, and in particular by the viscosity – resistance to flow – of the molten rock, or magma. This, in turn, depends on its chemical composition. The least viscous and fastest-flowing lavas are basalt lavas ejected by oceanic volcanoes, such as Kilauea and its sister volcano Mauna Loa in Hawaii. These have vast "shield" slopes with a gentle gradient. By contrast, classic, high cone-shaped volcanoes, such as those of the Pacific ring of fire, are more dangerous and highly unpredictable. Their magma is much more viscous, so that it does not flow easily.

The buildup of gas pressure ejects magma in a fountain of incandescent fragments. The heaviest pieces of magma solidify in flight, fall back to earth and, together with ash, form a steep-sided cinder cone.

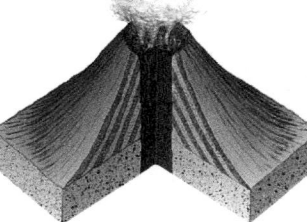

Cinder cone

Composite cone

Volcanic variety

Cinder cones (top) formed from ash and rock fragments are steeper sided than the composite cones formed from alternating layers of lava and cinder (above).

Power of destruction

Volcanic eruptions can release incredibly powerful blasts of ash, gas, and steam. The force of the eruption of Mount St. Helens in Washington State in 1980 was unexpected. On May 18, following two earthquakes, one side of the volcano collapsed, unleashing pent-up gas which vaporized the upper 1,350 ft. (410 m.) of the mountain and sent 8.8 billion tons (8 billion metric tons) of rock avalanching down the mountainside at a speed of 155 m.p.h. (250 km.p.h.).

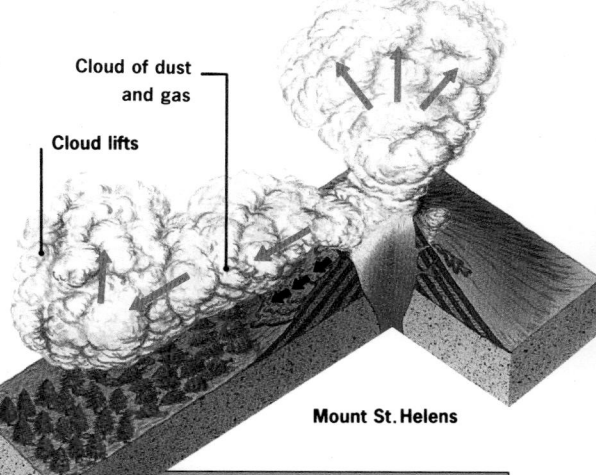

Cloud of dust and gas

Cloud lifts

Mount St. Helens

Liftoff

After the collapse of the volcanic flank of Mount St. Helens (right and above right), a cloud of gas and ash composed of pulverized rock and magma spread over a 155-sq.-mi. (400-sq.-km.) area, flattening whole forests and rising 15 mi. (24 km.) into the atmosphere.

THE RECORD OF THE ROCKS

Solid and changeless though it may appear, the rock of the earth's crust has been constantly in motion and recycling itself over the past 4.6 billion years. Over time rock can take many different forms. Igneous rocks, formed from cooling magma, are ground down over the ages by wind or water. Rivers carry the particles to the oceans and deposit them on the seabed. As yet more particles accumulate, pressure compacts them into sedimentary rock, which can be lifted into high mountain ranges by movements of the earth's tectonic plates. Heat from deep within the earth can transform sedimentary rock into metamorphic rock, turning chalky limestone, for example, into smooth marble. A more intense process converts the soft carbon of graphite into one of the hardest materials known – diamond. Further change can occur: tectonic movement may carry rocks into the earth's depths, where they are remelted into magma and become the raw material of new rock.

Earth's building blocks

All the types of rock found on earth – from the sky-grazing ramparts of the Himalayas to the hard, black pavements of Icelandic basalt or the sandstone towers of Monument Valley in Utah (the setting for countless Hollywood Westerns) – belong to one of three groups. The first is igneous rock, which has crystallized from magma (molten lava formed deep in the earth and often ejected in a volcanic eruption). Cooling takes place quickly and the rock thus formed has a fine-grained structure. Some masses of magma do not rise to the earth's surface; instead, they cool slowly underground to become much coarser-grained rocks.

Sedimentary rock, the second group, is formed by accumulations of sand, silt, mud, and other detritus that become compacted by pressure. Erosion by wind, water, ice, or heat can sculpt these rocks into dramatic landforms, such as the Grand Canyon in Arizona.

Metamorphic rock, the third group, consists of existing rock transformed by pressure and heat. Italy's Carrara marble was once sedimentary limestone. It was compressed in the tectonic movement that formed the Alps.

Riches below ground

The earth's crust is the source of all our mineral wealth. The most commonly used metals, such as iron and aluminum, are almost always found as ores – minerals in which the metal is in chemical compound with other elements. Rarer and more valuable are pure metals such as gold, which do not react with other elements. They are usually found in a native, uncombined state in veins deep underground.

Gemstones are much prized for their rarity and beauty. The most valuable have their origins deep in the earth's crust, where they were formed under extreme pressure and heat, which squeezed them into a compact crystal structure. This makes them extremely hard – diamond, for example, is the hardest material found in nature. Small, imperfect diamonds, unsuitable as gems, are used in industry for cutting or grinding.

Igneous outcrop

A granite outcrop (right) on the English coast is more resistant than surrounding rocks, but is still affected by weathering. Its crystal structure is revealed in polarized light (below).

Rock of fire

Igneous rock forms when molten rock solidifies. This can happen in either of two ways (right). In a volcano, magma forces its way to the surface from the mantle below. As it emerges, it can assume many forms, from glassy obsidian to spongelike pumice. Alternatively, molten rock trapped deep in the earth cools slowly into a large mass, or pluton, with large mineral crystals. The most common plutonic rock is granite.

— Rising magma

— Pluton (molten rock)

Volcanoes —

Glittering prizes

Diamonds are crystals of pure carbon, formed under intense pressure and heat. Valued for their durability and sparkling beauty, the colorless ones are particularly prized as gemstones. Ruby and sapphire are both forms of corundum, an oxide of aluminum. Their hues derive from traces of different metals trapped in the crystal structure. Emeralds are a form of the mineral beryl, colored green by chromium. Silicon, with other chemicals, forms the basis of both opals and jadeite. Precious metals such as gold, silver, and platinum are all found in a pure state within the earth's crust.

Diamond (cut)

Sapphire

Gold

Ruby

Emerald

Silver

Opal

Jadeite

Platinum

The composition of the earth

About 90 percent of the mass of the earth is made up of four elements: oxygen, silicon, aluminum, and iron. In the planet as a whole, iron is the most abundant element; it is believed to constitute about 90 percent of the earth's core. However, iron is only the fourth-most-common element in the crust, where oxygen is predominant. Silicon, the second-most-plentiful element, is found in virtually all rocks, as well as in sand, clays, and soils.

Crust laid bare

A mere nine elements account for more than 99 percent of the material in the earth's crust (right). Of these, two elements – silicon and oxygen – make up 75 percent of the crust. In chemical combination, these elements are the basis of many different forms of minerals, from clear crystals of quartz to darker hornblende.

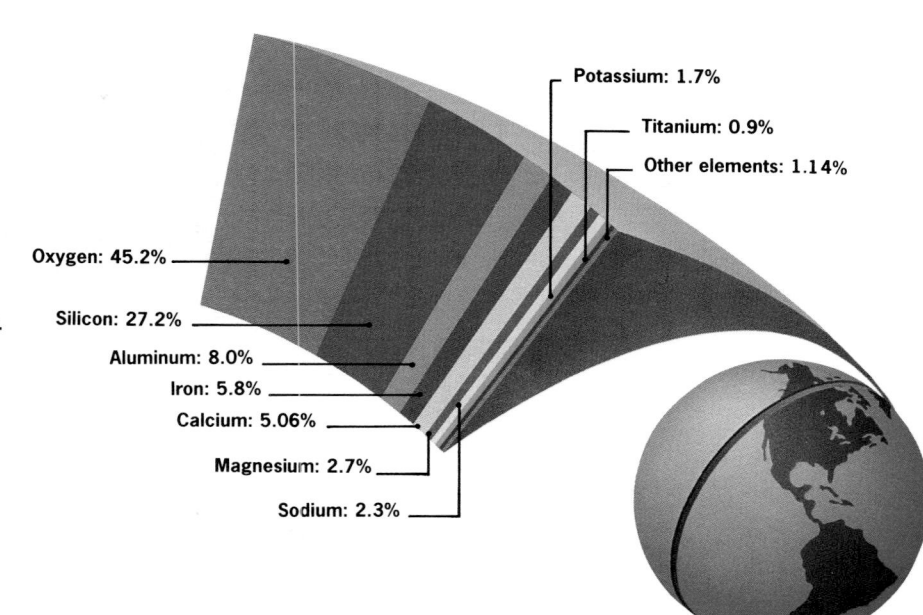

Potassium: 1.7%
Titanium: 0.9%
Other elements: 1.14%
Oxygen: 45.2%
Silicon: 27.2%
Aluminum: 8.0%
Iron: 5.8%
Calcium: 5.06%
Magnesium: 2.7%
Sodium: 2.3%

Rocks from the sea

The Badlands of South Dakota (above) are composed of soft sedimentary rocks, originally deposited on an ancient sea floor.

Color within

A quartz geode (above) is a mineral formation within a rock cavity. Colorful layers of the mineral grow inward from the cavity walls.

Soft strata

As layers of sediment are deposited on the sea floor (above), the cumulative pressure binds the particles together to form rock.

Magma
River delta
Layers of sediment

Streaked beauty

Marble forms when limestone is subjected to great heat or pressure. Impurities within create its characteristic streaks.

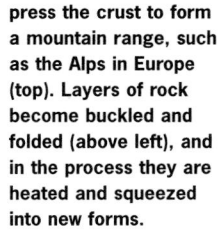

Folded layers
Mountain peaks

Changing states

Metamorphism occurs when extreme heat and pressure act on rock. This can happen when tectonic forces com- press the crust to form a mountain range, such as the Alps in Europe (top). Layers of rock become buckled and folded (above left), and in the process they are heated and squeezed into new forms.

The cycle of the rocks

Rocks are converted from one form to another through a process known as the rock cycle. A fragment can be carried far across the face of the earth, as well as up or down within its crust. Rocks on the surface are eroded by weathering, then carried away as sediment and compacted into new sedimentary rock. This can then be pressed and heated into metamorphic rock, which in turn may be melted into magma and thrown to the surface by volcanic activity. When the magma solidifies into igneous rock and is exposed to the atmosphere, the entire cycle starts over again.

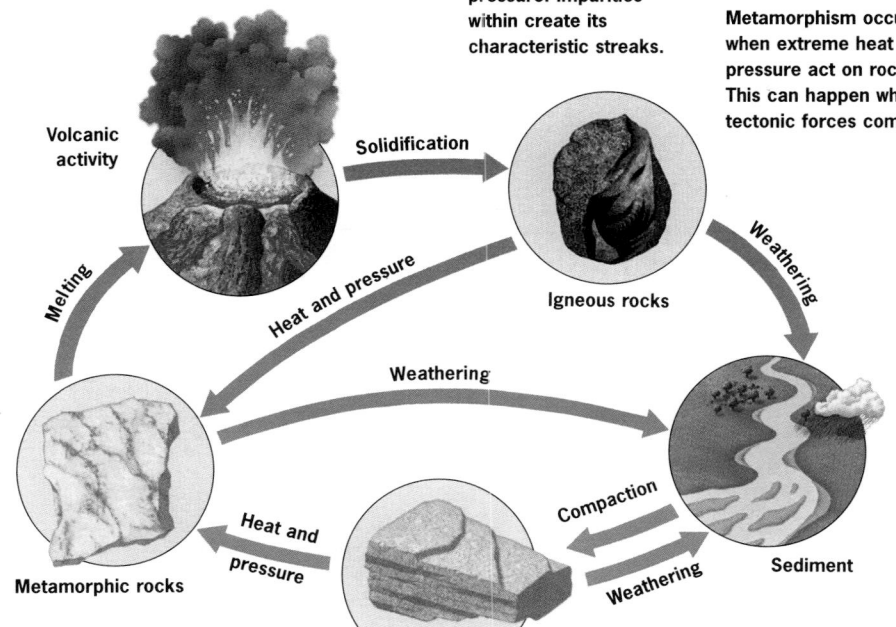

Volcanic activity
Solidification
Melting
Heat and pressure
Igneous rocks
Weathering
Weathering
Metamorphic rocks
Heat and pressure
Weathering
Compaction
Sediment
Weathering
Sedimentary rocks

Endless cycle

The many paths of the rock cycle (left) show how rocks are transformed from one type to another and recycled through the earth's crust.

17

The earth's atmosphere is a turbulent mix of gases, swirling in currents driven by the heat of the sun. If the earth did not spin on its axis, air would circulate in simple looping currents, or "cells," as it heated up and cooled. The currents would rise over the equator, sink down over the poles, and return low over the earth's surface to the equator. However, the rotation of the earth complicates these patterns, as any air currents moving across the earth will also start to spin. The uneven distribution of land and water over the globe is yet another factor, making it impossible to predict weather systems with complete precision. As air currents circulate around the globe, they tend to form vortexes − the high- and low-pressure areas familiar from weather forecasts. In some places these vortexes can intensify, growing into mighty tropical storms. In others they can spawn tornadoes, which can wreak havoc all along their narrow yet deadly paths.

Tropical tempest

An astronaut on board a space shuttle took this photograph (below) of Hurricane Elena as it approached the Caribbean Sea in 1985. The distinctive spiral structure of a tropical storm can be clearly seen.

Swirling destruction

Severe tropical storms have a variety of names, depending on where they occur. They are known as hurricanes over the Atlantic, typhoons over the Pacific, and cyclones over the Indian Ocean. All form in roughly the same manner. In summer the tropical sea surface warms. When it reaches 80°F (27°C), humid air evaporates from the surface and rises. The air cools as it lifts, and its water vapor condenses, forming huge thunderclouds. High-altitude winds deflect the air above the thunderclouds, and more air is drawn up to take its place. The earth's rotation sets the whole system of air currents and thunderclouds turning, producing huge spiral bands of clouds. The storm's most violent winds, which exceed 75 m.p.h. (120 km.p.h.), are concentrated around the center of the spiral. Most damage occurs when this section of the storm crosses land. The "eye" of a tropical storm is a region of very low air pressure. This forces the sea to bulge upward, magnifying tides in a stormy sea churning with waves.

Twister

A tornado forms inside a big thundercloud, where swirling air currents are rising and descending (right). As the spiral descends, the tornado narrows into a funnel shape, which intensifies the speed of the rotating air. Its wind speeds may reach 300 m.p.h. (480 km.p.h.).

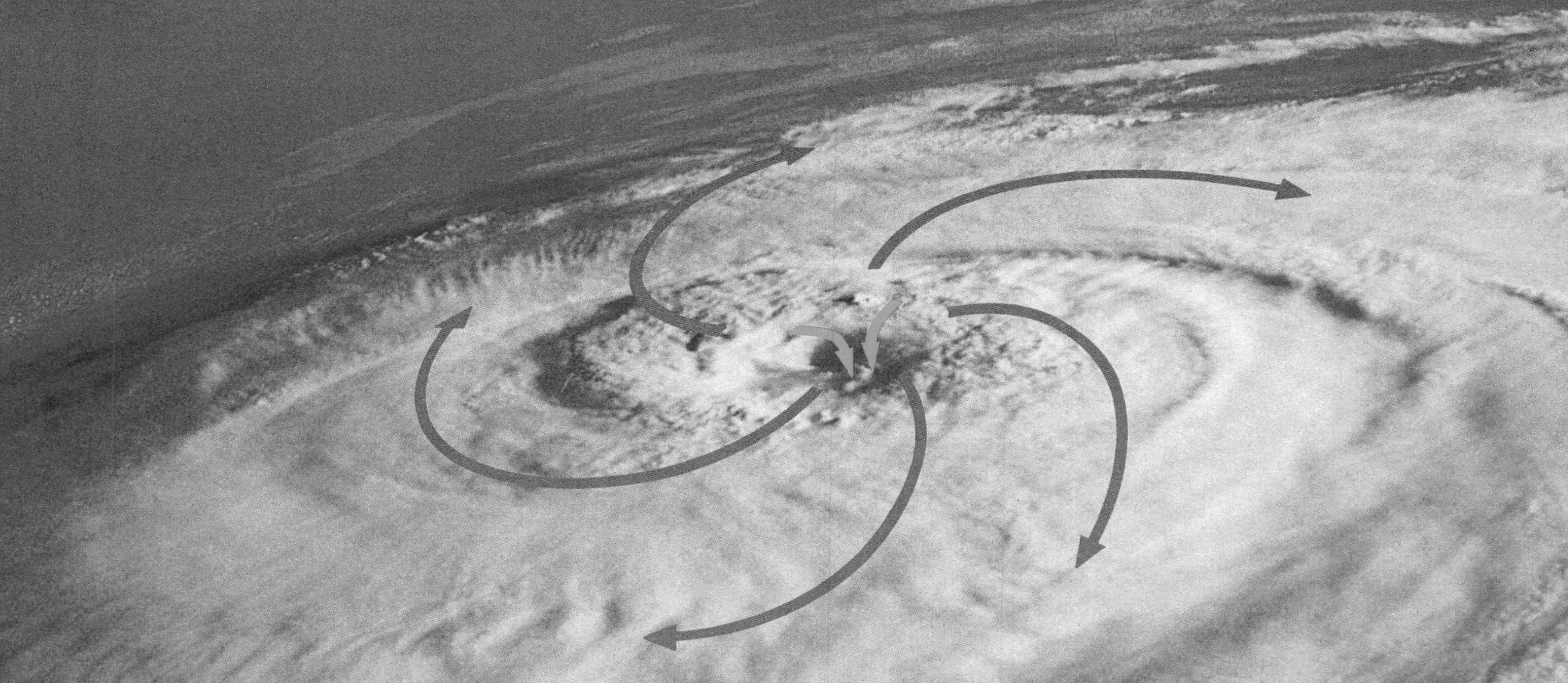

Stormy structure

A hurricane forms when water evaporates from the warm tropical seas, creating updrafts of hot, moist air (right). As the air cools, water vapor condenses into thick clouds, which are shaped into wide spirals by air sucked in from the sea's surface. Above the storm most winds flow outward, except for a small amount of air flowing downward in the calmer, cloud-free "eye."

Cold air sinks

Winds flow outwards

Eye

Warm air rises

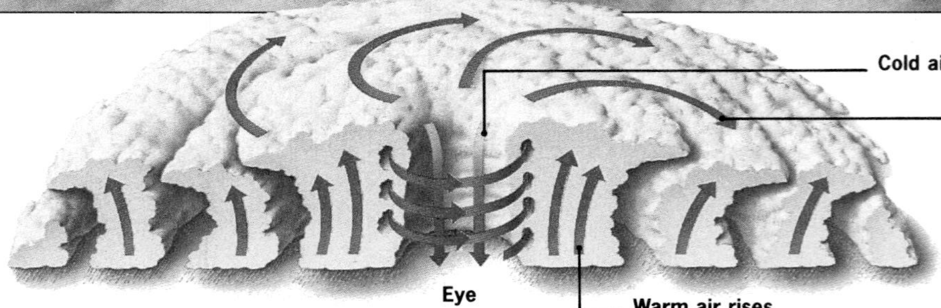

Weather zones

The seven continents are divided into different climatic zones, each with a characteristic annual pattern of temperature and rainfall. Many factors govern the particular climate found at any one place. Latitude determines the amount of heat that a region receives from the sun and is therefore a major influence on average temperatures. Distance from the ocean distinguishes dry continental interiors from moister coastal regions and islands. Ocean currents, which warm the air crossing over them, are also important. The mild climate of northwest Europe is partly caused by the passage of air over the warm waters of the Gulf Stream.

Physical features can also be significant – the "rain shadow" effect of a mountain range can create regions as diverse as desert and tropical rain forest on its opposite slopes.

The winds of the world

The systems of vertically circulating air around the world are known as cells. In Hadley cells, the looping air currents in the Northern and Southern Hemispheres, warm air rises at the equator and then cools and sinks again at a latitude of 30°N and 30°S. Most of the cooler air is sucked back toward the low-pressure area of the equator, but some of the air moves toward the poles, forming so-called Ferrel cells, which circulate in the opposite direction. Each loop of air is skewed by the earth's spin to form the lateral trade winds.

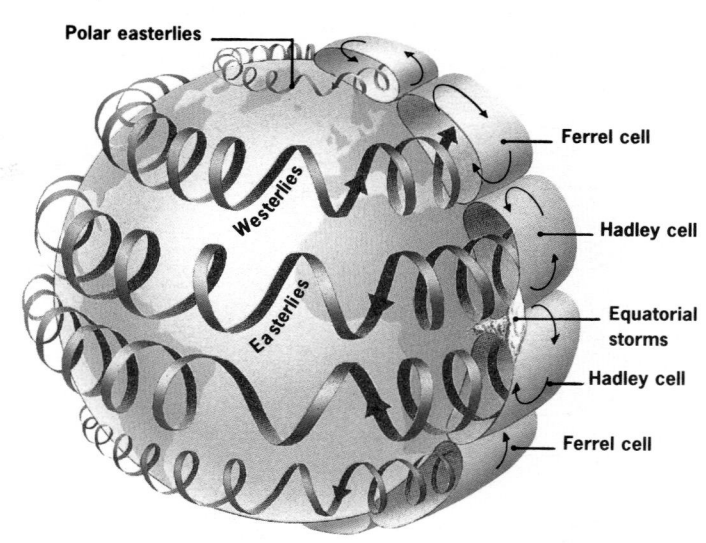

Polar easterlies — Ferrel cell — Hadley cell — Equatorial storms — Hadley cell — Ferrel cell — Westerlies — Easterlies

Atmospheric moves

A simplified diagram of the earth's atmospheric patterns (above) shows the Hadley and Ferrel cells in both hemispheres. The vertical circulation of these cells is partly responsible for the world's climates. The earth's rotation deflects these currents into belts of prevailing winds which blow horizontally over its surface. In the tropics, easterlies are known as trade winds.

- Tundra
- Taiga
- Temperate
- Mediterranean
- Desert
- Tropical rain forest
- Savanna
- Others

Polar

Eismitte in Greenland (below) has a polar climate, with freezing temperatures all year. Cold air cannot carry much moisture, so the area has the low rainfall of a desert.

Continental

Krasnoyarsk in Russia (left) has a typical continental climate, with bitterly cold winters and warm summers. Its distance from the sea gives the city a very low rainfall.

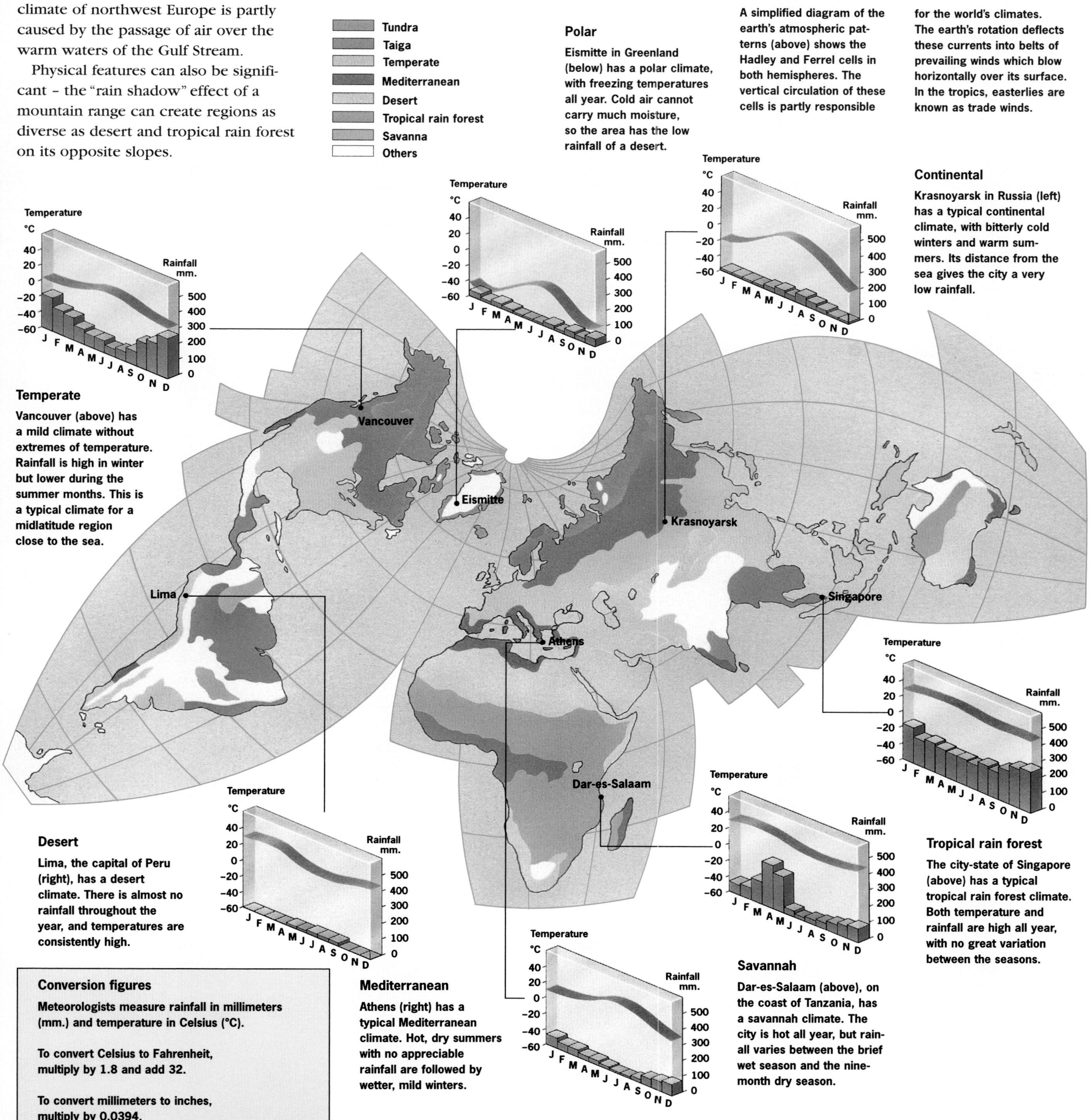

Temperate

Vancouver (above) has a mild climate without extremes of temperature. Rainfall is high in winter but lower during the summer months. This is a typical climate for a midlatitude region close to the sea.

Desert

Lima, the capital of Peru (right), has a desert climate. There is almost no rainfall throughout the year, and temperatures are consistently high.

Tropical rain forest

The city-state of Singapore (above) has a typical tropical rain forest climate. Both temperature and rainfall are high all year, with no great variation between the seasons.

Savannah

Dar-es-Salaam (above), on the coast of Tanzania, has a savannah climate. The city is hot all year, but rainfall varies between the brief wet season and the nine-month dry season.

Mediterranean

Athens (right) has a typical Mediterranean climate. Hot, dry summers with no appreciable rainfall are followed by wetter, mild winters.

Conversion figures

Meteorologists measure rainfall in millimeters (mm.) and temperature in Celsius (°C).

To convert Celsius to Fahrenheit, multiply by 1.8 and add 32.

To convert millimeters to inches, multiply by 0.0394.

THE BLUE PLANET

Where currents flow
A band of westward-flowing water at the equator is diverted north and south when it strikes the barrier formed by the continental shelves of landmasses (below). Surface currents form great loops, which are known as gyres. Beneath them flow the cold currents that transport icy water from the poles.

More than 70 percent of the earth's surface is covered by sea water. It extends to an average depth of 2.25 mi. (3.62 km.), and most of this territory remains unexplored. The great oceans interconnect to form a single global body of water in which the continents, for all their vastness, are – in effect – only islands. The waters are in constant motion. Tidal "bulges" are created by the gravitational pull of the moon and sun. At the same time, currents carry the oceans' waters about the planet in a complex, three-dimensional process driven by variations in water temperature and density, by the wind, and by the rotation of the earth. Deep in the oceans, cold water flows away from the poles; on the surface, winds push warm water, heated by the sun, from one part of the world to another in vast, meandering flows. The transfer of heat between ocean and atmosphere exerts an enormous influence on climate everywhere in the world, and on the distribution of life in the oceans.

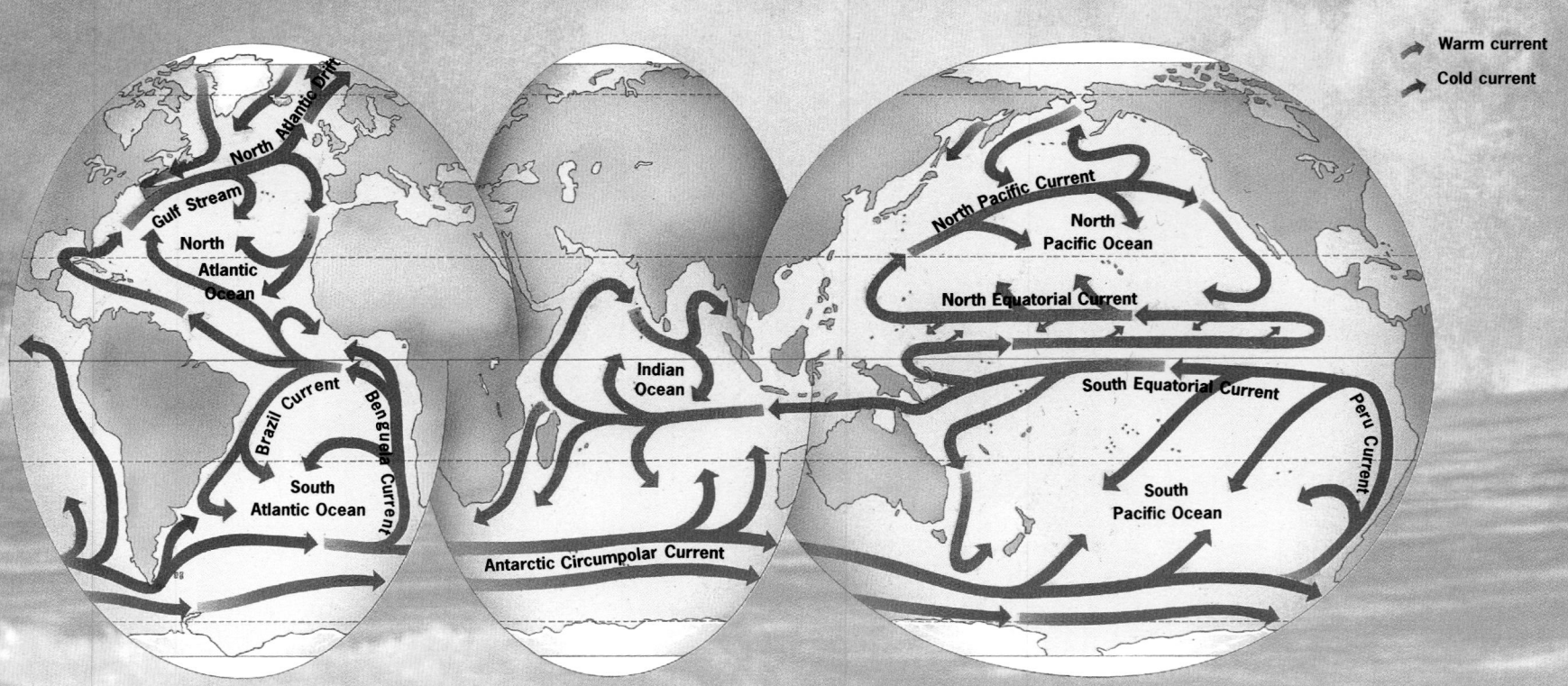

The global conveyor belt

There are "rivers" in the sea – powerful currents that move water in such prodigious volumes as to make the flow of even the mighty Amazon seem puny. The largest deep current, carrying cold water from the Arctic into the North Atlantic, moves 12 billion gallons (45 million kl.) – 25 times the volume of the Amazon.

Many of these currents are linked to a cycle that has been termed "the global conveyor belt." Warm surface water flows toward the North Atlantic Ocean. Between Florida and the Bahamas, the shape of the coast directs the water toward Europe. This current – the Gulf Stream – is driven by warm, moist, westerly winds that produce a warm, wet climate in northwest Europe. The water cools as it approaches the North Pole. At these latitudes ice forms on the surface of the sea. Because only fresh water freezes, the salinity of the remaining water is concentrated, which increases its density. It is this denser, colder, more saline water that feeds into the deep ocean currents, flowing more than 900 mi. (1,400 km.) into the South Atlantic and the Pacific.

Scourge of "The Child"

Every 10 years or so, a phenomenon known as El Niño occurs in the Pacific Ocean. During El Niño ("The Child" in Spanish, so called because it occurs around Christmas), the usual direction of the winds and ocean currents reverses – with disastrous effect. In 1982–83, the surface temperature of the Pacific Ocean at the equator rose almost 13°F (7°C) above normal. Peru's anchovy industry collapsed as fish fled to cooler waters. Indonesia and Australia were gripped by drought, while Ecuador and Peru were inundated by rainfall 300 times greater than normal. The causes of El Niño may be linked to higher sunspot activity occurring at similar intervals.

Good year

In a normal year (top right), easterly winds across the Pacific drive warm surface water to Oceania. Here storm clouds form, bringing heavy summer rains. Off South America cold, nutrient-rich water flows upward, creating rich fishing grounds.

Bad year

When El Niño occurs (bottom right), winds and ocean currents reverse. Warm currents and rain move eastward across the Pacific, creating drought in Oceania. The cold upwelling off South America is suppressed. Fish stocks diminish.

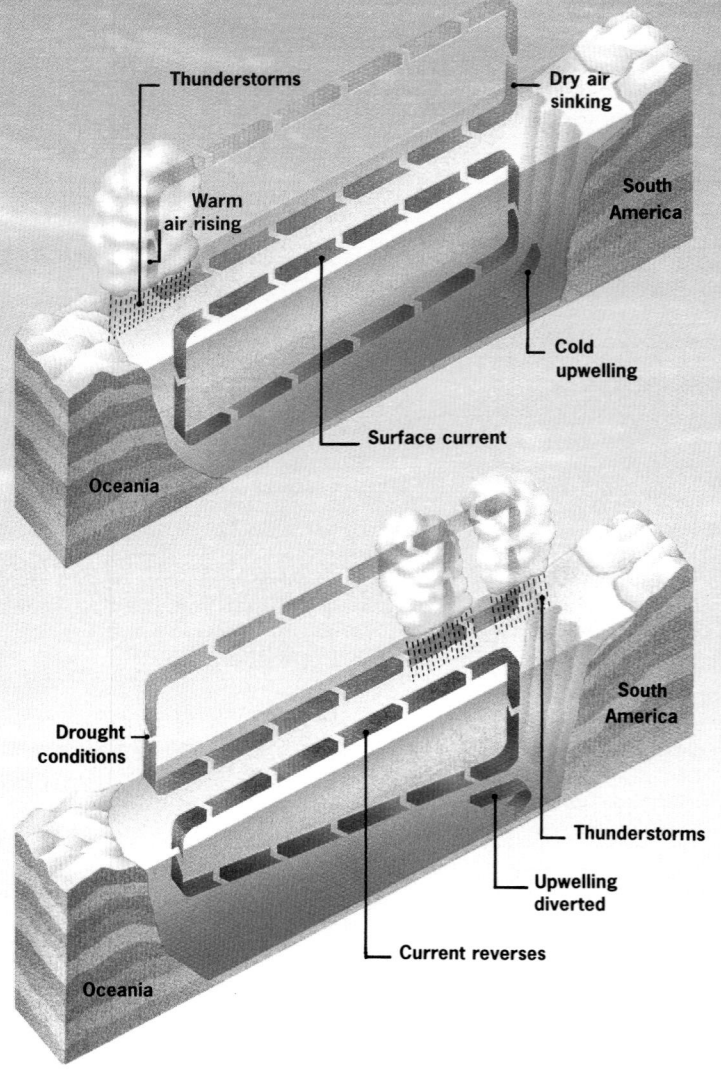

Warmer in the north

If the earth were a perfect sphere, the surface of the oceans would be warmest at the equator. However, surveys show that the highest temperatures occur a few degrees north of the equator. One explanation for this is that most of the world's sea water lies in the Southern Hemisphere – only 19 percent of which is land. As land heats faster than water, continents of the Northern Hemisphere make their surrounding seas warmer than those of the Southern Hemisphere.

Global turbulence

A computer simulation (left) of sea surface temperatures clearly shows the warm band of water (colored red) that stretches across equatorial seas. In the Pacific it can be seen breaking up into eddies. The model has been used to predict shifts in major currents, such as the Gulf Stream off North America.

How tides occur

Both the moon and sun exert a gravitational pull on the earth, but the sun, more distant, exerts a lesser pull. The pull of each body causes the oceans to bulge, producing tides.

Bulge due to the Moon

Bulge due to the Sun

Spring tide

Moon

Sun

Neap tide

Spring tide

Neap tide

Ebb and flow

The slow but constant rhythm of the tides is caused primarily by the gravitational pull of the moon, but the effect is not the same in all parts of the globe. The tidal range at any given place is influenced by such factors as the shape of a coastline, the depth of water, and the length of an inlet. The Mediterranean Sea is almost without tides, with a range of only 4 to 6 in. (10 to 15 cm.), yet the sea level in the Bay of Fundy on the east coast of Canada rises and falls by as much as 45 ft. (13.7 m.).

Spring tides

When the sun, moon, and earth are ranged along the same straight line (which occurs at either a new or a full moon), their tidal bulges coincide. This effect creates higher tides around the world, known as spring tides.

Opposite bulges

A tidal bulge forms on the side of the earth nearest to the moon (left). A second bulge – really a tail, or "wake" – occurs on the opposite side as the moon's pull on the earth is greater than its pull on the ocean on that side.

OCEANS AND SEAS OF THE WORLD	
Name	Area in sq. mi. (sq. km.)
Pacific Ocean	63,838,000 (165,340,000)
Atlantic Ocean	31,736,000 (82,196,000)
Indian Ocean	28,364,000 (73,462,000)
Arctic Ocean	5,426,000 (14,053,000)
South China Sea	1,148,500 (2,975,000)
Caribbean Sea	971,400 (2,516,000)
Mediterranean Sea	967,000 (2,505,000)
Bering Sea	876,000 (2,269,000)

Neap tides

Twice a month, the moon and sun are at right angles relative to the earth. The gravitational pulls of the sun and moon to some extent cancel each other out, making the lowest, or neap, tides.

LIFE IN THE SEAS AND OCEANS

Ocean wanderer

Blue-footed boobies sleep on the surface of the sea and rarely visit land, except to breed. They catch fish by diving steeply from the sky.

Blue-footed booby

It was in the primeval oceans that life began over 3 billion years ago. Today, the oceans cover two-thirds of the earth's surface and support as rich and varied a community of animal life as any that can be found on land. Ultimately, this community depends upon the plant life of the sea, which consists overwhelmingly of minute algae, known as phytoplankton. Like all other plants, these rely on light to produce energy. Below a depth of around 330 ft. (100 m.), light intensity is not sufficient to support energy production, so most phytoplankton are confined to the upper layers, as are the shoals of fish that feed on them and each other. Life does exist at depths of 2.5 mi. (4 km.) or more, but food there is scarce, consisting mainly of dead plants and animals and other detritus that sinks from above. In shallow waters and coral reefs, on the other hand, the sea floor supports some of the most varied and colorful animal species on earth.

Giant of the oceans

The main diet of the humpback whale (left) is krill, a shrimplike animal abundant in cold, polar waters. These whales travel to warmer waters only to breed.

Rulers of the oceans

The undisputed rulers of the seas are the fish, of which there are two main groups: the first, which includes the sharks and rays, have skeletons made of cartilage, while the second, which includes most other fish, have skeletons made of bone. Only bony fish have developed an air-filled buoyancy sac that enables them to hover in the water; cartilaginous fish must swim continuously, or else they would sink.

Just as on land, there are herbivores and carnivores. Efficient killers, such as sharks, tunas, and barracudas, feed voraciously on the vast shoals of anchovies, sardines, and herrings that graze the abundant plankton.

Killer colony

A Portuguese man-of-war (above left) is not a single jellyfish, but a colony of individual polyps. Some polyps sting, some reproduce, some feed, and others form the sail-like float.

Sargassum fish

Swimming serpent

The sea snake (left) secures its prey by injecting a fast-acting venom. This kills the victim before it has time to swim away.

Sea snake

Hiding out

The sargassum fish lives in the calm tropical waters of the Sargasso Sea. It is well camouflaged for lurking among the brown fronds of sargassum weed that form vast rafts in this sea.

Safety in numbers

Although shoals of anchovies (above) no doubt attract predators as a result of their sheer size, by massing together they can intimidate enemies and allow individual fish a much better chance of survival.

Deep headlights

One way to signal in the dark is to shine a light. Many deep-sea creatures, including the squid (below) and sea pen (right), have evolved clever ways to convert chemical energy into light energy. In order to trap prey without attracting predators, only part of the body is illuminated.

Fossil fan

The sea pen (right) represents an early phase of evolution: its fossilized remains have been found in rocks 500 million years old. It filters food through fan-shaped polyps.

Fishing with light

The deep-sea angler fish (below) uses a luminous lure to attract prey within reach of its mouth. These fish can live at depths of 2.5 mi. (4 km.).

Viper fish

The viper fish (right) has side lights to attract prey in the Pacific depths. At 12 in. (30 cm.) long, it has a huge gaping mouth and sharp teeth.

Luminous squid

Plankton soup

The ocean's food chain starts with billions of phytoplankton – microscopic plants – and equally vast numbers of zooplankton, the minute animals that feed on them. They multiply in the surface water, which is, in effect, a green "soup." Many marine species depend directly on this soup, from tiny fish and larvae to the largest living animal, the blue whale, which filters plankton through horny plates (baleen) suspended from the roof of its mouth.

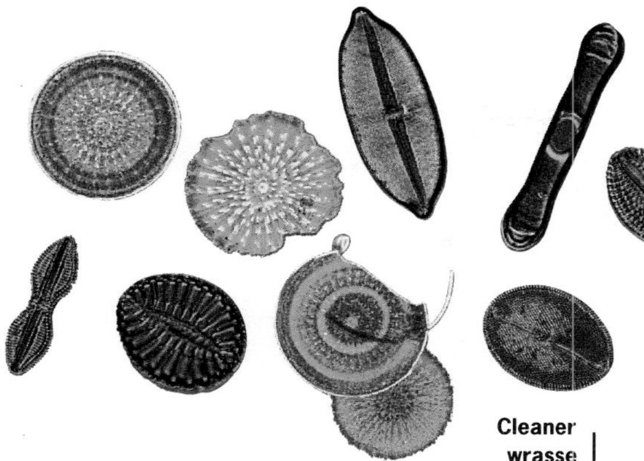

Eight open arms

Octopuses are highly evolved relatives of slugs and snails. They have tentacles with suckers to seize prey.

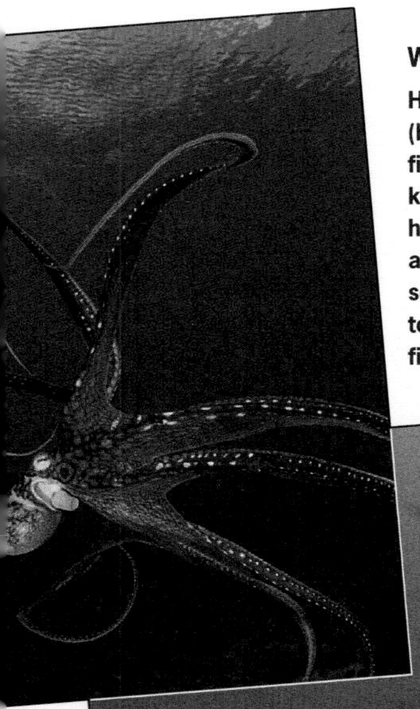

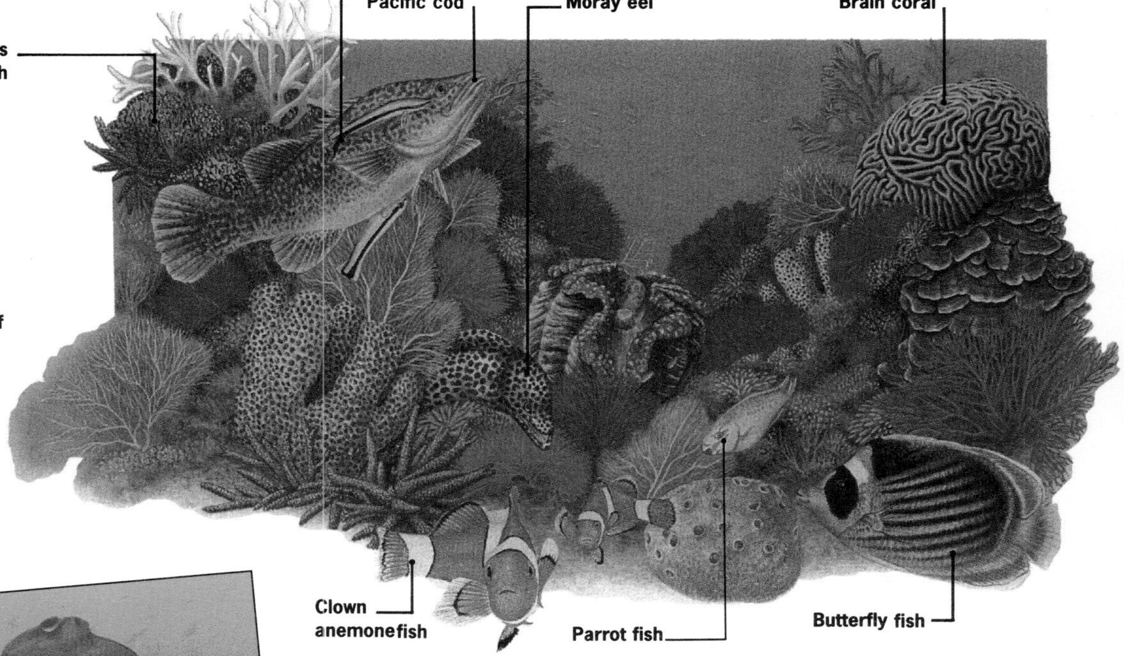

Wide-eyed hunter

Hammerhead sharks (below) have a wide field of vision and a keen sense of smell to help them hunt. They also use well-developed sensors on their heads to detect the electric field around their prey.

Coral community

Butterfly fish and parrot fish feed on coral, as does the voracious crown-of-thorns starfish. A single starfish can devastate 55 sq. ft. (5 sq. m.) of coral in a year. Moray eels lurk in holes to catch unwary prey. Anemone fish, such as clown fish, live protected among the stinging tentacles of sea anemones, which are fatal to other fish.

Floating plants

Diatoms (left) are one of the main groups of single-celled plants that make up phytoplankton (the term comes from Greek words meaning "wandering plants"). Magnification shows their elaborate and beautiful shells, made of silica or lime. All phytoplankton use the energy of sunlight to convert water and carbon dioxide into sugars and oxygen.

Cleaner wrasse

Crown-of-thorns starfish

Pacific cod

Moray eel

Brain coral

Clown anemonefish

Parrot fish

Butterfly fish

Flashing blade

The exact function of the swordfish's blade-like nose has yet to be determined. One possibility is that it is used to slash at prey.

Colonies of color

Coral reefs are home to a wider variety of sea creatures than any other marine habitat. All are attracted by the shelter and food sources that the reef creates. Coral itself is made up of huge communities of polyps – tiny creatures that filter out plankton from the sea. Each polyp builds its own hard limestone skeleton, and as each generation of polyps dies, it adds its skeletons to the foundations of the reef.

Coral will grow only where the water is clear, shallow, and warm, so reefs are found exclusively in tropical waters. The water temperature is most important – an average temperature lower than 68°F (20°C) would prevent the coral from flourishing.

Many reef residents are closely interdependent. Some small species of wrasse, for example, feed on the parasites attached to larger fish such as groupers and cods.

Hungry mouth

Deep-sea fish must grab what they can get, whatever the size, but may suffocate on a big mouthful. However, a fangtooth (below) can swallow and breathe at the same time.

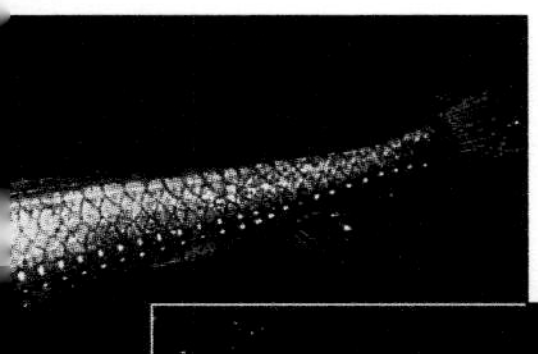

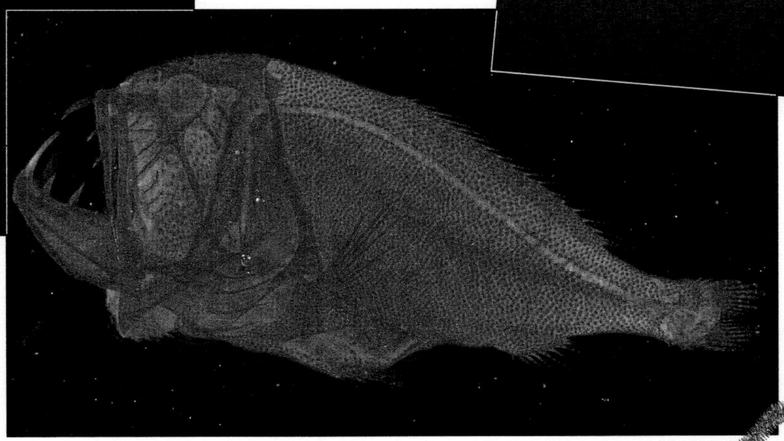

Sea cucumber

Sea spider

Brittle star

Long-term residents

Many of the ocean's inhabitants have changed little over hundreds of millions of years. Among them are sea cucumbers, sea urchins, brittle stars, jellyfish, sea anemones, and marine "worms." Crustaceans – including sea spiders, shrimps, lobsters, and crabs – are a primitive group that is as numerous in the world's seas as insects are on land. All these creatures have a constant food supply in the sediments of the seabed and the nutrient-rich waters of the ocean.

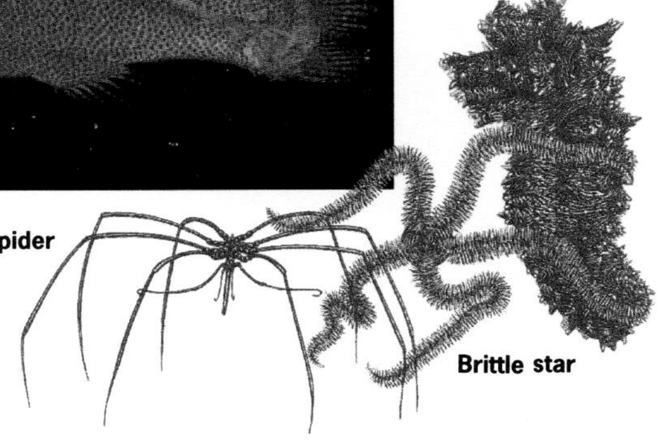

AT THE EDGES OF THE OCEANS

Where the restless waters of the oceans meet the land, their mighty sculpting power creates a dazzling variety of coastal formations. Surging waves carve magnificent arches and pillars out of cliff faces, for example, or grind rocks down into shifting patterns of fine sand. Such diverse features bring a range of challenges and opportunities for those life forms that make their home here. There are several different habitats, from the "splash zone" – beyond the highest tides but frequently soaked with salt spray – to the strip of beach closest to the sea and uncovered only at the lowest spring tides. The intertidal zone, submerged and then exposed twice daily by advancing and retreating tides, contains highly specialized communities of plants and animals. Sand and mud have a low oxygen content, which, combined with pounding waves, makes this a demanding environment for shore life. However, tide pools provide safe havens for many species as they await the returning tide.

The crumbling coast

The scouring power of water sweeping along a rocky coastline can create a natural gallery of dramatic features. Cliffs may contain areas of relatively soft rock, which waves erode, producing caves or cutting through a headland to form an arch. In time the roof of the arch may collapse, leaving a lonely stack separated from the shore.

Sand is driven along shorelines by currents, accumulating in places where the current is weaker. It may pile up into spits, which lengthen over time to create bars, as well as lines of barrier islands.

The power of water

As ocean currents beat against a coastline (right), rock is ground into sand while the waves cut an arch and stack from the solid rock of a headland.

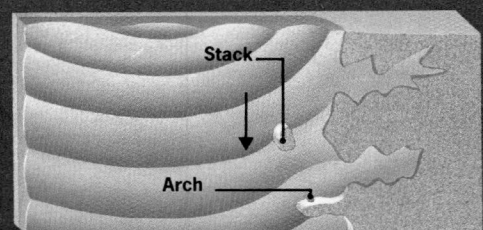

Further wear

Sand piles up into spits and tombolos, the latter linking rocks to the shore (left). The arch is eroded further until its roof collapses, leaving a second stack.

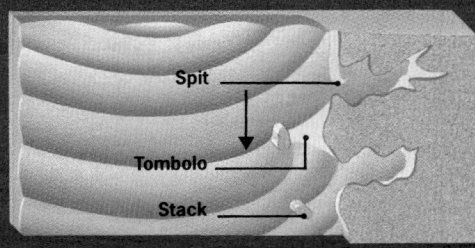

Reshaping the shore

As yet more sand accumulates (right), a spit gradually extends into a baymouth bar. The stacks and other rock features are now completely worn away.

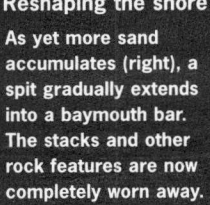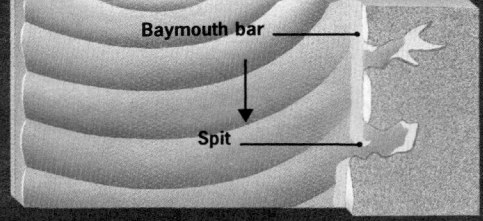

Shelter between the tides

For sea creatures a tide pool provides a safe "island" of water, surrounded at low tide by a "sea" of rock and sand. Yet it is still an exacting environment for aquatic life, with temperature fluctuations and periodic dilution by rainwater. It may be home to crabs and other crustaceans that can survive saltiness, rainfall acidity, and changes in temperature. Deeper pools may contain small fish, sea slugs, and even jellyfish from farther offshore. Around the pool's edge barnacles and mussels endure the low tides, their shells clamped tightly shut.

Refuge from the tide

A temperate tide pool (right) is home to many hundreds of species. The predators include hermit crabs, starfish, sea anemones, and blennies, which lurk near the bottom of the pool. Mussels anchor themselves firmly to the rock, filtering their food from the water. When high tides cover the pool, limpets roam the rock surface, grazing on algae. They return at low water to niches ground into the rock.

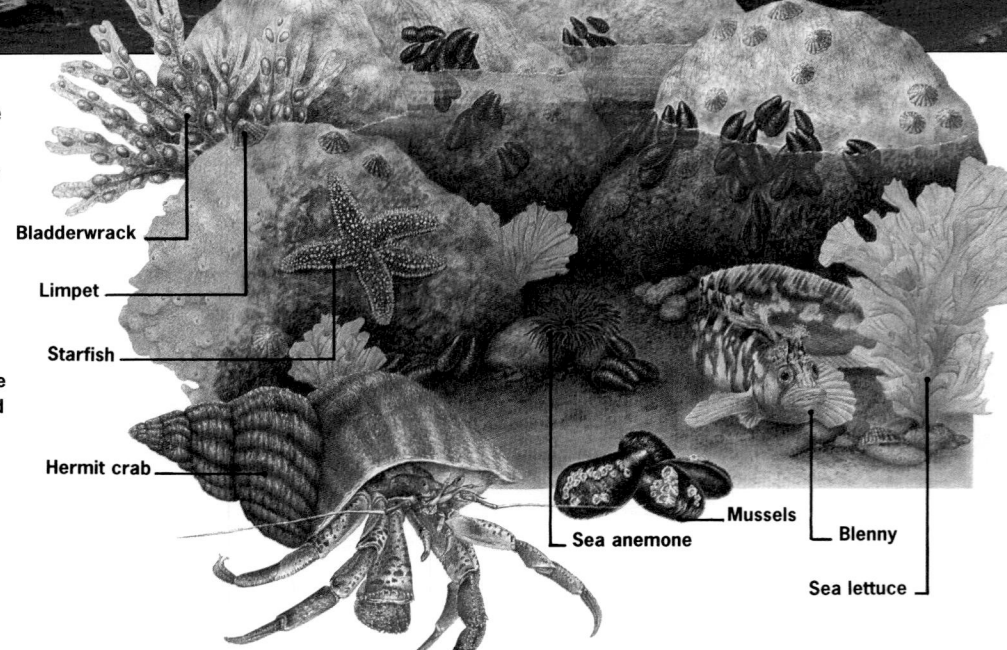

Bladderwrack

Limpet

Starfish

Hermit crab

Sea anemone

Mussels

Blenny

Sea lettuce

Life on the rocks

On a rocky shore thousands of seabirds nest high on cliffs, while lichens encrust the splash zone above high water. Kelp and seaweed forests growing underwater provide a habitat for shellfish and for fish and their predators, such as seals and sea otters. In the intertidal zone rocks may carry limpets, barnacles, and periwinkles and also form pools for other creatures.

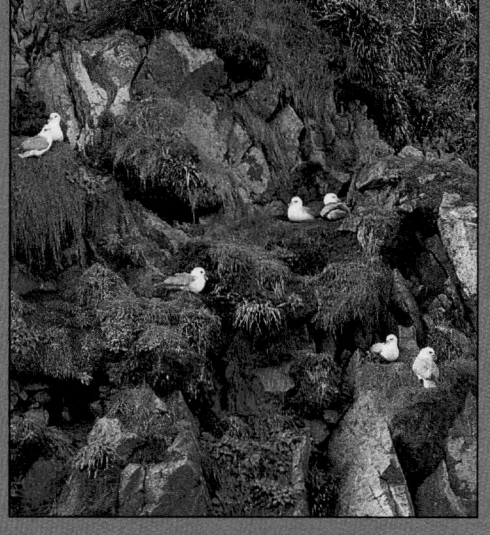

Cliff-nesting birds

Every spring, sea cliffs around the world become a temporary home for immense flocks of seabirds. Fulmars (left) breed on precarious cliff faces in the polar regions and along the coasts of northern Europe. Each pair lays a single white egg in a shallow dip on a ledge and incubates it for 50 days. The adult birds protect their only offspring ferociously, attacking any would-be predators with a volley of foul-smelling, half-digested food.

Sea-carved cliffs

The southern coast of Victoria in Australia (below) bears witness to the vast power of the sea, which has sculpted an assortment of lime-stone stacks, arches, and sandbars.

Ocean forest

Kelp is the "tree" of the ocean floor. Pacific kelp (below) grows to a length of 200 ft. (60 m.). It is anchored to the rocky seabed by a grasping holdfast. The many hundreds of life forms that hide within the cover of the kelp forest include sea urchins and abalones. The latter are feasted upon by sea otters.

Sandy shores

Sand is not the easiest of materials in which to make a home. At first, only marram grass takes root in the dry, salty dunes at the top of a beach, binding and compacting the sand for other plants, such as sea kale. Sand lower on the beach is equally inhospitable, being low in nutrients and regularly exposed to alternate wet and dry conditions. Rainfall may disturb its salt balance. Food supplies depend on the tides, which bring plankton to the burrowing shellfish and worms, whose presence is revealed by their casts left at low tide.

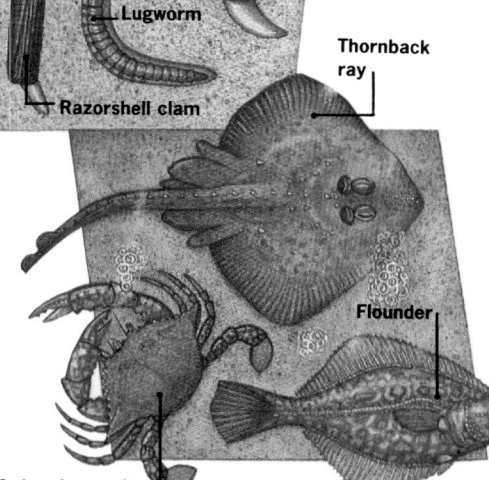

Cockle

Lugworm

Thornback ray

Razorshell clam

Flounder

Swimming crab

Filtering the sea

At high tide razorshell clams, lugworms, and cockles (top left) extend their filters or siphons into the water to feed on its harvest of microscopic plankton.

Beyond the tides

In the sandy shallows offshore are found the swimming crabs, whose flattened legs propel them along. On the seabed lurk "camouflaged" fish such as flounder and rays (left).

The River, from Source to Sea

Rivers most often start at a mountain spring or lake, whose cold, fast-flowing headstreams tumble down to gentler slopes, scouring into the earth to cut narrow valleys. Where streams join together, the river proper begins, its pace slowing as the landscape becomes flatter. In its lower reaches, a river may wind back and forth across its floodplain in a series of lazy meanders. Upon meeting the sea, it may fan out into a delta. As it passes through each of these different phases, a watercourse can play host to many forms of life – from mayfly and caddis fly larvae in the oxygen-rich mountain rills to the water snakes, caymans, crocodiles, and hippopotamuses that thrive in the muddy waters of a tropical meander.

North American dipper

Primrose

Mountain bloom

High in the Pyrenees between France and Spain, a rushing stream provides moisture for colorful plants (top). Among the plants growing at these heights is the bird's-eye primrose (above).

High cascade

As it plunges into a pool, this waterfall in Mt. Rainier National Park in Washington State provides a constant spray that promotes the growth of ferns, liverworts, and spongy mosses.

Riverbank vegetation

As well as watering the soil, rivers add moisture to the air through spray and evaporation. Even in dry mountain air, crevices beside a stream may contain rich greenery. Delicate ferns benefit from the constant mist of a waterfall, which is also an ideal habitat for plants such as liverworts and mosses.

In a dense forest a river provides a gap through which sunlight can reach the ground. Riverbanks in such regions are therefore colonized by a wide range of light-seeking shrubs.

White water

Rapids, like those on a river in Nepal (above), develop when a river flows down a steep valley. Boulders protruding from the riverbed force the water into a series of turbulent eddies.

Natural border

The Zambezi River (right), Africa's fourth longest, forms a natural border between Zambia and Zimbabwe. It winds through scattered scrub on its wide floodplain and ends its journey in a marshy delta.

Long-eared bat

Red lechwe

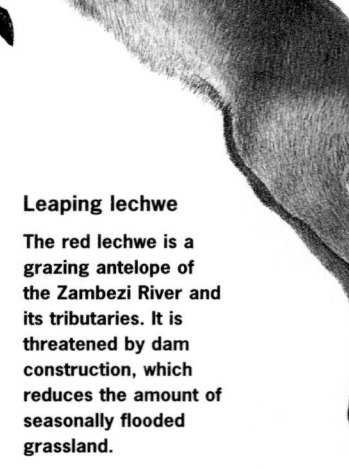

Underground sculpture

As raindrops fall through the air, they absorb carbon dioxide to become a very weak acid. If this rainwater falls on an area of limestone, it gradually dissolves the rock. Over millions of years this process of erosion enlarges cracks and creates caves and underground streams and rivers. Where water drips from the roof of a cave, it gives up its dissolved load of limestone. The solution is deposited – speck by speck – to form either a hanging stalactite or an upward-pointing stalagmite.

Safe shelter

Stalactites (left) hang in a cave carved by an underground river. The stable humidity and low, even temperature of such caves make them ideal hibernation sites for the long-eared bat. Caves also support their own specialized species of fungi, which feed on other cave-dwellers' waste as well as on detritus deposited by the river.

Leaping lechwe

The red lechwe is a grazing antelope of the Zambezi River and its tributaries. It is threatened by dam construction, which reduces the amount of seasonally flooded grassland.

Along the watercourse

Rivers are fed by rain falling on high terrain. The volume of water given to the river system depends partly on the underlying geology – porous rocks may absorb as much as 85 percent. Many rivers are dry for part of the year.

The fast water of a mountain stream scours away at the rock it passes over, carving out a steep-sided, V-shaped valley. Where the stream crosses an impervious layer of rock, its sculpting action is slowed. At a weak point in the rock, the river can cut through the hard layer, rapidly eating away softer rocks below to form a waterfall. In other places, patches of harder rock protrude into the riverbed, creating violent rapids.

The lowland, mature river winds through its own floodplain of alluvial soil, which is easily eroded. Slight bends in the river's course are exaggerated as the faster water on the outside of each bend cuts more quickly into the bank, while the slower water on the inside deposits sediment. In this way a loop in the river may eventually become cut off from the main stream, forming an oxbow lake.

As it approaches the ocean, a large river widens and its current slows down. Sediment is deposited to form sand-banks. These divide the river into the myriad channels of a delta or estuary, which provides a rich habitat for aquatic and bird life.

Dipper's dive

A North American dipper (left) is never far from water. It swims underwater in search of insect larvae and other invertebrates and can even walk along the riverbed. In places, these small birds have been seen to nest safely behind the constant protective curtain of a waterfall. The dipper is highly sensitive to acid rain. So while its presence is a sure sign of pure water, its sudden disappearance may be interpreted as an early warning of environmental threat.

Drawing breath

Slow, warm waters, such as those of the muddy, meandering Norman River in Queensland, Australia (bottom), contain little oxygen. The Australian lungfish (below) has coped with this problem by evolving a primitive lung as well as a set of gills. When the water at the bottom is too foul and stagnant to sustain life, the lungfish makes its way to the surface and draws in a gulp of air before diving again.

Australian lungfish

Traveling geese

The migration paths of Brent geese (below) are both long and complex. From summer breeding grounds inside the Arctic Circle, the geese fly to feeding grounds in the temperate river estuaries of Europe and North America.

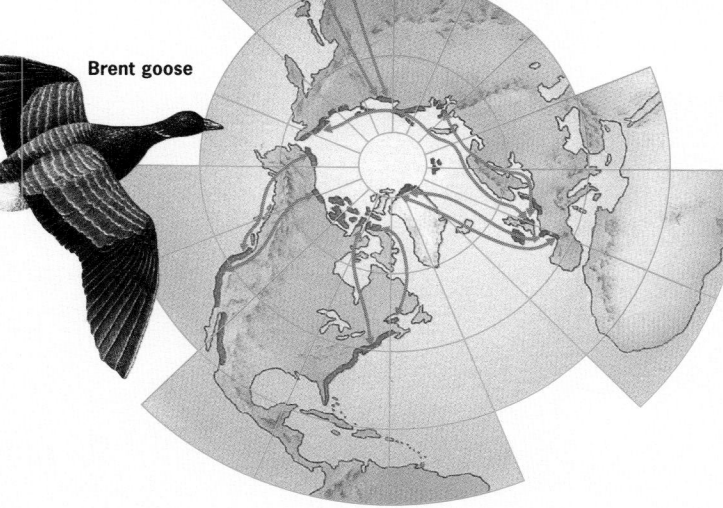

Brent goose

- ■ Winter
- ■ Summer
- ←→ Migration paths

Journey's end

The Blackwater Estuary in Essex, England (below), is one of the wintering grounds of the Brent goose. The fresh water of the river mixes with seawater in shifting channels that cut through the sediment deposited by the river as it slows.

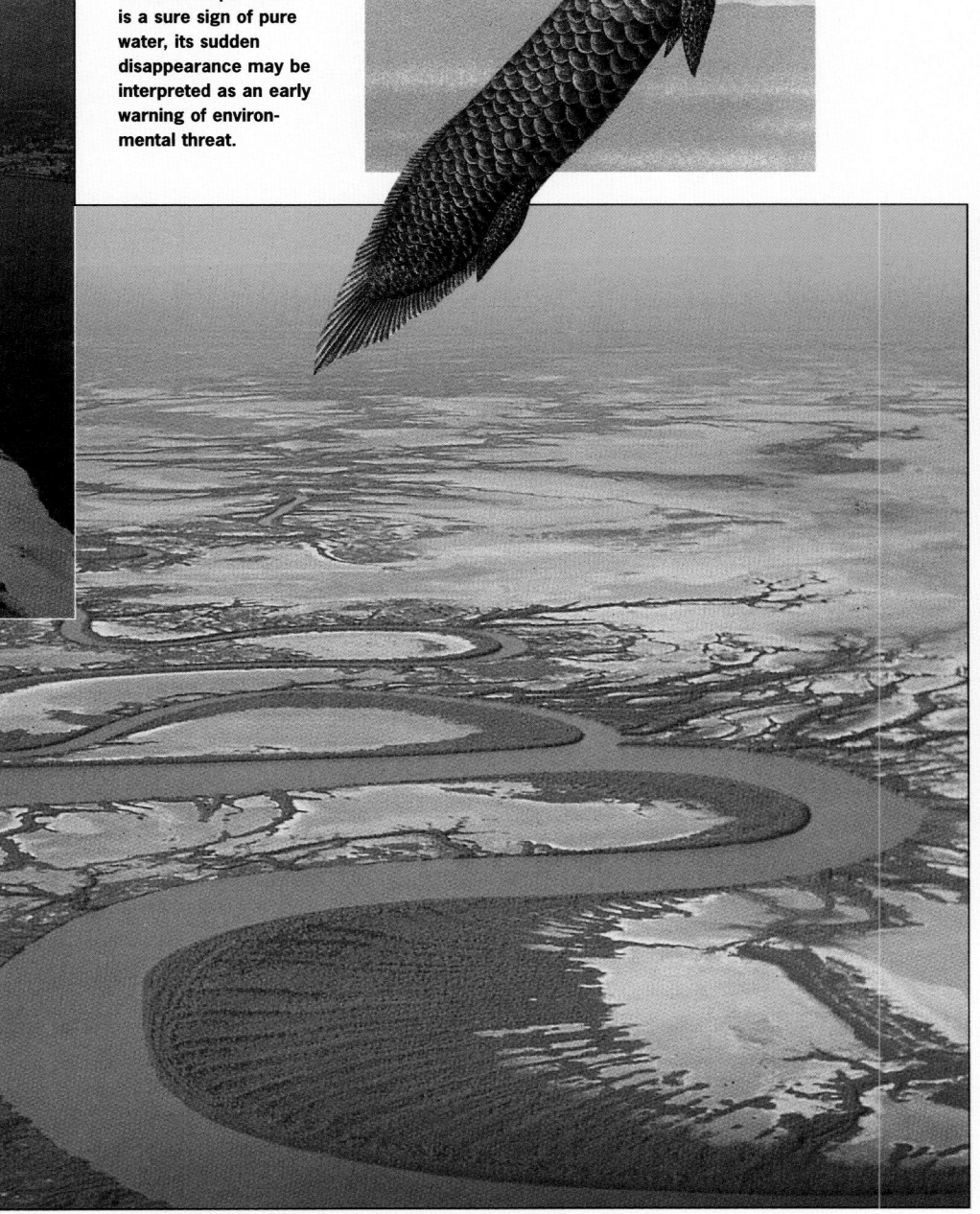

Vanishing waters

The Okavango River ends its journey in a landlocked basin in Botswana (above). The waters of the river are consumed by evaporation, forming a marshy delta – home for the Nile crocodile (right), Africa's largest reptile.

Nile crocodile

LAKES AND WETLANDS

The lakes and wetlands of the world are among the most valuable, yet most threatened, of our natural habitats. Lakes are formed either when hollows fill up with water or when natural drainage is obstructed. Some are the result of movements in the earth's crust; others are caused by glaciation or fill the craters of extinct volcanoes. Wetlands also take a variety of forms, from stagnant inland bogs to saltwater coastal mangrove swamps. Bodies of water may disappear altogether or acquire new features over time. Rivers can bring in silt and mud, which gradually build up into layers of sediment, reducing the water's depth. In some wetlands the level of nutrients increases slowly over thousands of years, accompanied by changes in the water's community of plants and animals. Sometimes the water will gradually silt up to become scrub and then woodland. Abrupt changes in the ecology can result when a lake becomes polluted by industry, acid rain, or intensive farming.

Snail kite

Pink wader

The roseate spoonbill probes with its beak to find food in the muddy waters of the Southern Everglades. An endangered species, it is being conserved at breeding sanctuaries on the island of Trinidad.

Roseate spoonbill

American alligator

Manatee

Garpike

Choosy eater

The main diet of the snail kite is the apple snail. Swamp drainage has reduced the snail population, so that only a thousand or so snail kites inhabit the U.S.

Rapacious reptile

Both crocodiles and alligators are found in the Everglades National Park. The two can be differentiated by their teeth: alligators have a distinct overbite.

Vanishing wilderness

The Florida Everglades was once an immense freshwater marsh, home of the Florida panther and American crocodile. Now both are threatened by human activities, in particular by drainage and water pollution. Only a handful of panthers and a few hundred crocodiles remain. The Everglades is sustained by fresh water filtering down to the sea from Lake Okeechobee, which collects water from the Florida Peninsula via the Kissimmee River. This river originally meandered but was straightened to create dry land for building and agricultural use. It must now be returned to its natural state if sufficient water is to reach Everglades National Park, the last remnant of this unique habitat.

Lurking carnivore

The wetlands, lakes, and rivers of North America are home to the gar. This carnivorous fish has large eyes and long jaws full of needlelike teeth for securing prey.

Hungry herbivore

The manatee is an herbivore that needs to eat 66 lbs. (30 kg.) of food a day to maintain its weight. Sadly, many of these rare creatures are maimed by whirring speedboat propellers.

Mangrove swamps

Red mangroves cope with the unstable, stagnant mud of a shallow river estuary on the Everglades' margins (left) by growing a tangle of arching prop roots. The roots form rafts that support the plants in the unstable mud. Pores in the roots allow the plants to "breathe" when the waters recede.

Dangerous interference

Lakes tend to develop specialized plant and animal communities that live together in a delicate balance. Disruption from direct pollution, acid rain, or an introduced species can be disastrous.

The introduction of perch into Lake Victoria in Africa in 1958 has caused the extinction of many of the lake's 170 species of cichlid – nearly all of which were unique to the lake. This has disturbed the ecology of the lake and the livelihood of people on its shoreline.

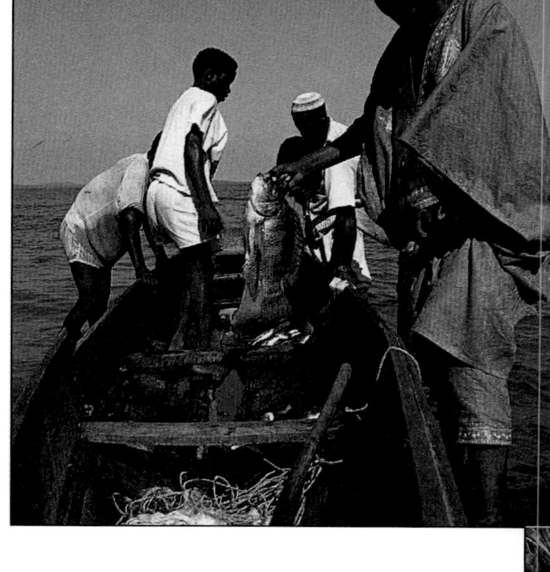

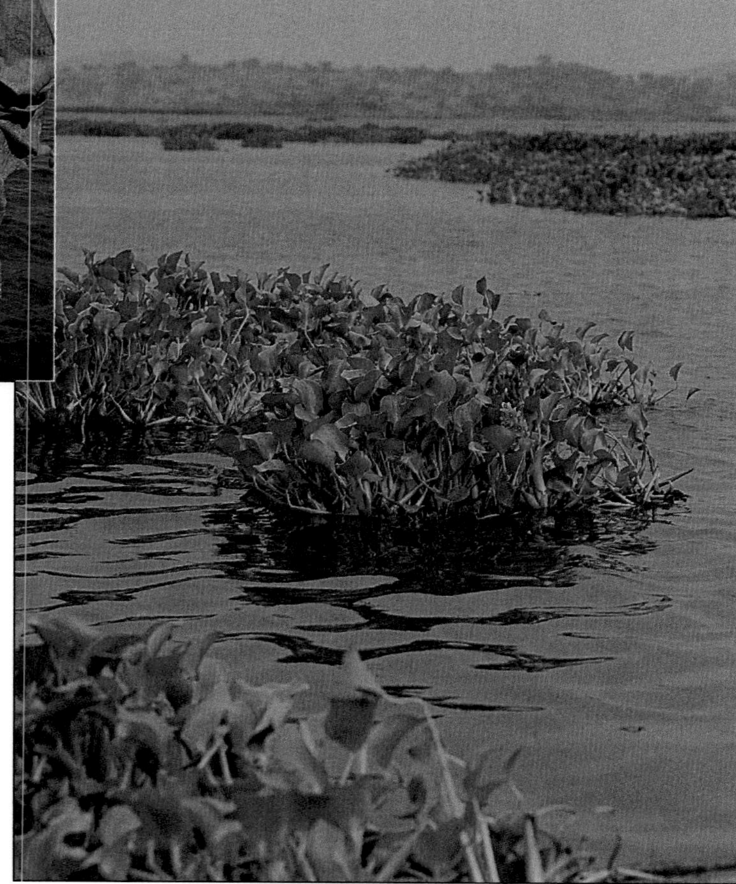

The jewel of Siberia

Lake Baikal in Russia contains one-fifth of the world's fresh water. The deepest lake on earth, it occupies a rift valley that is seven times as deep as the Grand Canyon and filled with 25 million years' accumulated sediment. The lake is fed by some 300 rivers but drained by only one. A complete change of water takes at least 400 years, so the lake is vulnerable to pollution. Rivers carry industrial waste, and pulp mills along the lakeshore add to the problem.

Lake Baikal

Lake Baikal (below) is literally a hotbed of life – its depths are stirred and heated by volcanic forces, creating swirling currents as warm water rises and cold water sinks. These currents prevent the stagnation usual in most deep lakes. At least half of the lake's 2,600 animal and plant species are unique, and all are under threat.

Meager catch

Before the Nile perch was brought to Lake Victoria (above), tilapia fish and cichlids fed the local people and sustained their economy.

Unwanted bloom

Water hyacinth is a weed found on Lake Victoria (right). It grows rapidly, forming dense rafts that cover the surface of the water.

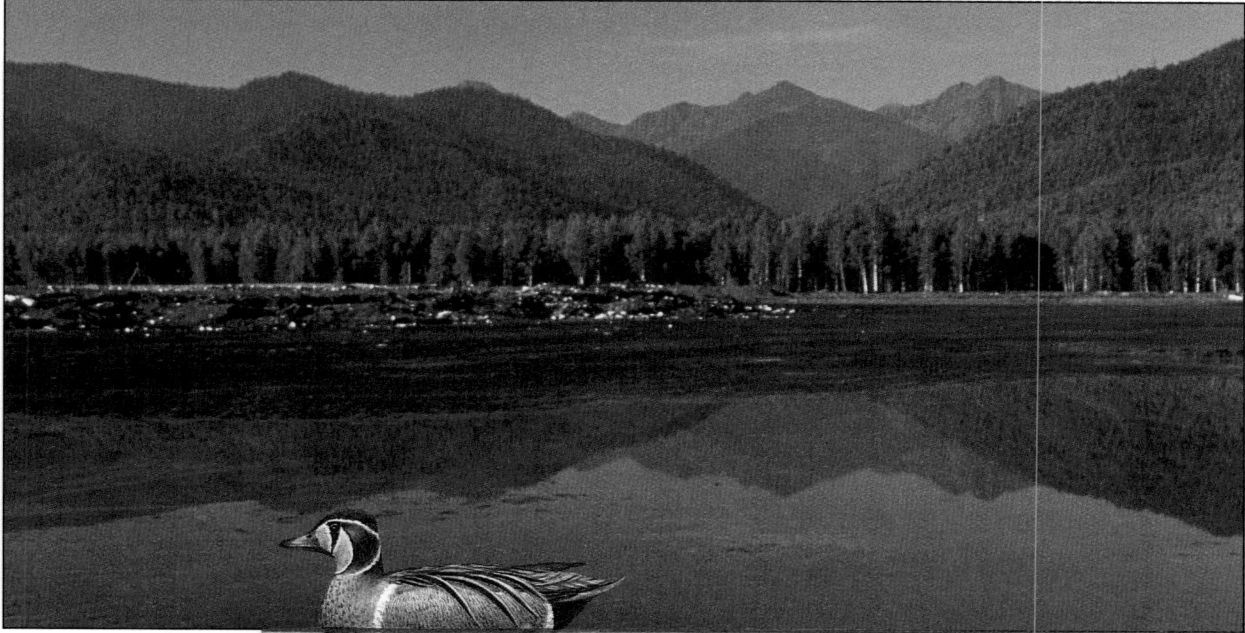

THE WORLD'S LARGEST LAKES

Name	Area sq. mi. (sq. km.)	Max. depth ft. (m.)
Caspian Sea	143,250 (371,020)	3,264 (996)
Superior	31,800 (82,360)	1,332 (406)
Victoria	26,800 (69,410)	279 (85)
Huron	23,010 (59,600)	748 (228)
Michigan	22,180 (57,450)	922 (281)
Aral Sea	14,280 (36,990)	223 (68)
Tanganyika	12,700 (32,890)	4,855 (1,481)
Baikal	12,160 (31,490)	5,315 (1,621)
Great Bear	12,100 (31,340)	1,355 (413)
Nyasa	9,000 (23,310)	2,224 (678)

FACTS ABOUT THE GREAT LAKES
• Lake Superior is the largest and deepest.
• Lake Ontario is the smallest.
• Lake Erie is the shallowest.
• Lake Michigan is the only one entirely in the U.S.

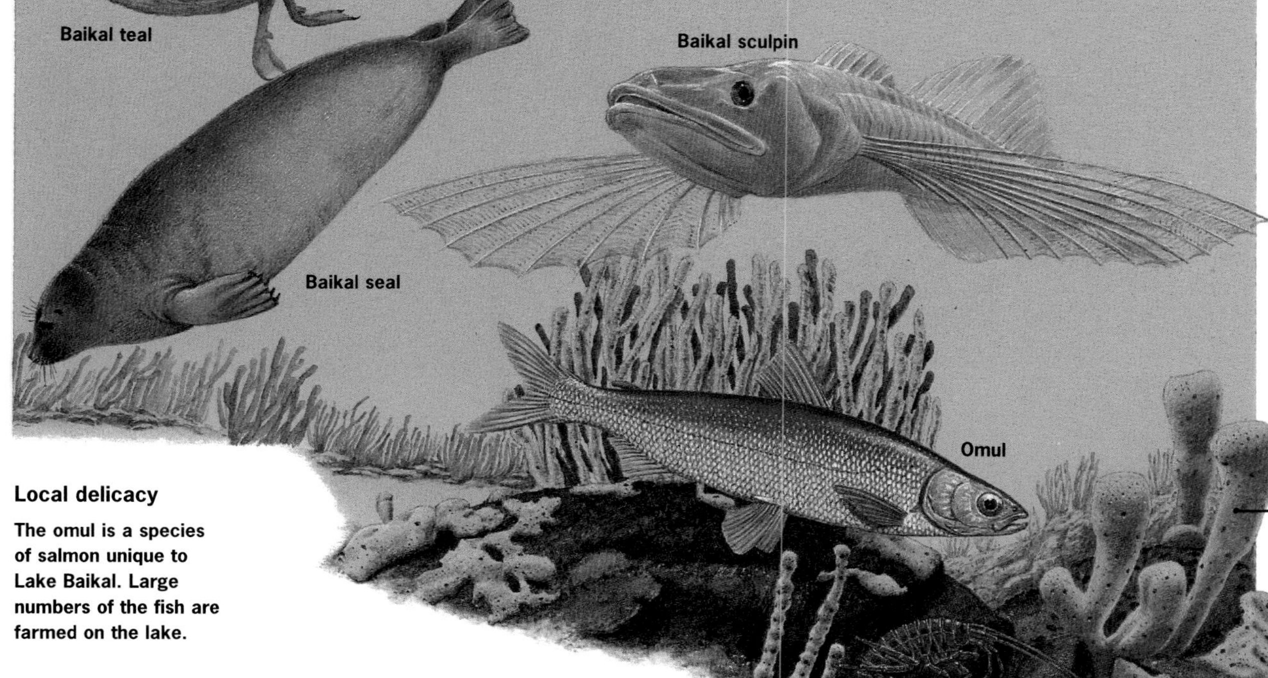

Bobbing about

The Baikal teal is a duck that breeds in and around Lake Baikal as well as other Siberian forest regions.

Siberian seal

The Baikal seal lives in Lake Baikal – 2,500 mi. (4,000 km.) from its nearest marine cousins. It is the only freshwater seal in the world, and the only mammal among the lake's 1,400 animal species. The greatest numbers of Baikal seals live in the lake's less-polluted northern part.

Local delicacy

The omul is a species of salmon unique to Lake Baikal. Large numbers of the fish are farmed on the lake.

Baikal teal

Baikal sculpin

Baikal seal

Omul

Upwardly mobile

The Baikal sculpin amazes biologists by its daily migrations from the depths to the shallows of the lake in search of food.

Sponges

Baikal is unique among deep lakes in having freshwater sponges that thrive on the lake floor, thanks to deep currents that carry both oxygen and nutrients to them.

Baikal sponge

THE POLAR REGIONS

At the North and South Poles, the sun's rays make only glancing contact with the surface of the earth, making these icy, remote regions the coldest places on the planet. Physically, the Arctic and Antarctic are quite dissimilar. The North Pole lies in the middle of the frozen expanse of the Arctic Ocean, while the South Pole sits on the frozen continent of Antarctica, which has mountain peaks that soar more than 13,200 ft. (4,030 m.) above the ice. Both regions are hugely inhospitable to life. Surprisingly, a lack of water (in its liquid form) is as much of a challenge as the intense cold. Few green plants can grow, as there are no soils to provide anchorage and nutrients. The animals that do live near the poles are all endothermic, or warm-blooded – there are no reptiles or amphibians on the ice caps – and most take their food from the sea. This means that the fauna of polar regions is concentrated in a narrow strip beside unfrozen stretches of the oceans.

Life in Antarctica

The animal life of Antarctica includes many bird species, particularly penguins, and millions of ticks and lice. Two of the seal species are named after Antarctic seas: the Weddell seal, an expert deep diver that can stay below water for as long as 70 minutes, and the Ross seal, a skillful swimmer that lives on the pack ice and catches squid and octopus. The most abundant Antarctic seal is the crab-eater, which has specialized teeth to filter krill from the water. The notorious leopard seal feeds on penguins, other sea birds, and even seals. The massive elephant seal takes its name from the male's flexible snout.

Both seals and penguins spend most of their life in the sea, coming ashore to produce offspring. Paddlelike limbs and heads merging smoothly into their bodies make them facile swimmers.

Emperors of the ice

Emperor penguins are the only species to breed on the ice during the harsh Antarctic winter. The female lays a single egg onto the ice. This is incubated by the male, who holds it on top of his feet, covered by a feathered fold of skin to keep it warm. Thousands of incubating males huddle together for warmth until the end of the winter, when the eggs hatch, whereupon both parents feed the chicks.

Polar hunter

Killer whales are the largest species of the dolphin family. Males can grow to more than 30 ft. (9 m.). Living in shoals of about 50 individuals, they feed on a wide range of prey, including seals and penguins, as well as fish and other dolphins.

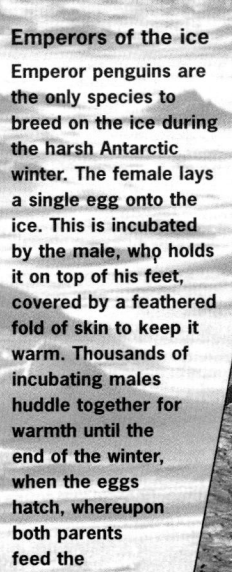

Sun at midnight

As the earth orbits the sun, its tilt remains constant. Across most of the world, the seasons make this apparent, with longer days in summer and shorter days in winter. But at the poles the effect is much more extreme. During a polar midwinter, when the Pole is pointing away from the sun, each day is a 24-hour "night." At midsummer, when the Pole is tilted toward the sun, continuous daylight occurs (right). At evening the sun sinks lower as if about to set, but at midnight, still above the horizon, it starts to rise again. The Arctic and Antarctic circles mark, respectively, the southern and northern limits of the regions where – for at least one day per year – the sun neither rises nor sets.

The ozone layer

Ultraviolet (UV) radiation from the sun can split molecules of oxygen into their constituent atoms, which recombine to form ozone, a colorless gas. The ozone layer in the earth's atmosphere is vital to life, as it absorbs damaging UV radiation. In the early 1980s a "hole" – a region of depleted ozone – was found above the South Pole. Research showed that this was due to reactions involving synthetic chemicals called CFCs. These are now being phased out, but it may take up to a century for the ozone to replenish itself.

Broken shield

The ozone layer, located some 5 to 30 mi. (8 to 48 km.) above the earth, screens out harmful UV radiation (right). CFCs, used in coolants and aerosols, are broken down by UV radiation into chlorine, which attacks the ozone shield. Winter wind patterns over Antarctica create a region of almost still air, where ozone-depleting chlorine builds up, before being unleashed in spring.

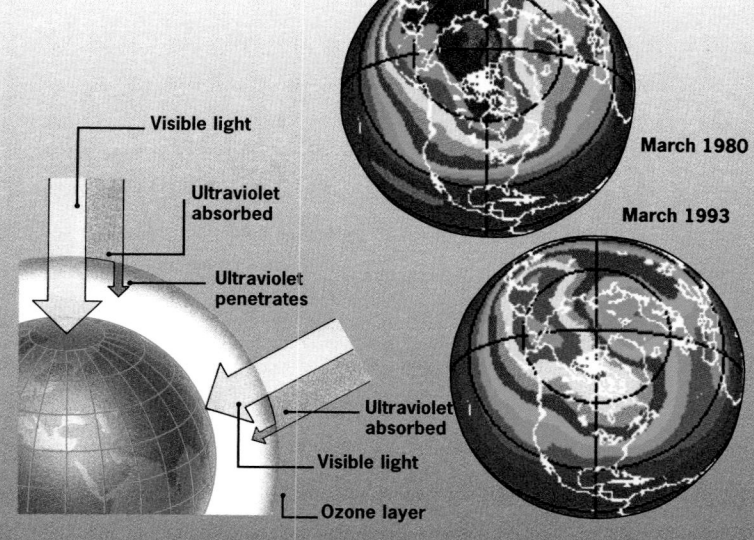

Visible light
Ultraviolet absorbed
Ultraviolet penetrates
March 1980
March 1993
Ultraviolet absorbed
Visible light
Ozone layer

Hole in the north

The ozone hole over the Arctic is smaller than that over the Antarctic, but still significant. The globe comparison (left) shows the enlargement of the ozone hole above the North Pole during a 13-year period. Areas of high ozone concentration are shown in red.

Life in the Arctic

The Arctic and Antarctic regions each contain a different set of mammals and birds, although seals as a group are common to both. In the Antarctic there is no counterpart of the northern polar bear, and the Arctic has no penguins.

The ringed seal is a small species common on the Arctic pack ice. Also native to the region are the harp seal, bearded seal, and hooded seal.

In addition to the polar bear, land mammals of the Arctic include the arctic hare, the ermine, and the arctic fox, which all retreat south to the tundra during the coldest months.

The edges of the Arctic ice cap provide a rich feeding ground for birds such as guillemots, razorbills, and puffins. Most breeding birds migrate to warmer climes at summer's end.

Seals and bears

Harp seals spend most of their time at sea, but climb onto the sea ice to mate and have pups, as well as to molt. They breed in large colonies in the Arctic. The pups are white at first, molting into a blotchy juvenile coat (bottom) before they acquire the adult pattern: light gray with a black head and harp-shaped flank patches (below). They are hunted by polar bears and the Inuit, who make use of their skin, flesh, and fat for food, clothing, and shelter.

Tusked titans

Like seals, walruses have to come onto land or solid ice to give birth. Both sexes have tusks (the males' slightly longer than the females'), used mainly in display to establish dominance. The mustache of stiff, sensitive bristles helps the walrus in its search for food, even in total darkness.

Lonely hunter

The polar bear hunts throughout the year on the Arctic pack ice. An accomplished swimmer, it is fast and agile on land, its hairy feet providing a good grip on the ice. Polar bears feed mostly on seals as they come up to breathe through holes in the ice. But they will eat anything available, including fish, young whales or walruses, and even carrion.

THE FRIGID FAR NORTH

For a few weeks each summer, the land in Alaska, Canada, Greenland, Scandinavia, and Siberia between the frozen Arctic Ocean and the northern fringes of the great forests bursts into life with fresh plant growth. This is the tundra, a region so cold that the ground just below the surface remains permanently frozen. Winter lasts eight to nine months, with temperatures falling to –22°F (–30°C). Only tough, low-growing plant species can survive on the acidic, waterlogged soils. Many of the animals, such as caribous, are migrants, drawn northward in herds from the forests toward the rich summer foraging. In their wake follow predators – namely, wolves. Perhaps the tundra's most populous summer inhabitants are mosquitoes. They emerge in such prodigious numbers that caribou may take refuge on the lingering snowfields, where cold air deters these blood-seeking insects. Only a few animal species stay put for the long winter, burrowing into deep snow for shelter.

Changing coats

In winter the tundra merges into the polar regions, hidden below a thick covering of snow. But in summer the snows melt to leave a landscape of greens, browns, and grays. A dark animal stands out against snow, while a white-coated animal is equally obvious against plants and rocks, so many residents of the tundra have evolved to change the color of their fur or feathers with the seasons. Among the birds that show such changes are the ptarmigan and the snow goose; among the mammals are the arctic hare and arctic fox.

Land carved by cold

Just below the surface of the tundra, at a depth of about 20 in. (51 cm.), is a frozen layer called permafrost, which – as its name implies – never thaws out. The soil above thaws in summer, but the water cannot drain away. It collects on the surface and forms marshy pools. The tundra is dotted with features that have been shaped by ice, such as domed polygons and ice hills. Of the earth's total land surface, 26 percent is permafrost. Global warming threatens the tundra: even a slight rise in temperature could melt some of the permafrost, flooding huge areas.

Clear of frost

The trans-Alaska pipeline, 4 ft. (1.2 m.) wide, carries oil from the state's northern shore to ice-free Valdez in the south. The pipe is raised on stilts to minimize freeze-thaw damage, to allow access for maintenance, and to limit damage to the sensitive permafrost beneath. The exploitation of oil and minerals continues to threaten the tundra.

Gray hunter

The gyrfalcon is a tundra predator. Specimens from the north have white feathers; farther south, feathers are gray.

Gyrfalcon

Polygons

Domed polygons (below) form when cracks in the ground fill with water. This water expands as it freezes, pushing the land upward. Cold passes through rock more easily than through soil, so the ice forms first beneath the stones. As they are pushed to the surface, they roll into the ditches surrounding the polygons.

Tundra plants

The tundra is a windswept, treeless plain. Plants are mostly ground hugging (such as moss, lichen, and dwarf willow) or else hummock forming (such as grass, sedge, and heather). Other plants, such as the arctic poppy, have thick, hairy stems that will not succumb to the fierce, icy winds. Plants survive the low winter temperatures beneath an insulating layer of snow. The soil is acidic, waterlogged, and often deficient in nutrients. To overcome this, some plants, such as butterworts, are carnivorous, feeding on the insects that swarm during the tundra summer.

Mountain avens

Arctic poppy

Dwarf willow

Sphagnum moss

Mosquito

Blood suckers

In spring mosquito larvae hatch from eggs in pools of melting snow. By summer adults throng the air, the females thirsty for blood to fuel egg production. The vast numbers of mosquitoes attract migrant birds.

The incredible journey

As the cold, dark days of winter approach, most large mammals leave the tundra for the protection of forests to the south. One exception is the musk ox, which builds up reserves of fat during summer. Other mammals, such as lemmings and ermines, are too small to make the journey. These remain through the winter, tunneling under the snow to find food. Most tundra birds are migrants, which fly south when their insect food supply runs out in autumn.

CANADA

Winter feeding grounds

Summer feeding grounds

The long trek

Caribous live in North American tundra regions. They are the same species as the Scandinavian reindeer but have not been domesticated. Adults of both sexes have well-developed antlers, but those of the males are larger. Great herds of up to 100,000 caribous migrate 6,200 mi. (10,000 km.) from the forests of Canada northward each summer to feed on the tundra (above). During their journey they often have to cross icy, fast-flowing rivers (right).

Ice hill

Ice mounds, or pingos, are common sights near tundra rivers or lakes (below). At the heart of each hill is a core of ice, gradually pushed upward by pressure from the surrounding land.

These strange hills can be as high as 230 ft. (70 m.). When cracks on the mound become deep enough to expose the ice core, it melts, collapsing the mound and leaving a circular rampart.

Hare of the north

The arctic hare (brown in summer, white in winter) is unlike other hares in that it digs a burrow, rather than sleeping in a shallow depression.

Arctic hare

Defensive formation

Shaggy-coated musk oxen (below) bunch together for protection from the cold. Facing outward, they use their horns to defend against hungry predators.

Arctic fox

Plumage

Ptarmigans (right) acquire white plumage during winter and so remain hidden from predators such as the gyrfalcon. They feed on buds, shoots, berries, insects, and worms.

Ptarmigan

Hidden hunter

Arctic foxes (right) feed on small mammals and birds, changing color through the year to remain camouflaged. In winter they sometimes feed from frozen stores of earlier kills.

WHERE RAIN SELDOM FALLS

With less than 10 in. (25.4 cm.) of rain per year, a desert is defined not by its heat but by its aridity. The Sahara, by day, is one of the hottest places on earth, with temperatures often exceeding 122°F (50°C), though heat loss under cloudless skies brings the mercury down dramatically at night. Other deserts, such as the Gobi, are hot in summer but in winter can be as cold as −4°F (−20°C). Typically, warm deserts receive less than 5 in. (12.7 cm.) of rain annually, and most of that evaporates. With such a scarcity of water, this environment might be expected to be completely lifeless. In fact, most animal groups have species that are adapted to these conditions. Despite the scant soil tough grasses, cacti, and other spiny shrubs succeed in pushing their roots down to reach any moisture lying beneath the surface of the sand. Other plants survive by having seeds that germinate and flower rapidly after seasonal rains, completing their life cycles within a few months.

King of the cacti

A saguaro cactus dominates a stretch of the Sonoran Desert of Arizona (right). These treelike plants are the largest of all cacti, reaching heights up to 57 ft. (17 m.) and living up to 200 years. They are topped with clusters of large, showy flowers that attract swarms of pollinating insects.

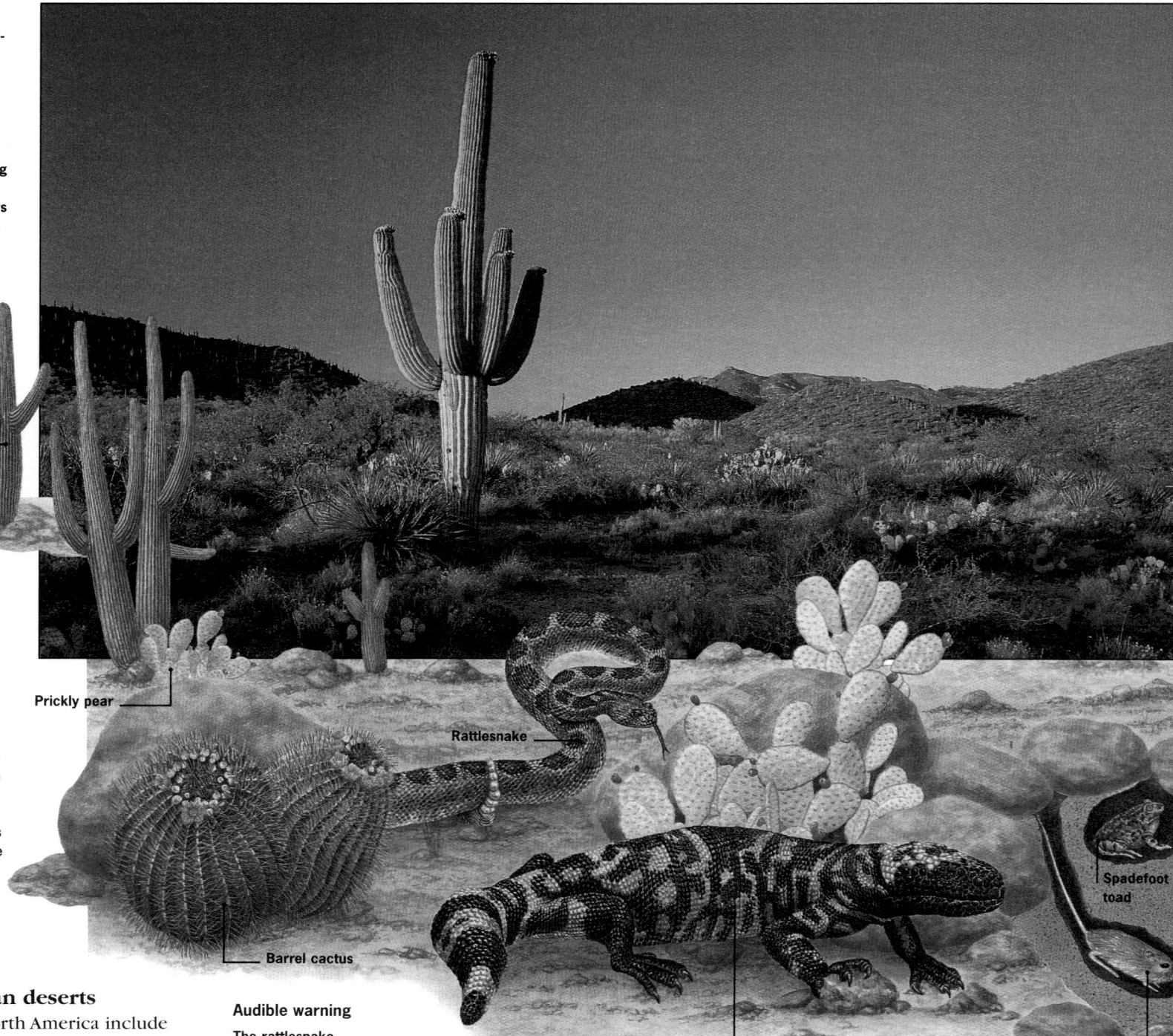

Saguaro cactus

Spiny sponge

Cacti are superbly adapted to harsh desert conditions. They have thick, fleshy stems where moisture is stored, and in place of leaves, they have sharp spines that deter grazers. The barrel cactus's rotund stem is adapted for storing water. The pads of the prickly pear face east-west, so that at midday only the edges catch the blistering heat of the sun.

Prickly pear

Rattlesnake

Barrel cactus

Gila monster

Spadefoot toad

Kangaroo rat

North American deserts

The deserts of North America include the Great Basin Desert of Nevada, Utah, and Oregon, and the Mojave, Sonoran, and Chihuahuan Deserts of the Southwest. These landscapes contain not golden dunes, but stony soils with rocky outcrops. There are two rainy periods, one in winter and one in summer. Most cacti and annual flowers bloom after the winter rains. The deciduous creosote bush, whose oldest specimens are some 11,500 years old, puts out leaves at this season but is able to flower at any time.

Audible warning

The rattlesnake belongs to a group called pit vipers. Heat-sensitive organs between the eye and nostril act like infrared "eyes," so that the snake can locate prey in total darkness by tracking its body heat. Horny interlocking segments at the end of the tail vibrate, making a rattling sound that warns would-be predators.

Lethal lizard

The gila monster (above) is a venomous reptile that feeds on small mammals and birds. Venom is produced by glands in its lower jaw and flows along grooves in its teeth. The motion of chewing increases the flow of poison.

Going underground

The spadefoot toad, like all amphibians, needs water for the tadpole stage of its life cycle. The toad survives the heat of the Sonoran Desert by remaining in a deep burrow for periods of up to nine months, emerging only when it rains. The kangaroo rat shelters from the sun in its burrow, where moisture loss is minimized. As it breathes, water vapor is absorbed by its store of seeds. The rat then regains the moisture by consuming the seeds. When it emerges to feed at night, it becomes vulnerable to many predators, such as owls and snakes.

Desert regions

Deserts and arid zones cover more than a quarter of the earth's land surface – mainly in the interiors of continents, where atmospheric pressure is high and rainfall low, or where distance from any ocean limits rainfall. Deserts also form in areas where offshore winds predominate, such as the Atacama Desert in South America. Here the air is nearly always cool and dry, the winds having lost most of their moisture as they passed over adjacent land masses.

Desert markers

A pair of date palm trees marks a point in the dunes of the Sahara Desert (below) where the ground water is at or near the surface. Date palms thrive in the hot desert climate, but they must have frequent water during their fruiting season.

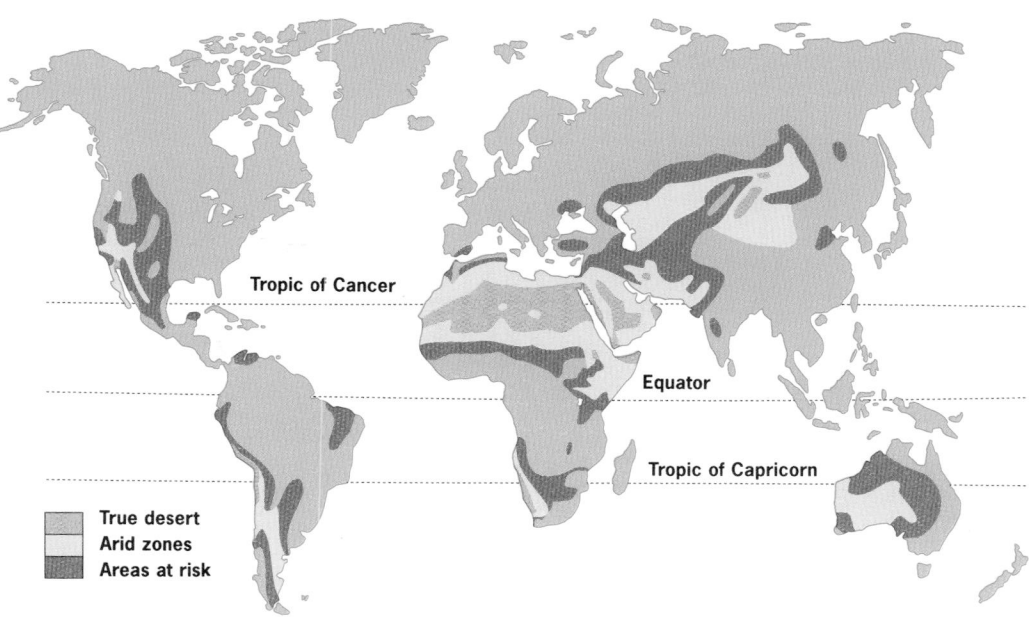

Tropic of Cancer

Equator

Tropic of Capricorn

- True desert
- Arid zones
- Areas at risk

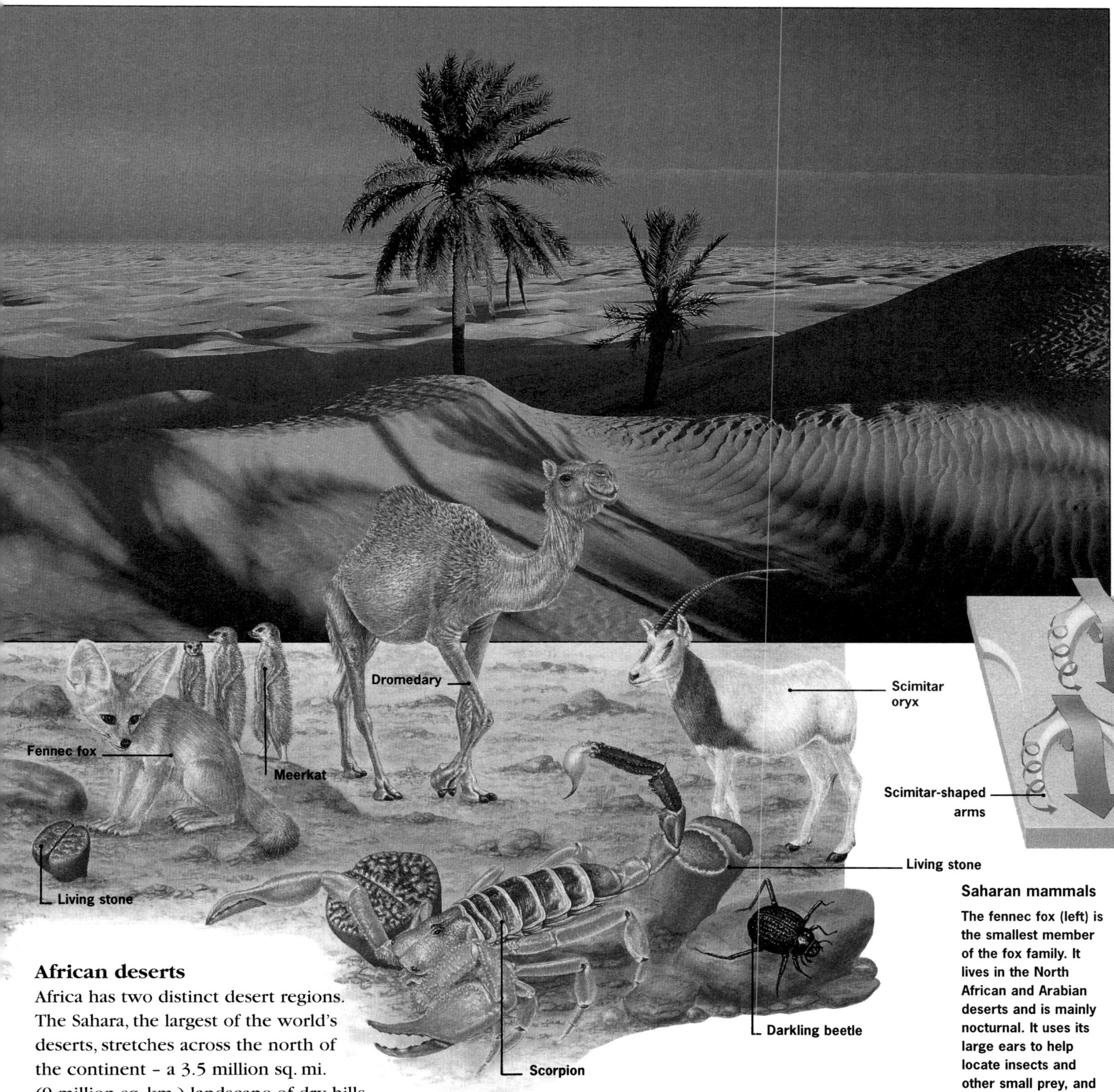

Spreading sands

Desertification – the spreading of deserts – is a problem in many areas (map above). It can be caused by climatic changes, tree felling, or the over-grazing of desert edges by animals.

Barchan dunes

When a wind blows constantly in one direction across an area of sand, it produces tapering barchan dunes (below). As wind passes over a hump, it divides into several eddies, some of which swirl sideways to pile sand into scimitar-shaped arms. Another eddy tucks backward, blowing sand upward to form the steep lee slope of the dune.

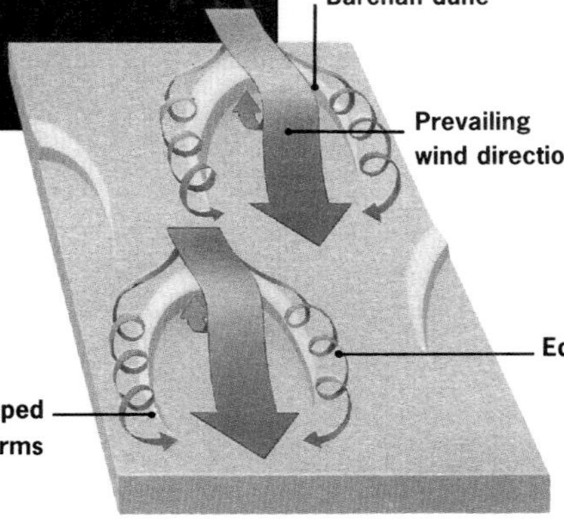

Barchan dune

Prevailing wind direction

Eddies

Scimitar-shaped arms

Dromedary

Scimitar oryx

Fennec fox

Meerkat

Living stone

Living stone

Living stone

Scorpion

Darkling beetle

African deserts

Africa has two distinct desert regions. The Sahara, the largest of the world's deserts, stretches across the north of the continent – a 3.5 million sq. mi. (9 million sq. km.) landscape of dry hills, rocks, and shifting sands. The sparse vegetation in this harsh environment supports few animals. Africa's other great arid area, in the southwest, is split in two. The Namib is a coastal strip that receives moisture from sea mists, while the Kalahari, farther inland, is an expanse of rolling sand dunes.

Living stones

Lithops, or living stones, are plants of the Kalahari Desert that closely resemble the rocks among which they grow – a clever bit of camouflage that protects them from animals.

Lethal sting

Androctonus australis (above) is a scorpion of the Sahara region. Its sting is used in defense and to subdue strug-gling prey. Unlike most scorpions, it has venom powerful enough to kill humans.

Early drinker

The darkling beetle (above) of the Namib Desert comes out at dawn, holding its abdomen high off the sand. Droplets of fog condense on the beetle's body and run down into its mouth.

Saharan mammals

The fennec fox (left) is the smallest member of the fox family. It lives in the North African and Arabian deserts and is mainly nocturnal. It uses its large ears to help locate insects and other small prey, and as radiators that prevent overheating.

Meerkats live in close-knit family groups. While some stand upright, alert for danger, others forage for insects, small rodents, and lizards.

The dromedary, or Arabian camel, was domesticated centuries ago and is now found mainly in eastern Africa and India. It has also been success-fully introduced into Australia's central desert. A dromedary's spreading feet allow it to walk steadily even on soft sand.

The scimitar oryx lives along the southern edge of the Sahara Desert. Like all oryxes, it can survive for long periods without water, relying solely on moisture in the grasses and other plants in its diet.

35

SEAS OF GRASS

Grasslands are found on all the continents – except Antarctica – as extensive plains, sometimes dotted with trees. There are two main kinds: the temperate grasslands, which include the prairies of North America, the steppes of Asia, and the pampas of South America; and the drier tropical and subtropical grasslands, or savannahs, found in East Africa, Australia, Venezuela, and Colombia. On the classic savannah landscape of East Africa roam herds of grazing animals, following the seasonal rains to take advantage of fresh grass. Predators, such as lightning-fast cheetahs, stalk the herds in search of a kill, usually an old or weak individual that can easily be separated from the other members of the group. The fertility of the plains has not escaped human attention. Vast areas of temperate grasslands have been cleared of their wildlife and given over to the farming of wheat or corn – themselves types of grass – or to the ranching of cattle or sheep.

Treetop browser
The giraffe's long neck allows it to reach into the trees for a year-round supply of green foliage not available to lower-level grazers. Its long legs make it a fast and graceful runner.

Powerful giants
The African elephant is the largest of all land mammals, weighing up to 7.2 tons (6.5 metric tons). Its main diet is grass, plus the bark and foliage of trees and shrubs. Elephants may appear destructive as they strip bark and push over trees. However, this natural thinning of trees actually allows the grassland to develop.

Cheetah

Struggle for survival

The greatest variety of grassland wildlife is found on the East African plains, where there is a constant battle between predators and prey. There are few hiding places, so grazing animals such as wildebeest and gazelles have evolved other strategies to avoid hunters. Safety lies in numbers: it is more difficult for a hunter to select a victim from a closely gathered herd. Lions, cheetahs, and hyenas all choose their kill when an individual animal strays from its companions. Speed also provides protection: some grass eaters can run at 32 m.p.h. (51 km.p.h.), and a hunter will not waste energy pursuing a lost cause.

Grassland records

Some of the world's biggest, most powerful animals inhabit the African grasslands. Lions are the largest predators. A pride of lions hunts as a team, but usually only the females take part. The adult male (above right), despite its strength and weight of up to 500 lbs. (230 kg.), does little of the killing.

The ostrich (center right) is the world's largest bird, up to 9 ft. (2.75 m.) tall. It also lays the largest eggs, measuring as long as 8 in. (20 cm.).

Race for life

A cheetah can sprint at 60 m.p.h. (97 km.p.h.), but only for a short time. At 32 m.p.h. (51 km.p.h.), the Thomson's gazelle is slower but may escape because of its greater stamina.

Rising from the flames

Fire has helped to create the open landscapes of the grasslands. It is vital for maintaining the ecological balance between the grasses, the trees, and the animals that graze and browse on them. Some fires are caused by lightning, but most are started by human activity. Grassland soils are not naturally fertile, yet burning adds nutrient-rich ash and encourages new growth of grasses, which can easily regenerate from their roots. Saplings are usually destroyed, but some savannah trees have mechanisms for surviving a fire. In southwest Australia, for example, the mallee eucalyptus survives by thrusting out new stems from its fire-resistant roots. Some birds also take advantage of a fire. African secretary birds and storks lurk at the edge of a blaze, waiting for rodents and other small animals to be driven out of hiding by the flames.

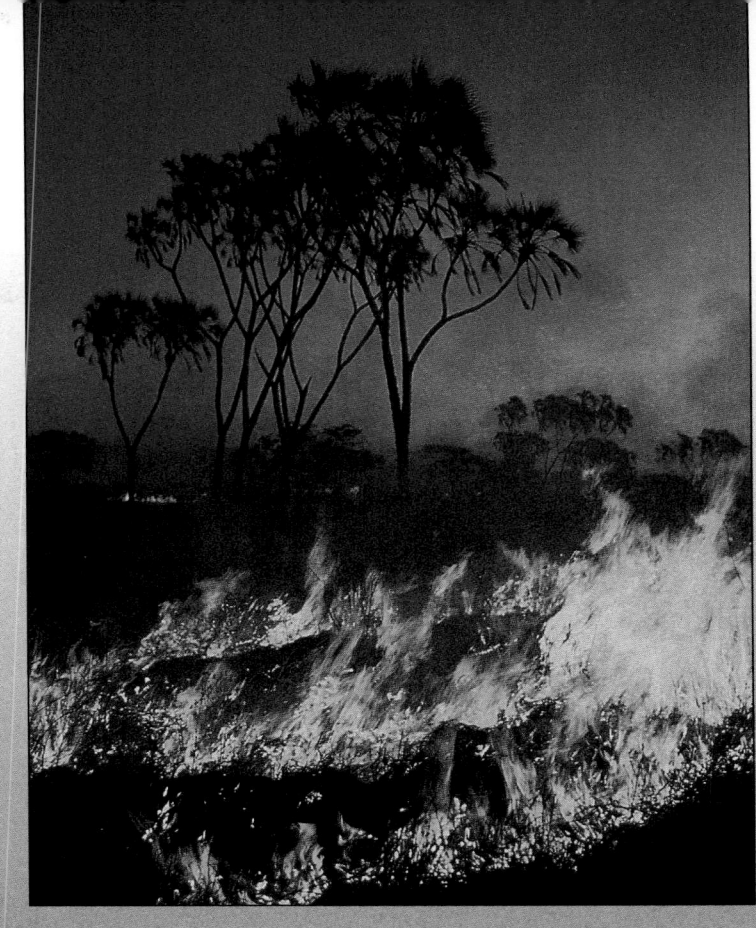

Following the rains

Wildebeest roam the African plains in huge herds (below). In the Serengeti National Park in Tanzania, their migration follows the clockwise path of the seasonal rains. All the pregnant females of a herd give birth within a few days of each other, so predators are able to take only a few of the vulnerable young.

Bush fire

A bush fire in Meru National Park, Kenya (above), rages out of control – but new grass will grow on soil enriched by the ash.

King of the prairies

Around 60 million bison roamed the American prairies before 1800. After being hunted almost to extinction, they have made a recovery and now number about 25,000.

Wild horse

Przewalski's horses once roamed the Asian steppes, but the species is now endangered. Tests have shown them to be the closest ancestors of the modern horse.

Thomson's gazelle

American bison

Przewalski's horse

Prairies

Asian steppe

Outback

© Bartholomew

Inhabitants of the grasslands

In similar environments around the world, animals and plants possess related characteristics that have evolved independently. The savannahs of South America, Africa, and Australia, for example, all contain large, plant-eating flightless birds – the rhea, ostrich, and emu respectively. Plant eaters are the dominant animals in all grassland areas and are preyed upon by only a few carnivores, such as the lion in Africa. In Australia the lion's role was once filled by the thylacine, a marsupial "lion," and in the Americas by the saber-toothed cat. Both animals are now extinct.

Guanaco

Pampas

African savannah

Red kangaroo

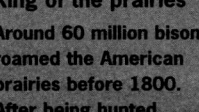

Zebra

Savannah
Semi-arid grasslands

Pampas native

The guanaco grazes on the tough grasses of the South American pampas. It is a type of llama, related to the camel. Both can survive on very little water.

Counterparts

Each of the world's grasslands is grazed by large grass-eating animals. The guanaco of South America has its counterparts in the African zebra and the Australian kangaroo.

The striped horse

The striped markings of zebras vary between individuals. When zebras move about, their patterns may help confuse predators.

Hopping herbivore

The red kangaroo is a pouched mammal, or marsupial. Its heavy tail acts as a counterbalance to its body when it hops.

TROPICAL RAIN FORESTS

The tropical rain forests of South America, central Africa, and Southeast Asia are among the earth's most vital resources. They contain by far the greatest diversity of plants and animals of any habitat, with as many as 200 species of trees and more than 60,000 species of insects and spiders in an area of 2 to 3 acres (0.8 to 1.2 ha.). Some trees are invaluable, such as the Amazonian liana tree, the source of a drug used to treat multiple sclerosis and Parkinson's disease. As producers of oxygen and absorbers of carbon dioxide, the forests make a huge contribution to the planet's ability to sustain life, yet they are being stripped at an alarming rate for logging and ranching purposes. The cleared land takes centuries to recover. However, vast areas of the Amazon, the Congo, and the East Indies are still virgin forest, and concerted efforts are being made in Brazil and Costa Rica to develop agriculture and forestry practices that preserve this precious environment.

Rain forest life

A permanently warm, damp climate ensures that plants grow larger and more luxuriantly in the rain forest than elsewhere. There is scarcely a tree that is not entwined with lianas and creepers. Bromeliads root themselves into trees, absorbing rainwater through their scales and trapping it amid their fleshy leaves in standing pools, inhabited by lizards, snakes, and even crabs and frogs.

The crowns of trees rise to more than 130 ft. (40 m.) to form the green canopy, while in places single trees, known as emergents, grow half as tall again. In these upper heights dwell insect-eating birds such as the massive-billed toucan, as well as huge birds of prey that swoop onto monkeys in the canopy below. Snakes and big cats lie in wait for their prey among the lower branches. Leaves near the forest floor provide foraging for tapirs, gorillas and other large mammals.

Treetop life

The leafy canopy (right) teems with animals, all adapted to life above the ground. Red tree frogs are found in Amazonia, while the birdwing butterfly is a brightly colored resident of the Southeast Asian forest.

On the floor

Many rain forest trees (right) spread strong buttresses up to 33 ft. (10 m.) from the bases of their trunks.

Okapi

Hunters and hunted

In each of the world's rain forests, the emergent layer that towers above the canopy (right) is home to a species of large eagle. In central Africa eagles prey on several species of red colobus monkey, eaters of leaves, flowers, and fruit. The harpy eagle of South America swoops through the treetops at 50 m.p.h. (80 km.p.h.) in pursuit of small monkeys such as the capuchin and the squirrel monkey.

Tree frog

Harpy eagle

Red colobus monkey

The middle layer

The blotched markings of the jaguar – South America's only big cat – provide good camouflage in the dense foliage of the middle layer of the forest. This layer is also home to many bird species, including the colorful scarlet macaw. Many rain forest plants, such as bromeliads, are known as epiphytes – plants that grow on the trunks and branches of forest trees but do not draw nutrients from their hosts as parasites do.

Jaguar

Asian birdwing butterfly

Scarlet macaw

Plant eaters

The abundant rainforest vegetation supports a wealth of species. In South American forests large quantities of leaves are taken by leaf-cutter ants, which cultivate them to grow fungi in huge underground nests. Some equatorial African forests are host to gorillas, which eat mainly leaves and the stems of shrubs and climbing plants. The okapi of central Africa is a shy, solitary, often nocturnal animal that browses on the leaves of tree saplings. Its finely tuned senses of smell and hearing enable it to detect and evade predators.

Leaf-cutter ant

Gorilla

Disappearing Eden

The luxuriance of the rain forest depends not on rich soils – the nutrient level is actually very low – but on the recycling of great quantities of leaf litter on the forest floor. Once trees have been removed and the ground cleared of vegetation, there is nothing to prevent heavy rains from washing away the soil, leaving in their wake a denuded landscape that can take several centuries to regenerate to mature forest.

An estimated 44.5 million acres (18 million ha.) of forest are cleared around the world each year, not only for timber and farmland but also for mining and settlement. To slow down the destruction, it is increasingly recognized that rain forest countries must be helped by the world community to develop effective forest management policies and alternative sources of income.

Lone survivor

A single tree is left standing in an area of Amazonian forest (right). After clearance the plot will be farmed for only a few years before the soil nutrients are exhausted. Only about 85 percent of the Amazonian rain forest remains. Preserving this natural heritage has become the focus of major international efforts.

Spreading scar

A huge clearing in the forest of northern Brazil (left) was made to allow oil prospecting. It is being enlarged by erosion as rainwater carries away fertile soil and cuts deep gulleys into exposed slopes.

Conditions of growth

Rain forests are restricted to a belt around the equator, between the tropics of Cancer and Capricorn. Here are constant temperatures of at least 75°F (24°C) and rainfall of 90 in. (229 cm.) or more per year – in some places the annual rainfall is as high as 300 in. (762 cm.). This creates humid conditions where plants grow rapidly. Because there are no seasons in the equatorial belt, the vegetation grows in abundance all year round. The climate need not be constantly wet, however: some of the world's rain forest regions show monsoon characteristics.

Lost heritage

A map of tropical rain-forest regions (below) shows the huge loss of habitat over the past 50 years. Almost half the original rain-forest acreage has already been destroyed.

Remaining tropical rain forest

Forest cleared since 1945

© Bartholomew

Raggiana bird of paradise

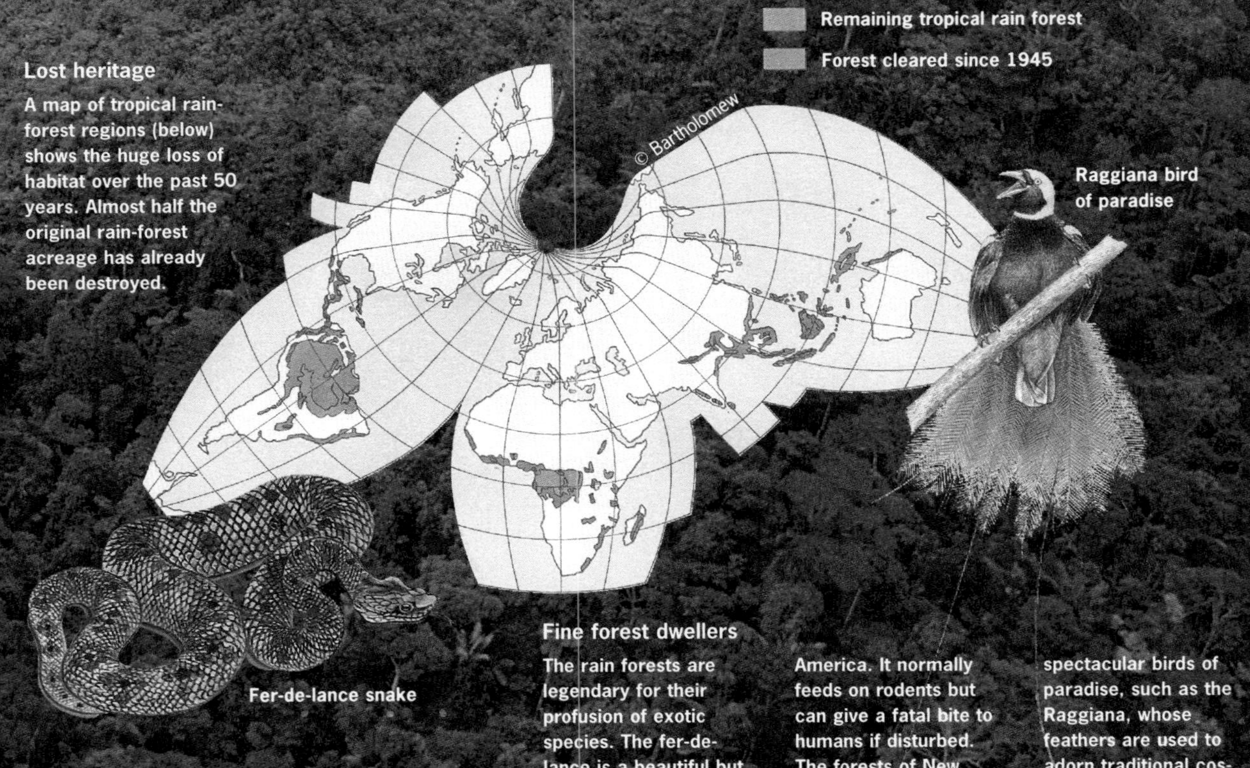

Fine forest dwellers

The rain forests are legendary for their profusion of exotic species. The fer-de-lance is a beautiful but feared snake of South America. It normally feeds on rodents but can give a fatal bite to humans if disturbed. The forests of New Guinea are home to spectacular birds of paradise, such as the Raggiana, whose feathers are used to adorn traditional costumes for festivals.

Fer-de-lance snake

39

THE GREAT FORESTS

Great gray owl

Cold-climate trees
Most coniferous forests are in the Northern Hemisphere. Farther south, mountain ranges such as the Andes in Chile (right) provide similar conditions.

Cone cruncher
Crossbills are a group of finches with beaks adapted for prying apart the scales of pine cones and extracting the seeds.

Crossbill

Broadleaf trees thrive wherever rainfall is spread evenly through the year and the summers are warm and not too short. Most of the world's temperate regions fall into this category, but because these areas are heavily populated, much of their ancient woodland has been cleared for agriculture. The fertility of the land derives from the trees that once grew there, dropping their leaves onto the ground year after year for thousands of years. If farming were to cease, the trees would slowly recolonize their natural territory. In regions where summers are short and the risk of frost is always present, evergreens predominate. Coniferous forests stretch across the upper reaches of North America, Scandinavia, and Russia in a broad swath known as the boreal (northern) forest. The term *taiga,* often used interchangeably with *boreal forest,* describes the marshy conifer forests of Siberia. The frontier between coniferous and broadleaf zones is determined by both climate and elevation.

Native browser
Moose (known as elks in Europe) are the largest deer. They live in the boreal forest and adjacent open country and swamps, feeding on bark, twigs, grasses, and water plants.

Tree feller
A North American beaver (above) fells trees by gnawing with its strong incisor teeth. The trees are used to build both dams and the lodge where the beaver lives. This is a complex construction, with underwater entrances in the center of the dammed pond.

Forest feline
The densely furred feet and short tail of the lynx (above) help it to stay warm in the forests of northern Europe. The lynx hunts at night, using its keen eyesight and sense of smell.

Coniferous forests

Evergreen forests grow in regions with long, hard winters. The boreal forest has no equivalent in the Southern Hemisphere because there is no landmass at the corresponding latitude.

The shape of many evergreen trees allows snow to slide off their branches, rather than building up and breaking them. Roots cannot extract water from frozen ground; evergreen leaves are therefore designed to conserve water. Leaves are reduced in size and are often needlelike, with a waxy coating to reduce evaporation. An evergreen tree can start to manufacture food as soon as the spring warmth comes because its leaves are in place already. It also conserves energy because it does not have to generate new leaves each year.

Acid rain

One of the major threats to woodlands comes from acid rain. Sulphur dioxide from the burning of fossil fuels and nitrogen oxides from motor vehicle exhausts combine with moisture in the air to form sulphuric and nitric acids. Clouds may travel 600 mi. (1,000 km.) or more before raining down their acid far from the original source.

The effect of acid rain is worst where the soil is already acidic in content – notably in the evergreen belt. Acids can release toxic metals in the soil and destroy soil bacteria on which trees depend. By the time the effects are seen, the soil may be irreversibly damaged. The trees start to shed their needles and become less resistant to drought, frost, and disease.

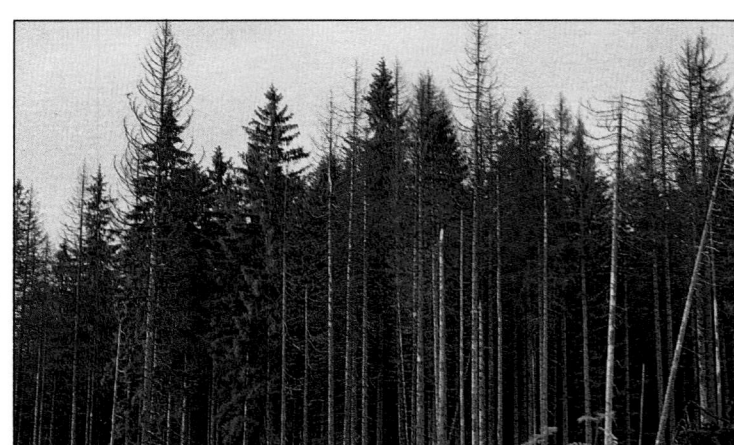

Death from above
These dying conifers (above) bear witness to the effects of acid rain, which can be 1,000 times more acidic than natural rain. Acid rain drains into rivers and lakes, carrying with it aluminum from the soil, which is poisonous to fish. The increased acidity of the water damages the entire community that depends on it, from tiny plankton to waterbirds and mammals at the top of the food chain.

The broadleaf forests

Deciduous trees are active in summer and dormant in winter. During the summer their broad leaves make full use of the abundant light. In winter, when roots are less able to replace water from the soil, evaporation through the leaves would be too great, so they are shed as the days shorten.

The fallen leaves are broken down by fungi and bacteria, and their nutrients are released back into the soil. Leaf fall allows light to penetrate to the forest floor during winter and spring, so that bulbs and other early plants can sprout before the trees grow new foliage. The floor of a deciduous wood is therefore richer in herbs and shrubs than either a tropical or evergreen forest.

The dominant tree species in a forest depends on soil, rainfall, and climate. Beeches grow on alkaline, well-drained soils. Oaks thrive on heavy clay; common oaks favor neutral soils, but sessile oaks can tolerate acid conditions.

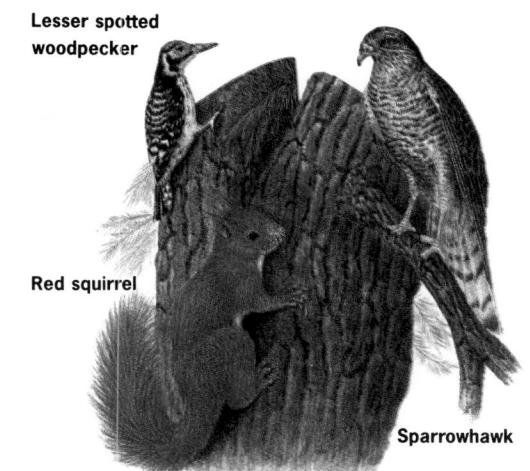

Lesser spotted woodpecker

Red squirrel

Sparrowhawk

Forest fellows

Deciduous woods support many small birds and mammals (left). Woodpeckers probe tree bark for grubs. Both red and gray squirrels feed on seeds, berries, and nuts; gray squirrels occasionally take birds' eggs. The swift flight of a sparrowhawk allows it to chase its songbird prey through the forest. In spring, sunlight reaching the forest floor when the trees are still leafless encourages flowers such as primroses, daffodils, and bluebells to bloom (left).

Eurasian jay

Careful cleaner

Jays clean themselves by "anting." They allow ants to run over their feathers, squirting formic acid, which acts as a natural pesticide, killing lice and mites.

Wild boar

Red fox

Longhorn beetle

Tree beetle

The longhorn beetle larva burrows into a tree to feed. It surfaces just before pupating, so that the weak-jawed adult (left) can emerge.

Woodland deer

The North American wapiti (above) is closely related to the red deer of western Europe and central Asia. Second in size only to the moose, these deer inhabit coniferous forests. The smaller, dappled fallow deer is found in deciduous woodlands throughout Eurasia.

Wild boar

The wild boar (above) is the ancestor of the domestic pig. It eats nuts, roots, fungi, worms, and snails.

Adaptable animal

The red fox, normally an animal of deciduous forests, is becoming a common sight in the cities of Europe and North America.

Mole

Tricholoma

Shaggy parasol

Horn of plenty

Leaf litter animals

The ground beneath the trees acts like an extensive compost heap. Fallen leaves support a complex community of life on the forest floor. The amount of warmth and moisture determines the level of activity: decomposition is normally faster in deciduous woodland than in evergreen forest. Most of the organisms are tiny, but they are present in enormous numbers. A handful of litter might contain hundreds of springtails. These tiny wingless insects, together with worms, snails, and woodlice, are preyed on by beetles, centipedes, and spiders. Fungi play an important part in decomposition and are eaten by small invertebrates, which themselves may be food for a mole. Mites are parasites of moles and other mammals.

Wood blewit

Chanterelle

Snail

Millipede

Centipede

Boletus

Life on the floor

Many fungi thrive in the shady warmth of the woodland floor. A network of fungal filaments spreads through the leaf litter, from which the fungi absorb nutrients.

Springtail

Earthworm

Mite

Plant or meat eater?

Millipedes are plant eaters with weak jaws, whereas centipedes are carnivores that can inflict a painful bite.

41

THE ROOF OF THE WORLD

The great mountain ranges of the world – the Alps, Himalayas, Rockies, and Andes – reach heights of more than 2.5 mi. (4 km.) above sea level. Because the temperature drops by approximately 3.5°F (2°C) for every 1,000 ft. (305 m.) of altitude gained, high mountains near the equator, such as Mount Kilimanjaro, have permanent snow and ice on their summits, while their lower slopes are bathed in tropical warmth. These magnificent ranges were created by collisions of the earth's crustal plates – the interlocking pieces that form the planet's outermost layer. Forces within the earth push one plate against another until the crumpled rocks in the crust are forced upward to form mountains. At the same time, some of the rocks are pushed down as far as 40 mi. (64 km.) into the earth's hot interior. At this depth the rocks melt and turn into hot, molten magma, which in due course may well up and rise above the earth's surface in the form of volcanic mountains.

Southern fjords

The Southern Alps of New Zealand's South Island lie in an active fault zone. Milford Sound (below) is in the Fjordland region at the island's western tip. Mitre Peak (left) is 5,548 ft. (1,691 m.) high. It is the only habitat of the kakapo, a flightless nocturnal parrot facing extinction. The Southern Alps' highest peak is Mount Cook at 12,350 ft. (3,764 m.), whose eastern slope carries the Tasman glacier. To the south of the chain, parallel ridges break up into complex, dissected terrain.

Life on the peaks

The ascent of any mountain climbs through a sequence of vegetation zones. In the Tropics this may resemble a journey from the equator to the poles, from rain forest in the foothills to tundra nearer the summit.

Plant and animal species vary not only according to vegetation zone, but also from sunny side to shady side. In spring, alpine meadows can be a blaze of color, with flowers such as gentians and campions. On the summits few mammals can survive. Those that do have thick coats to combat the cold, and agility and surefootedness to reach sparse grazing on ledges. Giant birds of prey, such as eagles and falcons, glide and soar on mountain winds.

Unbroken barrier

The 4,600 mi. (7,400 km.) of the Andes (right) form the longest mountain range, with 40 peaks over 20,000 ft. (6,100 m.).

Forested flanks

The Rockies (below) extend 3,000 mi. (4,800 km.) from Alaska to New Mexico. The tree line, above which no trees can grow, is clearly defined.

Porcupine

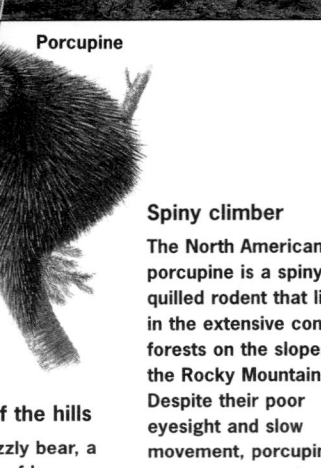

Spiny climber

The North American porcupine is a spiny-quilled rodent that lives in the extensive conifer forests on the slopes of the Rocky Mountains. Despite their poor eyesight and slow movement, porcupines climb high trees in search of nuts, bark, leaves, and twigs.

Giant of the hills

The grizzly bear, a species of brown bear, used to roam the length of the Rockies but now survives only in a few national parks in Alaska and Canada.

Grizzly bear

Kea

Threatened bird

The kea is a large, powerful parrot of New Zealand's Southern Alps. It uses its sharp, hooked beak to feed on fruit, insects, and plant buds. Its reputation for attacking sheep has led to its near eradication by farmers.

The magnificent Andes

The high plateaus and soaring peaks of the Andes stretch from South America's Caribbean coast, in the north, to the southern tip of the continent. They comprise a succession of mountain chains, or cordilleras, standing above a subduction zone, where the Pacific Plate is wedged under the South American Plate (right).

This belt of tectonic plate movement is the site of both earthquakes and active volcanoes. Aconcagua, in Argentina, is the highest peak in the Americas, topping off at 22,836 ft. (6,960 m.).

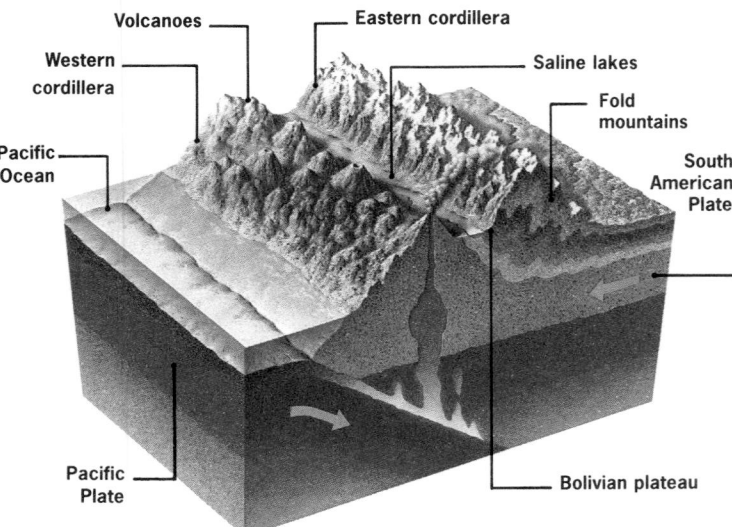

Volcanoes
Western cordillera
Pacific Ocean
Eastern cordillera
Saline lakes
Fold mountains
South American Plate
Pacific Plate
Bolivian plateau

Mountain building

A cross-section of the central Andes (left) shows the differing nature of the two main cordilleras. The western cordillera is volcanic. The eastern one, with its folds and faults, was pushed upward as the western margin of the South American Plate crumpled under the pressure of the Pacific Plate. Between them lies the high Bolivian plateau, with its string of saline lakes, including Lake Titicaca.

Patrolling the peaks

The Andean condor (below) is the world's heaviest bird of prey. It has a wingspan of 10 ft. (3 m.) and can soar to heights up to 23,000 ft. (7,000 m.). These giant scavengers are exceptionally long-lived: one survived in captivity at the Moscow Zoo for 72 years. They have been known to raid the nests of seabirds, taking young chicks and eggs.

Andean condor

Mountain cat

The snow leopard (right) is an extremely rare wild cat, found only in the Himalayan region. Despite official protection it is still hunted for its fur.

On top of the world

The Himalayan peaks (left) are the highest in the world. Few creatures can survive for long in this oxygen-starved, icy realm.

Snow leopard

Warm coats

Chinchillas, which shelter in burrows or rock crevices in the high Andes, have been extensively hunted for their fur, and only a few communities remain in the wild.

Chinchilla

Parched plains

Much of the Andes has a very dry climate with permanent snow only above 21,300 ft. (6,500 m.). Grassland plateaus in these mountains are suitable for grazers, such as the guanaco (above).

High water

Set 12,500 ft. (3,800 m.) above sea level, on the border of Peru and Bolivia, Lake Titicaca (right) is the world's highest navigable lake. It offers sanctuary to many waterbirds, amphibians, and fish.

Bills for sifting

Andean flamingos sift food from the salt waters of Lake Titicaca with their specially adapted beaks.

Andean flamingo

Scaling the peaks

A trajectory across Europe from the Canaries to the Caucasus (left) cuts through many types of mountains (below). Teide, on Tenerife, is a volcano. The Pyrenees, Alps, and Carpathians are young mountains created by the collision between tectonic plates. The Massif Central is an older highland, and El'brus is another volcano. High in the Swiss Alps stands the glacial pyramid of the Matterhorn (right).

Ranges of North America

The Appalachians extend for 1,550 mi. (2,500 km.) down the East Coast of the United States. In a pattern that started more than 600 million years ago, successive phases of folding constructed the mountains while continuing erosion reduced their height. Now no peak is higher than 6,683 ft. (2,037 m.).

West of the Great Plains rise the Rocky Mountains and, farther west, the Pacific Range. The latter contains, in eastern California, the Sierra Nevada, created only 15 million years ago, when a massive granite range was thrust upward. The tallest peak, Mount Whitney, is 14,495 ft. (4,418 m.) high.

To the north, in Washington State, are the Cascades, which are volcanic in origin. They include Mount St. Helens, which last erupted in May 1980.

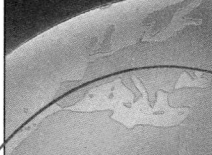

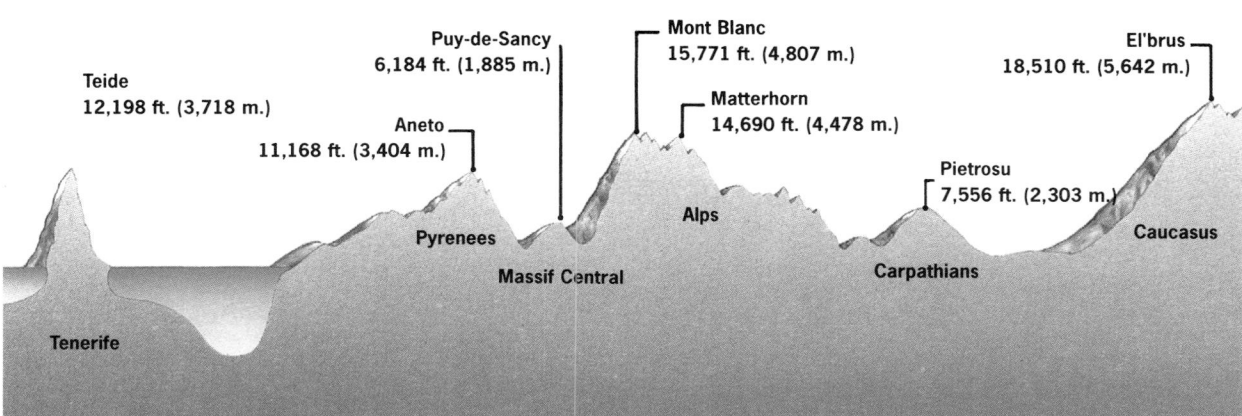

Teide
12,198 ft. (3,718 m.)

Aneto
11,168 ft. (3,404 m.)

Puy-de-Sancy
6,184 ft. (1,885 m.)

Mont Blanc
15,771 ft. (4,807 m.)

Matterhorn
14,690 ft. (4,478 m.)

Pietrosu
7,556 ft. (2,303 m.)

El'brus
18,510 ft. (5,642 m.)

Tenerife

Pyrenees

Massif Central

Alps

Carpathians

Caucasus

PEOPLING THE PLANET

One of the earliest surviving traces of the ancestors of our human species is a trail of footprints made by humanlike creatures walking upright some 3.7 million years ago, found at Laetoli, in present-day Tanzania. Most of the globe was populated by early humans walking from one place to another, perhaps as hunters following migratory herds or in search of new food supplies. The fossil record shows a complex story of evolution, with several species fanning out across the planet, probably from a single common ancestry in Africa. Our own subspecies, *Homo sapiens sapiens,* appeared in Africa more than 130,000 years ago and seems to have spread northward, reaching most parts of the world by 10,000 years ago. At that time the world's estimated population was between 5 and 10 million; today it is approximately 5.8 billion. People continue to migrate from place to place – whether in search of political freedom, religious tolerance, or better economic prospects.

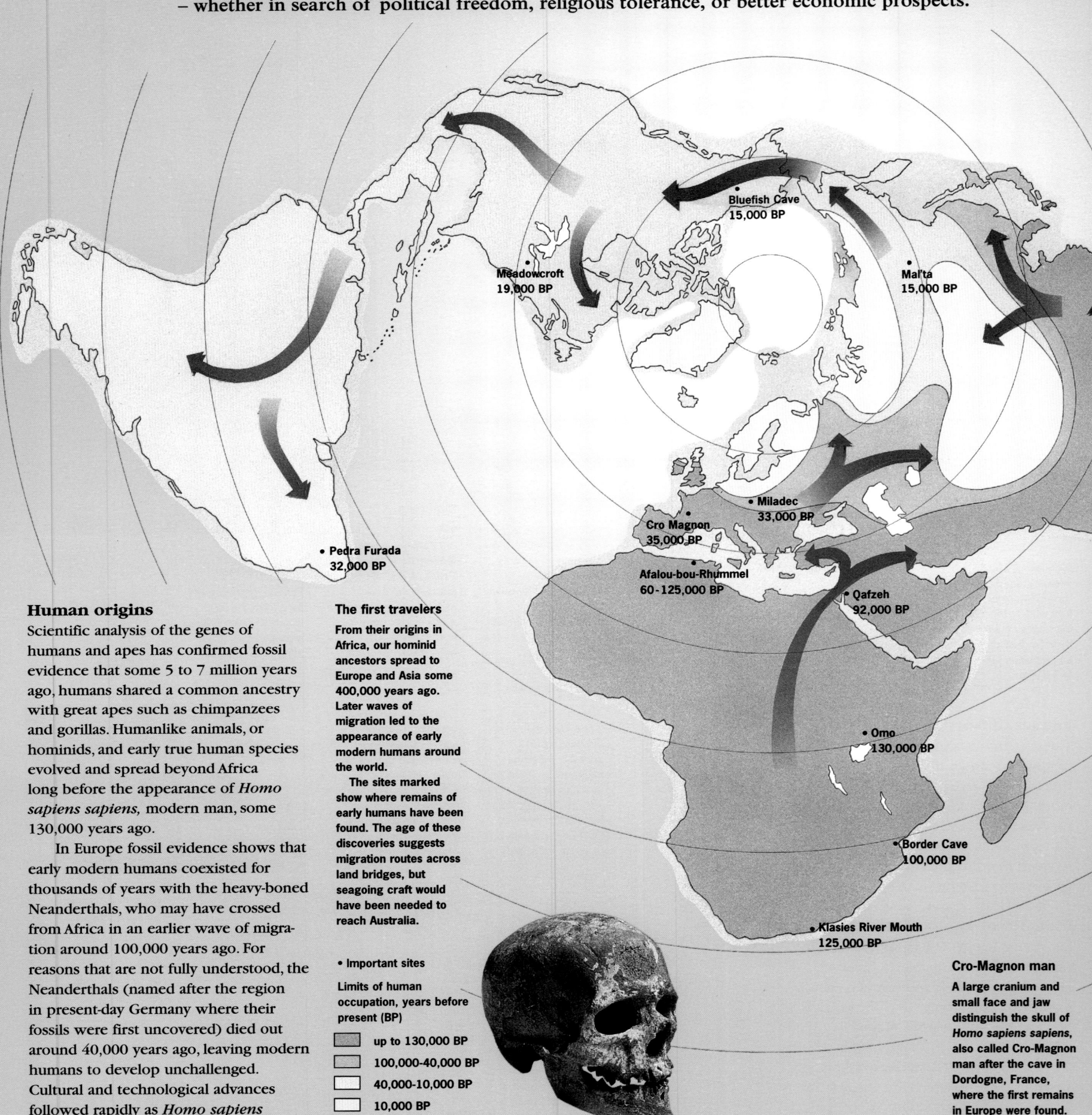

Human origins

Scientific analysis of the genes of humans and apes has confirmed fossil evidence that some 5 to 7 million years ago, humans shared a common ancestry with great apes such as chimpanzees and gorillas. Humanlike animals, or hominids, and early true human species evolved and spread beyond Africa long before the appearance of *Homo sapiens sapiens,* modern man, some 130,000 years ago.

In Europe fossil evidence shows that early modern humans coexisted for thousands of years with the heavy-boned Neanderthals, who may have crossed from Africa in an earlier wave of migration around 100,000 years ago. For reasons that are not fully understood, the Neanderthals (named after the region in present-day Germany where their fossils were first uncovered) died out around 40,000 years ago, leaving modern humans to develop unchallenged. Cultural and technological advances followed rapidly as *Homo sapiens sapiens* colonized the habitable world.

The first travelers

From their origins in Africa, our hominid ancestors spread to Europe and Asia some 400,000 years ago. Later waves of migration led to the appearance of early modern humans around the world.

The sites marked show where remains of early humans have been found. The age of these discoveries suggests migration routes across land bridges, but seagoing craft would have been needed to reach Australia.

- **Important sites**

Limits of human occupation, years before present (BP)

- up to 130,000 BP
- 100,000-40,000 BP
- 40,000-10,000 BP
- 10,000 BP
- Ice Age land masses

Meadowcroft 19,000 BP

Bluefish Cave 15,000 BP

Mal'ta 15,000 BP

Miladec 33,000 BP

Cro Magnon 35,000 BP

Afalou-bou-Rhummel 60-125,000 BP

Qafzeh 92,000 BP

Pedra Furada 32,000 BP

Omo 130,000 BP

Border Cave 100,000 BP

Klasies River Mouth 125,000 BP

Cro-Magnon man

A large cranium and small face and jaw distinguish the skull of *Homo sapiens sapiens,* also called Cro-Magnon man after the cave in Dordogne, France, where the first remains in Europe were found.

44

Historic movements

Throughout history peoples have moved overland from one place to another, aided by the horse and the camel, both domesticated some 6,000 years ago. The Aryans, thought to be the ancestors of most of the peoples of Europe, the Middle East, and the Indian subcontinent, probably came from the steppes of central Asia about 3,000 years ago. These areas are still linked by a group of related languages, from Celtic to Hindi, that are spoken by their inhabitants.

More recent migrations have included those of the barbarians, who swept from the steppes into the disintegrating Roman Empire during the 4th and 5th centuries, and the Mongols, who left Asia to conquer large swaths of the Middle East and Eastern Europe in the 13th century. Other peoples were seafarers, and the greatest of these were the Polynesians, who had spread their culture across the islands of the vast Pacific Ocean by AD 1000.

Lake Mungo
38,000 BP

Tabon Cave
30,000 BP

Devil's Lair
38,000 BP

Luijiang
67,000 BP

A modern mecca
The U.S. has long been a magnet to people seeking a new life (below). In the 19th century most immigrants came from Europe, spurred on by political unrest, economic hardship, or religious persecution in their homelands. Many workers from China and Japan were brought in through the ports of the West Coast to work on railroads.

Going west
Many of the great migrations of history originated in Asia (below). The Huns came from central Asia in the 4th century; the Mongols, 900 years later. In the 8th century the Arabs brought Islamic rule to Spain before being turned back. In the 9th and 10th centuries the Vikings traveled as far as Newfoundland.

→ Vikings
→ Huns
→ Arabs
→ Mongols

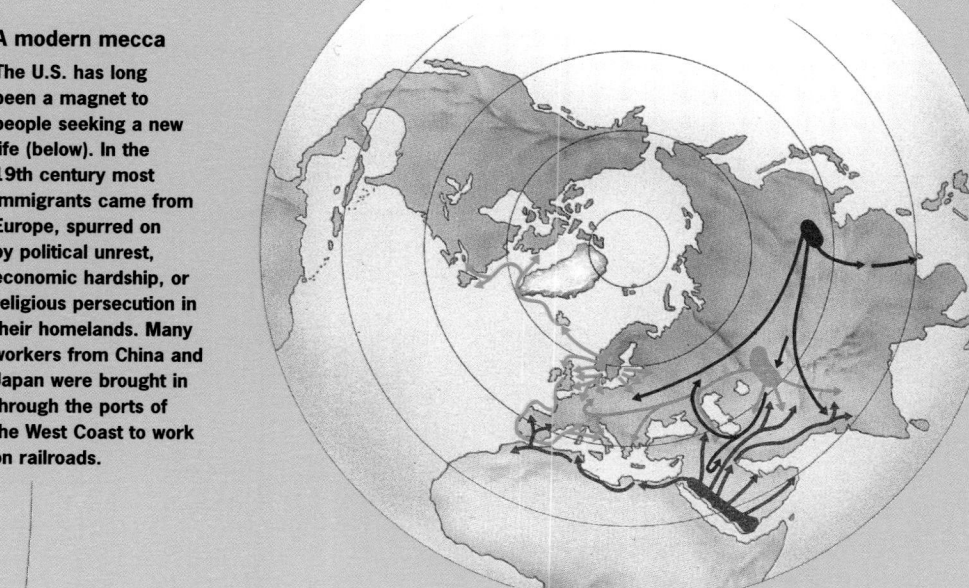

The peopling of America

No fossils of early *Homo sapiens* have been found in the Americas. The most ancient remains date from around 32,000 years ago. The ancestors of today's Native Americans are thought to have walked from northeast Asia across the Bering Strait, when a glacial period caused sea levels to fall and dry land to appear across the strait.

The first Europeans to set eyes on North America were Norsemen from Greenland and Iceland. Viking legends of a colony across the Atlantic are backed up by archeological evidence of a Norse settlement in Newfoundland around AD 1000. However, following Columbus's voyage to the New World in 1492, many European countries established colonies in the Americas. During the 19th century the United States became the destination for the greatest migration in human history, as millions of Europeans arrived to build new lives in a new land.

Ethnic pride
Chinese-American children in Los Angeles (above) show pride in both their ethnic origin and American citizenship.

Land of freedom
One of America's attractions to groups such as the Amish (above right) was the constitutional freedom to practice any religion.

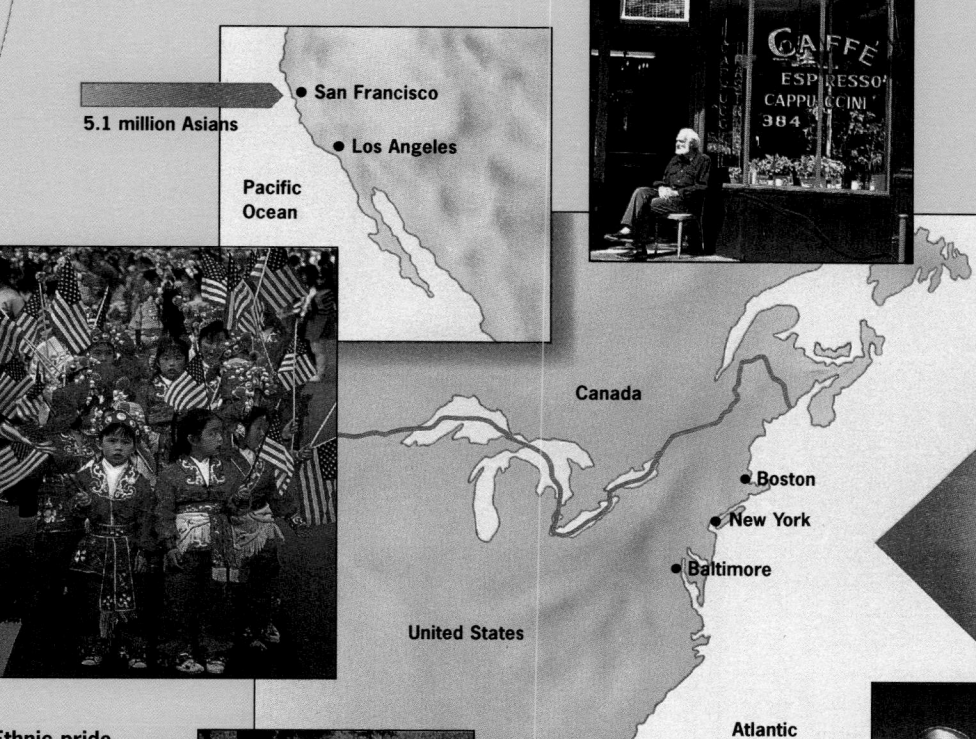

5.1 million Asians

San Francisco
Los Angeles
Pacific Ocean

Canada

Boston
New York
Baltimore

United States

Atlantic Ocean

Mexico

Home from home
New settlers often chose to live and work in the same neighborhood, such as New York's Little Italy (left).

1820–1990

8.1 million Eastern Europeans
7.0 million Germans
5.3 million Italians
5.1 million British
4.7 million Irish
2.5 million Scandinavians

All American
Three U.S. Navy sailors salute the flag (above) in a striking display of modern America's ethnic diversity.

PUTTING THE EARTH TO WORK

Our ability to harvest the natural resources of land and sea accounts for our very success as a species, motivating enterprises from small farms and fishing boats to the vast silver mines of Mexico and cattle ranges of Australia. Two-fifths of our planet's land surface has been "domesticated," primarily for crops and livestock. The yield is massive: every year, the earth provides over 551 million tons (500 million metric tons) of rice, 110 million tons (100 million metric tons) of fish, and 22 billion barrels of oil. Such exploitation often takes a toll: the excavation of ore, coal, and stone leaves huge scars on the landscape; industry pollutes air, rivers, seas, and land; chemical fertilizers and pesticides eventually impoverish the soil; and the clearing of forests for farms may have long-term climatic effects. The fossil fuels upon which the modern world depends are finite resources. Their husbanding, and eventual replacement, is one of the great challenges of the future.

Back to nature

Modern farming techniques enable the developed world to produce far more food than it needs, though at considerable cost to the environment and, potentially, to human health. Organic farming is being reintroduced as an alternative to intensive methods of producing food. Farm waste is better for soil structure and long-term fertility than chemicals, while regular rotation of crops – for example, alternately sowing cereals, roots, and legumes in the same field – ensures that all levels of the soil are used and protects it from becoming depleted. At the same time, pests find it harder to become established, reducing the need for pesticides.

The ocean's harvest

Fishing provides about a quarter of the world's protein and a livelihood for millions. The use of modern factory ships has quadrupled the total catch since 1950; it now stands at some 110 million tons (100 million metric tons) a year. In order to halt the alarming depletion of many species, including tuna and cod, governments have closed some fishing grounds and imposed quotas limiting catches. To help stocks recover, nets must have holes large enough for young fish to swim through.

The bread basket

In many cereal-growing areas such as Michigan (right), farmers have created vast fields to allow tractors and combine harvesters to operate freely. The eradication of trees and hedges can bring soil erosion and nutrient loss, which are controlled by the use of chemicals.

The rice bowl

In warm, wet areas of Asia such as India (left), the staple food is rice, planted and harvested using traditional – and often labor-intensive – methods.

How land is used

Many factors affect patterns of land use (below). Topography, soil, climate, social organization, and levels of investment in farming all play a part.

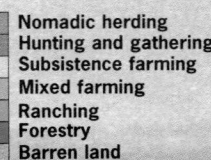

- Nomadic herding
- Hunting and gathering
- Subsistence farming
- Mixed farming
- Ranching
- Forestry
- Barren land

© Bartholomew

Floating factory

A modern fishing vessel (below) is a complete processing plant. Within its 377-ft. (115-m.) length, fish can be caught, filleted, frozen, and packed. Such a boat might tow a net 2,600 ft. (800 m.) long, which opens wide enough to engulf whole shoals of fish. Shoals are located using sonar and possibly even a spotter plane. Such efficient factory ships have decimated fish stocks around the world. In 30 years the proportion of different species caught off the Gulf of Maine has swung dramatically, from the traditional cod and flounder to the less popular dogfish and skate (see table below).

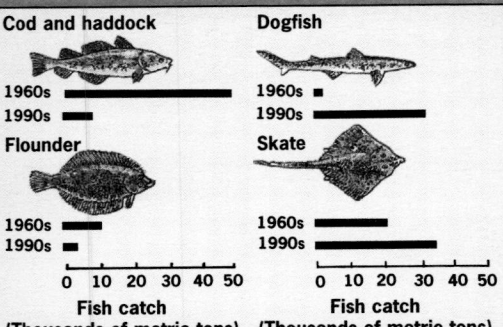

Cod and haddock	Dogfish
1960s	1960s
1990s	1990s
Flounder	**Skate**
1960s	1960s
1990s	1990s
0 10 20 30 40 50	0 10 20 30 40 50
Fish catch (Thousands of metric tons)	Fish catch (Thousands of metric tons)

Black gold

Oil is by far the most vital of the earth's fossil fuels, supplying some 40 percent of the world's energy needs. Together with natural gas, it is a by-product of the decomposition of microscopic plants and organisms deposited in ancient sedimentary rock. Despite the expense and technical difficulty of extracting oil from under the sea, reserves have been successfully tapped beneath the North Sea, the Gulf of Mexico, and the Arctic Ocean.

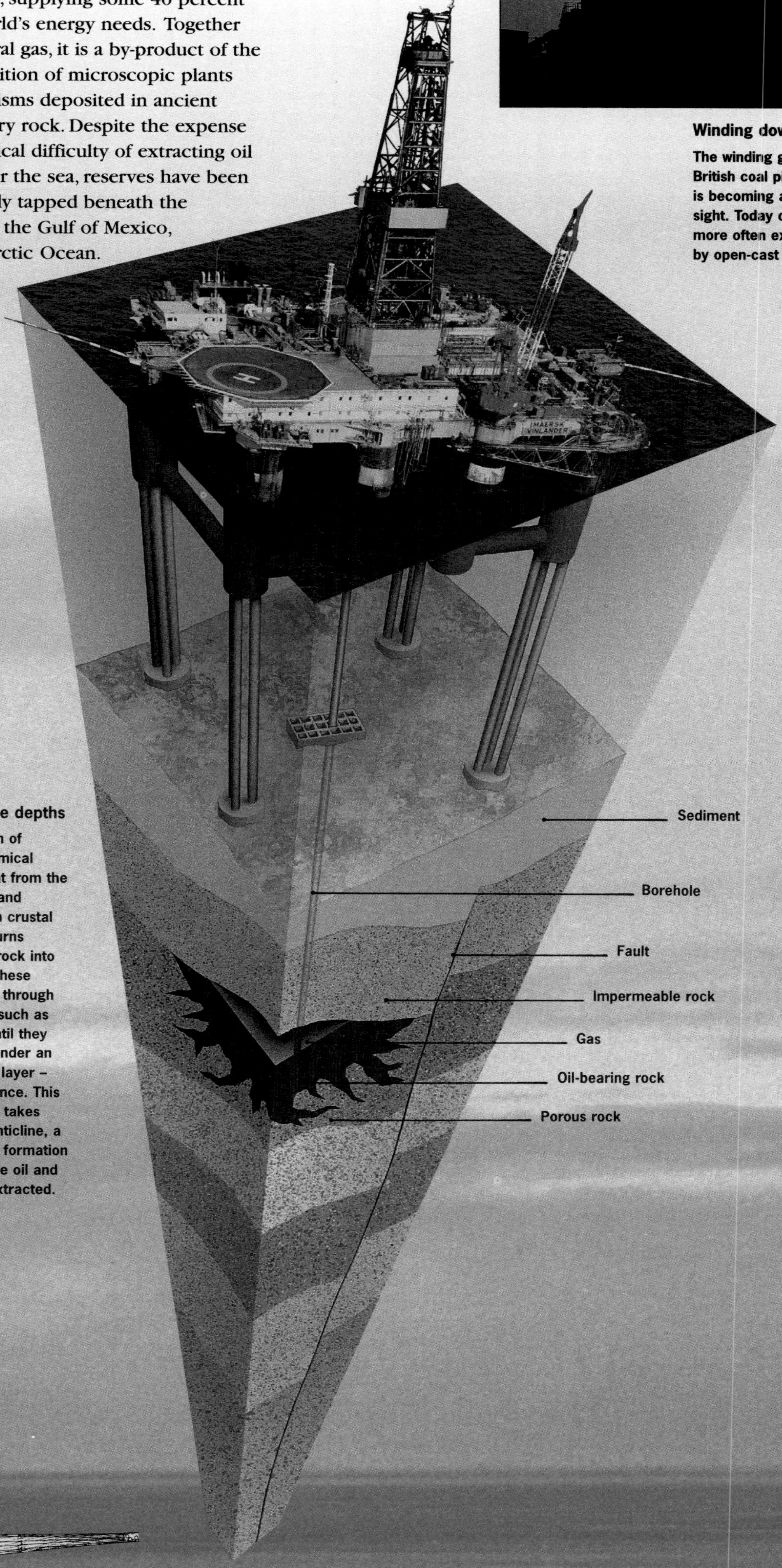

Winding down

The winding gear of a British coal pit (above) is becoming a rare sight. Today coal is more often extracted by open-cast methods.

The fuel formed from forests

Coal is the fossilized remains of extinct plants. Most of the 386 billion tons (350 billion metric tons) of coal reserves in Europe and the Americas were formed some 300 million years ago during the Upper Carboniferous, or Pennsylvanian, era, when large areas of the earth were covered by vast swampy forests.

Dead plant matter was attacked by microbes to form peatlike bogs. As layers of sediment accumulated above it, the peaty material was compressed: first into soft, brown lignite and then into harder, cleaner-burning bituminous coal. The most widely used type – brown coal – can be turned into industrial coke.

The increased cost of deep mining has led to the development of large-scale open-cast strip mines in the Americas, Australia, and China, which produce cheaper coal than the old-fashioned shaft-and-tunnel mines.

Plumbing the depths

A combination of bacteria, chemical catalysts, heat from the earth's core, and pressure from crustal movements turns sedimentary rock into oil and gas. These move upward through porous rock (such as sandstone) until they are trapped under an impermeable layer – clay, for instance. This process often takes place in an anticline, a dome-shaped formation from which the oil and gas can be extracted.

Sediment

Borehole

Fault

Impermeable rock

Gas

Oil-bearing rock

Porous rock

Open-cast mining

One of the world's largest copper mines, Bingham Canyon, near Salt Lake City, Utah, is the world's largest man-made hole. Covering 2.75 sq. mi. (7.1 sq. km.), it is 2,600 ft. (800 m.) deep. Over 1.1 billion tons (1 billion metric tons) of ore have been extracted, about a third of the total. Open-cast mines efficiently extract bauxite (aluminum ore), iron ore, and other minerals but have a greater environmental impact than deep-shaft mines.

THE POPULATION EXPLOSION

In the past 500 years the population of the earth has risen from about 300 million people to approximately 6 billion – a 20-fold increase. According to projections by the United Nations, continuing growth, though slower than expected a few years ago, will increase the world's population to 9.4 billion by the year 2050. Such an increase is the result of many factors, including improved sanitation and medical treatment, which allow more babies to survive their first year and go on to live longer lives. Until now, advances in technology have yielded sufficient food to feed the burgeoning population, but how much longer agriculture will be able to meet the demand remains uncertain. One of the consequences of increasing populations in developing countries is a steady drift of people from the country to the city in search of work. Such urbanization results in shantytowns appearing on the outskirts of cities; lacking proper services and amenities, they pose grave risks to health.

City of contrasts
Rio de Janeiro has a population of about 6 million, swollen by migrants from the countryside. Lack of both money and space forces people to live in favelas – shantytowns that cling to the hills surrounding the city.

© Bartholomew

Population Density
(people per sq. km.)

Less than 1
1 – 50
50 – 250
More than 250

● Largest conurbations

Los Angeles
Mexico City
New York
São Paulo
Buenos Aires
Rio de Janeiro
London
The Ruhr
Paris
Moscow
Cairo
Tehran
Delhi
Bombay
Calcutta
Tokyo/Yokohama
Osaka/Kobe
Seoul
Manila
Jakarta

1 sq. km. = 0.386 sq. mi.

Mapping the masses

The world's population is far from evenly distributed. A map of population density (above) shows that the areas with the heaviest concentrations are Europe, the Indian subcontinent, and China. No areas are now truly free of human settlement: even Antarctica contains permanent scientific bases, staffed for months or years by research teams.

Predicting the peak

The term *population explosion* describes the huge increase in the number of people on earth over the past 200 years. This explosion occurred at different times in different parts of the world; it is now most marked in developing countries. In West and Central Africa, for example, population is growing by more than 3 percent a year. By contrast, Europe's population, which increased most rapidly in the late 19th century, is now rising at only 0.4 percent and may soon decline. Many governments encourage birth control. China, for example, has tried to control population by restricting married couples to one child.

Too many people?

The chart (left) shows the historic pattern of world population increase. Fastest growth now occurs in the developing regions of Africa and Asia. The global population has increased by more than 10 times since 1750, and it may double again before a stable level is reached.

- Asia
- Americas
- Russia
- Africa
- Oceania
- Europe

(Global population (billions) chart — years: 1750, 1800, 1850, 1900, 1950, 2000; values 1, 2, 3)

Feeding the world

The most feared consequence of a rising global population is worldwide famine. Such a catastrophe was originally forecast by the English economist Thomas Malthus in 1798, when the population of the planet was around 600 million. Now it is nearly 6 billion, yet the predicted shortages have not arisen. Localized famines do occur but are almost always the consequence of human conflict. In recent times world food production, aided by new strains of rice and wheat, has increased at a greater rate than the population. Between 1980 and 1992 food production rose by 28 percent, while the increase in population was only 24 percent.

(Rice produced / consumed chart — countries: China, India, Indonesia, Bangladesh, Vietnam, Thailand, Myanmar (Burma), Brazil, Philippines, Japan)

1 metric ton = 1.102 tons

Rice production

The staple food of eastern Asia is rice, one of the most productive, though highly labor-intensive, of crops. Several of the world's most populous nations are in Asia, yet – as is shown in the above chart – all but one of these countries produce more rice than they consume annually. The exception is Japan, which, as the richest nation in the region, can afford to import its rice.

A picture of population

The scientific study of population is called demography. One of its most commonly used tools is a population pyramid – a graph that shows the numbers of men and women in each age group, the youngest at the bottom.

A great deal can be learned from a country's population pyramid. A truly pyramidal shape, with a wide base tapering toward the top, indicates a high birthrate and low life expectancy – characteristics of many countries in the developing world. Countries with a lower rate of population growth and longer life expectancies have a differently shaped pyramid, with a narrower base and much less tapering toward the top. In many developed countries, a wide waist to the pyramid reflects the large numbers born during the "baby boom" years after World War II. For every country the lopsided shape of the pyramid reflects the fact that women, on average, live longer than men.

Pyramids of people

The population pyramids (right) of two countries in the Far East correspond closely to their different economic and social circumstances. Vietnam is experiencing rapid growth after the strife-torn middle years of the 20th century. This growth is reflected in the wide base of its population pyramid. The diagram dwindles to a narrow peak, reflecting both the casualties of war and the low life expectancy in a country that has seen its health care facilities ravaged by conflict. Japan, by contrast, shows a population pyramid typical of a mature, industrialized economy. Many more people survive into old age, and a low birthrate is reflected in the relatively small number of children.

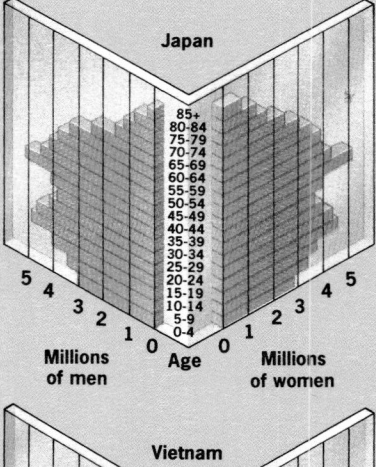

Japan. Millions of men — Age — Millions of women (age groups 0-4 to 85+)

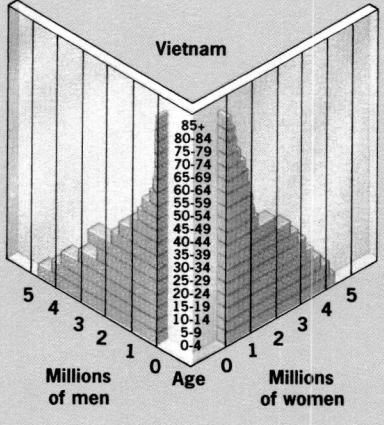

Vietnam. Millions of men — Age — Millions of women (age groups 0-4 to 85+)

THE ENERGY AUDIT

Much of the world's population aspires to the energy-hungry, affluent lifestyle that many of us in the Western Hemisphere simply take for granted – owning a car, living and working in heated or air-conditioned premises, and using labor-saving devices that depend on electricity. Countries of the developed world consume far more energy than those of the developing world. Even the intensive agriculture of the developed world uses significantly more energy than the subsistence farming of developing lands. The use of fossil fuels, however, pumps pollutants into the air and boosts the proportion of carbon dioxide in the atmosphere, trapping long-wave radiation and over-heating the earth's surface. As concern about this so-called greenhouse effect mounts, and as oil, coal, and other nonrenewable resources become scarcer and more expensive, the search for alternative sources of energy that harness sunlight, wind, and water becomes more urgent than ever.

Harvesting the wind
This forest of metal pylons topped by whirring blades (background) is one of many "wind farms" in the U.S. that convert the wind's energy into electricity. Hundreds of turbines, however, are needed to replace one small power station.

Alternative sources
People in the developed world consume fossil fuels at an alarming rate. In 1995 the average North American used the equivalent of 6.6 tons (6 metric tons) of oil – more than six times the world average for the same year. Even without an increase in consumption, the world's known oil reserves would run out in the year 2039, and natural gas would last only until 2061.

Alternative sources of energy bring their own disadvantages: reservoirs and tidal barrages created to harness hydro-electric power can engulf sensitive habitats; start-up costs for extracting worthwhile amounts of solar power are high; and wind farms are noisy and unsightly. Controlled nuclear fusion, which holds out the promise of releasing unlimited energy from sea water, is still in the experimental stage.

Energy-hungry earth
Throughout the world most of the energy used is derived from three principal fossil fuels: oil, coal, and gas. A graph of consumption in the main land areas (left) shows that in most places oil or gas is the predominant fuel. The graph also reveals the huge difference between developed and developing regions in the total amount of energy consumed. The gap, however, is narrowing, and in most parts of the world, consumption is rising. An exception is the group of countries that used to form the Soviet Union, where the political upheavals of the early 1990s actually resulted in reduced consumption.

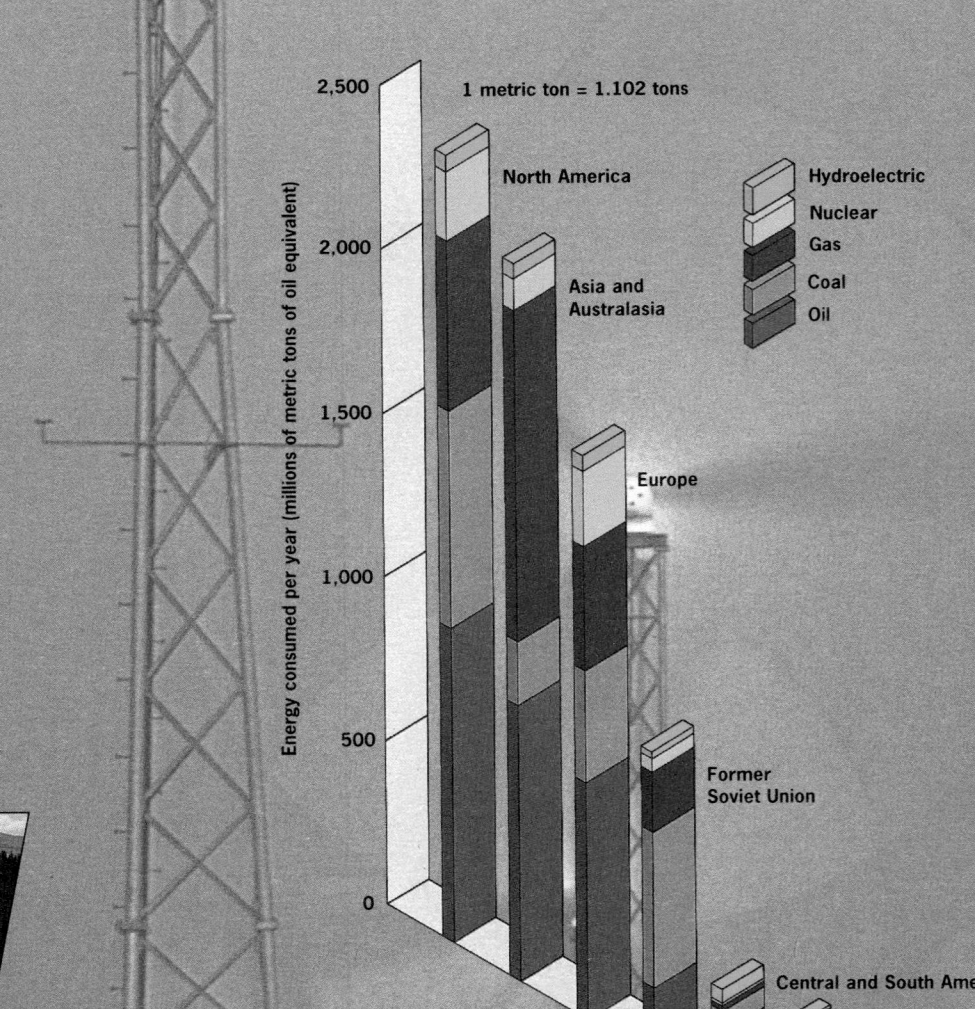

1 metric ton = 1.102 tons

Energy consumed per year (millions of metric tons of oil equivalent)

2,500
2,000
1,500
1,000
500
0

North America

Asia and Australasia

Europe

Former Soviet Union

Central and South America

Middle East

Africa

Hydroelectric
Nuclear
Gas
Coal
Oil

Water power
The dam at Loch Laggan in the Scottish Highlands (above) creates enough water pressure to drive a set of powerful turbines and generators. Hydroelectricity is the world's most common form of renewable energy.

Sun power
Solar cells (above) are made from layers of silicon that convert sunlight directly into electricity. Commonly used to power pocket calculators, they are too costly for large-scale power generation.

Steam power
More than half the homes in Iceland keep warm by using water heated by hot volcanic rocks. Natural steam from deep underground is also piped to the surface to drive power stations (right).

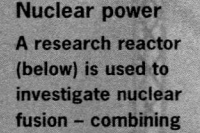

Nuclear power
A research reactor (below) is used to investigate nuclear fusion – combining atomic nuclei to release "clean" energy.

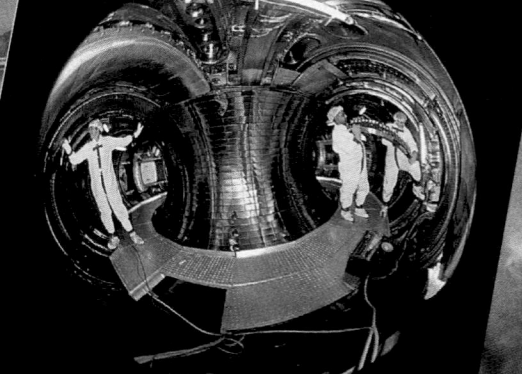

Choking the roads

There are more than 600 million motor vehicles on the world's roads. Vehicle registrations rose by 3.3 percent between 1982 and 1992 – along with an inevitable, steady increase in the amount of pollution pumped out by their engines. Some countries have passed legislation to limit exhaust emissions. California, for example, has set manufacturers the task of ensuring that by the year 2003, cars with "zero emissions" will account for 10 percent of all sales. This might make electric vehicles more common, but at present they have neither the performance nor the range of rivals powered by the internal combustion engine.

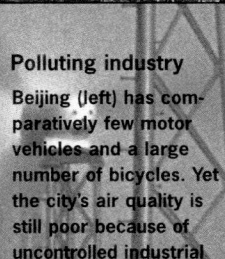

Polluting industry

Beijing (left) has comparatively few motor vehicles and a large number of bicycles. Yet the city's air quality is still poor because of uncontrolled industrial pollution.

Hands on the wheel

An examination of levels of automobile ownership around the world shows the stark divide between the developed and developing worlds. The U.S., for instance, has 147 million cars on the road – one vehicle for fewer than every two people. In contrast, Bangladesh has a population of over 125 million but only 43,000 cars.

600
500
400
300
200
100

Number of cars per 1,000 people

USA
Germany
Australia
UK
Japan
Ireland
Oman
Brazil
Zimbabwe
Indonesia
India
China
Bangladesh

Smog city

A ring of mountains shelters car-loving Los Angeles (above, left) from onshore breezes. As a result pollutants – especially smog formed by the action of sunlight on exhaust fumes – get trapped in a low-lying layer of hot air.

Power to the people

The energy sources used in developing countries vary enormously, depending on natural resources. Africa has few fossil fuels and limited ability to buy them, so wood and dried manure supply more than 80 percent of energy needs. Chinese homes and factories alike burn a lot of coal, of which China is the world's second-largest producer.

Although they consume less fuel per capita than their Western counterparts, developing countries face their own energy problems. The felling of trees for firewood can quickly strip an area of its stabilizing vegetation, leading to soil erosion. Gathering cattle dung for burning robs fields of valuable nutrients.

Alternative sources of energy are available but harnessed on a smaller scale than in the developed world. Solar electricity needs expensive equipment, but a simple reflecting dish can focus sunlight onto a pot to boil water. Building dams for hydroelectric power is also costly and can damage sensitive ecosystems, but a "microhydro" scheme can use a stream to drive a small turbine, providing local electricity with minimal disruption to the environment.

Daily harvest

In Vietnam and other developing countries, collecting wood for fuel is one of the day's most important tasks (left). However, the scale of felling is damaging many forests.

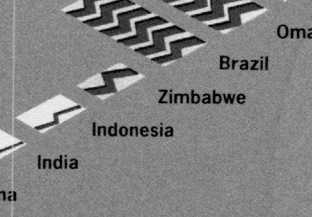

Animal traction

In Egypt oxen are still used to pull plows and to extract water from wells for irrigation (right). Plant-eating animals have less-exacting "fuel" needs than a petrol engine.

Sunbaked

A wide dish made from recycled metal sheets focuses the sun's rays onto a solar oven (right). In bright sunshine the energy concentrated on the oven can raise the temperature high enough to bake bread.

51

Remodeling our Planet

Seen from outer space, the face of the earth appears to be entirely the work of nature, sculpted by forces such as plate tectonics and erosion. A closer look, however, reveals how radically the land has been altered by human activity. Many major rivers have been diverted or dammed to prevent flooding, irrigate crops, regulate water supply, or generate electricity; vast areas of woodland have been cleared for agriculture, forever marring their pristine beauty; and new forests have been planted for timber and papermaking. Features of the landscape, such as ridges and hills, have been modified to create defensive structures to repel attack. Population pressure and land shortages have motivated the reclamation of marshland and the utilization of vertical space through terraces on steep hillsides, or skyscrapers in confined city centers. The clever skills of the engineer have given rise to canals and tunnels that slice through natural barriers, and bridges that span rivers and harbors.

Ancient barrier
The Great Wall of China (background) marked the ancient northern border of China. Portions that still stand date back to the Ming Dynasty (1368-1644).

Built for defense
From the days of the first cave dwellers, natural features have been exploited to provide protection against the elements, animals, and fellow humans. A mountain ridge, topped by a wall, becomes an impenetrable barrier; a hill is an easily defended stronghold. An acropolis, at the highest point of an ancient Greek city, was both citadel and sanctuary.

Winning more space
Humans have always shown ingenuity in putting seemingly inhospitable terrain to good use. If level land is at a premium, hillside terraces allow the cultivation of grapes in Europe and rice in Asia. In the 15th century the Aztecs used a system of dikes and ditches to convert the swampy Lake Chalco into productive farmland. Since 1900 reclamation of land from the sea has increased the area of the Netherlands by almost 650 sq. mi. (1,680 sq. km.).

Reach for the sky
The skyline of New York's financial district shows how architects have built upward to provide much-needed office space above the streets of crowded Manhattan Island.

Fortified temple
The Incas flattened a mountain ridge to create the fortress city of Machu Picchu. Its impregnable position is 2,000 ft. (610 m.) above the Urubamba river in the Andes.

Land from the sea
In a satellite image of the Netherlands, polders, or areas of reclaimed land, are seen as a green patchwork (below).

Across the divide

Natural features that once formed barriers between peoples and nations are crossed every day in the course of modern trade and travel. Advances in steel technology since the 1850s have revolutionized the construction of bridges, making it possible to span increasingly wide spaces. A planned bridge across the Akashi Strait in Japan, for example, will have a main span nearly 1.25 mi. (2 km.) long. Tunnels are now dug by huge machines that chew their way through rock like giant earthworms. Such dynamos excavated the 31 mi. (50 km.) tunnel under the English Channel, linking England to France in 1990. Major canals provide shortcuts for trade around peninsulas, and sometimes whole continents. The Suez Canal, opened in 1869, linked the Mediterranean with the Red Sea, allowing ships from Europe to avoid the trip around the Cape of Good Hope on their way to India and Australia.

Narrow passage

The Corinth Canal (left) cuts through the 4-mile (6 km.) isthmus that joins the Peloponnese Peninsula to mainland Greece, shortening the voyage from Piraeus to the Ionian Sea by over 200 mi. (320 km.).

Desert track

The city of Perth is separated from the rest of Australia by vast deserts. The Nullarbor Plain is crossed by a railway (below) with the longest straight section in the world.

Mountain fields

Man-made terraces, such as these rice paddies in the Philippines, allow steep hillsides to be used for growing food.

Graceful span

The Humber Bridge in England (left) has a central section of 4,626 ft. (1,410 m.). When completed in 1981, it included the world's longest single span. It cuts out a lengthy detour inland.

BUILDING IT BIG

Longest multispan bridge		
Lake Pontchartrain Causeway, Louisiana	24 mi. (38.4 km.)	
Longest railway tunnel		
Seikan Tunnel, Japan	33.5 mi. (53.9 km)	
Highest structure		
CN Tower, Toronto, Canada	1,814 ft. (553 m.)	
Longest canal for oceangoing vessels		
Suez Canal, Egypt	118 mi. (190 km.)	
Highest dam		
Nurek, on the Vakhsh River, Tajikistan	984 ft. (300 m.)	
Largest man-made lake		
Lake Volta, Ghana	3,274 sq. mi. (8,482 sq. km.)	

54 THE WORLD IN MAPS

CONTENTS

KEY TO MAPS

CITIES AND TOWNS

	MAP SCALES	MAP SCALES
	1:300,000-1:9,000,000	1:12,000,000-1:18,000,000
Major city	**Chicago**	Chicago
Large city	**Iquitos**	Iquitos
Towns	Tacna	Tacna
Other settlements	Old Crow	Old Crow
⬤ Urban areas		

CAPITALS OF POLITICAL UNITS

PARIS ORANJESTAD	Independent country and dependent territory
Winnipeg Pierre	State, province, etc.
Waukegan	County, oblast, etc.

POLITICAL BOUNDARIES

International

International disputed de jure

International disputed de facto

Demarcation line

Indefinite, undefined, over open water

Main administrative (state, province, etc.)

Other administrative (county, oblast, etc.)

AUSTRALIA MALAYSIA — Independent country

GREENLAND PUERTO RICO — Dependent territory

PARÁ COOK — Administrative area

NORMANDIE *ALENTEJO* — Cultural, historic region

TRANSPORTATION

Motorway, special highway

Main road

Other road

Track

Main railway

Other railway

Tunnel, road

Tunnel, rail

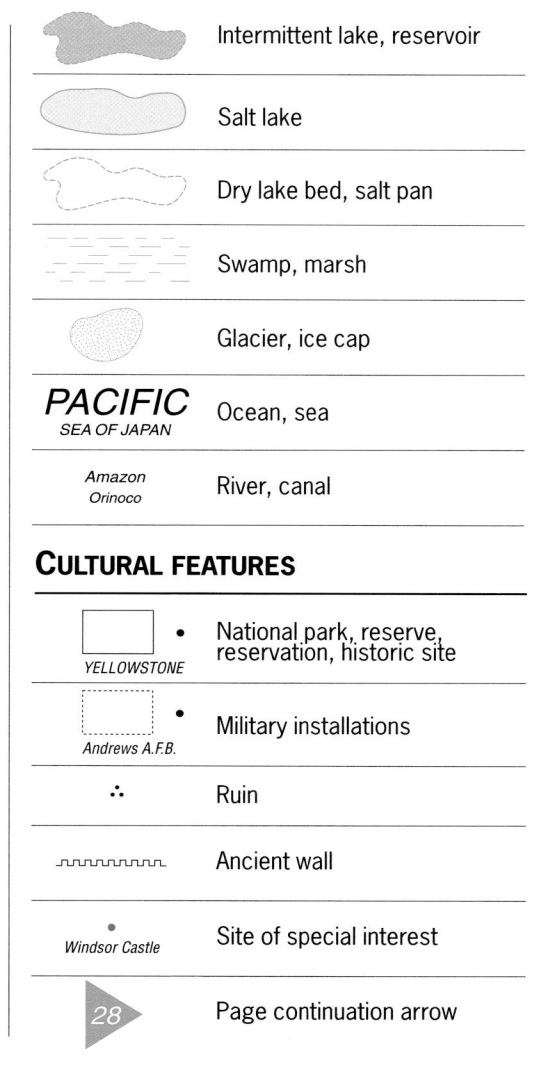

Bridge, road or rail

Car and rail ferries

International airport

Other airport

TOPOGRAPHIC FEATURES

Matterhorn 4478 m ▲ — **Elevation above sea level**

76 m ▼ — **Elevation below sea level**

Mount Fuji 3776 m ▲ — **Volcano**

≍ — **Mountain pass**

∗ — **Rock**

Lava

Sand desert, dunes

ANDES La Gran Sabana — **Mountain range, plateau, plain, etc.**

NEW GUINEA Hispaniola — **Island**

Cape York Pen. Lizard Point — **Peninsula, cape, point, etc.**

PATAGONIA *Barkly Tableland* — **Physical region, desert, forest, etc.**

Elevation & depth tints

HEIGHT

9,842ft. 3,000m.

6,562ft. 2,000m.

3,281ft. 1,000m.

1,640ft. 500m.

656ft. 200m.

Sea level

656ft. 200m.

6,562ft. 2,000m.

DEPTH

HYDROGRAPHIC FEATURES

River, stream

Intermittent river

Salto Ángel — **Falls**

764m ▽ — **Depth of water**

Navigable canal

Irrigation or drainage canal

Los Angeles Aqueduct — **Aqueduct**

Intracoastal waterway

Reef

Kumdah ○ — **Oasis, spring, geyser**

Cree Lake — **Lake, reservoir**

(395m) — **Height of lake above sea level**

Dam

Intermittent lake, reservoir

Salt lake

Dry lake bed, salt pan

Swamp, marsh

Glacier, ice cap

PACIFIC SEA OF JAPAN — **Ocean, sea**

Amazon Orinoco — **River, canal**

CULTURAL FEATURES

YELLOWSTONE — **National park, reserve, reservation, historic site**

Andrews A.F.B. — **Military installations**

∴ — **Ruin**

Ancient wall

Windsor Castle — **Site of special interest**

28 — **Page continuation arrow**

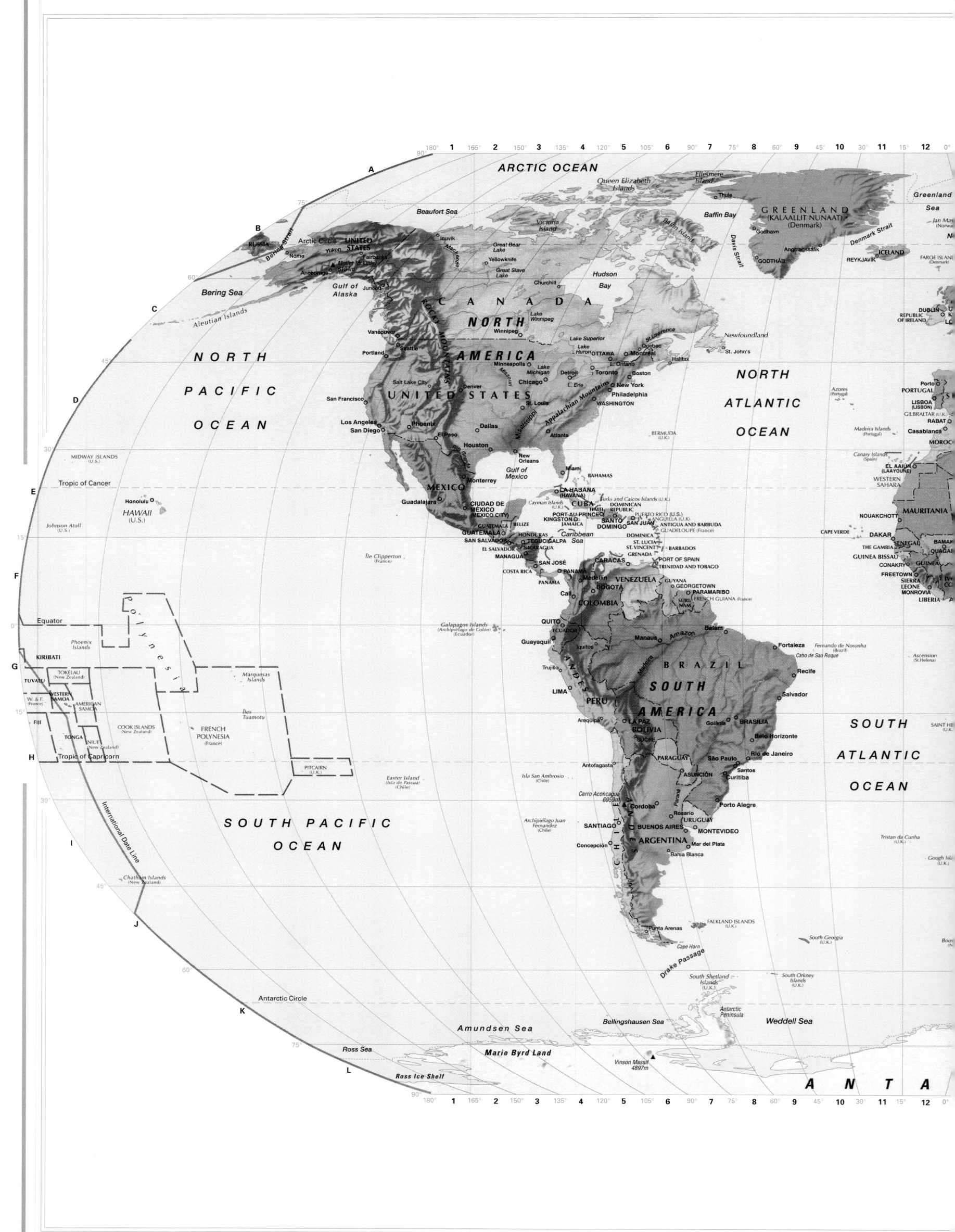

Scale 1:80,000,000

One centimeter represents 800 kilometers.

One inch represents approximately 1265 miles.

Of the earth's total surface area of some 197 million sq. mi. (510 million sq. km.), more than two-thirds is covered by oceans. The remaining 57 million sq. mi. (148 million sq. km.) – the world's seven continents and myriad islands, both large and small – amount to a mere 29 percent of the total. Yet these land areas encompass an astonishing array of landforms and habitats and are home to richly varied human cultures.

57

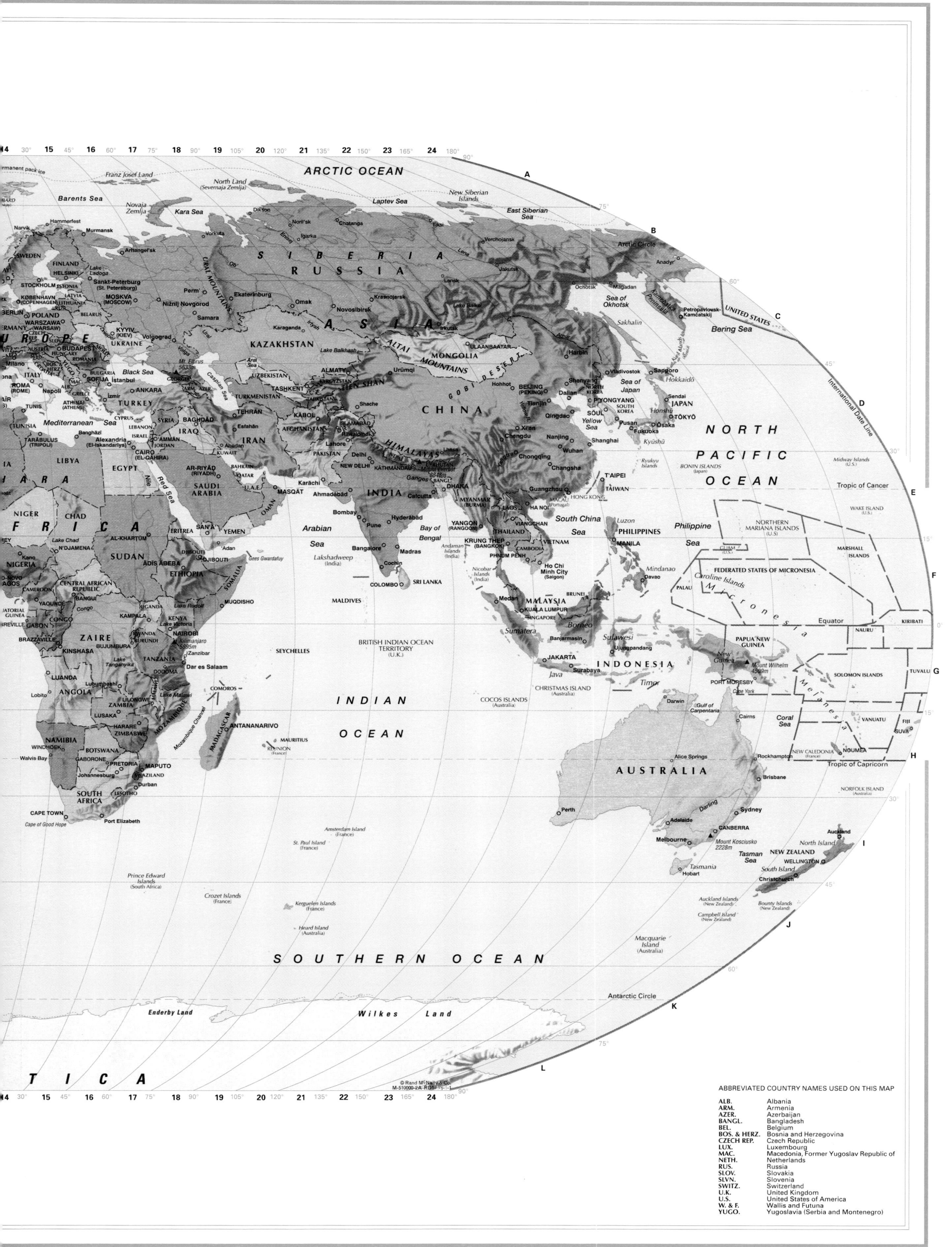

ABBREVIATED COUNTRY NAMES USED ON THIS MAP

ALB.	Albania
ARM.	Armenia
AZER.	Azerbaijan
BANGL.	Bangladesh
BEL.	Belgium
BOS. & HERZ.	Bosnia and Herzegovina
CZECH REP.	Czech Republic
LUX.	Luxembourg
MAC.	Macedonia, Former Yugoslav Republic of
NETH.	Netherlands
RUS.	Russia
SLOV.	Slovakia
SLVN.	Slovenia
SWITZ.	Switzerland
U.K.	United Kingdom
U.S.	United States of America
W. & F.	Wallis and Futuna
YUGO.	Yugoslavia (Serbia and Montenegro)

0	500	1000	2000	3000	4000	5000	6000	7000	8000 Kilometers

0	500	1000	2000	3000	4000	5000 Miles

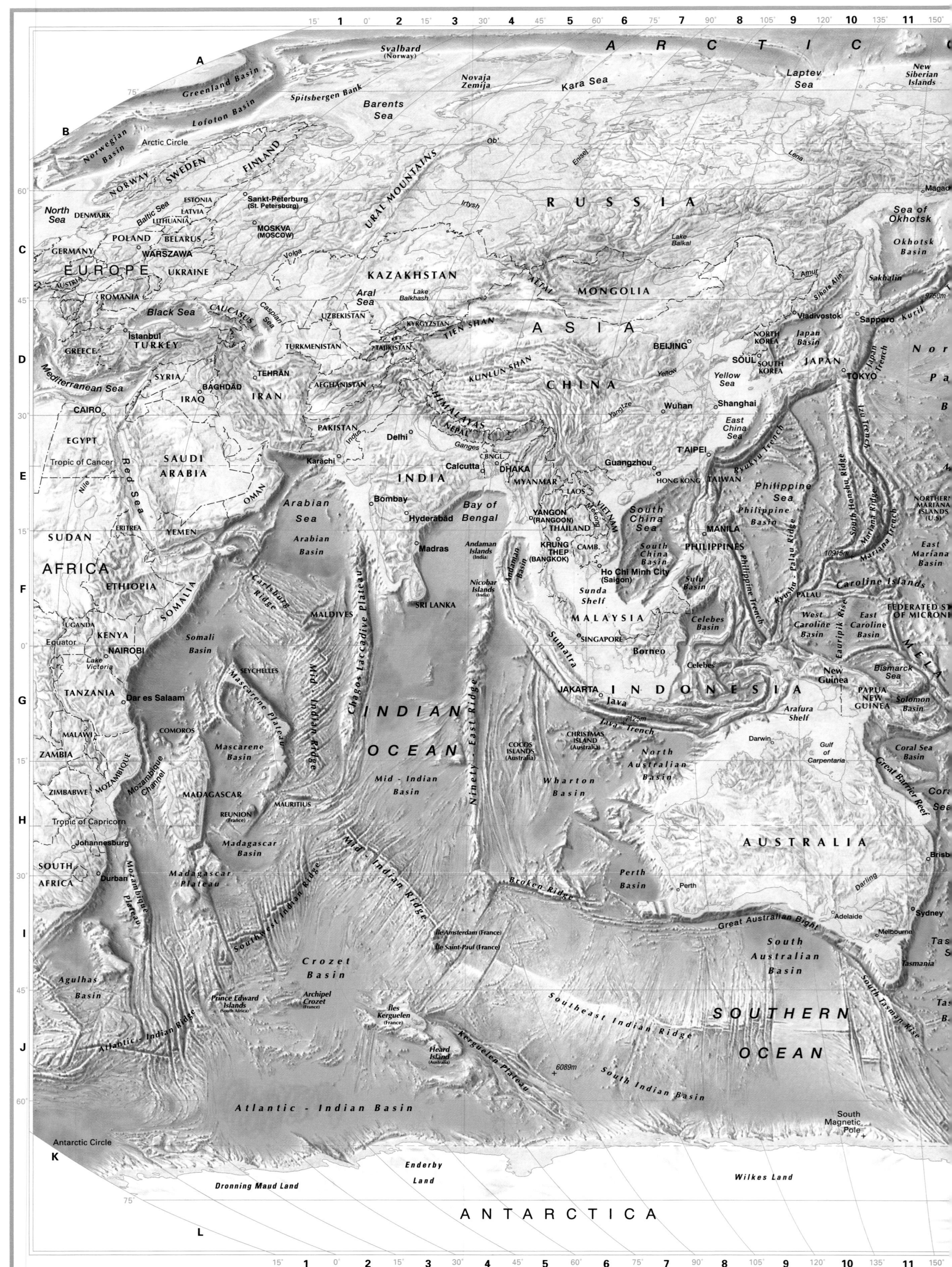

Lambert Conformal Conic Projection

Scale 1:60,000,000

One centimeter represents 600 kilometers.

One inch represents approximately 950 miles.

Named by its first European navigator, Magellan, who enjoyed calm weather there, the Pacific is the world's largest and deepest ocean. Covering one-third of the earth's surface, it occupies more territory than all seven continents combined. The greatest known ocean depth lies within its Mariana Trench, some 35,000 ft. (10,700 m.) deep. By contrast, the Indian Ocean bottoms out at 24,459 ft. (7,455 m.).

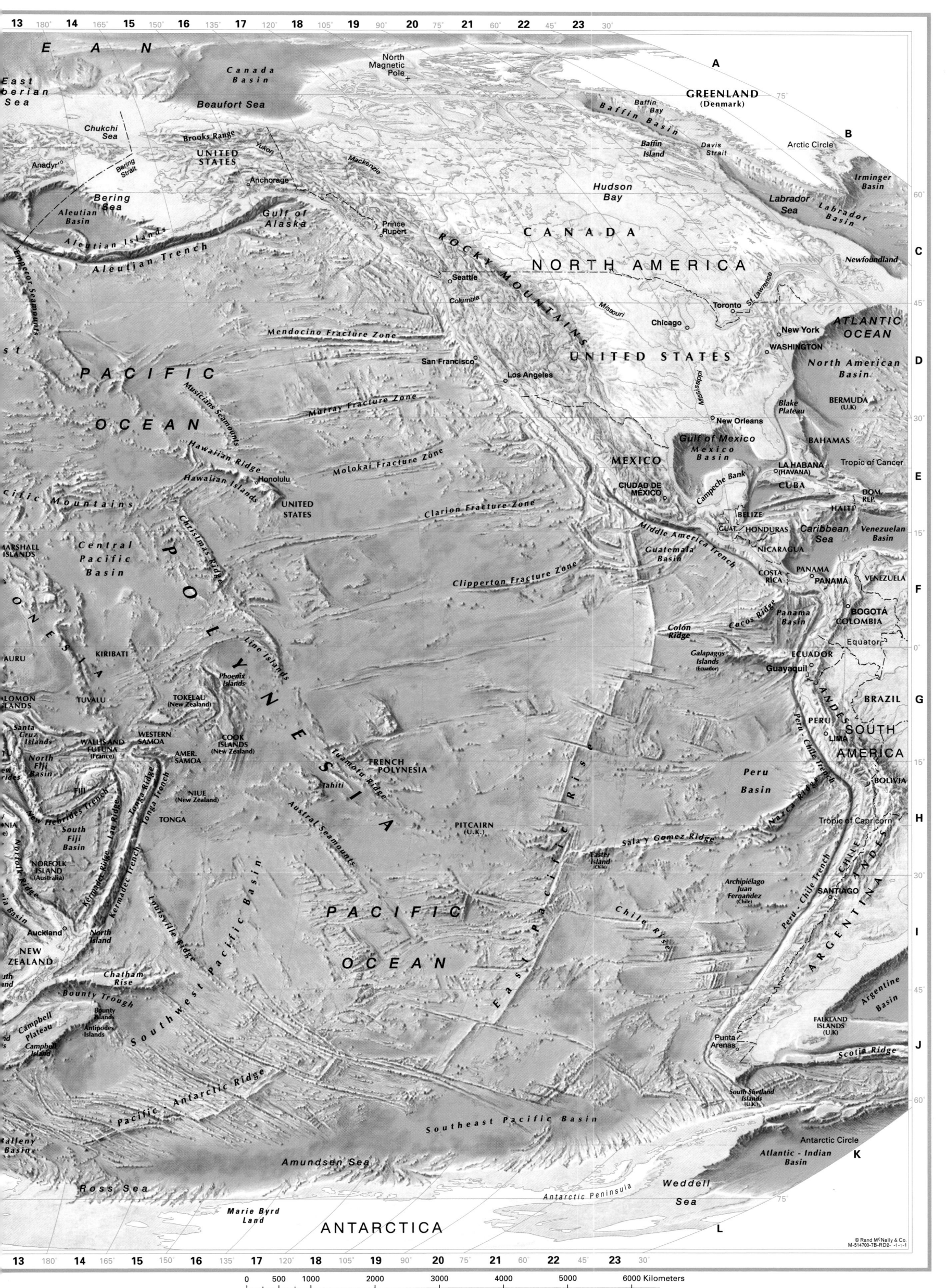

The world's second-largest ocean after the Pacific, the Atlantic has (on average) the warmest and saltiest waters of any ocean. It is named after Africa's Atlas Mountains, which, for the ancient Greeks, marked the western boundary between the known and the unknown world.

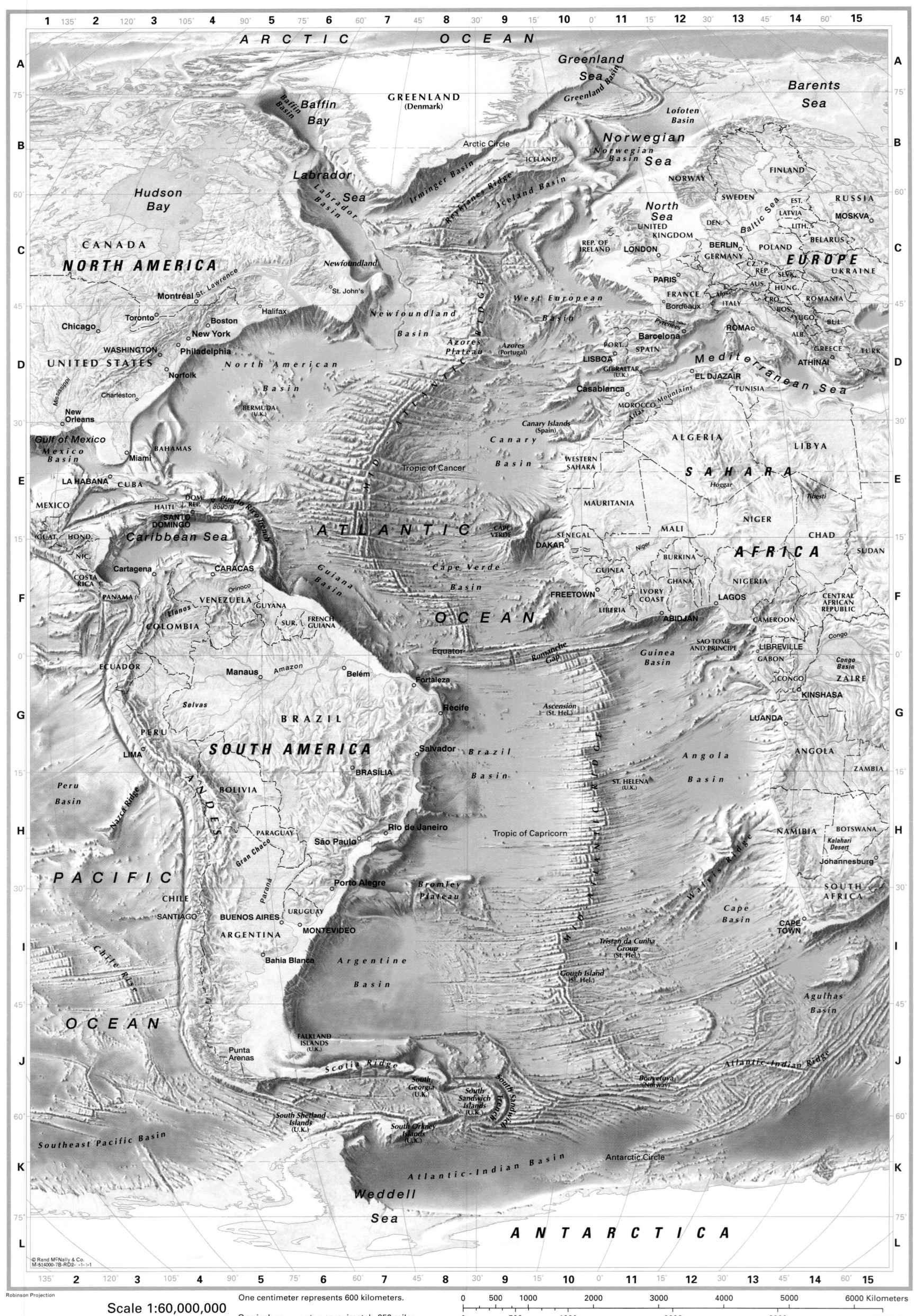

Robinson Projection

Scale 1:60,000,000

One centimeter represents 600 kilometers.

One inch represents approximately 950 miles.

| 0 | 500 | 1000 | 2000 | 3000 | 4000 | 5000 | 6000 Kilometers |

| 0 | 500 | 1000 | 2000 | 3000 | 4000 Miles |

Though the smallest of the world's oceans, the Arctic Ocean has the widest continental shelf on earth. The North Pole lies at the ocean's frozen center while Europe, Asia, and North America ring its waters, which in many spots are covered by 10-ft.-thick (3 m.) pack ice year-round.

PACIFIC OCEAN

Aleutian Trench

Aleutian Islands

Kuril Trench

(A)

Aleutian Basin

Bering Sea

Petropavlovsk-Kamčatskij

Gulf of Alaska Seamount Province

Okhotsk Basin

ostrov Sachalin (Sakhalin)

Sea of Okhotsk

Gulf of Alaska

Magadan

St. Lawrence Island

Anchorage

Nome

(B)

Anadyr

Juneau

Arctic Circle

Bering Strait

Čerskij Range

UNITED STATES

Chukchi Sea

Ambarčik

Kolyma

Jakutsk

Mackenzie Mountains

Brooks Range

Barrow

ostrov Vrangelja (Wrangel I.)

East Siberian Sea

Lena

Verhojansk Range

ASIA

Mackenzie

Inuvik

(C)

NEW SIBERIAN ISLANDS

NORTH AMERICA

Beaufort Sea

Mendeleyev Ridge

Tiksi

Sachs Harbour

Canada Basin

ARCTIC OCEAN

Makarov Basin

Laptev Sea

Nordvik

RUSSIA

Banks Island

Victoria Island

Cambridge Bay

Alpha Cordillera

(D)

Lomonosov Ridge

Fram Basin

Nansen Basin

Noril'sk

Enise

Parry Channel

QUEEN ELIZABETH ISLANDS

North Magnetic Pole

North Pole

Nansen Cordillera

NORTH LAND

Dikson

CANADA

Ellesmere Island

(D)

FRANZ JOSEF LAND

Etah

Alert

Lincoln Sea

Baffin Island

Baffin Basin

Baffin Bay

Kara Sea

Iqaluit

Davis Strait

Godhavn

NOVAJA ZEMLJA

Salehard

Ob'

SVALBARD (Norway)

Labrador Sea

GREENLAND (Denmark)

Greenland Sea

(C)

Spitsbergen Bank

Barents Sea

URAL MOUNTAINS

GODTHÅB

Arctic Circle

Greenland Basin

Hammerfest

Murmansk

White Sea

Arhangel'sk (Archangel)

Angmagssalik

Mohns Ridge

Tromsø

Kandalakša

Julianehåb

Jan Mayen (Norway)

Lofoten Basin

EUROPE

Denmark Strait

Jan Mayen Ridge

FINLAND

Norwegian Sea

SWEDEN

Sankt-Peterburg (St. Petersburg)

REYKJAVIK

ICELAND

Norwegian Basin

(B)

HELSINKI

ESTONIA

MOSKVA (MOSCOW)

Reykjanes Ridge

Trondheim

NORWAY

OSLO

STOCKHOLM

Baltic Sea

LATVIA

FAROE ISLANDS (Denmark)

Iceland Basin

Rockall Rise

(A)

North Sea

KØBENHAVN (COPENHAGEN)

LITHUANIA

BELARUS

ATLANTIC OCEAN

UNITED KINGDOM

DENMARK

GERMANY

POLAND

UKRAINE

© Rand McNally & Co.
M-513900-79-R-02-

Lambert Azimuthal Equal Area Projection

Scale 1:25,000,000

One centimeter represents 250 kilometers.

One inch represents approximately 390 miles.

0 250 500 1000 1500 2000 3000 4000 4500 Kilometers

0 250 500 1000 2000 Miles

EUROPE

ICELAND

NORWEGIAN SEA

FAROE ISLANDS (Denmark)

NORTH ATLANTIC OCEAN

REPUBLIC OF IRELAND

NORTHERN IRELAND

SCOTLAND

ENGLAND

UNITED KINGDOM

WALES

North Sea

NORWAY

SWEDEN

DENMARK

Baltic Sea

NETHERLANDS

BELGIUM

LUXEMBOURG

GERMANY

POLAND

CZECH REPUBLIC

FRANCE

SWITZERLAND

AUSTRIA

SLOVAKIA

HUNGARY

SLOVENIA

CROATIA

BOSNIA AND HERZEGOVINA

YUGOSLAVIA

ALBANIA

ITALY

SAN MARINO

MONACO

ANDORRA

PORTUGAL

SPAIN

PYRENEES

ALPS

Celtic Sea

Irish Sea

English Channel

Bay of Biscay

Gulf of Lions

Ligurian Sea

Adriatic Sea

Tyrrhenian Sea

Ionian Sea

Corse (Corsica) (France)

Sardegna (Sardinia) (Italy)

Sicilia (Sicily)

MALTA VALLETTA

Balearic Islands (Illes Balears)

Mallorca (Majorca)

MEDITERRANEAN SEA

MOROCCO

RABAT

Casablanca

ALGERIA

EL DJAZAÏR (ALGIERS)

ATLAS MOUNTAINS

TUNISIA

TUNIS

REYKJAVIK

PARIS

LONDON

DUBLIN

BRUXELLES

AMSTERDAM

BERLIN

WARSZAWA (WARSAW)

PRAHA (PRAGUE)

WIEN (VIENNA)

BRATISLAVA

BUDAPEST

LJUBLJANA

ZAGREB

SARAJEVO

BEOGRAD

TIRANE

ROMA (ROME)

Napoli (Naples)

MADRID

LISBOA (LISBON)

KØBENHAVN (COPENHAGEN)

STOCKHOLM

OSLO

Conic Equidistant Projection

© Rand McNally & Co.
DM-560000-7A-RD1-

Scale 1:12,000,000

One centimeter represents 120 kilometers.

One inch represents approximately 190 miles.

196

Europe is generally considered to be separated from Asia by the long north-south line of the Ural Mountains and, farther south, by the Caspian and Black Seas and the Caucasus Mountains. Although it is the second-smallest continent, Europe is the proud birthplace of many of Western civilization's greatest achievements, including democracy, parliamentary government, and the glories of the Renaissance.

Barents Sea
White Sea
West Siberian Plain
URAL MOUNTAINS (URAL'SKIE GORY)
KOMI
RUSSIA
FINLAND
KARELIJA
Murmansk
Arhangel'sk (Archangel)
Severodvinsk
Syktyvkar
Perm'
Ekaterinburg
Celjabinsk
Magnitogorsk
Omsk
Kurgan
Tjumen'
Niznij Tagil
UDMURTIJA
Izevsk
Kazan'
TATARIJA
BASKIRIJA
Ufa
Sankt-Peterburg (St. Petersburg) (Leningrad)
HELSINKI
Gulf of Finland
TALLINN
ESTONIA
LATVIA
Pskov
Novgorod
Vologda
Jaroslavl'
Kostroma
Niznij Novgorod (Gorky)
Nizni Novgorod
Ivanovo
Vladimir
MARIJ EL
Joskar-Ola
CUVASIJA
Ceboksary
Uljanovsk
Dimitrovgrad
Samara
Toljatti
Novokujbysevsk
MOSKVA (MOSCOW)
Tula
Rjazan'
Penza
Saransk
MORDOVIJA
Orenburg
Orsk
Novotroick
Tver'
Smolensk
Kaluga
Brjansk
Orel
Lipeck
Voronez
Tambov
Saratov
Engel's
Balakovo
MINSK
BELARUS
Homel' (Gomel')
Kursk
Belgorod
Volgograd (Stalingrad)
KALMYKIJA
CASPIAN DEPRESSION
KAZAKHSTAN
KYYIV (KIEV)
UKRAINE
Kharkiv (Khar'kov)
Poltava
Luhans'k
Donets'k
Rostov-na-Donu
Astrahan' (Astrakhan)
UST'URT PLATEAU
UZBEKISTAN
Aral Sea (41m)
Dnipropetrovs'k
Zaporizhzhya
Kryvyy Rih
Mykolaiv
Kherson
Odesa
MOLDOVA
CHISINAU
Mariupol'
Taganrog
Melitopol'
Berdyans'k
Stavropol'
Kara Kum (Garagum)
ROMANIA
BUCURESTI (BUCHAREST)
CRIMEA
Simferopol'
Sevastopol'
Yalta
Novorossijsk
Soci
Krasnodar
Majkop
Grozny
CEC
DAGESTAN
Mahackala
CASPIAN SEA (-28m)
TURKMENISTAN
BLACK SEA
Sea of Azov
CAUCASUS
Mt. Elbrus 5633m
Vladikavkaz
GEORGIA
TBILISI
AZERBAIJAN
BAKI (BAKU)
BULGARIA
Varna
Burgas
Istanbul
Sea of Marmara
Ankara
Batumi
Kutaisi
ARMENIA
YEREVAN
Samsun
Trabzon
Aegean Sea
Izmir
TURKEY
ASIA MINOR
Lake Urmia
Tabriz
TEHRAN
IRAN
Konya
Adana
Gaziantep
Sanliurfa
Diyarbakir
Mosul
Zagros Mountains
CYPRUS
NICOSIA
SYRIA
MESOPOTAMIA
IRAQ
BAGHDAD
LEBANON
Crete (Kriti)

0 200 400 600 800 1000 1200 Kilometers
0 200 400 600 800 Miles

Scandinavia

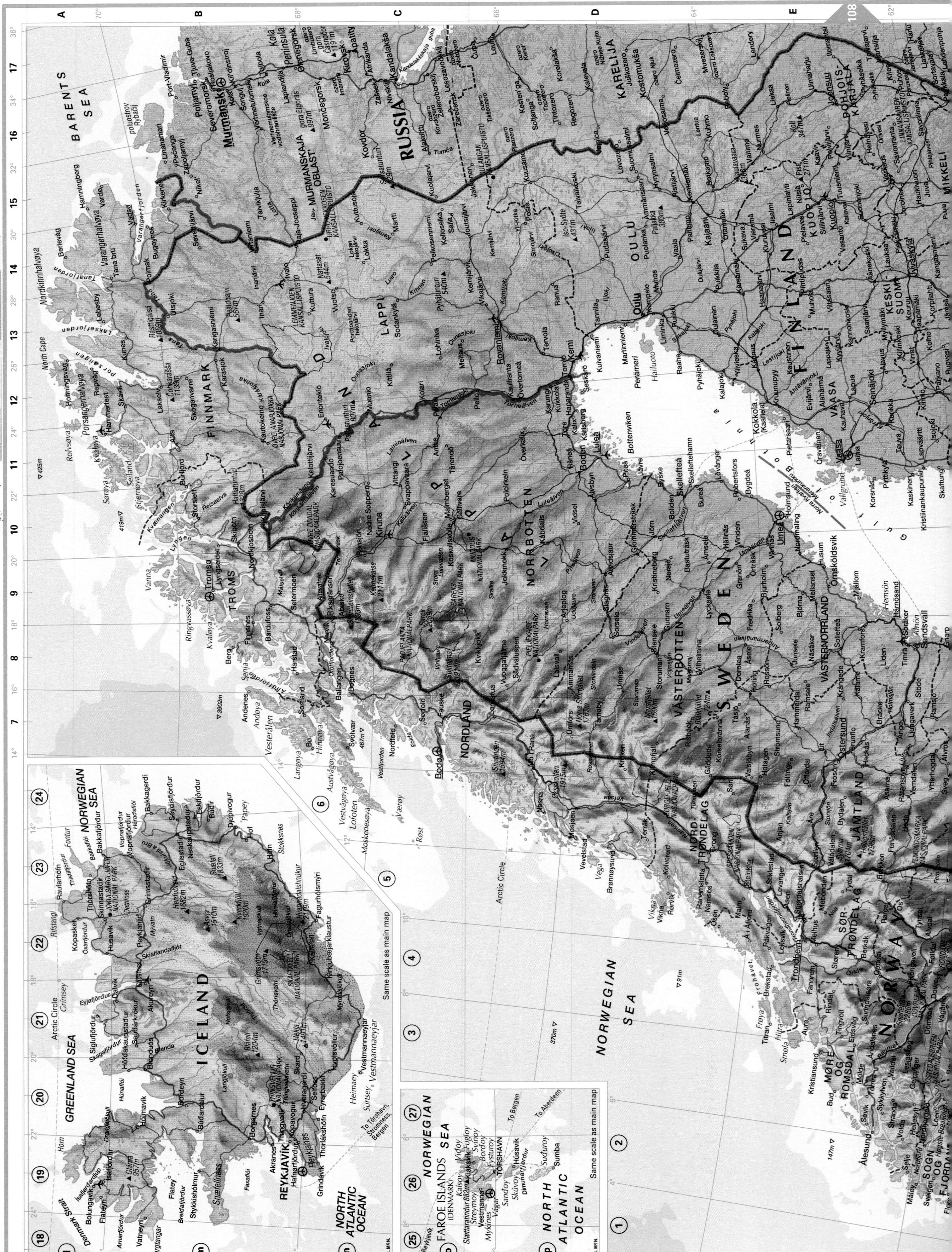

Scale 1:4,500,000

One centimeter represents 45 kilometers.

One inch represents approximately 71 miles.

Conic Equidistant Projection

Strictly speaking, the region known as Scandinavia encompasses only Norway and Sweden, which occupy the Scandinavian Peninsula, and nearby Denmark. But in the broader usage, it includes Finland and, far out in the Atlantic, Iceland and Denmark's Faroe Islands. Homeland of the ancient Vikings, this sea-girt region extends well north of the Arctic Circle into the Land of the Midnight Sun.

65

Southern Scandinavia and the Baltic States

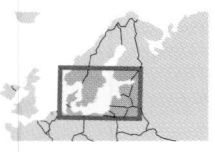

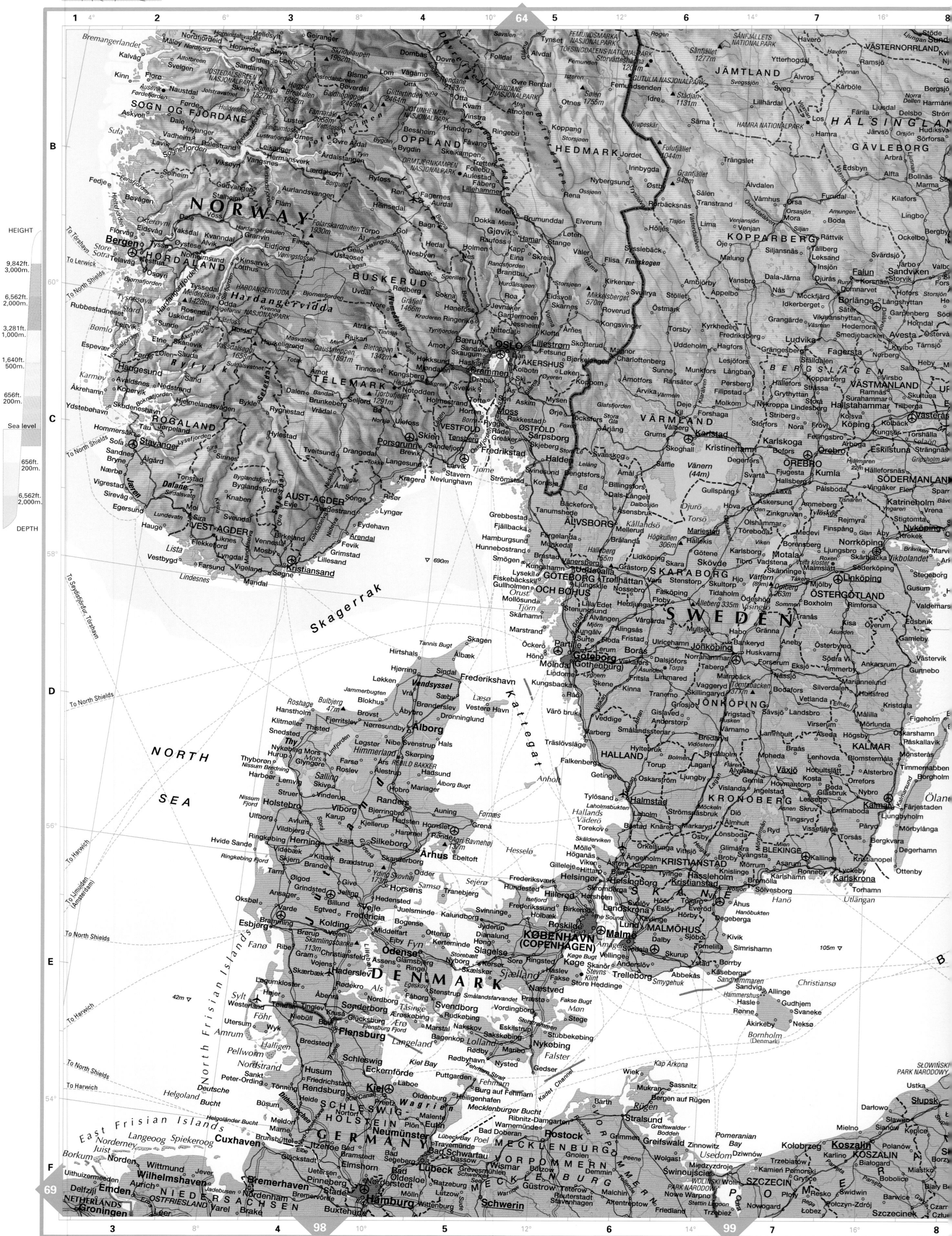

Conic Equidistant Projection

Scale 1:3,000,000

One centimeter represents 30 kilometers.

One inch represents approximately 47 miles.

Buried beneath an immense burden of ice during the Ice Age, the landscapes of this region abound with evidence of the bygone ice caps: the countless fjords etched into the coasts of Norway, the myriad lakes of southern Sweden and Finland, the glacier-honed lowlands of the Baltic states (Lithuania, Latvia, and Estonia), and the islands that emerge from the sea as the earth's crust, now free of ice, rebounds upward.

67

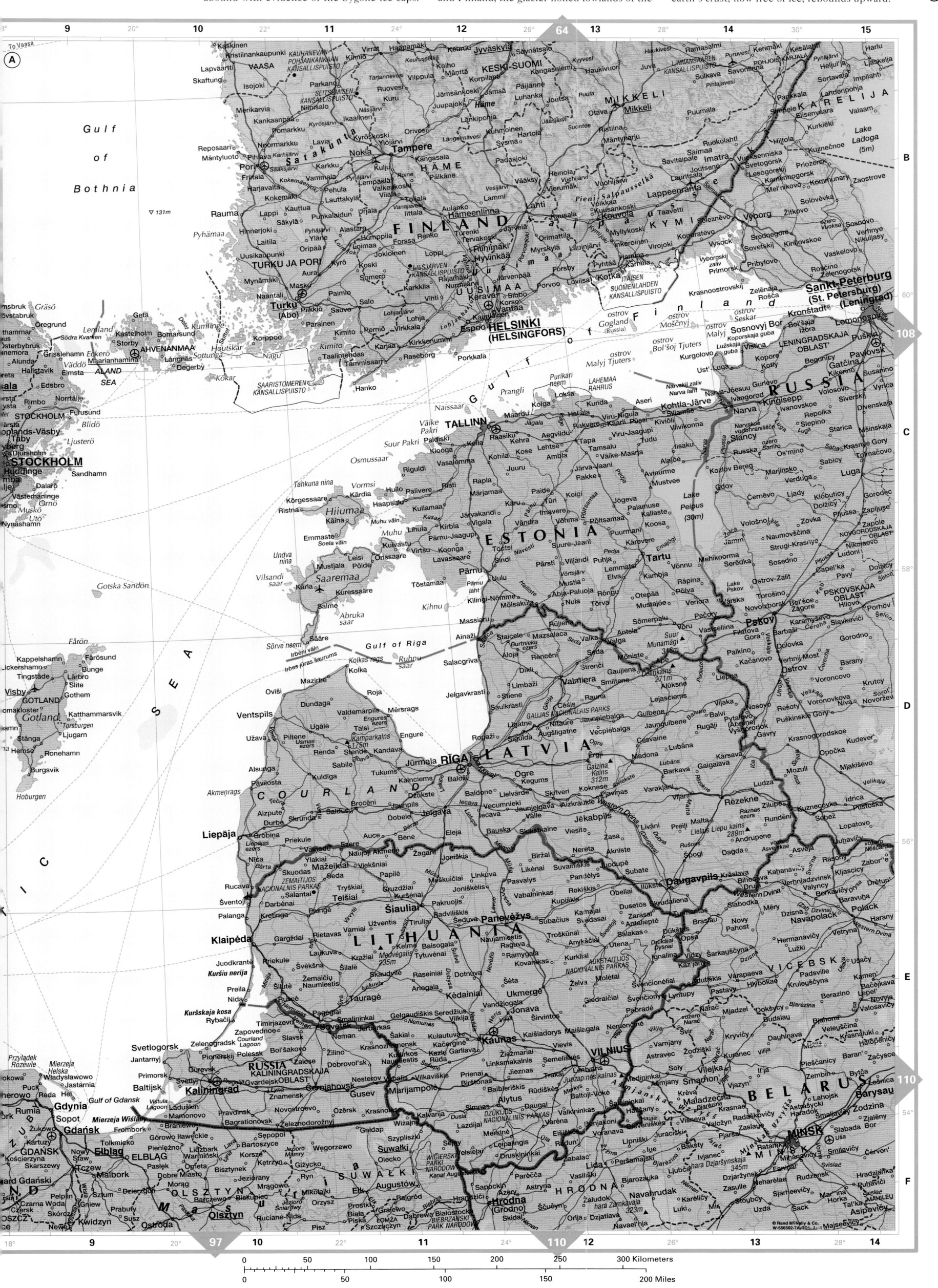

Denmark

A peninsula and some 400 neighboring islands make Denmark a stepping-stone between the European mainland and the Scandinavian peninsula. One of Europe's smallest states, Denmark has a 4,500-mile (7,200-km.) coastline and terrain that is among the flattest on earth.

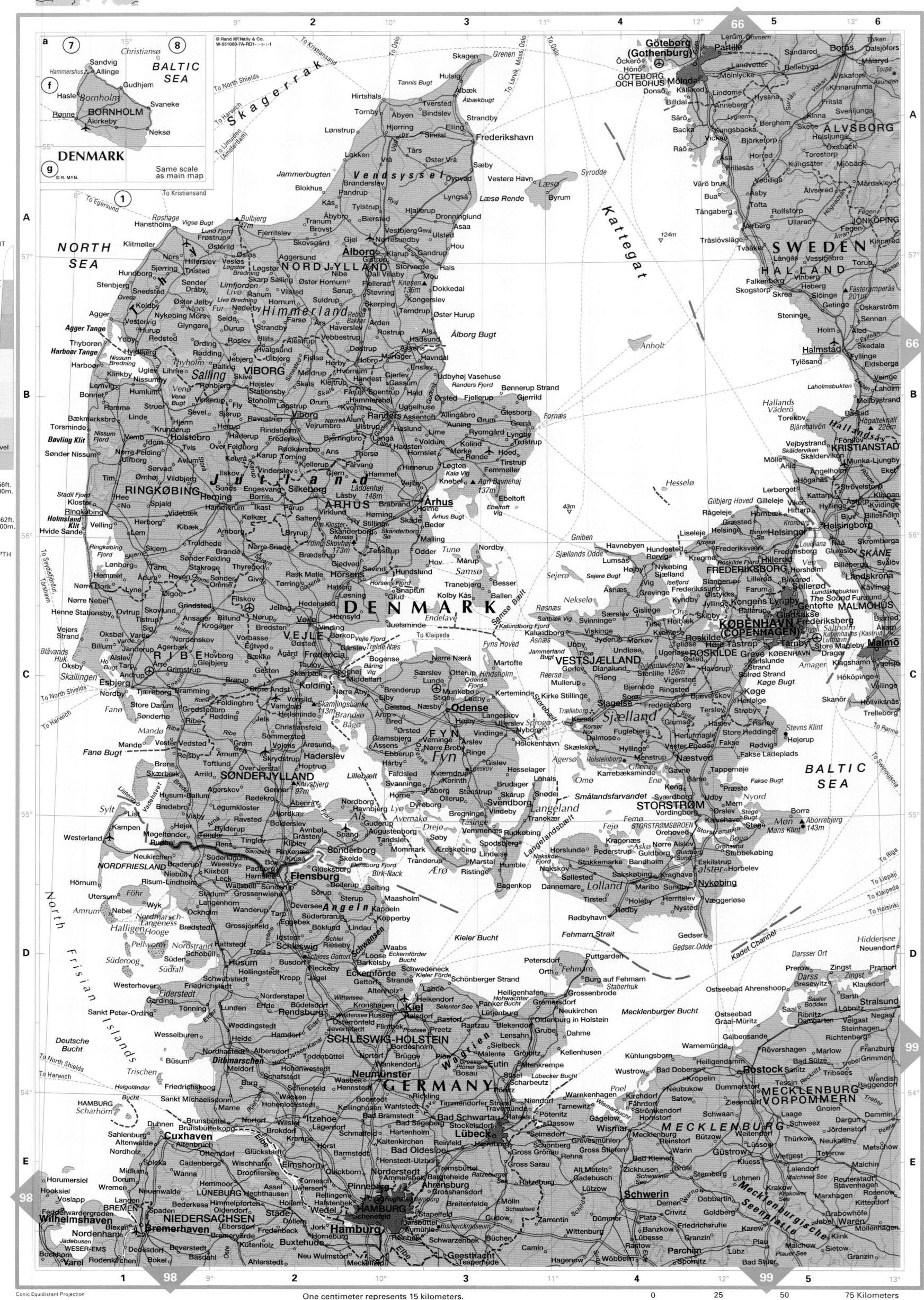

Scale 1:1,500,000

One centimeter represents 15 kilometers.

One inch represents approximately 24 miles.

Conic Equidistant Projection

| 0 | | 25 | | 50 | | 75 Kilometers |
| 0 | | 25 | | 50 Miles |

From the sandy heaths of Norfolk to the cliffs of the Dingle Peninsula in Ireland, from the deep red loams of Devon to the world's oldest known rocks near Loch Torridon, these western European islands offer a rich variety. The surrounding waters, never effective in deterring immigrants, are even less so now that a tunnel beneath the English Channel links Britain to the mainland for the first time since the Ice Age.

71

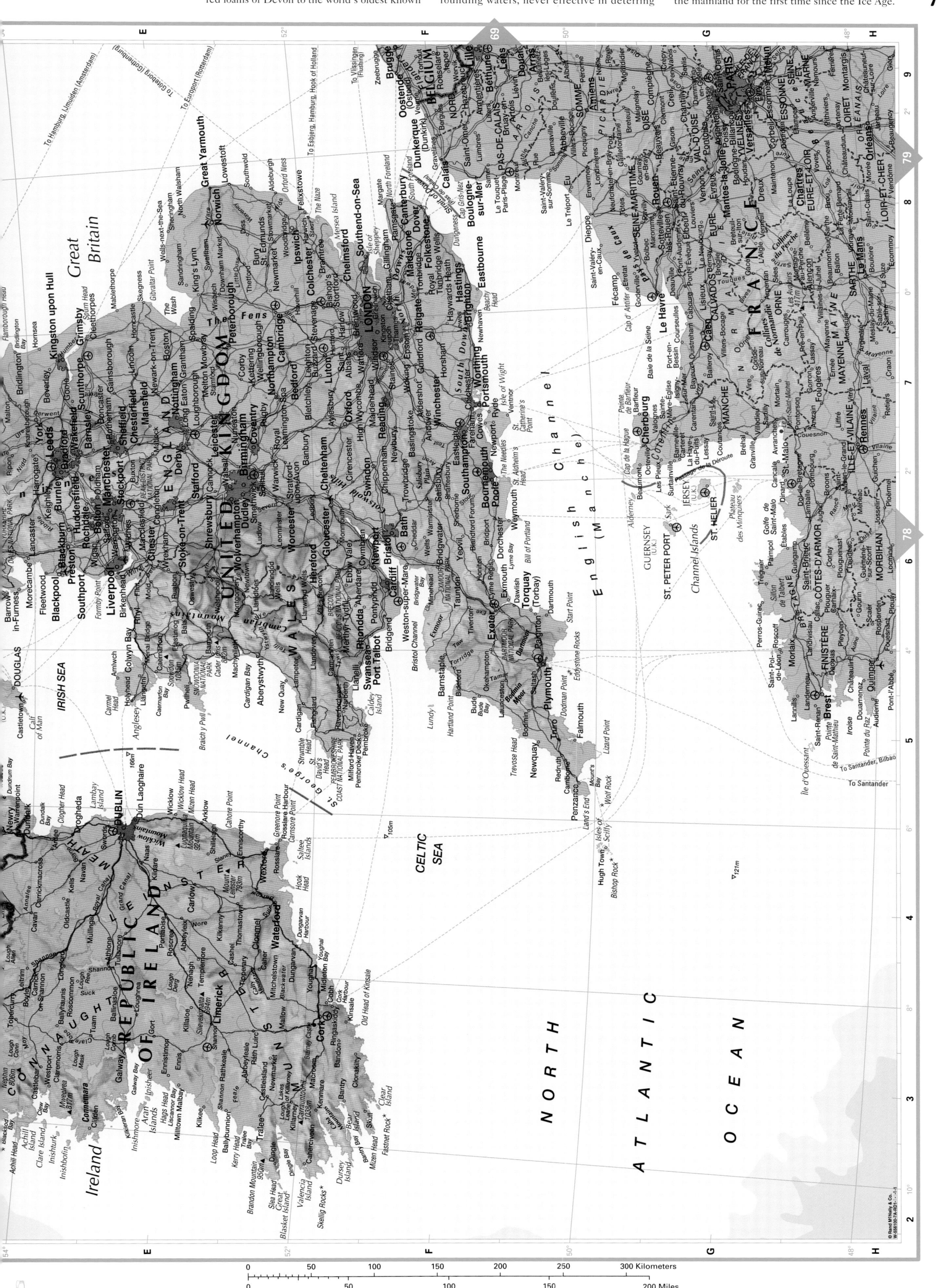

0   50   100   150   200   250   300 Kilometers

0   50   100   150   200 Miles

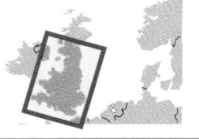

England and Wales

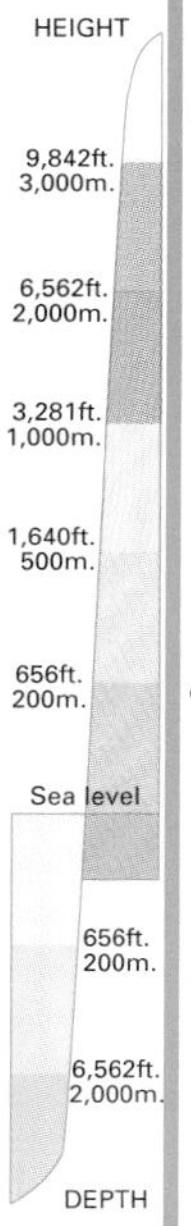

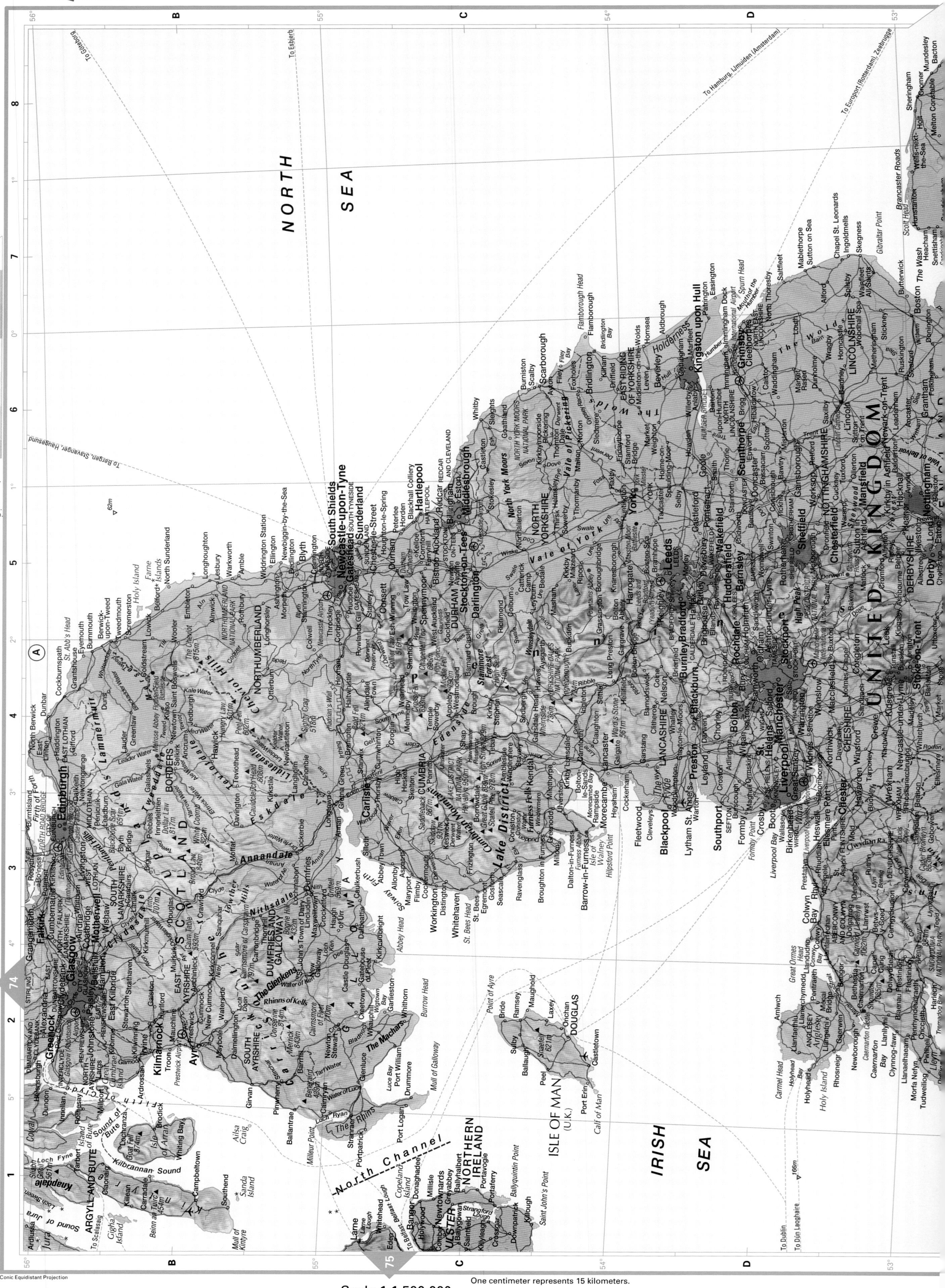

Scale 1:1,500,000

One centimeter represents 15 kilometers.

One inch represents approximately 24 miles.

Conic Equidistant Projection

Much of England and Wales has been shaped by human toil. But here and there the older bones of the land show through, as in the granite cap of Dartmoor and the splendors of Snowdonia. The principality of Wales, largely isolated from England until the Middle Ages, was finally incorporated into the larger country by Henry VIII in 1536. Yet it retains a distinct cultural identity with a unique language and literature.

73

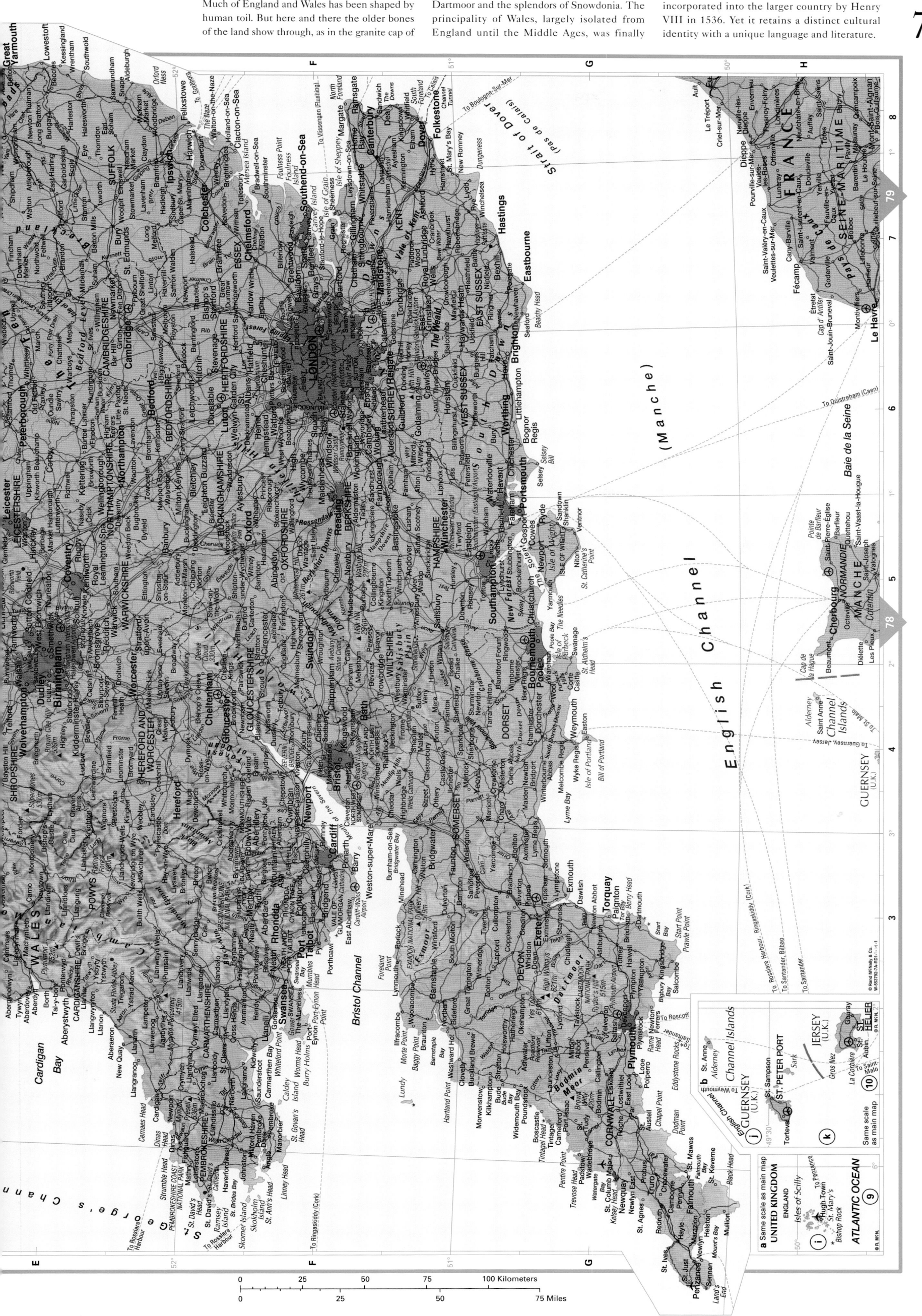

0   25   50   75   100 Kilometers

0   25   50   75 Miles

Scotland

Famed for its lush, misty beauty, Scotland is roughly divided into Highland and Lowland regions, with islands off to the west and north.

HEIGHT

9,842ft.
3,000m.

6,562ft.
2,000m.

3,281ft.
1,000m.

1,640ft.
500m.

656ft.
200m.

Sea level

656ft.
200m.

6,562ft.
2,000m.

DEPTH

NORTH ATLANTIC OCEAN

ORKNEY ISLANDS
Papa Westray, Westray, Pierowall, Rousay, Eday, Sanday, Sanday Sound, Wasbister, Stronsay, North Sound, North Ronaldsay, Dennis Head, Rapness, Whitehall, Shapinsay, Mull Head, Stromness, Kirkwall, Scapa Flow, Flotta, Burray, South Ronaldsay, Burwick, Hoy, South Walls, Pentland Firth, Stroma, Swona, Rora Head

SHETLAND ISLANDS
Fair Isle, Herma Ness, Haroldswick, Point of Fethaland, Isbister, Ronas Hill 450m., Burravoe, Hillswick, St. Magnus Bay, Mossbank, Whalsay, Papa Stour, Melby House, Walls, Foula, The Deeps, West Burra, Lerwick, Isle of Noss, Bressay, Sumburgh, Fitful Head, Sumburgh Head, Sumburgh Roost

UNITED KINGDOM
SCOTLAND
ATLANTIC OCEAN
NORTH SEA
Same scale as main map

HEBRIDES / WESTERN ISLES
Butt of Lewis, Port of Ness, Dell, Barvas, Carloway, Standing Stones, Stornoway, Broad Bay, Tiumpan Head, Portnaguran, Eye Peninsula, Isle of Lewis, Great Bernera, Gallan Head, Brenish, Loch Grunavat, Callanish, Laxay, Clisham 799m., West Loch Tarbert, Tarbert, Scalpay, Harris, Taransay, Toe Head, Leverburgh, Pabbay, Shiant Islands, North Uist, Lochmaddy, Bayhead, Sound of Monach, Baleshare, Monach Islands, Benbecula, Creagorry, Howmore, Beinn Mhòr 620m., South Uist, Lochboisdale, Kilbride, Eriskay, Sound of Barra, Barra, Borve, Vatersay, Sandray, Mingulay, Berneray

Outer Hebrides / The Little Minch / The Minch

Island of Skye
Kilmaluag, Staffin, Uig, Waternish Point, Dunvegan Castle, Portree, Raasay, Rona, Broadford, Kyleakin, Kyle of Lochalsh, Sgurr Alasdair 993m., Soay

HIGHLAND
Cape Wrath, Durness, Loch Eriboll, Whiten Head, Kyle of Tongue, Strathy Point, Tongue, Melvich, Reay, Thurso, Castletown, Dunnet Head, John o' Groats, Duncansby Head, Castle of Mey, Scrabster, Halkirk, Wick, Noss Head, Mybster, Lybster, Latheron, Dunbeath, Scourie, Ben Hope 927m., Ben Loyal, Loch Naver, Altnaharra, Syre, Kinbrace, Helmsdale, Drumbeg, Inchnadamph, Ben Klibreck 961m., Loch Shin, Lairg, Kildonan, Brora, Golspie, Lochinver, Ben More Assynt 998m., Loch Assynt, Oykel Bridge, Culrain, Bonar Bridge, Dornoch, Dornoch Firth, Tarbat Ness, Wilkhaven, Hill of Fearn, Ullapool, Ardcharnich, Tain, Invergordon, Cromarty, Moray Firth

NORTHWEST HIGHLANDS
Gairloch, Poolewe, An Teallach 1062m., Beinn Dearg 1081m., Sgurr Mor 1109m., Loch Maree, Torridon, Liathach 1053m., Kinlochewe, Achnasheen, Shieldaig, Lochcarron, Stromeferry, Plockton, Dornie, Kyle of Lochalsh, Sgurr na Lapaich 1151m., Cannich, Invermoriston, Fort Augustus, Loch Ness, Drumnadrochit, Inverness, Dingwall, Muir of Ord, Beauly, Black Isle, Fortrose, Nairn, Forres, Elgin, Lossiemouth, Burghead, Buckie, Cullen, Portknockie, Macduff, Banff, Rosehearty, Fraserburgh

MORAY
Keith, Huntly, Dufftown, Rothes, Ben Rinnes 840m., Grantown-on-Spey, Tomintoul, Rhynie, Insch, Alford, Inverurie, Oldmeldrum, Ellon, Peterhead, New Deer, Strichen, Mintlaw

ABERDEENSHIRE
Kintore, Westhill, **Aberdeen**, CITY OF ABERDEEN, Echt, Banchory, Stonehaven, Aboyne, Ballater, Balmoral Castle, Braemar, Strachan, Inverbervie

CAIRNGORM MOUNTAINS
Aviemore, Kingussie, Laggan, Ben Macdui 1309m., Cairn Gorm, Dalwhinnie, Glen Shee, Glas Maol 1068m., Forest of Atholl, Blair Atholl, Glenshee, Spittal of Glenshee

GRAMPIAN MOUNTAINS
Fort William, Ben Nevis 1343m., Glen Nevis, Loch Linnhe, Ballachulish, Loch Leven, Kinlochleven, Blackwater Reservoir, Loch Rannoch, Loch Laidon, Rannoch Moor, Bridge of Orchy, Loch Tulla, Tyndrum, Crianlarich, Ben More 1174m., Killin, Ben Lawers 1214m., Loch Tay, Aberfeldy, Kenmore, Dunkeld, Pitlochry, Blairgowrie, Coupar Angus

ANGUS
Kirriemuir, Forfar, Glamis Castle, Brechin, Montrose, Arbroath, Carnoustie

PERTHSHIRE AND KINROSS
Crieff, Comrie, Lochearnhead, Callander, Auchterarder, Perth, Scone, Bridge of Earn, Abernethy, Kinross, Cupar, St. Andrews, Crail

STIRLING
Aberfoyle, Loch Katrine, Loch Lomond, Doune, Dunblane, Bridge of Allan, Stirling, Bannockburn, Alloa, Clackmannan, Alva, Tillicoultry

ARGYLL AND BUTE
Ardnamurchan, Salen, Tobermory, Island of Mull, Ben More 967m., Iona, Oban, Connel, Dalmally, Inveraray, Lochgilphead, Ardrishaig, Tarbert, Kilmartin, Crinan, Jura, Islay, Bowmore, Port Ellen, Portnahaven, Mull of Oa, Gigha Island, Campbeltown, Southend, Mull of Kintyre, Kintyre, Colonsay, Scalasaig, Oronsay, Scarba

Island of Arran
Brodick, Whiting Bay, Lamlash

DUMBARTONSHIRE / WEST DUNBARTONSHIRE
Helensburgh, Garelochhead, Dumbarton, Clydebank, Bearsden, Alexandria, Cumbernauld

Glasgow, CITY OF GLASGOW, Paisley, RENFREWSHIRE, INVERCLYDE, Greenock, Port Glasgow, Gourock, Wemyss Bay, Largs, Rothesay, Island of Bute, Millport, Johnstone, Barrhead, NORTH LANARKSHIRE, Airdrie, Coatbridge, Motherwell, Wishaw, Bellshill, Hamilton, East Kilbride, SOUTH LANARKSHIRE, Lanark, Carluke, Carstairs, Biggar

NORTH AYRSHIRE / EAST AYRSHIRE / SOUTH AYRSHIRE
Saltcoats, Irvine, **Kilmarnock**, Troon, Prestwick, Prestwick Airport, **Ayr**, Mauchline, Cumnock, Auchinleck, New Cumnock, Maybole, Girvan, Dalmellington, Kirkconnel, Sanquhar

FIFE
Glenrothes, **Kirkcaldy**, **Dunfermline**, Leven, Anstruther, Kinghorn, Burntisland, East Wemyss, Buckhaven, Elie, Fife Ness

Dundee, CITY OF DUNDEE, Tayport, Newport-on-Tay, Firth of Tay, FORTH ROAD BRIDGE, Firth of Forth, **Falkirk**, FALKIRK, Grangemouth, Bo'ness, Polmont, Linlithgow, WEST LOTHIAN, Livingston, Bathgate, **Edinburgh**, CITY OF EDINBURGH, Holyrood Palace, MIDLOTHIAN, Dalkeith, Bonnyrigg, Penicuik, Gorebridge, Pentland Hills, Musselburgh, EAST LOTHIAN, Haddington, Tranent, North Berwick, Dunbar, Gifford

BORDERS
Galashiels, Melrose, Selkirk, Peebles, Innerleithen, Hawick, Jedburgh, Kelso, Coldstream, Eyemouth, Duns, Lauder, Greenlaw, Broad Law 840m., Lammermuir Hills

DUMFRIES AND GALLOWAY
Stranraer, Portpatrick, The Rhins, Newton Stewart, Wigtown, Whithorn, Kirkcowan, Gatehouse of Fleet, Creetown, Kirkcudbright, Castle Douglas, Dalbeattie, **Dumfries**, Lockerbie, Annan, Gretna, Moffat, Thornhill, Merrick 843m., Corserine 814m., Cairnsmore of Fleet, Lowther Hills, Nithsdale, Annandale, Eskdale, Liddesdale, Teviotdale

Cheviot Hills / The Cheviot 815m.

ENGLAND / CUMBRIA / NORTHUMBERLAND
Carlisle, Longtown, Brampton, Haltwhistle, Bewcastle, Hadrian's Wall, NORTHUMBERLAND NATIONAL PARK, Wooler, Rothbury, Otterburn, Kielder Water

NORTHERN IRELAND / ULSTER
REPUBLIC OF IRELAND, Moville, Inishowen Head, Giant's Causeway, Portrush, Coleraine, Macosquin, Ballymoney, Ballycastle, Cushendun, Cushendall, Red Bay, Garron Point, Parkmore, Carnlough, Larne, Carncastle, Ballymena, Broughshane, Dunloy, Trostan 551m., Newtown-Crommelin, Ahoghill, Mullaghmore 554m., Lough Foyle, Rathlin Island, Fair Head, Mull of Kintyre

NORTH CHANNEL
NORTH SEA
SEA OF THE HEBRIDES
Inner Hebrides
North Channel

To Belfast, To Aberdeen, To Bergen, To Lerwick and Torshavn

Conic Equidistant Projection

Scale 1:1,500,000

One centimeter represents 15 kilometers.

One inch represents approximately 24 miles.

0 25 50 75 Kilometers

0 25 50 Miles

Nourished by a mild, humid, yet fickle climate, Ireland is often carpeted in a lush shade of green, accounting for its colorful nickname, the Emerald Isle. Four-fifths of the island is ruled by the Republic of Ireland, while the remainder of it – Northern Ireland – is part of the U.K.

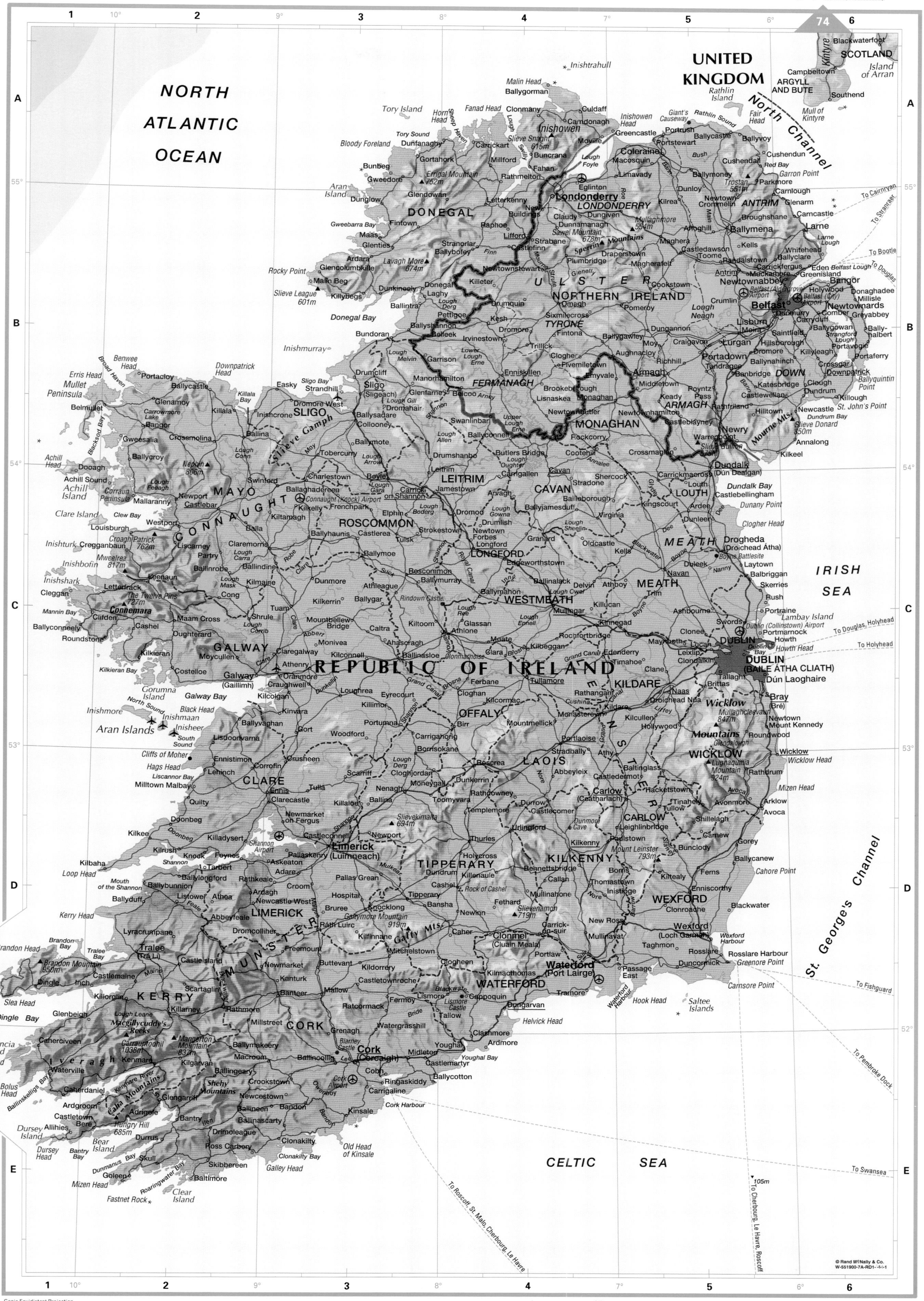

Ireland

NORTH ATLANTIC OCEAN

UNITED KINGDOM

REPUBLIC OF IRELAND

NORTHERN IRELAND

ULSTER

CONNAUGHT

MUNSTER

IRISH SEA

CELTIC SEA

St. George's Channel

North Channel

SCOTLAND

Scale 1:1,500,000

One centimeter represents 15 kilometers.

One inch represents approximately 24 miles.

Conic Equidistant Projection

| 0 | 25 | 50 | 75 | 100 Kilometers |

| 0 | 25 | 50 | 75 Miles |

© Rand McNally & Co.
W-551900-7A-RD1-⁴-¹-1

France

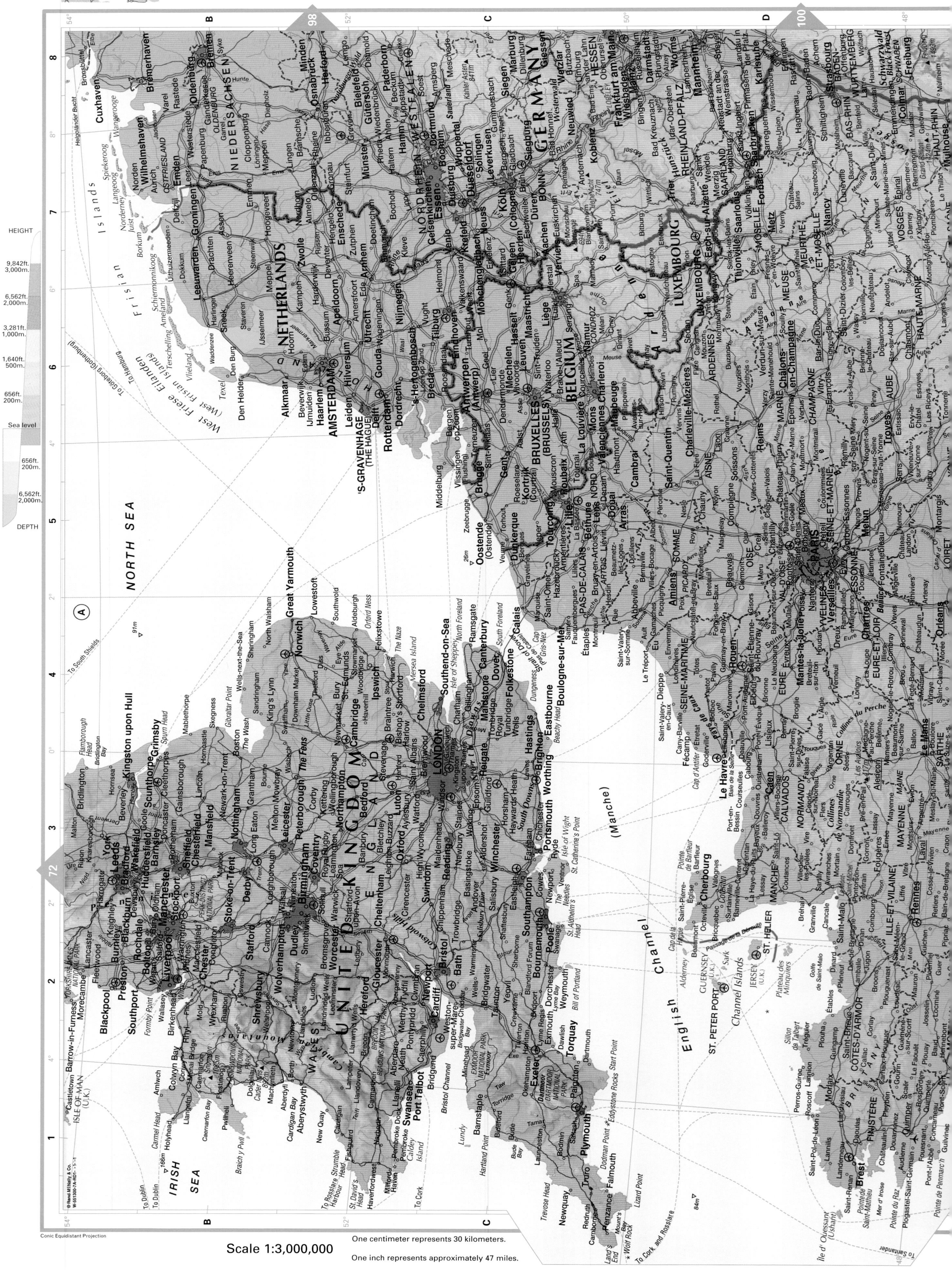

Scale 1:3,000,000

One centimeter represents 30 kilometers.

One inch represents approximately 47 miles.

Conic Equidistant Projection

While France is the largest country in western Europe, it is more sparsely populated than any of its neighbors; most of its 57 million inhabitants are scattered throughout rural areas, well beyond the epicenter of Paris. With more than half its land cultivated, France leads Europe in food exports, notably wine. One-quarter of the world's wine is produced by French vineyards, many located in the Loire and Rhone valleys.

77

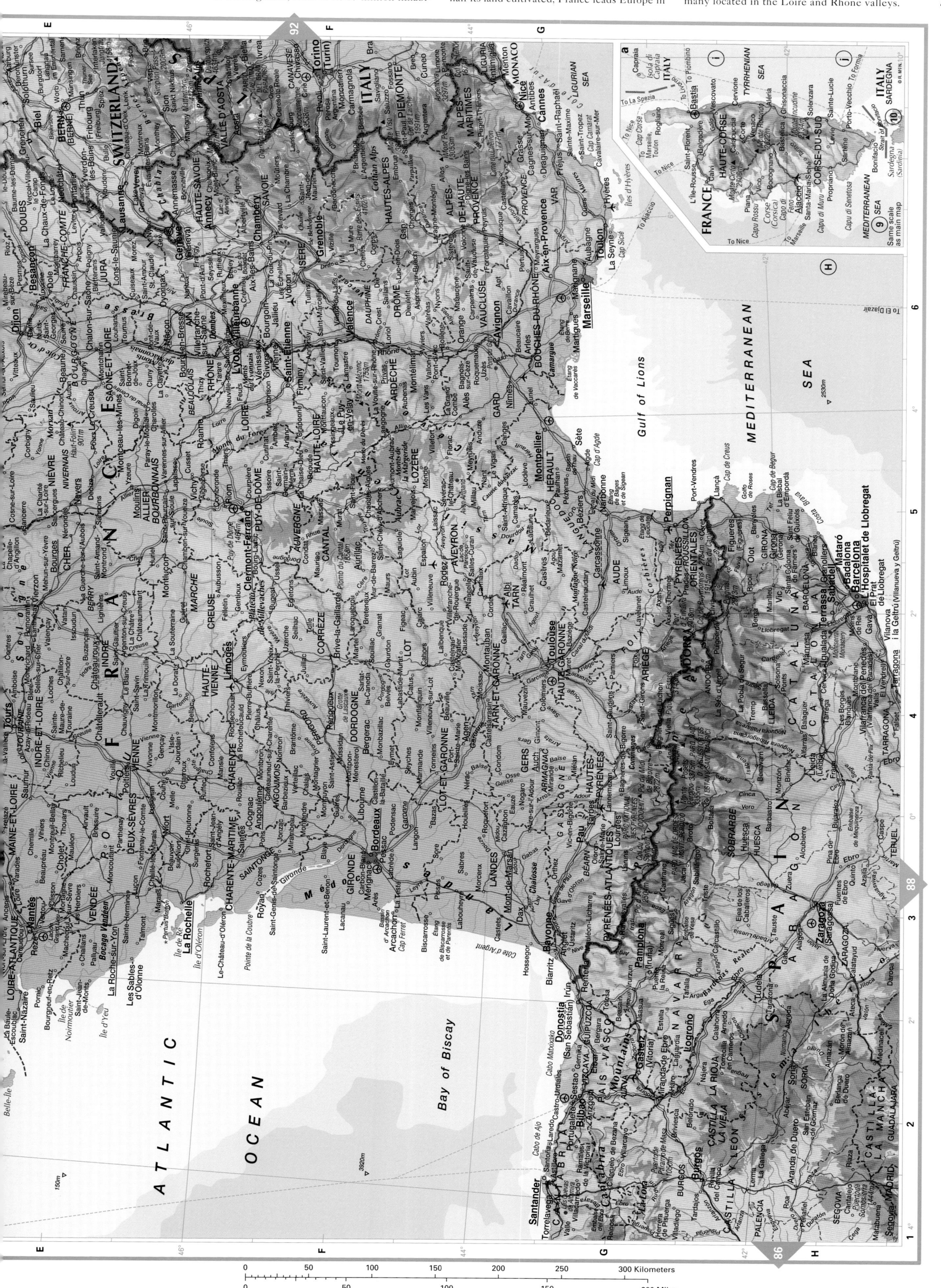

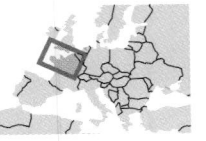

HEIGHT

9,842ft. 3,000m.
6,562ft. 2,000m.
3,281ft. 1,000m.
1,640ft. 500m.
656ft. 200m.
Sea level
656ft. 200m.
6,562ft. 2,000m.

DEPTH

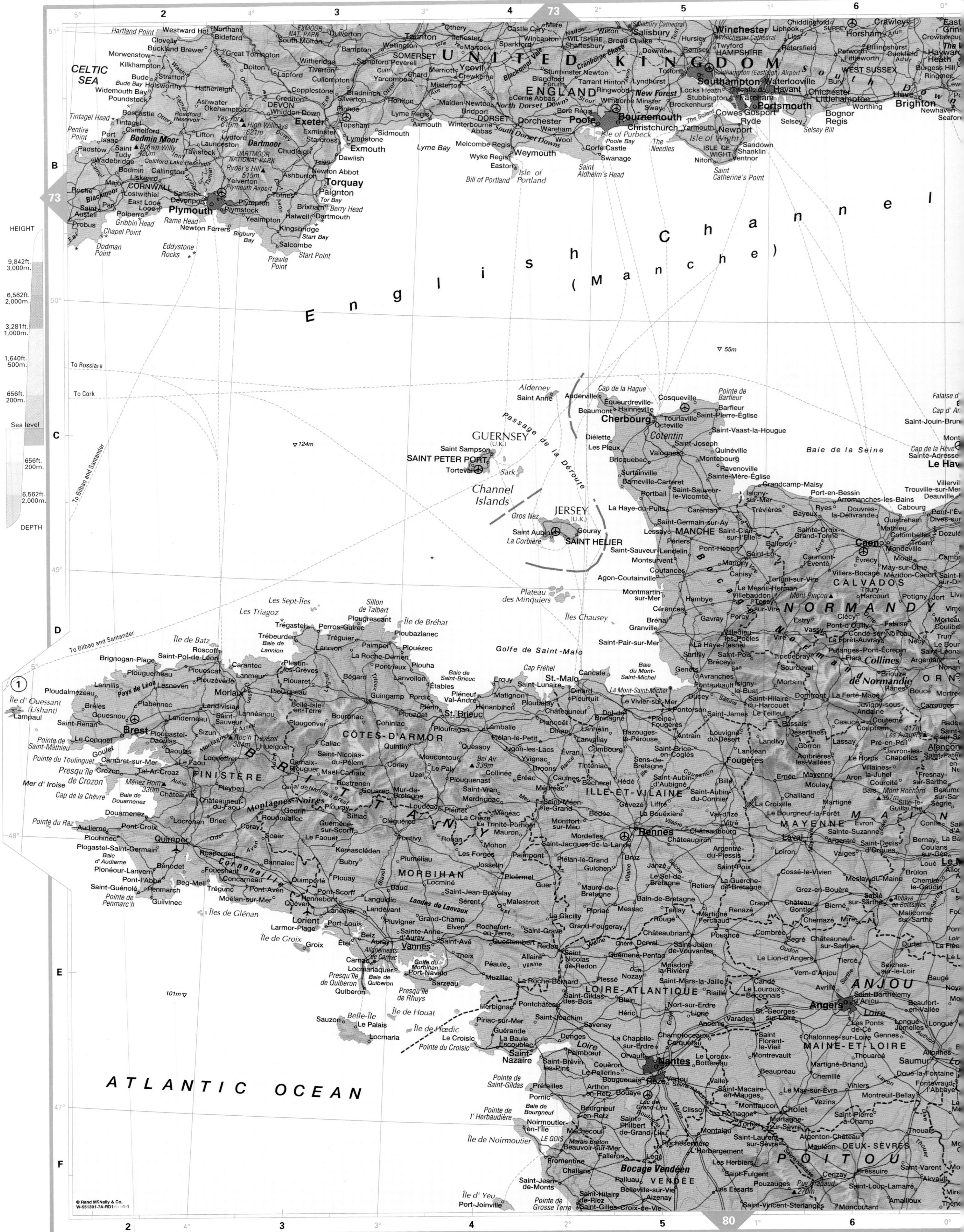

Conic Equidistant Projection

© Rand McNally & Co.
W-551391-7A-RD1-·-·-·1-1

Scale 1:1,500,000

One centimeter represents 15 kilometers.

One inch represents approximately 24 miles.

The fretted coast and many islands of Brittany, the region of northwest France forming a peninsula between the Bay of Biscay and the English Channel, make up one-third of the entire French seaboard. To the east lie the Loire Valley, home to many magnificent 15th- and 16th-century chateaux, and Normandy, a land of old ports, from which the Seine can be followed upstream to that most celebrated of capitals, Paris.

79

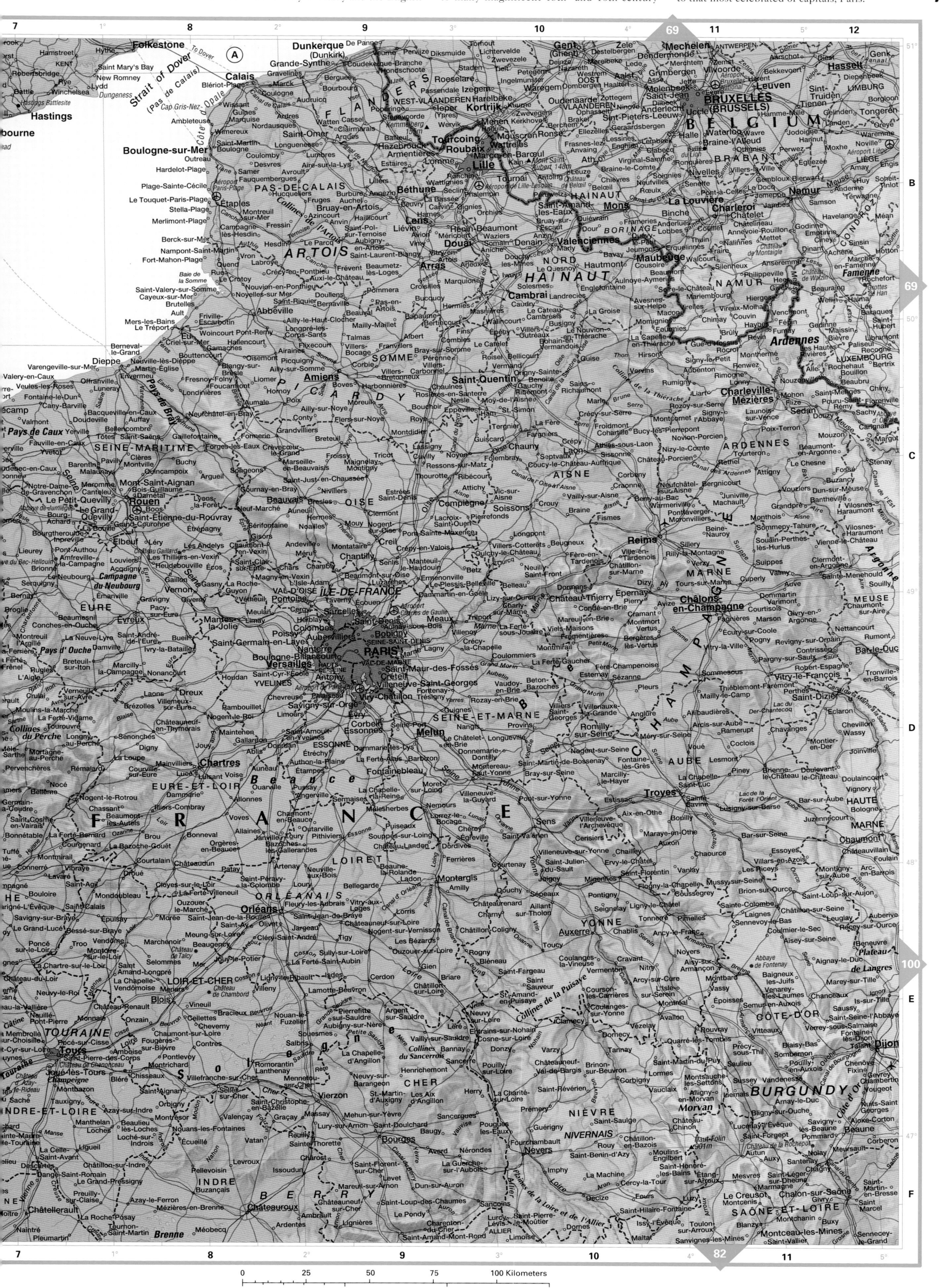

0   25   50   75   100 Kilometers

0   25   50   75 Miles

Southwest France

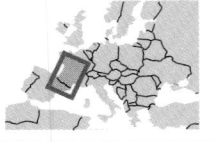

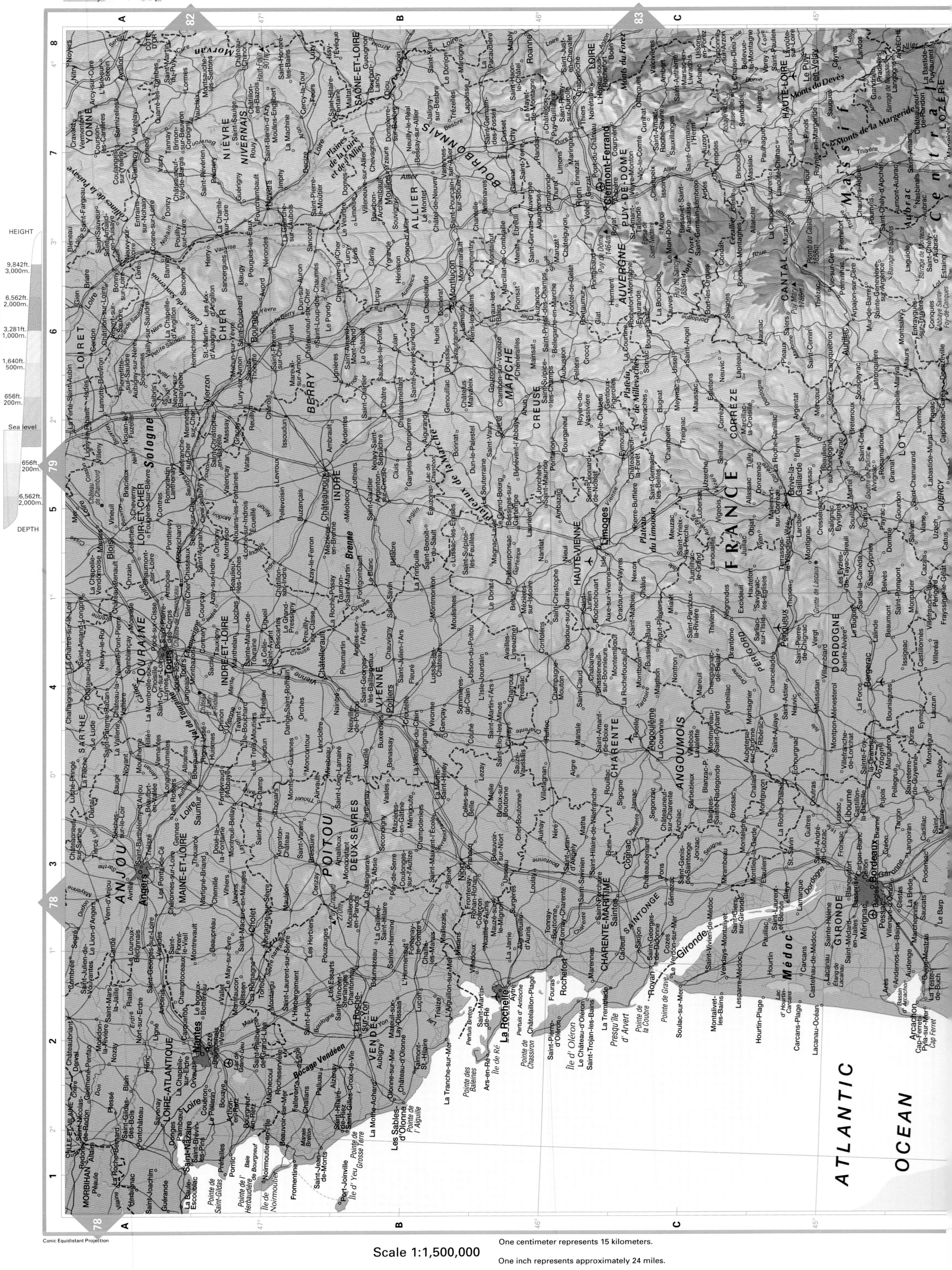
HEIGHT
9,842ft. 3,000m.
6,562ft. 2,000m.
3,281ft. 1,000m.
1,640ft. 500m.
656ft. 200m.
Sea level
656ft. 200m.
6,562ft. 2,000m.
DEPTH
ATLANTIC
OCEAN
FRANCE
Conic Equidistant Projection

Scale 1:1,500,000

One centimeter represents 15 kilometers.

One inch represents approximately 24 miles.

A low-lying landscape dominates most of France, as in the Aquitaine region, where the flat, fertile farmland around Bordeaux yields grapes used to make some of the finest wines in the world. Not far away, however, the landscape changes dramatically, as the vast granite Massif Central, to the east, reaches a middle elevation, and the lofty Pyrenees, to the south, form an upper tier rivaled only by the mighty Alps.

81

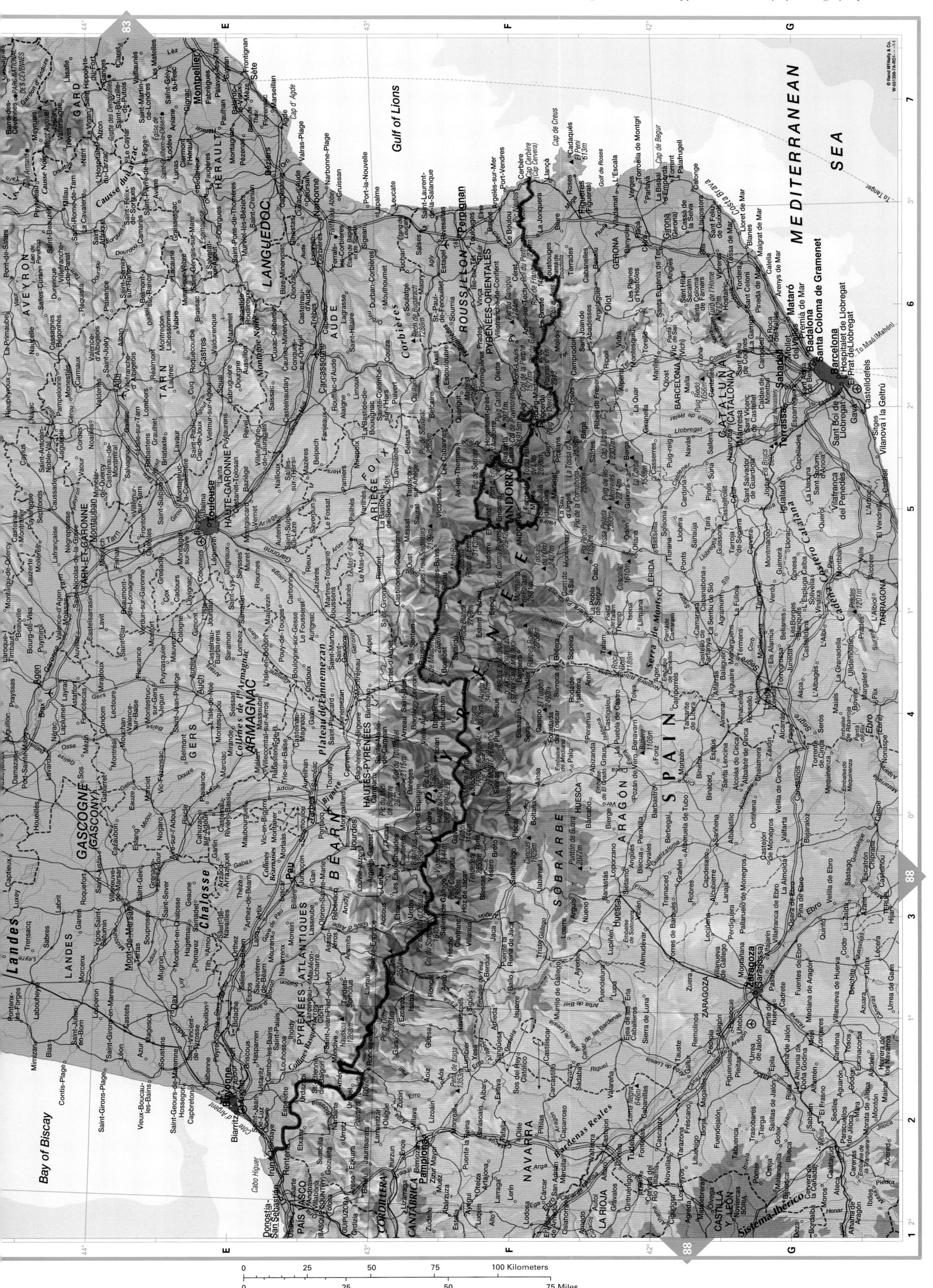

0   25   50   75   100 Kilometers

0   25   50   75 Miles

Southeast France

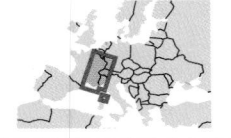

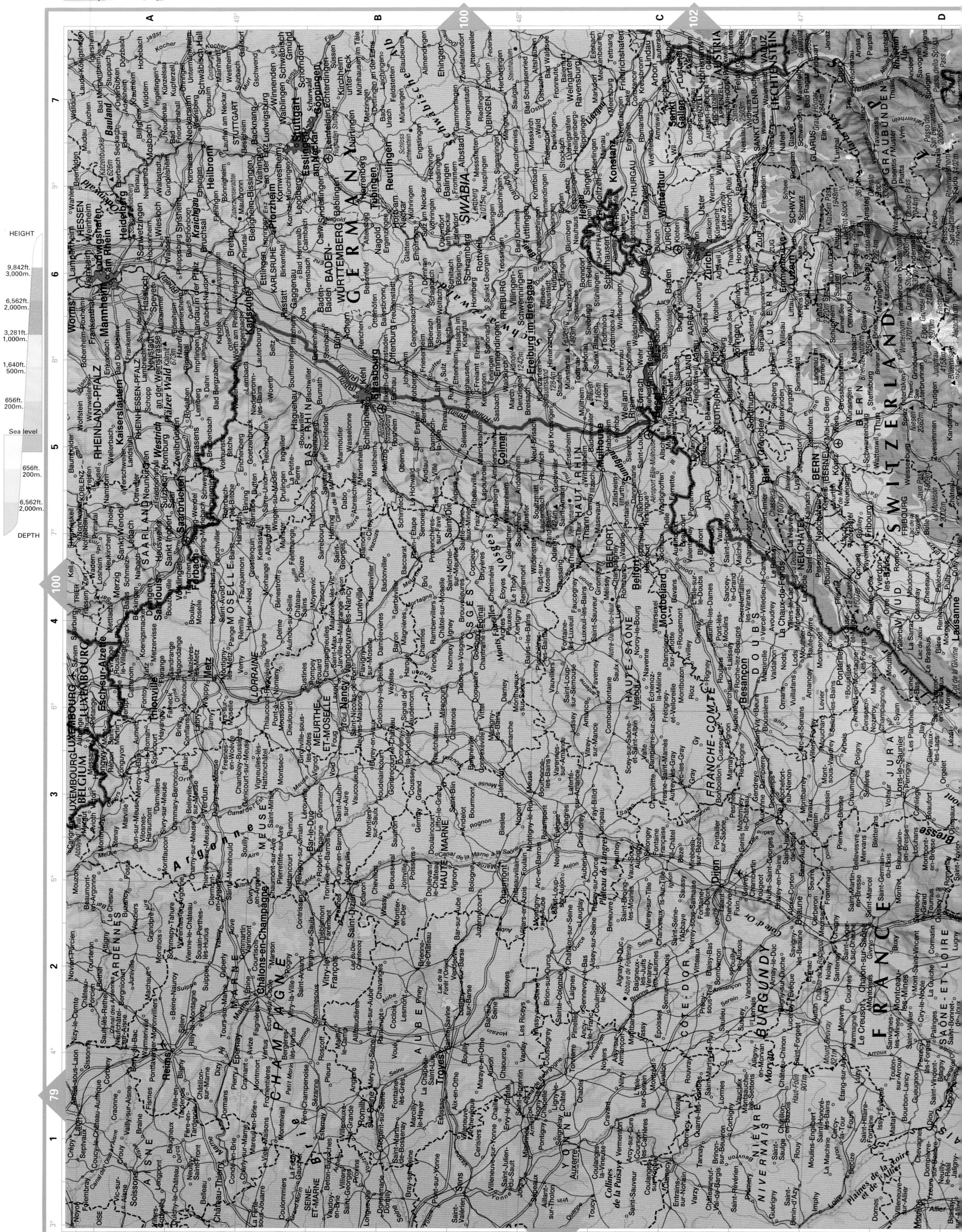
HEIGHT
9,842ft. 3,000m.
6,562ft. 2,000m.
3,281ft. 1,000m.
1,640ft. 500m.
656ft. 200m.
Sea level
656ft. 200m.
6,562ft. 2,000m.
DEPTH
GERMANY
SWITZERLAND
FRANCE
BURGUNDY
CHAMPAGNE

Conic Equidistant Projection

Scale 1:1,500,000

One centimeter represents 15 kilometers.

One inch represents approximately 24 miles.

The picturesque region of Provence is best known for its abundance of flowers, fruits, and vegetables. Along its southern coast stretches the French Riviera (Côte d'Azur), which in the late 19th century became a popular destination for the well-to-do, who flocked to posh resorts.

83

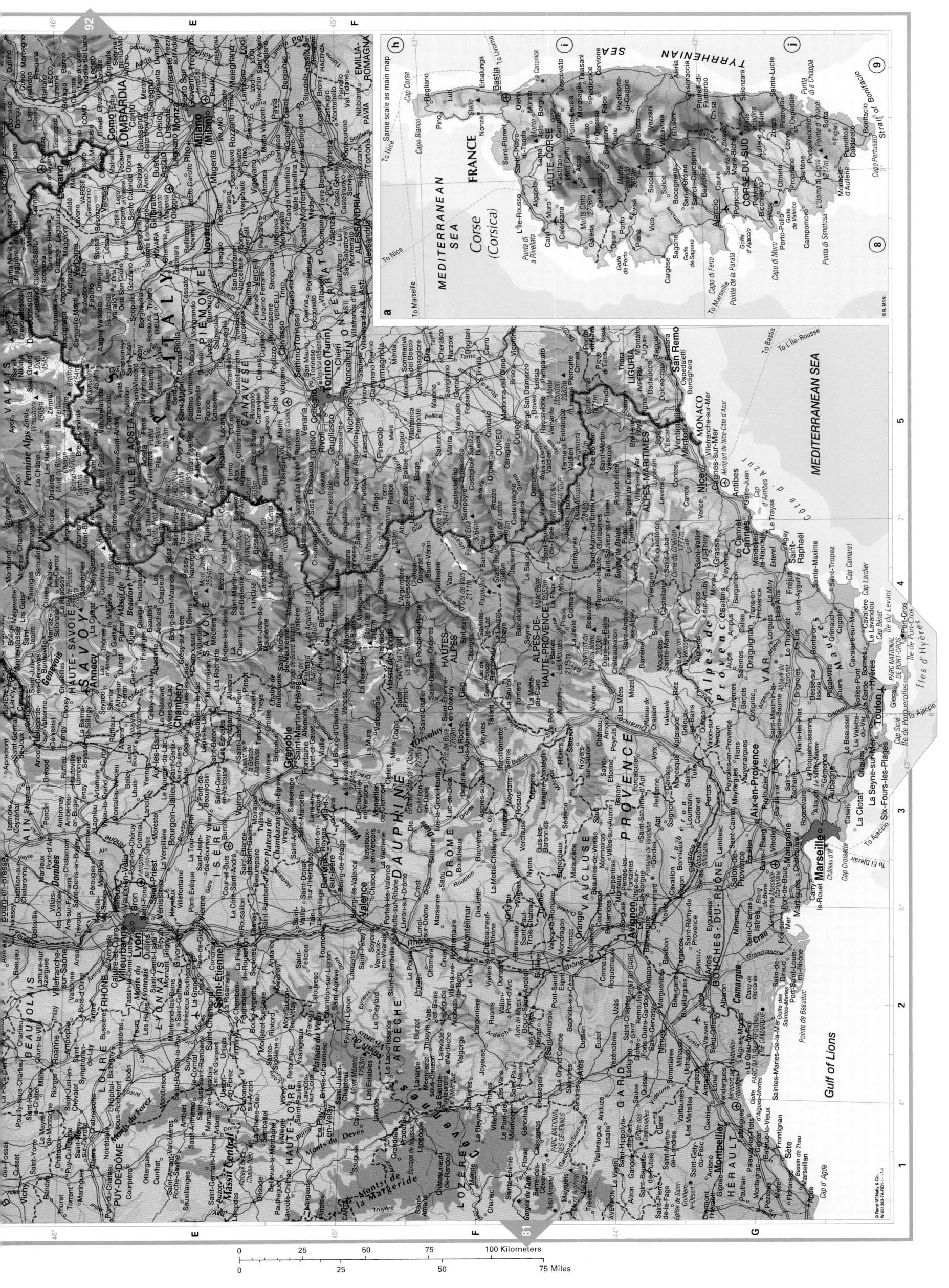

MEDITERRANEAN SEA

FRANCE

Corse (Corsica)

HAUTE-CORSE

CORSE-DU-SUD

TYRRHENIAN SEA

ITALY

LOMBARDIA

PIEMONTE

Milano (Milan)

Torino (Turin)

LIGURIA

MONACO

Nice

Cannes

MEDITERRANEAN SEA

Gulf of Lions

Marseille

Aix-en-Provence

PROVENCE

DAUPHINÉ

Grenoble

Lyon

Saint-Étienne

ALPES-DE-HAUTE-PROVENCE

HAUTES-ALPES

SAVOIE

HAUTE-SAVOIE

Annecy

Chambéry

VAUCLUSE

BOUCHES-DU-RHÔNE

VAR

ALPES-MARITIMES

Toulon

Avignon

Valence

DRÔME

ARDÈCHE

GARD

HÉRAULT

Montpellier

Nîmes

Îles d'Hyères

0   25   50   75   100 Kilometers

0   25   50   75 Miles

Spain and Portugal

HEIGHT

9,842ft. 3,000m.

6,562ft. 2,000m.

3,281ft. 1,000m.

1,640ft. 500m.

656ft. 200m.

Sea level

656ft. 200m.

6,562ft. 2,000m.

DEPTH

ATLANTIC OCEAN

Bay of Biscay

Golfe de Gascogne

Costa Verde

Costa Cantábrica

Rías Altas

Rías Bajas

CORDILLERA CANTÁBRICA

Sistema Central

Sierra de Gredos

Sierra de Guadarrama

Montes de Toledo

Sierra Morena

Cordillera Penibética

Sierra Nevada

Campiña

Campo de Montiel

Tierra de Campos

La Serena

La Alcarria

GALICIA

ASTURIAS

CANTABRIA

PAÍS VASCO

LA RIOJA

CASTILLA Y LEÓN

CASTILLA-LA MANCHA

EXTREMADURA

ANDALUCÍA

MADRID

PORTUGAL

SPAIN

Alentejo

Algarve

Estremadura

Trás-os-Montes

Minho

Costa Dourada

Costa do Algarve

Costa de la Luz

Costa del Sol

Costa Tropical

Costa de Almería

Strait of Gibraltar

ALBORAN SEA

ATLANTIC OCEAN

MOROCCO

Lisboa (Lisbon)

Porto (Oporto)

Madrid

Sevilla (Seville)

Córdoba (Cordova)

Granada

Málaga

Cádiz

Gibraltar (U.K.)

Ceuta (Spain)

Melilla (Spain)

Tanger (Tangier)

Tétouan

Conic Projection

198

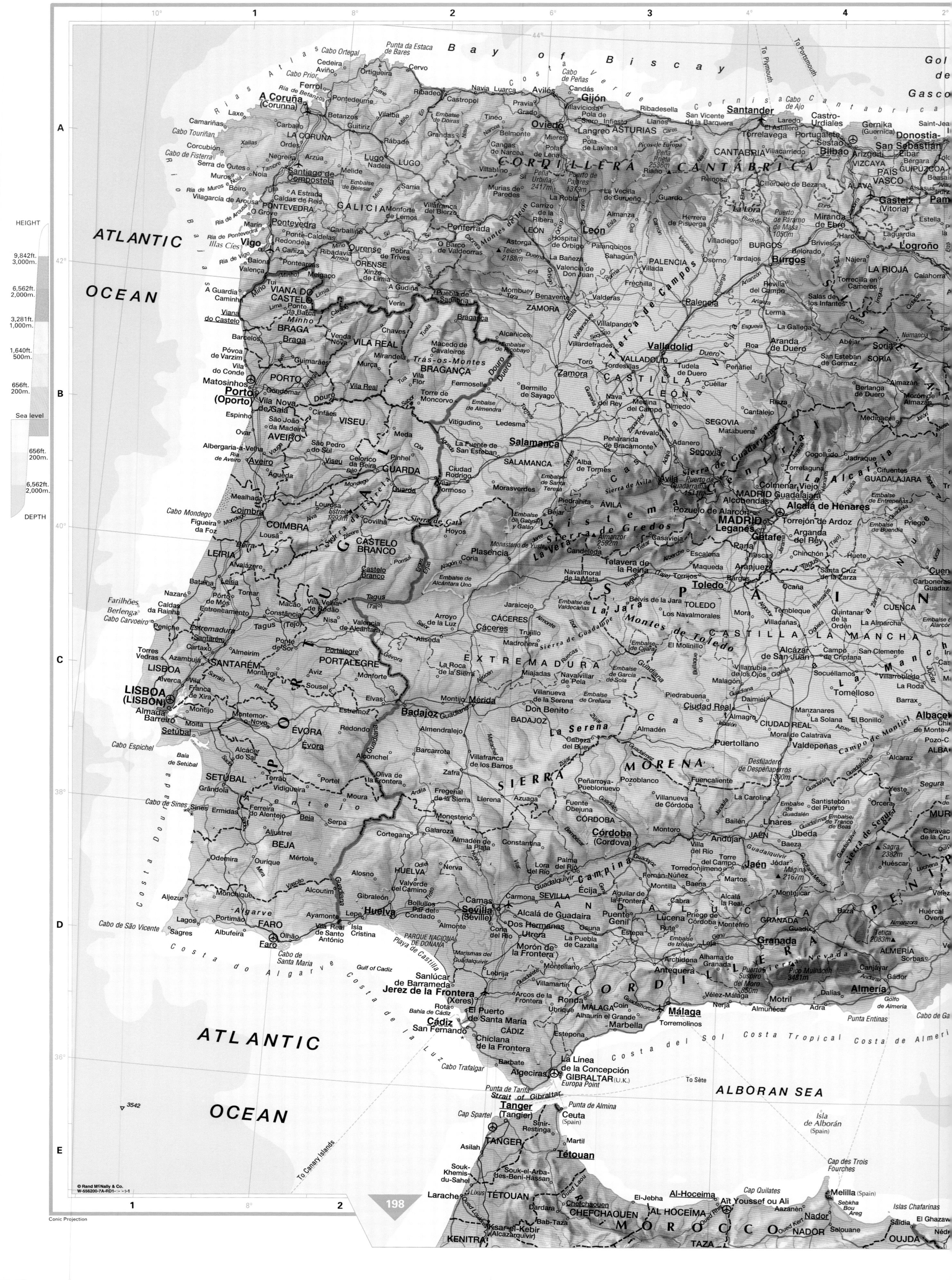

The Iberian Peninsula, embracing Spain, Portugal, and the tiny principality of Andorra, is cobbled roughly onto the remainder of Europe by the Pyrenees. Spain, the largest portion, is divided by mountain ranges, and over centuries its provinces have each evolved their own strong and particular character. Stretches of the north coast are rugged, damp, and green, while regions to the south can be as hot and dry as Morocco.

85

Scale 1:3,000,000

One centimeter represents 30 kilometers.

One inch represents approximately 47 miles.

0	50	100	150	200	250	300 Kilometers

0	50	100	150	200 Miles

Western Spain and Portugal

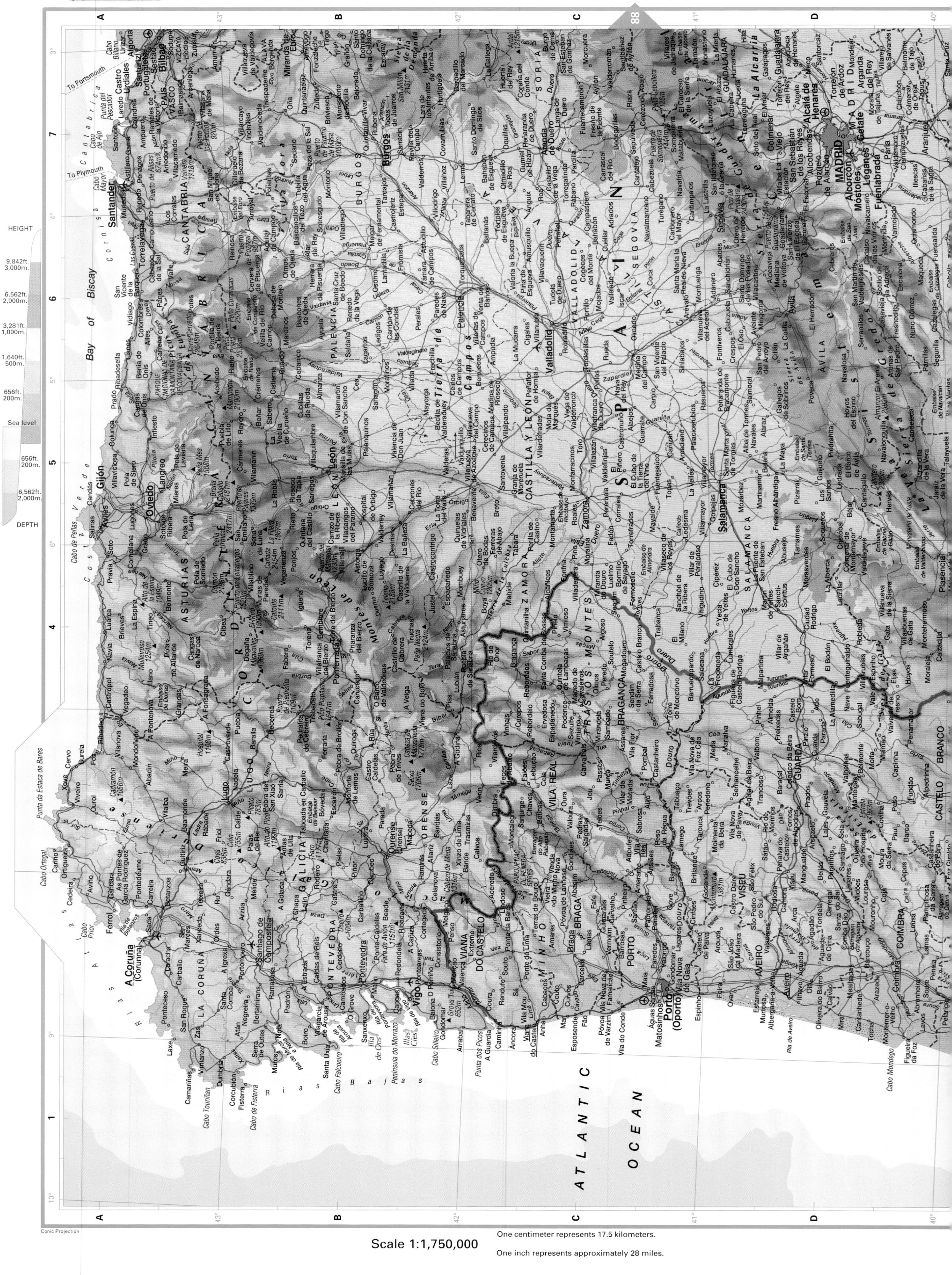

Scale 1:1,750,000

One centimeter represents 17.5 kilometers.

One inch represents approximately 28 miles.

Conic Projection

All of Portugal's coast faces the Atlantic, but south of the Tagus River, the feel of the country, with its orange groves, cork plantations, and sandy beaches, is distinctly Mediterranean. North of the Tagus lie tiny fields of maize and root crops. Far upstream on the river's 628-mile (1,010-km.) course through Spain is the Meseta, a treeless plateau – torrid in summer, frigid in winter – on which is set the capital, Madrid.

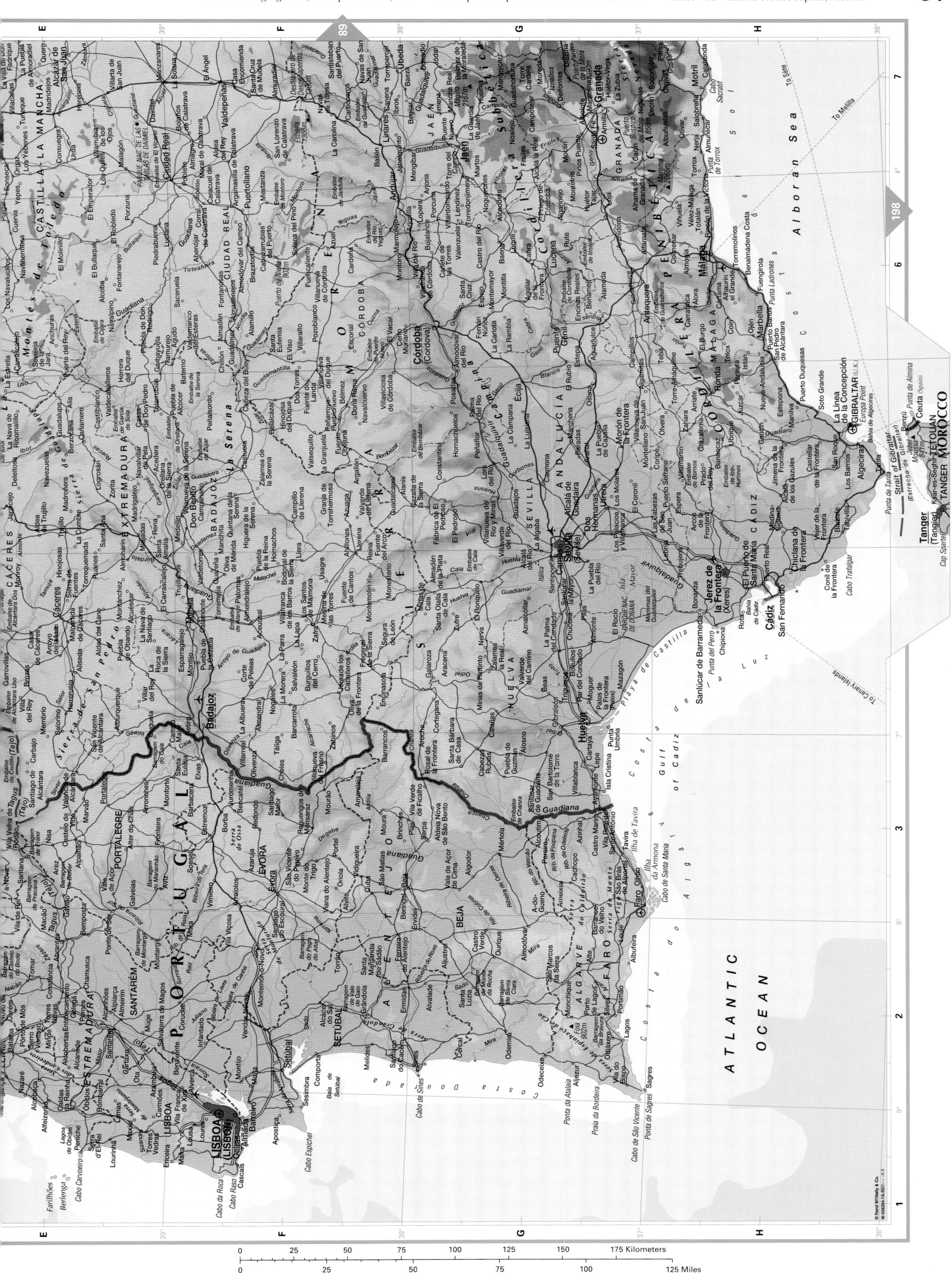

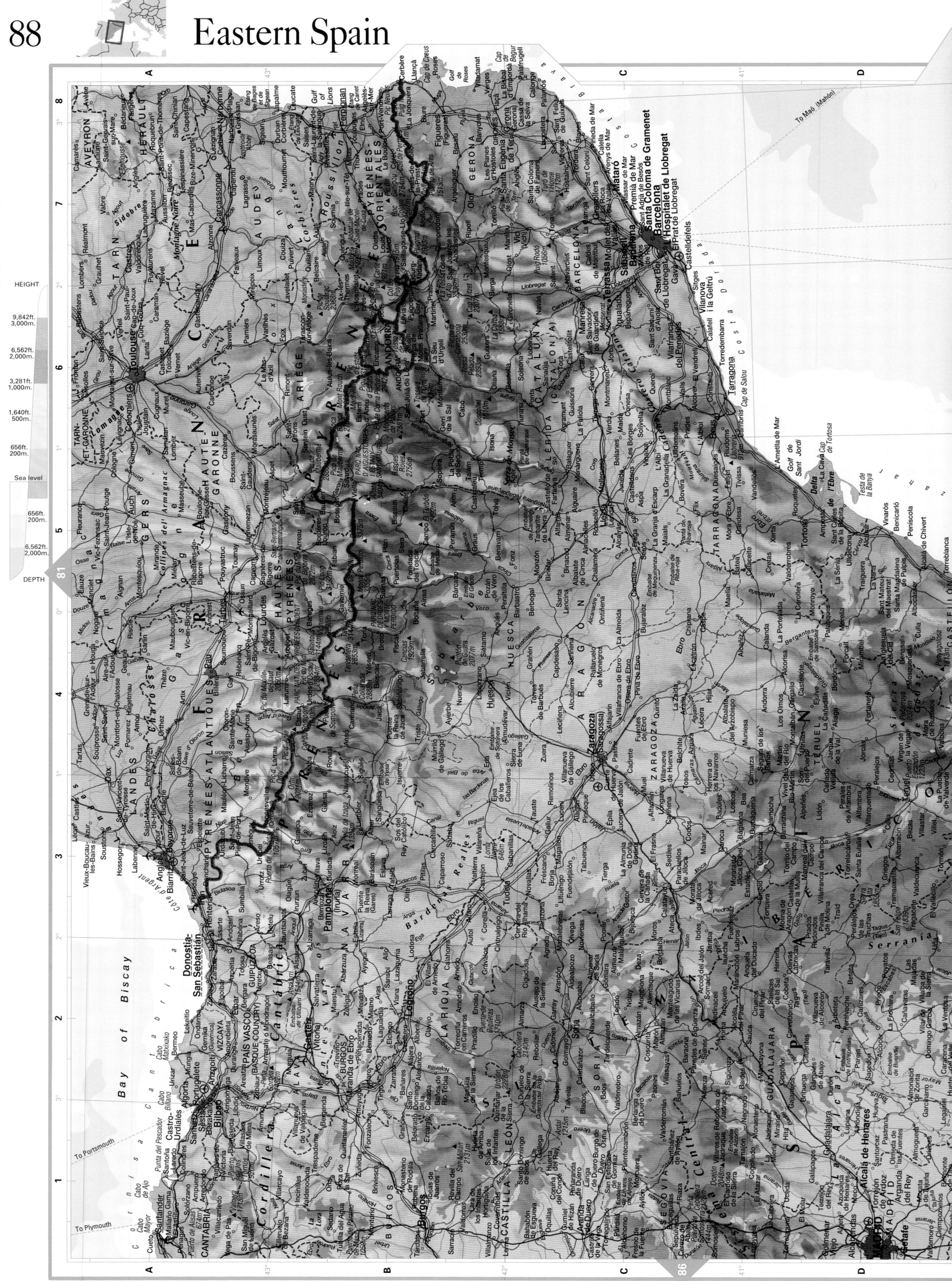

HEIGHT

9,842ft.
3,000m.

6,562ft.
2,000m.

3,281ft.
1,000m.

1,640ft.
500m.

656ft.
200m.

Sea level

656ft.
200m.

6,562ft.
2,000m.

DEPTH

Conic Equidistant Projection

Scale 1:1,750,000

One centimeter represents 17.5 kilometers.

One inch represents approximately 28 miles.

Ten legend-haunted mountain passes through the Pyrenees lead southward to the huge expanses of Castile, the heart of Spain, and to bustling Barcelona and the bays and inlets of the Costa Brava. Here, and offshore in the Balearic Islands, begins storied Spain, a popular haven for vacationers. Farther south, sunny Andalucía embraces the ice-capped Sierra Nevada and, at Almería, Europe's only true desert.

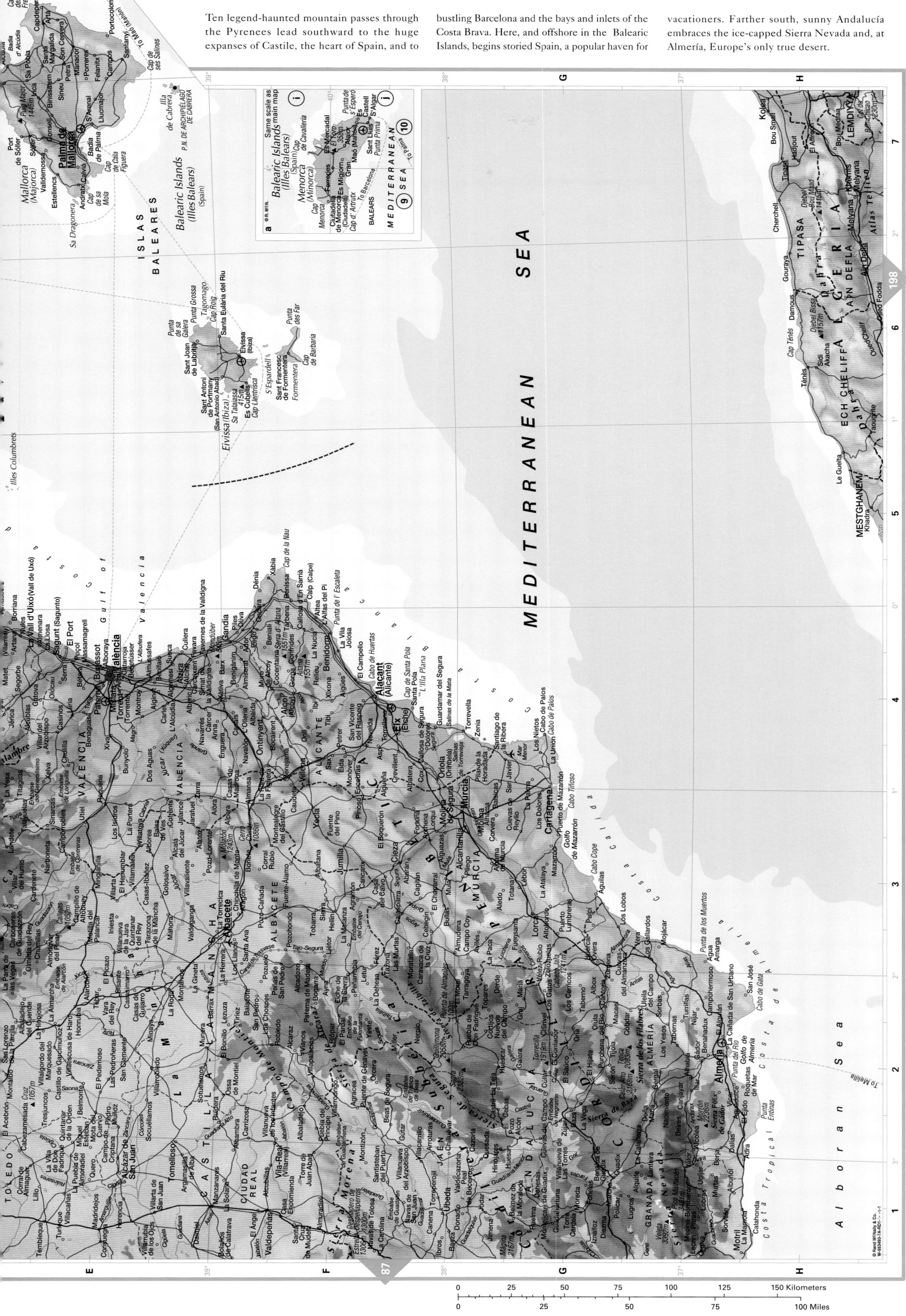

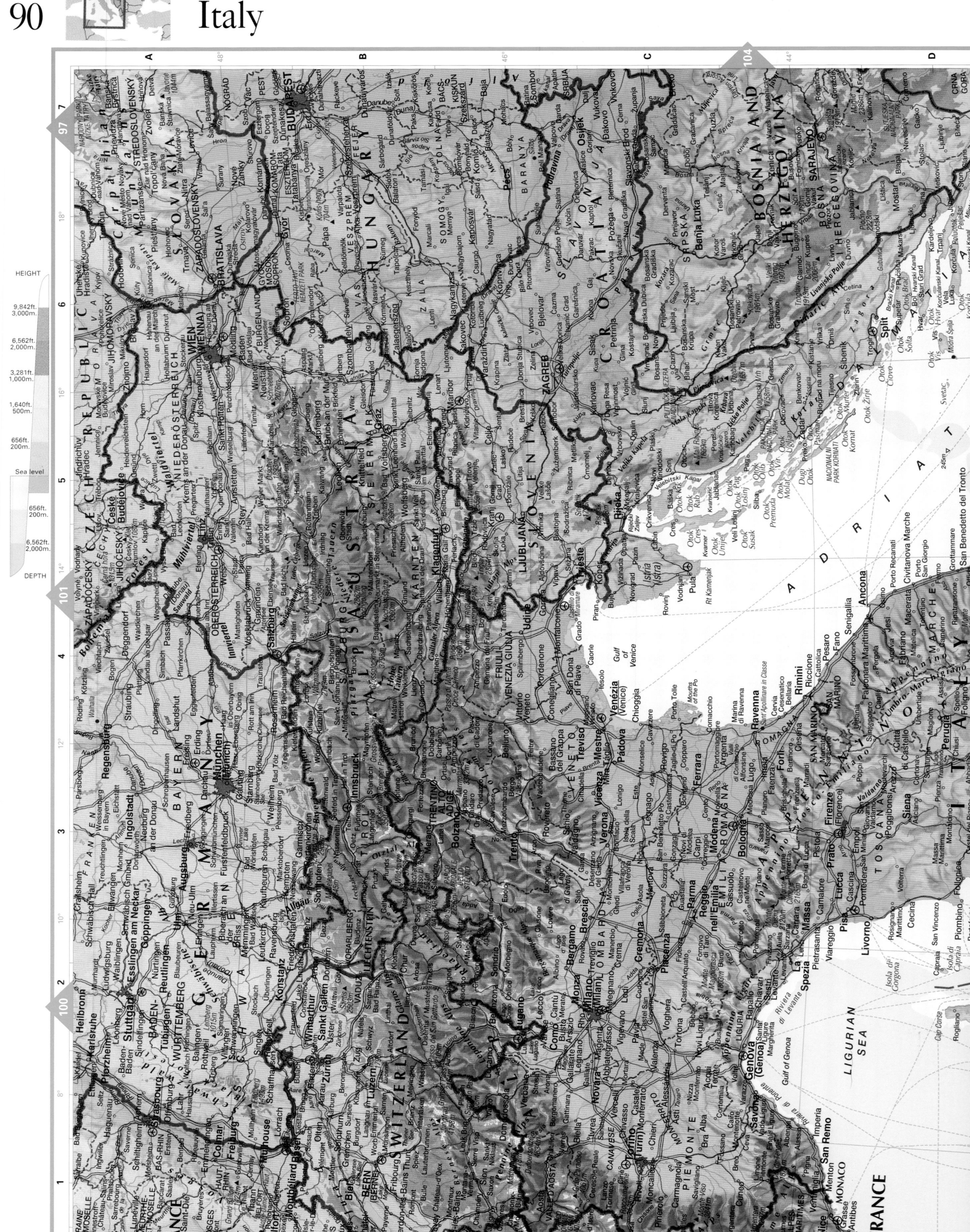
HEIGHT
9,842ft. 3,000m.
6,562ft. 2,000m.
3,281ft. 1,000m.
1,640ft. 500m.
656ft. 200m.
Sea level
656ft. 200m.
6,562ft. 2,000m.
DEPTH
Conic Equidistant Projection
ADRIATIC SEA
LIGURIAN SEA
Gulf of Venice
Gulf of Genoa
ITALY
FRANCE
SWITZERLAND
AUSTRIA
GERMANY
SLOVENIA
CROATIA
HUNGARY
BOSNIA AND HERZEGOVINA
CZECH REPUBLIC
SLOVAKIA
LIECHTENSTEIN
SAN MARINO
MONACO
Milano (Milan)
Venézia (Venice)
Genova (Genoa)
Torino (Turin)
Firenze (Florence)
Bologna
Verona
Trieste
Ljubljana
Zagreb
Wien (Wienna)
München (Munich)
Bratislava
Budapest
Sarajevo
Zürich
Bern (Berne)
Genève (Geneva)
Nice
Ancona
Rijeka
Split
To Toulon and Marseille

Comprised of a mountainous peninsula and several islands (the largest of which are Sicily and Sardinia), Italy was the center of the Roman Empire, and its landscape remains studded with roads, aqueducts, monuments, and other wonders of that civilization. Divided between the industrialized north and the agricultural south, the country draws some 60 million foreign visitors each year – more than any other.

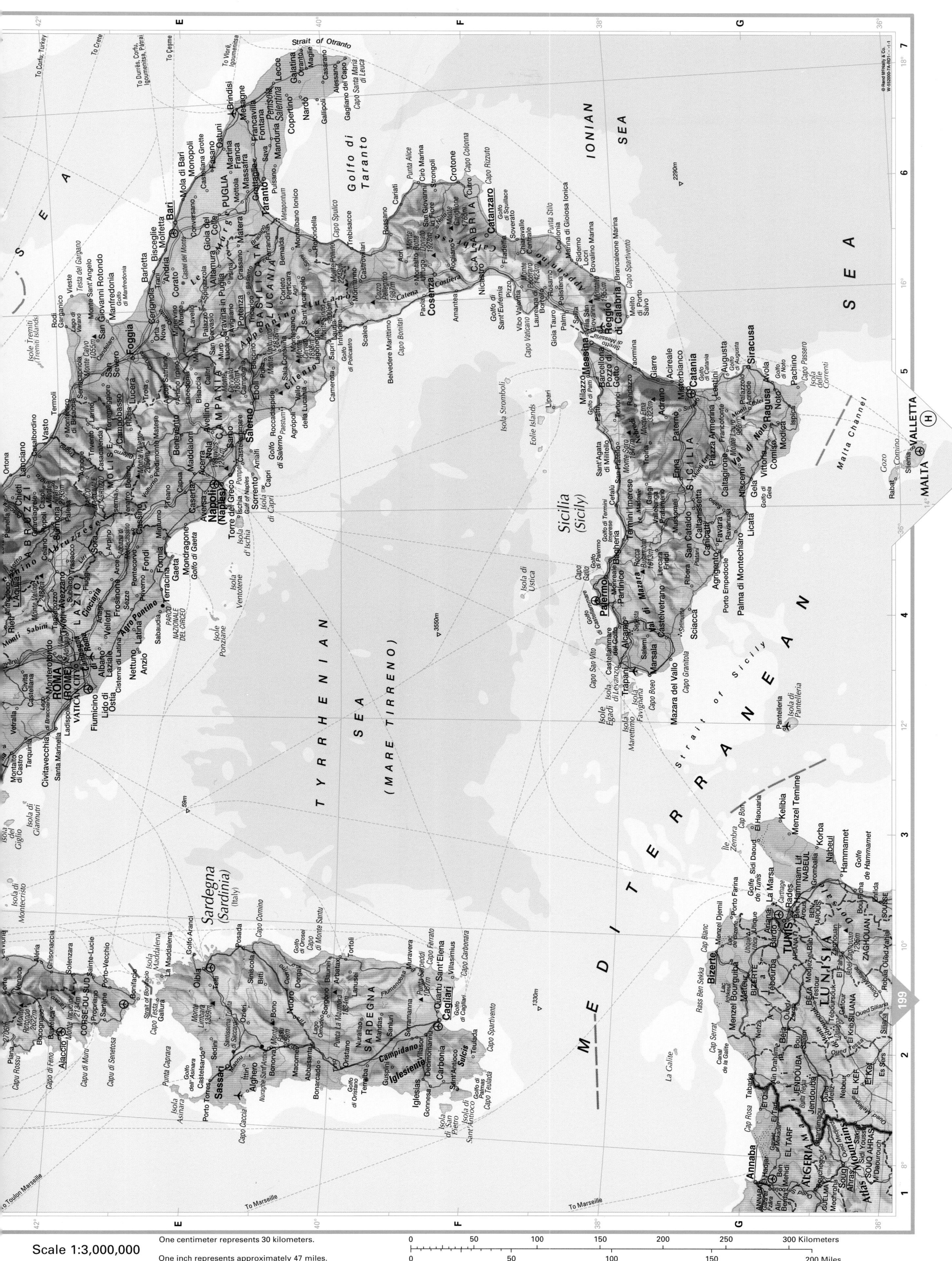

Scale 1:3,000,000

One centimeter represents 30 kilometers.

One inch represents approximately 47 miles.

0   50   100   150   200   250   300 Kilometers

0   50   100   150   200 Miles

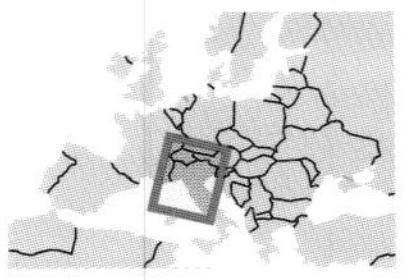

Northern Italy and Switzerland

HEIGHT

9,842ft.
3,000m.

6,562ft.
2,000m.

3,281ft.
1,000m.

1,640ft.
500m.

656ft.
200m.

Sea level

656ft.
200m.

6,562ft.
2,000m.

DEPTH

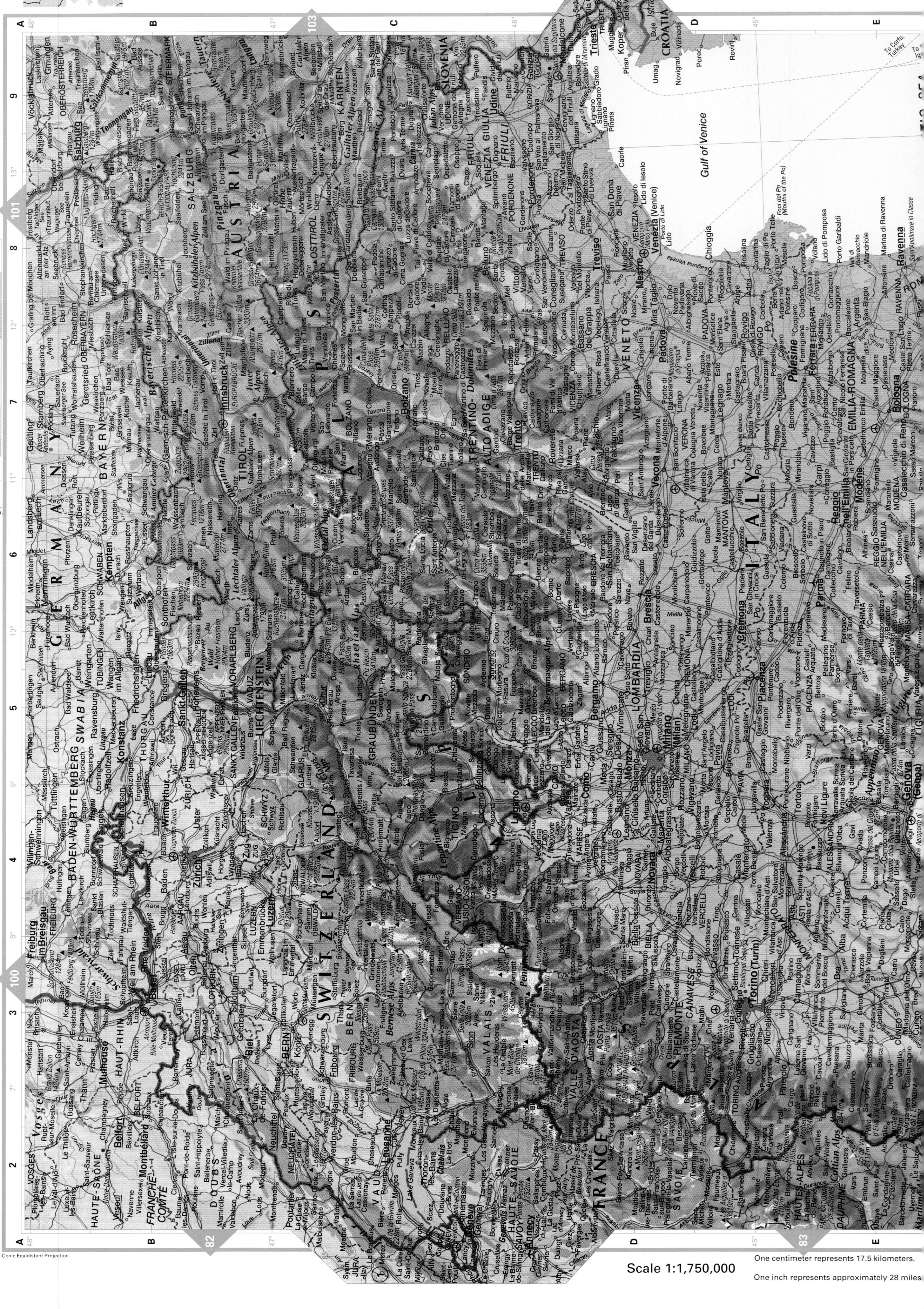

Conic Equidistant Projection

Scale 1:1,750,000

One centimeter represents 17.5 kilometers.

One inch represents approximately 28 miles.

The border regions of Italy and Switzerland are dominated by the towering Alps, whose inhabitants may speak French, German, Italian, Slovene, or Romansh. Southward lie Milan, the country's primary financial and commercial center; the fertile Po Valley; the artistic treasure troves of Venice, Verona, Siena, and Florence; the regions of Tuscany and Umbria, cradle of the Renaissance; and the Eternal City of Rome.

93

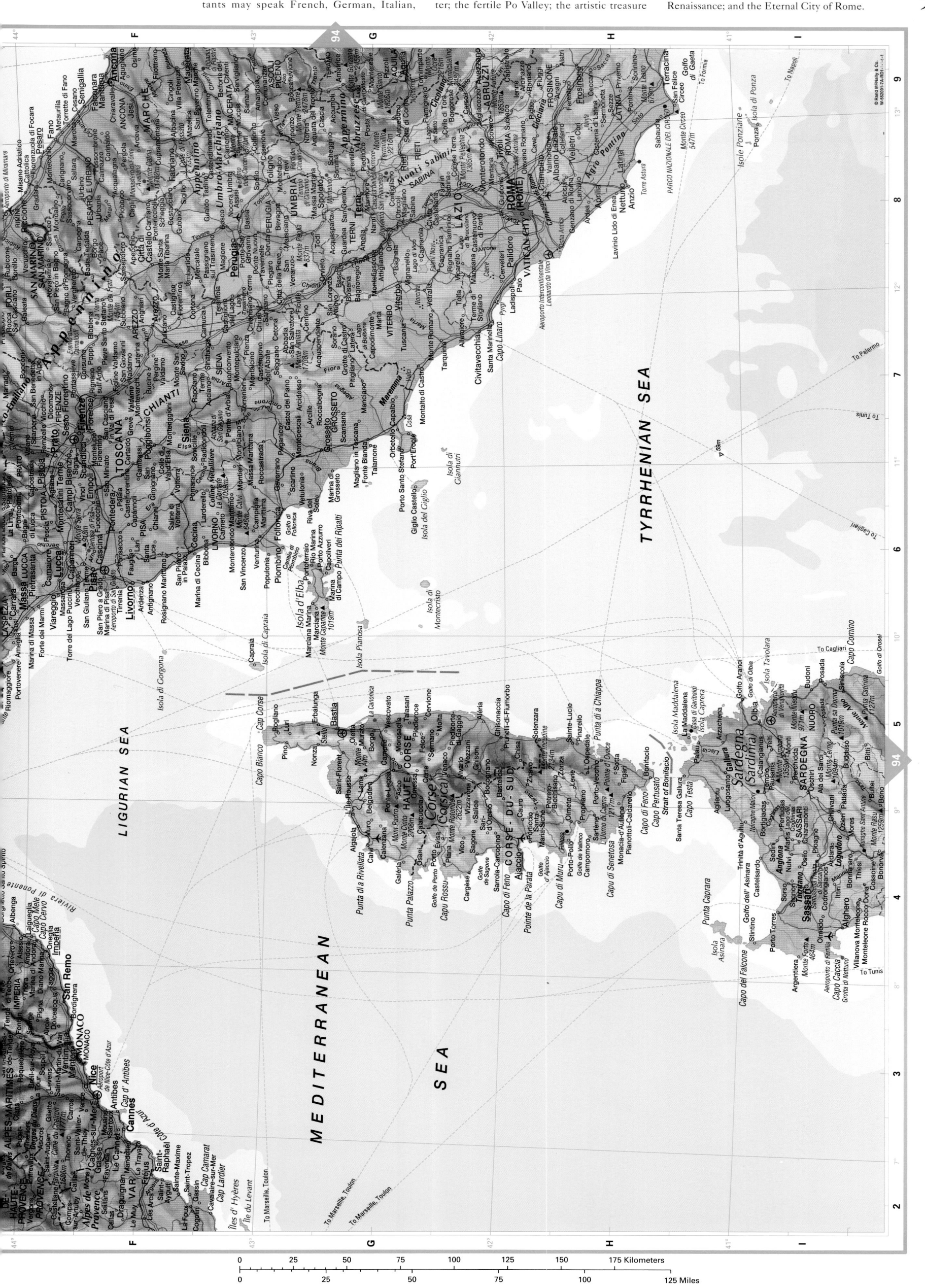

0   25   50   75   100   125   150   175 Kilometers

0   25   50   75   100   125 Miles

HEIGHT

9,842ft.
3,000m.

6,562ft.
2,000m.

3,281ft.
1,000m.

1,640ft.
500m.

656ft.
200m.

Sea level

656ft.
200m.

6,562ft.
2,000m.

DEPTH

BOSNIA AND HERZEGOVINA

CROATIA

DALMATIA

ADRIATIC SEA

ITALY

APPENNINO

ABRUZZI

MOLISE

CAMPANIA

PUGLIA

BASILICATA

LUCANIA

MARCHE

UMBRIA

TOSCANA

LAZIO

Pescara

Chieti

L'AQUILA

ROMA

VATICAN CITY

Napoli

SALERNO

AVELLINO

BENEVENTO

CAMPOBASSO

ISERNIA

FROSINONE

FOGGIA

Bari

Taranto

BRINDISI

LECCE

MATERA

POTENZA

Golfo di Taranto

MEDITERRANEAN SEA

FRANCE

CORSE-DU-SUD

SASSARI

Sardegna

Golfo di Taranto

Conic Equidistant Projection

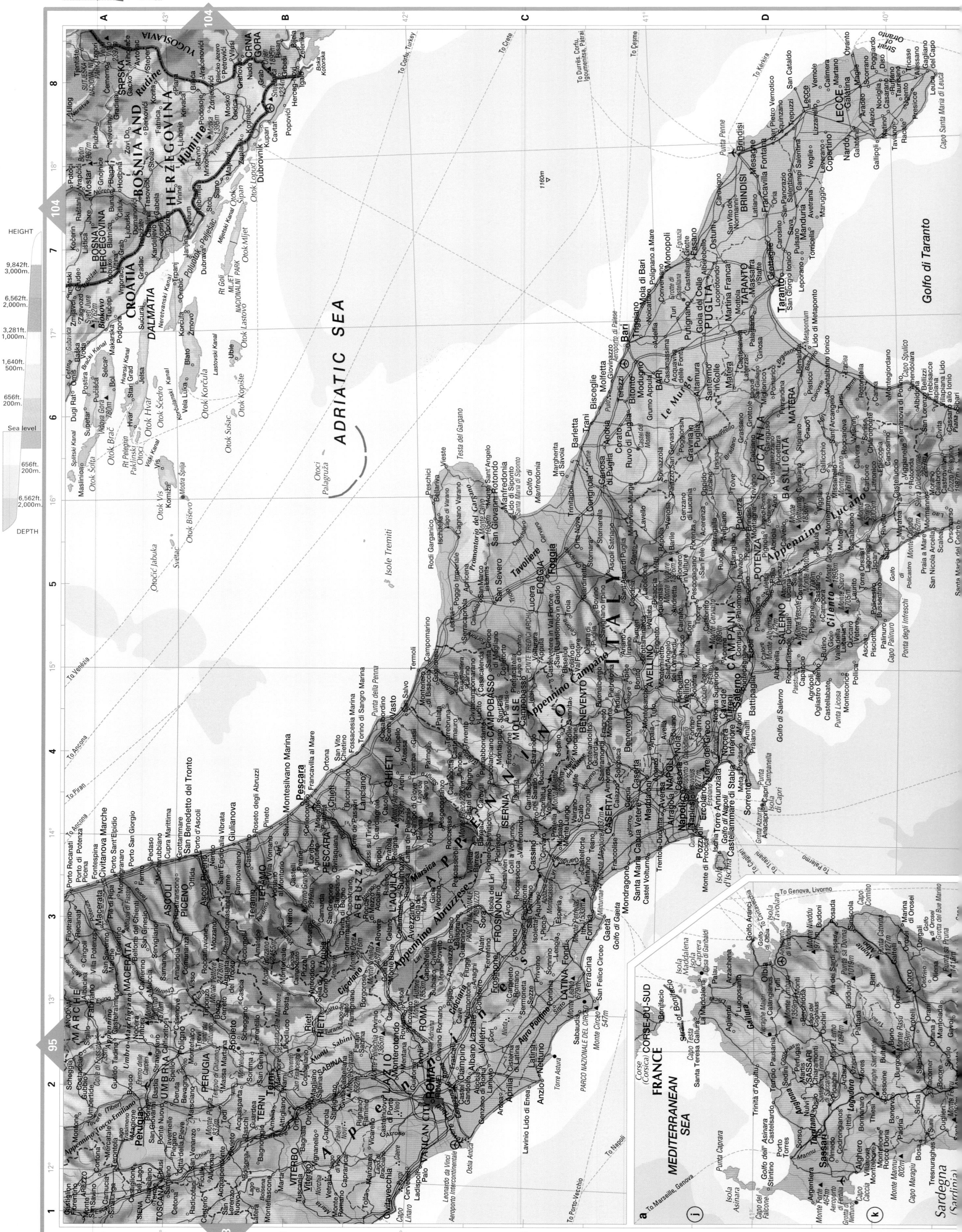

Scale 1:1,750,000

One centimeter represents 17.5 kilometers.

One inch represents approximately 28 miles.

South of Rome (once the capital of the mighty Roman Empire) lies an Italy that is hotter and craggier than its northern reaches – the so-called Mezzogiorno. In the Campania region reside ancient Pompeii and teeming Naples. The south has beckoned visitors since Roman emperors first went to Capri, and captivates them still with the splendor of the Amalfi coast. It is also home to two volcanoes, Mounts Etna and Vesuvius.

95

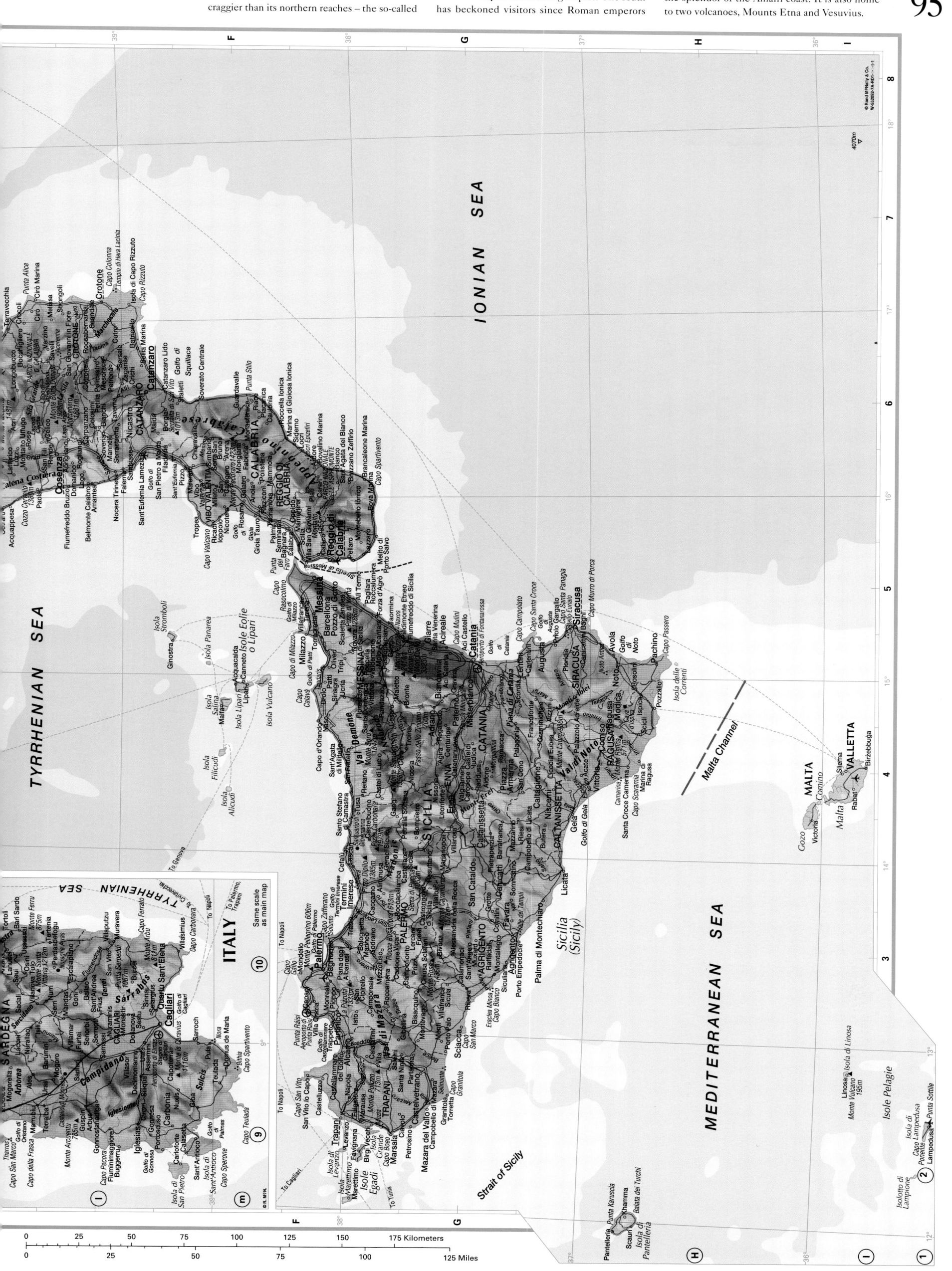

North-Central Europe

HEIGHT

9,842ft. 3,000m.

6,562ft. 2,000m.

3,281ft. 1,000m.

1,640ft. 500m.

656ft. 200m.

Sea level

656ft. 200m.

6,562ft. 2,000m.

DEPTH

NORTH SEA

NETHERLANDS

BELGIUM

LUXEMBOURG

GERMANY

DENMARK

FRANCE

SWITZERLAND

LIECHTENSTEIN

ITALY

68

79

82

83

93

Conic Equidistant Projection

With no mountain barriers along the North Sea and Baltic coasts, the broad sweep of the North European Plain, which rolls across Germany and Poland, has long provided a path for invaders, resulting in ever-shifting boundaries. To the south the land rises through the Bavarian Alps and the Carpathian Mountains. The Danube, a major transport artery, flows through no less than 8 countries on its course to the Black Sea.

97

Scale 1:3,000,000

One centimeter represents 30 kilometers.

One inch represents approximately 47 miles.

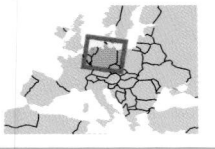
NORTH SEA

Scale 1:1,500,000

One centimeter represents 15 kilometers.

One inch represents approximately 24 miles.

Conic Equidistant Projection

© Rand McNally & Co.

Bordered by nine countries (Denmark, the Netherlands, Belgium, France, Luxembourg, Switzerland, Austria, the Czech Republic, and Poland), Germany is the second-most-populous country in Europe (after Russia) and its leading industrial power. Its northern territory is dominated by a wide plain traversed by the Rhine and other rivers and punctuated by such cities as Hamburg, Dresden, Cologne, and Berlin.

99

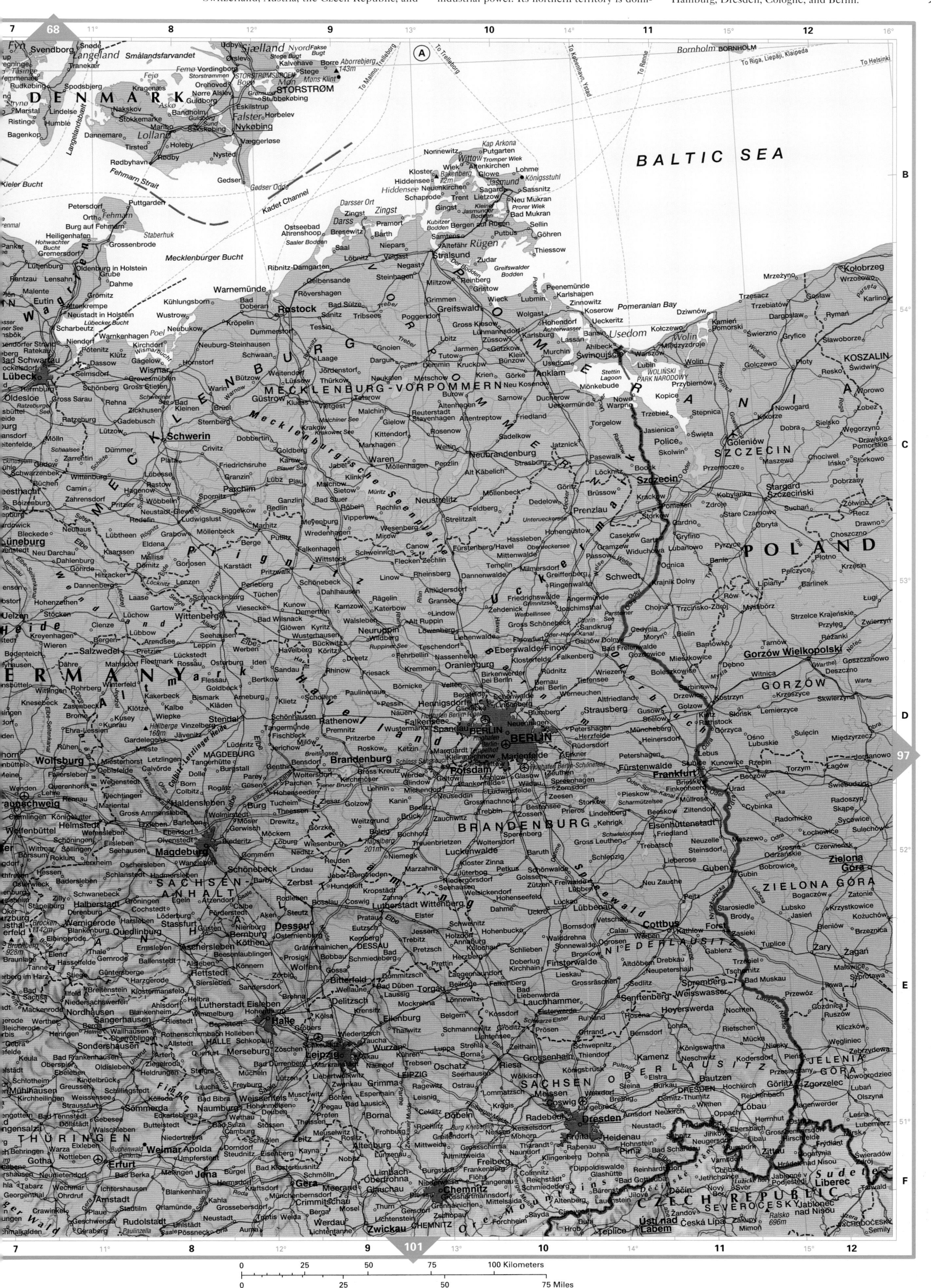

Scale 1:1,500,000

One centimeter represents 15 kilometers.

One inch represents approximately 24 miles.

As one heads south through Germany, plains give way to rolling hills in the midsection of the country before high alpine peaks dominate the landscape along the frontier with Switzerland and Austria. The states of southern Germany, Baden-Württemberg and Bavaria, are large and prosperous, embracing Stuttgart, maker of world-famous cars, and Munich, third largest of German cities, which grew from a monastery.

101

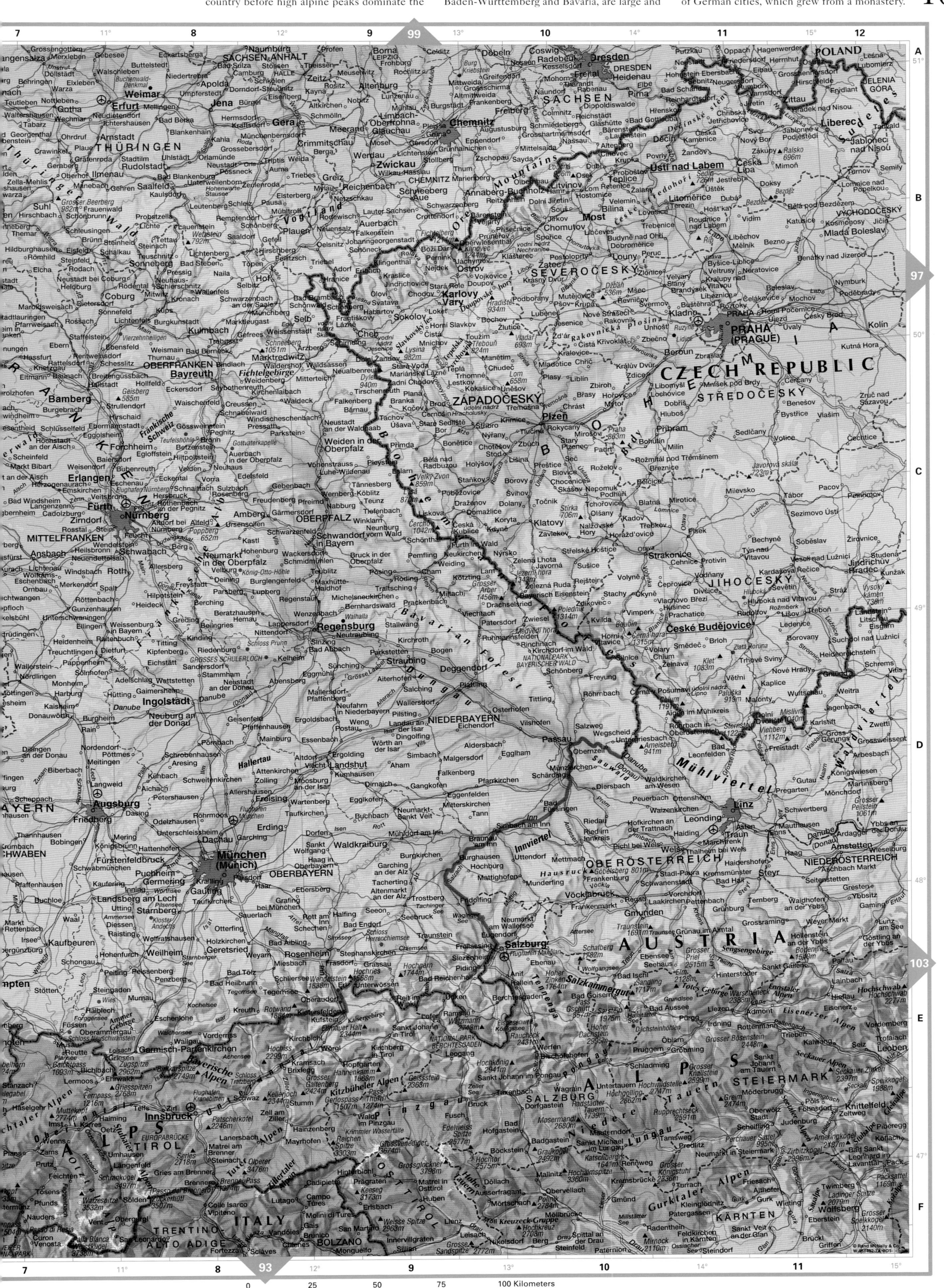

0   25   50   75   100 Kilometers

0   25   50   75 Miles

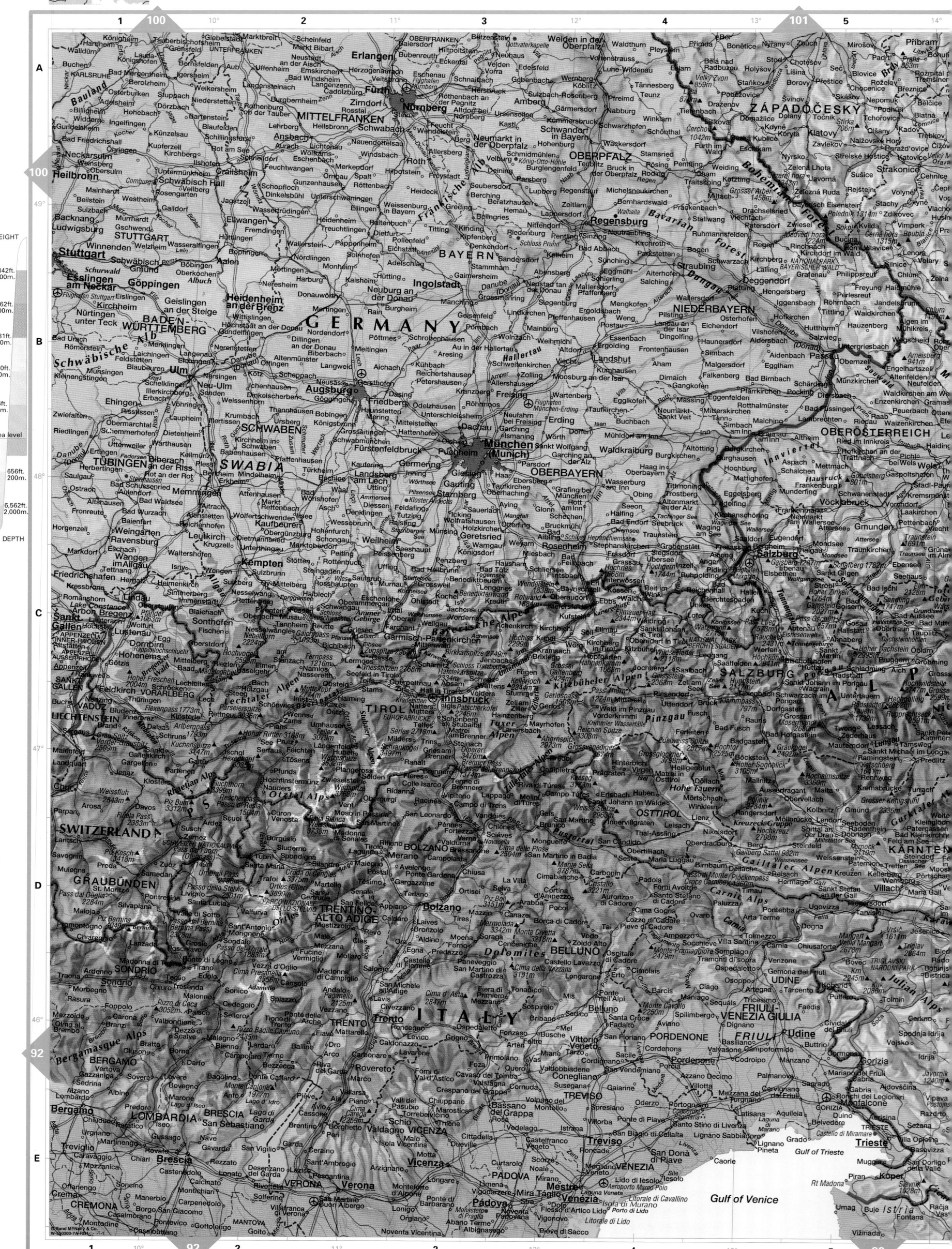

HEIGHT

9,842ft. 3,000m.

6,562ft. 2,000m.

3,281ft. 1,000m.

1,640ft. 500m.

656ft. 200m.

Sea level

656ft. 200m.

6,562ft. 2,000m.

DEPTH

Conic Equidistant Projection

Scale 1:1,500,000

One centimeter represents 15 kilometers.

One inch represents approximately 24 miles.

Once the hub of a great empire, this landlocked country in the heart of Europe is dominated by mountains. Indeed, though plains can be found in the east, it is the Alps that enhance Austria's economy as well as its scenery. Tourism is such a vital industry that farmland is government subsidized and a portion of the Alps is federally protected. Astride the majestic Danube is the capital, Vienna, designed on an imperial scale.

103

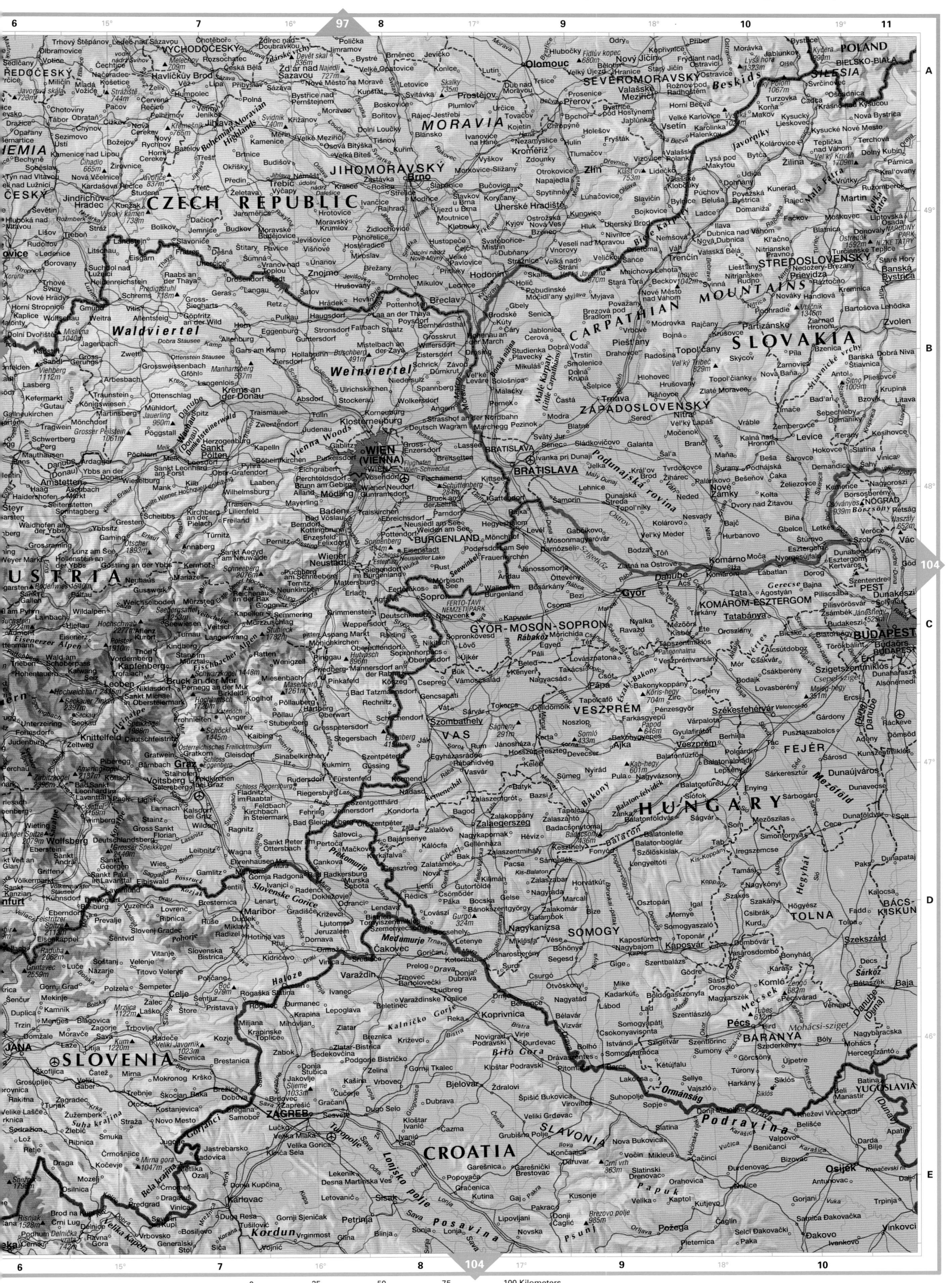

0   25   50   75   100 Kilometers

0   25   50   75 Miles

South-Central Europe

HEIGHT

9,842ft.
3,000m.

6,562ft.
2,000m.

3,281ft.
1,000m.

1,640ft.
500m.

656ft.
200m.

Sea level

656ft.
200m.

6,562ft.
2,000m.

DEPTH

Scale 1:3,000,000

One centimeter represents 30 kilometers.

One inch represents approximately 47 miles.

Conic Equidistant Projection

© Rand McNally & Co.
W-556000-7A-RD1-·-·-·-·1

| 0 | 50 | 100 | 150 | 200 | 250 | 300 Kilometers |

| 0 | 50 | 100 | 150 | 200 Miles |

Bordered by the Adriatic and Ionian seas in the west, the Aegean and Black seas in the east, and the Mediterranean in the south, the Balkan Peninsula is home to such varied peoples as Albanians, Romanians, Greeks, Serbs, Bulgars, and Turks. The former Yugoslavia has fallen apart, but other states in the region try, amid flareups of ethnic conflict, to assert their nationhood and preserve their distinctive cultures.

105

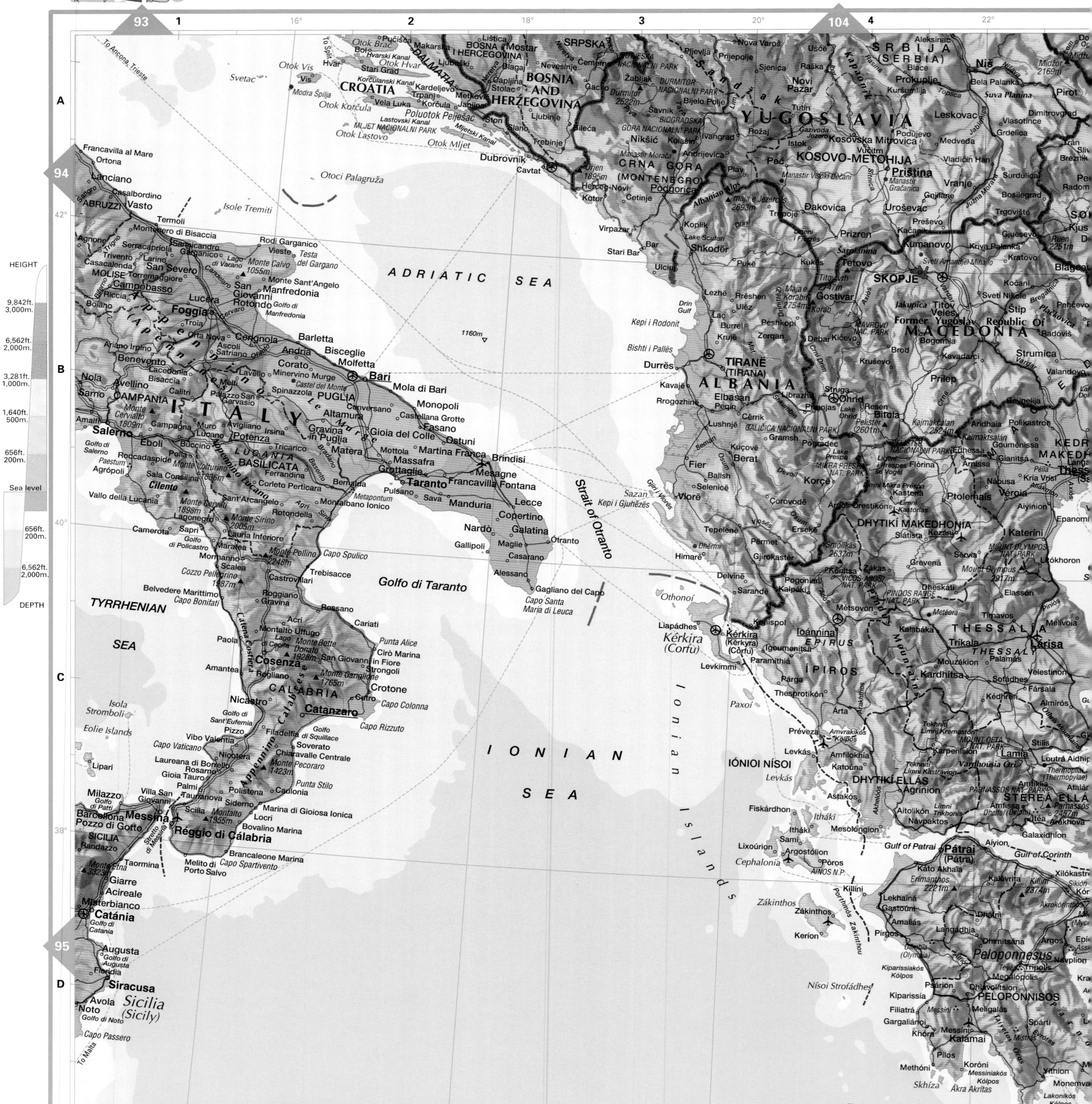

Scale 1:3,000,000

One centimeter represents 30 kilometers.

One inch represents approximately 47 miles.

Conic Equidistant Projection

Once the center of the Western world, Greece is the land where democracy was born. The southernmost nation of the Balkans, its territory is comprised of a large, mainly mountainous peninsula and a collection of more than 2,000 islands, separated by a vast network of bays, gulfs, channels, and lesser seas. In nearby Turkey, across the Aegean, the city of Istanbul remains the gateway between Europe and Asia.

107

0   50   100   150   200   250   300 Kilometers

0   50   100   150   200 Miles

Northwest Russia

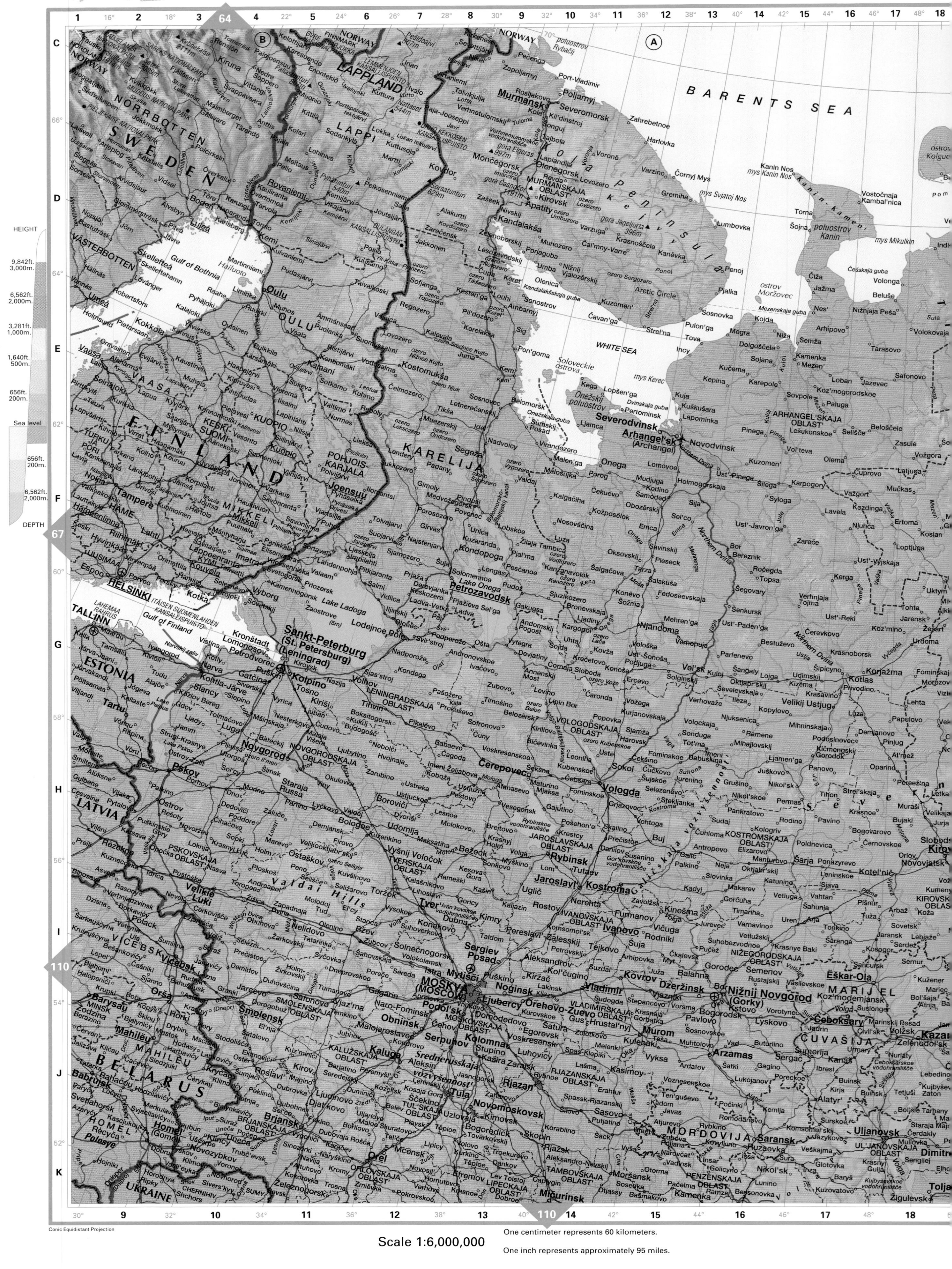

Conic Equidistant Projection

Scale 1:6,000,000

One centimeter represents 60 kilometers.

One inch represents approximately 95 miles.

Bounded by 13 countries and spanning 11 time zones, Russia is the world's largest country, with an area of some 6 million sq. mi. (16 million sq. km.) – a territory nearly twice the size of either the U.S. or China. Within its northwest corner, a land of rolling steppes, forests, and lakes, are three-quarters of its population and two of its major cities: St. Petersburg, the capital from 1712 to 1918, and Moscow, the current capital.

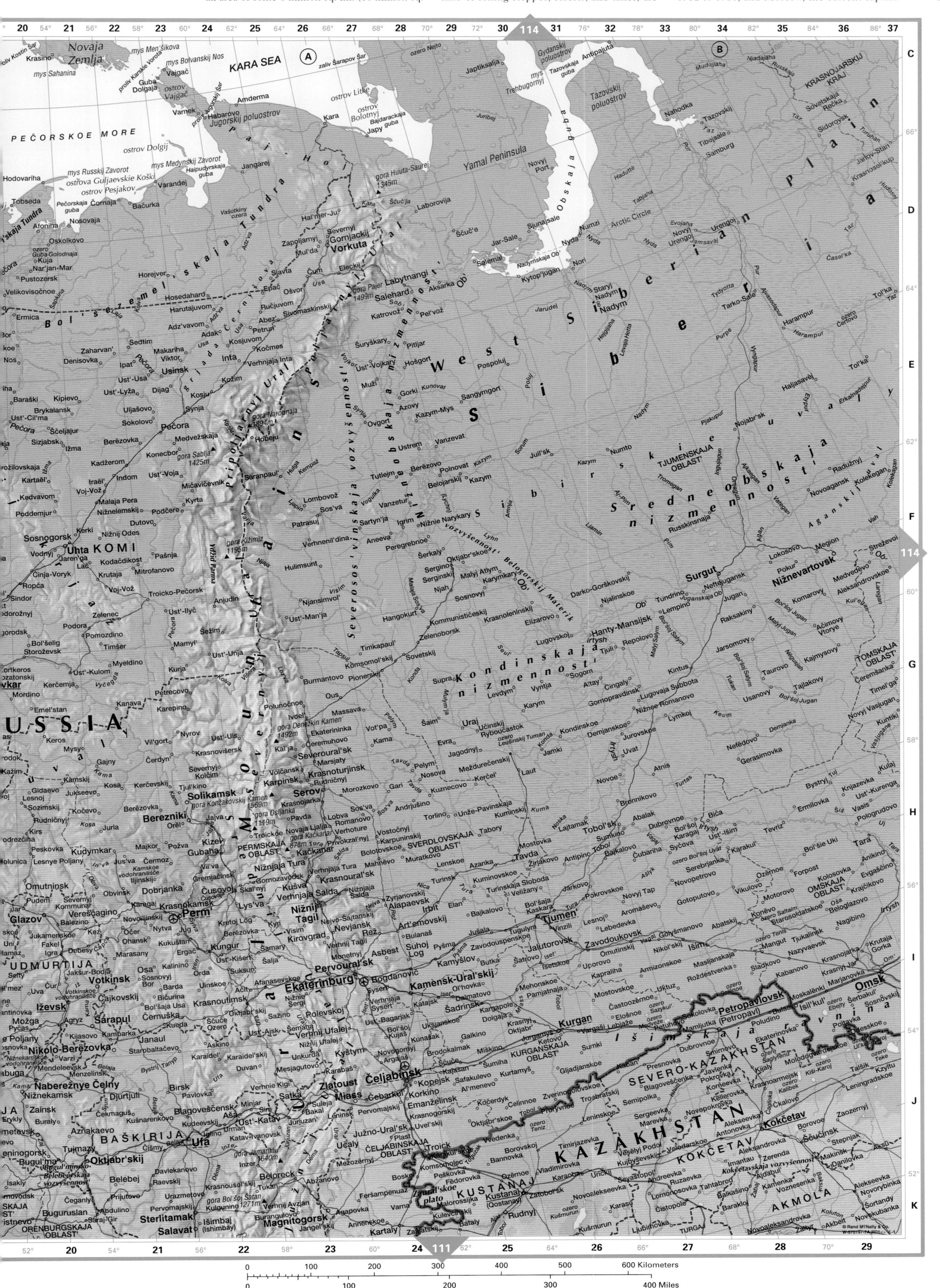

Scale 1:6,000,000

One centimeter represents 60 kilometers.

One inch represents approximately 95 miles.

Lambert Conformal Conic Projection

© Rand McNally & Co.
W-579900-7A-RD1-1

Ukraine means "frontier land," an apt description of Europe's second-largest country, for Ukraine's location has made it a meeting place between the former Ottoman Empire in the south, Russia in the east, and Poland in the west. The Carpathian Mountains rise in the west and the Crimean peaks in the south, but the country's most valuable natural resource is the fertile soil covering some three-quarters of its territory.

111

Largest of the continents, Asia contains one-third the world's landmass. Its 40-plus nations are home to more than half the people on earth.

The world's highest mountain (Mt. Everest), lowest elevation (the Dead Sea), and largest inland sea (the Caspian Sea) are all found here.

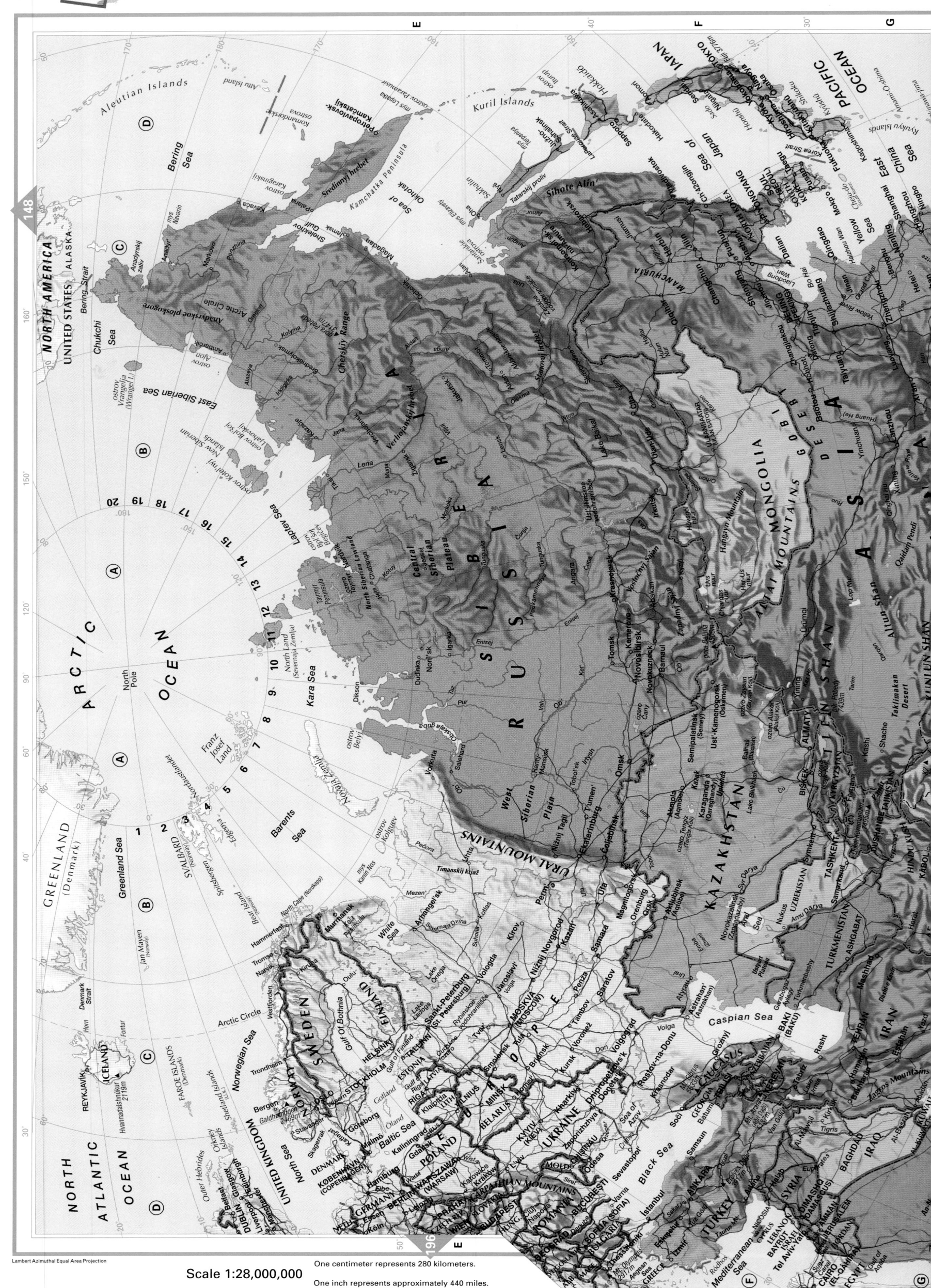

Lambert Azimuthal Equal Area Projection

Scale 1:28,000,000

One centimeter represents 280 kilometers.

One inch represents approximately 440 miles.

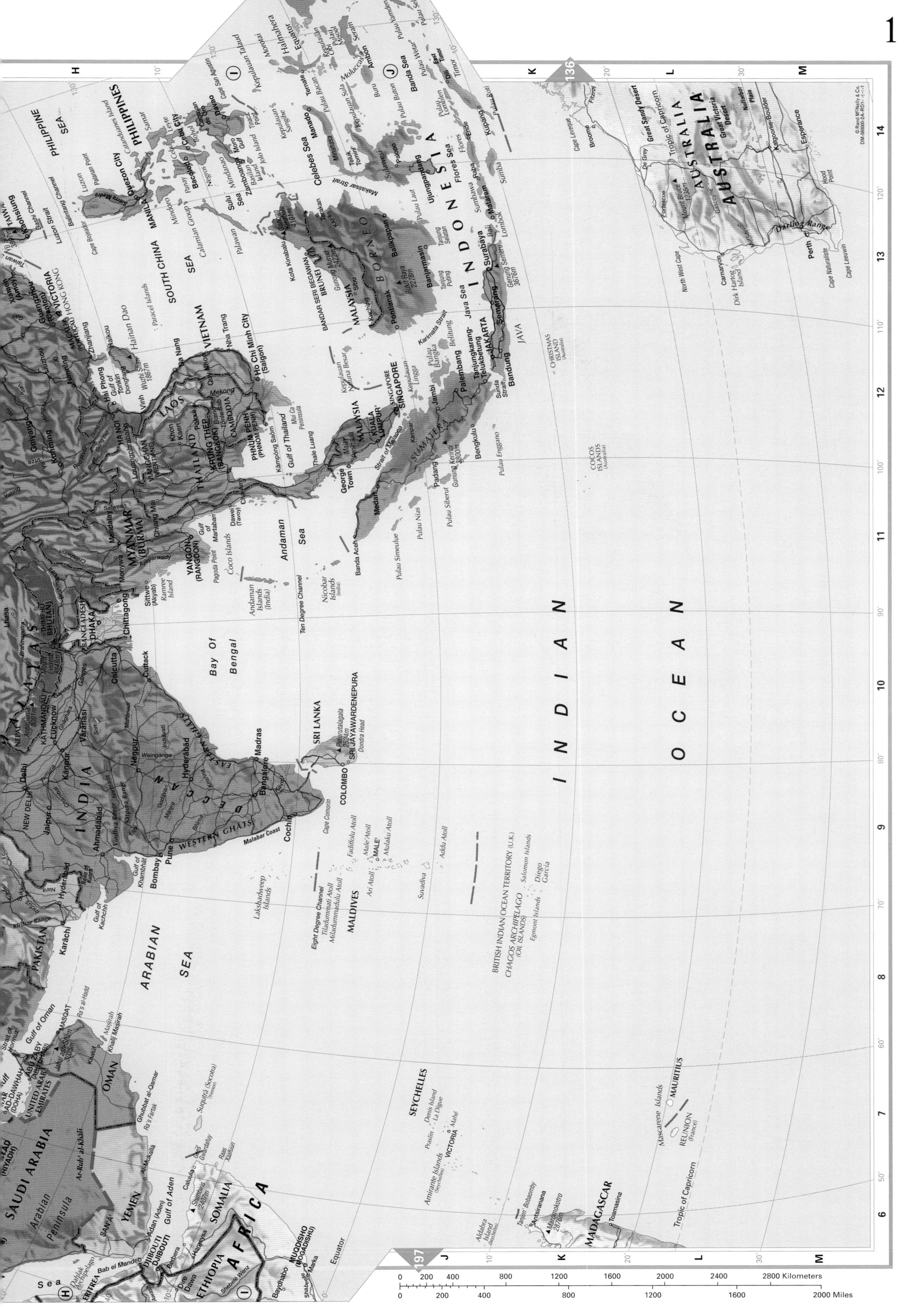

TAIWAN
Kaohsiung

PHILIPPINE
SEA

PHILIPPINES
Luzon
Quezon City
MANILA
Palawan Point
Cape Bojeador
Panay
Cebu CITY
Bacolod
Cebu
Leyte
Samar
Cape San Agustin
Negros
Mindanao
Zamboanga
Basilan
Island Jolo Island
Cagayan Sulu Island

Morotai
Halmahera
Kepulauan Talaud
Equator
Ternate
Kepulauan Sangihe
Pulau Yamdena
Pulau Selaru
Moluccas
Kepulauan Sula
Buru
Amboi
Banda Sea
Ceram
Timor
Dili
Pulau Wetar
Pulau Roti

Celebes Sea
Menado
Talud
Tomini
Sulawesi
Gulf of Tomini
Buton

INDONESIA
Ujungpandang
Flores Sea
Sumbawa
Raba
Ende
Flores
Kupang
Sumba

SOUTH CHINA
SEA

Paracel Islands

Hainan Dao
Haikou

VIETNAM
Da Nang
Nha Trang

Ho Chi Minh City
(Saigon)

BORNEO

Kota Kinabalu
BRUNEI
BANDAR SERI BEGAWAN
MALAYSIA
Gunung Murud 2438m
Tarakan

Pontianak
Banjarmasin
Bukit Raya 2278m
Balikpapan
Makassar Strait

Java Sea
Surabaya
JAKARTA
Bandung
Semarang
Gunung Semeru 3676m
JAVA

Tropic of Capricorn
Great Sandy Desert
Broome
Cape Leveque
De Grey
Fitzroy

AUSTRALIA

North West Cape
Great Victoria Desert
Nullarbor Plain
Kalgoorlie-Boulder

Perth
Darling Range
Cape Naturaliste
Cape Leeuwin
Esperance

CHRISTMAS ISLAND (Australia)

COCOS ISLANDS (Australia)

INDIAN

OCEAN

LAOS
THAILAND
KRUNG THEP (BANGKOK)
CAMBODIA
PHNUM PENH (PHNOM PENH)
Gulf of Thailand

MALAYSIA
KUALA LUMPUR
SINGAPORE
SINGAPORE

SUMATERA
Medan
George Town
Padang
Palembang
Tanjungkarang-Telukbetung
Sunda Strait

YANGON (RANGOON)
Andaman Sea
Coco Islands
Andaman Islands (India)
Nicobar Islands (India)
Ten Degree Channel

MYANMAR (BURMA)
Mandalay
Chiang Mai

Bay Of Bengal

Calcutta
Cuttack

EASTERN GHATS

SRI LANKA
COLOMBO
SRI JAYAWARDENEPURA
Pidurutalagala 2524m
Dondra Head

INDIA
NEW DELHI
Jaipur
Ahmadabad
Bombay
Pune
Hyderabad
Bangalore
Madras
Cape Comorin
Cochin
WESTERN GHATS
Malabar Coast

MALDIVES
MALE
Eight Degree Channel
Lakshadweep Islands

ARABIAN
SEA

PAKISTAN
Karachi
Hyderabad

OMAN
MASQAT
Gulf of Oman
Strait of Hormuz

SAUDI ARABIA
(RIYADH)
Ar-Rub' al-Khali
YEMEN
SANA
Gulf of Aden

AFRICA
SOMALIA
MUQDISHO (MOGADISHU)
ETHIOPIA
DJIBOUTI

BRITISH INDIAN OCEAN TERRITORY (U.K.)
CHAGOS ARCHIPELAGO (OIL ISLANDS)
Diego Garcia
Salomon Islands
Egmont Islands

SEYCHELLES
VICTORIA
Amirante Islands

Mascarene Islands
MAURITIUS
REUNION (France)

MADAGASCAR
Tropic of Capricorn

Equator

Stretching from the eastern edge of Europe to the Pacific Ocean, Russia and the other 14 republics that formerly constituted the Soviet Union dominate northern Asia. With over 6 mi lion sq. mi. (16 million sq. km.), their combin landmass, spanning 11 time zones and wrapp

HEIGHT

9,842ft.
3,000m.

6,562ft.
2,000m.

3,281ft.
1,000m.

1,640ft.
500m.

656ft.
200m.

Sea level

656ft.
200m.

6,562ft.
2,000m.

DEPTH

Numbers at E 7
(near Caucasus)
refer to the
corresponding
Russian republics
below:

1 ADYGEJA
2 KARAČAJEVO-
  ČERKESIJA
3 KABARDINO-
  BALKARIJA
4 SEVERNAJA
  OSETIJA
5 INGUŠETIJA
6 ČEČNJA

Lambert Azimuthal Equal Area

Scale 1:18,000,000

One centimeter represents 180 kilometers.

One inch represents approximately 284 miles.

way around the globe, is the largest of any
on. Much of this land is a wilderness rich in
imber, and other untapped resources.

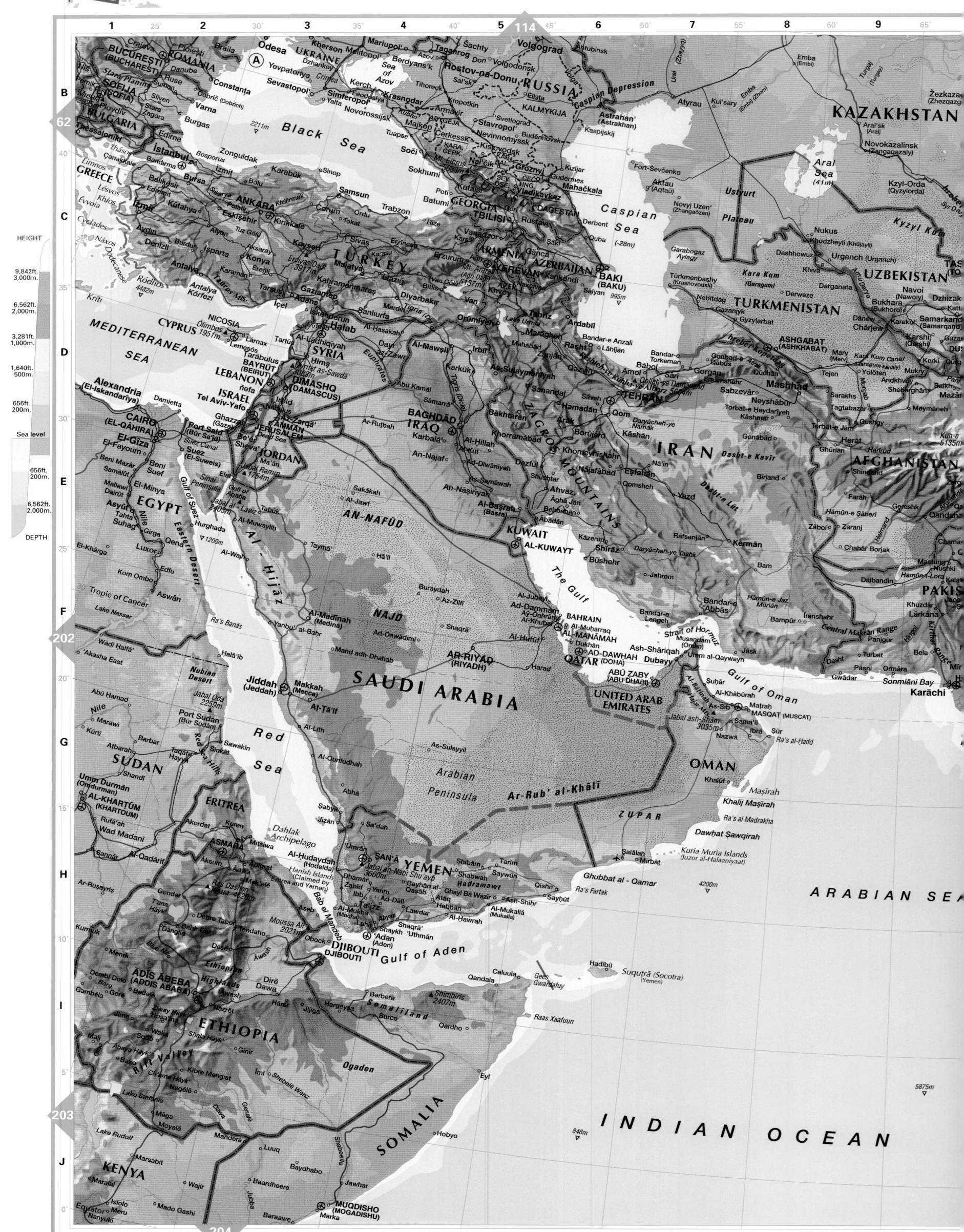

Scale 1:16,000,000

One centimeter represents 160 kilometers.

One inch represents approximately 250 miles.

Seamed by the craggy peaks of the Hindu Kush, Afghanistan is situated in the heart of southwest Asia. To the southwest is one subcontinent, Arabia, while to the southeast is another, India. A vast desert stretches from the Arabian Peninsula to western Pakistan, but irrigation is provided by the Jordan, Tigris-Euphrates, and Indus rivers. The oil wealth of the Persian Gulf makes the region a cornerstone of global power.

117

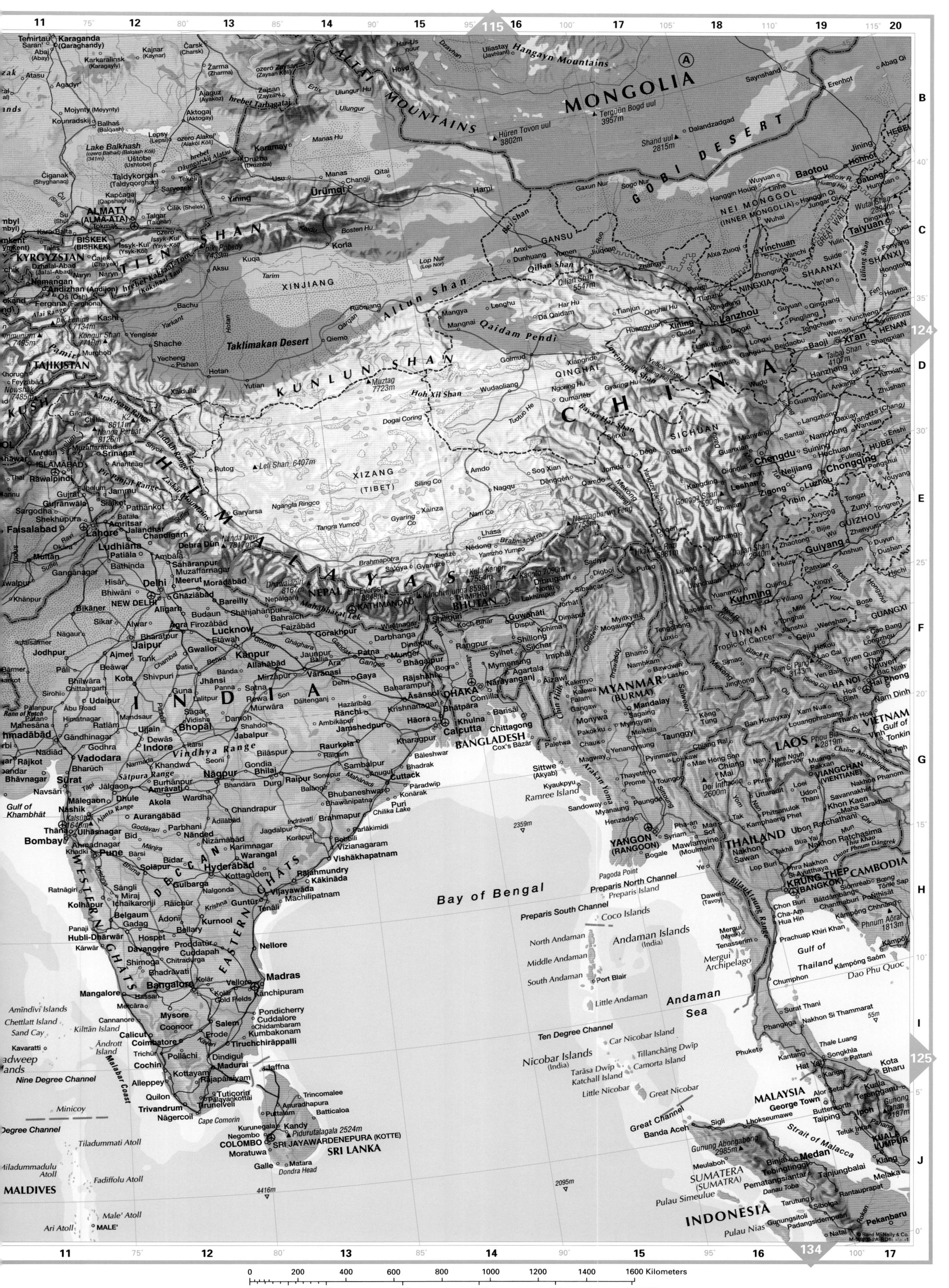

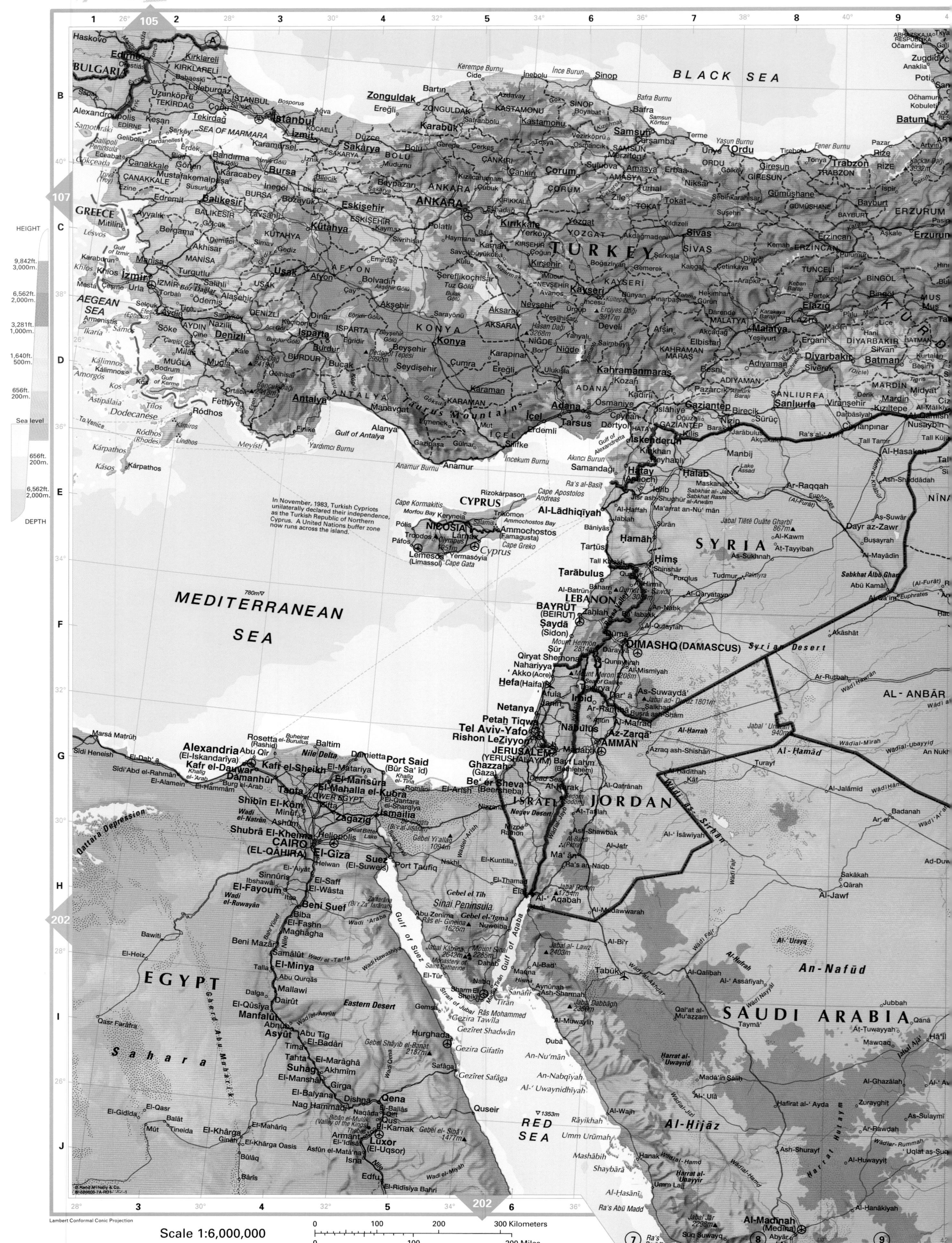

Scale 1:6,000,000

Lambert Conformal Conic Projection

In November, 1983, Turkish Cypriots unilaterally declared their independence, as the Turkish Republic of Northern Cyprus. A United Nations buffer zone now runs across the island.

Commonly identified as the region of southwest Asia between the Mediterranean and Pakistan, the Middle East is the birthplace of recorded human history. Arching over the Arabian Peninsula, the Fertile Crescent was the cradle of many early civilizations, including those of the Sumerians, Babylonians, and Assyrians. The 4,000-year-old city of Damascus, in Syria, is believed to be the oldest one in existence.

119

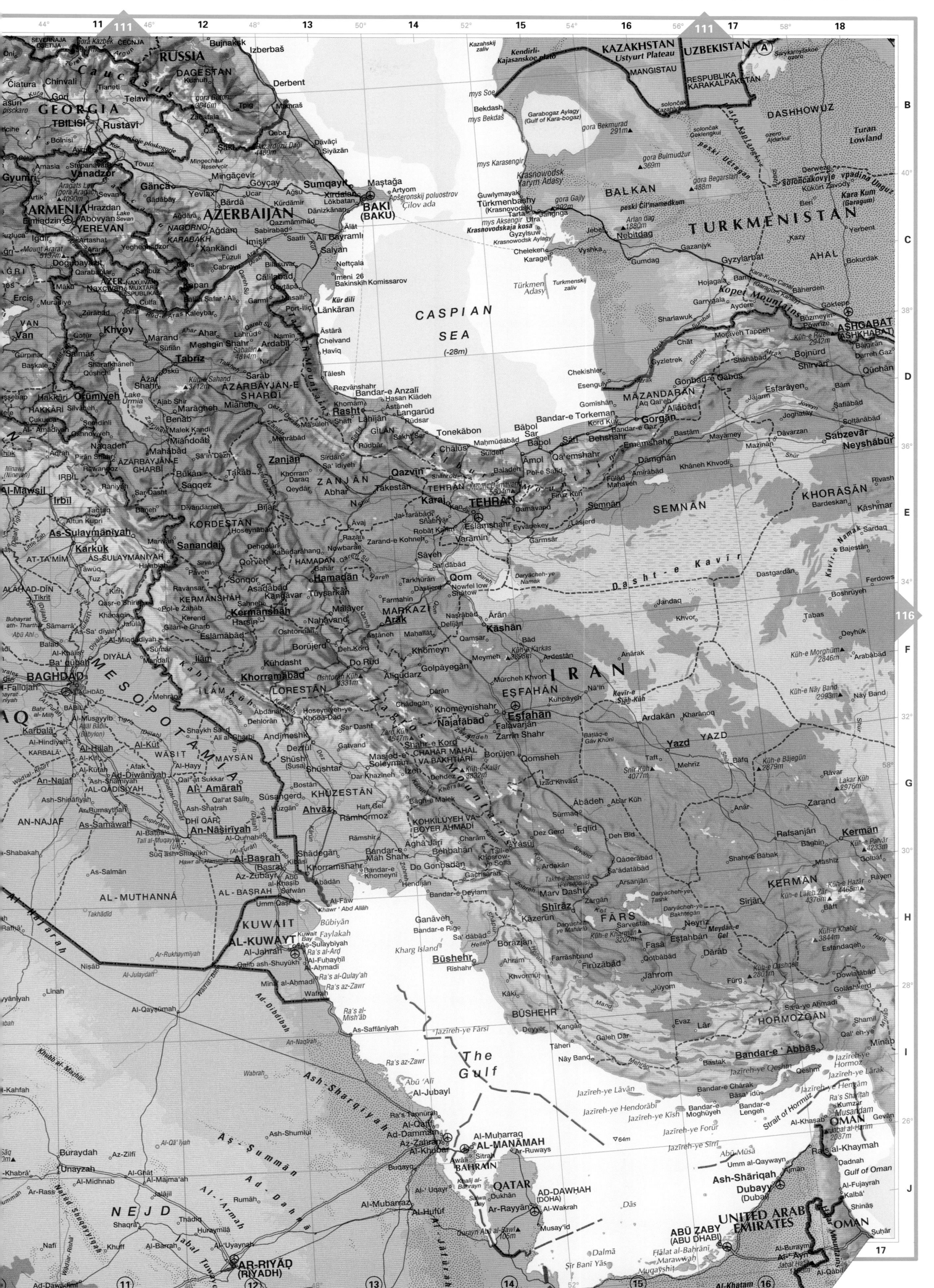

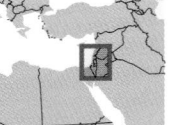

Israel and Southern Lebanon

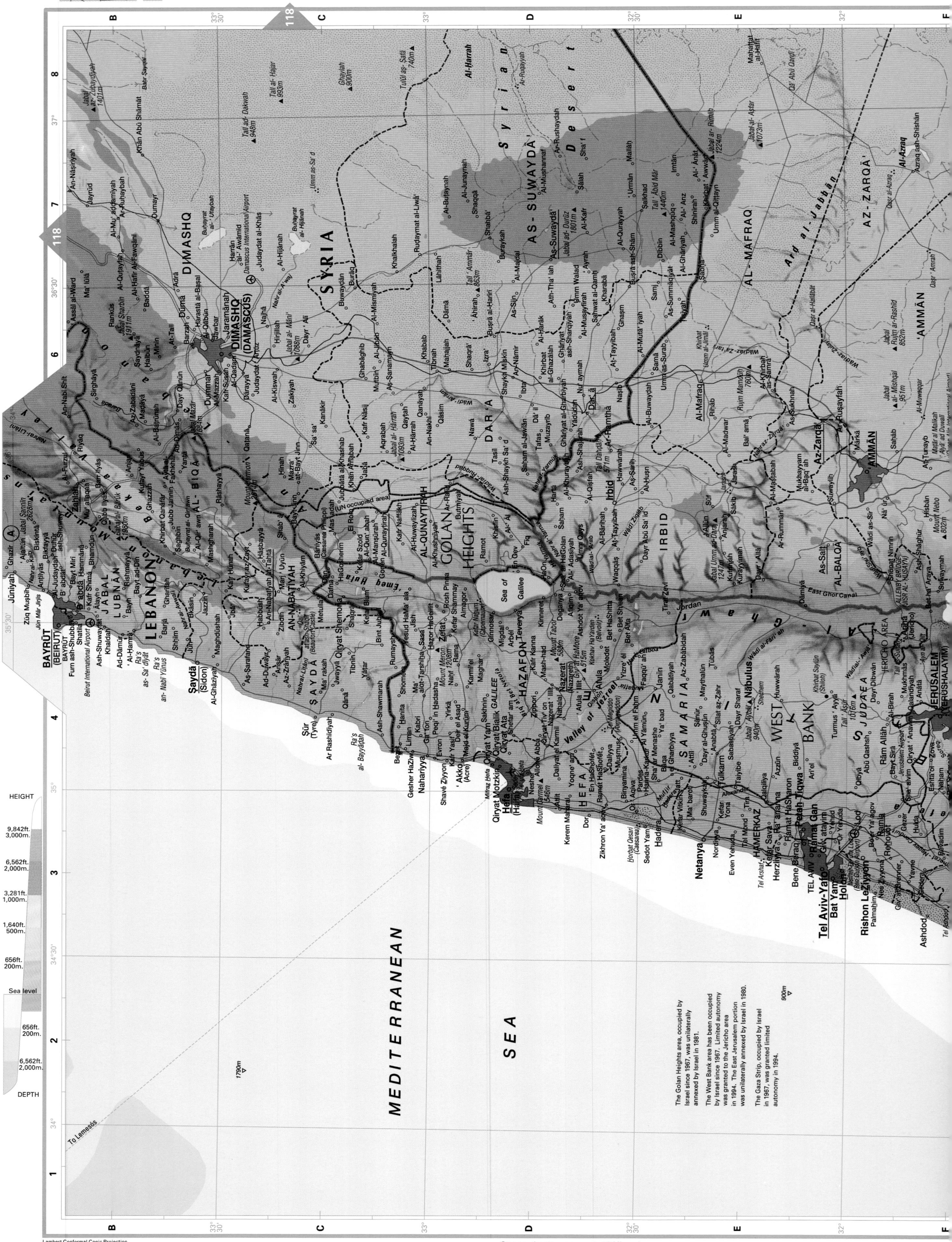
118
118
SYRIA
LEBANON
DIMASHQ
DIMASHQ (DAMASCUS)
BAYRŪT (BEIRUT)
Şaydā (Sidon)
Şūr (Tyre)
GOLAN HEIGHTS
Sea of Galilee
Jordan
WEST BANK
JERUSALEM (YERUSHALAYIM)
Tel Aviv-Yafo
Netanya
Hefa (Haifa)
Nazerat (Nazareth)
Irbid
'AMMĀN
AZ-ZARQĀ'
AL-MAFRAQ
AS-SUWAYDĀ'
DAR'Ā
AL-QUNAYṬIRAH
IRBID
AL-BALQĀ'
SAMARIA
JUDAEA
GALILEE
HAZAFON
HEFA
HAMERKAZ
TEL AVIV
Syrian Desert
MEDITERRANEAN SEA
To Lemesós
The Golan Heights area, occupied by Israel since 1967, was unilaterally annexed by Israel in 1981.
The West Bank area has been occupied by Israel since 1967. Limited autonomy was granted to the Jericho area in 1994. The East Jerusalem portion was unilaterally annexed by Israel in 1980.
The Gaza Strip, occupied by Israel in 1967, was granted limited autonomy in 1994.
HEIGHT
9,842ft. 3,000m.
6,562ft. 2,000m.
3,281ft. 1,000m.
1,640ft. 500m.
656ft. 200m.
Sea level
656ft. 200m.
6,562ft. 2,000m.
DEPTH

Lambert Conformal Conic Projection

Scale 1:1,000,000

One centimeter represents 10 kilometers.

One inch represents approximately 16 miles.

Bordered by Egypt, Jordan, Syria, and Lebanon, Israel is the traditional Holy Land shared by three of the world's great religions: Judaism, Christianity, and Islam. While much of the country's northern half is fertile, its southern half is dominated by the Negev Desert. Since attaining independence in 1948, Israel has experienced tremendous turbulence, marked by bitter conflicts with several of its Islamic neighbors.

121

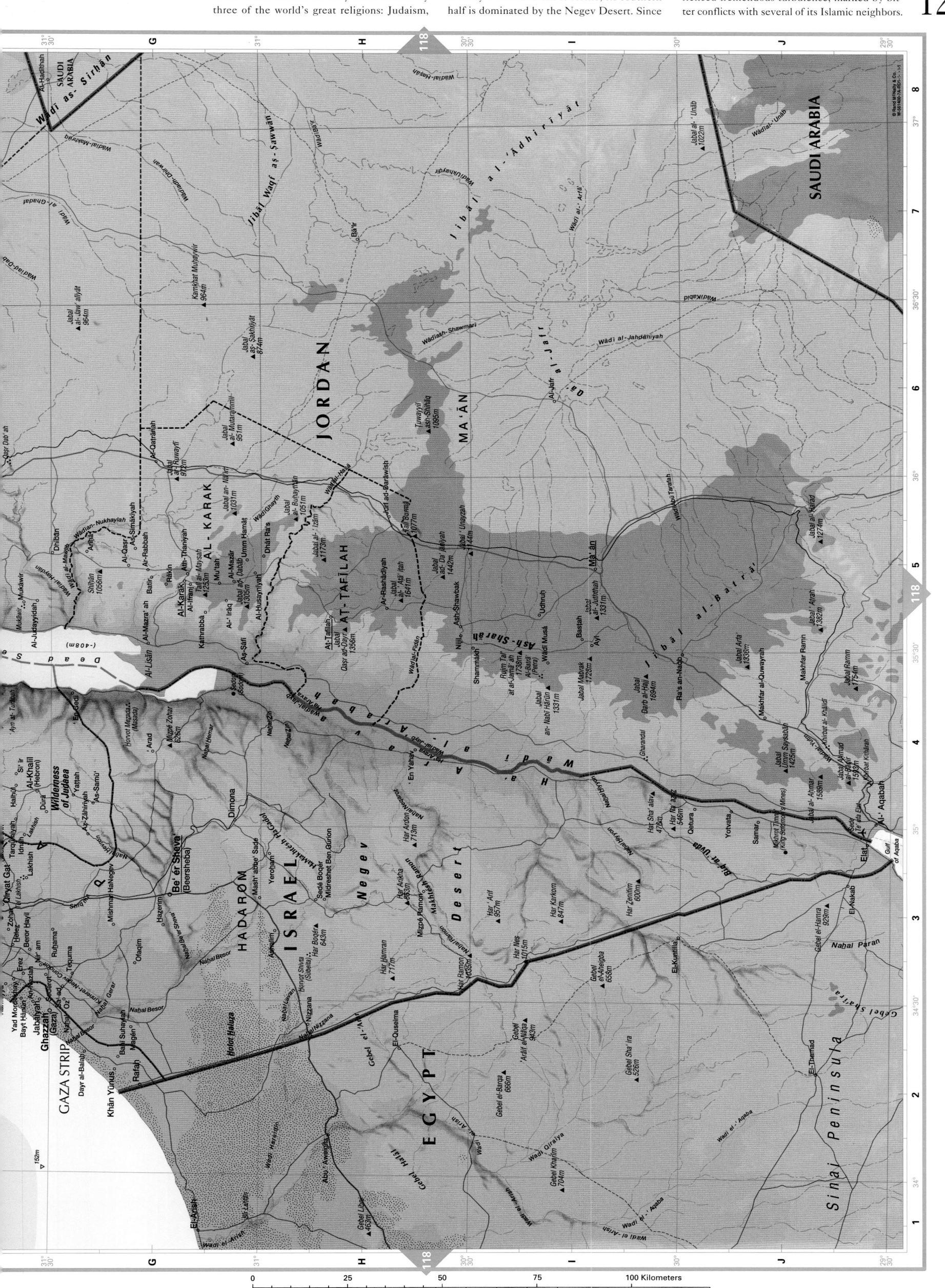

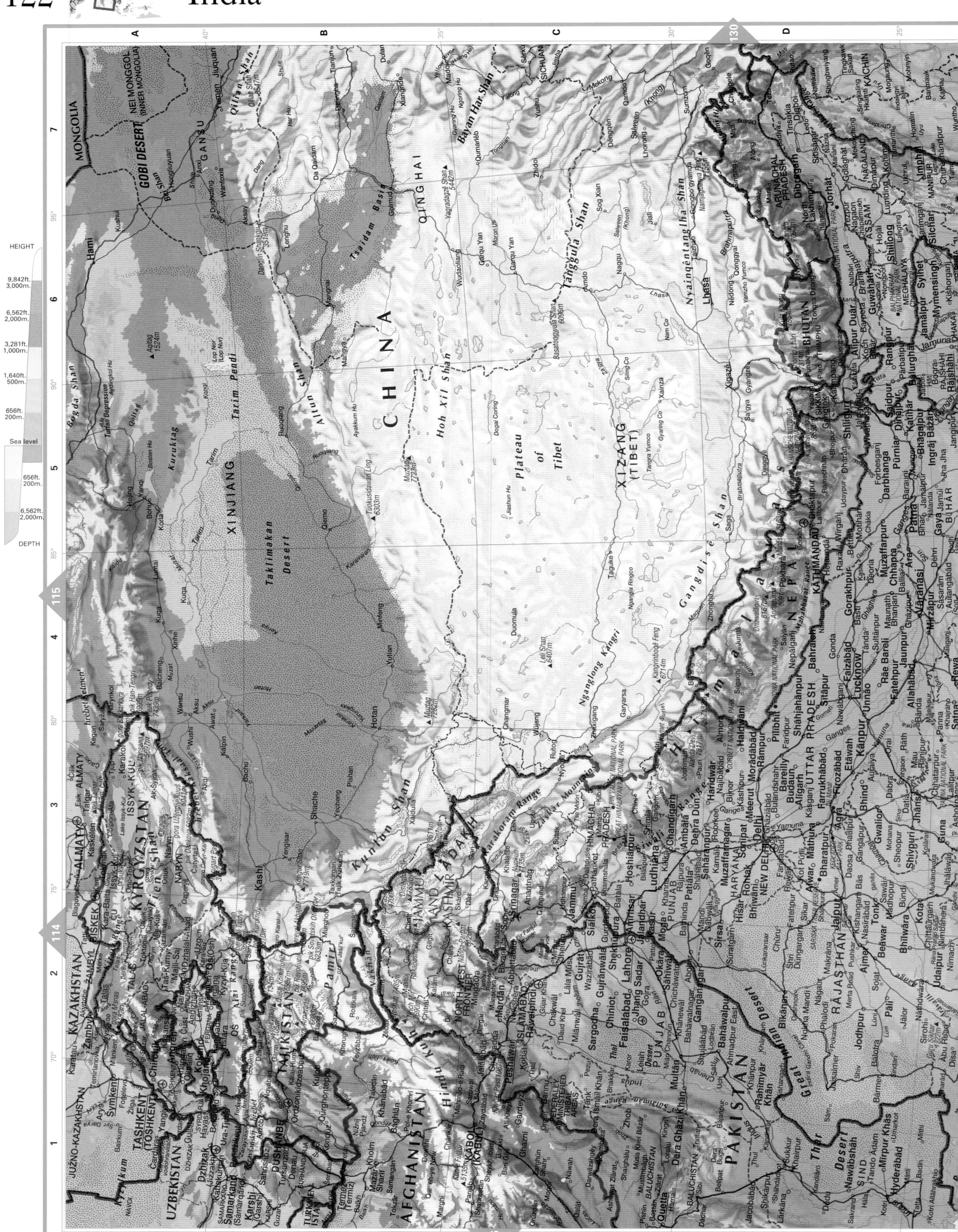

HEIGHT

9,842ft.
3,000m.

6,562ft.
2,000m.

3,281ft.
1,000m.

1,640ft.
500m.

656ft.
200m.

Sea level

656ft.
200m.

6,562ft.
2,000m.

DEPTH

Lambert Conformal Conic Projection

Scale 1:9,000,000

One centimeter represents 90 kilometers.

One inch represents approximately 142 miles.

A subcontinent as well as a nation, India is separated from the rest of Asia by the Himalaya Mountains, which include the loftiest peaks in the world. India's climate ranges from frigid in the Himalayas to arid in the desert plains of Rajasthan, but the region is dominated by tropical monsoons, which bring precious moisture to vital rice crops. By the year 2030 India's teeming population is expected to eclipse that of China.

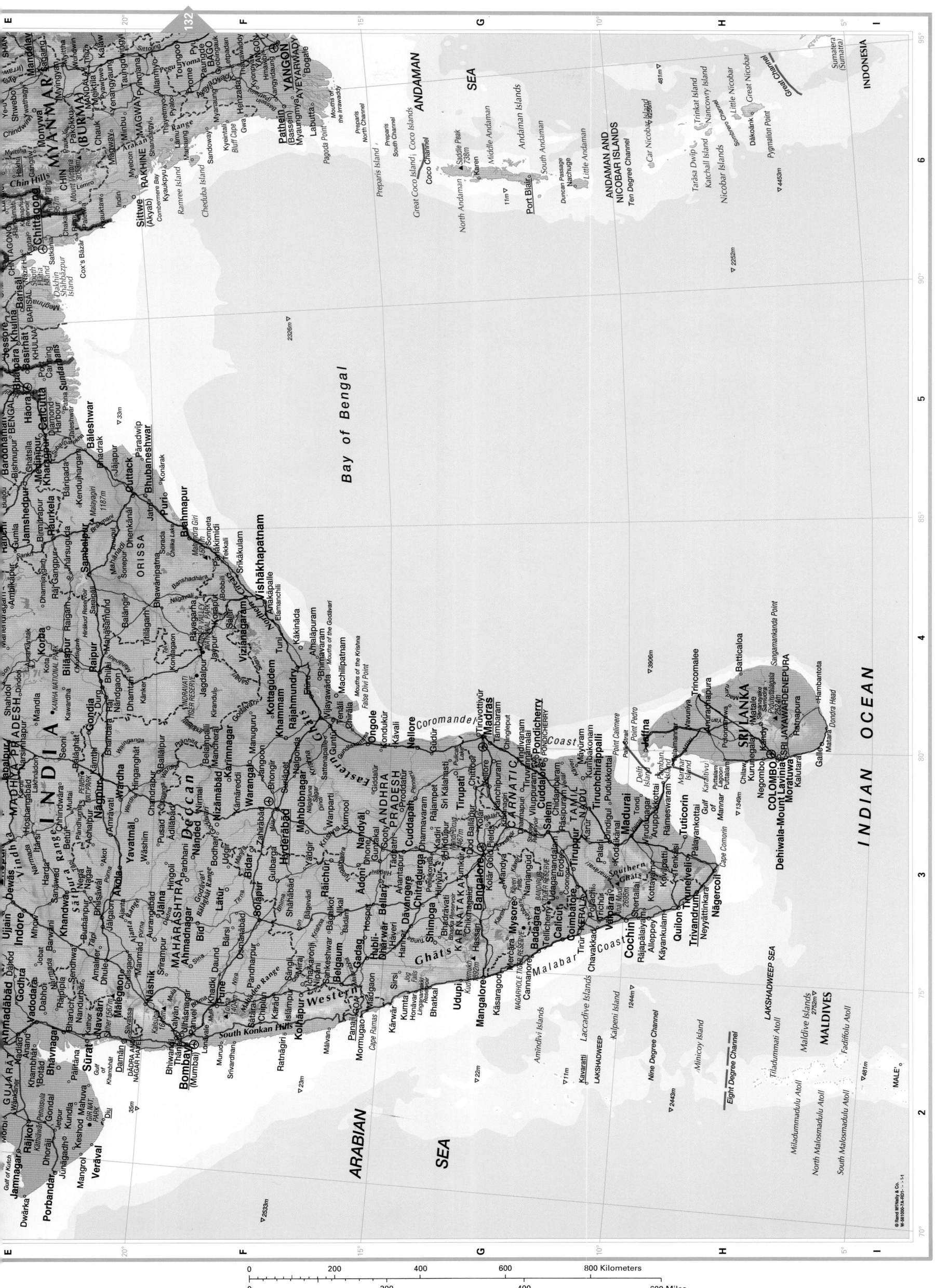

Eastern Asia

HEIGHT

9,842ft.
3,000m.

6,562ft.
2,000m.

3,281ft.
1,000m.

1,640ft.
500m.

656ft.
200m.

Sea level

656ft.
200m.

6,562ft.
2,000m.

DEPTH

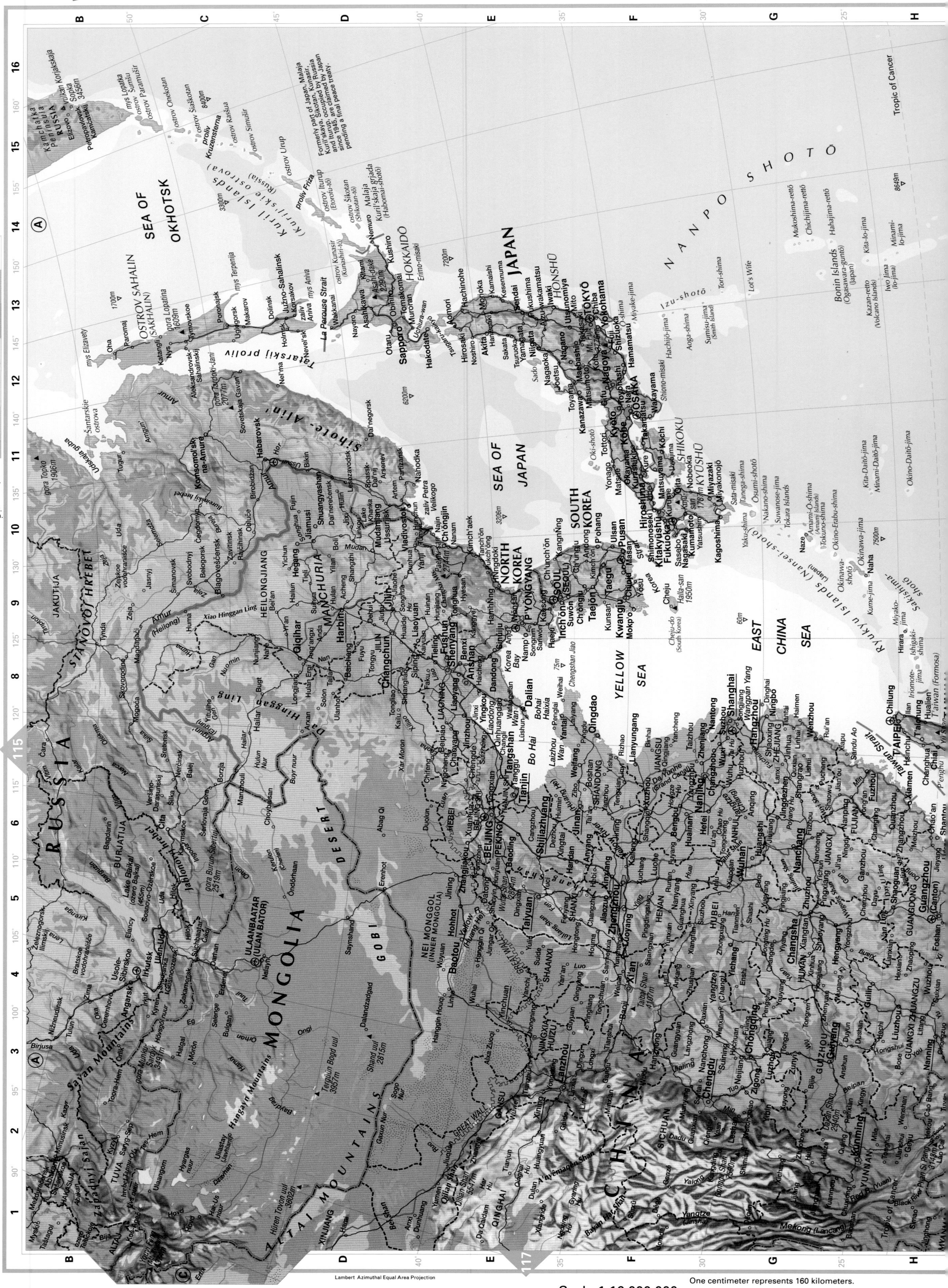

Lambert Azimuthal Equal Area Projection

Scale 1:16,000,000

One centimeter represents 160 kilometers.

One inch represents approximately 250 miles.

Bounded by the coast of China and such island nations as Taiwan, the Philippines, and Borneo, the South China Sea is ringed by ancient cultures. Rich with busy trade routes and thriving ports, this exotic region is home to Krakatoa, scene of the world's greatest volcanic explosion, in 1883.

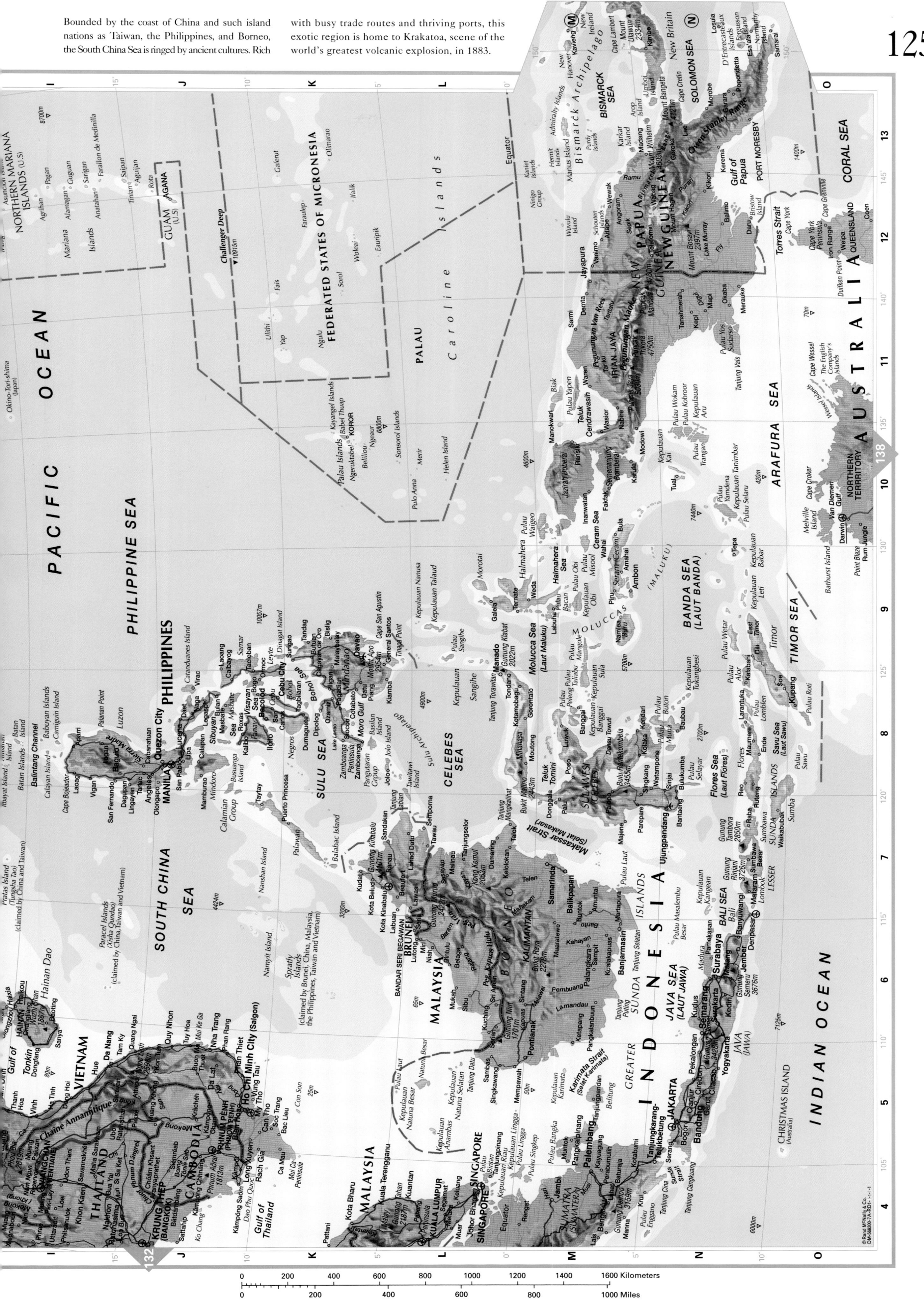

Japan

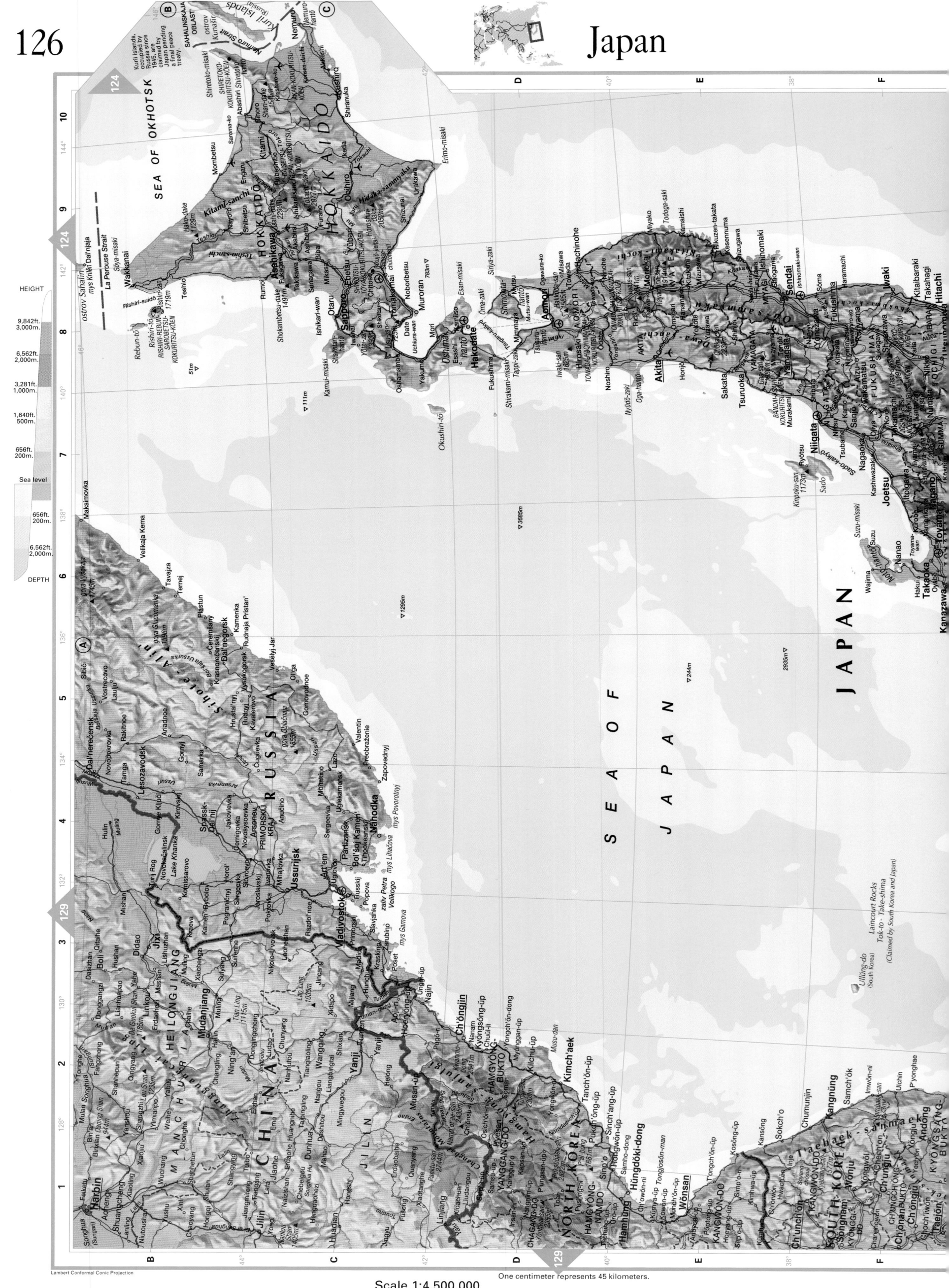

SEA OF OKHOTSK

HOKKAIDO

SEA OF JAPAN

JAPAN

RUSSIA

CHINA

NORTH KOREA

SOUTH KOREA

Kuril Islands (Russia)

SAHALINSKAJA OBLAST

HEIGHT

9,842ft. 3,000m.
6,562ft. 2,000m.
3,281ft. 1,000m.
1,640ft. 500m.
656ft. 200m.

Sea level

656ft. 200m.
6,562ft. 2,000m.

DEPTH

Lambert Conformal Conic Projection

Scale 1:4,500,000

One centimeter represents 45 kilometers.

One inch represents approximately 71 miles.

Located off the east Asian coast in the North Pacific, Japan is made up of four large islands (Honshū, Kyūshū, Shikoku, and Hokkaidō) and more than 3,000 smaller ones. The country's terrain is chiefly mountainous; industries, farms, and cities are concentrated on the remaining fertile coastal plains. Japan's location makes it vulnerable to two kinds of natural disasters – earthquakes and the tidal waves they may trigger.

127

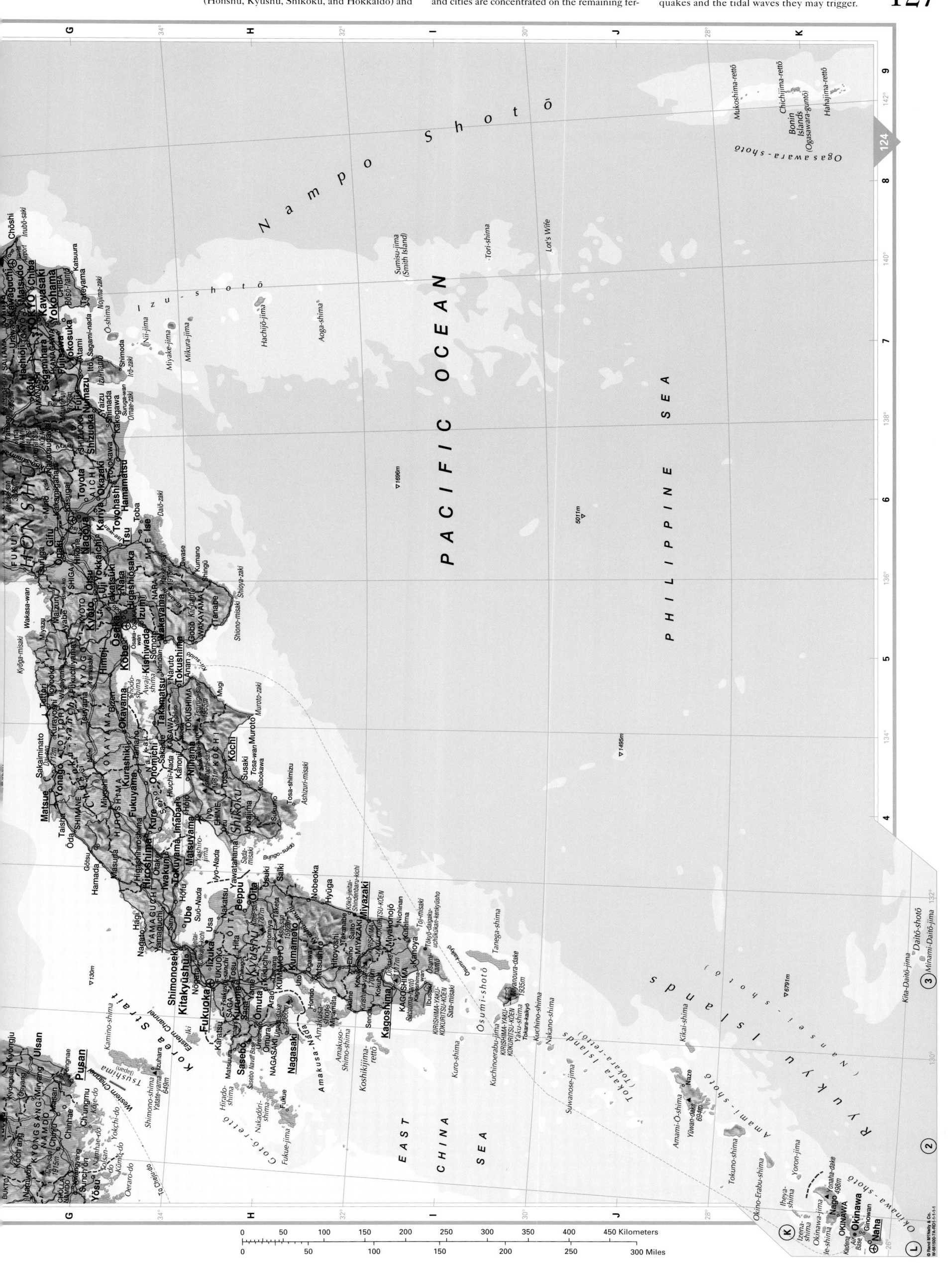

HEIGHT

9,842ft.
3,000m.

6,562ft.
2,000m.

3,281ft.
1,000m.

1,640ft.
500m.

656ft.
200m.

Sea level

656ft.
200m.

6,562ft.
2,000m.

DEPTH

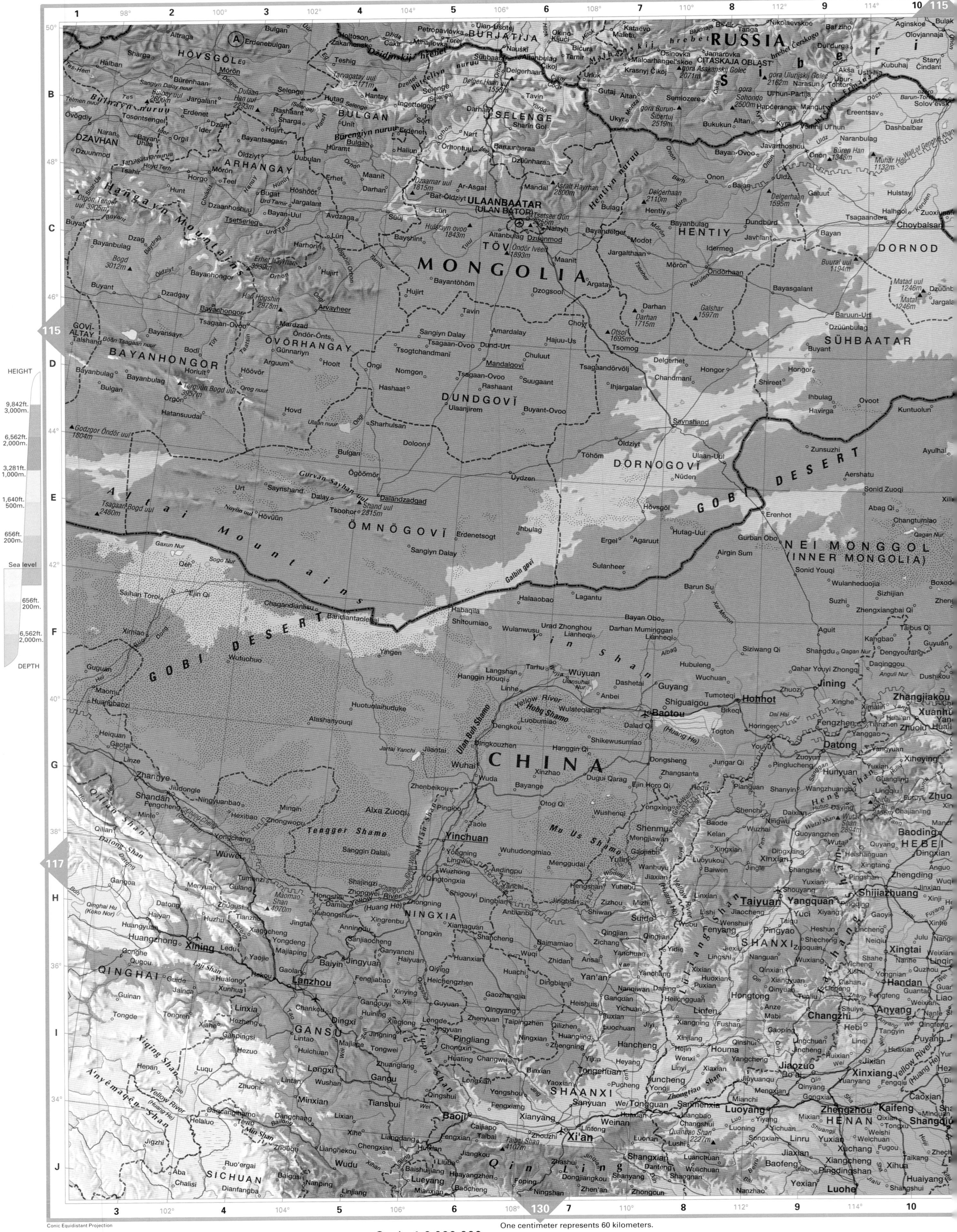

Conic Equidistant Projection

Scale 1:6,000,000

One centimeter represents 60 kilometers.

One inch represents approximately 95 miles.

Bordered by 14 countries, China, which is slightly smaller than Canada, is the world's third-largest country. Home to 1.2 billion people, it is the most populous nation on earth. About 90 percent of its citizens reside in one-sixth of its territory, mainly in the eastern lowlands. The adjoining Korean Peninsula is divided into the U.S.-dominated South and the communist North, which is largely isolated from the world.

HEIGHT

9,842ft. 3,000m.
6,562ft. 2,000m.
3,281ft. 1,000m.
1,640ft. 500m.
656ft. 200m.

Sea level

656ft. 200m.
6,562ft. 2,000m.

DEPTH

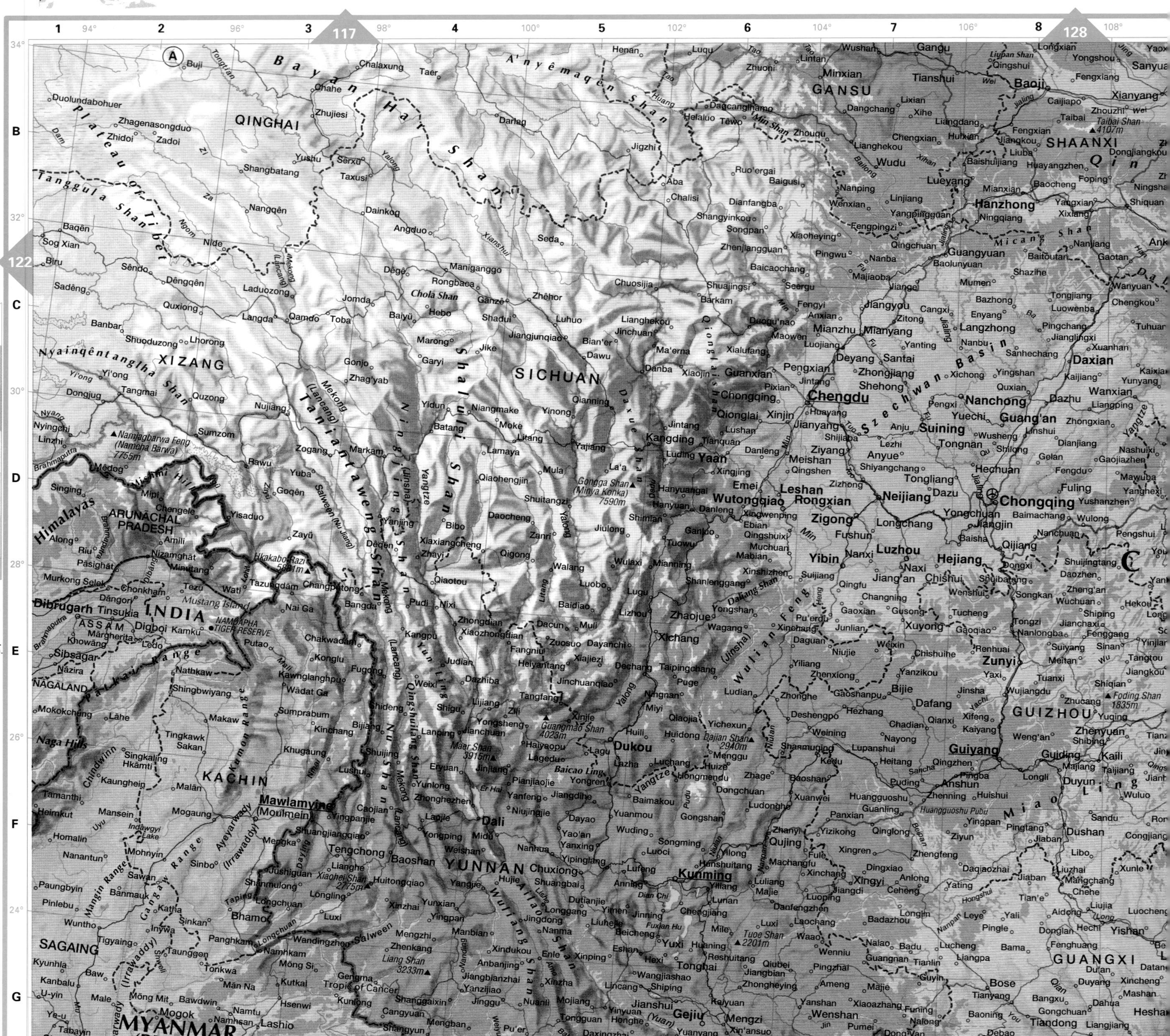

Conic Equidistant Projection

Scale 1:6,000,000

One centimeter represents 60 kilometers.

One inch represents approximately 95 miles.

Paddy fields and terraced hillsides in the agrarian south create the image of China that is most familiar to Western eyes. But in recent years the region has flourished, particularly in Guangzhou and Shenzhen, which owe their good fortune to their proximity to Hong Kong (back under Chinese rule as of July 1997). Nearby, the self-proclaimed island republic of Taiwan has developed into a major manufacturing center.

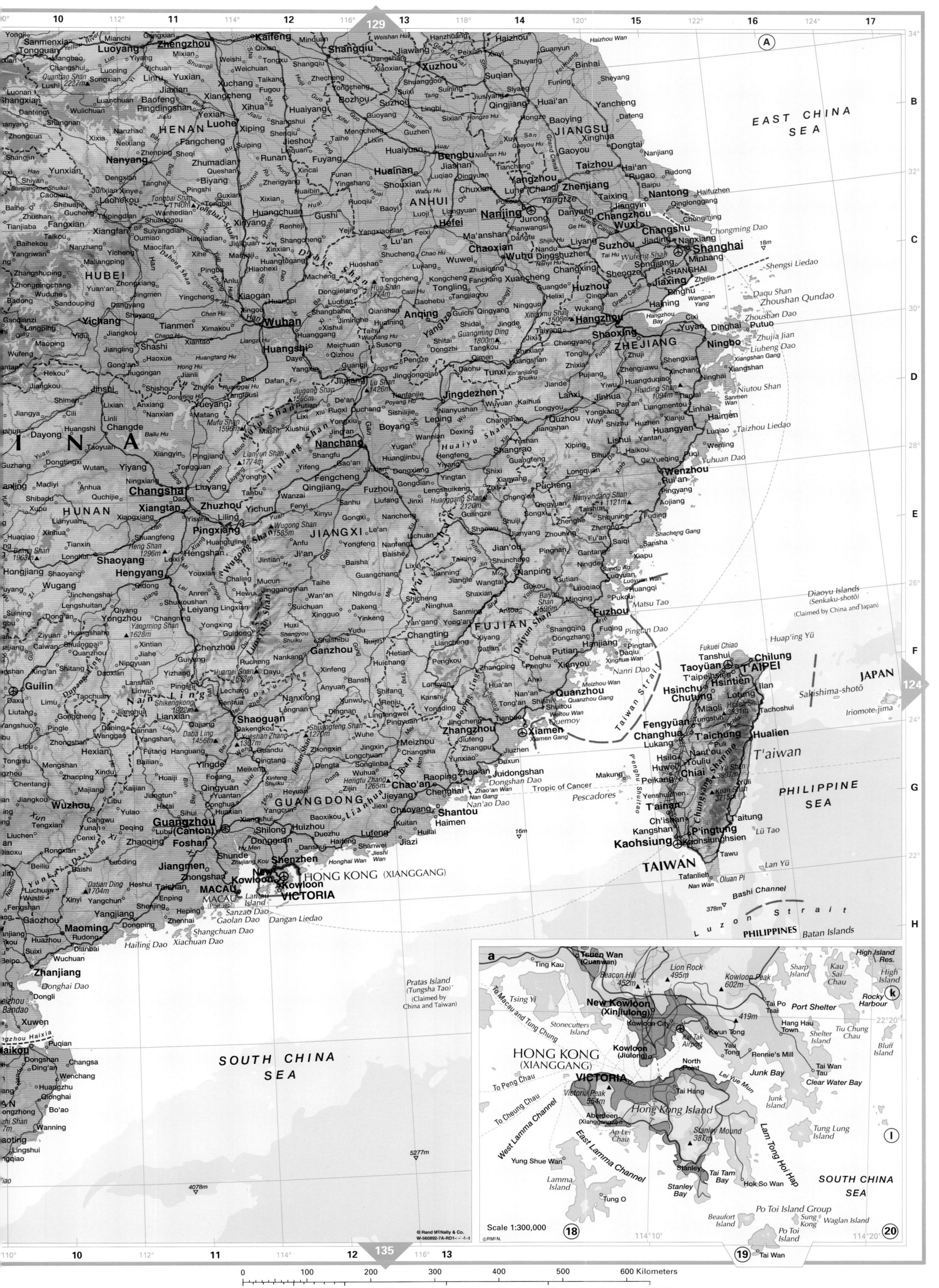

HEIGHT

9,842ft.
3,000m.

6,562ft.
2,000m.

3,281ft.
1,000m.

1,640ft.
500m.

656ft.
200m.

Sea level

656ft.
200m.

6,562ft.
2,000m.

DEPTH

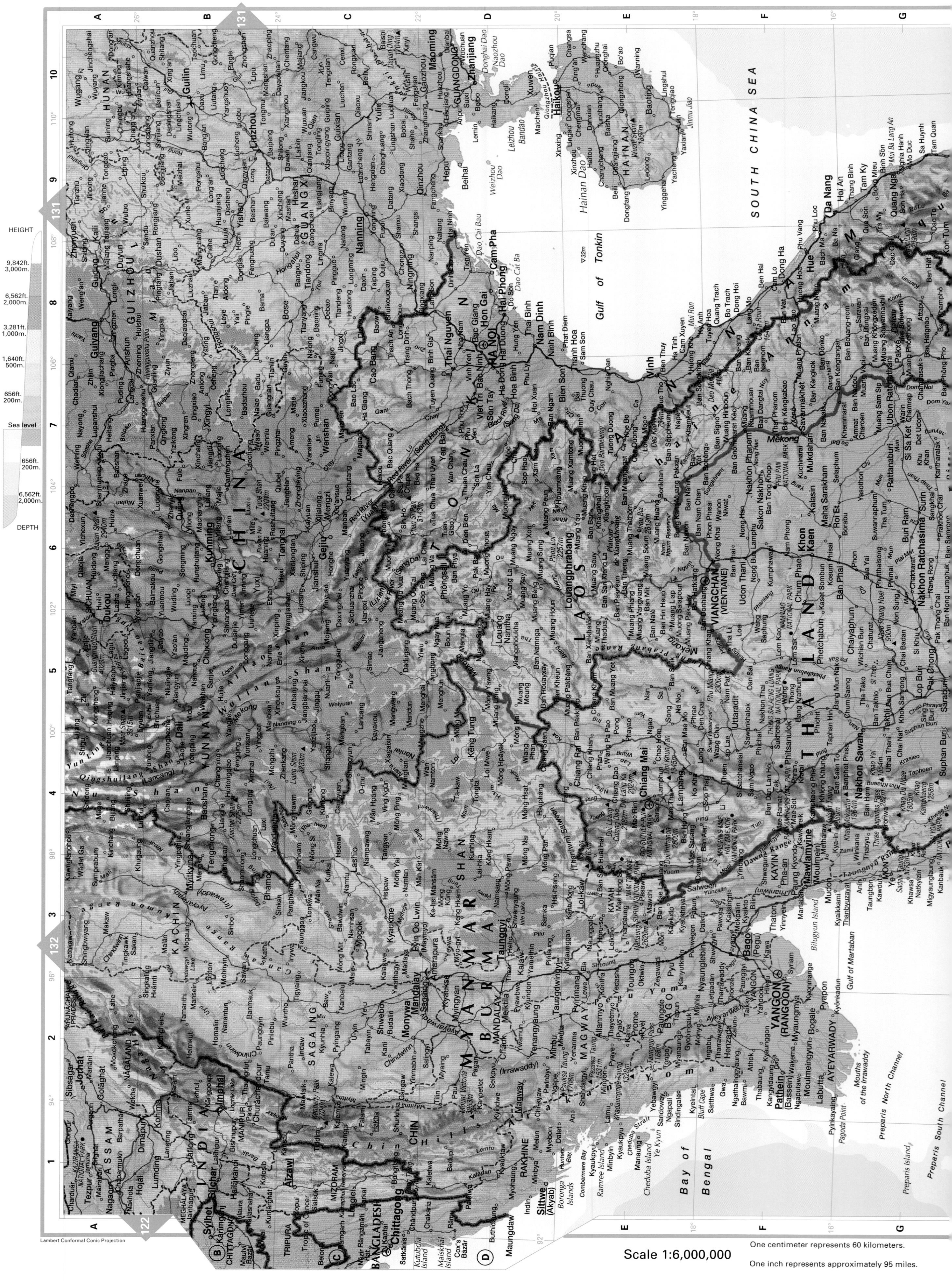

Lambert Conformal Conic Projection

Scale 1:6,000,000

One centimeter represents 60 kilometers.

One inch represents approximately 95 miles.

The Indochina Peninsula and its four main countries (Thailand, Cambodia, Laos, and Vietnam) first became familiar to many during the Vietnam War. Thailand has a vast, low-lying central plain and a mountainous region to the north. In Cambodia forests make up three-quarters of the territory. Laos, also heavily forested, is landlocked by its neighbors. Vietnam's terrain includes a flat, fertile south and a rugged north.

133

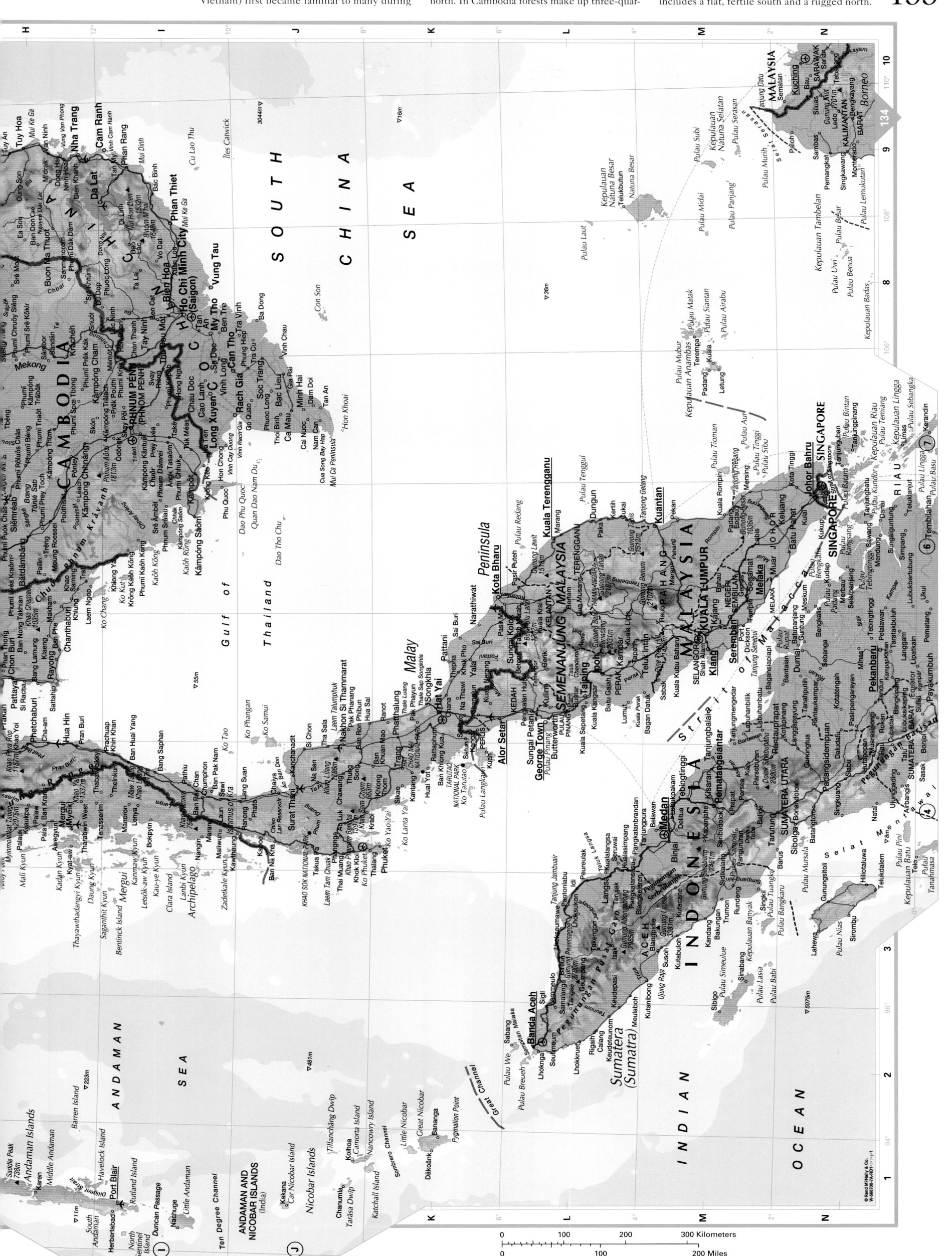

0   100   200   300 Kilometers

0   100   200 Miles

The more than 13,000 islands of Indonesia range from tiny, uninhabited islets to California-size Sumatra. They form the world's longest archipelago, stretching some 3,100 mi. (5,000 km.) across the Pacific. The Philippines – a mere 7,000 islands – is Southeast Asia's only Catholic nation. Malaysia, comprising three separate territories, extends for 1,200 mi. (1,900 km.) from the Malay Peninsula to the northeastern tip of Borneo.

135

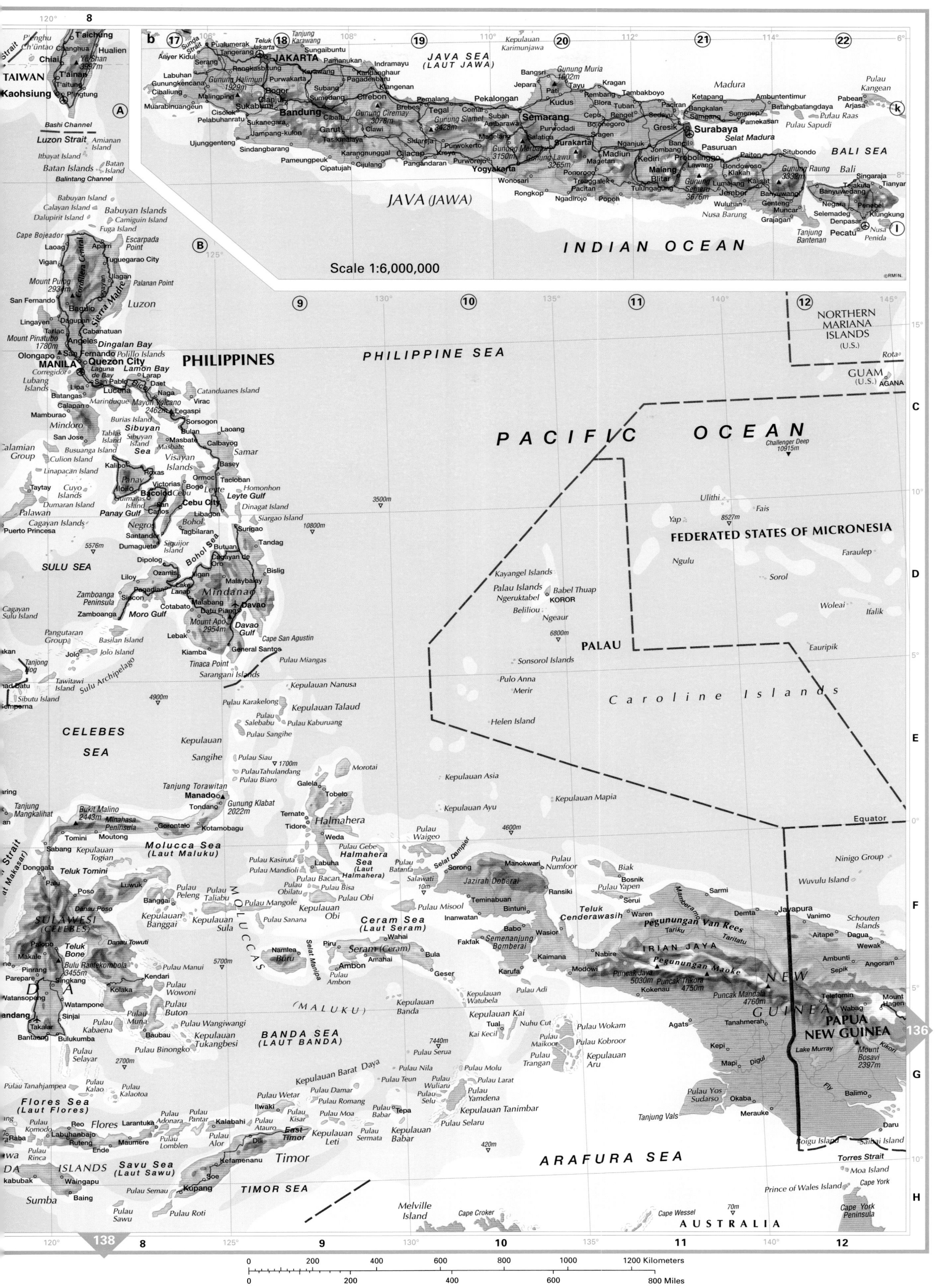

Scale 1:6,000,000

Lambert Azimuthal Equal Area Projection

Scale 1:24,000,000

One centimeter represents 240 kilometers.

One inch represents approximately 380 miles.

A fragmented "continent" scattered across vast expanses of the Pacific (from Palau in the west to Easter Island in the east, from Midway in the north to New Zealand in the south), Oceania encompasses Australia, New Zealand, and tens of thousands of islands. Only 3,000 of them have names, though many have been grouped as Micronesia, Melanesia, and Polynesia – the "Little," "Black," and "Many" islands.

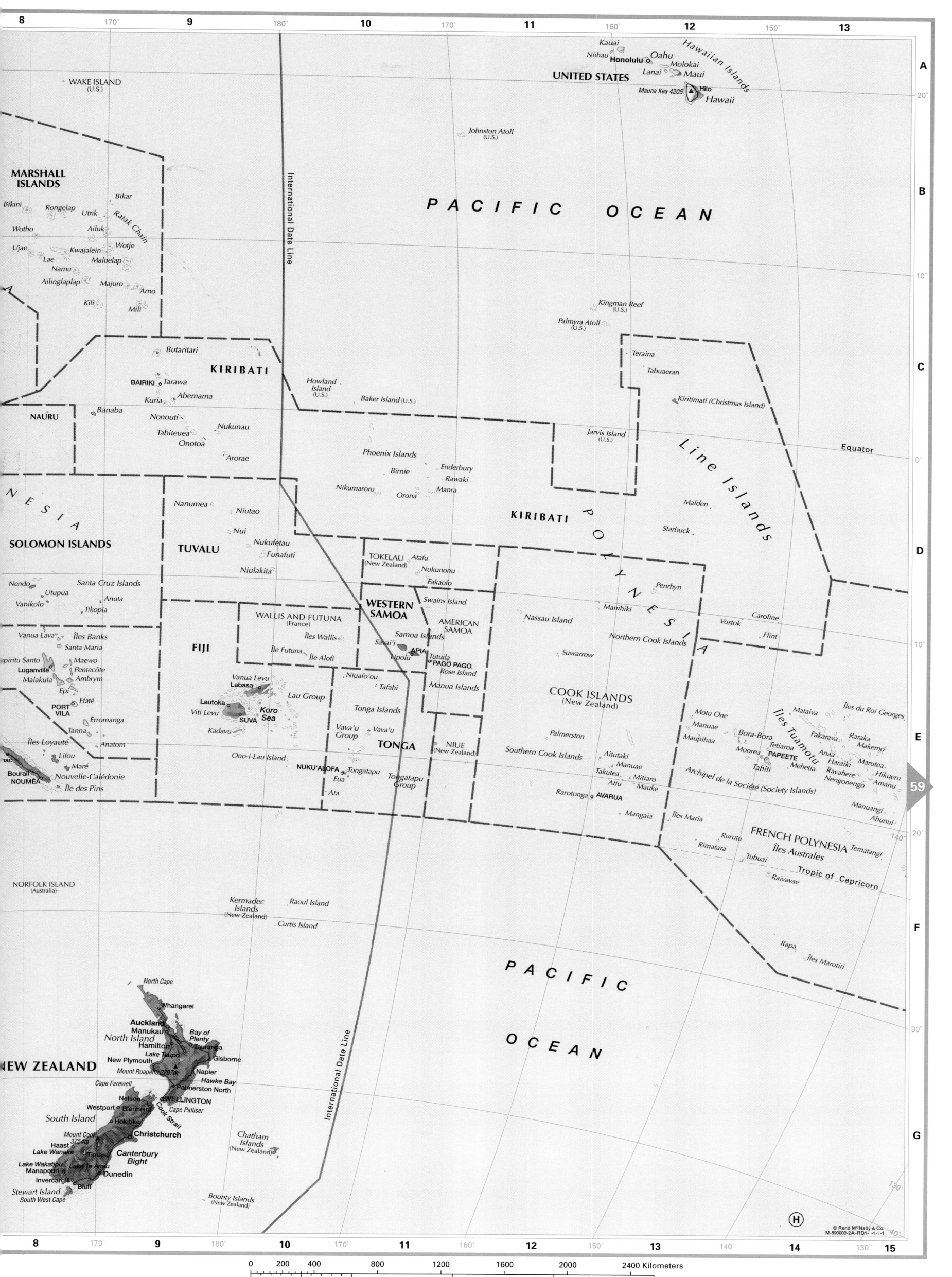

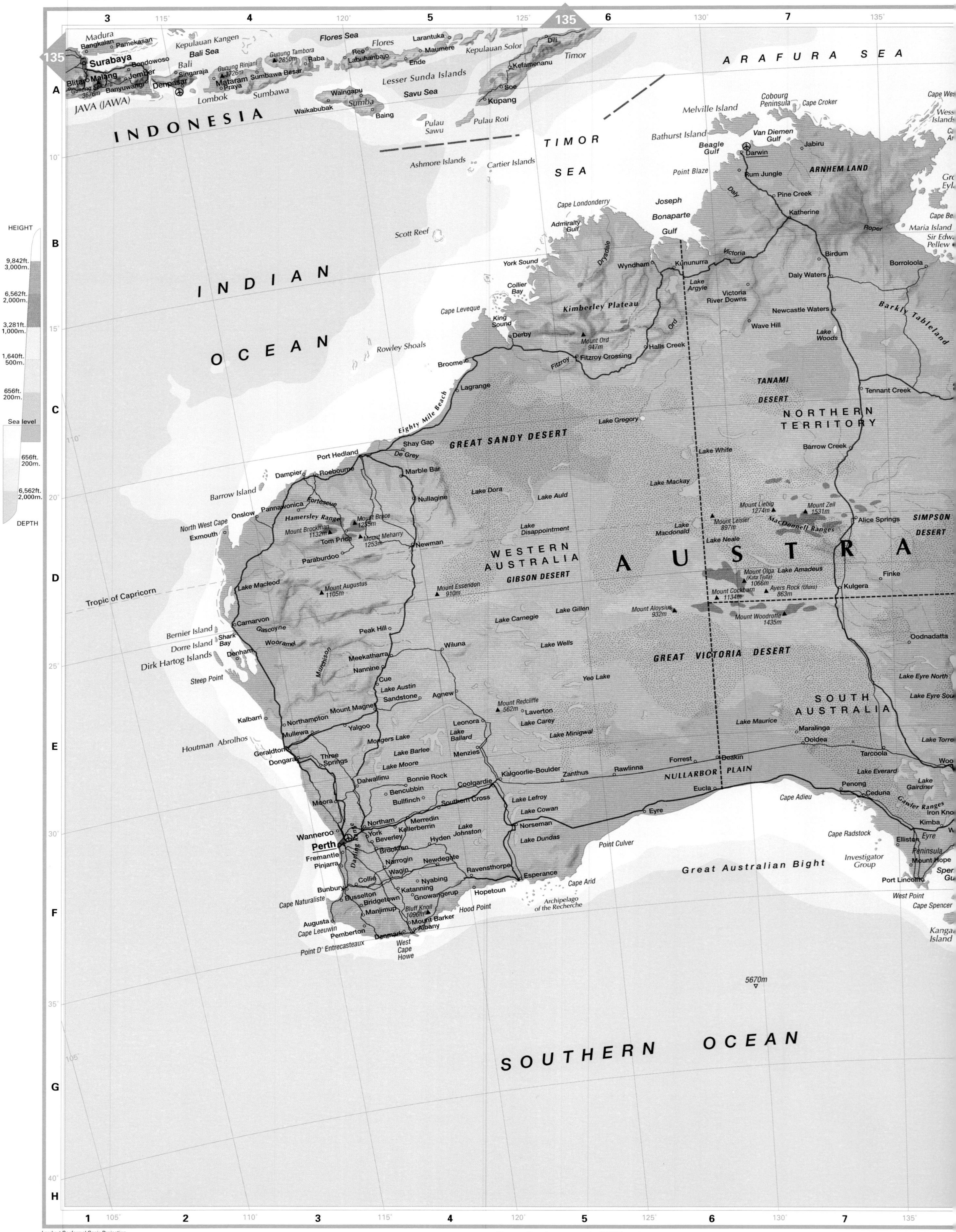

HEIGHT

9,842ft. 3,000m.

6,562ft. 2,000m.

3,281ft. 1,000m.

1,640ft. 500m.

656ft. 200m.

Sea level

656ft. 200m.

6,562ft. 2,000m.

DEPTH

INDONESIA

Madura
Bangkalan Pamekasan
Kepulauan Kangen
Flores Sea
Larantuka
Bali Sea
Reo Flores
Maumere
Kepulauan Solor
Dili
Timor
Gunung Tambora 2850m
Labuhanbajo
Surabaya Bondowoso
Bali
Blitar Malang Jember Singaraja
Gunung Rinjani 3726m
Raba
Ende
Kefamenanu
Gunung Semeru 3676m Banyuwangi Denpasar
Mataram Sumbawa Besar
Lombok Sumbawa
Praya
JAVA (JAWA)
Waingapu
Lesser Sunda Islands
Savu Sea
Waikabubak
Sumba
Baing
Kupang
Pulau Sawu
Pulau Roti

ARAFURA SEA

Cobourg Peninsula Cape Croker
Cape West
Melville Island
Bathurst Island
Van Diemen Gulf
Beagle Gulf
Darwin
Jabiru
ARNHEM LAND
Gro Eyla
Rum Jungle
Point Blaze
Cape Be
Maria Island
Sir Edwa
Pellew

TIMOR SEA

Ashmore Islands
Cartier Islands
Cape Londonderry
Joseph Bonaparte Gulf
Daly
Pine Creek
Katherine
Roper
Admiralty Gulf
Wyndham Kununurra
Victoria
Birdum
Daly Waters
Borroloola
Barkly Tableland

INDIAN OCEAN

Scott Reef
York Sound
Collier Bay
Kimberley Plateau
Lake Argyle
Victoria River Downs
Newcastle Waters
Drysdale
Cape Leveque
King Sound
Derby
Mount Ord 947m
Ord
Halls Creek
Wave Hill
Lake Woods
Rowley Shoals
Broome
Fitzroy
Fitzroy Crossing
TANAMI DESERT
Eighty Mile Beach
Lagrange
Lake Gregory
NORTHERN TERRITORY
Shay Gap
Lake White
Barrow Creek
GREAT SANDY DESERT
De Grey
Tennant Creek
Port Hedland
Marble Bar
Lake Dora
Lake Mackay
Dampier Roebourne
Nullagine
Mount Liebig 1274m
Mount Zeil 1531m
Barrow Island
Lake Auld
Alice Springs
SIMPSON DESERT
North West Cape Onslow Pannawonica Fortescue
Hamersley Range 1235m
Mount Bruce 1235m
Lake Disappointment
Mount Leisler 897m
MacDonnell Ranges
Exmouth
Mount Brockman 1132m Tom Price
Mount Meharry 1253m
Newman
Lake Macdonald
WESTERN AUSTRALIA
A U S T R A
Paraburdoo
GIBSON DESERT
Lake Neale
Mount Olga (Kata Tjuta) 1066m
Lake Amadeus
Finke
Lake Macleod
Mount Augustus 1105m
Mount Essendon 910m
Mount Cockburn 1134m
Ayers Rock (Uluru) 863m
Kulgera
Tropic of Capricorn
Mount Aloysius 932m
Oodnadatta
Bernier Island
Carnarvon
Gascoyne
Peak Hill
Lake Carnegie
Lake Gillen
Mount Woodroffe 1435m
Dorre Island Shark Bay
Wooramel
Lake Wells
GREAT VICTORIA DESERT
Lake Eyre North
Dirk Hartog Islands
Denham
Meekatharra
SOUTH AUSTRALIA
Lake Eyre Sou
Steep Point
Murchison
Nannine
Yeo Lake
Cue
Wiluna
Lake Austin
Sandstone
Agnew
Mount Redcliffe 562m
Kalbarri
Mount Magnet
Leonora
Laverton
Lake Maurice
Maralinga
Northampton
Yalgoo
Mongers Lake
Lake Carey
Ooldea
Lake Torre
Houtman Abrolhos
Geraldton
Lake Barlee
Menzies
Lake Minigwal
Tarcoola
Woo
Dongara
Three Springs
Lake Moore
Forrest
Deakin
Lake Everard
Lake Gairdner
Gawler Ranges
Iron Kno
Dalwallinu
Bonnie Rock
Kalgoorlie-Boulder
Zanthus
Rawlinna
NULLARBOR PLAIN
Penong
Ceduna
Meora Bencubbin
Coolgardie
Eucla
Kimba
Wanneroo Northam
Bullfinch
Southern Cross
Lake Lefroy
Eyre
Cape Adieu
Ellisto
Eyre
Perth Beverley
Merredin Kellerberrin
Lake Cowan
Cape Radstock
Mount Hope
Fremantle
York Hyden
Lake Johnston
Norseman
Investigator Group
Port Lincol
Pinjarra
Brookton
Narrogin Newdegate
Point Culver
Great Australian Bight
West Point
Collie Wagin
Ravensthorpe
Esperance
Cape Spencer
Bunbury Nyabing
Cape Arid
Busselton Katanning Gnowangerup Hopetoun
Archipelago of the Recherche
Kanga Island
Cape Naturaliste
Bridgetown
Bluff Knoll 1096m
Hood Point
Augusta Manjimup
Mount Barker
Cape Leeuwin Pemberton
Denmark Albany
Point D' Entrecasteaux
West Cape Howe

5670m

SOUTHERN OCEAN

Scale 1:12,000,000

One centimeter represents 120 kilometers.

One inch represents approximately 190 miles.

Though it may be the smallest continent, Australia is the world's sixth-largest country. Its six states and two territories include an astonish-ing array of landscapes – from tropical rain forests to bone-dry deserts, from rolling pastures to towering peaks. Some two-thirds of the country is occupied by the vast, arid Western Plateau, while the entire eastern seaboard is dominated by the heights of the Great Dividing Range.

139

0   200   400   600   800   1000   1200 Kilometers

0   200   400   600   800 Miles

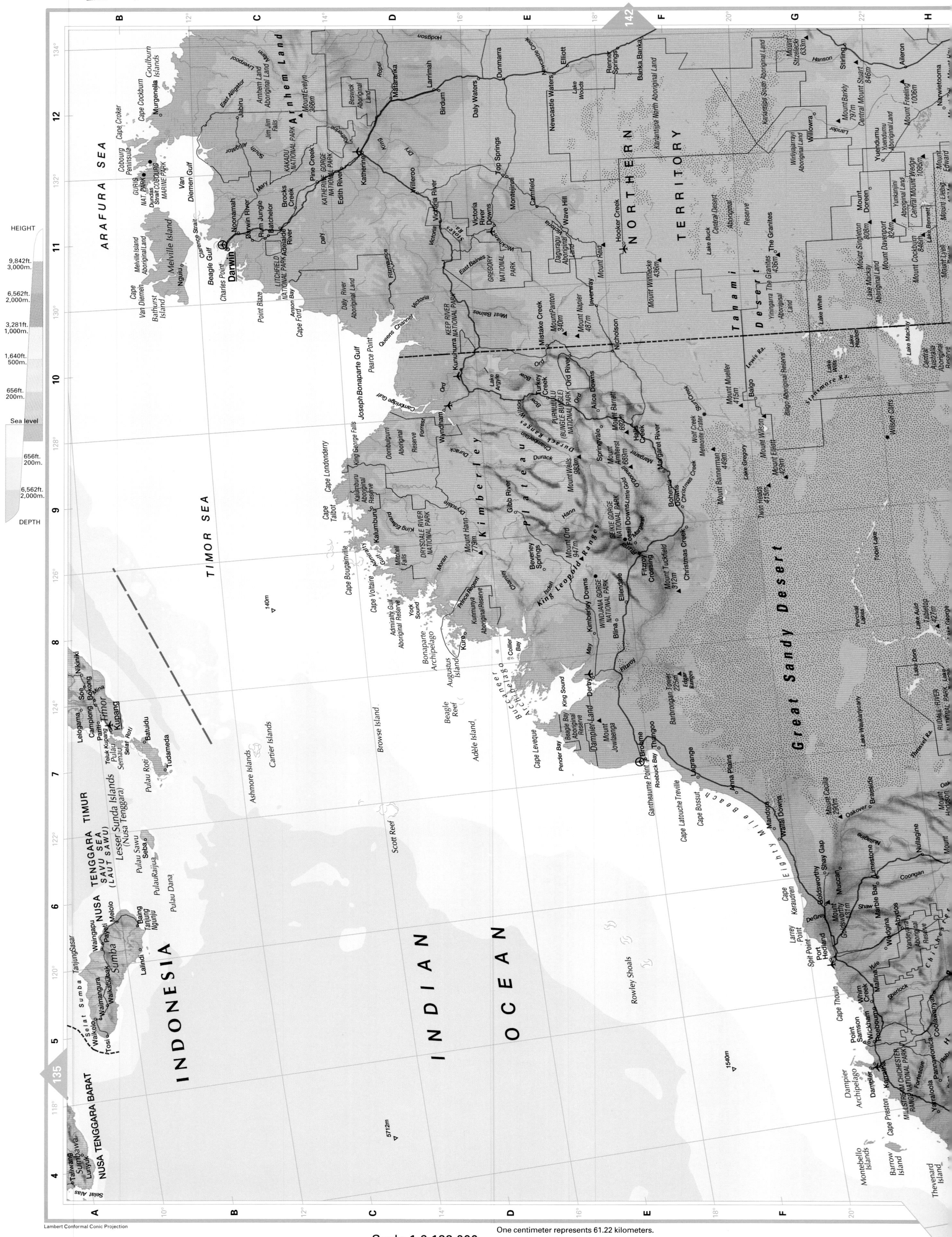

HEIGHT

9,842ft.
3,000m.

6,562ft.
2,000m.

3,281ft.
1,000m.

1,640ft.
500m.

656ft.
200m.

Sea level

656ft.
200m.

6,562ft.
2,000m.

DEPTH

Lambert Conformal Conic Projection

Scale 1:6,122,000

One centimeter represents 61.22 kilometers.

One inch represents approximately 97 miles.

Characteristic of Western Australia are the coastal farmlands, which give way to flat, arid, largely uninhabited spaces. The region's capital, Perth, for example, is about 1,300 mi. (2,090 km.) from its nearest urban neighbor, making it perhaps the most isolated city on earth. Deserts stretch toward the Indian Ocean, but there are forests, too. In the outback looms Ayers Rock, one of the largest monoliths in the world.

141

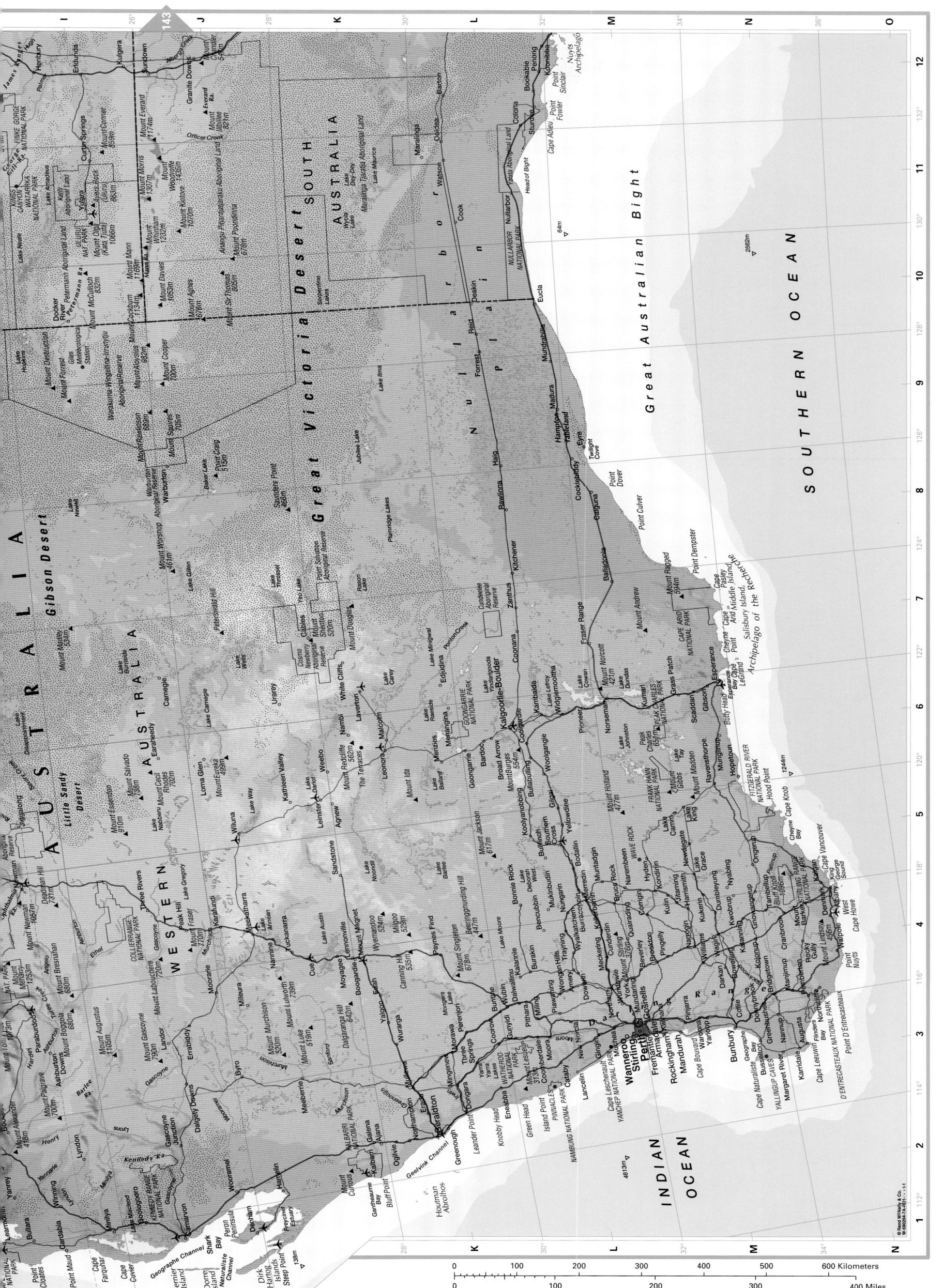

HEIGHT

9,842ft.
3,000m.

6,562ft.
2,000m.

3,281ft.
1,000m.

1,640ft.
500m.

656ft.
200m.

Sea level

656ft.
200m.

6,562ft.
2,000m.

DEPTH

CORAL SEA

CORAL SEA ISLANDS TERRITORY
(Australia)

Willis Group

Diamond Islets

Tregosse Islets

Chilcott Islet ▽ 850m

GREAT BARRIER REEF MARINE PARK

Gulf of Carpentaria

Cape York Peninsula

GREAT BARRIER REEF MARINE PARK

GREAT DIVIDING RANGE

QUEENSLAND

NORTHERN TERRITORY

Barkly Tableland

Tanami Desert

Tropic of Capricorn

Thursday Island
Prince of Wales Island

Rockhampton
Gladstone
Mackay
Townsville
Cairns
Cooktown
Mount Isa
Cloncurry
Tennant Creek
Alice Springs

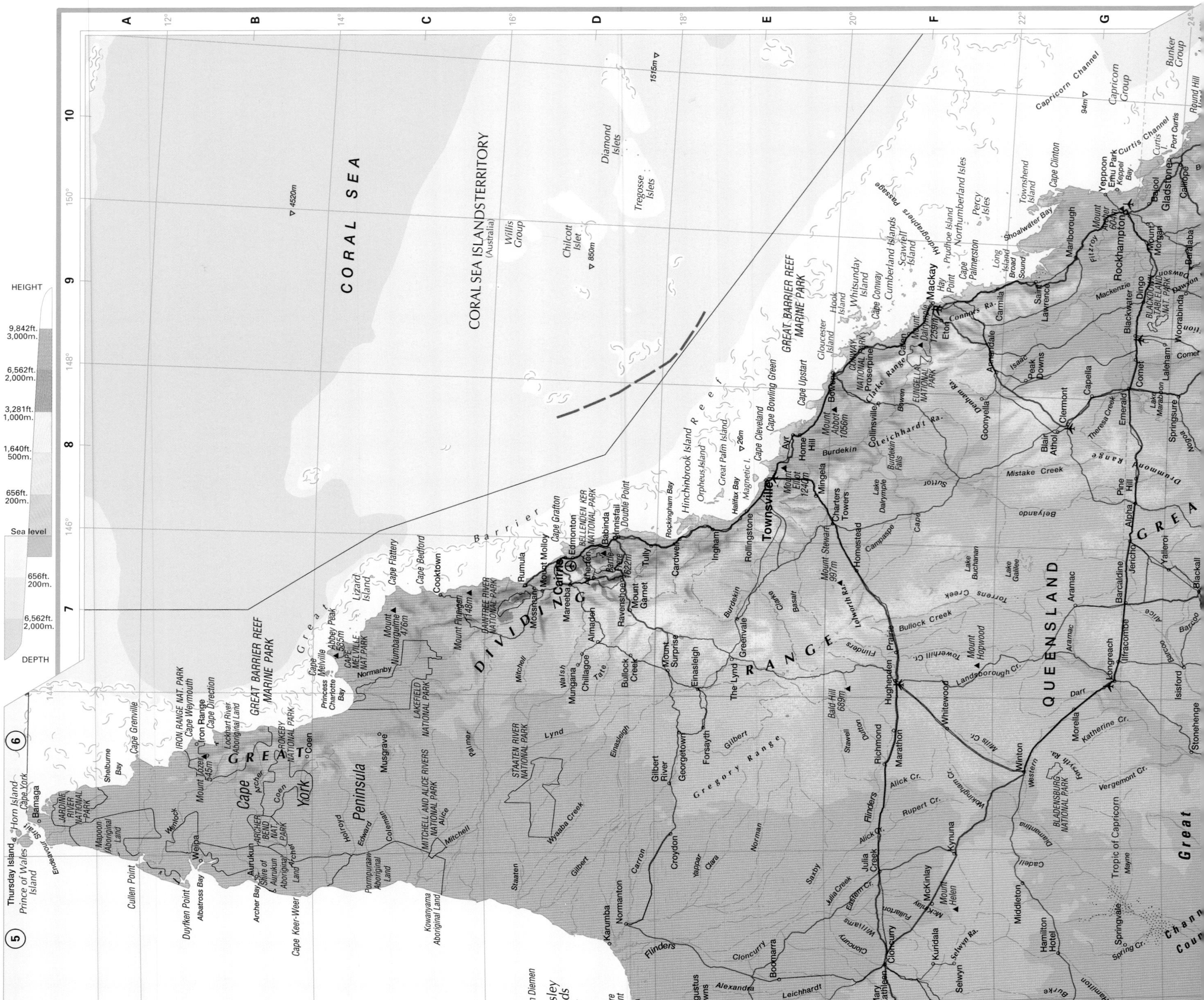

Lambert Conformal Conic Projection

Scale 1:6,122,000

One centimeter represents 61.22 kilometers.

One inch represents approximately 97 miles.

The Great Barrier Reef – the world's largest complex of coral islands, shoals, and atolls – runs along the coast for some 1,200 mi. (1,930 km).

143

AUSTRALIA

SOUTH AUSTRALIA

NEW SOUTH WALES

VICTORIA

QUEENSLAND

TASMAN SEA

SOUTHERN OCEAN

Great Australian Bight

GREAT DIVIDING RANGE

Great Victoria Desert

Sturt Stony Desert

Strzelecki Desert

Simpson Desert

Major cities and places

Brisbane, Gold Coast (Southport), Toowoomba, Ipswich, Redcliffe, Caloundra, Maryborough, Gympie, Nambour, Murwillumbah, Coolangatta, Lismore, Casino, Grafton, Coffs Harbour, Armidale, Tamworth, Port Macquarie, Taree, Newcastle, Gosford, Maitland, Sydney, Parramatta, Penrith, Campbelltown, Wollongong, Shellharbour, Kiama, Nowra, CANBERRA, Queanbeyan, Goulburn, Bathurst, Orange, Dubbo, Wagga Wagga, Albury, Wangaratta, Shepparton, Bendigo, Ballarat, Melbourne, Geelong, Warrnambool, Portland, Mount Gambier, Adelaide, Port Adelaide, Elizabeth, Salisbury, Gawler, Port Augusta, Port Pirie, Whyalla, Port Lincoln, Broken Hill, Bourke, Cobar, Dubbo, Moree, Goondiwindi, Roma, Charleville, Cunnamulla, Birdsville, Oodnadatta, Marree, Leigh Creek, Coober Pedy, Woomera, Ceduna, Streaky Bay

Lake Eyre North, Lake Eyre South, Lake Torrens, Lake Gairdner, Lake Frome, Lake Blanche, Lake Callabonna

Flinders Ranges, Grey Range, Barrier Range, McGregor Ranges

Fraser Island, Moreton Island, North Stradbroke Island, Kangaroo I., Wilsons Promontory

Murray, Darling, Murrumbidgee, Lachlan, Macquarie, Cooper Creek, Eyre Creek, Warrego

Spencer Gulf, Gulf Saint Vincent, Investigator Group, Yorke Peninsula, Eyre Peninsula

© Rand McNally & Co.

0 100 200 300 400 500 600 Kilometers

0 100 200 300 400 Miles

Southeast Australia

HEIGHT

9,842ft. 3,000m.

6,562ft. 2,000m.

3,281ft. 1,000m.

1,640ft. 500m.

656ft. 200m.

Sea level

656ft. 200m.

6,562ft. 2,000m.

DEPTH

SOUTH AUSTRALIA

AUSTRALIA

VICTORIA

SOUTHERN OCEAN

Great Australian Bight

Lambert Conformal Conic Projection

Scale 1:3,500,000

One centimeter represents 35 kilometers.

One inch represents approximately 55 miles.

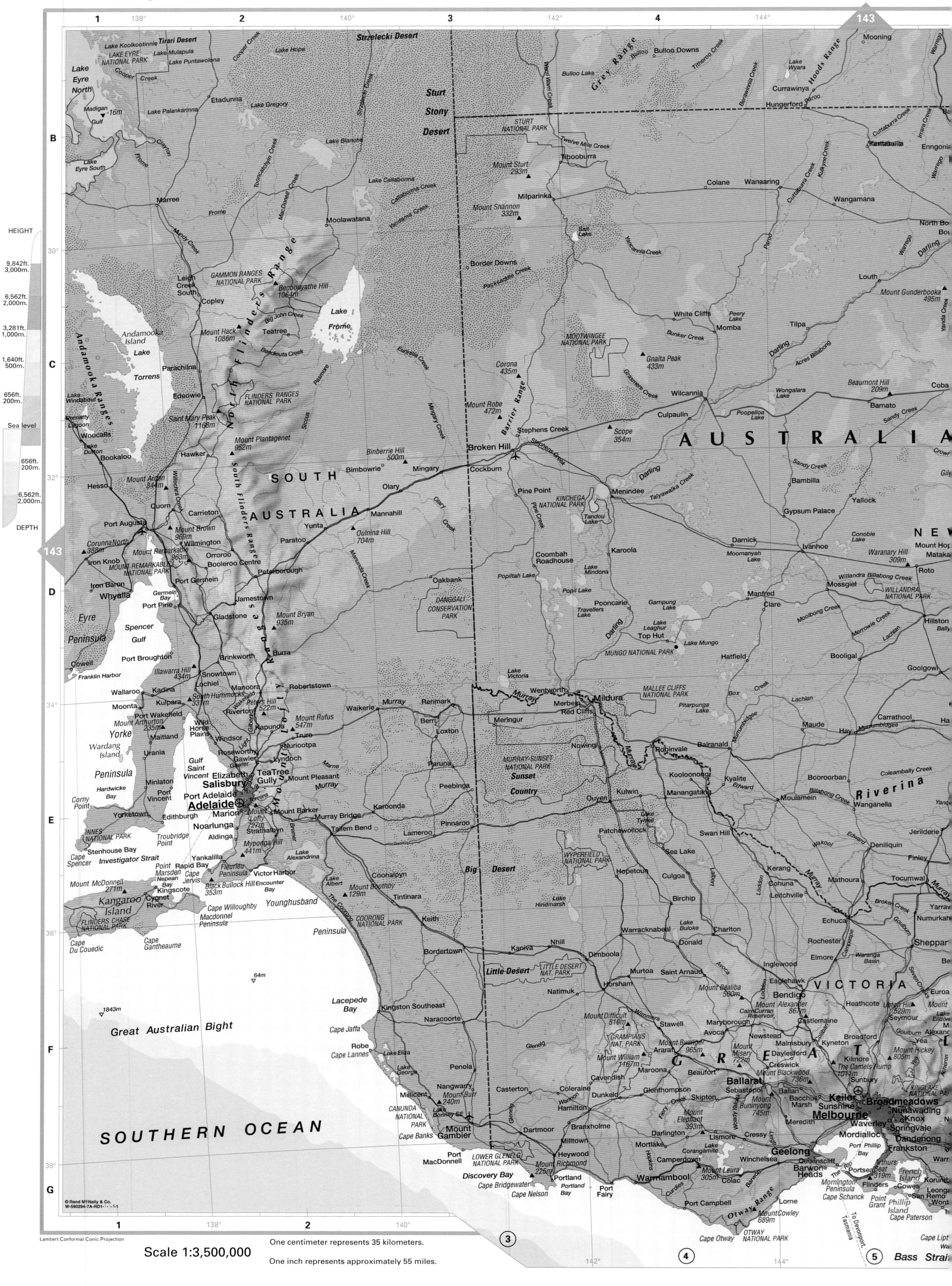

Most Australians live in the southeastern section of the continent, along a broad coastal arc that stretches south from Brisbane (the capital of Queensland), through Sydney (the capital of New South Wales), Canberra (the nation's capital), and Melbourne (the capital of Victoria).

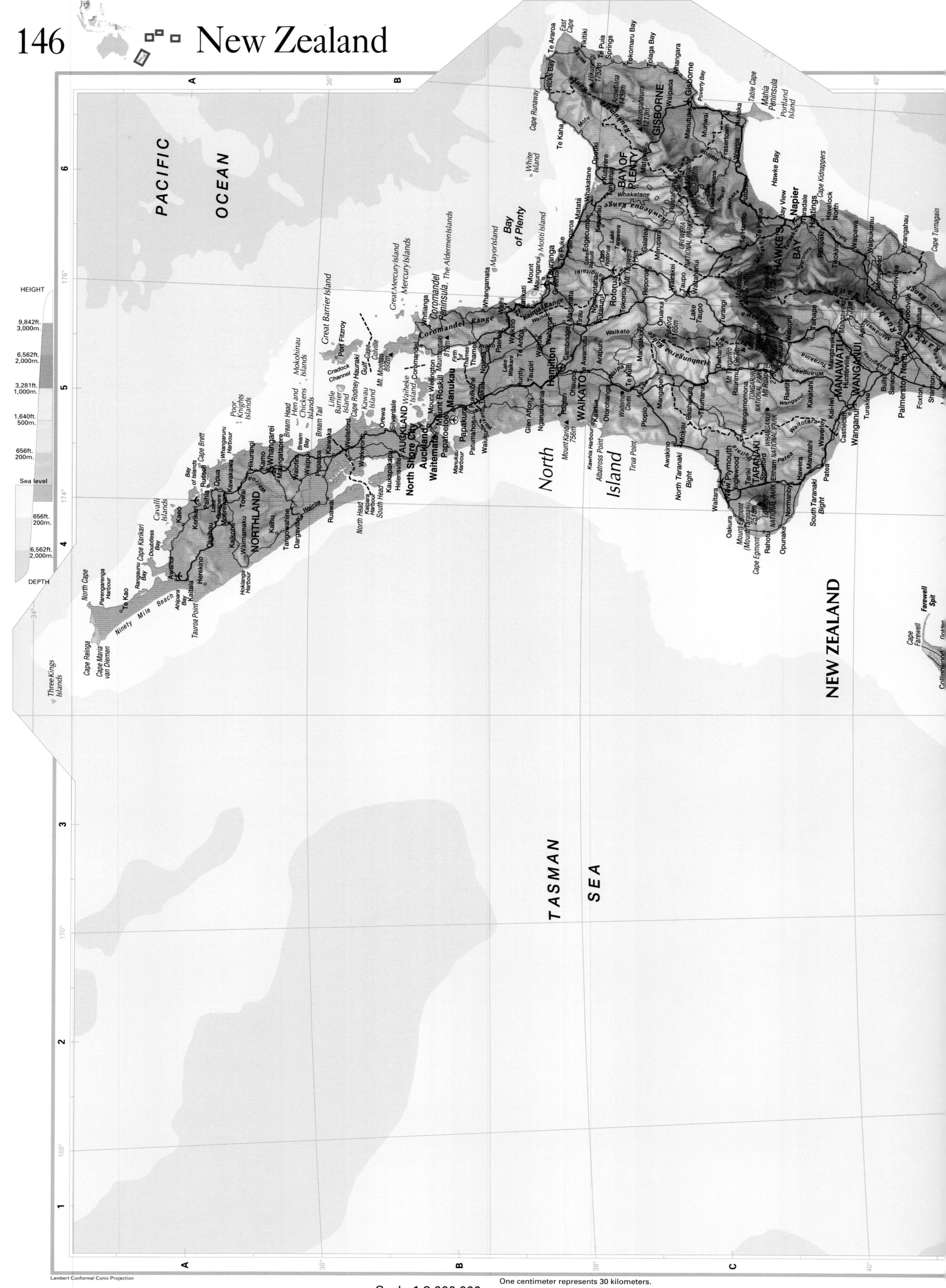

HEIGHT

9,842ft.
3,000m.

6,562ft.
2,000m.

3,281ft.
1,000m.

1,640ft.
500m.

656ft.
200m.

Sea level

656ft.
200m.

6,562ft.
2,000m.

DEPTH

PACIFIC

OCEAN

Three Kings Islands

North Cape
Cape Reinga
Parengarenga Harbour
Cape Maria van Diemen
Rangaunu Bay
Cape Karikari
Te Kao
Doubtless Bay
Awanui
Cavalli Islands
Taipa
Kaeo
Ninety Mile Beach
Taurea Point
Ahipara Bay
Herekino
Kaitaia
Bay of Islands
Kaikohe
Okaihau
Russell
Opua
Paihia
Kerikeri
Cape Brett
Whangaruru Harbour
Hikurangi
Whangarei
Hokianga Harbour
Waimamaku
Towai
Kaikohe
Mangakahia
Poor Knights Islands
Hen and Chickens Islands
Bream Head
Bream Tail
Bream Bay
Kaiwaka
Waipu
Maungaturoto
Dargaville
Tangowahine
Kairo
Kaihu
Rawene
Waipoua
Kaipara Harbour
North Head
Kaiaua Harbour
South Head
Helensville
Kaukapakapa
Orewa
Silverdale
Waiwera
Great Barrier Island
Port Fitzroy
Mokohinau Islands
Little Barrier Island
Kawau Island
Cape Rodney
Warkworth

NORTHLAND

NEW ZEALAND

TASMAN

SEA

Albatross Point
Kawhia Harbour

North
Island

AUCKLAND
North Shore City
Auckland
Waitemata
Manukau
Papatoetoe
Mount Roskill
Mount Wellington
Manukau Harbour
Papakura
Pukekohe
Patumahoe

WAIKATO
Hamilton
Cambridge
Te Awamutu
Otorohanga
Waitomo Caves
Te Kuiti
Piopio
Mangapehi
Awakino
Mokau

North Taranaki Bight

TARANAKI
New Plymouth
Inglewood
Waitara
Urenui
Okato
Oakura
Stratford
Eltham
Opunake
Hawera
Patea
Waverley
Rahotu
Kaponga
EGMONT NATIONAL PARK
Mount Egmont
(Mount Taranaki)
2518m

South Taranaki Bight

Coromandel
Peninsula
The Aldermen Islands
Whitianga
Coromandel
Tairua
Whangamata
Waihi
Paeroa
Thames
Firth of Thames
Te Aroha
Morrinsville
Matamata
Putaruru
Tokoroa
Mangakino

Bay
of Plenty

BAY OF PLENTY
Tauranga
Mount Maunganui
Te Puke
Whakatane
Matata
Edgecumbe
Kawerau
Opotiki
White Island
Mayor Island
Motiti Island

Rotorua
Lake Rotorua
Lake Taupo
Taupo
Turangi
TONGARIRO NATIONAL PARK
Mt Ruapehu
Mt Ngauruhoe
Mt Tongariro
Raetihi
Ohakune
Waiouru

UREWERA NATIONAL PARK

Kaingaroa Range

Kaimanawa Range

HAWKE'S
BAY
Napier
Hastings
Havelock North
Bay View
Clive
Cape Kidnappers
Hawke Bay

Te Araroa
East Cape
Hicks Bay
Te Kaha
Tikitiki
Te Puia Springs
Tokomaru Bay
Tolaga Bay
GISBORNE
Gisborne
Manutuke
Muriwai
Mahia Peninsula
Portland Island
Table Cape

Ruahine Range

MANAWATU
WANGANUI
Wanganui
Palmerston North
Marton
Feilding
Bulls
Foxton
Shannon

Scale 1:3,000,000

Lambert Conformal Conic Projection

One centimeter represents 30 kilometers.

One inch represents approximately 47 miles.

On this ruggedly beautiful island, sheepherding is a major source of revenue. Volcanoes, geysers, and thermal springs flank the fertile sheepgrazing land of North Island, while the peaks of the Southern Alps – some over 10,000 ft. (3,050 m.) – dominate the larger but less populated South Island. Their glaciers have forged a varied landscape, scooping out lakes, bringing forth tumbling rivers, and lacing the coast with fjords.

147

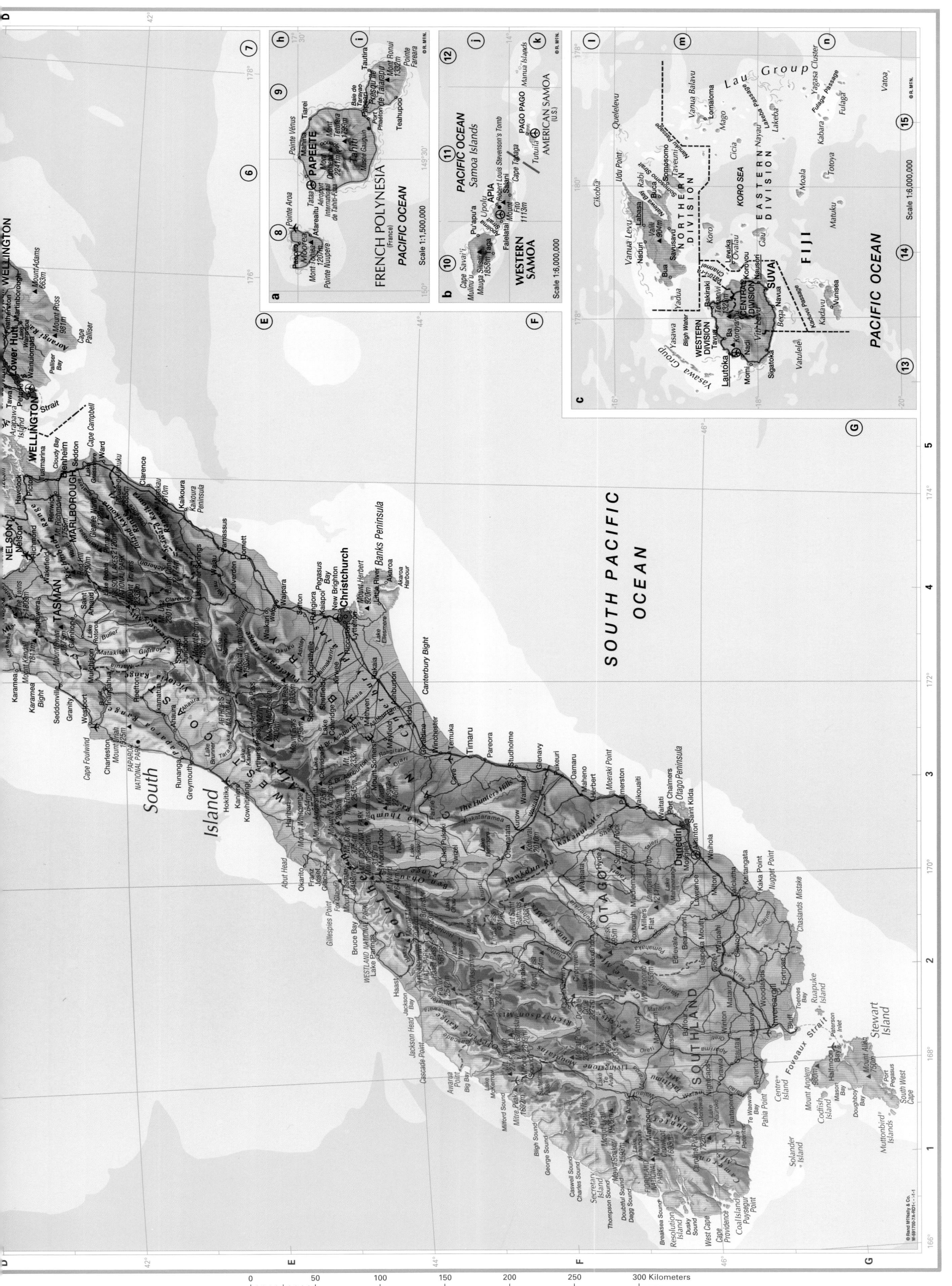

Lambert Azimuthal Equal Area Projection

Scale 1:24,000,000

One centimeter represents 240 kilometers.

One inch represents approximately 380 miles.

The northern half of the American landmass, North America is the third-largest continent, embracing Canada, the U.S., Mexico, Central America, and Greenland (a Danish province). Its climate ranges from the permafrost of the Arctic to the tropical rain forests of Central America.

0	200	400	800	1200	1600	2000	2400 Kilometers

0	200	400	800	1200	1600 Miles

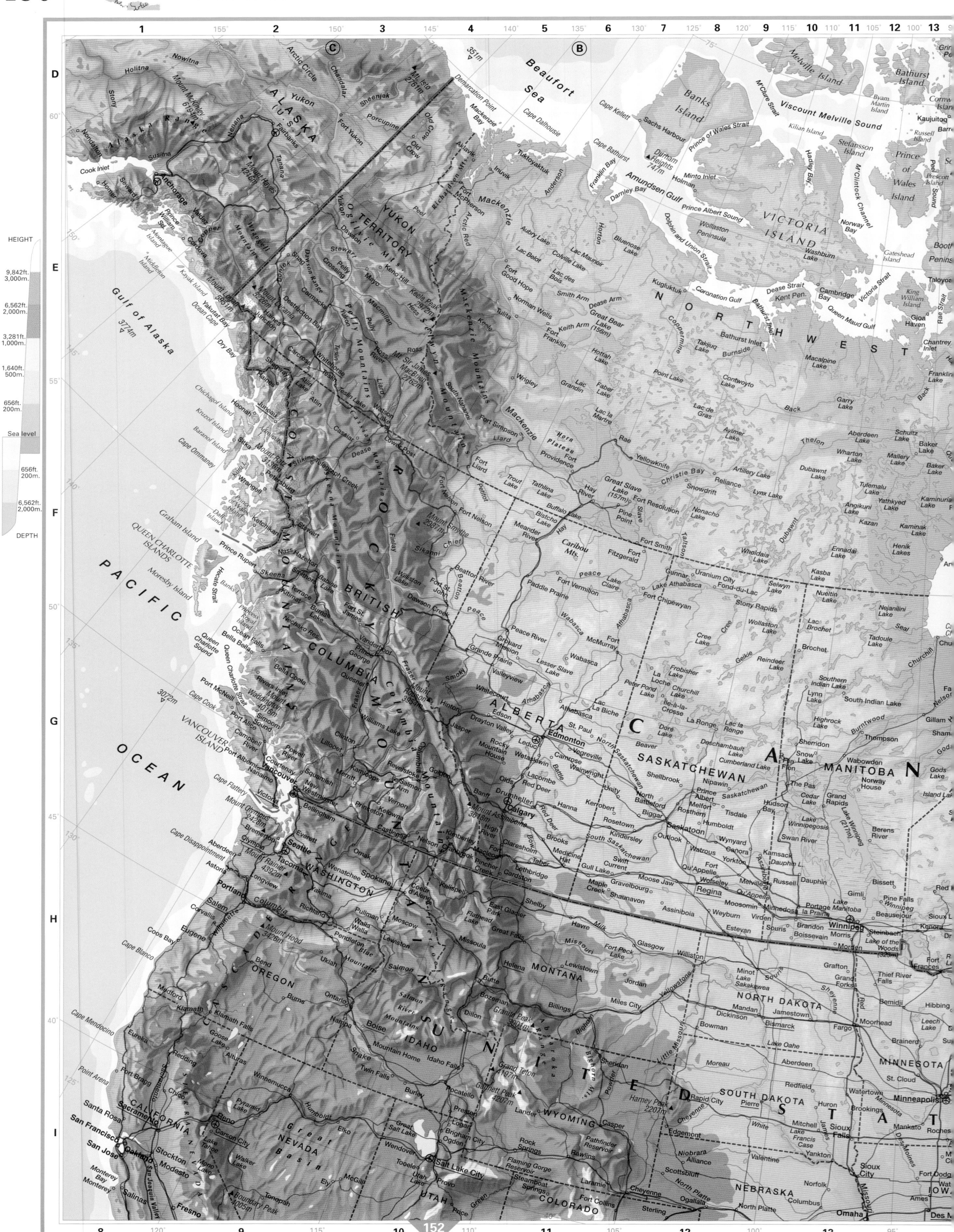

HEIGHT

9,842ft.
3,000m.

6,562ft.
2,000m.

3,281ft.
1,000m.

1,640ft.
500m.

656ft.
200m.

Sea level

656ft.
200m.

6,562ft.
2,000m.

DEPTH

Lambert Conformal Conic Projection

Scale 1:12,000,000

One centimeter represents 120 kilometers.

One inch represents approximately 190 miles.

The world's second-largest country (after Russia), Canada has a wide assortment of habitats: mountains, plains, lowlands, boreal forests, and tundra. Climate ranges from temperate in the south to arctic in the north. Though Canada is slightly larger than the U.S. (about 3.8 million sq. mi., or 9.9 million sq. km.), its population – some 29 million, concentrated close to the U.S. border – is only about one-tenth as large.

151

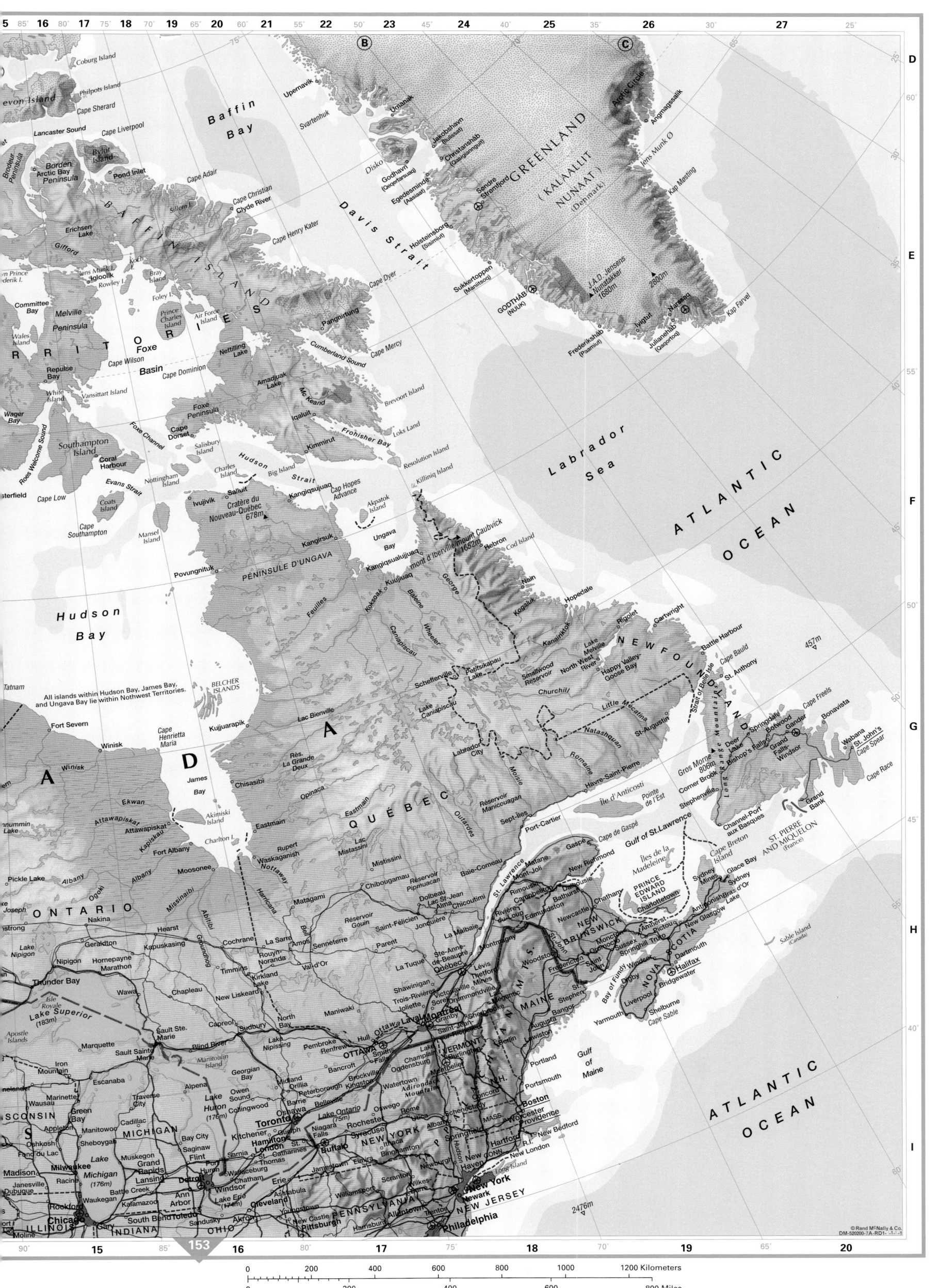

All islands within Hudson Bay, James Bay, and Ungava Bay lie within Nothwest Territories.

0	200	400	600	800	1000	1200 Kilometers

0	200	400	600	800 Miles

© Rand McNally & Co.
DM-520200-7A-RD1- -1- -1

United States and Mexico

HEIGHT
9,842ft. 3,000m.
6,562ft. 2,000m.
3,281ft. 1,000m.
1,640ft. 500m.
656ft. 200m.
Sea level
656ft. 200m.
6,562ft. 2,000m.
DEPTH

PACIFIC OCEAN

Albers Conic Equal Area Projection

0 200 400 600 800 1000 1200 Kilometers
0 200 400 600 800 Miles

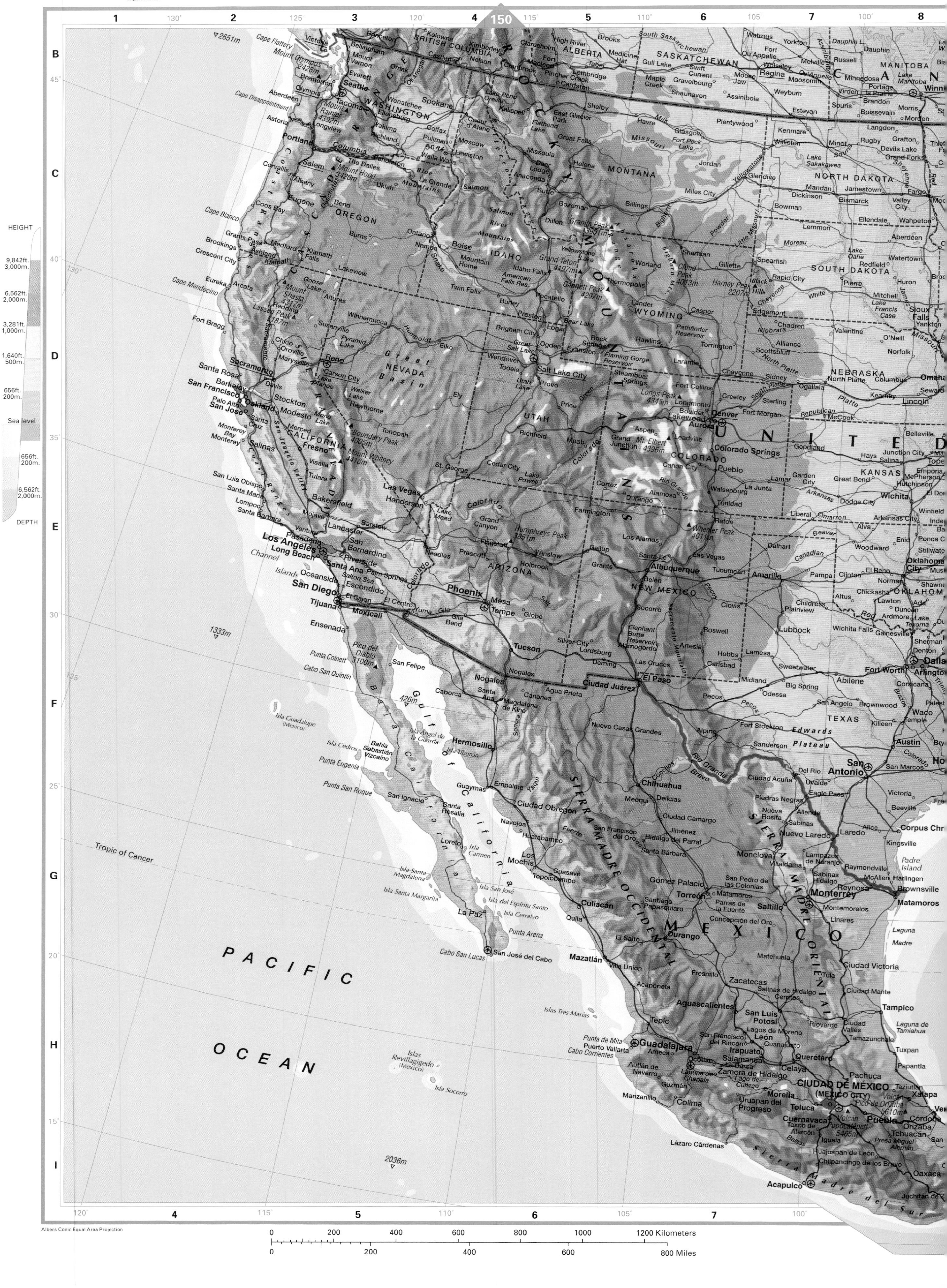

Comprised of 48 contiguous states and the outlying states of Alaska and Hawaii, the U.S. is blessed with a vast, varied landscape, abundant natural resources, and a wide range of climates. The result is a nation that is neither overpopulated (like India) nor underpopulated (like Australia) and seldom at the mercy of either climate or topography. Its neighbor, Mexico, boasts the world's biggest conurbation, Mexico City.

153

Scale 1:12,000,000

One centimeter represents 120 kilometers.

One inch represents approximately 190 miles.

© Rand McNally & Co.
M-520500-7A-RD1-.1-.1

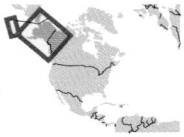
CHUKCHI SEA

RUSSIA

ČUKOTSKIJ AVTONOMNYJ OKRUG

Siberia (Sibir')

Anadyrskij zaliv

BERING SEA

Saint Lawrence Island

Hall Island

Saint Matthew Island

Saint Paul Island
Pribilof Islands
Saint George Island

Aleutian Islands

Islands of Four Mountains

Seguam Island

UNITED STATES

ALASKA

Brooks Range

Seward Peninsula

Norton Sound

Bristol Bay

Alaska Peninsula

Kodiak Island

PACIFIC OCEAN

Barrow
Point Barrow

HEIGHT

9,842ft. 3,000m.
6,562ft. 2,000m.
3,281ft. 1,000m.
1,640ft. 500m.
656ft. 200m.

Sea level

656ft. 200m.
6,562ft. 2,000m.

DEPTH

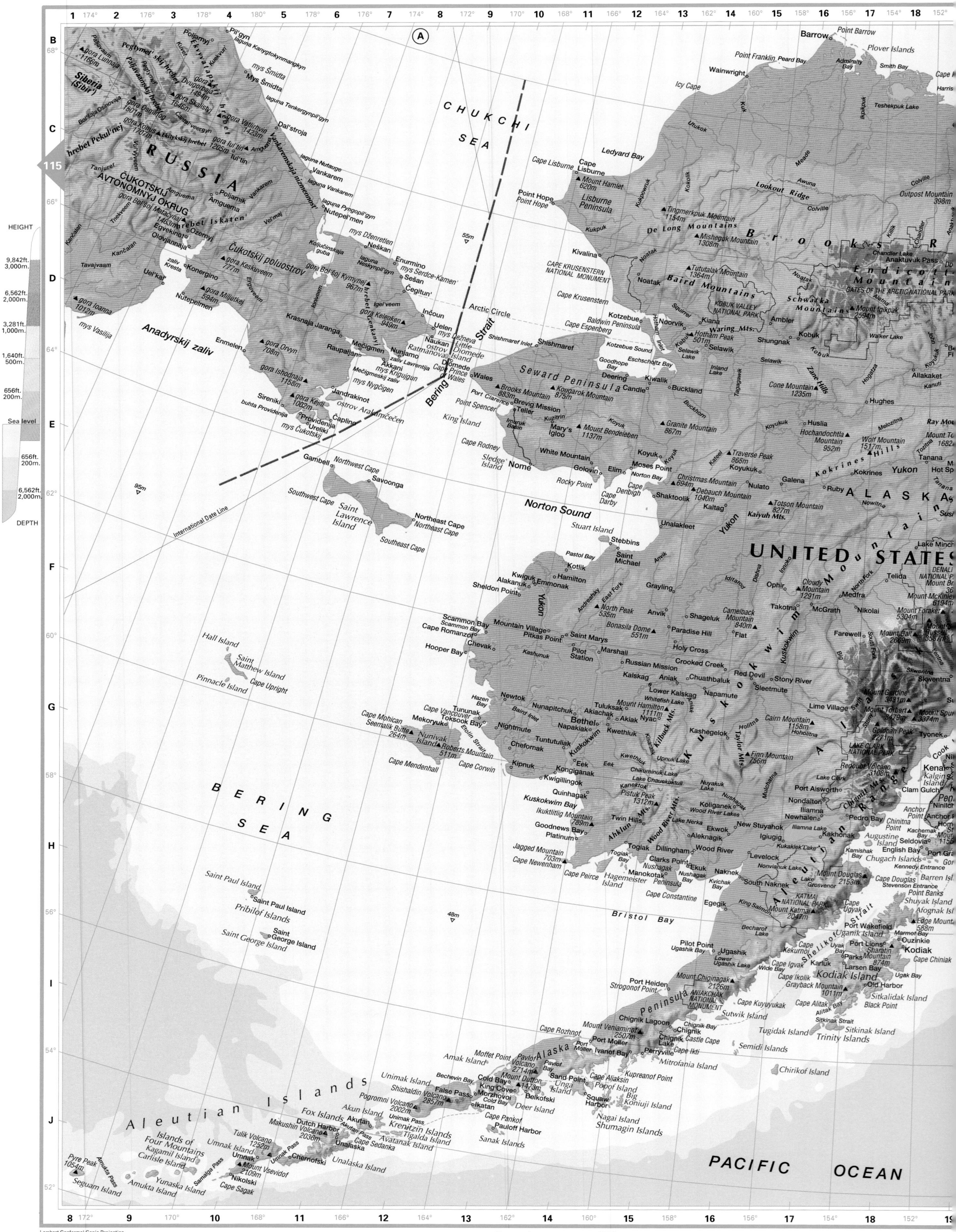

Lambert Conformal Conic Projection

Scale 1:6,000,000

One centimeter represents 60 kilometers.

One inch represents approximately 95 miles.

The largest state in the U.S., Alaska was shaped during the last Ice Age, when vast quantities of water were trapped within massive ice caps. As the world's sea and ocean levels sank, the land mass that is now Alaska was joined to Asia at the Bering Sea, providing a natural bridge for early ancestors of Native Americans. Both Alaska and its Canadian neighbor, the Yukon Territory, are rich in gold, silver, lead, zinc, and other minerals.

155

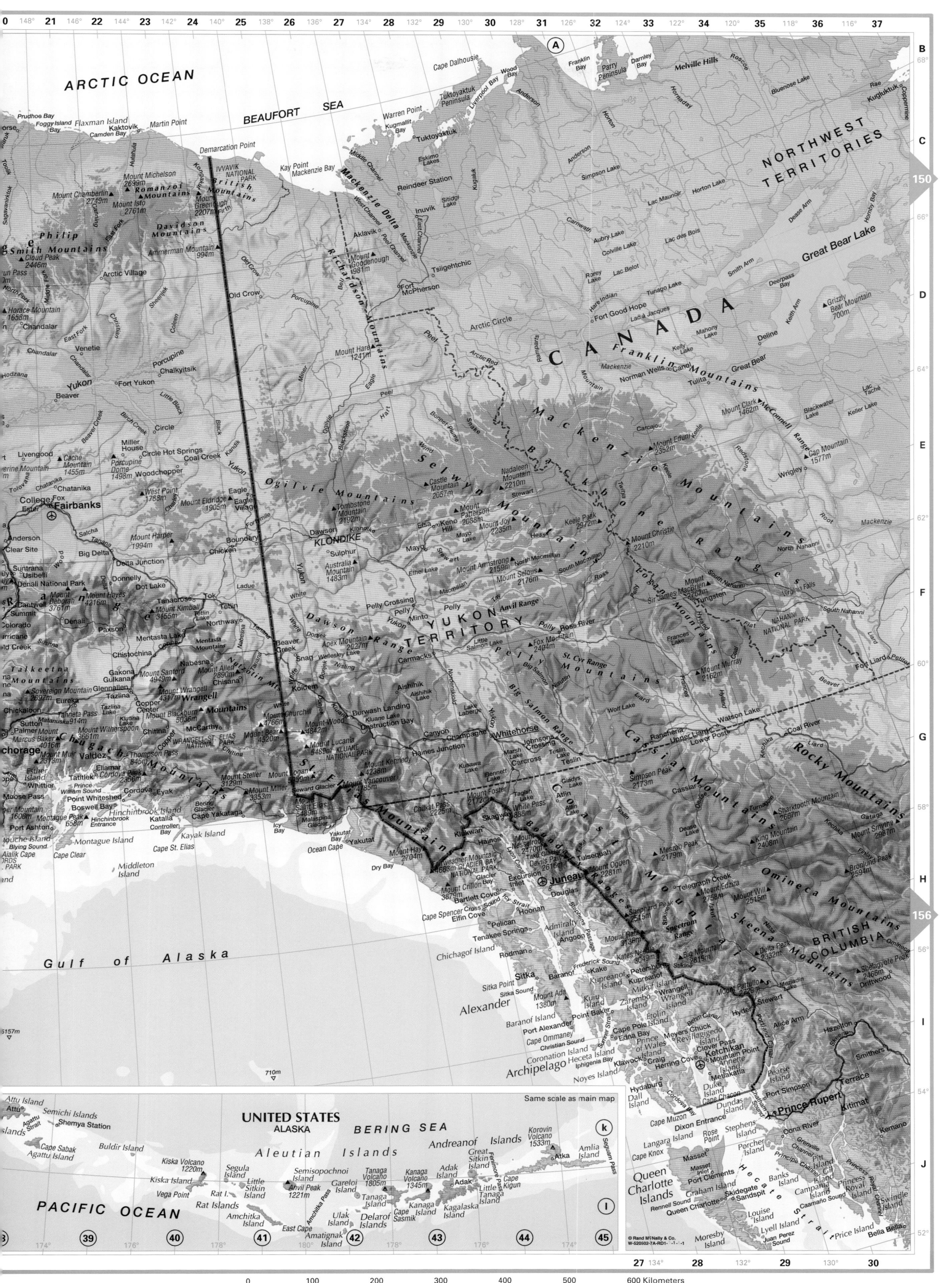

ARCTIC OCEAN

BEAUFORT SEA

NORTHWEST TERRITORIES

CANADA

YUKON TERRITORY

Gulf of Alaska

PACIFIC OCEAN

UNITED STATES
ALASKA

BERING SEA

Aleutian Islands

BRITISH COLUMBIA

Queen Charlotte Islands

Same scale as main map

© Rand M°Nally & Co.
W-S20502-7A-RD1-

| 0 | 100 | 200 | 300 | 400 | 500 | 600 Kilometers |

| 0 | 100 | 200 | 300 | 400 Miles |

155

HEIGHT

9,842ft.
3,000m.

6,562ft.
2,000m.

3,281ft.
1,000m.

1,640ft.
500m.

656ft.
200m.

Sea level

656ft.
200m.

6,562ft.
2,000m.

DEPTH

YUKON TERRITORY

UNITED STATES

ALASKA

BRITISH COLUMBIA

Juneau

Sitka

Ketchikan

Prince Rupert

Dixon Entrance

Queen
Charlotte
Islands

Moresby Island

Hecate Strait

Kitimat

Prince
George

PACIFIC

OCEAN

Queen
Charlotte
Sound

Queen Charlotte Strait

Vancouver
Island

Nanaimo

Vancouver

Burnaby

Richmond

Victoria

Seattle

Bellingham

Scale 1:4,500,000

One centimeter represents 45 kilometers.

One inch represents approximately 71 miles.

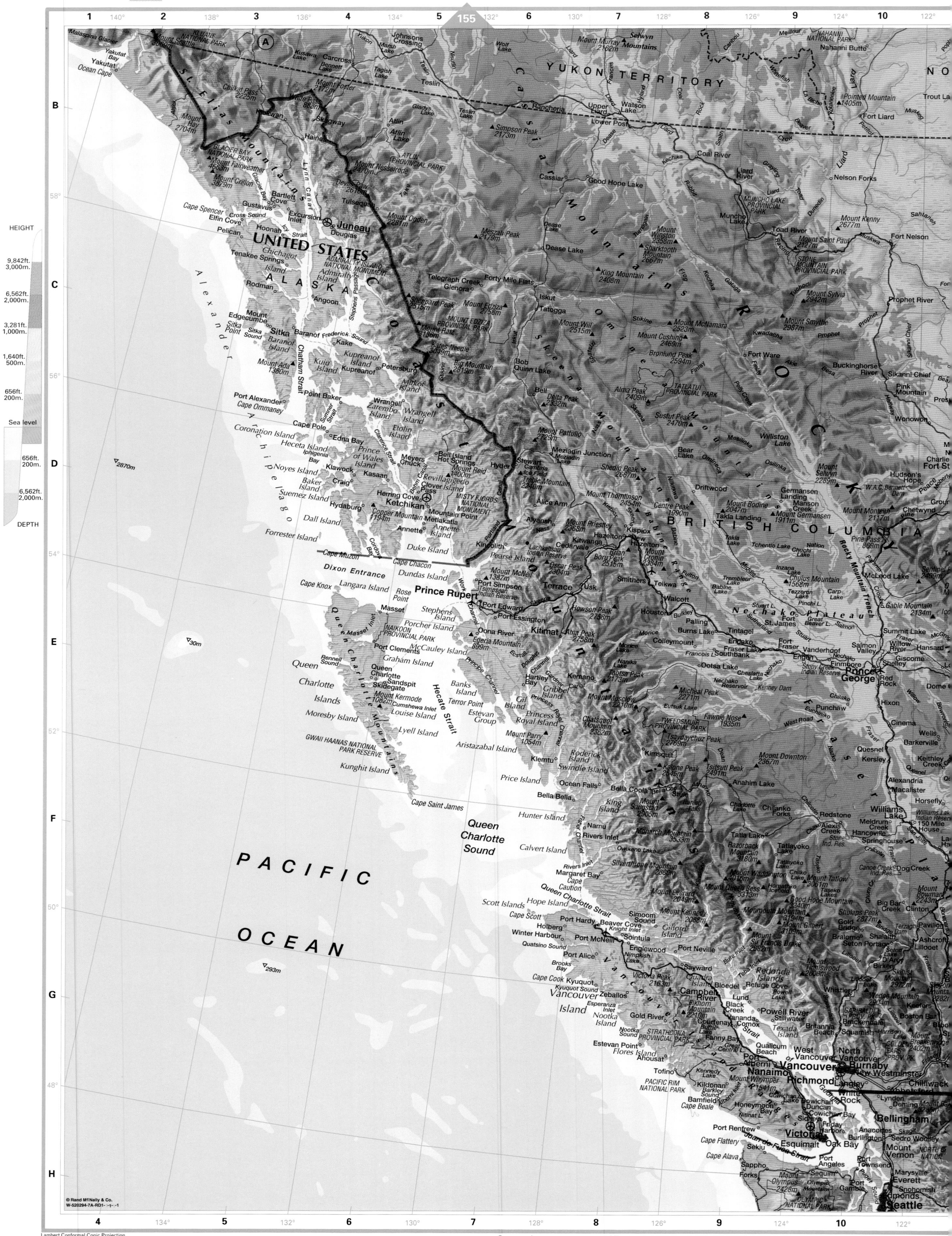

Lambert Conformal Conic Projection

© Rand McNally & Co.
W-520294-7A-RD1--:-:-1

British Columbia embraces coastal rain forest, interior plateau, and towering mountains. Vancouver is a prosperous port, and the provin- cial capital, Victoria, at the southern tip of Vancouver Island, is famed for its English ambi- ence. In the neighboring province of Alberta, where an expanse of ranches and farms spreads eastward from the high spine of the Rockies, oil and gas have spurred economic growth.

157

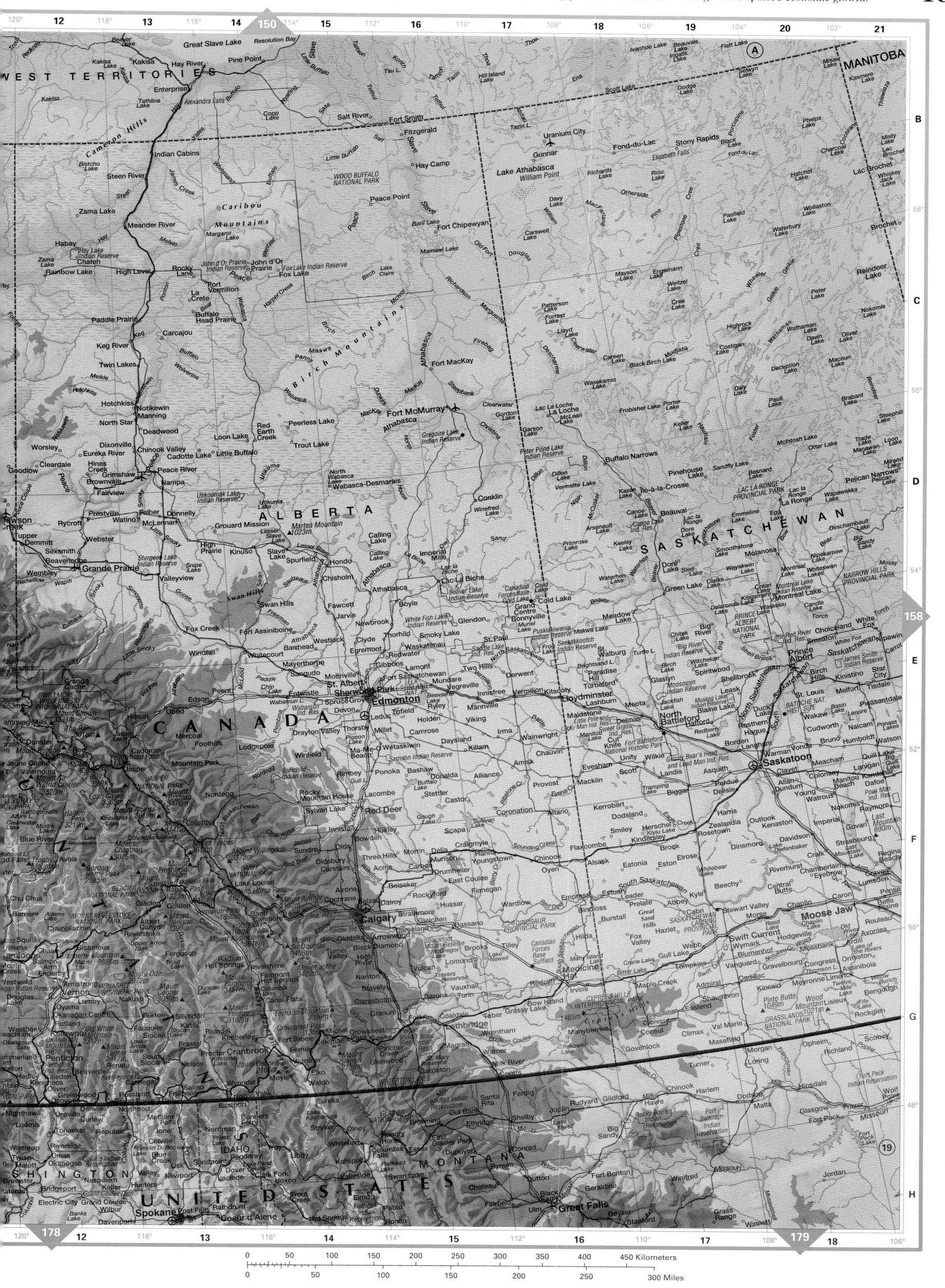

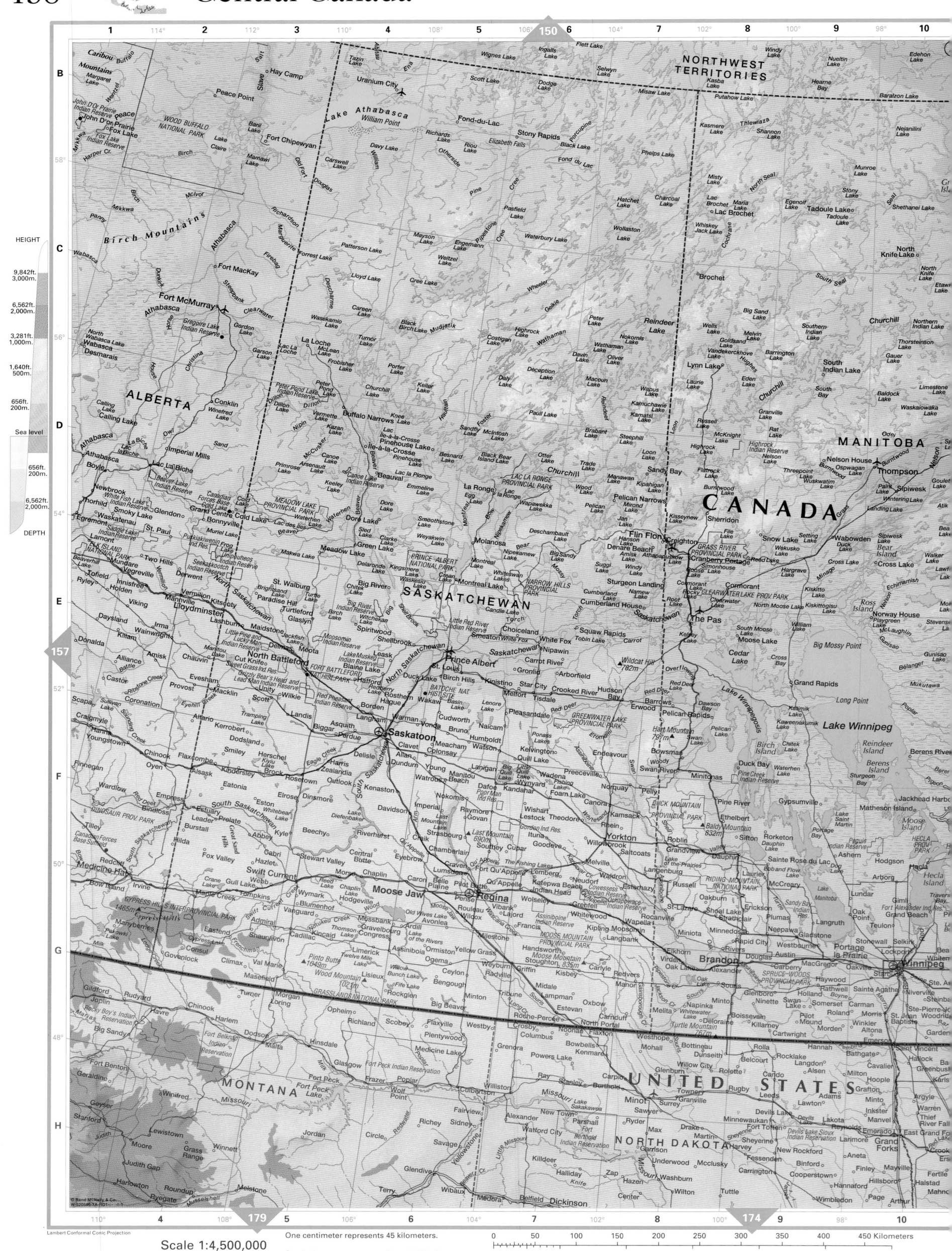

HEIGHT

9,842ft.
3,000m.

6,562ft.
2,000m.

3,281ft.
1,000m.

1,640ft.
500m.

656ft.
200m.

Sea level

656ft.
200m.

6,562ft.
2,000m.

DEPTH

Scale 1:4,500,000

Lambert Conformal Conic Projection

One centimeter represents 45 kilometers.

One inch represents approximately 71 miles.

© Rand McNally & Co.

Wheat, barley, and other profitable grains grow well on the fertile prairies of southern Saskatchewan and Manitoba. The region's largest city, Winnipeg, is situated roughly midway between the Atlantic and Pacific oceans. Northward, the prairies give way to the woods and waters of the rugged Canadian Shield, which extends eastward into northern Ontario, then to the tundra on the shores of Hudson Bay.

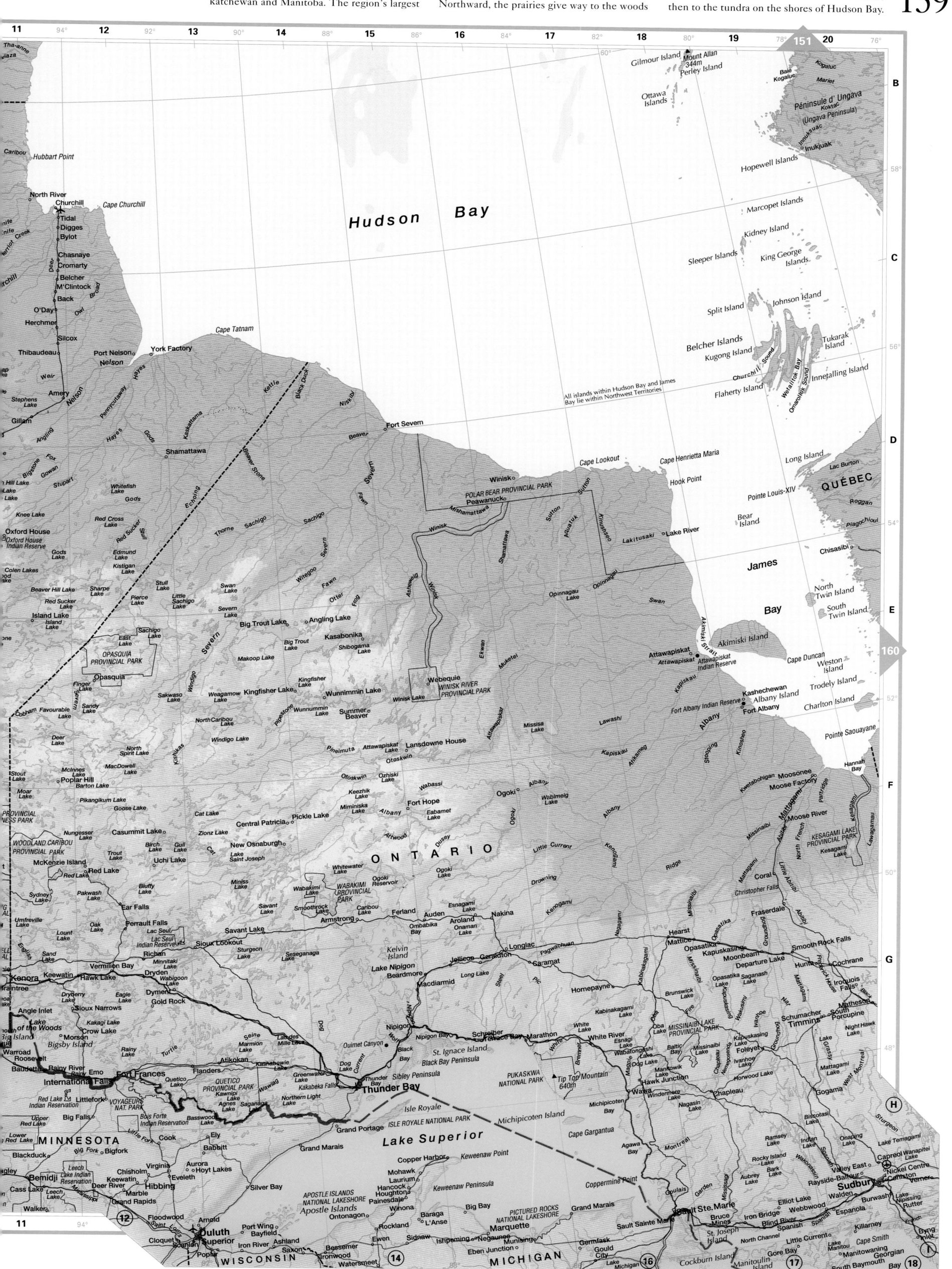

Eastern Canada

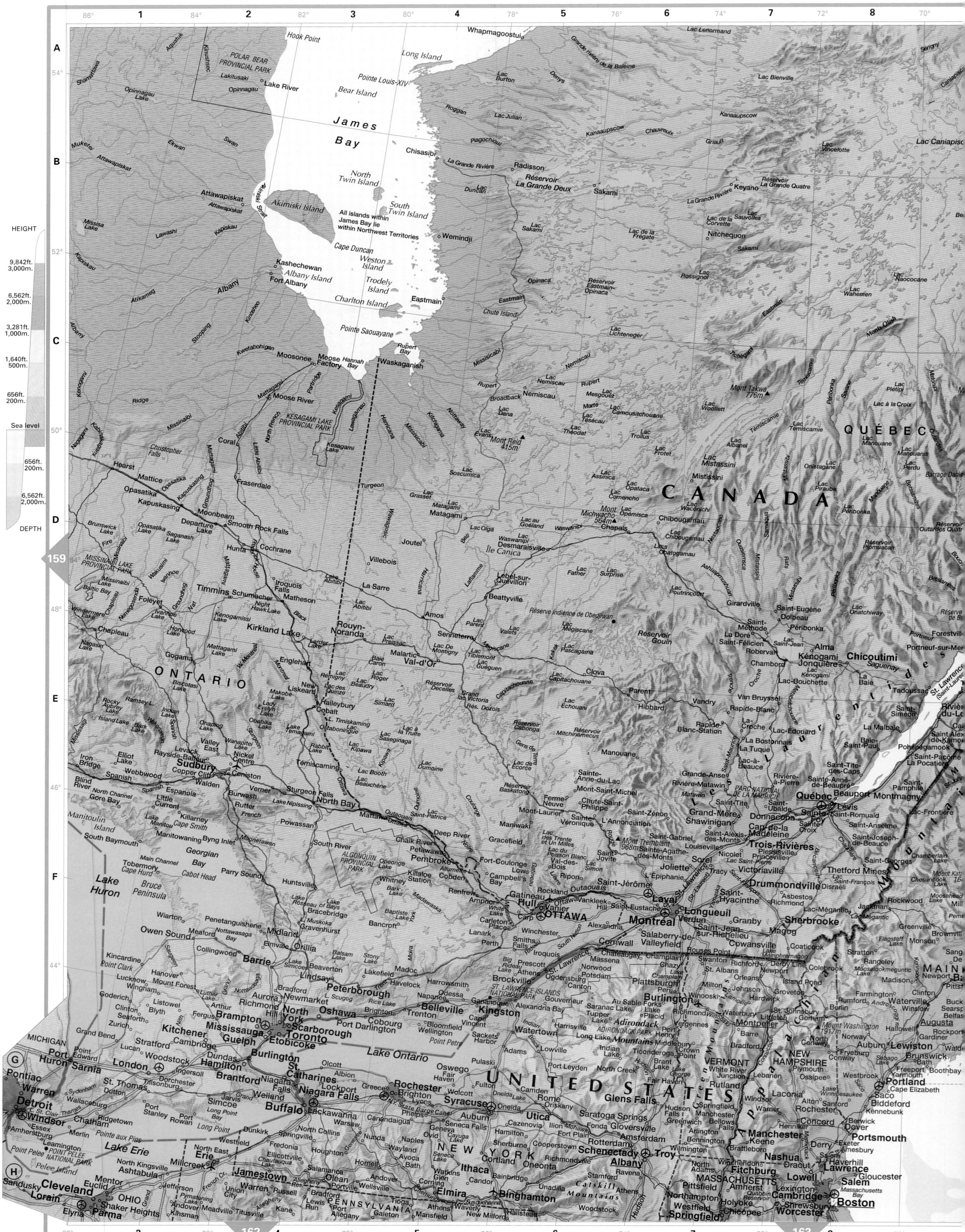

Scale 1:4,500,000

One centimeter represents 45 kilometers.

One inch represents approximately 71 miles.

Lambert Conformal Conic Projection

The heaviest concentration of industry in Canada lies between Windsor and Québec City. Situated in this densely populated region are Ottawa, Canada's capital; Toronto, the nation's largest city; and the French-speaking metropolis of Montréal. In the sparsely populated Atlantic region (New Brunswick, Prince Edward Island, Nova Scotia, and Newfoundland), fishing, farming, and forestry dominate the economy.

161

HEIGHT

9,842ft.
3,000m.

6,562ft.
2,000m.

3,281ft.
1,000m.

1,640ft.
500m.

656ft.
200m.

Sea level

656ft.
200m.

6,562ft.
2,000m.

DEPTH

Albers Conic Equal Area Projection

Scale 1:3,000,000

One centimeter represents 30 kilometers.

One inch represents approximately 47 miles.

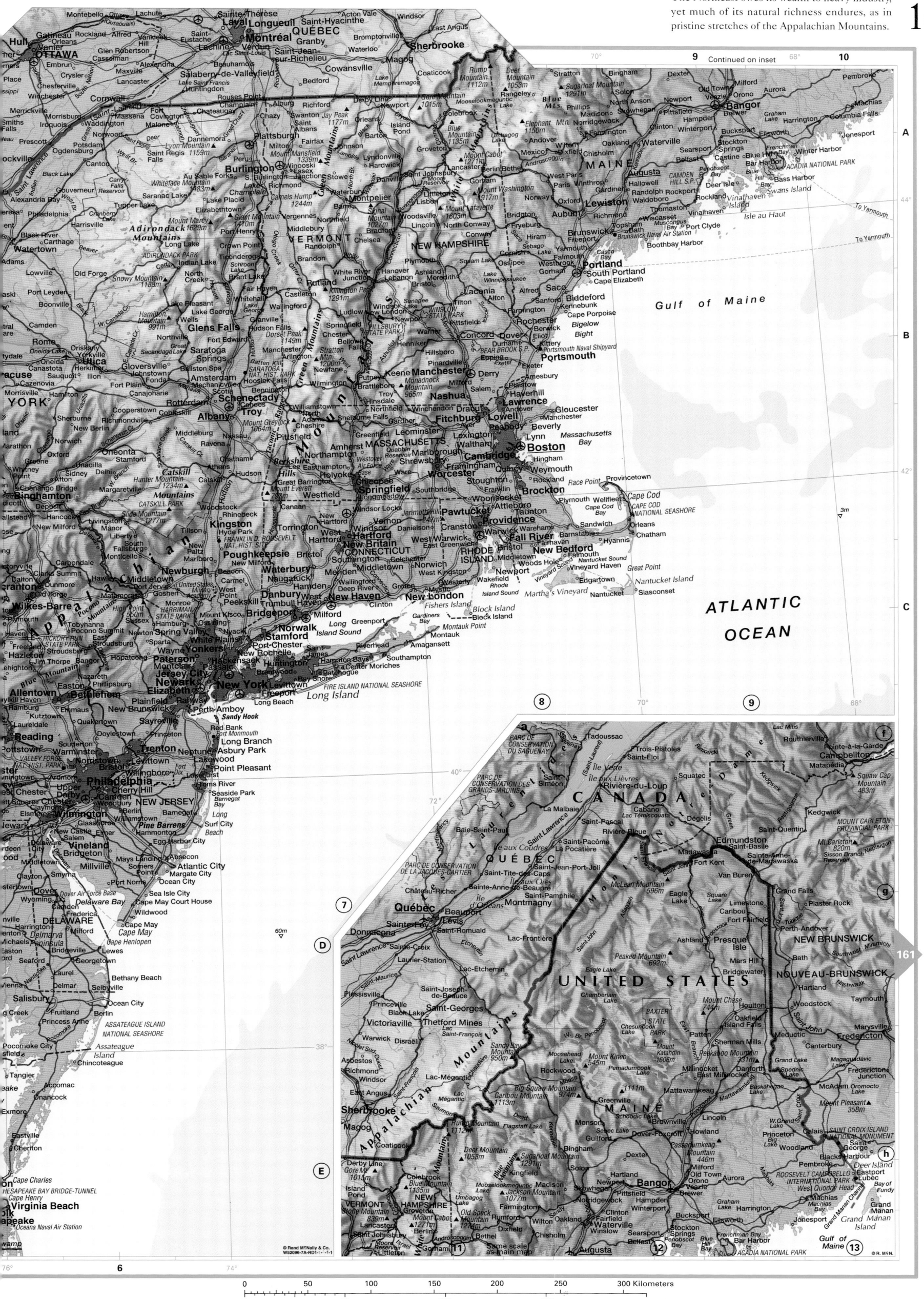

The Northeast owes its wealth to heavy industry, yet much of its natural richness endures, as in pristine stretches of the Appalachian Mountains.

163

ATLANTIC OCEAN

Gulf of Maine

CANADA

QUÉBEC

UNITED STATES

MAINE

NEW BRUNSWICK
NOUVEAU-BRUNSWICK

VERMONT

NEW HAMPSHIRE

MASSACHUSETTS

CONNECTICUT

RHODE ISLAND

NEW YORK

NEW JERSEY

DELAWARE

Appalachian Mountains

© Rand McNally & Co.
WS2096-7A-RD1- - - 1-1

0   50   100   150   200   250   300 Kilometers
0   50   100   150   200 Miles

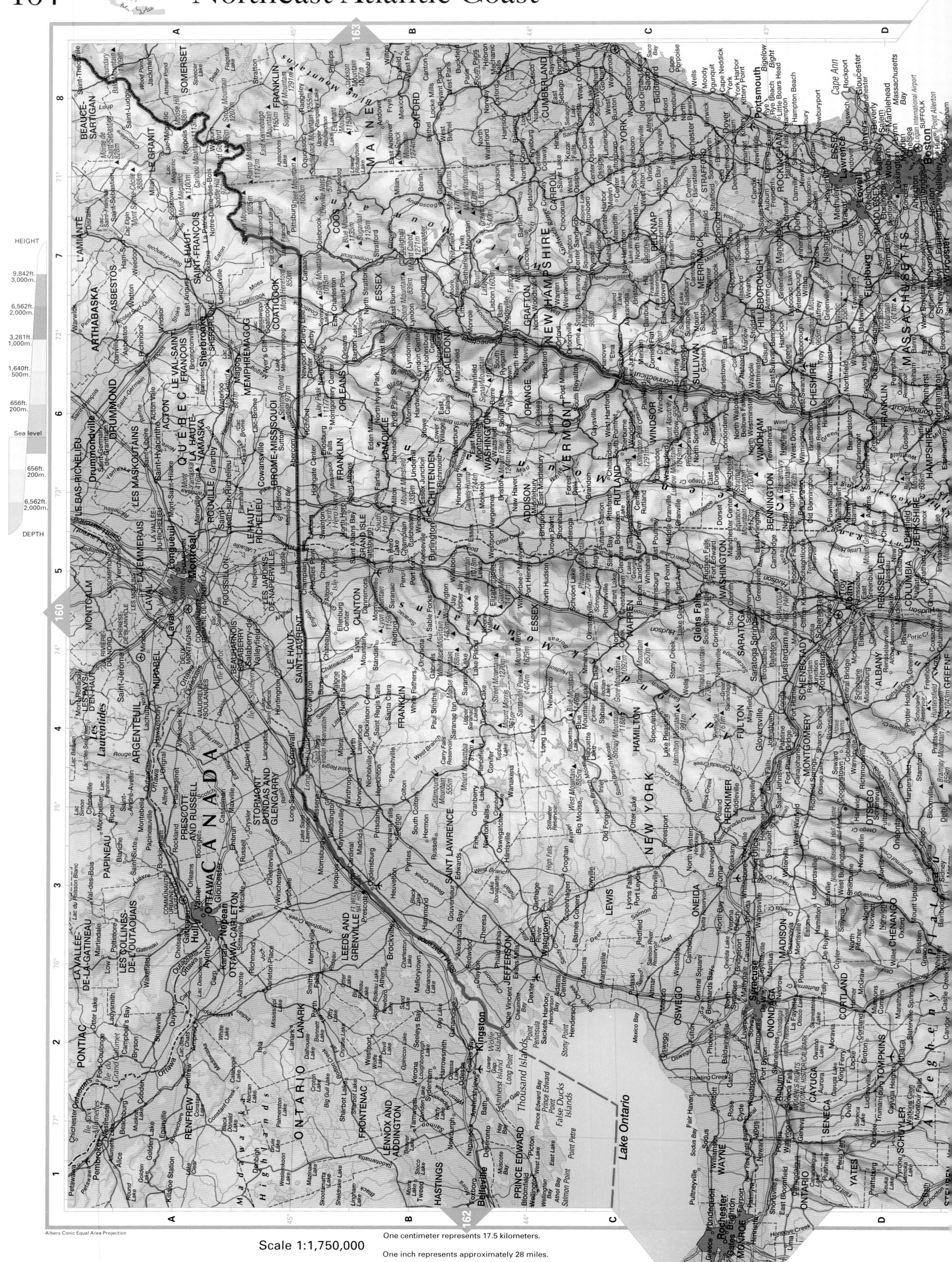

HEIGHT

9,842ft.
3,000m.

6,562ft.
2,000m.

3,281ft.
1,000m.

1,640ft.
500m.

656ft.
200m.

Sea level

656ft.
200m.

6,562ft.
2,000m.

DEPTH

Albers Conic Equal Area Projection

Scale 1:1,750,000

One centimeter represents 17.5 kilometers.

One inch represents approximately 28 miles.

To early European settlers this region was one of seemingly endless wilderness, but booming urban development between Boston and Washington, D.C., has created a 500-mile-long (800-km.) "megalopolis" with a population density that, in some places, exceeds that of India.

165

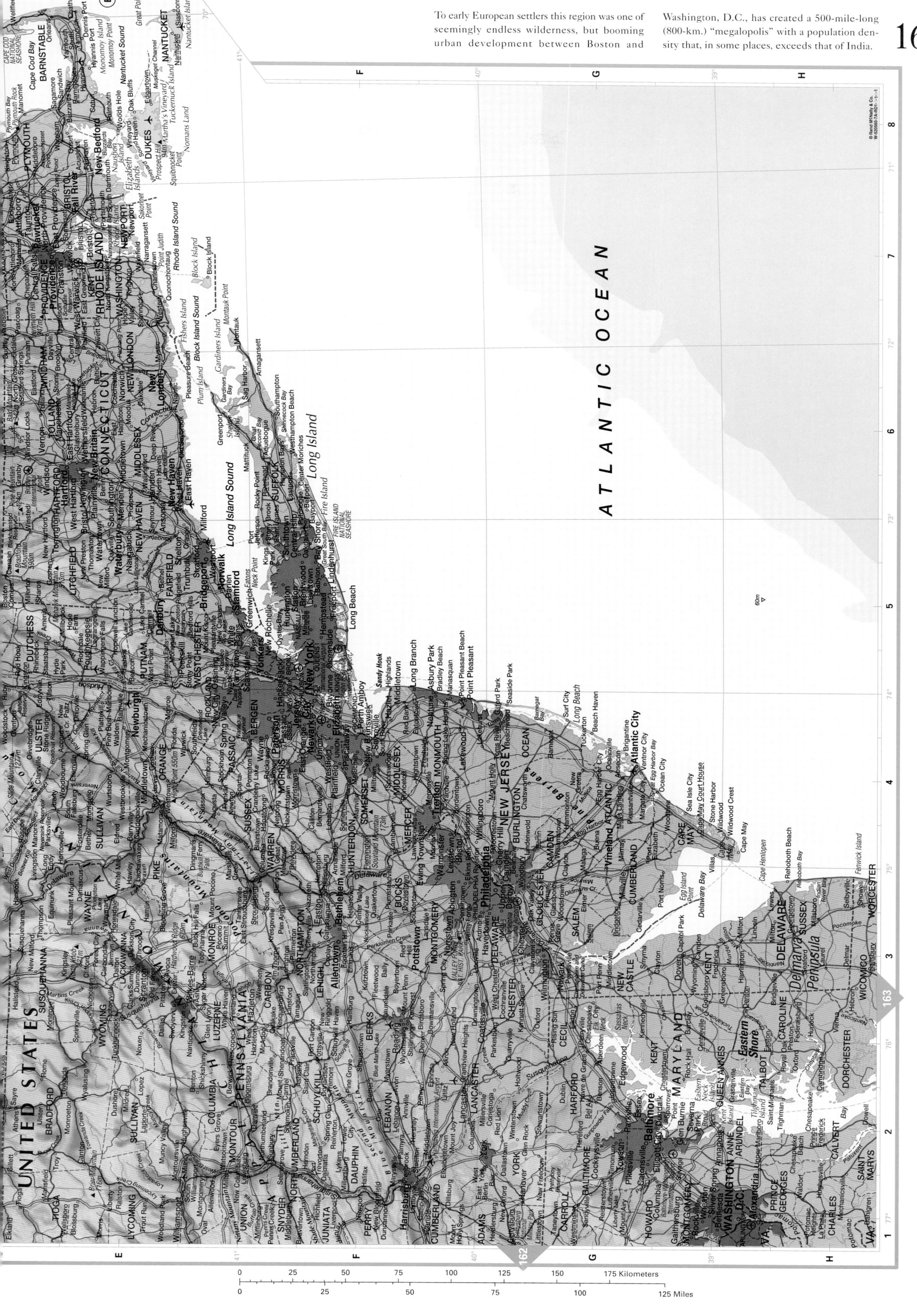

ATLANTIC OCEAN

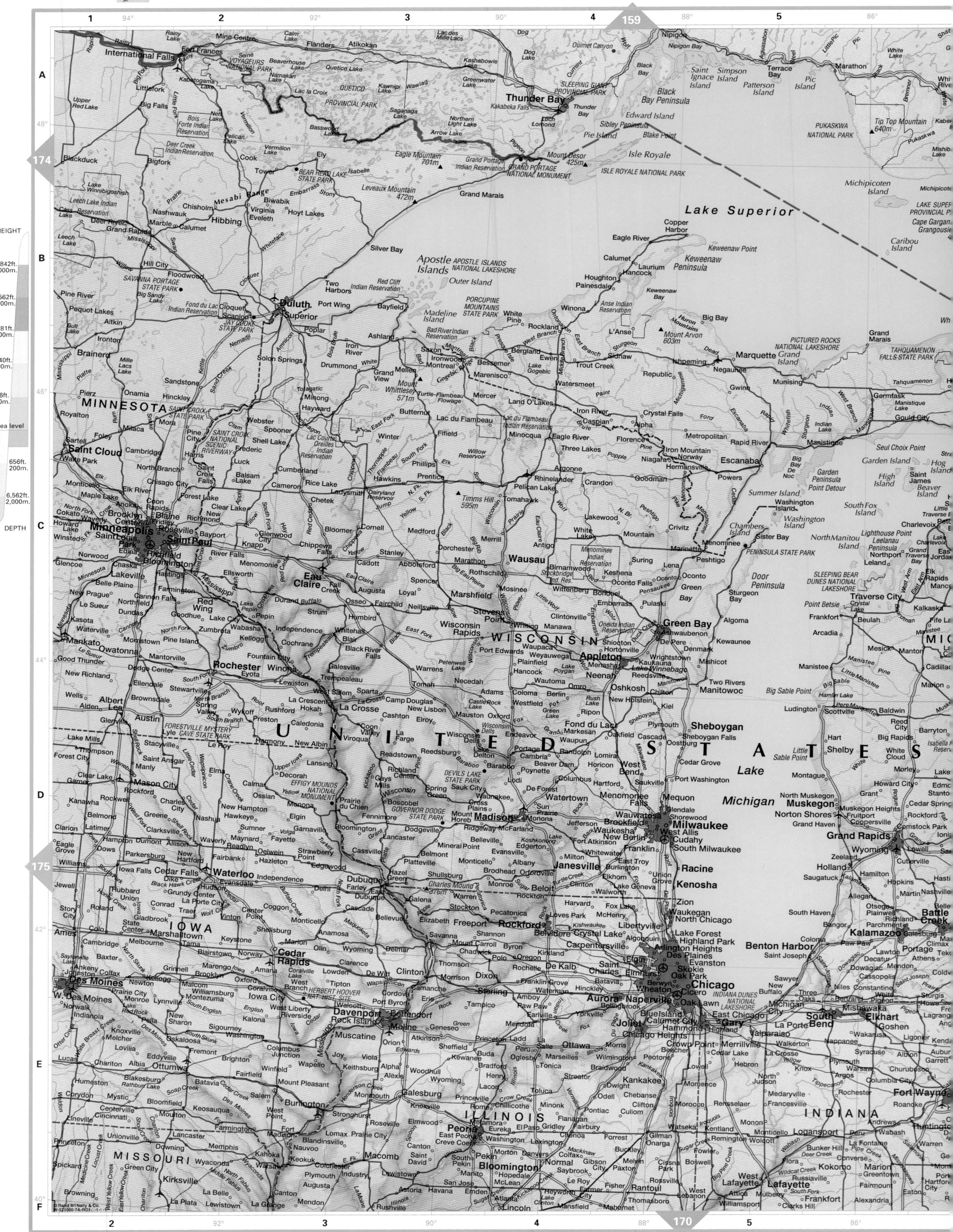

Scale 1:3,000,000

One centimeter represents 30 kilometers.

One inch represents approximately 47 miles.

Albers Conic Equal Area Projection

Straddling the U.S.-Canada border, the five interconnected bodies of water known as the Great Lakes – Lakes Superior, Michigan, Huron, Erie, and Ontario – form the largest expanse of fresh water in the world, covering a total surface area of 94,747 sq. mi. (245,395 sq. km.). Lake Superior (the biggest, deepest, and northernmost of them) is the largest lake in North America and the second largest in the world.

167

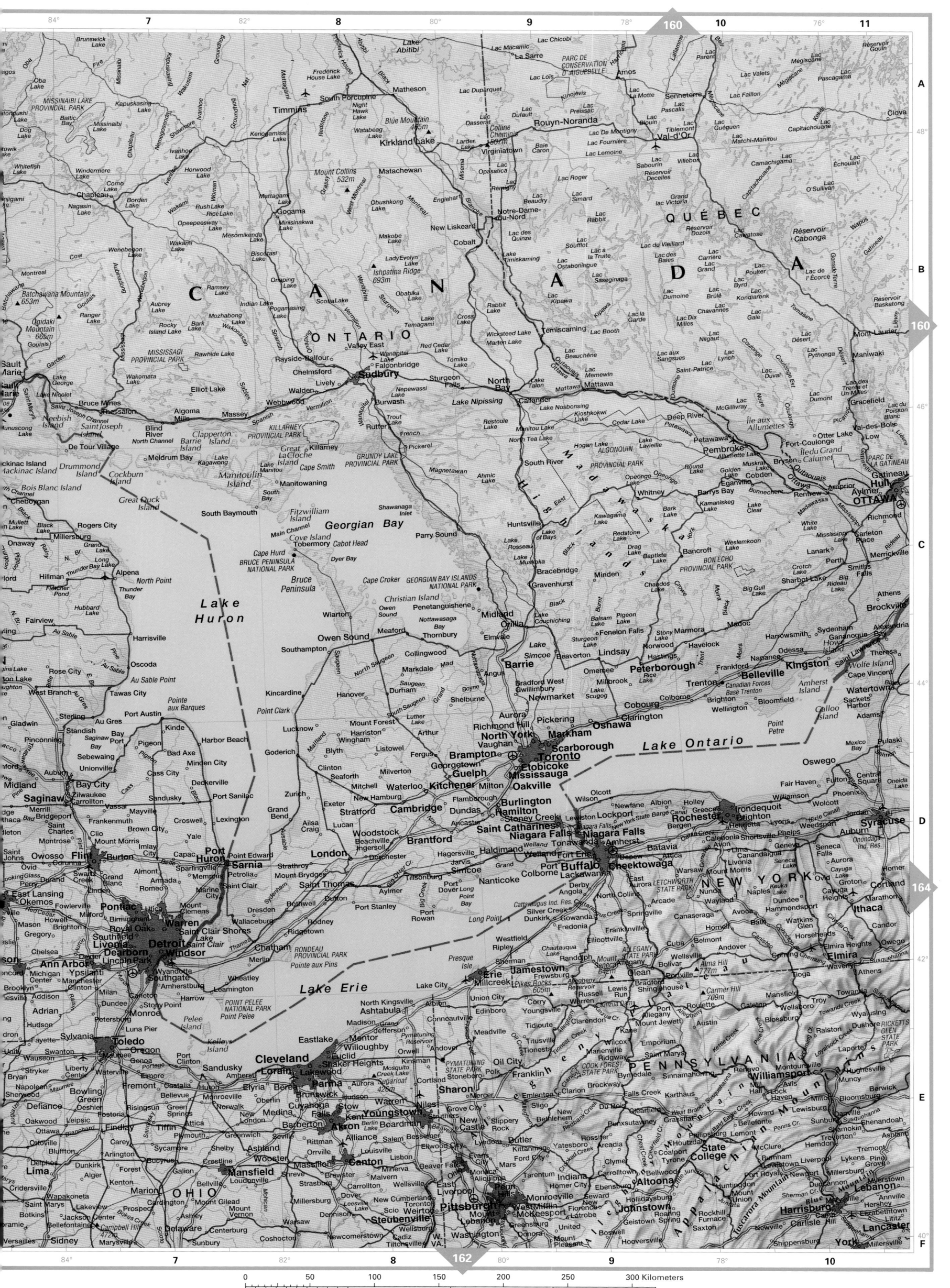

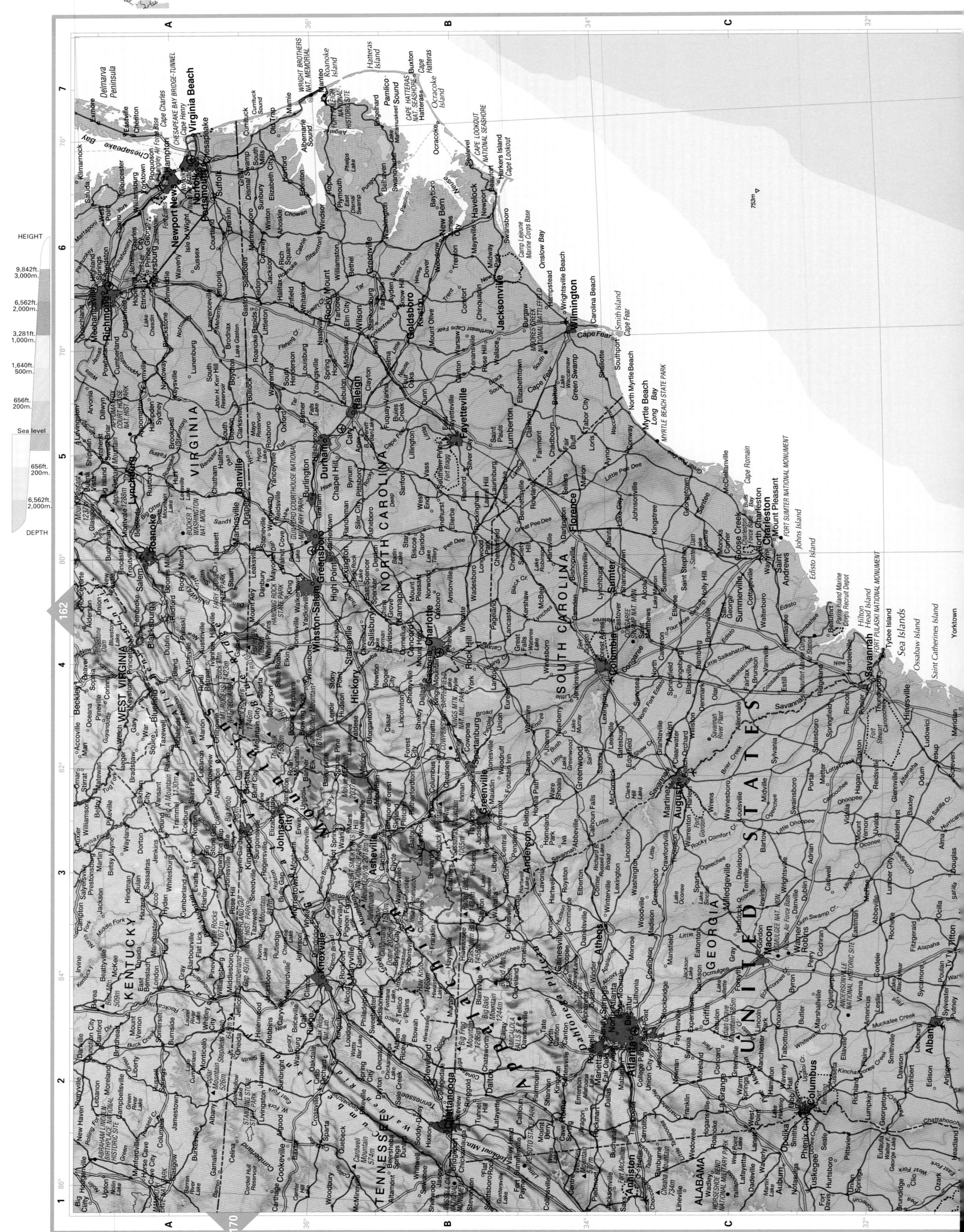

Scale 1:3,000,000

One centimeter represents 30 kilometers.

One inch represents approximately 47 miles.

Albers Conic Equal Area Projection

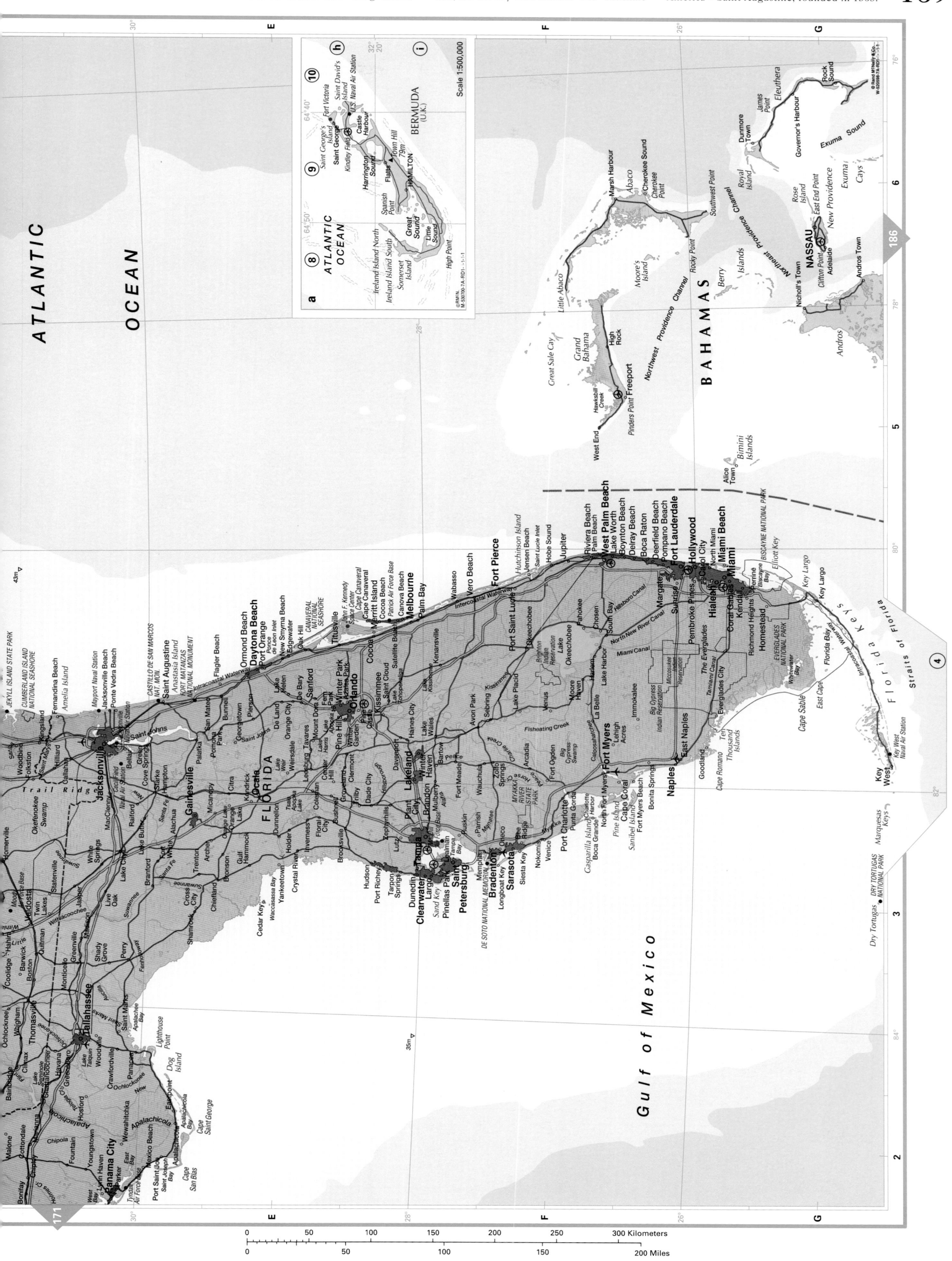

Left in ruins after the Civil War, the Southeast awoke slowly from its agrarian past. Economies once reliant on tobacco and "King Cotton" eventually turned to more modern industries. Florida, with its 8,000 mi. (12,900 km.) of coastline, led the way with tourism. The "Sunshine State" also boasts the unique Everglades and the oldest European settlement in North America – Saint Augustine, founded in 1565.

HEIGHT

| 9,842ft. 3,000m. |
| 6,562ft. 2,000m. |
| 3,281ft. 1,000m. |
| 1,640ft. 500m. |
| 656ft. 200m. |
| Sea level |
| 656ft. 200m. |
| 6,562ft. 2,000m. |

DEPTH

Albers Conic Equal Area Projection

Scale 1:3,000,000

One centimeter represents 30 kilometers.

One inch represents approximately 47 miles.

A vast and vital waterway, the 2,348-mile (3,778-km.) Mississippi River boasts over half a billion tons of traffic yearly. As the Mississippi snakes south, it touches 10 states, feeding fertile farmlands along its wide floodplain, which is protected from regular inundation by a series of levees. The "Big Muddy," as it's sometimes called, ends its meandering journey at the Gulf of Mexico near New Orleans, America's busiest port.

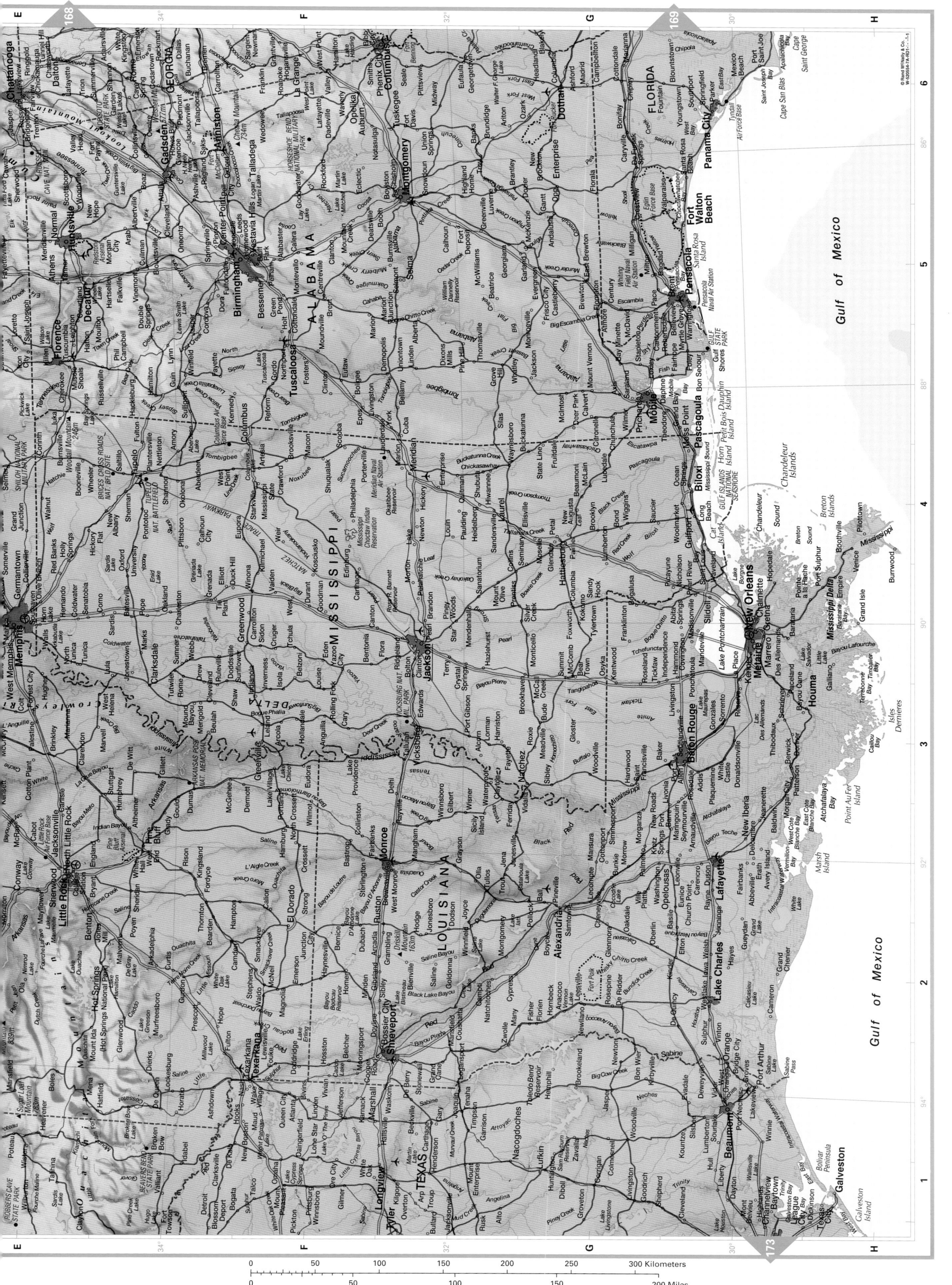

Gulf of Mexico

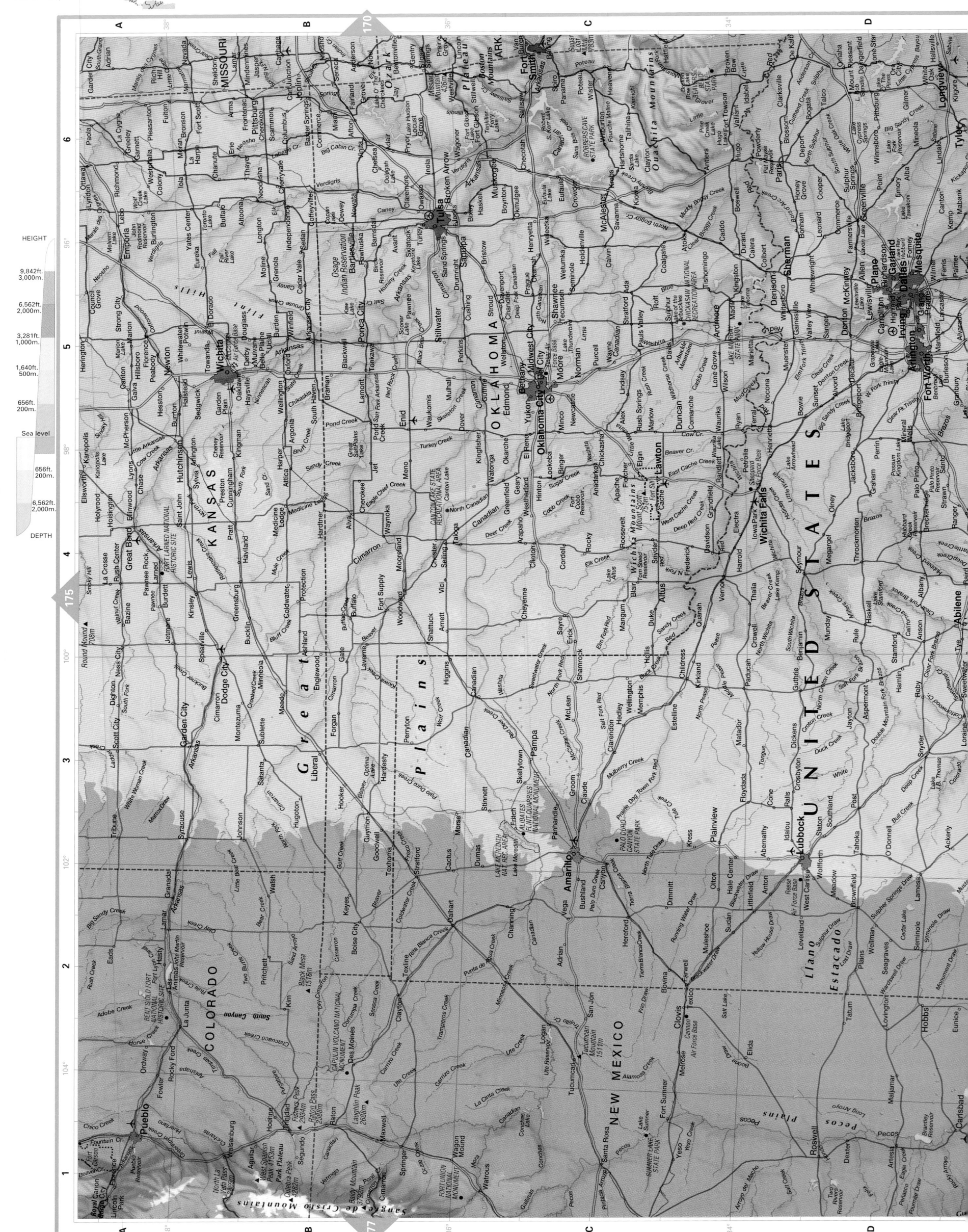

HEIGHT

9,842ft.
3,000m.

6,562ft.
2,000m.

3,281ft.
1,000m.

1,640ft.
500m.

656ft.
200m.

Sea level

656ft.
200m.

6,562ft.
2,000m.

DEPTH

Albers Conic Equal Area Projection

Scale 1:3,000,000

One centimeter represents 30 kilometers.

One inch represents approximately 47 miles.

A sovereign nation before its admission into the Union in 1845, Texas is a state as large as its legend. Within its borders – which encompass an area equivalent to one-twelfth of the lower 48 states – can be found deserts, swamps, gleaming skyscrapers, ancient adobe villages, vast oil fields, and a tropical coast. To the north is Oklahoma, a sprawling land of high desert buttes, fertile grasslands, and lush, rolling hills.

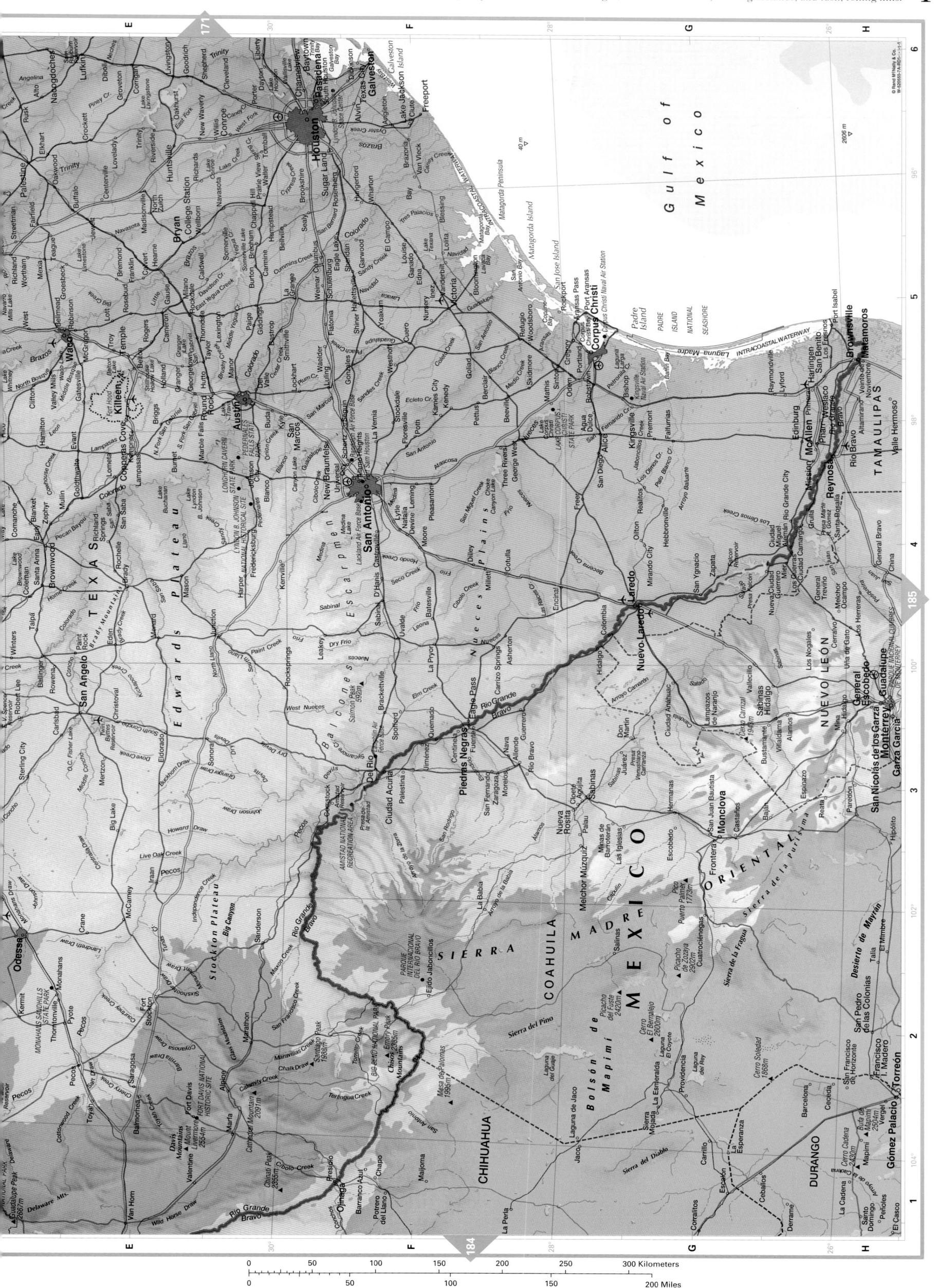

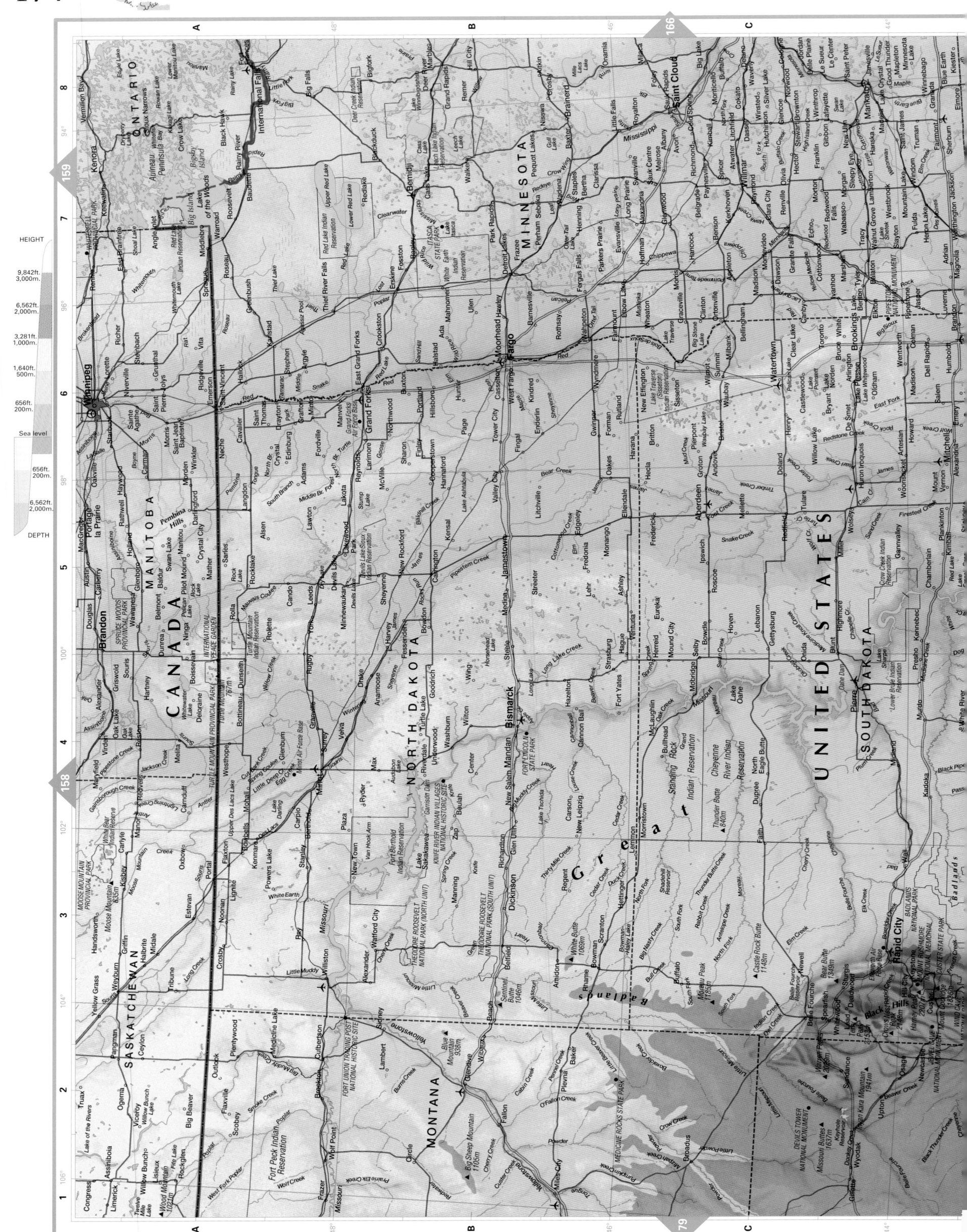

HEIGHT

9,842ft.
3,000m.

6,562ft.
2,000m.

3,281ft.
1,000m.

1,640ft.
500m.

656ft.
200m.

Sea level

656ft.
200m.

6,562ft.
2,000m.

DEPTH

Albers Conic Equal Area Projection

Scale 1:3,000,000

One centimeter represents 30 kilometers.

One inch represents approximately 47 miles.

Once dubbed "The Great American Desert," the Great Plains were transformed into the nation's breadbasket by the invention of the steel plow. The region now boasts record crops of wheat, corn, and soy beans, and a thriving livestock industry. Although it feeds the entire nation, the Great Plains remain one of the least populated areas in the U.S. Surprisingly, less than 3 percent of all Americans work on farms.

175

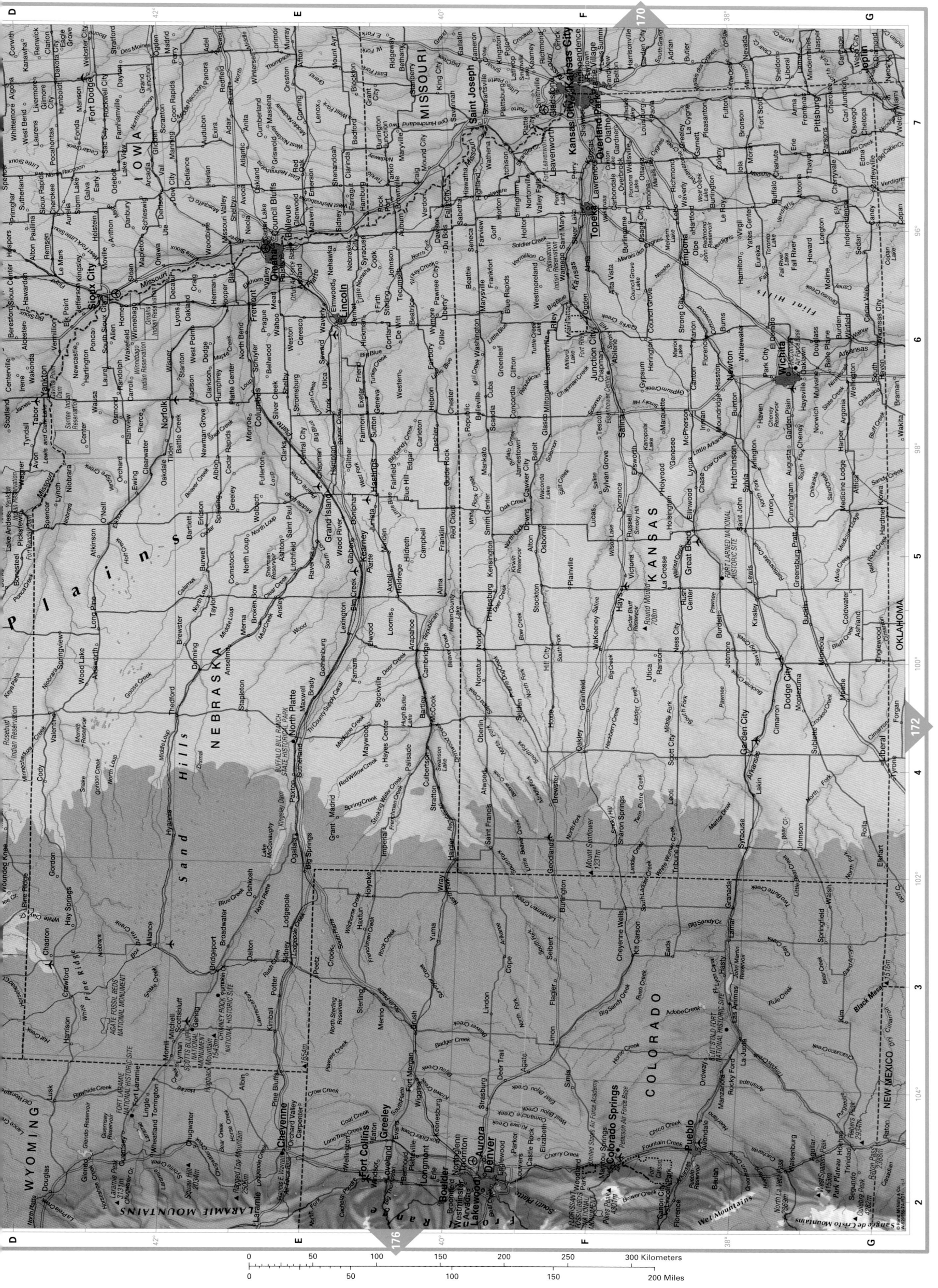

0 50 100 150 200 250 300 Kilometers

0 50 100 150 200 Miles

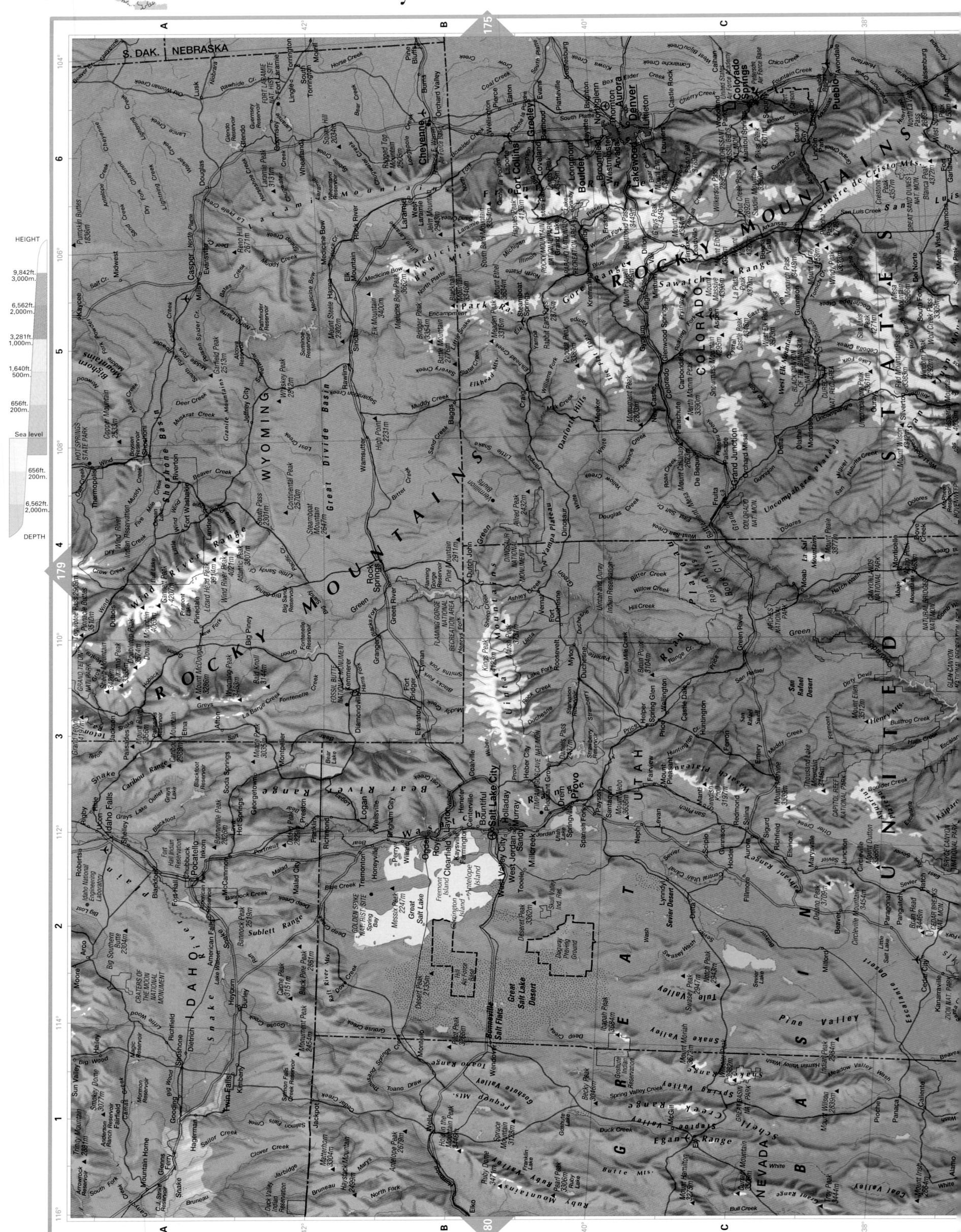

Albers Conic Equal Area Projection

Scale 1:3,000,000

One centimeter represents 30 kilometers.

One inch represents approximately 47 miles.

From the snowcapped heights of the Rockies to the dizzying depths of the Grand Canyon, this is one of the world's great natural showplaces. Visitors marvel at the fanciful formations of Zion National Park, the fiery red towers of Monument Valley, and the haunting beauty of Canyon de Chelly, where cliff houses, abandoned over 800 years ago by the mysterious Anasazis, stand in silent testament to a civilization long lost.

177

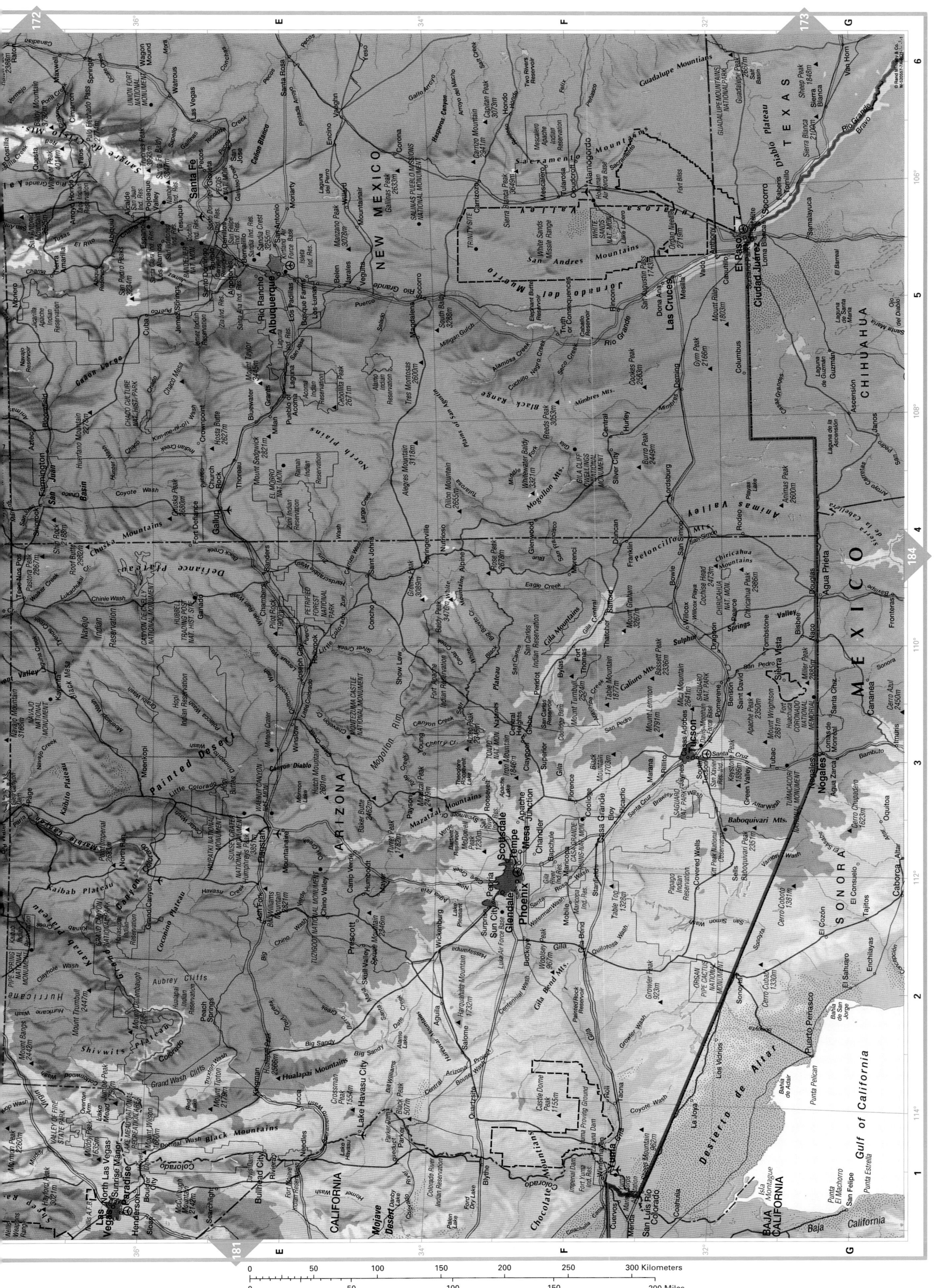

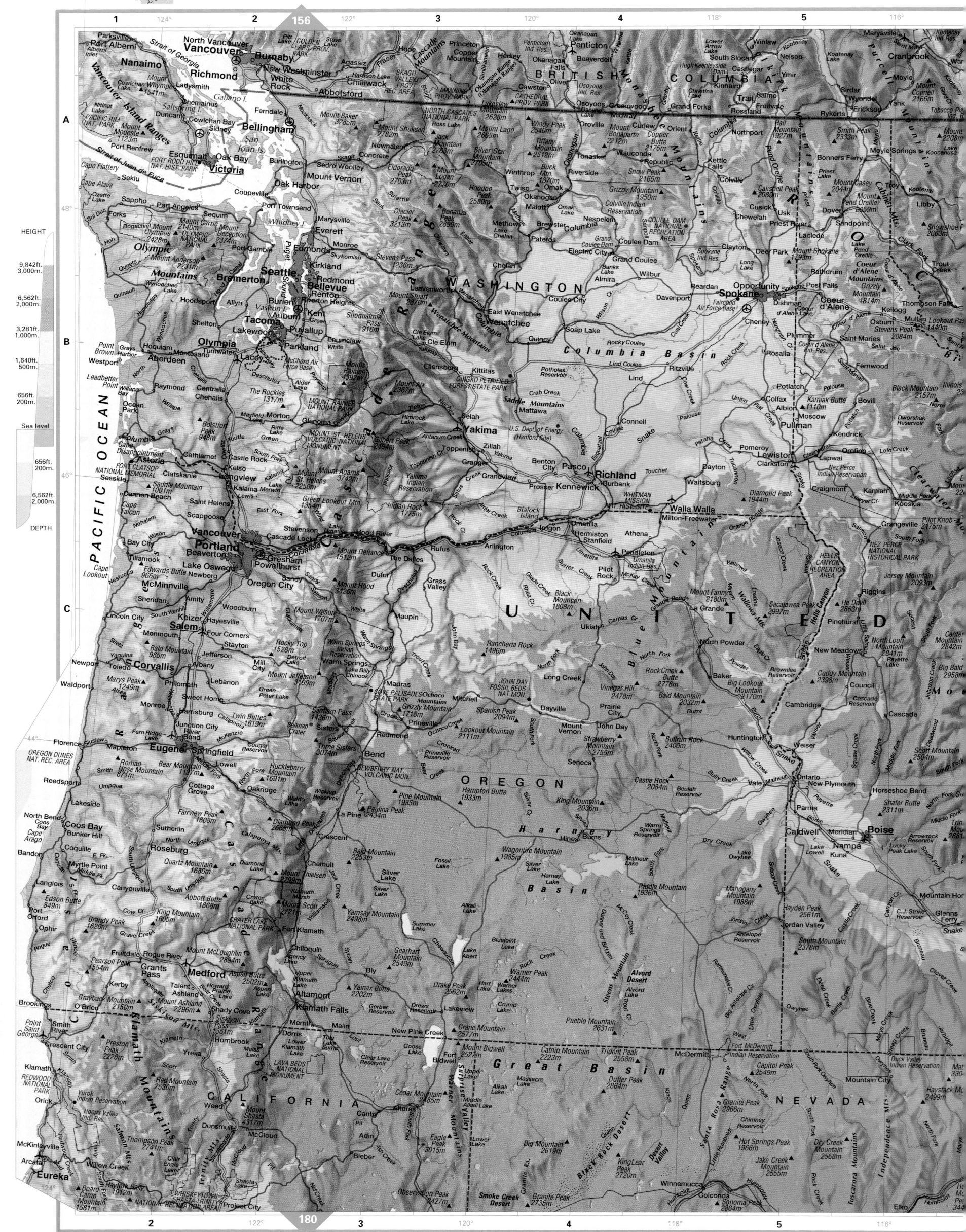

Scale 1:3,000,000

One centimeter represents 30 kilometers.

One inch represents approximately 47 miles.

Albers Conic Equal Area Projection

Looming large over a lushly forested landscape, the volcanic peaks of the Cascade Range reign supreme in the Pacific Northwest. Part of the Pacific "Ring of Fire," the region's mountains include the majestic 14,410-foot (4,392-m.) cone of Mt. Rainier and the jagged stump of Mt. St. Helens, which blew its top in 1980. Nearby Seattle, with its booming software and aerospace industries, is the urban jewel of the Northwest.

179

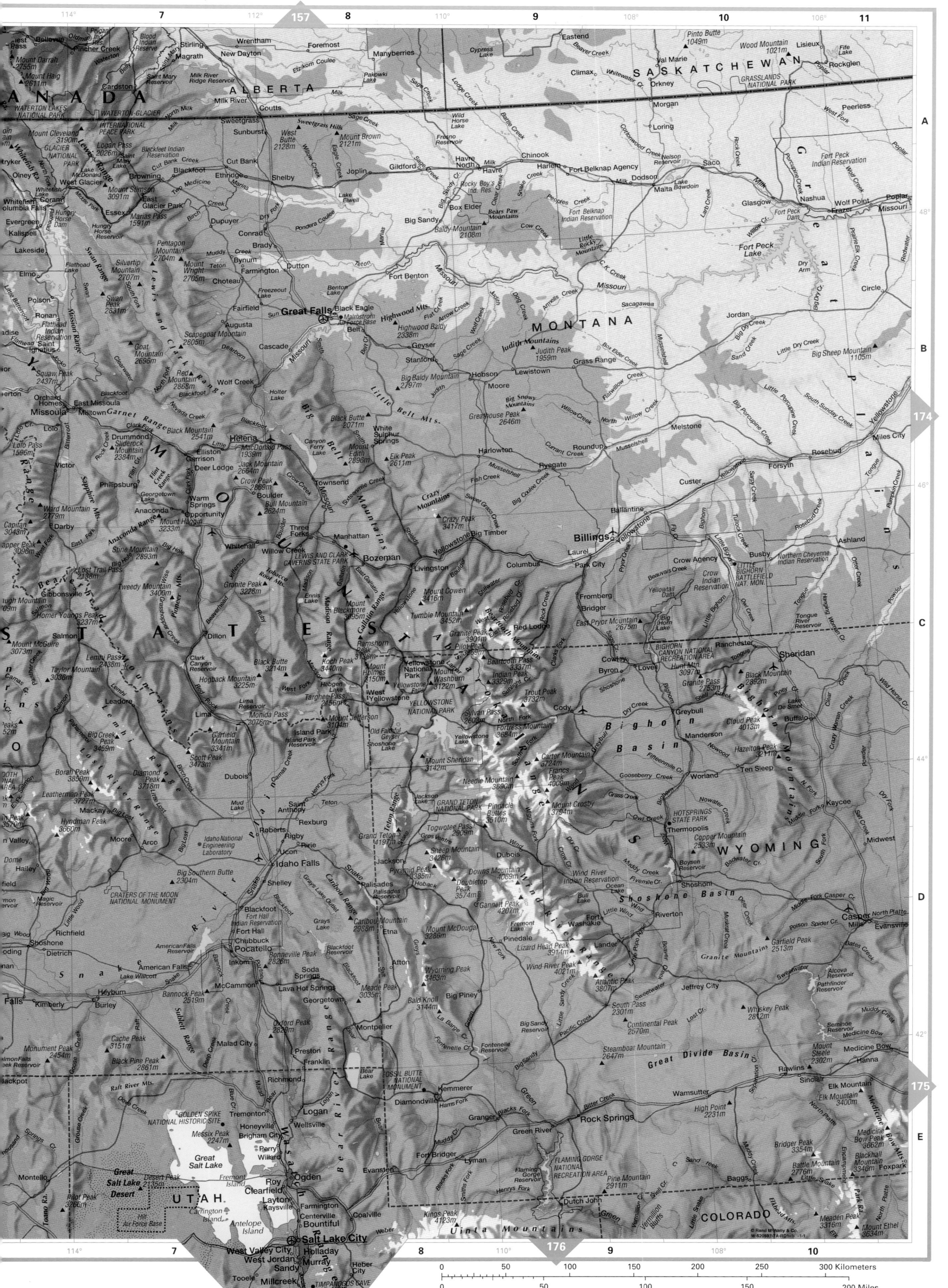

0   50   100   150   200   250   300 Kilometers

0   50   100   150   200 Miles

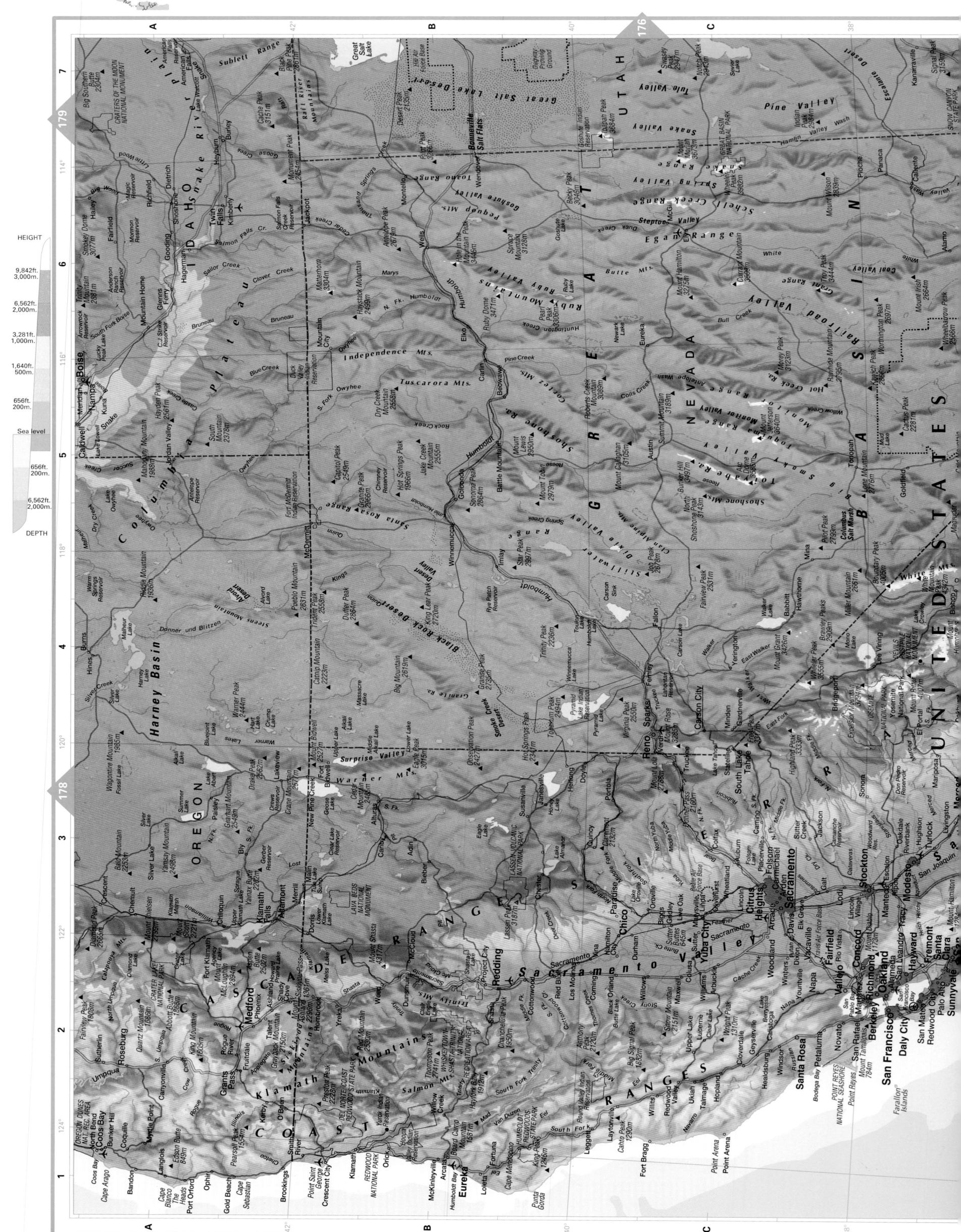

HEIGHT

9,842ft.
3,000m.

6,562ft.
2,000m.

3,281ft.
1,000m.

1,640ft.
500m.

656ft.
200m.

Sea level

656ft.
200m.

6,562ft.
2,000m.

DEPTH

Albers Conic Equal Area Projection

Scale 1:3,000,000

One centimeter represents 30 kilometers.

One inch represents approximately 47 miles.

A legend writ large on movie screens across the globe, the world's image of the U.S. is one centered firmly in the American West. Here is the empty sagebrush plain of Nevada, lit in one corner by the neon oasis of Las Vegas. Here, too, are the varied splendors of California, from its towering redwoods to the sunbaked basin of Death Valley. Still farther west, the island paradise of Hawaii beckons from the deep blue Pacific.

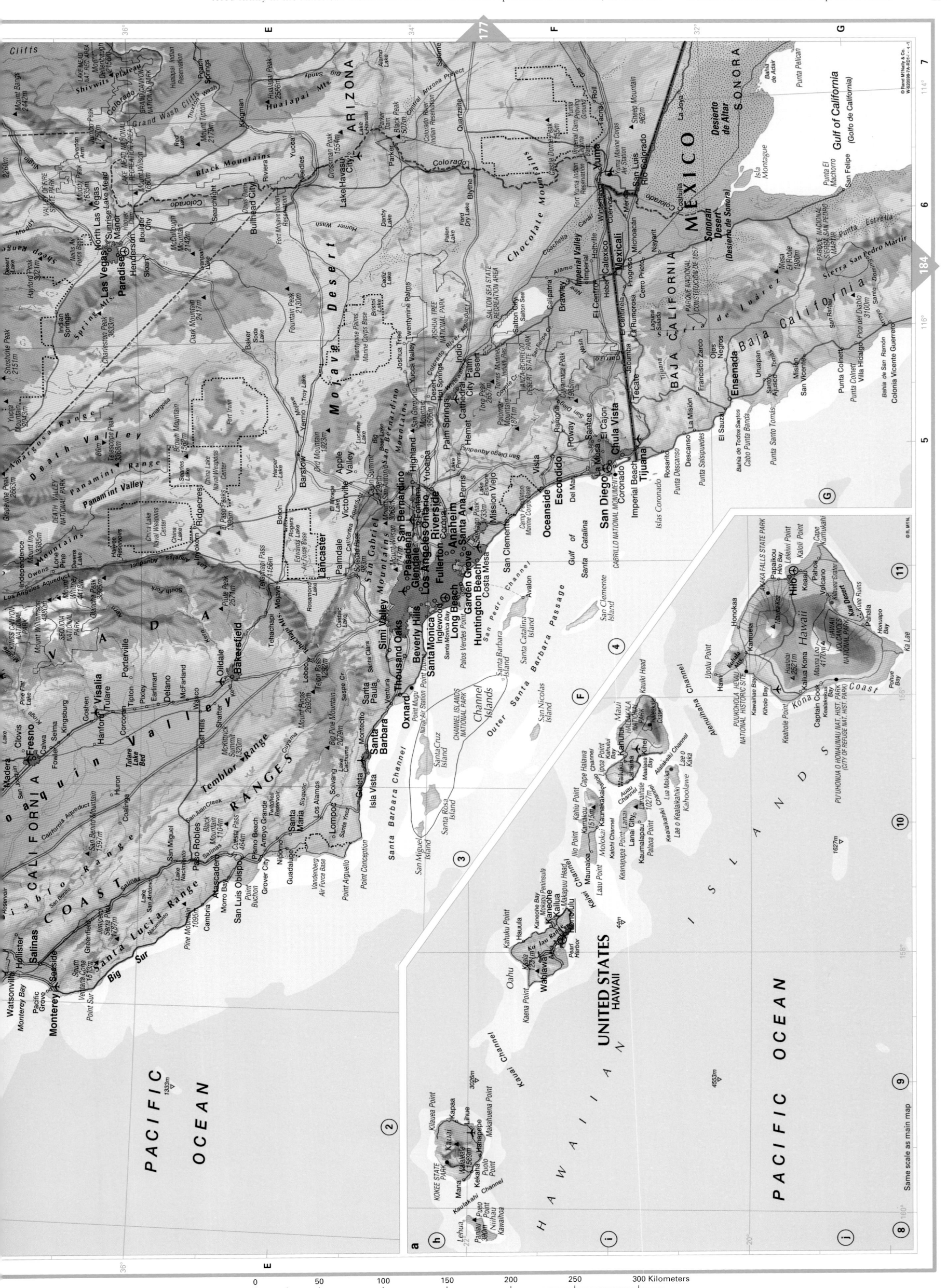

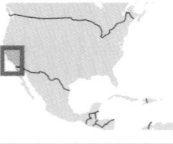

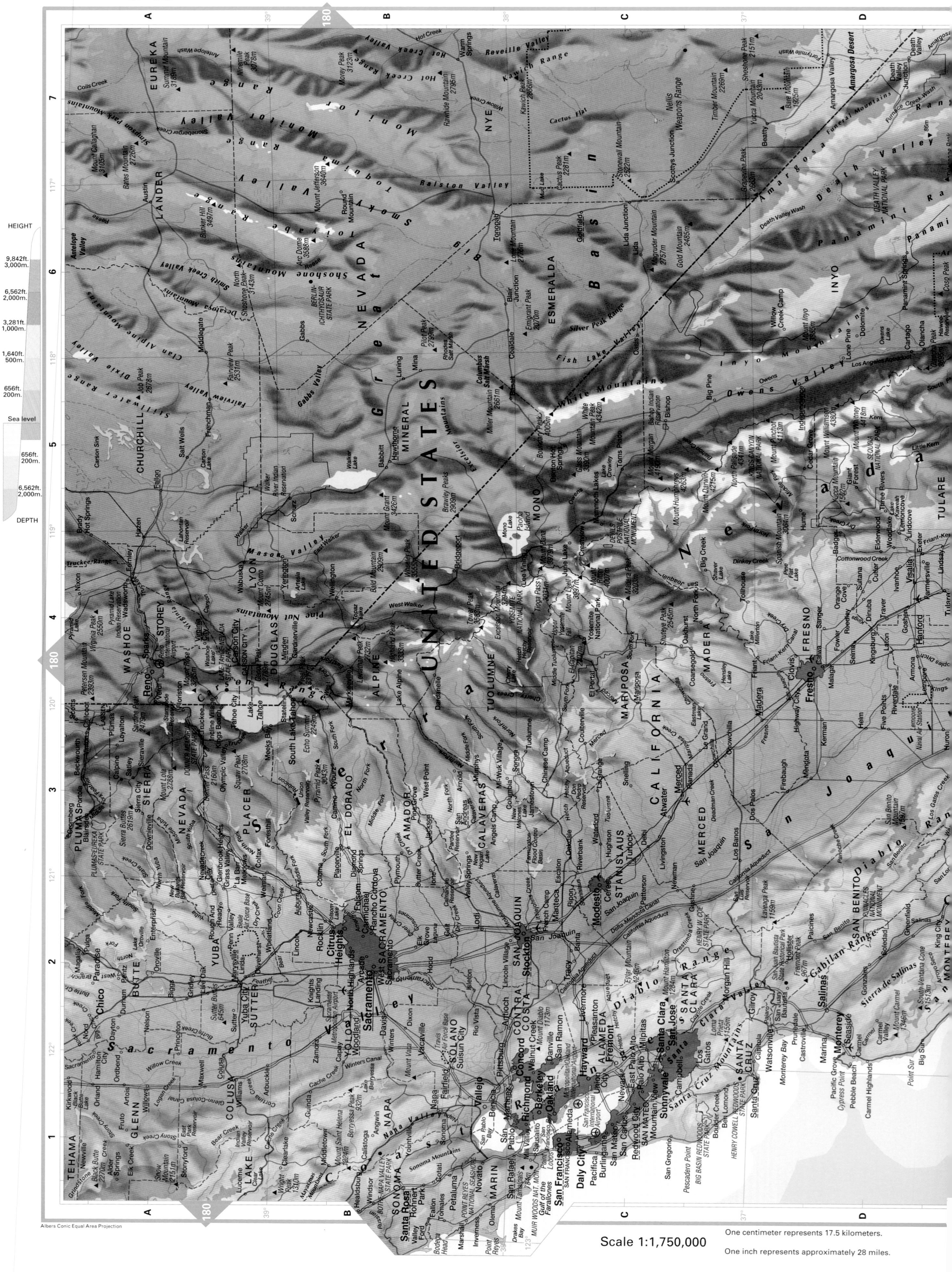

HEIGHT

9,842ft.
3,000m.

6,562ft.
2,000m.

3,281ft.
1,000m.

1,640ft.
500m.

656ft.
200m.

Sea level

656ft.
200m.

6,562ft.
2,000m.

DEPTH

Albers Conic Equal Area Projection

Scale 1:1,750,000

One centimeter represents 17.5 kilometers.

One inch represents approximately 28 miles.

From the foggy hills of San Francisco to the sun-drenched sprawl of Los Angeles, California is a study in contrasts. Its 760-mile (1,220-km.) coastline is a short drive from blistering deserts, shady forests, and lofty peaks, while its diverse industries range from agriculture and entertainment to fishing and computer science. The populace of the Golden State is equally varied, with one in four U.S. immigrants settling here.

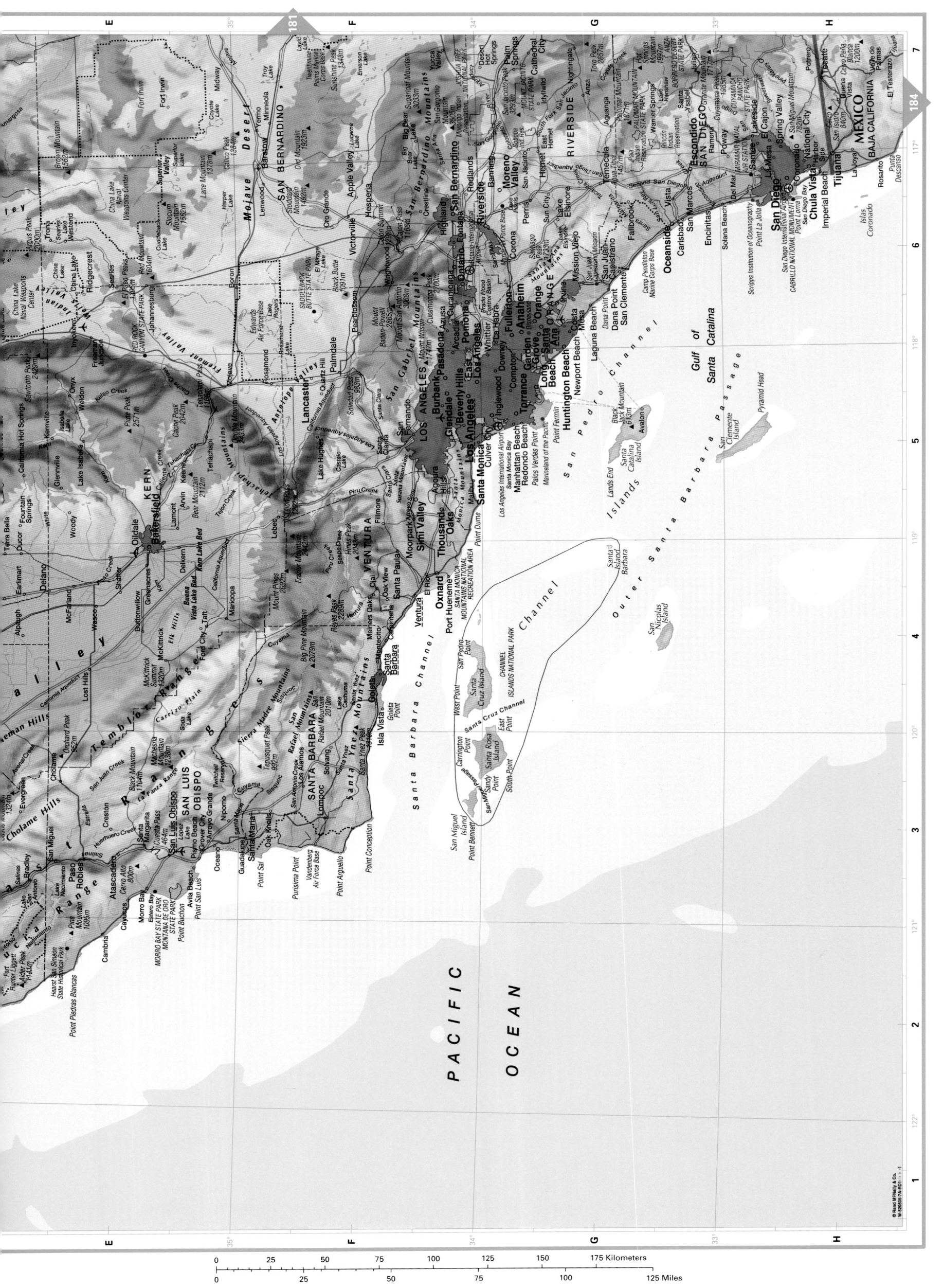

HEIGHT

9,842ft.
3,000m.

6,562ft.
2,000m.

3,281ft.
1,000m.

1,640ft.
500m.

656ft.
200m.

Sea level

656ft.
200m.

6,562ft.
2,000m.

DEPTH

Scale 1:6,000,000

One centimeter represents 60 kilometers.

One inch represents approximately 95 miles.

Lambert Conformal Conic Projection

© Rand McNally & Co.
W-532000-7A-RD1- - - -1-1

With a population of 95 million, Mexico is the world's largest Spanish-speaking nation, but it is also host to an array of Native American dialects, revealing the country's mixed heritage. In fact, Mexico City, the capital, was built over Tenochtitlán, the heart of the Aztec empire. Mexico's terrain is as diverse as its people – from the lonely heights of the Sierra Madre to the dense tropical forests of the Yucatán Peninsula.

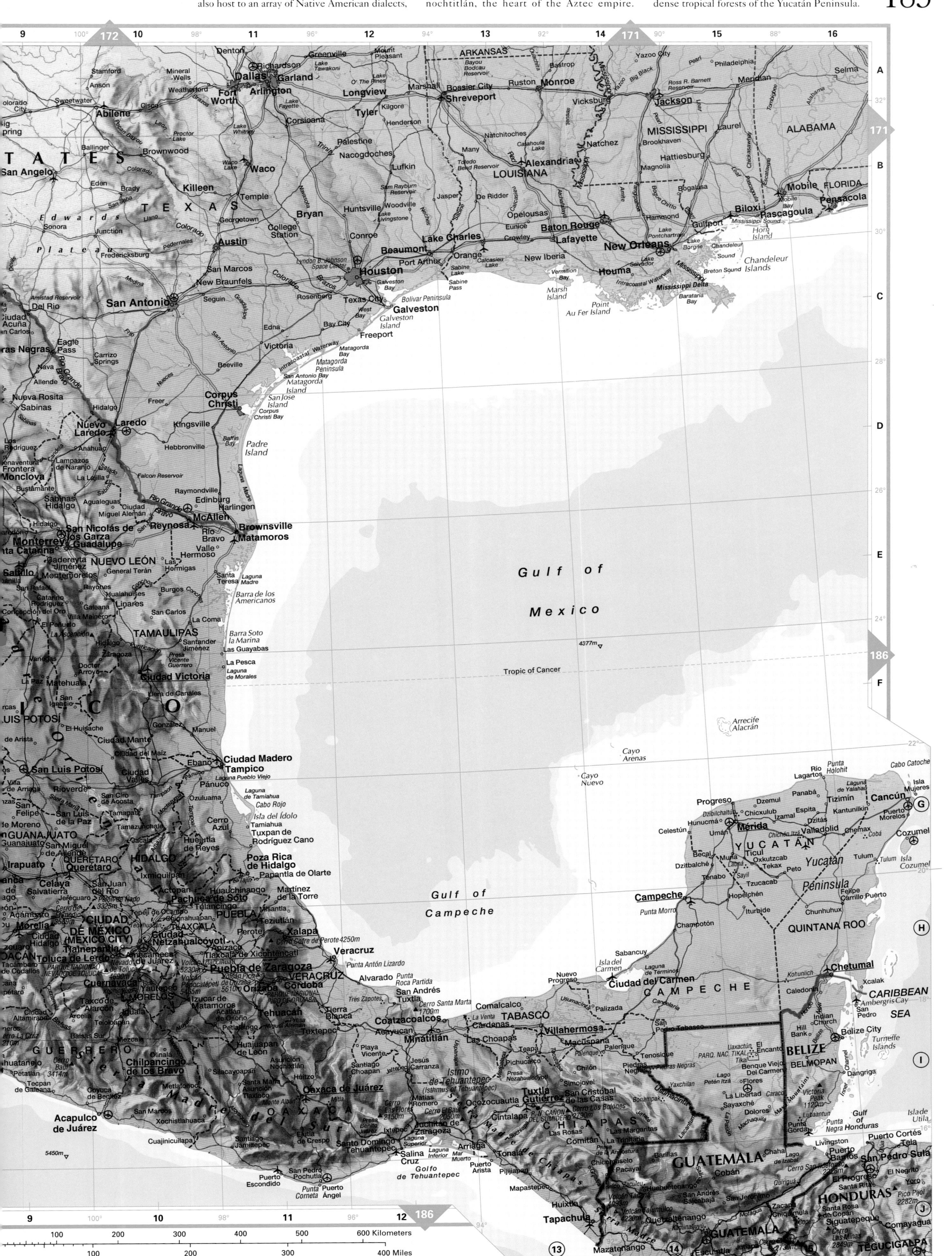

Central America and the Caribbean

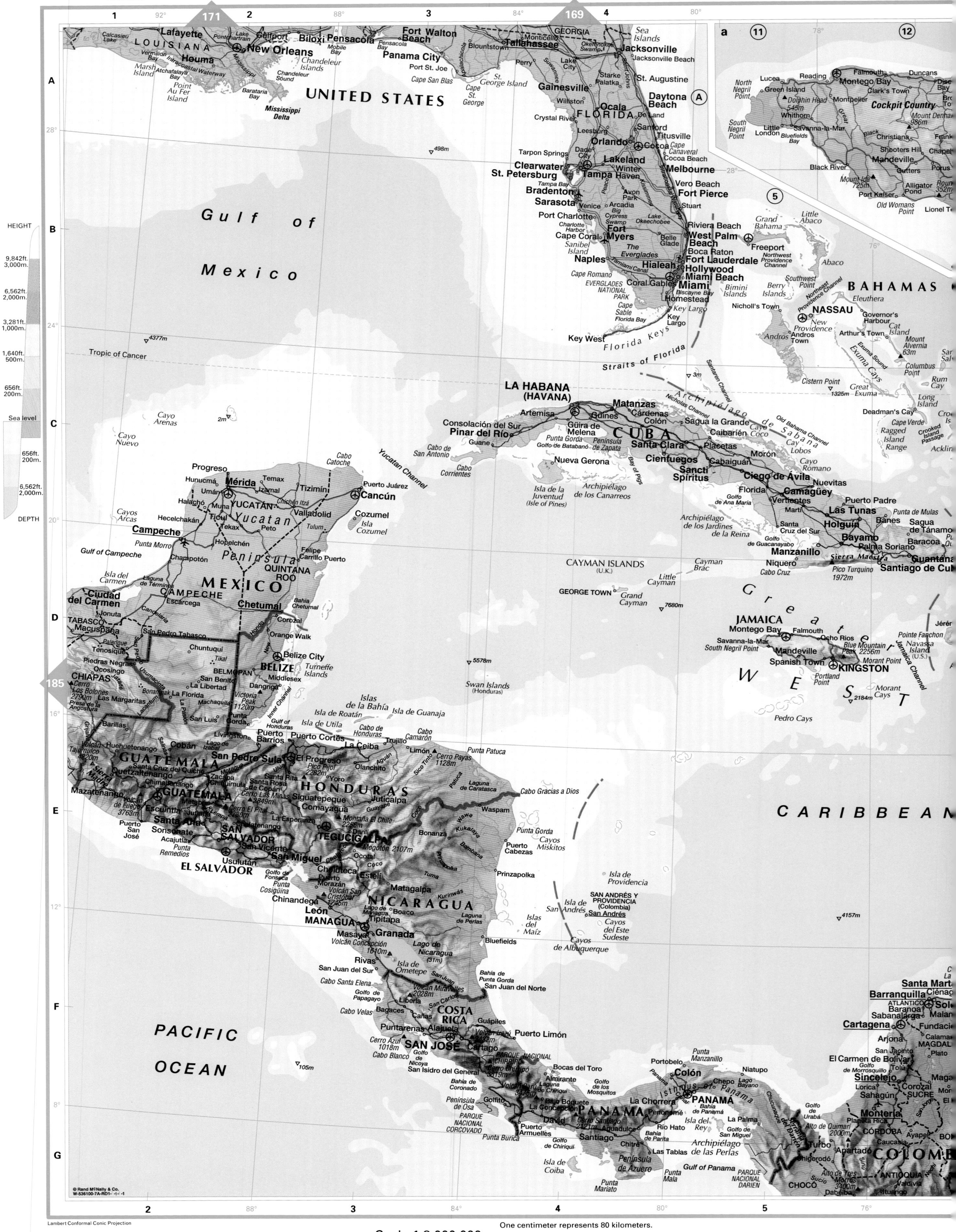

Lambert Conformal Conic Projection

Scale 1:8,000,000

One centimeter represents 80 kilometers.

One inch represents approximately 126 miles.

© Rand McNally & Co.
W-536100-7A-RD1- -1- -1

Linking North and South America, Central America extends from the southern border of Mexico to the northern one of Colombia. It includes seven republics (Guatemala, Belize, Honduras, El Salvador, Nicaragua, Costa Rica, and Panama) and is bisected by the Panama Canal. Among the largest islands of the Caribbean are Cuba, Jamaica, Hispaniola (Haiti and the Dominican Republic), and Puerto Rico.

187

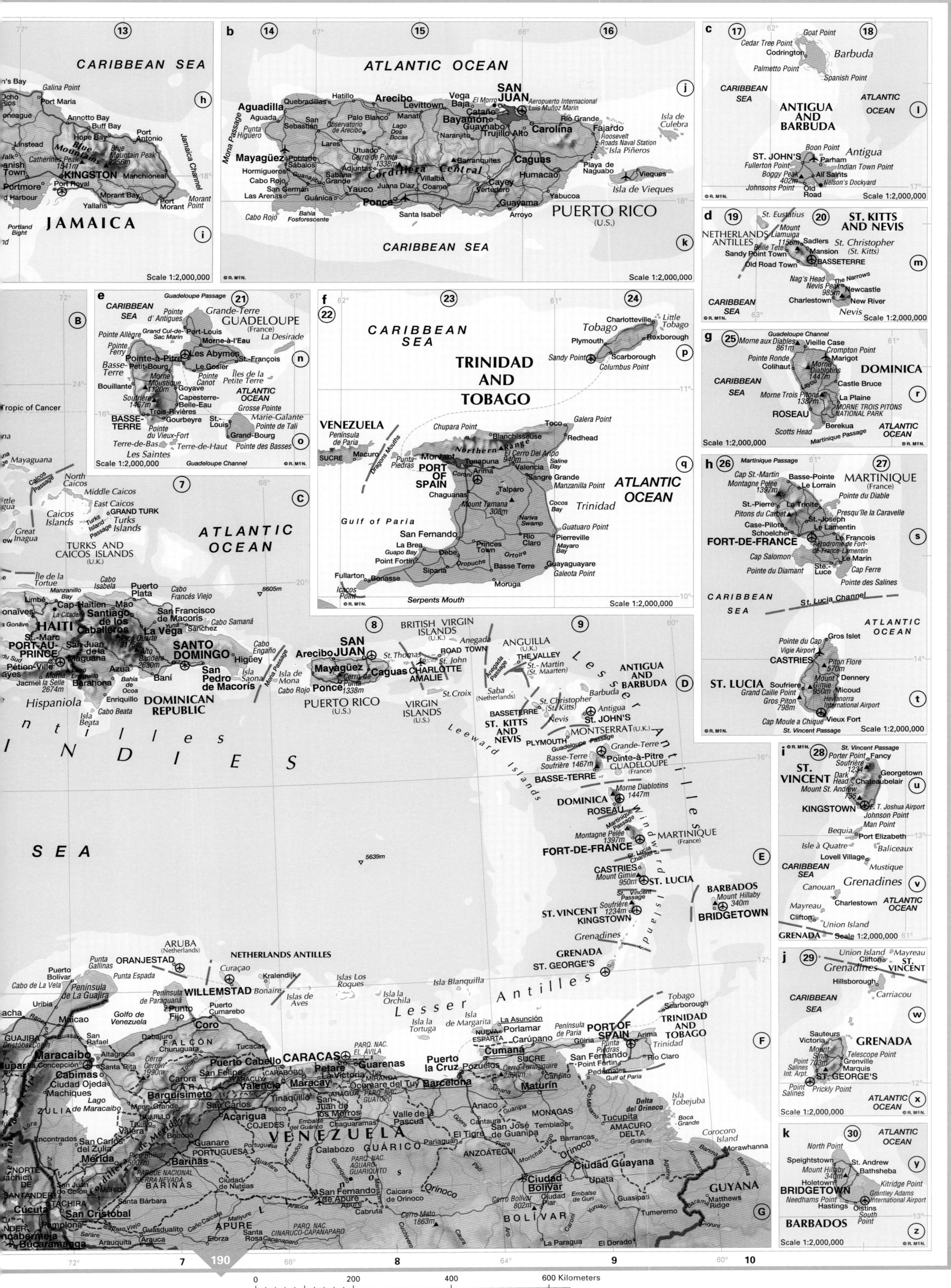

0   200   400   600 Kilometers

0   200   400 Miles

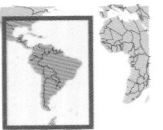

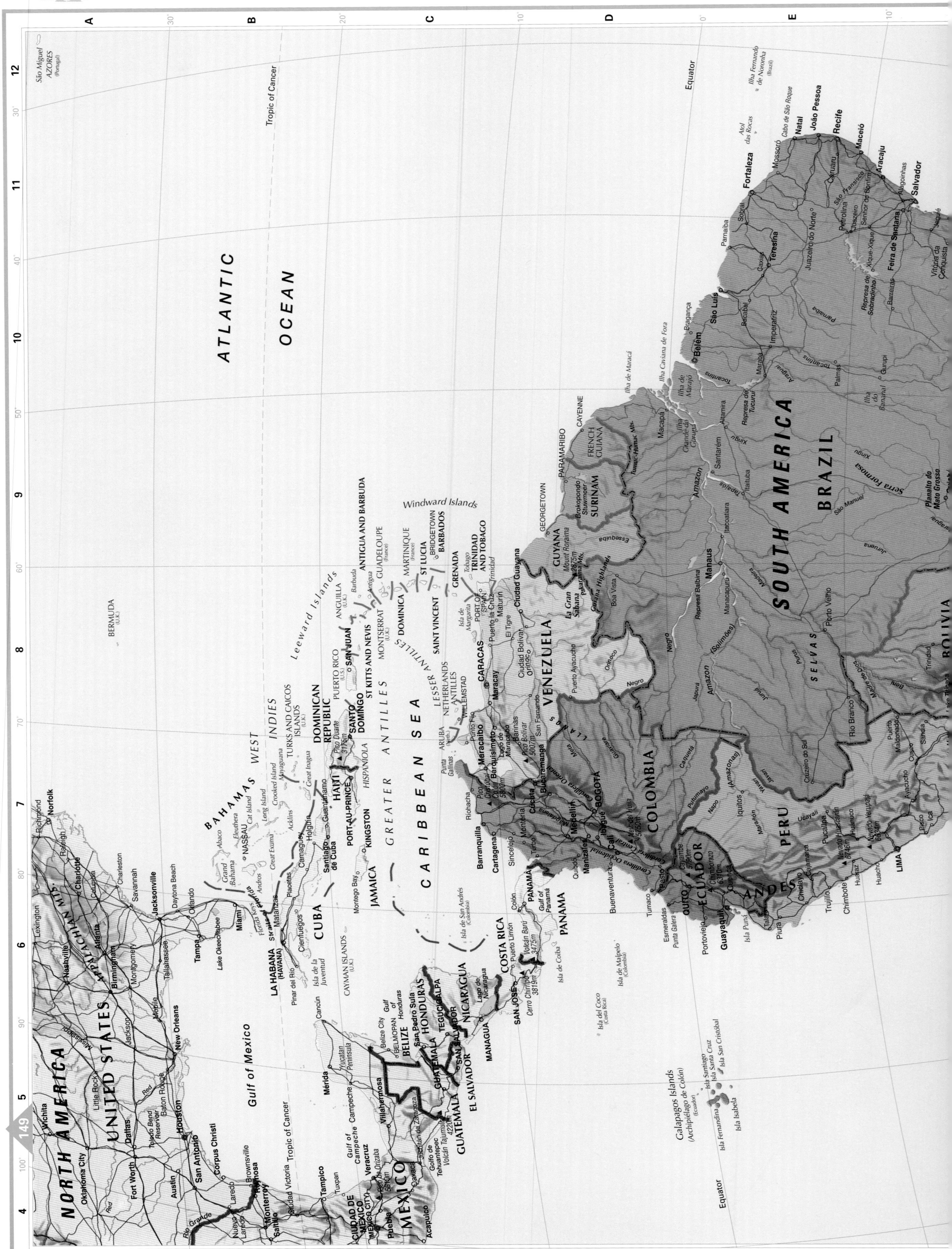

SOUTH AMERICA

Lambert Azimuthal Equal Area Projection

Scale 1:24,000,000

One centimeter represents 240 kilometers.

One inch represents approximately 380 miles.

South America has six regions: the Andes, a series of mountain ranges from Venezuela through Chile; the Guiana and Brazilian Highlands; the Orinoco Basin, a lowland between the Venezuelan Andes and Guiana Highlands; the Amazon Basin, between the Andean foothills and the Atlantic; the Pampas-Chaco plains of Argentina, Paraguay, and Bolivia; and the Patagonian Plateau.

189

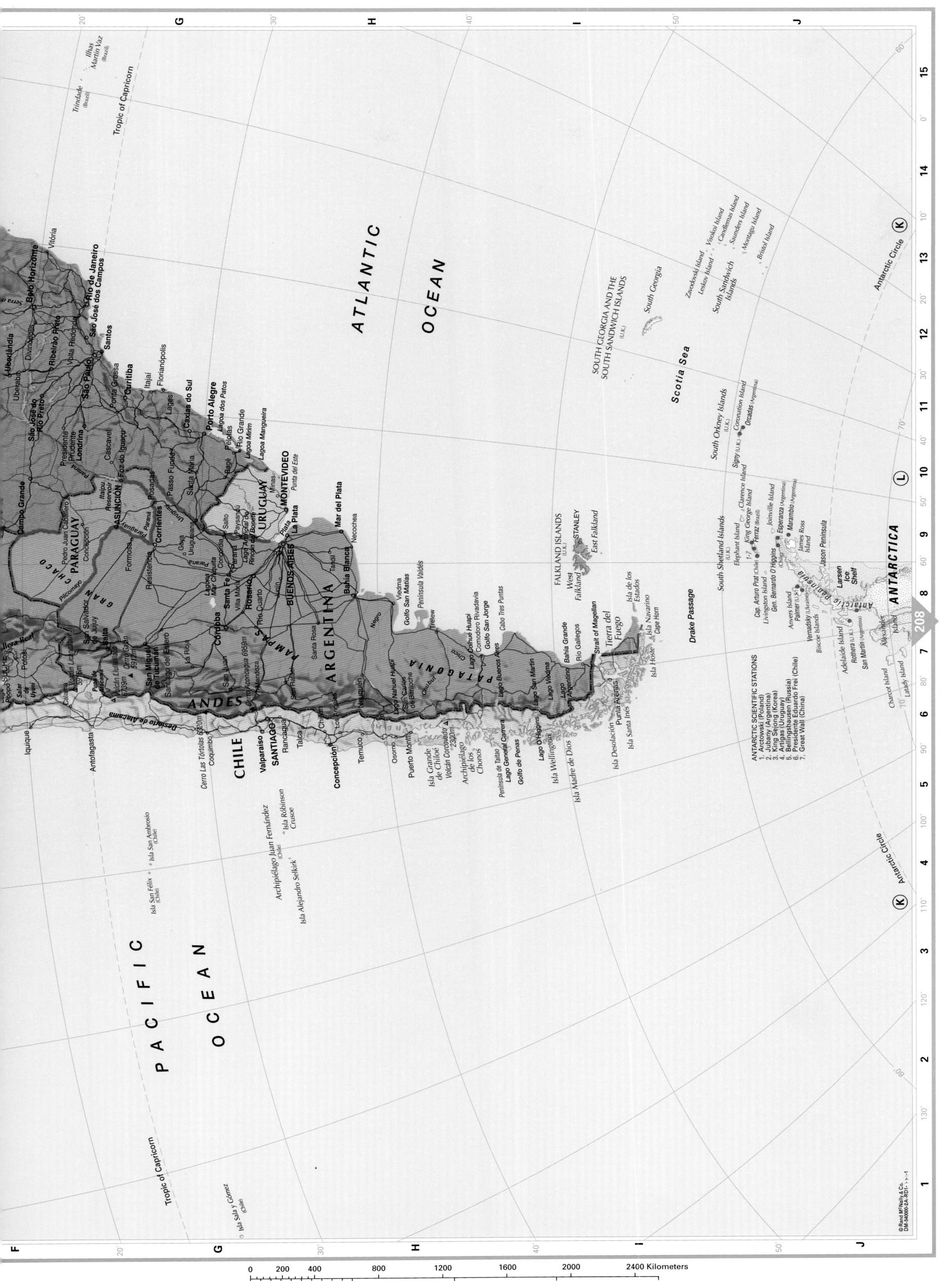

ANTARCTIC SCIENTIFIC STATIONS
1. Arctowski (Poland)
2. Jubany (Argentina)
3. King Sejong (Korea)
4. Artigas (Uruguay)
5. Bellingshausen (Russia)
6. Presidente Eduardo Frei (Chile)
7. Great Wall (China)

0   200   400   800   1200   1600   2000   2400 Kilometers

0   200   400   800   1200   1600 Miles

© Rand McNally & Co.
DM-580000-2A-RD1-↑-↓-1

Scale 1:12,000,000

One centimeter represents 120 kilometers.

One inch represents approximately 190 miles.

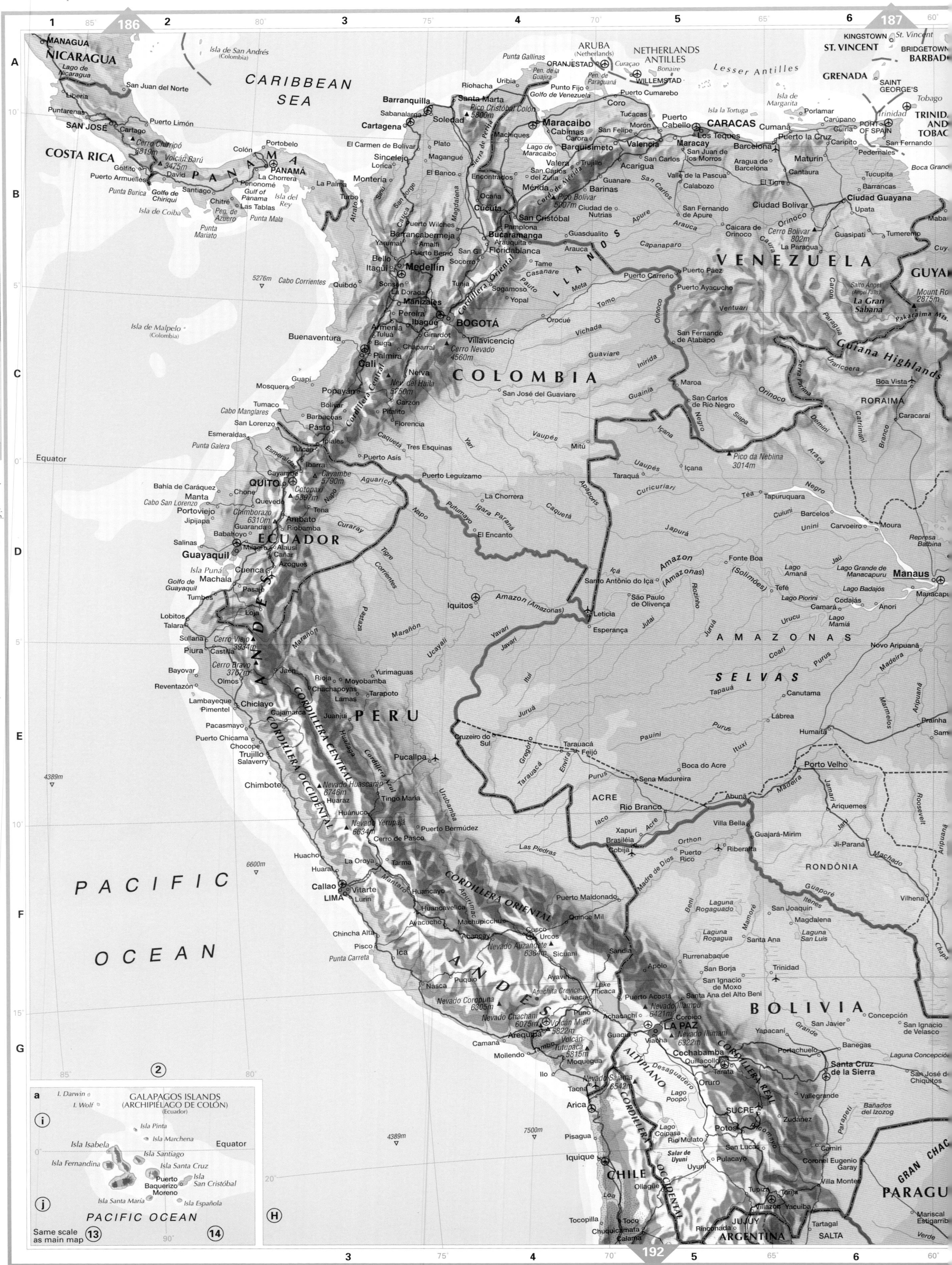

Bipolar Oblique Conic Conformal Projection

Capped with snow, the great bastion of the Andes runs for 4,600 mi. (7,400 km.) from Venezuela to Tierra del Fuego, stretching out in Bolivia to a width of 373 mi. (600 km.). Among the many rivers it gives birth to is the mighty Amazon, which – with its tributaries – drains a vast forest basin the size of Australia. In the Guiana Highlands, immense plateaus of sandstone rise abruptly out of grassland and jungle.

191

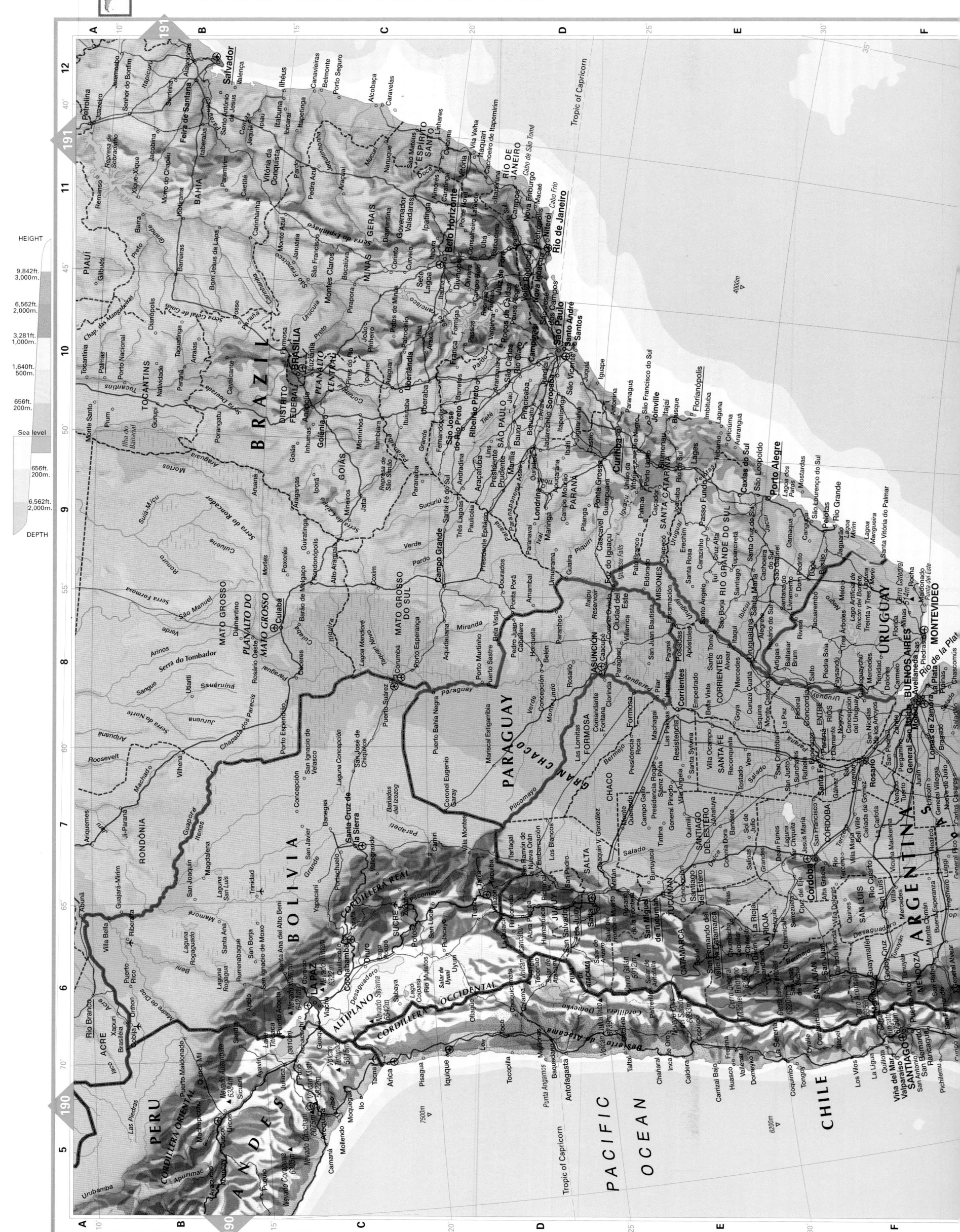

Chile, a long, thin curve defined by the Andes, is the backbone of South America, only 112 mi. (180 km.) wide but as long as the span between New York and Los Angeles. It encompasses lakes, volcanoes, and desert, and at its tip is Cape Horn, the continent's southernmost point. Aconcagua, straddling the Chile-Argentina border, rises nearly 23,000 ft. (7,020 m.), making it the loftiest peak in the Western Hemisphere.

193

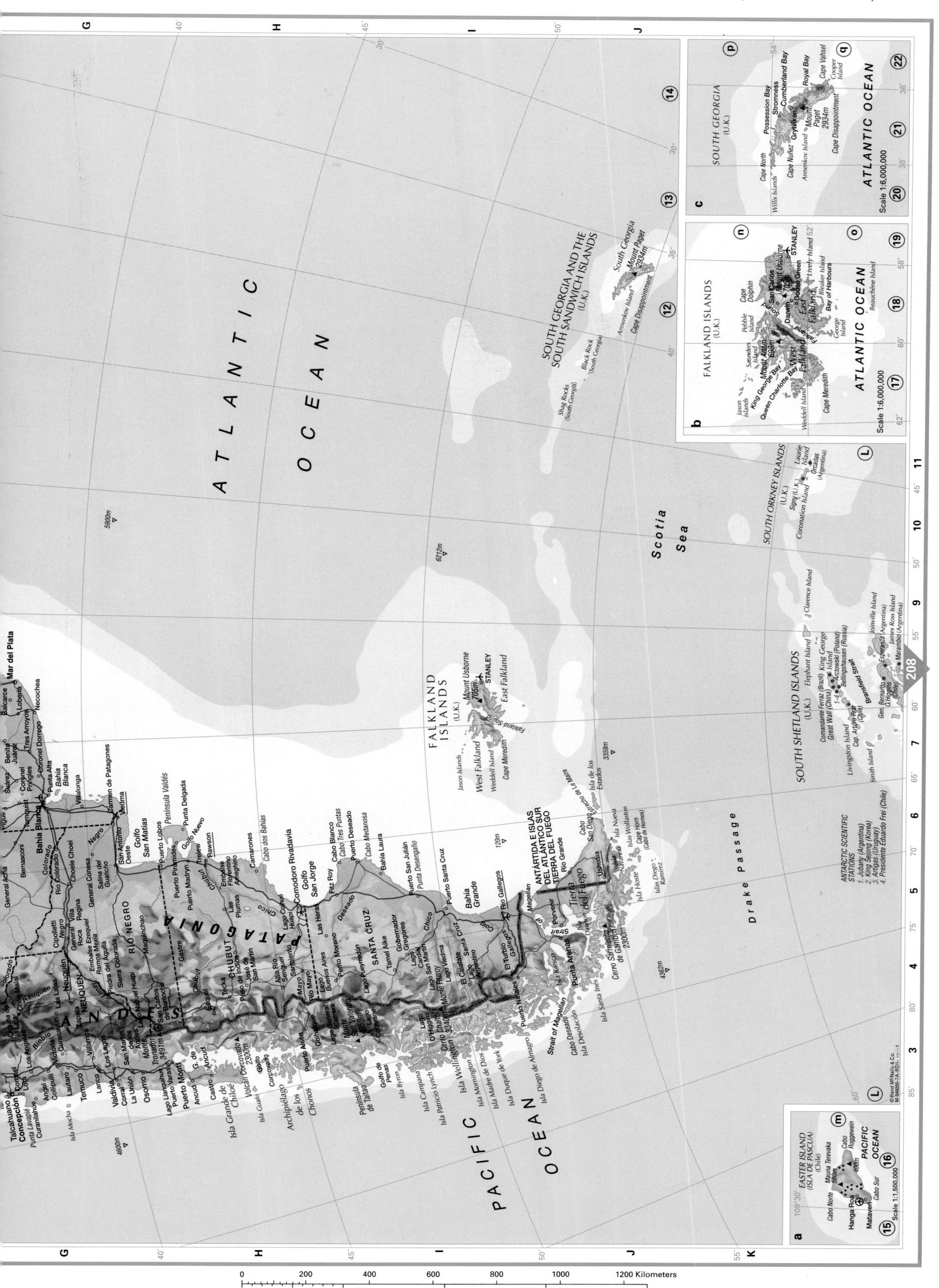

SOUTH GEORGIA (U.K.)

Possession Bay
Stromness
Cumberland Bay
Willis Islands
Cape North
Cape Nuñez
Annenkov Island
Grytviken
"Mount Paget 2934m"
Royal Bay
Cape Vahsel
Cooper Island

ATLANTIC OCEAN

Scale 1:6,000,000

FALKLAND ISLANDS (U.K.)

Jason Islands
Saunders Island
Pebble Island
King George Bay
Mount Adam 698m
Queen Charlotte Bay
Weddell Island
West Falkland
George Island
Cape Meredith
San Carlos
Mount Usborne 705m
Darwin
East Falkland
Goose Green
Bleaker Island
Lively Island
Beauchêne Island
STANLEY
Port Howard
Bay of Harbours
Cape Dolphin

ATLANTIC OCEAN

Scale 1:6,000,000

SOUTH ORKNEY ISLANDS (U.K.)
Spry (U.K.)
Coronation Island
Laurie Island
Orcadas (Argentina)

SOUTH GEORGIA AND THE SOUTH SANDWICH ISLANDS (U.K.)

South Georgia
Mount Paget 2934m
Annenkov Island
Cape Disappointment
Black Rock
Shag Rocks (South Georgia)

ATLANTIC OCEAN

Scotia Sea

5900m

6212m

FALKLAND ISLANDS (U.K.)

Mount Usborne 705m
STANLEY
East Falkland
West Falkland
Jason Islands
Weddell Island
Cape Meredith

SOUTH SHETLAND ISLANDS (U.K.)
Clarence Island
Elephant Island
Comandante Ferraz (Brazil)
Great Wall (China)
Livingston Island
Smith Island
King George Island
Arctowski (Poland)
Bellingshausen (Russia)
Gen. Bernardo O'Higgins (Chile)
Cap. Arturo Prat (Chile)
Esperanza (Argentina)
Joinville Island
James Ross Island
Marambio (Argentina)
Bransfield Strait

Drake Passage

ANTARCTIC SCIENTIFIC STATIONS
1. Jubany (Argentina)
2. King Sejong (Korea)
3. Artigas (Uruguay)
4. Presidente Eduardo Frei (Chile)

3358m

ATLANTIC OCEAN

PACIFIC OCEAN

Mar del Plata
Balcarce
Lobería
Benito Juárez
Necochea
Tres Arroyos
Coronel Dorrego
Punta Alta
Bahía Blanca
Coronel Pringles
Carmen de Patagones
Viedma
Golfo San Matías
Península Valdés
Punta Delgada
San Antonio Oeste
Puerto Lobos
Golfo Nuevo
Rawson
Trelew
Puerto Madryn
Península Valdés
Cabo dos Bahías
Camarones
RIO NEGRO
Río Negro
Colorado
Río Colorado
Choele Choel
Salina del Gualicho
Sierra Colorada
General Conesa
Puerto Pirámides
Florentino Ameghino
Gastre
CHUBUT
Chubut
Tecka
Gan Gan
PATAGONIA
Las Plumas
Comodoro Rivadavia
Golfo San Jorge
Cabo Blanco
Puerto Deseado
Cabo Tres Puntas
Cabo Blanco
Fitz Roy
Las Heras
Deseado
Puerto Deseado
Cabo Medanosa
SANTA CRUZ
Bahía Laura
Puerto San Julián
Punta Desengaño
Puerto Santa Cruz
Bahía Grande
Río Gallegos
ANDES
NEUQUÉN
Zapala
Río Mayo
Perito Moreno
Alto Río Senguer
José de San Martín
Gobernador Gregores
Tres Lagos
Lago Cardiel
Lago San Martín
Lago Viedma
El Calafate
Lago Argentino
Cerro Chaltén 3375m
Puerto Coig
Lago Buenos Aires
Lago Pueyrredón
Tamel Aike
Esquel
Lago Fontana
Lago General Carrera
Chico
Chico
Chico
Coig
Puerto Natales
Cerro Payne 3375m
ANTARTIDA E ISLAS DEL ATLANTICO SUR
TIERRA DEL FUEGO
Cabo San Diego
Isla de los Estados
Río Grande
Tierra del Fuego
Strait of Magellan
Estrecho de le Maire
Punta Arenas
Porvenir
El Turbio
Cabo San Pablo
Puerto Williams
Ushuaia
Isla Nueva
Islas Wollaston
Cabo de Hornos (Cape Horn)
Isla Navarino
Isla Hoste
Isla Diego Ramírez
Cerro Sarmiento de Gamboa 2300m
120m
4362m

Temuco
Valdivia
Corral
La Unión
Osorno
Puerto Montt
Castro
Ancud
Isla Grande de Chiloé
Golfo de Ancud
Golfo de Corcovado
Volcán Corcovado 2300m
Puerto Aisén
Coihaique
Puerto Chacabuco
Archipiélago de los Chonos
Península de Taitao
Golfo de Penas
Isla Wellington
Isla Mornington
Isla Campana
Isla Patricio Lynch
Isla Byron
Isla Madre de Dios
Isla Duque de York
Isla Diego de Almagro
Puerto Edén
Isla Desolación
Estrecho de Magallanes
Isla Santa Inés
Cabo Froward
Isla Santa Inés
Lago Llanquihue
Puerto Varas
San Carlos de Bariloche
Lanco
Villarrica
Angol
Collipulli
Los Ángeles
Concepción
Talcahuano
Curanilahue
Lota
Coronel
Lebu
Punta Lavapié
Isla Mocha
Isla Santa María
Los Lagos
Monte Tronador 3491m

PACIFIC OCEAN

EASTER ISLAND (ISLA DE PASCUA) (Chile)
109°30'
Cabo Norte
Maunga Terevaka 600m
Cabo Roggeween
Mauna Terevaka
Hanga Roa
Cabo Sur
Mataveri

Scale 1:1,500,000

© Rand McNally & Co.
M-M4500.7A-RD-1-1-1

194

Southeast Brazil

The largest and most industrialized country in
South America, Brazil is home to the world's
largest tropical rain forest – one-third its area.

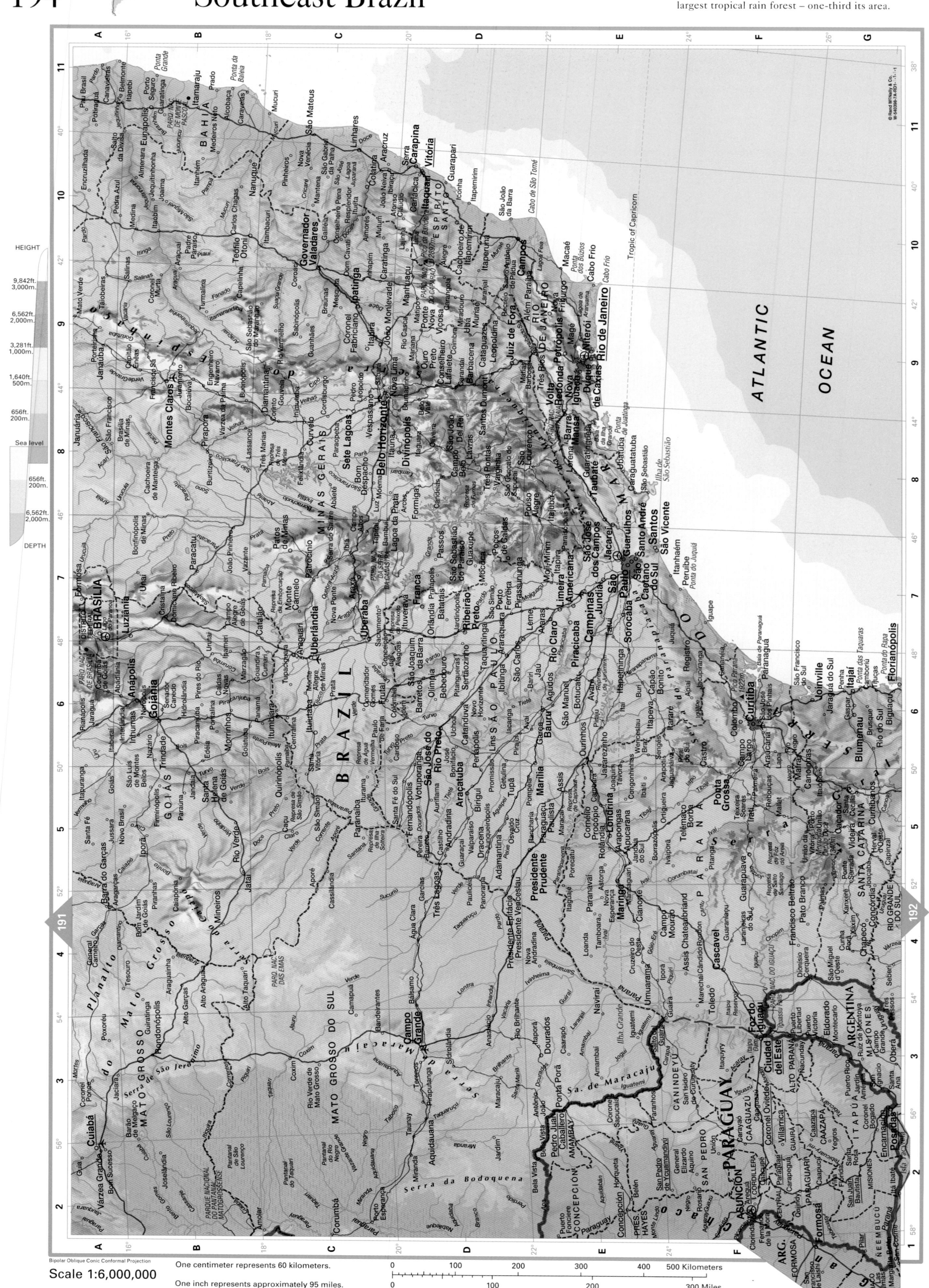

HEIGHT

9,842ft.
3,000m.

6,562ft.
2,000m.

3,281ft.
1,000m.

1,640ft.
500m.

656ft.
200m.

Sea level

656ft.
200m.

6,562ft.
2,000m.

DEPTH

Bipolar Oblique Conic Conformal Projection

Scale 1:6,000,000

One centimeter represents 60 kilometers.

One inch represents approximately 95 miles.

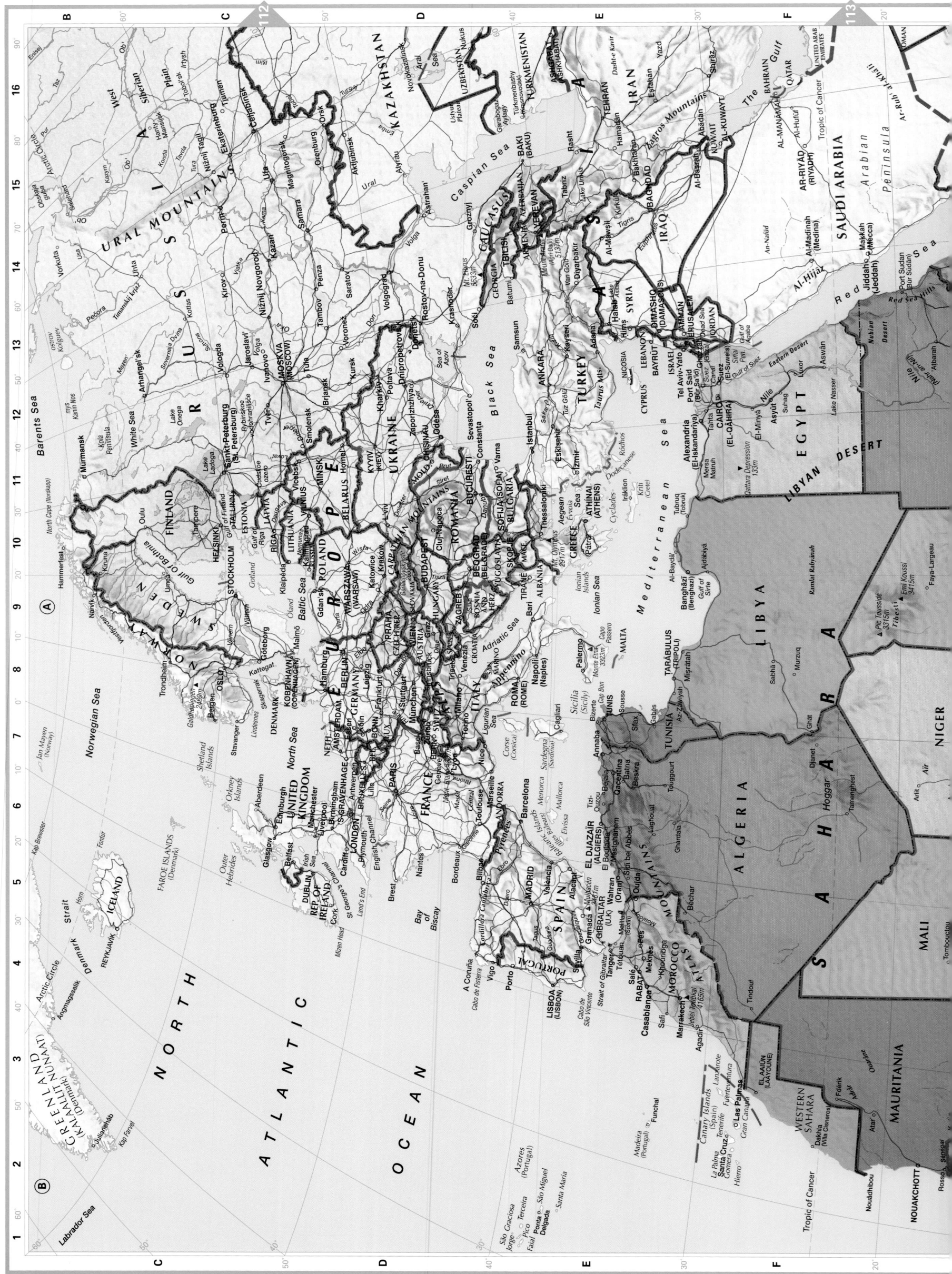

Lambert Azimuthal Equal Area Projection

Scale 1:24,000,000

One centimeter represents 240 kilometers.

One inch represents approximately 380 miles.

From the equator Africa's awesome bulk extends north and south through rain forests, tropical grasslands, and deserts. Some of its nations have old roots – indeed, the landmass is part of the Old World – but many trace their origins to European colonies gained in the 19th-century scramble for a chunk of the "Dark Continent." Hence, their borders are the arbitrary lines of mapmakers, with scant regard to nature.

197

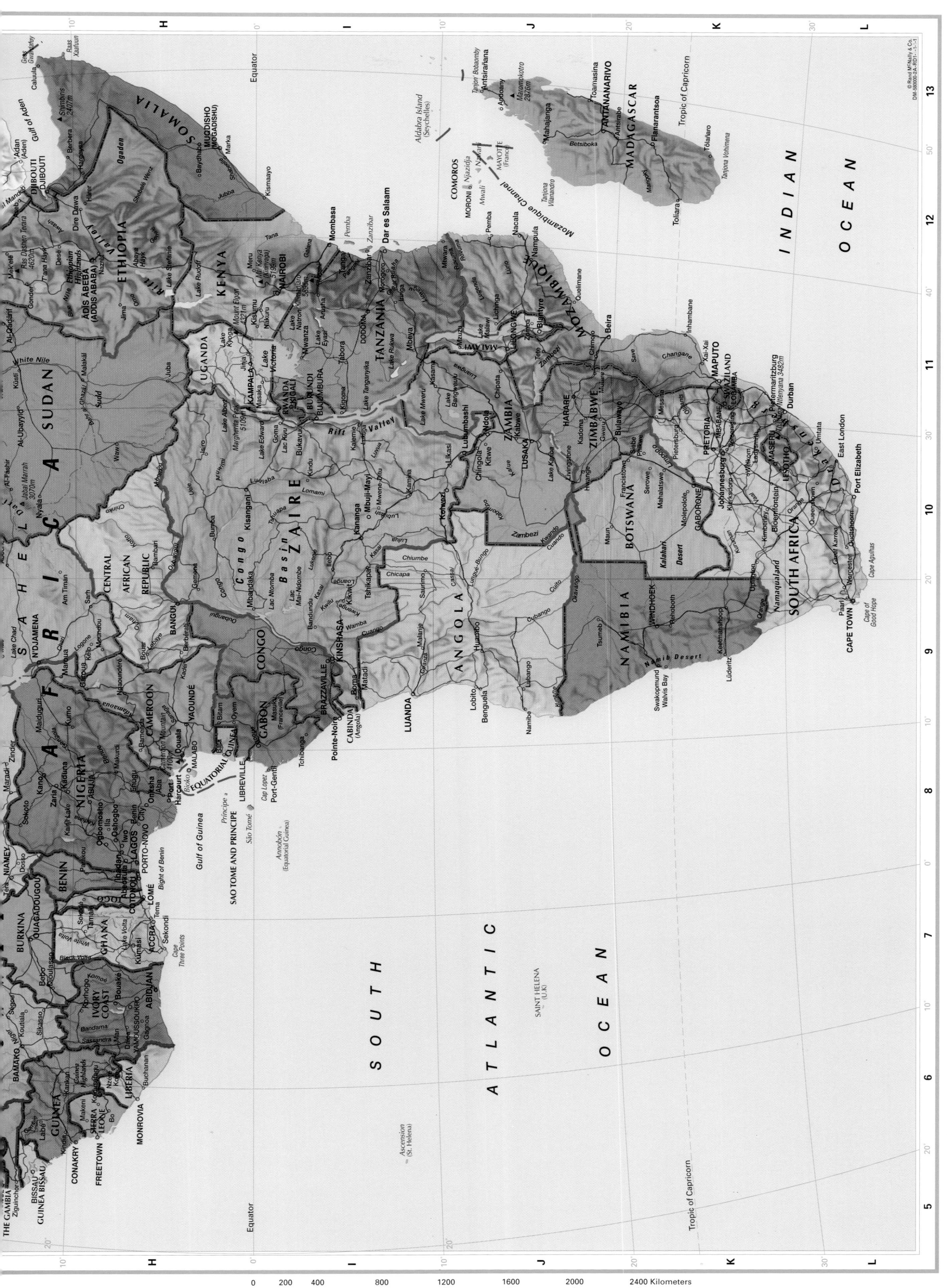

0   200   400   800   1200   1600   2000   2400 Kilometers

0   200   400   800   1200   1600 Miles

Northwest Africa

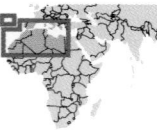

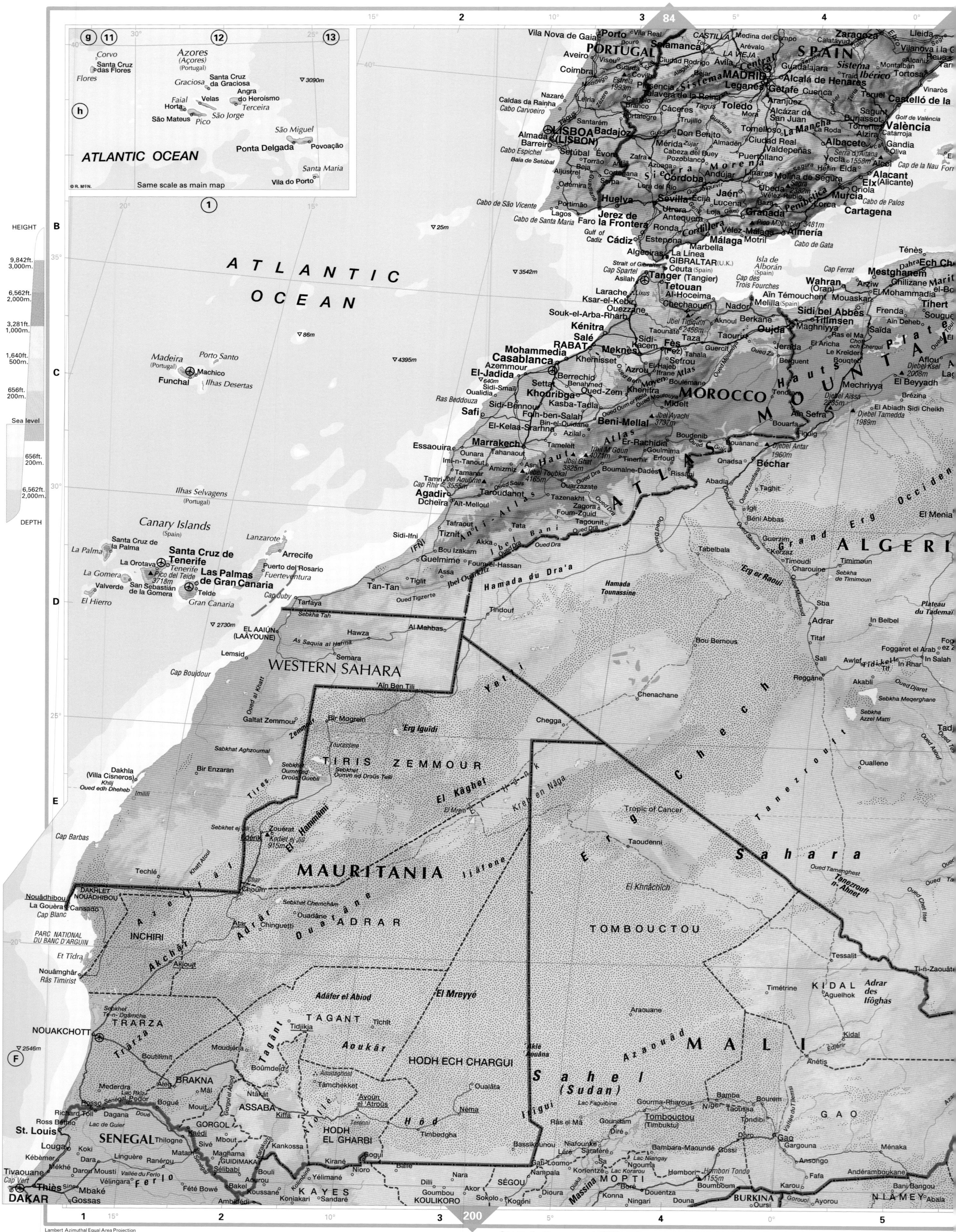

Lambert Azimuthal Equal Area Projection

Scale 1:9,000,000

One centimeter represents 90 kilometers.

One inch represents approximately 142 miles.

Some 10,000 years ago the region that is now the Sahara Desert began to dry out, cutting off North Africa's Mediterranean Coast from the rest of the continent. This coastal climate is not unlike that of southern Europe. Today, the Sahara – covering some 3½ million sq. mi. (about 9 million sq. km.) – is the world's largest desert. The Atlas Mountains capture much-needed moisture for the valleys of Algeria and Tunisia.

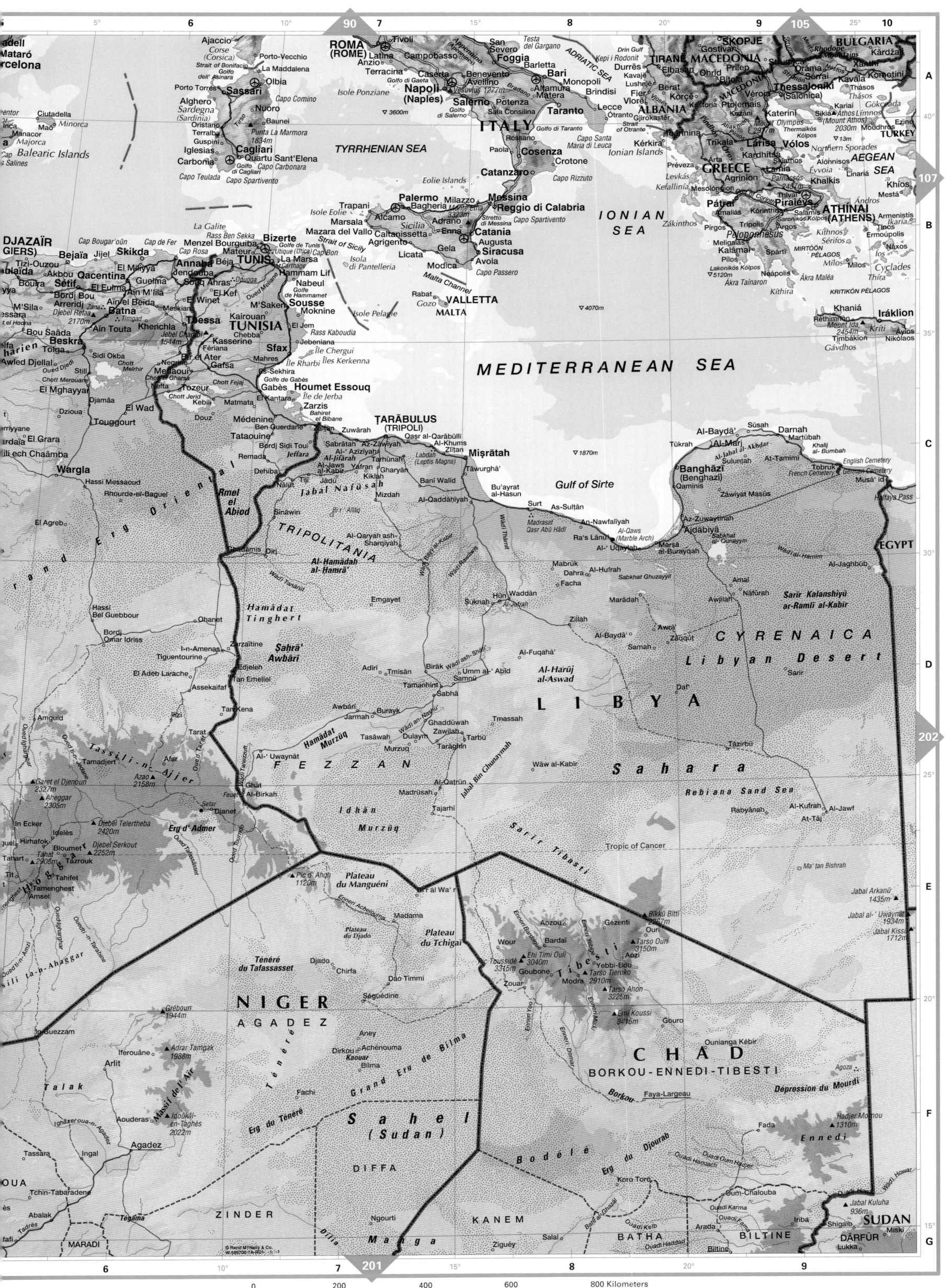

In an area about the size of the U.S., the West African mosaic hosts a greater range of cultural diversity than any comparable region on earth.

Scale 1:9,000,000

One centimeter represents 90 kilometers.

One inch represents approximately 142 miles.

Lambert Azimuthal Equal Area Projection

Tropic of Cancer

LIBYA

Sahara

Idhân Murzûq
Sarīr Tibesti

Plateau du Manguéni
Pic d'Ahon 1120m
Bir al Wa'ar
Madama

Plateau du Djado

Ténéré du Tafassasset
Djado
Chirfa
Dao Timmi

Tibesti
Ehi Timi Ouli 3040m
Bardaï
Tarso Ouri 3150m
Oun
Gézenti
Bikkû Bittî 2267m

Aozou
Goubone
Modra Tarso 2910m
Yebbi-Bou
Arkan-Ahon 3120m
Tarso Ahon 3225m
Émi Koussi 3415m
Gouro

BORKOU-ENNEDI-TIBESTI

Aney
Achénouma
Dirkou
Bilma

Fachi

Grand Erg de Bilma

Zouar
Tieroko 2910m

Ounianga Kébir

Dépression du Mourdi

AGADEZ

Ténéré du Talassasset

Gréboun 1944m

Adrar Tamgak 1988m
Iférouâne
Arlit

Massif de l'Aïr
Idoûkâl-en-Taghès 2022m

Aouderas

Agadez

NIGER

Sahel (Sudan)

Erg du Ténéré

Borkou
Faya-Largeau

Ennedi
Fada
Hadjer Mornou 1310m

Bodélé
Erg du Djourab

Koro Toro

CHAD

Ouadi Howa
Jabal Kuluha 936m
Betbetti

SUDAN

BILTINE

Biltine
Nieré
Guéréda
Iriba
Shigalb
Miski
Shibami

Kukâwa
Salal
Arada

KANEM

Mao
Bol
LAC

Lake Chad (Lac Tchad)

Massakory

BATHA

Ati
Oum-Hadjer
Abéché

OUADDAÏ

Am Dam
Adré
Goz Beïda

Al-Junaynah
DĀRFŪR

N'DJAMENA

CHARI-BAGUIRMI

Massenya

Bokoro

Mongo
Massif de Guéra 1613m

GUÉRA

Mongororo

Abou-Deïa

Mangueigne

MARADI

Maradi
Katsina

ZINDER

Zinder

Gouré
Diffa
DIFFA

Nguigmi
Ngourti

Manga

Maïduguri

Kano

Zaria
Kaduna

NIGERIA

ABUJA

Zuma Hill 771m

Jos

Bauchi

Gombe

Yola

Maroua

EXTRÊME NORD

Mora

Garoua
NORD

Moundou

LOGONE OCCIDENTAL

LOGONE ORIENTAL

Sarh
MOYEN-CHARI

SALAMAT

Am Timan

Melfi

TANDJILÉ

Kélo

Doba

MAYO KEBBI

Ngaoundéré

ADAMAOUA

Tchabal Mbabo 2490m
Tchabal Gangdaba 2419m

OUHAM

OUHAM-PENDE

Bozoum

NANA-MAMBÉRÉ

Bouar

CENTRAL AFRICAN REPUBLIC

Bambari

HAUTE-KOTTO

BAMINGUI-BANGORAN

VAKAGA

NORD-OUEST

Bamenda
Bafoussam
OUEST

Bafang

CAMEROON

CENTRE

EST

Bertoua

SUD-OUEST

Kumba
Buéa
Cameroon Mountain 4100m
Douala
LITTORAL

YAOUNDÉ

Mbalmayo

SUD

Sangmélima

Ebolowa

BANGUI

LOBAYE

OMBELLA-MPOKO

SANGHA-MBAÉRÉ

Nola

MBOMOU

Bangassou

MAMBÉRÉ-KADÉÏ

Berbérati

EQUATORIAL GUINEA

MALABO

Bata
RÍO MUNI

Pico de Santa Isabel 3008m
Bioko (Fernando Póo)

Bight of Biafra

SAO TOME AND PRINCIPE

Príncipe
Santo António

Pico de São Tomé 2024m
SÃO TOMÉ

Annobón (Pagalu)

LIKOUALA

Impfondo

HAUT-ZAIRE

Bumba
Lisala
Aketi

ZAIRE

ÉQUATEUR

Mbandaka

SANGHA

Ouesso

CUVETTE

Owando

CONGO

GABON

LIBREVILLE

ESTUAIRE

MOYEN-OGOOUÉ

Lambaréné

Mont Iboundji 972m
HAUT-OGOOUÉ

Franceville

NGOUNIÉ

OGOOUÉ-LOLO

OGOOUÉ-IVINDO

Makokou

OGOOUÉ-MARITIME

Port-Gentil

NYANGA

PLATEAUX

BANDUNDU

KASAI-OCCIDENTAL

KASAI-ORIENTAL

POOL

NIARI
LÉKOUMOU

BOUENZA
KOUILOU

Pointe-Noire

BRAZZAVILLE

KINSHASA (LEOPOLDVILLE)

BAS-ZAIRE

ANGOLA
CABINDA
Cabinda

Boma
Matadi

Muanda
Ponta do Padrão

0   200   400   600 Kilometers

0   200   400 Miles

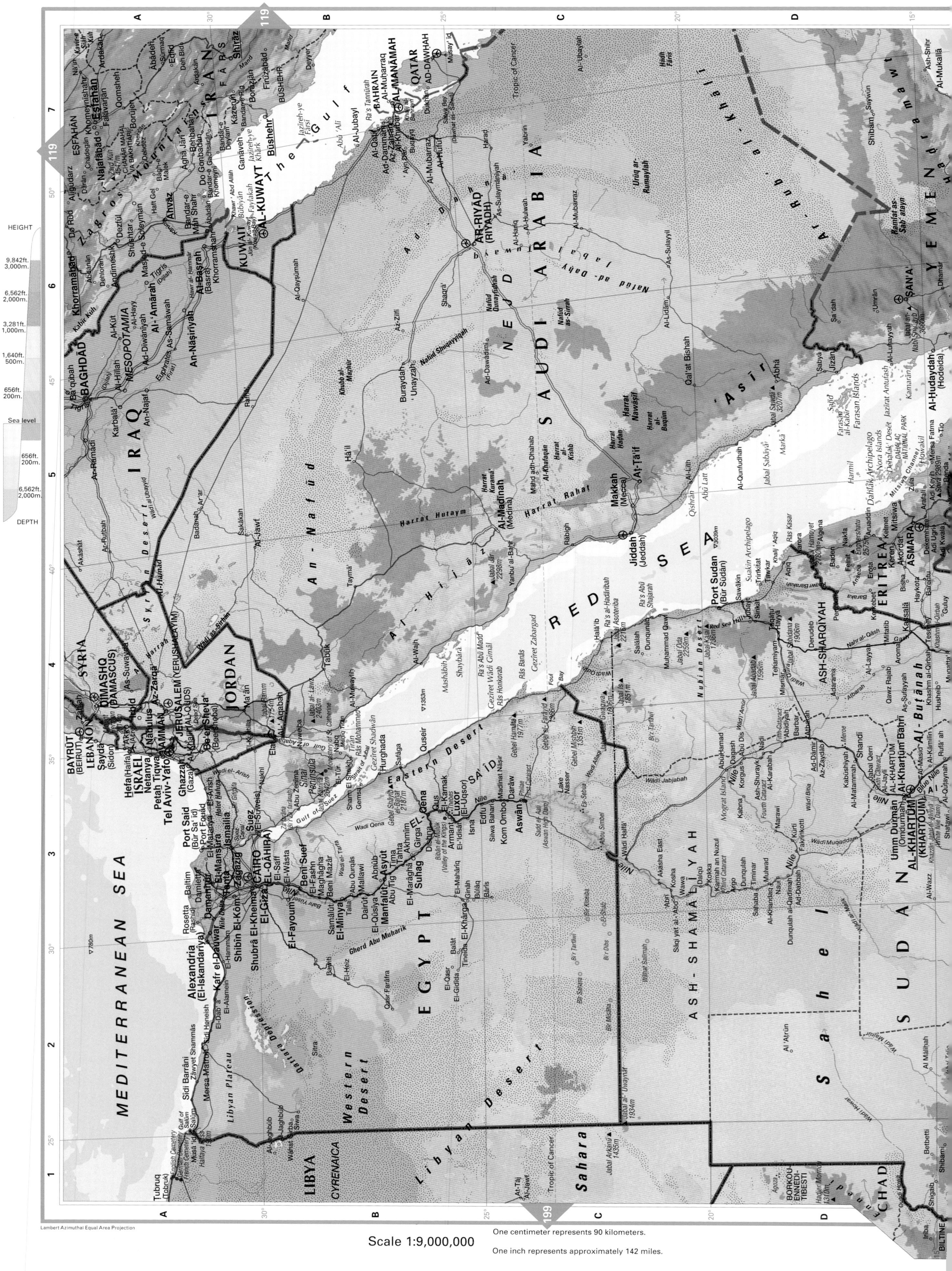

HEIGHT

9,842ft.
3,000m.

6,562ft.
2,000m.

3,281ft.
1,000m.

1,640ft.
500m.

656ft.
200m.

Sea level

656ft.
200m.

6,562ft.
2,000m.

DEPTH

Lambert Azimuthal Equal Area Projection

Scale 1:9,000,000

One centimeter represents 90 kilometers.

One inch represents approximately 142 miles.

For 6,000 years the source of life in Egypt (especially in the long, narrow oasis of its valley between the Sudan border and Cairo) has been the Nile, the world's longest river. Today, 96 percent of Egyptians live near the river – creating one of the world's highest population densities.

INDIAN OCEAN

SOMALIA

ETHIOPIA

KENYA

TANZANIA

UGANDA

ZAIRE

CENTRAL AFRICAN REPUBLIC

RWANDA

BURUNDI

DJIBOUTI

Gulf of Aden

DARFUR

KURDUFAN

SUDAN

MUQDISHO (MOGADISHU)

ADIS ABEBA

NAIROBI

KAMPALA

KIGALI

BUJUMBURA

DODOMA

Mombasa

Tanga

Lake Victoria

RIFT VALLEY

Ogaden

| 0 | 200 | 400 | 600 | 800 Kilometers |

| 0 | 200 | 400 | 600 Miles |

HEIGHT

9,842ft.
3,000m.

6,562ft.
2,000m.

3,281ft.
1,000m.

1,640ft.
500m.

656ft.
200m.

Sea level

656ft.
200m.

6,562ft.
2,000m.

DEPTH

Lambert Azimuthal Equal Area Projection

Scale 1:9,000,000

One centimeter represents 90 kilometers.

One inch represents approximately 142 miles.

INDIAN OCEAN

Tropic of Capricorn

MADAGASCAR

ANTANANARIVO

MAHAJANGA

TOAMASINA

TOLIARA

FIANARANTSOA

ANTSIRANANA

Mozambique Channel

MOZAMBIQUE

Nampula

ZAMBEZIA

Quelimane

Beira

SOFALA

MANICA

TETE

INHAMBANE

GAZA

MAPUTO

ZIMBABWE

HARARE (SALISBURY)

Bulawayo

MASHONALAND

MATABELELAND

MANICALAND

MASVINGO

MIDLANDS

ZAMBIA

LUSAKA

SOUTHERN

CENTRAL

WESTERN

NORTH WESTERN

BLANTYRE

ZOMBA

CAPRIVI STRIP

BOTSWANA

GABORONE

GHANZI

NGAMILAND

CENTRAL

KGALAGADI

KWENENG

SOUTHERN

Okavango Delta

Maun

Kalahari Desert

NAMIBIA

WINDHOEK

ERONGO

KHOMAS

HARDAP

KARAS

KUNENE

OSHIKOTO

OTJOZONDJUPA

OMAHEKE

KAVANGO

OHANGWENA

OMUSATI

OSHANA

Walvis Bay

Etosha Pan

Skeleton Coast

Namib Desert

SOUTH AFRICA

PRETORIA

Johannesburg

Soweto

GAUTENG

MPUMALANGA

LIMPOPO

NORTH-WEST

FREE STATE

Bloemfontein

NORTHERN CAPE

WESTERN CAPE

EASTERN CAPE

KWAZULU-NATAL

Durban

Pietermaritzburg

East London (Oos-Londen)

Port Elizabeth

CAPE TOWN (KAAPSTAD)

Cape of Good Hope

Cape Agulhas

Kimberley

Welkom

Newcastle

SWAZILAND

MBABANE

LESOTHO

MASERU

CUNENE

CUANDO CUBANGO

NAMIBE

ANGOLA

Tropic of Capricorn

ATLANTIC OCEAN

INDIAN OCEAN

Wild Coast

Victoria Falls

Livingstone

| 0 | 200 | 400 | 600 | 800 Kilometers |
| 0 | 200 | 400 | 600 Miles |

© Rand McNally & Co.

HEIGHT

9,842ft.
3,000m.

6,562ft.
2,000m.

3,281ft.
1,000m.

1,640ft.
500m.

656ft.
200m.

Sea level

656ft.
200m.

6,562ft.
2,000m.

DEPTH

a Ascension
(St. Helena)
M-584101-7A-RD1- -:-1--1
©RMN.

English Bay ★ North Point
Pyramid Point   East Crater ▲ 228m   Northeast Point
GEORGETOWN   Two Boats   Boatswain Bird Island
ⓘ Cross Hill   Village
263m   Green   White Hill
South West   Mountain   522m   Whale
Bay   850m   Point
Portland   Wideawake
Point   ⊕ Airfield   ★ ★ White Bluff
South Point   ★ ★   ATLANTIC
OCEAN
Scale 1:500,000 ⑫   14°20' ⑬

Ⓖ

b St. Helena
(U.K.)   Sugarloaf Point
JAMESTOWN   Barn Long Point
ⓙ   Longwood
Cathedral   Mount Actæon   Gill Point
820m
George Island
Egg Island   White Point   16°
694m
South   High Peak   ATLANTIC
West   798m
Point   OCEAN
Ⓚ Speery Island   Castle Rock Point
Manati Bay   Sandy Bay Point
Scale 1:500,000 ⑭   5°40' ⑮   Ⓗ

Lambert Azimuthal Equal Area Projection

© Rand McNally & Co.
W-584700-7A-RD1- -:-1--1

Scale 1:4,500,000

One centimeter represents 45 kilometers.

One inch represents approximately 71 miles.

NAMIBIA

BOTSWANA

SOUTH AFRICA

WINDHOEK

CAPE TOWN (KAAPSTAD)

ATLANTIC OCEAN

WESTERN CAPE

NORTHERN CAPE

KALAHARI

GHANZI

NAMIB DESERT

South Africa's central plateau, or veld, is bordered to the south and east by the Drakensberg Mountains. Though large sections remain poor, this grassland region is the richest on the continent in terms of natural resources. Its bounty includes gold, diamonds, and other prized minerals; teeming wildlife; white-sand beaches lapped by the waves of two oceans; and several species of flowers found nowhere else on earth.

207

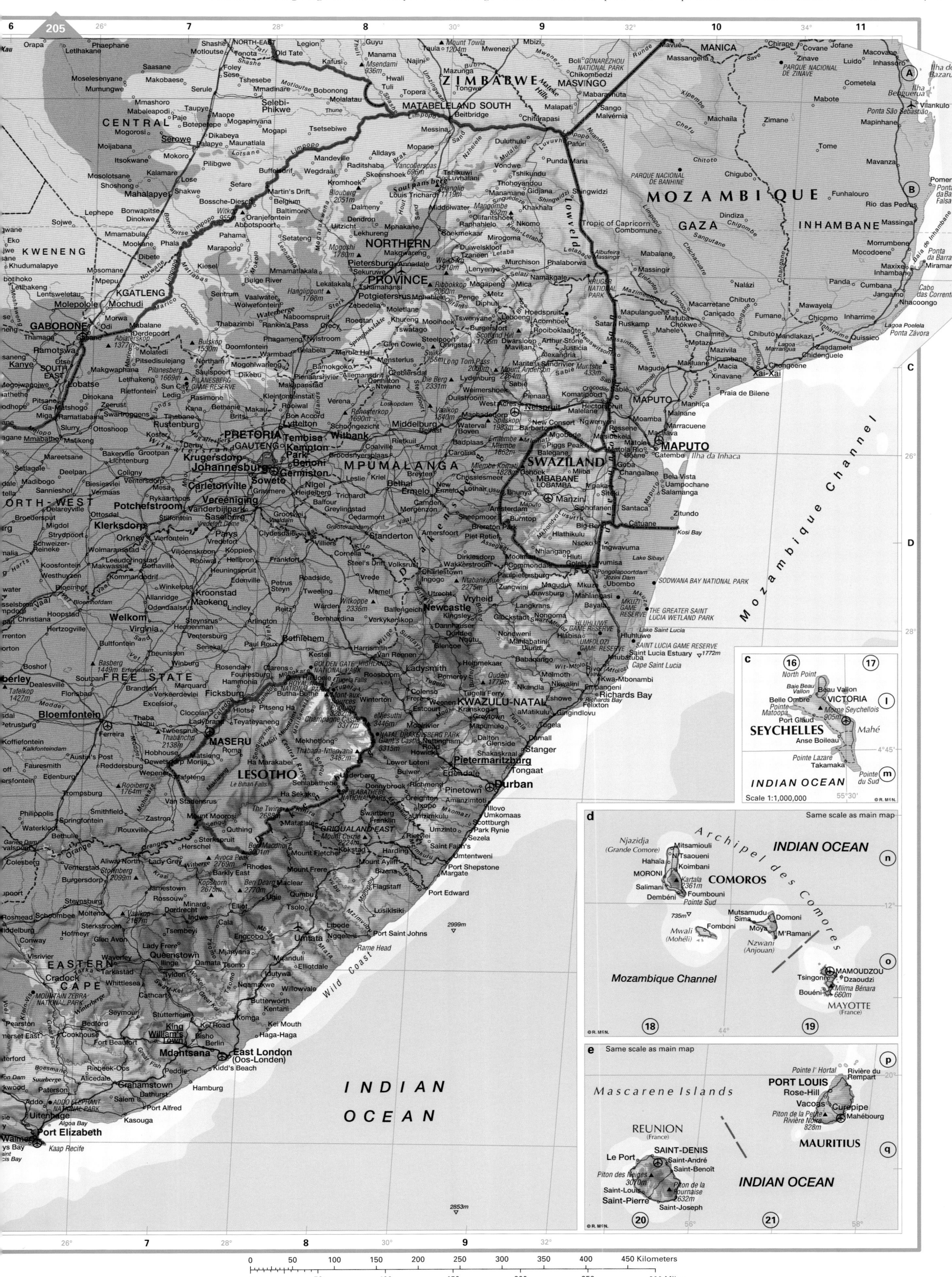

ANTARCTICA

Nearly covered by an ice sheet more than one mile thick, Antarctica contains 90 percent of the world's ice and 70 percent of its fresh water.

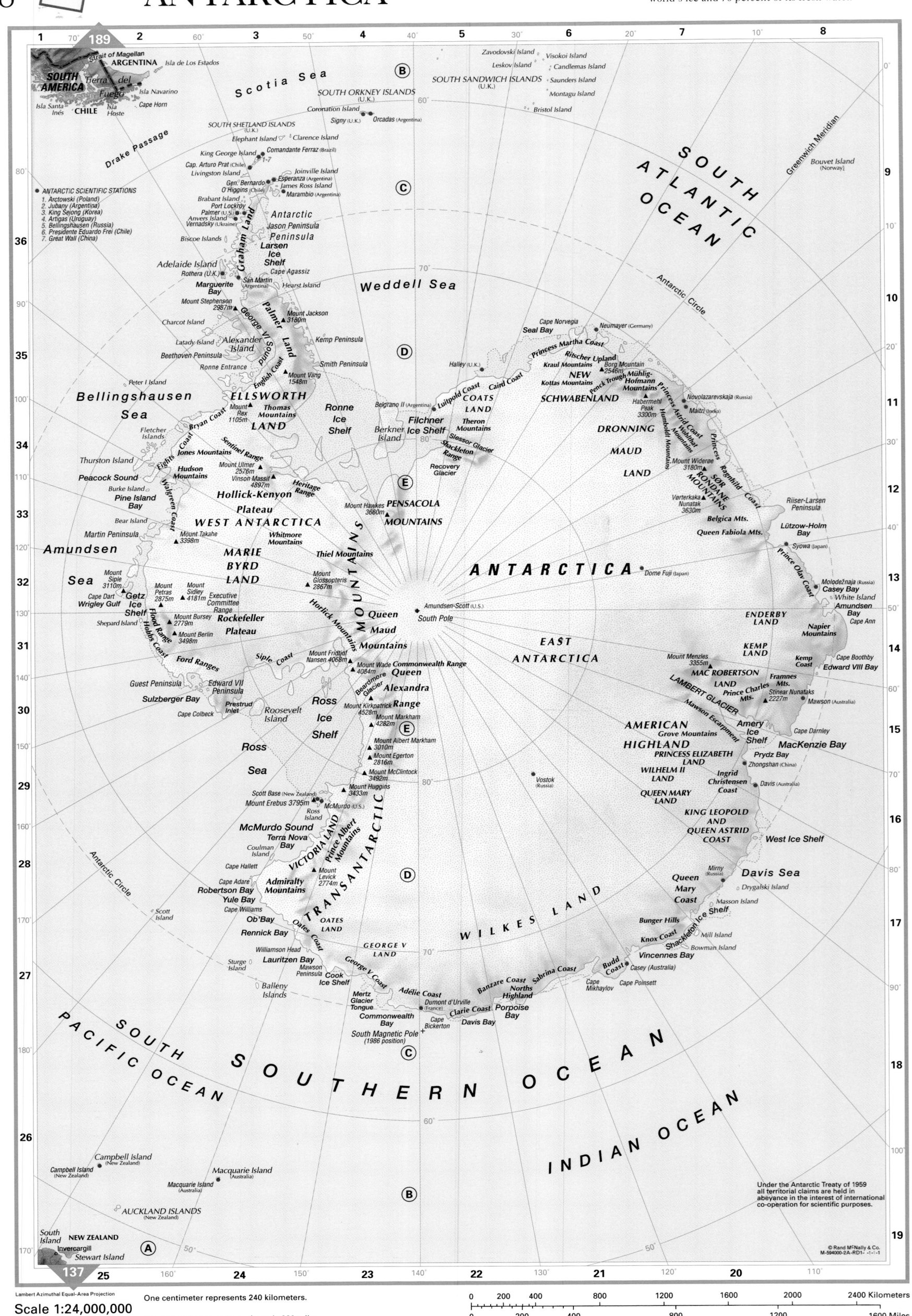

Lambert Azimuthal Equal-Area Projection

Scale 1:24,000,000

One centimeter represents 240 kilometers.

One inch represents approximately 380 miles.

Under the Antarctic Treaty of 1959 all territorial claims are held in abeyance in the interest of international co-operation for scientific purposes.

© Rand McNally & Co.
M-594000-2A-RD1-·|-·|-·1

| 0 | 200 | 400 | 800 | 1200 | 1600 | 2000 | 2400 Kilometers |
| 0 | 200 | 400 | 800 | | 1200 | | 1600 Miles |

NATIONS OF THE WORLD

This section offers a brief guide to all of the world's 192 independent countries. It gives a concise profile of each nation's geography, economy, politics, and history, as well as statistical information, national flags, and a regional map. Neighboring countries are grouped together, as shown below, enabling the reader to compare the different nations in a particular region.

Information is based on the following guidelines:

Capital city or town: The commonly accepted English version of the name is used, where available.

International organizations: Each country's profile includes a list of the most influential regional organizations to which the country belongs. Organizations to which almost all countries belong have been excluded. A nation can be assumed to be a member of the UN, for example, unless it is stated otherwise. Abbreviations are explained in the lower left-hand corner of each double-page spread.

Population: The figures cited are the most recent ones available for each country. They have been rounded off to the nearest thousandth. In cases where the most recent data available is several years old, the date of the figure has been specified. Population growth rates represent an average over recent years and may be subject to external influences, such as war or the influx or exodus of refugees.

Life expectancy: The figures are differentiated between males (m) and females (f) where this information is available.

Languages: The major or official language(s) of a country are shown in roman type. Other languages used within the country appear in italic type.

Adult literacy rates: Many developed countries do not supply this data. For such countries UNESCO estimates of "over 95%" have been provided.

Currency: The standard unit of currency has been provided. Since exchange rates fluctuate from day to day and from year to year, no attempt has been made to compare values between currencies.

GNP: The Gross National Product of a country represents the total value of all goods and services produced annually by the economy. GNP is the standard measure of a country's wealth and the basis upon which economic comparisons are made. This information is not available for every country.

Income per capita: This figure represents the GNP (subject to certain accounting adjustments) divided by the total population. While it serves as a standard measure of individual prosperity, it does not take into account income differences between residents.

Principal sources: the United Nations for demographic information and the World Bank for financial statistics.

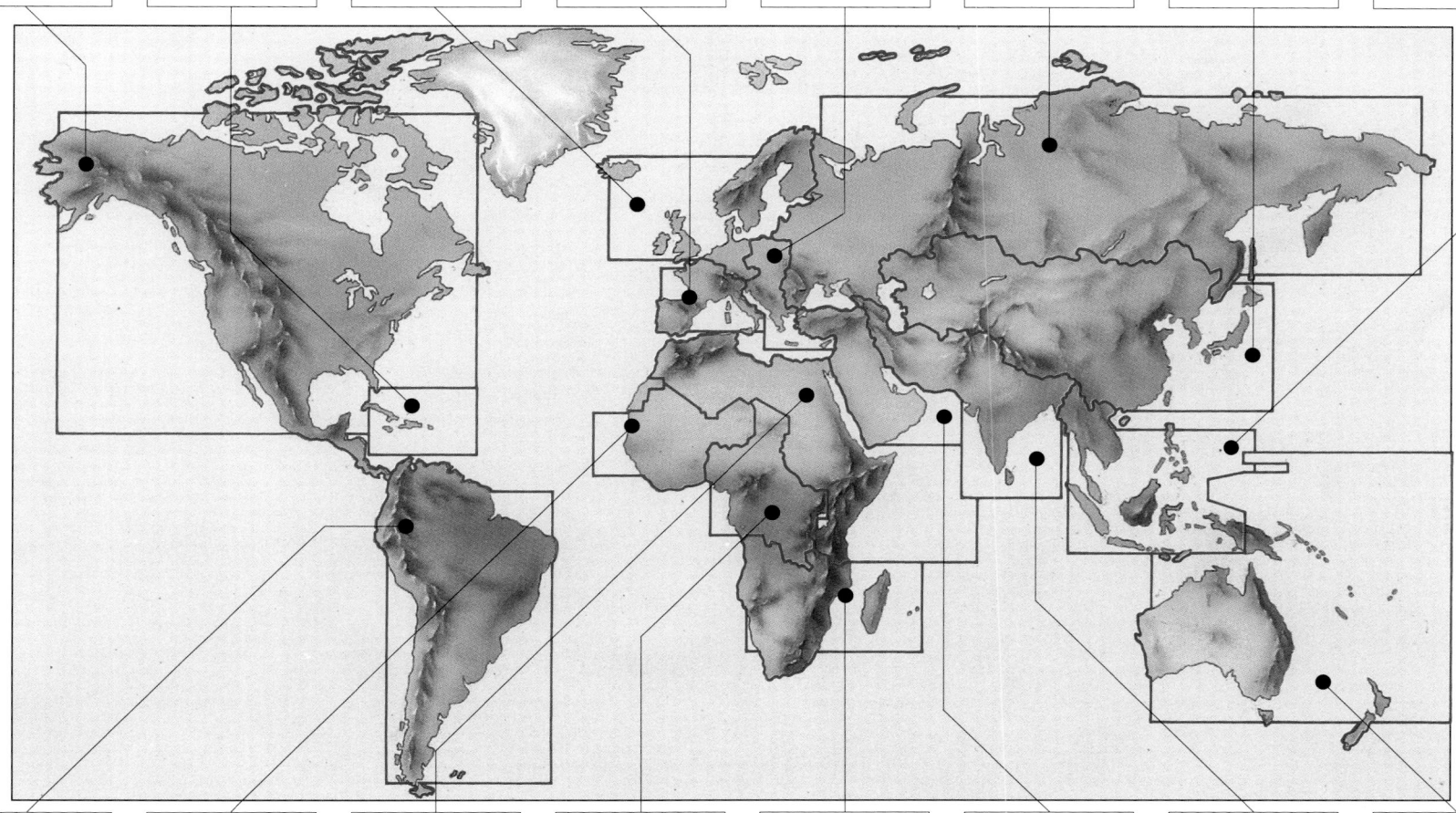

NORTH AMERICA
▶ *pages 228–29*
Belize
Canada
Costa Rica
El Salvador
Guatemala
Honduras
Mexico
Nicaragua
Panama
United States

THE CARIBBEAN
▶ *pages 230–31*
Antigua & Barbuda
The Bahamas
Barbados
Cuba
Dominica
Dominican Republic
Grenada
Haiti
Jamaica
St. Kitts & Nevis
St. Lucia
St. Vincent & the Grenadines
Trinidad & Tobago

NORTHERN EUROPE
▶ *pages 210–11*
Austria
Belgium
Denmark
Finland
Germany
Iceland
Ireland
Luxembourg
Netherlands
Norway
Sweden
United Kingdom

SOUTHERN EUROPE
▶ *pages 212–13*
Andorra
France
Italy
Liechtenstein
Malta
Monaco
Portugal
San Marino
Spain
Switzerland
Vatican City

CENTRAL EUROPE
▶ *pages 214–15*
Albania
Bosnia & Herzegovina
Croatia
Cyprus
Czech Republic
Greece
Hungary
Macedonia
Poland
Slovakia
Slovenia
Yugoslavia

RUSSIA AND WESTERN NEIGHBORS
▶ *pages 216–17*
Belarus
Bulgaria
Estonia
Latvia
Lithuania
Moldova
Romania
Russia
Ukraine

CENTRAL AND EASTERN ASIA
▶ *pages 222–23*
China
Japan
Kazakhstan
North Korea
South Korea
Kyrgyzstan
Mongolia
Taiwan
Tajikistan
Turkmenistan
Uzbekistan

SOUTHEAST ASIA
▶ *pages 224–25*
Brunei
Cambodia
Indonesia
Laos
Malaysia
Myanmar (Burma)
Philippines
Singapore
Thailand
Vietnam

SOUTH AMERICA
▶ *pages 232–33*
Argentina
Bolivia
Brazil
Chile
Colombia
Ecuador
Guyana
Paraguay
Peru
Surinam
Uruguay
Venezuela

WESTERN AFRICA
▶ *pages 236–37*
Benin
Burkina
Cape Verde
The Gambia
Ghana
Guinea
Guinea-Bissau
Ivory Coast
Liberia
Mali
Mauritania
Niger
Senegal
Sierra Leone
Togo

NORTHERN AFRICA
▶ *pages 234–35*
Algeria
Djibouti
Egypt
Eritrea
Ethiopia
Kenya
Libya
Morocco
Seychelles
Somalia
Sudan
Tanzania
Tunisia

CENTRAL AFRICA
▶ *pages 238–39*
Burundi
Cameroon
Central African Republic
Chad
Congo
Equatorial Guinea
Gabon
Nigeria
Rwanda
São Tomé & Príncipe
Uganda
Zaire

SOUTHERN AFRICA
▶ *pages 240–41*
Angola
Botswana
Comoros
Lesotho
Madagascar
Malawi
Mauritius
Mozambique
Namibia
South Africa
Swaziland
Zambia
Zimbabwe

THE MIDDLE EAST AND THE GULF
▶ *pages 218–19*
Bahrain
Iraq
Israel
Jordan
Kuwait
Lebanon
Oman
Qatar
Saudi Arabia
Syria
Turkey
United Arab Emirates
Yemen

INDIAN SUB-CONTINENT AND NEIGHBORS
▶ *pages 220–21*
Afghanistan
Armenia
Azerbaijan
Bangladesh
Bhutan
Georgia
India
Iran
Maldives
Nepal
Pakistan
Sri Lanka

OCEANIA
▶ *pages 226–27*
Australia
Fiji
Kiribati
Marshall Islands
Micronesia
Nauru
New Zealand
Palau
Papua New Guinea
Solomon Islands
Tonga
Tuvalu
Vanuatu
Western Samoa

NORTHERN EUROPE

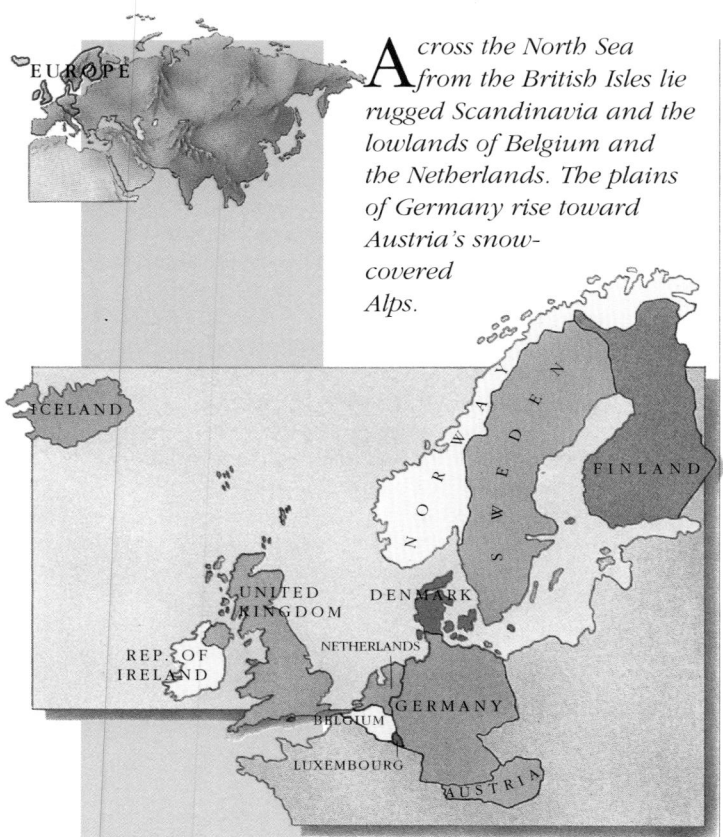

*A*cross the North Sea from the British Isles lie rugged Scandinavia and the lowlands of Belgium and the Netherlands. The plains of Germany rise toward Austria's snow-covered Alps.

Colonies and Dependent Territories

FAEROE ISLANDS
Parent country
DENMARK
Map page 64

GUERNSEY
Parent country
U.K.
Map page 73

ISLE OF MAN
Parent country
U.K.
Map page 72

JAN MAYEN
Parent country
NORWAY
Map page 56

JERSEY
Parent country
U.K.
Map page 73

SVALBARD
Parent country
NORWAY
Map page 57

Abbreviations
CE Council of Europe
COMM Commonwealth
EBRD European Bank for
  Reconstruction and
  Development
ECE Economic Commission
  for Europe
EFTA European Free Trade
  Association
EU European Union
G7 Group of Seven
NATO North Atlantic Treaty
  Organization

GNP Gross National Product

AUSTRIA

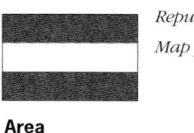
Republic of Austria
Map pages 102–3

Area	32,369 sq. mi.
	(83,858 sq. km.)
Capital	Vienna
Member of	CE, EBRD, ECE, EU

Population	8,031,000
Population growth rate	0.5%
Life expectancy	73 (m), 79 (f)
Language	German
Adult literacy rate	99%

Currency	Austrian schilling
GNP (U.S.$, in millions)	197,475
Income per capita (U.S.$)	24,950

As the feudal seat of the Hapsburg dynasty, Austria was the hub of a Central European empire that incorporated all or part of nearly a dozen future nations and held sway for more than 600 years. The Hapsburg possessions were dismantled after World War I, and modern Austria is the offspring of the German-speaking core of that Austro-Hungarian realm. It was annexed by Nazi Germany and partly occupied by the Soviet Union from 1945 to 1955.

Austria has emerged as a small but viable state with well-run industries, ample hydroelectric power, and a vigorous tourist economy based largely on its Alpine scenery and sports. Austrians have set an example of preserving farmland for both practical and aesthetic purposes, and they are justly proud of their magnificent imperial capital, Vienna, with its incomparable heritage of music, art, intellect, and graceful living.

BELGIUM

Kingdom of Belgium
Map page 69

Area	11,784 sq. mi.
	(30,528 sq. km.)
Capital	Brussels
Member of	CE, EBRD, ECE, EU, NATO

Population	10,101,000
Population growth rate	0.2%
Life expectancy	73 (m), 80 (f)
Languages	Flemish, French, German
Adult literacy rate	99%

Currency	Belgian franc
GNP (U.S.$, in millions)	231,051
Income per capita (U.S.$)	22,920

Brussels, the capital, is headquarters of the European Union, yet Belgium itself is deeply divided by language and culture. Ever since 1830, when it broke away from the Netherlands, it has been an uneasy federation of Flemish northerners and southern, French-speaking Walloons.

Though Belgium sits astride a well-worn invasion route between Germany and France, much of its architecture dates back to its medieval heyday as a textile and trading center. Modern industries still include textiles, as well as chemicals and steel. The seaport of Antwerp is the second busiest in Europe.

DENMARK

Kingdom of Denmark
Map page 68

Area	16,634 sq. mi.
	(43,094 sq. km.)
Capital	Copenhagen
Member of	CE, EBRD, ECE, EU, NATO

Population	5,215,700
Population growth rate	0.1%
Life expectancy	73 (m), 78 (f)
Language	Danish
Adult literacy rate	99%

Currency	Danish krone
GNP (U.S.$, in millions)	145,384
Income per capita (U.S.$)	28,110

Once a homeland of Viking warriors, Denmark occupies the Jutland Peninsula and hundreds of surrounding islands. Except for oil and natural gas from the North Sea, the low-lying, seagirt nation boasts few exploitable natural resources. But with 60 percent of its land under cultivation, agriculture helps contribute to Denmark's prosperity. Among its prized farm products are butter from 2 million cows and bacon from 4 million pigs.

In a post-World War II burst of industrialization, furniture and textile manufacturing benefited from the Danes' distinctive flair for design; oil refining and ship-building are other economic buttresses. Tourism is also significant, with attractions as diverse as Copenhagen's lively Tivoli Gardens, seaside resorts, and Kronborg Castle at Elsinore (the setting for Shakespeare's *Hamlet*). Denmark is widely admired for its rigorous environmental standards.

FINLAND

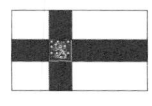
Republic of Finland
Map page 64

Area	117,573 sq. mi.
	(304,593 sq. km.)
Capital	Helsinki
Member of	CE, EBRD, ECE, EU

Population	5,098,800
Population growth rate	0.4%
Life expectancy	72 (m), 80 (f)
Languages	Finnish, Swedish, Lapp
Adult literacy rate	99%

Currency	markka
GNP (U.S.$, in millions)	95,817
Income per capita (U.S.$)	18,850

With nearly one-third of its land extending north of the Arctic Circle, Finland ranges from mountainous uplands in the frigid north to vast lowland tracts of coniferous forests accented by tens of thousands of lakes. Forest products have traditionally formed the sturdy backbone of its economy, but shipbuilding, manufacturing, and other industries have expanded dramatically since World War II. (Finland joined the European Union in 1995.) In the far north a small population of Lapps tends herds of reindeer, just as it always has.

GERMANY

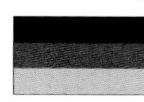
Federal Republic of Germany
Map pages 98–101

Area	137,792 sq. mi.
	(356,974 sq. km.)
Capital	Berlin
Member of	CE, EBRD, ECE, EU, G7

Population	81,339,000
Population growth rate	0.7%
Life expectancy	73 (m), 79 (f)
Language	German
Adult literacy rate	99%

Currency	deutsche mark
GNP (U.S.$, in millions)	2,075,452
Income per capita (U.S.$)	25,580

Economic titan of modern Europe, Germany engineered its postwar revival with the sleek precision of a Mercedes limousine. It was a founding member of the European Union, yet for much of the continent's history, German nationhood existed more as an idea than a reality.

For centuries German-speaking Europe was a hodgepodge of kingdoms, duchies, electorates, and minor states loosely grouped under the title of Holy Roman Empire. Yet German achievement was prodigious. The Hanseatic League, which dominated northern commerce; Johann Gutenberg's printing press; Martin Luther and the birth of Protestantism; Kepler and Leibnitz in mathematics; Kant and Hegel in philosophy; Goethe in literature; and such musical geniuses as Bach and Wagner – all belong to German culture, if not to a nation called Germany.

In 1871 Prussian chancellor Otto von Bismarck united the independent German states as the German Empire. The new nation inherited Prussia's militarism, inspiring Bismarck's successors to pursue policies that incited two world wars. In the second, Nazi führer Adolf Hitler led his country to near-total destruction and succeeded in bringing about the virtual extermination of European Jews and gypsies. Germany's penalty was partition, with Soviet Russia setting up East Germany as a Communist puppet state in 1949. Not until 1990, a year after the collapse of European Communism, were the two Germanys reunited in a single nation.

By then West Germany's economic juggernaut had become legendary, spewing out autos, steel, chemicals, optics, electronics, and machine tools for world consumption. The cost of integrating a formerly Communist populace into a thriving free-market system has been high in deutsch marks and social displacement alike, but no previous German incarnation has been welcomed with such high hopes and general thanksgiving by the world at large.

ICELAND

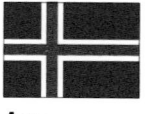
Republic of Iceland
Map page 64

Area	39,758 sq. mi.
	(103,000 sq. km.)
Capital	Reykjavik
Member of	CE, EBRD, ECE, EFTA, NATO

Population	268,000
Population growth rate	1.1%
Life expectancy	77 (m), 81 (f)
Language	Icelandic
Adult literacy rate	99%

Currency Icelandic krona
GNP (U.S.$, in millions) 6,545
Income per capita (U.S.$) 24,590

A barren volcanic island partially covered by glaciers and ice fields, Iceland relies on fishing for the bulk of its exports. Abundant geothermal and hydroelectric energy provides the country with economical heating and electric power.

IRELAND

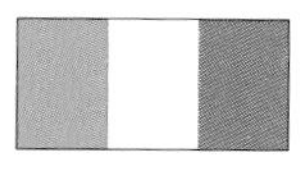

Republic of Ireland
Map page 75

Area 26,593 sq. mi. (68,895 sq. km.)
Capital Dublin
Member of CE, EBRD, ECE, EU

Population 3,582,000
Population growth rate 0%
Life expectancy 73 (m), 78 (f)
Languages Irish, *English*
Adult literacy rate 99%

Currency Irish pound
GNP (U.S.$, in millions) 48,275
Income per capita (U.S.$) 13,630

Ireland lies on Europe's fringe, yet its faith and tribulations have long been central to the European and American experience alike. Christianized by St. Patrick in the fifth century, Celtic Ireland harbored monasteries that were isolated lights of learning during the Dark Ages. Viking rovers frequently raided the island, but in 1170 Anglo-Norman invaders commenced eight centuries of British rule and suppression of Ireland's Catholic faith. The Irish Free State was established in 1922, although the island's northern six counties (settled by Protestants) remain part of the United Kingdom.

Along with the ongoing rebellion in Northern Ireland, another profound event in the island's modern history was the famine caused by a potato blight in the 1840s. Millions perished or emigrated, many to the United States. Today the nation's population is half that of 1845. Still an exporter of its citizens, Ireland boasts a strong tourist industry that reflects the homeward pull of what is, to many, their ancestral land.

LUXEMBOURG

Grand Duchy of Luxembourg
Map page 69

Area 998 sq. mi. (2,586 sq. km.)
Capital Luxembourg
Member of CE, EBRD, ECE, EU, NATO

Population 406,000
Population growth rate 1.0%
Life expectancy 76 (av. m/f)
Languages Letzeburgish, *French, German*
Adult literacy rate 99%

Currency Luxembourg franc
GNP (U.S.$, in millions) 15,973
Income per capita (U.S.$) 39,850

Compact but centrally located in western Europe, Luxembourg exerts an influence that belies its small size. (Its per capita income is the highest of any nation in the European Union.) Iron and steel production have traditionally fueled its economy. Today, though, Luxembourg is best known as a financial center – the home base of nearly 200 banks – and as the headquarters of many important international organizations.

NETHERLANDS

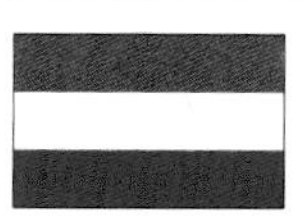

Kingdom of the Netherlands
Map page 69

Area 13,100 sq. mi. (33,939 sq. km.)
Capital Amsterdam
Member of CE, EBRD, ECE, EU, NATO

Population 15,385,000
Population growth rate 0.7%
Life expectancy 74 (m), 80 (f)
Language Dutch
Adult literacy rate 99%

Currency Netherlands guilder
GNP (U.S.$, in millions) 338,144
Income per capita (U.S.$) 21,970

Nearly half of the Netherlands – one of Europe's most densely populated nations – has been reclaimed from the North Sea by a system of dikes begun 800 years ago. As if turning the ocean bottom into dry land weren't enough, the industrious Dutch have also made tremendously profitable use of their position at the mouth of the Rhine: Rotterdam is the busiest port in the world.

After breaking away from Spanish control in the late 1500s, the Netherlands discovered commercial wealth and an overseas empire in Indonesia and the West Indies. The golden age of Dutch painting produced such renowned artists as Frans Hals and Rembrandt. Present-day Dutch prosperity rests not only upon shipping and manufacturing, but upon efficient cultivation of the land (including the famous tulip fields) by only 5 percent of the population.

NORWAY

Kingdom of Norway
Map page 64

Area 125,017 sq. mi. (323,877 sq. km.)
Capital Oslo
Member of CE, EBRD, ECE, EFTA, NATO

Population 4,348,000
Population growth rate 0.4%
Life expectancy 75 (m), 81 (f)
Languages Norwegian (Bokmål and Nynorsk, or neo-Norwegian), *Lapp*
Adult literacy rate 99%

Currency Norwegian krone
GNP (U.S.$, in millions) 114,328
Income per capita (U.S.$) 26,480

Because Norway's interior is so ruggedly inhospitable, settlement in this one-time Viking stronghold has always hugged the coast, and people have traditionally sustained themselves from the sea. Fishing remains a major pursuit, but today North Sea oil and natural gas are the main marine assets. (Norway is the leading European oil producer and enjoys one of the continent's highest standards of living.) Shipbuilding and a thriving merchant fleet round out Norway's reliance on the sea.

SWEDEN

Kingdom of Sweden
Map page 64

Area 173,686 sq. mi. (449,964 sq. km.)
Capital Stockholm
Member of CE, EBRD, ECE, EU

Population 8,816,000
Population growth rate 0.5%
Life expectancy 76 (m), 81 (f)
Languages Swedish, *Finnish, Lapp*
Adult literacy rate 99%

Currency Swedish krona
GNP (U.S.$, in millions) 206,419
Income per capita (U.S.$) 23,630

Sweden's proud neutrality – uninterrupted for nearly 200 years – belies the nation's past as the home of Viking raiders and King Gustavus Adolphus's 17th-century military machine. Today Sweden builds its reputation on precision manufacturing, a strong environmental stance, and a generous program of social welfare built on a mix of socialism and capitalism. Ample hydroelectric power, along with vast reserves of timber, help underwrite the Swedes' high standard of living.

UNITED KINGDOM

United Kingdom of Great Britain and Northern Ireland
Map pages 92–95

Area 93,316 sq. mi. (241,752 sq. km.)
Capital London
Member of CE, COMM, EBRD, ECE, EU, G7, NATO

Population 58,395,000
Population growth rate 0.3%
Life expectancy 74 (m), 79 (f)
Languages English, *Welsh*
Adult literacy rate 99%

Currency British pound
GNP (U.S.$, in millions) 1,069,457
Income per capita (U.S.$) 18,410

Builder of the largest empire in history, the United Kingdom is itself the product of conquest. By 1066, when the Normans made the last successful invasion, the British Isles had seen successive waves of Celts, Romans, Anglo-Saxons, and Vikings, all of whom contributed to their national character.

The United Kingdom – the term *Britain* is convenient shorthand for the union formalized in 1801 – comprises the island realms of England, Wales, Scotland, and Northern Ireland. From earliest times the British have been seafarers. Two great victories (against the Spanish Armada in 1588 and Napoleon at Trafalgar in 1805) secured Britain's stature as the world's dominant sea power. The unhindered trade made possible by such naval supremacy burgeoned in the 18th and 19th centuries with the industrial revolution. In the wake of mercantile adventure, Britain's worldwide empire grew far and wide. Meanwhile, it refined the concept of parliamentary government, which – along with the now-universal English language – is perhaps its greatest legacy to the world.

Victorious yet financially drained by two world wars, Britain granted independence to nearly all of its colonies. More problematic than divestiture of the empire was the decline of the nation's industries, centered in several smokestack cities in the Midlands. Britain has modernized its economy on the foundations of North Sea oil and gas and financial and service industries. Nevertheless, prosperity has been uneven, with the north failing to keep up with the south. The nation continues to grapple with the quest for peace in Northern Ireland, Scottish and Welsh nationalist movements, integration with the European Union and its new common currency, and the role of the ancient but increasingly challenged monarchy.

20TH-CENTURY LANDMARKS

1901 Finnish army disbanded; soldiers forced to join Russian army.

1910

1914–18 World War I sparked by assassination of Archduke Ferdinand. Belgium occupied by Germany.

1916 Easter rebellion in Dublin. Battle of Jutland.

1917–19 Finland gains independence but endures civil war before republic is declared.

1920

1926 General strike in Britain.

1929 Market crash triggers Great Depression.

1930

1933 Hitler becomes German chancellor.

1936 Germany and Italy sign Axis Pact.

1938 Austria annexed by Nazi Germany.

1939 World War II begins.

1940

1940 German rule in Luxembourg, Norway, Belgium, Denmark, and the Netherlands. Battle of Britain. London Blitz.

1941 Germany invades Soviet Union.

1944 D-Day landings. Belgium, Denmark, and Luxembourg liberated.

1945 Germany surrenders to Allies. Nuremberg trials begin.

1949 Germany divided into East and West.

1950

1957 Treaty of Rome: Belgium, France, Italy, West Germany, Luxembourg, and the Netherlands found the EEC.

1960

1961 Berlin Wall built.

1970

1972 U.K. imposes rule on Northern Ireland.

1972–76 Iceland and U.K. engage in Cod War.

1973 U.K., Ireland, and Denmark join EEC.

1980

1989 Berlin Wall razed.

1990

1990 Unification of East and West Germany.

1992 Single market between EC members.

1994 Northern Ireland peace process resumes.

1995 Austria, Finland, and Sweden become members of EU.

SOUTHERN EUROPE

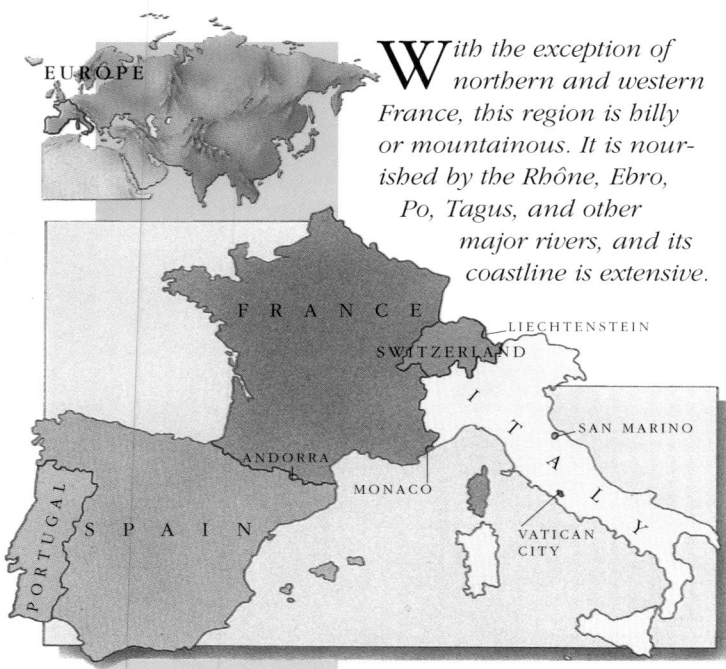

With the exception of northern and western France, this region is hilly or mountainous. It is nourished by the Rhône, Ebro, Po, Tagus, and other major rivers, and its coastline is extensive.

Colonies and Dependent Territories

GIBRALTAR
Parent country
U.K.
Map page 87

ANDORRA

Principality of Andorra
Map page 88

Area	181 sq. mi.
	(468 sq. km.)
Capital	Andorra la Vella
Member of	CE, ECE

Population	65,000
Population growth rate	5.3%
Life expectancy	79 (av. m/f)
Languages	Catalan, *French, Spanish*
Adult literacy rate	99%

Currency	French franc, Spanish peseta
GNP (U.S.$, in millions)	1,005
Income per capita (U.S.$)	15,411

Located high in the Pyrenees, this tiny nation was jointly governed by France and Spain from 1278 until 1993, when it adopted a constitution that set up a parliamentary government.

FRANCE

French Republic
Map pages 78–83

Area	209,970 sq. mi.
	(543,965 sq. km.)
Capital	Paris
Member of	CE, EBRD, ECE, EU, G7, NATO

Population	57,903,000
Population growth rate	0.5%
Life expectancy	73 (m), 81 (f)
Languages	French, *Breton, Basque*
Adult literacy rate	over 95%

Currency	French franc
GNP (U.S.$, in millions)	1,355,039
Income per capita (U.S.$)	23,470

The largest nation in western Europe and a founding member of the European Union, France owes its status as a leading world power to the cornerstones of high technology, extensive agriculture, an independent nuclear-based defense, and a strong sense of cultural and linguistic identity.

France's size and strategic location assured it a central role in history. Inhabited by Celts, the region was conquered by Julius Caesar and remained under Roman rule until the fifth century, when it fell to the Franks. Emerging as a powerful kingdom over the following centuries, France helped to develop the traditions of medieval feudalism that ended with the rise of an absolute monarchy in the 17th century. A century later the excesses of the French kings led to the revolution of 1789.

With its watchwords of "Liberty! Equality! Fraternity!" the French Revolution was a major watershed of European history, culminating in the rise of Napoleon, whose imperial ambitions plunged Europe into a cauldron of war. Nineteenth-century France witnessed an expansion of colonial power, along with a succession of dynastic restoration and republican fervor. The monarchy ended in 1870, and the colonies have since been liberated. Yet Napoleon's administrative and legal reforms have endured.

France's place in the 20th century was forged by Charles de Gaulle, leader of the resistance to Germany's World War II occupation and the embodiment of French pride and national sense of destiny. As the first president of the Fifth Republic, de Gaulle promoted many of the country's economic and technological advances.

From the heights of its southern and eastern mountains (including Mont Blanc, Europe's loftiest peak), the French landscape descends to fertile, well-drained lowlands. Home to a vigorous agricultural economy, France boasts the world's finest wines and a world-renowned cuisine. The country is heavily rural, with about half its citizens living in the countryside. Yet Paris, the capital, is a world symbol of sophistication in culture and fashion. Modern technology forms a bulwark of the French economy; no European nation relies as heavily upon nuclear power, and France's 186-m.p.h. (300-km.p.h.) TGV trains are the envy of the world.

French energies are currently focused on resolving political conflicts between the left and right wings, the absorption of immigrants from former colonies and the xenophobia they have sometimes aroused, and struggles with persistent separatist movements among the nation's Basque, Breton, and Corsican minorities.

ITALY

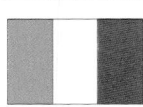

Italian Republic
Map pages 92–95

Area	116,311 sq. mi.
	(301,323 sq. km.)
Capital	Rome
Member of	CE, EBRD, ECE, EU, G7, NATO

Population	57,269,000
Population growth rate	0.1%
Life expectancy	74 (m), 80 (f)
Languages	Italian, *German, French, others*
Adult literacy rate	97.1%

Currency	Italian lira
GNP (U.S.$, in millions)	1,101,258
Income per capita (U.S.$)	19,840

Among Italians the first loyalty is to family and community. United under one flag only in the 1870s, Italians still harbor strong regional identities and a deep distrust of central government. Yet for all its fragmentation, Italy is cherished the world over for its people, landscape, and culture. It is, quite simply, one of the great glories of civilization, whose twin wellsprings were the Roman Empire and the Renaissance.

Remarkably different circumstances gave rise to these golden ages. Ancient Rome was a centralizing power that overwhelmed the competing cultures of Etruscans and Greeks and extended its boundaries northward into Europe. Its genius was for organization, lawgiving, and engineering: a vast network of masterfully designed and constructed roads and aqueducts survives to this day. In contrast, the Renaissance was the product of a splendid mosaic of independent city states that were often at war with each other. The great rebirth of classical traditions and humanist learning – of painting, sculpture, and architecture – was nurtured under the patronage of the rulers and merchant princes of these enclaves.

From the 16th to the 19th century, Italy was at the mercy of foreign opportunists. Their carved-out domains, along with the remainder of the Papal States, were unified between 1861 and 1870 by King Victor Emmanuel II of Sardinia and Giuseppe Garibaldi. In terms of territory, today's Italy is essentially their creation, but the country has experienced many political changes since then, including the Fascist dictatorship of Benito Mussolini and a string of fragile postwar coalition governments.

Although modern Italy has one of the world's most powerful economies, it remains hampered by social and regional fragmentation. The nation's rigid class structure contributed to the power of its Cold War-era Communist Party. Even more deeply rooted is the disparity in wealth and opportunity between the prosperous industrial north and the southern Mezzogiorno, a starkly beautiful land of hardscrabble agriculture and conservative traditions. Although mass unemployment and overpopulation plague the southern provinces, forcing many young people to seek jobs in the north and beyond, a separatist Northern League is opposing government subsidies to southern Italy.

LIECHTENSTEIN

Principality of Liechtenstein
Map page 102

Area	62 sq. mi.
	(160 sq. km.)
Capital	Vaduz
Member of	CE, EBRD, ECE, EFTA

Population	31,000
Population growth rate	1.4%
Life expectancy	72 (av. m/f)
Language	German, *Alemannic dialect*
Adult literacy rate	over 95%

Currency	Swiss franc
GNP (U.S.$, in millions)	1,140
Income per capita (U.S.$)	37,220

Though modest in size, this picturesque principality boasts a robust economy and one of the world's highest standards of living. Thanks to lenient tax laws and secretive banking practices, it is the home base for many foreign corporations. Although it is an independent nation, Liechtenstein has an economic alliance with Switzerland and shares the same currency.

MALTA

Republic of Malta
Map page 95

Area	122 sq. mi.
	(316 sq. km.)
Capital	Valletta
Member of	CE, EBRD, ECE

Population	370,000
Population growth rate	0.3%
Life expectancy	75 (m), 79 (f)
Languages	Maltese, English, *Italian*
Adult literacy rate	87.9%

Currency	Maltese lira
GNP (U.S.$, in millions)	2,606
Income per capita (U.S.$)	7,970

Abbreviations
CE *Council of Europe*
EBRD *European Bank for Reconstruction and Development*
ECE *Economic Commission for Europe*
EFTA *European Free Trade Association*
EU *European Union*
G7 *Group of Seven*
NATO *North Atlantic Treaty Organization*

GNP *Gross National Product*

This small but strategically located island-nation has been ruled through the centuries by a succession of foreign powers. Part of the United Kingdom from 1814 until it gained independence in 1964, Malta served as an allied naval base in both world wars. Blessed with a balmy climate, it is a popular tourist destination.

MONACO

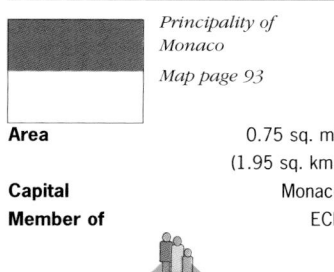

Principality of Monaco
Map page 93

Area	0.75 sq. mi.
	(1.95 sq. km.)
Capital	Monaco
Member of	ECE

Population	30,000
Population growth rate	1.3%
Life expectancy	78 (av. m/f)
Languages	French, Monégasque, Italian, English
Adult literacy rate	99%

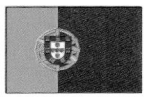

Currency	French franc
GNP (U.S.$, in millions)	not available
Income per capita (U.S.$)	not available

The micro-nation of Monaco (only Vatican City is smaller) is famed throughout the world as a posh resort. A Mediterranean climate, seaside scenery, luxury hotels, a gambling casino, and a host of social and sporting events all contribute to its éclat.

PORTUGAL

Portuguese Republic
Map pages 86–87

Area	35,447 sq. mi.
	(91,831 sq. km.)
Capital	Lisbon
Member of	CE, EBRD, ECE, EU, NATO

Population	9,900,000
Population growth rate	−0.1%
Life expectancy	71 (m), 78 (f)
Language	Portuguese
Adult literacy rate	85%

Currency	Portuguese escudo
GNP (U.S.$, in millions)	92,124
Income per capita (U.S.$)	9,370

The first European nation to carve out a great overseas empire, Portugal rose to power when its rugged, adventurous people turned from their poor farms and gazed out across the vast and promising Atlantic.

Prince Henry, "the Navigator," launched Portugal's era of exploration in the 15th century, inspiring captains who braved the treacherous waters off Africa's Cape of Good Hope to secure trade routes to the East. But Europe's larger maritime powers broke Portugal's trade monopolies, and by the 20th century one of western Europe's smallest and poorest nations was left ruling African colonies many times its size.

After the overthrow of an enfeebled right-wing dictatorship in 1974, Portugal liberated its colonies and refocused attention on issues closer to home. Its priorities include modernizing an antiquated agricultural sector (vital for its cork, citrus fruits, and port wine), developing industry, and accommodating ever more tourists, who are lured by Portugal's rugged mountains, rambling coastline, and 15th-century architecture.

SAN MARINO

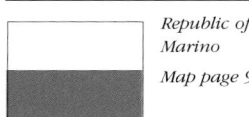

Republic of San Marino
Map page 93

Area	23 sq. mi.
	(60 sq. km.)
Capital	San Marino
Member of	CE, ECE

Population	25,000
Population growth rate	1.5%
Life expectancy	73 (m), 79 (f)
Language	Italian
Adult literacy rate	98.4%

Currency	Italian lira
GNP (U.S.$, in millions)	220
Income per capita (U.S.$)	8,626

San Marino traces its founding to the fourth century and so claims to be the world's oldest republic. Although completely surrounded by Italy, it is an independent state. Rugged terrain and imposing medieval fortresses (a major tourist draw) help explain its ability to thwart all attempts at conquest.

SPAIN

Kingdom of Spain
Map pages 86–89

Area	194,846 sq. mi.
	(504,782 sq. km.)
Capital	Madrid
Member of	CE, EBRD, ECE, EU, NATO

Population	39,188,000
Population growth rate	0.3%
Life expectancy	75 (m), 80 (f)
Languages	Castilian Spanish, others
Adult literacy rate	95.8%

Currency	peseta
GNP (U.S.$, in millions)	525,334
Income per capita (U.S.$)	13,280

Topography and history have set Spain apart from the rest of Europe. Isolated by the Pyrenees, the nation was also cut off from the progressive post-World War II mainstream by a rigid right-wing dictator.

Spain also owes a strong measure of its singularity to past conquest. Originally settled by Iberians, Basques, and Celts, and later ruled by Romans and Visigoths, Spain was eventually overwhelmed by a powerful new force: Islam. Beginning in 711, Moorish invaders overran nearly all of Iberia. From the Great Mosque at Córdoba to Granada's Alhambra citadel, southern Andalucía retains much of its Moorish flavor.

Modern Spain was born in 1492, with the expulsion of the Moors by King Ferdinand and Queen Isabella, and the first voyage of Christopher Columbus. Spain was unified under the Catholic monarchs, and Columbus's discoveries launched the Spanish empire. After 1500, conquistadors channeled the wealth of the Americas into imperial coffers, but fiscal mismanagement and corrupt administration led to a long decline. By 1898, when Spain lost its last major colonies in the Spanish-American War, the nation was shorn of its overseas glory and relegated to a second-class status within Europe. In 1936 Spain suffered its greatest national tragedy when the insurgency of General Francisco Franco against a left-leaning republic led to bloody civil war. Franco's triumph ushered in an era of authoritarianism that ended with his death in 1975.

With its monarchy restored under King Juan Carlos I, Spain began a new era of political and cultural liberalization. Integration with the European community has led to extensive industrial investment. Tourism, centered upon the coastal resorts favored by millions of middle-class Europeans, has burgeoned. Agriculture, still employing nearly one-third of the work force at the dawn of the 21st century, has also enjoyed an increase in productivity.

Restoring the public's confidence in a government riddled with corruption and scandal is one of Spain's primary concerns, but its greatest challenge may be the growing sense of regionalism that threatens to tear apart the national fabric. Ethnically distinct Basques continue to agitate for independence in the north, while the Catalonian population centered around Barcelona identifies increasingly with its own language and heritage. From Andalucía in the sunny south to Galicia in the green, rainy northwest, Spain has evolved into a land of no fewer than 17 ever more autonomous regions.

SWITZERLAND

Swiss Confederation
Map page 92

Area	15,936 sq. mi.
	(41,284 sq. km.)
Capital	Bern
Member of	CE, EBRD, ECE, EFTA

Population	7,019,000
Population growth rate	1%
Life expectancy	75 (m), 82 (f)
Languages	German, French, Italian, others
Adult literacy rate	99%

Currency	Swiss franc
GNP (U.S.$, in millions)	264,974
Income per capita (U.S.$)	37,180

Switzerland has long served as a model of political neutrality and smoothly-engineered prosperity. First cobbled together as an anti-Austrian alliance in the 13th century, the federation of Swiss cantons (provinces) has remained a cohesive yet remarkably heterogeneous state. It incorporates German, French, Italian, and a tiny minority of Romansh-speaking citizens, with languages often varying from one valley to another. The Swiss have built their clockwork economy on banking, precision technologies, and tourism. Alpine passes are still defended by an army relying on universal male conscription, and the Swiss commitment to neutrality is so strong that membership in both the UN and EU have been resolutely avoided.

VATICAN CITY

The Holy See
Map page 94

Area	0.17 sq. mi.
	(0.44 sq. km.)
Capital	not applicable
Member of	not applicable

Population	800
Population growth rate	not available
Life expectancy	not available
Languages	Italian, Latin
Adult literacy rate	100%

Currency	Vatican lira
GNP (U.S.$, in millions)	not available
Income per capita (U.S.$)	not available

Sovereigns of the Roman Catholic Church, the popes have lived in what is now Vatican City since the 14th century. The Vatican is all that remains of the once extensive Papal States, incorporated into Italy in the 1860s.

1904 France and U.K. sign Entente Cordiale.

— 1910 —

1910 Portugal declared a republic.

1914 World War I begins. Germany invades French territory.

1916 Battles of Somme and Verdun (France).

1918 World War I ends.

1919 Treaty of Versailles is signed.

— 1920 —

1922 Mussolini heads Italian government.

1923 Spanish military overthrows monarchy.

1926 Military coup in Portugal is followed by right-wing dictatorship.

— 1930 —

1931 Second Republic declared in Spain.

1936–39 Spanish Civil War; Nationalist general Franco defeats republican army.

1936 Italy and Germany sign Axis Pact.

1939 World War II begins.

— 1940 —

1940 France occupied by Germany.

1943 Mussolini overthrown; Italy surrenders.

1944 D-Day landings in northern France.

1945 World War II comes to an end.

1946 Italy becomes a republic.

1946–58 Fourth Republic in France.

— 1950 —

1957 Treaty of Rome: six European countries found the EEC.

1958 Fifth Republic declared in France.

— 1960 —

1962 France grants Algeria independence.

1968 Student unrest in France.

— 1970 —

1974 Dictatorship ends in Portugal.

1975 Death of General Franco; Juan Carlos becomes king of Spain.

1977 Democratic elections held in Spain.

— 1980 —

1986 Portugal and Spain join EEC.

— 1990 —

1992 Single market between EU members.

CENTRAL EUROPE

*B*ounded by the Baltic Sea to the north and the Mediterranean Sea to the south, this is a region of myriad landscapes. The broad, rolling plains of Hungary are among the most fertile in Europe, yet the imposing Carpathian Mountains vault to craggy, barren heights. The Balkan highlands sport a cloak of dense forest and thick mist, while the rocky beaches and crumbling ruins of Greece bake under the blazing Aegean sun.

ALBANIA

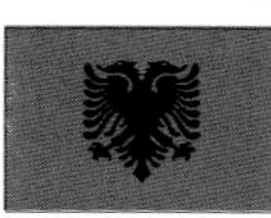

Republic of Albania
Map page 106

Area	10,576 sq. mi.
	(27,398 sq. km.)
Capital	Tiranë
Member of	CE, EBRD, ECE

Population	3,363,000
Population growth rate	1.6%
Life expectancy	69 (m), 75 (f)
Language	Albanian (dialects: Gheg in
	the north, Tosk in the south)
Adult literacy rate	95%

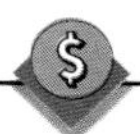

Currency	lek
GNP (U.S.$, in millions)	1,229
Income per capita (U.S.$)	360

Albania is emerging – ever so slowly – from half a century of alienation under dictator Enver Hoxha, who committed this agrarian country to a strict policy of industrialization and repression in the pursuit of a self-reliance that severed its ties with the world. But Hoxha's death in 1985 and the changes that rocked Eastern Europe in 1989 combined to end Albania's Communist rule by 1992.

Language and land still isolate this nation: Albanians speak a tongue unlike any other in Europe, and the country is shielded by rugged mountains. Horse-drawn wagons provide the main mode of transport; private cars were banned prior to 1991. Exports of chromium bring in foreign dollars, but riots and food shortages plague Albania, which remains the poorest nation in Europe.

BOSNIA & HERZEGOVINA

Republic of Bosnia and Herzegovina
Map page 104

Area	19,736 sq. mi.
	(51,129 sq. km.)
Capital	Sarajevo
Member of	ECE

Population	3,527,000
Population growth rate	−5.0%
Life expectancy	not available
Language	Serbo-Croat (Muslims and
	Croats use Roman script; Serbs, Cyrillic)
Adult literacy rate	93%

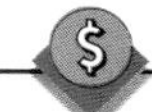

Currency	Bosnia and Herzegovina dinar
GNP (U.S.$, in millions)	not available
Income per capita (U.S.$)	not available

Of all the former Yugoslavian provinces, none descended into civil war as deeply as Bosnia and Herzegovina. Bosnian Muslims, descendants of Slavs converted to Islam under Turkish rule, battled a minority of Orthodox Serbs from 1992 to 1995, when a U.S.-brokered truce and UN troops imposed peace. In addition to the victims of warfare and "ethnic cleansing" campaigns, casualties included the manufacturing sector and Sarajevo – reduced to ruins just 10 years after hosting the 1984 Winter Olympics.

CROATIA

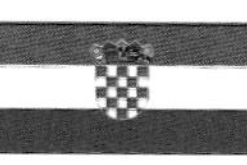

Republic of Croatia
Map page 104

Area	21,851 sq. mi.
	(56,610 sq. km.)
Capital	Zagreb
Member of	CE, EBRD, ECE

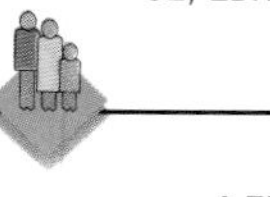

Population	4,779,000
Population growth rate	0.7%
Life expectancy	71 (m), 78 (f)
Language	Serbo-Croat
Adult literacy rate	93%

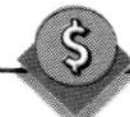

Currency	kuna
GNP (U.S.$, in millions)	12,093
Income per capita (U.S.$)	2,530

Favored with nearly 1,500 mi. (4,000 km.) of stunning Adriatic coastline, a healthy tourist economy, and thriving industries, Croatia declared itself a sovereign state in 1991. Serbia fought to keep the province in Yugoslavia, and Serbs within Croatia later tried to declare independence. With its economy and historic cities (such as Dubrovnik) damaged in the war, Croatia works to restore its old orientation toward western Europe and once again welcomes visitors to the islands and beaches of its scenic coast.

CYPRUS

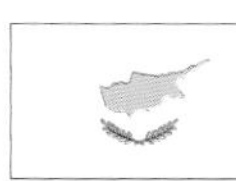

Republic of Cyprus
Map page 118

Area	3,571 sq. mi.
	(9,251 sq. km.)
Capital	Nicosia
Member of	COMM, EBRD, ECE

Population	730,000
Population growth rate	1.1%
Life expectancy	77 (av. m/f)
Languages	Greek, Turkish
Adult literacy rate	94%

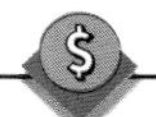

Currency	Cyprus pound
GNP (U.S.$, in millions)	7,539
Income per capita (U.S.$)	10,380

The isle of Cyprus, coveted in classical times for copper (which takes its name from the island), stands today a nation divided. Perched amid Europe, Asia, and Africa, Cyprus has survived invasions by Byzantines, Turks, and Britons. In 1974 Turkish troops returned to halt fighting between ethnic Turks and Greeks. A force of UN peacekeepers now mans the partition between the self-declared Turkish Republic of Northern Cyprus and the remainder of the island.

CZECH REPUBLIC

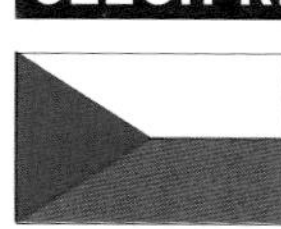

Czech Republic
Map page 97

Area	30,442 sq. mi.
	(78,864 sq. km.)
Capital	Prague
Member of	CE, EBRD, ECE

Population	10,331,000
Population growth rate	0.1%
Life expectancy	68 (m), 75 (f)
Languages	Czech, *German, others*
Adult literacy rate	99%

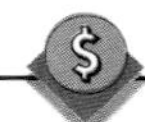

Currency	Czech koruna
GNP (U.S.$, in millions)	33,051
Income per capita (U.S.$)	3,210

Born at the close of World War I, Czechoslovakia, like Yugoslavia to the south, was a multiethnic concoction pieced out of the shattered Austro-Hungarian Empire. In the 1990s the Czechs and Slovaks managed an amicable divorce without the bloody fighting that accompanied the Yugoslav breakup.

Landlocked and ringed by mountains, the Czech Republic incorporates the medieval states of Bohemia and Moravia, ancient centers of commerce, learning, and religion. Its capital, Prague, is one of the most beautiful cities in the world; its baroque center and venerable university have weathered the centuries remarkably intact.

Struggle against powerful neighbors has defined the 20th-century Czech experience. Offered the largely German-speaking Czech Sudetenland as appeasement in 1938, Hitler gobbled up the entire country. In 1948 a Communist takeover brought Czechoslovakia into the Eastern Bloc. Liberalization was crushed by Soviet tanks in 1968, but the "Velvet Revolution" of 1989 was eastern Europe's smoothest unshackling of Communist fetters, putting formerly jailed dissident playwright Vaclav Havel in the president's chair. A few years later, Slovakian demands for independence met with scant resistance, and the split became effective in 1993. Of the two nations, the heavily industrialized Czech Republic is better poised to make economic headway, with rapid privatization and an eager resumption of its historic ties with western Europe.

GREECE

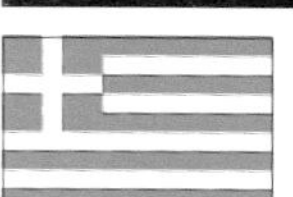

The Hellenic Republic
Map pages 106–7

Area	50,935 sq. mi.
	(131,957 sq. km.)
Capital	Athens
Member of	CE, EBRD, ECE, EU, NATO

Population	10,369,000
Population growth rate	0.5%
Life expectancy	75 (m), 80 (f)
Language	Greek
Adult literacy rate	95.2%

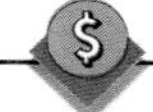

Currency	drachma
GNP (U.S.$, in millions)	80,194
Income per capita (U.S.$)	7,710

On a jagged peninsula in the southeastern corner of Europe, Western civilization was born some two and a half millennia ago. Greece will forever be associated with the golden age of Athens – the flowering of art, philosophy, and democratic government in the fifth century BC. Although the Parthenon still crowns the Acropolis, and visitors still seek the past from Macedonia to Rhodes, present-day Greece is primarily a product of the intervening centuries. Conquered by Alexander the Great, later a province of Rome and Byzantium, Greece was subject to Turkish rule until 1830 and entered the modern era as an agrarian backwater.

Since World War II and the bitter civil war that followed, Greece has become an urban, industrial society. The population of Athens increased six-fold

between 1945 and 1995, leading to such intense air pollution that classical monuments were threatened and cars were eventually banned from the city's center. Seafaring traditions also play out on a modern industrial scale; Greeks are the world's leading shipowners. Yet old rural ways live on, both on the mainland and in villages that dot some of Greece's 2,000 islands. Lemons, olives, and myriad fruits scent the countryside, and small-town life still revolves around the taverna and the square.

HUNGARY

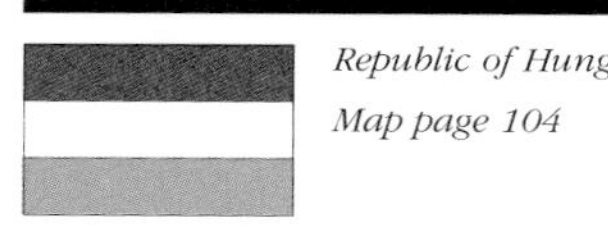

Republic of Hungary
Map page 104

Area	35,910 sq. mi. (93,030 sq. km.)
Capital	Budapest
Member of	CE, EBRD, ECE, EU (assoc.)
Population	10,277,000
Population growth rate	–0.4%
Life expectancy	65 (m), 74 (f)
Language	Hungarian
Adult literacy rate	99%

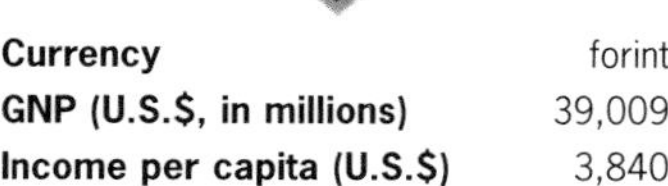

Currency	forint
GNP (U.S.$, in millions)	39,009
Income per capita (U.S.$)	3,840

Hungary was the first breach in the monolithic wall of European Communism. Opening its borders in 1989, the nation became a conduit for refugees from Soviet satellites, and a champion of the liberalization that culminated in the Soviet Union's own demise in 1991. Hungary's transformation reversed the dark legacy of 1956, when an anti-Communist uprising was crushed by Soviet tanks.

The fertile, landlocked plains of Hungary, drained by the glorious Danube, were settled in the ninth century by fiercely independent Magyars from the Asian steppes. A sovereign kingdom for centuries before succumbing to Turkish, then Austrian rule, Hungary carved out a semi-autonomous existence within the Hapsburg realm. The dual monarchy – Austria's emperor was also Hungary's king – lasted until World War I.

As a Soviet satellite after World War II, Hungary survived the failed 1956 uprising to follow a course away from political and economic repression, capped by the dissolution of its Communist Party in 1989. Despite the high cost of adopting a market economy, recent years have witnessed the debut of the first stock market in the former Eastern Bloc (in cosmopolitan Budapest), successful privatization of industries and agriculture, and free elections.

MACEDONIA

Former Yugoslav Republic of Macedonia
Map page 106

Area	9,925 sq. mi. (25,713 sq. km.)
Capital	Skopje
Member of	CE, EBRD, ECE
Population	1,937,000
Population growth rate	–1.5%
Life expectancy	70 (m), 74 (f)
Languages	Macedonian, *Albanian, Serbo-Croat*
Adult literacy rate	93%

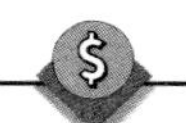

Currency	denar
GNP (U.S.$, in millions)	1,653
Income per capita (U.S.$)	790

Landlocked, mountainous, and independent since 1992, Macedonia shares a border – and its name – with a province in northern Greece. Resenting Macedonia's adoption of this name and fearing that it signified an intent to assimilate the province, Greece blockaded the former Yugoslav republic in 1994. A 1995 agreement stabilized relations, but the issue of Macedonia's name remains a source of tension.

POLAND

Republic of Poland
Map page 97

Area	120,696 sq. mi. (312,685 sq. km.)
Capital	Warsaw
Member of	CE, EBRD, ECE
Population	38,581,000
Population growth rate	0.3%
Life expectancy	68 (m), 76 (f)
Languages	Polish, *German*
Adult literacy rate	99%

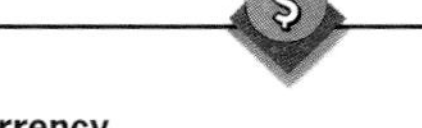

Currency	new zloty
GNP (U.S.$, in millions)	94,613
Income per capita (U.S.$)	2,470

Standing astride the Northern European Plain, Poland under its late-medieval kings was one of the region's great powers. The broad plain, however, offers no natural defenses, making the territory vulnerable to invaders from both east and west.

Poland's long history is one of subjugation and reemergence. It is the story of a brave nation fighting not only for independence, but for its very existence. In 1795 Poland was erased from the map – partitioned among Prussia, Austria, and Russia – not to return until the end of World War I. But the new Poland was again fair game for aggressive neighbors. Hitler and Stalin agreed to divide and swallow Poland, and the Nazi invasion in 1939 signaled the start of World War II. More than 6 million Poles, half of them Jews, died over the next six years.

After the war Poland became the largest nation of the Communist Eastern Bloc. With its map redrawn, Poland ceded eastern farmlands to the Soviets but came into possession of extensive German territories, including industrial Silesia and the Baltic port of Gdansk. Peace, however, brought Communist repression and inefficiency; Poles chafed under their Soviet-controlled regime and its suppression of their long-cherished Roman Catholic religion.

Fueled by increasing economic hardships, protests came to a head in 1980 with the founding of Solidarity, an independent trade union. After 10 years of struggle, Solidarity saw its leader, Lech Walesa, voted president of Poland in free elections. Since then, Poles have wrestled with the harsh reality of converting to a free-market economy and industrial privatization. The role of the now-liberated church also remains a lively topic of debate.

SLOVAKIA

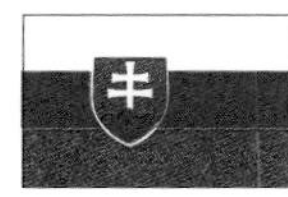

Slovak Republic
Map page 97

Area	18,928 sq. mi. (49,036 sq. km.)
Capital	Bratislava
Member of	CE, EBRD, ECE
Population	5,368,000
Population growth rate	0.4%
Life expectancy	67 (m), 75 (f)
Languages	Slovak, *Hungarian, Czech, others*
Adult literacy rate	93%

Currency	Slovak koruna
GNP (U.S.$, in millions)	11,914
Income per capita (U.S.$)	2,230

The two nations that linked themselves in 1918 to form Czechoslovakia peacefully split into separate republics in 1993. The division was partly a result of Czech dominance in political and economic spheres and Slovakian discontent with this state of affairs, but it also reflected distinct cultural differences between the two emergent nations: Slovakian culture is Hungarian in origin, while Czech culture bespeaks Germanic roots. Never as economically vibrant as its former partner, Slovakia faces the challenge of improving its outmoded factories and broadening its industrial base.

SLOVENIA

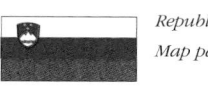

Republic of Slovenia
Map page 103

Area	7,818 sq. mi. (20,253 sq. km.)
Capital	Ljubljana
Member of	CE, EBRD, ECE
Population	1,990,000
Population growth rate	0.7%
Life expectancy	69 (m), 77 (f)
Languages	Slovene, *Hungarian, Italian*
Adult literacy rate	99%

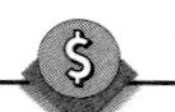

Currency	tolar
GNP (U.S.$, in millions)	14,246
Income per capita (U.S.$)	7,140

Long-standing ties to the West helped Slovenia forge the strongest, most peaceful bid for independence of all the former Yugoslav republics. Recognized by the UN in 1992, this young nation weathered rising crime and economic turmoil after the breakup of its mother country. With ample natural resources, a balanced economy, and high educational standards – its people rank eighth in literacy worldwide – Slovenia has the tools for a prosperous future.

YUGOSLAVIA

Federal Republic of Yugoslavia
Map page 104

Area	39,439 sq. mi. (102,173 sq. km.)
Capital	Belgrade
Member of	ECE
Population	10,482,000
Population growth rate	0.9%
Life expectancy	72 (av. m/f)
Language	Serbo-Croat (Cyrillic script)
Adult literacy rate	89%

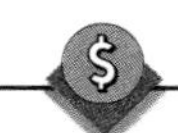

Currency	new Yugoslav dinar
GNP (U.S.$, in millions)	9,520
Income per capita (U.S.$)	900

Today's Yugoslavia is only a remnant of a larger nation assembled from Serbia and fragments of the Turkish and Austrian empires in 1918. Long held together by the charismatic dictator Tito, Yugoslavia's ethnic states grew restless after his death in 1980. In the early 1990s all but Serbia and Montenegro declared their independence. Serbia's futile war to prevent the breakaway of Croatia, and its support of the Serbian side in the Bosnian bloodbath incurred UN sanctions that devastated Yugoslavia's economy. Sanctions were lifted in 1995.

20TH-CENTURY LANDMARKS

1908 Bosnia and Herzegovina annexed by Austria-Hungary.

— 1910 —

1912–13 Balkan Wars.

1914–18 Assassination of Archduke Ferdinand by a Serbian nationalist sparks World War I.

1918 Czechoslovakia; Hungary; Kingdom of Serbs, Croats, and Slovenes; and Poland become republics.

— 1920 —

1928 King Zog, the former prime minister, is crowned in Albania.

— 1930 —

1939 Germany invades Poland, marking the start of World War II.

— 1940 —

1940 Hungary and Slovakia support the German-Italian Axis.

1941 Germany invades Yugoslavia and Greece.

1944 Soviet forces occupy Czechoslovakia, Hungary, and Poland.

1945 Marshal Tito declares Communist rule in Yugoslavia.

1947 Czechoslovakia, Hungary, and Poland become Communist.

— 1950 —

1956 Hungarian uprising suppressed by Soviet troops.

— 1960 —

1967 Greek colonels depose monarch.

1968 Prague Spring in Czechoslovakia crushed by Soviet troops.

— 1970 —

1973 Greece declared a republic.

1974 Northern Cyprus invaded by Turkey; the island is partitioned.

— 1980 —

1980 Solidarity trade union formed in Poland; martial law imposed (in 1981) after civil unrest.

1989 Czechoslovakia, Hungary, and Poland overthrow Communism.

— 1990 —

1991 Independence of Croatia, Macedonia, and Slovenia declared.

1992 Civil war begins in former Yugoslavia.

1993 Czechoslovakia divides into the Czech Republic and Slovakia.

1995 Fragile peace made in Croatia and in Bosnia and Herzegovina.

RUSSIA AND WESTERN NEIGHBORS

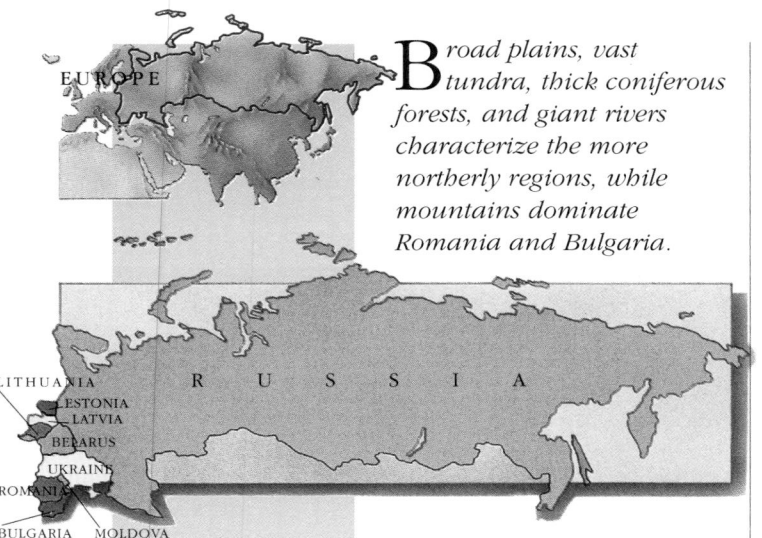

Broad plains, vast tundra, thick coniferous forests, and giant rivers characterize the more northerly regions, while mountains dominate Romania and Bulgaria.

BELARUS

Republic of Belarus
Map page 110

Area	80,132 sq. mi.
	(207,595 sq. km.)
Capital	Minsk
Member of	CIS, EBRD, ECE

Population	10,297,000
Population growth rate	0.2%
Life expectancy	64 (m), 74 (f)
Languages	Belarussian, Russian
Adult literacy rate	97.9%

Currency	Belarussian ruble
GNP (U.S.$, in millions)	21,937
Income per capita (U.S.$)	2,160

Kings and czars once hunted in the forests of western Belarus, a landlocked nation ruled in medieval times by Kiev, then Lithuania, Poland, and beginning in the late 1700s, Russia. Today this woodland, which shelters wild European bison, is part of Europe's oldest nature preserve. Forests still cover a third of Belarus (formerly known as Belorussia, or "White Russia").

World War II devastated Belarus, claiming a quarter of its people and reducing Minsk to rubble. After the war the Soviet Union set about industrializing Belarus, but this flat, marsh-covered country remains largely agricultural. In 1986 Belarus's agricultural vitality was threatened by an explosion at the Chernobyl nuclear power plant in neighboring Ukraine. Seventy percent of the fallout descended on Belarussian soil. The disaster still burdens the country, saddling it with enormous cleanup costs, endangering its citizens with rising cancer rates, and condemning a portion of its farm products.

Slow economic reform in the post-Soviet era and dependence on Russia for fuel, steel, and other raw materials also fetter progress. With a population that is 98 percent Slavic, however, Belarus has escaped the ethnic strife that troubles other former Soviet republics.

Abbreviations

BSEC *Black Sea Economic Cooperation Group*

CE *Council of Europe*

CIS *Commonwealth of Independent States*

EBRD *European Bank for Reconstruction and Development*

ECE *Economic Commission for Europe*

ESCAP *Economic and Social Commission for Asia and the Pacific*

GNP *Gross National Product*

BULGARIA

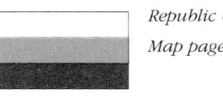

Republic of Bulgaria
Map page 105

Area	42,844 sq. mi.
	(110,994 sq. km.)
Capital	Sofia
Member of	BSEC, CE, EBRD, ECE

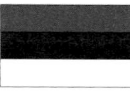

Population	8,427,000
Population growth rate	−0.2%
Life expectancy	68 (m), 74 (f)
Languages	Bulgarian, Turkish, others
Adult literacy rate	92%

Currency	lev
GNP (U.S.$, in millions)	10,255
Income per capita (U.S.$)	1,160

In 1878 the armies of the tsar helped liberate Bulgaria from five centuries of rule by the Ottoman Turks. Since then this mountainous, largely agricultural land has depended heavily on Russia for trade and support.

Before the collapse of the Soviet Union, land reforms and improved farming techniques quadrupled crop yields between 1950 and 1970. Bulgarian wines and tobacco have become known worldwide, and perfume oils from the Valley of Roses fetch thousands of dollars per pint. The economy, however, has turned down sharply in recent years. Bread shortages, unemployment, and ethnic tension between the Bulgarian majority and Turkish minority continue to vex the country.

The nation's leaders are attempting to expand trade with Western Europe and to develop the Black Sea beaches and ski slopes as tourist attractions. Nevertheless, Bulgaria remains one of the poorest countries in Europe, and for most citizens prosperous times are still a distant dream.

ESTONIA

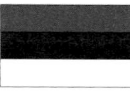

Republic of Estonia
Map page 67

Area	17,458 sq. mi.
	(45,227 sq. km.)
Capital	Tallinn
Member of	CE, EBRD, ECE

Population	1,492,000
Population growth rate	0.1%
Life expectancy	62 (m), 74 (f)
Languages	Estonian, Russian
Adult literacy rate	99.7%

Currency	kroon
GNP (U.S.$, in millions)	4,351
Income per capita (U.S.$)	2,820

Glacial ice scoured the land that is now Estonia, leaving behind a flat, marshy terrain pocked with lakes. As they melted, the glaciers also created the Baltic Sea, Estonia's gateway to the world. The main port is Tallinn, where tiled roofs and turrets adorn old buildings, evoking the city's medieval origins.

Estonia has known centuries of foreign rule, including two periods of domination by Russia – one ending in 1918, the other in 1991. Russians remain a large minority; only 60 percent of the population is made up of ethnic Estonians. Yet this was among the first of the 15 former Soviet republics to declare independence, and the quickest to benefit from a free-market economy. It is noted for its production of consumer goods, from electric motors and textiles to cross-country skis.

LATVIA

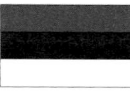

Republic of Latvia
Map page 67

Area	24,931 sq. mi.
	(64,589 sq. km.)
Capital	Riga
Member of	CE, EBRD, ECE

Population	2,530,000
Population growth rate	−0.1%
Life expectancy	62 (m), 74 (f)
Languages	Latvian, Russian
Adult literacy rate	98%

Currency	Latvian lats
GNP (U.S.$, in millions)	5,920
Income per capita (U.S.$)	2,290

Long a pawn of foreign powers, Latvia enjoyed a brief period of independence from 1918 until 1939, following two centuries of Russian rule. With the outbreak of World War II, it was annexed by the Soviet Union and did not regain its independence until 1991. These long periods of foreign domination have left their mark: ethnic Latvians account for only a bit more than half of the population. The largest minority is made up of Russians (about one-third of the total), many of whom moved in to man the country's factories during the rapid industrialization of recent decades.

A broad lowland plain with few natural resources, Latvia depends on its neighbors for energy: Russia for oil and natural gas, Estonia and Lithuania for electricity. But its industrial base is strong; it makes electrical appliances, automobiles, fertilizers, pharmaceuticals, textiles, and farm equipment. The capital city, Riga, once nicknamed "the Paris of the Baltic," remains one of the busiest ports on the Baltic Sea.

LITHUANIA

Republic of Lithuania
Map page 67

Area	25,206 sq. mi.
	(65,300 sq. km.)
Capital	Vilnius
Member of	CE, EBRD, ECE

Population	3,718,000
Population growth rate	0.7%
Life expectancy	63 (m), 75 (f)
Languages	Lithuanian, Russian, Polish, Yiddish
Adult literacy rate	98.4%

Currency	litas
GNP (U.S.$, in millions)	4,992
Income per capita (U.S.$)	1,350

Largest of the three Baltic States, Lithuania is also the least developed. Its low-lying, sandy coast affords no natural harbor, thus depriving the country of easy access to overseas markets. Yet prior to the 18th century, the well-preserved city of Vilnius was the capital of the Grand Duchy of Lithuania, which once extended across present-day Russia and Ukraine from the Baltic Sea all the way to the Black Sea.

Later annexed by Russia, a much-reduced Lithuania won two decades of freedom following World War I. It was taken over by the Soviet Union in 1940, and in 1990 became the first of the former Soviet republics to declare itself an independent nation.

Mostly lowlands dotted with lakes and fringed white-sand beaches, Lithuania's rich farmlands continue to produce meat and dairy products, as they have for centuries. Since the 1940s, industrial production has increased. One prized product – amber – is collected along the Baltic Coast just as it has been since Roman times.

MOLDOVA

Republic of Moldova
Map page 105

Area	13,008 sq. mi.
	(33,700 sq. km.)
Capital	Chisinău
Member of	BSEC, CE, CIS, EBRD, ECE

Population	4,350,000
Population growth rate	0.5%
Life expectancy	64 (m), 71 (f)
Languages	Moldovan (Romanian), Russian
Adult literacy rate	96.4%

Currency	Moldovan leu
GNP (U.S.$, in millions)	3,853
Income per capita (U.S.$)	870

Small and densely populated, the former Soviet republic of Moldova is a land of rolling plains graced with a mild climate. Its fields produce bumper crops of wheat, fruit, cotton, and tobacco; the grapes in its vineyards yield some of the world's finest wines.

Moldova's unique ethnic mix reflects its history as Bessarabia, a territory that endured periods of Romanian, Turkish, and Russian control. Nearly two-thirds of the population share a common ancestry with the people of neighboring Romania, which ruled much of Bessarabia before it was annexed by the Soviet Union in 1940. Despite this link reunification with Romania was voted down in 1994. Meanwhile, some of Moldova's minorities demand their own autonomous republics.

ROMANIA

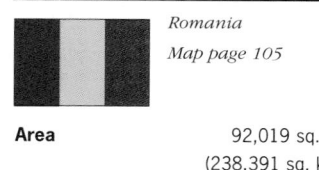

Romania
Map page 105

Area	92,019 sq. mi.
	(238,391 sq. km.)
Capital	Bucharest
Member of	BSEC, CE, EBRD, ECE

Population	22,731,000
Population growth rate	0.2%
Life expectancy	67 (m), 73 (f)
Languages	Romanian, *Hungarian,*
	German, others
Adult literacy rate	96.7%

Currency	Romanian leu
GNP (U.S.$, in millions)	27,921
Income per capita (U.S.$)	1,230

A Latin nation in a neighborhood of Slavs, Romania owes its name and language to a time when much of it was a colony of ancient Rome. Since then Romania's fertile Danube River lowlands and the fields and forests of its Transylvanian highlands have attracted occupation by – among others – Hungarians, Mongols, Austrians, Turks, and Russians.

The nation's dark history is reflected in the reputation of its most notorious figure, Vlad Tepes (1456-75), the so-called "Impaler" who became the model for literatures's most famous vampire, Count Dracula. During World War II Romania supplied Nazi Germany with oil from its Ploiesti oil fields. (The reserves are now severely depleted.) With the Allied victory, the country fell under control of the Soviet Union.

Under the oppressive 24-year rule of Communist dictator Nicolae Ceausescu, Romania saw an explosive burst of industrial development – largely at the expense of Romanian consumers. When the economy stalled in the 1980s, Ceausescu pushed exports of petroleum and agricultural products to pay off debts. Food and electricity ran short, even as the president poured money into building himself a palace in Bucharest.

In 1989 the people rebelled and Ceausescu was executed. Since then ethnic tension, recession, and foot-dragging by ex-Communist politicians has burdened Romania's transition to a free-market economy. There are signs of recovery, however. The nation welcomes foreign investment as it sets about privatizing its industries. Farm production, though lagging, is still substantial enough to create a surplus for export.

RUSSIA

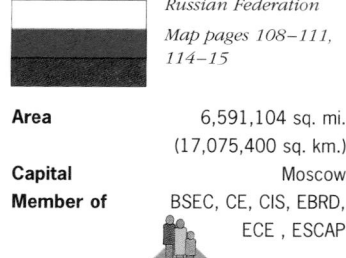

Russian Federation
Map pages 108–111,
114–15

Area	6,591,104 sq. mi.
	(17,075,400 sq. km.)
Capital	Moscow
Member of	BSEC, CE, CIS, EBRD,
	ECE , ESCAP

Population	148,100,000
Population growth rate	0.5%
Life expectancy	62 (m), 74 (f)
Languages	Russian, *Tatar, Yakut,*
	Chuvash, Bashkir, others
Adult literacy rate	99%

Currency	Russian ruble
GNP (U.S.$, in millions)	392,496
Income per capita (U.S.$)	2,650

Even stripped of its empire, Russia – in size alone – captures every superlative. Sprawled across the top of two continents, from the Baltic Sea in the west to the Bering Strait in the east, it spans 11 time zones and embraces roughly one-ninth of the world's land mass. Its climate ranges from Arctic ice field to Siberian forest, from grassy plains to sunbaked deserts and palm-fringed Black Sea beachfront. This giant landscape contains Europe's tallest peak, Mount Elbrus, at 18,510 ft. (5,642 m.); its longest river, the Volga, 2,292 mi. (3,689 km.) long; and the world's deepest lake, Baikal, which bottoms out at 5,315 ft. (1,621 m.) deep. The Trans-Siberian Railway, running 5,775 mi. (9,294 km.) from Moscow to Vladivostok (located near the Sea of Japan), is the world's longest stretch of track.

As a political entity, Russia still rivets the attention. Ranking sixth in population, it has an astonishing wealth of resources and a diversified industrial base. At the same time, it wields a Cold War legacy of nuclear weapons and an army that

remains strong in numbers. Not surprisingly, the collapse of Russia's militant Communist government in 1990 was met with near-universal rejoicing.

Russia came into being as medieval Slavic states coalesced around the principality of Muscovy, in a region of Eastern Europe influenced by the Byzantine Empire and the Orthodox Church. In the 16th century, following an era of Mongol domination, the first great Russian tsar, Ivan IV ("the terrible"), began pushing eastward across the steppes, over the Ural Mountains, and into Siberia. Then, beginning with Peter the Great (1682-1725), Russia turned its imperial eye toward Europe, spreading its borders into the Baltic States, Poland, Moldova, and south to the Caucasus.

In the course of expansion, Russia acquired huge resources of timber, furs, gold, diamonds, coal, iron, and other strategic minerals. Its oil reserves are among the world's largest. The nation also gathered in a vast polyglot population of ethnic groups; some, like the Tatars and Bashkirs, now inhabit their own autonomous republics within the Russian Federation.

The reign of the tsars ended with the Bolshevik revolution of 1917, which ushered in 73 years of Communist rule. Under Vladimir Lenin and his successor, Joseph Stalin, the Soviet Union (as the Russian empire was now recast) was hauled out of its feudal past and into a future built upon steel quotas, five-year plans, and huge collective farms. The process was ruthless. Stalin's labor camps, political purges, and the famine that accompanied his collective farm programs, accounted for some 20 million Russian deaths – a figure comparable to the losses sustained by the Soviets during World War II.

After victory over Germany in 1945, the Soviet Union emerged as a superpower locked in an ideological Cold War with its former ally, the United States. Pushing outward, the Soviets extended their control across Eastern Europe. But by the late 1980s, the numbing cost of the arms race, along with the restiveness of satellite nations and the liberal policies of Soviet President Mikhail Gorbachev, helped bring about the fall of Communism. Russia, dominant republic in the vanished Soviet empire, was left with the lion's share of its problems: inefficient systems of production and distribution, outmoded infrastructure, agricultural stagnation, and the dreary distinction of being one of the most polluted nations on earth. What is more, the move to open democracy has led to a state of political turmoil with no end in sight.

UKRAINE

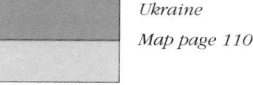

Ukraine
Map page 110

Area	233,028 sq. mi.
	(603,700 sq. km.)
Capital	Kiev
Member of	BSEC, CE, CIS, EBRD, ECE

Population	51,728,000
Population growth rate	0.1%
Life expectancy	64 (m), 69 (f)
Languages	Ukrainian (Cyrillic script),
	Russian, Romanian, Hungarian, Polish
Adult literacy rate	96%

Currency	hryvna
GNP (U.S.$, in millions)	80,921
Income per capita (U.S.$)	1,570

Largest and richest of the former Soviet republics (except for Russia itself), Ukraine is charged with a sense of national identity that dates back more than a millennium. Ukrainians trace their roots to the ninth century Slavic kingdom of Kievan Rus, centered on Kiev, which became the parent state of both Russia and the Ukraine.

Ukrainian sovereignty, though, has been painfully elusive. Centuries of foreign domination – by Mongols, Lithuanians, Poles, Austrians, and Russians – were relieved by only a brief era of Cossack self-rule during the 1600s. More recently a bid for independence from Russia after World War I was put down by Lenin's Red Army, and enforced farm collectivization (under Stalin in the 1930s) claimed some 5 million lives. During World War II Ukraine bore the brunt of the German army's onslaught and retreat, at a cost of 7.5 million lives. In 1991 Ukraine at last gained independence, a move that triggered the final breakup of the Soviet Union. It is now Europe's second-largest country.

The young nation's principal asset is a flat central plain – more than 600 miles across – that contains some of the world's richest soil. In years past this region (known as the breadbasket of Russia) produced more than 40 percent of the Soviet Union's agricultural output. The country is also rich in deposits of coal and iron, which feed a large and diverse industrial sector in the Donets Basin and elsewhere. Crimea, on the Black Sea, is a year-round tourist destination.

Still, Ukraine continues to be plagued by problems. Its ties to Moscow are close but contentious. Moreover, it still suffers contamination from the 1986 meltdown of its Chernobyl nuclear power plant – the world's worst nuclear disaster.

1904 Trans-Siberian railway completed.

— 1910 —

1914–18 World War I: Russia fights on Allies' side until 1917.

1917 Revolution in Russia: tsar abdicates. Lenin becomes leader.

1918–20 Civil war in Russia.

— 1920 —

1922 U.S.S.R. formed.

1924 Lenin dies. Stalin becomes leader.

1928 Collectivization of agriculture in U.S.S.R.

— 1930 —

1932–33 Millions die in Ukraine from famine created by Stalin to crush resistance.

1936 Millions killed or sent to labor camps in U.S.S.R.'s Great Purge.

1939 Stalin signs pact with Hitler. World War II begins.

— 1940 —

1941 Germany invades U.S.S.R. Battle of Kerch and Siege of Leningrad.

1941–44 Belorussia (Belarus), Latvia, and Lithuania occupied by Germany.

1942–43 Battle of Stalingrad.

1945 U.S.S.R. controls Eastern Europe at end of World War II.

1947 Cold War begins.

— 1950 —

1950 Chervenkov made Bulgarian prime minister.

1953 Stalin dies.

1955 Warsaw Pact.

— 1960 —

1962 Cuban missile crisis with U.S.

1965 Ceausescu gains power in Romania.

— 1970 —

1972 Dissidents and intellectuals arrested in Ukraine by U.S.S.R.

— 1980 —

1985 Mikhail Gorbachev made leader of U.S.S.R. *Perestroika* introduced.

1986 Chernobyl nuclear disaster in Ukraine.

1989 East European Communist regimes fall.

— 1990 —

1990 Bulgaria becomes a democratic republic.

1991 CIS established. Boris Yeltsin President of Russian Federation. Warsaw Pact dissolved.

THE MIDDLE EAST AND THE GULF

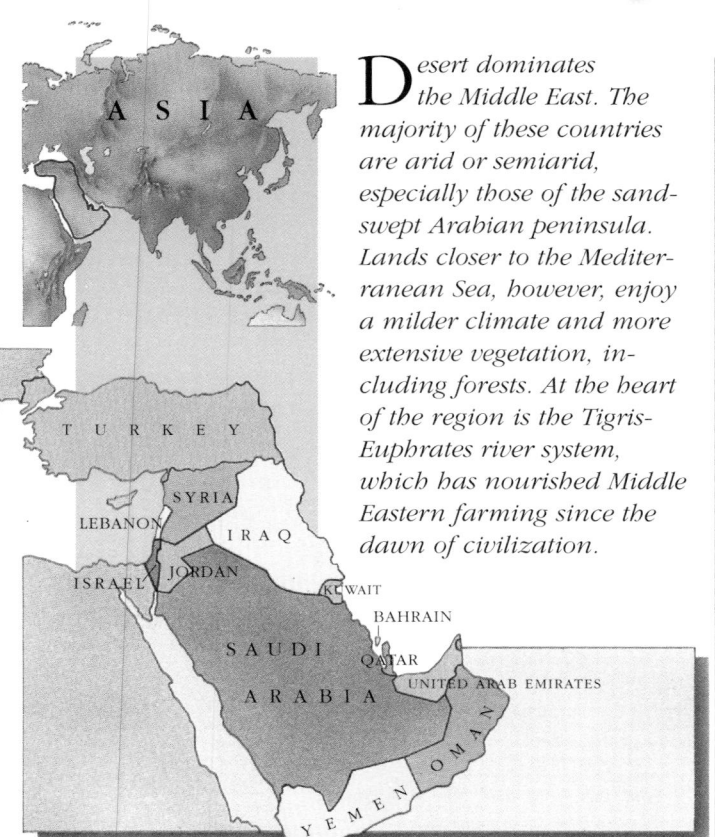

Desert dominates the Middle East. The majority of these countries are arid or semiarid, especially those of the sand-swept Arabian peninsula. Lands closer to the Mediterranean Sea, however, enjoy a milder climate and more extensive vegetation, including forests. At the heart of the region is the Tigris-Euphrates river system, which has nourished Middle Eastern farming since the dawn of civilization.

BAHRAIN

State of Bahrain
Map page 119

Area	268 sq. mi.
	(695 sq. km.)
Capital	Manama
Member of	CCASG, IDB, LAS, OAPEC, OIC

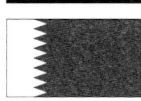

Population	568,000
Population growth rate	3.1%
Life expectancy	69 (m), 73 (f)
Languages	Arabic, English
Adult literacy rate	84.1%

Currency	Bahraini dinar
GNP (U.S.$, in millions)	4,114
Income per capita (U.S.$)	7,500

A tiny group of islands that serve as the center for trade in the Persian Gulf, Bahrain became an independent nation in 1971. Its economy relies on the refinery and export of oil, piped in from neighboring Saudi Arabia. Desalination plants provide much of the fresh water for this arid archipelago.

IRAQ

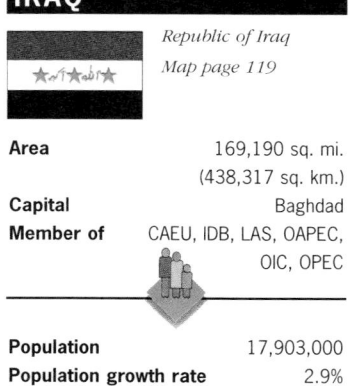

Republic of Iraq
Map page 119

Area	169,190 sq. mi.
	(438,317 sq. km.)
Capital	Baghdad
Member of	CAEU, IDB, LAS, OAPEC, OIC, OPEC

Population	17,903,000
Population growth rate	2.9%
Life expectancy	77 (m), 78 (f)
Languages	Arabic, Kurdish, Turkoman
Adult literacy rate	58%

Currency	Iraqi dinar
GNP (U.S.$, in millions)	15,000 (est.)
Income per capita (U.S.$)	882

An ancient land crippled by modern warfare, Iraq retains its two greatest resources: the fertile valleys of the Tigris and Euphrates rivers and an immense reserve of oil.

Around AD 750 Baghdad became the capital of the Islamic world. Wrested by the British from the Ottoman Empire during World War I, Iraq was a kingdom from 1921 until 1958, when a coup brought republican rule. Saddam Hussein assumed power in 1979.

Iraq's eight-year war against Iran, followed by defeat at the hands of multinational forces responding to its 1990 invasion of Kuwait, resulted in a massive drain of blood and treasure and a UN-sponsored trade embargo. A return to respectability and trade remains hampered by Iraq's suppression of minorities, including northern Kurds and southern Marsh Arabs.

ISRAEL

State of Israel
Map pages 120–21

Area	8,299 sq. mi.
	(21,501 sq. km.)
Capital	Jerusalem
Member of	EBRD, ECE

Population	5,473,000
Population growth rate	2.7%
Life expectancy	75 (m), 79 (f)
Languages	Hebrew, Arabic, many European languages
Adult literacy rate	97%

Currency	new shekel
GNP (U.S.$, in millions)	78,113
Income per capita (U.S.$)	14,410

In Israel religious history exerts a profound influence on present-day politics. The nation's boundaries contain the biblical homeland of the Jews, sites sacred to Muslims, and the birthplace of Christianity.

The modern nation of Israel came into existence in 1948, when a Jewish state in Palestine – already host to a substantial number of prewar Jewish settlers – was created under UN auspices. The new Israelis, their numbers swelled by immigration, made impressive progress in irrigated agriculture and created the most industrialized country in the Middle East.

Since its founding, Israel has struggled with the problem of coexistence between its Jewish population and Arabs living within and beyond its borders.

Israel has fought five major wars with its Arab neighbors, and internal relations between Jews and Palestinians remain tense. Treaties with Egypt and Jordan and cautious steps toward Palestinian self-rule have offered some glimmer of hope.

JORDAN

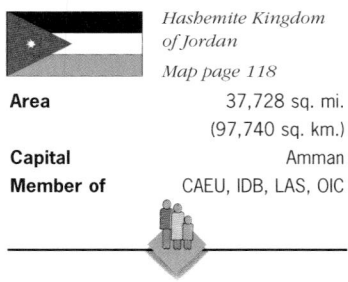

Hashemite Kingdom of Jordan
Map page 118

Area	37,728 sq. mi.
	(97,740 sq. km.)
Capital	Amman
Member of	CAEU, IDB, LAS, OIC

Population	5,198,000
Population growth rate	5.2%
Life expectancy	66 (m), 70 (f)
Language	Arabic
Adult literacy rate	86.6%

Currency	Jordanian dinar
GNP (U.S.$, in millions)	5,849
Income per capita (U.S.$)	1,390

Named for the biblical river along its western flank, Jordan shares the longest border with Israel of any Arab nation and has absorbed vast numbers of Palestinian refugees. Despite this Palestinian influx – which has swollen its capital, Amman – Jordan is fundamentally a nation of Bedouin Arabs.

An independent kingdom since 1946, Jordan has become a stable society with a record of nimble diplomacy under long-reigning King Hussein. Devoid of oil, it draws its revenue from petroleum refining, phosphate exports, tourism (the ruins at Petra are especially popular), and efficient agriculture in its small portion of arable terrain.

KUWAIT

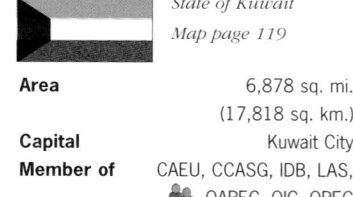

State of Kuwait
Map page 119

Area	6,878 sq. mi.
	(17,818 sq. km.)
Capital	Kuwait City
Member of	CAEU, CCASG, IDB, LAS, OAPEC, OIC, OPEC

Population	1,576,000
Population growth rate	–0.5%
Life expectancy	73 (m), 77 (f)
Languages	Arabic, English
Adult literacy rate	78.6%

Currency	Kuwaiti dinar
GNP (U.S.$, in millions)	31,433
Income per capita (U.S.$)	19,040

Despite its compact size, Kuwait lies atop an enormous reserve of oil, which tempted neighboring Iraq to seize the Persian Gulf state in 1990. Routed by a

multinational coalition of UN-backed forces, Iraqi troops blackened the skies with smoke from burning oil wells. Kuwait has rebuilt its infrastructure, however, and returned to a prosperity that supports extensive social welfare programs. An emirate under dynastic rule since the 18th century, the country has made moves toward political liberalization.

LEBANON

Republic of Lebanon
Map page 118

Area	4,034 sq. mi.
	(10,452 sq. km.)
Capital	Beirut
Member of	IDB, LAS, OIC

Population	2,915,000
Population growth rate	3.3% (est.)
Life expectancy	67 (m), 71 (f)
Languages	Arabic, French, Kurdish, Armenian
Adult literacy rate	92.4%

Currency	Lebanese pound
GNP (U.S.$, in millions)	not available
Income per capita (U.S.$)	not available

Some 3,000 years ago, Phoenician seafarers commanded a mighty empire of trade from the ports of Sidon and Tyre. Their legacy echoed in modern Lebanon's standing as a cosmopolitan financial capital – until civil war between Islamic and Christian factions, followed by Syrian and Israeli invasions, virtually tore the nation apart in the 1970s and 1980s. Rebuilding since peace was recovered in 1989, Lebanon still strives to regain its former prosperity, to restore tourism to its scenic mountains and sea-shores, and to return its French-influenced capital, Beirut, to its one-time status as "the Paris of the Middle East."

OMAN

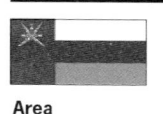

Sultanate of Oman
Map page 116

Area	119,467 sq. mi.
	(309,500 sq. km.)
Capital	Muscat
Member of	CCASG, IDB, LAS, OIC

Population	2,096,000
Population growth rate	4.4%
Life expectancy	67 (m), 68 (f)
Languages	Arabic, English
Adult literacy rate	41%

Currency	Omani rial
GNP (U.S.$, in millions)	10,779
Income per capita (U.S.$)	5,200

Perched on the eastern edge of the Arabian Peninsula, oil-rich Oman commands a strategic position near the mouth of the Persian Gulf and has long attracted invaders, such as the Portuguese and Persians. The present royal line was established in 1741. While southern Oman is mostly desert, its north enjoys enough rainfall to support modest agriculture.

QATAR

State of Qatar
Map page 119

Area	4,415 sq. mi.
	(11,437 sq. km.)
Capital	Doha
Member of	CCASG, IDB, LAS, OAPEC,
	OIC, OPEC

Population	593,000
Population growth rate	4.5%
Life expectancy	69 (m), 74 (f)
Languages	Arabic, *English*
Adult literacy rate	79%

Currency	Qatar riyal
GNP (U.S.\$, in millions)	7,810
GNP per head (U.S.\$)	14,540

Resting on a sunbaked knob of the Arabian Peninsula, the absolute monarchy of Qatar once relied on pearl diving, fishing, and camel breeding as its chief sources of revenue. The discovery of oil and natural gas reserves, however, transformed this impoverished land into one of the wealthiest nations on earth. Descended from three Bedouin tribes, most of Qatar's citizens are Sunni Muslims.

SAUDI ARABIA

Kingdom of Saudi Arabia
Map page 116

Area	864,640 sq. mi.
	(2,240,000 sq. km.)
Capital	Riyadh
Member of	CCASG, IDB, LAS, OAPEC,
	OIC, OPEC

Population	16,930,000
Population growth rate	3.6%
Life expectancy	68 (m), 71 (f)
Language	Arabic
Adult literacy rate	63%

Currency	Saudi riyal
GNP (U.S.\$, in millions)	126,597
Income per capita (U.S.\$)	7,240

Saudi Arabia is the creation of two vastly different forces: the global thirst for oil and the religious conservatism of a desert people. Arabia is the birthplace of Islam, and the Muslim faithful still flock annually to the holy city of Mecca.

The peninsular Arabs spread Islam throughout the Middle East and beyond in the seventh and eighth centuries, but their homeland fell back into tribal conflict and obscurity, eventually becoming part of the Turkish-ruled Ottoman Empire.

After Turkey's defeat in World War I, Arabia was united under King ibn Saud in 1932. The discovery of oil in the 1930s forever changed this land of nomadic herdsmen; since then, the House of Saud and the nation it rules through Islamic law have become synonymous with Arab petroleum wealth. As the world's biggest exporter of oil, Saudi Arabia enjoys a high standard of living and extensive state benefits. Such an economy, however, is vulnerable to shifting oil prices, and the cost of helping to defeat Iraq in the 1991 Gulf War was staggering, even by Saudi standards.

Today this kingdom balances itself between pressures from Islamic traditionalists wary of Western influences and from reformers favoring greater democracy and secularism.

SYRIA

Syrian Arab Republic
Map page 118

Area	71,043 sq. mi.
	(184,050 sq. km.)
Capital	Damascus
Member of	CAEU, IDB, LAS, OAPEC,
	OIC

Population	13,812,000
Population growth rate	3.5%
Life expectancy	64 (m), 68 (f)
Languages	Arabic, *Kurdish*
Adult literacy rate	70.8%

Currency	Syrian pound
GNP (U.S.\$, in millions)	14,607
Income per capita (U.S.\$)	1,170

Home to Damascus and Aleppo – two of the world's oldest continuously inhabited cities – Syria's history dates back some 4,500 years. In ancient times Syria sprawled over an area encompassing Jordan, Lebanon, and Israel. Its modern boundaries were formed during French colonial rule, which lasted from 1920 to 1946.

Most of Syria's population resides within 60 miles of its Mediterranean seacoast. Agriculture is bolstered by the Mediterranean climate (marked by wet, mild winters and hot, dry summers) and ample irrigation from the Euphrates River. Cotton is the main cash crop, but wheat, fruit, and vegetables are also grown. While increasingly industrialized, thanks largely to new oil discoveries

in the 1980s, development has been hindered by conflicts with Israel and tense relations with other neighbors, including Turkey, whose dams on the Euphrates threaten Syria's water supply.

TURKEY

Republic of Turkey
Map pages 107 & 118

Area	300,868 sq. mi.
	(779,452 sq. km.)
Capital	Ankara
Member of	CE, EBRD, ECE, IDB,
	NATO, OIC

Population	61,644,000
Population growth rate	2.1%
Life expectancy	65 (m), 69 (f)
Languages	Turkish, *Kurdish*
Adult literacy rate	82.3%

Currency	Turkish lira
GNP (U.S.\$, in millions)	149,002
Income per capita (U.S.\$)	2,450

Culturally and geographically, Turkey stands at the crossroads of Europe and Asia. As long as 9,000 years ago, the fabled city of Troy stood overlooking the Dardanelles. The Byzantine empire, with its glittering capital, Constantinople, was the eastern successor to Rome for over a thousand years. In 1453 the Ottoman Turks defeated the Byzantines. Their sultans established an empire that fought Venice and Genoa for Mediterranean supremacy and even hammered at the gates of Vienna. The sultans' rule lasted until 1922, following Turkey's defeat in World War I. An army officer named Mustafa Kemal (Ataturk) led the nationalist movement that created a Turkish republic in 1923.

Ataturk made Turkey the most westernized of Islamic nations. He separated mosque and state, romanized the Turkish alphabet, and moved the capital from imperial Constantinople (now Istanbul) to Ankara. Maintaining a secular republic has remained state policy, although Islamic parties have achieved increasing electoral success. Other political issues include Turkey's continued entanglement in Cyprus, where Turks have rebelled against the Greek majority, and internal clashes with Kurdish separatists. The nation boasts productive agriculture, growing industries, and a vigorous tourist economy centered around Mediterranean beaches and classical ruins.

Although patriarchal cultural traditions run deep, in 1993 Turkey became only the second nation in the Islamic world, after Pakistan, to be led by a woman prime minister.

UNITED ARAB EMIRATES

United Arab Emirates
Map page 116

Area	29,992 sq. mi.
	(77,700 sq. km.)
Capital	Abu Dhabi
Member of	CAEU, CCASG, IDB, LAS,
	OAPEC, OIC, OPEC

Population	2,377,700
Population growth rate	3.3%
Life expectancy	73 (m), 75 (f)
Languages	Arabic, *English*
Adult literacy rate	79.2%

Currency	Emirian dirham
GNP (U.S.\$, in millions)	38,700
Income per capita (U.S.\$)	21,420

Skirting the western shore of the Persian Gulf, the United Arab Emirates was created in 1971 by the unification of six independent sheikdoms; the seventh joined in 1972. Until oil was discovered in 1958, the main livelihoods were pearl diving, fishing, and date farming. Since the export of oil began in 1962, oil and gas have transformed this arid land into one of the world's wealthiest nations. Most of its inhabitants are immigrant workers in oil production and other industries.

YEMEN

Republic of Yemen
Map page 116

Area	207,231 sq. mi.
	(536,869 sq. km.)
Capital	San'a
Member of	CAEU, IDB, LAS, OIC

Population	14,561,330
Population growth rate	4.1%
Life expectancy	50 (m), 50 (f)
Language	Arabic
Adult literacy rate	38%

Currency	Yemeni rial
GNP (U.S.\$, in millions)	3,884
Income per capita (U.S.\$)	280

Towering to a height of 12,336 ft. (3,760 m.), the mountains of Yemen create a well-watered landscape in a region dominated by desert. Its climate and strategic location at the mouth of the Red Sea have long attracted settlers. Islamic since the seventh century, Yemen later came under Ottoman rule. The British arrived in the 19th century, occupying the port of Aden until 1967. Once divided into North and South Yemen, the nation was unified in 1990. A secessionist rebellion was suppressed in 1994.

1901–2 Abd al-Aziz, a member of the deposed Saudi family, regains his kingdom (Saudi Arabia).

— 1910 —

1914–18 Ottoman empire (Turkey) sides with Germany during World War I.

1917 British support for a Jewish national home in Palestine outlined in the Balfour Declaration.

— 1920 —

1920 Iraq and Jordan mandated to Britain by League of Nations.

1923 Turkey becomes a republic; President Ataturk initiates reforms.

— 1930 —

1939–45 Genocide of Jews during World War II increases international support for a Jewish homeland.

— 1940 —

1948–9 State of Israel proclaimed. After war with Arab neighbors, Israel emerges with 75% of western Palestine.

— 1950 —

1958 Iraqi monarchy overthrown by military. Syria merges with Egypt to form United Arab Republic (until 1961).

— 1960 —

1960 OPEC founded.

1964 PLO founded.

1967 Israel and Arab states fight Six-Day War.

— 1970 —

1970 Hafiz al-Assad seizes power in Syria.

1973 Egypt and Syria attack Israel to begin the Yom Kippur War.

1974 Turkish troops occupy northern Cyprus.

1975–89 Civil war in Lebanon.

1979 Saddam Hussein gains power in Iraq.

— 1980 —

1980–88 Iran-Iraq war ends in stalemate.

1982 Israel invades Lebanon.

1984 Separatist Kurds start guerrilla war in southeast Turkey.

1988 King Hussein of Jordan cedes claim to West Bank to PLO.

— 1990 —

1990–91 Iraq invades Kuwait; Kuwait liberated by multinational forces.

1993 Israel recognizes PLO as stage in peace negotiations.

INDIAN SUBCONTINENT AND NEIGHBORS

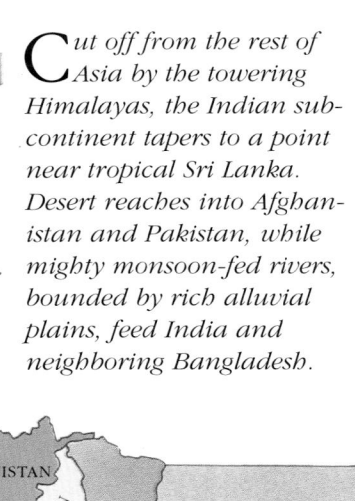

Cut off from the rest of Asia by the towering Himalayas, the Indian subcontinent tapers to a point near tropical Sri Lanka. Desert reaches into Afghanistan and Pakistan, while mighty monsoon-fed rivers, bounded by rich alluvial plains, feed India and neighboring Bangladesh.

AFGHANISTAN

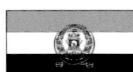

Islamic State of Afghanistan
Map page 116

Area	251,758 sq. mi.
	(652,225 sq. km.)
Capital	Kabul
Member of	ADB, ESCAP, IDB, OIC

Population	17,080,000
Population growth rate	−1%
Life expectancy	41 (m), 42 (f)
Languages	Pashtu, Dari (dialect
	of Farsi), many local languages
Adult literacy rate	29%

Currency	afghani
GNP (U.S.$, in millions)	3,156
Income per capita (U.S.$)	160

Afghanistan, a land whose politics have grown as forbidding as its craggy terrain, stands ravaged by two decades of civil war. Its landlocked perch atop the Khyber Pass has invited invasion by Persians, Arabs, Mongols, the British, and as recently as 1979, the Soviets. The Red Army's 10-year attempt to prop up a Communist regime in Kabul failed, leaving a shattered Afghanistan ruled by warring groups of Muslim guerrillas known as mujahideen. The war left over 1 million dead and sent millions of refugees pouring into Pakistan and Iran. Mountainous, parched, and cursed with the widest temperature range of any nation, Afghanistan's land yields just one dependable crop: opium.

Abbreviations
ADB *Asian Development Bank*
CIS *Commonwealth of Independent States*
COMM *Commonwealth*
EBRD *European Bank for Reconstruction and Development*
ECE *Economic Commission for Europe*
ESCAP *Economic and Social Commission for Asia and the Pacific*
IDB *Islamic Development Bank*
OIC *Organization of the Islamic Conference*
OPEC *Organization of Petroleum Exporting Countries*

GNP *Gross National Product*

ARMENIA

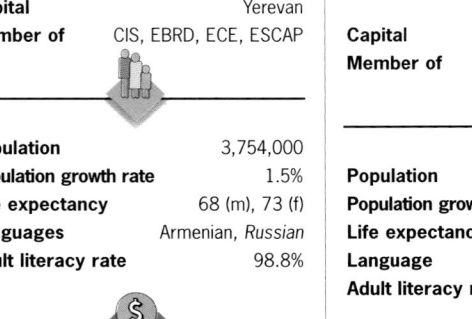

Republic of Armenia
Map page 111

Area	11,503 sq. mi.
	(29,800 sq. km.)
Capital	Yerevan
Member of	CIS, EBRD, ECE, ESCAP

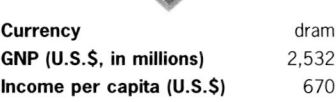

Population	3,754,000
Population growth rate	1.5%
Life expectancy	68 (m), 73 (f)
Languages	Armenian, *Russian*
Adult literacy rate	98.8%

Currency	dram
GNP (U.S.$, in millions)	2,532
Income per capita (U.S.$)	670

Violence has afflicted Armenia (smallest of the former Soviet republics) since the fourth century, when it became the world's first state to officially adopt Christianity. During World War I hundreds of thousands of Armenians were massacred by Turks, with whom Armenia has long been at odds. Bordered on three sides by Islamic countries, Armenia is engaged in an ongoing conflict with Azerbaijan over disputed territory.

AZERBAIJAN

Azerbaijan Republic
Map page 111

Area	33,428 sq. mi.
	(86,600 sq. km.)
Capital	Baku
Member of	CIS, EBRD, ESCAP, IDB, OIC

Population	7,499,000
Population growth rate	1.3%
Life expectancy	67 (m), 74 (f)
Language	Azerbaijani
Adult literacy rate	97.3%

Currency	Azerbaijani manat
GNP (U.S.$, in millions)	3,730
Income per capita (U.S.$)	500

The euphoria of independence in 1991 quickly turned to the despair of war as Azerbaijan battled Armenia for control of Nagorno-Karabakh, an enclave in southwestern Azerbaijan populated mainly by Armenians. A ceasefire signed in 1994 called a temporary halt to the fighting; Armenia currently controls the area. The country's economy has been hobbled by this conflict, but natural resources may boost it in the future. Azerbaijan's long coastline along the Caspian Sea harbors oil reserves that have been exploited for over 1,000 years, while its rivers irrigate crops of cotton, grain, and grapes in this largely dry land.

BANGLADESH

People's Republic of Bangladesh
Map pages 122–23

Area	56,962 sq. mi.
	(147,570 sq. km.)
Capital	Dhaka
Member of	ADB, COMM, ESCAP,
	IDB, OIC

Population	117,787,000
Population growth rate	2%
Life expectancy	57 (m), 56 (f)
Language	Bangla, *English*
Adult literacy rate	38%

Currency	taka
GNP (U.S.$, in millions)	26,636
Income per capita (U.S.$)	230

An immense yet fragile marshland, Bangladesh floats atop floodplains that are among the most fertile – and deadly – in the world. The country's fortunes rest on the fickle Ganges and Brahmaputra rivers: their silt-rich waters nourish three rice crops a year, but their periodic flooding destroys both crops and homes. Battered by this relentless cycle of flood and consequent famine, the world's most crowded nation – nearly half the population of the U.S. packed into a space no larger than Illinois – remains dirt poor.

The region became East Pakistan when British India was partitioned into Hindu and Muslim states in 1947, but 1,000 miles separated the more populous easterners from the politically dominant west Pakistanis. In 1971 eastern guerrillas, backed by India, won a brutal battle for independence.

Bangladesh has yet to recover from a civil war that left 1 million people dead and spawned a vicious famine. The female-dominated textile trade, which helped carry women to positions of power, has lifted the economy. Nevertheless, floods and other disasters continue to torment this nation, which, with only one hospital bed for every 5,000 people, does not have the means to cope.

BHUTAN

Kingdom of Bhutan
Map page 122

Area	17,949 sq. mi.
	(46,500 sq. km.)
Capital	Thimphu
Member of	ADB, ESCAP

Population	1,375,000
Population growth rate	2.2%
Life expectancy	46 (m), 47 (f)
Language	Dzongkha
Adult literacy rate	38.4%

Currency	ngultrum
GNP (U.S.$, in millions)	272
Income per capita (U.S.$)	under 200

Fiercely protective of its traditions, mountain-bound Bhutan began to build roads only in the 1960s. Except for nomads in the northern Himalayas, most Bhutanese are farmers who live in villages built around Buddhist monasteries. Bhutan's monarch has banned television, and a recent law mandates that residents wear customary attire.

GEORGIA

Republic of Georgia
Map page 111

Area	26,904 sq. mi.
	(69,7001 sq. km.)
Capital	Tbilisi
Member of	CIS, EBRD, ECE

Population	5,471,000
Population growth rate	0.4%
Life expectancy	68 (m), 76 (f)
Language	Georgian, *Russian*
Adult literacy rate	99%

Currency	lari
GNP (U.S.$, in millions)	3,071
Income per capita (U.S.$)	560

Wedged between Russia and the Caucasus Mountains in the north and Turkey in the south, Georgia has been wracked by ethnic fighting since the breakup of the Soviet Union. A proud people with a 5,000-year tradition and a deep devotion to the arts, Georgians resisted Soviet control until the Stalinist purges of the 1930s. Since independence in 1991, civil war and internal fighting with separatist minorities have crippled the mountainous nation.

INDIA

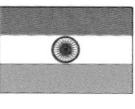

Republic of India
Map pages 122–23

Area	1,268,884 sq. mi.
	(3,287,263 sq. km.)
Capital	New Delhi
Member of	ADB, COMM, ESCAP

Population	920,000,000
Population growth rate	2%
Life expectancy	60 (m), 60 (f)
Languages	Hindi, *English, many local languages*
Adult literacy rate	52%

Currency	rupee
GNP (U.S.$, in millions)	278,739
Income per capita (U.S.$)	310

The world's largest democracy, India combines tremendous accomplishment with dire challenge. Despite its ethnic and cultural diversity – and daunting poverty – this paradox of a country has maintained a parliamentary government and established a solid middle class. Furthermore, it has attained self-sufficiency in agriculture (largely through the efforts of the small landholders who still make up the bulk of the population) and nurtured thriving industries. Yet the sheer number of people on this subcontinent – soon to climb beyond the 1 billion mark – threatens to overwhelm the nation's infrastructure, resources, and land.

India's civilization is one of the oldest in the world, dating back some 5,000 years. The fertile plains and vast plateaus that spread south of the Himalayas have enticed invaders since pre-historic times. Indo-Aryans, bringing the essentials of Hinduism, swept indigenous Dravidian peoples southward about 1500 BC. The arrival of Islam in the eighth century culminated in the great Mogul empire that produced the incomparable Taj Mahal. British commercial interest expanded into imperial domination by 1857, while independence – the goal of Mahatma Ghandi, legendary apostle of nonviolence – was finally achieved in 1947.

Modern India, a land of lilting voices and lemon-colored light, emerged as an independent state when the end of British rule saw the subcontinent partitioned into Islamic Pakistan and Hindu India. The division was accompanied by bitter strife, sending more than 12 million Muslim and Hindu refugees across the newly formed borders and resulting in some 200,000 deaths. Relations with Pakistan remain tense because of India's control of the largely Islamic Kashmir region and its assistance in establishing Bangladesh in 1971.

Internal discord remains an issue in India, where conflicts between Hindus and Sikhs have triggered riots and the assassinations of two prime ministers. The nation also struggles to escape the surviving fetters of an outlawed caste system. Home to some of the world's richest farmland, India must curb its population explosion if it is to take a secure place among the nations of the developed world.

IRAN

Islamic Republic of Iran
Map page 119

Area	636,128 sq. mi.
	(1,648,000 sq. km.)
Capital	Tehran
Member of	ESCAP, IDB, OIC, OPEC

Population	59,778,000
Population growth rate	3.3%
Life expectancy	65 (m), 66 (f)
Languages	Farsi, *Turkic*, *other local languages*
Adult literacy rate	78%

Currency	rial
GNP (U.S.$, in millions)	42,000
Income per capita (U.S.$)	2,230

Iran, whose name means "land of the Aryans," was the seat of the Persian empire of Cyrus the Great in the sixth century BC. Long a feudal land famous for its intricately woven carpets, Iran became, in the 20th century, an oil-producing powerhouse ruled by the autocratic Shah Reza Pahlevi. The Shah's attempts to use oil revenues to finance rapid westernization of his country created stark inequalities of wealth and bitter resentment among conservative Muslims.

In 1979 religious fundamentalists, led by the Ayatollah Ruhollah Khomeini, toppled the Shah, declaring Iran an Islamic republic (now the world's largest theocracy). Turning back the clock on social liberalism, however, entailed economic privation as well, especially when coupled with the tragic effects of Iran's long, bitter war with Iraq. Secular and religious elements continue to quarrel over the future of this nation, which, despite its tremendous reserves of oil and natural gas, is still largely dependent on subsistence farming.

MALDIVES

Republic of Maldives
Map page 58

Area	115 sq. mi.
	(298 sq. km.)
Capital	Male
Member of	ADB, COMM, ESCAP, IDB, OIC

Population	245,000
Population growth rate	3.2%
Life expectancy	67 (m), 67 (f)
Language	Divehi (Maldivian, *related to Sinhala*)
Adult literacy rate	98.2%

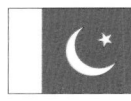

Currency	rufiyaa
GNP (U.S.$, in millions)	221
Income per capita (U.S.$)	900

A necklace of coral atolls dotting the Indian Ocean, Maldives lives by the sea – and may one day die by it. Only five feet above sea level (on average), the islands thrive on fishing, but even a slight rise in ocean levels could threaten their survival.

NEPAL

Kingdom of Nepal
Map page 122

Area	56,812 sq. mi.
	(147,181 sq. km.)
Capital	Kathmandau
Member of	ADB, ESCAP

Population	19,280,000
Population growth rate	2.6%
Life expectancy	54 (m), 53 (f)
Languages	Nepali, *local languages*
Adult literacy rate	27.5%

Currency	Nepalese rupee
GNP (U.S.$, in millions)	4,174
Income per capita (U.S.$)	200

Draped across the highest peaks on earth (the Himalayas), this tiny kingdom is poor in resources, yet dazzlingly rich in scenic beauty and culture. Nepal was the birthplace of Buddha, but Hindu invaders from India converted the population by the third century. More than 2,700 religious shrines now grace the Kathmandu Valley, helping to lure tourists.

Most Nepalese grow rice, maize, and wheat on terraced farms fed by seasonal monsoons. Despite economic liberalization and plans to develop hydroelectric power, more than 40 percent of the population remains undernourished, and Nepal's literacy rate ranks among the world's lowest.

PAKISTAN

Islamic Republic of Pakistan
Map pages 116–17

Area	307,293 sq. mi.
	(796,095 sq. km.)
Capital	Islamabad
Member of	ADB, COMM, ESCAP, IDB, OIC

Population	126,610,000
Population growth rate	2.8%
Life expectancy	61 (m), 63 (f)
Languages	Urdu, *Punjabi, Sindhi, Pashtu, Balochi, English*
Adult literacy rate	37.8%

Currency	Pakistani rupee
GNP (U.S.$, in millions)	55,565
Income per capita (U.S.$)	440

Home to one of history's oldest civilizations, Pakistan now struggles to forge itself into a truly modern Islamic nation. Its roots lie in the mighty Indus River, which flows south from the towering Hindu Kush. Around 2,000 BC the fertile alluvial plains of the Indus supported the Harappan civilization much as they support modern Pakistanis, who today use the world's most extensive irrigation system to produce cotton and rice for export.

The name *Pakistan* (meaning "land of the pure") was conjured in the late 1920s by exiled Indian Muslims who dreamed of their own Islamic state. They got their wish in 1947, when Pakistan was carved out of Hindu India to relieve religious tensions. (With periodic conflicts, the border region of Kashmir is still in dispute). While Pakistan is 97 percent Muslim, it remains an ethnically diverse nation in which the official language, Urdu, is not widely spoken.

With a thriving trade in textiles and food processing, Pakistan seeks foreign investment. Benazir Bhutto, the Islamic world's first woman prime minister, boasted of her nation's liberal society and rapidly developing economy. Nevertheless, more than half the population still toils on farms, and conservative Islamic law holds sway in much of the country. Nearly twice as many boys as girls go to school and an unusually low ratio of females to males hints at parental neglect and the practice of female infanticide.

SRI LANKA

Democratic Socialist Republic of Sri Lanka
Map page 123

Area	25,325 sq. mi.
	(65,610 sq. km.)
Capital	Colombo
Member of	ADB, COMM, ESCAP

Population	17,865,000
Population growth rate	1.3%
Life expectancy	70 (m), 74 (f)
Languages	Sinhala, Tamil, *English*
Adult literacy rate	90.2%

Currency	Sri Lanka rupee
GNP (U.S.$, in millions)	11,634
Income per capita (U.S.$)	640

Like an emerald pendant, the lush island nation of Sri Lanka dangles from the southern tip of India. Its current population – Sinhalese Buddhists, who form the majority, and Tamil Hindus – reflects Indian forebears who settled here 2,500 years ago.

Formerly known as Serendip, and later Ceylon, the island became a British Commonwealth in 1948 and gained full independence in 1972, when it adopted the name *Sri Lanka* (meaning "resplendent island"). Violence between Sri Lanka's two main ethnic groups has escalated steadily since 1983 as the Tamils agitate for an autonomous state in the northeast.

20TH-CENTURY LANDMARKS

1906 Muslim League is founded in India to demand independent Islamic state.

— 1910 —

1915–22 Ottomans kill or deport 1.5 million Armenians.

— 1920 —

1920–22 Armenia, Azerbaijan, and Georgia become part of Soviet Republic. Mahatma Gandhi leads India's first nonviolent campaign for independence.

— 1930 —

1930–33 Second nonviolent campaign for independence in India.

1939–45 India becomes important World War II manufacturing and military base.

— 1940 —

1947 India and Pakistan become independent.

1948 Mahatma Gandhi assassinated. India and Pakistan at war over ownership of Kashmir.

— 1950 —

1956 Pakistan is made an Islamic republic.

— 1960 —

1962 India and China fight over border.

1965 India and Pakistan enter second war over Kashmir.

— 1970 —

1971 East Pakistan secedes from Pakistan to form Bangladesh; India declares third war on Pakistan in support of Bangladesh.

1973 Afghanistan is made a republic. Start of mujaheddin rebellion.

1979 U.S.S.R. invades Afghanistan. Shah of Iran deposed; Ayatollah Khomeini leads Islamic fundamentalist regime.

— 1980 —

1980–88 Iran-Iraq war ends in stalemate.

1983 Civil war between Tamils and Sinhalese erupts in Sri Lanka.

1989 Soviet troops suppress riots in the Georgian city of Tbilisi. Further conflict in Afghanistan follows Soviet withdrawal.

— 1990 —

1991 Armenia, Azerbaijan, and Georgia gain independence when U.S.S.R. collapses.

1993 Armenia and Azerbaijan declare war over Nagorno-Karabakh.

CENTRAL AND EASTERN ASIA

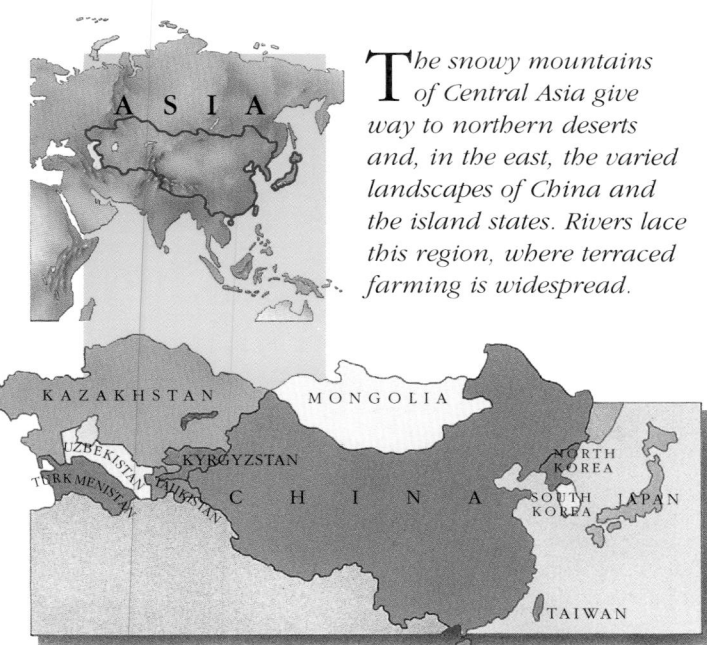

The snowy mountains of Central Asia give way to northern deserts and, in the east, the varied landscapes of China and the island states. Rivers lace this region, where terraced farming is widespread.

Colonies and Dependent Territories

MACAO
Parent country
Portugal
Map page 131

CHINA

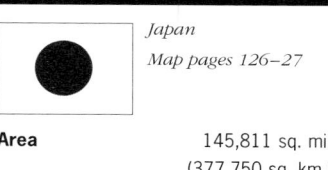

People's Republic of China
Map pages 128–131

Area	3,694,522 sq. mi.
	(9,571,300 sq. km.)
Capital	Beijing
Member of	ADB, APEC, ESCAP

Population	1,198,500,000
Population growth rate	1.4%
Life expectancy	68 (m), 71 (f)
Languages	Northern Chinese (Mandarin)
	others
Adult literacy rate	77.8%

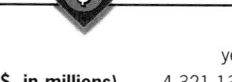

Currency	yuan
GNP (U.S.$, in millions)	630,202
Income per capita (U.S.$)	490

After 40 centuries of civilization, China remains a mighty paradox: a cultural monolith incorporating a welter of minority peoples; a Communist state that promotes capitalist entrepreneurship; an industrial powerhouse with a population that is three-quarters rural. Yet, despite these contradictions, the land once thought of as a "sleeping giant" now stands awake and aware of its vast potential for the 21st century.

For centuries China isolated itself, believing itself to be the "Middle Kingdom" between heaven and earth, and certain that those beyond its borders could offer little in the way of culture or trade. Indeed, China accomplished much during its millennia of self-imposed exile: the invention of paper, gunpowder, printing, and the compass, and the establishment of a remarkably stable society. Perhaps the greatest triumph of all was China's knack for absorbing any invaders who breached its Great Wall, and ultimately making them Chinese.

Preyed upon by European powers in the 19th century, a weakened China stood ripe for

Abbreviations

ADB *Asian Development Bank*

APEC *Asia-Pacific Economic Cooperation*

CIS *Commonwealth of Independent States*

EBRD *European Bank for Reconstruction and Development*

ECE *Economic Commission for Europe*

ESCAP *Economic and Social Commission for Asia and the Pacific*

G7 *Group of Seven*

GNP *Gross National Product*

---

change at the beginning of the 20th century. Following years of struggle against Japan and a bloody civil war between Communist forces and the nationalist army of Chiang Kai-shek, China emerged in 1949 as a Socialist state under the leadership of Mao Zedong, who reorganized Chinese society along radically collectivist lines and brutally purged dissident voices. During the Cold War, China maintained a stalwart independence, distancing itself from both the U.S. and the Soviet Union.

A visit from President Richard M. Nixon in 1972 began a thawing in relations with the West, and since Mao's death in 1976, China has reappeared as a presence on the world stage. Reformers led by Deng Xiaoping have guided the country toward a "socialist market economy," marrying Western-style profit incentives to the one-party control of state Communism and aggressively courting foreign markets. But in most ways China remains rigidly authoritarian. In 1989 the world's attention was captured by a peaceful student-led movement for democratic reform, centering on Beijing's Tiananmen Square. Despite international calls for restraint, the tanks rolled, protestors were arrested, and thousands were killed or injured.

The resources with which China carries out its great social experiments are enormous. The world's third-largest nation in size, it ranks first in coal reserves and has abundant minerals. But with over one-quarter of the world's population to feed, clothe, and shelter, China also has huge burdens. The one-child family is state policy, but stabilizing China's numbers has proven difficult. Other challenges that face the nation include establishing a rapprochement with the breakaway island of Taiwan and managing the 1997 absorption of the former British colony of Hong Kong.

JAPAN

Japan
Map pages 126–27

Area	145,811 sq. mi.
	(377,750 sq. km.)
Capital	Tokyo
Member of	ADB, APEC, EBRD,
	ESCAP, G7

Population	125,200,000
Population growth rate	0.4%
Life expectancy	77 (m), 83 (f)
Language	Japanese
Adult literacy rate	99%

Currency	yen
GNP (U.S.$, in millions)	4,321,136
Income per capita (U.S.$)	34,630

Twice in the past 150 years, this island nation has catapulted from a position of crippling disadvantage to one of international prominence. Opened to trade in 1854 after centuries of self-imposed isolation, Japan accomplished a near-overnight transformation from feudalism to an industrial society based on Western models. A century later, after a crushing defeat in World War II, the Japanese once again applied their discipline and determination to competition, peacefully rebuilding their shattered country into the world's second-largest economy.

Descendants of mainland Asians who migrated to the Japanese archipelago millennia ago, Japan's people were at one time heavily influenced by Chinese culture, which exported Buddhism to the islands in the seventh century. But for most of the last 1,000 years, the Japanese have managed to live in almost hermetic isolation from even their closest neighbors. European traders and missionaries, who began to appear in the 1500s, were expelled a century later. An unbroken line of Japanese emperors dates back some 2,500 years, although the real power of feudal Japan often lay with local shoguns, or warlords, while the emperors reigned as largely ceremonial figures revered as gods.

Japan has the dubious distinction of being the only nation to suffer a nuclear attack. With the bombings of Hiroshima and Nagasaki at the close of World War II, Japanese militarism effectively came to an end. Under a new, American-written constitution, Japan's defeated emperor gave up all claims to divinity, and the country renounced the right to wage war. Freed from the burdens of monarchy and military expansion, Japan commenced a massive program of economic reconstruction – with spectacular results. Though their homeland is favored with few natural resources, the Japanese have proven themselves adept at coordinating the efforts of government and private industry to transform imported raw materials with astonishing efficiency into steel, ships, and automobiles. The Japanese are no less skillful at finding new markets and have made their nation a leader in high technology. With just 3 percent of the world's population, this tiny country commands 10 percent of global income.

For all its business acumen, Japan has not forgotten its ancestral traditions. Ancient protocols of honor, respect, courtesy, and self-effacement govern even the most casual encounter. The result is a country where high population density coexists with a remarkable degree of civil order.

KAZAKHSTAN

Republic of Kazakhstan
Map page 114

Area	1,048,878 sq. mi.
	(2,717,300 sq. km.)
Capital	Almaty
Member of	ADB, CIS, EBRD, ECE,
	ESCAP

Population	16,763,000
Population growth rate	0.8%
Life expectancy	64 (m), 73 (f)
Languages	Kazakh, *Russian*
Adult literacy rate	97.5%

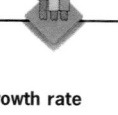

Currency	tenge
GNP (U.S.$, in millions)	18,896
Income per capita (U.S.$)	1,110

Home to both nomadic herders and a Russian rocket-launching facility, Kazakhstan is the ninth-largest country in the world and the second-largest former Soviet republic, stretching from the Caspian Sea in the west to the cold, rugged Altai Mountains in the east. Northern farmlands yield to central plains and finally to deserts in the south. Irrigation schemes implemented during the Soviet era make desert farming possible, but the diversion of rivers feeding the Aral Sea has caused it to recede, leaving coastal fishing villages high and dry.

The Soviet Union settled many Kazakh nomads by force in the 1930s, leaving nearly 1 million of them dead, then set out in the 1950s to turn grasslands into croplands – a venture that attracted a large number of Russian immigrants to the region. Today, Kazakhs barely outnumber Russians in their homeland. Since becoming independent in 1991, the nation has moved quickly to transform itself into a market economy, and its tremendous reserves of oil, gas, coal, gold, uranium, zinc, and iron promise growing prosperity.

NORTH KOREA

Democratic People's Republic of Korea
Map page 129

Area	46,528 sq. mi.
	(120,538 sq. km.)
Capital	Pyongyang
Member of	ESCAP

Population	23,483,000
Population growth rate	1.8%
Life expectancy	68 (m), 74 (f)
Language	Korean
Adult literacy rate	99%

Currency	North Korean won
GNP (U.S.$, in millions)	21,200
Income per capita (U.S.$)	923

Widely regarded as a relic of the Cold War, North Korea's regimented society struggles to match the economic success of its capitalist counterpart on the Korean peninsula. The North is heavily dependent on outmoded smokestack industries; in recent years roughly a quarter of the nation's gross national product has gone to the military.

Korea emerged as a unified empire during the seventh century but has been overshadowed for much of its history by neighboring China and Japan. North Korea became a distinct state in 1948, following 40 years of Japanese domination and the brief Soviet occupation that institutionalized Communism under Kim Il Sung. Two years later it embarked upon an invasion of South Korea that led to UN intervention and a continuing stalemate along a heavily patrolled border.

SOUTH KOREA

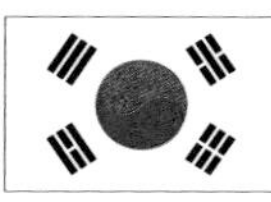

Republic of Korea
Map page 129

Area	38,365 sq. mi. (99,392 sq. km.)
Capital	Seoul
Member of	ADB, APEC, EBRD, ESCAP

Population	44,851,000
Population growth rate	1%
Life expectancy	69 (m), 77 (f)
Language	Korean
Adult literacy rate	96.3%

Currency	South Korean won
GNP (U.S.$, in millions)	366,484
Income per capita (U.S.$)	8,220

Although its common ethnic heritage with North Korea reaches back some 2,000 years, South Korea stands in marked political and economic contrast to its neighbor. In the aftermath of the 1950-53 Korean War, triggered by the North's military incursion across the 38th parallel, South Korea, with U.S. assistance, has built a powerhouse economy based on electronics, automobiles, steel, and textile manufacturing.

Commitment to developing the economy has not always been accompanied by liberal democratic ideals, however. After three decades of military rule by strongmen, the authoritarian climate began to change only after widespread protests in 1987. Despite hopes for eventual reunification - on South Korean terms - and a 1991 nonaggression pact, relations with the North remain tense. Particularly unsettling to South Koreans is the possibilty that North Korea is developing a nuclear arsenal.

KYRGYZSTAN

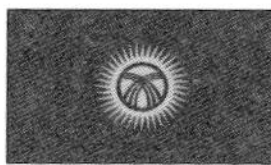

Republic of Kyrgyzstan
Map page 122

Area	76,621 sq. mi. (198,500 sq. km.)
Capital	Bishkek
Member of	ADB, CIS, EBRD, ECE, ESCAP

Population	4,476,000
Population growth rate	1.7%
Life expectancy	65 (m), 73 (f)
Languages	Kyrgyz (Cyrillic script; Latin script to be reintroduced), *Russian*
Adult literacy rate	97%

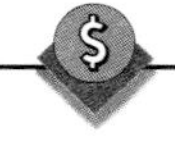

Currency	som
GNP (U.S.$, in millions)	2,825
Income per capita (U.S.$)	610

This ancient pastureland still supports livestock, though today few herders are nomadic. Among the poorest of former Soviet republics, mountainous Kyrgyzstan strives to increase trade, while keeping a cap on growing Kyrgyz nationalism.

MONGOLIA

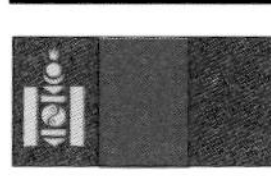

Mongolia
Map page 115

Area	604,669 sq. mi. (1,566,500 sq. km.)
Capital	Ulan Bator
Member of	ADB, ESCAP

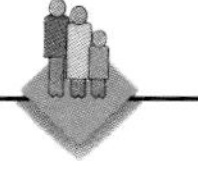

Population	2,317,000
Population growth rate	2.8%
Life expectancy	63 (av. m/f)
Languages	Khalkha Mongolian, *Kazakh*
Adult literacy rate	89%

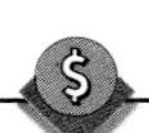

Currency	tugrik
GNP (U.S.$, in millions)	801
Income per capita (U.S.$)	340

One of the world's oldest countries, Mongolia was at the heart of the huge Mongol Empire that was created by Genghis Khan and ruled Asia from the Caspian Sea to the South China Sea during the 13th and 14th centuries. Today Mongolia is the world's largest landlocked country, encircled by Russia and China. Mountains ripple in the north and east; the Gobi Desert sprawls across the south. On the nation's vast plains, nomadic herders seek shelter from biting winds by living in sturdy felt tents. Livestock has long been the economy's foundation; domestic animals outnumber humans 15 to 1, and there are more horses per capita than in any other nation. Democracy returned to this country in 1990 after half a century under Communism.

TAIWAN

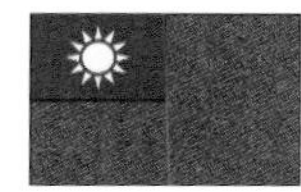

Republic of China
Map page 131

Area	13,896 sq. mi. (36,000 sq. km.)
Capital	Taipei
Member of	ADB, APEC

Population	21,240,000
Population growth rate	1.2%
Life expectancy	72 (m), 78 (f)
Languages	Northern Chinese (Mandarin), *Taiwanese*
Adult literacy rate	93.7%

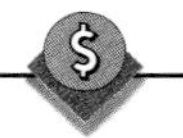

Currency	new Taiwan dollar
GNP (U.S.$, in millions)	243,934
Income per capita (U.S.$)	11,597

The island state of Taiwan retains an uncertain political status. To Chinese nationalists who fled offshore following defeat by the Communists in 1949, Taiwan is the Republic of China, the only legitimate Chinese nation. But to the Communist colossus just 80 miles west, Taiwan remains a renegade province. Most nations - and the UN - have ceased to recognize the Taiwan regime.

Despite questions of its legitimacy, Taiwan is an economic force to be reckoned with, a major producer of electronics and apparel. Ironically, Taiwanese capitalists now invest large shares of their profits in the rapidly expanding economy of the People's Republic.

TAJIKISTAN

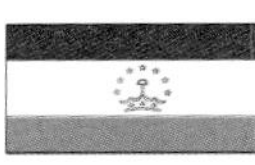

Republic of Tajikistan
Map page 122

Area	55,237 sq. mi. (143,100 sq. km.)
Capital	Dushanbe
Member of	CIS, EBRD, ECE, ESCAP

Population	5,751,000
Population growth rate	2.9%
Life expectancy	67 (m), 72 (f)
Languages	Tajik (Cyrillic script), *Russian*
Adult literacy rate	97.7%

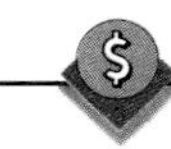

Currency	Tajik ruble
GNP (U.S.$, in millions)	2,075
Income per capita (U.S.$)	350

Violence and economic decline have marred Tajikistan's newly declared independence. Islamic militants vie with former Communists for control, while ethnic rivalry between Tajiks (of Persian origin) and Uzbeks (of Turkish origin) shadow this stark, mountainous nation, the poorest former Soviet republic.

TURKMENISTAN

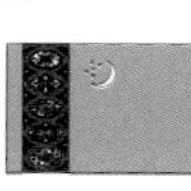

Republic of Turkmenistan
Map page 116

Area	188,407 sq. mi. (488,100 sq. km.)
Capital	Ashgabat
Member of	CIS, EBRD, ECE, ESCAP

Population	4,483,000
Population growth rate	2.5%
Life expectancy	62 (m), 68 (f)
Languages	Turkmen (Latin-based script), *Russian, Uzbek, Kazakh*
Adult literacy rate	98%

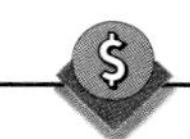

Currency	manat
GNP (U.S.$, in millions)	5,000
Income per capita (U.S.$)	1,380

Famed for Karakul sheep and rugs made from their wool, Turkmenistan is a dry land dominated by the Kara Kum Desert. Its population clusters in river valleys and oases. This former Soviet republic benefits from large oil and gas reserves and little ethnic conflict.

UZBEKISTAN

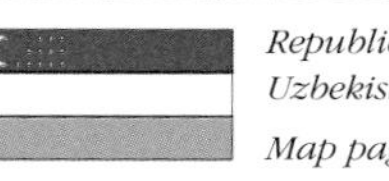

Republic of Uzbekistan
Map page 116

Area	172,696 sq. mi. (447,400 sq. km.)
Capital	Tashkent
Member of	CIS, EBRD, ECE, ESCAP

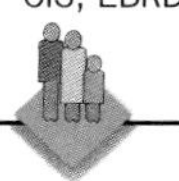

Population	22,098,000
Population growth rate	2.3%
Life expectancy	70 (av. m/f)
Languages	Uzbek (reverting to Latin script), *Russian, Kazakh*
Adult literacy rate	97%

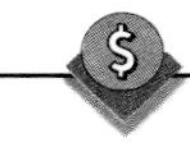

Currency	sum
GNP (U.S.$, in millions)	21,142
Income per capita (U.S.$)	950

Over 2,000 years ago, caravans following the Silk Road paused at cities near oases in Uzbekistan. Silk weaving remains an important industry in Samarkand, the oldest of these cities, but it is cotton that really drives Uzbekistan's economy, supported by a Soviet-era irrigation system that unfortunately contributes to the draining of the Aral Sea. Though transition to a market economy is proceeding very slowly, this flat, arid nation harbors abundant reserves of fossil fuels and sizable gold and uranium deposits, all of which bodes well for its future. An authoritarian government has stifled the growth of multiparty democracy, but also keeps in check the ethnic hostilities that currently rattle neighboring Tajikistan.

20TH-CENTURY LANDMARKS

1900–1 Boxer Rebellion in China.

1904–5 Russo-Japanese war: Russia defeated; Japan gains control of Korea and Formosa (Taiwan).

— 1910 —

1911 China overthows Manchu dynasty and becomes a republic under Sun Yat-sen.

1914 Japan declares war on Germany as World War I begins.

— 1920 —

1921 Communist Party founded in China.

1923 Earthquake destroys the Japanese city of Yokohama.

— 1930 —

1931 Japan invades Manchuria.

1934–35 Chinese Communist Party flees on Long March; Mao Zedong established as party leader.

1937 War between Japan and China begins.

— 1940 —

1941 Japan attacks U.S. fleet at Pearl Harbor, bringing U.S. fully into World War II.

1945 U.S. drops atomic bombs on Hiroshima and Nagasaki. Japan surrenders, losing all overseas possessions, including Korea and Taiwan.

1949 Chinese civil war ends in victory for Communists. Mao Zedong proclaims People's Republic of China.

— 1950 —

1950–51 China takes control of Tibet.

1950–53 Korean War.

1959 Dalai Lama flees Tibet.

— 1960 —

1962 China and India war over border.

1966 Mao Ze-dong leads Cultural Revolution in China.

— 1970 —

1971 Taiwan forced to relinquish UN seat in favor of China.

— 1980 —

1989 Chinese student protest crushed in Tiananmen Square.

— 1990 —

1991 U.S.S.R. dissolved. CIS formed.

1997 Hong Kong reverts to China.

SOUTHEAST ASIA

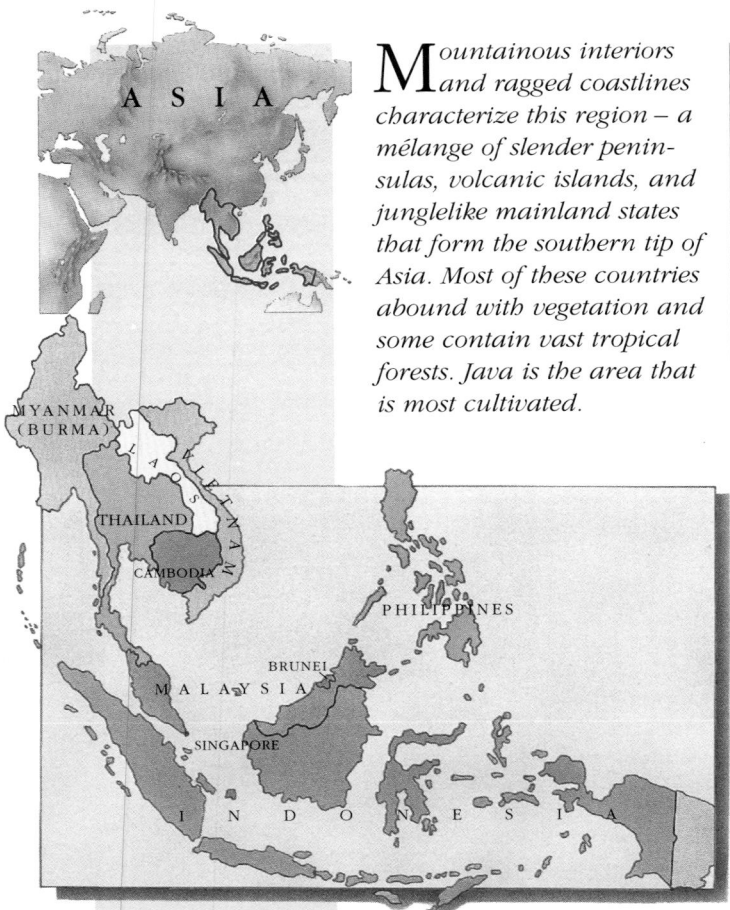

Mountainous interiors and ragged coastlines characterize this region – a mélange of slender peninsulas, volcanic islands, and junglelike mainland states that form the southern tip of Asia. Most of these countries abound with vegetation and some contain vast tropical forests. Java is the area that is most cultivated.

Colonies and Dependent Territories

CHRISTMAS ISLAND
Parent country
AUSTRALIA
Map page 134

COCOS (KEELING) ISLANDS
Parent country
AUSTRALIA
Map page 134

PARACEL ISLANDS
Parent country
Disputed among China,
Vietnam, and Taiwan
Map page 134

SPRATLY ISLANDS
Parent country
Disputed among China,
Malaysia, Taiwan,
Vietnam, Brunei, and the
Philippines
Map page 134

BRUNEI

Negara Brunei Darussalam
Map page 134

Area	2,226 sq. mi.
	(5,765 sq. km.)
Capital	Bandar Seri Begawan
Member of	APEC, ASEAN, COMM, ESCAP, IDB

Population	285,000
Population growth rate	3.0%
Life expectancy	70 (m), 73 (f)
Languages	Malay, *Chinese, English*
Adult literacy rate	89%

Currency	Brunei dollar
GNP (U.S.$, in millions)	4,000
Income per capita (U.S.$)	16,000

This tiny sultanate, a former British protectorate, struck it rich in 1929 when Shell Oil discovered an ocean of crude oil beneath its lush rain forest. Smaller than Delaware and drenched by equatorial monsoons for half the year, Brunei now produces 9 percent of the world's natural gas and 1 percent of its oil. The standard of living is exceptionally high: Brunei boasts one of the world's highest per-capita incomes (none of it taxed). Yet the wealth is not distributed equally and comes at great cost to political freedoms. The sultan (by most accounts, the world's richest man) rules his Islamic state by decree; political parties are banned, and a state of emergency declared in 1962 has yet to be lifted. Discriminatory laws deny citizenship to the Chinese minority, roughly one-fifth of the country's population.

CAMBODIA

Kingdom of Cambodia
Map page 133

Area	69,880 sq. mi.
	(181,035 sq. km.)
Capital	Phnom Penh
Member of	ADB, ESCAP

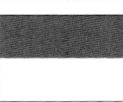

Population	9,568,000
Population growth rate	3.1%
Life expectancy	49 (m), 52 (f)
Language	Khmer
Adult literacy rate	35%

Currency	riel
GNP (U.S.$, in millions)	1,725
Income per capita (U.S.$)	200

Throughout the 1970s Cambodians lived a nightmare. Swept into the conflict between neighboring North and South Vietnam, Cambodia suffered massive U.S. bombing and a takeover by the Communist Khmer Rouge. During the ensuing regime, one of the most brutal in modern history, ideological extremists resettled Cambodia's entire urban population to the countryside, where mass executions and the hardships of forced labor claimed over a million Cambodian lives.

An invasion by Vietnamese forces unseated the Khmer regime in 1979, but Cambodia's woes continued. In the late 1970s and early 1980s, vast numbers of Cambodians fleeing Khmer Rouge guerillas, the Vietnamese, or both flowed across the border into Thailand. In the chaos thousands died of starvation. A UN-sponsored election in 1992 has brought some flickering hope for stability to this long-suffering nation. Armed factionalism, however, continues, and Cambodia's political future remains murky.

INDONESIA

Republic of Indonesia
Map pages 134–35

Area	740,856 sq. mi.
	(1,919,317 sq. km.)
Capital	Jakarta
Member of	ADB, APEC, ASEAN, ESCAP, IDB, OPEC

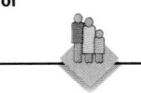

Population	195,283,000
Population growth rate	1.6%
Life expectancy	61 (m), 65 (f)
Languages	Bahasa Indonesia (a form of Malay), *many local languages*
Adult literacy rate	83.8%

Currency	rupiah
GNP (U.S.$, in millions)	167,632
Income per capita (U.S.$)	880

A hodgepodge of volcanic islands scattered like jewels along 3,100 mi. (5,000-km.) of the equator, Indonesia has purchased national cohesion among its hundreds of ethnic groups at the price of democracy. The country's 200 million people (the fourth-largest population in the world) are spread across some 13,000 islands; held together only by their religion (Islam), an autocratic central government, and an official language, they are in many ways the unlikeliest of countrymen.

Indonesia has long dominated the main trade routes between India and China and was a prize much sought by foreign powers in centuries past. Arab traders converted the archipelago to Islam in the 1600s; Dutch hegemony replaced Portugese power in the region a century later. A four-year Japanese occupation during World War II was the only major break from Dutch control until a nationalist uprising led Indonesia to independence in 1949.

Since then the Javanese, controlling the central government from the densely packed island of Java, have practiced an authoritarian rule while ruthlessly policing their wide-ranging state. Backed by a Russian-armed military, Indonesia's first president, Sukarno, suspended parliament in 1960 and was declared president-for-life in 1963; ousted by a coup four years later, he was replaced by military strongman General Suharto, who has further tightened the political reins.

Meanwhile, Indonesia's economy has taken off, fueled by a booming petroleum industry. Chinese businessmen are leading a new manufacturing sector into electronics and aerospace technology, while large plantations churn out rubber, coffee, tea, and sugarcane for export. Every year loggers harvest nearly half the world's tropical hardwood crop from Indonesia's hills, leading some environmentalists to predict that the nation's forests will be flattened in three decades.

Indonesia is blanketed by tropical forest and mangrove swamp, leaving just 10 percent of the land for farming. Buffeted by monsoons and earthquakes, it is punctuated by some 200 volcanoes, including Krakatoa, whose 1883 eruption is thought to be the largest natural explosion in recorded history.

Indonesia's greatest present-day disturbances come not from subterranean forces, however, but from smoldering ethnic conflicts in outlying areas like Irian Jaya and especially East Timor. Annexed in 1975, East Timor has been tormented by Indonesian troops, who have killed an estimated one-third of the island's population.

LAOS

Lao People's Democratic Republic
Map page 132

Area	91,405 sq. mi.
	(236,800 sq. km.)
Capital	Vientiane
Member of	ADB, ESCAP

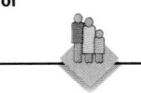

Population	4,581,000
Population growth rate	3.1%
Life expectancy	49 (m), 52 (f)
Languages	Lao, *French, many local languages*
Adult literacy rate	56.6%

Currency	kip
GNP (U.S.$, in millions)	1,496
Income per capita (U.S.$)	320

After two decades of Communist rule, Laos has yet to emerge from the contradictions that mark it as one of the poorest nations in the world. Only 10 percent of its mountainous terrain is arable, yet 85 percent of Laotians work the land, clinging to a ribbon of rice farms along the banks of the Mekong River. Efforts to extend central authority to the ethnically diverse, opium-producing mountain tribes have largely failed. The eastern jungle hides the remnants of the Ho Chi Minh Trail and still bears scars from a fierce U.S. bombing campaign intended to cripple Communist supply lines during the Vietnam War.

MALAYSIA

Malaysia
Map page 134

Area	127,287 sq. mi.
	(329,758 sq. km.)
Capital	Kuala Lumpur
Member of	ADB, APEC, ASEAN, COMM, ESCAP, IDB

Population	20,103,000
Population growth rate	2.5%
Life expectancy	69 (m), 74 (f)
Languages	Bahasa Malaysia, *English, Chinese, Tamil, Iban*
Adult literacy rate	74%

Currency	ringgit
GNP (U.S.$, in millions)	68,674
Income per capita (U.S.$)	3,520

Since 1987 Malaysia has turned a sprawling federation of states, carved from over a hundred thousand square miles of dense jungle, into one of Asia's most striking economic success stories. The largely urban Chinese minority has generated tin, timber, and palm oil exports that rank as the world's largest, while also developing heavy

industry, rubber production, and a robust business in foreign-produced semiconductors. The soaring skyline of Kuala Lumpur, site of the world's tallest office building, testifies to the country's towering 8 percent annual growth rate.

Long considered a vital trading route, the strategically located Malaysian peninsula was exploited by the Dutch, Portuguese, and British before the country became an independent federation in 1963. Tropical beaches on the peninsula's east coast and the ancient rain forests of Borneo lure more tourists to Malaysia than to any other country in Southeast Asia.

MYANMAR (BURMA)

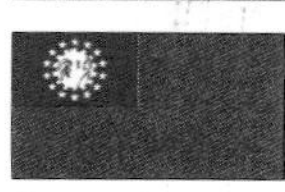

Union of Myanmar

Map page 132

Area	261,149 sq. mi. (676,553 sq. km.)
Capital	Yangôn (Rangoon)
Member of	ADB, ESCAP

Population	41,550,000
Population growth rate	2.1%
Life expectancy	56 (m), 60 (f)
Languages	Myanmar (Burmese), *other local languages*
Adult literacy rate	83.1%

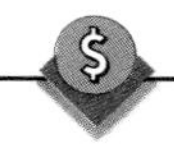

Currency	kyat
GNP (U.S.$, in millions)	7,450
Income per capita (U.S.$)	200

Captive to a ruling cadre of xenophobic military autocrats, this troubled nation makes precious little use of its abundant natural endowments. The wide, wet floodplains of the Irrawaddy River, which dominate the country's tropical interior, at one time yielded the world's most abundant rice crop. Today Myanmar (formerly known as Burma) has sunk to seventh in rice exports. Once Southeast Asia's richest nation, it has become one of its poorest.

The largely rural population inhabits a densely forested land hiding vast reserves of oil, lead, zinc, and rubies. The military government in Yangôn has paid scant attention to economic development, however, spending more than 35 percent of its budget on defense. The most significant threat to the ruling junta (in power since a 1988 coup) comes from a broad prodemocracy movement headed by Aung San Suu Kyi, who won international recognition for her cause by capturing the Nobel Peace Prize in 1991. (She remained under house arrest until 1995.) Walled off from India by the Arakan Mountains, Burma was settled by Tibetans in the ninth century. Overrun by Kublai Khan in the 13th century, it remained a part of China for the next four centuries. The British annexed this Buddhist nation in the 19th century but failed to leave a lasting cultural imprint before ceding control in 1948.

PHILIPPINES

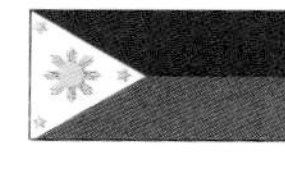

Republic of the Philippines

Map page 135

Area	115,800 sq. mi. (300,000 sq. km.)
Capital	Manila
Member of	ADB, APEC, ASEAN, ESCAP

Population	67,038,000
Population growth rate	2.1%
Life expectancy	63 (m), 67 (f)
Languages	Filipino (based on Tagalog), English, many local languages
Adult literacy rate	94.6%

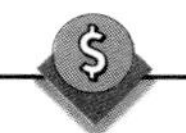

Currency	Philippine peso
GNP (U.S.$, in millions)	63,311
Income per capita (U.S.$)	960

The 7,000 islands of the Philippines are a regional oddity – an oasis of Hispanic, Roman Catholic culture perched on the rim of Asia's Islamic and Buddhist worlds. The nation's cultural singularity derives from some 300 years of rule by the Spanish, who arrived in the 16th century. In 1898 the islands passed to American hands – the richest prize of the Spanish-American War. Filipinos, however, proved no more content with their Yankee masters than they had been under the yoke of Spanish colonialism, and years of insurrection followed. The islands were granted self-governing status in 1935, suffered four years of Japanese occupation during World War II, and finally became an independent republic in 1946.

A legacy of plantation agriculture had carved a wide gap between rich and poor, and the newly independent Philippines became a battleground between propertied interests and a rural Communist insurgency. The corrupt, authoritarian rule of Ferdinand Marcos (1965-86) only deepened the nation's distress. Since the overthrow of the Marcos regime, democratic leaders have moved toward peace with separatist rebels and begun to rebuild the Philippines' economy and infrastructure.

SINGAPORE

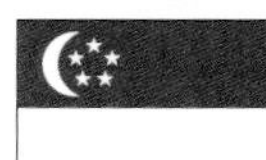

Republic of Singapore

Map page 134

Area	249 sq. mi. (646 sq. km.)
Capital	Singapore
Member of	ADB, ASEAN, COMM, ESCAP

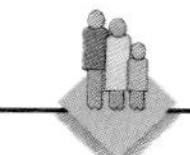

Population	2,930,000
Population growth rate	1.1%
Life expectancy	74 (m), 78 (f)
Languages	Malay, *Chinese (Mandarin), Tamil*, English
Adult literacy rate	91.1%

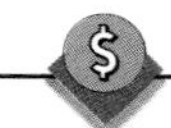

Currency	Singapore dollar
GNP (U.S.$, in millions)	65,842
Income per capita (U.S.$)	23,360

A city-state relentlessly driven by old-fashioned profit, tiny, entrepreneurial Singapore has achieved one of the world's highest standards of living, thanks in large part to its strategic natural harbor. In recent years it has also asserted itself as a world leader in computer hardware, telecommunications, and biotechnology.

In 1819 leases arranged by Sir Thomas Stamford Raffles of the East India Company brought the islands into the British colonial sphere. Eventually prominence as a merchant port led to Singapore's status as a British naval bastion and to an influx of Chinese immigrants; today, some three-quarters of the population is Chinese. Independent since 1965, Singapore is technically a democracy. Nevertheless, a single party dominates the government. Civil liberties are tightly reined on behalf of civic order and an efficient economy.

THAILAND

Kingdom of Thailand

Map page 132

Area	198,062 sq. mi. (513,115 sq. km.)
Capital	Bangkok
Member of	ADB, APEC, ASEAN, ESCAP

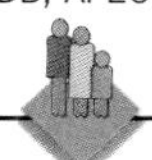

Population	59,095,000
Population growth rate	1.6%
Life expectancy	64 (m), 69 (f)
Languages	Thai, *Chinese, Malay*
Adult literacy rate	93.8%

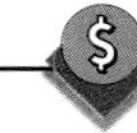

Currency	baht
GNP (U.S.$, in millions)	129,864
Income per capita (U.S.$)	2,210

Thailand (known as Siam until 1939) is the only country in southeast Asia that was never colonized by a European power. Since the 13th century, the Thai monarchy has been a unifying force in national affairs, and Thailand's kings adeptly steered a diplomatic path that kept empire builders at bay. The monarchy's influence has abated little in this overwhelmingly Buddhist nation, despite a revolving door of military and civilian governments during the last 100 years.

No less significant to modern Thailand is fast-track development. Textiles and high technology, along with a booming tourist trade, continue to modernize and diversify an economy that was once based largely on the processing of primary resources, including rubber, rice, and tin. Thailand's greatest challenge, though, is to export prosperity from the country's congested capital, Bangkok, to the rural provinces – especially the isolated north and the southern peninsula.

VIETNAM

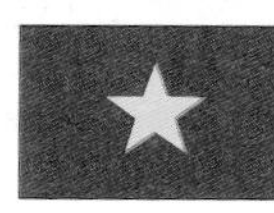

Socialist Republic of Vietnam

Map page 132

Area	127,810 sq. mi. (331,114 sq. km.)
Capital	Hanoi
Member of	ADB, ASEAN, ESCAP

Population	70,983,000
Population growth rate	2.1%
Life expectancy	63 (m), 67 (f)
Language	Vietnamese
Adult literacy rate	93.7%

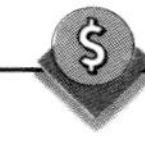

Currency	dông
GNP (U.S.$, in millions)	13,775
Income per capita (U.S.$)	190

Nearly 1,000 years of self-determination ended for Vietnam in 1883, when it fell under French colonial rule. Nationalist forces won independence in 1954, but the country was divided into a Chinese-backed Communist North and a Western-oriented South. Thus, the stage was set for one of the longest, costliest, and most agonizing conflicts in the history of another foreign power, the United States.

The 20-year war in Vietnam exacted a heavy toll for the U.S.: some 58,000 Americans lost their lives. But Vietnam was devastated. More than 1 million Vietnamese died, leaving behind a nation in tatters. U.S. forces pulled out of the region under a ceasefire agreement signed in 1973. Two years later South Vietnam fell to invading Communist forces.

Rebuilding has been slow. Burdened by conflicts with Cambodia and China and cut off from a major source of aid after the collapse of the Soviet Union, Vietnam's Communist leaders have turned to economic liberalization. For now their strategy seems to be working: Western investments have increased and collective agriculture has largely been abandoned. Full diplomatic relations with the U.S. were restored in 1995.

20TH-CENTURY LANDMARKS

1901 Dutch policies in Indonesia spark nationalist movement.

— 1910 —

1917 Thailand joins Allies in World War I.

— 1920 —

1929 Oil extraction begins in Brunei.

— 1930 —

1930 Indo-China Communist Party founded in Vietnam.

1937 Burma (Myanmar) is separated from India.

— 1940 —

1941–45 All countries in the region are occupied by Japan during World War II.

1945–54 Vietnam fights for independence from France.

— 1950 —

1954 Vietnam is divided into North Vietnam, supported by U.S.S.R., and South Vietnam, supported by U.S.

1959 Brunei becomes Islamic state.

— 1960 —

1961–73 Vietnam War: U.S. helps South Vietnam but eventually pulls out.

1962 Military coup in Myanmar sees start of isolationist policy.

1965 Ferdinand Marcos elected president of the Philippines.

— 1970 —

1975 Indonesia invades East Timor. Laos becomes Communist. Khmer Rouge assumes power in Cambodia: more than a million die under its rule.

1976 Pol Pot becomes prime minister of Kampuchea (Cambodia). Vietnam unites and becomes Communist.

1978 Vietnam invades Kampuchea and installs "friendly" government; Khmer Rouge starts guerrilla war.

1979 Vietnam enters Nine-Day War with China.

— 1980 —

1986 Marcos exiled to U.S. from Philippines.

1988 Student riots in Myanmar. Vietnam withdraws from Cambodia.

— 1990 —

1991 Aung San Suu Kyi raises awareness of conditions in Myanmar.

1993 UN oversees elections in Cambodia.

OCEANIA

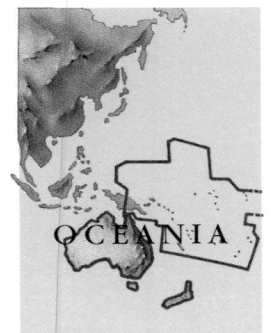

The thousands of islands scattered across the Pacific form three main groups: Melanesia, Micronesia, and Polynesia. Some are volcanic mountains rising from the sea; others – coral reefs called atolls – barely poke above the waves. Australia, the largest landmass, is mostly flat desert.

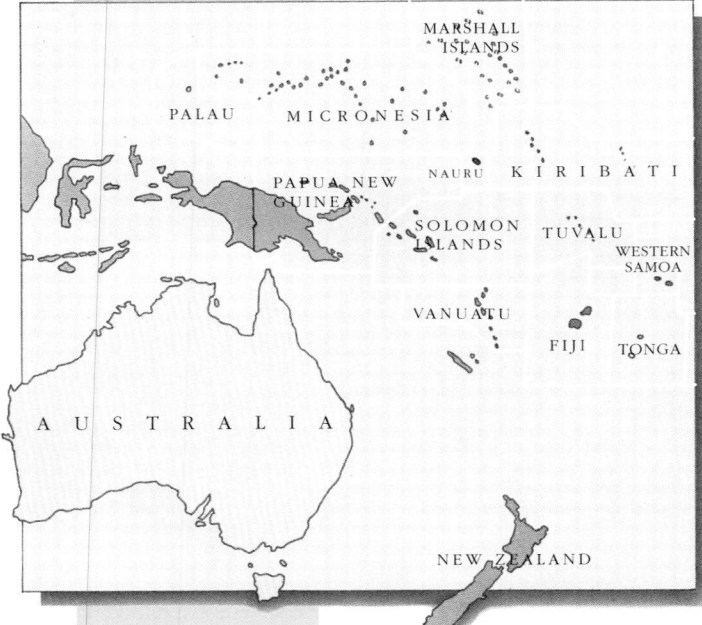

Cook, the celebrated explorer, its eastern shores began in 1788 to receive the overflow from England's crowded prisons. Sheer distance frequently made exile to Australia permanent, even if the sentence was relatively short. Freed convicts helped form the nucleus of a population whose numbers soared with the discovery of gold in 1851. In 1901, long after the era of the penal colony had ended, Australia became a self-governing British commonwealth. Today, Australians debate whether to declare a republic or keep their ties to the crown.

Despite Australia's relationship to Britain, patterns of immigration and trade have recently made it less an outpost of Europe than a partner of the Pacific Rim. Asian nations are now important customers for Australian exports, which include wool, bauxite, and coking coal. Half of all immigrants to Australia are Asian; like the European majority, most make their homes in cities along the southeastern coast. More remote areas of the country's interior are home to a quarter-million aborigines, the continent's sole inhabitants for more than 40,000 years. Nearly extirpated during pioneer days and denied citizenship until the 1960s, aborigines have been compensated for land but still lag in social and economic opportunity.

Colonies and Dependent Territories

AMERICAN SAMOA
Parent country U.S.
Map page 147

COOK ISLANDS
Parent country
NEW ZEALAND
Map page 137

FRENCH POLYNESIA
Parent country
FRANCE
Map page 147

GUAM
Parent country U.S.
Map page 125

NEW CALEDONIA
Parent country
FRANCE
Map page 139

NIUE
Parent country
NEW ZEALAND
Map page 137

MARIANA ISLANDS
Parent country U.S.
Map page 136

WALLIS AND FUTUNA ISLANDS
Parent country
FRANCE
Map page 137

Abbreviations
ADB *Asian Development Bank*
APEC *Asia-Pacific Economic Cooperation*
COMM *Commonwealth*
ESCAP *Economic and Social Commission for Asia and the Pacific*
SPC *South Pacific Commission*
SPF *South Pacific Forum*

GNP *Gross National Product*

AUSTRALIA

Commonwealth of Australia
Map pages 140–45

Area	2,965,368 sq. mi.
	(7,682,300 sq. km.)
Capital	Canberra
Member of	ADB, APEC, COMM, ESCAP, SPC, SPF

Population	17,657,000
Population growth rate	1.5%
Life expectancy	74 (m), 80 (f)
Languages	English, aboriginal languages
Adult literacy rate	over 95%

Currency	Australian dollar
GNP (U.S.$, in millions)	320,705
Income per capita (U.S.$)	17,980

Australia is a land of stark superlatives, a continent-size country of modern cities and vast deserts as lonely as any place on earth. The world's sixth-largest nation and the least-populated continent (except for Antarctica), Australia possesses numerous natural resources, some on an epic scale. Half the world's diamonds are mined here, for example, and one of Australia's many ranches is as large as Belgium. Ecologically isolated, this island continent harbors a number of animal species found nowhere else on earth, among them koala, emu, and of course, the kangaroo.

As a nation, Australia had humble beginnings. Claimed for Great Britain by Captain James

FIJI

Republic of Fiji
Map page 147

Area	7,093 sq. mi.
	(18,376 sq. km.)
Capital	Suva (on Viti Levu)
Member of	ADB, ESCAP, SPC, SPF

Population	784,000
Population growth rate	1.4%
Life expectancy	70 (m), 74 (f)
Languages	Fijian, Hindi, *English*
Adult literacy rate	87%

Currency	Fiji dollar
GNP (U.S.$, in millions)	1,785
Income per capita (U.S.$)	2,180

Fiji, an archipelago of two large islands and over 300 smaller ones, is located along major airline routes. Hence, tourism has long been a mainstay of its economy. The number of visitors dropped off precipitously, however, after Fiji's military staged a coup in 1987, preventing a newly elected, Indian-dominated government from taking office. Civilian government returned in 1996 with a new constitution that protected the rights of native Fijians. Sugar is the country's major export.

KIRIBATI

Republic of Kiribati
Map page 137

Area	313 sq. mi.
	(811 sq. km.)
Capital	Bairiki (on Tarawa Atoll)
Member of	ADB, COMM, ESCAP, SPC, SPF

Population	77,000
Population growth rate	1.5%
Life expectancy	56 (av. m/f)
Languages	I-Kiribati (Gilbertese), English
Adult literacy rate	not available

Currency	Australian dollar
GNP (U.S.$, in millions)	56
Income per capita (U.S.$)	730

The 33 atolls of Kiribati (pronounced *Kiribass*), strewn across 2 million square miles of the Pacific, lie on both sides of the Equator and the International Date Line. Originally a British protectorate called the Gilbert Islands, which included the Ellice Islands (later, independent Tuvalu), Kiribati won independence in 1979. Tarawa Atoll saw some of the fiercest fighting in the Pacific during World War II.

MARSHALL ISLANDS

Republic of the Marshall Islands
Map page 137

Area	69 sq. mi.
	(180 sq. km.)
Capital	Majuro Atoll
Member of	ADB, ESCAP, SPC, SPF

Population	52,000
Population growth rate	3%
Life expectancy	64 (m), 68 (f)
Languages	English, Marshallese, Japanese
Adult literacy rate	91%

Currency	U.S. dollar
GNP (U.S.$, in millions)	88
Income per capita (U.S.$)	1,680

Claimed by Japan during World War I and then captured by the U.S. in World War II, the Marshall Islands became independent in 1986 but still rely heavily on U.S. aid. Two of the nation's 34 atolls – Bikini and Eniwetok – were heavily contaminated by U.S. nuclear weapon tests between 1946 and 1958.

MICRONESIA

Federated States of Micronesia
Map page 136

Area	270 sq. mi.
	(700 sq. km.)
Capital	Kolonia
Member of	ADB, ESCAP, SPC, SPF

Population	105,000
Population growth rate	1.8%
Life expectancy	71 (av. m/f)
Languages	English, *Trukese*, *Pohnpeian*
Adult literacy rate	not available

Currency	U.S. dollar
GNP (U.S.$, in millions)	202
Income per capita (U.S.$)	1,890

Half of the land that constitutes Micronesia forms Pohnpei, an island at the eastern end of this 2,000-mile band of 607 islands. Some are volcanic, but most are low-lying atolls. Exports of copra and tuna are the economy's mainstays, along with U.S. aid.

NAURU

Republic of Nauru
Map page 137

Area	8 sq. mi.
	(21 sq. km.)
Capital	none
Member of	ADB, COMM, ESCAP, SPC, SPF

Population	10,000
Population growth rate	2.3%
Life expectancy	not available
Languages	Nauruan, *English*
Adult literacy rate	99%

Currency	Australian dollar
GNP (U.S.$, in millions)	80.7
Income per capita (U.S.$)	8,070

Luxury cars skim the 10-mile road ringing the tiny island of Nauru, the world's smallest republic and home to some of its wealthiest people. Their affluence is built upon the mining of phosphate, left behind by centuries of seabird droppings. Food and drinking water are imported.

NEW ZEALAND

New Zealand
Map pages 146–47

Area	104,426 sq. mi.
	(270,534 sq. km.)
Capital	Wellington
Member of	ADB, APEC, COMM, ESCAP, SPC, SPF

Population	3,643,000
Population growth rate	0.9%
Life expectancy	73 (m), 79 (f)
Languages	English, native Maori language
Adult literacy rate	99%

Currency	New Zealand dollar
GNP (U.S.$, in millions)	46,578
Income per capita (U.S.$)	13,190

New Zealand was one of the last empty spaces on the map to be filled in. The Polynesian Maoris arrived 1,700 years ago; Europeans discovered the islands in 1642, but the British ancestors of today's European population did not land until the 1840s. Relations between Maoris and white settlers were initially peaceful, but harmony did not last; the Maori Wars, a bloody struggle, ended in 1870, with the British victorious. Although Maoris still suffer economic disadvantage, progress has been made in land rights compensation, and interracial marriage is widely accepted. Recently there has been a revival of the Maori language.

Encouraged by the familiar green, temperate, and well-watered environment, English immigrants to New Zealand filled the islands' rich pastures with millions of cattle and sheep, and today the nation is the world's second-largest exporter of lamb. Although agriculture is still important - New Zealanders created the international market for kiwi fruit - diversification has led to efficient industries based on ample hydroelectric capacity, and the nation's closest trade ties have shifted from Britain to the U.S., Australia, and Asia. Tourism is an economic force, too. New Zealand's cities are known for their European flavor; dramatic mountain scenery on both of the country's two main islands attracts visitors from around the world. Among Kiwis, as New Zealanders call themselves, environmental consciousness is so high that the nation bans nuclear vessels from its harbors.

PALAU

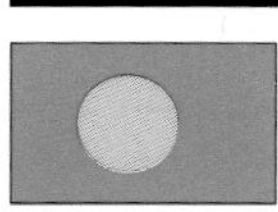

Republic of Palau
Map page 135

Area	196 sq. mi. (508 sq. km.)
Capital	Koror (on Koror Island)
Member of	ESCAP (associate), SPC, SPF

Population	16,000
Population growth rate	2.1%
Life expectancy	60 (m), 63 (f)
Languages	Palauan, English
Adult literacy rate	not available

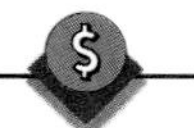

Currency	U.S. dollar
GNP (U.S.$, in millions)	not available
Income per capita (U.S.$)	not available

Only 8 of Palau's 200-plus islands are permanently inhabited. Claimed at various times by Spain, Germany, and Japan, the islands have been independent since 1994, after 47 years as a U.S. trust territory. Copra is the main export.

PAPUA NEW GUINEA

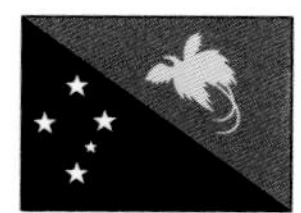

Independent State of Papua New Guinea
Map page 136

Area	178,656 sq. mi. (462,840 sq. km.)
Capital	Port Moresby
Member of	ADB, APEC, COMM, ESCAP, SPC, SPF

Population	3,997,000
Population growth rate	2.2%
Life expectancy	55 (m), 57 (f)
Languages	Pidgin English, Motu, *English, many local languages*
Adult literacy rate	72.2%

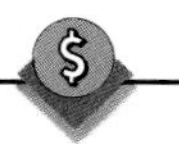

Currency	kina
GNP (U.S.$, in millions)	4,857
Income per capita (U.S.$)	1,160

Craggy mountains cloaked by rain forest run the length of the island of New Guinea, the eastern half of which is occupied by Papua New Guinea. Nearby volcanic islands form the rest of the nation.

The indigenous people of the mountain highlands belong to a multitude of tribes, speaking some 750 different languages. Many are so isolated by the island's rugged terrain that they have little or no contact with the outside world. In low-lying areas, agriculture employs about two-thirds of the nation's workers, with copra, coffee, and cocoa topping the list of food exports. Impassable mountains and rivers impede land travel; airplanes link Port Moresby with hundreds of airfields across the country. Independent since 1975 after 69 years of Australian administration, Papua New Guinea is rattled by political unrest, especially on Bougainville Island, where debate over the profits from the island's copper mining operation (one of the world's largest) has escalated into a violent separatist movement.

SOLOMON ISLANDS

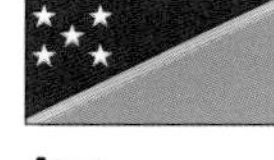

Solomon Islands
Map pages 136–37

Area	10,637 sq. mi. (27,556 sq. km.)
Capital	Honiara (on Guadalcanal)
Member of	ADB, COMM, ESCAP, SPC, SPF

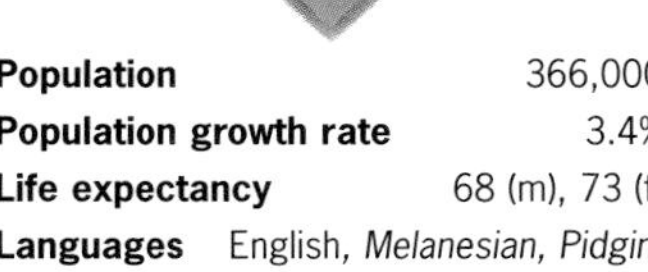

Population	366,000
Population growth rate	3.4%
Life expectancy	68 (m), 73 (f)
Languages	English, *Melanesian, Pidgin, other local languages*
Adult literacy rate	60%

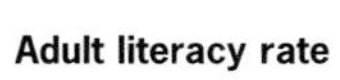

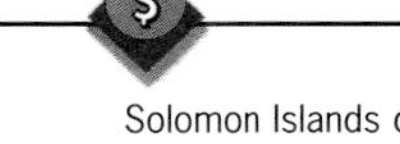

Currency	Solomon Islands dollar
GNP (U.S.$, in millions)	291
Income per capita (U.S.$)	800

Melanesia was the site of the first human settlements in the Pacific, some 3,000 years ago, and Melanesians remain the largest ethnic group in the Solomon Islands. In many ways, the lives of modern Solomon Islanders mirror their ancestors'; most reside in traditional villages and depend upon subsistence farming and fishing. The nation's chief exports are timber from the island's dense rain forests, and tuna. The six main islands, volcanic in origin, surround an area of water that cloaks the remains of dozens of sunken warships - silent witnesses to the fierce fighting that occurred here during World War II, when U.S. forces tried to wrest the country's largest island, Guadalcanal, from Japanese hands.

TONGA

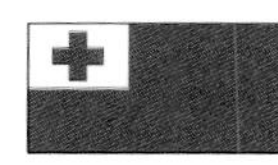

Kingdom of Tonga
Map page 137

Area	289 sq. mi. (748 sq. km.)
Capital	Nuku'alofa
Member of	ADB, COMM, ESCAP, SPC, SPF

Population	98,000
Population growth rate	0.8%
Life expectancy	66 (m), 70 (f)
Languages	Tongan, English
Adult literacy rate	93%

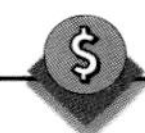

Currency	pa'anga
GNP (U.S.$, in millions)	160
Income per capita (U.S.$)	1,640

The same line of Polynesian monarchs has ruled Tonga for 1,000 years. Nevertheless, Tongans also support democracy. This South Pacific nation comprises 170 islands, with lofty volcanic peaks in the north and low-lying atolls in the south. Most Tongans reside on the largest isle, Tongatapu.

TUVALU

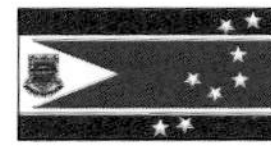

Tuvalu
Map page 137

Area	10 sq. mi. (26 sq. km.)
Capital	Funafuti Atoll
Member of	ADB, COMM, ESCAP, SPC, SPF

Population	9,000
Population growth rate	0%
Life expectancy	not available
Languages	Tuvaluan, English
Adult literacy rate	95%

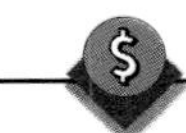

Currency	Australian dollar
GNP (U.S.$, in millions)	3
Income per capita (U.S.$)	326

Stamp collectors around the world know Tuvalu for its exquisite postage stamps. Copra production rounds out the economy. The country's tiny total land area comprises nine atolls spread across 360 sq. mi. (932 sq. km.) of ocean. Once a British territory, Tuvalu became independent in 1978.

VANUATU

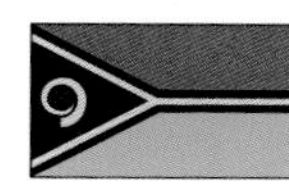

Republic of Vanuatu
Map page 136

Area	4,705 sq. mi. (12,190 sq. km.)
Capital	Port Vila
Member of	ADB, COMM, ESCAP, SPC, SPF

Population	165,000
Population growth rate	2.5%
Life expectancy	64 (m), 67 (f)
Languages	Bislama, English, French, *many local languages*
Adult literacy rate	53%

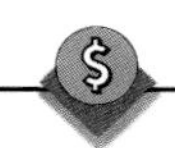

Currency	vatu
GNP (U.S.$, in millions)	189
Income per capita (U.S.$)	1,150

English, French, and Bislama are Vanuatu's three official languages, but the nation actually embraces some 105 native tongues. The first two reflect two centuries of contact with the British and French, who jointly ruled the islands as the New Hebrides from 1906 to 1980. There are 12 main islands and about 70 smaller ones.

WESTERN SAMOA

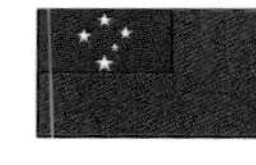

Independent State of Western Samoa
Map page 147

Area	1,093 sq. mi. (2,831 sq. km.)
Capital	Apia
Member of	ADB, COMM, ESCAP, SPC. SPF

Population	164,000
Population growth rate	0.5%
Life expectancy	64 (m,) 70 (f)
Languages	Samoan, English
Adult literacy rate	97%

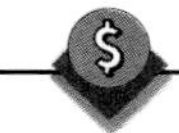

Currency	tala
GNP (U.S.$, in millions)	163
Income per capita (U.S.$)	970

A communal lifestyle predominates in the villages of Western Samoa, a nation of nine volcanic islands green with large banana and cocoa plantations and dense rain forests. New Zealand administered the islands prior to 1962, when Western Samoa became the first Polynesian nation to regain independence.

20TH-CENTURY LANDMARKS

1901 Commonwealth of Australia founded.

1905 Australia acquires Papua New Guinea.

— 1910 —

1914 World War II begins. Japan occupies Marshall Islands. New Zealand occupies Western Samoa.

1915 Battle of Gallipoli.

1916 British colony established on Gilbert and Ellice Islands (Kiribati and Tuvalu).

— 1920 —

1921 New Guinea mandated to Australia by League of Nations.

— 1930 —

1939 World War II starts. Australia and New Zealand join Allies.

— 1940 —

1941 Pacific becomes major war zone.

1942 Battle of Midway.

1942–45 Japanese occupy Kiribati, Papua New Guinea, and Nauru.

1946–58 Nuclear tests conducted by U.S. in Marshall Islands.

— 1950 —

1957 Nuclear tests carried out by Britain near Christmas Island.

— 1960 —

1968 Nauru (not in UN) made special member of Commonwealth.

— 1970 —

1975 Ellice Islands secede to form Tuvalu.

1975 Governor-general of Australia dismisses Labor government; calls for Australia to become a republic gain support.

— 1980 —

1985 *Rainbow Warrior*, Greenpeace flagship, sabotaged and sunk in Auckland Harbor.

1987 Military coup in Fiji establishes republic; Fiji suspended from Commonwealth.

— 1990 —

1990 Papua New Guinea blockades Bougainville Island, where rebels seek independence.

1994 Papua New Guinea agrees to cease-fire with rebels

1995 Large tracts of land in New Zealand returned to Maoris.

1995–96 French nuclear tests in Pacific cause widespread anger.

NORTH AMERICA

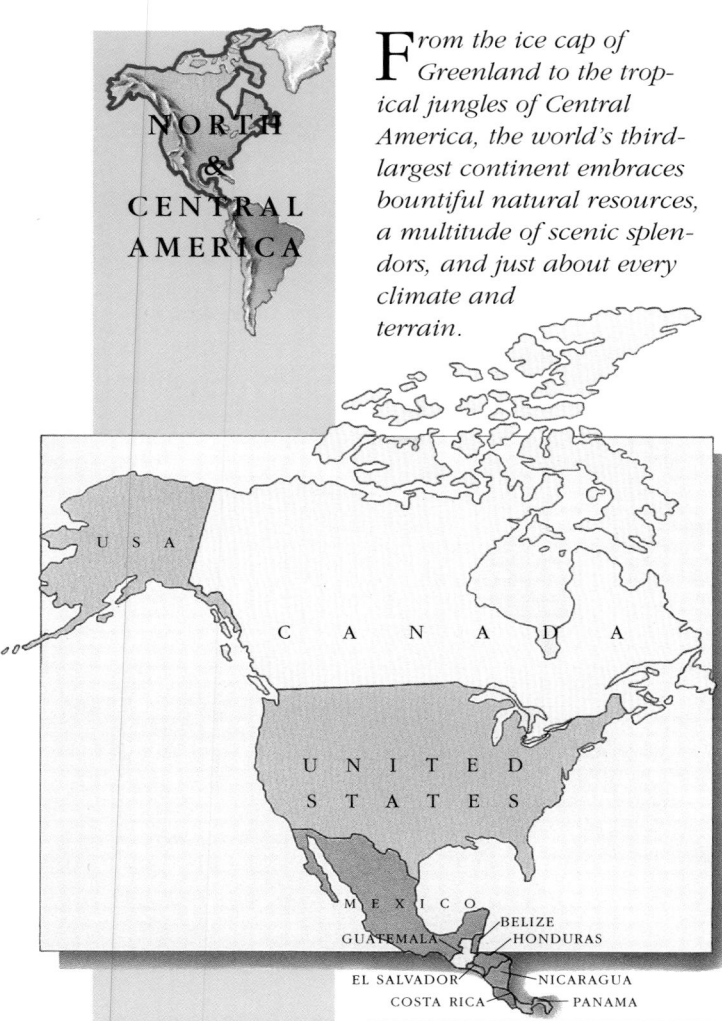

*F*rom the ice cap of Greenland to the tropical jungles of Central America, the world's third-largest continent embraces bountiful natural resources, a multitude of scenic splendors, and just about every climate and terrain.

Colonies and Dependent Territories

BERMUDA
Parent country
U.K.
Map page 169

GREENLAND
Parent country
DENMARK
Map page 151

MIDWAY ISLANDS
Parent country
U.S.
Map page 56

ST. PIERRE AND MIQUELON
Parent country
FRANCE
Map page 161

WAKE ISLAND
Parent country
U.S.
Map page 137

Abbreviations
COMM *Commonwealth*
EBRD *European Bank for Reconstruction and Development*
ECLAC *Economic Commission for Latin America and the Caribbean*
G7 *Group of Seven*
IABD *Inter-American Development Bank*
LAIA *Latin American Integration Association*
NAFTA *North American Free Trade Agreement*
NATO *North Atlantic Treaty Organization*
OAS *Organization of American States*

GNP *Gross National Product*

228

CANADA

Canada
Map pages 155–67

Area	3,843,911 sq. mi.
	(9,958,319 sq. km.)
Capital	Ottawa
Member of	COMM, ECLAC, G7, IADB, NATO, NAFTA, OAS

Population	29,248,000
Population growth rate	1.3%
Life expectancy	74 (m), 81 (f)
Languages	English, French
Adult literacy rate	99%

Currency	Canadian dollar
GNP (U.S.$, in millions)	569,949
Income per capita (U.S.$)	19,570

The largest country in the Western Hemisphere, Canada covers nearly 7 percent of the earth's surface. From a tumbled swath of western mountains, it stretches out through dense evergreen forest, across open plains and muskeg swamp, past a bleak northern tier of Arctic ice and permafrost, to the deeply indented bays and estuaries of the Atlantic coast. Nearly half the country rests on a giant slab of ancient rock – the so-called Canadian Shield – laced with lakes, rivers, and glacial debris. So vast is Canada's territory that Victoria on the Pacific Coast is 3,136 mi. (5,047 km.) from St. John's on the Atlantic.

Four-fifths of this expanse is wilderness – home to bears, wolves, and caribou. The majority of Canada's 29 million citizens occupy only 1 percent of the land, with the densest concentration in the industrial belt that stretches from Windsor to Québec City. Inuit seal hunters sparsely inhabit the Arctic regions.

Few nations can match the bounty from Canada's farms, forests, mines, and rivers. One of the world's major exporters of wheat and barley, Canada is also a leading producer of wood and paper products, oil and natural gas, and minerals such as gold, lead, and silver. Other exports include motor vehicles and telecommunications equipment. Fast-flowing rivers provide hydroelectric power for use at home and in the U.S.

French explorers and fur traders opened eastern Canada to settlement in the 17th century. France lost possession to the English in 1759, and the British North America Act of 1867 established the Dominion of Canada. By 1880 the nation had acquired its present boundaries (except for Newfoundland, which joined in 1949). Since the 1970s a separatist movement in French-speaking Québec has raised constitutional issues with the central government.

BELIZE

Belize
Map page 185

Area	8,864 sq. mi.
	(22,965 sq. km.)
Capital	Belmopan
Member of	COMM, ECLAC, IADB, OAS

Population	209,000
Population growth rate	2.6%
Life expectancy	70 (m), 74 (f)
Languages	English, Spanish, Creole, Garifuna, Maya, Ketchi, German dialect
Adult literacy rate	90%

Currency	Belizean dollar
GNP (U.S.$, in millions)	535
Income per capita (U.S.$)	2,550

Formerly known as British Honduras, tiny Belize changed its name in 1973 and achieved independence eight years later. Long before British settlement began in the 17th century, this least populated of all Central American nations was part of the ancient Mayan civilization. Mahogany and other fine woods are harvested in its inland forests as they have been for centuries, but the main exports are food crops – citrus fruits, bananas, and especially sugar. Tourism is also being promoted, based on a rich array of assets: a tropical climate tempered by sea breezes; Mayan ruins; toucans, jaguars, and other exotic wildlife; sandy beaches; and just offshore, the world's second-longest barrier reef.

COSTA RICA

Republic of Costa Rica
Map page 186

Area	19,725 sq. mi.
	(51,100 sq. km.)
Capital	San José
Member of	ECLAC, IADB, OAS

Population	3,266,000
Population growth rate	2.5%
Life expectancy	73 (m), 78 (f)
Language	Spanish
Adult literacy rate	92.8%

Currency	Costa Rican colón
GNP (U.S.$, in millions)	7,856
Income per capita (U.S.$)	2,380

Christopher Columbus sailed to the shores of Costa Rica in 1502 and Spanish colonization soon followed. Though the country gained independence from Spain in 1821, it remains the most European nation in Central America: little of its indigenous Indian population survives.

Swampy lowlands line both the Caribbean and Pacific coasts, so most citizens of Costa Rica (Spanish for "rich coast") live in the central highlands. Coffee and bananas are the chief exports, but among the imports are increasing numbers of tourists, who come from all over to behold the wonders of the tropical rain forest.

EL SALVADOR

Republic of El Salvador
Map page 186

Area	8,122 sq. mi.
	(21,041 sq. km.)
Capital	San Salvador
Member of	ECLAC, IADB, OAS

Population	5,058,000
Population growth rate	1.9%
Life expectancy	51 (m), 64 (f)
Language	Spanish
Adult literacy rate	71.5%

Currency	Salvadorean colón
GNP (U.S.$, in millions)	8,365
Income per capita (U.S.$)	1,480

The smallest and most densely populated of the nations of Central America, El Salvador continues to rebuild following a 12-year civil war that ended in 1992. Meanwhile it struggles to diversify an economy based largely on coffee exports and textile manufacturing. The nation won independence from Spain in 1821; ever since, its volatile politics have reflected towering inequalities in land ownership and distribution of wealth. Land clearing for plantation crops and subsistence farming has left only 2 percent of El Salvador's central plateau and mountain slopes forested – a sure recipe for soil erosion.

GUATEMALA

Republic of Guatemala
Map page 186

Area	42,031 sq. mi.
	(108,889 sq. km.)
Capital	Guatemala City
Member of	ECLAC, IADB, OAS

Population	10,621,000
Population growth rate	2.9%
Life expectancy	60 (m), 64 (f)
Languages	Spanish, many local languages
Adult literacy rate	55.1%

Currency	quetzal
GNP (U.S.$, in millions)	12,237
Income per capita (U.S.$)	1,190

Guatemala's ancient Mayan civilization fell to Spanish conquistadors in 1523, but the Mayan way of life still brightens the country's impoverished villages. The local Indians, who make up the national majority, weave vividly-colored clothing of precolonial design. Tourists flock to Mayan ruins like Tikal, whose lofty pyramids push above the jungle canopy. While most people live in poverty, large plantations on the Pacific Coast offer up coffee, sugar, and bananas for export and support a small group of wealthy elite.

The country's political life is as volatile as its volcano-studded landscape. More than 100,000 Guatemalans were killed – and half a million displaced – in decades of civil violence. A 1996 peace accord between the government and leftist rebels holds out promise for greater stability in the future.

HONDURAS

Republic of Honduras
Map page 186

Area	43,266 sq. mi.
	(112,088 sq. km.)
Capital	Tegucigalpa
Member of	ECLAC, IADB, OAS

Population	5,770,000
Population growth rate	3.0%
Life expectancy	65 (m), 70 (f)
Language	Spanish
Adult literacy rate	72.7%

Currency	lempira
GNP (U.S.$, in millions)	3,162
Income per capita (U.S.$)	580

The second-largest country in Central America, Honduras also ranks as one of the poorest in the hemisphere. Bananas have been the country's signature export for decades, but significant amounts of coffee, flowers, shrimp, beef, and other goods are produced here as well. Gold deposits in this mountainous land were what attracted Spanish conquistadors in the 16th century, and the country's underexploited mineral resources could very well enhance future development. Independent since 1821, Honduras has endured repeated military coups and changes of government.

MEXICO

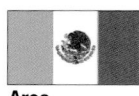

United Mexican States
Map pages 184–85

Area	755,866 sq. mi.
	(1,958,201 sq. km.)
Capital	Mexico City
Member of	ECLAC, IADB, LAIA,
	NAFTA, OAS

Population	93,008,000
Population growth rate	2.2%
Life expectancy	68 (m), 74 (f)
Languages	Spanish,
	local languages
Adult literacy rate	87.6%

Currency	new Mexican peso
GNP (U.S.$, in millions)	368,679
Income per capita (U.S.$)	4,010

Forged in a clash of warring cultures, Mexico was Europe's first great New World conquest. A succession of highly developed indigenous societies once dominated the region. Ruined cities and precisely engineered pyramids bear testimony to the Maya, who thrived after the fourth century. Later the fierce Aztecs ruled from Tenochtitlán, a city steeped in human sacrifice. In 1521 their empire was overthrown by Spanish conquistador Hernando Cortés.

Mexico won independence in 1821, but lost its northern half to the U.S. in a war fought from 1846 to 1848. Always volatile, Mexico's politics sank into near anarchy during the revolution of 1910 to 1921. In recent years stability has meant single-party domination of Mexico's democratic system.

Mexico is the world's largest producer of silver, and its oil reserves are immense. Yet an export economy based on primary resources has proven perilous; falling oil prices in the 1980s led to debt crisis and currency devaluation. Free trade with the U.S. has brought a proliferation of American-owned factories, yet opportunities lag for the rapidly growing population. As Mexico City mushrooms

into the world's largest city, it chokes in its own air pollution, and many Mexicans continue to emigrate illegally to the U.S.

Mexico's most deep-seated problems, however, stem from stark inequalities in the distribution of wealth and land, and from the economic hardships of its Indian population in a society dominated by *mestizo* (mixed race) citizens and a European-descended elite.

NICARAGUA

Republic of Nicaragua
Map page 186

Area	46,418 sq. mi.
	(120,254 sq. km.)
Capital	Managua
Member of	ECLAC, IADB, OAS

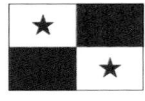

Population	4,401,000
Population growth rate	3.1%
Life expectancy	65 (m), 69 (f)
Languages	Spanish, *English*
Adult literacy rate	65.6%

Currency	gold cordoba
GNP (U.S.$, in millions)	1,395
Income per capita (U.S.$)	330

Central America's most thinly populated nation, Nicaragua is prone to violence born of long-standing inequality. A century of independence – and instability – was capped by the rise of the Somoza dictatorship in the 1930s. The leftist Sandinistas seized power in 1979 and were challenged in turn by rightist guerrillas, backed by the U.S. Fighting ended in 1990, and a freely elected government now is trying to rebuild and diversify a plantation-based economy. The Hispanic population is concentrated in western uplands; along the Caribbean plain live the Miskito Indians and descendants of African slaves.

PANAMA

Republic of Panama
Map page 186

Area	29,150 sq. mi.
	(75,517 sq. km.)
Capital	Panama City
Member of	ECLAC, IADB, OAS

Population	2,631,000
Population growth rate	2.0%
Life expectancy	71 (m), 75 (f)
Language	Spanish
Adult literacy rate	88.8%

Currency	balboa
GNP (U.S.$, in millions)	6,905
Income per capita (U.S.$)	2,670

Panama's defining characteristic is the passage it offers between the Caribbean Sea and Pacific Ocean across the narrow isthmus where Balboa, the Spanish conquistador, first spied the Pacific Ocean. The country acquired a unique global importance in 1914 with the opening of the Panama Canal, built by the U.S. after Panama's secession from Colombia. Vital to the country's economy, and world shipping as well, the canal reverts by treaty to Panamanian control at the end of 1999.

Like its neighbors, Panama has had a tumultuous political history. An invasion by American troops in 1989 achieved the capture of dictator Manuel Noriega, who was extradited to the U.S., tried in a federal court, and convicted of drug smuggling. Elected governments have since abolished the army and boosted the economy by promoting international banking. Panama benefits from a large merchant shipping fleet; it also exports coffee, sugar, and bananas, along with prized mahogany from its ever-diminishing rain forests.

UNITED STATES

United States
of America
Map pages 162–83

Area	3,786,333 sq. mi.
	(9,809,155 sq. km.)
Capital	Washington, D.C.
Member of	ECLAC, G7, IADB, NAFTA,
	NATO, OAS

Population	260,341,000
Population growth rate	1.0%
Life expectancy	72 (m), 79 (f)
Languages	English, *Spanish*
Adult literacy rate	over 95%

Currency	U.S. dollar
GNP (U.S.$, in billions)	6,737,367
Income per capita (U.S.$)	25,860

In little more than 200 years, the U.S. has grown from a narrow cluster of farming villages and Colonial seaports into the richest, most powerful nation on earth. The sweep of its land, the strength of its economy, the diversity of its people – along with its ideals of personal liberty and material promise – have no rival. Its influence extends, for better or worse, throughout the globe.

The nation came into being after 13 British Colonies along the Atlantic seaboard declared their independence in 1776. The U.S. quickly expanded, through purchase, treaty, and conquest. Pioneers moved westward past the forested Appalachians into the Indian lands of the Ohio Valley, across the Mississippi River and through an ocean of prairie destined to ripple with grain

(today feeding much of the world), and toward the Rocky Mountains. Farther west, on land taken from Spanish-ruled Mexico in 1848, they settled in the temperate valleys of the Pacific Coast. The U.S. later extended its reach as far north as Alaska and as far west as the Hawaiian Islands.

This celebrated "melting pot" is flavored with cultures from around the globe. The Colonial British stock of the East Coast was joined by the French colonists of Louisiana, the Spanish who populated the Southwest, and the blacks who were brought from Africa to work the plantations of the South. Newcomers from Germany and Scandinavia moved into the Midwest, and Asians helped build California. Today more than one in four citizens belongs to a minority group, including 33 million African-Americans, 27 million Hispanics, and 9 million Asians and Pacific Islanders.

The American economy turns out a prodigious potpourri of goods and services. The U.S. grows 70 percent of the world's corn exports, 66 percent of its soybeans, and 36 percent of its wheat. A leading producer of phosphates, gypsum, sulphur, lead, and other raw materials, it has the world's largest oil-refining capacity. American workshops and laboratories have delivered a steady flood of inventions – from the steel plow to the microprocessor. Manufactures include aircraft, machinery, automobiles, textiles, steel, and chemicals. The vitality of the nation's polyglot population has given rise to one of its most marketable and distinctive exports: American culture, as typified by television and film.

A strong democratic tradition – underpinned by a constitution that is one of mankind's great civic documents – has brought enviable stability to public life. Still, in 1860 a Civil War erupted between North and South over the issues of slavery and states' rights, claiming some 500,000 lives. The Great Depression of the 1930s revealed an ever-widening chasm between economic classes. For all its resources and idealism, the U.S. has yet to resolve the problems of racism and poverty. In fact the income spread between rich and poor is one of the largest in the industrialized world.

America's armed forces played a vital role in securing Allied victories in two world wars. The nation emerged from World War II with an arsenal of atomic weapons and a frontline position in world affairs. Since then it has resolved 40 years of Cold War confrontation with the Communist Bloc, and it now remains the only nuclear superpower in the world.

The Caribbean

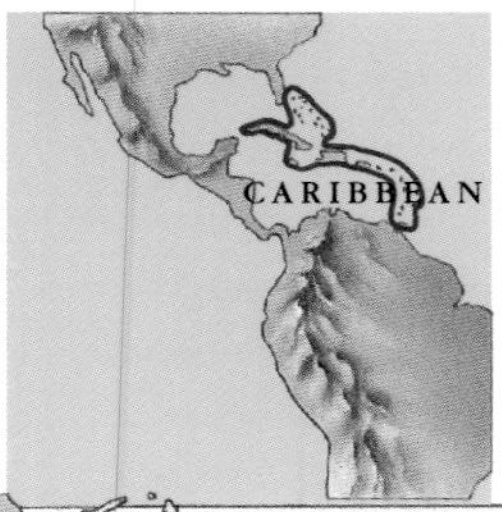

Once a pirates' haven and the scene of fierce clashes between colonial powers, the Caribbean now draws tourists from all over the world to its sunny islands and warm seas.

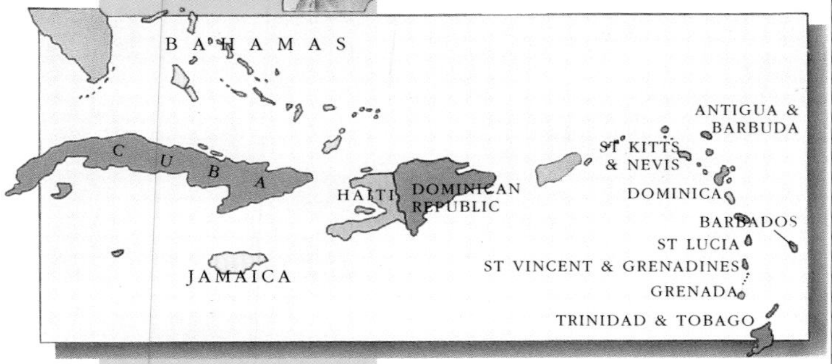

Colonies and Dependent Territories

ANGUILLA
Parent country U.K.
Map page 187

ARUBA
Parent country NETHERLANDS
Map page 187

BRITISH VIRGIN ISLANDS
Parent country U.K.
Map page 187

CAYMAN ISLANDS
Parent country U.K.
Map page 186

GUADELOUPE
Parent country FRANCE
Map page 187

MARTINIQUE
Parent country FRANCE
Map page 187

MONTSERRAT
Parent country U.K.
Map page 187

NAVASSA ISLAND
Parent country U.S.
Map page 186

NETHERLANDS ANTILLES
Parent country NETHERLANDS
Map page 187

PUERTO RICO
Parent country U.S.
Map page 187

TURKS AND CAICOS ISLANDS
Parent country U.K.
Map page 187

VIRGIN ISLANDS (U.S.)
Parent country U.S.
Map page 187

ANTIGUA & BARBUDA

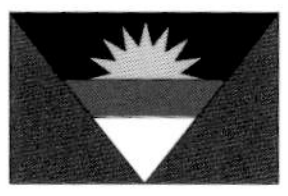

Antigua and Barbuda
Map page 187

Area	171 sq. mi. (442 sq. km.)
Capital	St John's
Member of	COMM, ECLAC, OAS
Population	64,200
Population growth rate	0.5%
Life expectancy	74 (av. m/f)
Languages	English, *English patois*
Adult literacy rate	90%
Currency	East Caribbean dollar
GNP (U.S.$, in millions)	453
Income per capita (U.S.$)	6,970

A British colony from the 1600s until its independence in 1981, this nation is comprised of three islands: Antigua, the most heavily populated; Barbuda, a low-lying game reserve; and Redonda, an uninhabited rock. Sugar plantations long dominated the economy, but it is Antigua's dry, tropical climate, numerous sandy beaches, and splendidly scenic interior that have made the country a vacation haven and a yachting and boating paradise.

THE BAHAMAS

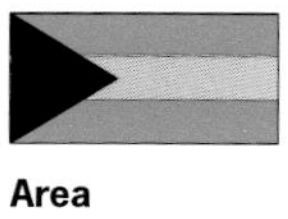

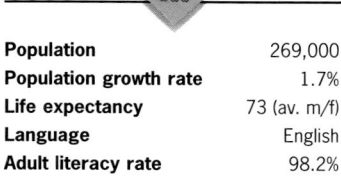

Commonwealth of the Bahamas
Map page 186

Area	5,382 sq. mi. (13,939 sq. km.)
Capital	Nassau
Member of	COMM, ECLAC, IADB, OAS
Population	269,000
Population growth rate	1.7%
Life expectancy	73 (av. m/f)
Language	English
Adult literacy rate	98.2%
Currency	Bahamian dollar
GNP (U.S.$, in millions)	3,207
Income per capita (U.S.$)	11,790

The Bahamas, located north of the Caribbean, were Columbus's first landfall in the New World, but it was not until after the British arrived in the mid-17th century that these islands became a colony. Though briefly occupied by both American and Spanish forces in the late 18th century, the archipelago was primarily under British rule until it gained independence in 1973. It consists of some 2,000 islets and 700 islands, only 29 of which are inhabited. Because the soil of these coral-limestone islands is not arable, the economy – thanks to the glorious subtropical climate – is heavily based on tourism.

BARBADOS

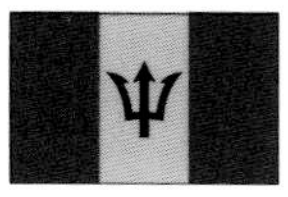

Barbados
Map page 187

Area	166 sq. mi. (430 sq. km.)
Capital	Bridgetown
Member of	COMM, ECLAC, IADB, OAS
Population	264,000
Population growth rate	0.3%
Life expectancy	72 (m), 77 (f)
Language	English
Adult literacy rate	98%
Currency	Barbados dollar
GNP (U.S.$, in millions)	1,704
Income per capita (U.S.$)	6,530

This easternmost island in the Caribbean is among the world's most densely populated nations. With a fortuitous combination of fertile soil, warm climate, and nonmountainous terrain, it has excelled in sugar production ever since it was first settled by Great Britain in the 1600s. Fine pink-and-white sand beaches and fringing coral reefs make tourism the cornerstone of the economy, however. Though independent since 1966, Barbados was under British rule for over 300 years and retains such a distinctly British flavor that residents of other Caribbean islands often refer to it as "little England."

CUBA

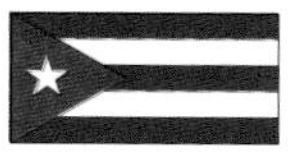

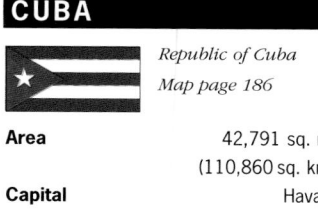

Republic of Cuba
Map page 186

Area	42,791 sq. mi. (110,860 sq. km.)
Capital	Havana
Member of	ECLAC
Population	10,901,000
Population growth rate	0.9%
Life expectancy	74 (m), 77 (f)
Language	Spanish
Adult literacy rate	94%
Currency	Cuban peso
GNP (U.S.$, in millions)	not available
Income per capita (U.S.$)	not available

Cuba, the largest of the Caribbean islands, is home to the most enduring experiment with Communism in the Western Hemisphere. Located just 90 miles off the coast of the U.S., it has figured as friend, foe, and flashpoint in the 20th-century history of its giant neighbor.

After Christopher Columbus claimed Cuba for Spain in 1492, Spanish colonial rulers established sugar and tobacco plantations and imported African slaves whose descendants remain a significant factor in Cuba's racial makeup. In the late 19th century, Cubans fought two rebellions against Spain, but the colony continued under Spanish rule until the Spanish-American War of 1898, when the U.S. secured its independence. American troops withdrew from Cuba in 1902, but U.S. involvement in the island's economy extended into the mid-20th century.

Decades of corruption resulted in the 1959 triumph of a revolutionary insurgency commanded by Fidel Castro. Incensed by the new regime's seizure of foreign assets, the U.S. backed an exile-led invasion, which collapsed at Cuba's Bay of Pigs. Professing himself a Communist and turning to the Soviet Union, Castro nearly precipitated a war with the U.S. in 1962 when he accepted a plan to install Soviet missiles in Cuba. After a tense standoff with President John F. Kennedy, the missiles were removed.

For three decades, as a client state of the Soviet Union, Cuba was heavily dependent on the U.S.S.R. for weapons and economic aid. With the fall of Soviet Communism in 1991, however, the U.S.S.R. withdrew its support. Ideologically isolated, Cuba was left with a severely weakened economy and became increasingly susceptible to the damage inflicted by a long-standing U.S. trade embargo.

Regardless of which country softens its posture first, Cuba's potential – for a revival of tourism, modernization of agriculture, and development of its mineral resources – will most likely be unlocked as relations thaw with its powerful neighbor and sometime adversary, the United States.

DOMINICA

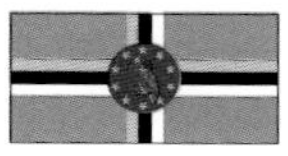

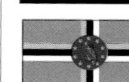

Commonwealth of Dominica
Map page 187

Area	290 sq. mi. (750 sq. km.)
Capital	Roseau
Member of	COMM, ECLAC, OAS
Population	71,000
Population growth rate	– 0.2%
Life expectancy	72 (av. m/f)
Languages	English, *Creole*
Adult literacy rate	94.4%
Currency	East Caribbean dollar
GNP (U.S.$, in millions)	201
Income per capita (U.S.$)	2,830

A mountainous volcanic island endowed with relatively little arable land, Dominica relies on the production of bananas, coconuts, and tropical fruits. Though it boasts few beaches, it has other natural assets that could nurture a growth in the tourism industry: spectacular scenery, lush tropical rain forests (with substantial tracts protected in national parks), rushing rivers and waterfalls, and exotic wildlife.

DOMINICAN REPUBLIC

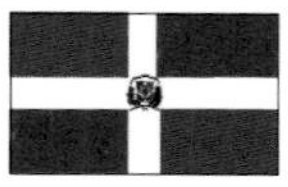

Dominican Republic
Map pages 186–87

Area	18,691 sq. mi. (48,422 sq. km.)
Capital	Santo Domingo
Member of	ECLAC, IADB, OAS
Population	7,769,000
Population growth rate	2.1%
Life expectancy	68 (m), 72 (f)
Language	Spanish
Adult literacy rate	83.3%
Currency	Dominican Republic peso
GNP (U.S.$, in millions)	10,109
Income per capita (U.S.$)	1,320

Claimed by Columbus for Spain in 1492, the island of Hispaniola is now shared by the Dominican Republic and Haiti. The entire island was known as the Republic of Haiti for over two decades (1822-44), until the Dominican Republic gained independence.

Like Haiti, the Dominican Republic has a history of plantation agriculture and political volatility. From 1930 until his assassination in 1961, the nation was held in the iron grip of Gen. Rafael Trujillo. Tenuously democratic since 1965, when the U.S. intervened to end a civil war, the country still suffers political and economic instability. A great disparity exists between the rich and the poor in this multiracial society. Wealth is dominated by the landed white minority, while black farmers (descendants of slaves brought to work the plantations) are at the bottom of the social ladder.

Abbreviations
COMM Commonwealth
ECLAC Economic Commission for Latin America and the Caribbean
IABD Inter-American Development Bank
OAS Organization of American States
GNP Gross National Product

GRENADA

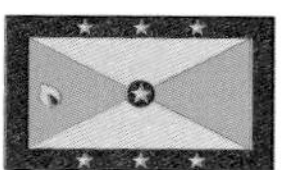

Grenada
Map page 187

Area	133 sq. mi.
	(344 sq. km.)
Capital	St. George's
Member of	COMM, ECLAC, OAS

Population	94,800
Population growth rate	0.2%
Life expectancy	71 (av. m/f)
Languages	English, *French patois*
Adult literacy rate	90%

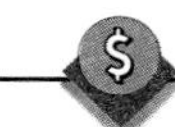

Currency	East Caribbean dollar
GNP (U.S.$, in millions)	241
Income per capita (U.S.$)	2,620

Long known as the Isle of Spice, this scenic gem is the world's second-largest producer of nutmeg and also exports mace, bananas, and a number of other food crops. Grenada, which relies heavily on tourism, gained independence from Great Britain in 1974. Nearly a decade later an invasion by troops from the U.S. and several neighboring islands suceeded in ousting a pro-Marxist administration and restoring democracy.

HAITI

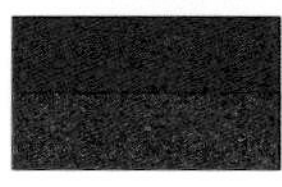

Republic of Haiti
Map page 186

Area	10,712 sq. mi.
	(27,750 sq. km.)
Capital	Port-au-Prince
Member of	ECLAC, IADB, OAS

Population	7,041,000
Population growth rate	2%
Life expectancy	55 (m), 58 (f)
Languages	French, Creole
Adult literacy rate	45%

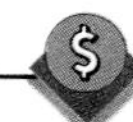

Currency	gourde
GNP (U.S.$, in millions)	1,542
Income per capita (U.S.$)	220

Few nations bear as grim a legacy as Haiti. Under French colonial rule Haiti developed a slave-based sugar economy. The slaves successfully rebelled in 1804, but the nation's politics descended into repression, culminating in the mid-1990s in the decades-long tyranny of the Duvaliers and their vicious "Tonton Macoute" secret police. Jean-Claude Duvalier's 1986 overthrow brought little relief; military strongmen dominated Haiti until the U.S. intervened in 1994 and restored a previously-elected government. A land of subsistence farmers tilling a treeless and eroded landscape,

Haiti has an economy based on coffee, sisal, and sugar production. As the poorest nation in the Western Hemisphere, though, even a politically stable Haiti faces daunting challenges.

JAMAICA

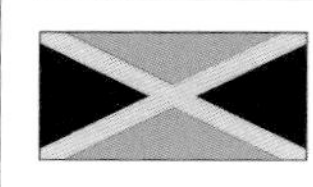

Jamaica
Map page 186

Area	4,243 sq. mi.
	10,991 sq. km.
Capital	Kingston
Member of	COMM, ECLAC, IADB, OAS

Population	2,374,200
Population growth rate	0.9%
Life expectancy	71 (m), 76 (f)
Languages	English, *local patois*
Adult literacy rate	85%

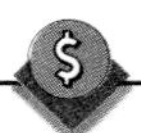

Currency	Jamaican dollar
GNP (U.S.$, in millions)	3,553
Income per capita (U.S.$)	1,420

Once a Caribbean jewel in Britain's crown, Jamaica was initially claimed by Columbus for Spain in 1494 but was seized by the British in the 17th century. Like other arable islands in the Caribbean, colonial Jamaica was divided into great sugar plantations worked by African slaves. After emancipation in 1838, most of the former slaves – ancestors of the bulk of today's population – began to till small landholdings. Although the agriculture-based economy of plantation days has been replaced by the mining of bauxite (the base ore of aluminum), rural Jamaica is still home to some 150,000 subsistence farmers, and Jamaica is still known for its production of Blue Mountain coffee, and also for sugar and its time-honored by-product, dark Jamaican rum.

In 1962 Jamaica became the first Caribbean nation to achieve independence in the postwar era. Three centuries of British colonial rule had, however, left its imprint: though many Jamaicans speak Creole, the island is the most populous English-speaking nation in the West Indies and the majority of its population is Protestant.

Jamaican politics during the first decades of independence have been marked by sharp polarization between socialist and conservative elements, frequently with violent overtones at election times. More recently a measure of free-market consensus has been achieved. The country is the third-largest supplier of bauxite in the world but is susceptible to volatile markets. Tourism also figures prominently in the economy, although its influence is more pervasive along the north and west coasts than among the

villages of the mountainous interior and bustling streets of Kingston, the capital. But Kingston is perhaps best known for the infectious lilt of reggae music that developed in its poor districts during the 1960s.

ST. KITTS & NEVIS

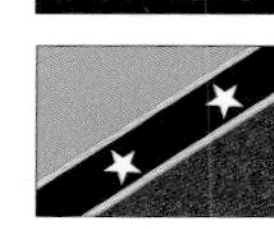

Federation of St. Kitts and Nevis
Map page 187

Area	101 sq. mi.
	(261 sq. km.)
Capital	Basseterre
Member of	COMM, ECLAC, OAS

Population	44,400
Population growth rate	– 0.5%
Life expectancy	66 (m), 71 (f)
Language	English
Adult literacy rate	97.3%

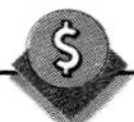

Currency	East Caribbean dollar
GNP (U.S.$, in millions)	195
Income per capita (U.S.$)	4,760

Site of the first successful British settlement in the West Indies (in 1623), volcanic St. Kitts and its smaller neighboring island, Nevis, became a fully independent state in 1983. As on many Caribbean islands, tourism is supplanting agriculture (mainly sugar cane production, but also sea-island cotton and other crops) as the mainstay of the economy. Nevis is known as "the Spa of the Caribbean."

ST. LUCIA

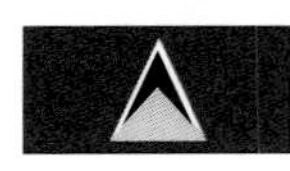

St. Lucia
Map page 187

Area	238 sq. mi.
	(616 sq. km.)
Capital	Castries
Member of	COMM, ECLAC, OAS

Population	157,862
Population growth rate	1.7%
Life expectancy	69 (m), 75 (f)
Languages	English, *French*
Adult literacy rate	81.5%

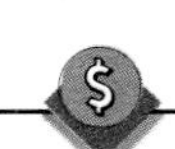

Currency	East Caribbean dollar
GNP (U.S.$, in millions)	501
Income per capita (U.S.$)	3,450

During the colonial era St. Lucia was the pawn in a fierce tug of war between France and England, but ultimately became a British possession until it gained independence in 1979. A dramatically beautiful volcanic island much beloved by tourists, its signature landmarks are the twin Pitons, a pair of conical volcanic plugs that flank a bay and rise to awesome heights at the very edge of the water.

ST. VINCENT & THE GRENADINES

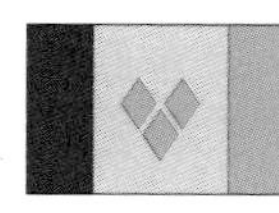

St. Vincent and the Grenadines
Map page 187

Area	150 sq. mi.
	(389 sq. km.)
Capital	Kingstown
Member of	COMM, ECLAC, OAS

Population	111,000
Population growth rate	0.9%
Life expectancy	72 (av. m/f)
Language	English
Adult literacy rate	82%

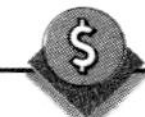

Currency	East Caribbean dollar
GNP (U.S.$, in millions)	235
Income per capita (U.S.$)	2,120

St. Vincent is the main island of this former British colony and the home of most of its people. Relying on a combination of tourism and agriculture, it is the world's leading producer of arrowroot starch. The Grenadines, an archipelago of about 100 islands trailing off to the south like a string of pearls, is sparsely populated but has become the Caribbean playground of the rich and famous.

TRINIDAD & TOBAGO

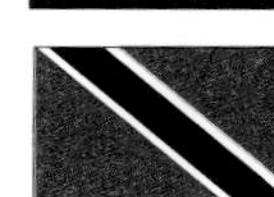

Republic of Trinidad and Tobago
Map page 187

Area	1,979 sq. mi.
	(5,128 sq. km.)
Capital	Port of Spain
Member of	COMM, ECLAC, IADB, OAS

Population	1,249,700
Population growth rate	1.2%
Life expectancy	72 (av. m/f)
Languages	English, *French, Spanish, Hindi, Chinese*
Adult literacy rate	94.9

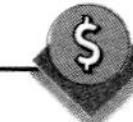

Currency	Trinidad and Tobago dollar
GNP (U.S.$, in millions)	4,838
Income per capita (U.S.$)	3,740

Although they form one country, in some ways the large island of Trinidad and tiny one of Tobago are a study in contrasts. The majority of Trinidad's inhabitants are of black African and East Indian descent, while most Tobagans are black. Trinidad's economy is fueled by oil, natural gas, and the world's largest source of asphalt; Tobago relies on tourism and agriculture. The pace on Trinidad is fast; on Tobago (claimed to be the inspiration for Robinson Crusoe's isle), life is more tranquil. But both are renowned for their wealth of wildlife.

SOUTH AMERICA

The Andes run the length of the west coast behind a narrow coastal plain, while the Guiana highlands, to the north, face the Atlantic. The forested Amazon basin covers one-third of Brazil, whose southern plateau extends to the great plains, or pampas, of Uruguay and Argentina.

ARGENTINA

Argentine Republic
Map pages 192–93

Area	1,068,019 sq. mi.
	(2,766,889 sq. km.)
Capital	Buenos Aires
Member of	ECLAC, IADB, OAS

Population	34,180,000
Population growth rate	1.4%
Life expectancy	68 (m), 74 (f)
Language	Spanish
Adult literacy rate	95.3%

Currency	nuevo peso
GNP (U.S.$, in millions)	275,657
Income per capita (U.S.$)	8,060

Argentina was colonized by Spanish adventurers who struck south from Peru in the 1500s. Lacking precious metals, the province remained a colonial backwater, but settlers soon recognized the potential of its vast pampas for grazing and agriculture. Declaring its independence in 1816, the nation was embroiled in a civil war until 1853. By 1900 Argentina was attracting large numbers of European immigrants. With a robust economy based on meat and grain exports, it soon developed into a cosmopolitan society.

Two world wars disrupted trade with Europe, and a succession of military coups weakened Argentina's social and economic stability. In the 1940s and early 1950s a populist president Juan Perón and his wife, Eva, gained widespread support among poor urban workers. During the 1970s military dictators suppressed dissidents, some 10,000 of whom were "disappeared"; military rule ended after Argentina failed to seize the Falkland Islands from Britain in a 1982 war. (Argentina now seeks to aquire the islands through diplomatic channels.)

Subsequent civilian governments have tamed hyperinflation, privatized unprofitable state industries, and sought to develop a stronger manufacturing component to the heavily agricultural economy. Nearly 40 percent of Argentinians live in the capital, Buenos Aires, while in the desolate south, Patagonia remains a barren, thinly-populated frontier.

Colonies and Dependent Territories

FALKLAND ISLANDS
Parent country
U.K.
Map page 193

FRENCH GUIANA
Parent country
FRANCE
Map page 191

SOUTH GEORGIA AND SOUTH SANDWICH ISLANDS
Parent country
U.K.
Map page 193

Abbreviations
COMM *Commonwealth*
ECLAC *Economic Commission for Latin America and the Caribbean*
IADB *Inter-American Development Bank*
OPEC *Organization of the Petroleum Exporting Countries*
OAS *Organization of American States*

GNP *Gross National Product*

BOLIVIA

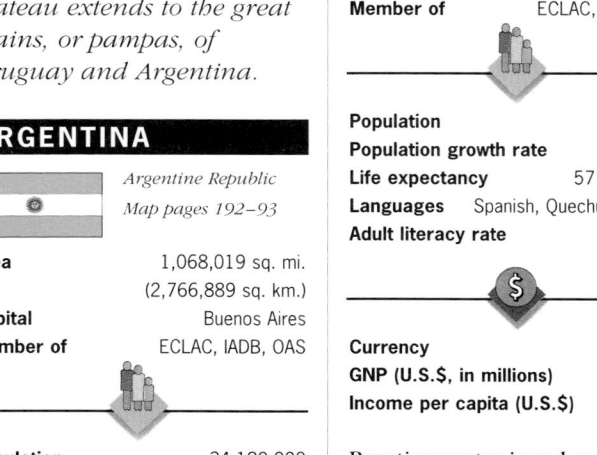

Republic of Bolivia
Map page 192

Area	424,052 sq. mi.
	(1,098,581 sq. km.)
Capitals	La Paz and Sucre
Member of	ECLAC, IADB, OAS

Population	7,237,000
Population growth rate	2.2%
Life expectancy	57 (m), 61 (f)
Languages	Spanish, Quechua, Aymará
Adult literacy rate	79.1%

Currency	boliviano
GNP (U.S.$, in millions)	5,601
Income per capita (U.S.$)	770

Boasting vast mineral resources, Bolivia leads the world in tin production, and its lowland plain is the site of recently discovered deposits of oil and natural gas. Yet, hampered by its landlocked location and political instability, this nation is the poorest in South America. The majority of Bolivia's people live on the altiplano, a high plateau perched at approximately 12,000 ft. (3,600 m.) above sea level between two north-south chains of the Andes. Most are employed in subsistence agriculture, including extensive (if illegal) cultivation of coca, the source of cocaine.

BRAZIL

Federative Republic of Brazil
Map pages 191–92

Area	3,285,630 sq. mi.
	(8,511,996 sq. km.)
Capital	Brasília
Member of	ECLAC, IADB, OAS

Population	155,822,000
Population growth rate	1.8%
Life expectancy	63 (m), 70 (f)
Language	Portuguese
Adult literacy rate	82.8%

Currency	real
GNP (U.S.$, in millions)	536,309
Income per capita (U.S.$)	3,370

Brazil projects two popular images: Rio de Janiero, with its postcardlike harbor and carnival charm, and the mystical Amazon rain forest, once impenetrable but ever more threatened by logging and ranching. Somewhere between these extremes, however, lies another Brazil, a giant in every respect.

Occupying nearly half of South America, Brazil shares borders with every country on the continent except Ecuador and Chile. The result of a 1494 compromise between Portugal and Spain, it is the only Portuguese-speaking nation in South America. Tiny Portugal employed its huge colony to develop sugar plantations worked by slaves, and a strong African racial and cultural component still characterizes the country.

Independent since 1822, Brazil has been mired in corruption and bureaucracy for much of its history; its most recent constitution was adopted in 1988. Economically, the country has fared better, with ample crops and resources, including rubber, cattle ranching, and the world's largest coffee harvests. The land yields not only iron, bauxite, chrome, nickel, and gold, but a wealth of diamonds.

Manufacturing lures many to the cities: greater São Paulo is home to some 20 million people, and Rio is as vibrant as ever. At Brasília, a capital carved out of wilderness in the late 1950s, officials wrestle with issues such as land reform and the destruction of Brazil's rain forest, which contains a greater number and variety of wildlife species than any habitat on earth. As Brazil looms larger in the global economy, it faces growing protest – and pressure – from nations that consider the Amazon a worldwide resource.

CHILE

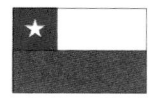

Republic of Chile
Map pages 192–93

Area	292,057 sq. mi.
	(756,626 sq. km.)
Capital	Santiago
Member of	ECLAC, IADB, OAS

Population	14,210,000
Population growth rate	1.7%
Life expectancy	70 (m), 77 (f)
Language	Spanish
Adult literacy rate	94.3%

Currency	Chilean peso
GNP (U.S.$, in millions)	50,051
Income per capita (U.S.$)	3,560

Stretching some 2,700 mi. (4,300 km.) from north to south like a long, narrow ribbon, Chile can claim truly remarkable variations in both topography and climate. The north is dominated by the bleak Atacama Desert, while the fertile central region, which enjoys a Mediterranean-like climate, is noted for its extensive farmlands. By contrast, the country's storm-swept southern reaches consist of forests and grazing lands but also include a stretch of intricately convoluted coastline known for its spectacular fjords and glaciers.

Chile has suffered extreme political and economic turmoil in recent decades, but with the restoration of a democratic government in 1989 – following 16 years of brutally repressive dictatorship – both stability and prosperity have returned. Endowed with rich mineral resources, Chile owes its economic success to the production of copper. The northern desert is the site of one of the world's largest copper mines, and the country is rapidly becoming a leading producer of gold. Nevertheless, agriculture remains an important sector of the nation's thriving economy.

COLOMBIA

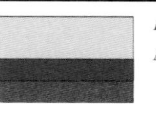

Republic of Colombia
Map page 190

Area	440,714 sq. mi.
	(1,141,748 sq. km.)
Capital	Bogotá
Member of	ECLAC, IADB, OAS

Population	35,886,000
Population growth rate	2.2%
Life expectancy	66 (m), 72 (f)
Language	Spanish
Adult literacy rate	85.2%

Currency	Colombian peso
GNP (U.S.$, in millions)	58,935
Income per capita (U.S.$)	1,620

A treasure trove for Spanish conquistadors, Colombia still supplies more than half of the world's emeralds, along with gold, silver, platinum, and less lustrous riches – coal and oil. Yet the country's modern economy is overshadowed by the influence of cocaine cartels, whose illicit product is said to be the nation's most lucrative export.

Along with its neighbors on the northwestern shoulder of South America, Colombia declared independence from Spain beneath the banner of Simón Bolívar in 1819. Its later history was often violent: revolution split the nation from 1899 to 1902, and a tumultuous period in the 1940s and 1950s called La Violencia claimed over 200,000 lives. Following four years of military dictatorship, a multiparty democracy was established in 1957.

While Colombia is largely an urban nation – its eastern plains are barely populated – fertile croplands yield bananas, cotton, sugar, and in the Andean foothills, world-renowned Colombian coffee beans. Peasant farmers, long the victims of starkly uneven land distribution, are often all too eager to supply the drug cartels with the raw materials of their outlawed but highly profitable trade.

ECUADOR

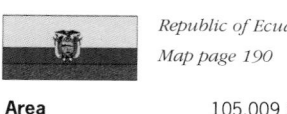

Republic of Ecuador
Map page 190

Area	105,009 sq. mi.
	(272,045 sq. km.)
Capital	Quito
Member of	ECLAC, IADB, OAS,

Population	11,460,000
Population growth rate	2.3%
Life expectancy	66 (m), 71 (f)
Languages	Spanish, *Quechua, other*
	local languages
Adult literacy rate	87.3%

Currency	sucre
GNP (U.S.$, in millions)	14,703
Income per capita (U.S.$)	1,310

Conquered by the Inca empire in the 1400s and by Spain in 1533, the territory now known as Ecuador gained independence in 1830. The country's history is still apparent in the makeup of its people: over half the population is *mestizo* (of mixed Spanish and Indian descent) and a quarter is Indian.

Most Ecuadorians live well below the poverty line. While the development of oil and natural gas in the 1970s gave the economy a boost, fluctuating oil prices in the 1980s caused severe hardship. Today flourishing farmlands on the populous Pacific coastal lowlands supplement the country's modest economy.

GUYANA

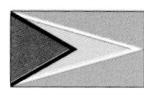

The Cooperative Republic of Guyana
Map page 190

Area	82,978 sq. mi.
	(214,969 sq. km.)
Capital	Georgetown
Member of	COMM, ECLAC, IADB, OAS

Population	740,000
Population growth rate	0.5%
Life expectancy	62 (m), 68 (f)
Languages	English, *Hindi, Urdu,*
	Amerindian dialects
Adult literacy rate	96.4%

Currency	Guyanese dollar
GNP (U.S.$, in millions)	434
Income per capita (U.S.$)	530

Densely forested and sparsely settled throughout its spacious interior, Guyana has been populated primarily along its narrow coastal plain. Ethnic tensions sometimes flare between the Asian and African communities, whose ancestors were brought in to work on sugar plantations. Sugar remains a major export, along with bauxite, rice, and seafood.

PARAGUAY

Republic of Paraguay
Map page 192

Area	157,006 sq. mi.
	(406,752 sq. km.)
Capital	Asunción
Member of	ECLAC, IADB. OAS

Population	4,643,000
Population growth rate	3%
Life expectancy	68 (m), 72 (f)
Languages	Spanish, *Guarani*
Adult literacy rate	92.1%

Currency	guarani
GNP (U.S.$, in millions)	7,606
Income per capita (U.S.$)	1,570

Though landlocked and isolated, Paraguay is linked to the sea by two rivers, the Paraguay and the Parana. The Paraguay divides the country into two contrasting regions. To the east are rich ranchlands and farmlands, seat of Paraguay's agriculture-based economy. To the west are the nearly deserted marshes and scrublands of the Gran Chaco, home of the nation's indigenous Indian minority. An impressive hydroelectric power project at Itaipu on the Parana River is the largest one of its kind in the world. This and similar facilities enable Paraguay to export an excess of electric power.

PERU

Republic of Peru
Map page 190

Area	494,080 sq. mi.
	(1,280,000 sq. km.)
Capital	Lima
Member of	ECLAC, IADB, OAS

Population	23,088,000
Population growth rate	2%
Life expectancy	63 (m), 67 (f)
Languages	Spanish, *Quechua, Aymara*
Adult literacy rate	88.7%

Currency	nuevo sol
GNP (U.S.$, in millions)	44,110
Income per capita (U.S.$)	1,890

Peru's Andean highlands were once the heartland of the flourishing Inca empire, which was destroyed by the Spanish conquistadors in the 1530s. Spanish domination continued for nearly three centuries, but Indians remain the largest ethnic group in Peru, comprising some 45 percent of the population. Many still live in the Andes, where they eke a meager existence from the soil. Rivers rushing down from the Andes

provide the irrigation that supports the cultivation of cotton, coffee, and other crops. (The coca plant, lifeblood of a thriving, illegal cocaine trade, is also extensively cultivated.)

East of the Andes, the terrain descends to the tropical lowlands of the Amazon basin. Clothed in a lush rainforest, this sparsely populated region occupies nearly half the country's total land area and is the source of oil reserves that are transported to the coast by a trans-Andean pipeline. Along with oil refining, such industries as textile manufacturing, fish processing, copper production, and metal refining also play an important role in the economy.

SURINAME

Republic of Suriname
Map page 191

Area	63,020 sq. mi.
	(163,265 sq. km.)
Capital	Paramaribo
Member of	ECLAC, IADB, OAS

Population	418,000
Population growth rate	1.1%
Life expectancy	68 (m), 73 (f)
Languages	Dutch, *English, Hindustani,*
	Javanese, Sranang Tongo
Adult literacy rate	93%

Currency	Suriname guilder
GNP (U.S.$, in millions)	364
Income per capita (U.S.$)	870

With most of its interior covered by tropical rain forest (at present a virtually unexploited resource), Suriname's population is concentrated along its narrow Atlantic coastal strip. Bauxite and aluminum are the major exports of this former Dutch colony, which has been independent since 1975.

URUGUAY

Oriental Republic of Uruguay
Map page 195

Area	68,019 sq. mi.
	(176,215 sq. km.)
Capital	Montevideo
Member of	ECLAC, IADB, OAS

Population	3,167,000
Population growth rate	0.6%
Life expectancy	69 (m), 76 (f)
Language	Spanish
Adult literacy rate	96.3%

Currency	Uruguayan peso
GNP (U.S.$, in millions)	14,725
Income per capita (U.S.$)	4,650

Although Uruguay's population, mainly of white European ancestry, is overwhelmingly urban, the keystone of the economy is agriculture. The landscape is dominated by fertile, well-watered grasslands that are ideal for grazing sheep and cattle – both raised by the millions. Meat, hides, and wool are the chief exports; only Australia produces more wool. The economy is further enriched by banking, manufacturing, and tourism, which is on the upswing thanks to the country's mild climate and sandy beaches.

VENEZUELA

Republic of Venezuela
Map page 190

Area	352,051 sq. mi.
	(912,050 sq. km.)
Capital	Caracas
Member of	ECLAC, IADB, OAS, OPEC

Population	21,377,000
Population growth rate	2.5%
Life expectancy	69 (m), 75 (f)
Language	Spanish
Adult literacy rate	91.1%

Currency	bolívar
GNP (U.S.$, in millions)	59,025
Income per capita (U.S.$)	2,760

Venezuela is South America's most urbanized country, with the greatest share of its population concentrated in cities along the Caribbean coast. Deep within the densely forested interior are hauntingly beautiful plateaus, native tribes that have barely encountered modern civilization, and Angel Falls, which at over 3,212 ft. (979 m.) is the highest waterfall on earth.

Spain was Venezuela's master until Simón Bolívar liberated the colony in 1821. Independent since 1830, Venezuela endured more than a century of dictatorships, with democracy emerging only in 1958.

It was the 1914 discovery of oil beneath Lake Maracaibo – the largest such reserves outside the Middle East – that led to Venezuela's most radical transformation. Petroleum income has enriched elites, created a middle class, and turned the capital, Caracas, into a high-rise metropolis. This founding member of OPEC has, however, neglected its once-vital agricultural sector and has experienced the perils of fluctuating oil prices, most recently during the 1980s. Venezuela now seeks to exploit other resources, such as aluminum, and to manage a more even distribution of wealth between its cities and developing regions.

1903 Colombia loses Panama as a territory.

— 1910 —

1916 Hipólito Irigoyen becomes first freely elected president of Argentina.

— 1920 —

1928–35 Chaco Wars between Bolivia and Paraguay.

— 1930 —

1930 Military coups in Argentina and Brazil.

1932 Civilian rule restored to Argentina.

1936 Fascist regime established in Paraguay.

— 1940 —

1942 Brazil enters World War II on the side of the Allies.

1943 Military rule in Argentina.

1946–55 Juan Perón is president of Argentina.

1948–58 In Colombia La Violencia claims 200,000 lives.

— 1950 —

1952 Eva (Evita) Perón, the popular wife of Juan Perón, dies.

1954 Military coup in Paraguay.

1955 Juan Perón overthrown in military coup.

— 1960 —

1964 Bloodless, right-wing coup in Brazil.

— 1970 —

1973 Military coup in Chile; junta, led by General Pinochet, aims to eradicate Marxism. Perón returned to power in Argentina.

1974 Juan Perón dies.

1976 Military junta in Argentina; thousands of alleged left-wing activists are "disappeared."

— 1980 —

1982 Falklands War between Argentina and Britain.

1983 Free elections held in Argentina.

1985 Free elections held in Brazil, Uruguay.

1989 Free elections held in Chile.

— 1990 —

1991 Argentina, Brazil, Paraguay, and Uruguay sign trade agreement.

1992 Peru gives Bolivia access to Pacific port of Ilo. Earth Summit held in Rio de Janeiro.

1993 Free elections held in Paraguay.

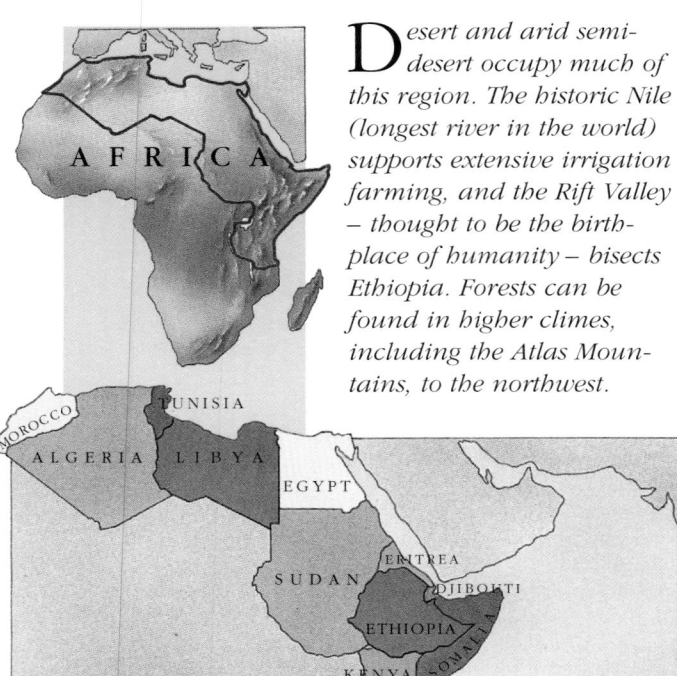

*D*esert and arid semi-desert occupy much of this region. The historic Nile (longest river in the world) supports extensive irrigation farming, and the Rift Valley – thought to be the birthplace of humanity – bisects Ethiopia. Forests can be found in higher climes, including the Atlas Mountains, to the northwest.

Colonies and Dependent Territories

BRITISH INDIAN OCEAN TERRITORY
Parent country
U.K.
Map page 113

MAYOTTE
Parent country
FRANCE
Map page 197

Abbreviations
AfDB African Development Bank
COMM Commonwealth
ECA Economic Commission for Africa
IDB Islamic Development Bank
IMF International Monetary Fund
LAS League of Arab States
NAM Non-Aligned Movement
OAPEC Organization of Arab Petroleum Exporting Countries
OAU Organization of African Unity
OPEC Organization of Petroleum Exporting Countries

GNP Gross National Product

ALGERIA

Democratic and Popular Republic of Algeria
Map pages 198–99

Area	919,352 sq. mi.
	(2,381,741 sq. km.)
Capital	Algiers
Member of	AfDB, ECA, OAU, OPEC

Population	26,581,000
Population growth rate	2.5%
Life expectancy	63 (m), 65 (f)
Languages	Arabic, French, Berber
Adult literacy rate	57.4%

Currency	Algerian dinar
GNP (U.S.$, in millions)	46,115
Income per capita (U.S.$)	1,690

Nine in 10 Algerians make their homes on a small, fertile strip of Mediterranean coastline, sheltered from the Sahara's parching winds by the Atlas Mountains. The economic engine of this tumultuous Arab republic, however, lies deep below the sands of its vast desert, which hides one of the world's largest reserves of oil and natural gas.

A founding member of OPEC, Algeria waged a bitter guerrilla war for independence against French colonial rule in the late 1950s. After France grudgingly ceded its claims in 1962, a Soviet-style regime won the postwar scuffle for power. Since 1988, liberalization has raised the lid on a cauldron of religious and ethnic hostilities. Tens of thousands have died in a protracted struggle between the military-controlled government and Islamic militants. Largely isolated from this bloody feud, a semi-nomadic Berber minority raises sheep, cattle, and goats in the mountainous Kabylia region, just as it has for nearly 5,000 years.

DJIBOUTI

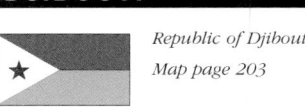

Republic of Djibouti
Map page 203

Area	8,955 sq. mi.
	(23,200 sq. km.)
Capital	Djibouti
Member of	ECA, LAS, OAU

Population	519,000
Population growth rate	4.1%
Life expectancy	47 (m), 50 (f)
Languages	Arabic, French
Adult literacy rate	46.2%

Currency	Djibouti franc
GNP (U.S.$, in millions)	448
Income per capita (U.S.$)	780

Most people in this small, brutally hot horseshoe of sand cling to the port city of Djibouti, which serves as a commercial gateway to Ethiopia. The rest of the population ekes out a living herding livestock in the desert. The country's economy relies heavily on French aid.

EGYPT

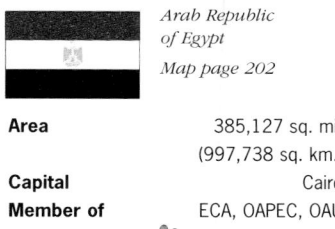

Arab Republic of Egypt
Map page 202

Area	385,127 sq. mi.
	(997,738 sq. km.)
Capital	Cairo
Member of	ECA, OAPEC, OAU

Population	57,851,000
Population growth rate	2.0%
Life expectancy	63 (m), 66 (f)
Languages	Arabic, English, French
Adult literacy rate	48.4%

Currency	Egyptian pound
GNP (U.S.$, in millions)	40,950
Income per capita (U.S.$)	710

Nurtured since time immemorial by the Nile, Egypt is both a modern nation and an abiding symbol of antiquity. The Egypt of the pharaohs emerged more than 5,000 years ago, when agriculture began to thrive along the Nile. The pyramids, the Sphinx, and the tombs of the Valley of the Kings all bear testimony to the ingenuity of a civilization that flourished well before the time of Christ.

Egypt has long suffered the domination of foreign powers, including the Greeks, Persians, Romans, Byzantines, British, and Arabs (who brought Islam to the country in the seventh century). It finally gained independence in the middle of the 20th century. The nation's first strong modern leader was pan-Arabist Gamal Ab-del Nasser, who waged war on Israel and

nationalized the Suez Canal. Nasser's successor, Anwar Sadat, negotiated peace with Israel but was assassinated in 1981.

Egypt's greatest contemporary struggle is against the poverty spawned by overpopulation; 99 percent of its people reside on just 4 percent of its land, and Cairo is by far the continent's largest metropolis. Industry, especially textiles, relieves some of the pressure, but most Egyptians are subsistence farmers who use methods as old as the pyramids. Meanwhile, Egypt's leaders must find ways to cope with a growing Islamic fundamentalist movement opposed to Western influences.

ERITREA

State of Eritrea
Map page 202

Area	46,762 sq. mi.
	(121,144 sq. km.)
Capital	Asmara
Member of	AfDB, ECA, OAU

Population	3,436,000
Population growth rate	2.7%
Life expectancy	49 (m), 52 (f)
Languages	Arabic, Tigre, English
Adult literacy rate	20%

Currency	Ethiopian birr
GNP (U.S.$, in millions)	393 (est.)
Income per capita (U.S.$)	500

The conclusion in 1991 of a bitter 30-year struggle for independence from Ethiopia has left this tiny, drought-prone nation mired in poverty. Mine-laced beaches on the arid Red Sea coast have stalled the planned development of tourist resorts, while a lack of investment capital leaves rich mineral veins in the inland mountains largely untouched. Nearly three in four Eritreans rely on food aid to survive.

ETHIOPIA

Federal Democratic Republic of Ethiopia
Map page 203

Area	437,485 sq. mi.
	(1,133,380 sq. km.)
Capital	Addis Ababa
Member of	AfDB, ECA, OAU

Population	56,677,000
Population growth rate	2.9%
Life expectancy	46 (m), 49 (f)
Languages	Amharic, English, many local languages
Adult literacy rate	77%

Currency	Ethiopian birr
GNP (U.S.$, in millions)	6,947
Income per capita (U.S.$)	130

Cradle of a 3,000-year-old civilization, Ethiopia has a long history of independence, but this proud tradition has been overshadowed by more recent troubles – namely, famine and civil war – that have vexed the country for the last two decades. Christian since the fourth century, Ethiopia resisted the spread of Islam in medieval times. It surprised the world by repelling an Italian invasion in the 1890s. When the Italians returned in 1935, they ruled for just six years, turning Ethiopian Emperor Haile Selassie I into a symbol of colonial resistance.

Famine and army mutiny led to Selassie's dethronement in 1974; civil war followed, virtually destroying the country's infrastructure. When drought returned in the 1980s, sparking a worldwide relief effort, the country reached rock bottom. An end to hostilities in 1991, after 17 years, has given Ethiopians a chance to repair their ravaged land. Still, the population remains largely illiterate, scattered among 40 ethnic groups that share 286 languages. Vulnerable to droughts, some 7 million Ethiopians are threatened by starvation.

KENYA

Republic of Kenya
Map page 203

Area	224,022 sq. mi.
	(580,367 sq. km.)
Capital	Nairobi
Member of	AfDB, COMM, ECA, OAU

Population	29,292,000
Population growth rate	2.9%
Life expectancy	54 (m), 57 (f)
Languages	Kiswahili, English, Kikuyu, Luo
Adult literacy rate	78.1%

Currency	Kenya shilling
GNP (U.S.$, in millions)	6,643
Income per capita (U.S.$)	260

Kenya's abundant natural resources, modified free market economy, and relative political stability have enshrined it in the Western mind as a model African nation. Since independence from England in 1963, Kenyan leaders have courted foreign investment, building East Africa's most diversified economy. Outside the cities agriculture dominates, with 80 percent of the population crowded onto the highlands of the southwest, where Masai tribesmen herd livestock and farmers grow coffee and tea for export. Game reserves like Tsavo National Park support a thriving tourist trade.

But rifts between the haves and the have-nots deeply divide

contemporary Kenya. Within sight of modern Nairobi, thousands huddle beneath tin shacks in the Amarthi Valley, one of Africa's worst slums. Tribal warfare, high inflation, political corruption, and the rapid spread of AIDS also challenge Kenya's legacy of stability.

LIBYA

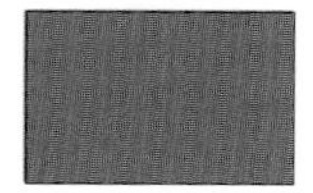

Socialist People's Libyan Arab Jamahiriya

Map page 199

Area	685,343 sq. mi. (1,775,500 sq. km.)
Capital	Tripoli
Member of	AfDB, ECA, IDB, OPEC
Population	4,899,000
Population growth rate	3.6%
Life expectancy	62 (m), 65 (f)
Languages	Arabic, *English, Italian*
Adult literacy rate	64.5%

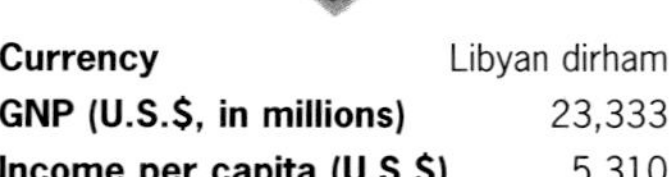

Currency	Libyan dirham
GNP (U.S.$, in millions)	23,333
Income per capita (U.S.$)	5,310

Libya – independent since 1951 after centuries of domination by foreign powers – occupies a large portion of North Africa but is essentially a narrow strip of arable land set against a background of desert. Most Libyans live along the Mediterranean coast, where agriculture and industry are assisted by piped-in Saharan groundwater. Oil gives Libya the highest per-capita income in Africa, yet the nation has suffered in recent years from international sanctions imposed as a result of the terrorism campaign sponsored by dictator Muammar Gaddafi.

MOROCCO

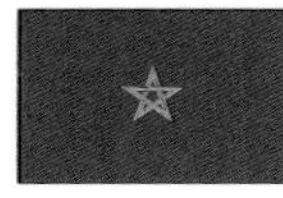

Kingdom of Morocco

Map page 198

Area	274,388 sq. mi. (710,850 sq. km.)
Capital	Rabat
Member of	AfDB, ECA, IDB, LAS
Population	26,074,000
Population growth rate	2.2%
Life expectancy	62 (m), 65 (f)
Languages	Arabic, Berber, *Spanish, French*
Adult literacy rate	43.7%

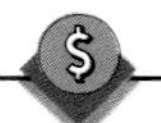

Currency	Moroccan dirham
GNP (U.S.$, in millions)	30,330
Income per capita (U.S.$)	1,150

A mere hour from the southern tip of Spain, Morocco remains a world apart from Europe. In the old trading quarters of Fez and Tangier, labyrinths of bustling streets date back to the 11th century, when a Moroccan empire stretched from Senegal to northern Spain. French and Spanish colonialism lasted only from 1912 to 1956, leaving modern Moroccans to build a strong economy around textile manufacturing, phosphate mining, and citrus cultivation. Illicit farms supply 30 percent of the marijuana sold in Europe.

Some 3 million tourists visit Morocco each year, lured by its dramatic desert and mountain scenery and liberal society. The only Arab state to offer its Jewish minority full political freedom, Morocco has banned Islamic political groups while preserving a deeply Islamic culture. Despite a long tradition of learning, its literacy rate is among the lowest in the world.

SEYCHELLES

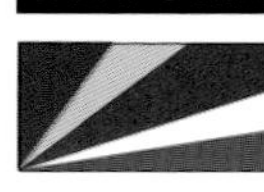

Republic of Seychelles

Map page 207

Area	175 sq. mi. (454 sq. km.)
Capital	Victoria (on Mahé)
Member of	AfDB, COMM, ECA, OAU
Population	74,000
Population growth rate	1.3%
Life expectancy	65 (m), 74 (f)
Languages	Creole, *English, French*
Adult literacy rate	85%

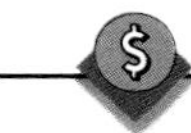

Currency	Seychelles rupee
GNP (U.S.$, in millions)	453
Income per capita (U.S.$)	6,210

Home to an exotic array of flora and fauna, including the giant tortoise, this chain of granite and coral islands was once a haven for pirates. First claimed by France and later by Britain, the Seychelles declared independence in 1976.

SOMALIA

Somali Democratic Republic

Map page 203

Area	246,136 sq, mi. (637,657 sq. km.)
Capital	Mogadishu
Member of	AfDB, ECA, LAS, OAU
Population	7,114,000
Population growth rate	1.6%
Life expectancy	45 (m), 49 (f)
Languages	Somali, *Arabic, English, Italian*
Adult literacy rate	24.1%

Currency	Somali shilling
GNP (U.S.$, in millions)	946
Income (U.S.$)	150

A nation of wandering Muslim herders, unusually homogeneous in language and culture, Somalia was torn apart in the 1990s by interclan rivalries and famine. In July 1992 the UN declared Somalia a country without a government; a two-year U.S.-led intervention failed to restore order, and the country slid further into chaos, with armed bandits constituting the sole political authority. Somalians consume fewer calories than citizens of any other nation; the infant mortality rate is among the world's five highest.

SUDAN

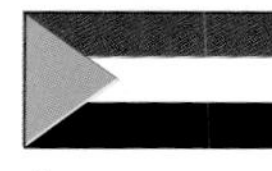

Republic of Sudan

Map pages 202–3

Area	967,244 sq. mi. (2,505,813 sq. km.)
Capital	Khartoum
Member of	AfDB, ECA, LAS, OAU
Population	24,941,000
Population growth rate	2.9%
Life expectancy	52 (m), 54 (f)
Languages	Arabic, *English, and local languages*
Adult literacy rate	46.1%

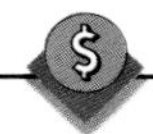

Currency	Sudanese pound
GNP (U.S.$, in millions)	10,107
Income per capita (U.S.$)	400

Stretched precariously across the boundary between Africa's Arab north and black south, the continent's largest nation is a tragic catalogue of its most destructive woes. Vast stretches of desert have pushed most Sudanese into the fertile valleys of the Blue and the White Niles, where irrigation coaxes cotton, sugarcane, and sorghum out of the soil. There, subsistence farmers live in dread of the twin perils: flood and drought.

Since 1956, when Sudan threw off Anglo-Egyptian rule, political unrest has deepened the danger from natural disaster. Arabs in the north control the country from the city of Khartoum, which is laid out in the pattern of a British flag. Their attempts to impose Islamic law on the Bantu and Nuba tribal minorities in the south ignited bitter civil war in the 1980s and 1990s. In that time war and famine have combined to displace some 3 million and take a third as many Sudanese lives.

TANZANIA

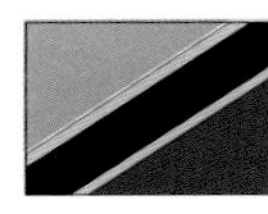

United Republic of Tanzania

Map page 204

Area	364,804 sq. mi. (945,087 sq. km.)
Capital	Dodoma
Member of	AfDB, COMM, ECA, OAU
Population	30,340,000
Population growth rate	3.1%
Life expectancy	52 (m), 55 (f)
Languages	Swahili, *English, many local languages*
Adult literacy rate	67.8%

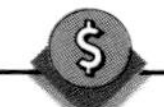

Currency	Tanzanian shilling
GNP (U.S.$, in millions)	2,521
Income per capita (U.S.$)	100

The 2-million-year-old remains of mankind's earliest ancestors were uncovered in 1964 by Dr. Louis Leakey in Tanzania's Olduvai Gorge, cradled there by some of the continent's most majestic scenery. The nearby Serengeti Plain, graced by lions, elephants, rhinos, and other distinctively African wildlife, rolls to the base of snowcapped Kilimanjaro, Africa's highest peak.

Despite the luxuriant national parks that cover one-third of the country, the rest of Tanzania is largely barren; cursed by dryness or tsetse flies, it remains virtually undeveloped. Nearly 80 percent of its people claw out a living farming cassava, corn, beans, coffee, and cashews. Its 120 ethnic Bantu groups live in remarkable harmony, united by their common language, Swahili.

TUNISIA

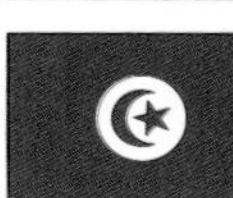

Republic of Tunisia

Map page 199

Area	59,649 sq. mi. (154,530 sq. km.)
Capital	Tunis
Member of	COMM, ECA, NAM
Population	8,947,000
Population growth rate	2.3%
Life expectancy	67 (m), 69 (f)
Languages	Arabic, *Berber, French*
Adult literacy rate	66.7%

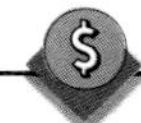

Currency	Tunisian dinar
GNP (U.S.$, in millions)	15,873
Income per capita (U.S.$)	1,800

The Arab world's most liberal nation, Tunisia has used family planning to engineer the lowest birthrate in the region, while maintaining a high standard for women's rights unheard of in most Islamic countries. Magnificent Roman ruins – the amphitheater at El Jem rivals the Colosseum in size – and the battered remains of ancient Carthage testify to a long culture of urban settlement. Bolstered by a diverse economy, the Tunisian government has dealt severely with Muslim militants and keeps a wary eye on the conflict in neighboring Algeria.

20TH-CENTURY LANDMARKS

1900–1918 White settlement of Kenya.

1910

1911 Libya conquered by Italy.

1914 Egypt comes under British rule.

1917 Railway links Ethiopia and Djibouti.

1918 Tanganyika made a British mandate.

1920

1920 Interior of Kenya made a British colony.

1923 Ethiopia joins League of Nations.

1930

1935 Ethiopia invaded by Italy.

1936 Egypt becomes independent, but British forces remain to guard Suez Canal.

1940

1940–41 Italians expelled from Somalia, Eritrea, and Ethiopia.

1942 Allies defeat Germans at Battle of el-Alamein, Egypt.

1942 Allies land in Morocco and Algeria.

1945–91 Superpowers compete for influence during Cold War; "proxy wars" fought in Ethiopia, Eritrea, and Somalia.

1950

1952–60 The Mau Mau revolt against British rule in Kenya.

1956 Suez Crisis.

1960

1963 Organization of African Unity founded.

1967 Egypt and Israel fight Six-Day War.

1970

1972–74 Droughts in Ethiopia and Sudan cause mass starvation.

1974 Emperor Haile Selassie of Ethiopia deposed.

1979 Peace treaty signed between Egypt and Israel.

1980

1981 President Sadat of Egypt assassinated.

1984 One million die in Ethiopian drought.

1985 Libya expels 30,000 foreign workers.

1986 U.S. bombs Libya in retaliation for alleged terrorist activities.

1990

1992 UN peacekeeping force sent to Somalia. UN imposes sanctions on Libya.

WESTERN AFRICA

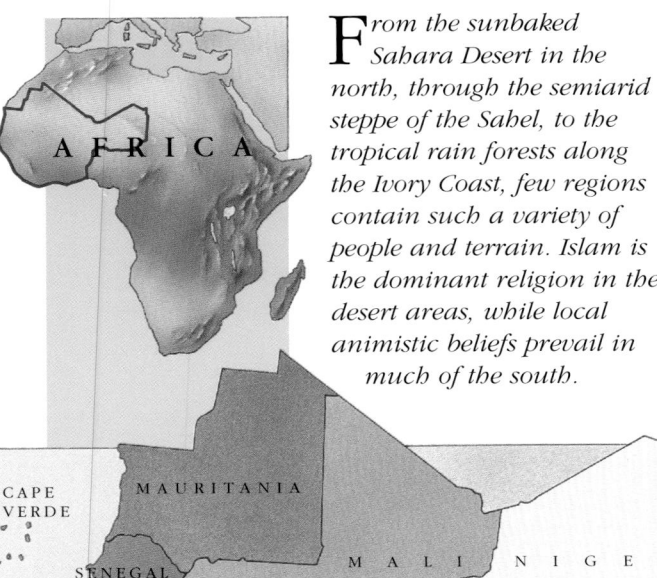

From the sunbaked Sahara Desert in the north, through the semiarid steppe of the Sahel, to the tropical rain forests along the Ivory Coast, few regions contain such a variety of people and terrain. Islam is the dominant religion in the desert areas, while local animistic beliefs prevail in much of the south.

BENIN

Republic of Benin
Map page 200

Area 43,472 sq. mi.
(112,622 sq. km.)

Capital Porto-Novo

Member of AfDB, ECA, ECOWAS, FZ

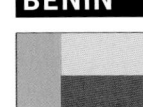

Population 5,215,000

Population growth rate 3.0%

Life expectancy 44 (m), 47 (f)

Languages French, *Bariba, Fulani, Fon, Yoruba*

Adult literacy rate 37.0%

Currency CFA franc

GNP (U.S.$, in millions) 1,954

Income per capita (U.S.$) 370

Millions of slaves were shipped from here to the New World in the 17th and 18th centuries, bringing wealth to the tribal monarchs who operated the slave trade. After a 70-year period of rule by France, and a 17-year experiment with Marxism that ended in 1989, Benin moved on to free-market democracy. Its interior wildlife parks and sparkling coastal beaches attract an ever-increasing number of visitors.

BURKINA

Burkina Faso
Map page 200

Area 105,841 sq. mi.
(274,200 sq. km.)

Capital Ouagadougou

Member of AfDB, ECA, FZ, OAU

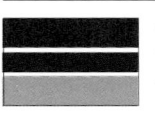

Population 9,889,000

Population growth rate 2.7%

Life expectancy 45 (m), 49 (f)

Languages French, *Mossi, other local languages*

Adult literacy rate 19.2%

Currency CFA franc

GNP (U.S.$, in millions) 2,982

Income per capita (U.S.$) 300

Decades of low rainfall, along with overgrazing and unsound farming practices, have spelled ecological disaster for this already arid land, once the French colony of Upper Volta. Dust storms from the Sahara sweep across the northern plains. To the south malaria and river blindness (caused by the simulium fly) limit cultivation of the river valleys. Even so, most of the country's inhabitants depend on subsistence farming. More than half the population belongs to the Mossi tribe, whose warrior ancestors controlled one of Africa's most powerful precolonial empires.

CAPE VERDE

Republic of Cape Verde
Map page 200

Area 1,557 sq. mi.
(4,033 sq. km.)

Capital Praia

Member of AfDB, ECA, ECOWAS, OAU

Population 341,500

Population growth rate 2.3%

Life expectancy 64 (m), 71 (f)

Languages Portuguese, *Creole*

Adult literacy rate 62.9%

Currency Cape Verde escudo

GNP (U.S.$, in millions) 346

Income per capita (U.S.$) 910

These 15 volcanic islands are notable for their array of stark mountains, dazzling beaches, and consistently cloudless skies – and therein lies their tragedy. Crippling droughts have caused 75,000 deaths since 1900. The islands were a colony of Portugal until 1975.

THE GAMBIA

Republic of the Gambia
Map page 200

Area 4,360 sq. mi.
(11,295 sq. km.)

Capital Banjul

Member of AfDB, COMM, ECOWAS, OAU

Population 1,025,900

Population growth rate 4.1%

Life expectancy 43 (m), 47 (f)

Languages English, *Mandinka, Fula Wolof, other local languages*

Adult literacy rate 27.2%

Currency dalasi

GNP (U.S.$, in millions) 384

Income per capita (U.S.$) 360

Africa's smallest nation hugs the banks of the Gambia River, cutting deep into neighboring Senegal. Fishing, farming, peanut growing, and coastal tourism are the main activities of this former British colony, along with ferry service up and down the river.

GHANA

Republic of Ghana
Map page 200

Area 92,075 sq. mi.
(238,537 sq. km.)

Capital Accra

Member of AfDB, COMM, ECOWAS, OAU

Population 15,400,000

Population growth rate 3.1%

Life expectancy 54 (m), 58 (f)

Languages English, *many local languages*

Adult literacy rate 64.5%

Currency new cedi

GNP (U.S.$, in millions) 7,311

Income per capita (U.S.$) 430

Led by the charismatic Kwame Nkrumah, Ghana became the first black African state to win independence from Great Britain in 1957. Only now is it beginning to achieve economic and political stability.

Seat of the once-powerful Ashanti empire, Ghana was a prime source of slaves and precious metals for European traders from the 15th to 19th centuries. It became known as the Gold Coast.

Ghana is still rich in natural resources, with gold, diamonds, palm oil, hardwoods, bauxite, and manganese ore composing its major exports. For many years this tropical country produced the world's largest cocoa crop. Mismanagement and corruption in the early days of independence, however, ran the country deep into debt.

A military coup in 1966 sent Nkrumah into exile, and fierce clashes erupted among the country's more than 50 tribal groups. Stability returned in the early 1990s, along with hopes for a revitalized economy.

GUINEA

Republic of Guinea
Map page 200

Area 94,901 sq. mi.
(245,857 sq. km.)

Capital Conakry

Member of AfDB, ECOWAS, IDB, OAU

Population 5,600,000

Population growth rate 2.9%

Life expectancy 44 (m), 45 (f)

Languages French, *Soussou, Manika, other local languages*

Adult literacy rate 28.0%

Currency franc guinéen

GNP (U.S.$, in millions) 3,310

Income per capita (U.S.$) 510

The first independent state in French-speaking Africa, Guinea endured 26 years of oppressive rule under socialist President Sekou Touré, who took power in 1958. Withdrawal of foreign aid sank the economy into recession. With Touré's death in 1984, the new military regime moved to liberalize trade and develop the country's diamond, bauxite, and iron resources. Thanks to a tropical climate, the land is well watered and fertile.

GUINEA-BISSAU

Republic of Guinea-Bissau
Map page 200

Area 13,944 sq. mi.
(36,125 sq. km.)

Capital Bissau

Member of AfDB, ECOWAS, IDB, OAU

Population 1,050,000

Population growth rate 2.1%

Life expectancy 42 (m), 45 (f)

Languages Portuguese, *Creole*

Adult literacy rate 54.9%

Currency Guinea peso

GNP (U.S.$, in millions) 253

Income per capita (U.S.$) 240

Among the least developed countries in the world when it gained independence from Portugal in 1974, Guinea-Bissau was then plagued by a decade of civil war. Its resources, still largely unexploited, are fishing and forestry. Nearly all its people live in the capital, Bissau.

IVORY COAST

Republic of Ivory Coast
Map page 200

Area 124,470 sq. mi.
(322,462 sq. km.)

Capital Yamoussoukro

Member of AfDB, ECA, ECOWAS, OAU

Population 13,695,000

Population growth rate 3.6%

Life expectancy 50 (m), 54 (f)

Languages French, *many local languages*

Adult literacy rate 34.1%

Currency	CFA franc
GNP (U.S.$, in millions)	7,070
Income per capita (U.S.$)	510

Despite back-to-back recessions in the 1980s – the result of falling cocoa prices and high foreign debt – the Ivory Coast (named for one of its most prized commodities) is one of black Africa's most prosperous countries. Besides its cocoa exports it markets large crops of coffee and palm oil, along with cotton, rubber, bananas, and pineapples. Recent discoveries of oil and gas may make it self-sufficient in energy.

Trade in elephant tusks and slaves drew Europeans to the Ivory Coast as early as 1483. French missionaries arrived in 1637, and efforts at colonization and development began in the mid-1800s. Under French colonial rule the Ivory Coast acquired roads, railroads, electricity, and – with marine improvements at Abidjan in 1950 – one of West Africa's few deepwater seaports. Abidjan, with 3 million inhabitants, is the largest city and home to thousands of French expatriates. Since its independence in 1960, the Ivory Coast has followed a pro-Western, free-market economy. It remains one of the most politically stable nations in tropical Africa.

LIBERIA

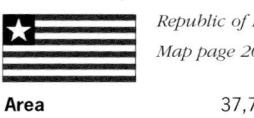

Republic of Liberia
Map page 200

Area	37,733 sq. mi.
	(97,754 sq. km.)
Capital	Monrovia
Member of	AfDB, ECA, ECOWAS, OAU

Population	2,700,000
Population growth rate	3.2%
Life expectancy	54 (m), 57 (f)
Languages	English, *many local*
	languages and dialects
Adult literacy rate	38.3%

Currency	Liberian dollar
GNP (U.S.$, in millions)	1,051
Income per capita (U.S.$)	450

A brutal civil war has devastated Liberia, Africa's first independent republic. An estimated 150,000 people have died since fighting broke out in 1989 and some 800,000 others – over half the population – have fled.

Founded in 1847 by freed slaves from the United States, Liberia enjoyed more than a century of stable constitutional government. A military coup in 1980 displaced the African-American political elite, opening the way to fierce intertribal bloodshed.

MALI

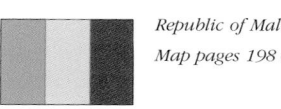

Republic of Mali
Map pages 198 & 200

Area	478,714 sq. mi.
	(1,240,192 sq. km.)
Capital	Bamako
Member of	AfDB, ECA, ECOWAS, OAU

Population	8,156,000
Population growth rate	2.8%
Life expectancy	44 (m), 48 (f)
Languages	French, *many local*
	languages
Adult literacy rate	31.0%

Currency	CFA franc
GNP (U.S.$, in millions)	2,421
Income per capita (U.S.$)	250

The desert city of Timbuktu was once the glory of Western Africa – a center of Islamic culture that grew prosperous through the trans-Saharan caravan trade. Today, however, catastrophic drought has thrust all of Mali into poverty, causing widespread invasion by desert sands and forcing nomadic herders into former farm areas. Under French rule until 1960, Mali is now a multiparty democracy.

MAURITANIA

Islamic Republic of Mauritania
Map page 198

Area	397,850 sq. mi.
	(1,030,700 sq. km.)
Capital	Nouakchott
Member of	AfDB, ECA, ECOWAS, OAU

Population	2,211,000
Population growth rate	2.5%
Life expectancy	50 (m), 53 (f)
Languages	Arabic, French, *many local*
	languages
Adult literacy rate	37.7%

Currency	ouguiya
GNP (U.S.$, in millions)	1,063
Income per capita (U.S.$)	480

Mostly desert, Mauritania relies heavily on foreign aid to feed its people. The country's resources include high-grade iron ore and rich offshore fishing, but ethnic and religious tensions continue to hamper its development.

NIGER

Republic of Niger
Map page 201

Area	489,062 sq. mi.
	(1,267,000 sq. km.)
Capital	Niamey
Member of	AfDB, ECOWAS, IDB, OAU

Population	8,361,000
Population growth rate	3.2%
Life expectancy	45 (m), 48 (f)
Languages	French, *many local*
	languages
Adult literacy rate	13.6%

Currency	CFA franc
GNP (U.S.$, in millions)	2,040
Income per capita (U.S.$)	230

The encroaching Sahara Desert has brought severe hardship to Niger, a landlocked nation whose only reliable water sources are a corner of Lake Chad (in the southeast) and a 200-mile stretch of the Niger River (in the southwest). Camel-riding Tuareg herdsman range the arid northern region; the rest of the population (some 90 percent) lives in the south.

Uranium, mined in the Aïr Mountains, has replaced peanuts as the main export, but the economy is still heavily dependent on foreign aid. The cafés and restaurants of Niamey, the capital, reflect 70 years of French colonial rule, which ended in 1960.

SENEGAL

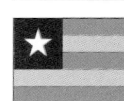

Republic of Senegal
Map page 200

Area	75,935 sq. mi.
	(196,722 sq. km.)
Capital	Dakar
Member of	AfDB, ECA, ECOWAS, OAU

Population	8,152,000
Population growth rate	2.7%
Life expectancy	48 (m), 50 (f)
Languages	French, *many local*
	languages
Adult literacy rate	33.1%

Currency	CFA franc
GNP (U.S.$, in millions)	4,952
Income per capita (U.S.$)	610

Formerly a part of France's possessions in Western Africa, Senegal is a largely rural land with a veneer of urban polish. The bustling port of Dakar, on Africa's westernmost point, is home to 20 percent of the population. Elsewhere, the main activity is subsistence farming – either in the moist, tropical southwest or on the semiarid plains of the interior. Coastal fishing is also important. The main exports are peanut oil, fish products, and phosphates. A moderate socialist government, in place since independence in 1960, has given the country political stability and encourages private enterprise.

SIERRA LEONE

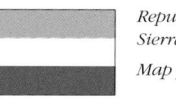

Republic of Sierra Leone
Map page 200

Area	27,692 sq. mi.
	(71,740 sq. km.)
Capital	Freetown
Member of	AfDB, COMM, ECA, ECOWAS

Population	4,509,000
Population growth rate	2.5%
Life expectancy	38 (m), 41 (f)
Languages	English, *Krio (Creole), other*
	local languages
Adult literacy rate	31.4%

Currency	leone
GNP (U.S.$, in millions)	698
Income per capita (U.S.$)	150

The British government founded Freetown, the capital, in 1787 as a refuge for freed slaves from North America; independence was gained in 1961. The nation's mineral resources – diamonds, iron ore, and bauxite – have yet to be systematically developed. Most inhabitants remain subsistence farmers. High inflation and mismanagement plague the economy, along with crippling disruptions that have spilled over from the civil war in Liberia. As a result, Sierra Leone remains very poor.

TOGO

Republic of Togo
Map page 200

Area	21,919 sq. mi.
	(56,785 sq. km.)
Capital	Lomé
Member of	ECA, ECOWAS, FZ, OAU

Population	3,928,000
Population growth rate	3.1%
Life expectancy	53 (m), 57 (f)
Languages	French, Kabiye, Ewe
Adult literacy rate	51.7%

Currency	CFA franc
GNP (U.S.$, in millions)	1,267
Income per capita (U.S.$)	320

Scientific farming methods, adopted in a "green revolution" in 1977, have made this largely agricultural country all but self-sufficient in basic foods. Cocoa, coffee, and peanuts are the main cash crops. Togo also has some of the largest phosphate reserves in the world.

Ethnic tension between the urbanized, coastal-dwelling Ewe and the Kabré farmers in the north, who dominate the army and government, erupted into violence during the 1994 multiparty elections.

1901 Ashanti (Ghana) annexed by Britain.

1903–35 Railway built between Ivory Coast and Upper Volta (Burkina).

— 1910 —

1914 Togo invaded by Britain and France.

1915 Guinea-Bissau interior effectively subdued by Portuguese.

1919 Liberia cedes large inland areas to French control.

— 1920 —

1920 Mauritania made a French colony.

1926 Liberia grants 1 million acres (405,000 ha.) to Firestone Tire and Rubber Co.

— 1930 —

1931 Liberia examined by League of Nations after charges of forced labor and slavery.

— 1940 —

1940–42 Vichy government rules Ivory Coast.

1947 Upper Volta made part of the French Union.

— 1950 —

1959 Mali and Senegal form federation.

— 1960 —

1960 Senegal withdraws from federation with Mali.

1966 Military coups in Upper Volta and Ghana.

1968 Military coup in Mali; uranium mined in Niger.

— 1970 —

1970 Guinean exiles and Portuguese troops try to invade Guinea.

1973 Mali and Niger suffer droughts.

1974 Military coup in Niger.

— 1980 —

1980 Military coup in Liberia.

1982 The Gambia and Senegal form limited federation.

1984 Military coup in Guinea; drought in Niger.

1985 Mali and Burkina fight six-day war.

1987 Blaise Compaoré seizes power in Burkina.

— 1990 —

1990 Start of civil war in Liberia.

1992 Ghana and Mali hold multiparty elections.

1993 Niger holds democratic elections.

CENTRAL AFRICA

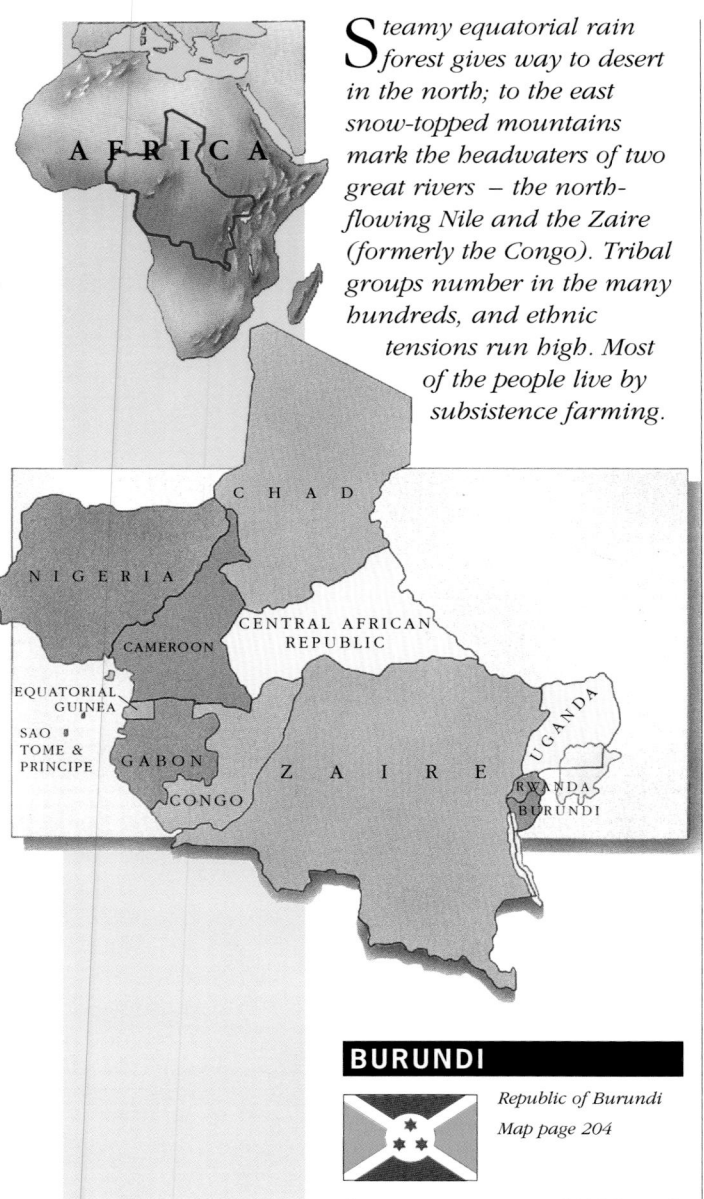

*S*teamy equatorial rain forest gives way to desert in the north; to the east snow-topped mountains mark the headwaters of two great rivers – the north-flowing Nile and the Zaire (formerly the Congo). Tribal groups number in the many hundreds, and ethnic tensions run high. Most of the people live by subsistence farming.

BURUNDI

Republic of Burundi
Map page 204

Area	10,744 sq. mi.
	(27,834 sq. km.)
Capital	Bujumbura
Member of	AfDB, ECA, OAU

Population	6,134,000
Population growth rate	3%
Life expectancy	48 (m), 52 (f)
Languages	French, *Kirundi, Swahili*
Adult literacy rate	50%

Currency	Burundian franc
GNP (U.S.$, in millions)	904
Income per capita (U.S.$)	150

The history of Burundi is one that is steeped in ethnic conflict. Settled by Hutu people nearly 1,000 years ago, the country was conquered by the Tutsis, who in the 16th century established feudal authority. Four years after Burundi gained independence in 1962, a coup resulted in a Tutsi-led military government. A failed 1972 Hutu rebellion left more than 150,000 people dead, and widespread ethnic violence, beginning in 1993, forced an estimated 1 million people into refugee camps in Zaire and Tanzania.

This mountainous, well-watered nation is intensively farmed to feed its dense population, but continuing ethnic strife has hampered further development of resources.

CAMEROON

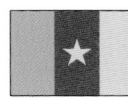

Republic of Cameroon
Map page 201

Area	183,570 sq. mi.
	(475,442 sq. km.)
Capital	Yaoundé
Member of	AfDB, COMM, ECA, OAU

Population	11,540,000
Population growth rate	2.8%
Life expectancy	52 (m), 55 (f)
Languages	English, French, *many local languages*
Adult literacy rate	63.4%

Currency	CFA franc
GNP (U.S.$, in millions)	8,735
Income per capita (U.S.$)	680

Mountains and high plateaus dominate central Cameroon. In its northern reaches these uplands are covered with savannah, which merges into arid plains bordering Lake Chad. The southern hills and coastal lowlands are hot and steamy, in many parts covered with dense forest. Some 200 ethnic groups, sharing 80 different languages, inhabit Cameroon, with the greatest concentration of people living in the southwest.

Politically stable, Cameroon enjoys a prosperity rare in central Africa. Aluminum, bauxite, cocoa, coffee, gas, oil, and timber make up most of its exports. Yaoundé is a solidly middle-class city. Elsewhere most people farm, and in the remote forests pygmies still live in a traditional manner.

A German protectorate before World War I, Cameroon was divided between France and Britain. After independence in 1960 part of the British sector opted for union with Nigeria, while the rest joined the French sector to form today's republic.

CENTRAL AFRICAN REPUBLIC

Central African Republic
Map page 201

Area	240,458 sq. mi.
	(622,948 sq. km.)
Capital	Bangui
Member of	AfDB, ECA, FZ, OAU

Population	2,464,000
Population growth rate	2.5%
Life expectancy	47 (m), 52 (f)
Languages	French, *Sango*
Adult literacy rate	37.7%

Currency	CFA franc
GNP (U.S.$, in millions)	1,191
Income per capita (U.S.$)	370

Landlocked in the arid heart of the continent, much of the Central African Republic is covered by a vast savannah that supports fewer than 2 percent of its inhabitants. The bulk of the population resides along the nation's equatorial southern border, which is blanketed by lush rain forest and drained by the mighty Ubangi River.

The republic gained independence in 1960, and five years later a coup brought President Jean-Bedel Bokassa to power, beginning a 14-year reign marked by brutal authoritarianism and economic ruin. The nation remained under military rule until 1986, when a new constitution instituted civilian government. The first multiparty elections were held in 1993.

While diamonds, cotton, and iron are significant exports, forestry and subsistence farming remain the backbone of the largely agricultural economy.

CHAD

Republic of Chad
Map page 201

Area	486,051 sq. mi.
	(1,259,200 sq. km.)
Capital	N'Djamena
Member of	AfDB, ECA, FZ, OAU

Population	6,214,000
Population growth rate	2.3%
Life expectancy	44 (m), 47 (f)
Languages	French, Arabic, *many local languages*
Adult literacy rate	29.8%

Currency	CFA franc
GNP (U.S.$, in millions)	1,153
Income per capita (U.S.$)	190

Civil conflict between the Islamic north and the largely animist black south has plunged this former French colony into decades of turmoil. After independence in 1960 the southerners gained political control, prompting an Arab revolt. With his eye on possible oil deposits, Libya's Muammar Gaddafi sent in troops to occupy northern Chad. Soon after an international tribunal confirmed the rights of the central government in 1994, Libya withdrew, but Chad remains in political flux.

Plagued by two decades of drought, this landlocked country is stricken by poverty. Chad has no railroads and only 160 miles of paved road. Most of its land is desert or arid scrub, with a strip of savannah in the south. The main crops are cotton and millet. Lake Chad, its waters shrunk by more than half since 1970, yields an ever-diminishing catch of fish.

CONGO

Republic of the Congo
Map page 201

Area	132,012 sq. mi.
	(342,000 sq. km.)
Capital	Brazzaville
Member of	AfDB, ECA, FZ, OAU

Population	1,843,000
Population growth rate	3%
Life expectancy	49 (m), 52 (f)
Languages	French, *Kikongo, Lingala, other local languages*
Adult literacy rate	56.6%

Currency	CFA franc
GNP (U.S.$, in millions)	1,607
Income per capita (U.S.$)	640

Swampy, river-cut plains dominate northern Congo, while dense tropical forest shrouds the south. Oil is the country's chief export, accounting for nearly 90 percent of its economy and giving this equatorial nation one of the highest per capita GNPs in the region. Timber, sugar, coffee, and tobacco are also important sources of revenue.

Originally settled by Bantu-speaking tribes in the 15th century, Congo became a French colony in the late 1800s. It gained independence in 1960 and established a Marxist government three years later. In 1991 a new constitution was approved; democratic elections followed the next year.

EQUATORIAL GUINEA

Republic of Equatorial Guinea
Map page 201

Area	10,828 sq. mi.
	(28,051 sq. km.)
Capital	Malabo
Member of	AfDB, ECA, FZ, OAU

Population	356,000
Population growth rate	2.5%
Life expectancy	46 (m), 50 (f)
Languages	Spanish, *Fang, other local languages*
Adult literacy rate	50%

Currency	CFA franc
GNP (U.S.$, in millions)	167
Income per capita (U.S.$)	430

Cocoa, coffee, and timber once brought prosperity to Equatorial Guinea, but brutal dictatorship and bankruptcy followed its 1968 independence from Spain. Although efforts to revitalize agriculture have failed, exploration for oil and natural gas have shown some promise.

GABON

Gabonese Republic
Map page 201

Area	103,319 sq. mi. (267,667 sq. km.)
Capital	Libreville
Member of	AfDB, ECA, FZ, OAU
Population	1,011,710
Population growth rate	1.8%
Life expectancy	52 (m), 55 (f)
Languages	French, *Fang, Bantu dialects*
Adult literacy rate	60.7%

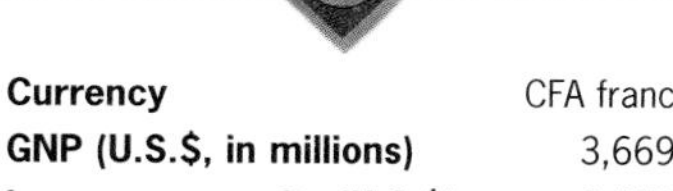

Currency	CFA franc
GNP (U.S.$, in millions)	3,669
Income per capita (U.S.$)	3,550

Founded in 1849 as a refuge for freed African slaves, Libreville is home to one-quarter of Gabon's population. Since winning independence from France in 1960, this tiny equatorial nation has generated wealth with its uranium, manganese, and oil.

NIGERIA

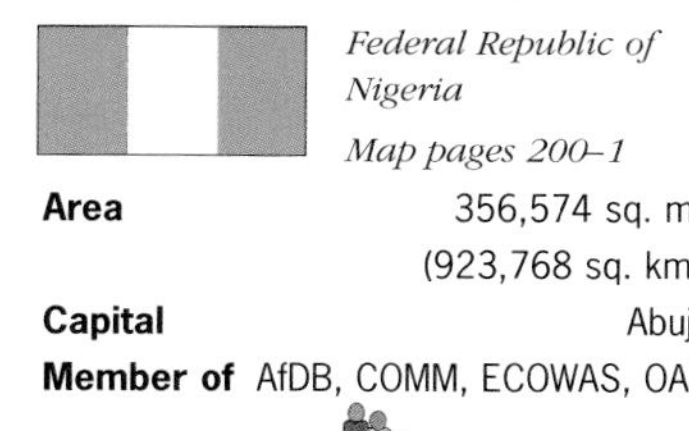

Federal Republic of Nigeria
Map pages 200–1

Area	356,574 sq. mi. (923,768 sq. km.)
Capital	Abuja
Member of	AfDB, COMM, ECOWAS, OAU
Population	88,515,000
Population growth rate	2.9%
Life expectancy	49 (m), 52 (f)
Languages	English, *Hausa, Yoruba*
Adult literacy rate	57.1%

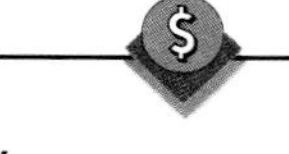

Currency	naira
GNP (U.S.$, in millions)	29,995
Income per capita (U.S.$)	280

The most populous country in Africa, Nigeria contains nearly 100 million inhabitants and some 250 different ethnic groups. Some of its cultural roots date back more than 2,000 years. Muslim traders brought Islam to the northern plains and deserts, where it still prevails. To the south, where mountains give way to tropical jungle and river delta, most inhabitants are Christian. Not until 1914, when the British established a protectorate, were Nigeria's regions and peoples combined into a single political entity.

Soon after independence in 1960, Nigeria threatened to break apart. The Ibo, who inhabit the southeast, proclaimed the separatist state of Biafra in 1967. The resulting civil war lasted four years and claimed an estimated 1 million lives, mostly through starvation. The years following Biafra's defeat have seen a succession of military and civilian regimes. Since 1991 Nigeria has been divided into 30 provinces.

Corruption and political turmoil continue to afflict Nigeria's economy, potentially one of the strongest in Africa. Vast petroleum reserves in the Niger River delta led to an oil boom in the 1970s. Lagos, the former capital, swelled to 6 million people, its glittering skyscrapers juxtaposed with appalling slums. The country's agricultural base – peanuts and animal hides in the north; cocoa, cotton, palm oil, and rubber in the south – declined. The subsequent collapse in oil prices left Nigera with huge foreign debts and a sharply eroded standard of living.

Despite its considerable woes Nigeria remains a cultural leader. In 1986, for example, writer Wole Soyinka became the first African to win a Nobel Prize in literature.

RWANDA

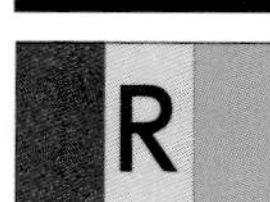

Republic of Rwanda
Map page 204

Area	10,166 sq. mi. (26,338 sq. km.)
Capital	Kigali
Member of	AfDB, ECA, OAU
Population	7,165,000
Population growth rate	2.7%
Life expectancy	45 (m), 48 (f)
Languages	French, English, Kinyarwanda, *Kiswahili*
Adult literacy rate	60.5%

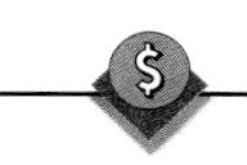

Currency	Rwandan franc
GNP (U.S.$, in millions)	1,499
Income per capita (U.S.$)	201

Centuries-old enmity between the Tutsi minority and the Hutu majority has diminished any benefits of Rwanda's independence from Belgium in 1962. In 1994 more than 1 million Hutus fled from Tutsi rebels to refugee camps in eastern Zaire and Tanzania. Two years later, some 600,000 of the refugees returned to Rwanda.

A nation of grassy, volcanic highlands, Rwanda is well watered and dotted with lakes. Most people are subsistence farmers, and cash crops, such as pyrethrum, coffee, and tea, are of lesser importance. The scarcity of level terrain prompts the terracing of many hillsides.

Despite a large influx of foreign aid, civil strife and lack of nonagricultural resources have left Rwanda's population impoverished and the economy at a virtual standstill.

SAO TOME & PRINCIPE

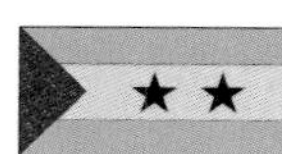

Democratic Republic of São Tomé and Príncipe
Map page 201

Area	386 sq. mi. (1,001 sq. km.)
Capital	São Tomé
Member of	AfDB, ECA, OAU
Population	125,000
Population growth rate	2.1%
Life expectancy	67 (av. m/f)
Languages	Portuguese, *many local dialects*
Adult literacy rate	25%
Currency	dobra
GNP (U.S.$, in millions)	31
Income per capita (U.S.$)	250

Discovered by Portugal in 1741, this archipelago was first settled by convicts and exiled Jews. Now almost totally dependent on cocoa production, this tiny republic's priorities have become crop diversification and tourism development.

UGANDA

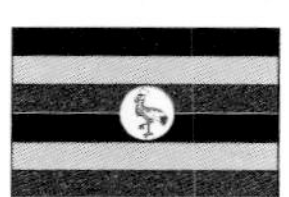

Republic of Uganda
Map page 203

Area	76,064 sq. mi. (197,058 sq. km.)
Capital	Kampala
Member of	AfDB, COMM, ECA, OAU
Population	16,672,000
Population growth rate	3.2%
Life expectancy	44 (m), 46 (f)
Languages	English, *Luganda, other local languages*
Adult literacy rate	61.8%

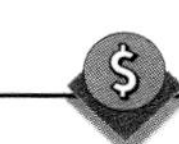

Currency	shilling
GNP (U.S.$, in millions)	3,718
Income per capita (U.S.$)	200

"The pearl of Africa" is how Winston Churchill described this former British protectorate, high in the mountains above Lake Victoria. With its temperate climate, fertile soils, cascading rivers, and a newly revived economy, Uganda may soon live up to its lustrous image.

Trouble between Uganda's tribal kingdoms began shortly after independence in 1962. The first president, Milton Obote, was overthrown in 1971 by army commander Idi Amin. The result was sheer disaster.

Short of funds, Amin expelled all foreigners and seized their assets. Murdering and torturing to stay in power, he became a world symbol of government brutality. By 1986, when he was deposed, more than 300,000 people had been put to death.

The new government curbed inflation, reformed the currency, and privatized industry. Production of coffee and cotton (the main exports) shot up, foreign investment returned, and by 1994 Uganda's fledgling industrial sector was growing by a healthy 7 percent.

ZAIRE

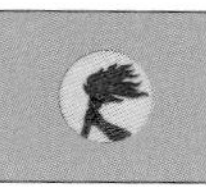

Republic of Zaire
Map page 204

Area	905,126 sq. mi. (2,344,885 sq. km.)
Capital	Kinshasa
Member of	AfDB, ECA, OAU
Population	36,672,000
Population growth rate	3.3%
Life expectancy	50 (m), 54 (f)
Languages	French, *many Sudanese and Bantu dialects*
Adult literacy rate	77.3%

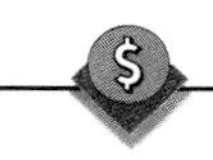

Currency	new zaire
GNP (U.S.$, in millions)	8,123
Income per capita (U.S.$)	220

Watered by the mighty Zaire River and its tributaries, the former Belgian Congo is Africa's third-largest nation. Vast equatorial jungles hold mahogany, ebony, and other valuable hardwoods. There are plantations of rice, coffee, cocoa, tea, cotton, rubber, and sugar cane. The mountains contain copper, gold, silver, tin, and 65 percent of the world's cobalt. Yet, for all its resources, Zaire is in a state of economic collapse due to widespread governmental corruption. Most people live on subsistence crops, and one-quarter of the nation's food must be imported.

At the time of first European contact – with the Portuguese in 1482 – much of Zaire was ruled by the powerful Kongo kingdom, which sold slaves for export to the Americas. Direct European investment in mining and agriculture began in the late 19th century, when the country became the economic fief of Belgium's King Leopold II.

With independence (in 1960), came civil disorder. A revolt in the Shaba region required intervention by UN troops. In 1965 Mobutu Sese Seko, a dictatorial former army general, seized power.

Under Mobutu's lengthy, self-serving regime, economic problems multiplied. In the early 1990s inflation reached 2,000 percent. Civil war in Rwanda and Burundi brought a flood of refugees, and a 1996 revolt in Zaire's eastern region compounded the nation's troubles.

20TH-CENTURY LANDMARKS

1900 Britain establishes Protectorate of Northern Nigeria.

1908 Belgium grants the Congo Free State (Zaire) a colonial charter.

— 1910 —

1914 British Protectorates of Northern and Southern Nigeria merge to form Nigeria.

1916 Urundi (Burundi) occupied by Belgium during World War I.

1919 Cameroon divided by French and British.

— 1920 —

1923 Ruanda-Urundi (Rwanda and Burundi) made Belgian mandate by League of Nations.

— 1930 —

1939–45 World War II disrupts trade.

— 1940 —

1940 Free French troops take over Gabon from Vichy government.

1946 Ruanda-Urundi made UN trusteeship.

— 1950 —

1958 Central African Republic gains autonomy from France.

— 1960 —

1962 Ruanda-Urundi divides into Rwanda and Burundi.

1965 Military coups in Central African Republic (led by Bokassa) and Zaire (led by Mobutu).

1966 Burundi deposes monarch and becomes a republic. Military coup in Nigeria.

1967–70 Civil war in Nigeria.

1968 Equatorial Guineau gains independence from Spain.

— 1970 —

1971–79 Idi Amin leads military coup in Uganda.

1972 Some 100,000 Hutus massacred by Tutsis in Burundi.

1973 "Auzou strip" in Chad occupied by Libya.

1979–82 Civil war in Chad between Muslims and Christians.

— 1980 —

1988 Further mass slaughter of Tutsis and Hutus in Burundi.

— 1990 —

1990–97 Thousands killed in war between Hutus and Tutsis in Burundi, Rwanda, and Zaire. Many also die of sickness or starvation in refugee camps.

SOUTHERN AFRICA

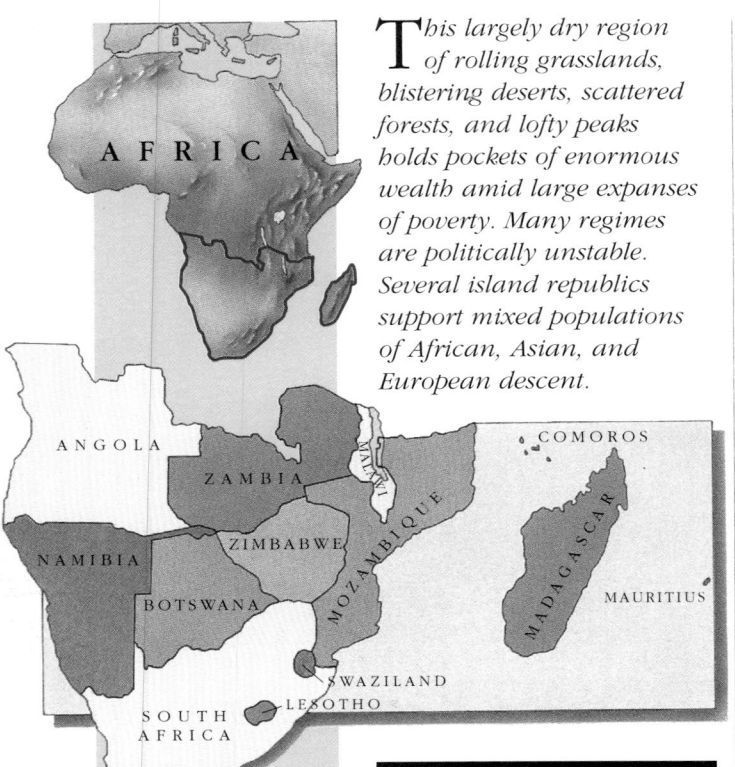

AFRICA

COMOROS
ANGOLA
ZAMBIA
ZIMBABWE
NAMIBIA
MOZAMBIQUE
MADAGASCAR
BOTSWANA
MAURITIUS
SWAZILAND
LESOTHO
SOUTH AFRICA

*T*his largely dry region of rolling grasslands, blistering deserts, scattered forests, and lofty peaks holds pockets of enormous wealth amid large expanses of poverty. Many regimes are politically unstable. Several island republics support mixed populations of African, Asian, and European descent.

Colonies and Dependent Territories

BOUVET ISLAND
Parent country
NORWAY
Map page 208

REUNION
Parent country
FRANCE
Map page 207

ST. HELENA AND DEPENDENCIES
Parent country
U.K.
Map page 206

Abbreviations
AfDB African Development Bank
COMM Commonwealth
ECA Economic Commission for Africa
FZ The Franc Zone
OAU Organization of African Unity
SADC Southern African Development Community

GNP Gross National Product

ANGOLA

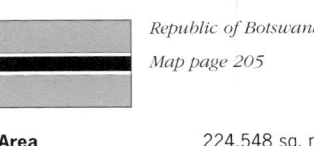

Republic of Angola
Map page 204

Area	481,226 sq. mi.
	(1,246,700 sq. km.)
Capital	Luanda
Member of	AfDB, ECA, OAU, SADC

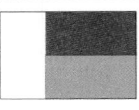

Population	10,609,000
Population growth rate	3.2%
Life expectancy	45 (m), 48 (f)
Languages	Portuguese, *Umbundo, Kimbundo, Chokwe, Ganguela*
Adult literacy rate	41.7%

Currency	readjusted kwanza
GNP (U.S.$, in millions)	5,996
Income per capita (U.S.$)	620

Though blessed with abundant natural riches – including diamond mines, forests, farmlands, and oil reserves – Angola has yet to find its place in the sun. Some 35 years of rebellion and civil war have left its economy in a state of shambles.

Colonized by the Portuguese in the 16th century, Angola became an important center of the lucrative African slave trade; by the mid-19th century, an estimated 2 million captive tribesmen had been shipped to the Americas from Benguela and Luanda, the colonial capital.

Angola won independence in 1975 after 14 years of hard-fought guerrilla warfare; some 300,000 Portuguese colonists departed in haste. Rival guerrilla leaders, backed by military aid from foreign powers, then plunged the country into further bloodshed. Ceasefire accords in 1991 and 1994 both collapsed, and by the middle of the decade, the death toll stood at well over half a million, with millions more left homeless.

BOTSWANA

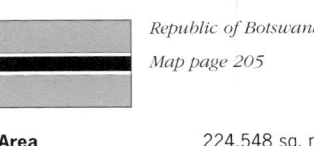

Republic of Botswana
Map page 205

Area	224,548 sq. mi.
	(581,730 sq. km.)
Capital	Gaborone
Member of	AfDB, COMM, OAU, SADC

Population	1,442,700
Population growth rate	3.3%
Life expectancy	56 (m), 62 (f)
Languages	English, *Setswana*
Adult literacy rate	73.7%

Currency	pula
GNP (U.S.$, in millions)	4,037
Income per capita (U.S.$)	2,800

A British protectorate until 1966, this sparsely populated nation embraces the bleak Kalahari Desert and one of the world's most spectacular marshes – the Okavango Basin, a vast swamp teeming with lions, elephants, and other large game. A stable democratic government, substantial diamond exports, and cattle ranching combine to give Botswana a measure of prosperity.

COMOROS

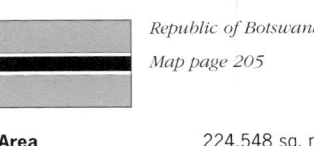

Federal Islamic Republic of the Comoros
Map page 207

Area	719 sq. mi.
	(1,862 sq. km.)
Capital	Moroni
Member of	AfDB, ECA, FZ, OAU

Population	446,800
Population growth rate	2.7%
Life expectancy	55 (av. m/f)
Languages	Comorian (Swahili and Arabic), French, Arabic
Adult literacy rate	61%

Currency	Comorian franc
GNP (U.S.$, in millions)	249
Income per capita (U.S.$)	510

Three of these volcanic "perfume isles" (Grande Comoro, Anjouan, and Mohéli) became an Islamic state in 1975, while the fourth, Mayotte, voted to remain a French dependency. The main cash crops are vanilla, cloves, and perfume essences.

LESOTHO

Kingdom of Lesotho
Map page 207

Area	11,717 sq. mi.
	(30,355 sq. km.)
Capital	Maseru
Member of	AfDB, COMM, OAU, SADC

Population	1,700,000
Population growth rate	2.7%
Life expectancy	58 (m), 63 (f)
Languages	English, Sesotho
Adult literacy rate	71.3%

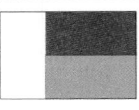

Currency	loti
GNP (U.S.$, in millions)	1,398
Income per capita (U.S.$)	700

A snowcapped realm of sky-high peaks and little arable land, this landlocked country – independent since 1966 – relies heavily on wages sent home by emigrants working in the gold and coal mines of neighboring South Africa. Future hopes lie in tourism – the casinos of Maseru and a developing ski industry – and in a huge new hydroelectric dam on the Orange River.

MADAGASCAR

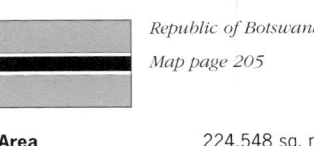

Republic of Madagascar
Map page 205

Area	226,598 sq. mi.
	(587,041 sq. km.)
Capital	Antananarivo
Member of	AfDB, ECA, OAU

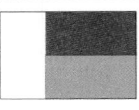

Population	11,493,000
Population growth rate	3%
Life expectancy	55 (m), 58 (f)
Languages	Malagasy, French, *Hova,* other local languages
Adult literacy rate	80.2%

Currency	Malagasy franc
GNP (U.S.$, in millions)	3,058
Income per capita (U.S.$)	230

More than 150,000 unique varieties of plants and animals – including several species of timid, nocturnal lemurs – inhabit Madagascar, the world's fourth-largest island. The human population is a blend of Africa and Asia, with people of Arabic, Indonesian, Bantu, Chinese, and Indian descent. Rice is the staple food in the central highlands; cassava, a starchy root, in more heavily African areas. Six decades of French occupation (ending in 1960) have given the capital, Antananarivo, a distinct European air.

Largely an agricultural nation, Madagascar produces two-thirds of the world's vanilla. Even so, the island remains gripped in poverty. Deforestation, overgrazing, and intensive agriculture – combined with an exploding population – have devastated the landscape. The institution of multiparty politics in 1990, along with recent mineral discoveries, suggests a brighter future.

MALAWI

Republic of Malawi
Map page 204

Area	45,735 sq. mi.
	(118,484 sq. km.)
Capital	Lilongwe
Member of	AfDB, COMM, ECA, SADC

Population	10,032,600
Population growth rate	4.5%
Life expectancy	45 (m), 46 (f)
Languages	English, *Chichewa*
Adult literacy rate	56.4%

Currency	Malawian kwacha
GNP (U.S.$, in millions)	1,560
Income per capita (U.S.$)	140

Tall, wooded mountainsides, grassy parklands, plunging waterfalls, Africa's third-largest lake – Malawi contains a lion's share of natural wonders. Scenic riches notwithstanding, it is one of the poorest nations in the world, with virtually no industry and a peasant population that subsists on tiny plots, farming millet, cassava, and peanuts. A small plantation-owning elite raises export crops of tea, tobacco, and sugar.

For some 30 years Malawi endured the autocratic rule of President-for-life Hastings Banda, who led the country to independence from Britain in 1964 and charted a pro-Western but increasingly repressive political course. The people voted him out of office in 1994 in the country's first democratic multiparty election.

MAURITIUS

Republic of Mauritius
Map page 207

Area	787 sq. mi.
	(2,040 sq. km.)
Capital	Port Louis
Member of	AfDB, COMM, OAU, SADC

Population	1,112,600
Population growth rate	0.9%
Life expectancy	71 (av. m/f)
Languages	English, *Creole,* other local languages
Adult literacy rate	82.9%

Currency	Mauritian rupee
GNP (U.S.$, in millions)	3,514
Income per capita (U.S.$)	3,180

A volcanic island surrounded by coral reefs, Mauritius was discovered by the Portuguese in the 16th century. Its economy benefits from tourism and sugar exports. The country has been independent since 1968.

MOZAMBIQUE

Republic of
Mozambique
Map page 204-5

Area	308,561 sq. mi.
	(799,380 sq. km.)
Capital	Maputo
Member of	AfDB, COMM, OAU, SADC

Population	17,423,000
Population growth rate	2%
Life expectancy	45 (m), 48 (f)
Languages	Portuguese, many local languages
Adult literacy rate	40.1%

Currency	metical
GNP (U.S.$, in millions)	1,328
Income per capita (U.S.$)	80

When Mozambique won freedom from Portuguese colonial rule in 1975, virtually every professional post was held by Europeans. As the foreigners fled, the economy collapsed; cotton plantations, cashew groves, sugar cane spreads, and food processing plants lay abandoned. The new Marxist government appealed to the Soviet Union and received major substantive help, but ruinous droughts in the 1980s and 1990s, followed by floods that wiped out the crops and devastated the economy, inflicted tremendous hardships. In addition, a rebel army backed by South Africa waged civil war against the central regime, causing an estimated 600,000 deaths and leaving 5.7 million people homeless.

A new constitution in 1990 led the way to multiparty government, and a peace accord ended the fighting. Since then, the nation has made progress in settling refugees, attracting foreign investment, and restoring the ravaged land.

NAMIBIA

Republic of Namibia
Map page 205

Area	318,177 sq. mi.
	(824,292 sq. km.)
Capital	Windhoek
Member of	AfDB, COMM, OAU, SADC

Population	1,594,000
Population growth rate	2.7%
Life expectancy	58 (m), 60 (f)
Languages	English, Afrikaans, German, local languages
Adult literacy rate	62%

Currency	Namibian dollar
GNP (U.S.$, in millions)	3,045
Income per capita (U.S.$)	2,030

Sand dunes reach 1,000 feet high in Namibia's coastal desert, one of the most arid places on earth and the site of huge diamond reserves. The interior mountains hold uranium, copper, and other minerals. Mining has enriched the elite, but left the majority in poverty. Namibia gained independence from South Africa in 1990 after a long guerrilla war.

SOUTH AFRICA

Republic of
South Africa
Map pages 206-7

Area	470,565 sq. mi.
	(1,219,080 sq. km.)
Capitals	Pretoria (administrative),
	Cape Town (legislative),
	Bloemfontein (judicial)
Member of	COMM, ECA, OAU, SADC

Population	41,244,500
Population growth rate	2.4%
Life expectancy	60 (m), 66 (f)
Languages	Afrikaans, English, nine African languages
Adult literacy rate	70%

Currency	rand
GNP (U.S.$, in millions)	125,225
Income per capita (U.S.$)	2,910

The swift transition of South Africa from white minority rule to multiracial democracy after the introduction of reforms in the 1990s was one of the most remarkable political dramas of the 20th century.

Five hundred years ago South Africa's Cape of Good Hope was a landmark for India-bound Portuguese explorers. In their wake came Dutch settlers, foundation stock of the Afrikaner, or "Boer," farmers who staked their claim to a long-inhabited land. In the 19th century the Boers were displaced from the Cape by the British. Fabulous discoveries of gold and diamonds eventually led the British to claim all of South Africa, but despite the Afrikaners' 1902 defeat in the Boer War, they remained politically dominant in the self-governing Union of South Africa that emerged in 1910.

In 1948 the ruling white minority (today roughly 14 percent of the population) made official the draconian system of racial segregation called apartheid. Its cornerstones were registration by race; identification papers circumscribing residence, work, and travel; denial of voting rights; and forced settlement of blacks in resource-poor "homelands." By the 1980s, however, world opposition to apartheid led to boycotts of the South African economy, and exclusion of the nation from international organizations and events. Taking office in 1989, President F. W. de Klerk acknowledged that apartheid must end. Within weeks black nationalist leader Nelson Mandela was released from prison after nearly three decades of confinement. Race separation laws were dismantled in 1991, and the framework for multiracial elections was approved, leading to Mandela's election in 1994 as South Africa's first black president.

South Africa still faces challenges. Its new leaders were left with a legacy of racial inequality in land distribution and economic opportunity, as well as agitation for Zulu autonomy. But bars to global investment are down, and the nation that is already Africa's most developed retains plentiful mineral reserves, rich farmlands, and the makings of a lucrative tourist trade.

SWAZILAND

Kingdom of
Swaziland
Map page 207

Area	6,702 sq. mi.
	(17,363 sq. km.)
Capital	Mbabane
Member of	AfDB, COMM, OAU, SADC

Population	879,000
Population growth rate	3.4%
Life expectancy	55 (m), 60 (f)
Languages	English, siSwati
Adult literacy rate	67.3%

Currency	lilangeni
GNP (U.S.$, in millions)	1,048
Income per capita (U.S.$)	1,160

One of Africa's last ruling dynasties, the proud kingdom of Swaziland – its royal house dates back 400 years – is closely tied to the economy of South Africa. Cash crops include sugar, citrus fruits, cotton, and wood pulp.

ZAMBIA

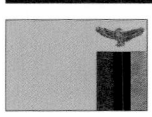

Republic of Zambia
Map pages 204-5

Area	290,509 sq. mi.
	(752,614 sq. km.)
Capital	Lusaka
Member of	AfDB, COMM, OAU, SADC

Population	8,023,000
Population growth rate	3.3%
Life expectancy	48 (m), 50 (f)
Languages	English, Nyanja, Bemba, Tonga, Lozi, Lunda, Luvale
Adult literacy rate	72.8%

Currency	Zambian kwacha
GNP (U.S.$, in millions)	3,206
Income per capita (U.S.$)	350

For more than a century, the fortunes of Zambia have depended on its immense copper reserves. The Copperbelt, centered in Ndola and other cities, brings in more than 90 percent of the nation's foreign exchange. In 1964, when Zambia won independence from Britain, copper prices were high and the future seemed assured. A decade later, the price plummeted; it has yet to recover. At the same time, political turmoil severed rail links with neighboring Angola and Mozambique, increasing transportation costs.

The government hopes to expand the economic base. With ample water resources and vast tracts of fertile land, Zambia is ripe for agricultural development. Victoria Falls and other scenic sites bring in increasing tourist income. Nevertheless, recovery may take decades.

ZIMBABWE

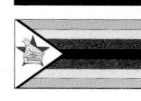

Republic of Zimbabwe
Map page 205

Area	150,833 sq. mi.
	(390,759 sq. km.)
Capital	Harare
Member of	AfDB, COMM, OAU, SADC

Population	11,150,000
Population growth rate	3%
Life expectancy	52 (m), 55 (f)
Languages	English, Chishona, Sindebele
Adult literacy rate	80.3%

Currency	Zimbabwe dollar
GNP (U.S.$, in millions)	5,424
Income per capita (U.S.$)	490

The English adventurer Cecil Rhodes obtained rights to mine this rich land in 1888 and soon began extracting its gold and other minerals. The region's fertile soil and temperate climate attracted European farmers, who raised tobacco as the main cash crop. As Southern Rhodesia, it became one of Britain's best-paying colonies.

Independence came in stages. As nearby African states won release from colonial rule, Southern Rhodesia's all-white government – determined to stay in power – unilaterally quit the British empire in 1965. International sanctions and civil war eventually forced its resignation, and in 1980 the new nation of Zimbabwe elected its first black president.

The new government, led by the scholarly Robert Mugabe, weathered the economic storms of independence. Despite problems with land reform, Zimbabwe remains the most highly developed southern African state after South Africa.

1899–1902 Boer War between Britain and South Africa.

1903 Swaziland made British protectorate.

— 1910 —

1910 Union of South Africa formed.

1912 ANC founded.

1914 South African forces enter German-occupied Southwest Africa (Namibia).

— 1920 —

1920 Southwest Africa becomes South African mandate.

1925 Black majority banned from skilled jobs in South Africa.

— 1930 —

1939–45 World War II disrupts trade.

— 1940 —

1948 National Party gains power in South Africa and introduces apartheid.

— 1950 —

1950 South Africa refuses to hand Southwest Africa mandate to UN.

1953 Southern and Northern Rhodesia (Zimbabwe and Zambia) and Nyasaland (Malawi) are federated.

— 1960 —

1960 South Africa becomes a republic.

1964 Armed struggle for independence starts in Mozambique.

1965 Guerrilla war against Southern Rhodesia's white rulers.

1966 South Africa's apartheid laws extended to Southwest Africa; resistance movement begins.

— 1970 —

1975 Civil war breaks out in Angola.

1976 Mozambique closes border with Southern Rhodesia.

— 1980 —

1980 Black majority wins independence for Zimbabwe.

1985 International sanctions imposed on South Africa.

1989 Civil war in Mozambique.

— 1990 —

1992 Peace accord in Mozambique.

1994 ANC wins first democratic elections in South Africa.

INDEX TO MAPS

The following index contains more than 40,000 names of places and physical features that appear in the maps on pages 56 to 208. Each name is followed by a map reference key and a page reference.

Names: Local official names are used for most features on the maps and in the index. The names are shown in full, complete with accents and other diacritical marks. Features that extend beyond the boundaries of one country and have no single official name are usually named in English. Many conventional English names and former names are cross-referenced to the official names.

Transliteration: For names in languages not written in the Latin alphabet, the locally official transliteration system has been used where one exists. Thus the transliteration for mainland Chinese names follows the pinyin system, which has been officially adopted in mainland China. For languages with no single locally accepted system, transliteration closely follows systems developed by the United States Board on Geographic Names.

Abbreviation and Capitalization: Abbreviations of names on the maps have been standardized as much as possible. Names that are abbreviated on the maps are generally spelled out in full in the index. Periods are used after abbreviations, regardless of local practice. The abbreviation *St.* is used only for *Saint. Sankt* and other forms of this term are spelled out.

Most initial letters of names are capitalized, except for generic terms in Russia and a number of other countries (mostly in eastern Europe and central Asia) and a few Dutch names, such as s-Gravenhage. Capitalization of noninitial words in a name generally follows local practice.

Alphabetization: Names of features are alphabetized in the order of the letters of the English alphabet. Accents and other diacritical marks are disregarded in alphabetization. For example, the German or Scandinavian *ä* or *ö* are treated as *a* or *o;* the Spanish *ñ* is treated as *n*.

The names of physical features may be listed in an inverted form, since they are always alphabetized under the proper, not the generic, part of the name (e.g., *Gibraltar, Strait of*). Every entry, whether it consists of one word or more, is alphabetized letter by letter, not word by word. For example, *Lakeland* appears after *La Crosse* but before *La Salle.* Names beginning with articles other than *The* (e.g., *Le Havre, Den Helder, Al-Madinah*) are not inverted. Names beginning with *St.* and *Sainte* are alphabetized as *Saint.*

In the case of identical names, towns are listed first, followed by political divisions, then physical features. Entries that are completely identical (including symbols, which are discussed below) are distinguished by abbreviations of their English country names. The country abbreviations used for places in the United States, Canada, and the United Kingdom indicate the state, province, or political division in which the feature is located. (See the List of Abbreviations below.)

Symbols: The names of cities and towns are not followed by symbols. The names of all other features, however, are followed by symbols that graphically represent broad categories. For example, "ʌ" is used to denote mountain (*Everest, Mount* ʌ). Superior numbers indicate finer distinctions. For example, "ʌ¹" is used to denote volcano (*Fuji, Mount* ʌ¹). A complete list of symbols, including those with superior numbers, follows the List of Abbreviations.

All cross-references are indicated by the word *see.*

Map reference keys and page references: The map reference keys and page references are found in the last two columns of each entry.

Each map reference key consists of a letter followed by a number. Corresponding letters and numbers appearing along the edges of the maps mark bands of latitude and longitude, respectively.

The map reference key for a point feature (such as a town, city, or mountain peak) indicates the location of the feature's symbol. For an extensive feature (such as a country, mountain range, or river), the key provides the position of the name.

The page number generally refers to the map that shows the feature at the best scale. Countries, mountain ranges, and other extensive features are usually indexed to maps that show the features completely and in their relationship to broad areas. Two-page maps are always referenced by the left-hand page. If a map contains several insets, each inset is identified by a lowercase letter.

List of Abbreviations

Ab., Can.	Alberta, Can.	Czech Rep.	Czech Republic	Kir.	Kiribati	Nic.	Nicaragua	Sol. Is.	Solomon Islands
Afr.	Africa	D.C., U.S.	District of Columbia, U.S.	Ks., U.S.	Kansas, U.S.	Nig.	Nigeria	Som.	Somalia
Ak., U.S.	Alaska, U.S.	De., U.S.	Delaware, U.S.	Kuw.	Kuwait	N. Ire., U.K.	Northern Ireland, U.K.	Sp. N. Afr.	Spanish North Africa
Al., U.S.	Alabama, U.S.	Den.	Denmark	Ky., U.S.	Kentucky, U.S.	N.J., U.S.	New Jersey, U.S.	Sri L.	Sri Lanka
Alb.	Albania	Dji.	Djibouti	Kyrg.	Kyrgyzstan	N. Kor.	North Korea	St. Hel.	St. Helena
Alg.	Algeria	Dom.	Dominica	La., U.S.	Louisiana, U.S.	N.M., U.S.	New Mexico, U.S.	St. K./N.	St. Kitts and Nevis
Am. Sam.	American Samoa	Dom. Rep.	Dominican Republic	Lat.	Latvia	N. Mar. Is.	Northern Mariana Islands	St. Luc.	St. Lucia
And.	Andorra	Ec.	Ecuador	Leb.	Lebanon	Nmb.	Namibia	S. Tom./P.	Sao Tome and Principe
Ang.	Angola	El Sal.	El Salvador	Leso.	Lesotho	Nor.	Norway	St. P./M.	St. Pierre and Miquelon
Ant.	Antarctica	Eng., U.K.	England, U.K.	Lib.	Liberia	Norf. I.	Norfolk Island	St. Vin.	St. Vincent and the
Antig.	Antigua and Barbuda	Eq. Gui.	Equatorial Guinea	Liech.	Liechtenstein	N.S., Can.	Nova Scotia		Grenadines
Ar., U.S.	Arkansas, U.S.	Erit.	Eritrea	Lith.	Lithuania	N.T., Can.	Northwest Territories,	Sur.	Surinam
Afg.	Afghanistan	Est.	Estonia	Lux.	Luxembourg		Can.	Swaz.	Swaziland
Arg.	Argentina	Eth.	Ethiopia	Ma., U.S.	Massachusetts, U.S.	Nv., U.S.	Nevada, U.S.	Swe.	Sweden
Arm.	Armenia	Eur.	Europe	Mac.	Former Yugoslav Republic	N.Y., U.S.	New York, U.S.	Switz.	Switzerland
Aus.	Austria	Falk. Is.	Falkland Islands		of Macedonia	N.Z.	New Zealand	Tai.	Taiwan
Austl.	Australia	Far. Is.	Faroe Islands	Madag.	Madagascar	Oc.	Oceania	Taj.	Tajikistan
Az., U.S.	Arizona, U.S.	Fin.	Finland	Malay.	Malaysia	Oh., U.S.	Ohio, U.S.	Tan.	Tanzania
Azer.	Azerbaijan	Fl., U.S.	Florida, U.S.	Mald.	Maldives	Ok., U.S.	Oklahoma, U.S.	T./C. Is.	Turks and Caicos Islands
Bah.	Bahamas	Fr.	France	Marsh. Is.	Marshall Islands	On., Can.	Ontario, Can.	Thai.	Thailand
Bahr.	Bahrain	Fr. Gu.	French Guiana	Mart.	Martinique	Or., U.S.	Oregon, U.S.	Tn., U.S.	Tennessee, U.S.
Barb.	Barbados	Fr. Poly.	French Polynesia	Maur.	Mauritania	Pa., U.S.	Pennsylvania, U.S.	Tok.	Tokelau
B.C., Can.	British Columbia, Can.	Ga., U.S.	Georgia, U.S.	May.	Mayotte	Pak.	Pakistan	Trin.	Trinidad and Tobago
Bdi.	Burundi	Gam.	Gambia, The	Mb., Can.	Manitoba, Can.	Pan.	Panama	Tun.	Tunisia
Bel.	Belgium	Gaza	Gaza Strip	Md., U.S.	Maryland, U.S.	Pap. N. Gui.	Papua New Guinea	Tur.	Turkey
Bela.	Belarus	Geor.	Georgia	Me., U.S.	Maine, U.S.	Para.	Paraguay	Turk.	Turkmenistan
Ber.	Bermuda	Ger.	Germany	Mex.	Mexico	P.E., Can.	Prince Edward Island,	Tx., U.S.	Texas, U.S.
Bhu.	Bhutan	Gib.	Gibraltar	Mi., U.S.	Michigan, U.S.		Can.	U.A.E.	United Arab Emirates
B.I.O.T.	British Indian Ocean	Golan	Golan Heights	Micron.	Micronesia, Federated	Phil.	Philippines	Ug.	Uganda
	Territory	Grc.	Greece		States of	Pit.	Pitcairn	U.K.	United Kingdom
Bngl.	Bangladesh	Gren.	Grenada	Mid. Is.	Midway Islands	Pol.	Poland	Ukr.	Ukraine
Bol.	Bolivia	Gmld.	Greenland	Mn., U.S.	Minnesota, U.S.	Port.	Portugal	Ur.	Uruguay
Bos.	Bosnia and Herzegovina	Guad.	Guadeloupe	Mo., U.S.	Missouri, U.S.	P.Q., Can.	Quebec, Can.	U.S.	United States
Bots.	Botswana	Guat.	Guatemala	Mol.	Moldova	P.R.	Puerto Rico	Ut., U.S.	Utah, U.S.
Braz.	Brazil	Gui.	Guinea	Mon.	Monaco	Reu.	Reunion	Uzb.	Uzbekistan
Bru.	Brunei	Gui.-B.	Guinea-Bissau	Mong.	Mongolia	R.I., U.S.	Rhode Island, U.S.	Va., U.S.	Virginia, U.S.
Br. Vir. Is.	British Virgin Islands	Guy.	Guyana	Monts.	Montserrat	Rom.	Romania	Vat.	Vatican City
Bul.	Bulgaria	Hi., U.S.	Hawaii, U.S.	Mor.	Morocco	Rw.	Rwanda	Ven.	Venezuela
Ca., U.S.	California, U.S.	H.K.	Hong Kong	Moz.	Mozambique	S.A.	South America	Viet.	Vietnam
Cam.	Cameroon	Hond.	Honduras	Mrts.	Mauritius	S. Afr.	South Africa	V.I.U.S.	Virgin Islands of the U.S.
Camb.	Cambodia	Hung.	Hungary	Ms., U.S.	Mississippi, U.S.	Sau. Ar.	Saudi Arabia	Vt., U.S.	Vermont, U.S.
Can.	Canada	Ia., U.S.	Iowa, U.S.	Mt., U.S.	Montana, U.S.	S.C., U.S.	South Carolina, U.S.	Wa., U.S.	Washington, U.S.
C.A.R.	Central African Republic	I.C.	Ivory Coast	Mwi.	Malawi	Scot., U.K.	Scotland, U.K.	Wake I.	Wake Island
Cay. Is.	Cayman Islands	Ice.	Iceland	Myan.	Myanmar	S.D., U.S.	South Dakota, U.S.	Wal./F.	Wallis and Futuna
Christ. I.	Christmas Island	Id., U.S.	Idaho, U.S.	N.A.	North America	Sen.	Senegal	W.B.	West Bank
Co., U.S.	Colorado, U.S.	Il., U.S.	Illinois, U.S.	N.B., Can.	New Brunswick, Can.	Sey.	Seychelles	Wi., U.S.	Wisconsin, U.S.
Cocos Is.	Cocos (Keeling) Islands	In., U.S.	Indiana, U.S.	N.C., U.S.	North Carolina, U.S.	S. Geor.	South Georgia and the	W. Sah.	Western Sahara
Col.	Colombia	Indon.	Indonesia	N. Cal.	New Caledonia		South Sandwich Islands	W. Sam.	Western Samoa
Com.	Comoros	I. of Man	Isle of Man	N. Cyp.	North Cyprus	Sing.	Singapore	W.V., U.S.	West Virginia, U.S.
Cook Is.	Cook Islands	Ire.	Republic of Ireland	N.D., U.S.	North Dakota, U.S.	Sk., Can.	Saskatchewan, Can.	Wy., U.S.	Wyoming, U.S.
C.R.	Costa Rica	Isr.	Israel	Ne., U.S.	Nebraska, U.S.	S. Kor.	South Korea	Yk., Can.	Yukon Territory, Can.
Cro.	Croatia	Jam.	Jamaica	Neth.	Netherlands	S.L.	Sierra Leone	Yugo.	Yugoslavia
Ct., U.S.	Connecticut, U.S.	Jer.	Jericho Area	Neth. Ant.	Netherlands Antilles	Slvk.	Slovakia	Zam.	Zambia
C.V.	Cape Verde	Jord.	Jordan	Nf., Can.	Newfoundland, Can.	Slvn.	Slovenia	Zimb.	Zimbabwe
Cyp.	Cyprus	Kaz.	Kazakhstan	N.H., U.S.	New Hampshire, U.S.	S. Mar.	San Marino		

Key to Symbols

ʌ	Mountain	ⲩ	Cape	⪬³	Isthmus	↘	Strait	ⲧ¹	Ocean	▫	Political Unit	▫⁸	Miscellaneous	■	Military Installation
ʌ¹	Volcano	ⲩ¹	Peninsula	⪬⁴	Cliff	⊂	Bay, Gulf	ⲧ²	Sea	▫¹	Independent Nation	▫⁹	Historical	✦	Miscellaneous
ʌ²	Hill	ⲩ²	Spit, Sand Bar	⪬⁵	Cave, Caves	⊂¹	Estuary	ⲧ³	Anchorage	▫²	Dependency			✦¹	Region
				⪬⁶	Crater	⊂²	Fjord	ⲧ⁴	Oasis, Well, Spring	▫³	State, Canton,	ⵄ	Cultural Institution	✦²	Desert
ⲭ	Mountains	Ι	Island	⪬⁷	Depression	⊂³	Bight				Republic	ⵄ¹	Religious Institution	✦³	Forest, Moor
ⲭ¹	Plateau	Ι¹	Atoll	⪬⁸	Dunes					▫⁴	Province, Region,	ⵄ²	Educational	✦⁴	Reserve,
ⲭ²	Hills	Ι²	Rock	⪬⁹	Lava Flow	⊜	Lake, Lakes	✦	Submarine Features		Oblast		Institution		Reservation
)(	Pass	ΙΙ	Islands			⊜¹	Reservoir	✦¹	Depression	▫⁵	Department,	ⵄ³	Scientific, Industrial	✦⁵	Transportation
⋁	Valley, Canyon	ΙΙ¹	Rocks	⪦	River	⁛	Swamp	✦²	Reef, Shoal		District, Prefecture		Facility	✦⁶	Dam
≃	Plain	⪩	Other Topographic	⪦¹	River Channel	⊠	Ice Features, Glacier	✦³	Mountain,	▫⁶	County	⊥	Historical Site	✦⁷	Mine, Quarry
≃¹	Basin		Features	≊	Canal				Mountains	▫⁷	City, Municipality	✦	Recreational Site	✦⁸	Neighborhood
≃²	Delta	⪩¹	Continent	≊¹	Aqueduct	ⲧ	Other Hydrographic	✦⁴	Slope, Shelf			⊗	Airport		
		⪩²	Coast, Beach	∟	Waterfall, Rapids		Features								

242

Name	Map Ref.	Page

A

Aachen F 3 98
Aalen D 7 100
Aali, Sadd el- (Aswan High Dam) ➜[6] C 3 202
A'āli an-Nīl □[3] F 3 202
Aalsmeer B 3 69
Aalst D 3 69
Aalten C 5 69
Aalter C 2 69
Aansluit D 5 206
Aarau C 5 82
Aarburg C 5 82
Aare ≃ C 6 82
Aareschlucht ✦ D 6 82
Aargau □[3] C 6 82
Aarschot D 3 69
Aasiaat
  see Egedesminde C 22 150
Aba, China B 6 130
Aba, Nig. D 6 200
Abā al-Bawl, Qurayn ʌ[2] J 14 118
Abaco I F 6 168
Ābādān G 13 118
Ābādeh G 15 118
Abadla C 4 198
Abaeté C 8 194
Abaetetuba D 9 190
Abag Qi E 10 128
Abaj (Abay) A 11 116
Abakaliki D 6 200
Abakan B 2 124
Abakan ≃ B 1 124
Abala C 5 200
Abalak G 28 108
Abancay F 4 190
Abano Terme D 7 92
Abarán F 3 88
Abar Küh G 15 118
Abashiri B 10 126
Abashiri B 10 126
Ābaya Hāyk' F 4 202
Abbadia San Salvatore G 7 92
Abbasanta E 2 90
Abbeville, Fr. B 8 78
Abbeville, Ga., U.S. C 3 168
Abbeville, La., U.S. H 2 170
Abbey F 17 156
Abbeyleix D 4 75
Abbiategrasso D 4 92
Abbotsford G 10 156
Abbotspoort B 7 206
Abbottābād C 2 122
'Abd al-Kūrī I E 7 202
'Abd Allāh, Khawr ṳ H 13 118
Abdulino J 20 108
Abéché C 2 88
Abéjar C 2 88
Abel Tasman National Park ✦ D 4 146
Abemama I[1] V 9 136
Abengourou D 4 200
Abenrā C 2 68
Abensberg D 8 100
Abeokuta D 5 200
Aber G 3 202
Abercarn F 3 72
Aberchirder C 6 74
Aberconwy and Colwyn □[6] D 3 72
Abercrombie ≃ D 7 144
Aberdare F 3 72
Aberdare National Park ✦ H 4 202
Aberdeen, Austl. B 8 144
Aberdeen, Md., U.S. G 2 164
Aberdeen, Scot., U.K. C 6 74
Aberdeen, S.D., U.S. C 5 174
Aberdeen, Wa., U.S. B 2 178
Aberdeen, City of □[6] C 6 74
Aberdeen Lake ⊜ D 13 150
Aberdeenshire □[6] C 6 74
Aberdovey E 2 72
Abergavenny F 3 72
Abergele D 3 72
Abertillery F 3 72
Aberystwyth E 2 72
Abetone E 6 92
Abhā D 5 202
Abhar D 13 118
Abhazskaja Respublika □[3] H 12 110
Ābhē Bid Hāyk' ⊜ E 5 202
Abidjan G 2 202
Abiengama G 2 202
Abilene, Ks., U.S. F 6 174
Abilene, Tx., U.S. D 4 172
Abingdon, Eng., U.K. F 3 72
Abingdon, Va., U.S. B 2 166
Abington G 3 164
Abinsk G 11 110
Abiod, Rmel el- ➜[1] C 6 198
Abisko B 9 64
Abitau ≃ B 17 156
Abitibi ≃ C 3 160
Abitibi, Lac (Abitibi, Lake) ⊜ D 3 160
Abitibi, Lake (Abitibi, Lac) ⊜ D 3 160
Ābīy Ādī E 4 202
Ābīyata Hāyk' F 4 202
Abja-Paluoja C 12 66
Abnūb I 4 118
Abo
  see Turku B 11 66
Abohar C 2 122
Abomey D 5 200
Abong Abong, Gunung ʌ L 3 132
Abong Mbang E 7 200
Abony B 6 104
Aborigen, pik ʌ C 17 114
Abou G 5 202
Abou-Deïa C 8 200
Abou Simbel ⊥ I 4 118
Abovyan (Abovjan) I 14 110
Abraham Lincoln Birthplace National Historic Site ✦ D 6 170
Abrantes E 2 86
Abra Pampa D 6 192
Abrene
  see Pytalovo H 7 108
'Abrī E 3 202
Abruzzi □[3] B 3 94
Abruzzo, Parco Nazionale d' ✦ C 3 94
Absaroka Range ʌ G 4 164
Absecon G 4 164
Abū 'Alī I G 12 118
Abū al-Khasīb G 12 118
Abu Dhabi
  see Abū Zaby J 16 118
Abū 'Alī □[3] D 3 202
Abuja D 5 200
Abū Jubayhah F 2 202
Abū Kamāl E 9 118
Abū Kulaywāt E 2 202

Abū Madd, Ra's ⧫ J 7 118
Abunā E 5 190
Abu Qīr ➜[8] G 4 118
Abu Qurqās I 4 118
Ābu Road E 2 122
Abū Shajarah, Ra's ⧫ C 4 202
Abū Shanab E 2 202
Abū Sunbul
  see Abou Simbel ⊥ C 3 202
Abu Tīg I 4 118
Abū Zabad E 2 202
Abu Zaby (Abu Dhabi) J 16 118
Abwong F 3 202
Aby, Lagune ⊜ D 4 200
Abyad E 2 202
Abyei F 2 202
Acadia National Park ✦ A 9 162
Acajutla E 2 186
Acámbaro H 9 184
A Cañiza B 2 86
Acaponeta F 7 184
Acaponeta ≃ F 7 184
Acapulco de Juárez I 9 184
Acaraí Mountains ʌ C 7 190
Acaraú D 10 190
Acaraú ≃ D 10 190
Acaray ≃ F 3 194
Acari A 8 194
Acarigua F 7 186
Acàş B 7 104
Acatlán de Osorio H 10 184
Acayucan H 12 184
Accoville A 4 168
Accra D 4 200
Acerentia ⊥ E 6 94
Acerra E 5 90
Aceuchal F 4 86
Achacachi G 5 190
Achalpur E 3 122
Acheng D 16 128
Achénouma B 7 200
Achern D 4 100
Achill Head ⧫ B 1 75
Achill Island I C 1 75
Achim C 6 98
Achwa ≃ B 5 204
Aci Castello G 5 94
Aci Catena G 5 94
Acinsk D 12 114
Ackerly D 3 172
Acklins I C 6 186
Acoma Indian Reservation ➜[4] E 5 176
Aconcagua, Cerro ʌ C 3 195
Aconibe E 7 200
A Coruña (Corunna) A 3 86
Acquapendente G 7 92
Acquaviva delle Fonti D 6 94
Acqui Terme E 4 92
Acraman, Lake ⊜ L 2 142
Acre
  see 'Akko D 4 120
Acre □[3] E 5 190
Acre ≃ F 5 190
Acri E 6 94
Acton □[6] A 6 164
Acton Vale A 6 164
Actopan G 10 184
Ada, Ok., U.S. C 5 172
Ada, Yugo. C 6 104
Adaffer el Abiod ➜[1] F 2 198
Adailo E 5 202
Adair D 1 170
Adair, Cape ⧫ B 18 150
Adairville D 5 170
Adak I 43 155a
Adam, Mount ʌ n 18 193b
Adamantina D 5 194
Adamaoua □[3] D 7 200
Adamawa □[3] D 7 200
Adamello ʌ C 6 92
Adamów C 12 96
Adams, N.D., U.S. A 5 174
Adams, N.Y., U.S. C 2 164
Adams ≃[6] G 1 164
Adams, Mount ʌ B 3 178
Adams Lake ⊜ F 12 156
'Adan (Aden) E 6 202
Adana D 6 118
Adana □[3] D 6 118
Adanero D 6 86
Adare, Cape ⧫ D 20 208
Adavale H 7 142
Adda ≃ D 5 92
Ad-Dabbah D 3 202
Ad-Dahnā' ➜[2] D 5 202
Ad-Dāmir D 3 202
Ad-Dammām I 13 118
Ad-Dawhah (Doha) J 14 118
Ad-Dibdibah ➜[1] H 12 118
Addis Ababa
  see Ādīs Ābeba F 4 202
Addison B 1 162
Addison □[6] B 5 164
Ad-Dīwānīyah F 11 118
Addo Elephant National Park ✦ G 6 206
Ad-Du'ayn F 2 202
Ad-Duwaym F 3 202
Adébour C 7 200
Adel B 1 170
Adelaide E 2 144
Adelaide Island I C 2 208
Adelaide River C 11 140
Adèle Island I D 7 140
Adelfia D 6 94
Adélie Coast ≃[2] C 23 208
Adelong E 6 144
Aden
  see 'Adan E 6 202
Aden, Gulf of c G 6 206
Adendorp G 6 206
Adi, Pulau I F 10 134
Adige (Etsch) ≃ D 8 92
Ādīgrat E 4 202
Adıgüzel Baraji ⊜[1] C 8 106
Adi Keyih E 4 202
Adi Kwala E 4 202
Adīlābād F 3 122
Adilang D 7 198
Adīrī D 7 198
Adirondack Mountains ʌ C 4 164
Adıyaman D 8 118
Adıyaman □[3] D 8 118
Adler H 11 110
Adliswil C 6 82
Admiral G 17 156
Admiralty Bay c A 16 154
Admiralty Gulf c D 9 140
Admiralty Gulf Aboriginal Reserve ✦ D 8 140
Admiralty Island I H 27 154

Admiralty Islands II M 13 124
Admiralty Mountains ʌ D 25 208
Adolfo Gonzales Chaves E 8 195
Adolfo López Mateos, Presa ⊜[1] E 6 184
Adonara, Pulau I G 8 134
Ādoni F 3 122
Adorf B 9 100
Adour ≃ E 2 80
Adra H 1 88
Adrano G 4 94
Adrar D 4 198
Adrar □[3] E 2 198
Adrār ➜[1] E 2 198
Adré C 9 200
Adria D 8 92
Adrian, Mi., U.S. C 1 162
Adrian, Mn., U.S. D 7 174
Adrian, Mo., U.S. C 1 170
Adrian, W.V., U.S. D 3 162
Adrianople
  see Edirne B 7 106
Adriatic Sea ≃[2] G 11 62
A Dun ≃ H 9 132
Ādwa E 4 202
Adyča ≃ C 16 114
Adygeja □[3] G 12 110
Adyk G 14 110
Adžarskaja Respublika □[3] I 13 110
Adzopé D 4 200
Aegean Sea ≃[2] C 6 106
Aegina
  see Aíyina D 5 106
Aegviidu C 12 66
Ærø I D 3 68
Ærøskøbing D 3 68
A Estrada B 2 86
Afade C 7 200
Afar □[3] D 6 198
Afféry D 4 200
Afghanistan □[1] G 6 202
Afgoye G 6 202
Afikpo D 6 200
Aflao D 5 200
Aflou C 5 198
Afognak Island I G 18 154
Afoniha B 20 108
A Fonsagrada A 3 86
Afragola D 4 94
Africa ≃[1] G 8 196
Afrikanda C 16 64
Afşin C 7 118
Afton, N.Y., U.S. D 3 164
Afton, Ok., U.S. D 1 170
'Afula D 4 120
Afyon C 9 106
Afyon □[3] C 4 118
Agadez B 6 200
Agadez □[3] B 6 200
Agadez, Ighazer oua-n- ≃ B 6 200
Agadir A 11 116
Agadyr' A 11 116
Agaie D 6 200
Agan ≃ F 31 108
Agana C 12 134
Agano ≃ F 7 126
Agapovka J 23 108
Āgaro F 4 202
Agartala E 6 122
Agassiz Pool ⊜ A 6 174
Agate G 3 82
Agate Fossil Beds National Monument ✦ D 3 174
Agats G 11 134
Agattu Strait ṳ k 38 155a
Agboville D 4 200
Agde G 1 82
Agen D 4 80
Aggeneys E 3 206
Aggteleki Nemzeti Park ✦ A 6 104
Āghā Jārī G 13 118
Aghzoumal, Sabkhat ⊜ A 3 198
Aginskoe A 10 128
Agira G 4 94
Agliana F 6 92
Agnibilékrou D 4 200
Agnita C 8 104
Agogo D 4 200
Agou, Mont ʌ D 5 200
Agoura Hills F 5 182
Agoza ⊥ B 9 200
Āgra D 3 122
Agreda C 3 88
Ağrı C 10 118
Ağrı □[3] C 10 118
Agrigento G 3 94
Agrigento □[6] G 3 94
Agrihan I I 13 124
Agrínion C 4 106
Agrópoli D 4 94
Agro Pontino ➜[1] H 8 92
Agryz H 20 108
Ağsu I 16 110
Aguachica F 6 186
Aguadilla j 14 187b
Aguadulce, Pan. F 4 186
Aguadulce, Spain H 2 88
Agualeguas D 10 184
Aguán ≃ E 3 186
Aguanaval ≃ E 8 184
Aguanish ≃ C 12 160
Agua Prieta B 5 184
A Guardia C 2 86
Aguarico ≃ D 3 190
Aguaro-Guariquito, Parque Nacional ✦ F 8 186
Aguas Santas C 2 86
Água Vermelha, Represa de ⊜[1] F 5 194
Agua Zarca B 3 86
A Gudiña B 3 86
Agudos E 6 194
Aguijan I M 13 124
Aguilar E 6 86
Aguilar de Campoo B 6 86
Aguilar de la Frontera G 3 88
Águilas G 3 88
Aguit F 9 128
Agujita F 9 128? C 7 200
Aguja, Punta ⧫ A 1 122
Ahangaran A 1 122

Ahar C 12 118
Āhaus D 4 98
Ahipara Bay c A 4 146
Ahlat C 10 118
Ahlbeck C 11 98
Ahlen E 4 98
Ahmadābād E 2 122
Ahmadnagar F 2 122
Ahmadpur East D 2 122
Ahmar Mountains ʌ F 5 202
Ahmeti C 7 106
Ahon, Tarso ʌ A 8 200
Ahoskie A 6 168
Ahrensbök B 7 98
Ahrensburg C 7 98
Ahtuba ≃ F 15 110
Ahtubinsk E 15 110
Ahumada B 6 184
Ahunui I[1] E 13 136
Åhus E 7 66
Ahvāz G 13 118
Ahvenanmaa □[3] B 10 66
Aichach D 8 100
Aichi □[3] G 6 126
Aiea i 9 181a
Aigen im Mühlkreis B 5 102
Aigle D 4 82
Aiguebelle, Parc de conservation d' ✦ A 9 166
Aigueperse B 7 80
Aiguestortes i Estany Sant Maurici, Parque Nacional d' ✦ B 5 88
Aigurande B 5 80
Aiken C 4 168
Ailao Shan ʌ F 5 130
Ailinglaplap I[1] C 8 136
Ailuk I[1] B 8 136
Aimorés C 10 194
Ain □[3] D 3 82
Ain ≃ D 3 82
Aïn Defla H 6 88
Aïn Deheb G 2 198
Aïn Draham G 2 198
Aïn el Beïda B 6 198
Aïn M'lila B 6 198
Ainos National Park ✦ C 4 106
Ainring C 4 102
Ainslie Lake ⊜ E 13 160
Ainsworth D 4 174
Aïn Témouchent B 4 198
Aïn Témouchent □[3] E 5 84
Aïn Touta B 6 198
Aïn Wessara B 5 198
Aiora E 3 88
Aïr, Massif de l' ʌ B 6 200
Airdrie, Ab., Can. F 14 156
Airdrie, Scot., U.K. B 3 72
Aire-sur-l'Adour E 3 80
Aire-sur-la-Lys B 9 78
Air Force Island I D 18 150
Airolo D 6 82
Aishihik F 26 154
Aishihik Lake ⊜ F 26 154
Aisne □[3] C 10 78
Aisne ≃ C 9 78
Aïssa, Djebel ʌ C 4 198
Aitape M 12 124
Aitkin B 2 174
Aït-Melloul C 3 198
Aitutaki I[1] E 12 136
Aiud B 7 104
Aix-en-Provence G 3 82
Aix-La-Chapelle
  see Aachen F 2 98
Aix-les-Bains E 3 82
Aiyínion B 5 106
Aíyion C 5 106
Aïzawl E 6 122
Aizkraukle D 12 66
Aizu-wakamatsu F 7 126
Aj B 21 110
'Ajab Shīr D 11 118
Ajaccio j 8 83a
Ajaguz (Ayakoz) A 13 116
Ajana E 3 122
Ajanta Range ʌ E 3 122
Ajasse D 5 200
Ajdābīyā B 9 198
Ajdarkul', ozero ⊜ I 20 110
Ajdovščina D 9 92
Ajjer, Tassili-n- ʌ[1] D 6 198
Ajka B 4 104
Ajke, ozero ⊜ D 22 110
'Ajlūn D 4 120
'Ajmān J 16 118
Ajni D 12 122
Ajo K 4 176
Ajon, ostrov I C 19 114
Ajtos D 9 104
Akaba D 5 200
Akabira C 10 126
Akagera ≃ C 5 204
Akagera, Parc National de l' ✦ C 5 204
Akaka Falls State Park ✦ j 11 181a
Akan-kokuritsu-kōen ✦ C 10 126
Akaroa E 4 146
'Akāshāt F 8 118
Akbou B 5 198
Akbulak D 19 110
Akçadağ C 7 118
Akçakale D 8 118
Akçakoca B 9 106
Akchār ➜ F 2 198
Akdağmadeni C 6 118
Aken E 8 98
Akershus □[3] C 5 66
Aketi B 3 204
Akharnaí C 5 106
Akhdar, Wādī al- ≃ H 7 118
Akhisar C 7 106
Akhmīm I 4 118
Akiachak F 14 154
Akimiski Island I F 3 160
Ākirkeby f 7 68a
Akita E 7 126
Akita □[3] E 7 126
Akjoujt A 5 198
Akka H 3 198
Akkani C 9 154
Akkeshi C 11 126
'Akko (Acre) C 4 120
Aklavik B 27 154
Akmola D 11 114
Akmola □[3] B 11 114
Akmolinsk
  see Akmola J 28 108
Akō G 7 126
Akobo (Akūbū) F 3 202
Akok C 7 200
Akola C 3 122
Akonolinga D 7 200
Akordat E 3 202
Akosombo Dam ➜[6] D 5 200
Akot D 4 202
Akoupé D 4 200
Akpatok Island I D 19 150

Akranes m 19 64a
Åkrehamn C 2 66
Akrítas, Ákra ⧫ D 4 106
Akrokórinthos ⊥ D 5 106
Akron, Oh., U.S. C 3 162
Akron, Pa., U.S. F 2 164
Aksaj A 9 128
Aksaray C 5 118
Aksaray □[3] C 5 118
Akşehir C 9 106
Akşehir Gölü ⊜ C 9 106
Akshatau
  see Akšatau E 19 110
Aksu A 4 122
Aksu ≃ D 9 106
Aksubaevo I 19 108
Aktanyš B 19 110
Aktaū (Aqtaū) H 17 110
Aktjubinsk (Aqtöbe) D 20 110
Aktogaj (Aktogay) A 12 116
Aktyubinsk
  see Aqtöbe D 20 110
Aku D 6 200
Akūbū (Ākobo) ≃ F 3 202
Akune H 3 126
Akure D 5 200
Akureyri m 21 64a
Akutan I 11 154
Akutan Pass ṳ I 11 154
Akwanga D 6 200
Akyab
  see Sittwe D 1 132
Akyazı B 9 106
Al B 4 66
Ala A 5 122
Al-Butānah ➜[1] D 3 202
Alabama □[3] E 10 152
Alabama ≃ D 1 168
Alabaster F 5 170
Alacant (Alicante) F 4 88
Alaçam B 6 118
Alachua E 3 168
Aladža manastir ⊥[1] D 10 104
Alagoas □[3] E 11 190
Alagoinhas F 11 190
Alagón C 3 88
Alagón ≃ E 4 86
Alai Range ʌ B 2 122
Alajärvi C 13 66
Alajuela F 3 186
Alakol', ozero (Alaköl Köli) ≃ A 13 116
Alamagan I I 13 124
Al-'Amārah G 12 118
Ālamat'ā E 4 202
Alameda C 2 182
Alameda □[6] D 1 176
Alamo D 6 82
Alamo ≃ D 6 184
Alamogordo F 6 176
Alamo Indian Reservation ➜[4] E 5 176
Álamos D 5 184
Alamosa C 15 176
Åland Islands II F 10 64
Åland Sea ≃[2] B 9 66
Alanson D 5 166
Alanya D 4 118
Alaotra, Farihy ⊜ k 9 205a
Alapaevsk H 24 108
Alapaha ≃ D 3 168
Alaplı B 9 106
Al-'Aqabah E 3 120
Alarcón E 3 88
Alarcón, Embalse de ⊜ E 3 88
Alas, Selat ṳ A 4 140
Alaşehir C 8 106
Alaska □[3] D 18 154
Alaska, Gulf of c G 21 154
Alaska Peninsula ⧫[1] H 15 154
Alaska Range ʌ E 20 154
Alassio E 4 92
Alastaro B 11 66
Alāt I 16 110
Alatna ≃ C 18 154
Alatri H 9 92
Alatyr' I 17 108
Alatyr' ≃ I 16 108
Alausí D 3 190
Alava □[6] B 2 88
Alava, Cape ⧫ A 1 178
Alawa Aboriginal Land ✦ C 2 142
Alba, Italy E 4 92
Alba, Tx., U.S. D 6 172
Alba □[3] B 7 104
Albacete F 3 88
Albacete □[6] F 4 88
Albaida F 4 88
Alba Iulia B 7 104
Albal F 2 88
Al-Balqā' □[3] E 5 120
Albanel, Lac ⊜ B 5 160
Albania □[1] G 11 62
Albano Laziale H 7 92
Albany, Austl. N 4 140
Albany, Ga., U.S. D 2 168
Albany, N.Y., U.S. D 7 164
Albany, Oh., U.S. D 3 162
Albany, Or., U.S. E 2 178
Albany, Tx., U.S. C 8 172
Albany ≃ F 16 150
Albany □[6] D 4 164
Al-Barrah C 3 202
Al-Basrah (Basra) G 12 118
Albatera F 4 88
Al-Bāṭinah ➜[1] D 6 202
Al-Batrā' (Petra) ⊥ I 4 120
Al-Baydā', Libya B 9 198
Al-Baydā', Libya B 9 198
Albemarle Sound ☍ A 7 168
Albenga E 4 92
Alberga Creek ≃ I 2 142
Alberic F 3 88
Alberobello D 7 94
Albert D 9 78
Albert, Lake ⊜, Afr. B 5 204
Albert, Lake ⊜, Austl. F 5 144

Alberta, Mount ʌ E 13 156
Albertirsa B 5 104
Albertkanaal ≊ C 4 69
Albert Lea D 2 166
Albert Markham, Mount ʌ E 24 208
Albert Nile ≃ B 5 204
Alberton E 11 160
Albertville, Al., U.S. E 5 170
Albertville, Fr. E 4 82
Albertville
  see Kalemie, Zaire D 4 204
Albi E 6 80
Al Bidia C 9 200
Albina B 8 190
Albino D 5 92
Albion, Mi., U.S. B 1 162
Albion, Ne., U.S. E 5 174
Albion, Pa., U.S. C 3 162
Albion Park B 8 144
Al-Biqā' ≃[3] E 5 120
Al-Birkah F 4 120
Alblasserdam C 3 69
Albocácer D 7 86
Albolote G 7 86
Aborán Sea ≃[2] D 4 84
Alboraya E 4 88
Albox G 2 88
Albstadt G 5 100
Álbū Gharz, Sabkhat ⊜ E 9 118
Albufeira H 1 88
Albuñol H 3 88
Albuquerque E 5 176
Albury F 6 144
Al-Buṭānah ➜[1] D 3 202
Alcácer do Sal F 2 86
Alcalá de Guadaíra G 5 86
Alcalá de Henares D 7 86
Alcalá del Río G 4 86
Alcalá la Real D 5 176
Alcamo E 2 94
Alcanar D 5 88
Alcañiz C 4 88
Alcântara E 4 86
Alcântara D 5 176
Alcantarilla G 3 88
Alcaudete G 6 86
Alcázar de San Juan E 3 88
Alcester D 6 174
Alcira
  see Alzira F 4 88
Alcoa D 1 168
Alcobaça, Braz. B 11 194
Alcobaça, Port. E 1 86
Alcobendas D 7 86
Alcoi (Alcoy) D 7 86
Alcolu D 6 168
Alcora D 4 88
Alcorcón D 6 86
Alcorn □[6] H 3 170
Alcoutim G 3 170
Alcúdia E 8 88
Alcúdia, Badia d' c E 8 88
Aldabra Island II I 12 196
Aldan D 15 114
Aldan Plateau
  see Aldanskoe nagor'e ʌ[1] D 15 114
Aldanskoe nagor'e ʌ[1] D 15 114
Alderney I j 10 73b
Aldershot F 6 72
Alderson A 4 168
Aleg F 2 198
Alegre D 10 194
Alegrete F 10 194
Alejandro Selkirk, Isla I H 6 188
Aleksandro-Nevskaja H 14 110
Aleksandrov H 13 108
Aleksandrovskij D 10 110
Aleksandrovsk-Sahalinskij B 12 124
Aleksandrów Kujawski B 10 96
Alekseevka, Kaz. J 29 108
Alekseevka, Kaz. J 28 108
Alekseevka, Russia D 11 110
Aleksin I 12 108
Aleksinac D 6 104
Além Paraíba D 9 194
Alençon D 6 78
Alenquer D 8 190
Alentejo □[9] F 2 86
Aleppo
  see Halab D 7 118
Alès F 2 82
Aleşd B 7 104
Aleškovo D 12 110
Alessándria E 4 92
Alessano D 12 94
Alēşişkē D 4 202
Aleutian Basin ⤲[1] A 4 61
Aleutian Trench ⤲[1] C 14 58
Alevina, mys ⧫ D 18 114
Alexander E 8 158
Alexander Archipelago II H 26 154
Alexander Bay C 2 206
Alexander Island I C 1 208
Alexandra Falls ↳ A 13 156
Alexandretta
  see İskenderun D 7 118
Alexandria, B.C., Can. E 10 156
Alexandria (El-Iskandarīya), Egypt G 3 118
Alexandria, La., U.S. G 3 170
Alexandria, Mn., U.S. C 7 174
Alexandria, On., Can. C 7 160
Alexandria, Ro. B 8 104
Alexandria, S. Afr. H 5 206
Alexandria, Va., U.S. H 1 164
Alexandria, Lake ⊜ E 3 144
Alexándroúpolis B 8 106
Alexis Creek E 10 156
Alfaro B 9 88
Al-Fāshir E 2 202
Alfatar C 4 104
Al-Fayyūm I 4 118
Alfeld, Niedersachsen D 8 100
Alfeld (Great Alfold) ≊ D 8 100
Alfonsine D 7 92
Alford C 6 74
Alfreton D 6 72
Alfta F 8 66
Al-Fuhayhīl H 13 118

Al-Fuqahā' D 8 198
Alga E 20 110
Algarve □[9] G 2 86
Algarve, Costa do ≃[2] H 3 86
Algeciras H 5 86
Algemesí E 4 88
Alger E 7 166
Algeria □[1] F 8 196
Algete D 7 86
Al-Ghawr V E 5 120
Alghero I 4 92
Algiers
  see El Djazair B 5 198
Alginet E 4 88
Algoa Bay c G 6 206
Algoma C 5 166
Algona D 7 174
Algonquin D 4 166
Algonquin Provincial Park ✦ F 4 160
Algorta, Spain A 7 86
Algorta, Ur. C 9 195
Alhambra F 1 88
Al-Harīq C 6 202
Al-Harrah ʌ[9] F 7 118
Al-Harūj al-Aswad ʌ[2] D 9 198
Al-Hasakah D 9 118
Alhaurín el Grande H 6 86
Al-Hawrah E 6 202
Al-Hijāz □[9] B 4 202
Al-Hillah F 11 118
Al-Hoceima B 4 198
Al-Hoceima □[3] E 3 84
Al-Hudayb C 7 202
Al-Hudaydah (Hodeida) E 5 202
Al-Hufrah ➜[1] H 8 118
Al-Hufūf I 13 118
Aliaga, Spain D 4 88
Aliaga, Tur. C 7 106
Aliákmon ≃ B 5 106
Alibates Flint Quarries National Monument ✦ C 3 172
Āli Bayrami I 16 110
Alibey, ozero ⊜ C 10 104
Alicante
  see Alacant F 4 88
Alicante □[6] F 4 88
Alice G 4 172
Alice Arm D 7 156
Alice Springs G 1 142
Alice Town E 6 168
Alicurá, Embalse de ⊜[1] G 2 195
Aligarh D 3 122
Alíkovo B 15 110
Alima ≃ C 2 204
Alingsås D 6 66
Ālīpur Duār D 5 122
Aliquippa C 3 162
Al-'Istiwā'īyah □[3] F 3 202
Alitak Bay c H 17 154
Alivérion C 6 106
Alix E 14 156
Al-Jabalayn F 3 202
Al-Jaghbūb D 9 198
Al-Jahrah H 12 118
Al-Jalāmīd G 8 118
Al-Jawf, Libya E 9 198
Al-Jawf, Sau. Ar. H 8 118
Al-Jawlān
  see Golan Heights □[2] D 5 120
Al-Jaylī D 3 202
Al-Jazīrah ➜[1] D 3 202
Aljezur G 2 86
Al-Jubayl H 13 118
Al-Junaynah E 1 202
Al-Kahfah I 10 118
Aikamari C 7 200
Al-Karabah D 3 202
Al-Karak G 5 120
Al-Karak □[3] G 5 120
Al-Kawm E 8 118
Al-Khābūrah E 8 118
Al-Khafjī H 13 118
Al-Khalīl (Hebron) E 5 120
Al-Khamsīn D 3 202
Al-Khārijah K 16 118
Al-Khartūm (Khartoum) D 3 202
Al-Khartūm □[3] D 3 202
Al-Khartūm Bahrī D 3 202
Al-Khatam ➜[1] K 16 118
Al-Khubar I 13 118
Al-Khums C 7 198
Al-Kūfah F 11 118
Al-Küt F 11 118
Al-Kuwayt H 12 118
Al-Lādhiqīyah D 6 118
Al-Lagowa E 2 202
Alhambād E 2 202
Allan F 18 156
Allanmyo D 3 132
Allanridge F 8 206
Allanton D 7 206
'Allāq, Bi'r ➜[4] C 7 198
Allaqi, Wadi ≃ D 4 195
Allatoona Lake ⊜[1] B 2 168
Allauch D 5 176
Alldays B 8 206
Allegany State Park ✦ B 4 162
Allegheny Mountains ʌ D 7 118
Allegheny Plateau ʌ[1] E 10 152
Allegheny Reservoir ⊜[1] B 5 162
Allemands, Lac Des ⊜ E 5 170
Allen, Arg. G 4 195
Allen □[6] D 6 174
Allen, Tx., U.S. D 5 172
Allenby Bridge (Husayn, Jisr al-) ➜[5] F 5 120
Allendale D 4 168
Allende C 3 168
Allentown F 3 164
Allevard E 5 160
Allier □[3] B 7 80
Allier ≃ B 7 80
Alliance, Ne., U.S. D 3 174
Alliance, Oh., U.S. C 5 202
Al-Lişān ⧫[1] E 5 120
Al-Līth D 5 202
Alloa B 4 74
Allora F 9 144
Allschwil C 4 100
Allumette Lake ⊜ F 5 160
Allumettes, Île aux I A 1 164
Allyn B 2 178

Alma — Arkansas

Name | Map Ref. | Page

Alma, Ks., U.S. F 6 174
Alma, P.Q., Can. D 8 160
Alma-Ata see Almaty A 3 122
Almacelles C 5 88
Almada F 1 86
Almaden, Austl. D 7 142
Almadén, Spain F 6 86
Al-Madīnah (Medina) J 8 118
Al-Mafraq E 6 120
Al-Mafraq □[3] E 7 120
Almagro F 7 86
Al-Manāmah I 14 118
Al-Manāqil E 3 202
Almansa F 3 88
Almanza B 5 86
Al-Marj C 9 198
Almassora E 4 88
Al-Matammah D 3 202
Almaty A 3 122
Almaty □[3] A 3 122
Al-Mawṣil D 10 118
Almeida D 4 86
Almejas, Bahía ⊂ E 4 184
Almelo B 5 69
Almenara B 10 194
Almenar de Soria C 2 88
Almendra, Embalse de ⊜[1] C 4 86
Almendralejo F 4 86
Al'menevo I 25 108
Almería H 2 88
Almería □[6] G 2 88
Almería, Costa de ⊥[2] H 3 88
Almería, Golfo de ⊂ H 2 88
Al'metevsk I 19 108
Al-Mijlad E 2 202
Al-Miqdādīyah E 11 118
Almira B 4 178
Almirante Latorre A 2 195
Almodôvar G 2 86
Almodóvar del Campo F 6 86
Almonte, On., Can. A 2 164
Almonte, Spain G 4 86
Almora D 3 122
Al-Mubarraz J 13 118
Al-Mudawwarah H 7 118
Almudévar B 4 88
Al-Muḥarraq I 14 118
Al-Mukallā E 6 202
Al-Mukhā E 5 202
Almuñécar H 7 86
Almussafes E 4 88
Al-Muthanná □[3] G 11 118
Al-Muwaqqar ⊥ F 6 120
Al-Muwayliḥ I 6 118
Alnön I E 8 64
Alnwick B 5 72
Alofi, Île I E 10 136
Aloi G 3 202
Along D 6 122
Alónnisos C 5 106
Alor, Pulau I G 8 134
Alor Setar K 5 132
Alosno G 3 86
Aloysius, Mount ∧ I 10 140
Alpen E 3 98
Alpena, Ar., U.S. D 2 170
Alpena, Mi., U.S. A 2 162
Alpes-de-Haute-Provence □[3] F 4 82
Alpes-Maritimes □[3] G 5 82
Alpha B 3 170
Alpharetta B 2 168
Alphen aan den Rijn B 3 69
Alpine E 2 172
Alpine □[6] B 4 182
Alpine National Park ♦ F 6 144
Alps ⩕ F 10 62
Al-Qābil K 16 118
Al-Qaḍārif E 4 202
Al-Qādisīyah □[3] G 11 118
Al-Qalībah H 7 118
Al-Qāmishlī D 9 118
Al-Qaṭīf I 13 118
Al-Qaṭrūn D 7 198
Al-Qaws (Marble Arch) ⊥ C 8 198
Al-Qunayṭirah C 5 120
Al-Qunayṭirah □[3] C 5 120
Al-Qunfudhah D 5 202
Al-Qurnah G 12 118
Al-Quṭayfah B 7 120
Al-Quṭaynah E 3 202
Alroy Downs E 2 142
Als I C 2 68
Alsasua B 2 88
Alsdorf F 3 98
Alsek ≃ B 2 156
Alsen A 5 174
Alsfeld F 6 98
Alsunga D 10 66
Alta Gracia B 5 195
Altai Mountains ⩕ D 2 124
Altamaha ≃ D 4 168
Altamira D 8 190
Altamirano H 5 172
Altamont D 3 178
Altamura D 6 94
Altanbulag A 6 128
Altar ≃ G 3 176
Altar, Desierto de ◆[2] B 3 184
Altario F 16 156
Alta Vista F 6 174
Altay F 28 108
Altdorf, Ger. D 9 100
Altdorf, Switz. D 6 82
Altea F 4 88
Altena E 4 98
Altenberge D 4 98
Altenburg E 9 98
Altenesch C 5 98
Altenholz B 7 98
Altensteig D 5 100
Altentreptow C 10 98
Altevatnet ⊜ B 9 64
Altheimer E 3 170
Altınoluk C 7 106
Altiplano ⩕[1] G 5 190
Altkirch C 5 82
Altmark ◆[1] D 8 98
Alto Ligonha F 6 204
Alton, Eng., U.K. F 6 72
Alton, Ia., U.S. D 6 174
Alton, Il., U.S. C 3 170
Alton, Mo., U.S. D 3 170
Altona C 11 156
Altoona C 4 162
Alto Paraná □[3] F 3 194
Alto Parnaíba A 9 190
Alto Río Senguer I 5 192
Altötting D 7 96
Altstätten C 7 82
Altuhovo J 11 108
Altun Shan ⩕ C 14 116
Alturas E 3 178
Altus C 4 172
Al-'Ubaylah C 7 202
Al-Ubayyiḍ E 3 202
Al-Uḍayyah E 2 202
Aluk F 2 202
Alūksne D 13 66
Aluminé ≃ F 2 195
Aluminé, Lago ⊜ F 2 195
Al-'Uqaylah C 8 198
Al-'Urayq ◆[1] J 10 118
Alushta G 9 110
Al-'Uwaynāt D 7 198
Alva B 4 172
Älvängen C 6 66
Alvarado H 12 184
Álvaro Obregón, Presa ⊜[1] D 5 184
Alvdal A 5 66
Alverca F 1 86
Alvernia, Mount ∧[2] B 6 186
Alvesta D 7 66
Alvin F 6 172
Alvito F 3 86
Alvord D 5 172
Älvsborg □[3] C 6 66
Älvsbyn D 10 64
Al-Wakrah J 14 118
Alwar D 3 122
Al-Wusṭā □[3] E 3 202
Alxa Zuoqi G 5 128
Alyawarra Aboriginal Land ◆[4] F 2 142
Alytus E 12 66
Alzano Lombardo D 5 92
Alzey C 5 100
Alzira (Alcira) E 4 88
Amadeus, Lake ⊜ I 11 140
Amadjuak Lake ⊜ C 18 150
Amador □[6] B 3 182
Amahai F 9 134
Amajac ≃ G 10 184
Ama Keng i 14 134a
Amakuso-Shimo-shima I H 2 126
Amal D 9 198
Amalāpuram F 4 122
Amalfi, Col. B 3 190
Amalfi, Italy D 4 94
Amalia D 6 206
Amaliás D 4 106
Amalner E 2 122
Amambaí E 3 194
Amambay □[3] E 2 194
Amami-Ō-shima I J 2 126
Amami-shotō II K 2 126
Amán F 6 120
Amana B 3 170
Amaná, Lago ⊜ D 6 190
Amantea E 5 94
Amanu I[1] E 13 136
Amanzimtoti F 9 206
Amapá C 8 190
Amapá □[3] C 8 190
Amarapura D 3 132
Amarāvati ≃ G 3 122
Amareleja F 3 86
Amargosa ≃ E 5 180
Amargosa Range ⩕ D 7 182
Amarillo C 2 172
'Amar Jadīd E 2 202
Amarkantak E 4 122
Amasia B 10 118
Amasya B 6 118
Amasya □[3] B 6 118
Amatrice G 9 92
Amawbia Awka D 6 200
Amay D 4 69
Amazon (Amazonas) (Solimões) ≃ D 8 190
Amazonas □[3] D 6 190
Ambahikily I 8 205a
Ambāla C 3 122
Ambalavao I 9 205a
Ambam E 7 200
Ambanja j 9 205a
Ambarawa k 20 135b
Ambarčik C 19 114
Ambargasta, Salinas de ≚ A 5 195
Ambarnyj C 11 108
Ambaro, Helodrano ⊂ j 9 205a
Ambato D 3 190
Ambatolampy k 9 205a
Ambatondrazaka k 9 205a
Ambatosoratra k 9 205a
Ámbelos, Ákra > C 5 106
Amberg C 8 100
Ambérieu-en-Bugey E 3 82
Ambert E 1 82
Ambikāpur E 4 122
Ambilobe j 9 205a
Amble B 5 72
Ambler C 16 154
Ambohimitombo I 9 205a
Amboise E 8 78
Ambon F 9 134
Ambon, Pulau I F 9 134
Amboseli National Park ♦ H 4 202
Ambositra I 9 205a
Amboy B 4 170
Ambre, Cap d' see Bobaomby, Tanjona > j 9 205a
Ambrym I E 8 136
Ambuntentimur k 21 135b
Amchitka Island I I 41 155a
Amchitka Pass)(I 42 155a
Amded, Oued ≃ E 5 198
Amderma B 24 108
Ameca G 8 184
Amecameca de Juárez H 10 184
Amelia G 8 92
Āmer D 3 122
American ≃ B 2 182
Americana E 7 194
American Falls D 7 178
American Falls Reservoir ⊜[1] D 7 178
American Highland ⩕[1] D 16 208
Americanos, Barra de los I E 11 184
American Samoa □[2] E 10 136
Americus C 2 168
Amersfoort B 4 69
Amery C 11 158
Amery Ice Shelf ⊓ C 16 208
Ames E 2 166
Amesbury, Eng., U.K. F 5 72
Amesbury, Ma., U.S. D 8 164
Amfíklia C 5 106
Ámfissa C 5 106
Amga ≃ C 16 114
Amguema ≃ C 6 154
Amgun' ≃ B 11 124
Amherst, Ma., U.S. D 6 164
Amherst, N.S., Can. F 11 160
Amherst, N.Y., U.S. B 4 162
Amherst, Oh., U.S. C 2 162
Amherst, Va., U.S. E 4 162
Amherstburg G 2 160
Amianan Island I A 8 134
Amiata, Monte ∧[1] G 7 92
Amicalola Falls State Park ♦ B 2 168
Amidon B 3 174
Amiens C 9 78
Amilly E 9 78
Amīndīvi Islands II G 2 122
Aminuis B 3 206
Amirante Islands II J 7 112
Amisk E 16 156
Amisk Lake ⊜ D 7 158
Amistad, Presa de la see Amistad Reservoir ⊜[1] F 3 172
Amistad National Recreation Area ♦ F 3 172
Amistad Reservoir (Amistad, Presa de la) ⊜[1] F 3 172
Amiterno ⊥ G 9 92
Am Loubia C 9 200
Amlwch D 2 72
'Ammān F 5 120
Ammanford F 2 72
Ammarnäs C 8 64
Åmmeberg C 7 66
Ammeloe B 5 69
Ammerbuch D 5 100
Ammerland ◆[1] C 4 98
Ammochostos (Famagusta) E 5 118
Ammochostos Bay ⊂ E 6 118
Āmol D 15 118
Amorebieta A 2 88
Amory E 4 170
Amos D 4 160
Åmot C 4 66
Ampanihy I 8 205a
Ampasindava, Helodrano ⊂ j 9 205a
Amper D 6 200
Amposta D 5 88
Ampoza I 8 205a
Amraoti see Amrāvati E 3 122
Amrāvati E 3 122
Amriswil C 7 82
Amritsar C 2 122
Amsel E 6 198
Amstelveen B 3 69
Amsterdam, Neth. B 3 69
Amsterdam, N.Y., U.S. D 4 164
Amsterdam, S. Afr. D 9 206
Amstetten B 6 102
Am Timan C 9 200
Amu Darya ≃ B 9 116
Amukta Pass)(J 8 154
Amundsen Bay ⊂ C 13 208
Amundsen Gulf ⊂ B 8 150
Amundsen-Scott ⊛[3] E 13 208
Amundsen Sea ⊤[2] D 3 208
Amungen ⊜ B 7 66
Amuntai F 7 134
Amur (Heilong) ≃ B 9 124
Amuria G 3 202
Amurrio A 7 86
Amurskaja oblast' □[6] A 17 128
Amvrakikós Kólpos ⊂ C 4 106
Amwom, Khawr ≃ F 3 202
Amzi, Oued ti-n- ≃ E 6 198
Anaa I[1] E 13 136
Anabar ≃ B 14 114
'Anabtā E 4 120
Anaco F 8 186
Anaconda B 7 178
Anaconda Range ⩕ C 7 178
Anacortes G 10 156
Anadarko C 4 172
Anadyr' C 20 114
Anadyr' ≃ C 20 114
Anadyrskij zaliv ⊂ C 21 114
Anadyrskoe ploskogor'e ⩕[1] C 19 114
Anagni H 9 92
'Ānah E 9 118
Anaheim G 6 182
Anáhuac D 9 184
Ānai Mudi ∧ G 3 122
Anakāpalle F 4 122
Anaklia H 12 110
Anaktuvuk ≃ B 19 154
Analalava j 9 205a
Analavoka I 9 205a
Ana María, Golfo de ⊂ C 5 186
Anambas, Kepulauan II M 7 132
Anamosa D 3 166
Anamur D 5 118
Anamur Burnu > E 5 118
Anan H 5 126
Ānand E 2 122
Anangu Pitjantjatjaraku Aboriginal Land ◆[4] J 11 140
Anantapur G 3 122
Anantnāg C 3 122
Anan'yiv B 10 104
Anapa G 10 110
Anápolis B 6 194
Anapu ≃ D 8 190
Anastácio D 3 194
Anatahan I I 13 124
Anatolikí Makedhonía kaí Thráki □[3] B 6 106
Anatom I F 8 136
Añatuya E 7 192
Anbanjing G 5 130
Anbyŏn-ŭp G 16 128
Ancaster B 3 162
Anchau C 6 200
Anchorage F 20 154
Anchuras E 6 86
Ancona F 9 92
Ancona □[6] F 9 92
Ancud H 5 192
Ancud, Golfo de ⊂ H 5 192
Ancy-le-Franc E 11 78
Anda C 15 128
Åndalsnes E 3 64
Andalucía □[3] D 3 84
Andalusia G 5 170
Andaman and Nicobar Islands □[3] H 6 122
Andaman Islands II G 6 122
Andaman Sea ⊤[2] I 2 132
Andara F 3 204
Andechs, Kloster ⊛[1] E 8 100
Andenes B 7 64
Andenne D 4 69
Anderlecht D 3 69
Anderlues D 3 69
Andernach B 4 100
Anderson, Ak., U.S. D 20 154
Anderson, In., U.S. B 6 170
Anderson, S.C., U.S. B 3 168
Anderson ≃ B 30 154
Andersonville National Historic Site ♦ C 2 168
Anderstorp D 6 66
Andes ⩕ G 8 188
Andfjorden ⊻ B 8 64
Andhra Pradesh □[3] F 3 122
Andilamena k 9 205a
Andīmeshk F 12 118
Andizhan A 2 122
Andizhan □[6] A 2 122
Andkhvoy C 9 116
Andoain A 2 88
Andoany j 9 205a
Andomskij Pogost F 12 108
Andong H 17 128
Andorra, And. B 6 88
Andorra, Spain D 4 88
Andorra □[1] G 8 62
Andorra-la-Vella see Andorra B 6 88
Andover, Eng., U.K. F 5 72
Andover, Me., U.S. B 8 164
Andover, Oh., U.S. C 3 162
Andøya I B 7 64
Andradina D 5 194
Andranopasy I 8 205a
Andreanof Islands II k 43 155a
Andreapol' H 9 108
André Félix, Parc National ♦ D 9 200
Andrews D 2 172
Andria C 6 94
Andriamena k 9 205a
Andriba k 9 205a
Andriyevo-Ivanivka B 11 104
Andrijušino G 25 108
Ándros D 6 106
Ándros I, Bah. B 5 186
Ándros I, Grc. D 6 106
Āndrott Island I H 11 116
Andrupene D 13 66
Andrychów D 10 96
Andújar F 6 86
Aneby D 7 66
Aneeva E 25 108
Anegada, Bahía ⊂ G 6 195
Anegada Passage ⊻ D 9 186
Anèho D 5 200
Anenii Noi B 10 104
Aneta H 10 158
Aneto ∧ B 5 88
Aney B 7 200
Anfu E 12 130
Angamos, Punta > D 5 192
Ang'angxi C 14 128
Angara ≃ D 12 114
Angarapa Aboriginal Land ◆[4] G 2 142
Angarsk B 4 124
Ángel, Salto (Angel Falls) ⌞ B 6 190
Ángel de la Guarda, Isla I C 3 184
Angeles B 8 134
Ängelholm D 6 66
Angelina ≃ G 1 170
Angeln ◆[1] B 6 98
Angels Camp B 3 182
Ångermanälven ≃ D 8 64
Angermünde C 10 98
Angers E 6 78
Angikuni Lake ⊜ D 13 150
Angkor Wat ⊥ H 6 132
Ângk Tasaôm I 7 132
Angle Inlet A 7 174
Anglesey □[6] D 2 72
Anglesey I D 2 72
Anglet E 2 80
Angleton F 6 172
Anglona ◆[1] I 4 92
Angmagssalik C 25 150
Angoche F 6 204
Angoche, Ilha I F 7 204
Angol E 1 195
Angola B 4 162
Angola □[1] J 9 196
Angola Basin ✦[1] G 11 60
Angora see Ankara B 5 118
Angoram M 12 124
Angostura, Presa de la ⊜[1] J 13 184
Angoulême C 4 80
Angoumois □[9] C 3 80
Angra do Heroísmo h 12 198a
Angren A 2 122
Angu B 3 204
Anguang D 14 128
Anguilla F 3 170
Anguilla □[2] D 9 186
Anguo G 10 128
Angus A 3 162
Angus □[6] D 6 74
Anhalt □[9] E 8 98
Anhua D 10 130
Anhui □[3] B 13 130
Aniak F 15 154
Aniakchak National Monument ♦ H 16 154
Aniche B 10 78
Anina C 6 104
Añisoc E 7 200
Aniva, mys > C 12 124
Aniva, zaliv ⊂ C 12 124
Anjan E 6 64
Anjār E 2 122
Anjiabe j 9 205a
Anjou □[9] E 6 78
Anjujskij hrebet ⩕ C 19 114
Anju-ŭp G 15 128
Anka C 6 200
Ankaboa, Tanjona > I 8 205a
Ankang B 9 130
Ankara B 5 118
Ankara □[3] B 5 118
Ankarsrum D 8 66
Ankeny B 2 170
Ankilimivony I 8 205a
Anklam C 10 98
Ankpa D 6 200
Anloga D 5 200
Anlong F 7 130
Anlu C 11 130
Ann, Cape > C 14 208
Ann, Cape >[1] D 8 164
Anna, Il., U.S. D 4 170
Anna, Russia D 12 110
Anna, Lake ⊜[1] D 5 162
Annaba B 6 198
Annaba □[3] G 1 90
An-Nabaṭīyah □[3] C 5 120
An-Nabaṭīyah at-Taḥtā C 5 120
Annaberg-Buchholz B 10 100
An-Nabk E 7 118
Annadale B 8 206
An-Nafūd ◆[2] H 9 118
An-Najaf G 10 118
An-Najaf □[3] G 10 118
Annam □[9] F 8 132
Annamitique, Chaîne ⩕ F 8 132
Annan C 3 72
Annapolis H 2 164
Annapolis Royal F 11 160
Annapūrṇa ∧ D 4 122
Ann Arbor B 1 162
An-Nāṣirīyah G 12 118
Annean, Lake ⊜ J 5 140
Anne Arundel □[6] H 2 164
Annecy E 4 82
Annecy, Lac d' ⊜ E 4 82
Annemasse D 4 82
Annenkov Island I q 21 193c
Annenskoe J 23 108
Annette D 6 156
Annette Island I I 29 154
Annezin B 9 78
Anning F 6 130
Anniston F 6 170
Annobón (Pagalu) I F 6 200
Annonay E 2 82
Annotto Bay h 13 186a
An-Nuhūd E 2 202
Anoka C 2 166
Anori D 6 190
Anorontany, Tanjona > j 9 205a
Anpu H 9 130
Anqing C 13 130
Anqiu H 12 128
Anren E 11 130
Ans B 2 100
Ansbach C 7 100
Anseba ≃ D 4 202
Anselmo E 4 174
Anshan F 14 128
Anshun E 7 130
Ansley E 5 174
Ansoáin B 3 88
Anson Bay ⊂ C 10 140
Ansongo B 5 200
Ansonia E 5 164
Antakya see Hatay D 7 118
Antalaha j 9 205a
Antalieptė E 12 66
Antalya D 9 106
Antalya □[3] D 4 118
Antalya, Gulf of ⊂ D 4 118
Antanambao-Manampotsy k 9 205a
Antananarivo k 9 205a
Antananarivo □[3] k 9 205a
Antanetibe k 9 205a
Antanimora I 9 205a
Antarctica ⊥[1] E 12 208
Antarctic Peninsula >[1] C 3 208
Antártida e Islas del Atlántico Sur, Tierra del Fuego □[3] J 6 192
Antelope Island I E 7 178
Antequera G 6 86
Antetikireja j 9 205a
Anthony F 5 176
Anti-Atlas ⩕ D 3 198
Antibes G 5 82
Anticosti, Île d' I D 12 160
Antietam National Battlefield ♦ D 5 162
Antigo C 4 166
Antigonish F 13 160
Antigua I I 18 187c
Antigua and Barbuda □[1] D 9 186
Anti-Lebanon ⩕ B 6 120
Antioch, Ca., U.S. B 2 182
Antioch see Hatay, Tur. D 7 118
Antioquia □[3] G 6 186
Antipino H 27 108
Antipodes Islands II J 13 58
Antofagasta D 5 192
Antofalla, Salar de ≚ E 6 192
Anton D 2 172
Antongila, Helodrano ⊂ k 9 205a
Antonina E 10 192
Antonio Amaro E 8 184
Antonito D 5 176
Antony D 9 78
Antrain D 5 78
Antrim □[8] B 5 75
Antrodoco G 9 92
Antsaidoha-Bebao k 8 205a
Antsiafabositra k 9 205a
Antsirabe k 9 205a
Antsirabe Avaratra j 9 205a
Antsirañana j 9 205a
Antsirañana □[3] j 9 205a
Anttis C 11 64
Antwerp see Antwerpen C 3 69
Antwerpen (Antwerp) C 3 69
Antwerpen □[3] C 3 69
Anugul E 4 122
Anula I E 8 136
Anuradhapura H 4 122
Anvers see Antwerpen C 3 69
Anvik E 14 154
Anxi, China A 7 122
Anxi, China F 14 130
Anxian C 7 130
Anxiang D 11 130
Anxious Bay ⊂ L 2 142
Anyama D 4 200
Anyang, China H 10 128
Anyang, S. Kor. H 16 128
A'nyêmaqên Shan ⩕ E 3 124
Anyer Kidul k 17 135b
Anykščiai E 12 66
Anyuan F 12 130
Anyue C 7 130
Anza-Borrego Desert State Park ♦ F 5 180
Anze H 9 128
Anžero-Sudžensk D 11 114
Anzin B 10 78
Anzio H 8 92
Anzoátegui □[3] F 8 186
Anzob B 1 122
Aoga-shima I H 7 126
Aohan Qi E 12 128
Aoiz B 3 88
Aojiang E 15 130
Aoji-ri E 18 128
Aomen see Macau G 11 130
Aomen see Macau □[2] G 11 130
Aomori D 8 126
Aomori □[3] D 8 126
Aóös (Vjosës) ≃ C 4 106
Aôral, Phnum ∧ I 7 132
Aosta D 3 92
Aosta □[6] D 3 92
Aoudaghost ⊥ F 2 198
Aouk, Bahr ≃ D 8 200
Aoukâr ◆[1] F 3 198
Aourou B 2 200
Aozou A 8 200
Apa ≃ E 2 194
Apache Junction F 3 176
Apachita Crevice ◆ G 4 190
Apalachicola E 2 168
Apalachicola ≃ E 2 168
Apaporis ≃ D 5 190
Aparri B 8 134
Apartadó G 5 186
Apatin C 5 104
Apatity C 10 108
Apatzingán de la Constitución H 8 184
Apeldoorn B 4 69
Apen C 4 98
Apennines see Appennino ⩕ D 3 90
Apex B 5 168
Api ∧ C 4 122
Apia j 11 147b
Apiacás, Serra dos ⩕[1] E 7 190
Apiaí F 6 194
Apiti C 5 146
Apizaco H 10 184
Apo, Mount ∧ D 9 134
Apolda E 8 98
Apolo F 5 190
Aporé ≃ C 5 194
Apostle Islands II B 3 166
Apostle Islands National Lakeshore ♦ B 3 166
Apóstoles E 8 192
Apostolos Andreas, Cape > E 6 118
Appalachian Mountains ⩕ C 12 152
Appen C 6 98
Appennino (Apennines) ⩕ D 3 90
Appenzell C 7 82
Appenzell Ausser-Rhoden □[3] C 7 82
Appenzell Inner-Rhoden □[3] C 7 82
Appingedam A 5 69
Appleby D 5 206
Appleton, Mn., U.S. C 6 174
Appleton, Wi., U.S. C 4 166
Apple Valley F 6 182
Appomattox E 4 162
Appomattox Court House National Historical Park ♦ E 4 162
Aprelevka I 12 108
Apricena C 5 94
Aprilia H 8 92
Apšeronsk G 11 110
Apt G 3 82
Apucarana E 5 194
Apure □[3] G 7 186
Apure ≃ B 5 190
Apurímac ≃ F 4 190
Aqaba, Gulf of ⊂ H 6 118
'Aqīq, Khalīj ⊂ D 4 202
Aq Qal'eh D 16 118
Aqtöbe (Aktjubinsk) D 20 110
Aquidauana D 2 194
Aquila H 8 184
Ara D 4 122
'Arab, Baḥr al- ≃ F 2 202
'Arab, Khalîg el- ⊂ G 3 118
'Arab, Shaṭṭ al- see Shatt al-Arab ≃ G 12 118
'Arabah, Wādī al- (Ha'Arava) V H 4 120
Arabian Basin ✦[1] F 6 58
Arabian Peninsula >[1] G 6 116
Arabian Sea ⊤[2] H 8 112
Araçá ≃ C 6 190
Aracaju F 11 190
Aracati D 11 190
Araçatuba D 5 194
Aracena G 4 86
Aracruz C 10 194
Araçuaí B 9 194
'Arad, Isr. G 4 120
Arad, Rom. B 6 104
Arad □[3] B 6 104
Arada B 9 200
Arafura Sea ⊤[2] N 10 124
Aragarças A 4 194
Aragats Lerr ∧ I 13 110
Aragon B 2 168
Aragón □[3] C 4 88
Aragón ≃ B 4 88
Aragua □[3] F 8 186
Araguacema A 9 190
Aragua de Barcelona B 6 190
Araguaia ≃ E 9 190
Araguari C 6 194
Araguari ≃, Braz. C 8 190
Araguari ≃, Braz. C 7 194
Araguatins A 9 190
Arahal G 5 86
Ârak, Alg. D 5 198
Arāk, Iran E 13 118
Arakan Yoma (Arakan Range) ⩕ E 2 132
Arákhova C 5 106
Araks see Aras, Rūd-e ≃ C 12 118
Aral see Aral'sk A 9 116
Aral Sea ⊤[2] A 8 116
Aral'sk (Aral) A 9 116
Aralsor, ozero ⊜ E 18 110
Ārān E 14 118
Aranda de Duero C 7 86
Aranđelovac C 6 104
Aran Islands II C 2 75
Aranjuez D 7 86
Aranos C 3 206
Aranyaprathet H 6 132
Arao H 3 126
Arapahoe E 5 174
Arapaho National Recreation Area ♦ B 5 176
Arapiraca E 11 190
Arapkir C 8 118
Arapongas E 5 194
Arapoti F 5 194
Ar'ar G 9 118
Araranguá E 10 192
Araraquara D 6 194
Araras E 7 194
Ararat, Arm. J 14 110
Ararat, Austl. F 4 144
Ararat, Mount ∧ C 10 118
Araruama, Lagoa de ⊂ E 9 194
Aras, Rūd-e (Aras) (Araz) ≃ C 12 118
Ar-Asgat B 5 128
Áratos B 6 106
Arauca G 7 186
Arauca ≃ B 5 190
Araucária F 6 194
Arauco, Bahía de ⊂ E 1 195
Arāvalli Range ⩕ E 2 122
Araxá C 7 194
Araz see Aras, Rūd-e ≃ C 12 118
Ārba F 5 202
Ārba Minch' F 4 202
Arboga C 7 66
Arbois D 3 82
Arbon C 7 82
Arborea ◆[1] I 9 94a
Arborg F 10 158
Arbroath D 6 74
Arbuckle A 1 182
Arcachon D 2 80
Arcade B 2 182
Arcadia, Ca., U.S. F 6 182
Arcadia, La., U.S. F 2 170
Arcadia, Mi., U.S. C 5 166
Arcadia, S.C., U.S. B 3 168
Arcata E 1 178
Arce C 3 94
Arcelia H 9 184
Archangel see Arhangel'sk D 13 108
Archena F 3 88
Archer E 3 168
Archer ≃ B 5 142
Archer Bay ⊂ B 5 142
Archer Bend National Park ♦ B 6 142
Arches National Park ♦ C 4 176
Archiac C 3 80
Archidona G 6 86
Arcisate D 4 92
Arcis-sur-Aube D 11 78
Arco D 6 92
Arcola F 3 170
Arcos D 8 194
Arcos de la Frontera H 5 86
Arcoverde E 11 190
Arctic Bay B 15 150
Arctic Ocean ⊤[1] D 3 61
Arctic Red ≃ C 28 154
Arctic Red River see Tsiigehtchic C 28 154
Arctowski ⊛[3] L 8 192
Ardabīl C 13 118
Ardahan B 10 118
Ardakān F 15 118
Årdalstangen B 3 66
Ardèche □[3] F 2 82
Ardee C 5 75
Arden C 3 180
Ardenne ◆[1] D 4 69
Ardennes □[3] D 6 76
Ardestān F 15 118
Ardila ≃ F 3 86
Ardill G 19 156
Ardlethan E 6 144
Ardmore, Ok., U.S. C 5 172
Ardmore, Pa., U.S. F 3 164
Ardnamurchan >[1] D 3 74
Ardoch I 7 142
Ardrossan B 2 72
Arecibo j 15 187b
Arecibo, Observatorio de ⊛[3] j 15 187b
Areguá F 2 194
Areia ≃ A 8 194
Areia Branca D 11 190
Arena, Point > C 2 180
Arena, Punta > F 5 184
Arenas de San Pedro D 5 86
Arendal C 4 66
Arendonk C 4 69
Arenys de Mar C 7 88
Arenzano E 4 92
Arequipa G 4 190
Arévalo C 6 86
Arezzo F 7 92
Arezzo □[6] F 7 92
Argajaš I 24 108
Argamasilla de Alba E 1 88
Argamasilla de Calatrava F 6 86
Arganda del Rey D 7 86
Argedeb F 5 202
Argelès-sur-Mer F 7 80
Argent, Côte d' ⊥[2] E 2 80
Argenta E 7 92
Argentan D 6 78
Argentat C 5 80
Argenteuil G 8 70
Argenteuil □[6] A 4 164
Argentia E 17 160
Argentina □[1] F 7 192
Argentine Basin ✦[1] I 7 60
Argentino, Lago ⊜ J 5 192
Argenton-sur-Creuse B 5 80
Argeș □[3] C 8 104
Argeș ≃ C 8 104
Arghandāb ≃ D 10 116
Argo D 3 202
Argolikós Kólpos ⊂ D 5 106
Argonne C 4 166
Argonne ◆[1] A 3 82
Árgos D 5 106
Árgos Orestikón B 4 106
Argostólion C 4 106
Argun H 14 110
Argun' (Ergun) ≃ B 7 124
Argungu C 5 200
Argyle, Lake ⊜ E 10 140
Argyll and Bute □[6] B 1 72
Arhangay □[3] B 3 128
Arhangel'sk (Archangel) D 13 108
Arhangel'skaja oblast' □[6] D 16 108
Arhara B 18 128
Arhara ≃ B 18 128
Arhéa Epídavros ⊥ D 5 106
Arhipo-Osipovka G 10 110
Arhipovo C 16 108
Århus B 3 68
Århus □[3] B 2 68
Ariana G 3 90
Ariana □[3] G 2 90
Ariano Irpino C 5 94
Aribinda C 4 200
Arica C 5 192
Ariccia H 8 92
Arid, Cape > N 7 140
Ariège □[3] E 5 80
Arīḥā (Jericho) F 4 120
Arima q 23 187f
Arinos ≃ F 7 190
Arinthod D 3 82
Ario de Rosales H 9 184
Ariogala E 11 66
Aripuanã ≃ E 6 190
Ariquemes E 6 190
Arish, Wadi el- ≃ G 5 118
Ariton G 6 170
Arizaro, Salar de ≚ D 6 192
Arizgoiti A 2 88
Arizona G 6 192
Arizona □[3] E 5 152
Arja H 17 108
Arjasa k 22 135b
Arjeplog C 9 64
Arjona, Col. F 6 186
Arjona, Spain G 6 86
Arkadak D 13 110
Arkadelphia E 2 170
Arkalyk E 21 62
Arkansas □[3] E 9 152
Arkansas ≃ D 9 152

Symbols in the index entries represent the broad categories identified in the key at the right. Symbols with superior numbers (⩕[1]) identify subcategories (see complete key on page 242).

∧ Mountain ⩕ Mountains)(Pass V Valley ≚ Plain > Cape I Island II Islands ⊥ Other Topographic Feature ≃ River ≡ Canal

Name	Map Ref.	Page
Arkansas City	G 6	174
Arkansas Post National Memorial ♦	F 3	170
Arklow	D 5	75
Arkoma	E 1	170
Arkona, Kap ⊁	B 10	98
Arkul'	H 19	108
Arlbergpass)(	C 2	102
Arles	G 2	82
Arli	C 5	200
Arlington, Ky., U.S.	D 4	170
Arlington, Ma., U.S.	D 7	164
Arlington, S. Afr.	D 8	206
Arlington, S.D., U.S.	C 6	174
Arlington, Tn., U.S.	E 4	170
Arlington, Tx., U.S.	D 5	172
Arlington, Va., U.S.	D 5	162
Arlington □⁶	H 1	164
Arlington Heights	A 5	170
Arlit	B 6	200
Arlon	E 4	69
Arluno	D 4	92
Arma	D 1	170
Armadale	M 3	140
Armageddon see Tel Megiddo ⊥	D 4	120
Armagh	B 5	75
Armagh □⁸	B 5	75
Armagnac □⁹	E 4	80
Armançon ≃	E 11	78
Armant	J 5	118
Armavir	G 12	110
Armenia	C 3	190
Armenia □¹	G 16	62
Armeniş	C 7	104
Armentières	B 9	78
Armidale	C 8	144
Armilla	G 7	86
Armizonskoe	H 28	108
Armstrong, Ia., U.S.	D 7	174
Armstrong, On., Can.	F 14	158
Armstrong, Mount ⋀	E 27	154
Armyans'k	F 8	110
Arnarfjördur c	m 18	64a
Arnaudville	G 3	170
Arnedo	B 2	88
Årnes	B 5	66
Arnhem	C 4	69
Arnhem, Cape ⊁	B 3	142
Arnhem Bay c	B 3	142
Arnhem Land →¹	B 7	138
Arnhem Land Aboriginal Land →⁴	B 2	142
Árnissa	B 4	106
Arno I ¹	C 9	136
Arno ≃	F 6	92
Arno Bay	L 3	142
Arnold, Eng., U.K.	D 5	72
Arnold, Mn., U.S.	H 12	158
Arnold, Mo., U.S.	C 3	170
Arnprior	F 5	160
Arnsberg	E 4	98
Arnsberg □⁶	E 4	98
Arnsdorf	E 10	98
Arnstadt	F 7	98
Aroab	D 3	206
Aroland	F 15	158
Arolsen	E 5	98
Aromaševo	H 28	108
Arona	D 4	92
Aroostook ≃	g 12	163a
Arop Island I	M 13	124
Arorae I	D 9	136
Arp	F 1	170
Arquata Scrivia	E 4	92
Arques	B 9	78
Arrah	D 4	200
Ar-Rahad	E 3	202
Arraias	F 9	190
Ar-Ramādī	F 10	118
Ar-Ramthā	D 6	120
Ar-Rank	E 3	202
Ar-Raqqah	D 8	118
Arras	B 9	78
Arras, Nuraghe ⊥	B 5	94
Arrasate o Mondragón	A 2	88
Ar-Rawdah	I 9	118
Ar-Rayyān	J 14	118
Arrecife	i 17	85b
Arrecifes	D 7	195
Arriaga	I 12	184
Arrigorriaga	A 2	88
Ar-Riyāḍ (Riyadh)	J 12	118
Arroio Grande	C 11	195
Arronches	E 3	86
Arros ≃	E 4	80
Arroyito	k 15	187b
Arroyo de la Luz	E 4	86
Arroyo Grande	E 3	182
Arroyo Hondo	C 2	184
Ar-Rub' al-Khālī (Empty Quarter) →²	G 6	116
Ar-Ruqayyah	D 8	120
Ar-Rusayfah	E 6	120
Ar-Rusayris	E 3	202
Ar-Rutbah	F 8	118
Arsanjān	H 15	118
Arsenault Lake ⊜	D 17	156
Arsenev	B 4	126
Arsenevka ≃	B 4	126
Ars-en-Ré	B 2	80
Ārsī □³	F 4	202
Arsk	H 18	108
Ars-sur-Moselle	A 3	82
Árta, Grc.	C 4	106
Artà, Spain	E 8	88
Artashat	J 14	110
Arteaga	H 8	184
Art'em	C 4	126
Artemisa	C 4	186
Art'emovskij	H 24	108
Artern	E 8	98
Artesia	D 7	172
Artesian	C 6	174
Arthabaska □⁶	A 7	164
Arthur	H 10	158
Arthur's Lake ⊜¹	i 12	145a
Arthur's Pass)(	E 3	146
Arthur's Pass National Park ♦	E 3	146
Arthur Stone ⊥	C 9	206
Arthur's Town	B 5	186
Artigas	B 9	195
Artigas 〕³	L 8	192
Artik	I 13	110
Artillery Lake ⊜	D 11	150
Artois □⁹	B 9	78
Artsyz	B 10	104
Artvin	B 10	118
Artvin □³	B 10	118
Artyom	I 17	110
Aru, Kepulauan II	G 10	134
A Rúa, Spain	B 3	86
Arua, Ug.	G 3	202
Aruanã	F 8	190
Aruba □²	E 7	186
Arucas	i 15	85b
Arufu	D 6	200
Arunáchal Pradesh □³	D 6	122

Arun Qi	B 14	128
Aruppukkottai	H 3	122
Arusha	C 6	204
Arusha □³	C 6	204
Arusha National Park ♦	C 6	204
Aruvi ≃	H 4	122
Aruwimi ≃	B 3	204
Arvada	F 2	174
Arviat	D 14	150
Arvidsjaur	D 9	64
Arvika	C 6	66
Arvon, Mount ⋀	B 4	166
Arvonia	E 4	162
Arxan	C 13	128
Arys'	A 1	122
Arzamas	I 15	108
Arzew see Arziw	B 4	198
Arzgir	G 14	110
Arzignano	D 7	92
Arziw (Arzew)	B 4	198
Ås	C 5	66
Aša	I 22	108
Asaba	D 6	200
Asadābād	E 12	118
Asahan ≃	M 4	132
Asahi-dake ⋀¹	C 9	126
Asahikawa	C 8	126
Asale ≃	E 4	202
Asamankese	D 4	200
Asankranguaa	D 4	200
Asan-man c	H 16	128
Āsānsol	E 5	122
Åsarna	E 7	64
Asbest	H 24	108
Asbestos	F 8	160
Asbestos □⁶	A 7	164
Asbestos Range National Park ♦	i 12	145a
Asbury Park	F 5	164
Ascensión	B 6	184
Ascension I	I 6	196
Aschaffenburg	C 6	100
Ascheberg	E 4	98
Aschendorf	C 4	98
Aschersleben	E 8	98
Ascó	E 4	88
Ascoli Piceno	B 3	94
Ascoli Piceno □⁶	B 3	94
Ascoli Satriano	C 5	94
Ascona	D 6	82
Aseb	E 5	202
Āsela	F 4	202
Åsele	D 8	64
Asenovgrad	D 8	104
Aseri	C 13	66
Asfûn el-Matâ'na	J 5	118
Ashbourne	D 5	72
Ashburton	E 3	146
Ashburton ≃	H 3	140
Ashburton Downs	D 4	140
Ashby-de-la-Zouch	E 5	72
Ashdod	F 3	120
Ashdod, Tel ⊥	F 3	120
Asheboro	B 5	168
Asherton	F 4	172
Asheville	B 3	168
Asheweig ≃	D 15	158
Ashford, Al., U.S.	G 6	170
Ashford, Eng., U.K.	F 7	72
Ash Fork	I 5	178
Ashgabat	J 21	110
Ashibetsu	C 9	126
Ashikaga	F 7	126
Ashington	B 5	72
Ashland, Ks., U.S.	G 5	174
Ashland, Ky., U.S.	D 2	162
Ashland, Me., U.S.	g 12	163a
Ashland, Mo., U.S.	C 2	170
Ashland, Mt., U.S.	C 10	178
Ashland, Oh., U.S.	C 2	162
Ashland, Or., U.S.	D 3	178
Ashland, Wi., U.S.	B 3	166
Ashley, Austl.	B 7	144
Ashley, N.D., U.S.	B 5	174
Ashoknagar	E 3	122
Ashqelon	F 3	120
Ash-Shamālīyah □³	C 2	202
Ash-Shāmīyah	G 11	118
Ash-Sharāh →¹	I 5	120
Ash-Shāriqah	J 16	118
Ash-Sharqāt	E 10	118
Ash-Sharqīyah □³	D 4	202
Ash-Sharqīyah →¹	I 13	118
Ash-Shatrah	G 12	118
Ash-Shihr	E 6	202
Ash-Shināfīyah	G 11	118
Ashtabula	C 3	162
Ashtead	F 6	72
Ashton, Ia., U.S.	D 7	174
Ashton, S. Afr.	G 4	206
Ashton-under-Lyne	D 4	72
Ashuanipi Lake ⊜	B 11	160
Ashville	D 4	118
Ashwaubenon	C 4	166
'Āsī ≃	E 7	118
Asia, Kepulauan II	E 10	134
Asia Minor □⁹	H 14	62
Asilah	B 3	198
Asinara, Golfo dell' c	I 4	92
Asino	D 11	114
Asipovičy	F 14	66
'Asīr →¹	D 5	202
Aşkale	C 21	110
Askham	G 4	206
Askja ⋀¹	m 22	64a
Askvoll	B 2	66
Asmara	D 4	202
Asmera see Asmara	D 4	202
Ašmjany	E 12	66
Åsnæs	D 7	66
Åsnen ⊜	D 6	92
Asola	E 3	202
Asosa	D 5	198
Asouf, Oued ≃	F 4	198
Asp	C 5	176
Aspendos ⊥	D 9	106
Aspiring, Mount ⋀	B 5	166
As Pontes de García Rodríguez	A 3	86
Aspres-sur-Buëch	F 3	82
Aspromonte, Parco Nazionale dell' ♦	F 6	94
Assa	D 3	198
Assab see Aseb	E 5	202
Assaba □³	F 2	198
Assad, Lake ⊜¹	D 8	118
As-Salţ	E 5	120
Assam □³	D 7	122
As-Samāwah	G 11	118
Assateague Island I	D 6	162
Assateague Island National Seashore ♦	D 6	162
Asse	D 3	69
Assemini	J 4	92
Assen	A 5	69

Assenede	C 2	69
Assens	C 2	68
Asseria ⊥	C 3	104
As-Sīb	F 8	116
Assini ⊥	D 5	106
Assiniboine ≃	G 9	158
Assiniboine, Mount ⋀	F 13	156
Assiniboine Indian Reserve →⁴	F 7	158
Assinica, Lac ⊜	C 6	160
Assis	E 5	194
Assis Chateaubriand	F 4	194
Assisi	A 2	104
Asslar	B 5	100
As-Sulaymānīyah, Iraq	E 11	118
As-Sulaymānīyah, Sau. Ar.	C 6	202
As-Sulaymānīyah □³	E 11	118
As-Sulayyil	C 6	202
As-Summān →¹	I 12	118
Assumption	C 4	170
As-Suwaydā'	D 7	120
As-Suwaydā' □³	D 7	120
Astakós	C 4	106
Āstāneh	D 14	118
Āstārā	C 13	118
Asten	E 4	98
Asti	E 4	92
Asti □⁶	E 4	92
Astillero	A 7	86
Astorga, Braz.	E 5	194
Astorga, Spain	B 4	86
Astoria, Il., U.S.	B 3	170
Astoria, Or., U.S.	B 2	178
Åstorp	D 6	66
Astrachanskaja oblast' □⁶	F 15	110
Astrahan (Astrakhan)	F 16	110
Astravec	E 12	66
Astudillo	B 6	86
Astura, Torre ⊥	H 8	92
Asturias □³	A 4	86
Asunción	F 2	194
Asunción Island I	I 13	124
Åsunden ⊜	D 7	66
Asveja ⊜	D 14	66
Aswān	C 3	202
Aswan High Dam see Aali, Sadd el- →⁶	C 3	202
Asyūt	I 4	118
Aszód	B 5	104
Ata I	F 10	136
Atacama □³	C 3	192
Atacama, Desierto de →²	D 6	192
Atacama, Puna de ⋌¹	D 6	192
Atacama, Salar de ≃	D 6	192
Atafu I ¹	D 10	136
Atakpamé	D 5	200
Atalándi	C 5	106
Atami	G 7	126
Atar	E 2	198
Atascadero	E 3	182
Atasu	A 11	114
Atatürk Baraji ⊜¹	D 8	118
Atauro, Pulau I	G 9	134
Atbara see 'Atbarah ≃	D 3	202
'Atbarah ≃	D 3	202
'Atbarah □³	D 3	202
Atbasar	E 21	62
Atchafalaya ≃	G 3	170
Atchafalaya Bay c	H 3	170
Atchison	C 1	170
Atebubu	D 4	200
Aterno ≃	B 3	94
Ath	D 2	69
Athabasca	D 15	156
Athabasca ≃	C 16	156
Athabasca, Lake ⊜	B 17	156
Athapapuskow Lake ⊜	D 7	158
Athena	C 4	178
Athens, Al., U.S.	E 5	170
Athens, Ga., U.S.	B 3	168
Athens (Athínai), Grc. see Athínai	D 5	106
Athens, Mi., U.S.	D 6	166
Athens, N.Y., U.S.	D 7	162
Athens, Oh., U.S.	D 2	162
Athens, Tn., U.S.	D 2	168
Athens, Tx., U.S.	D 6	172
Atherton	D 7	142
Athi ≃	H 4	202
Athínai (Athens)	D 5	106
Athi River	H 4	202
Athol	E 2	146
Áthos (Athos, Mount) ⋀	B 6	106
Athos, Mount see Áthos ⋀	B 6	106
Athus	E 4	69
Ati	E 4	75
Atienza	C 2	88
Atikaki Provincial Wilderness Park ♦	F 11	158
Atik Lake ⊜	D 10	158
Atikokan	G 13	158
Atikonak Lake ⊜	B 11	160
Atiu I	F 12	136
Atkarsk	D 14	110
Atkins	E 2	170
Atkinson	D 5	174
Atlanta, Ga., U.S.	C 2	168
Atlanta, Tx., U.S.	F 1	170
Atlantic	J 2	174
Atlantic □⁶	G 4	164
Atlantic City	F 4	164
Atlantic-Indian Basin →¹	K 4	58
Atlantic Ocean ▾¹	F 6	58
Atlántida □³	G 3	186
Atlas, Rias ±²	A 2	86
Atlas Mountains ⋌	C 4	198
Atlas Saharien ⋌	C 5	198
Atlas Tellien (Maritime Atlas) ⋌	H 7	83
Atlin ≃	B 5	156
Atlin Lake ⊜	B 5	156
Atlin Provincial Park ♦	B 5	156
Atmore	G 5	170
Atnarko ≃	B 9	150
Atoka	E 5	172
Atoui, Khatt ≃	E 2	198
Atoyac ≃	H 10	184
Atrā ⋀¹	B 8	195
Atrak (Atrek) ≃	D 5	66
Ātran ≃	D 6	66
Atrato ≃	B 3	190
Atrek (Atrak) ≃	D 16	118
Atri	B 3	94
Atripalda	D 4	94
At-Tafīlah	H 5	120
At-Tafīlah □³	H 5	120
At-Ta'if	C 5	202
At-Ta'mīm □³	E 10	118
Attapu	G 8	132
Attawapiskat	D 3	92

Attawapiskat ≃	E 17	158
Attawapiskat Indian Reserve →⁴	E 17	158
Attawapiskat Lake ⊜	E 14	158
Attica, Ks., U.S.	G 5	174
Attica, N.Y., U.S.	D 9	166
Attica, Oh., U.S.	C 2	162
Attikí □³	C 5	106
Attleboro	E 7	164
Attu Island I	k 38	155a
At-Tuwayyah	I 9	118
Atuel ≃	D 4	195
Atuel, Bañados del ⊞	D 4	195
Åtvidaberg	G 8	64
Atwater	C 3	182
Atwood, Ks., U.S.	F 4	174
Atwood, Tn., U.S.	E 4	170
Atyrau	F 17	110
Atyrau □³	F 17	110
Aubagne	G 3	82
Aube □³	D 11	78
Aubenas	F 2	82
Aubervilliers	D 9	78
Aub-Ghos	C 3	206
Aubigny-sur-Nère	E 9	78
Aubinadong ≃	B 7	166
Aubry Lake ⊜	C 31	154
Auburn, Al., U.S.	F 6	170
Auburn, Ca., U.S.	B 2	184
Auburn, In., U.S.	B 6	170
Auburn, Ma., U.S.	D 7	164
Auburn, Me., U.S.	A 8	162
Auburn, Mi., U.S.	B 1	162
Auburn, N.Y., U.S.	B 5	162
Auburn, Wa., U.S.	B 3	178
Auburn ≃	H 10	142
Aubusson	C 6	80
Auch	E 4	80
Auchterarder	D 5	74
Auckland	B 5	146
Auckland □³	B 5	146
Aude □³	E 4	80
Aude ≃	F 15	158
Audierne	D 2	78
Audincourt	C 4	82
Audubon Lake ⊜¹	B 4	174
Aue	E 7	98
Auerbach	E 7	98
Augathella	H 8	142
Auge, Pays d' →¹	C 7	78
Augrabies	E 4	206
Augrabies Falls National Park ♦	E 4	206
Augsburg	D 7	100
Augusta, Austl.	N 3	140
Augusta, Ga., U.S.	C 3	168
Augusta, Il., U.S.	B 3	170
Augusta, Italy	A 9	162
Augusta, Wi., U.S.	C 3	166
Augustdorf	A 3	164
Augustów	B 12	96
Augustus, Mount ⋀	I 4	140
Augustus Downs	E 4	142
Aukstaitijos nacionalinis parkas ♦	E 12	66
Aulanko	B 12	66
Auld, Lake ⊜	H 7	140
Aulendorf	E 6	100
Aulla	E 5	92
Aulnay	B 3	80
Aulnoye-Aymeries	B 10	78
Aumale	C 8	78
Aumance ≃	B 6	80
Aumühle	C 7	98
Auna	B 3	68
Auob ≃	D 4	206
Auraiya	D 3	122
Aurangābād, India	E 4	122
Aurangābād, India	E 3	78
Auray	D 4	98
Aurich	D 2	194
Aurilândia	F 2	174
Aurillac	D 6	80
Aurora, Co., U.S.	F 2	174
Aurora, Il., U.S.	A 9	162
Aurora, Me., U.S.	C 3	164
Aurora, Oh., U.S.	C 3	162
Aurora, On., Can.	D 4	162
Aurora, W.V., U.S.	B 5	142
Aurukun	B 5	142
Au Sable ≃	A 2	162
Au Sable Forks	F 2	164
Auschwitz see Oświęcim	C 10	96
Ausevik ⊥	B 2	66
Ausnek	D 2	206
Aust-Agder □³	C 4	66
Austerlitz see Slavkov u Brna	A 8	102
Austin, In., U.S.	C 6	170
Austin, Mn., U.S.	B 1	162
Austin, Pa., U.S.	C 6	170
Austin, Tx., U.S.	B 5	172
Austin, Lake ⊜	J 5	140
Austinville	E 3	162
Australes, Îles II	F 13	136
Australia □¹	D 7	138
Australian Capital Territory □³	G 6	138
Austria □¹	F 10	62
Autlán de Navarro	H 7	184
Autun	F 11	78
Auvergne □⁹	C 6	80
Auxerre	E 10	78
Auxier	C 3	162
Auxvasse	C 3	170
Auzangate, Nevado ⋀	F 4	190
Avakubi	A 4	204
Avallon	E 10	78
Avalon Peninsula ⊁¹	E 17	160
Avanos	C 4	118
Avaré	B 5	194
Avarua	F 12	136
Avebury Stone Circle ⊥	F 5	72
Aveiro	E 2	86
Avella	D 4	94
Avellaneda	D 4	195
Avellino	D 4	94
Avellino □⁶	D 4	94
Avenal	E 3	182
Averbode, Abbaye d' ♦¹	C 3	69
Aversa	D 4	94
Avesnes-sur-Helpe	B 10	78
Avesta	F 6	64
Aveyron □³	E 6	80
Aveyron ≃	D 5	80
Avezzano	B 3	94
Aviano	C 8	92
Aviemore	C 5	74
Avigliana	D 3	92

Avignon	G 2	82
Ávila	D 6	86
Ávila □⁶	D 5	86
Avilés	A 5	86
Avinurme	C 13	66
Avion	B 9	78
Aviz	E 3	86
Avoca, Ia., U.S.	B 1	170
Avoca, N.Y., U.S.	B 5	162
Avola	H 5	94
Avon ≃	C 7	174
Avon, N.Y., U.S.	A 2	162
Avon ≃	E 5	72
Avondrust	H 4	206
Avon Park	F 4	168
Avontuur	G 5	206
Avranches	G 5	126
Awaji-shima I	H 9	126
Awakino	C 5	146
Āwasa	F 4	202
Āwash	F 4	202
Āwash ≃	F 4	202
Āwash Bihērawī Kilil ♦	E 5	202
Awbārī	D 7	198
Awbārī, Ṣaḥrā' →¹	D 7	198
Awdal □³	E 5	202
Awled Djellal	C 5	198
Awlef	D 5	198
'Awrā	D 8	198
Axel Heiberg Island I	B 10	148
Axim	E 4	200
Axiós (Vardar) ≃	E 7	104
Axis	G 4	170
Ax-les-Thermes	F 5	80
Axminster	G 3	72
Ayabe	G 8	126
Ayacucho, Arg.	E 8	195
Ayacucho, Peru	F 4	190
Ayakkum Hu ⊜	B 5	122
Ayamé	D 4	200
Ayamonte	F 6	186
Ayapel	F 4	190
Ayaviri	F 4	190
Aydar ≃	E 11	110
Aydın	D 7	106
Aydın □³	D 7	106
Ayer	E 5	164
Ayer Chawan, Pulau I	j 14	134a
Ayer Merbau, Pulau I	j 14	134a
Ayers Rock (Uluru) ⋀	I 11	140
Ayeyarwady ≃	F 2	132
Ayia Paraskeví	C 7	106
Ayina ≃	B 1	204
Áyion Óros □³	B 6	106
Áyios Kírikos	D 7	106
Áyios Nikólaos	C 6	106
Ayíou Órous, Kólpos c	B 5	106
Aylesbury	F 6	72
Aylmer, On., Can.	D 8	166
Aylmer, P.Q., Can.	A 3	164
Aylmer Lake ⊜	D 11	150
Ayon Island I	A 13	138
Ayon, ostrov I	A 13	138
Ayon, ostrov see Ajon, ostrov I	O 19	114
Ayos	E 7	200
'Ayoûn el 'Atroûs	F 3	198
Ayr, Austl.	E 8	142
Ayr, Scot., U.K.	B 2	72
Ayre, Point of ⊁	C 2	72
Ayrum	I 14	110
Ayu, Kepulauan II	E 10	134
Ayvalık	C 7	106
Azahar, Costa del ±²	D 5	88
Azalea Park	E 4	168
Azamatovo	C 18	110
Azanka	A 26	108
Azaouad →¹	B 4	200
Azaouagh ≃	B 5	200
Azärbaycan see Azerbaijan □¹	G 17	62
Äzärbāyjān-e Gharbī □³	C 13	118
Äzärbāyjān-e Sharqī □³	D 13	118
Azare	B 7	200
Āzar Shahr	D 11	118
Azay-le-Rideau, Château d' ⊥	E 7	78
Azeffâl →⁸	A 2	198
Azemmour	C 3	198
Azerbaijan □¹	G 17	62
Azéry	F 12	66
Azgir	F 15	110
Azilal	C 3	198
Aznakaevo	I 20	108
Azogues	D 3	190
Azores II	h 12	198a
Azoum, Bahr ('Azūm, Wādī) ≃	C 9	200
Azov	F 10	110
Azov, Sea of ▾²	F 10	110
Azovs'ke	G 9	110
Azraq ash-Shīshān	F 12	120
Azrou	C 3	198
Azua	E 8	186
Azuaga	F 5	86
Azuero, Península de ⊁¹	G 4	186
Azuga	C 8	104
Azul	E 8	195
Azul, Cordillera ⋌	E 3	162
'Azūm, Wādī (Azoum, Bahr) ≃	C 9	200
Azur, Côte d' ±²	G 5	82
Az-Zabadānī	D 6	120
Az-Zāhran	I 13	118
Az-Zarqā'	F 7	120
Az-Zarqā' □³	F 7	120
Az-Zāwiyah	D 3	202
Az-Zaydab	D 3	202
Azzel Matti, Sebkha ⊞	D 5	198
Az-Zubayr	G 12	118
Azzurra, Grotta ±⁵	D 4	94
Az-Zuwaytīnah	C 9	198

B

Ba ≃, China	m 13	147c
Ba ≃, China	C 8	130
Ba ≃, China	C 12	130
Ba ≃, Viet.	H 9	132
Baar	C 6	82
Baarle-Hertog	B 3	69
Baarn	B 6	69
Baba Burnu ⊁	C 6	106
Babadag	D 11	104
Babaeski	B 11	106
Babahoyo	D 3	190
Babana	D 5	200
Babanka	A 11	104

Babanūsah	E 2	202
Babar, Kepulauan II	G 9	134
Babar, Pulau I	G 9	134
Babbitt	H 13	158
B'abdā	B 5	120
Bab el Mandeb see Mandeb, Bab el ⊔	E 5	202
Babel Thuap I	D 10	134
Bābia, Arroyo de la ≃	F 3	172
Babian ≃	G 5	130
Bābil □³	F 11	118
Bābil, Atlāl (Babylon) ⊥	F 11	118
Babina Greda	D 8	156
Babine ≃	D 9	156
Babine Lake ⊜	C 2	204
Babiogórski Park Narodowy ♦	D 10	96
Babo	F 10	134
Bābol	D 15	118
Bābol Sar	C 6	110
Babuyan Island I	B 8	134
Babuyan Islands II	B 8	134
Babylon	F 5	164
Babylon see Bābil, Atlāl ⊥	F 11	118
Bacaadweyn	F 6	202
Bacabal	D 10	190
Bacan, Pulau I	F 9	134
Bacău	B 9	104
Bacău □³	B 9	104
Bac Binh	I 9	132
Baccarat	B 4	82
Bacchus Marsh	F 5	144
Bačėjkava	E 14	66
Bac Giang	D 8	132
Bachiniva	C 6	184
Bach Thong	C 13	150
Back ≃	C 5	104
Bačka →¹	C 5	104
Bačka Palanka	C 5	104
Bačka Topola	D 4	162
Back Creek ≃	D 6	100
Bäckefors	D 6	200
Backnang	J 7	132
Bac Lieu	C 8	134
Bac Ninh	B 5	186
Bacolod	B 5	104
Bácsalmás	B 5	104
Bács-Kiskun □³	F 3	202
Bačurka	B 22	108
Bad ≃	B 1	162
Badagara	G 3	122
Bad Aibling	E 8	100
Badajós, Lago ⊜	D 6	190
Badajoz	F 4	86
Badajoz □⁶	F 5	86
Badalona	C 7	88
Bādāmi	F 3	122
Badanah	G 9	118
Badanga	C 8	200
Bad Aussee	F 3	202
Bad Bergzabern	C 4	100
Bad Berleburg	E 5	98
Bad Bevensen	C 7	98
Bad Blankenburg	B 8	100
Bad Bramstedt	C 6	98
Baddeck	E 13	160
Bad Doberan	B 8	98
Bad Driburg	E 6	98
Bad Düben	E 9	98
Bad Dürkheim	A 6	82
Bad Dürrenberg	E 9	98
Bad Dürrheim	B 6	82
Bad Ems	B 4	100
Baden, Aus.	B 8	102
Baden, Switz.	C 5	100
Baden-Baden	B 5	100
Bad Endbach	F 5	98
Baden-Powell, Mount ⋀	F 6	182
Badenweiler	B 6	82
Baden-Württemberg □³	D 11	98
Bad Frankenhausen	E 7	98
Bad Freienwalde	D 11	98
Bad Friedrichshall	C 6	100
Bad Gastein	G 4	86
Badger	D 15	160
Bad Hall	B 6	102
Bad Harzburg	E 7	98
Bad Hersfeld	F 6	98
Bad Homburg vor der Höhe	B 5	100
Bad Honnef	B 4	100
Badia Polesine	D 7	92
Badīar, Parc National du ♦	C 2	200
Bad Iburg	D 5	98
Bad Ischl	C 5	102
Bad Kissingen	B 7	100
Bad König	C 5	100
Bad Kreuznach	E 4	100
Bad Krozingen	E 10	190
Badlands →², S.D., U.S.	D 3	174
Badlands →², U.S.	B 3	174
Badlands National Park ♦	D 3	174
Bad Langensalza	E 7	98
Bad Lausick	E 9	98
Bad Lauterberg im Harz	E 7	98
Bad Liebenstein	F 7	98
Bad Liebenwerda	E 10	98
Bad Lippspringe	E 5	98
Bad Mergentheim	C 6	100
Bad Muskau	B 6	120
Bad Nauheim	E 5	98
Bad Neuenahr-Ahrweiler	B 4	100
Bad Neustadt an der Saale	B 7	100
Bad Oeynhausen	E 5	98
Bad Oldesloe	C 7	98
Badong	C 10	130
Bad Orb	B 6	100
Bad Pyrmont	D 6	98
Bad Ragaz	D 6	92
Bad Reichenhall	E 9	100
Bad River Indian Reservation →⁴	B 3	166
Bad Sachsa	E 7	98
Bad Säckingen	E 11	100
Bad Sauzlfuen	C 7	98
Bad Salzungen	F 7	98
Bad Sanktt Leonhard im Lavanttal	G 15	100
Bad Schmiedeberg	E 9	98
Bad Schussenried	E 6	100
Bad Schwalbach	C 5	100
Bad Schwartau	C 7	98
Bad Segeberg	C 7	98
Bad Sooden-Allendorf	E 6	98
Bad Urach	C 6	100
Bad Vöslau	B 8	102
Bad Waldsee	E 6	100

Bad Wildbad im Schwarzwald	D 5	100
Bad Wildungen	E 5	98
Bad Windsheim	C 7	100
Bad Wörishofen	E 6	96
Bad Wurzach	E 6	100
Bad Zwischenahn	C 4	98
Baena	G 6	86
Bærum	C 5	66
Baeza	G 7	86
Bafang	D 7	200
Bafatá	C 2	200
Baffin Basin →¹	B 29	61
Baffin Bay c, N.A.	B 13	148
Baffin Bay c, Tx., U.S.	G 5	172
Baffin Island I	C 19	150
Bafia	E 7	200
Bafilo	D 5	200
Bafoulabé	C 2	200
Bafoussam	D 7	200
Bāfq	G 16	118
Bāft	H 17	118
Bafwasende	B 4	204
Bagaces	F 3	186
Bāgalkot	F 3	122
Bagan Siapiapi	M 5	132
Bagata	C 2	204
Bagawi	E 3	202
Bagdad see Baghdād	F 11	118
Bagdarin	B 10	195
Bagé	D 3	68
Bāgēvādi	F 3	122
Baghdād	F 11	118
Baghdād □³	F 11	118
Bāgh-e Malek	G 13	118
Bagheria	F 3	94
Baghlān	B 1	122
Bagnara Cálabra	F 5	94
Bagnères-de-Bigorre	E 4	80
Bagnères-de-Luchon	F 4	80
Bagni di Lucca	E 6	92
Bagnols-sur-Cèze	F 2	82
Bago (Pegu)	F 3	132
Bago □³	E 2	132
Bagoé ≃	C 3	200
Bagolino	D 6	92
Bagrationovsk	E 10	66
Baguio	B 8	134
Bahamas □¹	B 6	186
Bahār	E 5	122
Baharampur	E 5	122
Bahau	M 6	132
Bahāwalnagar	C 2	122
Bahāwalpur	D 6	190
Bāherden	J 20	110
Baherove	G 9	110
Bahia, Islas de la II	D 3	186
Bahia Bianca	F 6	195
Bahía de Caráquez	D 2	190
Bahía Kino	C 4	184
Bahia Laura	I 6	192
Bahir Dar	E 4	202
Bahraich	D 4	122
Bahrain □¹	E 7	116
Bahrayn, Khalīj al- c	J 14	118
Bahušėusk	F 7	110
Bai ≃	B 11	130
Baia de Aramă	C 7	104
Baia Mare	B 7	104
Baia Sprie	B 7	104
Baicheng, China	A 4	122
Baicheng, China	D 14	128
Baidoa see Baydhabo	G 5	202
Baie-Comeau	D 9	160
Baie-Johan-Beetz	C 12	160
Baiesbronn	B 6	82
Baie-Saint-Paul	B 8	160
Baie-Trinité	B 8	160
Baikal, Lake (Bajkal, ozero) ⊜	B 5	124
Báile Govora	C 8	104
Bailén	F 7	86
Bäilești	C 7	104
Baileborough	C 4	75
Bailleul	B 9	78
Ba-Illi	C 8	200
Bailong ≃	D 8	130
Bainbridge, Ga., U.S.	D 2	168
Bainbridge, N.Y., U.S.	D 3	164
Baing, Indon.	H 8	134
Baing, Indon.	B 6	140
Bains-les-Bains	B 4	82
Baipu	B 15	130
Baird Inlet c	C 16	128
Baird Inlet c	F 12	154
Bairiki	C 9	136
Bairkum	A 1	122
Bairnsdale	G 6	144
Baisha, China	D 8	132
Baisha, China	E 9	132
Baishuijiang	F 2	204
Baixo Longa	H 5	128
Baiyin	C 4	130
Baiyu	C 5	200
Baiz̄o	D 10	132
Baja	F 6	202
Baja California □³	B 2	184
Baja California (Lower California) ⊁¹	C 2	184
Baja California Sur □³	D 3	184
Bajas, Rias ±²	A 2	86
Bajdaracakga guba c	B 27	108
Bajina Bašta	C 5	104
Bajkalovo	H 27	108
Bajmak	C 21	110
Bajo Boquete	G 6	186
Bakacak	B 7	106
Bakal	I 23	108
Bakel	B 2	200
Baker, La., U.S.	G 3	170
Baker, Mount ⋀	A 2	178
Baker Island I	C 10	136
Baker Island I, Austl.	J 9	140
Baker Lake ⊜, N.T., Can.	E 14	150
Bakersfield	E 4	182
Bakerstown	D 7	166
Bakhchysaray	G 4	110
Bakhmach	D 4	110
Bākhtarān see Kermānshāh	E 12	118
Bakhtegān, Daryāchehye ⊜	H 16	118
Baki (Baku), Azer.	I 16	110
Baki, Som.	E 6	202
Bakituba	H 4	202
Bakkafjói ≃	I 23	64a
Bakkagerdi	m 24	64a
Bakony ≃	F 4	102
Bakool □³	F 5	202
Bakool ≃	C 8	110
Bakouma	D 9	200

⊾ Waterfall ⊔ Strait c Bay, Gulf ⊜ Lake ⊞ Swamp ⊠ Ice Feature ▾ Other Hydrographic Feature → Submarine Feature □ Political Unit 〕 Cultural Institution ⊥ Historical Site ♦ Recreational Site ⊠ Airport ▪ Military Installation ⋌ Miscellaneous

245

Bakovensfontein — Belmonte

Name	Map Ref.	Page
Bakovensfontein	G 5	206
Bakoy ≃	C 2	200
Baksan	H 13	110
Baksan ≃	H 13	110
Bakšty	F 13	66
Baku see Bakı	I 16	110
Bakwanga see Mbuji-Mayi	D 3	204
Balâ, Tur.	C 5	118
Bala, Wales, U.K.	E 3	72
Balabac Island I	D 7	134
Balabac Strait ⋓	D 7	134
Ba'labakk	F 7	118
Balad	F 10	118
Bālāghāt	E 3	122
Balaguer	C 5	88
Balahna	H 15	108
Balaklava	G 8	110
Balakliya	E 10	110
Balakovo	C 15	110
Balambangan, Pulau I	D 7	134
Balāngīr	E 4	122
Balaši	D 16	110
Balašov	D 13	110
Balassagyarmat	A 5	104
Balaton	C 7	174
Balaton ⊜	D 9	102
Balbieriškis	E 11	66
Balbina, Reprêsa ⊜[1]	D 7	190
Balcad	G 6	202
Balcarce	E 8	195
Balclutha	G 2	146
Bald Knob	E 3	170
Baldock	E 6	72
Baldock Lake ⊜	C 10	158
Baldone	D 12	66
Bald Rock National Park ♦	B 9	144
Baldwin	D 6	166
Baldwin City	C 1	170
Baldy Mountain ∧	F 8	158
Baldy Peak ∧	E 4	176
Bâle see Basel	C 5	82
Balē □[3]	F 5	202
Balearic Islands see Balears, Illes II	C 7	84
Balearic Sea ▾[2]	E 6	88
Balears, Illes (Balearic Islands) II	C 7	84
Baleine ≃	E 19	150
Baleine, Grande rivière de la ≃	A 5	160
Balej	B 7	124
Bale Mountain National Park ♦	F 4	202
Balen	C 4	69
Bāleshwar	E 5	122
Balestrand	B 3	66
Balezino	G 20	108
Balfour	D 8	206
Balfour Downs	H 6	140
Balgo	G 9	140
Balgo Aboriginal Reserve ➔[4]	G 10	140
Balhaš (Balqash)	A 12	116
Bali I	k 22	135b
Bali, Selat ⋓	G 6	134
Balige	M 4	132
Balıkesir	C 7	106
Balıkesir □[3]	C 7	106
Balikpapan	F 7	134
Balikumbat	D 6	200
Balimo	N 12	124
Balingen	D 5	100
Balintang Channel ⋓	B 8	134
Bali Sea (Bali, Laut) ▾[2]	G 7	134
Balkan □[3]	B 16	118
Balkan Mountains (Stara Planina) ⋏	D 8	104
Balkh	B 1	122
Balkh ≃	B 1	122
Balkhash, Lake (Balhaš, ozero) (Balqash Köli) ⊜	A 12	116
Ballachulish	D 3	74
Ballālpur	F 3	122
Ballan	F 5	144
Ballangen	B 8	64
Ballarat	F 4	144
Ballard, Lake ⊜	K 6	140
Ballater	C 5	74
Ballenas, Bahía de ⊂	D 3	184
Ballengeich	D 8	206
Balleny Islands II	C 25	208
Ballerup	C 5	68
Balleza ≃	D 6	184
Ballia	D 4	122
Ballina, Austl.	B 9	144
Ballina, Ire.	B 2	75
Ballinasloe	C 3	75
Ballincollig	E 3	75
Ballinrobe	C 2	75
Ballston Spa	C 5	164
Ballycastle	A 5	75
Ballymena	B 5	75
Ballymoney	A 5	75
Ballymote	B 3	75
Ballyrogan, Lake ⊜	D 5	144
Balma	E 5	80
Balmaseda	A 7	86
Balmoral Castle ⊥	C 5	74
Balmorhea	E 2	172
Balonne ≃	B 7	144
Bālotra	D 2	122
Balphakram National Park ♦	D 6	122
Balqash see Balhaš	A 12	116
Balranald	E 4	144
Balsam Lake	C 2	166
Balsas	A 9	190
Balsas ≃, Braz.	E 9	190
Balsas ≃, Mex.	H 9	184
Balsas Sur	H 9	184
Bålsta	C 8	66
Balsthal	C 5	82
Balta	B 10	104
Baltasar Brum	B 9	195
Baltasi	H 18	108
Bălţi	B 9	104
Baltic Sea ▾[2]	D 11	62
Baltijsk	B 1	110
Baltijskaja kosa (Wiślany, Mierzeja) ›[2]	A 10	96
Baltim	G 4	118
Baltimore, Md., U.S.	G 2	164
Baltimore, S. Afr.	B 8	206
Baltimore □[6]	G 2	164
Ba Lu ≃	G 9	132
Baluchistan □[9]	C 1	122
Baluchistān □[3]	D 1	122
Bālurghāt	D 5	122
Balvi	D 13	66
Balykši	F 17	110
Balyn	A 9	104
Bam	E 8	116
Bama	F 8	130
Bamaga	A 6	142
Bamako	C 3	200
Bambari	D 9	200
Bamberg, Ger.	C 7	100
Bamberg, S.C., U.S.	C 4	168
Bambesa	B 4	204
Bambio	E 8	200
Bambouti	F 2	202
Bambuí	C 7	194
Bambuto ≃	G 3	176
Bamenda	D 6	200
Bamfield	G 9	156
Bamingui ≃	D 8	200
Bamingui-Bangoran □[3]	D 9	200
Bamingui-Bangoran, Parc National du ♦	D 8	200
Bamokgoko	C 8	206
Bampūr	A 9	116
Bamy	J 20	110
Bana	E 5	204
Banaba I	D 8	136
Banalia	B 4	204
Banamba	C 3	200
Bananal, Ilha do I	F 8	190
Banaras see Vārānasi	D 4	122
Banarlı	B 7	106
Banās ≃	D 3	122
Banâs, Râs ›	C 4	202
Banat □[9]	C 6	104
Banaz	C 8	106
Banbridge	B 5	75
Banbury	E 5	72
Banc d'Arguin, Parc National du ♦	E 1	198
Banchory	C 6	74
Bancroft see Chililabombwe	E 4	204
Bānda, India	D 4	122
Banda, Zaire	B 4	204
Banda, Kepulauan II	F 9	134
Banda Aceh	L 2	132
Bandai-Asahi-kokuritsu-kōen ♦	E 7	126
Bandama ≃	D 4	200
Bandama Blanc ≃	D 3	200
Bandama Rouge ≃	D 3	200
Bandarbeyla	F 7	202
Bandar-e 'Abbās	I 16	118
Bandar-e Anzalī	D 13	118
Bandar-e Deylam	H 14	118
Bandar-e Gaz	D 15	118
Bandar-e Khomeynī	G 13	118
Bandar-e Lengeh	I 16	118
Bandar-e Māh Shahr	G 13	118
Bandar-e Shāhpūr see Bandar-e Khomeynī	G 13	118
Bandar-e Torkeman	D 15	118
Bandar Murcaayo	E 6	202
Bandar Seri Begawan	D 6	134
Banda Sea (Banda, Laut) ▾[2]	F 9	134
Bandeira, Pico da ∧	D 10	194
Bandeirantes	C 3	194
Bandelier National Monument ♦	E 5	176
Bandera	E 7	192
Banderas, Bahía de ⊂	G 7	184
Bandhavgarh National Park ♦	E 4	122
Bandiagara	C 4	200
Bandiantaolehai	F 5	128
Bandingilo National Park ♦	F 3	202
Bandipur Tiger Reserve ➔[4]	G 3	122
Bandırma	B 8	106
Bandon	E 3	75
Ban Don, Ao ⊂	J 4	132
Bandundu	C 2	204
Bandundu □[3]	C 2	204
Bandung, Indon.	k 18	135b
Bandung, Indon.	k 18	135b
Băneasa	C 9	104
Banegas	G 6	190
Bāneh	E 11	118
Banes	C 6	186
Banff	F 14	156
Banff National Park ♦	F 13	156
Banfora	C 4	200
Bangalore	G 3	122
Bangassou	E 9	200
Bangeta, Mount ∧	N 13	124
Banggai	F 8	134
Banggai, Kepulauan II	F 8	134
Banggi, Pulau I	D 7	134
Banghāzī (Benghazi)	C 9	198
Banghiang ≃	F 7	132
Bangil	k 21	135b
Bangka, Pulau I	F 5	134
Bangka, Selat ⋓	F 5	134
Bangkalan	k 21	135b
Bangkinang	N 5	132
Bangkok see Krung Thep	H 5	132
Bangladesh □[1]	F 14	116
Bang Mun Nak	F 5	132
Bangolo	D 3	200
Bangor, Me., U.S.	A 9	162
Bangor, N. Ire., U.K.	B 6	75
Bangor, Wales, U.K.	D 2	72
Bangsri	k 20	135b
Bangui	E 8	200
Bangweulu, Lake ⊜	E 5	204
Bangweulu Swamps ≣	E 5	204
Banhine, Parque Nacional de ♦	B 10	206
Bani, C.A.R.	D 9	200
Baní, Dom. Rep.	D 7	186
Bania	E 8	200
Bani Bangou	B 5	200
Banie	B 8	96
Banifing ≃	C 3	200
Banima	D 9	200
Banio, Lagune ⊜	F 7	200
Bāniyās	E 6	118
Banja Luka	C 4	104
Banjarmasin	F 6	134
Banjul (Bathurst)	C 1	200
Bankass	C 4	200
Bankilaré	C 5	200
Bankja	D 7	104
Banks, Îles II	E 8	136
Banks Island I, B.C., Can.	E 6	156
Banks Island I, N.T., Can.	B 8	150
Banks Lake ⊜[1]	B 4	178
Banks Peninsula ›[1]	E 4	146
Banks Strait ⋓	i 13	145a
Bankstown	D 8	144
Bankumuna	C 2	204
Bann ≃	A 5	75
Ban Nadou	G 7	132
Ban Namnga	D 5	132
Banner Elk	A 4	168
Banning	G 6	182
Banningville see Bandundu	C 2	204
Bannockburn Battlesite ⊥	D 5	74
Bannu	C 2	122
Bánokszentgyörgy	D 8	102
Ban Pakneun	E 5	132
Ban Phai	F 6	132
Ban San Xieng La	E 6	132
Banská Bystrica	B 11	102
Banská Štiavnica	B 10	102
Ban Songkhon	E 7	132
Banstead	F 6	72
Bantaeng	G 7	134
Bantenan, Tanjung ›	I 22	135b
Ban Thabôk	I 6	130
Banyo	D 7	200
Banyoles	B 7	88
Banyuwangi	I 22	135b
Banyuwedang	I 22	135b
Baode	G 8	128
Baoding	G 10	128
Baofeng	B 11	130
Bao Ha	C 7	132
Baoji	A 8	130
Baojing	D 9	130
Bao Lac	I 8	132
Baoning	G 8	130
Baoqing	C 18	128
Baoshan	F 4	130
Baoting	I 9	130
Baotou	F 8	128
Baoulé ≃	C 3	200
Baoying	B 14	130
Bapaume	B 9	78
Bāqa el Gharbiyya	E 4	120
Ba'qūbah	F 11	118
Baquedano	D 5	192
Baraawe	G 5	202
Baraboo	D 4	166
Baracoa	C 6	186
Baradero	C 8	195
Baradine	C 7	144
Baragoi	G 4	202
Bārah	E 3	202
Barahona	D 7	186
Barāk ≃	E 6	122
Baraka (Barakah, Khawr) ≃	D 4	202
Barakah, Khawr (Baraka) ≃	D 4	202
Barakaldo	A 1	88
Baraki	C 1	122
Barakloj	J 27	108
Baram ≃	E 6	134
Barama ≃	G 9	186
Bāramūla	C 2	122
Baran'	E 14	66
Baranavičy	J 13	64
Baranoa	F 6	186
Baranof Island I	H 27	154
Baranya □[3]	D 10	102
Baraolt	B 8	104
Baraški	D 20	108
Barataria	H 3	170
Barat Daya, Kepulauan II	G 9	134
Barauni	D 5	122
Baravuha	E 14	66
Barbacena	D 9	194
Barbacoas	C 3	190
Barbados □[1]	E 10	186
Barbar	D 3	202
Barbas, Cap ›	E 1	198
Barbastro	B 5	88
Barbate	H 5	86
Barbeau Peak ∧	A 12	148
Barberton, Oh., U.S.	C 3	162
Barberton, S. Afr.	C 9	206
Barbezieux	C 3	80
Barbuda I	I 18	187c
Barby	E 8	98
Bârca	C 7	104
Barcaldine	G 7	142
Barcău (Berettyó) ≃	B 7	104
Barcellona Pozzo di Gotto	F 5	94
Barcelona, Mex.	D 8	184
Barcelona, Spain	C 7	88
Barcelona, Ven.	F 8	186
Barcelona □[6]	C 6	88
Barcelos, Braz.	D 6	190
Barcelos, Port.	C 2	86
Barcoo ≃	H 6	142
Barcs	E 9	102
Bärdä, Azer.	I 15	110
Barda, Russia	H 21	108
Bardai	C 9	200
Barddhamān	E 5	122
Bardejov	D 11	96
Bardeskan	E 17	118
Bardo	G 3	90
Bardoc	L 6	140
Bardstown	D 6	170
Bardwell	D 4	170
Bareilly	D 3	122
Barentin	C 7	78
Barentsøya I	B 5	114
Barents Sea ▾[2]	B 6	114
Barentu	D 4	202
Barga	E 6	92
Barge	F 5	82
Bargnop	F 2	202
Bargoed	F 3	72
Bargteheide	C 7	98
Barguzin ≃	B 5	124
Bar Harbor	A 9	162
Bari, Italy	C 6	94
Bari, Zaire	B 2	204
Bari □[6]	D 6	94
Bari □[3]	E 7	202
Barikiwa	D 6	204
Baril Lake ⊜	B 16	156
Barinas	F 7	186
Barinas □[3]	F 7	186
Bāripada	E 5	122
Bariri	E 6	194
Bârîs	J 4	118
Barisāl	E 6	122
Barisāl □[3]	E 6	122
Barisan, Pegunungan ⋏, Indon.	N 5	132
Barisan, Pegunungan ⋏, Indon.	F 4	134
Barito ≃	F 6	134
Barjac	F 2	82
Barjols	G 4	82
Barkam	C 6	130
Barkava	D 13	66
Barkley, Lake ⊜[1]	D 5	170
Barkley Sound ⋓	G 9	156
Barkly East	F 7	206
Barkly Tableland ⋏[1]	E 2	142
Barla	C 9	106
Bârlad	B 9	104
Barleben	D 8	98
Bar-le-Duc	D 12	78
Barlee, Lake ⊜	K 5	140
Barletta	C 6	94
Barling	E 1	170
Bārmer	D 2	122
Barmstedt	C 6	98
Barnard ≃	C 8	144
Barnard Castle	C 4	72
Barnato	C 5	144
Barnaul	D 11	114
Barnesville	B 6	174
Barnet □[6]	F 6	72
Barneveld	B 4	69
Barneville-Carteret	C 5	78
Barnim ➔[1]	D 10	98
Barnoldswick	D 4	72
Barnsley	D 5	72
Barnsley □[6]	D 5	72
Barnstable	E 8	164
Barnstable □[6]	E 8	164
Barnstaple	F 2	72
Barnstaple Bay ⊂	F 2	72
Baro ≃	F 3	202
Baroua	C 7	200
Barpeta	D 6	122
Barques, Pointe aux ›	A 2	162
Barquisimeto	F 7	186
Barra	F 10	190
Barra, Ponta da ›	B 11	206
Barrackville	D 3	162
Barra do Cuanza	D 1	204
Barra do Garças	A 4	194
Barra Falsa, Ponta da ›	B 11	206
Barrafranca	G 4	94
Barra Mansa	E 8	194
Barrancabermeja	G 6	186
Barrancas	F 9	186
Barranco do Velho	G 2	86
Barranquilla	F 6	186
Barrax	E 2	88
Barre	B 6	164
Barreiras	F 10	190
Barreiro	F 1	86
Barretos	D 6	194
Barrhead	D 14	156
Barrie	F 4	160
Barrière	F 11	156
Barrier Range ⋏	C 3	144
Barrington Lake ⊜	C 8	158
Barrington Tops National Park ♦	D 8	144
Barringun	B 5	144
Barrow, Ak., U.S.	A 16	154
Barrow, Arg.	F 7	195
Barrow ≃	D 5	75
Barrow, Point ›	A 16	154
Barrow-in-Furness	C 3	72
Barrow Island I	G 3	140
Barrows	E 8	158
Barrow Strait ⋓	B 14	150
Barry	F 3	72
Barrydale	G 4	206
Barryton	D 6	166
Barsakel'mes, ostrov I	G 21	110
Barsbüttel	C 7	98
Bārsi	F 3	122
Barsinghausen	D 6	98
Barssel	C 4	98
Barstow	F 6	182
Bar-sur-Seine	D 11	78
Barth	B 9	98
Bartholomew, Bayou ≃	F 3	170
Bartibougou	C 5	200
Bartica	B 7	190
Bartın	B 5	118
Bartle Frere ∧	D 7	142
Bartlesville	B 5	172
Bartlett, N.H., U.S.	B 7	164
Bartlett, Tn., U.S.	E 4	170
Bartley	E 4	174
Barton-upon-Humber	D 6	72
Bartoszyce	A 11	96
Bartow, Fl., U.S.	F 4	168
Bartow, Ga., U.S.	C 3	168
Barú, Volcán ∧[1]	F 4	186
Barumun ≃	M 5	132
Barung, Nusa I	I 21	135b
Barun-Torej, ozero ⊜	B 10	128
Barus	N 4	132
Baruun-Urt	C 9	128
Barwāni	E 2	122
Barwice	B 9	96
Barwon ≃	C 6	144
Barwon Heads	G 5	144
Baryš	J 17	108
Barysau	E 14	66
Basankusu	B 2	204
Basarabeasca	B 10	104
Basatongwula Shan ∧	C 6	122
Basavilbaso	C 8	195
Basel (Bâle)	C 5	82
Basel-Land □[3]	C 5	82
Basey	C 9	134
Bashaw	E 15	156
Bashi Channel ⋓, Asia	H 15	130
Bashi Channel ⋓, Asia	A 8	134
Basilan Island I	D 8	134
Basildon	F 7	72
Basile	G 2	170
Basiliano	C 8	92
Basilicata □[3]	D 6	94
Basílio	F 9	192
Basingstoke	F 5	72
Basīrhāt	E 5	122
Başkale	C 10	118
Baskatong, Réservoir ⊜[1]	E 6	160
Baškirija □[3]	B 19	110
Baskomutan Milli Parkı ♦	C 9	106
Bašmakovo	J 15	108
Bāsoda	E 3	122
Basoko	B 3	204
Basque Country see Vasco, País □[3]	A 2	88
Basra see Al-Başrah	G 12	118
Bas-Rhin □[3]	B 5	82
Bassano del Grappa	D 7	92
Bassar	D 5	200
Bassein see Pathein	F 2	132
Bassein (Pathein) ≃	F 6	122
Basse-Kotto □[3]	D 9	200
Bassella	B 6	88
Basse-Terre, Guad.	o 21	187e
Basseterre, St. K./N.	m 20	187d
Basse Terre, Trin.	q 23	187f
Basse-Terre I	n 21	187e
Bassikounou	F 3	198
Bass River	F 12	160
Bass Strait ⋓	G 5	144
Bassum	D 5	98
Basswood Lake ⊜	A 3	166
Bastak	I 16	118
Bastelica	j 8	83a
Basti	D 4	122
Bastia, Fr.	i 9	83a
Bastia, Italy	F 8	92
Bastogne	D 4	69
Bastrop	F 2	170
Bas-Zaïre □[3]	D 2	204
Bata	E 6	200
Batabanó, Golfo de ⊂	C 4	186
Batajsk	F 11	110
Batala	C 3	122
Batalha	E 2	86
Batang	C 4	130
Batangas	C 8	134
Batangbatangdaya	k 21	135b
Batan Island I	A 8	134
Batan Islands II	A 8	134
Batanta, Pulau I	F 10	134
Batatais	D 7	194
Batavia, Ia., U.S.	B 2	170
Batavia, Il., U.S.	B 4	170
Batavia, N.Y., U.S.	B 4	162
Batchelor	C 11	140
Bătdâmbâng	H 6	132
Bateckij	G 9	108
Batemans Bay	E 8	144
Bate Pito ≃	G 4	176
Batesville, Ar., U.S.	E 3	170
Batesville, In., U.S.	C 6	170
Batesville, Tx., U.S.	F 4	172
Bath, Eng., U.K.	F 4	72
Bath, Me., U.S.	B 9	162
Bath, N.Y., U.S.	D 1	164
Batha □[3]	C 8	200
Bath and North East Somerset □[6]	F 4	72
Bathgate	G 10	158
Bathinda	C 2	122
Bathurst, Austl.	D 7	144
Bathurst see Banjul, Gam.	C 1	200
Bathurst, N.B., Can.	E 11	160
Bathurst, S. Afr.	G 7	206
Bathurst, Cape ›	B 7	150
Bathurst Inlet	C 11	150
Bathurst Inlet ⊂	C 11	150
Bathurst Island I, Austl.	B 10	140
Bathurst Island I, N.T., Can.	A 12	150
Batī	E 5	202
Batié	D 4	200
Bāṭin, Wādī al- ≃	H 12	118
Batley	D 5	72
Batman	D 9	118
Batman □[3]	C 9	118
Batna	B 6	198
Batoche National Historic Site ♦	E 19	156
Baton Rouge	G 3	170
Batouala	E 7	200
Batouri	E 7	200
Battambang see Bătdâmbâng	H 6	132
Batticaloa	H 4	122
Battipaglia	D 4	94
Battle ≃	E 16	156
Battle Creek, Mi., U.S.	B 1	162
Battle Creek, Ne., U.S.	E 6	174
Battlefields	F 4	204
Battle Mountain	B 5	180
Battonya	B 6	104
Batu ∧	F 4	202
Batu, Kepulauan II	F 3	134
Batu Gajah	L 5	132
Batumi	I 12	110
Batu Pahat	N 6	132
Baturaja	F 4	134
Baturité	D 11	190
Bat Yam	E 3	120
Baubau	G 8	134
Bauchi	C 6	200
Baud	E 4	78
Bauland ➔[1]	C 6	100
Bauld, Cape ›	C 16	160
Baume-les-Dames	C 4	82
Baunatal	E 6	98
Baure	C 6	200
Bauru	E 6	194
Bauska	D 12	66
Bautzen	E 11	98
Bavaria see Bayern □[3]	D 7	100
Bavarian Forest ⋏	C 9	100
Båven ⊜	C 8	66
Bavispe ≃	B 5	184
Baw Baw National Park ♦	F 6	144
Bawean, Pulau I	G 6	134
Bawiti	H 3	118
Bawku	C 4	200
Baxian	G 11	128
Baxter, Mn., U.S.	B 7	174
Baxter, Tn., U.S.	A 2	168
Baxter State Park ♦	g 12	163a
Bay	E 3	170
Bay □[3]	G 5	202
Bay, Laguna de ⊜	C 8	134
Bayamo	C 5	186
Bayamón	j 15	187b
Bayan	C 16	128
Bayanga	E 8	200
Bayan Har Shan ⋏	D 16	116
Bayanhongor	C 3	128
Bayanhongor □[3]	D 2	128
Bayano, Lago ⊜[1]	F 5	186
Bayan Obo	E 7	128
Bayan-Ovoo	B 8	128
Bayan-Uhaa	B 2	128
Bayan-Uul	C 3	128
Bayard	B 1	170
Bayasgalant	C 9	128
Bayboro	B 6	168
Bayburt	B 9	118
Bayburt □[3]	B 9	118
Bay City, Mi., U.S.	B 2	162
Bay City, Or., U.S.	C 2	178
Bay City, Tx., U.S.	F 5	172
Baydhabo	G 5	202
Baydrag ≃	C 2	128
Bayerische Alpen ⋏	E 8	100
Bayerischer Wald, Nationalpark ♦	D 10	100
Bayern □[3]	D 7	100
Bayeux	C 6	78
Bayfield	B 3	166
Bayhān	H 6	116
Bayındır	C 7	106
Bay Minette	G 5	170
Bay of Plenty □[3]	C 6	146
Bayonne, Fr.	E 2	80
Bayonne, N.J., U.S.	F 4	164
Bayou Bodcau Reservoir ⊜[1]	F 2	170
Bayou Cane	H 3	170
Bayou D'Arbonne Lake ⊜[1]	F 2	170
Bayovar	E 2	190
Bayport, Mn., U.S.	C 2	166
Bayport, N.Y., U.S.	F 5	164
Bayramiç	C 7	106
Bayreuth	C 8	100
Bay Roberts	E 17	160
Bayrūt (Beirut)	B 4	120
Bayrūt □[3]	B 4	120
Bays, Lake of ⊜	F 4	160
Bay Saint Louis	G 4	170
Bay Shore	F 5	164
Bay Springs Lake ⊜[1]	E 4	170
Bayt al-Faqīh	E 5	202
Bayt Jālā	F 4	120
Bayt Laḥm (Bethlehem)	F 4	120
Baytown	H 1	170
Bayy al-Kabīr, Wādī ≃	C 7	198
Baza	G 2	88
Bazardüzü Daği ∧	I 15	110
Bazaruto, Ilha do I	A 11	206
Bazas	D 3	80
Bazhong	C 8	130
Bazine	A 4	172
Be, Nosy I	j 9	205a
Beach	B 2	174
Beachville	B 3	162
Beacon	E 5	164
Beaconsfield	F 6	72
Beagle Bay Aboriginal Reserve ➔[4]	E 7	140
Beagle Gulf ⊂	C 11	140
Bealanana	j 9	205a
Bear ≃	E 7	178
Bear Brook State Park ♦	C 7	164
Bearden	F 2	170
Beardmore Glacier ⊓	E 26	208
Beardstown	B 3	170
Bear Head Lake State Park ♦	B 2	166
Bear Island I	D 33	208
Bear Lake	C 8	156
Bear Lake ⊜, Mb., Can.	D 10	158
Bear Lake ⊜, U.S.	E 8	178
Béarn □[9]	E 3	80
Bear River Range ⋏	E 8	178
Bearsden	E 4	74
Beartooth Mountains ⋏	C 9	178
Beās ≃	C 3	122
Beasain	A 2	88
Beata, Cabo ›	D 7	186
Beata, Isla I	D 7	186
Beatrice	E 6	174
Beatton ≃	C 11	156
Beatton River	C 11	156
Beattyville	E 2	162
Beaucaire	G 2	82
Beauce ➔[1]	D 8	78
Beauce-Sartigan □[6]	A 8	164
Beauchêne Island I	o 18	193b
Beaudesert	A 9	144
Beaufort, Austl.	F 4	144
Beaufort, Malay.	D 7	134
Beaufort, N.C., U.S.	B 6	168
Beaufort Castle see Qal'at ash-Shaqīf ⊥	C 4	120
Beaufort Sea ▾[2]	B 6	148
Beaufort West	G 5	206
Beaugency	E 8	78
Beauharnois	A 7	162
Beauharnois-Salaberry □[6]	A 5	164
Beaujolais □[9]	D 2	82
Beaumetz-lès-Loges	B 9	78
Beaumont, Ms., U.S.	G 4	170
Beaumont, Tx., U.S.	G 1	170
Beaumont-sur-Oise	C 9	78
Beaumont-sur-Sarthe	D 6	78
Beaune	E 11	78
Beauport	E 8	160
Beaupréau	E 6	78
Beausejour	F 10	158
Beauvais	C 8	78
Beauvais Lake ⊜	A 19	156
Beauvallon	E 2	206
Beauvoir-sur-Mer	F 4	78
Beaver, Pa., U.S.	C 3	162
Beaver, Ut., U.S.	C 2	176
Beaver, W.V., U.S.	E 3	162
Beaver ≃, Can.	A 9	156
Beaver ≃, Can.	D 18	156
Beaver ≃, U.S.	B 4	172
Beaver Creek ≃, Ak., U.S.	D 21	154
Beaver Creek ≃, Mt., U.S.	A 9	178
Beaver Dam	D 4	166
Beaverdell	G 12	156
Beaver Falls	C 3	162
Beaverhead ≃	C 7	178
Beaverhead Mountains ⋏	C 7	178
Beaver Hill Lake ⊜	D 11	158
Beaver Island I	C 6	166
Beaver Lake Indian Reserve ➔[4]	D 16	156
Beavers Bend State Park ♦	E 1	170
Beaverton	C 2	178
Beāwar	D 2	122
Bebedouro	D 6	194
Béboto	D 8	200
Bebra	F 6	98
Bécancour ≃	E 8	160
Beccles	E 8	72
Bečej	C 5	104
Beceni	C 9	104
Béchar	C 4	198
Becharof Lake ⊜	H 16	154
Bec-Hellouin, Abbaye du ◗[1]	C 7	78
Bechet	D 7	104
Bechevin Bay ⊂	I 12	154
Beckingen	C 3	100
Beckley	E 3	162
Beckum	E 4	98
Beckville	F 1	170
Bedale	C 5	72
Bedford, Eng., U.K.	E 6	72
Bedford, In., U.S.	C 5	170
Bedford, Ma., U.S.	D 7	164
Bedford, Pa., U.S.	C 4	162
Bedford, P.Q., Can.	A 5	164
Bedford, Va., U.S.	E 4	162
Bedfordshire □[6]	E 6	72
Bédi	C 8	200
Bedlington	B 5	72
Bedok	j 15	134a
Bedourie	H 4	142
Beech Creek	D 5	170
Beech Grove	C 5	170
Beechy	F 18	156
Beek	F 2	98
Beelitz	D 9	98
Beenleigh	A 9	144
Beerse	C 3	69
Be'ér Sheva'	G 3	120
Beeskow	D 11	98
Beeston	E 5	72
Beethoven Peninsula ›[1]	D 1	208
Beeville	F 5	172
Befale	B 3	204
Bega	F 7	144
Begna ≃	B 5	66
Begoro	D 4	200
Behbahān	G 14	118
Behm Canal ⋓	I 29	154
Behshahr	D 15	118
Bei ≃	G 11	130
Bei'an	B 16	128
Beicheng	F 6	130
Beihai	H 9	130
Beijing (Peking)	G 11	128
Beijing □[3]	F 11	128
Beiliu	G 10	130
Beipan ≃	F 7	130
Beipiao	F 13	128
Beira	F 5	204
Beira □[9]	C 1	84
Beirut see Bayrūt	B 4	120
Beiseker	F 15	156
Bei Shan ⋏	A 7	122
Beitbridge	B 9	206
Beizhen	F 13	128
Beja, Port.	F 3	86
Béja, Tun.	B 6	198
Beja □[3], Port.	G 2	86
Béja □[3], Tun.	G 2	90
Bejaïa	B 6	198
Béjar	D 5	86
Bejneu	G 19	110
Béka	D 7	200
Bekaa Valley V	E 7	118
Bekabad	A 1	122
Békés	B 6	104
Békés □[3]	B 6	104
Békéscsaba	B 6	104
Bekily	I 9	205a
Bekodoka	k 8	205a
Bekwai	D 4	200
Bekyem	D 4	200
Bela	E 10	116
Bélabo	E 7	200
Bela Crkva	C 6	104
Belaga	E 6	134
Bel Air	G 2	164
Belaja ≃	B 19	110
Belaja Berëzka	C 8	110
Belaja Holunica	G 19	108
Belaja Kalitva	E 12	110
Belalcázar	F 5	86
Belampalli	F 3	122
Bela Palanka	D 7	104
Belarus □[1]	E 13	62
Bela Vista, Ang.	D 1	204
Bela Vista, Braz.	E 2	194
Belawan	M 4	132
Belbubulo	F 3	202
Bełchatów	C 10	96
Belcher	C 11	158
Belcher Islands II	C 18	158
Belebej	I 21	108
Belecke	E 5	98
Beledweyne	G 5	202
Belel	D 7	200
Belém	D 9	190
Belén, Arg.	E 6	192
Belen, N.M., U.S.	E 5	176
Belén de Escobar	D 8	195
Belene	D 8	104
Bélep, Îles II	C 13	138
Beles ≃	E 4	202
Belet Uen see Beledweyne	G 5	202
Belëv	J 12	108
Belfast, Me., U.S.	A 9	162
Belfast, N. Ire., U.K.	B 5	75
Belfast (City) Airport ⊠	B 6	75
Belfield	B 3	174
Belfort	C 4	82
Belfort □[3]	C 4	82
Belgaum	F 2	122
Belgium	B 8	206
Belgium □[1]	E 8	62
Belgorod	D 10	110
Belgorodskaja oblast' □[6]	D 10	110
Belgrade, Mn., U.S.	C 7	174
Belgrade see Beograd, Yugo.	C 6	104
Belgrano II ◗[3]	D 5	208
Beliliou I	D 10	134
Beli Manastir	E 10	102
Belin-Beliet	D 3	80
Belington	D 4	162
Belitung I	F 5	134
Belize □[1]	I 15	184
Belize City	I 15	184
Belknap □[6]	C 7	164
Bell	C 7	156
Bell ≃, P.Q., Can.	D 5	160
Bell ≃, Yk., Can.	C 26	154
Bella Bella	E 7	156
Bellac	B 4	80
Bella Coola ≃	E 8	156
Bellair	D 4	168
Bellaria	E 8	92
Bellary	F 3	122
Bella Unión	B 9	195
Bella Vista	E 8	192
Bellé	C 2	200
Bellefontaine	C 2	162
Bellefonte	C 5	162
Belle Fourche ≃	C 3	174
Bellegarde-sur-Valserine	D 3	82
Belle Glade	B 4	186
Belle-Île I	E 3	78
Belle Isle, Strait of ⋓	C 15	160
Bellenden Ker National Park ♦	D 7	142
Belle Plaine, Mn., U.S.	C 2	166
Belle-Plaine, Sk., Can.	F 19	156
Belleview	G 5	170
Belleville, Il., U.S.	C 3	170
Belleville, Ks., U.S.	F 6	174
Belleville, On., Can.	F 5	160
Bellevue, Ab., Can.	A 6	178
Bellevue, Ne., U.S.	B 1	170
Bellevue, Oh., U.S.	C 2	162
Bellevue, Wa., U.S.	B 2	178
Belley	E 3	82
Bellingham, Mn., U.S.	C 6	174
Bellingham, Wa., U.S.	A 2	178
Bellingshausen ◗[3]	L 8	192
Bellingshausen Sea ▾[2]	C 35	208
Bellinzago Novarese	E 6	82
Bellinzona	D 7	82
Bellmawr	G 3	164
Bellmead	E 5	172
Bello	B 3	190
Bellpat	D 1	122
Bells Corners	A 5	162
Bellshill	B 2	72
Belluno	C 8	92
Belluno □[6]	C 7	92
Bell Ville, Arg.	C 6	195
Bellville, S. Afr.	G 3	206
Bellville, Tx., U.S.	F 5	172
Bellwood	C 4	162
Belmond	D 2	166
Belmont, N.Y., U.S.	B 4	162
Belmont, Wi., U.S.	D 3	166
Belmonte, Braz.	A 11	194
Belmonte, Port.	D 3	86
Belmonte, Spain	E 2	88

Symbols in the index entries represent the broad categories identified in the key at the right. Symbols with superior numbers (⋏[1]) identify subcategories (see complete key on page 242).

∧ Mountain ⋏ Mountains)(Pass V Valley ≂ Plain › Cape I Island II Islands ⊥ Other Topographic Feature ≃ River ≋ Canal

Belmopan — Bolhov

Name	Map Ref.	Page
Belmopan	I 15	184
Beloe, ozero ⊜	F 12	108
Belœil, Château de ◗	D 2	69
Belogorsk	B 9	124
Beloha	m 8	205a
Belo Horizonte	C 8	194
Beloit	D 4	166
Belojarskij	E 27	108
Belomorsk	D 11	108
Belomorsko-Baltijskij kanal ⊼	E 11	108
Belorado	B 7	86
Beloreč‌ensk	G 11	110
Beloreck	I 22	108
Beloščele	D 17	108
Belo sur Mer	I 8	205a
Belot, Lac ⊜	C 31	154
Belo Vale	D 8	194
Belovo	D 11	114
Belozërsk	F 12	108
Belper	D 5	72
Belt	B 8	178
Belton, Mo., U.S.	C 1	170
Belton, Tx., U.S.	E 5	172
Beluha, gora ∧	E 11	114
Belukha, Mount see Beluha, gora ∧	E 11	114
Belvedere Marittimo	E 5	94
Belvidere, Il., U.S.	A 4	170
Belvidere, N.J., U.S.	F 3	164
Belvís de la Jara	E 6	86
Belvoir see Kokhav HaYarden ⊥	D 4	120
Belyando ≃	G 8	142
Belyj, ostrov I	B 10	114
Belyj Jar	D 11	114
Belyy Island see Belyj, ostrov I	B 10	114
Belz	C 12	96
Belzig	D 9	98
Belzoni	F 3	170
Bembèrèkè	C 5	200
Bembibre	B 4	86
Bemidji	B 7	174
Bemis	E 4	170
Bena	C 6	200
Benaadir □[3]	G 6	202
Benāb	D 12	118
Benahmed	C 3	198
Benalla	F 5	144
Benalmádena Costa	H 6	86
Benares see Vārānasi	D 4	122
Ben Arous	G 3	90
Ben Arous □[3]	G 3	90
Benavarri	B 5	88
Benavente	C 5	86
Benbecula I	C 1	74
Ben Boyd National Park ♦	F 8	144
Bencubbin	L 4	140
Bend	C 3	178
Bendigo	F 5	144
Bendorf	B 4	100
Běne	D 11	66
Bene Beraq	E 3	120
Benešov	C 11	100
Benetússer	E 4	88
Bénévent-l'Abbaye	B 5	80
Benevento	C 4	94
Benevento □[6]	C 4	94
Bengal, Bay of ⊂	F 6	122
Bengbis	E 7	200
Bengbu	B 13	130
Benghazi see Banghāzī	C 9	198
Bengkalis	N 5	132
Bengkayang	N 9	132
Bengkulu	F 4	134
Bengo □[3]	D 1	204
Bengtsfors	C 5	66
Benguela	E 1	204
Benguela □[3]	E 1	204
Ben Guerdane	C 7	198
Beni	B 4	204
Beni ≃	F 5	190
Béni Abbas	C 4	198
Benicarló	D 5	88
Benicasim see Benicàssim	D 5	88
Benicàssim (Benicasim)	D 5	88
Benicia	B 1	182
Benidorm	F 4	88
Benifaió	E 4	88
Benigànim	F 4	88
Beni Mazâr	H 4	118
Beni-Mellal	C 3	198
Benin □[1]	G 8	196
Benin, Bight of ⊂	E 5	200
Benin City	D 6	200
Beni Saf	E 5	84
Benissa	F 5	88
Beni Suef	H 4	118
Benito Juárez	E 8	195
Benito Juárez, Presa ⊜[1]	I 12	184
Benjamin Hill	B 4	184
Benkovac	C 3	104
Ben Lomond	C 1	182
Ben Lomond National Park ♦	i 12	145a
Ben Mehidi	G 1	90
Benmore, Lake ⊜[1]	F 3	146
Bennebroek	B 3	69
Bennett, Lake ⊜	H 11	140
Bennett Lake ⊜	A 4	156
Bennettsville	B 5	168
Bennington	D 5	164
Bennington □[6]	C 5	164
Benoni	D 8	206
Bénoué (Benue) ≃	D 7	200
Bénoué, Parc National de la ♦	D 7	200
Bénoy	D 8	200
Ben Sekka, Rass ›	B 6	198
Bensheim	C 5	100
Benson	G 3	176
Bentiaba	E 1	204
Bentiaba ≃	E 1	204
Bentinck Island I	D 4	142
Bentley	D 5	72
Bento Gonçalves	A 11	195
Bentol	D 2	200
Benton, Ar., U.S.	E 2	170
Benton, Il., U.S.	C 4	170
Benton City	B 4	178
Benton Harbor	D 5	166
Bentonville	D 1	170
Ben Tre	I 8	132
Bent's Old Fort National Historic Site ♦	F 3	174
Benue (Bénoué) ≃	D 6	200
Benxi	F 14	128
Benza	D 1	204
Beograd (Belgrade)	C 6	104
Béoumi	D 3	200
Beppu	H 3	126
Bérandjoko	B 2	204
Berat	B 3	106
Berazino, Bela.	E 14	66
Berazino, Bela.	C 6	110
Berbegal	C 5	88
Berbera	E 6	202
Berbérati	E 8	200
Berchtesgaden	E 10	100
Berchtesgaden, Nationalpark ♦	E 9	100
Berčogur	E 21	110
Berdaale	G 5	202
Berdyans'k	F 10	110
Berdychiv	E 6	110
Berea, Ky., U.S.	E 1	162
Berea, Oh., U.S.	C 3	162
Berehove	A 7	104
Berekua	r 25	187g
Berekum	D 4	200
Berens ≃	E 10	158
Berens River	E 10	158
Beresford	D 6	174
Berettyó (Barcău) ≃	B 6	104
Berettyóújfalu	B 6	104
Berevo-Ranobe	k 8	205a
Berezhany	E 4	110
Berezivka	B 11	104
Bereznik	E 15	108
Berezniki	G 22	108
Berëzovka, Russia	D 21	108
Berëzovka, Russia	G 21	108
Berg	B 8	64
Berga	B 6	88
Bergama	C 7	106
Bergamo	D 5	92
Bergamo □[6]	D 5	92
Bergara	A 2	88
Bergen, Ger.	D 6	98
Bergen, Ger.	D 7	98
Bergen, Nor.	B 2	66
Bergen, N.Y., U.S.	B 4	163a
Bergen □[6]	F 4	164
Bergen auf Rügen	B 10	98
Bergen-Belsen-Denkmal ⊥	D 6	98
Bergen op Zoom	C 3	69
Bergerac	D 4	80
Bergheim	B 3	100
Bergisch Gladbach	F 4	98
Bergland	B 2	206
Bergsche Maas ≃	C 4	69
Bergsjö	A 8	66
Bergslagen □[9]	C 7	66
Bergues	B 9	78
Berhala, Selat ⊔	F 4	134
Beri	J 21	110
Beringa, ostrov I	D 19	114
Bering Glacier ⊠	F 23	154
Bering Sea ⊂	D 2	148
Bering Strait ⊔	C 10	154
Berja	H 1	88
Berkane	C 4	198
Berkeley	C 1	182
Berkeley Springs	D 4	162
Berkhamsted	F 6	72
Berkner Island I	D 4	208
Berks □[6]	F 3	164
Berkshire □[6], Eng., U.K.	F 5	72
Berkshire □[6], Ma., U.S.	D 5	164
Berkshire Hills ⋏[2]	D 5	164
Berland ≃	E 12	156
Berlevåg	A 14	64
Berlin, Ger.	D 10	98
Berlin, Md., U.S.	D 6	162
Berlin, N.H., U.S.	B 7	164
Berlin, Pa., U.S.	D 4	162
Berlin □[3]	D 10	98
Berlin, Mount ∧	D 31	208
Berlin-Ichthyosaur State Park ♦	B 6	182
Bermejillo	E 8	184
Bermejo ≃, Arg.	F 6	192
Bermejo ≃, S.A.	E 7	192
Bermejo, Paso del)(	C 3	195
Bermen, Lac ⊜	B 9	160
Bermeo	A 2	88
Bermuda □[2]	i 9	168
Bern (Berne)	D 5	82
Bern □[3]	D 5	82
Bernalda	D 6	94
Bernau bei Berlin	D 10	98
Bernaville	B 9	78
Bernay	C 7	78
Bernburg	E 8	98
Berne, Ger.	C 5	98
Berne see Bern, Switz.	D 5	82
Berner Alpen (Bernese Alps) ⋏	E 7	76
Bernese Alps see Berner Alpen ⋏	E 7	76
Bernhardina	D 8	206
Bernier Island I	I 2	140
Bernina, Piz ∧	D 1	102
Bernkastel-Kues	C 3	100
Bernsdorf	E 11	98
Beromünster	C 6	82
Beroun	C 11	100
Berovo	E 7	104
Berra	E 7	92
Berrechid	C 3	198
Berre-l'Étang	G 3	82
Berriozar	B 3	88
Berry □[9]	F 9	78
Berryessa, Lake ⊜[1]	B 1	182
Berseba	D 2	206
Bershad'	A 10	104
Bersut	I 19	108
Berté, Lac ⊜	C 9	160
Bertha	B 7	174
Berthoud	E 2	174
Berthoud Pass)(	C 5	176
Bertoua	F 7	200
Bertrand	B 5	170
Berwick, Me., U.S.	C 8	164
Berwick, Pa., U.S.	E 2	164
Berwick-upon-Tweed	B 5	72
Berwyn	B 5	170
Beryslav	F 8	110
Besançon	C 4	82
Bešankovičy	E 13	66
Besigheim	C 6	100
Beşiri	D 9	118
Beskids ⋏	D 10	96
Beskra	C 6	198
Beslan	H 14	110
Besnard Lake ⊜	D 18	156
Besni	D 7	118
Besozzo	E 6	82
Bessacarr	D 5	72
Bessarabia □[9]	B 10	104
Bessèges	F 2	82
Bessemer, Al., U.S.	F 5	170
Bessemer, Mi., U.S.	B 3	166
Bessheim	B 4	66
Bestuževo	F 15	108
Bestwig	E 5	98
Beswick Aboriginal Land ✦[4]	D 12	140
Betamba	C 3	204
Betanzos	A 2	86
Betbetti	D 1	202
Bétera	E 4	88
Bétérou	D 5	200
Bethal	D 8	206
Bethanien	D 2	206
Bethany, Mo., U.S.	B 1	170
Bethany, Ok., U.S.	C 5	172
Bethel, Ak., U.S.	F 13	154
Bethel, Ct., U.S.	E 5	164
Bethel, N.C., U.S.	B 6	168
Bethesda	H 1	164
Bethlehem, Pa., U.S.	F 3	164
Bethlehem, S. Afr.	E 8	206
Bethlehem, S. Afr.	D 6	206
Bethlehem see Bayt Lahm, W.B.	F 4	120
Bethulie	F 6	206
Béthune	B 9	78
Betong	L 5	132
Bétou	B 2	204
Bet Sh'ean	D 4	120
Bet Shemesh	F 4	120
Betsiamites	D 9	160
Betsiamites ≃	D 9	160
Betsiamites, Réserve indienne de ✦[4]	D 9	160
Betsiboka ≃	k 9	205a
Betta	C 2	206
Bettendorf	B 3	170
Bettiah	D 4	122
Betūl	B 2	122
Betuwe ✦[1]	C 4	69
Betwa ≃	D 4	122
Beulah	B 4	174
B. Everett Jordan Lake ⊜[1]	B 5	168
Beverley	D 6	72
Beverley Springs	E 8	140
Beverlo	E 2	98
Beverly	D 8	164
Beverly Hills	F 5	182
Beverungen	E 6	98
Beverwijk	B 3	69
Bewdley	E 4	72
Bexbach	C 4	100
Bexhill	G 7	72
Bexley	D 2	162
Bexley □[6]	F 7	72
Beycuma	B 9	106
Beydağları Olimpos Milli Parkı ♦	D 9	106
Beyla	D 3	200
Beypazarı	B 4	118
Beyra	F 6	202
Beyşehir	D 4	118
Beyşehir Gölü ⊜	D 4	118
Bezaha	I 8	205a
Bezděz ⊥	B 11	100
Bežeck	H 12	108
Béziers	E 7	80
Bhadrak	E 5	122
Bhadra Reservoir ⊜[1]	G 3	122
Bhadrāvati	G 3	122
Bhāgalpur	D 5	122
Bhakkar	C 2	122
Bhaktapur	D 5	122
Bhamo	B 3	132
Bhandāra	B 3	122
Bharatpur	D 3	122
Bharūch	E 2	122
Bhatkal	G 2	122
Bhātpāra	E 5	122
Bhāvnagar	E 2	122
Bhawānipatna	E 4	122
Bhilai	E 4	122
Bhīlwāra	D 2	122
Bhīma ≃	F 3	122
Bhīmavaram	F 4	122
Bhind	D 3	122
Bhiwandi	F 2	122
Bhiwāni	D 3	122
Bhongīr	F 3	122
Bhopāl	E 3	122
Bhubaneshwar	E 5	122
Bhuj	E 1	122
Bhunya	D 9	206
Bhusāwal	E 3	122
Bhutan □[1]	E 15	116
Bia, Phou ∧	E 6	132
Biafra, Bight of ⊂	E 6	200
Biak I	F 11	134
Biała Piska	B 12	96
Biała Podlaska	B 12	96
Biała Podlaska □[3]	C 12	96
Białobrzegi	C 11	96
Białogard	A 9	96
Białowieski Park Narodowy ♦	B 12	96
Białystok	B 12	96
Białystok □[3]	B 12	96
Biancavilla	G 4	94
Biaro, Pulau I	E 9	134
Biarritz	E 2	80
Biasca	E 9	82
Biba	H 4	118
Bibai	C 16	126
Bibane, Bahiret el ⊂	C 7	198
Bibân el-Mulûk (Valley of the Kings) ⊥	B 3	202
Bibbiena	F 7	92
Biberach an der Riss, Ger.	D 5	96
Biberach an der Riss, Ger.	D 6	100
Bibiani	D 4	200
Biblis	C 5	100
Biča	H 29	108
Bicaz	B 8	104
Bicester	F 5	72
Biche, Lac la ⊜	D 15	156
Bichena	E 4	202
Bicheno	i 13	145a
Bicol ›[1]	C 8	134
Bicuari, Parque Nacional do ♦	F 1	204
Bičura	A 6	128
Bīd	F 3	122
Bida	D 6	200
Bīdar	F 3	122
Biddeford	C 8	164
Bideford	F 2	72
Bidwell	D 2	162
Bié □[3]	E 2	204
Bieber	E 3	178
Biebrzański Park Narodowy ♦	B 12	96
Biel	C 5	82
Biel, Lake see Bielersee ⊜	C 5	82
Bielawa	C 9	96
Bielefeld	D 5	98
Bielersee (Biel, Lake) ⊜	C 5	82
Biella	D 4	92
Biella □[6]	D 4	92
Bielsk	B 10	96
Bielsko-Biała	D 10	96
Bielsko-Biała □[3]	D 10	96
Bielsk Podlaski	B 12	96
Bien Hoa	I 8	132
Bienne see Biel	C 5	82
Bien Son	D 7	132
Bienville, Lac ⊜	A 7	160
Bierné	E 6	78
Biesiesvlei	D 6	206
Bieszczadzki Park Narodowy ♦	D 12	96
Bietigheim-Bissingen	D 6	100
Biga	B 7	106
Bigadiç	C 8	106
Big Bar Creek	F 10	156
Big Basin Redwoods State Park ♦	C 1	182
Big Bear Lake	F 7	182
Big Belt Mountains ⋏	B 8	178
Big Bend	D 9	206
Big Bend National Park ♦	F 2	172
Big Bonito Creek ≃	F 4	176
Big Clifty	A 1	168
Big Cypress Indian Reservation ✦[4]	F 4	168
Big Cypress Swamp ⊞	F 4	168
Big Delta	D 21	154
Big Desert ✦[2]	E 3	144
Bigfork	B 2	166
Biggar	E 17	156
Biggleswade	E 6	72
Bighorn ≃	C 10	178
Bighorn Canyon National Recreation Area ♦	C 9	178
Big Horn Lake ⊜[1]	C 9	178
Bighorn Mountains ⋏	C 10	178
Big Island	A 5	168
Big Island I	D 18	150
Big Lake	E 3	172
Big Lake ⊜	h 13	163a
Big Muddy Creek ≃	A 2	174
Bignasco	D 6	82
Bignona	C 1	200
Bigorre ✦[1]	E 4	80
Big Piney	D 8	178
Big Prairie Creek ≃	F 5	170
Big Quill Lake ⊜	F 6	158
Big Rapids	D 6	166
Big Rideau Lake ⊜	F 5	160
Big River Indian Reserve ✦[4]	E 18	156
Big Salmon ≃	F 28	154
Big Sand Lake ⊜	C 8	158
Big Sandy	A 8	178
Big Sandy ≃	D 2	162
Big Sandy Creek ≃	F 3	174
Big Sandy Lake ⊜	D 20	156
Big Sioux ≃	D 6	174
Big Spring	D 3	172
Bigstone ≃	D 11	158
Big Stone Gap	E 2	162
Bigstone Lake ⊜	E 11	158
Big Sur ✦[1]	D 2	182
Big Thompson ≃	B 6	176
Big Trout Lake ⊜	E 14	158
Biguaçu	G 6	194
Big Warrambool, The ≃	B 6	144
Bihać	C 3	104
Bīhar	D 5	122
Bihār □[3]	E 5	122
Biharamulo	C 5	204
Bihor □[3]	B 7	104
Bihoro	C 10	126
Bihu	D 14	130
Bija ≃	D 11	114
Bijagós, Arquipélago dos (Bissagos) II	C 1	200
Bījār	E 12	118
Bijeljina	C 5	104
Bijelo Polje	D 5	104
Bijiang	E 4	130
Bijie	E 7	130
Bijnor	D 3	122
Bijsk	D 11	114
Bīkāner	D 2	122
Bikar I[1]	B 9	136
Bikié	C 1	204
Bikin	C 20	128
Bikin ≃	C 20	128
Bikini I[1]	B 8	136
Bīkkū Bīttī ∧	E 8	198
Bilanga	C 4	200
Bilāspur, India	C 3	122
Bilāspur, India	E 4	122
Biläsuvar	J 16	110
Bila Tserkva	E 7	110
Bilauktaung Range ⋏	H 4	132
Bilbao	A 7	86
Bilbilis ⊥	C 3	88
Bilecik	B 8	106
Bilecik □[3]	B 8	106
Biłgoraj	C 12	96
Bilhorod-Dnistrovs'kyy	B 11	104
Bili	B 4	204
Bilin	F 3	132
Bilin ≃	F 3	132
Bílina	B 10	100
Billabong Creek ≃	E 5	144
Billerbeck	D 4	98
Billère	E 3	80
Billericay	F 7	72
Billingham	C 5	72
Billings	C 9	178
Billingsfors	C 6	66
Bill Williams ≃	E 2	176
Biloela	H 10	142
Bilohirs'k	G 9	110
Bilopillya	D 9	110
Biloxi	G 4	170
Biltine	C 9	200
Biltine □[3]	C 9	200
Biltmore Forest	B 3	168
Bilzen	D 4	69
Bimberi Peak ∧	E 7	144
Bimbila	D 4	200
Bimbo	E 8	200
Bimbowrie	D 2	144
Bimini Islands II	G 5	168
Bīna-Etāwa	E 3	122
Binche	D 3	69
Bindloss	F 16	156
Bindura	F 5	204
Binéfar	C 5	88
Bin-el-Ouidane	C 3	198
Binga	B 3	204
Bingen	C 4	100
Binghamton	D 3	164
Bingöl	C 9	118
Bingöl □[3]	C 9	118
Binhai	A 14	130
Binjai	M 4	132
Binongko, Pulau I	G 8	134
Bintimani ∧	D 2	200
Bint Jubayl	C 4	120
Bintulu	E 6	134
Bintuni	F 10	134
Binxian, China	H 11	128
Binxian, China	I 7	128
Binxian, China	D 16	128
Binyang	G 9	130
Bin-Yauri	C 5	200
Bio Addo	F 6	202
Biobío □[3]	E 1	195
Biobío ≃	G 5	192
Biograd na moru	D 3	104
Biogradska Gora Nacionalni Park ♦	D 5	104
Bioko (Fernando Póo) I	E 6	200
Bira ≃	B 19	128
Birāk	D 7	198
Bi'r al Wa'r	E 7	198
Birao	C 9	200
Bircao see Buur Gaabo	H 5	202
Birch ≃	B 15	156
Birch Creek ≃	C 22	154
Birch Lake ⊜	F 12	158
Birch Mountains ⋏[2]	C 15	156
Birch Run	B 2	162
Birchy Bay	D 16	160
Birdum	D 12	140
Birecik	D 8	118
Bir el Ater	C 6	198
Bir Enzaran	E 2	198
Birigui	D 5	194
Biriljussy	D 12	114
Bīrjand	D 8	116
Birjusa ≃	D 12	114
Birkeland	C 4	66
Birkenfeld, Ger.	D 5	100
Birkenfeld, Ger.	C 4	100
Birkenhead	D 3	72
Birkenwerder bei Berlin	D 10	98
Birkerød	C 5	68
Birkfeld	C 7	102
Birmingham, Al., U.S.	F 5	170
Birmingham, Eng., U.K.	E 4	72
Birmingham, Mi., U.S.	B 2	162
Birmitrapur	E 4	122
Birnie I[1]	D 10	136
Birnin Gaouré	C 5	200
Birnin-Kebbi	C 5	200
Birnin Konni	C 6	200
Birnin Kudu	C 6	200
Birobidžan	B 19	128
Birsk	I 21	108
Birungu, Pac des ♦	C 4	204
Biržai	D 12	66
Bisa, Pulau I	F 9	134
Bisaccia	C 5	94
Bisbee	G 4	176
Biscarrosse	D 2	80
Biscay, Bay of ⊂	G 7	62
Biscayne National Park ♦	G 4	168
Bisceglie	C 6	94
Bischofshofen	C 5	102
Bischwiller	B 5	82
Bisha	D 4	202
Bishnupur	E 5	122
Bisho	G 7	206
Bishop	G 5	172
Bishop Auckland	C 5	72
Bishop Indian Reservation ✦[4]	C 5	182
Bishop Rock II[1]	i 9	73a
Bishop's Stortford	F 7	72
Bishrah, Ma'tan ⊤[4]	E 9	198
Bisina, Lake ⊜	G 3	202
Biškek	A 2	122
Biskupiec	B 11	96
Bislig	D 9	134
Bismarck	B 4	174
Bismarck Archipelago II	M 13	124
Bismarckmuseum ◗	C 7	98
Bismarck Range ⋏	N 12	124
Bismarck Sea ⊤[2]	M 13	124
Bismo	B 4	66
Bissau	C 1	200
Bissett	F 11	158
Bistcho Lake ⊜	B 12	156
Bistineau, Lake ⊜[1]	F 2	170
Bistrica	D 2	102
Bistrita	B 8	104
Bistrita-Năsăud □[3]	B 8	104
Bitam	E 7	200
Bitburg	C 3	100
Bitche	A 5	82
Bitéa, Ouadi ≃	C 9	200
Bithia ⊥	m 9	94a
Bitkin	C 8	200
Bitlis	C 10	118
Bitlis □[3]	C 10	118
Bitola	E 6	104
Bitonto	C 6	94
Bitou	C 4	200
Bitterfeld	E 9	98
Bitterroot ≃	B 7	178
Bitterroot, West Fork ≃	C 6	178
Bitterroot Range ⋏	B 6	178
Bitti	I 5	92
Biu	C 7	200
Biwabik	B 2	166
Biwa-ko ⊜	G 5	126
Biyang	B 11	130
Bizana	F 8	206
Bizen	G 5	126
Bizerte	B 6	198
Bizerte □[3]	G 2	90
Bizerte, Lac de ⊜	G 2	90
Bjala Slatina	D 7	104
Bjalyničy	B 6	110
Bjarèzina ≃	C 6	110
Bjargtangar ›	m 18	64a
Bjaroza	J 12	64
Bjarozauka	F 12	66
Bjärred	C 6	68
Bjelovar	E 8	102
Bjerringbro	B 2	68
Björna	E 9	64
Bjuv	D 6	66
Bla	C 3	200
Black ≃, Ak., U.S.	D 24	154
Black ≃, La., U.S.	G 3	170
Black ≃, N.Y., U.S.	B 3	164
Black ≃, U.S.	E 3	170
Blackall	H 7	142
Black Bear Island Lake ⊜	D 6	158
Black Birch Lake ⊜	C 18	156
Blackburn	D 4	72
Blackburn, Mount ∧	F 22	154
Black Canyon of the Gunnison National Monument ♦	C 5	176
Black Creek	G 9	156
Blackdown Tableland National Park ♦	G 9	142
Black Duck ≃	C 14	158
Black Eagle	B 8	178
Blackfeet Indian Reservation ✦[4]	A 7	178
Blackfoot	D 7	178
Blackfoot Indian Reserve ✦[4]	F 15	156
Black Forest see Schwarzwald ⋏	D 5	100
Black Hills ⋏	C 3	174
Black Lake	g 11	163a
Black Lake ⊜	B 19	156
Black Mesa ∧	G 3	174
Blackmoor ✦[3]	B 2	78
Black Mountain ⋏	E 2	162
Black Nossob ≃	B 3	206
Blackpool	D 3	72
Black River	B 3	164
Black River (Da, Song) (Lixian) ≃	D 7	132
Black River Falls	C 3	166
Black Rock II[1]	J 11	192
Black Rock Desert ✦[2]	E 4	178
Blacksburg	E 3	162
Black Sea ⊤[2]	H 6	110
Blacks Fork ≃	E 9	178
Blacks Harbour	h 13	163a
Blackstone	E 5	162
Blackstone ≃	D 26	154
Black Tickle	B 16	160
Blacktown	D 8	144
Black Volta (Mouhoun) ≃	D 4	200
Blackwater	G 9	142
Blackwater ≃	D 4	75
Blackwater Draw ≃	C 2	172
Blackwater Lake ⊜	D 33	154
Blackwell	B 5	172
Blackwood ≃	M 4	140
Bladensburg National Park ♦	G 6	142
Bladgrond	E 3	206
Blaenau Gwent □[6]	F 3	72
Blagnac	E 5	80
Blagodarnyj	G 13	110
Blagodatovka	C 16	110
Blagoevgrad	D 7	104
Blagoveščensk, Russia	I 21	108
Blagoveščensk, Russia	A 16	128
Blaine	C 2	166
Blaine Lake	E 18	156
Blair	E 6	174
Blair Athol	G 8	142
Blairstown	B 2	170
Blaj	B 7	104
Blakely	G 6	170
Blanc, Cap ›	A 1	200
Blanc, Mont ∧	E 4	82
Blanca, Bahía ⊂, Arg.	G 7	192
Blanca, Bahía ⊂, Arg.	G 7	192
Blanca, Costa ⊥[2]	F 4	88
Blanca Peak ∧	D 6	176
Blanche, Lake ⊜, Austl.	H 7	140
Blanche, Lake ⊜, Austl.	B 2	144
Blanchisseuse	q 23	187f
Blanco ≃	A 3	195
Blanco, Cabo ›	F 3	186
Blanco, Cape ›	A 1	180
Blanc-Sablon	C 15	160
Bland	E 3	162
Blandinsville	B 3	170
Blanes	C 7	88
Blankenberge	C 1	69
Blankenburg	E 7	98
Blankenfelde	D 10	98
Blankenheim	B 3	100
Blanquilla, Isla I	F 8	186
Blansko	A 8	102
Blantyre	F 5	204
Blarney Castle ⊥	E 3	75
Blasdell	B 4	162
Blatná	C 10	100
Blaubeuren	D 6	100
Blaye	C 3	80
Bleaker Island I	o 18	193b
Bled, Lake ⊜	B 2	104
Bleiburg	D 6	102
Bleicherode	E 7	98
Blekinge □[3]	D 7	66
Blenheim	D 4	146
Blenheim Palace ◗	F 5	72
Blerick	C 5	69
Blessing	F 5	172
Bletchley	F 6	72
Bleus, Monts ⋏	B 5	204
Bligh Water ⊔	m 13	147c
Blina	E 8	140
Blind River	E 2	160
Blitar	I 21	135b
Block Island	E 7	164
Block Island I	E 7	164
Bloed ≃	D 9	206
Bloedel	F 9	156
Bloemendaal	B 3	69
Bloemfontein	E 6	206
Bloemhofdam ⊜[1]	D 6	206
Blois	E 8	78
Blokhus	A 2	68
Blomberg	E 6	98
Blönduós	m 20	64a
Blood Indian Reserve ✦[4]	G 15	156
Bloodvein ≃	F 10	158
Bloomfield, Ia., U.S.	B 2	170
Bloomfield, In., U.S.	C 5	170
Bloomington, Il., U.S.	B 4	170
Bloomington, In., U.S.	C 5	170
Bloomington, Mn., U.S.	C 2	166
Bloomington, Wi., U.S.	D 3	166
Bloomsburg	F 2	164
Blora	k 20	135b
Blossburg	E 1	164
Bloumet	E 6	198
Blountsville	E 5	170
Blowering Reservoir ⊜[1]	E 7	144
Blowing Rock	A 4	168
Bludenz	C 1	102
Blue ≃	F 4	176
Bluebush Swamp ⊞	F 3	142
Blue Earth	D 7	174
Bluefield	E 3	162
Bluefields	F 4	186
Blue Island	B 5	170
Blue Knob State Park ♦	C 4	162
Blue Lagoon National Park ♦	F 4	204
Blue Mound	C 4	170
Blue Mountain ⋏	C 5	162
Blue Mountain Peak ∧	h 13	186a
Blue Mountains ⋏, Austl.	D 8	144
Blue Mountains ⋏, Jam.	h 13	186a
Blue Mountains ⋏, Me., U.S.	h 11	163a
Blue Mountains ⋏, U.S.	C 4	178
Blue Mountains National Park ♦	D 7	144
Blue Mud Bay ⊂	B 2	142
Blue Nile (Azraq, Al-Baḥr al-) ≃	D 3	202
Bluenose Lake ⊜	B 35	154
Blue Ridge ⋏	E 3	162
Blue Ridge Parkway ♦	E 3	66
Blue River	E 12	156
Bluestone Dam ✦[6]	A 4	168
Bluff, N.Z.	G 2	146
Bluff, Ut., U.S.	D 4	176
Bluff Knoll ∧	N 4	140
Bluff Park	F 5	170
Bluffton	B 6	170
Blumberg	E 5	100
Blumenau	G 6	194
Blumenhof	F 18	156
Bly	D 3	178
Blying Sound ⊔	G 20	154
Blyth	B 5	72
Blythe	F 1	176
Blytheville	E 4	170
Bø, Nor.	B 7	64
Bo, S.L.	D 2	200
Boaco	E 3	186
Boa Esperança, Represa ⊜[1]	E 10	190
Bo'ai	I 9	128
Boane	D 10	206
Boardman	C 3	162
Boa Vista	C 6	190
Boa Vista I	h 11	200a
Bobai	G 9	130
Bobaomby, Tanjona ›	j 9	205a
Bobbili	F 4	122
Bobenheim-Roxheim	C 5	100
Bobigny	D 9	78
Bobingen	D 7	100
Böblingen	D 6	100
Bobo-Dioulasso	C 4	200
Bob Quinn Lake	C 6	156
Bobr	B 6	110
Bobrov	D 11	110
Bobrynets'	E 8	110
Boby ∧	I 9	205a
Boca do Acre	E 5	190
Boca Grande	F 3	168
Bocairent	F 4	88
Bocaiúva	B 8	194
Boca Raton	F 4	168
Bocas del Toro	F 4	186
Bochnia	D 11	96
Bocholt, Bel.	C 4	69
Bocholt, Ger.	E 3	98
Bochum	E 4	98
Bockhorn	C 4	98
Bocognano	i 8	83a
Boconó	F 7	186
Bocșa	C 6	104
Boda	E 8	200
Boda Glasbruk	D 7	66
Bodajbo	D 14	114
Bodalangi	B 3	204
Bodallin	L 5	140
Bodélé ✦[1]	B 8	200
Boden	D 10	64
Bodhan	F 3	122
Bodh Gaya	E 4	122
Bodī	D 3	128
Bodmin	G 2	72
Bodmin Moor ✦[3]	G 2	72
Bodø	C 7	64
Bodoukpa	D 8	200
Bodrum	D 7	106
Boën, Fr.	C 7	80
Boën, Fr.	E 1	82
Boende	C 3	204
Boeo, Capo ›	G 2	94
Boetsap	D 6	206
Boffa	C 2	200
Bofors	C 7	66
Bofossou	D 3	200
Bogal, Lagh ≃	G 4	202
Bogale	F 2	132
Bogalusa	G 4	170
Bogan ≃	C 6	144
Bogan Gate	D 6	144
Bogata	F 1	170
Bogatynia	F 11	98
Boğazlıyan	C 6	118
Bogdanovič	H 24	108
Bogda Shan ⋏	A 5	122
Bogen	D 9	100
Bogense	C 2	68
Boggy Peak ∧	I 18	187c
Bognes	B 8	64
Bognor Regis	G 6	72
Bogo	C 8	134
Bogong, Mount ∧	F 6	144
Bogor	k 18	135b
Bogorodick	J 13	108
Bogorodsk, Russia	H 15	108
Bogorodsk, Russia	E 19	108
Bogorodskoe	F 13	110
Bogotá	C 4	190
Bogou	C 5	200
Bogra	E 5	122
Bogué	F 2	198
Bogue Chitto ≃	G 3	170
Bohai Haixia ⊔	G 13	128
Bohain-en-Vermandois	C 10	78
Bohemia see Čechy □[9]	D 8	96
Bohemian Forest ⋏	C 10	100
Bohicon	D 5	200
Bohinjska Bistrica	D 5	102
Böhlen	E 9	98
Bohol	F 6	202
Bohol I	D 8	134
Bohol Sea ⊤[2]	D 8	134
Bohongou	C 5	200
Bohu	A 5	122
Boiano	C 4	94
Boiestown	E 10	160
Boiro	B 2	86
Bois ≃	C 5	194
Bois, Lac des ⊜	C 32	154
Bois Blanc Island I	C 6	166
Bois de Sioux ≃	C 6	174
Boise	D 5	178
Boise ≃	D 5	178
Boise, Middle Fork ≃	D 6	178
Boise, South Fork ≃	D 6	178
Bois Forte Indian Reservation ✦[4]	A 2	166
Bois-Guillaume	C 8	78
Boissevain	G 8	158
Boizenburg	C 7	98
Bojeador, Cape ›	B 8	134
Bojnūrd	D 17	118
Bojonegoro	k 20	135b
Boju	D 6	200
Bokāro Steel City	E 5	122
Bokatola	C 2	204
Boké	C 2	200
Boki	D 7	200
Boknafjorden ⊔	C 2	66
Bokondo	B 3	204
Bokoro	C 8	200
Bokovskaja	E 12	110
Boksitogorsk	G 10	108
Bokungu	C 3	204
Bokurdak	J 21	110
Bol	C 7	200
Bolama	B 3	204
Bolaños ≃	G 8	184
Bolaños de Calatrava	F 7	86
Bolayır	B 7	106
Bolbec	C 7	78
Bolekhiv	A 7	104
Boles	E 1	170
Bolesławiec	C 8	96
Boleszkowice	B 8	96
Bolgatanga	C 4	200
Bolhov	C 9	110

⌞ Waterfall ⊔ Strait ⊂ Bay, Gulf ⊜ Lake ⊞ Swamp ⊠ Ice Feature ⊤ Other Hydrographic Feature ✦ Submarine Feature □ Political Unit ◗ Cultural Institution ⊥ Historical Site ♦ Recreational Site ✈ Airport ■ Military Installation ✦ Miscellaneous

Symbols in the index entries represent the broad categories identified in the key at the right. Symbols with superior numbers (∦¹) identify subcategories (see complete key on page 242).

∧ Mountain   ∧ Mountains   )(Pass   v Valley   ≃ Plain   ≻ Cape   I Island   II Islands   ⊥ Other Topographic Feature   ≃ River   ≃ Canal

Burco — Casas Grandes

Name	Map Ref.	Page
Burco	F 6	202
Burdekin ≃	F 8	142
Burden	G 6	174
Burdur	D 9	106
Burdur □[3]	D 9	106
Burdur Gölü ⊜	D 9	106
Burē	E 4	202
Bureinskij hrebet ⋏	B 10	124
Bureja ≃	B 10	124
Büren	E 5	98
Bürenhaan	B 2	128
Burfjord	B 11	64
Burg	D 8	98
Burgas	D 9	104
Burgas □[3]	D 9	104
Burgaski Zaliv c	D 9	104
Burg auf Fehmarn	B 8	98
Burgdorf, Ger.	D 7	98
Burgdorf, Switz.	C 5	82
Burgenland □[3]	C 8	102
Burgeo	E 15	160
Burgersfort	C 9	206
Burgess Hill	G 6	72
Burghausen	D 9	100
Burghead	C 5	74
Burglengenfeld	C 8	100
Burgo de Osma	C 7	86
Burgos	B 7	86
Burgos □[6]	A 4	84
Burgstädt	F 9	98
Burgsvik	D 9	66
Burgundy		
see Bourgogne □[9]	E 6	76
Burhaniye	C 7	106
Burhānpur	E 3	122
Burias Island I	C 8	134
Burica, Punta ›	G 4	186
Burien	B 2	178
Burin	E 16	160
Buri Ram	G 6	132
Buritizeiro	B 8	194
Burjassot	E 4	88
Burjatija □[3]	B 6	124
Burke ≃	G 5	142
Burkesville	D 6	170
Burketown	D 4	142
Burkina □[1]	G 7	196
Burlada	B 3	88
Burladingen	D 6	100
Burleigh Heads	B 9	144
Burleson	D 5	172
Burley	D 7	178
Burlin	C 22	110
Burlingame	C 1	182
Burlington, Ia., U.S.	B 3	170
Burlington, Ma., U.S.	D 7	164
Burlington, N.C., U.S.	A 5	168
Burlington, N.J., U.S.	F 4	164
Burlington, On., Can.	G 4	160
Burlington, Vt., U.S.	B 5	164
Burlington, Wa., U.S.	A 2	178
Burlington □[6]	G 4	164
Burlit	C 20	128
Burma		
see Myanmar □[1]	F 16	116
Burnaby	G 10	156
Burnet	E 4	172
Burnett ≃	H 11	142
Burnham	E 10	166
Burnham-on-Sea	F 3	72
Burnie	i 11	145a
Burnley	D 4	72
Burns	D 4	178
Burnside ≃	C 11	150
Burnside, Lake ⊜	I 7	140
Burns Lake	D 8	156
Burnsville, Al., U.S.	F 5	170
Burnsville, W.V., U.S.	D 3	162
Burntisland	A 3	72
Burntwood	E 4	72
Burntwood ≃	D 10	158
Burntwood Lake ⊜	D 8	158
Burra	D 2	144
Burracoppin	L 5	140
Burragorang, Lake ⊜[1]	E 8	144
Burrel	B 3	106
Burrendong, Lake ⊜[1]	D 7	144
Burren Junction	C 7	144
Burrinjuck Reservoir ⊜[1]	E 7	144
Burrowa-Pine Mountain		
National Park ♦	F 6	144
Burruyacú	E 7	192
Burrwood	H 4	170
Bursa	B 8	106
Bursa □[3]	B 8	106
Burscheid	E 4	98
Burshtyn	E 4	110
Burslem	D 4	72
Bürstadt	C 5	100
Burt Lake ⊜	C 6	166
Burton, Mi., U.S.	B 2	162
Burton, Tx., U.S.	E 5	172
Burton upon Trent	E 5	72
Buru I	F 9	134
Buruc	E 6	202
Burullus, Buheirat el- ⊜	G 4	118
Burundi □[1]	I 11	196
Burun-Šibertuj, gora ∧	B 7	128
Burwell	E 5	174
Bury	D 4	72
Bury □[6]	D 4	72
Bury Saint Edmunds	E 7	72
Busanga	C 3	204
Busby	C 10	178
Buseck	B 5	100
Bushbush ≃	H 5	202
Būshehr	H 14	118
Būshehr □[3]	H 14	118
Bushenyi	H 3	202
Bushland	C 2	172
Bushmanland ◆[1]	E 3	206
Bushtyna	A 7	104
Busia	G 3	202
Businga	B 3	204
Busira ≃	C 2	204
Bus'k	D 4	110
Buskerud □[3]	B 4	66
Busko-Zdrój	C 11	96
Busovača	C 4	104
Busselton	M 3	140
Bussolengo	D 6	92
Bussoleno	D 3	92
Bussum	B 4	69
Bustamante	D 9	184
Busto Arsizio	D 4	92
Busto Garolfo	E 6	82
Busuanga Island I	C 8	134
Büsum	B 5	98
Buta	B 3	204
Butan	D 7	104
Butare	C 4	204
Butaritari I[1]	C 9	136
Bute Inlet c	F 9	156
Butemba	G 3	202
Butembo	B 4	204
Butha-Buthe	E 8	206
Buthidaung	D 1	132
Butiá	B 11	195
Butler, In., U.S.	B 6	170
Butler, Pa., U.S.	C 4	162
Buton, Pulau I	F 8	134
Butru	F 4	142
Butsha	B 4	204
Butte □[6]	A 2	182
Butte du Lion ⊥	D 3	69
Butterworth, Malay.	L 5	132
Butterworth, S. Afr.	G 8	206
Butuan	D 9	134
Buturlino	I 16	108
Buturlinovka	D 12	110
Butzbach	B 5	100
Bützow	C 8	98
Buulobarde	G 6	202
Buurgplaatz ∧	D 5	69
Buxtehude	C 6	98
Buxton, Eng., U.K.	D 5	72
Buxton, N.C., U.S.	B 7	168
Buxton, S. Afr.	D 6	206
Buyant ≃	C 2	128
Buyat	C 1	128
Buyo	D 3	200
Buyo, Barrage de ◆[6]	D 3	200
Buyr nuur		
see Buir Nur ⊜	C 11	128
Büyükçekmece	B 8	106
Büyükkale	C 7	106
Büyükmenderes ≃	D 7	106
Buzançais	F 8	78
Buzău	C 9	104
Buzău □[3]	C 9	104
Buzău ≃	C 9	104
Búzi ≃	F 5	204
Buziaș	C 6	104
Büzmeyin	C 17	118
Buzuluk	C 18	110
Byam Martin Island I	A 12	150
Bychawa	C 12	96
Bydalen	E 6	64
Bydgoszcz	B 10	96
Bydgoszcz □[3]	B 9	96
Bygdeå	D 10	64
Bykovo	E 14	110
Bylnice	A 10	102
Bylot Island I	B 17	150
Byng Inlet	F 3	160
Bynum	B 5	168
Byrnedale	E 9	166
Byrock	C 6	144
Byron	A 4	170
Byron, Cape ›	B 9	144
Byron, Isla I	I 4	192
Byrranga, gory ⋏	B 13	114
Byske	D 10	64
Bystřice pod Hostýnem	A 9	102
Bystrzyca Kłodzka	C 9	96
Bytča	E 14	66
Bytom	C 10	96
Bytów	A 9	96
Byxelkrok	D 8	66
Byzantium		
see İstanbul	B 8	106
C		
Ca ≃	I 7	130
Caacupé	F 2	194
Caaguazú □[3]	F 2	194
Caála	E 2	204
Caapucú	G 2	194
Caarapó	E 3	194
Caazapá	G 2	194
Caazapá □[3]	G 2	194
Cabaiguán	C 5	186
Caballo Reservoir ⊜[1]	F 5	176
Cabanatuan	B 8	134
Cabano	E 9	160
Cabeza del Buey	F 5	86
Cabimas	F 7	186
Cabinda	D 1	204
Cabinda □[3]	D 1	204
Cabo Blanco	I 6	192
Cabo Delgado □[3]	E 6	204
Cabo Frio	E 10	194
Cabonga, Réservoir ⊜[1]	E 5	160
Caboolture	I 11	142
Caborca	B 3	184
Cabo Rojo	j 14	187b
Cabot	E 3	170
Cabot Strait ⊔	E 13	160
Cabourg	C 6	78
Cabo Verde,		
Arquipélago de II	h 11	200a
Cabra	G 6	86
Cabrayıl	J 15	110
Cabrera, Parc National		
de Archipiélago ♦	E 7	88
Cabriel ≃	E 3	88
Cabrillo National		
Monument ♦	H 6	182
Cabruta	G 8	186
Caçador	G 5	194
Čačak	D 6	104
Caçapava do Sul	B 11	195
Cacequi	A 10	195
Cáceres, Braz.	G 7	190
Cáceres, Spain	E 4	86
Cáceres □[6]	E 4	86
Čačèvičy	C 6	110
Cache	C 4	172
Cache Creek ≃	B 1	182
Cache la Poudre ≃	B 6	176
Cacheu	C 1	200
Cachimbo, Serra do ⋏	E 7	190
Cachingues	E 2	204
Cachoeira do Sul	B 11	195
Cachoeiro de		
Itapemirim	D 10	194
Cacín ≃	G 7	86
Căciulați	C 9	104
Cacolo	F 2	204
Cactus	B 2	172
Cactus Flat ≚	C 7	182
Cacuaco	D 1	204
Caculuvar ≃	F 1	204
Cacuri	D 2	204
Cadaqués	F 7	80
Čadca	A 10	102
Caddo Lake ⊜[1]	F 2	170
Cadereyta Jiménez	E 9	184
Cadibarrawirracanna,		
Lake ⊜	J 2	142
Cadillac, Fr.	D 3	80
Cadillac, Mi., U.S.	A 1	162
Cádiz	H 4	86
Cádiz □[6]	H 5	86
Cadiz, Gulf of (Cádiz,		
Golfo de) c	H 3	86
Cadiz Lake ⊜	E 6	180
Cadomin	E 13	156
Cadotte Lake	C 13	156
Caen	C 6	78
Caengo (Kwenge) ≃	D 2	204
Caere ⊥	G 8	92
Caernarfon	D 2	72
Caernarfon Bay c	D 2	72
Caernarfon Castle ⊥	D 2	72
Caernarfonshire and		
Merionethshire □[6]	E 2	72
Caernarvon		
see Caernarfon	D 2	72
Caerphilly	F 3	72
Caerphilly □[6]	F 3	72
Caesarea		
see Qesari, Horbat ⊥	D 3	120
Caetité	F 10	190
Cafima	F 2	204
Cagayan ≃	B 8	134
Cagayan de Oro	D 8	134
Cagayan Islands II	D 8	134
Cagayan Sulu Island I	D 7	134
Cagli	F 8	92
Cagliari	F 2	90
Cagliari □[6]	I 10	94a
Cagliari, Golfo di c	F 2	90
Čaglinka ≃	J 28	108
Cagnano Varano	C 5	94
Cagnes-sur-Mer	G 5	82
Caguas	j 15	187b
Cahama	F 1	204
Caherciveen	E 1	75
Cahokia	C 3	170
Cahora Bassa,		
Albufeira ⊜[1]	F 5	204
Cahors	D 5	80
Cahul	C 10	104
Caianda	E 3	204
Caiapó, Serra do ⋏	G 8	190
Caibarién	C 5	186
Caicara de Orinoco	G 8	186
Caicó	E 11	190
Caicos Islands II	C 6	186
Caicos Passage ⊔	C 6	186
Caiguna	M 8	140
Caijiapo	A 8	130
Caimanero, Laguna del		
⊜	F 6	184
Caird Coast ⌓[2]	D 7	208
Cairns	D 7	142
Cairo (El-Qâhira), Egypt	G 4	118
Cairo, Il., U.S.	D 4	170
Cairofa	E 1	204
Cairo Montenotte	E 4	92
Caiundo	F 2	204
Cajamarca	E 3	190
Cajarc	D 5	80
Čajek (Chayek)	A 2	122
Čajkovskij	H 21	108
Cajon Pass)(	F 6	182
Čakovec	D 8	102
Cala	F 7	206
Calabar	D 6	200
Calabozo	F 8	186
Calabria □[3]	F 6	94
Calabria, Parco		
Nazionale d' ♦	E 6	94
Calafat	C 7	104
Calafell	C 6	88
Calafquén, Lago ⊜	F 1	195
Calahorra	B 2	88
Calais	B 8	78
Calais, Pas de		
see Dover, Strait of ⊔	F 8	70
Calama	D 6	192
Calamian Group II	C 8	134
Calamonte	F 4	86
Calañas	G 4	86
Calandula	D 2	204
Calangianus	I 5	92
Calapan	C 8	134
Călărași, Mol.	B 10	104
Călărași, Rom.	C 9	104
Călărași □[3]	C 9	104
Calasparra	F 3	88
Calatafimi	G 2	94
Calatayud	C 3	88
Calau	E 10	98
Calaveras □[6]	B 3	182
Calayan Island I	B 8	134
Calbayog	C 8	134
Calbe	E 8	98
Calcasieu Lake ⊜	H 2	170
Calcinato	E 2	102
Calcutta	E 5	122
Caldas da Rainha	E 1	86
Caldas de Reis	B 2	86
Caldas Novas	B 6	194
Caldera	E 5	192
Caldera de Taburiente,		
Parque Nacional de		
la ♦	i 13	85b
Calderdale □[6]	D 4	72
Caldes de Montbui	C 7	88
Caldicot	F 4	72
Caldwell, Id., U.S.	D 5	178
Caldwell, Oh., U.S.	D 3	162
Caledon	H 3	206
Caledon (Mohokare) ≃	E 7	206
Caledonia, Belize	H 15	184
Caledonia, Mn., U.S.	D 3	166
Caledonia □[6]	B 6	164
Caledonian Canal ≍	D 3	74
Calella	C 7	88
Calen	F 9	142
Calera	D 5	172
Calexico	F 6	180
Calgary	F 14	156
Calhoun, Al., U.S.	F 5	170
Calhoun, Ga., U.S.	B 2	168
Calhoun Falls	B 3	168
Cali	C 3	190
Calicut	G 3	122
Calida, Costa ⌓[2]	G 3	88
Caliente	D 1	176
California □[3]	D 4	152
California, Golfo de		
(California, Gulf of) c	C 3	184
California, Gulf of		
see California, Golfo		
de c	C 3	184
California Aqueduct ≍[1]	F 5	182
Cälilabad	J 16	110
Călimănești	C 8	104
Calimere, Point ›	G 3	122
Calion	F 2	170
Calitzdorp	G 4	206
Callabonna, Lake ⊜	B 3	144
Callahan	D 4	168
Callander	D 4	74
Callao	F 3	190
Callaquén, Volcán ∧[1]	E 2	195
Calling Lake	D 15	156
Callosa de Segura	F 4	88
Calmar	D 3	166
Calne	F 5	72
Calolziocorte	D 5	92
Calonga ≃	F 2	204
Calonge	C 8	88
Calore ≃	C 4	94
Caloundra	I 11	142
Calp (Calpe)	F 5	88
Caltagirone	G 4	94
Caltanissetta	G 4	94
Caltanissetta □[6]	G 4	94
Çaltılıbük	C 8	106
Calucinga	E 2	204
Caluire-et-Cuire	E 2	82
Calulo	E 2	204
Calumet	B 2	166
Calumet City	B 5	170
Calunda	E 3	204
Caluso	E 5	82
Caluula	E 7	202
Calvados □[3]	C 6	78
Calvert	G 4	170
Calvert □[6]	H 2	164
Calvert Island I	F 7	156
Calvi	i 8	83a
Calvià	E 7	88
Calvillo	G 8	184
Calvinia	F 3	206
Calw	D 5	100
Camagüey	C 5	186
Camaiore	F 6	92
Camaldoli, Eremo di ▶[1]	F 7	92
Camaná	G 4	190
Camanche	B 3	170
Camapuã	C 3	194
Camaquã	B 11	195
Camaquã ≃	B 12	195
Camará	D 6	190
Camarès	E 6	80
Camargue ◆[1]	G 2	82
Camargue, Parc Naturel		
Regional de ♦	G 2	82
Camarina ⊥	H 4	94
Camarones	H 6	192
Camas	G 4	86
Ca Mau	J 7	132
Ca Mau, Mui ›	J 7	132
Camaxilo	D 2	204
Cambados	B 2	86
Cambará	E 5	194
Camberley	F 6	72
Cambodia □[1]	H 7	132
Cambooya	A 8	144
Camboriú	G 6	194
Camborne	G 1	72
Cambrai	B 10	78
Cambria	D 4	166
Cambrian Mountains ⋏	E 3	72
Cambridge, Eng., U.K.	E 6	72
Cambridge, Il., U.S.	B 3	170
Cambridge, Ma., U.S.	D 7	164
Cambridge, Md., U.S.	H 2	164
Cambridge, Mn., U.S.	C 2	166
Cambridge, N.Y., U.S.	C 5	164
Cambridge, N.Z.	B 5	146
Cambridge, Oh., U.S.	C 3	162
Cambridge, On., Can.	G 3	160
Cambridge Bay	C 11	150
Cambridge Gulf c	D 10	140
Cambridgeshire □[6]	E 7	72
Cambrils	C 6	88
Cambundi-Catembo	E 2	204
Camden, Ar., U.S.	F 2	170
Camden, Austl.	E 8	144
Camden, De., U.S.	G 3	164
Camden, N.J., U.S.	G 3	164
Camden, S. Afr.	D 8	206
Camden □[6]	G 4	164
Camden Bay c	A 22	154
Camden Hills State		
Park ♦	A 9	162
Camenca	A 10	104
Cameri	D 4	92
Camerino	F 8	92
Cameron, La., U.S.	H 2	170
Cameron, Wi., U.S.	C 3	166
Cameron Hills ⋏[2]	A 13	156
Cameroon □[1]	H 9	196
Cameroon Mountain ∧[1]	E 6	200
Cametá	D 9	190
Camfield	E 11	140
Çamiçi Gölü ⊜	D 7	106
Camiguin Island I	B 8	134
Caminha	C 2	86
Camiri	H 6	190
Camissombo	D 3	204
Cam Lo	F 8	132
Camocim	D 10	190
Camooweal	E 4	142
Camousitchouane, Lac		
⊜	C 6	160
Campagna	E 5	90
Campagna di Roma ◆[1]	H 8	92
Campana	D 8	195
Campana, Isla I	I 4	192
Campanario	F 5	86
Campania □[3]	D 5	94
Campania Island I	J 30	154
Campbell, Ca., U.S.	C 1	182
Campbell, Mo., U.S.	D 3	170
Campbell, Ne., U.S.	E 5	174
Campbell Hill ∧[2]	C 2	162
Campbell Island I	J 13	58
Campbell River	F 9	156
Campbellsville	D 6	170
Campbellton	D 10	160
Campbelltown	E 8	144
Campbeltown	B 1	72
Campeche	H 14	184
Campeche □[3]	H 14	184
Campeche, Gulf of c	H 12	184
Câmpeni	B 7	104
Camperdown	G 4	144
Cam Pha	D 8	132
Camp Hill	F 1	164
Câmpia Turzii	B 7	104
Campi Bisenzio	F 6	92
Campiglia Marittima	F 6	92
Campillos	G 6	86
Câmpina	C 8	104
Campina ◆[1]	G 5	86
Campina Grande	E 11	190
Campinas	E 7	194
Campi Salentina	D 7	94
Camplong	A 7	140
Campo	F 6	204
Campobasso	C 4	94
Campobasso □[6]	C 4	94
Campobello di Licata	G 3	94
Campobello di Mazara	G 2	94
Campo Belo	D 8	194
Campo de Criptana	E 1	88
Campo Gallo	E 7	192
Campo Grande, Arg.	G 3	194
Campo Grande, Braz.	D 3	194
Campo Largo	F 6	194
Campo Maior	D 10	190
Campo Mourão	F 4	194
Campos, Braz.	D 10	194
Campos, Spain	E 8	88
Campos Altos	C 7	194
Campotosto, Lago di		
⊜[1]	G 9	92
Camp Point	B 3	170
Câmpulung	C 8	104
Câmpulung		
Moldovenesc	B 8	104
Campuzano	A 6	86
Cam Ranh	I 9	132
Cam Ranh, Vinh c	I 9	132
Camrose	E 15	156
Çan	B 7	106
Canaan	D 5	164
Canada □[1]	E 13	150
Canada Basin ✦[1]	C 36	61
Cañada de Gómez	C 7	195
Cañada Honda	F 6	192
Canadian ≃	C 6	172
Canajoharie	D 4	164
Çanakkale	B 7	106
Çanakkale □[3]	C 7	106
Canals	F 4	88
Canal Winchester	D 2	162
Canandaigua	D 1	164
Cananea	B 4	184
Cañar	D 3	190
Canarias □[3]	i 15	85b
Canarias, Islas (Canary		
Islands) II	h 15	85b
Canary Islands		
see Canarias, Islas II	h 15	85b
Cañas	F 3	186
Canastota	C 3	164
Canatlán	E 7	184
Canaveral, Cape ›	E 4	168
Canaveral National		
Seashore ♦	E 4	168
Canavese □[9]	D 3	92
Canavieiras	A 11	194
Canbelego	C 6	144
Canberra	E 7	144
Canby	C 6	174
Cancon	D 4	80
Cancún	G 16	184
Candás	A 5	86
Candelaria ≃	H 14	184
Candle	D 13	154
Candle Lake ⊜	E 19	156
Candlemas Islands II	J 12	188
Cando	A 5	174
Candor	B 5	168
Canelli	E 4	92
Canelones	D 9	195
Cañete	E 1	195
Caney	G 7	174
Cangas	B 2	86
Cangas de Narcea	A 4	86
Canginge	E 3	204
Cangkuang, Tanjung ›	G 5	134
Cangongo	D 2	204
Canguçu	B 11	195
Cangxi	C 7	130
Cangyuan	G 4	130
Cangzhou	G 11	128
Caniapiscau ≃	E 19	150
Caniapiscau, Lac ⊜[1]	A 8	160
Caniçado	C 10	206
Canicattì	G 3	94
Canim Lake ⊜	F 11	156
Canindeyú □[3]	F 3	194
Canjáyar	G 2	88
Çankırı	B 5	118
Çankırı □[3]	B 5	118
Canmore	F 14	156
Cannanore	G 2	122
Canne ⊥	C 6	94
Cannes	G 4	82
Canning ≃	B 22	154
Cannington	A 4	162
Cannock	E 4	72
Cannonball ≃	B 4	174
Cannon Beach	C 2	178
Canoas	A 12	195
Canoas ≃	G 5	194
Canoe Creek Indian		
Reserve ◆[4]	F 10	156
Canoe Lake ⊜	D 17	156
Canoe Lake Indian		
Reserve ◆[4]	D 18	156
Canoinhas	G 5	194
Canol	D 31	154
Canon City	F 2	174
Cañon del Sumidero,		
Parque Nacional ♦	I 13	184
Canonica, La ▶[1]	i 9	83a
Canosa di Púglia	C 6	94
Canova Beach	E 4	168
Canso	F 13	160
Cantabria □[3]	A 7	86
Cantábrica, Cordillera ⋏	A 3	84
Cantabrica, Cornisa ⌓[2]	A 2	88
Cantal □[3]	C 6	80
Cantanhede	D 2	86
Cantaura	F 8	186
Canteleu	C 7	78
Canterbury	F 8	72
Canterbury □[3]	E 3	146
Canterbury Bight c	F 3	146
Canterbury Cathedral		
▶[1]	F 7	72
Canterbury Plains ≚	E 3	146
Can Tho	I 7	132
Canton		
see Guangzhou,		
China	G 11	130
Canton, Ga., U.S.	B 2	168
Canton, Il., U.S.	B 3	170
Canton, Ks., U.S.	F 6	174
Canton, Ms., U.S.	F 3	170
Canton, N.C., U.S.	B 3	168
Canton, N.Y., U.S.	B 3	164
Canton, Oh., U.S.	C 3	162
Canton Lake ⊜[1]	B 4	172
Canton Lake State		
Recreational Area ♦	B 4	172
Cantù	D 5	92
Cantwell	E 20	154
Cañuelas	D 8	195
Canunda National Park		
♦	F 3	144
Canutama	E 6	190
Čany, ozero ⊜	D 10	114
Cany-Barville	C 7	78
Canyon	C 2	172
Canyon de Chelly		
National Monument ♦	D 4	176
Canyon Lake ⊜[1]	F 4	172
Canyonlands National		
Park ♦	C 4	176
Canyonville	D 2	178
Cao Bang	C 7	132
Cao Lanh	I 7	132
Caombo	D 2	204
Caorle	D 8	92
Caoxian	I 10	128
Čapaevo	D 17	110
Čapaevsk	C 16	110
Capala	E 1	204
Capanaparo ≃	B 5	190
Capannori	F 6	92
Capão Bonito	F 6	194
Caparaó, Parque		
Nacional do ♦	D 9	194
Capata	E 3	204
Cap-Chat	D 10	160
Cap-de-la-Madeleine	E 7	160
Cape ≃	F 8	142
Cape Arid National		
Park ♦	M 7	140
Cape Barren Island I	i 13	145a
Cape Basin ✦[1]	I 11	60
Cape Breton Highlands		
National Park ♦	E 13	160
Cape Breton Island I	E 13	160
Cape Canaveral	E 4	168
Cape Coast	D 4	200
Cape Cod Bay c	E 8	164
Cape Cod National		
Seashore ♦	E 8	164
Cape Coral	F 3	168
Cape Dorset	D 17	150
Cape Fear ≃	C 6	168
Cape Girardeau	D 4	170
Cape Hatteras National		
Seashore ♦	B 7	168
Cape Henlopen State		
Park ♦	H 3	164
Cape Krusenstern		
National Monument ♦	C 11	154
Capelinha	B 9	194
Cape Lisburne	B 11	154
Capella	G 9	142
Capelle aan de IJssel	C 3	69
Cape Lookout National		
Seashore ♦	B 6	168
Cape May	H 4	164
Cape May □[6]	G 4	164
Cape May Court House	G 4	164
Cape Melville National		
Park ♦	C 7	142
Cape Pole	H 28	154
Cape Range National		
Park ♦	H 2	140
Capernaum		
see Kefar Nahum ⊥	D 5	120
Cape Romanzof	F 11	154
Capertee ≃	D 8	144
Capesterre-Belle-Eau	n 21	187e
Cape Town (Kaapstad)	G 2	206
Cape Verde □[1]	h 11	200a
Cape Verde Basin ✦[1]	F 8	60
Cape Vincent	B 2	164
Cape York Peninsula ›[1]	B 6	142
Cap-Haïtien	D 6	186
Capim ≃	D 9	190
Capistrello	H 9	92
Capitán Arturo Prat ▶[3]	L 7	192
Capitão Enéas	B 9	194
Capitola	D 2	182
Capitol Reef National		
Park ♦	C 3	176
Capivara, Represa de		
⊜[1]	E 5	194
Capiz		
see Roxas	C 8	134
Čapljina	D 4	104
Čaplygin	J 14	108
Capo d'Orlando	F 4	94
Capoterra	I 9	94a
Capraia	F 5	92
Caprarola	G 8	92
Capreol	H 18	158
Capri	D 4	94
Capri, Isola di I	D 4	94
Capricorn Channel ⊔	G 11	142
Caprivi □[3]	F 3	204
Caprivi Strip □[9]	F 3	204
Cap Saint Jacques		
see Vung Tau	I 8	132
Captieux	D 3	80
Capua	C 4	94
Capulin Volcano		
National Monument ♦	B 2	172
Capuna	F 2	204
Caquetá (Japurá) ≃	D 4	190
Čara	A 7	124
Čara ≃	D 14	114
Carabobo □[3]	F 7	186
Caracal	C 8	104
Caracaraí	C 6	190
Caracas	F 8	186
Caracol ⊥	I 15	184
Caraguatatuba	E 8	194
Carajás, Serra dos ⋏[2]	E 8	190
Caramat	G 15	158
Carandaí	D 9	194
Carangola	D 9	194
Caransebeș	C 7	104
Carapina	D 10	194
Caraquet	E 11	160
Caraș-Severin □[3]	C 6	104
Caratasca, Laguna de		
c	E 3	186
Carate Brianza	E 7	82
Caratinga	C 9	194
Caravaca de la Cruz	F 3	88
Caravaggio	E 1	102
Carayaó	F 2	194
Carazinho	E 9	192
Carballiño	B 2	86
Carballo	A 2	86
Carbo	C 4	184
Carbon □[6]	F 3	164
Carbon-Blanc	D 3	80
Carbondale, Il., U.S.	D 4	170
Carbondale, Ks., U.S.	C 1	170
Carbondale, Pa., U.S.	E 3	164
Carbonear	E 17	160
Carbonia	F 2	90
Carcaixent	E 4	88
Carcajou	C 13	156
Carcajou ≃	D 31	154
Carcarañá ≃	C 6	195
Carcassonne	E 6	80
Carceri, Eremo delle ▶[1]	F 8	92
Carcross	A 4	156
Čardara	A 1	122
Čardarinskoe		
vodohranilišče ⊜[1]	A 1	122
Cardedeu	G 6	80
Cárdenas, Cuba	C 4	186
Cárdenas, Mex.	H 13	184
Cardiel, Lago ⊜	I 5	192
Cardiff	F 3	72
Cardiff □[6]	F 3	72
Cardigan	E 2	72
Cardigan Bay c	E 2	72
Cardiganshire □[6]	E 2	72
Cardigan State Park ♦	C 6	164
Cardington	D 5	206
Cardona, Spain	G 5	80
Cardona, Ur.	C 9	195
Cardston	G 15	156
Cardwell	E 7	142
Careen Lake ⊜	C 17	156
Carei	B 7	104
Carentan	C 5	78
Carey, Lake ⊜	K 7	140
Careysburg	D 2	200
Cariacica	D 10	194
Caribbean Sea ⊤[2]	D 3	186
Cariboo ≃	E 11	156
Caribou, Me., U.S.	g 12	163a
Caribou, N.S., Can.	F 12	160
Caribou ≃	B 11	158
Caribou Mountains ⋏	B 14	156
Carignan	C 12	78
Carinhanha	F 10	190
Carinhanha ≃	F 10	190
Caripito	F 9	186
Carlentini	G 5	94
Carlet	E 4	88
Carleton	E 6	174
Carleton, Mount ∧	E 10	160
Carleton Place	F 5	160
Carletonville	D 7	206
Carlin	B 5	180
Carlisle, Eng., U.K.	C 3	72
Carlisle, In., U.S.	C 5	170
Carlisle, Pa., U.S.	F 1	164
Carl Junction	D 1	170
Carlos Casares	G 7	192
Carlos Chagas	B 10	194
Carlos Tejedor	D 6	195
Carlow (Ceatharlach)	D 4	75
Carlow □[3]	D 5	75
Carlsbad, Ca., U.S.	G 6	182
Carlsbad		
see Karlovy Vary,		
Czech Rep.	B 9	100
Carlsbad, N.M., U.S.	D 1	172
Carlsbad, Tx., U.S.	E 3	172
Carlsbad Caverns		
National Park ♦	D 1	172
Carlyle Lake ⊜[1]	C 4	170
Carmagnola	E 3	92
Carman	G 10	158
Carmarthen	F 2	72
Carmarthenshire □[6]	F 2	72
Carmaux	D 6	80
Carmel, In., U.S.	C 5	170
Carmel, N.Y., U.S.	E 5	164
Carmel, Mount ∧	D 3	120
Carmel Head ›	D 2	72
Carmelo	C 8	195
Carmel Valley	D 2	182
Carmen ≃	A 2	195
Carmen, Isla I	E 4	184
Carmen de Patagones	G 6	195
Carmichael	B 2	182
Carmila	F 9	142
Carmona	G 5	86
Carnarvon, Austl.	I 2	140
Carnarvon, S. Afr.	F 5	206
Carnarvon		
see Caernarfon,		
Wales, U.K.	D 2	72
Carnarvon National		
Park ♦	H 8	142
Carnatic □[9]	G 3	122
Carndonagh	A 4	75
Carnegie	I 7	140
Carnegie, Lake ⊜	J 7	140
Carnia ◆[1]	C 8	92
Carnoustie	D 6	74
Carnsore Point ›	D 5	75
Carnwath ≃	C 30	154
Carol City	G 4	168
Carolina, Braz.	A 9	190
Carolina, P.R.	j 16	187b
Carolina Beach	B 6	168
Caroline □[6]	H 3	164
Caroline I[1]	D 12	136
Caroline Islands II	C 6	136
Caron	F 19	156
Caroní ≃	B 6	190
Carora	F 7	186
Carouge	D 4	82
Carovigno	D 7	94
Carp	F 5	160
Carpathian Mountains ⋏	F 12	62
Carpații Meridionali ⋏	F 12	62
Carpenedolo	D 6	92
Carpentaria, Gulf of c	B 4	142
Carpentersville	A 4	170
Carpentras	F 3	82
Carpi	E 6	92
Cărpineni	B 10	104
Carpineto Romano	C 3	94
Carpinteria	F 4	182
Carp Lake ⊜	D 10	156
Carquefou	E 5	78
Carrara	E 6	92
Carrauntoohil ∧	E 2	75
Carreta, Punta ›	F 3	190
Carrick ◆[1]	B 2	72
Carrickfergus	B 6	75
Carrick on Shannon	C 3	75
Carrick-on-suir	D 4	75
Carrillo	D 8	184
Carrión de los Condes	B 6	86
Carrizal Bajo	E 5	192
Carrizo Creek ≃	B 2	172
Carrizo Springs	F 3	172
Carroll	C 8	144
Carroll □[6], Md., U.S.	G 1	164
Carroll □[6], N.H., U.S.	C 7	164
Carrollton, Ga., U.S.	F 6	170
Carrollton, Ky., U.S.	C 6	170
Carrollton, Mi., U.S.	B 2	162
Carrollton, Mo., U.S.	C 2	170
Carrollton, Tx., U.S.	D 5	172
Carrolltown	C 4	162
Carron ≃	D 5	142
Carrot ≃	E 7	158
Carrouges	D 6	78
Carry Falls Reservoir		
⊜[1]	B 4	164
Çarşamba	B 7	118
Čarsk (Charsk)	A 13	116
Carsoli	G 9	92
Carson	B 4	174
Carson, East Fork ≃	B 4	182
Carson City	A 4	182
Carson City □[6]	A 4	182
Carson Range ⋏	A 4	182
Carson Sink ⊜	C 4	180
Cartagena, Col.	F 5	186
Cartagena, Spain	G 3	88
Cartago	F 4	186
Cartaxo	E 2	86
Cartaya	G 3	86
Cartersville	B 2	168
Carterton, Eng., U.K.	F 5	72
Carterton, N.Z.	D 5	146
Carthage, Mo., U.S.	D 1	170
Carthage, N.Y., U.S.	B 3	164
Carthage, Tx., U.S.	F 1	170
Carthage ⊥	B 7	198
Cartwright	B 15	160
Caruaru	E 11	190
Carúpano	F 9	186
Carutapera	D 9	190
Carvin	B 9	78
Carvoeiro	D 6	190
Cary	B 5	168
Caryville	G 6	170
Casablanca	C 3	198
Casacalenda	C 4	94
Casa de Piedra,		
Embalse ⊜[1]	F 4	195
Casa Grande	F 3	176
Casa Grande Ruins		
National Monument ♦	F 3	176
Casalecchio di Reno	E 7	92
Casale Monferrato	D 4	92
Casalpusterlengo	D 5	92
Casamance ≃	C 1	200
Casamassima	D 6	94
Casanare ≃	B 4	190
Casar	B 4	168
Casarano	D 8	94
Casas Adobes	F 3	176
Casas Grandes ≃	B 6	184

⌞ Waterfall ⊔ Strait c Bay, Gulf ⊜ Lake ≋ Swamp ⊼ Ice Feature ⊤ Other Hydrographic Feature ✦ Submarine Feature □ Political Unit ▶ Cultural Institution ⊥ Historical Site ♦ Recreational Site ⊠ Airport ■ Military Installation ◆ Miscellaneous

Casas-Ibáñez — Chiredzi

Name | Map Ref. | Page

Casas-Ibáñez E 3 88
Casavieja D 6 86
Cascade, Ia., U.S. D 3 166
Cascade, Wi., U.S. D 4 166
Cascade Locks C 2 178
Cascade Mountains (Cascade Range) ⋏ B 3 178
Cascade Range (Cascade Mountains) ⋏ A 3 178
Cascais F 1 86
Cascavel F 4 194
Cascina F 6 92
Caserta C 4 94
Caserta □[6] C 4 94
Casey B 1 170
Casey ◗[3] C 19 208
Cashiers B 3 168
Casilda C 7 195
Casimcea C 10 104
Casino B 9 144
Čáslav D 8 96
Čašniki B 6 110
Casoria D 4 94
Časovo E 19 108
Caspe C 4 88
Casper D 10 178
Caspian Depression ≐ F 18 110
Caspian Sea ⊤[2] B 6 116
Cassà de la Selva C 7 88
Cassai (Kasai) ≃ E 3 204
Cassamba E 3 204
Cassanje ≃ B 2 194
Cassano allo Ionio E 6 94
Cass City B 2 162
Cassiar Mountains ⋏ G 30 154
Cassilândia C 4 194
Cassinga F 2 204
Cassino C 3 94
Cass Lake ⊜ B 7 174
Cassoalala D 1 204
Cassopolis E 6 166
Cassville D 2 170
Castalia C 2 162
Castaños G 3 172
Castelbuono G 4 94
Castel del Piano G 7 92
Castelfiorentino F 6 92
Castelfranco Emilia E 7 92
Castelfranco Veneto D 7 92
Castellammare del Golfo F 2 94
Castellammare di Stabia D 4 94
Castellana Grotte D 7 94
Castellane G 4 82
Castellaneta D 6 94
Castelldefels C 6 88
Castelleone D 5 92
Castelló de la Plana D 5 88
Castellote D 4 88
Castelnaudary E 5 80
Castelnau-Montratier D 5 80
Castelo Branco E 3 86
Castelo Branco □[3] D 3 86
Castelo de Paiva C 2 86
Castel San Giovanni D 5 92
Castel San Pietro Terme E 7 92
Castelsarrasin D 4 80
Castelvetrano G 2 94
Castenedolo D 6 92
Casterton F 3 144
Castiglione del Lago F 7 92
Castiglion Fiorentino F 7 92
Castilho D 5 194
Castilla E 2 190
Castilla-La Mancha □[3] C 4 84
Castilla la Nueva □[9] C 4 84
Castilla la Vieja □[9] B 3 84
Castilla y León □[3] G 2 76
Castillo de San Marcos National Monument ♦ E 4 168
Castillon-la-Bataille D 3 80
Castine A 9 162
Castlebar C 2 75
Castleblayney B 5 75
Castlecliff C 5 146
Castleford D 5 72
Castlegar G 13 156
Castlemaine F 5 144
Castle Mountain ∧ D 27 154
Castlepoint D 6 146
Castlereagh ≃ C 6 144
Castle Rock F 2 174
Castleton C 5 164
Castletown B 5 74
Castletown Bere E 1 75
Castor E 15 156
Castres E 6 80
Castricum B 3 69
Castries s 26 187h
Castro, Braz. F 6 194
Castro, Chile H 5 192
Castro Daire D 2 86
Castro del Río G 6 86
Castronuño C 5 86
Castro-Urdiales A 7 86
Castro Verde G 2 86
Castrovillari E 6 94
Castroville D 2 182
Castuera F 5 86
Casummit Lake F 12 158
Cataguazes D 9 194
Çatak C 10 118
Catalana, Cadena Costero ⋏ C 6 88
Catalão C 7 194
Çatalca B 8 106
Catalina E 6 192
Catalonia see Cataluña □[3] C 6 88
Cataluña (Catalonia) □[3] C 6 88
Catalunya see Cataluña □[3] C 6 88
Catamarca □[3] E 6 192
Catanduanes Island I C 8 134
Catanduva D 6 194
Catania G 5 94
Catania □[6] G 4 94
Catania, Golfo di c G 5 94
Cataño j 15 187b
Catanzaro F 6 94
Catanzaro □[6] F 6 94
Catarino Rodríguez E 9 184
Catarroja E 4 88
Catawba ≃ B 4 168
Catedral, Cerro ∧[2] F 9 192
Catembe D 10 206
Caterham F 6 72
Cathedral City G 7 182
Cathedral Provincial Park ♦ A 3 178
Cathedral Rock National Park ♦ C 8 144
Cat Island I B 6 186
Cat Lake ⊜ F 13 158
Catoche, Cabo > G 16 184
Catonsville G 2 164
Catonto E 3 204
Catrimani ≃ C 6 190
Catskill D 5 164
Catskill Mountains ⋏ D 4 164
Catskill Park ♦ D 4 164
Cattaraugus Indian Reservation ◆[4] B 4 162
Cattolica F 8 92
Catuane D 10 206
Catur E 6 204
Čatyrtaš A 3 122
Cau ≃ D 7 132
Caubvick, Mount (Iberville, Mont d') ∧ E 20 150
Cauca ≃ B 3 190
Caucasia F 6 186
Caucasus ⋏ H 14 110
Caucete B 3 195
Caudete F 3 88
Caudry B 10 78
Caungula D 2 204
Cauquenes D 1 195
Caura ≃ B 6 190
Căuşani B 10 104
Caussade D 5 80
Cauterets F 3 80
Cauvery see Kāveri ≃ G 3 122
Caux, Pays de ◆[1] C 7 78
Cava de' Tirreni D 4 94
Cavaillon G 3 82
Cavalcante F 9 190
Cavalese B 3 90
Cavalla (Cavally) ≃ D 3 200
Cavally see Cavalla ≃ D 3 200
Cavan B 4 75
Cavan □[3] C 4 75
Čavan'ga C 12 108
Cavarzere D 8 92
Cave H 8 92
Cave City E 3 170
Cave Spring E 6 170
Caviana de Fora, Ilha I C 9 190
Cavtat D 5 104
Cawker City F 5 174
Cawston A 4 178
Caxias D 10 190
Caxias do Sul A 12 195
Caxito D 1 204
Çay C 9 106
Cayambe C 3 190
Cayambe ∧[1] C 3 190
Cay Duong, Vinh c I 7 132
Cayenne C 8 190
Cayey j 15 187b
Caylus D 5 80
Cayman Brac I D 5 186
Cayman Islands □[2] D 4 186
Cayuga □[6] D 2 164
Cayuga Lake ⊜ D 2 164
Cazage E 3 204
Căzănești C 9 104
Cazaux et de Sanguinet, Étang de ⊜ D 2 80
Cazenovia D 3 164
Cazin C 3 104
Cazombo E 3 204
Cazorla G 1 88
Cchinvali see Chinvali H 14 110
Ceará □[3] D 11 190
Ceará-Mirim E 11 190
Čebarkul' I 24 108
Čeboksarskoe vodohranilišče ⊜[1] I 18 108
Čeboksary H 17 108
Cebollar A 4 195
Cebollas F 7 184
Cebollatí ≃ C 10 195
Cebreros D 6 86
Čebsara G 13 108
Cebu City C 8 134
Ceccano H 9 92
Čechtice C 12 100
Čechy □[9] D 8 96
Cecil □[6] G 3 164
Cecil Lake C 11 156
Cecina F 6 92
Čečnja □[3] H 14 110
Cedar ≃ E 3 166
Cedar Breaks National Monument ♦ D 2 176
Cedar City D 2 176
Cedar Creek Reservoir ⊜[1] D 5 172
Cedar Falls D 2 166
Cedar Grove D 3 162
Cedar Hill D 5 170
Cedar Lake B 5 170
Cedar Lake ⊜[1] E 8 158
Cedarmont D 8 206
Cedar Rapids E 3 166
Cedars of Lebanon State Park ♦ D 5 170
Cedar Springs D 6 166
Cedeira A 2 86
Cedillo, Embalse de ⊜[1] E 3 86
Cedros, Isla I C 2 184
Ceduna L 1 142
Ceek F 6 202
Ceelbuur G 6 202
Ceel Dheere F 6 202
Ceel Gaal E 5 202
Ceerigaabo E 6 202
Cefalù F 3 94
Čegdomyn B 10 124
Cegléd B 5 104
Cehegín F 3 88
Ceheng F 7 130
Čehov I 12 108
Çekerek ≃ B 6 118
Čekmaguš I 21 108
Čekuevo E 13 108
Čelákovice B 11 100
Celano B 3 94
Celanova B 2 86
Celaya G 9 184
Celebes see Sulawesi I F 8 134
Celebes Sea ⊤[2] E 8 134
Celina B 6 170
Celinograd see Akmola D 10 114
Čeljabinsk I 24 108
Čeljabinskaja oblast' □[6] I 24 108
Celje D 7 102
Čelkar F 21 110
Celldömölk C 9 102
Celle D 7 98
Celorico da Beira D 3 86
Celtic Sea ⊤[2] F 4 70
Čemerno D 5 104
Cenderawasih, Teluk c F 11 134
Cenovo D 8 104
Centelles G 6 80
Centenario F 3 195
Center B 4 174
Center Hill E 4 168
Center Hill Lake ⊜[1] D 6 170
Center Point F 5 170
Centerville, In., U.S. C 6 170
Centerville, Pa., U.S. C 3 162
Centerville, S.D., U.S. D 6 174
Centerville, Ut., U.S. E 8 178
Cento E 7 92
Central, N.M., U.S. F 4 176
Central, S.C., U.S. B 3 168
Central □[3], Bots. G 4 204
Central □[3], Kenya H 4 202
Central □[3], Mwi. E 5 204
Central □[3], Para. F 2 194
Central □[3], Zam. E 4 204
Central, Cordillera ⋏, Col. C 3 190
Central, Cordillera ⋏, Peru E 3 190
Central, Cordillera ⋏, Phil. B 8 134
Central, Cordillera ⋏, P.R. j 15 187b
Central, Massif ⋏ F 5 76
Central, Planalto ⋏[1] G 9 190
Central, Sistema ⋏ B 3 84
Central African Republic □[1] H 9 196
Central Australia Aboriginal Reserve ◆[4] H 10 140
Central City, Ky., U.S. D 5 170
Central City, Ne., U.S. E 6 174
Central Desert Aboriginal Reserve ◆[4] F 11 140
Central Division □[3] m 14 147c
Central Falls E 7 164
Central Heights F 3 176
Centralia, Il., U.S. C 4 170
Centralia, Wa., U.S. B 2 178
Centralina C 6 194
Central Islip F 5 164
Central Kalahari Game Reserve ◆[4] G 3 204
Central Makrān Range ⋏ E 9 116
Central Pacific Basin ✦[1] F 13 58
Central Siberian Plateau ⋏[1] C 13 114
Central Square C 2 164
Centre E 6 170
Centre □[3] E 7 200
Centre, Canal du ≡ D 2 82
Centreville G 2 164
Centuripe G 4 94
Century G 5 170
Čepca ≃ H 21 108
Čepelare E 8 104
Cephalonia see Kefallinía I B 9 198
Cepu k 20 135b
Ceram Sea (Seram, Laut) ⊤[2] F 9 134
Cerano E 6 82
Čerčany C 11 100
Čerdakly I 18 108
Čerdyn' F 22 108
Cerea D 7 92
Čeremhovo B 4 124
Čeremšany B 5 126
Čerepovec G 12 108
Ceres, Arg. A 7 195
Ceres, Ca., U.S. C 2 182
Ceres, S. Afr. G 3 206
Ceresco E 6 174
Cergy C 9 78
Cerignola C 5 94
Cérilly B 6 80
Çerkeş B 5 118
Čerkessek G 13 110
Çerkezköy B 7 106
Cerknica E 6 102
Čerlak D 10 114
Cermei B 6 104
Cerna C 10 104
Cernavodă C 9 104
Cernay C 5 82
Černigovka B 4 126
Černjahovsk B 2 110
Černjanka D 10 110
Černuška H 21 108
Cerralvo, Isla I E 5 184
Cerrillos E 5 176
Cerro Azul G 10 184
Cerro de Pasco F 3 190
Cerro Gordo C 4 170
Cerros Colorados, Embalse ⊜[1] F 3 195
Cerro Tololo, Observatorio Astronómico ◗[3] B 2 195
Čerskij C 19 114
Čerskogo, hrebet ⋏ A 9 128
Certaldo F 7 92
Čèrven' F 14 66
Červen Brjag D 8 104
Červený Kostelec C 8 96
Cervera C 6 88
Cervera del Río Alhama C 3 88
Cerveteri H 8 92
Cervia E 8 92
Cervignano del Friuli D 9 92
Červlënnaja H 14 110
Cervo A 3 86
Čèrykau C 7 110
Cesar □[3] F 6 186
Cesar ≃ F 6 186
Cesena E 8 92
Cesenatico E 8 92
Cēsis D 12 66
Česká Lípa B 11 100
Česká Třebová D 9 96
České Budějovice D 11 100
Český Brod B 11 100
Český Krumlov B 6 102
Český Těšín D 10 96
Çeşme C 7 106
Češskaja guba c C 16 108
Cessnock D 8 144
Cestos ≃ D 3 200
Cesvaine D 13 66
Cetinje D 5 104
Çetinkaya C 7 118
Ceuta I 5 86
Cévennes ◆[1] F 1 82
Cévennes, Parc National des ♦ F 1 82
Ceyhan D 6 118
Ceylanpınar D 9 118
Cha-am H 4 132
Chabeuil F 3 82
Chablais ◆[1] D 4 82
Chacabuco D 7 195
Chachani, Nevado ∧ G 4 190
Chachapoyas E 3 190
Chachimbemba E 2 204
Chaco □[3] E 7 192
Chaco ≃ D 4 176
Chaco Culture National Historical Park ♦ D 5 176
Chad □[1] G 9 196
Chad, Lake (Tchad, Lac) ⊜ C 7 200
Chādegān F 14 118
Chadron D 3 174
Chagang-do □[3] F 16 128
Chagos Archipelago (Oil Islands) II J 9 112
Chagos-Laccadive Plateau ✦[3] G 6 58
Chaguanas q 23 187f
Chahal J 15 184
Chahār Borjak D 9 116
Chahār Maḥāl va Bakhtīārī □[3] F 14 118
Chaihe D 17 128
Chaimite C 10 206
Chai Nat G 4 132
Chaiyaphum G 5 132
Chajarí B 8 195
Chakaria E 6 122
Chākia D 5 122
Chakwadām E 4 130
Chakwāl C 2 122
Chalais C 3 80
Chalatenango E 2 186
Chalbi Desert ◆[2] G 4 202
Chaleur Bay c E 11 160
Chaling E 11 130
Chālisgaon E 2 122
Chalk River E 5 160
Challans F 5 78
Challenger Deep ✦[1] C 12 134
Chalmette H 4 170
Châlons-en-Champagne (Châlons-sur-Marne) D 11 78
Châlons-sur-Marne see Châlons-en-Champagne D 11 78
Chalon-sur-Saône F 11 78
Chalosse ◆[1] E 3 80
Chalt B 2 122
Chaltel, Cerro (Monte Fitzroy) ∧ I 5 192
Châlus, Fr. C 4 80
Chālūs, Iran D 14 118
Cham C 6 82
Chama ≃ D 5 176
Chaman D 10 116
Chamba E 6 204
Chambal ≃ D 3 122
Chamberlain D 5 174
Chamberlain ≃ E 9 140
Chambers E 4 176
Chambersburg D 5 162
Chambéry E 3 82
Chambi, Jebel ∧ B 6 198
Chambly C 9 78
Chambon-sur-Voueize B 6 80
Chambord, Château de ⊥ E 8 78
Chamchawib C 2 206
Chamical B 4 195
Ch'amo Hāyk' ⊜ F 4 202
Chamonix-Mont-Blanc E 4 82
Champagne F 26 154
Champagne □[9] D 11 78
Champagne Castle ∧ E 8 206
Champagnole D 3 82
Champaign B 4 170
Champaquí, Cerro ∧ B 5 195
Champasak G 7 132
Champigneulles B 4 82
Champlain A 5 164
Champlain □[6] A 5 164
Champlain, Lake ⊜ B 5 164
Champlain Canal ≡ C 5 164
Champotón H 14 184
Chamusca E 2 86
Chañaral E 5 192
Chancelade C 4 80
Chandalar C 20 154
Chandalar ≃ C 21 154
Chandalar, East Fork ≃ C 21 154
Chandalar, North Fork ≃ C 20 154
Chandeleur Islands II H 4 170
Chandeleur Sound ∪ H 4 170
Chandīgarh C 3 122
Chandler, Az., U.S. F 3 176
Chandler, Ok., U.S. C 5 172
Chandler, P.Q., Can. D 11 160
Chandler Lake ⊜ B 17 154
Chāndpur E 6 122
Chandrapur E 3 122
Chang ≃, China C 9 130
Chang see Yangtze ≃, China B 14 130
Changalane D 10 206
Changane ≃ C 10 206
Changbai Mountains (Changbai Shan) ⋏ D 2 126
Chang Cheng (Great Wall) ◆ G 8 128
Changchun D 15 128
Changde D 10 130
Changhowŏn F 1 126
Changhua F 15 130
Changi i 15 134a
Changji B 14 116
Changjiang I 9 130
Changli G 12 128
Changling D 14 128
Changmar C 3 122
Changning, China E 11 130
Changning, China B 4 132
Changping F 11 128
Changsan-got > G 15 128
Changsha D 11 130
Changshan D 14 130
Changshu C 15 130
Changting, China D 17 128
Changting, China F 13 130
Changwŏn I 17 128
Changwu, China I 6 128
Changwu, China D 15 128
Changxing C 14 130
Changyi H 12 128
Changyŏn-ŭp G 15 128
Changzhi H 9 128
Changzhou C 15 130
Channel Country ◆[1] H 5 142
Channel Islands II, Ca., U.S. G 4 182
Channel Islands II, Eur. j 10 73b
Channel-Port aux Basques E 14 160
Channel Tunnel ◆[5] F 8 72
Channelview H 1 170
Chantada B 3 86
Chanthaburi H 5 132
Chantilly C 9 78
Chantrey Inlet c C 13 150
Chany, Lake see Čany, ozero ⊜ D 10 114
Chao'an G 13 130
Chao Hu ⊜ C 13 130
Chao Phraya ≃ G 5 132
Chaoxian C 13 130
Chaoyang, China F 12 128
Chaoyang, China G 13 130
Chapala, Laguna de ⊜ G 8 184
Chāparmukh D 6 122
Chaparral C 3 190
Chapayevsk see Čapaevsk C 16 110
Chapecó G 4 194
Chapel Hill B 5 168
Chapelton h 12 186a
Chapin C 3 170
Chapleau E 2 160
Chaplin Lake ⊜ F 18 156
Chaplynka F 8 110
Chapman E 5 174
Chapmanville E 2 162
Chappal, Waddi ∧ D 7 200
Chappell Hill E 5 172
Chá Pungana E 2 204
Charcas F 9 184
Charcoal Lake ⊜ B 20 156
Charcot Island I C 1 208
Chard G 4 72
Charente □[3] C 4 80
Charente ≃ C 3 80
Charente-Maritime □[3] C 3 80
Chari ≃ C 7 200
Chari-Baguirmi □[3] C 8 200
Chārīkār B 1 122
Chariton B 2 170
Chariton ≃ C 2 170
Charity B 7 190
Chärjew C 9 116
Char'kov see Kharkiv E 10 110
Charleroi D 3 69
Charles □[6] H 1 164
Charles, Cape > E 6 162
Charles City E 5 162
Charles Island I D 18 150
Charles Mound ∧[2] D 3 166
Charleston, Il., U.S. C 4 170
Charleston, Mo., U.S. D 4 170
Charleston, N.Z. D 3 146
Charleston, S.C., U.S. C 5 168
Charleston, W.V., U.S. D 3 162
Charlestown, Austl. D 8 144
Charlestown, S. Afr. D 8 206
Charleville I 8 142
Charleville-Mézières C 11 78
Charlevoix, Lake ⊜ C 6 166
Charley ≃ D 23 154
Charlie Lake C 11 156
Charlotte B 4 168
Charlotte Amalie D 8 186
Charlotte Harbor c F 3 168
Charlotte Lake ⊜ E 9 156
Charlottenberg C 6 66
Charlottesville D 4 162
Charlottetown E 12 160
Charlotteville p 24 187f
Charly-sur-Marne D 10 78
Charolles D 2 82
Charron Lake ⊜ E 11 158
Charroux B 4 80
Chārsadda C 2 122
Charsk see Čarsk A 13 116
Charters Towers F 8 142
Chartres D 8 78
Chascomús D 8 195
Chase E 19 154
Chasefu E 5 204
Chaska C 2 166
Chatanika ≃ D 21 154
Châteaubriant E 5 78
Château-Chinon E 10 78
Château-d'Oex D 5 82
Château-du-Loir E 7 78
Châteaudun D 8 78
Château-la-Vallière E 7 78
Châteauneuf-de-Randon F 1 82
Châteauneuf-sur-Loire E 9 78
Châteaurenard G 2 82
Château-Renault E 7 78
Châteauroux F 8 78
Château-Salins B 4 82
Château-Thierry C 10 78
Chateh B 12 156
Châtelet D 3 69
Châtelineau D 3 69
Châtellerault F 7 78
Châtelus-Malvaleix B 6 80
Chatham, Eng., U.K. F 7 72
Chatham, Ma., U.S. E 9 164
Chatham, N.B., Can. E 11 160
Chatham, N.Y., U.S. D 5 164
Chatham, On., Can. G 2 160
Chatham Islands II I 2 136
Chatham Strait ∪ C 4 156
Châtillon-Coligny E 9 78
Châtillon-sur-Chalaronne D 2 82
Châtillon-sur-Seine E 11 78
Chats, Lac des ⊜ A 2 164
Chatsworth E 6 170
Chatsworth House ◗ D 5 72
Chattahoochee D 2 168
Chattahoochee ≃ D 2 168
Chattanooga E 6 170
Chatteris E 6 72
Chaúa D 2 204
Chau Doc I 7 132
Chauekuktuli, Lake ⊜ F 14 154
Chauk D 2 132
Chaumont D 12 78
Chaumont-en-Vexin C 8 78
Chauny C 10 78
Chaussin D 3 82
Chautauqua Lake ⊜ B 4 162
Chavakkad G 3 122
Chaves C 3 86
Chay ≃ D 7 132
Chayek see Čajek A 2 122
Cheaha Mountain ∧ F 6 170
Cheat ≃ D 4 162
Cheat, Shavers Fork ≃ D 4 162
Cheb B 9 100
Chebanse B 5 170
Chebba B 6 198
Cheboksary see Čeboksary H 17 108
Cheboygan C 6 166
Chech, 'Erg ◆[2] E 4 198
Chechaouen B 3 198
Chechaouen □[3] E 3 84
Chechnya see Čečnja □[3] H 14 110
Chech'on F 2 126
Chęciny C 11 96
Cheddar F 4 72
Cheduba Island I E 1 132
Cheduba Strait ∪ E 1 132
Cheektowaga B 4 162
Chef-Boutonne B 3 80
Chegga D 3 198
Chegutu F 5 204
Chehalis B 2 178
Chehalis ≃ B 2 178
Cheju J 16 128
Cheju-do □[3] J 16 128
Cheju-do I J 16 128
Chelan B 3 178
Chelan, Lake ⊜[1] A 3 178
Cheleken J 18 110
Chelif, Oued ≃ B 5 198
Chełm C 12 96
Chełm □[3] C 12 96
Chełmno B 10 96
Chelmsford, Eng., U.K. F 7 72
Chelmsford, Ma., U.S. D 7 164
Chelmsford, On., Can. B 8 166
Chełmża B 10 96
Chelsea, Ma., U.S. D 7 164
Chelsea, Mi., U.S. B 1 162
Chelsea, Vt., U.S. C 6 164
Cheltenham F 4 72
Chelyabinsk see Čeljabinsk I 24 108
Chemainus A 2 178
Chemba F 5 204
Chemchâm, Sebkhet ⊜ E 2 198
Chemillé E 6 78
Chemnitz F 9 98
Chemnitz □[6] F 9 98
Chemung □[6] D 2 164
Chemung ≃ B 5 162
Chenāb ≃ D 2 122
Chenango □[6] D 3 164
Chenango Valley State Park ♦ D 3 164
Chen Barag Qi B 12 128
Chenderoh, Tasik ⊜ L 5 132
Chenele E 3 204
Cheney B 5 178
Cheneyville G 2 170
Chengde F 11 128
Chengdu C 7 130
Chenghai G 13 130
Chengjiang F 6 130
Chengmai I 9 130
Chengshan Jiao > H 14 128
Chengxian B 7 130
Chengzitan G 14 128
Chenonceau, Château de ⊥ E 7 78
Chenôve E 11 78
Chenxi E 9 130
Chenxiangtun F 14 128
Chenzhou F 11 130
Chepes B 4 195
Chepstow F 4 72
Cher □[3] A 6 80
Cheranchi C 6 200
Cherbourg C 5 78
Cherchell H 7 88
Cherepovets see Čerepovec G 12 108
Chergui, Chott ech ⊜ C 4 198
Cheriton E 6 162
Cherkasy E 8 110
Cherkasy □[6] A 11 104
Cherlen see Kerulen ≃ B 10 128
Chernihiv D 7 110
Chernihiv □[6] D 7 110
Chernivtsi, Ukr. A 10 104
Chernivtsi, Ukr. A 8 104
Chernivtsi □[6] A 8 104
Chernobyl see Chornobyl' D 6 110
Chernyakhiv D 6 110
Cherokee, Al., U.S. E 5 170
Cherokee, Ia., U.S. D 7 174
Cherokee Lake ⊜[1] A 3 168
Cherokees, Lake O' The ⊜[1] D 1 170
Cherokee Sound F 6 168
Cherry Hill G 3 164
Cherskiy Range (Čerskogo, hrebet) ⋏ C 17 114
Chervone D 9 110
Chervonohrad D 4 110
Chesapeake E 5 162
Chesapeake Bay c E 5 162
Chesapeake Bay Bridge-Tunnel ◆[5] E 5 162
Chesapeake Beach H 2 164
Cheshire D 5 164
Cheshire □[6], Eng., U.K. D 4 72
Cheshire □[6], N.H., U.S. D 6 164
Cheshunt F 6 72
Chest Creek ≃ C 4 162
Chester, Ca., U.S. B 3 180
Chester, Eng., U.K. D 4 72
Chester, Il., U.S. D 4 170
Chester, Ok., U.S. B 4 172
Chester, Pa., U.S. G 3 164
Chester □[6] G 3 164
Chesterfield, Eng., U.K. D 5 72
Chesterfield, S.C., U.S. B 4 168
Chesterfield, Îles II C 12 138
Chesterfield, Nosy I k 8 205a
Chesterfield Inlet D 14 150
Chester-le-Street C 5 72
Chestertown G 2 164
Chesterville A 3 164
Chetopa D 1 170
Chettlatt Island I H 11 116
Chetumal H 15 184
Chetumal, Bahia c D 2 186
Chevak F 12 154
Cheviot D 1 162
Cheviot Hills ⋏[2] B 4 72
Cheyenne, Ok., U.S. C 4 172
Cheyenne, Wy., U.S. B 6 176
Cheyenne ≃ C 4 174
Cheyenne River Indian Reservation ◆[4] C 4 174
Cheyne Bay c N 5 140
Chhapra D 4 122
Chhatarpur E 3 122
Chhay Arêng ≃ I 6 132
Chhindwāra E 3 122
Chi ≃, China B 13 130
Chi ≃, Thai. G 7 132
Chiai G 15 130
Chianciano Terme F 7 92
Chiang Kham E 5 132
Chiang Khan F 5 132
Chiang Mai E 4 132
Chiang Rai E 4 132
Chianti □[9] F 7 92
Chiapas □[3] I 13 184
Chiaravalle F 9 92
Chiari D 5 92
Chiasso E 6 82
Chiavari E 5 92
Chiavenna C 5 92
Chiba G 8 126
Chiba □[3] G 8 126
Chibango E 3 204
Chibia F 1 204
Chibuto C 10 206
Chibwe E 4 204
Chicago B 5 170
Chicago Heights B 5 170
Chicapa ≃ D 3 204
Chichagof Island I H 26 154
Chīchāwatni C 2 122
Chicheng F 10 128
Chichén Itzá ⊥ G 15 184
Chichester G 6 72
Chichijima-rettō II K 9 126
Chickamauga E 6 170
Chickamauga Lake ⊜[1] E 6 170
Chickasawhay ≃ G 4 170
Chickasaw National Recreation Area ♦ C 5 172
Chickasaw State Park ♦ E 4 170
Chickasha C 4 172
Chiclana de la Frontera H 4 86
Chiclayo E 3 190
Chico A 2 182
Chico ≃, Arg. H 6 192
Chico ≃, Arg. I 6 192
Chicomo C 11 206
Chicономо E 6 204
Chicopee, Ga., U.S. B 3 168
Chicopee, Ma., U.S. D 6 164
Chicoutimi D 8 160
Chicumbane C 10 206
Chicxulub G 15 184
Chidambaram G 3 122
Chiefland E 3 168
Chiemsee ⊜ E 9 100
Chieo Lan Reservoir ⊜[1] J 4 132
Chieri D 3 92
Chieti B 4 94
Chieti □[6] B 4 94
Chifeng E 12 128
Chiginagak, Mount ∧[1] H 16 154
Chignahuapan H 10 184
Chignik H 15 154
Chignik Bay c H 15 154
Chignik Lake H 15 154
Chigwell F 7 72
Chihuahua C 6 184
Chihuahua □[3] C 6 184
Chikmagalūr G 3 122
Chikowa Estate Mission E 5 204
Chikuma ≃ F 7 126
Chikuminuk Lake ⊜ F 14 154
Chilanga F 4 204
Chilanko Forks E 9 156
Chilaw H 3 122
Chilcotin ≃ F 10 156
Chilcott Islet I D 9 142
Childress C 3 172
Chile □[1] F 5 192
Chilecito A 4 195
Chilhowie E 3 162
Chilia, Braţul ≃ C 10 104
Chilika Lake ⊜ F 4 122
Chililabombwe E 4 204
Chilin see Jilin E 16 128
Chilko ≃ E 10 156
Chilko Lake ⊜ F 9 156
Chillán E 1 195
Chillicothe D 2 162
Chilliwack G 11 156
Chillon, Château de ⊥ D 4 82
Chiloé, Isla Grande de I H 5 192
Chilón I 13 184
Chiloquin D 3 178
Chilpancingo de los Bravo I 10 184
Chiltern Hills ⋏[2] F 6 72
Chiluage D 3 204
Chilumba E 5 204
Chilung F 15 130
Chilwa, Lake ⊜ F 6 204
Chimakela F 2 204
Chimaltenango E 2 186
Chimanimani National Park ♦ F 5 204
Chimbas B 3 195
Chimbiringua F 3 204
Chimborazo ∧[1] D 3 190
Chimbote E 3 190
Chimkent see Šymkent A 1 122
Chimney Rock National Historic Site ♦ E 3 174
Chimoio F 5 204
Chin □[3] C 1 132
China H 4 172
China □[1] D 9 130
China Lake ⊜ E 6 180
Chinandega E 3 186
Chincha Alta F 3 190
Chinchilla I 10 142
Chinchilla de Monte-Aragón F 3 88
Chincoteague E 6 162
Chinde F 6 204
Chindo I 16 128
Chindwinn ≃ C 2 132
Chingleput G 3 122
Chingola E 4 204
Chinguetti E 2 198
Chinhae I 17 128
Chin Hills ⋏[2] C 1 132
Chinhoyi F 4 204
Chiniot C 2 122
Chinizíua F 6 204
Chinju I 16 128
Chinko ≃ H 10 196
Chinon E 7 78
Chinook F 16 156
Chinook Valley C 13 156
Chinsali E 5 204
Chinunje E 6 204
Chinvali H 14 110
Chioggia D 8 92
Chios see Khíos I C 7 106
Chipata E 5 204
Chipera F 5 204
Chipili E 4 204
Chipiona H 4 86
Chip Lake ⊜ E 14 156
Chipley G 6 170
Chiplūn F 2 122
Chipogolo D 6 204
Chippenham F 4 72
Chippewa ≃ C 2 166
Chippewa, East Fork ≃ B 3 166
Chippewa Falls C 3 166
Chipping Norton F 5 72
Chipping Sodbury F 4 72
Chiquimula J 15 184
Chiquita D 2 204
Chīrāla F 4 122
Chirape A 10 206
Chirchik A 1 122
Chire see Shire ≃ F 6 204
Chiredzi G 5 204

Symbols in the index entries represent the broad categories identified in the key at the right. Symbols with superior numbers (⋏[1]) identify subcategories (see complete key on page 242).

∧ Mountain ⋏ Mountains)(Pass V Valley ≐ Plain > Cape I Island II Islands ⊥ Other Topographic Feature ≃ River ≡ Canal

Name	Map Ref.	Page

∟ Waterfall   ⋃ Strait   ⊂ Bay, Gulf   ⊜ Lake   ≃ Swamp   ⊠ Ice Feature   ▼ Other Hydrographic Feature   ⁺ Submarine Feature   □ Political Unit   ⅃ Cultural Institution   ⊥ Historical Site   ⁎ Recreational Site   ⊠ Airport   ♦ Military Installation   ◆ Miscellaneous

251

Symbols in the index entries represent the broad categories identified in the key at the right. Symbols with superior numbers (⋋[1]) identify subcategories (see complete key on page 242).

⋀ Mountain ⋌ Mountains ⋊ Pass V Valley ≈ Plain ⊁ Cape I Island II Islands ⋈ Other Topographic Feature ≃ River ⊖ Canal

◡ Waterfall ॥ Strait c Bay, Gulf ◎ Lake ≋ Swamp ⊠ Ice Feature ▽ Other Hydrographic Feature ◆ Submarine Feature □ Political Unit ▮ Cultural Institution ⊥ Historical Site ◆ Recreational Site ≍ Airport ■ Military Installation ◄ Miscellaneous

Name	Map Ref.	Page

Symbols in the index entries represent the broad categories identified in the key at the right. Symbols with superior numbers (⋌¹) identify subcategories (see complete key on page 242).

⋀ Mountain ⋌ Mountains ⋋ Pass V Valley = Plain ➤ Cape I Island II Islands ⊥ Other Topographic Feature ≈ River ≋ Canal

254

Name	Map Ref.	Page

ⱶ Waterfall   ⱴ Strait   c Bay, Gulf   ⱸ Lake   ⱬ Swamp   ⱬ Ice Feature   ⱴ Other Hydrographic Feature   ✦ Submarine Feature   □ Political Unit   ⱶ Cultural Institution   ⱶ Historical Site   ✦ Recreational Site   ⱬ Airport   ■ Military Installation   ⱴ Miscellaneous

Symbols in the index entries represent the broad categories identified in the key at the right. Symbols with superior numbers (⬈¹) identify subcategories (see complete key on page 242).

⋀ Mountain ⬈ Mountains ⋋ Pass V Valley ≃ Plain ⊁ Cape I Island II Islands ⊥ Other Topographic Feature ≃ River ⊜ Canal

Gisors — Guanling

Name | Map Ref. | Page

Gisors C 8 78
Gistel C 1 69
Gitambo B 3 204
Gitega C 4 204
Giulianova B 3 94
Giurgiu D 8 104
Giurgiu □[3] C 9 104
Giussano D 5 92
Giv'atayim E 3 120
Givet B 11 78
Givors E 2 82
Givry F 11 78
Giyon F 4 202
Gizo A 12 138
Giżycko A 11 96
Gjirokastër B 4 106
Gjoa Haven C 13 150
Gjøvik B 5 66
Gjuhëzës, Kepi i > B 3 106
Glace Bay E 14 160
Glacier F 13 156
Glacier Bay ⊂ G 26 154
Glacier Bay National Park ♦ G 26 154
Glacier National Park ♦, B.C., Can. F 12 156
Glacier National Park ♦, Mt., U.S. A 6 178
Glacier Peak ∧[1] A 3 178
Gladenbach F 5 98
Gladsakse C 5 68
Gladstone, Austl. G 10 142
Gladstone, Mb., Can. F 9 158
Gladstone, Mo., U.S. C 1 170
Gladwin A 1 162
Gladys Lake ⊜ B 5 156
Glafsfjorden ⊜ C 6 66
Glåma ≃ F 5 64
Glamis Castle ⊥ D 6 74
Glamorgan, Vale of □[6] F 3 72
Glamsbjerg C 3 68
Glan ⊜ C 7 66
Glanum ⊥ G 2 82
Glaris see Glarus C 7 82
Glaris see Glarus □[3] D 7 82
Glarus C 7 82
Glarus □[3] D 7 82
Glasgow, Ky., U.S. D 6 170
Glasgow, Mo., U.S. C 2 170
Glasgow, Scot., U.K. B 2 72
Glasgow, Va., U.S. E 4 162
Glasgow, City of □[6] B 2 72
Glassboro G 3 164
Glastonbury F 4 72
Glauchau F 9 98
Glazov G 20 108
Glazunovka C 10 110
Gleisdorf C 7 102
Gleiwitz see Gliwice C 10 96
Glenboro G 9 158
Glen Burnie G 2 164
Glen Canyon V D 3 176
Glen Canyon Dam →[6] D 3 176
Glen Canyon National Recreation Area ♦ D 3 176
Glencoe, Al., U.S. F 6 170
Glencoe, Mn., U.S. C 1 166
Glendale, Az., U.S. F 2 176
Glendale, Ca., U.S. F 5 182
Glendale, Ms., U.S. G 4 170
Glendale, Wi., U.S. D 5 166
Glendalough ⊥ C 5 75
Glendo D 2 174
Glenelg ≃ F 3 144
Glenfield E 5 72
Glengyle H 4 142
Glen Innes B 8 144
Glen Lyon E 2 164
Glenmora G 2 170
Glenn □[6] A 1 182
Glennallen E 21 154
Glennville D 3 168
Glenora C 6 156
Glen Rock G 2 164
Glenrothes D 5 74
Glens Falls C 5 164
Glenthompson F 4 144
Glen Ullin B 3 174
Glenville D 2 166
Glenwood, Ia., U.S. B 1 170
Glenwood, Mn., U.S. C 7 174
Glenwood, Nf., Can. D 16 160
Glenwood Springs C 5 176
Glienicke D 10 98
Glífa C 5 106
Glina E 8 102
Glinde C 7 98
Glittertinden ∧ B 4 66
Gliwice C 10 96
Gljadjanskoe I 26 108
Globe F 3 176
Glodeanu-Siliștea C 9 104
Glodeni B 9 104
Glogau see Głogów C 8 96
Głogów C 8 96
Głogów Małopolski C 12 96
Glorieta E 6 176
Glotovka J 17 108
Gloucester, Eng., U.K. F 4 72
Gloucester, Ma., U.S. D 8 164
Gloucester, On., Can. A 3 164
Gloucester, Va., U.S. E 5 162
Gloucester □[6] G 3 164
Gloucestershire □[6] F 4 72
Glouster D 2 162
Gloversville C 4 164
Głowno C 10 96
Glubokoe see Hlybokae E 13 66
Głuchołazy C 9 96
Glücksburg B 6 98
Glückstadt C 6 98
Glyngøre B 1 68
Gmünd, Aus. D 5 102
Gmünd, Aus. B 6 102
Gmunden C 5 102
Gnesen see Gniezno B 9 96
Gniew B 10 96
Gniezno B 9 96
Gnjilane D 6 104
Gnosjö D 6 66
Goa □[3] F 2 122
Goba, Eth. F 4 202
Goba, Moz. D 10 206
Gobabis B 3 206
Gobernador Gregores I 5 192
Gobi Desert →[2] D 5 124
Gobō H 5 126
Goce Delčev E 7 104
Goch E 3 98
Godalming F 6 72
Godāvari ≃ F 4 122
Godāvari, Mouths of the ≃[1] F 4 122
God Colow G 5 202
Goderich G 3 160
Godfrey C 3 170
Godhavn (Qeqertarsuaq) C 22 150
Godhra E 2 122
Gödöllő B 5 104
Godoy Cruz C 3 195
Gods ≃ C 12 158
Gods Lake ⊜ D 11 158
Godthåb (Nuuk) D 22 150
Godwin Austen, Mount see K2 ∧ B 3 122
Goéland, Lac au ⊜ D 5 160
Goélands, Lac aux ⊜ A 11 160
Goeree →[1] C 2 69
Goes C 2 69
Goff G 5 202
Goffstown C 7 164
Göggingen D 6 96
Gogrial F 2 202
Goiânia B 6 194
Goiás A 5 194
Goiás □[3] G 8 190
Goiatuba B 6 194
Goirle C 4 69
Gois, Le →[5] F 4 78
Gojam □[3] E 4 202
Gojeb ≃ F 4 202
Gojra C 2 122
Gökçeada I B 6 106
Gokçekaya Baraji ⊜[1] B 9 106
Gökçen C 7 106
Gökova Körfezi (Kerme, Gulf of) ⊂ D 7 106
Göksu ≃ D 5 118
Göktepe J 20 110
Gokwe F 4 204
Golāghāt D 6 122
Gołańcz B 9 96
Golan Heights □[2] D 5 120
Gölcük, Tur. B 8 106
Gölcük, Tur. C 8 106
Gołdap A 12 96
Goldbey B 4 82
Gold Bridge F 10 156
Gold Coast (Southport) A 9 144
Gold Coast ⏉[2] E 4 200
Golden F 13 156
Golden Bay ⊂ D 4 146
Golden City D 1 170
Golden Ears Provincial Park ♦ G 10 156
Golden Gate Highlands National Park ♦ E 8 206
Golden Spike National Historic Site ♦ E 7 178
Goldfield C 6 182
Gold River G 8 156
Goldsand Lake ⊜ C 8 158
Goldsboro B 6 168
Goldsworthy G 5 140
Goldthwaite E 4 172
Goleniów B 8 96
Goleta F 4 182
Golfito F 4 186
Golfo Aranci H 5 92
Gölhisar D 8 106
Goliad F 5 172
Golina B 10 96
Gölköy B 7 118
Gollnow see Goleniów B 8 96
Gölmarmara C 7 106
Golodnaja Guba, ozero ⊜ C 20 108
Golovin D 13 154
Golpāyegān F 14 118
Golyšmanovo H 28 108
Goma C 4 204
Gomati ≃ D 4 122
Gombe C 7 200
Gombi C 7 200
Gomel (Homel') C 7 110
Gómez Palacio E 7 184
Gomīshān D 15 118
Gommern D 8 98
Gonābād D 8 116
Gonaïves D 6 186
Gonarezhou National Park ♦ G 5 206
Gonâve, Golfe de la ⊂ D 6 186
Gonâve, Île de la I D 6 186
Gonbad-e Qābūs D 16 118
Gonda D 4 122
Gondal E 2 122
Gonder E 4 202
Gonder □[3] E 4 202
Gondia E 4 122
Gondola F 5 204
Gondomar C 2 86
Gönen B 7 106
Gonesse G 9 70
Gong ≃ F 12 130
Gong'an C 10 130
Gongbo'gyamda D 6 122
Gongcheng F 10 130
Gongga Shan (Minya Konka) ∧ D 5 130
Gonghe H 3 128
Gongola ≃ C 7 200
Gongolon C 6 144
Gongxi E 12 130
Gongxian A 11 130
Gongzhuling E 15 128
Goñi C 9 195
Goniri C 7 200
Gonnesa F 2 90
Gonzales, Ca., U.S. D 2 182
Gonzales, La., U.S. G 3 170
Gonzales, Tx., U.S. F 5 172
González F 10 184
Goochland E 5 162
Goodeve F 7 158
Good Hope, Cape of > H 3 206
Goodhope Bay ⊂ C 13 154
Good Hope Mountain ∧ F 9 156
Goodhouse E 3 206
Gooding D 6 178
Goodland F 4 174
Goodman C 4 166
Goodnews Bay G 13 154
Goodrich G 1 170
Goodwater F 5 170
Goole D 6 72
Goolgowi D 5 144
Goondiwindi B 8 144
Goongarrie L 6 140
Goongarrie National Park ♦ L 6 140
Goor B 5 69
Goose Creek C 4 168
Goose Green n 18 193b
Goose Lake ⊜, Mb., Can. D 8 158
Goose Lake ⊜, U.S. E 3 178
Gooty F 3 122
Göppingen D 6 100
Goqên D 3 130
Góra C 9 96
Gorakhpur D 4 122
Gorczański Park Narodwy ♦ D 11 96
Gorda, Punta >, Ca., U.S. B 1 180
Gorda, Punta >, Cuba C 4 186
Gordo F 5 170
Gordon D 3 174
Gordon ≃ j 11 145a
Gordon, Lake ⊜[1] j 12 145a
Gordon Indian Reserve →[4] F 6 158
Gore, Austl. B 8 144
Gore, N.Z. G 2 146
Gorebridge E 5 74
Goreloe C 12 110
Gore Range ⋀ B 5 176
Goreville D 4 170
Gorgān D 16 118
Gorgān ≃ D 16 118
Gorges D 2 206
Gorgol □[3] F 2 198
Gorgol el Abioḍ ≃ F 2 198
Gorgota C 8 104
Gorham C 8 164
Gori H 14 110
Gorica see Gorizia D 9 92
Goricy H 12 108
Gorinchem C 3 69
Goris J 15 110
Göritz see Górzyca D 11 98
Gorizia (Gorica) D 9 92
Gorizia □[6] D 9 92
Gorj □[3] C 7 104
Gorkhā D 4 122
Gor'kovskoe vodohranilišče ⊜[1] H 15 108
Gorky see Nižnij Novgorod H 16 108
Gorlice D 11 96
Görlitz E 11 98
Gorna Orjahovica D 8 104
Gornjackij C 26 108
Gornja Radgona D 7 102
Gornji Milanovac C 6 104
Gorno-Altajsk D 11 114
Gornopravdinsk F 28 108
Gornozavodsk G 23 108
Gornye Ključi B 4 126
Gorodec, Russia C 14 66
Gorodec, Russia H 15 108
Gorodišče see Haradzišča J 12 64
Gorodno D 14 66
Goroka N 13 124
Gorontalo E 8 134
Górowo Iławeckie A 11 96
Gorseinon F 2 72
Gór Stołowych, Park Narodowy ♦ C 9 96
Gort C 3 75
Görz see Gorizia D 9 92
Gorzów □[3] B 8 96
Gorzów Wielkopolski B 8 96
Gosford D 8 144
Gosforth C 3 72
Goshen, In., U.S. B 6 170
Goshen, N.S., Can. F 13 160
Goshen, N.Y., U.S. E 4 164
Goshute Indian Reservation →[4] C 1 176
Goslar E 7 98
Gosnells M 4 140
Gosport, Eng., U.K. G 5 72
Gosport, In., U.S. C 5 170
Gossas C 1 200
Gossau C 7 82
Gossinga F 2 202
Gostivar E 6 104
Gostyń C 9 96
Gostynin B 10 96
Göta ≃ D 6 66
Göta kanal ≊ C 7 66
Göteborg (Gothenburg) D 6 66
Göteborg och Bohus □[3] C 5 66
Gotești B 10 104
Gotha F 7 98
Gothenburg, Ne., U.S. E 4 174
Gothenburg see Göteborg, Swe. D 6 66
Gotland □[3] D 9 66
Gotland I D 9 66
Gotō-rettō II H 2 126
Gōtsu G 4 126
Göttingen E 6 98
Gottorf, Schloss ⊥ B 6 98
Gottvaterkapelle ⊳[1] C 8 100
Gottwaldov see Zlín A 9 102
Götzis C 1 102
Goubangzi F 13 128
Goubone A 8 200
Gouda C 3 69
Goudoumaria C 7 200
Gouéké D 3 200
Gough Island I I 10 60
Gouin, Réservoir ⊜[1] D 6 160
Goulais ≃ H 16 158
Goulburn E 7 144
Goulburn ≃ F 5 144
Goulburn River National Park ♦ D 7 144
Gould City B 6 166
Gouldsboro State Park ♦ E 3 164
Goulmima C 4 198
Goumbati ∧[2] C 2 200
Gouménissa B 5 106
Goundam B 4 200
Goundi D 8 200
Gounou-Gaya D 7 200
Gourbassi C 2 200
Gourcy C 4 200
Gouré C 7 200
Gourits ≃ H 4 206
Gouro B 8 200
Gouverneur B 3 164
Govenlock G 17 156
Governador Valadares C 10 194
Governor Dodge State Park ♦ D 3 166
Govĭ-Altay □[3] D 2 128
Govind Ballabh Pant Sāgar ⊜[1] E 4 122
Gowanda B 4 162
Goya A 8 195
Göyçay I 15 110
Goz Beïda C 9 200
Gozo I H 4 94
Graaff-Reinet G 6 206
Graafwater G 3 206
Grabow C 8 98
Grabowiec C 12 96
Gračanica C 5 104
Gračanica, Manastir ⊳[1] D 6 104
Graçay E 8 78
Graceville C 6 174
Gracias a Dios, Cabo > E 4 186
Graciosa I E 5 196
Gradačac C 5 104
Gradaús E 8 190
Grado D 9 92
Grad Sofija □[3] D 7 104
Grady E 3 170
Grafenau B 5 102
Gräfenhainichen E 9 98
Grafham Water ⊜[1] E 6 72
Grafing bei München D 8 100
Grafton B 9 144
Grafton □[6] B 7 164
Grafton Lakes State Park ♦ D 5 164
Graham, N.C., U.S. A 5 168
Graham, Tx., U.S. D 4 172
Graham, Mount ∧ F 4 176
Graham Island I E 6 156
Graham Land →[1] C 2 208
Grahamstown G 7 206
Grajagan I 22 135b
Grajaú A 9 190
Grajaú ≃ D 9 190
Grajewo B 12 96
Gram C 2 68
Gramado A 12 195
Gramat D 5 80
Grammichele G 4 94
Grammont see Geraardsbergen D 2 69
Grampian Mountains ⋀ D 5 74
Grampians National Park ♦ F 4 144
Gran see Esztergom C 10 102
Grana ≃ E 3 92
Granada, Mn., U.S. D 7 174
Granada, Nic. F 3 186
Granada, Spain G 7 86
Granada □[6] D 4 84
Granadella see La Granadella C 5 88
Granbury D 5 172
Granby, Ct., U.S. E 6 164
Granby, P.Q., Can. F 7 160
Granby ≃ G 12 156
Gran Canaria I j 15 85b
Gran Chaco →[1] D 7 192
Grand ≃, Mi., U.S. D 6 166
Grand ≃, On., Can. G 4 160
Grand ≃, S.D., U.S. C 4 174
Grand ≃, U.S. C 2 170
Grand, East Fork ≃ B 1 170
Grand, North Fork ≃ C 3 174
Grandas A 4 86
Grand Bahama I F 5 168
Grand Ballon ∧ C 5 82
Grand Bank E 15 160
Grand-Bassam D 4 200
Grand Bay F 10 160
Grand Beach F 10 158
Grand Béréby E 3 200
Grand Bruit E 14 160
Grand Calumet, Île du I A 2 164
Grand Canal see Da Yunhe ≊, China C 14 130
Grand Canal ≊, Ire. C 4 75
Grand Canyon D 2 176
Grand Canyon V D 2 176
Grand Canyon National Park ♦ D 2 176
Grand Cayman I D 4 186
Grand Centre D 16 156
Grand Chenier H 2 170
Grand Coulee Dam →[6] A 4 178
Grand-Couronne C 8 78
Grande ≃, Bol. G 6 190
Grande ≃, Braz. F 10 190
Grande ≃, Braz. G 9 190
Grande ≃, Chile B 2 195
Grande ≃, Ven. F 9 186
Grande, Bahía ⊂ J 6 192
Grande, Boca ≃[1] B 6 190
Grande, Ilha I E 3 194
Grande, Rio (Bravo) ≃ F 7 152
Grande-Anse E 7 160
Grande Chartreuse, Couvent de la ⊳[1] E 3 82
Grande de Manacapuru, Lago ⊜ D 6 190
Grande de Santiago ≃ G 7 184
Grande do Gurupá, Ilha I D 8 190
Grande Prairie D 12 156
Grand Erg de Bilma →[2] B 7 200
Grand Erg Occidental →[2] C 5 198
Grand Erg Oriental →[2] C 6 198
Grande Rivière, La ≃ B 4 160
Grande Ronde ≃ C 5 178
Grandes, Salinas ≚ E 7 192
Grande-Synthe A 9 78
Grande-Terre I n 21 187e
Grand Falls (Grand Sault) E 10 160
Grand Falls-Windsor D 16 160
Grandfield C 4 172
Grand Forks, B.C., Can. G 12 156
Grand Forks, N.D., U.S. B 6 174
Grand-Fougeray E 5 78
Grand Haven D 5 166
Grandin, Lac ⊜ D 9 150
Grand Island E 5 174
Grand Isle H 4 170
Grand Isle □[6] B 5 164
Grand Junction, Co., U.S. C 4 176
Grand Junction, Tn., U.S. E 4 170
Grand Lake ⊜, La., U.S. H 2 170
Grand Lake ⊜, N.A. h 13 163a
Grand Lake (Grand Lac) ⊜, N.B., Can. F 11 160
Grand Lake ⊜, Nf., Can. D 15 160
Grand Ledge B 1 162
Grand'Maison, Barrage de →[6] E 4 82
Grand Manan Island I F 10 160
Grand Marais B 3 166
Grand-Mère E 7 160
Grand Portage H 14 158
Grand Portage Indian Reservation →[4] B 3 166
Grand Portage National Monument ♦ B 4 166
Grand Prairie D 5 172
Grand Rapids, Mb., Can. E 9 158
Grand Rapids, Mi., U.S. D 5 166
Grand Rhône ≃ G 2 82
Grandrieu F 1 82
Grands-Jardins, Parc de conservation des ♦ g 11 163a
Grand Teton ∧ D 8 178
Grand Teton National Park ♦ D 8 178
Grand Traverse Bay ⊂ C 6 166
Grand Turk C 7 186
Grandview, Mo., U.S. C 1 170
Grandview, Wa., U.S. B 3 178
Grand Wash Cliffs ⏉[4] E 2 176
Graneros D 2 195
Grangemouth A 3 72
Granger, Wa., U.S. B 3 178
Granger, Wy., U.S. E 8 178
Granger Draw ≃ E 3 172
Granges see Grenchen C 5 82
Grängesberg B 7 66
Granite City C 3 170
Granite Downs I 1 142
Granite Peak ∧ C 8 178
Granite Range ⋀ E 4 178
Graniteville C 4 168
Granki I 9 108
Grankulla see Kauniainen B 12 66
Granollers C 7 88
Granön D 9 64
Gran Paradiso ∧ D 3 92
Gran Paradiso, Parco Nazionale del ♦ D 3 92
Gran Rio ≃ C 7 190
Gransee C 10 98
Grant D 6 166
Grantham E 6 72
Grants E 5 176
Grants Pass D 2 178
Grantsville D 3 162
Granum G 15 156
Granville, Fr. D 5 78
Granville, Oh., U.S. C 2 162
Granville Lake ⊜ C 8 158
Granvin B 3 66
Gras, Lac de ⊜ D 10 150
Grasmere D 7 206
Grass ≃ D 9 158
Grassano D 6 94
Grasse G 4 82
Grasset, Lac ⊜ D 4 160
Grasslands National Park ♦ G 18 156
Grass Patch M 6 140
Grass River Provincial Park ♦ D 8 158
Grass Valley A 2 182
Grassy Lake G 16 156
Grästorp C 6 66
Graubünden □[3] C 5 92
Graudenz see Grudziądz B 10 96
Graulhet E 5 80
Gravelines A 9 78
Gravenhage, 's- see 's-Gravenhage B 3 69
Gravenhurst F 4 160
Gravina G 4 94
Gravina in Puglia D 6 94
Gray, Fr. C 3 82
Gray, Ga., U.S. C 3 168
Grayling A 1 162
Grays F 7 72
Grays Harbor ⊂ B 1 178
Grayson F 2 170
Grays Peak ∧ C 6 176
Graz C 7 102
Grdelica D 7 104
Great Alfold see Alföld ≚ B 7 90
Great Artesian Basin ≚[1] H 5 142
Great Australian Bight ⊂ F 6 138
Great Barrier Island I B 5 146
Great Barrier Reef ✢[2] D 8 142
Great Barrier Reef Marine Park ♦ E 9 142
Great Barrington D 5 164
Great Basin ≚[1] D 4 152
Great Basin National Park ♦ C 1 176
Great Bear ≃ D 32 154
Great Bear Lake ⊜ C 34 154
Great Bend F 5 174
Great Bitter Lake ⊜ G 5 118
Great Britain I E 8 70
Great Channel ⋓ K 2 132
Great Dismal Swamp ∷ A 6 168
Great Divide Basin ≚[1] E 9 178
Great Dividing Range ⋀ H 8 142
Greater Antilles II D 7 186
Greater Saint Lucia Wetland Park, The ♦ D 10 206
Greater Sunda Islands II F 5 134
Great Exuma I C 5 186
Great Falls, Mt., U.S. B 8 178
Great Falls, S.C., U.S. B 4 168
Great Fish ≃ G 7 206
Great Grimsby see Grimsby D 6 72
Great Himalayan National Park ♦ C 3 122
Great Inagua I C 6 186
Great Indian Desert (Thar Desert) →[2] D 1 122
Great Karoo ⋀[1] G 5 206
Great Kei ≃ G 7 206
Great La Cloche Island I C 8 166
Great Lake ⊜[1] i 12 145a
Great Malvern E 4 72
Great Miami ≃ D 1 162
Great Nicobar I H 6 122
Great Ouse ≃ E 7 72
Great Pee Dee ≃ C 5 168
Great Plains ≚ B 3 172
Great Ruaha ≃ D 6 204
Great Sacandaga Lake ⊜[1] C 4 164
Great Saint Bernard Pass)(E 5 82
Great Salt Lake ⊜ E 7 178
Great Salt Lake Desert →[2] B 2 176
Great Sand Dunes National Monument ♦ D 6 176
Great Sandy Desert →[2] G 7 140
Great Sandy National Park ♦ H 11 142
Great Sankey D 4 72
Great Scarcies (Kolenté) ≃ D 2 200
Great Slave Lake ⊜ D 10 150
Great Smoky Mountains ⋀ B 3 168
Great Smoky Mountains National Park ♦ B 3 168
Great Tenasserim ≃ H 4 132
Great Valley V A 3 168
Great Victoria Desert →[2] K 9 140
Great Wall ⊳[3] L 8 192
Great Wall see Chang Cheng → G 8 128
Great Yarmouth E 8 72
Great Zab ≃ C 11 118
Gréboun ∧ A 6 200
Greece C 1 164
Greece □[1] H 12 62
Greeley, Co., U.S. E 2 174
Greeley, Ks., U.S. C 1 170
Greeley, Ne., U.S. E 5 174
Green ≃, Ky., U.S. D 5 170
Green ≃, N.D., U.S. B 3 174
Green ≃, U.S. C 4 176
Green Bay C 5 166
Green Bay ⊂ C 5 166
Green Brier D 5 170
Greenbush A 6 174
Greencastle C 5 170
Green Cove Springs D 4 168
Greene D 2 166
Greene □[6] D 4 164
Greeneville A 3 168
Greenfield, Ca., U.S. D 2 182
Greenfield, Ma., U.S. D 6 164
Greenfield, Oh., U.S. D 2 162
Greenisland B 6 75
Green Lake D 18 156
Greenland (Kalaallit Nunaat) □[2] C 16 148
Greenland Basin ✢[1] C 23 61
Greenland Sea ⫟[2] C 23 61
Green Mountains ⋀ C 6 164
Greenock B 2 72
Greenough K 3 140
Greenough ≃ K 3 140
Green River, Ut., U.S. C 3 176
Green River, Wy., U.S. E 9 178
Greensboro, Fl., U.S. D 2 168
Greensboro, Md., U.S. H 3 164
Greensboro, N.C., U.S. A 5 168
Greensburg, In., U.S. C 6 170
Greensburg, Ky., U.S. D 6 170
Greensburg, Pa., U.S. C 4 162
Greenup C 4 170
Greenvale E 7 142
Green Valley G 3 176
Greenville, Al., U.S. G 5 170
Greenville, Il., U.S. C 4 170
Greenville, Lib. D 3 200
Greenville, Me., U.S. h 12 163a
Greenville, Ms., U.S. F 3 170
Greenville, N.C., U.S. B 6 168
Greenville, Oh., U.S. B 6 170
Greenville, S.C., U.S. B 3 168
Greenville, Tx., U.S. D 5 172
Greenwater Lake Provincial Park ♦ E 7 158
Greenwich, Ct., U.S. E 5 164
Greenwich, N.Y., U.S. C 5 164
Greenwood, B.C., Can. G 12 156
Greenwood, In., U.S. C 5 170
Greenwood, Ms., U.S. F 3 170
Greenwood, S.C., U.S. B 3 168
Greers Ferry Lake ⊜[1] E 2 170
Grefrath E 3 98
Gregbe D 3 200
Gregoire Lake Indian Reserve →[4] C 16 156
Gregório ≃ E 4 190
Gregory G 5 172
Gregory ≃ E 4 142
Gregory, Lake ⊜, Austl. F 9 140
Gregory, Lake ⊜, Austl. I 5 140
Gregory, Lake ⊜, Austl. B 2 144
Gregory National Park ♦ E 11 140
Gregory Range ⋀ E 6 142
Greifenhagen see Gryfino B 8 96
Greifswald B 10 98
Greifswalder Bodden ⊂ B 10 98
Greiz B 9 100
Gremiha B 13 108
Gremjačinsk G 22 108
Grenada F 4 170
Grenada □[1] E 9 186
Grenada Lake ⊜[1] F 4 170
Grenadines II E 9 186
Grenchen C 5 82
Grenen > A 3 68
Grenfell, Austl. D 7 144
Grenfell, Sk., Can. F 7 158
Grenoble E 3 82
Gréoux-les-Bains G 3 82
Gresham C 2 178
Gresik, Indon. k 21 135b
Gresik, Indon. k 21 135b
Gressåmoen Nasjonalpark ♦ D 5 64
Gresten C 7 102
Gretna H 3 170
Greve, Den. C 5 68
Greve, Italy F 7 92
Grevelingendam →[5] C 3 69
Greven D 4 98
Grevená B 4 106
Grevenbroich E 3 98
Grevesmühlen C 8 98
Greve Strand see Greve C 5 68
Grey ≃ E 15 160
Greybull C 9 178
Grey Islands II C 16 160
Greylock, Mount ∧ D 5 164
Greymouth E 3 146
Grey Range ⋀ I 6 142
Greytown, N.Z. D 5 146
Greytown, S. Afr. E 9 206
Gribanovskij D 12 110
Gribbel Island I E 7 156
Gridley E 4 166
Griesheim C 5 100
Griffin, Ga., U.S. C 2 168
Griffin, Sk., Can. G 7 158
Griffith E 5 144
Grignan F 2 82
Grigny E 2 82
Grigoriopol B 10 104
Grijalva (Cuilco) ≃ J 13 184
Grillenthal D 1 206
Grim, Cape > i 11 145a
Grimari D 9 200
Grimbergen D 3 69
Grimma E 9 98
Grimmen B 10 98
Grimnitzsee ⊜ D 10 98
Grimsby D 6 72
Grimsel Pass)(D 6 82
Grímsstaðir m 22 64a
Grímsvötn ∧[1] m 22 64a
Grindavík n 19 64a
Grindsted C 1 68
Grinnell B 2 170
Grinnell Peninsula >[1] A 14 150
Gripsholm slott ⊥ C 8 66
Griqualand East □[9] F 8 206
Griqualand West □[9] E 5 206
Grischun see Graubünden □[3] C 5 92
Gris-Nez, Cap > B 8 78
Grisons see Graubünden □[3] C 5 92
Griswold A 4 174
Grizzly Bear Mountain ∧ D 34 154
Grizzly Bear's Head and Lead Man Indian Reserve →[4] E 18 156
Grjazi C 11 110
Grjazovec G 14 108
Grobblershoop E 4 206
Groblersdal C 8 206
Gröditz E 10 98
Grodno see Hrodna F 11 66
Grodzisk Mazowiecki B 11 96
Groen ≃ F 5 206
Groenlo B 5 69
Grójec C 11 96
Grombalia G 3 90
Gronau, Ger. D 4 98
Gronau, Ger. D 6 98
Grondneus E 4 206
Grong Grong E 6 144
Groningen A 5 69
Groningen □[3] A 5 69
Groom C 3 172
Groot ≃ G 6 206
Groot-Berg ≃ G 3 206
Grootdraaidam ⊜[1] D 8 206
Groote Eylandt I B 3 142
Grootfontein F 2 204
Grootpan D 7 206
Groot-Swartberge ⋀ G 5 206
Grootvloer ≚ E 4 206
Gropeni C 9 104
Gros Morne ∧ D 15 160
Gros Morne National Park ♦ D 14 160
Grossenhain E 10 98
Grossenkneten D 5 98
Grosser Arber ∧ C 10 100
Grosses Schulerloch ♦ D 8 100
Grosseto G 7 92
Grosseto □[6] G 7 92
Gross-Gerau C 5 100
Grossglockner ∧ C 4 102
Grosshansdorf C 7 98
Grossostheim C 6 100
Grossräschen E 10 98
Grossvenediger ∧ C 4 102
Gross-Zimmern C 5 100
Grosvenor, Lake ⊜ G 17 154
Groswater Bay ⊂ A 14 160
Groton C 5 174
Grottaglie D 7 94
Grottaminarda C 5 94
Grottammare B 3 94
Grouard Mission D 13 156
Groundhog ≃ D 2 160
Grove D 1 170
Grove City D 2 162
Grove Hill G 5 170
Grover City E 3 182
Groves H 2 170
Groveton B 7 164
Growa Point > E 3 200
Groznyj H 14 110
Grubišno Polje E 9 102
Grudziądz B 10 96
Grugliasco D 3 92
Gruia C 7 104
Grumo Appula C 6 94
Grums C 6 66
Grüna B 9 100
Grünberg B 5 100
Grundy Center D 2 166
Grundy Lake Provincial Park ♦ C 8 166
Grunthal A 6 174
Gruzdžiai D 11 66
Gryfice B 8 96
Gryfino B 8 96
Grythyttan C 7 66
Grytviken q 21 193c
Guacanayabo, Golfo de ⊂ C 5 186
Guadalajara, Mex. G 8 184
Guadalajara, Spain D 7 86
Guadalajara □[6] D 2 88
Guadalcanal I A 13 138
Guadalimar ≃ F 7 86
Guadalmena ≃ F 2 88
Guadalope ≃ C 4 88
Guadalquivir ≃ H 4 86
Guadalquivir, Marismas del ∷ H 4 86
Guadalupe, Ca., U.S. F 3 182
Guadalupe, Mex. F 8 184
Guadalupe, Mex. E 9 184
Guadalupe ≃ F 5 172
Guadalupe, Isla I F 4 152
Guadalupe Mountains National Park ♦ G 6 176
Guadalupe Peak ∧ E 1 172
Guadarrama D 6 86
Guadeloupe □[2] D 9 186
Guadeloupe Channel ⋓ o 21 187e
Guadeloupe Passage ⋓ D 9 186
Guadiana ≃ G 3 86
Guadiana Menor ≃ G 1 88
Guadix G 1 88
Guafo, Isla I H 5 192
Guaíba B 12 195
Guainía ≃ C 5 190
Guaíra F 3 194
Guairá □[3] F 2 194
Guajará-Mirim F 5 190
Guaje, Laguna del ⊜ C 8 184
Gualdo Tadino F 8 92
Gualeguay C 8 195
Gualeguay ≃ C 8 195
Gualeguaychú C 8 195
Gualicho, Salina del ≚ H 6 192
Guam □[2] C 12 134
Guaminí E 6 195
Guamúchil E 5 184
Gua Musang L 5 132
Guanajuato G 9 184
Guanajuato □[3] G 9 184
Guanambi F 10 190
Guanare F 7 186
Guandacol A 3 195
Guane C 3 186
Guang'an C 8 130
Guangchang E 12 130
Guangde C 14 130
Guangdong □[3] G 12 130
Guangfeng D 14 130
Guangji D 12 130
Guangling G 10 128
Guangxi □[3] F 8 130
Guangyuan B 7 130
Guangze E 13 130
Guangzhou (Canton) G 11 130
Guanhães C 9 194
Guánica j 15 187b
Guanipa ≃ F 9 186
Guanling F 7 130

∟ Waterfall ⋓ Strait ⊂ Bay, Gulf ⊜ Lake ∷ Swamp ⊓ Ice Feature ⫟ Other Hydrographic Feature ✢ Submarine Feature □ Political Unit ⊳ Cultural Institution ⊥ Historical Site ♦ Recreational Site ⊠ Airport ■ Military Installation → Miscellaneous

Symbols in the index entries represent the broad categories identified in the key at the right. Symbols with superior numbers (∧[1]) identify subcategories (see complete key on page 242).

∧ Mountain	∧ Mountains	)(Pass	V Valley	≃ Plain	≻ Cape	I Island	II Islands	∴ Other Topographic Feature	≃ River	≃ Canal

Henderson — Ídolo

Name | Map Ref. | Page

Henderson, Ky., U.S. D 5 170
Henderson, Nv., U.S. D 1 176
Henderson, Tn., U.S. E 4 170
Henderson, Tx., U.S. F 1 170
Hendersonville D 5 170
Hendījān G 13 118
Hengdaohezi E 16 128
Hengelo B 5 69
Hengfeng D 13 130
Hengshan, China H 7 128
Hengshan, China E 11 130
Hengshui H 10 128
Hengxian G 9 130
Hengyang E 11 130
Heniches'k F 9 110
Hénin-Beaumont B 9 78
Henley-on-Thames F 6 72
Henlopen, Cape > H 3 164
Hennebont E 3 78
Hennef F 4 98
Hennenman E 7 206
Hennigsdorf D 10 98
Henniker C 7 164
Henning E 4 170
Henrietta D 4 172
Henrietta Maria, Cape > D 17 158
Henry B 4 170
Henry, Cape > E 6 162
Henry Cowell Redwoods State Park ♦ C 1 182
Henry Kater, Cape > C 19 150
Henry W. Coe State Park ♦ C 2 182
Henstedt-Ulzburg C 6 98
Hentiy □[3] C 8 128
Henty E 6 144
Henzada F 2 132
Heppenheim C 5 100
Hepu H 9 130
Heqing A 5 132
Hequ G 8 128
Héraðsflói c m 23 64a
Hera Lacinia, Tempio di ⊥ E 7 94
Herāt D 9 116
Hérault □[3] G 5 76
Herbert F 3 146
Herbert Hoover National Historic Site ♦ B 3 170
Herbignac E 4 78
Herblay D 9 78
Herborn B 5 100
Herchmer C 11 158
Herculaneum see Ercolano ⊥ D 4 94
Hércules C 7 184
Herðubreið ∧[1] m 22 64a
Hereford, Eng., U.K. E 4 72
Hereford, Tx., U.S. C 2 172
Hereford and Worcester □[6] E 4 72
Hereke B 8 106
Herencia E 7 86
Herent D 3 69
Herentals C 3 69
Herford D 5 98
Héricourt C 4 82
Herington F 6 174
Herisau C 7 82
Herkimer C 3 164
Herkimer □[6] C 4 164
Herlen see Kerulen ≃ B 10 128
Herlong B 3 180
Herman E 6 174
Hermanavičy E 13 66
Hermanns-Denkmal ⊥ E 5 98
Hermansverk B 3 66
Hermansville C 5 166
Hermidale C 6 144
Hermiston C 4 178
Hermitage E 15 160
Hermit Islands II M 13 124
Hermon, Mount ∧ C 5 120
Hermosillo C 4 184
Hermsdorf F 8 98
Hermus see Gediz ≃ C 7 106
Hernando, Arg. C 5 195
Hernando, Ms., U.S. E 4 170
Herne E 4 98
Herne Bay F 8 72
Herning B 1 68
Heron Lake D 7 174
Herrenberg D 5 100
Herrenchiemsee, Schloss ⊥ E 9 100
Herrin D 4 170
Herring Cove I 28 154
Herrljunga C 6 66
Herschel F 7 206
Herscher B 4 170
Hershey F 2 164
Herstal D 4 69
Herten E 4 98
Hertford F 6 72
Hertfordshire □[6] F 6 72
Hertsa A 9 104
Herval d'Oeste G 5 194
Hervey Bay c H 11 142
Herzberg E 10 98
Herzberg am Harz C 5 96
Herzebrock E 5 98
Herzliyya E 3 120
Herzogenaurach C 7 100
Herzogenrath F 3 98
Hesdin B 8 78
Heshan G 9 130
Heshun H 9 128
Hesperia F 6 182
Hess ≃ E 28 154
Hessen □[3] C 5 96
Hesso D 1 144
Heswall D 3 72
Heta ≃ B 12 114
Hetaundā D 4 122
Hetch Hetchy Aqueduct ≚[1] C 2 182
Hetch Hetchy Reservoir ⊜[1] C 4 182
Het Loo, Paleis ◗ B 4 69
Hettinger B 3 174
Hettstedt E 8 98
Heung (Huang) ≃ F 5 132
Heusweiler E 5 69
Heuvelton B 3 164
Heves B 6 104
Heves □[3] B 6 104
Hexham C 4 72
Hexian F 10 130
Hexigten Qi E 11 128
Heyang I 7 128
Heyrieux E 3 82
Heysham C 3 72
Heyuan G 12 130
Heze I 10 128
Hialeah G 4 168
Hian C 4 200
Hiawassee B 3 168
Hibbard E 6 160
Hibbing B 2 166
Hickory, Ms., U.S. F 4 170
Hickory, N.C., U.S. B 4 168
Hickory Run State Park ♦ F 3 164
Hicks, Point > F 7 144
Hicks Bay B 7 146
Hico D 5 172
Hidalgo, Mex. D 9 184
Hidalgo, Mex. E 10 184
Hidalgo □[3] G 10 184
Hidalgo del Parral D 7 184
Hieflau C 6 102
Hierapolis see Pamukkale ⊥ D 8 106
Higashihiroshima G 4 126
Higashiōsaka G 5 126
Higgins B 3 172
Highland, Ca., U.S. F 6 182
Highland, In., U.S. B 5 170
Highland □[6] C 4 74
Highland Home G 5 170
Highland Park, Il., U.S. A 5 170
Highland Park, Tx., U.S. D 5 172
Highlands H 1 170
Highland Springs E 5 162
High Level B 13 156
High Peak ◆[1] D 5 72
High Point B 4 168
High Point ∧ E 4 164
High Point State Park ♦ E 4 164
High River F 14 156
High Rock F 5 168
Highrock Indian Reserve ◆[4] D 8 158
Highrock Lake ⊜, Mb., Can. D 8 158
Highrock Lake ⊜, Sk., Can. C 19 156
High Rock Lake ⊜[1] B 4 168
High Wycombe F 6 72
Higüero, Punta > j 14 187b
Higüey D 7 186
Hiiraan □[3] G 6 202
Hiiumaa I C 11 66
Híjar C 4 88
Hikone G 6 126
Hikueru I[1] E 13 136
Hilda F 16 156
Hildburghausen B 7 100
Hilden C 5 69
Hildesheim D 6 98
Hill City, Mn., U.S. B 2 166
Hill City, S.D., U.S. D 3 174
Hillerød C 5 68
Hilliard D 4 168
Hillingdon □[6] F 6 72
Hill Island Lake ⊜ A 17 156
Hills D 6 174
Hillsboro, Ks., U.S. A 5 172
Hillsboro, N.H., U.S. C 7 164
Hillsboro, Oh., U.S. D 2 162
Hillsborough □[6] C 7 164
Hillston D 5 144
Hilo j 11 181a
Hilok B 6 124
Hilok ≃ B 5 124
Hilovo D 14 66
Hilton Head Island I C 4 168
Hiltrup E 4 98
Hilversum B 4 69
Hima A 3 168
Himāchal Pradesh □[3] C 3 122
Himalayas ⨳ D 4 122
Himatnagar E 2 122
Himeji G 5 126
Ḥimṣ E 7 118
Hinchinbrook Entrance ʉ F 21 154
Hinchinbrook Island I E 8 142
Hinckley, Eng., U.K. E 5 72
Hinckley, Il., U.S. B 4 170
Hindman E 2 162
Hindmarsh, Lake ⊜ E 3 144
Hindu Kush ⨳ B 2 122
Hindupur G 3 122
Hinesville D 4 168
Hinganghāt E 3 122
Hingham D 8 164
Hingol ≃ E 10 116
Hingoli F 3 122
Hınıs C 9 118
Hinnøya I B 7 64
Hinojosa del Duque F 5 86
Hinsdale G 18 156
Hinterrhein ≃ D 7 82
Hinton, Ab., Can. E 13 156
Hinton, Ok., U.S. C 4 172
Hīrākud Reservoir ⊜[1] E 4 122
Hiram C 8 164
Hiraman ≃ H 4 202
Hirara H 8 124
Hiriyūr G 3 122
Hirnyk C 13 96
Hirosaki D 8 126
Hiroshima G 4 126
Hiroshima □[3] G 4 126
Hirschaid C 8 100
Hirson C 11 78
Hisār D 3 122
Hispaniola I D 6 186
Hita H 3 126
Hitachi F 8 126
Hitchin F 6 72
Hitchins D 2 162
Hither Hills State Park ♦ E 7 164
Hitoyoshi H 3 126
Hitra I E 4 64
Hiwannee G 4 170
Hiwassee ≃ B 2 168
Hixson E 6 170
Ḥiyyon, Naḥal ≃ I 4 120
Hjälmaren ⊜ C 7 66
Hjo C 7 66
Hjørring A 2 68
Hkakabo Razi ∧ D 3 130
Hkok (Kok) ≃ H 4 130
Hlathikulu D 9 206
Hlohovec B 9 102
Hlotse E 7 206
Hluboká ⊥ C 11 100
Hluboká nad Vltavou C 11 100
Hluhluwe E 10 206
Hluhluwe Game Reserve ◆[4] E 9 206
Hlukhiv D 8 110
Hluti D 9 206
Hlybokae E 13 66
Ho D 5 200
Hoa Binh D 7 132
Hoanib ≃ F 1 204
Hobart j 12 145a
Hobbs D 2 172
Hobbs Coast ⊻[2] D 31 208
Hobe Sound F 4 168
Hobro B 2 68
Hobyo F 6 202
Hocalar C 8 106
Höchberg C 6 100
Hochfeld A 2 206
Hochheim B 5 100
Ho Chi Minh City (Saigon) I 8 132
Hochkönig ∧ C 5 102
Höchst C 6 100
Höchstadt an der Aisch C 7 100
Hockenheim A 6 82
Hôḍ ◆[1] F 3 198
Hodeida see Al-Ḥudaydah E 5 202
Hodge F 2 170
Hodgeville F 18 156
Hodh ech Chargui □[3] F 3 198
Hodh el Gharbi □[3] F 2 198
Hódmezővásárhely B 6 104
Hodmo ≃ E 6 202
Hodna, Chott el ⊜ B 5 198
Hodonín B 9 102
Hodovariha B 20 108
Hoedspruit C 9 206
Hoek van Holland (Hook of Holland) C 2 69
Hoeryŏng-ŭp E 17 128
Hoeyang-ŭp G 16 128
Hof, Ger. B 8 100
Hof, Ice. m 23 64a
Hoffman C 7 174
Hofgeismar E 6 98
Hofmeyr F 6 206
Hofors B 8 66
Hofsjökull ⍓ m 21 64a
Hōfu H 3 126
Hog, Tanjong > D 7 134
Höganäs D 6 66
Hogansville F 6 170
Hoge Veluwe, Nationaal Park de ♦ B 4 69
Hoggar ⨳ E 6 198
Hohenau an der March B 8 102
Hohenems C 1 102
Hohenmölsen E 8 98
Hohensyburg ⊥ E 4 98
Hohenwald E 5 170
Hohenwarte-Stausee ⊜[1] B 8 100
Hohe Tauern ⨳ D 4 102
Hohhot F 8 128
Hohoe D 5 200
Hoh Xil Shan ⨳ B 5 122
Hoi An G 9 132
Hoi Xuan D 7 132
Hojāi D 6 122
Høje Tåstrup C 5 68
Hojniki D 7 110
Hōjō H 4 126
Hokah D 3 166
Hokitika E 3 146
Hokkaidō □[3] C 9 126
Hokkaidō I C 9 126
Hokksund C 4 66
Hola Prystan' F 8 110
Holbæk C 4 68
Holbeach E 7 72
Holberg F 7 156
Holbrook E 3 176
Holden, Mo., U.S. C 1 170
Holden, W.V., U.S. E 2 162
Holder E 3 168
Holderness >[1] D 6 72
Holešov A 9 102
Holguín C 5 186
Holíč B 9 102
Hollabrunn B 8 102
Holladay E 8 178
Holland, Mi., U.S. D 5 166
Holland, Tx., U.S. E 5 172
Holland □[9] B 3 96
Hollandale F 3 170
Holland-on-Sea F 8 72
Hollandsbird Island I C 1 206
Hollick-Kenyon Plateau ⨳[1] D 35 208
Hollidaysburg C 4 162
Hollis C 4 172
Hollister D 2 182
Holly River State Park ♦ D 3 162
Holly Springs E 4 170
Hollywood F 4 168
Holm H 9 108
Holman B 9 150
Holmen B 5 66
Holmfirth D 5 72
Holmsjön ⊜ E 7 64
Holmsk C 12 124
Holm-Žirkovskij I 10 108
Holod B 6 104
Ḥolon E 3 120
Holovanivs'k A 11 104
Holroyd ≃ C 6 142
Holstebro B 1 68
Holsteinborg ⊥ C 4 68
Holsteinsborg (Sisimiut) C 22 150
Holston ≃ A 3 168
Holston, North Fork ≃ E 3 162
Holsworthy G 2 72
Holton A 15 160
Holts Summit C 2 170
Holy Cross E 15 154
Holyhead D 2 72
Holyoke D 6 164
Holyrood F 5 174
Holyrood Palace ◗ B 3 72
Holzkirchen E 8 100
Holzminden E 6 98
Hom ≃ E 3 206
Homalin B 2 132
Homathko ≃ F 9 156
Homathko Icefield ⍓ F 9 156
Homberg E 6 98
Hombori Tondo ∧ B 4 200
Hombourg-Haut A 4 82
Hombre Muerto, Salar del ≚ E 6 192
Homburg C 4 100
Home Hill E 8 142
Homel' see Gomel C 7 110
Homel' □[3] C 6 110
Homeland Park B 3 168
Homer, Ak., U.S. G 19 154
Homer, La., U.S. F 2 170
Homer, Ne., U.S. D 6 174
Homerville D 3 168
Homestead G 4 168
Homewood F 5 170
Hommersåk C 2 66
Homonhon I C 9 134
Homutovo J 12 108
Honāvar G 2 122
Hondo H 3 126
Hondo ≃, N.A. I 15 184
Hondo ≃, N.M., U.S. F 6 176
Honduras □[1] E 3 186
Honduras, Gulf of c I 15 184
Honea Path B 3 168
Hønefoss B 5 66
Honesdale E 3 164
Honey Lake ⊜ B 3 180
Honeymoon Bay G 9 156
Honfleur C 7 78
Høng C 4 68
Hong, Song (Red River) (Yuan) ≃ C 7 132
Honga E 2 204
Hon Gai D 8 132
Honghe G 6 130
Hong Hu ⊜ D 11 130
Hongjiang E 9 130
Hong Kong see Victoria G 12 130
Hong Kong □[2] G 12 130
Hongshui ≃ F 8 130
Hongtong H 8 128
Honguedo, Détroit d' ʉ D 11 160
Hongwŏn-ŭp D 2 126
Hongze B 14 130
Hongze Hu ⊜ B 14 130
Honiara A 12 138
Honiton G 3 72
Honjō E 7 126
Hönö D 5 66
Honolulu i 10 181a
Hon Quan I 8 132
Honshū I G 6 126
Hood, Mount ∧[1] C 3 178
Hood Canal c B 2 178
Hood River C 3 178
Hoogeveen B 5 69
Hoogezand A 5 69
Hooker B 3 172
Hook of Holland see Hoek van Holland C 2 69
Hooks F 1 170
Hoolt D 4 128
Hoop B 3 206
Hoopa Valley Indian Reservation ◆[4] E 2 178
Hoople G 10 158
Höör E 6 66
Hoorn B 4 69
Hoover Dam ◆[6] D 1 176
Hooversville C 4 162
Hopatcong F 4 164
Hope, Ar., U.S. F 2 170
Hope, B.C., Can. G 11 156
Hope, In., U.S. C 6 170
Hope, Point > B 11 154
Hopedale B 4 170
Hopelchén H 15 184
Hopër ≃ D 13 110
Hopes Advance, Cap > D 19 150
Hopetoun M 6 140
Hopetown E 5 206
Hope Valley E 7 164
Hopewell E 5 162
Hopi Indian Reservation ◆[4] E 3 176
Hopkins, Lake ⊜ I 10 140
Hopkinsville D 5 170
Hopland C 2 180
Hoquiam B 2 178
Hor C 20 128
Hor ≃ C 11 124
Horatio F 1 170
Horb am Neckar D 5 100
Hörby E 6 66
Hordaland □[3] B 3 66
Horden C 5 72
Horgen C 6 82
Hořice C 8 96
Horinger F 8 128
Horiult D 3 128
Horki B 7 110
Horley F 6 72
Horlick Mountains ⨳ E 31 208
Horlivka E 10 110
Hormigueros j 14 187b
Hormozgān □[3] I 16 118
Hormuz, Strait of ʉ I 16 118
Horn B 7 102
Horn > I 19 64a
Horn, Cape (Hornos, Cabo de) > K 6 192
Hornaday ≃ B 33 154
Hornafjörður c m 22 64a
Hornavan ⊜ C 8 64
Hornby Bay c C 35 154
Horndal B 8 66
Hornell B 5 162
Hornindal B 3 66
Horní Počernice B 11 100
Horní Slavkov B 9 100
Horn Lake E 3 170
Horn Plateau ⨳[1] D 9 150
Hornsea D 6 72
Horodenka A 8 104
Horodkivka A 10 104
Horodnya K 9 108
Horodok, Ukr. E 3 110
Horodok, Ukr. E 5 110
Hořovice C 10 100
Horqin Youyi Zhongqi D 13 128
Horqin Zuoyi Houqi E 13 128
Horse Cave A 2 168
Horseheads D 2 164
Horsens C 2 68
Horseshoe Bend D 5 178
Horseshoe Bend National Military Park ♦ F 6 170
Horsham, Austl. F 4 144
Horsham, Eng., U.K. F 6 72
Hørsholm C 5 68
Hörstel D 4 98
Horta h 12 198a
Horten C 5 66
Hortobágy ◆[1] B 6 104
Hortobágyi Nemzeti Park ♦ B 6 104
Horton C 1 170
Horton ≃ B 32 154
Horton Lake ⊜ C 33 154
Horw C 6 82
Horwood Lake ⊜ D 2 160
Hory B 7 110
Hosa'ina F 4 202
Hösbach C 6 100
Hoséré Vokré ∧ D 7 200
Hoševtovo F 15 110
Hoshangābād E 3 122
Hoshiārpur C 3 122
Höshööt B 4 128
Hosmer A 6 178
Hospet F 3 122
Hospital de Órbigo B 5 86
Hosston F 2 170
Hoste, Isla I K 6 192
Hotan B 3 122
Hotan ≃ C 13 116
Hotarele C 9 104
Hotchkiss C 13 156
Hot Creek Range ⨳ B 7 182
Hotham Inlet c C 14 154
Hot Springs (Hot Springs National Park), Ar., U.S. E 2 170
Hot Springs, Mt., U.S. H 14 156
Hot Springs see Truth or Consequences, N.M., U.S. F 5 176
Hot Springs National Park see Hot Springs E 2 170
Hot Springs State Park ♦ D 9 178
Hottah Lake ⊜ C 9 150
Hottentotsbaai c D 1 206
Hottentotskloof G 3 206
Houdan D 8 78
Houghton G 4 160
Houghton Lake A 1 162
Houghton Lake ⊜ A 1 162
Houghton-le-Spring C 5 72
Houlton g 13 163a
Houma, China I 8 128
Houma, La., U.S. H 3 170
Houmet Essouq C 7 198
Housatonic D 5 164
Housatonic ≃ E 5 164
Houston, Mo., U.S. D 3 170
Houston, Tx., U.S. F 6 172
Houston, Lake ⊜[1] F 6 172
Hout ≃ B 8 206
Houthalen C 4 69
Hovd, Mong. C 2 124
Hovd, Mong. D 4 128
Hovd ≃ C 2 124
Hove G 6 72
Hövelhof E 5 98
Hoven C 5 174
Hovenweep National Monument ♦ D 4 176
Hoverla, hora ∧ A 8 104
Hövsgöl □[3] B 2 128
Hovsgol Lake see Hövsgöl nuur ⊜ B 4 124
Hövsgöl nuur ⊜ B 4 124
Hövüün E 4 128
Howa, Ouadi (Howar, Wādī) ≃ D 1 202
Howar, Wādī (Howa, Ouadi) ≃ D 2 202
Howard, Ks., U.S. G 6 174
Howard, S.D., U.S. D 6 174
Howard □[6] G 1 164
Howard Lake C 1 166
Howe, Cape > F 7 144
Howeke E 3 200
Howick E 9 206
Howland Island I C 10 136
Howrah see Hāora E 5 122
Hoxie D 3 170
Höxter E 6 98
Høyanger B 3 66
Hoyerswerda E 11 98
Hoyos D 4 86
Hradec Králové C 8 96
Hrádek nad Nisou B 11 100
Hrandziči F 11 66
Hranice, Czech Rep. B 9 100
Hranice, Czech Rep. A 9 102
Hrazdan I 14 110
Hrebinka D 8 110
Hriňová D 10 96
Hrodna (Grodno) F 11 66
Hrodna □[3] J 12 64
Hromtau D 21 110
Hron ≃ C 10 102
Hronov C 9 96
Hrubieszów C 12 96
Hsian see Xi'an A 9 130
Hsilo G 15 130
Hsinchu F 15 130
Hsintien F 15 130
Hsipaw C 3 132
Hua'an F 13 130
Huacho F 3 190
Huaco B 3 195
Huadian E 16 128
Hua Hin H 4 132
Huai ≃ B 13 130
Huai'an, China F 10 128
Huai'an, China B 14 130
Huaibin B 12 130
Huaidezhen E 15 128
Huaiji G 11 130
Huailai F 10 128
Huainan B 13 130
Huaining C 13 130
Huairou F 11 128
Huaiyang B 12 130
Huai Yot K 4 132
Huaiyuan B 13 130
Huajuapan de León I 11 184
Hualahuises E 10 184
Hualalai ∧[1] j 11 181a
Hualapai Indian Reservation ◆[4] E 2 176
Hualien F 15 130
Huallaga ≃ E 3 190
Huambo E 2 204
Huambo □[3] E 2 204
Huanan C 18 128
Huancavelica F 4 190
Huancayo F 3 190
Huang (Heung) ≃ F 5 132
Huangchuan B 12 130
Huanggai Hu ⊜ D 11 130
Huanggang C 12 130
Huang He see Yellow River ⊜ D 17 116
Huanghua G 11 128
Huangjinbu D 13 130
Huangling I 7 128
Huangnihe E 17 128
Huangpi C 12 130
Huangqi E 14 130
Huangshan D 14 130
Huangshi C 12 130
Huangtang Hu ⊜ C 11 130
Huangyan D 15 130
Huangyuan H 3 128
Huangzhong H 3 128
Huaning F 6 130
Huanjiang B 9 132
Huanren F 15 128
Huánuco E 3 190
Huanxian H 6 128
Huaral F 3 190
Huaraz E 3 190
Huascarán, Nevado ∧ E 3 190
Huasco E 5 192
Huatabampo D 5 184
Huatong F 13 128
Huauchinango G 10 184
Huaxian, China I 10 128
Huaxian, China G 11 130
Huaxian, China A 9 130
Huaynamota ≃ F 7 184
Huazamota F 7 184
Huazhou H 10 130
Hubbard Creek Reservoir ⊜[1] D 4 172
Hubbell Trading Post National Historic Site ♦ E 4 176
Hubei □[3] C 10 130
Hubli-Dhārwār F 3 122
Hückelhoven E 3 98
Hückeswagen E 4 98
Hucknall D 5 72
Huddersfield D 5 72
Huddinge C 9 66
Hude C 5 98
Huder B 13 128
Hudiksvall B 8 66
Hudson, Fl., U.S. E 3 168
Hudson, Ia., U.S. D 2 166
Hudson, Ma., U.S. D 7 164
Hudson, N.H., U.S. D 7 164
Hudson, N.Y., U.S. B 7 162
Hudson □[6] F 5 164
Hudson ≃ E 5 164
Hudson Bay E 7 158
Hudson Bay c D 15 150
Hudson Falls C 5 164
Hudson's Hope C 10 156
Hudson Strait ʉ D 18 150
Hue F 8 132
Huechulafquen, Lago ⊜ F 2 195
Huehuetenango J 14 184
Huejutla de Reyes G 10 184
Huelgoat D 3 78
Huelva G 4 86
Huelva □[6] G 4 86
Huentelauquén B 2 195
Huércal-Overa G 3 88
Huesca B 4 88
Huesca □[6] B 4 88
Huéscar G 2 88
Huétor Tájar G 6 86
Ḥufrat an-Naḥās F 1 202
Huggins, Mount ∧ D 24 208
Hughenden F 7 142
Hughes C 17 154
Hughesville E 2 164
Hugh Keenleyside Dam ◆[6] G 12 156
Hugli ≃ E 5 122
Hugus B 3 206
Huichang F 12 130
Hŭich'ŏn F 16 128
Huichuan I 4 128
Huidong E 6 130
Huíla □[3] E 2 204
Huila, Nevado del ∧ C 3 190
Huilai G 13 130
Huili E 6 130
Huimin H 11 128
Huinan E 16 128
Huishui E 8 130
Huissen E 2 98
Huitong E 9 130
Huixian B 8 130
Huixtla J 13 184
Huize E 6 130
Huizen B 4 69
Huizhou G 12 130
Ḥukūmah E 4 202
Hulan C 16 128
Hulan ≃ C 16 128
Hulan Ergi C 14 128
Hulbert B 6 166
Hulga ≃ D 24 108
Hulin D 19 128
Hull, Il., U.S. C 3 170
Hull, Ma., U.S. D 8 164
Hull, P.Q., Can. F 6 160
Hull, Tx., U.S. G 1 170
Hülscheid E 4 98
Hulst C 3 69
Hultsfred D 7 66
Hulun Nur ⊜ B 11 128
Hulyaypole F 10 110
Huma B 9 124
Huma ≃ B 8 124
Humacao j 16 187b
Humahuaca D 6 192
Humaitá, Braz. E 6 190
Humaitá, Para. E 8 192
Humansville D 2 170
Humber ≃ D 6 72
Humber Bridge ◆[5] D 6 72
Humbird C 3 166
Humboldt, Il., U.S. C 4 170
Humboldt, Sk., Can. E 19 156
Humboldt, Tn., U.S. E 4 170
Humboldt ≃ B 4 180
Humboldt, North Fork ≃ E 6 178
Humboldt Redwoods State Park ♦ B 2 180
Hume, Lake ⊜[1] F 6 144
Humenné D 11 96
Humine ◆[1] B 8 94
Humpata E 1 204
Humphrey E 3 170
Humphreys Peak ∧ E 3 176
Humppila B 11 66
Hun ≃, China F 15 128
Hun ≃, China F 14 128
Húnaflói c m 20 64a
Hunan □[3] E 10 130
Hunchun E 18 128
Hundested C 4 68
Hundred D 3 162
Hunedoara C 7 104
Hunedoara □[3] C 7 104
Hünfeld B 6 100
Hungary □[1] F 11 62
Hŭngdŏki-dong G 16 128
Hungen B 5 100
Hungerford B 5 144
Hungry Horse G 14 156
Hungry Horse Dam ◆[6] A 6 178
Hungry Horse Reservoir ⊜[1] A 7 178
Hunjiang E 16 128
Hunnebostrand C 5 66
Hunsberge ⨳ D 2 206
Hunstanton E 7 72
Hunter B 6 174
Hunter ≃ D 8 144
Hunterdon □[6] F 4 164
Hunter Island I, Austl. i 11 145a
Hunter Island I, B.C., Can. F 7 156
Hunters Bay c E 1 132
Hunterville C 5 146
Huntingdon, Eng., U.K. E 6 72
Huntingdon, Pa., U.S. C 5 162
Huntingdon, Tn., U.S. E 4 170
Huntington, Eng., U.K. D 5 72
Huntington, In., U.S. B 6 170
Huntington, N.Y., U.S. C 7 162
Huntington, Or., U.S. C 5 178
Huntington, Ut., U.S. C 3 176
Huntington, W.V., U.S. D 2 162
Huntington Beach G 5 182
Huntington Station F 5 164
Huntly B 5 146
Huntsville, Al., U.S. E 5 170
Huntsville, On., Can. F 4 160
Huntsville, Tx., U.S. E 6 172
Hunucmá G 14 184
Hunyuan G 9 128
Huong Hoa F 8 132
Huoqiu B 13 130
Huoshan C 13 130
Huoxian H 8 128
Hüramt B 4 128
Hurd, Cape > F 3 160
Hüren Tovon uul ∧ D 3 124
Hure Qi E 13 128
Hurghada I 5 118
Huriel B 6 80
Hurlock H 3 164
Huron, Oh., U.S. C 2 162
Huron, S.D., U.S. C 5 174
Huron, Lake ⊜ A 2 162
Hurricane D 2 162
Hurtado ≃ B 2 195
Hürth F 3 98
Hurtsboro C 2 168
Húsavík I 22 64a
Huși B 9 104
Huslia D 16 154
Husum B 6 98
Hutaym, Ḥarrat ⊻[9] J 9 118
Hutchinson, Ks., U.S. F 5 174
Hutchinson, Mn., U.S. C 7 174
Hutchinson, S. Afr. F 5 206
Hutuo ≃ G 9 128
Huwei G 15 130
Huy D 4 69
Hūzgān G 12 118
Huzhen D 15 130
Huzhou C 14 130
Huzhu H 4 128
Hvalynsk C 16 110
Hvannadalshnúkur ∧ m 22 64a
Hvar, Otok I D 4 104
Hveragerði m 20 64a
Hvolsvöllur n 20 64a
Hwali A 8 206
Hwange F 4 204
Hwange National Park ♦ F 4 204
Hwanghae-bukto □[3] G 16 128
Hwanghae-namdo □[3] G 15 128
Hyannis, Ma., U.S. E 8 164
Hyannis, Ne., U.S. D 4 174
Hyargas Lake see Hyargas nuur ⊜ C 2 124
Hyargas nuur ⊜ C 2 124
Hyde F 3 146
Hyden, Austl. M 5 140
Hyden, Ky., U.S. E 2 162
Hyde Park, N.Y., U.S. E 5 164
Hyde Park, Vt., U.S. B 6 164
Hyderābād, India F 3 122
Hyderābād, Pak. D 1 122
Hydrographers Passage ʉ F 10 142
Hyères G 4 82
Hyères, Îles d' II H 4 82
Hyesan F 17 128
Hyland ≃ F 30 154
Hylestad C 3 66
Hyndman Peak ∧ D 6 178
Hyōgo □[3] G 5 126
Hyrynsalmi D 14 64
Hythe F 8 72
Hyūga H 3 126
Hyvinkää B 12 66

I

Iaco ≃ F 5 190
Iakora I 9 205a
Ialomița □[3] C 9 104
Ialomița ≃ C 9 104
Ianantsony I 8 205a
Iași B 9 104
Iași □[3] B 9 104
Ibadan D 5 200
Ibagué C 3 190
Ibaiti E 5 194
Ibaka C 3 204
Ibaraki □[3] F 8 126
Ibarra C 3 190
Ibb E 5 202
Ibba G 2 202
Ibbenbüren D 4 98
Ibérico, Sistema ⨳ C 3 88
Iberville, Mont d' (Caubvick, Mount) ∧ E 20 150
Ibeto C 5 200
Ibi F 4 88
Ibiá C 7 194
Ibiapaba, Serra da ⨳[2] D 10 190
Ibicaraí F 11 190
Ibicuí ≃ E 8 192
Ibiraçu C 10 194
Ibitinga D 6 194
Ibiza see Eivissa I F 5 88
Ibondo C 5 204
Ibotirama F 10 190
Ibrā F 8 116
Ibrah, Wādī ≃ E 2 202
İbriktepe B 7 106
Ibros F 7 86
Ibshawâi H 4 118
Ibusuki I 3 126
Ica F 3 190
Içá (Putumayo) ≃ D 5 190
Icacos Point > q 22 187f
Içana C 5 190
Içana ≃ C 5 190
İçel D 6 118
İçel □[3] D 5 118
Iceland □[1] C 4 62
Ichaikaronji F 2 122
Ichkeul, Lac ⊜ G 2 90
Ichnya D 8 110
Ichtegem C 1 69
Ičinskaja Sopka, vulkan ∧[1] D 18 114
Icy Bay c G 24 154
Icy Cape > A 13 154
Icy Strait ʉ G 27 154
Ida, Mount ∧ E 6 106
Idah D 6 200
Idaho □[3] C 5 152
Idaho Falls D 7 178
Idaho National Engineering Laboratory ◗[3] D 7 178
Idanha-a-Nova E 3 86
Idar-Oberstein C 4 100
Idelès E 6 198
Ider ≃ B 2 128
Idi L 3 132
Idiofa D 2 204
Iditarod ≃ E 15 154
Idlib E 7 118
Idodi D 5 204
Ídolo, Isla del I G 11 184

⌊ Waterfall ʉ Strait c Bay, Gulf ⊜ Lake ≍ Swamp ⍓ Ice Feature ⊤ Other Hydrographic Feature ⊻ Submarine Feature □ Political Unit ◗ Cultural Institution ⊥ Historical Site ♦ Recreational Site ⊠ Airport ▪ Military Installation ◆ Miscellaneous

Idoûkâl-en-Taghès — Jequié

Name	Map Ref.	Page
Idoûkâl-en-Taghès ∧	B 6	200
Idrija	E 5	102
Idstein	B 5	100
Iecava	D 12	66
Ieper	D 1	69
Ierisós	B 5	106
Ie-shima I	K 1	126
Iesolo	D 8	92
If, Château d' ⊥	G 3	82
Ifalik I[1]	D 12	134
Ifanadiana	I 9	205a
Ife	D 5	200
Ifni □[9]	D 2	198
Ifôghas, Adrar des ⋀	B 5	200
Ifon	D 6	200
Ifrane	C 3	198
Igalula	D 5	204
Iganga	G 3	202
Igara Paraná ≃	D 4	190
Igarka	C 11	114
Igarra	D 6	200
Igawa	D 5	204
Igboho	D 5	200
Iğdır	C 10	118
Iggesund	B 8	66
Igharghar, Oued ≃, Afr.	E 6	198
Igharghar, Oued ≃, Alg.	D 6	198
Iglesias	F 2	90
Iglesiente ◆[1]	F 2	90
Igli	C 4	198
Iglino	I 22	108
Igloolik	C 16	150
Ignalina	E 13	66
Igombe ≃	C 5	204
Igra	H 20	108
Igrim	E 26	108
Iguaçu ≃	E 9	192
Iguaçu, Parque Nacional do ♠	F 4	194
Iguala	H 10	184
Igualada	C 6	88
Iguape	F 7	194
Iguape ≃	F 6	194
Iguassu Falls ⌊	E 9	192
Iguatu	E 11	190
Iguéla	F 6	200
Iguéla, Lagune ⊜	F 6	200
Iguîdi, 'Erg ⊥[8]	D 3	198
Iharaña	j 9	205a
Iheya-shima I	K 2	126
Ihiala	D 6	200
Ihosy ≃	I 9	205a
Ih Tal	E 14	128
Ihugh	D 6	200
Iisalmi	E 13	64
Iiyama	F 7	126
Iizuka	H 3	126
Ijâfene ◆[2]	E 3	198
Ijebu-Ode	D 5	200
IJmuiden	B 3	69
IJsselmeer ⊜	B 4	69
Ijuí	A 9	192
Ik ≃	B 18	110
Ikara	C 6	200
Ikaría I	D 7	106
Ikast	B 2	68
Ikeda	G 4	126
Ikela	C 3	204
Ikerre	D 6	200
Ikire	D 5	200
Iko	C 2	204
Ikopa ≃	k 9	205a
Ikorodu	D 5	200
Ikot-Ekpene	D 6	200
Ikozi	C 4	204
Ila	D 5	200
Ilagala	D 4	204
Ilagan	B 8	134
Īlām	F 12	118
Īlām □[3]	F 12	118
Ilan	F 15	130
Ilanskij	D 12	114
Ilanz	D 7	82
Iława	B 10	96
Île-à-la-Crosse, Lac ⊜	D 5	158
Ilebo	C 3	204
Île-de-France □[9]	C 9	78
Ilek ≃	D 18	110
Ileret	G 4	202
Ilesha	D 5	200
Ileza	F 15	108
Ilford	C 11	158
Ilfracombe	F 2	72
Ilha de Moçambique	F 7	204
Ilha Grande, Baía da ⊂	E 8	194
Ilha Solteira, Represa de ⊜[1]	C 5	194
Ilhavo	D 2	86
Ilhéus	F 11	190
Iliamna	G 17	154
Iliamna Lake ⊜	G 17	154
Iligan	D 8	134
Ilinge	F 7	206
Ilion	C 3	164
Ilium see Truva ⊥	C 7	106
Ilizi	D 6	198
Il'ja	E 13	66
Iljinskij	G 21	108
Ilkal	F 3	122
Ilkeston	E 5	72
Ill ≃	B 5	82
Illampu, Nevado ∧	G 5	190
Illapel	B 2	195
Ille-et-Vilaine □[3]	D 5	78
Illéla	C 6	200
Illertissen	D 6	96
Illichivs'k	B 11	104
Illiers-Combray	D 8	78
Illimani, Nevado ∧	G 5	190
Illinois □[3]	D 10	152
Illinois ≃	C 3	170
Illkirch-Graffenstaden	B 5	82
Illovo	F 9	206
Illzach	C 5	82
Ilma, Lake ⊜	K 9	140
Il'men', ozero ⊜	G 9	108
Ilmenau	B 7	100
Ilo	G 4	190
Iloilo	C 8	134
Ilondola	E 5	204
Ilorin	D 5	200
Ilovlja	E 14	110
Īlubabor □[3]	F 3	202
Ilulissat see Jakobshavn	C 22	150
Ilwaki	G 9	134
İlyasbey	B 8	106
Imabari	G 4	126
Imandra, ozero ⊜	C 10	108
Imantau	J 28	108
Imari	H 2	126
Imatra	B 14	66
Imbituba	E 10	192
Imeni Babuškina	G 15	108
Imeni Stepana Razina	B 14	110
Imeni Željabova	G 11	108
Imera ⊥	G 3	94
Imese	B 2	204
Imi-n-Tanout	C 3	198
İmişli	J 15	110
Imlay	B 4	180
Immenstadt	E 7	100
Immingham	D 6	72
Immingham Dock	D 6	72
Immokalee	F 4	168
Imola	E 7	92
Impé	C 2	204
Imperatriz	A 9	190
Imperia	F 4	92
Imperia □[6]	E 3	92
Imperial	E 4	174
Imperial Beach	H 6	182
Imperial Dam ◆[6]	F 1	176
Imperial de Aragón, Canal ≋	G 2	80
Imperial Mills	D 15	156
Imperial Valley V	F 6	180
Impfondo	B 2	204
Imphāl	E 6	122
Impilahti	F 9	108
Imst	C 2	102
Imuruk Basin ⊜	D 11	154
Imwŏn-ni	F 2	126
Ina, Il., U.S.	C 4	170
Ina, Japan	G 6	126
Inanwatan	F 10	134
Inari	B 13	64
Inarijärvi ⊜	B 13	64
Inawashiro-ko ⊜	F 8	126
In Belbel	D 5	198
Inca	E 7	88
Inca de Oro	E 5	192
İnce Burun ≻	A 6	118
İncesu	C 6	118
Inchiri □[3]	E 1	198
Inch'ŏn	H 16	128
İncirliova	D 7	106
Indaiá ≃	C 8	194
Indalsälven ≃	E 7	64
Inda Silasē	E 4	202
Indaw	C 2	132
Indawgyi Lake ⊜	B 2	132
Independence, Ca., U.S.	D 5	182
Independence, Ia., U.S.	D 3	166
Independence, Ks., U.S.	G 7	174
Independence, Ky., U.S.	C 6	170
Independence, La., U.S.	G 3	170
Independence, Mo., U.S.	C 1	170
Inder, ozero ⊜	E 17	110
Inderborskij	E 17	110
India □[1]	F 12	116
Indiana	C 4	162
Indiana □[3]	D 10	152
Indiana Dunes National Lakeshore ♠	B 5	170
Indianapolis	C 5	170
Indian Cabins	B 13	156
Indian Head	F 7	158
Indian Ocean ⊤[1]	G 7	58
Indianola, Ia., U.S.	B 2	170
Indianola, Ms., U.S.	F 3	170
Indian River	C 6	166
Indigirka ≃	B 17	114
Inđija	C 5	104
Indio	F 5	180
Indira Gandhi Canal ≋	D 2	122
Indispensable Reefs ≃[1]	B 13	138
Indom	D 21	108
Indonesia □[1]	F 8	134
Indore	E 3	122
Indragiri ≃	F 4	134
Indramayu	K 19	135b
Indrāvati ≃	F 4	122
Indravati Tiger Reserve ♠	F 4	122
Indre □[3]	B 5	80
Indre-et-Loire □[3]	E 7	78
Indura	B 12	96
Indus ≃	E 10	116
Indwe	F 7	206
İnegöl	B 8	106
Ineu	B 6	104
Inez	E 2	162
Inferior, Laguna ⊂	I 12	184
Infiernillo, Presa del ⊜[1]	H 8	184
Ingelheim	C 5	100
Ingelmunster	D 2	69
Ingelstad	D 7	66
Ingeniero Luiggi	G 7	192
Ingersoll	G 3	160
Ingettolgoy	B 5	128
Ingham	E 7	142
Inglewood, Austl.	B 8	144
Inglewood, Ca., U.S.	G 5	182
Inglewood, N.Z.	C 5	146
Ingoda ≃	B 6	124
Ingolstadt	D 8	100
Ingonish	E 13	160
Ingrāj Bāzār	D 5	122
In Guezzam	F 6	198
Inguri ≃	H 12	110
Ingušetija □[3]	H 14	110
Ingwe	E 4	204
Inhaca, Ilha da I	D 10	206
Inhafenga	G 5	204
Inhambane	B 11	206
Inhambane □[3]	G 5	206
Inhambane, Baia de ⊂	B 11	206
Inhanduí ≃	D 4	194
Inharrime ≃	C 11	206
Inhassoro	A 11	206
Inhulets'	F 8	110
Inhumas	B 6	194
Iniesta	E 3	88
Inírida ≃	C 5	190
Inis see Ennis	D 3	75
Inis Córthaidh see Enniscorthy	D 5	75
Inje	E 2	126
Injune	H 9	142
Inkster	G 10	158
Inland Lake ⊜	C 15	154
Inle Lake ⊜	D 3	132
Inman	B 3	168
Inn ≃	D 10	100
Innbygda	B 6	66
Inner Channel ʉ	I 15	184
Inner Hebrides II	D 2	74
Inner Mongolia see Nei Monggol □[3]	E 9	128
Innes National Park ♠	E 1	144
Innisfail, Ab., Can.	E 14	156
Innisfail, Austl.	D 8	142
Innoko ≃	E 16	154
Innsbruck	C 3	102
Innviertel ◆[1]	B 5	102
Inola	D 1	170
Inongo	C 2	204
İnönü	C 9	106
Inowrocław	B 9	96
In Salah	D 5	198
Insar	J 16	108
Inshar	D 6	200
Ińsko	B 8	96
Inta	C 23	108
Interlaken	D 5	82
International Falls	A 2	166
International Peace Garden ♠	A 4	174
Inthanon, Doi ∧	E 4	132
Intracoastal Waterway ≋	G 4	168
Inubō-saki ≻	G 8	126
Inuvik	B 28	154
Inverbervie	D 6	74
Invercargill	G 2	146
Inverclyde □[6]	B 2	72
Inverell	B 8	144
Inverloch	G 5	144
Invermere	F 14	156
Inverness, Ms., U.S.	F 3	170
Inverness, Scot., U.K.	C 4	74
Inverurie	C 6	74
Investigator Group II	L 2	142
Investigator Strait ʉ	M 3	142
Inyangani ∧	F 5	204
Inyathi	F 4	204
Inyo □[6]	D 6	182
Inyonga	D 5	204
Inza	J 17	108
Inzer	I 22	108
Ioánnina	C 4	106
Iō-jima see Iwo Jima I	H 12	124
Iona	F 13	160
Ionaivo ≃	I 9	205a
Ione	G 13	156
Iongo	D 2	204
Ionian Islands II	C 3	106
Ionian Sea ⊤[2]	H 11	62
Iónioi Nísoi □[3]	C 4	106
Ioniveem ≃	C 7	154
Íos	D 6	106
Iowa □[3]	C 9	152
Iowa ≃	E 3	166
Iowa City	B 3	170
Iowa Falls	D 2	166
Ipala	C 5	204
Ipameri	B 6	194
Ipatinga	C 9	194
Ipatovo	G 13	110
Ipel' (Ipoly) ≃	A 5	104
Iphigenia Bay ⊂	I 27	154
Ipiales	C 3	190
Ipiaú	F 11	190
Ípiros □[3]	C 4	106
Ipoh	L 5	132
Ipokera	D 6	204
Ipoly (Ipel') ≃	A 5	104
Iporã, Braz.	B 5	194
Iporã, Braz.	F 4	194
Ipswich, Austl.	A 9	144
Ipswich, Eng., U.K.	E 8	72
Ipswich, S.D., U.S.	C 5	174
Ipu	D 10	190
Iqaluit	D 19	150
Iquique	D 5	192
Iquitos	D 4	190
Iraan	E 3	172
Irákleio see Iráklion	E 6	106
Iráklion (Irákleio)	E 6	106
Iran □[1]	D 7	116
Iran, Pergunungan ⋀	E 6	134
Īrānshahr	A 9	116
Irapuato	G 9	184
Iraq □[1]	D 5	116
Irati	F 5	194
Irazú, Volcán ∧[1]	F 4	186
Irbeni väin (Irbes jūras šaurums) ʉ	D 10	66
Irbes jūras šaurums (Irbeni väin) ʉ	D 10	66
Irbid	D 5	120
Irbid □[3]	E 5	120
Irbīl	D 11	118
Irbīl □[3]	D 11	118
Irbit	H 25	108
Irebu	F 8	200
Ireland I	E 2	70
Ireland, Republic of □[1]	E 6	62
Iren' ≃	H 22	108
Irgiz	E 22	110
Irgiz ≃	E 22	110
Iri	I 16	128
Irian Jaya □[3]	F 11	134
Iriba	B 9	200
Irîgui ◆[1]	B 3	200
Iringa	D 6	204
Iringa □[3]	D 6	204
Iriomote-jima I	F 16	130
Iriri ≃	D 8	190
Irish Sea ⊤[2]	E 5	70
Irkut ≃	B 4	124
Irkutsk	B 4	124
Iro, Lac ⊜	C 8	200
Iroise, Mer d' (Iroise) ⊂	D 1	78
Iron Baron	D 1	144
Iron City	E 5	170
Irondale	F 5	170
Irondequoit	C 1	164
Iron Gate V	C 7	104
Iron Gate Reservoir ⊜[1]	C 6	104
Iron Knob	D 1	144
Iron Mountain	C 4	166
Iron Range National Park ♠	B 6	142
Iron River	B 3	166
Ironton, Mn., U.S.	B 2	166
Ironton, Oh., U.S.	D 2	162
Ironwood	B 3	166
Iroquois	C 6	174
Iroquois Falls	D 3	160
Irpin'	D 6	110
Irrawaddy see Ayeyarwady ≃	F 2	132
Irrawaddy, Mouths of the ≃[1]	G 2	132
Irshava	A 7	104
Irsina	D 6	94
Irtysh ≃	C 9	114
Irtyšsk	D 10	114
Irún	A 3	88
Iruña see Pamplona	B 3	88
Irurzun	B 3	88
Irvine, Ca., U.S.	G 6	182
Irvine, Ky., U.S.	E 1	162
Irvine, Scot., U.K.	B 2	72
Irving	D 5	172
Irwin ≃	K 3	140
Irwinton	C 3	168
Isa	C 6	200
Isaac ≃	G 9	142
Isabela, Isla I	j 13	190a
Isabella Indian Reservation ◆[4]	B 1	162
Ísafjarðardjúp ⊂	I 19	64a
Ísafjörður	I 19	64a
Isak	L 3	132
Isaka	C 5	204
Isakly	I 19	108
Isalo, Parc National de l' ♠	I 8	205a
Isandja	C 3	204
Isangano National Park ♠	E 5	204
Isar ≃	D 9	100
Isarco (Eisack) ≃	C 7	92
Íscar	C 6	86
İscehisar	C 9	106
Iščerskaja	H 14	110
Ischia	D 3	94
Ischia, Isola d' I	D 3	94
Ischitella	C 5	94
Ise	G 6	126
Isenyela	D 5	204
Iseo	E 2	102
Iseo, Lago d' ⊜	D 5	92
Isère □[3]	E 3	82
Iserlohn	E 4	98
Isernia	C 4	94
Isernia □[6]	C 4	94
Iset' ≃	H 26	108
Isetskoe	H 26	108
Ise-wan ⊂	G 6	126
Iseyin	D 5	200
Isfahan see Eṣfahān	F 14	118
Isfara	A 2	122
Ishikari ≃	C 9	126
Ishikari-wan ⊂	C 8	126
Ishikawa □[3]	F 6	126
Ishimbay see Išimbaj	J 22	108
Ishinomaki	E 8	126
Ishioka	F 8	126
Ishizuchi-san ∧	H 4	126
Ishpatina Ridge ∧	B 8	166
Ishpeming	B 5	166
Isil'kul'	I 29	108
Išim	H 28	108
Išim ≃	D 10	114
Išimbaj (Ishimbay)	J 22	108
Išimskaja ravnina ≚	I 28	108
Isiolo	G 4	202
Isiro	B 4	204
Isisford	H 7	142
Iskăr ≃	D 7	104
İskenderun	D 7	118
Iskut ≃	C 6	156
Isla Cristina	G 3	86
İslâhiye	D 7	118
Islāmābād	C 2	122
Islāmpur	F 2	122
Isla Mujeres	G 16	184
Island Beach State Park ♠	G 4	164
Island Falls	D 7	158
Island Lagoon ⊜	K 3	142
Island Lake	D 11	158
Island Lake ⊜	E 11	158
Islands, Bay of ⊂	D 14	160
Islas Baleares □[3]	C 7	84
Isla Vista	F 4	182
Islay I	E 2	74
Isle-aux-Morts	E 14	160
Isle of Man □[1]	E 7	62
Isle of Wight □[6]	G 5	72
Isle Royale National Park ♠	B 4	166
Isleta Indian Reservation ◆[4]	E 5	176
Islón	A 2	195
Ismailia	G 5	118
Isna	J 5	118
Isny	E 7	100
Isoanala	I 9	205a
Isoka	E 5	204
Isola	F 3	170
Isola della Scala	D 6	92
Isola del Liri	C 3	94
Isola di Capo Rizzuto	F 7	94
Isparta	D 9	106
Isparta □[3]	D 4	118
Ispica	H 4	94
İspir	B 9	118
Israel □[1]	D 3	116
Issia	D 3	200
Issigeac	D 4	80
Issoire	C 7	80
Issoudun	F 8	78
Issyk-Kul'	A 3	122
Issyk-Kul' □[3]	A 3	122
Issyk-Kul', ozero ⊜	A 3	122
İstanbul (Constantinople)	B 8	106
İstanbul □[3]	B 8	106
Istiaía	C 5	106
Isto, Mount ∧	B 22	154
Istra	H 12	108
Istra see Istria ≻[1]	C 4	90
Istres	G 2	82
Istria (Istra) ≻[1]	C 4	90
Itabaiana	E 11	190
Itaberaba	F 10	190
Itaberaí	A 6	194
Itabira	C 9	194
Itabuna	F 11	190
Itacoatiara	D 7	190
Itagüí	B 3	190
Itaí	E 6	194
Itaipu Dam ◆[6]	F 3	194
Itaipu Reservoir ⊜[1]	E 9	192
Itäisen Suomenlahden kansallispuisto ♠	B 13	66
Itaituba	D 7	190
Itajaí	G 6	194
Itajubá	E 8	194
Itaka	D 5	204
Itálica ⊥	G 4	86
Italy □[1]	G 10	62
Itamaraju	B 11	194
Itambacuri	C 10	194
Itampolo	I 8	205a
Itānagar	D 6	122
Itanhaém	F 7	194
Itaobim	B 10	194
Itapecuru-Mirim	D 10	190
Itapemirim	D 10	194
Itaperuna	D 10	194
Itapetinga	G 10	190
Itapetininga	E 6	194
Itapeva	E 6	194
Itapicuru ≃	F 11	190
Itapira	E 7	194
Itapúa □[3]	G 3	194
Itapuranga	A 5	194
Itaquari	D 10	194
Itaqui	A 9	195
Itaquyry	F 3	194
Itararé	F 6	194
Itārsi	E 3	122
Itasca, Lake ⊜	B 7	174
Itasca State Park ♠	B 7	174
Itata ≃	E 1	195
Itatiaia, Parque Nacional de ♠	E 8	194
Itaúna	D 8	194
Itbayat Island I	A 8	134
Itéa	C 5	106
Itenes (Guaporé) ≃	F 5	190
Ithaca see Itháki, Grc.	C 4	106
Ithaca, N.Y., U.S.	D 2	164
Itháki	C 4	106
Itimbiri ≃	B 3	204
Itiquira ≃	G 7	190
Itkillik ≃	B 19	154
Itō	G 7	126
Itobo	C 5	204
Itoigawa	F 6	126
Itri	C 3	94
Itsokwane	B 7	206
Ituango	G 6	186
Ituí ≃	E 4	190
Ituiutaba	C 6	194
Itula	C 4	204
Itumbiara	C 6	194
Iturama	C 5	194
Iturbide	H 15	184
Ituri ≃	B 4	204
Iturup, ostrov (Etorofu-tō) I	D 13	124
Ituverava	D 7	194
Ituxi ≃	E 5	190
Itzehoe	C 6	98
Iul'tin	C 5	154
Iva	B 3	168
Ivacèvičy	J 12	64
Ivaí ≃	D 9	192
Ivaiporã	F 5	194
Ivalo	B 13	64
Ivalojoki ≃	B 12	64
Ivanava	C 4	110
Ivanec	D 8	102
Ivangorod	G 7	108
Ivangrad	D 5	104
Ivanhoe, Austl.	D 5	144
Ivanhoe, Mn., U.S.	C 6	174
Ivanhoe Lake ⊜	A 18	156
Ivanivka	B 11	104
Ivanjica	D 6	104
Ivan'kovskoe vodohranilišče ⊜[1]	H 12	108
Ivanof Bay	I 15	154
Ivano-Frankivs'k	E 3	110
Ivano-Frankivs'k □[6]	A 8	104
Ivanovo	H 14	108
Ivanovskaja oblast' □[6]	H 14	108
Ivanovskoe	C 14	66
Ivato	I 9	205a
Ivdel'	F 24	108
Iveragh ◆[1]	E 1	75
Ivigtut	D 23	150
Ivindo ≃	F 7	200
Ivinheíma ≃	E 4	194
Ivory Coast □[1]	H 7	196
Ivory Coast ⊥[2]	E 3	200
Ivösjön ⊜	D 7	66
Ivrea	D 3	92
İvrindi	C 7	106
Ivujivik	D 17	150
Ivvavik National Park ♠	B 25	154
Iwaki	F 8	126
Iwaki-san ∧[1]	D 8	126
Iwakuni	G 3	126
Iwanai	C 8	126
Iwate □[3]	E 8	126
Iwate-san ∧[1]	E 8	126
Iwo	D 5	200
Iwo Jima (Iō-jima) I	H 12	124
Ixmiquilpan	G 10	184
Ixtapa	I 9	184
Ixtepec	I 12	184
Iyo	H 4	126
Izabal, Lago de ⊜	J 15	184
Izamal	G 15	184
Izberbaš	H 15	110
Izbica	C 12	96
Izděškovo	B 8	110
Izegem	D 2	69
Īzeh	G 13	118
Iževsk	H 20	108
Ižma	D 20	108
Ižma ≃	C 8	114
Izmayil	C 10	104
İzmir	C 7	106
İzmir □[3]	C 7	106
İzmir Körfezi ⊂	C 7	106
İzmit	B 8	106
İznik	B 8	106
İznik Gölü ⊜	B 8	106
Izozog, Bañados del ≡	G 6	190
Izra'	D 6	120
Izsák	B 5	104
Iztaccíhuatl, Volcán ∧[1]	H 10	184
Izucar de Matamoros	H 10	184
Izuhara	G 2	126
Izumi	G 5	126
Izu-shotō II	H 7	126
Izu Trench ⊹[1]	E 11	58
Izyum	E 10	110

J

Name	Map Ref.	Page
Jääsjärvi ⊜	B 13	66
Jabal al-Awliyā', Khazzān (White Nile Dam) ◆[6]	D 3	202
Jabal Lubnān □[3]	B 5	120
Jabalpur	E 3	122
Jabal Qerri	D 3	202
Jabālyah	F 2	120
Jabbān, Arḍ al- ◆[1]	E 7	120
Jabbū', Qā' ⊜	J 6	120
Jabbūl, Sabkhat al- ⊜	E 7	118
Jabjabah, Wādī ≃	C 3	202
Jablah	E 6	118
Jablanac	C 3	104
Jablaničko jezero ⊜[1]	D 4	104
Jablonec nad Nisou	B 12	100
Jablonica	B 9	102
Jablonovyj hrebet ⋀	B 6	124
Jabłonowo Pomorskie	B 10	96
Jaboatão	E 11	190
Jaca	B 4	88
Jacala	G 10	184
Jacareí	E 7	194
Jacarezinho	E 6	194
Jaceel ≃	E 7	202
Jáchal ≃	B 3	195
Jaciara	A 3	194
Jackadgeryo	B 9	144
Jackfish Lake ⊜	E 17	156
Jackman	A 8	164
Jackson, Al., U.S.	G 5	170
Jackson, Ca., U.S.	B 3	182
Jackson, Ky., U.S.	E 2	162
Jackson, Mi., U.S.	B 1	162
Jackson, Mo., U.S.	D 4	170
Jackson, Ms., U.S.	F 3	170
Jackson, Oh., U.S.	D 2	162
Jackson, Tn., U.S.	E 4	170
Jackson ≃	D 4	162
Jackson, Mount ∧	D 2	208
Jackson Center	C 1	162
Jacksonville, Al., U.S.	F 6	170
Jacksonville, Ar., U.S.	E 2	170
Jacksonville, Fl., U.S.	D 4	168
Jacksonville, Il., U.S.	C 3	170
Jacksonville, N.C., U.S.	B 6	168
Jacksonville, Tx., U.S.	G 1	170
Jacksonville Beach	D 4	168
Jacmel	D 6	186
Jaco	D 7	184
Jacobābād	D 1	122
Jacobina	F 10	190
Jacques, Lac à ⊜	C 31	154
Jacques-Cartier, Détroit de ʉ	D 12	160
Jacques-Cartier, Mont ∧	D 11	160
Jacques-Cartier, Parc de conservation de la ♠	g 11	163a
Jacquet River	D 11	160
Jacuí ≃	F 9	192
Jadebusen ⊂	C 4	98
J.A.D. Jensens Nunatakker ∧	D 23	150
Jadotville see Likasi	E 4	204
Jadrin	I 17	108
Jādū	C 7	198
Jaén, Peru	E 3	190
Jaén, Spain	G 7	86
Jaén □[6]	C 4	84
Jæren ◆[1]	C 2	66
Jaffna	H 4	122
Jagdalpur	F 4	122
Jagel	D 2	68
Jagersfontein	E 6	206
Jagodina	D 6	104
Jagodnoe	C 17	114
Jaguarão	C 11	195
Jaguarão (Yaguarón) ≃	C 11	195
Jaguariaíva	F 5	194
Jaguaribe ≃	E 11	190
Jahrom	H 15	118
Jainca	I 3	128
Jaipur	D 3	122
Jaipur Hāt	D 5	122
Jaisalmer	D 2	122
Jājapur	E 5	122
Jājarm	D 17	118
Jajce	C 4	104
Jajva	G 22	108
Jajva ≃	G 22	108
Jakarta, Indon.	k 18	124
Jakarta, Indon.	k 18	135b
Jakarta, Teluk ⊂	k 18	135b
Jakobshavn (Ilulissat)	C 22	150
Jakovlevo	D 10	110
Jakšur-Bodja	H 20	108
Jakutsk	C 15	114
Jalaid Qi	C 14	128
Jalālābād	C 2	122
Jalal-Abad □[3]	A 2	122
Jalandhar	C 2	122
Jalan Kayu	i 15	134a
Jaleshwar	E 5	122
Jālgaon	E 3	122
Jalingo	D 7	200
Jalisco □[3]	G 7	184
Jalizava	J 8	108
Jālna	F 3	122
Jalón ≃	C 3	88
Jālor	D 2	122
Jalostotitlán	G 8	184
Jalpa	G 8	184
Jalpāiguri	D 5	122
Jalta see Yalta	G 9	110
Jalūlā'	E 11	118
Jalutorovsk	H 26	108
Jamaame	H 5	202
Jamaare ≃	C 7	200
Jamaica □[1]	D 5	186
Jamaica Channel ʉ	D 5	186
Jamālpur, Bngl.	D 6	122
Jamālpur, India	D 5	122
Jamantau, gora ∧	I 22	108
Jamanxim ≃	E 7	190
Jamari ≃	E 6	190
Jamašurma	H 19	108
Jambes	D 3	69
Jambi	F 4	134
Jambol	D 9	104
Jambongan, Pulau I	D 7	134
James ≃, U.S.	D 6	174
James ≃, Va., U.S.	E 5	162
James Bay ⊂	F 16	150
James Ross Island I	L 8	192
James Smith Indian Reserve ◆[4]	E 19	156
Jamestown, Austl.	D 2	144
Jamestown, Ks., U.S.	F 5	174
Jamestown, Ky., U.S.	D 6	170
Jamestown, N.D., U.S.	B 5	174
Jamestown, N.Y., U.S.	B 4	162
Jamestown, St. Hel.	j 14	206b
Jamestown, Tn., U.S.	D 6	170
Jamestown ⊥	E 5	162
Jamm	G 8	108
Jammu	C 2	122
Jammu and Kashmīr □[2]	B 3	122
Jamnagar	E 1	122
Jampang-kulon	k 18	135b
Jämsänkoski	B 12	66
Jamshedpur	E 5	122
Jämtland □[3]	E 6	64
Jamūi	E 5	122
Jamuna ≃	E 5	122
Jana ≃	B 16	114
Janaúba	A 9	194
Janaul	H 21	108
Janavičy	I 9	108
Jandaia do Sul	E 5	194
Janesville, Ca., U.S.	B 3	180
Janesville, Wi., U.S.	D 4	166
Jangarej	B 24	108
Jangi-Bazar	A 2	122
Jangīpur	E 5	122
Jangnga	I 18	110
Jangoon	F 3	122
Janīn	E 4	120
Janisjarvi, ozero ⊜	F 9	108
Janjina	D 4	104
Jan Lake ⊜	D 7	158
Jan Mayen I	B 2	114
Jánosháza	C 9	102
Janów Lubelski	C 12	96
Jantra ≃	D 8	104
Januária	A 8	194
Janzé	E 5	78
Jaora	E 2	122
Japan □[1]	E 12	124
Japan, Sea of ⊤[2]	E 10	124
Japan Basin ⊹[1]	D 10	58
Japan Trench ⊹[1]	D 11	58
Japurá (Caquetá) ≃	D 5	190
Japy	B 27	108
Jar	G 19	108
Jār, Jabal ∧	J 8	118
Jaraguá	A 6	194
Jaraguá do Sul	G 6	194
Jaraíz de la Vera	D 5	86
Jarales	E 5	176
Jarama ≃	D 7	86
Jaramānah	C 6	120
Jaransk	H 17	108
Jarash	E 5	120
Jarash ⊥	E 5	120
Järbo	B 8	66
Jarcevo	I 10	108
Jardim	D 2	194
Jardín América	G 3	194
Jardine River National Park ♠	A 6	142
Jardines de la Reina, Archipiélago de los II	C 5	186
Jardinópolis	D 7	194
Jaren'ga, Russia	E 20	108
Jarenga, Russia	E 18	108
Jargeau	E 9	78
Jari ≃	D 8	190
Jarkovo	H 27	108
Jarnac	C 3	80
Jarny	A 3	82
Jarocin	B 9	96
Jaroměř	C 8	96
Jaroslavl'	H 13	108
Jaroslavskaja oblast' □[6]	G 13	108
Jaroslavskij	B 3	126
Jarosław	C 12	96
Jartai Yanchi ⊜	G 5	128
Jaru ≃	F 6	190
Jarud Qi	D 13	128
Järva-Jaani	C 12	66
Järvelä	B 12	66
Järvenpää	B 12	66
Jarville-la-Malgrange	B 4	82
Jarvis	G 3	160
Jaša Tomić	C 6	104
Jāsk	E 8	116
Jasło	D 11	96
Jasnogorsk	I 12	108
Jasnyj, Russia	D 21	110
Jasnyj, Russia	B 9	124
Jason Islands II	n 17	193b
Jason Peninsula ≻[1]	C 3	208
Jasper, Ab., Can.	E 12	156
Jasper, Al., U.S.	F 5	170
Jasper, In., U.S.	C 5	170
Jasper, Mn., U.S.	D 6	174
Jasper, Mo., U.S.	D 1	170
Jasper National Park ♠	E 13	156
Jastarnia	A 10	96
Jastrowie	B 9	96
Jászapáti	B 6	104
Jászberény	B 5	104
Jász-Nagykun-Szolnok □[3]	B 6	104
Jataí	B 5	194
Jatate ≃	I 14	184
Jatni	E 5	122
Jaú	E 6	194
Jaú ≃	D 6	190
Jaungulbene	D 13	66
Jaunjelgava	D 12	66
Jaunpils	D 11	66
Jaunpur	D 4	122
Jauru ≃	C 3	194
Java (Jawa) I	k 19	135b
Javari (Yavarí) ≃	D 4	190
Javas	I 15	108
Java Sea (Jawa, Laut) ⊤[2]	F 5	134
Java Trench ⊹[1]	G 9	58
Javlenka	I 28	108
Jawbar	B 6	120
Jawhar	G 6	202
Jawor	C 9	96
Jaworzno	C 10	96
Jay	D 1	170
Jaya, Puncak ∧	F 11	134
Jayapura	F 12	134
Jayb, Wādī al- (Ha'Arava) ≃	H 4	120
Jayceyl Bid see Jaceel ≃	E 7	202
Jay Cooke State Park ♠	B 2	166
Jaypur	F 4	122
Jayrūd	B 7	120
Jazevec	D 17	108
Jaz Mūrīān, Hāmūn-e ⊜	E 8	116
Jazykovo	I 17	108
Jebba	D 5	200
Jebeniana	B 7	198
Jeddah see Jiddah	C 4	202
Jeddore Lake ⊜	D 16	160
Jedepo	D 3	200
Jędrzejów	C 11	96
Jefferson, N.C., U.S.	E 3	162
Jefferson, S.D., U.S.	D 6	174
Jefferson □[6]	B 3	164
Jefferson ≃	C 7	178
Jefferson, Mount ∧	C 8	178
Jefferson, Mount ∧[1]	C 2	178
Jefferson City, Mo., U.S.	C 2	170
Jefferson City, Tn., U.S.	A 3	168
Jeffersontown	C 6	170
Jeffersonville	C 6	170
Jeffrey City	D 10	178
Jega	C 5	200
Jēkabpils	D 12	66
Jekaterinovka see Ekaterinovka	I 29	108
Jekyll Island State Park ♠	D 4	168
Jelenia Góra	C 8	96
Jelenia Góra □[3]	C 8	96
Jelgava	D 11	66
Jelgavkrasti	D 12	66
Jellico	E 1	162
Jelling	C 2	68
Jember	I 21	135b
Jemez Canyon Reservoir ⊜[1]	E 5	176
Jemez Indian Reservation ◆[4]	E 5	176
Jemez Springs	E 5	176
Jemnice	A 7	102
Jena	F 8	98
Jenašimskij Polkan, gora ∧	D 12	114
Jenbach	C 3	102
Jendouba	B 6	198
Jendouba □[3]	G 2	90
Jenkins	E 2	162
Jenkintown	F 3	164
Jennersdorf	D 8	102
Jennings	G 2	170
Jenolan Caves ♠	D 8	144
Jens Munk Island I	C 17	150
Jens Munks Ø I	D 24	150
Jepara	k 20	135b
Jequié	F 10	190

Symbols in the index entries represent the broad categories identified in the key at the right. Symbols with superior numbers (⋀[1]) identify subcategories (see complete key on page 242).

∧ Mountain ⋀ Mountains)(Pass V Valley ≚ Plain ≻ Cape I Island II Islands ⊥ Other Topographic Feature ≃ River ≋ Canal

Jequitinhonha — Karlstad

Name	Map Ref.	Page
Jequitinhonha	B 10	194
Jequitinhonha ≃	G 10	190
Jerada	C 4	198
Jerba, Île de I	C 7	198
Jerbar	F 3	202
Jérémie	D 6	186
Jeremoabo	F 11	190
Jerez de la Frontera (Xeres)	H 4	86
Jerez de los Caballeros	F 4	86
Jericho, Austl.	G 7	142
Jericho see Arīḥā, Gaza	F 4	120
Jericho Area □[2]	F 4	120
Jerid, Chott ⊜	C 6	198
Jerimoth Hill ∧[2]	E 7	164
Jersey □[1]	F 7	62
Jersey City	F 4	164
Jerusalem (Yerushalayim) (Al-Quds)	F 4	120
Jervis Bay	E 8	144
Jervis Bay ⊂	E 8	144
Jervis Bay Territory □[6]	E 8	144
Jesenice, Czech Rep.	B 10	100
Jesenice, Slvn.	D 5	102
Jesenice, vodní nádrź ⊜[1]	B 9	100
Jesi	F 9	92
Jessen	E 9	98
Jessheim	B 5	66
Jessore	E 5	122
Jésus, Île I	A 5	164
Jesús Carranza	I 12	184
Jesús María	B 5	195
Jetmore	F 5	174
Jetpur	E 2	122
Jette	D 3	69
Jeumont	B 11	78
Jever	F 3	66
Jevnaker	B 5	66
Jewel Cave National Monument ♦	D 2	174
Jewett	C 4	170
Jewett City	E 7	164
Jeziorany	A 11	96
Jha Jha	E 5	122
Jhālāwār	E 3	122
Jhang Sadar	C 2	122
Jhānsi	D 3	122
Jhārsuguda	E 4	122
Jhelum	C 2	122
Jhelum ≃	C 2	122
Jiading	C 15	130
Jiahe	F 11	130
Jialing ≃	D 8	130
Jiamusi	C 18	128
Ji'an, China	F 15	128
Ji'an, China	E 12	130
Jian ≃	E 14	130
Jianchang	F 12	128
Jianchuan	E 4	130
Jiande	D 14	130
Jiang'an	D 7	130
Jiangcheng	G 5	130
Jiange	B 7	130
Jiangjin	D 8	130
Jiangkou, China	E 9	130
Jiangkou, China	G 10	130
Jiangle	E 13	130
Jiangling	C 10	130
Jiangmen	G 11	130
Jiangmifeng	D 16	128
Jiangshan	D 14	130
Jiangsu □[3]	B 14	130
Jiangxi □[3]	E 12	130
Jiangyin	C 15	130
Jiangyou	C 7	130
Jianli	D 11	130
Jianning	E 13	130
Jian'ou	E 14	130
Jianping	F 12	128
Jianshi	C 9	130
Jianshui	G 6	130
Jianyang, China	E 14	130
Jianyang, China	C 7	130
Jiaocheng	H 8	128
Jiaohe	E 16	128
Jiaolai ≃	E 13	128
Jiaonan	I 12	128
Jiaoxian	H 12	128
Jiaozhou Wan ⊂	I 13	128
Jiaozuo	I 9	128
Jiashan	B 13	130
Jiashun Hu ⊜	C 5	122
Jiawang	A 13	130
Jiaxian, China	G 8	128
Jiaxian, China	A 11	130
Jiaxing	C 15	130
Jiazi	G 13	130
Jibagalle	F 6	202
Jibiya	C 6	200
Jicarilla Apache Indian Reservation ➤[4]	D 5	176
Jičín	B 12	100
Jiddah (Jeddah)	C 4	202
Jieshou	B 12	130
Jiexi	G 12	130
Jiexiu	H 8	128
Jieyang	G 13	130
Jieznas	E 12	66
Jigalong Aboriginal Reserve ➤[4]	H 6	140
Jigzhi	B 5	130
Jihlava	A 7	102
Jihočeský □[3]	A 6	102
Jihomoravský □[3]	A 8	102
Jiiqley	G 6	202
Jijel	B 6	198
Jijiga	F 5	202
Jilib	G 5	202
Jilin	E 16	128
Jilin □[3]	E 16	128
Jill, Kediet ej ∧	E 2	198
Jill, Sebkhet ej ⊜	E 2	198
Jīma	F 4	202
Jimbolia	C 6	104
Jimena de la Frontera	H 5	86
Jiménez (Ciudad Jiménez)	D 7	184
Jiménez del Téul	F 8	184
Jimeta	D 7	200
Jimo	H 13	128
Jim Thorpe	F 3	164
Jin (Gam) ≃, Asia	G 7	130
Jin ≃, China	E 13	130
Jinan	H 11	128
Jincheng	I 9	128
Jindřichův Hradec	C 12	100
Jing ≃	I 7	128
Jing'an	D 12	130
Jingbohu ⊜[1]	E 17	128
Jingde	C 14	130
Jingdezhen	D 13	130
Jingdong	F 5	130
Jinggangshan	E 12	130
Jinghai	G 11	128
Jinghong	G 5	130
Jingmen	C 11	130
Jingning	I 5	128
Jingxi	G 8	130
Jingxian, China	H 11	128
Jingxian, China	E 9	130
Jingxing	C 14	128
Jingyu	E 16	128
Jingyuan, China	H 5	128
Jingyuan, China	I 6	128
Jingzhi	H 12	128
Jinhua	D 14	130
Jining, China	I 11	128
Jining, China	F 9	128
Jinja	G 3	202
Jinmu Jiao ›	I 9	130
Jinning	F 6	130
Jinping	E 9	130
Jinsha	E 8	130
Jinsha ≃	E 6	130
Jinshi	D 10	130
Jintang	C 7	130
Jinxi, China	F 13	128
Jinxi, China	E 13	130
Jinxian, China	G 10	128
Jinxian, China	D 13	130
Jinzhou, China	G 13	128
Jinzhou, China	F 13	128
Ji-Paraná	F 6	190
Jipijapa	D 2	190
Jiri ≃	D 6	122
Jirkov	B 10	100
Jishou	D 9	130
Jisr ash-Shughūr	E 7	118
Jitarning	M 5	140
Jiu ≃	C 7	104
Jiufeng	F 13	130
Jiujiang	D 12	130
Jiulian Shan ⋏	F 12	130
Jiuling Shan ⋏	D 12	130
Jiulong ≃	F 13	130
Jiuquan	B 7	122
Jiutai	D 15	128
Jiuzhen	F 13	130
Jiwen	A 14	128
Jixi, China	D 18	128
Jixi, China	C 14	130
Jixian, China	I 10	128
Jixian, China	C 18	128
Jixian, China	F 11	128
Jīzān	D 5	202
Jizl, Wādī al- ≃	I 7	118
Joaçaba	G 5	194
Joaíma	B 10	194
João Monlevade	C 9	194
João Pessoa	E 12	190
João Pinheiro	B 7	194
Joaquin	G 1	170
Joaquín V. González	E 7	192
Jódar	G 7	86
Jodhpur	D 2	122
Joensuu	E 14	64
Joetsu	F 7	126
Jõgeva	C 13	66
Jog Falls ∟	G 2	122
Jogjakarta	G 6	134
Johannesburg	D 7	206
Johanngeorgenstadt	B 9	100
John ≃	C 18	154
John Day	C 4	178
John Day ≃	C 3	178
John Day, Middle Fork ≃	C 4	178
John Day, North Fork ≃	C 4	178
John Day Fossil Beds National Monument ♦	C 4	178
John D'Or Prairie Indian Reserve ➤[4]	B 14	156
John F. Kennedy Space Center ◗[3]	E 4	168
John H. Kerr Reservoir ⊜[1]	A 5	168
John o' Groats	B 5	74
Johns Island I	C 5	168
Johnson, Ks., U.S.	G 4	174
Johnson, Vt., U.S.	B 6	164
Johnson City, N.Y., U.S.	D 3	164
Johnson City, Tn., U.S.	A 3	168
Johnsondale	E 5	182
Johnsonville	C 5	168
Johnston, Lake ⊜	M 6	140
Johnston Atoll I[1]	B 11	136
Johnston City	D 4	170
Johnstone	B 2	72
Johnstown, N.Y., U.S.	C 4	164
Johnstown, Pa., U.S.	C 4	162
Johor □[3]	M 6	132
Johor ≃	i 16	134a
Johor, Selat Ʉ	i 15	134a
Johor Bahru	N 6	132
Joigny	D 10	78
Joiner	E 3	170
Joinville	G 6	194
Joinville Island I	L 9	192
Jokau	F 3	202
Jokkmokk	C 9	64
Jökulsá á Brú ≃	m 23	64a
Jökulsárgljúfur National Park ♦	I 22	64a
Joliet	B 4	170
Joliette	E 7	160
Jolo	D 8	134
Jolo Island I	D 8	134
Jombang	k 21	135b
Jomda	C 4	130
Jonava	E 12	66
Jonesboro, Ar., U.S.	E 3	170
Jonesboro, La., U.S.	F 2	170
Jones Mill	E 2	170
Jonesport	A 10	162
Jonesville, La., U.S.	G 3	170
Jonesville, N.C., U.S.	A 4	168
Jong ≃	D 2	200
Joniškėlis	D 12	66
Joniškis	D 11	66
Jönköping	D 6	66
Jönköping □[3]	D 7	66
Jonquière	D 8	160
Jonzac	C 3	80
Joplin	D 1	170
Joppa	D 4	170
Joppatowne	G 2	164
Jordan	B 10	178
Jordan □[1], Asia	D 4	116
Jordan ≃, Asia	E 5	120
Jordan ≃, Ut., U.S.	B 3	176
Jordan Valley	D 5	178
Jordet	B 6	66
Jorhāt	D 6	122
Jornado del Muerto ➤[2]	F 5	176
Joroinen	E 13	64
Jos	C 6	200
José Batlle y Ordóñez	C 10	195
José Bonifácio	D 6	194
José de San Martín	H 5	192
Joseph, Lac ⊜	B 11	160
Joseph Bonaparte Gulf ⊂	D 10	140
Joseph City	E 3	176
Joshīmath	C 3	122
Jōshin-Etsu-kōgen-kokuritsu-kōen ♦	F 7	126
Joshua Tree National Park ♦	F 5	180
Josselin	E 4	78
Jostedalsbreen ⩍	B 3	66
Jostedalsbreen Nasjonalpark ♦	B 3	66
Jotunheimen Nasjonalpark ♦	B 4	66
Joué-lès-Tours	E 7	78
Joure	B 4	69
Joutel	D 4	160
Joutseno	B 14	66
Joveyn ≃	D 17	118
Joy	B 3	170
Jozini Dam (Pongolapoortdam) ⊜[1]	D 9	206
J. Percy Priest Lake ⊜[1]	D 5	170
Juana Díaz	j 15	187b
Juan de Fuca, Strait of Ʉ	A 1	178
Juan Fernández, Archipiélago II	H 6	188
Juanjuí	E 3	190
Juan L. Lacaze	D 9	195
Juárez, Sierra de ⋏	B 2	184
Juazeiro	E 10	190
Juazeiro do Norte	E 11	190
Juba see Jubba	G 3	202
Jubal, Strait of Ʉ	I 6	118
Jubany ◗[3]	L 8	192
Jubayt	D 4	202
Jubba (Juba) (Genale)	G 3	202
Jubba (Genalē) (Juba) ≃	G 5	202
Jubbada Dhexe □[3]	G 5	202
Jubbada Hoose □[3]	H 5	202
Jubilee Lake ⊜	K 9	140
Juby, Cap ›	D 2	198
Júcar (Xúquer) ≃	E 4	88
Juchipila	G 8	184
Juchitán de Zaragoza	I 12	184
Jucurucu ≃	B 10	194
Judaea □[9]	F 4	120
Judea see Judaea □[9]	F 4	120
Judenburg	C 6	102
Judith ≃	B 9	178
Judith Gap	H 4	158
Judith Mountains ⋏	B 9	178
Juelsminde	C 3	68
Jug ≃	G 16	108
Jugon-les-Lacs	D 4	78
Juhnov	I 11	108
Juidongshan	G 13	130
Juil'sk	E 28	108
Juiz de Fora	D 9	194
Jujuy □[3]	D 6	192
Jukseevo	G 20	108
Juliaca	G 4	190
Julia Creek	F 5	142
Julianakanaal ≋	C 4	69
Julian Alps ⋏	D 5	102
Juliana Top ∧	C 7	190
Julianehåb (Qaqortoq)	D 23	150
Julia Pfeiffer Burns State Park ♦	D 2	182
Jülich	F 3	98
Julimes	C 7	184
Júlio de Castilhos	A 11	195
Juma	D 10	108
Jumièges, Abbaye de ◗[1]	C 7	78
Jumilla	F 3	88
Jumlā	D 4	122
Jūnāgadh	E 1	122
Junction	C 2	176
Junction City, Ks., U.S.	F 6	174
Junction City, Ky., U.S.	D 6	170
Junction City, Or., U.S.	C 2	178
Jundiaí	E 7	194
Juneau	G 27	154
Junee	E 6	144
June Lake	C 4	182
Jungar Qi	G 8	128
Jungfrau ∧	D 5	82
Juniata □[6]	F 1	164
Juniata ≃	F 1	164
Junín	D 7	195
Junín de los Andes	F 2	195
Jūniyah	A 5	120
Junlian	D 7	130
Junqueirópolis	D 5	194
Juodkrantė	E 10	66
Juozapinės kalnas ∧[2]	E 12	66
Juparanã, Lagoa ⊜	C 10	194
Jupille	D 4	69
Jupiter	F 4	168
Juquiá	F 7	194
Jur ≃	F 2	202
Jura	B 10	104
Jura □[3], Fr.	D 3	82
Jura □[3], Switz.	C 5	82
Jura ⋏	C 5	82
Jura I	D 3	74
Jura, Sound of Ʉ	E 3	74
Jurbarkas	E 11	66
Jurevec	H 15	108
Jurgamyš	I 26	108
Jurino	A 14	110
Jurja	G 18	108
Jurjuzan'	I 23	108
Jurla	G 21	108
Jūrmala	D 11	66
Jurong, China	C 14	130
Jurong, Sing.	j 14	134a
Jurong ≃	j 14	134a
Juruá ≃	D 5	190
Juruena ≃	E 7	190
Jurumirim, Represa de ⊜[1]	E 6	194
Jušala	H 25	108
Juškovo	G 16	108
Juškozero	D 15	64
Jussey	C 3	82
Justo Daract	C 5	195
Jutaí ≃	D 5	190
Jüterbog	E 10	98
Jutiapa	J 15	184
Juticalpa	E 3	186
Jutland ➤[1]	B 2	68
Juupajoki	B 12	66
Juva	B 13	66
Juventud, Isla de la (Pines, Isle of) I	C 4	186
Juxian	I 12	128
Juye	I 10	128
Juža	H 15	108
Južna Morava ≃	D 7	104
Južno-Kazakhstan □[3]	A 1	122
Južno-Sahalinsk	C 12	124
Južno-Suhokumsk	G 14	110
Južno-Ural'sk	I 24	108
Južnyj	F 12	110
Jwaneng	C 6	206
Jwayyā	C 4	120
Jyväskylä	A 12	66
K		
K2 ∧	B 3	122
Kaabong	G 3	202
Kaala ∧	i 9	181a
Kaarlela	E 11	64
Kaarli	C 13	66
Kaarst	C 5	69
Kabaena, Pulau I	G 8	134
Kabala	D 2	200
Kabale	H 2	202
Kabalega Falls (Murchison Falls) ∟	G 3	202
Kabalo	D 4	204
Kabambare	C 4	204
Kaban'	I 27	108
Kabanjahe	M 4	132
Kabardino-Balkarija □[3]	H 13	110
Kabba	D 6	200
Kabbani ≃	G 3	122
Kåbdalis	C 9	64
Kabinda	D 3	204
Kabīr Kūh ⋏	F 12	118
Kableškovo	D 9	104
Kabo	D 8	200
Kābol (Kabul)	C 1	122
Kabompo ≃	E 3	204
Kabongo	D 4	204
Kabou	D 9	200
Kabūdarāhang	E 13	118
Kabul see Kābol ≃	C 2	122
Kaburuang, Pulau I	E 9	134
Kabūshīyah	D 3	202
Kabwe	E 4	204
Kačanik	D 6	104
Kachchh, Gulf of ⊂	F 10	116
Kachemak Bay ⊂	G 18	154
Kachin □[3]	F 3	130
Kačkanar	G 23	108
Kadaingti	F 3	132
Kadan Kyun I	H 3	132
Kadavu I	E 9	136
Kadéï ≃	D 7	200
Kading ≃	E 7	132
Kadiri	G 3	122
Kadirli	D 7	118
Kadja, Ouadi (Kaja, Wādī) ≃	E 1	202
Kado	D 6	200
Kadom	I 15	108
Kadoma	F 4	204
Kaduna	C 6	200
Kaduna ≃	D 6	200
Kāduqlī	E 2	202
Kaduvu Passage Ʉ	n 13	147c
Kadžerom	D 21	108
Kaédi	F 2	198
Kaélé	C 7	200
Kaesŏng	H 16	128
Kafanchan	D 6	200
Kafin	D 6	200
Kafr el-Dauwar	G 3	118
Kafr el-Sheikh	G 4	118
Kafue	F 4	204
Kafue ≃	E 4	204
Kafue National Park ♦	E 4	204
Kafulwe Mission	D 4	204
Kafusi	A 8	206
Kaga	F 6	126
Kaga Bandoro	D 8	200
Kagawa □[3]	G 4	126
Kagera ≃	C 5	204
Kagitumba	C 5	204
Kağızman	B 10	118
Kagoshima	I 3	126
Kagoshima □[3]	I 3	126
Kagoshima-wan ⊂	I 3	126
Kahama	C 5	204
Kahayan ≃	F 6	134
Kahe	H 4	202
Kahemba	D 2	204
Kahla	F 8	98
Kahoka	B 3	170
Kahramanmaraş	D 7	118
Kahraman Maraş □[3]	C 7	118
Kahului	i 10	181a
Kahurangi National Park ♦, N.Z.	D 3	146
Kahurangi National Park ♦, N.Z.	D 4	146
Kahuzi-Biega, Parc National de ♦	C 4	204
Kai, Kepulauan II	G 10	134
Kaiapoi	E 4	146
Kaibab Indian Reservation ➤[4]	D 2	176
Kaidu ≃	A 4	122
Kaiedin	F 3	202
Kaifeng	A 12	130
Kaihua	D 14	130
Kaijiang	C 8	130
Kai Kecil I	G 10	134
Kaikohe	A 4	146
Kaikoura	E 4	146
Kailahun	D 2	200
Kailāshahar	B 1	132
Kaili	E 8	130
Kailu	E 13	128
Kailua	i 10	181a
Kailua Kona	j 11	181a
Kaimana	F 10	134
Kainji Lake ⊜[1]	C 5	200
Kaipara Harbour ⊂	B 4	146
Kairouan	B 6	198
Kaiserslautern	C 4	100
Kaišiadorys	E 12	66
Kaitaia	A 4	146
Kaitangata	G 2	146
Kaiwaka	B 5	146
Kaixian	C 9	130
Kaiyuan, China	E 15	128
Kaiyuan, China	G 6	130
Kaiyuancheng	E 15	128
Kaja, Wādī (Kadja, Ouadi) ≃	E 1	202
Kajaani	D 13	64
Kajabbi	E 4	142
Kajang	M 5	132
Kajiado	H 4	202
Kajnar (Kaynar)	A 12	116
Kajuru	C 6	200
Kaka	E 3	202
Kakabeka Falls ∟	G 14	158
Kakadu National Park ♦	C 12	140
Kakamas	E 4	206
Kakamega	G 3	202
Kakamigahara	G 6	126
Kakata	D 2	200
Kake	H 28	154
Kakegawa	G 7	126
Kakenge	F 9	200
Kakhovka	F 8	110
Kakhovs'ke vodoskhovyshche ⊜[1]	F 9	110
Kākināda	F 4	122
Kakisa Lake ⊜	A 12	156
Kakoaka	F 3	204
Kakšaal-Too, hrebet ⋏	A 3	122
Kaktovik	A 22	154
Kala ≃	G 11	108
Kalaallit Nunaat see Greenland □[2]	C 16	148
Kalabahi	G 8	134
Kalabo	E 3	204
Kalač	D 12	110
Kalač-na-Donu	E 13	110
Kaladan ≃	D 1	132
Ka Lae ›	j 11	181a
Kalahari Desert ➤[2]	B 5	206
Kalahari Gemsbok National Park ♦	C 4	206
Kalai-Humb	B 2	122
Kalām	B 2	122
Kalámai	D 4	106
Kalamare	B 7	206
Kalamazoo	D 6	166
Kalamazoo ≃	D 5	166
Kalanguj	A 11	128
Kalan-Kalan	C 3	200
Kalao, Pulau I	G 8	134
Kalaotoa, Pulau I	G 8	134
Kalar ≃	A 7	124
Kälarne	E 8	64
Kalasin	F 6	132
Kalašnikovo	H 11	108
Kalāt	E 10	116
Kalávrita	C 5	106
Kalaw	D 3	132
Kalb, Ra's al- ›	E 6	202
Kalbarri	J 3	140
Kalbarri National Park ♦	J 3	140
Kale, Tur.	D 8	106
Kale, Tur.	D 8	106
Kalemie	D 4	204
Kalemyo	C 1	132
Kaletwa	D 1	132
Kalevala	D 9	108
Kaleybar	C 12	118
Kalga	A 12	128
Kalgan	N 5	140
Kalgoorlie-Boulder	L 6	140
Kaliakra, nos ›	D 10	104
Kalibek, ozero ⊜	J 29	108
Kalibo	C 8	134
Kalima	C 4	204
Kalimantan I	F 6	134
Kalimantan Barat □[3]	N 9	132
Kálimnos	D 7	106
Kālimpang	D 5	122
Kaliningrad (Königsberg)	B 2	110
Kaliningradskaja oblast' □[6]	B 2	110
Kalinino, Russia	H 22	108
Kalinino, Russia	G 11	110
Kalininsk	D 14	110
Kalinkavičy	C 6	110
Kalinovik	D 5	104
Kaliro	G 3	202
Kalisat	I 21	135b
Kāli Sindh ≃	E 3	122
Kalispell	A 6	178
Kalisz	C 10	96
Kalisz □[3]	C 9	96
Kalisz Pomorski	B 8	96
Kalix	D 11	64
Kalixälven ≃	C 10	64
Kal'ja	F 23	108
Kaljazin	H 12	108
Kālka	C 3	122
Kalkar	E 3	98
Kalkaska	A 1	162
Kalkfonteindam ⊜[1]	E 6	206
Kalkhügel	C 2	206
Kalkmond	E 4	206
Kalkstasie	E 3	206
Kall	D 5	69
Kallang ≃	j 15	134a
Kallaste	C 13	66
Kallavesi ⊜	E 13	64
Kallsjön ⊜	E 6	64
Kalmar	D 8	66
Kalmar □[3]	D 8	66
Kalmarsund Ʉ	D 8	66
Kalmthout	C 3	69
Kalmykija □[3]	F 14	110
Kalnciems	D 11	66
Kalocsa	D 10	102
Kaloko	D 4	204
Kalomo	F 4	204
Kalsūbai ∧	F 2	122
Kaltag	D 15	154
Kaltenkirchen	C 6	98
Kaluga	I 11	108
Kalulushi	E 4	204
Kalumburu	D 9	140
Kalumburu Aboriginal Reserve ➤[4]	D 9	140
Kalundborg	C 3	68
Kalungwishi ≃	D 4	204
Kalush	A 8	104
Kałuszyn	B 11	96
Kalutara	H 3	122
Kalužskaja oblast' □[6]	I 11	108
Kalvarija	E 11	66
Kalyān	F 2	122
Kalynivka	E 6	110
Kama	F 25	108
Kama ≃	D 8	114
Kamaishi	E 8	126
Kamajai	E 12	66
Kaman	C 5	118
Kamanjab	F 1	204
Kamarān I	D 5	202
Kāmāreddi	F 3	122
Kamariótissa	B 6	106
Kamatsi Lake ⊜	C 7	158
Kambalda	L 6	140
Kambarka	H 21	108
Kambia	D 2	200
Kambolé	D 5	200
Kamčatka ≃	D 18	114
Kamčatskij poluostrov ›[1]	D 19	114
Kamchatka Peninsula ›[1]	D 19	114
Kamen', gora ∧	C 12	114
Kameng ≃	D 6	122
Kamenjak, Rt ›	C 2	104
Kamenka, Russia	J 15	108
Kamenka, Russia	D 11	110
Kamen'-na-Obi	D 11	114
Kamennogorsk	F 8	108
Kamenolomni	F 12	110
Kamen'-Rybolov	B 3	126
Kamensk-Šahtinskij	E 12	110
Kamensk-Ural'skij	H 24	108
Kamenz	E 11	98
Kāmet ∧	C 3	122
Kamiah	B 5	178
Kamień Pomorski	A 8	96
Kamieńsk	C 10	96
Kamiiso	D 8	126
Kamina	D 4	204
Kaminak Lake ⊜	D 13	150
Kaminaljuyú ⊥	J 14	184
Kaminuriak Lake ⊜	D 13	150
Kámiros ⊥	D 7	106
Kamishak Bay ⊂	G 17	154
Kamituga	C 4	204
Kamjanec	B 12	96
Kamloops	F 11	156
Kamloops Indian Reserve ➤[4]	F 11	156
Kamnik	D 6	102
Kamo	F 7	126
Kampala	G 3	202
Kampar	L 5	132
Kampar ≃	N 6	132
Kampar Kanan ≃	N 5	132
Kampen	B 4	69
Kamphaeng Phet	F 4	132
Kampinoski Park Narodowy ♦	B 10	96
Kâmpóng Cham	H 7	132
Kâmpóng Chhnăng	H 7	132
Kâmpóng Saôm	I 6	132
Kâmpóng Saôm, Chhâk ⊂	I 6	132
Kâmpóng Thum	H 7	132
Kâmpôt	I 6	132
Kampti	C 4	200
Kâmpŭchéa see Cambodia □[1]	H 7	132
Kamskij	F 20	108
Kamskoe vodohranilišče ⊜[1]	G 21	108
Kāmthi	E 3	122
Kamuchawie Lake ⊜	C 7	158
Kamuela	j 11	181a
Kamwandu	D 3	204
Kam'yanets'-Podil's'kyy	A 9	104
Kamyšin	D 14	110
Kamyšlov	H 25	108
Kamyšnoe	C 22	110
Kamyzjak	F 16	110
Kanaaupscow ≃	A 6	160
Kanafis	F 2	202
Kanaga Volcano ∧[1]	k 43	155a
Kanagawa □[3]	G 7	126
Kanairiktok ≃	A 12	160
Kananga	D 3	204
Kanaš	I 17	108
Kanata	A 3	164
Kanava	F 21	108
Kanawha ≃	D 3	162
Kanazawa	F 6	126
Kanbalu	C 2	132
Kanbauk	G 3	132
Kančalan ≃	D 3	154
Kanchanaburi	G 4	132
Kānchenjunga ∧	D 5	122
Kānchipuram	G 3	122
Kandahar	F 19	156
Kandalakša	C 10	108
Kandalakšskaja guba ⊂	C 10	108
Kandangan	F 7	134
Kandanghaur	k 19	135b
Kandé	C 5	200
Kandel	C 5	100
Kandhkot	D 1	122
Kandiāro	D 1	122
Kandıra	B 9	106
Kandy	H 4	122
Kane	C 4	162
Kanem □[3]	C 8	200
Kaneohe	i 10	181a
Kanëvka	C 13	108
Kangaba	C 3	200
Kangal	C 7	118
Kangān	I 15	118
Kangar	K 5	132
Kangaroo Island I	M 3	142
Kangasala	B 12	66
Kangāvar	E 12	118
Kangbao	F 10	128
Kangding	C 6	130
Kangean, Kepulauan II	G 7	134
Kangean, Pulau I	k 22	135b
Kangen ≃	F 3	202
Kanger Valley National Park ♦	F 4	122
Kanggye	F 16	128
Kangiqsualujjuaq	E 19	150
Kangiqsujuaq	D 18	150
Kangirsuk	D 18	150
Kangjinjing	C 16	128
Kangnŭng	H 17	128
Kango	E 7	200
Kangongo	F 3	204
Kangrinboqê Feng ∧	C 4	122
Kangshan	G 14	130
Kangsŏ	G 15	128
Kangto ∧	D 6	122
Kangwŏn-do □[3], N. Kor.	G 16	128
Kangwŏn-do □[3], S. Kor.	H 17	128
Kangyidaung	F 2	132
Kanha National Park ♦	E 4	122
Kani	D 3	200
Kaniama	D 3	204
Kanibadam	A 2	122
Kaniet Islands II	M 13	124
Kanin, poluostrov ›[1]	C 16	108
Kanin Nos	B 15	108
Kanin Nos, mys ›	C 7	114
Kaniv	E 7	110
Kaniva	F 3	144
Kanjiža	B 6	104
Kankakee	B 5	170
Kankakee ≃	E 5	166
Kankan	C 3	200
Kankéla	C 3	200
Kānker	E 4	122
Kanmaw Kyun I	I 4	132
Kannapolis	B 4	168
Kano	C 6	200
Kano ≃	C 6	200
Kanokovo	G 12	110
Kanonji	G 4	126
Kanoya	I 3	126
Kānpur	D 3	122
Kansas □[3]	D 8	152
Kansas ≃	F 7	174
Kansas City, Ks., U.S.	C 1	170
Kansas City, Mo., U.S.	C 1	170
Kansau	C 1	132
Kansk	D 12	114
Kant	A 2	122
Kantang	K 4	132
Kantchari	C 5	200
Kantishna ≃	D 19	154
Kantō-heiya ≚	F 7	126
Kantubek	G 21	110
Kanturk	D 3	75
Kanye	C 6	206
Kanygtokynmangkyn, laguna ⊂	F 4	154
Kanyu	G 3	204
Kanzanavolok	E 12	108
Kaohsiung	G 14	130
Kaohsiunghsien	G 15	130
Kaoko Otavi	F 1	204
Kaoko Veld ⋏[1]	F 1	204
Kaolack	C 1	200
Kaoma	E 3	204
Kaouar ➤[1]	B 7	200
Kapan	J 15	110
Kapanga	D 3	204
Kapatu Mission	D 5	204
Kapčagaj	B 12	116
Kapellen	C 3	69
Kapfenberg	C 7	102
Kapiri Mposhi	E 4	204
Kapiskau ≃	E 17	158
Kapit	E 6	134
Kapitanivka	E 7	110
Kaposvár	D 9	102
Kapp	B 5	66
Kappeln	B 6	98
Kapsan-ŭp	D 2	126
Kaptai	E 6	122
Kapuas ≃	E 6	134
Kapuas Hulu, Pegunungan ⋏	E 6	134
Kapulo	D 4	204
Kapuskasing	D 2	160
Kapuskasing ≃	D 2	160
Kapuvár	C 9	102
Kara, Russia	B 26	108
Kara, Togo	D 5	200
Kara-Balta	A 2	122
Karabaš	I 23	108
Kara-Bogaz-Gol Gulf see Garabogaz Aylagy ⊂	I 18	110
Karabük	B 5	118
Karaburun	C 7	106
Karabutak	E 22	110
Karacabey	B 8	106
Karačaevo-Čerkesija □[3]	H 12	110
Karačaevsk	H 12	110
Karacaköy	B 8	106
Karačev	J 11	108
Karāchi	F 10	116
Karād	F 2	122
Karaganda (Qaraghandy)	A 11	116
Karagayly see Karkaralinsk	A 12	116
Karagin Island see Karaginskij, ostrov I	D 19	114
Karaginskij, ostrov I	D 19	114
Karaidel'skij	I 22	108
Karaj	E 14	118
Karakalpakstan, Respublika □[3]	G 20	110
Karakax ≃	B 4	122
Karakaya Barajı ⊜[1]	C 8	118
Karakelong, Pulau I	E 9	134
Karakol	A 3	122
Karakoram Range ⋏	C 3	122
Karakul'	C 9	116
Karakul'skoe	I 25	108
Kara Kum (Garagum) ➤[2]	B 8	116
Kara Kum Canal ≋	C 9	116
Karaman	D 5	118
Karaman □[3]	D 5	118
Karamay	A 13	116
Karamea Bight ⊂	D 3	146
Karamürsel	B 8	106
Karangnungal	k 19	135b
Karapınar	D 5	118
Karas	D 2	206
Karas □[3]	D 2	206
Kara Sea (Karskoe more) ⫧[2]	B 10	114
Karasjok	B 12	64
Karasu, Kaz.	D 23	110
Kara-Su, Kyrg.	A 2	122
Karasu, Tur.	B 9	106
Karasu ≃	C 9	118
Karatau	A 1	122
Karatau, hrebet ⋏	B 10	116
Karaton	F 18	110
Karatsu	H 2	126
Karawang	k 18	135b
Karawang, Tanjung ›	k 18	135b
Karažal (Qarazhal)	A 11	116
Karbalā'	F 10	118
Karbalā' □[3]	F 10	118
Kårböle	A 7	66
Karcag	E 11	96
Kardhámaina	D 7	106
Kardhítsa	C 4	106
Kärdla	C 11	66
Kărdžali	E 8	104
Karelija □[3]	E 10	108
Karema	D 5	204
Karepino	F 22	108
Karepole	D 15	108
Kärevere	C 13	66
Kargalinskaja	H 15	110
Kargapole	H 25	108
Kargopol'	F 13	108
Kariaí	B 6	106
Kariba	F 4	204
Kariba, Lake ⊜[1]	F 4	204
Karibib	A 1	206
Kariega ≃	G 5	206
Karijini National Park ♦	H 5	140
Karimata, Kepulauan II	F 5	134
Karimata Strait (Karimata, Selat) Ʉ	F 5	134
Karīmganj	E 6	122
Karīmnagar	F 3	122
Karimunjawa, Kepulauan II	G 6	134
Karin	E 6	202
Karisimbi, Volcan ∧[1]	C 4	204
Kariya	G 6	126
Karkams	F 2	206
Karkaralinsk (Karagayly)	A 12	116
Karkar Island I	M 13	124
Karkheh ≃	F 12	118
Karkinits'ka zatoka ⊂	G 8	110
Karkkila	B 11	66
Karkonoski Park Narodowy ♦	C 8	96
Karkūk	E 11	118
Kärla	C 11	66
Karlantijpa North Aboriginal Land ➤[4]	F 12	140
Karlantijpa South Aboriginal Land ➤[4]	G 12	140
Karlino	A 8	96
Karl-Marx-Stadt see Chemnitz	F 9	98
Karlovac	E 7	102
Karlovo	D 8	104
Karlovy Vary	B 9	100
Karlsborg	C 7	66
Karlshamn	D 7	66
Karlskoga	C 7	66
Karlskrona	D 7	66
Karlsruhe	C 5	100
Karlsruhe □[6]	D 5	100
Karlstad, Mn., U.S.	A 6	174
Karlstad, Swe.	C 6	66

∟ Waterfall Ʉ Strait ⊂ Bay, Gulf ⊜ Lake ≋ Swamp ⩍ Ice Feature ⫧ Other Hydrographic Feature ✢ Submarine Feature □ Political Unit ◗ Cultural Institution ⊥ Historical Site ♦ Recreational Site ⊠ Airport ■ Military Installation ➤ Miscellaneous

Name	Map Ref.	Page
Karlstadt	C 6	100
Karma	C 5	200
Karmi'el	D 4	120
Karnack	F 1	170
Karnāl	D 3	122
Karnāli	D 4	122
Karnaphuli Reservoir ⊚¹	E 6	122
Karnātaka □³	G 3	122
Karnobat	D 9	104
Kärnten □³	D 5	102
Karoi	F 4	204
Karoli	E 3	122
Karonga	D 5	204
Karoo National Park ♦	G 5	206
Karoonda	F 2	144
Karora	D 4	202
Karotho Post	E 7	106
Kárpathos	E 7	106
Kárpathos I	E 7	106
Kárpats'kyy Pryrodnyy Natsional'nyy Park ♦	A 8	104
Karpenision	C 4	106
Karpinsk	G 23	108
Karratha	G 4	140
Karridale	N 3	140
Kars	B 10	118
Kars □³	B 10	118
Kārsava	D 13	66
Karshi (Qarshi)	B 1	122
Karshi □⁶	B 1	122
Karskie Vorota, proliv ⋃	B 8	114
Karskoe more see Kara Sea ⨓²	B 10	114
Karsun	B 15	110
Kartala ʌ¹	n 18	207d
Kartaly	J 24	108
Kartuzy	A 10	96
Käru	C 12	66
Karufa	F 10	134
Karumba	D 5	142
Kārūn ⨓	G 13	118
Karungu	H 3	202
Karūr	G 3	122
Karviná	D 10	96
Kārvār	G 2	122
Karym	F 27	108
Karymskoe	B 6	124
Kas	E 1	202
Kasaan	D 5	156
Kasabonika	E 14	158
Kasai (Cassai) ⨓	C 2	204
Kasai-Occidental □³	C 3	204
Kasai-Oriental □³	C 3	204
Kasama	E 5	204
Kasane	F 3	204
Kasanga	D 5	204
Kasanka National Park ♦	E 5	204
Kasansai	A 2	122
Kasar, Ras ⟩	D 4	202
Kāsaragod	G 2	122
Kasba Lake	D 12	150
Kasba-Tadla	C 3	198
Kaščukoúka	C 7	110
Kāseberga	E 7	66
Kasese, Ug.	G 2	202
Kasese, Zaire	C 4	204
Kāsganj	D 3	122
Kāshān	F 14	118
Kashechewan	B 3	160
Kashi	B 3	122
Kāshīpur	D 3	122
Kashitu	E 4	204
Kashiwazaki	F 7	126
Kāshmar	E 18	118
Kashunuk ⨓	F 12	154
Kasimov	I 14	108
Kašin	H 12	108
Kasinga	D 4	204
Kašira	I 13	108
Kasiruta, Pulau I	F 9	134
Kaskaskia ⨓	C 4	170
Kaskattama ⨓	C 13	158
Kaskelen	A 3	122
Kasongo	D 2	204
Kasongo-Lunda	D 2	204
Kasouga	G 7	206
Kaspijsk	H 15	110
Kaspijskij	G 15	110
Kassalá	D 4	202
Kassándras, Kólpos c	B 5	106
Kassel	E 6	98
Kassel □⁶	E 6	98
Kasserine	B 6	198
Kastamonu	B 5	118
Kastamonu □³	B 5	118
Kastanéai	B 7	106
Kastl	C 8	100
Kastoria	B 4	106
Kastornoe	D 11	110
Kasugai	E 6	126
Kasungu	E 5	204
Kasungu National Park ♦	E 5	204
Kasupe	F 6	204
Kasūr	C 2	122
Kaszuby □⁹	B 2	96
Kataba	E 4	204
Katahdin, Mount ʌ	h 12	163a
Katajsk	H 25	108
Katale	E 5	204
Katanda	D 4	204
Katanga □⁹	C 2	114
Katanga ⨓	B 12	124
Katanti	M 4	140
Katav-Ivanovsk	I 22	108
Katchiungo	E 2	204
Katerini	B 5	106
Kates Needle ʌ	C 6	156
Katete	E 5	204
Katha	B 3	132
Katherine	D 11	140
Katherine ⨓	D 12	140
Katherine Gorge National Park ♦	C 12	140
Kathiawār Peninsula ⟩¹	E 2	122
Kathleen Valley	J 6	140
Kāthmāndu ⋆ see Kāthmāndū	D 4	122
Káto Akhaḯa	C 4	106
Katonga ⨓	G 3	202
Katoomba	D 8	144
Katopa	C 3	204
Katowice	C 10	96
Katowice □³	C 10	96
Katrineholm	C 8	66
Katsina	C 6	200
Katsina-Ala	D 6	200
Katsina Ala ⨓	D 6	200
Katsuta	F 8	126
Katsuura	G 8	126
Kattakurgan	B 1	122
Kattegat ⋃	D 5	66
Katthammarsvik	D 9	66
Katwijk aan Zee	B 3	69
Katwitwi	F 2	204
Kauai I	h 9	181a
Kaufbeuren	E 7	100
Kaufungen	E 6	98
Kauhajoki	E 11	64
Kauhanevan-Pohjankankaan kansallispuisto ♦	A 11	66
Kaujuitoq	B 14	150
Kaukapakapa	B 5	146
Kaukauna	C 4	166
Kaukau Veld ⤳¹	F 3	204
Kaumalapau	i 10	181a
Kaunas	E 11	66
Kaunghein	B 2	132
Kaura-Namoda	C 6	200
Kaustinen	E 11	64
Kauttua	B 11	66
Kavača	C 19	114
Kavadarci	E 6	104
Kavajë	B 3	106
Kavála	B 6	106
Kavalerovo	B 5	126
Kāvali	G 4	122
Kavaratti	G 2	122
Kāveri ⨓	G 3	122
Kavieng	M 14	124
Kavimba	D 3	204
Kavir, Dasht-e ⇒²	D 8	118
Kavungo	D 5	204
Kavuu ⨓	D 5	204
Kawaguchi	G 7	126
Kawakawa	A 5	146
Kawardha	E 4	122
Kawasaki	G 7	126
Kaweenakumik Lake ⊚	E 9	158
Kawerau	C 6	146
Kawhia Harbour c	C 5	146
Kawkareik	F 4	132
Kaw Lake ⊚¹	B 5	172
Kawludo	E 3	132
Kawnipi Lake ⊚	G 13	158
Kawthaung	I 4	132
Kaya	C 4	200
Kayah □³	E 3	132
Kayak Island I	G 22	154
Kayan ⨓	D 10	134
Kayangel Islands II	D 10	134
Kāyankulam	H 3	122
Kaycee	D 10	178
Kayenta	D 3	176
Kayes	C 2	200
Kayes □³	C 2	200
Kayin □³	F 3	132
Kayın çı	C 8	106
Kaynar see Kajnar	A 12	116
Kayseri	C 6	118
Kayseri □³	C 6	118
Kaysville	E 7	178
Kayuagung	F 4	134
Kayuyu	C 4	204
Kazakeviçevo	B 20	128
Kazakhstan □¹	J 27	108
Kazak Uplands ⤳²	A 11	116
Kazan'	I 18	108
Kazan	D 13	150
Kazan	F 8	110
Kazan Lake ⊚	D 8	104
Kazan-rettō (Volcano Islands) II	G 12	124
Kazbek, gora ʌ¹	A 11	118
Kazembe	E 5	204
Kāzerūn	H 14	118
Kazimierza Wielka	C 11	96
Kazincbarcika	A 6	104
Kaziranga National Park ♦	D 6	122
Kazlų Rūda	E 1	66
Kazłovka	E 16	110
Kazuma Pan National Park ♦	F 4	204
Kazym	E 27	108
Kazym ⨓	E 27	108
Kazyr ⨓	B 2	124
Kdyně	C 10	100
Kea, Mauna ʌ¹	j 11	181a
Kearney, Mo., U.S.	C 1	170
Kearney, Ne., U.S.	E 5	174
Keban Baraji ⊚¹	C 5	200
Kebbe	B 1	200
Kébémer	D 7	200
Kebili	B 7	198
Kébir, Mayo ⨓	D 7	200
Kebnekaise ʌ	B 9	64
Kebri Dehar	G 5	202
Kecel	B 8	156
Kechika ⨓	B 8	156
Keçiborlu	D 4	106
Kecskemét	B 5	104
Kedah □³	L 5	132
Kedgwick	B 8	162
Kédainiai	E 11	66
Kedong	B 16	128
Kédougou	C 2	200
Kędzierzyn-Koźle	C 9	96
Keefers	F 11	156
Keele ⨓	D 31	154
Keele Peak ʌ	E 29	154
Keeley Lake ⊚	D 17	156
Keene	E 11	162
Keep River National Park ♦	D 10	140
Keeseville	B 5	164
Keetmanshoop	D 3	206
Keewatin	C 3	158
Kefallinía (Cephalonia) I	B 9	198
Kefamenanu	F 8	134
Kefar Nahum (Capernaum) ⊥	D 5	120
Kefar Sava	D 6	200
Keffi	D 6	200
Ke Ga, Mui ⟩	H 9	132
Kegaska	C 13	160
Keg River	D 12	156
Kegums	D 12	66
Kehl	D 5	72
Keighley	D 5	72
Keila	C 12	66
Keilor	F 5	144
Keimoes	E 4	206
Kei Mouth	G 8	206
Keith	H 3	144
Keith Arm c	C 8	150
Keithley Creek	E 11	156
Keizer	C 2	178
Kejimkujik National Park ♦	F 11	160
Kékes ʌ	B 6	104
Kelantan □³	L 6	132
Kelantan ⨓	L 6	132
Kelb, Ouadi ⨓	B 8	200
Keles	B 1	122
Kelheim	D 8	100
Kelibia	G 3	90
Kelkit ⨓	E 3	98
Keller	G 12	156
Kellerberrin	L 4	140
Keller Lake ⊚	E 34	154
Kellett, Cape ⟩	B 7	150
Kellinghusen	C 6	98
Kellogg, Ia., U.S.	B 2	170
Kellogg, Id., U.S.	B 5	178
Kells	C 5	75
Kelly Lake ⊚	D 31	154
Kelmé	E 11	66
Kelmet	D 4	202
Kélo	D 8	200
Kelolokan	E 7	134
Kelowna	G 12	156
Kelsey Lake ⊚	E 8	158
Kelso, Scot., U.K.	B 4	72
Kelso, Wa., U.S.	B 2	178
Keluang	N 6	132
Keluo ⨓	B 16	128
Kelvington	E 7	158
Kem' ⨓	D 11	108
Kemah	C 8	118
Kemalpaşa	C 7	106
Kembé	D 9	106
Kemer	D 8	106
Kemer Baraji ⊚¹	D 11	114
Kemerovo	D 12	64
Kemi	C 13	64
Kemijärvi	C 13	64
Kemijärvi ⊚	C 12	64
Kemijoki ⨓	E 8	178
Kemmerer	D 8	200
Kēmo □³	D 4	172
Kemp, Lake ⊚	E 4	172
Kempele	D 12	64
Kempen	E 3	98
Kempen ⤅¹	C 4	69
Kemp Land ⤳	D 14	208
Kempsey	C 9	144
Kempston	E 6	72
Kempten	E 7	100
Kempton Park	C 8	206
Kemul, Kong ʌ	E 7	134
Kenai	F 19	154
Kenai Fjords National Park ♦	F 19	154
Kenai Peninsula ⟩¹	F 19	154
Kenansville	B 5	168
Kendal	C 4	72
Kendall, Austl.	C 9	144
Kendall, Fl., U.S.	G 4	168
Kendari	F 8	134
Kendrew	G 6	206
Kendrick	E 3	168
Kendujhargarh	E 5	122
Kenema	D 2	200
Kēneurgenč	H 21	110
Kenge	C 2	204
Kēng Tung	D 4	132
Kenia	C 2	204
Kenilworth	E 5	72
Kénitra	C 3	198
Kénitra □³	E 2	84
Kenly	B 5	168
Kenmare	A 3	174
Kennebec ⨓	A 9	162
Kennebunk	C 8	164
Kennedy	F 4	204
Kennedy, Cape see Canaveral, Cape ⟩	E 4	168
Kennedy, Mount ʌ	F 25	154
Kennedy Entrance ⋃	G 18	154
Kennedy Lake ⊚	G 9	156
Kennedy Range National Park ♦	I 3	140
Kennemerduinen, Nationaal Park de ♦	B 3	69
Kenner	D 5	170
Kennett	D 7	170
Kennewick	B 4	178
Kenney Dam ⤅⁸	E 9	156
Kénogami	D 8	160
Kénogami ⨓	F 16	158
Kénogami, Lac ⊚¹	D 8	160
Keno Hill	E 27	154
Kenora	G 11	158
Kenosha	D 5	166
Kenozero, ozero ⊚	E 12	108
Kensal	B 5	174
Kensington	F 5	174
Kent, Oh., U.S.	C 3	162
Kent, Wa., U.S.	G 3	164
Kent □⁶, De., U.S.	E 4	164
Kent □⁶, Eng., U.K.	F 7	72
Kent □⁶, Md., U.S.	G 2	164
Kent □⁶, R.I., U.S.	D 4	170
Kenton	D 1	162
Kent Peninsula ⟩¹	C 11	150
Kentucky □³	D 10	152
Kentucky ⨓	C 6	170
Kentucky, North Fork ⨓	D 1	162
Kentucky Lake ⊚	D 4	170
Kentville	F 11	160
Kenya □¹	H 11	196
Kenya, Mount (Kirinyaga) ʌ	H 4	202
Kenzou	E 7	200
Keokuk	B 3	170
Keoladeo National Park ♦	D 3	122
Keowee, Lake ⊚¹	B 3	168
Kepi	G 11	134
Kepice	A 9	96
Kepno	C 10	96
Keppel Bay c	D 9	142
Kerala □³	G 3	122
Kerang, Parc National de ♦	C 5	200
Kerang	E 4	144
Keravat	B 12	66
Kerby	D 2	178
Kerčevskij	F 20	108
Kerch	G 10	110
Kerch Strait ⋃	G 10	110
Kéré	F 2	104
Kerema	N 13	124
Keremeos	G 12	156
Keren	D 4	202
Keret	C 10	108
Keret', ozero ⊚	D 10	108
Kerga	D 18	108
Kerguelen Islands II	J 17	56
Kerikeri	A 4	146
Kerinci, Gunung ʌ	F 4	134
Kerio ⨓	G 4	202
Kerion	D 4	106
Keriya ⨓	B 4	122
Kerkenna, Îles II	C 7	198
Kerkhoven	C 10	174
Kerki	C 10	116
Kérkira (Kérkyra)	C 3	106
Kérkira (Corfu) I	C 3	106
Kerkrade	D 4	69
Kermadec Islands II	F 10	136
Kermadec Trench ⫣¹	I 14	58
Kerman, Ca., U.S.	D 3	182
Kermān, Iran	G 17	118
Kermān □³	H 17	118
Kermānshāh	E 12	118
Kermānshāh □³	E 12	118
Kermit	E 2	172
Kern ⨓	E 5	182
Kern □⁶	E 5	182
Kernforschungszentrum ▮³	C 5	100
Kern Lake Bed ⤅¹	E 4	182
Keros	F 20	108
Kérouané	D 3	200
Kerpen	F 3	98
Kerrville	E 4	172
Kerry □³	D 2	75
Kersley	E 11	156
Kertih	L 6	132
Keru,len ⨓	B 10	128
Kesagami Lake ⊚	C 3	160
Kesagami Lake Provincial Park ♦	C 3	160
Kesālāhti	B 14	66
Kesan	B 7	106
Kesennuma	E 8	126
Keshan	B 15	128
Keshod	E 2	122
Keski-Suomi □³	E 12	64
Keskozero	F 10	108
Kestell	E 8	206
Keswick	C 3	72
Keszthely	D 9	102
Ket' ⨓	D 11	114
Ketapang, Indon.	E 5	134
Ketapang, Indon.	k 21	135b
Kemp Land	D 14	208
Ketchikan	I 29	154
Kete-Krachi	D 4	200
Kétou	D 5	200
Ketovo	I 26	108
Kętrzyn	A 11	96
Kettering, Eng., U.K.	E 6	72
Kettering, Oh., U.S.	D 1	162
Kettle ⨓	C 12	156
Kettle Falls	A 4	178
Kettle Hills ⤳²	L 2	132
Keudeteunom	B 3	69
Keukenhof ♦	B 3	69
Keuruu	A 12	66
Keurusselkä ⊚	A 12	66
Kevelaer	E 3	98
Kewanee	B 4	170
Keweenaw Peninsula ⟩¹	B 4	166
Keweenaw Point ⟩	B 5	166
Keyala	G 3	202
Keyes	B 2	172
Key Largo	G 4	168
Key Largo I	G 4	168
Keynsham	F 4	72
Keyser	D 4	162
Keystone, Ia., U.S.	D 2	166
Keystone, W.V., U.S.	E 3	162
Key West	G 4	168
Kez	D 20	108
Kežma	D 13	114
Kežmarok	C 8	164
Kennedy, Cape see Canaveral, Cape	F 4	204
Khomeynīshahr	F 14	118
Khomodimo	B 5	206
Khon Kaen	E 6	132
Khorāsān □³	E 17	118
Khorol	E 8	110
Khorramābād	G 13	118
Khorramshahr	F 12	118
Khorugh	B 2	122
Khotyn	A 9	104
Khouribga	C 3	198
Khowai	B 1	132
Khrystynivka	A 10	104
Khudumalapye	B 6	206
Khudzhand see Khojand	A 1	122
Khŭjayli see Khodzheyli	H 21	110
Khu Khan	E 6	132
Khulna	G 13	122
Khulna □³	E 5	122
Khŭnjerāb Pass ⊁	B 2	122
Khureng	A 7	104
Khust	A 7	104
Khuzdār	B 2	122
Khūzestān □³	G 13	118
Khvor	F 16	118
Khvoy	C 11	118
Khwae Noi (Kwai) ⨓	G 4	132
Khyber Pass ⊁	C 1	122
Khyriv	D 12	96
Kiama	E 8	144
Kiamba	D 8	134
Kiana	C 14	154
Kiangara	k 9	205a
Kiangarow, Mount ʌ	I 10	142
Kibaha	B 6	204
Kibamba	C 4	204
Kibasi □³	G 12	118
Kibila	D 4	204
Kibombo	C 4	204
Kibre Mengist	H 2	202
Kibumbu	H 4	202
Kibwezi	H 4	202
Kičevo	E 6	104
Kicking Horse Pass ⊁	F 13	156
Kidal	F 3	200
Kidal □³	D 5	204
Kidatu	D 6	204
Kidderminster	E 5	72
Kidepo National Park ♦	G 3	202
Kidete	D 6	204
Kidira	C 2	200
Kidsgrove	E 5	72
Kiefersfelden	E 9	100
Kiel	B 7	98
Kiel Bay see Kieler Bucht c	B 7	98
Kiel Canal see Nord-Ostsee-Kanal ⨘	A 5	96
Kielce	C 11	96
Kielce □³	C 11	96
Kieler Bucht (Kiel Bay) c	B 7	98
Kiembara	C 4	200
Kiesel	B 7	206
Kieta	C 9	96
Kietrz	C 9	96
Kiev see Kyyiv	D 7	110
Kiffa	C 5	106
Kifisiá	C 5	106
Kigali	C 5	204
Kigoma	C 5	204
Kigoma □³	C 5	204
Kihei	i 10	181a
Kihniö	A 11	66
Kijev see Kyyiv	D 7	110
Kikagati	H 3	202
Kikinda	C 6	104
Kikori	N 12	124
Kikori ⨓	N 12	124
Kikuchi	H 3	126
Kikwit	D 2	204
Kil	D 7	64
Kilauea Crater ⊾⁶	j 11	181a
Kilchu-ŭp	F 17	128
Kildare	F 5	75
Kildare □³	F 5	75
Kildonan	F 1	170
Kili I	D 1	136
Kilian Island I	D 6	136
Kilibo	D 5	200
Kilima	D 5	204
Kilimanjaro □³	C 6	204
Kilimanjaro Game Reserve ⤳⁴	H 4	202
Kilimli	B 9	106
Kilindoni	D 5	204
Kiliya	D 7	118
Kiliya	C 10	104
Kilkee	D 3	75
Kilkenny	D 5	75
Kilkenny □³	D 5	75
Kilkis	B 5	106
Killala	D 3	75
Killaloe	D 4	75
Killam	E 16	156
Killarney, Ire.	D 2	75
Killarney, On., Can.	F 3	160
Killarney, Lakes of ⊚	E 3	70
Killarney Provincial Park ♦	B 8	162
Killeen	E 5	172
Killiniq Island I	D 20	150
Killinkoski	A 5	164
Kilmarnock	B 5	72
Kil'mez'	H 19	108
Kilmichael	A 3	170
Kiloli	D 5	204
Kilombero ⨓	D 5	204
Kilpisjärvi	B 10	116
Kilrush	D 3	75
Kilwa	C 5	204
Kilwinning	B 2	204
Kim	F 7	172
Kim see Kenya, Mount	H 4	202
Kimba	F 7	144
Kimball, Mn., U.S.	E 1	174
Kimball, S.D., U.S.	D 7	174
Kimbe	N 14	124
Kimberley, B.C., Can.	G 18	156
Kimberley, S. Afr.	G 7	206
Kimberley Downs	D 4	140
Kimberley Plateau ⤳⁹	C 5	140
Kimberly	F 6	178
Kimch'aek	F 17	128
Kimch'ŏn	H 15	128
Kimhwa-ŭp	F 16	128
Kim Kim ⨓	i 15	134a
Kim-me-ni-oli Wash ⨓	E 5	176
Kimovsk	I 13	108
Kimry	H 12	108
Kimsquit	E 8	156
Kinabalu, Gunung ʌ	E 17	118
Kinbasket Lake ⊚	E 12	156
Kincaid	G 18	156
Kincardine	F 3	160
Kinda	D 4	204
Kindberg	C 7	102
Kindeje	D 1	204
Kindersley	F 17	156
Kindia	C 2	200
Kindred	B 6	174
Kinel'	C 4	204
Kineshma	H 15	108
King	A 4	168
Kingaroy	I 10	142
King City	B 1	170
King Edward ⨓	D 9	140
Kingfisher	D 5	162
King George c	D 5	162
King George Bay c	n 17	193 I
King George Island I	B 8	192
King George Sound ⋃	N 5	140
Kingisepp	C 14	66
Kinglake National Park ♦	F 5	144
King Leopold and Queen Astrid Coast ⤳	C 17	208
King Leopold Ranges ⤳	E 8	140
Kingman, Az., U.S.	H 4	176
Kingman, Ks., U.S.	B 8	172
Kingman Reef ⫣²	C 11	136
Kingoonya	K 2	142
Kingri	C 1	122
Kings ⨓	D 5	182
Kings □⁶, Ca., U.S.	F 5	182
Kings □⁶, N.Y., U.S.	F 5	164
Kings Canyon ⋁	I 11	140
Kings Canyon National Park ♦	D 5	182
Kingscote	F 7	144
Kings Mountain	D 5	182
Kings Mountain National Military Park ♦	B 4	168
King Solomon's Mines see Mikhrot Timna' ⊥	J 3	120
Kings Park	F 5	164
Kings Peak ʌ	B 6	178
Kingsport	E 2	162
Kingston, Austl.	j 12	145a
Kingston, Jam.	h 13	186a
Kingston, Ma., U.S.	B 8	164
Kingston, N.S., Can.	F 11	160
Kingston, N.Y., U.S.	F 2	164
Kingston, Oh., U.S.	D 2	162
Kingston, On., Can.	F 5	160
Kingston Southeast	F 2	144
Kingston upon Hull	D 6	72
Kingston upon Thames	E 7	72
Kingstown	u 28	187i
Kingstree	D 6	168
Kingsville	F 4	172
Kingswood	F 4	72
King William Island I	C 13	150
King William's Town	G 7	206
Kinik	E 5	106
Kinistino	E 19	156
Kinkala	B 2	204
Kinna	H 2	64
Kinnaird, B.C., Can.	A 5	178
Kinnaird, B.C., Can.	G 18	156
Kinnaird Head ⟩	C 7	74
Kinneret-Negev Conduit ⨘	F 3	120
Kinojévis ⨓	A 9	166
Kinross	D 5	74
Kinsarvik	B 3	66
Kinshasa (Léopoldville)	C 3	204
Kinsman	C 4	162
Kinston	B 6	168
Kintampo	D 4	200
Kintyre ⟩¹	B 1	72
Kintyre, Mull of ⟩	B 1	72
Kinuso	D 14	156
Kinzua Dam ⤅⁶	E 7	162
Kiowa	A 6	172
Kipahigan Lake ⊚	D 7	158
Kipawa	E 4	160
Kipawa, Lac ⊚¹	D 20	108
Kipievo	D 20	108
Kipili	C 5	204
Kipling	F 7	158
Kipushia	D 5	204
Kirakira	C 10	124
Kirandul	D 5	204
Kirauné	C 6	110
Kirbyville	G 2	172
Kirchbach in Steiermark	D 7	102
Kirchdorf an der Krems	C 7	102
Kirchhain	E 5	98
Kirchheim unter Teck	C 8	100
Kirchmöser	D 9	98
Kirenga ⨓	D 13	114
Kirgiz Range ⤳	A 11	96
Kiribati □¹	D 7	136
Kirikhan	E 4	106
Kirikkale	C 5	118
Kirikkale □³	C 5	118
Kirillov	G 12	108
Kirinyaga □³	H 4	202
Kirishima-Yaku-Kokuritsu-kōen ♦	I 3	126
Kirishima-yama ʌ¹	I 3	126
Kiritimati (Christmas Island) I	D 7	136
Kiriwina Islands II	A 11	138
Kirkby in Ashfield	F 3	113
Kirkcaldy	C 5	74
Kirkcudbright	A 3	72
Kirkenær	B 6	66
Kirkjubøur	n 26	64b
Kirkkonummi	F 11	64
Kirkland, Il., U.S.	A 4	170
Kirkland, Wa., U.S.	B 2	178
Kirkland Lake	D 3	160
Krklareli	B 7	106
Kirklareli □³	B 7	106
Kirklees □⁶	D 5	72
Kirkpatrick, Mount ʌ	E 25	208
Kirksville	B 2	170
Kirkwall	B 5	74
Kirkwood	C 3	170
Kirn	C 4	100
Kirov, Russia	G 18	110
Kirov, Russia	I 11	108
Kirovabad see Gäncä	I 15	110
Kirovgrad	H 23	108
Kirovo-Čepeck	G 19	108
Kirovohrad	E 7	110
Kirovohrad □⁶	A 11	104
Kirovsk, Russia	G 9	108
Kirovsk, Russia	C 10	108
Kirovskaja oblast' □⁶	H 18	108
Kirovskij	B 4	126
Kirrlemuir	D 5	74
Kirs	G 20	108
Kirsanov	C 13	110
Kirşehir	C 6	118
Kirşehir □³	C 6	118
Kirthar Range ⤳	E 10	116
Kiruna	C 10	64
Kirwee	E 4	146
Kiryū	F 7	126
Kiržač	H 13	108
Kisaki	D 6	204
Kisangani	B 4	204
Kisar, Pulau I	G 9	134
Kisaran	M 4	132
Kisbér	C 9	102
Kish, Jazīreh-ye I	I 15	118
Kishangarh Bās	D 2	122
Kishb, Harrat al- ⤳⁹	D 5	200
Kishi	D 5	200
Kishinev see Chişinău	B 10	104
Kishiwada	G 5	126
Kishorganj	E 6	122
Kiši-Karoj, ozero ⊚	J 29	108
Kisiwani	C 6	204
Kiska Island I	k 40	155a
Kiskatinaw ⨓	D 11	156
Kiska Volcano ʌ¹	k 40	155a
Kiskittogisu Lake ⊚	D 9	158
Kiskitto Lake ⊚	D 9	158
Kiskörös	B 5	104
Kiskunfélegyháza	B 5	104
Kiskunhalas	B 5	104
Kiskunsági Nemzeti Park ♦	B 5	104
Kislovodsk	H 13	110
Kismaayo	H 5	202
Kiso ⨓	G 6	126
Kiso-sammyaku ⤳	F 6	164
Kissamos	E 5	106
Kissidougou	E 4	168
Kissimmee	E 5	168
Kissimmee ⨓	F 4	168
Kistigan Lake ⊚	D 12	158
Kisújszállás	B 6	104
Kisumu	H 3	202
Kisvárda	A 6	104
Kiswere	D 6	204
Kita	C 3	200
Kita-Daitō-jima I	K 3	136
Kitaibaraki	F 8	126
Kita-Iō-jima I	G 12	124
Kitakami	F 7	126
Kitakata	F 7	126
Kitakyūshū	H 3	126
Kitale	G 3	202
Kitanda	D 5	204
Kitangari	D 6	204
Kitaya	C 9	126
Kitchener	G 3	160
Kitgum	E 15	64
Kithárah, Khirbat ⊥	J 4	120
Kithira	D 5	106
Kithira I	D 5	106
Kitimat	D 7	156
Kitinen ⨓	C 13	64
Kitscoty	E 16	156
Kitsman'	C 7	110
Kittanning	C 4	162
Kittilä	C 12	66
Kitt Peak National Observatory ▮³	F 3	176
Kitu	D 5	204
Kitunda	D 5	204
Kitwanga	D 7	156
Kitwe	C 4	204
Kitzbühel	C 4	102
Kitzingen	C 8	100
Kiuruvesi	C 7	100
Kivertsi	E 13	64
Kivik	E 7	66
Kivijärvi	C 13	66
Kivu, Lac ⊚	C 4	204
Kiyev see Kyyiv	D 7	110
Kizel	G 22	108
Kizema	F 16	108
Kizil Adalar II	B 8	106
Kizilcahamam	I 8	110
Kizildağ Milli Parkı ♦	E 13	110
Kizil'irmak ⨓	D 9	118
Kiziltepe	D 9	118
Kizljar	H 15	110
Kjustendil	C 7	104
Klaarstroom	G 5	206
Klabat, Gunung ʌ	E 9	134
Kladno	B 10	100
Kladovo	C 7	104
Klagenfurt	C 10	100
Klaipėda	E 10	66
Klaksvík	n 26	64b
Klamath ⨓	B 2	178
Klamath Falls	H 4	178
Klamath Mountains ⤳	C 3	178
Klang	k 21	135b
Klarälven (Trysilelva) ⨓	C 1	132
Klatovy	C 1	132
Klawock	I 28	154
Kleczew	B 2	206
Kleinmachnow	H 3	206
Klein Nauas	B 2	206
Klemtu	D 7	156
Klerksdorp	D 7	206
Kletnja	B 7	102
Kletskij	E 13	110
Kleve	B 3	98
Klimavičy	J 10	108
Klimovo	J 10	108
Klimpfjäll	D 7	64
Klin	J 10	108
Klinaklini ⨓	F 9	156
Klincy	I 10	108

Name	Map Ref.	Page

Klingenthal B 9 100
Klintehamn D 8 66
Klippan D 6 66
Klipplaat G 6 206
Klishkivtsi A 9 104
Kljaz'ma ≃ I 13 108
Ključ C 4 104
Kłobuck C 10 96
Kłodawa B 10 96
Kłodzko C 9 96
Kłomnice C 10 96
Klondike □⁹ D 25 154
Klondike ≃ D 26 154
Klostermansfeld E 8 98
Klosterneuburg B 8 102
Klosters C 5 92
Kloten C 6 82
Klötze D 8 98
Kluane ≃ F 25 154
Kluane Lake ⊜ F 25 154
Kluane National Park ♦ F 25 154
Kluczbork C 10 96
Klungkung I 22 135b
Klutina Lake ⊜ F 22 154
Knaben C 3 66
Knapdale ✦¹ E 3 74
Knäred D 6 66
Knaresborough C 5 72
Knee Lake ⊜, Mb., Can. D 11 158
Knee Lake ⊜, Sk., Can. D 5 158
Kneža D 8 104
Knife River Indian Villages National Historic Site ♦ B 4 174
Knight Inlet c F 8 156
Knights Landing B 2 182
Knik Arm c F 20 154
Knin C 4 104
Knislinge D 7 66
Knittelfeld C 6 102
Knjaževac D 7 104
Knob Lake Junction A 10 160
Knokke-Heist C 2 69
Knossós (Cnossus) ⊥ E 6 106
Knowsley □⁶ D 4 72
Knox F 5 144
Knox, Cape ► D 5 156
Knox Coast ±² C 19 208
Knoxville, Ga., U.S. C 2 168
Knoxville, Il., U.S. B 3 170
Knoxville, Tn., U.S. A 3 168
Knysna G 5 206
Koani D 6 204
Kobayashi H 3 126
Kobe G 5 126
Kobelyaky E 9 110
København (Copenhagen) C 5 68
København □³ C 5 68
Koblenz B 4 100
Koblenz □⁶ B 4 100
K'obo E 4 202
Kobroor, Pulau I G 10 134
Kobryn J 12 64
Kobuk C 16 154
Kobuk ≃ C 14 154
Kobuk Valley National Park ♦ C 12 110
Kobuleti I 12 110
Kocaali B 9 106
Kocaavşar ≃ C 7 106
Kocaeli □³ B 8 106
Kočani E 7 104
Koçarlı D 7 106
Kočečum ≃ C 12 114
Kočerdyk I 25 108
Kočevo G 20 108
Kōch'ang G 1 126
Koch Bihār D 5 122
Kōchi H 4 126
Kōchi □³ H 4 126
Koch Island I C 17 150
Kock C 12 96
Kočubej G 15 110
Kodačdikost E 21 108
Kodaikānal G 3 122
Kodarma E 5 122
Kodiak H 18 154
Kodiak Island I H 18 154
Kodok E 3 202
Kodyma A 10 104
Koës C 3 206
Koffiefontein E 6 206
Köflach C 7 102
Koforidua D 4 200
Kōfu G 7 126
Koga F 7 126
Kogaluc ⊜ B 20 158
Kogaluc, Baie ⊜ B 19 158
Kogaluk ≃ E 20 150
Køge C 5 68
Kogin Baba D 7 200
Kohāt C 2 122
Kohila C 12 66
Kohīma D 6 122
Kohkīlūyeh va Boyer Ahmadī □³ G 14 118
Kohtla-Järve H 15 184
Kohunlich ⊥ H 15 184
Koide F 7 126
Koidu-Sefagu D 2 200
Koigi C 12 66
Koimbani n 18 207d
Koindu D 2 200
Koiva see Gauja ≃ D 12 66
Kojda C 15 108
Kojgorodok F 19 108
Kojonup M 4 140
Kok (Hkok) ≃ H 4 130
Kokčetav J 28 108
Kokčetav □³ J 28 108
Kokee State Park ♦ h 9 181a
Kokemäenjoki ≃ B 11 66
Kokenau F 11 134
Ko Kha E 4 132
Kokhav HaYarden (Belvoir) ⊥ D 4 120
Kokka D 3 202
Koko C 5 200
Kokoda A 10 138
Kokomo B 5 170
Kokong C 5 206
Koko Nor see Qinghai Hu ⊜ H 2 124
Kokrines D 17 154
Koksan-üp G 16 128
Koksoak ≃ E 19 150
Kokstad F 8 206
Kokubu I 3 126
Kokžar E 22 108
Kola B 10 108
Kolaka F 8 134
Kola Peninsula ►¹ B 12 108
Kolár G 3 122
Kolāras D 3 122
Kolār Gold Fields G 3 122
Kolárovo D 4 200
Kolašin D 5 104

Kolbotn C 5 66
Kol'čugino H 13 108
Kolda C 1 200
Kolding C 2 68
Kole B 4 204
Kolea H 7 88
Kolèntèn C 2 200
Kolguev, ostrov I B 18 108
Kolhāpur F 2 122
Kolho A 12 66
Koliba (Corubal) ≃ C 2 200
Koliganek G 16 154
Kolín B 12 100
Koljučinskaja guba c C 7 154
Kolka D 11 66
Kolkas rags ► D 11 66
Kölleda E 8 98
Kollo C 5 200
Kołobrzeg A 8 96
Kologriv G 16 108
Kolokani C 3 200
Kolombangara I A 12 138
Kolomna I 13 108
Kolomyya A 8 104
Kolondiéba C 3 200
Kolonia C 7 136
Kolosib B 1 132
Kolosovka H 30 108
Kolpa (Kupa) ≃ E 6 102
Kolpaševo D 11 114
Kolpino G 9 108
Kol'skij poluostrov see Kola Peninsula ►¹ B 12 108
Koluszki C 10 96
Kolva ≃ C 22 108
Kolwezi E 4 204
Kolyma ≃ C 18 114
Kolyšlej C 14 110
Kom see Qom E 14 114
Kom ≃ E 7 200
Komadugu Yobe (Komadugu Yobé) ≃ C 7 200
Komandorskie ostrova II D 19 114
Komandorski Islands see Komandorskie ostrova II D 19 114
Komárno C 10 102
Komarnyky A 7 104
Komárom C 10 102
Komárom-Esztergom □³ C 10 102
Kornati (Incomati) ≃ D 10 206
Komatipoort C 9 206
Komatsu F 6 126
Kombissiri C 4 200
Komering ≃ F 4 134
Komi □³ E 21 108
Komin-Yanga C 5 200
Komló D 10 102
Kommandokraal G 5 206
Kommunističeskij F 26 108
Kommunizm, Qullai ▲ B 2 122
Kommunizma, pik see Kommunizm, Qullai ▲ B 2 122
Komo ≃ E 7 200
Komodo, Pulau I G 7 134
Komoé ≃ D 4 200
Kom Ombo C 3 202
Komotiní B 6 106
Kompasberg ▲ F 6 206
Komrat see Comrat B 10 104
Komsomolec C 22 110
Komsomolec, ostrov I A 12 114
Komsomolec, zaliv c G 17 110
Komsomol'sk H 13 108
Komsomol'skij I 16 108
Komsomol'sk-na-Amure B 11 124
Komyshuvakha F 9 110
Kona Coast ±² j 10 181a
Konakovo H 12 108
Konan D 3 200
Koňārak F 5 122
Konda ≃ G 27 108
Kondagaon F 4 122
Kondinin M 5 140
Kondinskoe G 27 108
Kondoa C 6 204
Kondopoga E 11 108
Kondrovo I 11 108
Kondukūr F 3 122
Kondūz B 1 122
Koněvo E 13 108
Konfara C 3 200
Kong ≃ H 8 132
Kongakut ≃ B 24 154
Kongbo E 9 200
Kongcheng C 13 130
Kongens Lyngby C 5 68
Kongolo, Zaire D 3 204
Kongolo, Zaire C 4 200
Kongoussi C 4 200
Kongsvinger F 7 66
Kongur Shan ▲ B 3 122
Kongwa D 6 204
Konice D 11 96
Königsberg see Kaliningrad B 2 110
Königsbrück E 10 98
Königsbrunn D 7 100
Königsfelden ♪¹ C 6 82
Königslutter D 7 98
Königssee ⊜ E 9 100
Königswinter F 4 98
Konin B 10 96
Konin □³ B 10 96
Konispol D 5 104
Koňitsa B 4 106
Konjic D 5 82
Konkepe ≃ D 2 206
Konkouré ≃ C 2 200
Konna D 4 200
Konoša F 13 108
Konotop E 10 110
Konqi ≃ A 5 122
Konsankoro D 3 200
Końskie C 11 96
Konstantinovka C 11 96
Konstantinovsk F 12 110
Konstanz E 6 100
Kontagora D 7 200
Kontcha D 7 200
Kontich D 3 69
Kontiomäki E 11 66
Kon Tum G 8 132
Kontum, Plateau du ✗¹ H 8 132
Konya B 5 118
Konya □³ C 5 118
Konz F 4 98
Konžakovskij Kamen', gora ▲ D 8 114

Koocanusa, Lake ⊜¹ A 6 178
Koog aan de Zaan B 3 69
Koolau Range ✗ i 10 181a
Koonga C 12 66
Koopan-Suid D 4 206
Koorawatha E 7 144
Koosa C 13 66
Kooskia A 6 178
Kootenai (Kootenay) ≃ G 13 156
Kootenay (Kootenai) ≃ G 13 156
Kootenay Indian Reserve ✦⁴ A 6 178
Kootenay Lake ⊜ G 13 156
Kootenay National Park ♦ F 13 156
Kopanovka F 15 110
Kópavogur m 20 64a
Kopayhorod A 9 104
Koper E 5 102
Kopervik C 2 66
Kopetdag, hrebet ✗ C 8 116
Köping C 7 66
Koppang B 5 66
Kopparberg □³ B 7 66
Koppies D 7 206
Koprivnica D 8 102
Köprülü Kanyon Milli Parkı ♦ D 9 106
Köprüören C 8 106
Kopylovo F 16 108
Kor ≃ H 15 118
Korab (Korabit, Maja e) ▲ E 6 104
Korabit, Maja e (Korab) ▲ E 6 104
Korablino I 14 108
Kora National Park ♦ H 4 202
Korāput F 4 122
Korarou, Lac ⊜ F 4 198
Korba, India E 4 122
Korba, Tun. G 3 90
Korbach E 5 98
Korbol C 8 200
Korçë B 4 106
Kordestān □³ E 12 118
Kord Kūy D 15 118
Korea, North □¹ E 9 124
Korea, South □¹ E 10 124
Korea Bay c G 14 128
Korea Strait ⋃ G 2 126
Korem E 4 202
Koré Maïroua C 5 200
Korenovsk G 11 110
Korgus D 3 202
Korhogo D 3 200
Korinthiakós Kólpos see Corinth, Gulf of c C 5 106
Kórinthos D 5 106
Kōriyama F 8 126
Korjakskaja Sopka, vulkan ▲ B 15 124
Korjakskoe nagor'e ✗ C 20 114
Korjažma F 17 108
Korkino I 24 108
Korkuteli D 9 106
Korla A 5 122
Körmend C 8 102
Kornati, Nacionalni Park ♦ D 3 104
Kornelimünster F 3 98
Korneuburg B 8 102
Kornsjø C 5 66
Korntal-Münchingen B 6 82
Kornwestheim D 6 100
Koro C 4 200
Koroleve A 7 104
Koronowo B 9 96
Koror D 10 134
Koro Sea ⊼² E 9 136
Korosten' D 6 110
Korostyshiv D 6 110
Koro Toro B 8 200
Korovin Volcano ▲¹ k 44 155a
Korovou m 14 147c
Korpélé E 8 200
Korppoo B 10 66
Korsakov C 12 124
Korselbränna D 7 64
Korsnäs B 7 66
Korso B 12 66
Korsør C 4 68
Korsun'-Shevchenkivs'kyy E 7 110
Kortkeros F 19 108
Kortrijk (Courtrai) D 2 69
Korumburra G 5 144
Korup National Park ♦ B 6 200
Kos D 7 106
Kos I D 7 106
Kosa G 21 108
Koš-Agač B 1 124
Kosaja Gora I 12 108
Koščagyl F 18 110
Košino B 9 96
Kościan C 3 200
Kościerzyna A 10 96
Kosciusko, Mount ▲ F 7 144
Kosciusko National Park ♦ F 7 144
Kose F 12 66
Kōshoku F 7 126
Kosi Bay c D 10 206
Kosju B 11 66
Kösko D 23 108
Koslan E 18 108
Kosong-üp G 17 128
Kosovo-Metohija □⁶ E 6 104
Kosovska Mitrovica D 6 104
Kossindi E 8 200
Kossou, Lac de ⊜¹ D 3 200
Koster C 4 104
Kostomukša D 9 108
Kostopil' D 5 110
Kostroma H 14 108
Kostroma ≃ G 14 108
Kostromskaja oblast' □⁴ G 16 108
Kostrzyn E 10 110
Kostyantynivka C 11 96
Koszalin D 9 96
Koszalin □³ B 9 96
Köszeg B 8 96
Kota, India C 9 122
Kota, India G 23 108
Kota Belud D 7 134
Kota Bharu F 4 132
Kotabumi K 4 134
Kota Kinabalu D 7 134
Kotamobagu F 7 134
Kotari ✦¹ C 3 104
Kota Tinggi N 6 132
Kotcho Lake ⊜ B 11 156
Kotcho ≃ B 11 156
Kotel'nič G 17 108
Kotel'nikovo F 13 110
Kotelny ostrov see Kotel'nyj, ostrov I B 16 114

Kotel'nyj, ostrov I B 16 114
Köthen E 8 98
Kotido G 3 202
Kotka B 13 66
Kotlas F 17 108
Kotlik E 13 154
Koton-Karifi D 6 200
Kotor Varoš C 4 104
Kotouba D 4 200
Kotovo D 14 110
Kotovsk, Russia C 12 110
Kotovs'k, Ukr. B 10 104
Kot Pütli D 3 122
Kotri D 1 122
Kottagüdem F 4 122
Kottayam H 3 122
Kotte see Sri Jayawardenepura H 3 122
Kotto ≃ D 9 200
Kotuj ≃ B 13 114
Kotzebue Sound ⋃ C 13 154
Kötzting C 9 100
Koubia C 2 200
Kouchibouguac National Park ♦ E 11 160
Koudougou C 4 200
Kouéré C 4 200
Kougnohou D 5 200
Kouilou □³ C 1 204
Kouilou ≃ C 1 204
Koulamoutou F 7 200
Koulikoro C 3 200
Koulikoro □³ C 3 200
Koumac D 13 138
Koumameyong E 7 200
Koumbia, Burkina C 4 200
Koumbia, Gui. C 2 200
Koumpentoum C 1 200
Koumra D 8 200
Koundára C 2 200
Koundougou C 3 200
Kounradskij A 11 116
Kountze G 1 170
Koupéla C 4 200
Kouri C 3 200
Kourou B 8 190
Kourouma C 3 200
Kouroussa C 3 200
Koussané C 7 200
Kousséri C 7 200
Koussi, Emi ▲ B 8 200
Koutia Ba C 2 200
Koutiala C 3 200
Kouvola B 13 66
Kovada Milli Parkı ♦ E 12 66
Kovarskas E 12 66
Kovdor C 8 108
Kovdozero, ozero ⊜¹ D 4 110
Kovel' D 4 110
Kovilpatti H 3 122
Kovrov H 14 108
Kovylkino I 15 108
Kovža ≃ F 13 108
Kowalewo Pomorskie B 10 96
Kowanyama Aboriginal Land ✦⁴ C 5 142
Kowie see Port Alfred G 7 206
Kowkcheh ≃ B 2 122
Kowloon G 12 130
Kowŏn-úp G 16 128
Köycegiz Gölü ⊜ D 8 106
Koyuk D 14 154
Koyukuk D 16 154
Koyukuk ≃ D 16 154
Koyukuk, North Fork ≃ C 20 154
Koyukuk, South Fork ≃ C 20 154
Koža H 18 108
Kozan D 6 118
Kozáni B 4 106
Kozara, Nacionalni Park ♦ D 19 114
Kozdinga E 17 108
Kozel'sk I 11 108
Kozienice C 11 96
Kožim D 23 108
Kozlu B 9 106
Koźmin C 9 96
Koz'modemjansk H 17 108
Kožposëlok E 13 108
Kozyatyn E 6 110
Kpalimé D 5 200
Kra, Isthmus of ±³ I 4 132
Kraai ≃ F 7 206
Krabi K 4 132
Krâchéh H 8 132
Kragan k 20 135b
Kragerø C 4 66
Kragujevac C 6 104
Kraichgau ✦¹ B 9 96
Krajenka B 9 96
Krakovets' D 12 96
Kraków C 10 96
Kraków □³ C 10 96
Kraljevica C 3 104
Kraljevo D 6 104
Kralupy nad Vltavou B 11 100
Kramfors E 8 64
Kranenburg E 2 98
Kranídhion D 5 106
Kranj D 10 102
Kranji Reservoir ⊜ i 14 134a
Krapina D 7 102
Krasavino F 16 108
Krasino A 20 108
Kraslava E 13 66
Kraslice E 8 100
Krasnaja Gorbatka I 14 108
Krasnaja Zarja D 11 110
Kraśnik C 12 96
Kraśnik Fabryczny C 12 96
Krasnoarmejsk J 28 108
Krasnoarmejsk F 13 110
Krasnoarmejsk'k C 11 110 (?)
Krasnoarmejskoe H 17 108
Krasnoarmijs'k E 10 110
Krasnobród C 13 66
Krasnodar G 11 110
Krasnodarskij kraj □⁶ G 11 110
Krasnogorskij J 13 108
Krasnogvardejsk I 24 108
Krasnoilsk B 9 104
Krasnojarka G 23 108
Krasnojarsk D 21 110
Krasnojarskij kraj □⁶ C 35 108
Krasnojarskoe vodohranilišče ⊜¹ D 13 114
Krasnokamsk G 21 108
Krasnolesnyj D 11 110
Krasnosel'kupsk A 13 114
Krasnoslobodsk I 16 108
Krasnoturjinsk E 24 108

Krasnoufimsk H 22 108
Krasnoural'sk G 24 108
Krasnousol'skij J 22 108
Krasnovišersk F 22 108
Krasnovodsk see Türkmenbashy B 15 118
Krasnowodsk Aylagy c J 18 110
Krasnoznamensk E 11 66
Krasnye Baki H 16 108
Krasnye Gory C 14 66
Krasnyj Čikoj A 7 128
Krasnyj Guljaj J 17 108
Krasnyj Holm G 12 108
Krasnyj Jar I 30 108
Krasnyj Kut D 15 110
Krasnyj Oktjabr' I 26 108
Krasnyj Sulin F 12 110
Krasnystaw C 12 96
Krasnyj Luch E 11 110
Krasnyy Lyman E 10 110
Kražiai E 11 66
Krbava ✦¹ C 3 104
Krečetovo F 13 108
Krefeld E 3 98
Kremastón, Tekhnití Límni ⊜¹ C 4 106
Kremenchuk E 8 110
Kremenets' D 4 110
Kremenchuk'ke vodoskhovyshche ⊜¹ E 8 110
Kremina E 11 110
Krems an der Donau B 7 102
Kress E 6 100
Kressbronn C 6 82
Kresta, zaliv c D 5 154
Kretinga E 10 66
Kreuzau F 3 98
Kreuzlingen C 7 82
Kreuztal F 4 98
Krēva E 13 66
Kribi E 6 200
Kriebstein, Burg ⊥ E 10 98
Kriel D 8 206
Kriens C 6 82
Křimice C 10 100
Krishna ≃ F 3 122
Krishna, Mouths of the ≃¹ F 4 122
Krishnagiri G 3 122
Krishnanagar E 5 122
Kristiania see Oslo C 5 66
Kristianopel D 8 66
Kristiansand C 4 66
Kristianstad D 6 66
Kristianstad □³ D 6 66
Kristiansund A 10 64
Kristiinankaupunki A 10 66
Kríti (Crete) I E 6 106
Kríti (Crete) □³ E 6 106
Kriva Palanka D 7 104
Krivoj Rog see Kryvyy Rih F 8 110
Krivoye see Kryvyy Rih F 8 110
Križevci D 8 102
Krk, Otok I C 9 96
Krnov C 9 96
Krokek C 8 66
Krokowa A 9 96
Krolevets' D 8 110
Kröller-Müller, Rijksmuseum ♪ A 9 102
Kroměříž C 9 96
Kromhoek B 8 206
Kronach E 8 100
Kronberg ⊥ B 5 68
Kröng Kaôh Kŏng I 6 132
Kronoberg □³ D 7 66
Kronockaja Sopka, vulkan ▲¹ D 19 114
Kronshtadt F 8 108
Kroonstad D 7 206
Kropotkin G 12 110
Krośniewice B 10 96
Krosno D 11 96
Krosno □³ D 12 96
Krotoszyn C 9 96
Krotz Springs G 3 170
Kroya k 19 135b
Kruger National Park ♦ D 9 206
Krugersdorp D 7 206
Krui G 4 134
Kruisfontein H 5 206
Krumbach B 9 100
Krung Thep (Bangkok) H 5 132
Krupka B 10 100
Kruševac D 6 104
Kruševo D 6 104
Krutaja E 21 108
Krutcy D 14 66
Kruzenstern, proliv ⋃ C 14 124
Krychaw H 14 108
Krylbo B 7 66
Krym, Respublika □³ G 9 110
Krymsk G 10 110
Krynica D 11 96
Krynki D 13 66
Kryvyy Rih F 8 110
Kryzhopil' A 10 104
Krzepice C 10 96
Krzeszowice C 10 96
Krzyż B 8 96
Ksar-el-Kebir (Alcazarquivir) D 3 98
Kšenskij D 10 110
Kstovo H 16 108
Kuah K 4 132
Kuala Kangsar L 6 132
Kuala Krai L 6 132
Kuala Kubu Baharu M 5 132
Kuala Lipis L 5 132
Kuala Lumpur M 5 132
Kuala Rompin L 6 132
Kuala Sepetang L 5 132
Kuala Terengganu K 6 132
Kuandian F 12 128
Kuantan M 6 132
Kuban' ≃ G 11 110
Kubenskoe, ozero ⊜ G 13 108
Kuboes B 2 206
Kubokawa H 4 126
Kučema H 14 108
Kuchelbau E 11 98 (?)
Kuching N 10 132
Kuçové B 3 106
Kudat D 7 134
Kudirkos Naumiestis E 11 66
Kudus k 20 135b

Kudymkar G 20 108
Kueda H 21 108
Kuee Ruins ⊥ j 11 181a
Kufrinjah E 5 120
Kufstein C 4 102
Kugaluk ≃ B 29 154
Kugmallit Bay c B 27 154
Kühdasht F 12 118
Kühlungsborn B 8 98
Kuhmo D 14 64
Kuikkol', ozero ⊜ D 22 110
Kuiseb ≃ B 1 206
Kuito D 3 204
Kuiu Island I G 13 130 (?)
Kuivastu C 11 66
Kuja ≃ C 20 108
Kujang-úp G 16 128
Kujawy ✦¹ B 10 96
Kujbyševskij Zaton I 18 108
Kujbyševskoe vodohranilišče ⊜¹ C 16 110
Kujjuarapik see Whapmagoostui A 4 160
Kujū-san ▲¹ H 3 126
Kukaklek Lake ⊜ G 16 154
Kukawa C 7 200
Kukkola C 11 64
Kukmor H 19 108
Kukup N 6 132
Kula, Tur. C 8 106
Kula, Yugo. C 5 104
Kulai N 6 132
Kula Kangri ▲ D 6 122
Kulautuva E 11 66
Kuldīga D 11 66
Kulebaki I 15 108
Kulevčinskij J 24 108
Kulgunino J 22 108
Kulim L 5 132
Kulju B 11 66
Kulmbach B 8 100
Kŭlob C 10 116
Kuloj F 15 108
Kuloj ≃ D 15 108
Kulpawn ≃ D 4 200
Kul'sary F 18 110
Kültepe ⊥ C 6 118
Kulu C 5 118
Kulumadau A 11 138
Kulundinskoe, ozero ⊜ D 11 114
Kum see Qom E 14 114
Kuma ≃ G 14 110
Kumagaya F 7 126
Kumamoto H 3 126
Kumamoto □³ H 3 126
Kumano H 6 126
Kumanovo D 6 104
Kumārghāt B 1 132
Kumasi D 4 200
Kumba B 6 200
Kumbakonam G 3 122
Kumbarilla I 10 142
Kumdanli D 12 106
Kŭm-gang ≃ H 16 128
Kümhwa G 16 128
Kumi G 3 202
Kuminovskoe H 26 108
Kumla C 7 66
Kumluca D 9 106
Kumo D 7 200
Kumskoj G 15 110
Kumta G 2 122
Kümya-úp G 16 128
Kumzār B 1 132
Kunašak I 25 108
Kunašir, ostrov (Kunashiri-tō) I D 13 124
Kunashiri-tō see Kunašir, ostrov I D 13 124
Kunda C 13 66
Kundelungu, Parc National de ♦ E 4 204
Kunene □³ E 2 206
Kunene (Cunene) ≃ F 1 204
Kungälv D 8 66
Kunghit Island I E 8 156
Kungrad H 21 108
Kungsbacka C 5 66
Kungshamn C 5 66
Kungsör C 7 66
Kungur G 22 108
Kunlong C 3 132
Kunlun Shan ✗ C 13 130
Kunming B 7 130
Kunsan G 1 126
Kunszentmárton B 5 104
Kunyu k 20 135b (?)
Kunzelsau B 9 100
Kuolajarvi C 13 64
Kuopio E 13 64
Kuopio □³ E 13 64
Kupang, Indon. H 8 134
Kupang, Teluk c H 8 134
Kupiškis C 12 66
Kupreanof H 28 154
Kupreanof Island I H 28 154
Kup'yans'k-Vuzlovyy E 10 110
Kup'yans'k E 10 110
Kuqa, China A 4 122
Kur ≃, Asia C 13 118
Kur ≃, Russia B 20 128
Kur ≃ (Kür) A 10 118
Kuramata', Harrat ✗⁹ C 5 202
Kurašasaj H 21 110
Kurayoshi L 2 126
Kurčatov D 11 66
Kürdämir C 4 204 (?)
Kurdistan ✦¹ ...

Kurkiëki B 14 66
Kurkliai E 12 66
Kurnool F 3 122
Kurobe F 6 126
Kurort Schmalkalden F 7 98
Kurow F 3 146
Kurovskoe I 13 108
Kurri Kurri D 8 144
Kuršiu nerija (Kuršskaja kosa) ►² E 10 66
Kursk D 10 110
Kurskaja G 14 110
Kurskaja oblast' □⁶ D 9 110
Kuršskaja kosa (Kuršiu nerija) ►² E 10 66
Kurtalan C 9 118
Kürtí I 26 108
Kuruktag ✗ A 5 122
Kuruman D 5 206
Kuruman ≃ D 4 206
Kurume H 3 126
Kurun ≃ F 3 202
Kurunegala H 3 122
Kurunzulaj A 11 128
Kusa B 21 110
Kuşadası D 7 106
Kuş Cenneti Milli Parkı ♦ B 8 106
Kusel C 4 100
Kuş Gölü ⊜ B 7 106
Kushima I 3 126
Kushiro C 10 126
Kushtia E 5 122
Kushui A 6 122
Kusiyārā ≃ F 13 154
Kuskokwim ≃ E 18 154
Kuskokwim, North Fork ≃ E 18 154
Kuskokwim, South Fork ≃ E 18 154
Kuskokwim Bay c G 13 154
Kuskokwim Mountains ✗ E 16 154
Kušmurun J 26 108
Kušmurun, ozero ⊜ J 26 108
Kušnacht C 6 82
Kušnarenkovo I 21 108
Kussharo-ko ⊜ C 10 126
Küssnacht am Rigi E 5 100
Kustanaj (Qostanay) C 23 110
Kustanaj □³ C 23 110
Küstí E 3 202
Kušva G 23 108
Kutabuloh M 3 132
Kütahya C 9 106
Kütahya □³ C 9 106
Kutaisi H 13 110
Kutaradja see Banda Aceh L 2 132
Kutch, Rann of ✦¹ E 8 122
Kutina E 8 102
Kutkai C 3 132
Kutná Hora C 12 100
Kutno B 10 96
Kutse Game Reserve ♦ B 5 206

Kuttusoja C 14 64
Kutu C 2 204
Kuty A 8 104
Kuujjuaq E 19 150
Kuurne D 2 69
Kuusamo C 14 64
Kuusankoski B 13 66
Kuvandyk D 20 110
Kuvšinovo H 10 108
Kuwait □¹ E 6 118
Kuwait, Jün al- (Kuwayt, Jün al-) c B 6 202
Kuwait Bay see Kuwayt, Jün al- c B 6 202
Kuwayt, Jün al- (Kuwait Bay) c B 6 202
Kuyal'nyts'kyy lyman c B 11 104
Kuye ≃ G 8 128
Kuyucak D 8 106
Kuzaranda D 11 108
Kuženkino H 11 108
Kuzneck C 15 110
Kuznečnoe B 14 66
Kuzneckij Alatau ✗ B 11 114
Kuznecovo C 25 108
Kuzomen' G 12 108
Kvænangen ✗ A 10 64
Kvam C 3 66
Kverkfjöll ▲ m 22 64a
Kvichak Bay c G 16 154
Kvikkjokk C 9 64
Kwai see Khwae Noi G 4 132
Kwajalein I¹ C 8 136
Kwakoegron B 7 190
Kwale I 4 202
Kwa Mtoro C 6 204
Kwando (Mashi) ≃ E 4 206
Kwangju G 1 126
Kwango (Cuango) ≃ C 2 204
Kwangyang ... I 16 128
Kwania, Lake ⊜ E 6 204
Kwara □³ D 6 200
KwaZulu-Natal □³ E 9 206
Kwekwe B 9 206
Kweneng □³ C 6 206
Kwenge (Caengo) ≃ C 2 204
Kwesimintim D 4 200
Kwidzyn B 10 96
Kwilu (Cuilo) ≃ C 2 204
Kwinana F 2 140
Kyabé C 8 200
Kyabram F 5 144
Kya-in F 3 132
Kyancutta J 2 144
Kyaukme C 3 132
Kyaukpyu, Myan. D 2 132
Kyaukse B 3 132
Kyeburn F 3 146
Kyeintali D 2 132
Kyiv see Kyyiv D 7 110
Kyjov G 12 100
Kyle F 3 146
Kymijoki ≃ B 13 66
Kyn G 22 108
Kyoga, Lake ⊜ A 6 204
Kyŏnggi-do □³ F 14 128
Kyŏnggi-man c H 16 128
Kyŏngju H 16 128
Kyŏngsang-bukto □³ H 17 128

⌐ Waterfall ⋃ Strait c Bay, Gulf ⊜ Lake ⋿ Swamp ⊠ Ice Feature ⊤ Other Hydrographic Feature ✦ Submarine Feature □ Political Unit ♪ Cultural Institution ⊥ Historical Site ♦ Recreational Site ⊞ Airport ■ Military Installation ✦ Miscellaneous

Symbols in the index entries represent the broad categories identified in the key at the right. Symbols with superior numbers (⋋[1]) identify subcategories (see complete key on page 242).

⋀ Mountain   ⋋ Mountains   )(Pass   ⋁ Valley   ≈ Plain   ► Cape   I Island   II Islands   ◆ Other Topographic Feature   ≃ River   ⇌ Canal

Lenhovda — Los Santos de Maimona

Name **Map Ref. Page**

Lenhovda D 7 66
Leninabad see Khojand A 1 122
Leninakan see Gyumri I 13 110
Leningrad see Sankt-Peterburg F 9 108
Leningradskaja oblast' □6 G 10 108
Leningradskoe J 29 108
Leninogorsk, Kaz. D 11 114
Leninogorsk, Russia I 19 108
Lenin Peak ∧ B 2 122
Leninsk, Russia I 23 108
Leninsk, Uzb. A 2 122
Leninskij I 12 108
Leninskoe, Kaz. I 26 108
Leninskoe, Russia B 19 128
Lennestadt E 5 98
Lennonville J 4 140
Lennox and Addington □6 B 1 164
Lennoxville A 7 164
Lenoir B 4 168
Lenore Lake ⊜ E 19 156
Lenormand, Lac ⊜ A 6 160
Lenox, Ga., U.S. D 3 168
Lenox, Tn., U.S. D 4 170
Lens B 9 78
Lensk C 14 114
Lenskoe G 25 108
Lenti D 8 102
Lentini G 5 94
Lentsweletau C 6 206
Lentua ⊜ D 14 64
Lentvaris E 12 66
Lenyenye B 9 206
Lenzburg C 6 82
Léo C 4 200
Leoben C 7 102
Leominster, Eng., U.K. E 4 72
Leominster, Ma., U.S. D 7 164
Léon, Fr. E 2 80
León, Mex. G 9 184
León, Nic. E 3 186
León, Spain B 5 86
León □6 B 5 86
Leon ≃ E 5 172
Léon, Pays de ✢1 D 2 78
Leonardville F 6 174
Leonberg D 5 100
Leonding B 6 102
Leonforte G 4 94
Leongatha G 5 144
Leonora K 6 140
Leonville G 2 170
Léopold II, Lac see Mai-Ndombe, Lac ⊜ C 2 204
Leopoldina D 9 194
Leopoldsburg C 4 69
Léopoldville see Kinshasa C 2 204
Leova B 10 104
Le Palais E 3 78
Lepanto see Návpaktos C 4 106
Lepe G 3 86
Le Péage-de-Roussillon E 2 82
Lepel' E 14 66
Le Petit-Quevilly C 7 78
Lephepe B 6 206
Leping D 13 130
L'Épiphanie F 7 160
Le Pont-de-Beauvoisin E 3 82
Le Port q 20 207e
Lepsy (Lepsi) A 12 116
Le Puy E 1 82
Léraba ≃ D 4 200
Léré, Chad D 7 200
Lere, Nig. C 6 200
Lerici C 2 90
Lérida see Lleida C 5 88
Lérida (Lleida) □6 C 6 88
Lerma B 7 86
Le Roy F 7 174
Lerum D 6 66
Lerwick g 9 74a
Les Abymes n 21 187e
Les Andelys C 8 78
Les Borges Blanques C 5 88
Lésbos I C 7 106
L'Escala F 7 80
Lescar E 3 80
Les Cayes D 6 186
Les Collines-de-l'Outaouais □6 A 3 164
Lesdiboderi D 7 200
Les Échelles E 3 82
Leshan D 6 130
Les Herbiers F 5 78
Lesina C 5 94
Les Jardins-de-Napierville □6 A 5 164
Lesjaskog E 3 64
Lesko D 12 96
Leskovac D 6 104
Leskov Island I J 12 188
Les Laurentides see Laurentides, Les ✢1 E 8 160
Leslie, Mi., U.S. B 1 162
Leslie, S. Afr. D 8 206
Les Maskoutains □6 A 6 164
Les Matelles E 7 80
Les Moulins □6 A 5 164
Lesneven D 2 78
Lesnoe G 11 108
Lesnoj H 27 108
Lesopil'noe C 19 128
Lesosibirsk D 12 114
Lesotho □1 K 10 196
Lesozavodsk B 4 126
Lesozavodskij C 10 108
Les Pays-d'en-Haut □6 A 4 164
Les Riceys D 11 78
Les Sables-d'Olonne B 2 80
Lessebo D 7 66
Lesser Antilles II D 9 186
Lesser Caucasus ∧ B 12 118
Lesser Slave ≃ D 14 156
Lesser Slave Lake ⊜ D 14 156
Lesser Sunda Islands II, Indon. G 8 134
Lesser Sunda Islands see Tenggara, Nusa II, Indon. B 7 140
Lessines D 2 69
Lestijoki ≃ E 12 64
Le Sueur C 2 166
Leszno C 9 96
Leszno □3 C 9 96
Letaba ≃ B 9 206
Letchworth F 6 72
Letchworth State Park ♦ B 4 162
Le Teil F 2 82
Lethbridge G 15 156
Leti, Kepulauan II G 9 134
Leticia D 5 190
Letka G 18 108
Letlhakane A 6 206
Letlhakeng C 7 206
Letpadan F 2 132
Le Trayas G 4 82
Le Tréport B 8 78
Letter D 6 98
Letterkenny B 4 75
Letychiv E 5 110
Leu C 8 104
Leuk D 5 82
Leuser, Gunung ∧ M 3 132
Leušinskij Tuman, ozero ⊜ G 26 108
Leutkirch E 7 100
Leuven D 3 69
Leuze D 2 69
Levack E 3 160
Levádhia C 5 106
Le Val-Saint-François □6 A 6 164
Levan C 3 176
Levante, Riviera di ✢2 E 5 92
Levanto E 5 92
Levelland D 2 172
Levelock G 16 154
Leveque, Cape > E 7 140
Leverano D 7 94
Leverkusen E 4 98
Levice B 10 102
Levier D 4 82
Levin D 5 146
Lévis E 8 160
Levisa Fork ≃ E 2 162
Levittown, N.Y., U.S. F 5 164
Levittown, Pa., U.S. F 4 164
Levittown, P.R. j 15 187b
Lévka Óri ∧ E 6 106
Levkás C 4 106
Levkás I C 4 106
Levkímmi C 3 106
Lévki Óri National park ♦ E 5 106
Levkosia see Nicosia E 5 118
Levroux F 8 78
Levuka m 14 147c
Lewe E 2 132
Lewes H 3 164
Lewis G 5 174
Lewis □6 C 3 164
Lewis, Butt of > B 2 74
Lewis, Isle of I B 2 74
Lewis and Clark Caverns State Park ♦ C 8 178
Lewis and Clark Lake ⊜1 D 6 174
Lewis and Clark Range ∧ B 7 178
Lewisburg, Pa., U.S. F 2 164
Lewisburg, Tn., U.S. E 5 170
Lewisporte D 16 160
Lewis Range ∧ A 7 178
Lewiston, Id., U.S. B 5 178
Lewiston, Me., U.S. A 8 162
Lewiston, Mi., U.S. A 1 162
Lewistown, Il., U.S. B 3 170
Lewistown, Mt., U.S. B 9 178
Lewistown, Pa., U.S. C 5 162
Lewisville D 5 172
Lewisville Lake ⊜1 D 5 172
Lexington, Ga., U.S. C 3 168
Lexington, Ky., U.S. C 6 170
Lexington, Ma., U.S. D 7 164
Lexington, Mo., U.S. C 2 170
Lexington, N.C., U.S. B 4 168
Lexington, S.C., U.S. B 4 168
Lexington, Tx., U.S. E 5 172
Lexington, Va., U.S. E 4 162
Lexington Park D 5 162
Leyden see Leiden B 3 69
Leye F 8 130
Leyland D 4 72
Leyte I C 8 134
Leyte Gulf c C 9 134
Lezhi C 7 130
Lëzna B 7 110
L'gov D 9 110
Lhasa D 6 122
Lhasa ≃ C 6 122
Lhokna L 2 132
Lhokseumawe L 3 132
Lhorong C 3 130
L'Hospitalet de Llobregat C 7 88
Li I 4 132
Li ≃ D 9 130
Liamuiga, Mount ∧1 m 20 187d
Lian ≃ F 11 130
Liancheng F 13 130
Liangbao A 10 130
Liangdang B 7 130
Liangping C 8 130
Liangyuan B 13 130
Lianjiang H 10 130
Liannan F 11 130
Lianxian F 11 130
Lianyuan E 10 130
Lianyungang I 12 128
Liao ≃ F 14 128
Liaocheng H 10 128
Liaodong Bandao >1 G 14 128
Liaodong Wan c F 13 128
Liaoning □3 F 14 128
Liaoyang F 14 128
Liaoyuan E 15 128
Liaozhong F 14 128
Liapádhes C 3 106
Liard ≃ D 8 150
Libagon C 9 134
Libby A 6 178
Libby Dam ✢6 A 6 178
Liberal, Ks., U.S. G 4 174
Liberal, Mo., U.S. G 7 174
Liberec B 12 100
Liberia F 3 186
Liberia □1 H 6 196
Libertador General Bernardo O'Higgins □3 D 2 195
Liberty, Ky., U.S. A 2 168
Liberty, Mo., U.S. C 1 170
Liberty, S.C., U.S. B 3 168
Liberty, Tx., U.S. G 1 170
Libertyville A 4 170
Libibi E 2 204
Libo F 8 130
Liboi G 5 202
Libourne D 3 80
Libramont E 4 69
Libreville E 6 200
Libya □1 F 9 196
Libyan Desert ✢2 D 6 196
Licancábur, Volcán ∧1 D 6 192
Licantén D 1 195
Licata G 3 94
Lice C 9 118
Lich B 5 100
Licheng H 9 128
Lichfield E 5 72
Lichinga E 6 204
Lichtenau E 6 98
Lichtenburg D 7 206
Lichtenfels B 8 100
Lichtenstein F 9 98
Lichtenstein, Schloss ⫸ D 6 100
Lichtervelde C 2 69
Lichuan, China E 13 130
Lichuan, China C 9 130
Lickershamn D 9 66
Licking ≃ D 1 162
Licungo ≃ F 6 204
Lida F 12 66
Liden E 8 64
Lidice ♦ B 11 100
Lidköping C 6 66
Lido di Ostia ✢8 E 4 90
Lidzbark B 10 96
Lidzbark Warmiński A 11 96
Liebertwolkwitz E 9 98
Liebig, Mount ∧ H 11 140
Liechtenstein □1 F 9 62
Liège (Luik) D 4 69
Liège □3 D 4 69
Lielvārde D 12 66
Lienen D 4 98
Lienz D 4 102
Liepāja D 10 66
Lier C 3 69
Liesjärven kansallispuisto ♦ B 11 66
Liestal C 5 82
Liévin B 9 78
Lièvre ≃ F 6 160
Liezen C 6 102
Lifanga B 3 204
Lifford B 4 75
Lifoku F 9 200
Lifou I D 14 138
Ligasa B 3 204
Lightning Ridge B 7 144
Lignières F 9 78
Ligny-en-Barrois B 3 82
Ligonha ≃ F 6 204
Ligonier B 6 170
Liguria □3 E 5 92
Ligurian Sea ⫪2 F 4 92
Lihoslavl' H 11 108
Lihue h 9 181a
Lihuel Calel, Parque Nacional ♦ E 5 195
Lihula C 11 66
Lijiang E 5 130
Likasi E 4 204
Likimi B 3 204
Likoma Island I E 5 204
Likouala □3 B 2 204
Likouala ≃ C 2 204
Lilanga C 3 204
L'Île-Rousse i 8 83a
Lilienthal C 5 98
Liling E 11 130
Lilla Edet C 6 66
Lille B 10 78
Lillebælt (Little Belt) ꞩ C 2 68
Lillebonne C 7 78
Lillehammer B 5 66
Lillerød C 5 68
Lillers B 9 78
Lillestrøm C 5 66
Lillhärdal B 7 66
Lillo E 7 86
Lillooet ≃ G 10 156
Lilongwe E 5 204
Liloy D 8 134
Lilydale i 12 145a
Lim ≃ D 5 104
Lima, N.Y., U.S. D 1 164
Lima, Oh., U.S. C 1 162
Lima, Peru F 3 190
Limarí ≃ B 2 195
Limassol see Lemesós E 5 118
Limavady A 5 75
Limay D 8 78
Limay ≃ G 6 192
Limbach-Oberfrohna F 9 98
Limbe, Cam. E 6 200
Limbe, Mwi. F 6 204
Limbueta E 2 204
Limburg □3, Bel. D 4 69
Limburg □3, Neth. C 4 69
Limburg an der Lahn B 5 100
Limburgerhof C 5 100
Lim Chu Kang i 14 134a
Limeira E 7 194
Limerick (Luimneach), Ire. D 3 75
Limerick, Sk., Can. G 18 156
Limerick □3 D 3 75
Limestone g 12 163a
Limestone ≃ C 11 158
Limestone, Lake ⊜1 E 5 172
Limfjorden ⊜ B 2 68
Limmared D 6 66
Limmen Bight c C 2 142
Límnos I C 6 106
Limoges C 5 80
Limon F 3 174
Limone Piemonte E 3 92
Limons C 7 80
Limoux E 6 80
Limpopo ≃ C 10 206
Linahamari B 15 64
Linapacan Island I C 7 134
Linares, Chile D 2 195
Linares, Mex. E 10 184
Linares, Spain F 7 86
Lincang G 6 130
Lincoln, Ar., U.S. E 1 170
Lincoln, Arg. D 7 195
Lincoln, Eng., U.K. D 6 72
Lincoln, Il., U.S. B 4 170
Lincoln, Ne., U.S. E 6 174
Lincoln Boyhood National Memorial ♦ C 5 170
Lincoln Cathedral ⫸1 D 6 72
Lincoln City C 2 178
Lincoln Park, Ga., U.S. C 2 168
Lincoln Park, Mi., U.S. B 2 162
Lincoln Sea ⫪2 A 14 148
Lincolnshire □6 D 6 72
Lincoln's New Salem State Park ♦ B 4 170
Lincolnton C 3 168
Lind B 4 178
Linda A 2 182
Lindau E 6 100
Linden, Guy. B 7 190
Linden, Mi., U.S. D 7 166
Linden, Tn., U.S. E 5 170
Lindenhurst F 5 164
Lindenwold G 4 164
Lindesberg C 7 66
Lindesnes > D 3 66
Lindhos D 8 106
Lindhos ⊥ D 7 106
Lindi D 6 204
Lindi □3 D 6 204
Lindi ≃ B 4 204
Lindian C 15 128
Lindome D 5 66
Lindsay, Ca., U.S. D 4 182
Lindsay, On., Can. F 4 160
Line Islands II D 12 136
Lineville C 2 168
Linfen H 8 128
Linganamakki Reservoir ⊜1 G 2 122
Lingao I 9 130
Lingayen B 8 134
Lingbi B 13 130
Lingbo B 8 66
Lingchuan I 9 128
Lingen D 4 98
Lingfengwei F 12 130
Lingga, Kepulauan II, Indon. N 7 132
Lingga, Kepulauan II, Indon. F 4 134
Lingolsheim D 4 100
Lingqiu G 10 128
Lingshan C 9 132
Lingshi H 8 128
Lingshui I 10 130
Linguère B 1 200
Lingwu G 6 128
Lingxian E 11 130
Lingyuan F 12 128
Linh, Ngoc ∧ G 8 132
Linhai D 15 130
Linhares C 10 194
Linhe F 6 128
Linjiang F 16 128
Linköping C 7 66
Linkou D 18 128
Linkuva D 12 66
Linnansaaren kansallispuisto ♦ E 14 64
Linqing H 10 128
Linqu H 12 128
Linquan B 12 130
Linru A 11 130
Lins D 6 194
Linstead h 12 186a
Lintan A 6 130
Lintao I 4 128
Linté D 7 200
Lintong A 9 130
Lintorf E 3 98
Linwu F 11 130
Linxi E 11 128
Linxia I 4 128
Linxian H 8 128
Linyi, China H 11 128
Linyi, China I 12 128
Linz, Aus. B 6 102
Linz, Ger. B 4 100
Linzgau ✢1 E 6 100
Linzolo F 7 200
Lio Matoh E 7 134
Lion, Golfe du (Lion, Gulf of) c A 8 84
Lion, Gulf of see Lion, Golfe du c A 8 84
Lionel Town i 12 186a
Liouesso B 2 204
Lipa C 8 134
Lipari F 4 94
Lipcani A 9 104
Lipeck C 11 110
Lipeckaja oblast' □6 C 11 110
Lipicy J 12 108
Liping E 9 130
Lipniški E 12 66
Lipno J 9 64
Lipno, údolní nádrž ⊜1 D 10 100
Lipova B 6 104
Lippe ≃ E 5 98
Lippstadt E 5 98
Liptovský Mikuláš D 10 96
Lipu F 10 130
Lira G 3 202
Liranga C 2 204
Liri ≃ C 3 94
Lisakovsk C 23 110
Lisala B 3 204
Lisboa (Lisbon) F 1 86
Lisbon, Oh., U.S. C 3 162
Lisbon see Lisboa, Port. F 1 86
Lisbonne □3 F 1 86
Lisburn B 5 75
Lisburne, Cape > B 11 154
Lisburne Peninsula >1 B 12 154
Lishe ≃ F 5 130
Lishi H 8 128
Lishu E 15 128
Lishui D 14 130
Lishuzhen D 18 128
Lisieux C 7 78
Lisitu D 5 204
Liski D 11 110
L'Isle-Adam C 9 78
L'Isle-sur-le-Doubs C 4 82
Lismore, Austl. B 9 144
Lismore, Austl. G 4 144
Lismore Castle ⊥ D 4 75
Lisse B 3 69
Lissone E 7 82
Listowel G 3 160
Lit E 7 64
Litang C 5 130
Litang ≃ D 5 130
Līṭānī, Nahr al- ≃ C 4 120
Litchfield, Mn., U.S. C 7 174
Litchfield, Ne., U.S. E 5 174
Litchfield □6 E 5 164
Litchfield National Park ♦ C 11 140
Lithgow D 8 144
Lithonia C 2 168
Lithuania □1 D 12 62
Lititz F 2 164
Litoměřice B 11 100
Litomyšl D 9 96
Litovko B 20 128
Littau C 6 82
Little ≃ E 5 172
Little Abaco I F 6 168
Little Andaman I G 6 122
Little Belt see Lillebælt ꞩ C 2 68
Little Bighorn ≃ C 10 178
Little Bighorn Battlefield National Monument ♦ C 10 178
Little Billabong E 6 144
Little Buffalo ≃ A 15 156
Little Cayman I D 4 186
Little Churchill ≃ C 11 158
Little Colorado ≃ E 3 176
Little Current E 3 160
Little Current ≃ F 16 158
Little Deschutes ≃ D 3 178
Little Desert ✢2 F 3 144
Little Desert National Park ♦ F 3 144
Little Diomede Island I D 10 154
Little Falls C 4 164
Littlefield D 2 172
Little Gold ≃ F 9 140
Littlehampton G 6 72
Little Inagua I C 6 186
Little Kanawha ≃ D 3 162
Little Karoo ✢1 G 4 206
Little Lake ⊜ H 3 170
Little London h 11 186a
Little Mecatina (Petit Mécatina) ≃ B 13 160
Little Minch, The see The Little Minch ꞩ C 2 74
Little Missouri ≃, Ar., U.S. F 2 170
Little Missouri ≃, U.S. B 3 174
Little Nicobar I H 6 122
Little Pine and Lucky Man Indian Reserve ✢4 E 17 156
Little Powder ≃ C 2 174
Little Rann of Kachchh ✢1 E 2 122
Little Red River Indian Reserve ✢4 E 19 156
Little Rock E 2 170
Little Sable Point > D 5 166
Little Sachigo Lake ⊜ D 12 158
Little Salmon Lake ⊜ E 27 154
Little Sandy Creek ≃ D 9 178
Little Scarcies ≃ D 2 200
Little Sioux ≃ E 7 174
Little Smoky ≃ D 13 156
Littlestown G 1 164
Littleton, Co., U.S. C 6 176
Littleton, W.V., U.S. D 3 162
Little Zab ≃ E 10 118
Littoral □3 E 7 200
Litvínov B 10 100
Liu ≃ F 9 130
Liuaniua see Ontong Java I1 D 7 136
Liucheng F 9 130
Liuhe E 15 128
Liuku B 4 132
Liuwa Plain National Park ♦ E 3 204
Liuyang D 11 130
Liuzhou F 9 130
Livada B 7 104
Līvāni D 13 66
Lively B 8 166
Lively Island I o 18 193b
Live Oak A 2 182
Livermore, Ca., U.S. C 2 182
Livermore, Ia., U.S. D 7 174
Liverpool, Eng., U.K. D 4 72
Liverpool, Pa., U.S. F 1 164
Liverpool, Cape > B 17 150
Liverpool Bay c B 29 154
Livigno C 6 92
Livingston, Ca., U.S. C 3 182
Livingston, Guat. J 15 184
Livingston, Scot., U.K. B 3 72
Livingston, Tx., U.S. G 1 170
Livingstone, Nf., Can. B 10 160
Livingstone, Zam. F 4 204
Livingstone, Lake ⊜1 E 6 172
Livingstone Falls ⌊ C 1 204
Livingston Island I L 7 192
Livno D 4 104
Livny C 10 110
Livonia, Mi., U.S. B 2 162
Livonia, N.Y., U.S. B 5 162
Livorno F 6 92
Livorno □6 F 6 92
Liwan G 4 202
Liwonde National Park ♦ F 5 204
Lixian, China D 10 130
Lixian, China A 7 130
Lixin B 13 130
Lixoúrion C 4 106
Lixus ⊥ B 3 198
Liyang C 14 130
Lizarra see Estella B 3 88
Ljadiny F 13 108
Ljamca D 12 108
Ljamin ≃ E 29 108
Ljan C 5 66
Ljuban' G 9 108
Ljubča F 13 66
Ljubercy I 12 108
Ljubimec E 9 104
Ljubinje D 5 104
Ljubljana D 6 102
Ljubohna J 10 108
Ljubuški D 14 104
Ljudinovo J 11 108
Ljungby D 6 66
Ljungbyholm D 8 66
Ljungskile C 5 66
Ljusina J 13 64
Ljusnan ≃ F 7 64
Ljutomer D 8 102
Llaima, Volcán ∧1 F 2 195
Llancanelo, Laguna ⊜ D 3 195
Llandaff Cathedral ⫸1 F 3 72
Llandrindod Wells E 3 72
Llandudno D 3 72
Llanelli F 2 72
Llanfyllin E 3 72
Llangollen E 3 72
Llano E 4 172
Llano Estacado see Estacado, Llano ≃ D 2 172
Llanos ≃ B 4 190
Llanquihue, Lago ⊜ H 5 192
Llantrisant F 3 72
Llanwrtyd Wells E 3 72
Lleida (Lérida) C 5 88
Llerena F 5 86
Lleulleu, Lago ⊜ F 1 195
Lleyn Peninsula >1 E 2 72
Llíria E 4 88
Llivia B 6 88
Llodio A 7 86
Lloret de Mar G 6 80
Lloyd Lake ⊜ C 17 156
Lloydminster E 17 156
Llucena D 4 88
Llucmajor E 7 88
Llullaillaco, Cerro ∧1 D 6 192
Lo ≃ H 7 130
Loa ≃ D 5 192
Loa, Mauna ∧1 j 11 181a
Loanda see Luanda, Ang. D 1 204
Loanda, Braz. E 4 194
Loange (Luangue) ≃ D 3 204
Loango D 1 204
Loano E 4 92
Lobamba D 9 206
Loban D 16 108
Lobatse C 6 206
Löbau E 11 98
Lobaye □3 E 8 200
Lobaye ≃ E 8 200
Lobería F 8 195
Łobez B 8 96
Lobito E 1 204
Lobitos D 2 190
Lobos D 8 195
Lobos, Isla de I D 10 195
Lobva G 24 108
Locarno D 6 82
Locate Triulzi E 7 82
Lochem B 5 69
Loch Garman see Wexford D 5 75
Lochgilphead D 3 74
Lochinvar National Park ♦ F 4 204
Lochmaben B 3 72
Lochristi C 2 69
Lochsa ≃ B 6 178
Lock L 2 142
Lockerbie B 3 72
Lockhart F 5 172
Lockhart River Aboriginal Land ✢4 B 6 142
Lock Haven C 5 162
Löcknitz C 11 98
Lockport B 4 162
Locks Heath G 5 72
Locminé E 4 78
Loc Ninh I 8 132
Locri Epizefiri ⊥ F 6 94
Locust Fork ≃ E 5 170
Locust Grove D 1 170
Lod F 3 120
Loddon ≃ E 4 144
Lodejnoe Pole F 10 108
Löderburg E 8 98
Lodge Creek ≃ G 17 156
Lodgepole E 14 156
Lodhrān D 2 122
Lodi, Ca., U.S. B 2 182
Lodi, Italy D 5 92
Lodi, Wi., U.S. D 4 166
Lodi □6 D 5 92
Lodja C 3 204
Lodwar G 4 202
Łódź C 10 96
Łódź □3 C 10 96
Loei F 5 132
Lofa ≃ D 2 200
Lofer C 4 102
Lofoten II B 6 64
Log E 13 110
Loga C 4 98
Logan, Austl. A 9 144
Logan, N.M., U.S. C 2 172
Logan, Ut., U.S. E 8 178
Logan, W.V., U.S. E 3 162
Logan, Mount ∧ F 24 154
Logan Martin Lake ⊜1 F 5 170
Logan Mountains ∧ F 30 154
Logan Pass)(A 7 178
Logansport B 5 170
Logirim G 3 202
Logone ≃ D 8 200
Logone Gana C 7 200
Logone-Occidental □3 D 8 200
Logone-Oriental □3 D 8 200
Logroño B 2 88
Logrosán E 5 86
Logtāk Lake ⊜ E 6 122
Logudoro ✢1 I 4 92
Løgumkloster C 1 68
Lohiniva C 12 64
Lohit ≃ D 3 130
Lohmar F 4 98
Lohne, Ger. J 4 64
Löhne, Ger. D 5 98
Lohr am Main C 6 100
Loi (Nanlei) ≃ H 5 130
Loi-kaw E 3 132
Loimaa B 11 66
Loimijoki ≃ B 11 66
Loir ≃ D 8 78
Loire □3 E 2 82
Loire ≃ E 3 76
Loire-Atlantique □3 E 5 78
Loiret □3 D 9 78
Loir-et-Cher □3 E 8 78
Loitz C 10 98
Loja, Ec. D 3 190
Loja, Spain G 6 86
Loka B 2 204
Lokan tekojärvi ⊜1 C 13 64
Lökbatan I 16 110
Løken C 5 66
Lokeren C 3 69
Lokhvytsya D 8 110
Lokichar G 4 202
Lokitaung G 4 202
Lokofa-Bokolongo B 2 204
Lokoja D 6 200
Lokoro ≃ C 3 204
Loks Land I D 20 150
Lol F 2 202
Lol ≃ F 2 202
Lolengi F 9 200
Loliondo C 6 204
Lolland I D 4 68
Lollar B 5 100
L'Olleria F 4 88
Lolo B 6 178
Lolodorf E 7 200
Lolo Pass)(B 6 178
Lom, Bul. D 7 104
Lom, Czech Rep. B 10 100
Lom, Nor. B 4 66
Lom ≃ D 7 200
Loma, Point > H 6 182
Lomagne ✢1 A 6 88
Lomami ≃ C 3 204
Lomas de Monreal G 3 176
Lomas de Zamora D 8 195
Lombardia □3 D 5 92
Lombe D 2 204
Lomblen, Pulau I G 8 134
Lombok I G 7 134
Lomé D 5 200
Lomela C 3 204
Lomela ≃ C 3 204
Lomié E 7 200
Lommatzsch E 10 98
Lomme B 9 78
Lommel C 4 69
Lomond, Loch ⊜ D 4 74
Lomonosov G 8 108
Lomonosovka J 27 108
Lomovoe D 14 108
Lompoc F 3 182
Lom Sak F 5 132
Łomża B 12 96
Łomża □3 B 12 96
Lonato D 6 92
Lonāvale F 2 122
Loncoche F 1 195
London, Eng., U.K. F 6 72
London, Ky., U.S. E 1 162
London, On., Can. G 3 160
Londonderry, N.H., U.S. D 7 164
Londonderry, N. Ire., U.K. B 4 75
Londonderry □8 B 4 75
Londonderry, Cape > C 9 140
Londrina E 5 194
Lone Grove C 5 172
Lone Star F 1 170
Long ≃ F 9 130
Longa ≃ E 1 204
Longarone C 8 92
Longaví D 2 195
Long Beach, Ca., U.S. G 5 182
Long Beach, Ms., U.S. G 4 170
Long Beach, N.Y., U.S. F 5 164
Long Branch F 5 164
Longchang D 7 130
Longchuan, China F 3 130
Longchuan, China F 12 130
Longchuan (Shweli) ≃ G 3 130
Long Creek C 4 178
Long Eaton E 5 72
Longford, Austl. G 6 144
Longford, Ire. C 4 75
Longford □3 C 4 75
Longhorn Cavern State Park ♦ E 4 172
Long Hu ⊜ D 13 130
Longhua F 11 128
Longido C 6 204
Longiram F 7 134
Long Island I, Bah. C 6 186
Long Island I, N.Y., U.S. F 6 164
Long Island Sound ꞩ E 5 164
Longjiang C 14 128
Longleat ⫸ F 4 72
Longli E 8 130
Longling F 4 130
Longmeadow D 6 164
Longmont E 2 174
Longnan F 12 130
Longnawan E 6 134
Longny-au-Perche D 7 78
Long Prairie C 7 174
Longquan D 14 130
Long Range Mountains ∧ D 15 160
Longreach G 7 142
Long Reef ✣2 B 11 138
Longsheng F 9 130
Longs Peak ∧ B 6 176
Long Tom ≃ C 2 178
Longton G 6 174
Longuenesse B 9 78
Longueuil F 7 160
Longuyon A 3 82
Longview, Tx., U.S. F 1 170
Longview, Wa., U.S. B 2 178
Longwood Park B 5 168
Longwy A 3 82
Longxi I 5 128
Longxian A 8 130
Long Xuyen I 7 132
Longyan F 13 130
Longyou D 14 130
Longzhou G 8 130
Lonigo D 7 92
Löningen D 4 98
Lonquimay, Volcán ∧1 F 2 195
Lönsboda D 7 66
Lons-le-Saunier D 3 82
Lonton B 3 132
Loogootee C 5 170
Lookout, Cape > B 6 168
Lookout Mountain ∧ E 6 170
Lookout Pass)(B 6 178
Loolmalassin ∧1 C 6 204
Loomis E 5 174
Loon Lake C 14 156
Loon Lake ⊜ D 7 158
Lopatina, gora ∧ B 12 124
Lopatka, Cape see Lopatka, mys > B 15 124
Lopatka, mys > B 15 124
Lopatovo D 14 66
Lop Buri G 5 132
Lopez, Cap > F 6 200
Lop Nor see Lop Nur ⊜ A 6 122
Lop Nur (Lop Nor) ⊜ A 6 122
Lopori ≃ B 3 204
Lopšen'ga D 12 108
Lopuhovka D 14 110
Łopuszno C 11 96
Lora, Hāmūn-i- ⊜ E 10 116
Lora Creek ≃ J 2 142
Lora del Río G 5 86
Lorain C 2 162
Loralai C 1 122
Lorca G 3 88
Lord Howe Island I G 7 136
Lordsburg F 4 176
Loreley ♦ B 4 100
Lorena E 8 194
Lorenzo Geyres C 9 195
Lorestān □3 F 13 118
Loreto A 9 190
Loretto E 5 170
Lorian Swamp ⩩ G 4 202
Lorica F 5 186
Lorient E 3 78
Lőrinci B 5 104
Loriol-sur-Drôme F 2 82
Lorman G 3 170
Lorn, Firth of c D 3 74
Lorna Glen J 6 140
Lorne G 4 144
Loronyo G 3 202
Lorquí F 3 88
Lörrach E 4 100
Lorraine □9 A 4 82
Lorris E 9 78
Los Alamos, Ca., U.S. F 3 182
Los Alamos, N.M., U.S. E 5 176
Los Andes C 2 195
Los Angeles, Ca., U.S. F 5 182
Los Angeles, Chile E 1 195
Los Angeles □6 F 5 182
Los Angeles Aqueduct ⫪1 F 5 182
Los Banos C 3 182
Los Barrios H 5 86
Los Blancos D 7 192
Los Corrales A 6 86
Los Fresnos G 5 172
Los Gatos C 2 182
Losheim C 3 100
Los Herreras H 4 172
Loskopdam ⊜1 C 8 206
Los Lagos F 1 195
Los Lagos □3 F 1 195
Los Llanos de Aridane i 12 85b
Los Mochis E 5 184
Los Navalmorales E 6 86
Lošnica E 14 66
Los Padillas E 5 176
Los Palacios y Villafranca G 4 86
Los Santos de Maimona F 4 86

⌊ Waterfall ꞩ Strait c Bay, Gulf ⊜ Lake ⩩ Swamp ⩍ Ice Feature ⫪ Other Hydrographic Feature ✣ Submarine Feature □ Political Unit ⫸ Cultural Institution ⊥ Historical Site ♦ Recreational Site ⌗ Airport ■ Military Installation ✢ Miscellaneous

Los Sauces — Mammola

Name — Map Ref. — Page

Los Sauces F 1 195
Losser D 4 98
Los Teques A 5 190
Lost Hills E 4 182
Lost River Range ⩘ C 7 178
Lost Trail Pass)(C 7 178
Losuia N 14 124
Los Yébenes E 7 86
Lot □[3] D 5 80
Lot ≃ D 4 80
Lota E 1 195
Lot-et-Garonne □[3] D 4 80
Lothair D 9 206
Loto C 3 204
Lot's Wife I[2] J 8 126
Lotta (Lutto) ≃ B 8 108
Lotung F 15 130
Louang Namtha D 5 132
Louangphrabang E 6 132
Loubetsi C 1 204
Loubomo C 1 204
Loudon B 2 168
Loudun E 7 78
Loue ≃ C 3 82
Louga B 1 200
Loughborough E 5 72
Loughrea C 3 75
Louin F 4 170
Louisa D 5 162
Louisbourg E 14 160
Louisbourg National Historic Site ♦ F 14 160
Louisburg A 5 168
Louise F 5 172
Louiseville E 7 160
Louisiade Archipelago II B 11 138
Louisiana C 3 170
Louisiana □[3] E 9 152
Louisiana ◗ C 5 68
Louisville, Ga., U.S. C 3 168
Louisville, Ky., U.S. C 6 170
Louis-XIV, Pointe > A 3 160
Loum E 6 200
Lount Lake ⊜ F 11 158
Louny B 10 100
Loup ≃ E 6 174
Lourdes E 3 80
Lourenço Marques see Maputo C 10 206
Lourinhã E 1 86
Lousã D 2 86
Louth, Austl. C 5 144
Louth, Eng., U.K. D 6 72
Louth □[3] C 5 75
Louvain see Leuven D 3 69
Louviers, Co., U.S. F 2 174
Louviers, Fr. C 8 78
Lövånger D 10 64
Lovat' ≃ H 9 108
Loveč D 8 104
Loveč □[3] D 8 104
Loveland E 2 174
Lovell C 9 178
Lovere D 6 92
Loves Park D 4 166
Loviisa B 13 66
Lovingston E 4 162
Lovosice B 11 100
Lovozero B 11 108
Lovozero, ozero ⊜ C 11 108
Lovrenc D 7 102
Lóvua E 3 204
Low F 5 160
Low, Cape > D 15 150
Lowa ≃ C 4 204
Lowden B 3 170
Lowell, Ma., U.S. D 7 164
Lowell, Mi., U.S. B 1 162
Lowell, Or., U.S. D 2 178
Lower Arrow Lake ⊜[1] G 12 156
Lower Brule Indian Reservation ✦[4] C 4 174
Lower California see Baja California >[1] C 2 184
Lower Egypt □[9] G 4 118
Lower Glenelg National Park ♦ G 3 144
Lower Hutt D 5 146
Lower Loteni E 8 206
Lower Manitou Lake ⊜ A 8 174
Lower Peirce Reservoir ⊜[1] i 14 134a
Lower Red Lake ⊜ B 7 174
Lower Trajan's Wall ✦ C 10 104
Lower Ugashik Lake ⊜ H 16 154
Lower Woods Harbour G 10 160
Lowestoft E 8 72
Łowicz B 10 96
Lowville C 3 164
Loxley G 5 170
Loxstedt C 5 98
Loxton E 3 144
Loyal C 3 166
Loyalty Islands see Loyauté, Îles II D 14 138
Loyauté, Îles (Loyalty Islands) II D 14 138
Loyoro G 3 202
Lozère □[3] F 5 76
Loznica C 5 104
Lozova E 9 110
Loz'va ≃ F 23 108
Luacano E 3 204
Luala ≃ F 6 204
Lualaba ≃ I 10 196
Luama ≃ C 4 204
Luambe National Park ♦ E 5 204
Lu'an C 13 130
Luan ≃ G 12 128
Luanda D 1 204
Luanda □[3] D 1 204
Luando ≃ E 2 204
Luang, Thale ⊜ K 5 132
Luanginga (Luanguinga) ≃ E 3 204
Luang Prabang Range ⩘ I 5 130
Luangue D 2 204
Luangue (Loange) ≃ D 2 204
Luangwa ≃ E 5 204
Luanping F 11 128
Luanshya E 4 204
Luanxian G 12 128
Luapula □[3] E 4 204
Luapula ≃ E 4 204
Luarca A 4 86
Luati E 3 204
Luau E 3 204
Luba E 6 200
Lubaantun ⊥ I 15 184
Lubań C 8 96
Lubāna D 13 66
Lubang Islands II C 8 134
Lubango E 1 204
Lubāns ⊜ D 13 66
Lubao D 4 204
Lubawa B 10 96
Lübbecke D 5 98
Lübben E 10 98
Lübbenau E 10 98
Lubbock D 3 172
Lübeck C 7 98
Lubefu ≃ C 3 204
Lubembe ≃ D 3 204
Lubień Kujawski B 10 96
Lubilash ≃ D 3 204
Lubin C 9 96
Lublin C 12 96
Lublin □[3] C 12 96
Lubliniec C 10 96
Lubny D 8 110
Lubomierz C 8 96
Lubondaie D 3 204
Lubraniec B 10 96
Lubsko C 8 96
Lubudi E 4 204
Lubudi ≃, Zaire D 3 204
Lubudi ≃, Zaire C 3 204
Lubukbertubung N 6 132
Lubuklinggau F 4 134
Lubuksikaping N 5 132
Lubumbashi E 4 204
Lübz C 9 98
Lucania □[9] D 6 94
Lucania, Mount ∧ F 24 154
Lucapa D 3 204
Lucas B 2 170
Lucasville D 2 162
Lucca F 6 92
Lucca □[6] E 6 92
Lucé D 8 78
Lucedale G 4 170
Lucena, Phil. C 8 134
Lucena, Phil. C 8 134
Lucena, Spain G 6 86
Luc-en-Diois F 3 82
Lučenec D 10 96
Luceque E 2 204
Lucera C 5 94
Lucerne see Luzern C 6 82
Lucerne, Lake ⊜ D 6 82
Luchang E 6 130
Lüchow D 8 98
Lucira E 1 204
Luckau E 10 98
Luckenwalde D 10 98
Lucknow D 4 122
Luçon B 2 80
Lucusse E 3 204
Lüda see Dalian G 13 128
Lüdenscheid E 4 98
Lüderitz D 1 206
Ludhiāna C 3 122
Lüdinghausen E 4 98
Ludington D 5 166
Ludlow, Eng., U.K. E 4 72
Ludlow, Ma., U.S. D 6 164
Ludogorie ✦[1] D 9 104
Ludowici D 4 168
Ludvika B 7 66
Ludwigsburg D 6 100
Ludwigsfelde D 10 98
Ludwigshafen am Rhein C 5 100
Ludwigslust C 8 98
Ludwigsort see Laduškin E 10 66
Ludwigstein, Burg ⊥ E 6 98
Ludza D 13 66
Luebo D 3 204
Lueki C 4 204
Luena, Ang. E 2 204
Luena, Zaire D 4 204
Luena ≃, Ang. E 3 204
Luena ≃, Zam. E 3 204
Lueyang B 7 130
Lufeng, China G 12 130
Lufeng, China F 6 130
Lufico D 1 204
Lufira ≃ D 4 204
Lufkin G 1 170
Lufubu ≃ D 5 204
Luga G 8 108
Lugano E 6 82
Lugano, Lago di see Lugano, Lake ⊜ C 2 90
Lugano, Lake (Lugano, Lago di) ⊜ C 2 90
Luganville E 8 136
Lugela F 6 204
Lugenda ≃ E 6 204
Lugo, Italy E 7 92
Lugo, Spain A 3 86
Lugo □[6] B 3 86
Lugoj C 6 104
Lugones A 5 86
Lugovaja Subbota G 28 108
Luhanka B 12 66
Luhans'k E 11 110
Luhans'k □[6] E 11 110
Luhe B 14 130
Luhit see Lohit ≃ D 3 130
Luhovicy I 13 108
Luia D 3 204
Luia ≃ F 5 204
Luiana ≃ F 3 204
Luik see Liège D 4 69
Luimneach see Limerick D 3 75
Luino C 4 92
Luitpold Coast ⊥[2] D 5 208
Luiza D 3 204
Luján de Cuyo C 3 195
Lujiang C 13 130
Lukang F 15 130
Lukanga Swamp ≡ E 4 204
Lukenie ≃ C 3 204
Luki F 13 66
Lukojanov I 16 108
Lukolela, Zaire C 2 204
Lukolela, Zaire D 3 204
Lukovit D 8 104
Łuków C 12 96
Lukuga ≃ D 4 204
Lukula D 1 204
Lukuledi ≃ E 6 204
Lukumburu D 6 204
Lukusashi ≃ E 5 204
Lukusuzi National Park ♦ E 5 204
Lula E 3 170
Lulaka ≃ C 3 204
Luleå D 11 64
Luleälven ≃ C 10 64
Lüleburgaz B 7 106
Luliang F 6 130
Lüliang Shan ⩘ H 8 128
Lulonga ≃ B 2 204
Lulu ≃ B 3 204
Lulua ≃ D 3 204
Lumajang I 21 135b
Lumana C 4 204
Lumbala N'guimbo E 3 204
Lumberport D 3 162
Lumberton, Ms., U.S. G 4 170
Lumberton, N.C., U.S. B 5 168
Lumbovka C 14 108
Lumbres B 9 78
Lumding D 6 122
Lumpkin C 2 168
Lumsden F 19 156
Lumut L 5 132
Lumut, Tanjung > F 5 134
Luna Pier C 2 162
Lund, B.C., Can. F 9 156
Lund, Swe. E 6 66
Lunda Norte □[3] D 2 204
Lunda Sul □[3] E 3 204
Lüneburg C 7 98
Lüneburg □[6] C 6 98
Lüneburger Heide ✦[1] D 7 98
Lunel G 2 82
Lünen E 4 98
Lunenburg E 4 162
Lunéville B 4 82
Lunga ≃ E 4 204
Lungau ✦[1] C 5 102
Lungi D 2 200
Lunglei E 6 122
Lungué-Bungo ≃ E 3 204
Lūni ≃ D 2 122
Luni ⊥ E 6 92
Luninec J 13 64
Lunino J 16 108
Lunna B 13 96
Lunsar D 2 200
Lunsemfwa ≃ E 4 204
Luo ≃, China I 7 128
Luo ≃, China A 10 130
Luobei C 18 128
Luoding G 10 130
Luohe B 11 130
Luojiang C 7 130
Luonan A 10 130
Luoning A 10 130
Luoping F 7 130
Luotian C 12 130
Luoyang A 11 130
Luoyuan E 14 130
Lupane F 4 204
Lupanshui E 7 130
Lupembe D 6 204
Lupeni C 7 104
Luputa D 3 204
Luqiao, China D 15 130
Luqiao, China B 13 130
Luqu A 6 130
Lūrah ≃ C 1 122
Luray D 4 162
Lure C 4 82
Lurgan B 5 75
Lurin F 3 190
Lúrio E 7 204
Lúrio ≃ E 6 204
Lusaka F 4 204
Lusaka □[3] F 4 204
Lusambo C 3 204
Lusangi C 4 204
Lusenga Plain National Park ♦ D 4 204
Luserna San Giovanni E 3 92
Lushan C 6 130
Lu Shan ∧ D 13 130
Lushnjë B 3 106
Lushoto C 6 204
Lüshun G 13 128
Lusignan B 4 80
Lusk D 2 174
Lussac-les-Châteaux B 4 80
Lustenau C 1 102
Lusutfu (Usutu) (Maputo) ≃ D 9 206
Lūt, Dasht-e ✦[2] D 8 116
Lutherstadt Eisleben E 8 98
Lutherstadt Wittenberg E 9 98
Lutherville-Timonium G 2 164
Lütjenburg B 7 98
Luton F 6 72
Lutong E 6 134
Luts'k D 4 110
Lutto (Lotta) ≃ B 7 108
Lutz E 3 168
Lützow C 8 98
Lutzow-Holm Bay c C 12 208
Luuq G 5 202
Luverne G 5 170
Luvua D 4 204
Luvua ≃ D 4 204
Luwegu ≃ D 6 204
Luwuk F 8 134
Luxembourg E 4 69
Luxembourg □[1] F 9 62
Luxembourg □[3] E 4 69
Luxemburg see Luxembourg □[3] E 4 69
Luxeuil-les-Bains C 4 82
Luxi, China F 4 130
Luxi, China F 6 130
Luxor (El-Uqsor) J 5 118
Luz C 8 194
Luz, Costa de la ⊥[2] H 4 86
Luza, Russia F 17 108
Luza, Russia E 12 108
Luzarches C 9 78
Luzern C 6 82
Luzern □[3] C 6 82
Luzerne □[6] E 3 164
Luzhou D 7 130
Luziânia B 7 194
Luzon I B 8 134
Luzon Strait ʊ, Asia H 15 130
Luzon Strait ʊ, Asia A 8 134
Luzy F 10 78
L'viv E 4 110
L'viv □[6] E 3 110
L'vov see L'viv E 4 110
Lwów see L'viv E 4 110
Lwówek Śląski C 8 96
Lyallpur see Faisalabad C 2 122
Lybster B 5 74
Lyck see Ełk B 12 96
Lyčkovo G 10 108
Lycoming □[6] E 1 164
Lydd G 7 72
Lydda see Lod F 3 120
Lyford G 5 172
Lyle D 2 166
Lymans'ke B 10 104
Lyme Bay c G 3 72
Lyme Regis G 3 72
Lynch D 5 174
Lynchburg, Tn., U.S. E 5 170
Lynchburg, Va., U.S. E 4 162
Lynd ≃ D 6 142
Lyndoch E 2 144
Lyndon H 3 140
Lyndon ≃ H 3 140
Lyndon B. Johnson National Historical Site ♦ E 4 172
Lyndon B. Johnson Space Center ◗[3] F 6 172
Lyndora C 3 162
Lyngen c A 10 64
Lyngør C 4 66
Lynn, Al., U.S. E 5 170
Lynn, Ma., U.S. D 8 164
Lynn Canal c G 27 154
Lynn Garden E 2 162
Lynn Lake C 8 158
Lynnville B 2 170
Lynx Lake ⊜ D 11 150
Lyon E 2 82
Lyon □[6] A 4 182
Lyon Mountain B 4 164
Lyonnais □[9] E 2 82
Lyons, Mi., U.S. B 1 162
Lyons, N.Y., U.S. C 2 164
Lyons ≃ I 3 140
Lysá pod Makytou A 10 102
Lysets' A 8 104
Lyskovo H 16 108
Lyss C 5 82
Lys'va G 22 108
Lysychans'k E 11 110
Lytham Saint Anne's D 3 72
Lyttelton E 4 146
Lyttelton ✦[8] C 8 206
Lyuboml' D 3 110
Lyubotyn E 9 110

M

Ma ≃ H 7 130
Ma'ān I 5 120
Ma'ān □[3] H 6 120
Maanit B 4 128
Ma'anshan C 14 130
Maar F 3 202
Maardu C 12 66
Maarianhamina B 9 66
Ma'arrat an-Nu'mān E 7 118
Maarssen B 3 69
Maas (Meuse) ≃ C 7 76
Maaseik C 4 69
Maasmechelen D 4 69
Maassluis C 3 69
Maastricht D 4 69
Mabalane B 10 206
Mabaravhuta A 9 206
Mabaruma B 7 190
Mabeleapodi G 3 204
Mabel Lake ⊜ F 12 156
Mabian D 6 130
Mableton C 2 168
Mabote A 11 206
Mabrūk D 8 198
Mabuasehube Game Reserve ✦[4] C 5 206
Mabwe D 4 204
Macaé E 10 194
Macaloge E 6 204
MacAlpine Lake ⊜ C 12 150
Macapá C 8 190
Macarretane C 10 206
Macau, Braz. E 11 190
Macau, Macau G 11 130
Macau □[2] G 11 130
Macclesfield D 4 72
Macdiarmid G 14 158
Macdonald, Lake ⊜ H 10 140
MacDonald Pass)(B 7 178
MacDonnell Range ⩘ H 12 140
MacDowell Lake ⊜ E 12 158
Macdui, Ben ∧ C 5 74
Macedo de Cavaleiros C 4 86
Macedonia □[9] E 7 104
Macedonia □[1] G 12 62
Maceió E 11 190
Macenta D 3 200
Macerata F 9 92
Macerata □[6] A 3 94
MacFarlane ≃ B 18 156
Macfarlane, Lake ⊜ L 3 142
Macgillycuddy's Reeks ⩘ D 2 75
Machado ≃ F 6 190
Machadodorp C 9 206
Machagai E 8 192
Machala D 2 190
Machalí D 2 195
Machaquilá ≃ I 15 184
Machattie, Lake ⊜ H 4 142
Machaze G 5 204
Macheng C 12 130
Machias A 10 162
Machico g 11 85a
Machili ≃ F 4 204
Machilīpatnam F 4 122
Machiques F 6 186
Macho, Arroyo del ≃ D 1 172
Machupicchu (Machu Picchu) F 4 190
Macia C 10 206
Macina see Massina ✦[1] C 4 200
Macintyre ≃ B 7 144
Mackay, Austl. F 9 142
Mackay, Id., U.S. D 7 178
MacKay ≃ C 16 156
Mackay, Lake ⊜ H 10 140
Mackenzie ≃, Austl. G 9 142
Mackenzie ≃, N.T., Can. C 6 150
MacKenzie Bay c, Ant. C 16 208
Mackenzie Bay c, Can. B 26 154
Mackenzie Delta ≚[2] B 27 154
Mackenzie Mountains ⩘ D 30 154
Mackinac, Straits of ʊ C 6 166
Mackinac Island C 6 166
Mackinac Island I C 6 166
Mackinaw City C 6 166
Mačkovci D 8 102
Macksville C 9 144
Maclean B 9 144
Macleay ≃ C 9 144
Macleod, Lake ⊜ I 2 140
Macmillan ≃ E 27 154
Macolo D 2 204
Macomb B 3 170
Macomer E 2 90
Mâcon, Fr. E 6 76
Macon, Ga., U.S. C 3 168
Macon, Il., U.S. C 4 170
Macon, Ms., U.S. F 4 170
Macossa F 5 204
Macoun Lake ⊜ C 20 156
Macquarie ≃, Austl. C 6 144
Macquarie ≃, Austl. i 12 145a
Macquarie, Lake ⊜ D 8 144
Macquarie Harbour c j 11 145a
Macquarie Marshes ≡ C 6 144
MacRitchie Reservoir ⊜[1] i 14 134a
Mac Robertson Land ✦[1] D 15 208
Macroom E 2 75
Macumba ≃ I 3 142
Macuspana I 13 184
Macusse F 3 204
Mada ≃ D 6 200
Mādabā F 5 120
Madagascar □[1] K 12 196
Madagascar Basin ✦[1] H 5 58
Madama A 7 200
Madang N 13 124
Madaoua C 6 200
Madawaska g 12 163a
Madawaska ≃ F 5 160
Madaya C 3 132
Maddaloni C 4 94
Madeira □[3] g 11 85a
Madeira I g 10 85a
Madeira II C 1 198
Madeira ≃ E 6 190
Madeleine, Îles de la II E 12 160
Madelia C 7 174
Madeline Island I B 3 166
Maden C 8 118
Madera, Ca., U.S. D 3 182
Madera, Mex. C 5 184
Madera □[6] C 4 182
Madgaon F 2 122
Madhya Pradesh □[3] E 3 122
Madibogo D 6 206
Madill C 5 172
Madimba D 2 204
Madinani D 3 200
Madīnat ash-Sha'b E 5 202
Madingou C 1 204
Madison, Fl., U.S. D 3 168
Madison, In., U.S. C 6 170
Madison, Mo., U.S. C 2 170
Madison, Ne., U.S. E 6 174
Madison, Oh., U.S. C 3 162
Madison, Va., U.S. D 4 162
Madison, Wi., U.S. D 4 166
Madison □[6] D 3 164
Madison ≃ C 8 178
Madison Range ⩘ C 8 178
Madisonville, Ky., U.S. D 5 170
Madisonville, La., U.S. G 3 170
Madisonville, Tx., U.S. E 5 172
Madiun k 20 135b
Madjingo B 1 204
Mado Gashi G 4 202
Madoi C 7 122
Madona D 13 66
Madonna della Guardia ◗[1] E 4 92
Madonna del Sasso ◗[1] D 6 82
Madrakah, Ra's al- > G 8 116
Madras, India G 4 122
Madras, Or., U.S. C 3 178
Madras see Tamil Nādu □[3] G 3 122
Madrasat Qasr Abū Hādī ⊥ C 8 198
Madre, Laguna c G 5 172
Madre, Laguna ⊜ E 11 184
Madre, Sierra ⩘, Phil. B 8 134
Madre, Sierra ⩘, Phil. J 14 184
Madre de Chiapas, Sierra ⩘ I 13 184
Madre de Dios ≃ F 5 190
Madre de Dios, Isla I J 4 192
Madre del Sur, Sierra ⩘ I 10 184
Madre Occidental, Sierra ⩘ D 6 184
Madre Oriental, Sierra ⩘ F 9 184
Madrid, Ne., U.S. E 4 174
Madrid, Spain D 7 86
Madrid □[3] B 4 84
Madridejos E 7 86
Madrigalejo E 5 86
Madrūsah E 7 198
Madura see Madurai G 3 122
Madura I k 21 135b
Madura, Selat ʊ k 21 135b
Madurai G 3 122
Maduru ≃ H 4 122
Maebashi F 7 126
Mae Hong Son E 3 132
Mae Klong ≃ E 5 132
Mae Ping Mae Hat Mae Kor National Park ♦ F 4 132
Mae Sot F 4 132
Maestra, Sierra ⩘ C 5 186
Maevatanana k 9 205a
Maewo I E 8 136
Mafeking see Mafikeng C 6 206
Mafeteng E 7 206
Mafia Channel ʊ D 6 204
Mafia Island I D 6 204
Mafikeng C 6 206
Mafra G 5 194
Magadan D 18 114
Magadi H 4 202
Magadi, Lake ⊜ H 4 202
Magangué F 6 186
Magaria C 6 200
Magazine Mountain ∧ E 2 170
Magburaka D 2 200
Magdagači B 9 124
Magdalena, Bol. F 6 190
Magdalena, Mex. G 7 184
Magdalena, N.M., U.S. E 5 176
Magdalena □[3] F 6 186
Magdalena ≃, Col. B 4 190
Magdalena ≃, Mex. B 4 184
Magdalena, Bahía c E 3 184
Magdeburg D 8 98
Magdeburg □[6] D 8 98
Magé E 9 194
Magelang k 20 135b
Magellan, Strait of ʊ J 5 192
Magenta D 4 92
Magetan k 20 135b
Maggiore, Lago see Maggiore, Lake ⊜ C 2 90
Maggiore, Lake (Maggiore, Lago) ⊜ C 2 90
Maghāgha H 4 118
Maghama F 2 198
Maghniyya C 4 198
Maghull D 4 72
Maglaj C 4 104
Maglić ∧ D 5 104
Maglie D 8 94
Magnetawan ≃ F 3 160
Magnitogorsk J 23 108
Magnolia, Ar., U.S. F 2 170
Magnolia, Mn., U.S. D 6 174
Magog F 7 160
Magoro G 3 202
Magpie ≃, On., Can. G 16 158
Magpie ≃, P.Q., Can. C 11 160
Magpie, Lac ⊜ C 11 160
Magpie Ouest ≃ C 11 160
Magrath G 15 156
Magude C 10 206
Magumeri C 7 200
Magway D 2 132
Magway □[3] E 2 132
Mahābād D 11 118
Mahabharat Range ⩘ D 4 122
Mahabo I 8 205a
Mahačkala H 15 110
Mahagi B 5 204
Mahajamba ≃ k 9 205a
Mahajanga k 9 205a
Mahajanga □[3] k 9 205a
Mahakam ≃ E 7 134
Mahalapye B 7 206
Maḥallāt F 14 118
Mahānadi ≃ E 4 122
Mahanoy City C 5 162
Mahārāshtra □[3] F 3 122
Mahārlū, Daryācheh-ye ⊜ H 15 118
Mahāsamund E 4 122
Maha Sarakham F 6 132
Mahasoa I 9 205a
Mahavavy ≃, Madag. j 9 205a
Mahavavy ≃, Madag. k 9 205a
Mahavelona k 9 205a
Mahbūbnagar F 3 122
Mahé I J 7 112
Mahébourg q 21 207e
Mahele C 10 206
Mahendra Giri ∧ F 4 122
Mahenge D 6 204
Maheriv C 12 96
Mahesāna E 2 122
Mahilëu C 6 110
Mahilëu □[3] C 7 110
Mahlangasi D 9 206
Mahlow D 10 98
Maḥmūdābād D 14 118
Mahomet B 4 170
Mahón see Maó C 8 84
Mahony Lake ⊜ D 32 154
Mahora E 3 88
Mahres C 7 198
Mahuta E 6 204
Mahuva E 2 122
Maicao F 6 186
Maîche C 4 82
Maicuru ≃ D 8 190
Maidenhead F 6 72
Maidstone, Eng., U.K. F 7 72
Maidstone, Sk., Can. E 17 156
Maiduguri C 7 200
Maigatari C 6 200
Maiko ≃ C 4 204
Maiko, Parc National de la ♦ C 4 204
Maikoor, Pulau I G 10 134
Main ≃ C 6 100
Mainburg D 8 100
Main Channel ʊ F 3 160
Mai-Ndombe, Lac ⊜ C 2 204
Main-Donau-Kanal ≅ C 8 100
Maine □[9] D 6 78
Maine □[3] B 14 152
Maine, Gulf of c C 14 152
Maine-et-Loire □[3] E 6 78
Mainhardt C 6 100
Mainland I, Scot., U.K. A 5 74
Mainland I, Scot., U.K. g 9 74a
Maintal B 5 100
Maintirano k 8 205a
Mainvilliers D 8 78
Mainz C 5 100
Maio I h 11 200a
Maiori D 4 94
Maiori, Nuraghe ⊥ I 4 92
Maipo ≃ C 2 195
Maipo, Volcán ∧[1] D 3 195
Maipú C 3 195
Maipú ✦[8] C 2 195
Maišiagala E 12 66
Maitland, Austl. E 1 144
Maitland, Austl. D 8 144
Maitri ◗[3] D 10 208
Maíz, Islas del II E 4 186
Maizières-lès-Metz A 4 82
Maizuru G 5 126
Maja ≃ C 16 114
Majeigha E 1 202
Majene F 7 134
Majkain D 10 114
Majkop G 11 110
Majli-Saj A 2 122
Majn ≃ C 20 114
Major, Puig ∧ E 7 88
Majorca see Mallorca I E 7 88
Majrūr E 3 202
Majrūr, Wādī ≃ D 2 202
Majskij H 14 110
Majuro I[1] C 9 136
Makabana C 1 204
Makalamabedi G 3 204
Makale F 7 134
Makapanstad C 8 206
Makarakomburu, Mount ∧ A 13 138
Makarewa G 2 146
Makariha C 22 108
Makarov C 12 124
Makassar Strait (Makasar, Selat) ʊ F 7 134
Makat F 18 110
Makaya C 2 204
Makemo I[1] E 13 136
Makeni D 2 200
Makgadikgadi ≚ G 4 204
Makgwaphana C 6 206
Maki National Park ♦ F 4 202
Makinsk J 29 108
Makiyivka E 10 110
Makkah (Mecca) C 4 202
Makkovik A 14 160
Makó B 6 104
Makobaese A 7 206
Makokou E 7 200
Makoop Lake ⊜ E 13 158
Makopong C 5 206
Makoua F 8 200
Maków Mazowiecki B 11 96
Makrāna D 2 122
Maksatiha H 11 108
Maktau H 4 202
Mākū C 11 118
Makuliro D 6 204
Makumbi D 3 204
Makung G 14 130
Makurdi D 6 200
Makushin Volcano ∧[1] J 11 154
Makwassie D 7 206
Mala, Punta > G 4 186
Malabang D 8 134
Malabar Coast ⊥[2] G 3 122
Malabo E 6 200
Malacca see Melaka M 6 132
Malacca, Strait of ʊ M 5 132
Malacky B 9 102
Mala Divytsya D 7 110
Maladzečna E 13 66
Málaga H 6 86
Málaga □[6] H 6 86
Malagón E 7 86
Malaimbandy I 9 205a
Malaita I A 13 138
Malaja Kuril'skaja grjada (Habomai-shotō) II D 13 124
Malaja Pera D 21 108
Malaja Višera G 9 108
Malaka, Sempitan ʊ L 2 132
Malakāl F 3 202
Malakula I E 8 136
Malambo F 6 186
Malang k 21 135b
Malangali D 5 204
Malanje D 2 204
Malanje □[3] D 2 204
Malapati B 9 206
Mälaren ⊜ C 8 66
Malargüe D 3 195
Malaryta K 12 64
Malaspina Glacier ⊓ G 24 154
Malatya C 8 118
Malatya □[3] C 7 118
Mala Vyska E 7 110
Malawi □[1] J 11 196
Malawi, Lake ⊜ E 5 204
Malaybalay D 9 134
Malāyer E 13 118
Malay Peninsula >[1] K 6 132
Malaysia □[1] E 6 134
Malazgirt C 10 118
Malbooma K 1 142
Malbork A 10 96
Mal'čevskaja E 11 110
Malchin C 9 98
Malchow C 9 98
Malcolm K 6 140
Malczyce C 9 96
Maldegem C 2 69
Malden D 7 164
Malden I D 12 136
Maldive Islands see Maldives □[1] H 2 122
Maldive Islands II H 2 122
Maldives □[1] H 2 122
Maldon F 7 72
Maldonado D 10 195
Male', Mald. I 2 122
Male', Myan. C 2 132
Maléa, Ákra > D 5 106
Male' Atoll I[1] J 11 116
Mālegaon E 2 122
Malema E 6 204
Malemort-sur-Corrèze C 5 80
Malen'ga E 12 108
Malente B 7 98
Maleshe C 5 206
Malgrat de Mar G 6 80
Malheur ≃ C 5 178
Malheur, South Fork ≃ D 4 178
Mali C 2 200
Mali □[1] G 7 196
Mali ≃ E 3 130
Malibu F 5 182
Malik, Wādī al- ≃ D 2 202
Målilla D 7 66
Malinau E 7 134
Malindi H 5 202
Malingping k 18 135b
Malin Head > A 4 75
Malino, Bukit ∧ E 8 134
Malinyi D 6 204
Malka Mari National Park ♦ G 4 202
Malkara B 7 106
Malko Tărnovo D 9 104
Mallaig D 3 74
Mallawi I 4 118
Mallee Cliffs National Park ♦ E 4 144
Mallery Lake ⊜ D 13 150
Mallet F 5 194
Mallnitz D 5 102
Mallorca (Majorca) I E 7 88
Malmbäck D 7 66
Malmberget C 10 64
Malmédy D 5 69
Malmesbury G 3 206
Malmö E 6 66
Malmöhus □[3] E 6 66
Malmslätt C 7 66
Malmyž H 19 108
Malnate D 4 92
Malo D 7 92
Maloba D 4 204
Maloelap I[1] C 9 136
Maloe Skuratovo J 12 108
Malojaroslavec I 11 108
Malone, Fl., U.S. D 2 168
Malone, N.Y., U.S. B 4 164
Małopolska ✦[1] C 11 96
Malošujka E 12 108
Maloti Mountains ⩘ E 8 206
Małowice C 8 96
Malozemel'skaja Tundra ✦[1] C 19 108
Malpartida de Plasencia E 4 86
Malpelo, Isla de I C 2 190
Malprabha ≃ F 2 122
Malsch D 5 100
Malta □[1] H 10 62
Malta I I 4 94
Malta Channel ʊ H 4 94
Maltahöhe C 2 206
Malton C 6 72
Malume D 4 200
Malūṭ E 3 202
Mālvan F 2 122
Malvern see Great Malvern, Eng., U.K. E 4 72
Malvern, Ia., U.S. B 1 170
Malvérnia B 9 206
Malý Dunaj ≃ B 9 102
Malyj Anjuj ≃ C 19 114
Malyj Atlym E 27 108
Malyj Uzen' ≃ E 16 110
Malyn D 6 110
Mamadyš I 19 108
Mamberamo ≃ F 11 134
Mambéré ≃ E 8 200
Mambéré-Kadéï □[3] E 8 200
Mambili ≃ B 2 204
Mamburao C 8 134
Ma-Me-O Beach E 15 156
Mamers D 7 78
Mamfe D 6 200
Mamiá, Lago ⊜ D 6 190
Mamljutka I 28 108
Mammola F 6 94

Symbols in the index entries represent the broad categories identified in the key at the right. Symbols with superior numbers (⩘[1]) identify subcategories (see complete key on page 242).

∧ Mountain ⩘ Mountains)(Pass V Valley ≚ Plain > Cape I Island II Islands ⊥ Other Topographic Feature ≃ River ≅ Canal

Name	Map Ref.	Page

Mammoth Cave National Park ♦ — D 5 — 170
Mamonovo — E 9 — 66
Mamoré ≃ — F 5 — 190
Mamou — C 2 — 200
Mamoudzou — o 19 — 207d
Mampong — D 4 — 200
Mamraš — I 16 — 110
Mamry, Jezioro — A 11 — 96
Mamuno — B 4 — 206
Mamyl' — E 22 — 108
Man — D 3 — 200
Manacapuru — D 6 — 190
Manacor — E 8 — 88
Manado — E 8 — 134
Managua — E 3 — 186
Managua, Lago de — E 3 — 186
Manakara — I 9 — 205a
Manāli — C 3 — 122
Manamane — B 9 — 206
Manambaho ≃ — k 8 — 205a
Manambolo ≃ — k 8 — 205a
Mánamo, Caño ≃ — F 9 — 186
Mananara ≃ — I 9 — 205a
Manangatang — E 4 — 144
Mananjary — I 9 — 205a
Manapire ≃ — G 8 — 186
Mana Pools National Park ♦ — F 4 — 204
Manapouri — F 1 — 146
Manas — B 14 — 116
Manās ≃ — D 6 — 122
Manas Hu — A 14 — 116
Manāslu ∧ — D 4 — 122
Manassas — D 5 — 162
Manassas National Battlefield Park ♦ — D 5 — 162
Mânăstirea — C 9 — 104
Manatí — j 15 — 187b
Manaus — D 6 — 190
Manavgat — D 4 — 118
Manawa — C 4 — 166
Manawan Lake ☒ — D 20 — 156
Manawatu-Wanganui □³ — C 5 — 146
Manbij — B 4 — 170
Mancha Real — G 7 — 86
Manche □³ — C 5 — 78
Manche see English Channel ⊔ — F 6 — 70
Mancheng — G 10 — 128
Mancherāl — D 5 — 122
Manchester, Ct., U.S. — E 6 — 164
Manchester, Eng., U.K. — D 4 — 72
Manchester, Ga., U.S. — C 2 — 168
Manchester, Ky., U.S. — C 2 — 168
Manchester, N.H., U.S. — D 7 — 164
Manchester, Oh., U.S. — C 2 — 162
Manchester, Vt., U.S. — C 5 — 164
Manchioneal — h 13 — 186a
Manchuria □⁹ — E 15 — 128
Manciano — G 7 — 92
Mand ≃ — H 15 — 118
Manda — D 8 — 200
Mandabe — I 9 — 205a
Mandaguari — E 4 — 194
Mandala, Puncak ∧ — F 12 — 134
Mandalay — C 2 — 132
Mandalay □³ — D 2 — 132
Mandalgovi — D 6 — 128
Mandalī — F 11 — 118
Mandan — B 4 — 174
Mandara Mountains ⋌ — C 7 — 200
Mandeb, Bab el ⊔ — E 5 — 202
Mandelieu — G 4 — 82
Mandello del Lario — D 5 — 92
Mandera — G 5 — 202
Mandeville, Jam. — h 12 — 186a
Mandeville, La., U.S. — G 3 — 170
Mandi — C 3 — 122
Mandiana — C 3 — 200
Mandi Dabwāli — D 2 — 122
Mandimba — E 6 — 204
Mandioli, Pulau I — F 9 — 134
Mandioré, Lagoa ☒ — G 7 — 190
Mandji — F 7 — 200
Mandla — E 4 — 122
Mandora — F 6 — 140
Mandrare ≃ — I 9 — 205a
Mandronarivo — I 9 — 205a
Mandsaur — E 2 — 122
Mandurah — M 3 — 140
Manduria — D 7 — 94
Māndvi — E 1 — 122
Mandya — G 3 — 122
Manendragarh — E 4 — 122
Manerbio — D 6 — 92
Manfalūṭ — I 4 — 118
Manfred — D 4 — 144
Manfredonia — C 5 — 94
Manfredonia, Golfo di C — C 4 — 94
Manga — C 4 — 200
Manga ≃¹ — B 7 — 200
Mangabeiras, Chapada das ⋌² — F 9 — 190
Mangaia I — F 12 — 136
Mangakino — C 5 — 146
Mangalia — D 10 — 104
Mangalmé — C 8 — 200
Mangalore — G 2 — 122
Mangaweka — C 5 — 146
Mange — D 2 — 200
Mangham — F 3 — 170
Mangistau □³ — H 18 — 110
Mangkalihat, Tanjung ⋋ — E 7 — 134
Manglares, Cabo ⋋ — C 2 — 122
Mangla Reservoir ☒¹ — C 2 — 122
Mangochi — E 6 — 204
Mangoky ≃ — I 8 — 205a
Mangole, Pulau I — F 9 — 134
Mangoro ≃ — k 9 — 205a
Mangotsfield — F 4 — 72
Mangrol — F 1 — 202
Mangueira, Lagoa c — F 9 — 192
Mangungu — E 4 — 204
Manhattan — F 6 — 174
Manhattan Beach — G 5 — 182
Manhiça — C 10 — 206
Manhuaçu — D 9 — 194
Mania ≃ — k 9 — 205a
Maniago — D 7 — 92
Manica — F 5 — 204
Manica □³ — F 5 — 204
Manicaland □³ — F 5 — 204
Manic Deux, Réservoir ☒¹ — D 9 — 160
Manicouagan ≃ — C 9 — 160
Manicouagan, Réservoir ☒ — C 9 — 160
Manic Trois, Réservoir ☒¹ — D 9 — 160
Maniema □³ — C 4 — 204
Manihiki I¹ — E 11 — 136
Manitsoq see Sukkertoppen — C 22 — 150
Mānikpur — D 4 — 122
Manila — D 3 — 134
Maningrida — B 2 — 142

Manipa, Selat ⊔ — F 9 — 134
Manipur □³ — E 6 — 122
Manisa — B 1 — 132
Manisa □³ — C 7 — 106
Manisa □³ — C 7 — 106
Manito — B 4 — 170
Manitoba □³ — F 13 — 150
Manitoba, Lake ☒ — F 9 — 158
Manitou ∧ — A 8 — 174
Manitou, Lake ☒ — F 3 — 160
Manitou Beach — F 19 — 156
Manitoulin Island I — F 2 — 160
Manitowaning — F 3 — 160
Manitowoc — C 5 — 166
Manizales — B 3 — 190
Manja — I 8 — 205a
Manjimup — N 4 — 140
Mānjra ≃ — F 3 — 122
Mankanza — B 2 — 204
Mankato, Ks., U.S. — F 5 — 174
Mankato, Mn., U.S. — C 2 — 166
Mankono — D 3 — 200
Manley Hot Springs — D 19 — 154
Manlleu — B 7 — 88
Manmād — E 2 — 122
Manna — F 4 — 134
Mannahill — D 3 — 144
Mannar, Gulf of C — H 3 — 122
Männedorf — C 6 — 82
Mannheim — C 5 — 100
Manning ≃ — C 9 — 144
Manning Provincial Park ♦ — G 11 — 156
Mannington — D 3 — 162
Manokotak — G 15 — 154
Manokwari — F 10 — 134
Manono — D 4 — 204
Manoora — D 2 — 144
Manor — E 5 — 172
Manosque — G 3 — 82
Manouane, Lac ☒¹ — C 8 — 160
Manp'o — F 16 — 128
Manra I¹ — D 10 — 136
Manresa — C 6 — 88
Mansa — E 4 — 204
Mansabá — C 1 — 200
Mānsehra — C 2 — 122
Mansel Island I — D 17 — 150
Mansfield, Austl. — A 13 — 138
Mansfield, Eng., U.K. — D 5 — 72
Mansfield, Ga., U.S. — C 3 — 168
Mansfield, Il., U.S. — B 4 — 170
Mansfield, Mo., U.S. — D 2 — 170
Mansfield, Oh., U.S. — C 2 — 162
Mansfield, Mount ∧ — B 6 — 164
Mansôa — C 1 — 200
Manson — H 11 — 156
Mansura — G 2 — 170
Manta — D 2 — 190
Manteca — D 2 — 190
Mantena — C 10 — 194
Mantes-la-Jolie — D 8 — 78
Manti — C 3 — 176
Mantiqueira, Serra da ⋌ — E 8 — 194
Mantorville — C 2 — 166
Mántova — D 6 — 92
Mantova □⁶ — D 6 — 92
Manturovo — G 16 — 108
Mäntyharju — B 13 — 66
Manuae I¹ — E 11 — 136
Manua Islands II — E 11 — 136
Manuangi I¹ — E 13 — 136
Manuel — F 10 — 184
Manuguru — F 4 — 122
Manui, Pulau I — F 8 — 134
Manukau — B 5 — 146
Manukau Harbour C — B 5 — 146
Manus Island I — M 13 — 124
Manutahi — C 5 — 146
Manvel — A 6 — 174
Manville — F 4 — 164
Manyame ≃ — F 5 — 204
Manyana — B 4 — 206
Manyara, Lake ☒ — C 6 — 204
Manyč-Gudilo, ozero ☒ — F 13 — 110
Many Island Lake ☒ — F 16 — 156
Manyoni — D 5 — 204
Manzanares — E 7 — 86
Manzanillo, Cuba — C 5 — 186
Manzanillo, Mex. — H 7 — 184
Manzanillo, Punta ⋋ — F 5 — 186
Manzanillo Bay C — D 6 — 186
Manzanola — F 2 — 174
Manzhouli — B 11 — 128
Manzini — D 9 — 206
Mao, Chad — C 8 — 200
Mao, Dom. Rep. — D 7 — 186
Maó (Mahón), Spain — C 8 — 84
Maokeng — D 7 — 206
Maoke, Pegunungan ⋌ — F 11 — 134
Maoming — H 10 — 130
Maouri, Dallol ≃ — C 6 — 130
Maowen — C 6 — 130
Mapanza — F 4 — 204
Mapastepec — J 13 — 184
Mapi ≃ — G 11 — 134
Mapia, Kepulauan II — E 9 — 134
Mapimí, Bolsón de ⋍² — D 7 — 184
Maple Lake — C 2 — 166
Mapleton — D 7 — 174
Mapoi — F 2 — 202
Mapoon Aboriginal Land ⋋⁴ — A 6 — 142
Mapuera ≃ — D 7 — 190
Mapumulo — E 9 — 206
Maputo — C 10 — 206
Maputo □³ — C 10 — 206
Maputo (Lusutfu) ≃ — D 9 — 206
Maquan ≃ — C 4 — 122
Maquela do Zombo — C 3 — 204
Maquinchao — H 6 — 192
Mar, Serra do ⋌ — F 7 — 194
Mara □³ — C 5 — 204
Mara ≃ — A 5 — 204
Marabá — A 9 — 190
Maraboon, Lake ☒¹ — G 8 — 142
Maracá, Ilha de I — A 9 — 190
Maracaibo — B 6 — 190
Maracaibo, Lago de — B 3 — 190
Maracaju — F 8 — 194
Maracay — B 7 — 190
Maracena — G 7 — 86
Maradi — C 6 — 200
Maradi □³ — C 6 — 200
Marādah — C 9 — 200
Marāgheh — D 12 — 118
Marahoué, Parc National de la ♦ — D 3 — 200
Marais des Cygnes ≃ — F 7 — 174
Marajó, Baía de C — D 9 — 190
Marajó, Ilha de I — D 8 — 190
Maralaleng — C 5 — 206
Maralinga — L 11 — 140

Maralinga Tjarutja Aboriginal Land ⋋⁴ — K 11 — 140
Maramasike I — A 13 — 138
Marambio B³ — L 8 — 192
Marampa — D 2 — 200
Maramureş □³ — B 7 — 104
Maran — M 6 — 132
Maranata — C 3 — 206
Marand — C 11 — 118
Marang, Malay. — L 6 — 132
Marang, Myan. — I 4 — 132
Maranhão □³ — A 9 — 190
Marano, Laguna di C — D 9 — 92
Maranoa ≃ — I 9 — 142
Marañón ≃ — D 3 — 190
Marapong — B 7 — 206
Marasany — H 21 — 108
Marathón, Grc. — C 5 — 106
Marathon, N.Y., U.S. — D 2 — 164
Marathon, On., Can. — G 15 — 158
Marathon, Tx., U.S. — E 2 — 172
Marawī — D 3 — 202
Marbella — H 6 — 86
Marble — B 2 — 166
Marble Bar — G 5 — 140
Marble Canyon V — D 3 — 176
Marble Hall — C 8 — 206
Marblehead — D 8 — 164
Marburg — F 5 — 98
Marca, Ponta da ⋋ — F 1 — 204
March — E 7 — 72
March (Morava) ≃ — B 8 — 102
Marche — B 2 — 170
Marche □⁹ — E 7 — 92
Marche □³ — D 4 — 90
Marchegg — B 8 — 102
Marchena — G 5 — 86
Marchena, Isla I — i 13 — 190a
Marchesato ⋋¹ — E 6 — 94
Mar Chiquita, Laguna ☒ — F 7 — 192
Marcillac-Vallon — D 6 — 80
Marcos Juárez — C 6 — 195
Marcq-en-Barœul — B 10 — 78
Marcus Baker, Mount ∧ — F 20 — 154
Marcy, Mount ∧ — B 5 — 164
Mardān — C 2 — 122
Mardarivka — B 10 — 104
Mar del Plata — E 9 — 195
Mardin — D 9 — 118
Mardin □³ — D 9 — 118
Maré I — D 14 — 138
Marechal Cândido Rondon — F 3 — 194
Mareeba — D 7 — 142
Maremma ⋋¹ — G 7 — 92
Marengo, Il., U.S. — B 2 — 170
Marengo, In., U.S. — E 4 — 92
Marennes — C 2 — 80
Marevo — H 9 — 108
Marfa — E 1 — 172
Margaree Harbour — E 13 — 160
Margaret Lake ☒ — B 14 — 156
Margaret River, Austl. — F 9 — 140
Margaret River, Austl. — M 3 — 140
Margarita, Isla de I — A 6 — 190
Margate, Eng., U.K. — F 8 — 72
Margate, Fl., U.S. — F 4 — 168
Margate City — D 4 — 164
Märgherita — E 2 — 130
Margherita di Savoia — C 6 — 94
Margherita Peak ∧ — B 4 — 204
Marghita — B 7 — 104
Margilan — A 2 — 122
Margny-lès-Compiègne — E 1 — 69
Marguerite Bay C — C 1 — 208
Marha ≃ — C 14 — 114
Marhanets' — F 9 — 110
Maria, Îles II — F 12 — 136
Maria Gail — D 5 — 102
Mariager — B 3 — 68
Maria Island National Park ♦ — j 13 — 145a
Maria Laach B³ — B 4 — 100
Maria Madre, Isla I — B 8 — 158
Mariana — G 6 — 184
Mariana Islands II — I 13 — 124
Mariana Trench ⋌¹ — F 11 — 58
Marian Guwaay ≃ — S 5 — 202
Mariāni — D 6 — 122
Marianna — I 2 — 168
Mariannelund — D 7 — 66
Mariánské Lázně — C 9 — 100
Mariano ≃ — k 9 — 205a
Marias ≃ — A 8 — 178
Marias Pass X — A 7 — 178
Mariato, Punta ⋋ — G 4 — 186
Maribo — D 4 — 68
Maribor — D 7 — 102
Marica (Évros) (Meriç) ≃ — E 9 — 104
Marico ≃ — D 7 — 206
Maricopa — F 5 — 176
Maricopa Indian Reservation ⋋⁴ — F 2 — 176
Marīdī — F 2 — 202
Marie Byrd Land ⋋¹ — C 33 — 208
Mariec — H 18 — 108
Marie-Galante I — o 21 — 187e
Marienbad see Mariánské Lázně — C 9 — 100
Marienberg — B 10 — 100
Marienburg see Malbork — A 10 — 96
Marienfelde ⋋⁸ — D 10 — 98
Mariental — C 3 — 206
Marienville — A 5 — 164
Mariënwerder see Kwidzyn — B 10 — 96
Mariestad — C 6 — 66
Marietta, Ga., U.S. — C 2 — 168
Marietta, Oh., U.S. — D 3 — 162
Marieville — A 5 — 164
Mariga ≃ — C 6 — 200
Marignane — G 3 — 82
Marigot — r 25 — 187g
Mariinsk — D 11 — 114
Marijampolė — F 6 — 66
Marij □³ — H 17 — 108
Marília — E 5 — 194
Marimba — C 3 — 204
Marín — B 1 — 86
Marina di Ravenna — E 7 — 92
Mar''ina Horka — F 13 — 66
Marinduque I — C 8 — 134
Marine-Ehrenmal ⊥ — B 7 — 98
Marine of the Pacific B³ — G 5 — 182
Marinette — C 5 — 166
Maringá — E 4 — 194
Maringá ≃ — B 3 — 204
Maringue — G 3 — 170
Marinha Grande — E 2 — 86
Marinskij Posad — H 17 — 108
Marion, Al., U.S. — D 3 — 168
Marion, Austl. — E 2 — 144
Marion, Il., U.S. — D 4 — 170
Marion, In., U.S. — B 3 — 162
Marion, Ks., U.S. — F 6 — 174

Marion, Ky., U.S. — D 4 — 170
Marion, Oh., U.S. — C 2 — 162
Marion, S.D., U.S. — D 7 — 166
Marion, Lake ☒¹ — C 4 — 168
Marion Bay — j 12 — 145a
Marion Downs — G 4 — 142
Marion Reef ⋋² — F 7 — 136
Marionville — D 2 — 170
Mariposa — C 4 — 182
Mariposa ≃ — C 4 — 182
Mariscal Estigarribia — D 7 — 192
Marissa — C 4 — 170
Maritime Alps ⋌ — C 1 — 90
Maritime Atlas see Atlas Tellien ⋌ — H 7 — 88
Mariupol' — F 10 — 110
Marīvān — E 11 — 118
Marka — G 5 — 202
Markala — C 3 — 200
Markaryd — D 6 — 66
Markazī □³ — E 14 — 118
Markdorf — E 6 — 100
Marked Tree — B 16 — 160
Markermeer ☒ — B 4 — 69
Markerwaarddijk (Afsluitdijk) ⋋⁵ — B 4 — 69
Market Drayton — E 5 — 72
Market Harborough — E 7 — 72
Market Weighton — D 6 — 72
Markgröningen ⋋³ — S 5 — 100
Markham — B 4 — 162
Markham, Mount ∧ — E 24 — 208
Markleeville — B 4 — 182
Markovo — C 20 — 114
Markoy — C 4 — 200
Markranstädt — E 9 — 98
Marks — D 15 — 110
Marktheidenfeld — E 6 — 100
Marktoberdorf — E 6 — 96
Marktredwitz — B 8 — 100
Mark Twain Lake ☒¹ — C 3 — 170
Markundi — E 4 — 98
Marl — E 4 — 98
Marlborough, Austl. — G 9 — 142
Marlborough, Eng., U.K. — F 5 — 72
Marlborough, Ma., U.S. — D 7 — 164
Marlborough □³ — D 4 — 146
Marlborough Sounds ⊔, N.Z. — D 5 — 146
Marlborough Sounds ⊔, N.Z. — D 5 — 146
Marle — B 11 — 66
Marma — B 8 — 66
Marmande — D 4 — 80
Marmara, Sea of ⊤² — B 8 — 106
Marmara Ereğlisi — B 7 — 106
Marmaris — D 3 — 106
Marmelos ≃ — E 6 — 190
Marmolada ∧ — B 3 — 90
Marmolejo — F 6 — 86
Marmora — A 5 — 162
Marmot Bay C — G 18 — 154
Marne — E 6 — 98
Marne ≃ — C 2 — 75
Marne □³ — C 11 — 78
Marne à la Saône, Canal de la ≃ — B 3 — 82
Marne au Rhin, Canal de la ≃ — B 5 — 82
Maroa — C 5 — 190
Maroantsetra — k 9 — 205a
Maroelabosom — D 2 — 204
Maromme — C 7 — 78
Maromokotro ∧ — j 9 — 205a
Marondera — F 5 — 204
Maroni (Marowijne) ≃ — C 8 — 190
Maros — B 6 — 104
Maroua — B 7 — 200
Marovato ≃ — k 9 — 205a
Marovoay — k 9 — 205a
Marowijne (Maroni) ≃ — C 8 — 190
Marpingen — F 3 — 132
Marquard — D 8 — 206
Marquette — B 5 — 166
Marquise — B 8 — 78
Marradi — E 7 — 92
Marrah, Jabal ∧² — C 2 — 200
Marrakech — C 3 — 200
Marree — B 2 — 144
Marrero — H 3 — 170
Marrupa — D 6 — 204
Marsabit — G 4 — 202
Marsabit National Park ♦ — G 4 — 202
Marsala — G 2 — 94
Marsberg — E 5 — 98
Marsciano — G 7 — 92
Marseille — G 3 — 82
Marseille-en-Beauvaisis — C 8 — 78
Marshall, Il., U.S. — C 5 — 170
Marshall, Mi., U.S. — C 5 — 170
Marshall, Mn., U.S. — C 7 — 174
Marshall, Mo., U.S. — C 2 — 170
Marshall, Tx., U.S. — F 1 — 170
Marshall Islands □² — B 8 — 136
Marshalltown — C 2 — 166
Marshfield, Mo., U.S. — D 2 — 170
Marshfield, Wi., U.S. — D 3 — 166
Marsh Harbour — A 4 — 186
Marsh Hill — g 12 — 163a
Marsh Island I — H 4 — 170
Marsh Lake ☒ — A 2 — 156
Mārsta — C 3 — 66
Marstal — C 8 — 66
Marston Moor Battlesite ⊥ — D 5 — 72
Martaban — F 3 — 132
Martaban, Gulf of C — F 3 — 132
Martapura — F 6 — 134
Marte — C 7 — 200
Marte R. Gómez, Presa ☒¹ — G 4 — 172
Martha's Vineyard I — E 8 — 164
Martí — C 5 — 186
Martigny — C 3 — 82
Martigues — G 3 — 82
Martil — C 5 — 84
Martin, Mi., U.S. — D 6 — 166
Martin, Tn., U.S. — A 10 — 170
Martin, Slvk. — F 14 — 96
Martina Franca — E 7 — 94
Martinengo — D 5 — 92
Mārtineşti — C 9 — 104
Martinez, Ca., U.S. — E 3 — 182
Martinez, Ga., U.S. — D 3 — 168
Martínez de la Torre — G 11 — 184
Martinique □² — E 10 — 186
Martinique Passage ⊔ — F 6 — 170
Martin Peninsula ⋋¹ — D 33 — 208
Martinsberg — B 7 — 102
Martinsburg — D 4 — 162

Martin's Drift — B 7 — 206
Martins Ferry — C 3 — 162
Martinsville, In., U.S. — C 5 — 170
Martinsville, Va., U.S. — E 4 — 162
Martin Vaz, Ilhas ⋌ — G 12 — 188
Martos — G 7 — 86
Martre, Lac la ☒ — D 9 — 150
Martūbah — C 9 — 198
Maru — C 5 — 204
Marungu — C 5 — 204
Marutea I¹ — E 13 — 136
Marv Dasht — H 15 — 118
Marvell — E 3 — 170
Mary (Merv) — C 9 — 112
Mary ≃ — H 11 — 142
Maryborough, Austl. — H 11 — 142
Maryborough, Austl. — F 4 — 144
Mary Kathleen — F 5 — 142
Maryland □³ — D 12 — 152
Marynivka — B 11 — 104
Maryport — C 3 — 72
Mary's Harbour — B 16 — 160
Marystown — E 16 — 160
Marysville, Ca., U.S. — A 2 — 182
Marysville, Ks., U.S. — E 6 — 174
Marysville, N.B., Can. — E 10 — 160
Marysville, Pa., U.S. — F 5 — 162
Marysville, Wa., U.S. — A 2 — 178
Maryville, Mo., U.S. — E 7 — 174
Maryville, Tn., U.S. — B 3 — 168
Masada see Meẕada, Horvot — G 4 — 120
Masai — i 15 — 134a
Masai Mara Game Reserve ♦ — H 3 — 202
Masai Steppe ⋋¹ — C 6 — 204
Masalembu Besar, Pulau I — G 6 — 134
Masallı — J 16 — 110
Masan — I 17 — 128
Masasi — E 6 — 204
Masaya — F 3 — 186
Masbate — C 8 — 134
Masbate I — C 8 — 134
Mascarene Islands II — L 7 — 112
Maseru — E 7 — 206
Mashan, China — D 18 — 128
Mashan, China — G 9 — 130
Mashar — F 2 — 202
Mashhad — C 8 — 116
Mashi (Kwando) ≃ — F 3 — 204
Mashonaland Central □³ — F 5 — 204
Mashonaland East □³ — F 5 — 204
Mashonaland West □³ — F 5 — 204
Masindi — G 3 — 202
Maşīrah I — F 8 — 116
Maşīrah, Khalīj C — G 8 — 116
Mask, Lough C — C 2 — 75
Masku — B 11 — 66
Masoala ⋋ — k 9 — 205a
Masoala, Saikanosy ⋋¹ — k 9 — 205a
Mason, Tn., U.S. — B 1 — 170
Mason, Tx., U.S. — E 4 — 172
Mason City — D 2 — 166
Masqaṭ (Muscat) — F 8 — 116
Massa — E 6 — 92
Massa-Carrara □⁶ — E 6 — 92
Massachusetts □³ — C 13 — 152
Massachusetts Bay C — D 8 — 164
Massafra — D 7 — 94
Massakory — C 8 — 200
Massamagrell — E 4 — 88
Massa Marittima — F 6 — 92
Massara — F 5 — 204
Massarosa — F 6 — 92
Massawa see Mitsiwa — D 4 — 202
Massena, Ia., U.S. — B 1 — 170
Massena, N.Y., U.S. — B 4 — 164
Masset — D 5 — 156
Masset Inlet C — E 5 — 156
Massiac — F 8 — 78
Massillon — C 3 — 162
Massina ⋋¹ — C 4 — 200
Massive, Mount ∧ — C 5 — 176
Maştağa — J 17 — 110
Masterton — D 5 — 146
Mastung — D 10 — 118
Masty — C 7 — 110
Masuda — G 3 — 126
Masuku (Franceville) — B 2 — 204
Masuria ⋋¹ — B 11 — 96
Masvingo — G 5 — 206
Masvingo □³ — G 5 — 206
Mata — C 4 — 200
Matabeleland North □³ — F 4 — 204
Matachewan — D 5 — 160
Matadi — D 1 — 204
Matagalpa — E 8 — 186
Matagami — D 5 — 160
Matagorda Bay C — F 5 — 172
Matagorda Island I — F 5 — 172
Mataiva I¹ — E 13 — 136
Matala — H 4 — 122
Matale — H 4 — 122
Matam — A 2 — 200
Matamey — C 6 — 200
Matamoros, Mex. — E 11 — 184
Matamoros, Mex. — E 8 — 184
Matandu ≃ — D 6 — 204
Matane — D 10 — 160
Matanuska ≃ — F 21 — 154
Matanzas — C 4 — 186
Matapa — B 6 — 206
Matapédia, Lac ☒ — D 10 — 160
Matara — H 4 — 122
Mataram — G 6 — 134
Mataró — D 14 — 88
Mataura — A 2 — 146
Mataveri — m 16 — 193a
Matehuala — F 9 — 184
Matera — D 7 — 94
Mateur — B 9 — 94
Matha — C 3 — 80
Matheson — D 5 — 160
Mathis — F 5 — 172
Mathura — C 3 — 122
Mati — D 8 — 134
Matías Barbosa — F 5 — 194
Matías Romero — I 12 — 184
Matignon — D 4 — 78

Matino — D 8 — 94
Mātli — E 1 — 122
Matlock — D 5 — 72
Mato — D 3 — 204
Mato, Cerro ∧ — G 8 — 186
Mato Grosso — F 7 — 190
Mato Grosso, Planalto do ⋌¹ — G 7 — 190
Mato Grosso do Sul □³ — G 8 — 190
Matola — C 10 — 206
Matosinhos — C 2 — 86
Mbé — D 7 — 200
Maṭraḥ — C 9 — 116
Matsap — E 5 — 206
Matsena — C 7 — 200
Matsudo — G 7 — 126
Matsue — G 4 — 126
Matsumoto — F 6 — 126
Matsu Tao I — E 14 — 130
Matsutō — F 6 — 126
Matsuura — H 2 — 126
Matsuyama — H 4 — 126
Mattagami ≃ — C 3 — 160
Mattawamkeag — h 12 — 163a
Mattawamkeag ≃ — h 12 — 163a
Matterhorn (Cervino) ∧ — C 8 — 102
Matthews Ridge — G 9 — 186
Mattighofen — B 5 — 102
Mattoon — C 4 — 170
Matuba — C 10 — 206
Maturín — F 9 — 186
Matusadona National Park ♦ — F 4 — 204
Mau — E 6 — 204
Mauban — C 3 — 134
Maubeuge — B 10 — 78
Maud — F 1 — 170
Mauès — D 7 — 190
Mauès ≃ — D 7 — 190
Mauganj — E 4 — 122
Mauga Silisili ∧ — j 10 — 147b
Maug Islands II — H 13 — 124
Maui I — i 10 — 181a
Mauke I — F 12 — 136
Mauldin — B 3 — 168
Maule □³ — D 2 — 195
Maule, Laguna del ☒ — D 2 — 195
Mauléon — F 6 — 78
Maumee — C 2 — 162
Maumee ≃ — E 7 — 166
Maumere — G 8 — 134
Maun — F 3 — 204
Maunath Bhanjan — D 4 — 122
Maunatlala — D 1 — 132
Maunoir, Lac ☒ — C 32 — 154
Maupihaa I¹ — E 12 — 136
Maupin — C 3 — 178
Mau Rānīpur — D 3 — 122
Maurepas, Lake ☒ — G 3 — 170
Mauriac — C 6 — 80
Maurice, Lake ☒ — K 11 — 140
Mauritania □¹ — G 6 — 196
Mauritius □¹ — L 7 — 112
Maurs — D 6 — 80
Mauston — D 3 — 166
Mauthausen — B 6 — 102
Mauvezin — E 4 — 80
Mavengue — F 2 — 204
Mavinga — F 3 — 204
Mavonde — F 5 — 204
Mavrovo Nacionalni Park ♦ — E 6 — 104
Mawchi — D 3 — 132
Mawlaik — B 2 — 132
Mawlamyine (Moulmein) ♦ — F 3 — 132
Mawson B³ — C 15 — 208
Mawson Escarpment ⋌⁴ — D 16 — 208
Maxixe — B 11 — 206
Maxwell, Ca., U.S. — A 1 — 182
Maxwell, N.M., U.S. — B 1 — 172
May — E 8 — 140
May ≃ — E 8 — 140
May, Cape ⋋ — H 4 — 164
Maya I — C 6 — 186
Mayaguana I — C 6 — 186
Mayaguana Passage ⊔ — C 6 — 186
Mayagüez — j 14 — 187b
Mayahi — C 6 — 200
Mayang — E 9 — 130
Maych'ew — E 6 — 202
Maydh — F 6 — 202
Mayen — D 6 — 78
Mayenne — D 6 — 78
Mayenne □³ — D 7 — 78
Mayenne ≃ — D 6 — 78
Mayerthorpe — E 14 — 156
Mayflower — D 3 — 170
Maynardville — A 3 — 168
Mayo — E 26 — 154
Mayo □³ — C 2 — 75
Mayo ≃, Arg. — I 5 — 192
Mayo ≃, Mex. — D 5 — 184
Mayo-Kébbi □³ — D 7 — 200
Mayo Lake ☒ — E 27 — 154
Mayon Volcano ∧¹ — C 8 — 134
Mayotte □² — j 12 — 196
May Pen — h 12 — 186a
Mayrhofen — C 4 — 96
Maysān □³ — F 12 — 118
Mays Landing — G 4 — 164
Mayumba — F 7 — 200
Māyūram — D 7 — 166
Mayville — D 7 — 166
Mazabuka — B 4 — 182
Mazagan see El-Jadida — C 3 — 198
Mazagão — D 8 — 190
Mazamet — E 9 — 80
Mazānderān □³ — D 16 — 118
Mazara, Val di ⋋¹ — G 3 — 94
Mazara del Vallo — G 2 — 94
Mazār-e Sharīf — B 1 — 124
Mazarrón — G 7 — 84
Mazatenango — J 14 — 184
Mazatlán — E 6 — 184
Mažeikiai — D 11 — 66
Mazira — E 6 — 204
Mazoe — E 5 — 204
Mazowe — E 5 — 204
Mazyr — C 6 — 110
Mbalmayo — E 7 — 200
Mbandaka — C 3 — 204
Mbanga — E 6 — 200
M'banza Congo — D 1 — 204
Mbanza-Ngungu — D 1 — 204
Mbarara — H 3 — 202
Mbari ≃ — D 9 — 200
Mbashe ≃ — E 8 — 206
Mbassany — D 8 — 200
M'batto — D 4 — 200
Mbé — D 7 — 200
Mbembesi — F 4 — 204
Mbereshi — D 4 — 204
Mbeya — D 5 — 204
Mbinda — E 6 — 204
Mbinga — E 6 — 204
Mbini — E 7 — 200
Mbizi — D 4 — 204
Mbomou □³ — H 2 — 126
Mbomou (Bomu) ≃ — D 9 — 200
Mboro — F 2 — 202
Mbotou — D 6 — 200
Mbour — C 1 — 200
Mbout — F 2 — 198
Mbridge ≃ — F 2 — 198
Mbuji-Mayi — D 3 — 204
Mbulu — C 6 — 204
Mbwemkuru ≃ — D 6 — 204
McAdam — F 10 — 160
McAlester — C 6 — 172
McAllen — G 4 — 172
McArthur — D 2 — 162
McArthur ≃ — D 3 — 142
McBee — B 4 — 168
McCamey — E 2 — 172
McCarthy — F 23 — 154
McClellan Creek ≃ — C 3 — 172
McClintock, Mount ∧ — E 23 — 208
McCloud — E 2 — 178
McClure — D 4 — 170
McComas — E 3 — 162
McComb — G 3 — 170
McConnellsburg — D 4 — 162
McCook — E 4 — 174
McCormick — C 3 — 168
McCrory — E 3 — 170
McDermitt — E 7 — 178
McDonald, Lake ☒ — A 7 — 178
Mcensk — J 12 — 108
McFarland — E 4 — 182
McGill — C 1 — 176
McGraw — D 2 — 164
McGregor — G 3 — 206
McGregor ≃ — D 11 — 156
McHenry — A 4 — 166
McIntosh — G 4 — 170
McIntosh Lake ☒ — D 19 — 156
McKeand ≃ — D 19 — 150
McKeesport — C 4 — 162
McKenzie — G 5 — 170
McKenzie ≃ — D 2 — 178
McKenzie Island — F 11 — 158
McKinlay ⋌ — F 5 — 142
McKinley, Mount ∧ — E 19 — 154
McKinleyville — B 1 — 178
McKinney — D 5 — 172
McKnight Lake ☒ — C 8 — 158
McLain — G 4 — 170
McLean — C 3 — 172
McLennan — D 13 — 156
McLeod — E 14 — 156
M'Clintock Channel ⊔ — B 12 — 150
McLoughlin, Mount ∧ — E 3 — 178
McLure — F 11 — 156
M'Clure Strait ⊔ — B 9 — 150
McMinnville, Or., U.S. — C 2 — 178
McMinnville, Tn., U.S. — B 3 — 168
McMurdo B³ — D 25 — 208
McMurdo Sound ⊔ — D 26 — 208
McPherson — F 6 — 174
McRae — E 3 — 168
McVille — B 5 — 174
Mdantsane — G 7 — 206
M'Daourouch — G 1 — 90
Mead, Lake ☒ — D 1 — 176
Meadow — D 2 — 172
Meadow Lake — D 17 — 156
Meadow Lake Provincial Park ♦ — D 4 — 158
Meadow Valley Wash ≃ — D 1 — 176
Meadview — D 1 — 176
Meadville, Mo., U.S. — C 2 — 162
Meadville, Pa., U.S. — C 3 — 162
Medford, Or., U.S. — E 3 — 178
Méan — D 4 — 69
Meander River — B 13 — 156
Meath — C 5 — 75
Meath □⁹ — C 5 — 75
Meaux — C 9 — 78
Mecca see Makkah — C 4 — 202
Mechanicsburg — C 2 — 162
Mechanicsville — E 5 — 162
Mechara — F 5 — 202
Mechelen — C 4 — 69
Mechernich — D 4 — 98
Mechriyya — D 8 — 154
Meckenbeuren — C 7 — 82
Mecklenburg — B 4 — 100
Mecklenburg □⁹ — C 9 — 98
Mecklenburg Bay see Mecklenburger Bucht — B 8 — 98
Mecklenburger Bucht (Mecklenburg Bay) C — B 8 — 98
Mecklenburgische Seenplatte ⋋¹ — C 8 — 98
Mecklenburg-Vorpommern □³ — C 9 — 98
Meconta — C 7 — 204
Mecula — D 6 — 204
Medan — M 4 — 132
Medanosa, Punta ⋋ — I 6 — 192
Mede — D 5 — 92
Medellín — B 3 — 190
Médenine — B 8 — 104 — Médéa...
Mederdra — F 1 — 198
Medford, Or., U.S. — E 3 — 178
Medford, Wi., U.S. — C 3 — 166
Medgidia — C 10 — 104
Media — B 3 — 164
Mediaş — B 8 — 104
Medicina — E 7 — 92
Medicine Bow Mountains ⋌ — B 5 — 176
Medicine Hat — F 16 — 156
Medicine Lake — A 2 — 174

⌐ Waterfall   c Strait   c Bay, Gulf   ☒ Lake   ⊞ Swamp   ≋ Ice Feature   ⊤ Other Hydrographic Feature   ⋌ Submarine Feature   □ Political Unit   ♦ Cultural Institution   ⊥ Historical Site   ♦ Recreational Site   ⊠ Airport   ⊥ Military Installation   ∼ Miscellaneous

267

Name	Map Ref.	Page

Symbols in the index entries represent the broad categories identified in the key at the right. ◣ Mountain ◣ Mountains ⋗ Pass ⌄ Valley ≡ Plain ► Cape I Island II Islands ⊥ Other Topographic Feature ≈ River ⊞ Canal
Symbols with superior numbers (◄¹) identify subcategories (see complete key on page 242).

Moma — Mutsu-wan

Name | Map Ref. | Page

Moma C 3 204
Momba C 4 144
Mombasa H 4 202
Mombetsu B 9 126
Mombo C 6 204
Momboyo ≐ C 2 204
Mombuey B 4 86
Momi m 13 147c
Mompós F 6 186
Momskij hrebet ∧∧ C 17 114
Mon □[3] G 3 132
Møn I D 5 68
Mona, Isla de I D 8 186
Monaco □[1] G 9 62
Monadhliath Mountains ∧∧ C 4 74
Monadnock Mountain ∧ D 6 164
Monagas □[3] F 9 186
Monaghan B 4 75
Monaghan □[3] B 4 75
Monahans E 2 172
Monahans Sandhills State Park ♦ E 2 172
Monango B 5 174
Mona Passage ʯ D 8 186
Mona Quimbundo E 3 204
Monarch Pass)(C 5 176
Monashee Mountains ∧∧ A 4 178
Monashee Provincial Park ♦ F 12 156
Monastery ⊥ B 6 88
Monastyrys'ka A 8 104
Mona Vale D 8 144
Monbazillac F 4 76
Moncalieri E 3 92
Mončegorsk B 9 108
Mönchengladbach E 3 98
Moncks Corner C 5 168
Monclova D 9 184
Moncoutant F 6 78
Moncton E 11 160
Mondego ≐ D 2 86
Mondello F 3 94
Mondjamboli B 3 204
Mondoro C 4 200
Mondragone C 3 94
Monemvasía D 5 106
Monessen C 3 162
Monesterio F 4 86
Monetnyj H 24 108
Monette E 3 170
Monfalcone D 9 92
Monferrato □[9] E 4 92
Monforte E 3 86
Monforte de Lemos B 3 86
Mongadjo B 3 204
Mongeri D 2 200
Mongers Lake ◎ K 4 140
Möng Hawm C 4 132
Möng Hsat D 4 132
Mongibello see Etna, Monte ∧[1] G 5 94
Möng Küng D 3 132
Möng Mit C 3 132
Mongo C 8 200
Mongolia □[1] C 4 124
Mongomo E 7 200
Mongororo C 9 200
Möng Pawn D 3 132
Mongu F 3 204
Monheim, Ger. C 5 69
Monheim, Ger. D 7 100
Monida Pass)(C 7 178
Monimpébougou C 3 200
Monistrol-sur-Loire E 2 82
Monitor Range ∧∧ B 7 182
Mońki B 12 96
Monmouth, Or., U.S. C 2 178
Monmouth, Wales, U.K. F 4 72
Monmouth □[6] F 4 164
Monmouthshire □[6] F 4 72
Mono □[6] C 5 182
Mono ≐ D 5 200
Mono Lake ◎ B 5 182
Monona, Ia., U.S. D 3 166
Monona, Wi., U.S. D 4 166
Monongahela ≐ D 3 162
Monopoli D 7 94
Monor B 5 104
Monòver F 4 88
Monreal del Campo D 3 88
Monreale F 3 94
Monreale, Castello di ⊥ I 9 94a
Monroe, La., U.S. F 2 170
Monroe, Mi., U.S. C 2 162
Monroe, Ne., U.S. E 6 174
Monroe, Wa., U.S. B 3 178
Monroe, Wi., U.S. D 4 166
Monroe □[6], N.Y., U.S. C 1 164
Monroe □[6], Pa., U.S. E 3 164
Monroe Lake ◎[1] C 5 170
Monroeville, Al., U.S. G 5 170
Monroeville, Pa., U.S. C 4 162
Monrovia D 2 200
Mons D 2 69
Monschau B 3 100
Monsec, Serra de ∧∧ F 4 80
Monselice D 7 92
Mönsterås D 8 66
Montabaur B 4 100
Montagnana D 7 92
Montagne d'Ambre, Parque National de la ♦ j 9 205a
Montagrier C 4 80
Montague Island I G 21 154
Montagu Island I J 12 188
Montaigle, Château de ⊥ D 3 69
Montaigu F 5 78
Montalbano Ionico D 6 94
Montalegre C 3 86
Montalto Uffugo E 6 94
Montana D 7 104
Montana □[3], Bul. D 7 104
Montana □[3], U.S. B 5 152
Montaña de Covadonga, Parque Nacional de la ♦ A 6 86
Montana de Oro State Park ♦ E 2 182
Montana-Vermala D 5 82
Montargil E 2 86
Montargis D 9 78
Montataire C 9 78
Montauban D 5 80
Montauk State Park ♦ D 3 170
Montbard E 11 78
Montbarrey C 3 82
Montbéliard C 4 82
Mont Belvieu H 1 170
Montblanc C 6 88
Montbrison E 1 82
Montcalm □[6] A 5 164
Montceau-les-Mines F 11 78
Montchanin F 11 78
Montclair C 6 162
Mont-de-Marsan E 3 80
Montdidier C 9 78
Monte, Castel del ⊥ C 6 94
Monte, Laguna del ◎ E 6 195
Monteagle E 6 170
Monte Albán ⊥ I 11 184
Monte Alegre D 8 190
Monte Alegre de Minas C 6 194
Monte Azul G 10 190
Montebello Iónico G 5 94
Montebelluna D 7 92
Montecarlo G 3 194
Monte Carmelo C 7 194
Monte Caseros B 8 195
Montecassino, Abbazia di ◗[1] C 3 94
Montecatini Terme F 6 92
Monte Comán F 6 192
Montecuccolo ◗[1] E 6 92
Monte di Procida D 3 94
Montefalco G 8 92
Montefiascone G 8 92
Monteforte d'Alpone D 7 92
Montego Bay h 12 186a
Montegranaro A 3 94
Montejicar G 7 86
Montélimar F 2 82
Monte Lindo ≐ D 8 192
Montella D 5 94
Montellano G 5 86
Montello E 6 178
Monteluco ◗[1] G 8 92
Montelupo Fiorentino F 7 92
Montemorelos E 9 184
Montemor-o-Velho D 2 86
Montenegro A 12 195
Montenegro see Crna Gora □[3] D 5 104
Montenero di Bisaccia C 4 94
Monte Pascoal, Parque Nacional de ♦ B 11 194
Monte Patria B 2 195
Montepuez E 6 204
Montepulciano F 7 92
Monte Quemado E 7 192
Montereale G 9 92
Montereau-Faut-Yonne D 9 78
Monterey, Ca., U.S. D 2 182
Monterey, Va., U.S. D 4 162
Monterey □[6] D 2 182
Monterey Bay c D 1 182
Montería F 6 186
Monterotondo G 8 92
Monterrey E 9 184
Montesano B 2 178
Monte Sant'Angelo C 5 94
Monte Santo, Braz. E 9 190
Monte Santo, Braz. E 9 190
Montesarchio C 4 94
Montes Claros B 8 194
Montesilvano Marina B 4 94
Montevallo F 5 170
Montevarchi F 7 92
Montevideo D 9 195
Montezie, Barrage de ✦[6] D 6 80
Montezuma, In., U.S. C 5 170
Montezuma, Ks., U.S. G 4 174
Montezuma Castle National Monument ♦ E 3 176
Montgomery, Al., U.S. F 5 170
Montgomery, La., U.S. G 2 170
Montgomery see Sāhīwāl, Pak. C 2 122
Montgomery □[6], Md., U.S. G 1 164
Montgomery □[6], N.Y., U.S. D 4 164
Montgomery □[6], Pa., U.S. F 3 164
Montguyon C 3 80
Monthey D 4 82
Monthois C 11 78
Monticello, In., U.S. B 5 170
Monticello, Ky., U.S. A 2 168
Monticello, Ms., U.S. G 3 170
Monticello, N.Y., U.S. E 4 164
Monticello, Wi., U.S. D 4 166
Monticello ⊥ D 4 162
Montichiari D 6 92
Montigny-le-Roi B 3 82
Montigny-lès-Metz A 4 82
Montijo, Pan. F 2 86
Montijo, Port. C 1 84
Montijo, Spain F 4 86
Montilla G 6 86
Montivilliers C 7 78
Mont-Joli D 9 160
Mont-Louis F 6 80
Montluçon B 6 80
Montmagny E 8 160
Montmédy A 3 82
Montmirail D 10 78
Montmorillon B 4 80
Montney C 11 156
Monto H 10 142
Montorio al Vomano B 3 94
Montoro F 6 86
Montour □[6] E 2 164
Montoursville E 2 164
Mont Peko, Parc National du ♦ D 3 200
Montpelier, In., U.S. B 6 170
Montpelier, Vt., U.S. B 6 164
Montpellier G 1 82
Montréal, P.Q., Can. F 7 160
Montreal, Wi., U.S. B 3 166
Montreal ≐, On., Can. E 3 160
Montreal ≐, Sk., Can. D 6 158
Montréal, Île de I A 5 164
Montreal Lake ◎ D 19 156
Montreal Lake Indian Reserve ✦[4] D 19 156
Montrésor E 8 78
Montreuil-sur-Mer B 8 78
Montreux D 4 82
Montrichard E 8 78
Montrose, Co., U.S. C 4 176
Montrose, Pa., U.S. E 3 164
Montrose, Scot., U.K. D 6 74
Mont-Saint-Aignan C 8 78
Mont-Saint-Hilaire A 5 164
Mont-Saint-Martin A 3 82
Mont-Saint-Michel, Baie du c D 5 78
Mont-Saint-Michel, Le ◗[1] D 5 78
Mont Sangbé, Parc National du ♦ D 3 200
Montserrat □[2] D 9 186
Montserrat Monastery ◗[1] C 6 88
Montuenga C 6 86
Monument Valley V D 3 176
Monyo E 2 132
Monywa C 2 132
Monza D 5 92
Monze F 4 204
Monzón C 5 88
Mooi ≐ E 9 206
Mooihoek C 8 206
Mookane B 7 206
Moolman D 9 206
Moonie I 10 142
Moonie ≐ B 7 144
Moonta E 1 144
Moora L 3 140
Moorarie I 4 140
Moore, Id., U.S. D 7 178
Moore, Mt., U.S. B 9 178
Moore, Ok., U.S. C 5 172
Moore ≐ L 3 140
Moore, Lake ◎ L 4 140
Moorea I E 13 136
Moores Creek National Battlefield ♦ B 5 168
Moorestown G 4 164
Mooresville C 5 170
Moorhead B 6 174
Moornanyah Lake ◎ D 4 144
Moorpark F 5 182
Moorreesburg G 3 206
Moosburg an der Isar D 8 100
Moose Factory C 3 160
Moosehead Lake ◎ h 11 163a
Moose Jaw F 18 156
Moose Lake E 8 158
Mooselookmeguntic Lake ◎[1] A 8 162
Moose Mountain Provincial Park ♦ G 7 158
Moose River C 3 160
Moosomin Indian Reserve ✦[4] E 17 156
Moosonee C 3 160
Mootwingee National Park ♦ C 4 144
Mopipi G 3 204
Mopti C 4 200
Mopti □[3] C 4 200
Moquegua G 4 190
Mór C 10 102
Mora, Cam. C 7 200
Mora, Spain E 7 86
Mora, Swe. B 7 66
Morača, Manastir ◗[1] D 5 104
Morādābād D 3 122
Móra d'Ebre C 5 88
Mora de Rubielos D 4 88
Morąg B 10 96
Moral de Calatrava F 7 86
Morales, Laguna de c F 11 184
Moramanga k 9 205a
Moran D 1 170
Morant Bay i 13 186a
Morant Point > i 13 186a
Moratalla F 3 88
Moratuwa H 3 122
Morava □[9] D 9 96
Morava (March) ≐ B 8 102
Morāveh Tappeh D 16 118
Moravské Budějovice A 7 102
Morawa K 4 140
Morawhanna F 10 186
Moray □[6] C 5 74
Moray Firth c C 5 74
Morbach C 4 100
Morbegno C 5 92
Morbi E 2 122
Morbihan □[3] E 4 78
Morcenx D 3 80
Morden G 9 158
Mordialloc F 5 144
Mordovija □[3] I 15 108
Moreau ≐ C 4 174
Moreau, North Fork ≐ C 3 174
Morecambe C 3 72
Morecambe Bay c C 3 72
Moree, Austl. B 7 144
Morée, Fr. E 8 78
Morehouse D 4 170
Moreland C 2 168
Morelia H 9 184
Morella D 4 88
Morelos F 3 172
Morelos □[3] H 10 184
Morena, Sierra ∧∧ C 3 84
Morenci F 4 176
Moreni C 8 104
Moreno Valley G 6 182
Møre og Romsdal □[3] E 3 64
Moresby Island I E 5 156
Morestel E 3 82
Moreton Island I I 11 142
Morez D 4 82
Morfou Bay c E 5 118
Morgan A 10 178
Morgan City, Al., U.S. E 5 170
Morgan City, La., U.S. H 3 170
Morgan Hill C 2 182
Morgantina ⊥ G 4 94
Morganton B 4 168
Morgantown D 4 162
Morganza G 3 170
Morges D 4 82
Morgongåva C 8 66
Moriarty E 5 176
Morice ≐ D 8 156
Morice Lake ◎ D 8 156
Morija E 7 206
Moriki C 6 200
Morin Dawa B 15 128
Morino H 9 108
Morinville E 15 156
Morioka E 8 126
Morīri, Tso ◎ C 3 122
Morkoka ≐ C 14 114
Morlaix D 3 78
Morlanwelz D 3 69
Morley D 5 72
Mormal' C 6 110
Mormugao F 2 122
Morne-à-l'Eau n 21 187e
Morne Trois Pitons National Park ♦ r 25 187g
Morney H 5 142
Mornington, Isla I I 4 192
Mornington Island I D 4 142
Morobe N 13 124
Morocco B 5 170
Morocco □[1] E 7 196
Morogoro D 6 204
Morogoro □[3] D 6 204
Moro Gulf c D 8 134
Moroleón G 9 184
Morombe I 8 205a
Morón, Arg. D 8 195
Morón, Cuba C 5 186
Mörön, Mong. B 3 128
Morón, Ven. A 5 190
Mörön ≐ C 7 128
Morondava I 8 205a
Morón de la Frontera G 5 86
Morongo Indian Reservation ✦[4] F 7 182
Moroni n 18 207d
Moron Us ≐ C 6 122
Morotai I E 9 134
Moroto G 3 202
Morouba D 8 200
Morozovsk E 12 110
Morozovskaja F 18 108
Morpeth B 5 72
Morrilton E 2 170
Morrinhos B 6 194
Morris, Il., U.S. B 4 170
Morris, Mn., U.S. C 7 174
Morris □[6] F 4 164
Morrisburg B 3 164
Morris Jesup, Kap > A 16 148
Morrison B 4 170
Morristown, Mn., U.S. C 2 166
Morristown, N.J., U.S. F 4 164
Morristown, Tn., U.S. A 3 168
Morrisville, N.Y., U.S. D 3 164
Morrisville, Pa., U.S. F 4 164
Morro Bay E 3 182
Morro Bay State Park ♦ E 2 182
Morro do Chapéu F 10 190
Morrosquillo, Golfo de c F 5 186
Morrumbala F 6 204
Mörrumsån ≐ D 7 66
Moršansk J 14 108
Morse F 18 156
Morson G 11 158
Mortagne ≐ B 4 82
Mortagne-sur-Sèvre E 6 78
Mortara D 4 92
Morteau C 4 82
Morteros B 6 195
Mortes ≐ F 8 190
Mortesoro E 3 202
Mortlock Islands II C 7 136
Morton, Il., U.S. B 4 170
Morton, Ms., U.S. F 4 170
Morton, Wa., U.S. B 2 178
Morton National Park ♦ E 8 144
Mortsel C 3 69
Moruya E 8 144
Morvant q 23 187f
Morwa C 7 206
Morwell G 6 144
Moryń B 8 96
Mosaneng C 6 206
Mosbach C 6 100
Mosborough D 5 72
Moscow, Id., U.S. B 5 178
Moscow see Moskva, Russia I 12 108
Mosel (Moselle) ≐ B 4 100
Moselesenyane A 6 206
Moselle □[3] A 4 82
Moselle (Mosel) ≐ C 3 100
Moses Point D 13 154
Mosgiel F 3 146
Moshaweng ≐ D 5 206
Mosheim A 3 168
Moshi C 6 204
Moshi ≐ D 5 200
Mosinee C 4 166
Moskalënki I 29 108
Moskovskaja oblast' □[6] I 12 108
Moskva (Moscow) I 12 108
Moskva ≐ B 11 110
Mosonmagyaróvár C 9 102
Mospyne F 11 110
Mosquera C 3 190
Mosquitos, Golfo de los c F 4 186
Moss C 5 66
Mossbank F 18 156
Mosselbaai H 5 206
Mossel Bay see Mosselbaai H 5 206
Mossendjo C 1 204
Mossgiel D 5 144
Mössingen D 6 100
Mossman D 7 142
Mossoró E 11 190
Moss Point G 4 170
Moss Vale E 8 144
Most B 10 100
Mostar D 4 104
Mostardas F 9 192
Møsting, Kap > D 24 150
Móstoles D 7 86
Mostovka G 26 108
Mosul see Al-Mawṣil D 10 118
Motaba ≐ B 2 204
Mota del Cuervo E 2 88
Mota del Marqués C 5 86
Motagua ≐ J 15 184
Motala C 7 66
Motaze C 10 206
Motherwell B 3 72
Motihāri D 4 122
Motloutse A 7 206
Motril H 7 86
Motru C 7 104
Mottola D 7 94
Motueka D 4 146
Motu One I[1] E 12 136
Mouaskar B 4 198
Mouaskar □[3] E 6 84
Moúdhros C 6 106
Mouding B 5 132
Moudjéria F 2 198
Mougdi C 8 200
Mouhoun see Black Volta ≐ D 4 200
Mouila F 7 200
Mouit F 2 198
Moulamein E 5 144
Moulins D 1 82
Moulins-la-Marche D 7 78
Moulmein see Mawlamyine F 3 132
Moulmeingyun F 2 132
Moulouya, Oued ≐ C 4 198
Moulton E 5 170
Moultrie D 3 168
Moultrie, Lake ◎[1] C 5 168
Mound City, Il., U.S. D 4 170
Mound City, S.D., U.S. C 4 174
Moundou D 8 200
Mounds D 4 170
Moundsville D 3 162
Mountain C 4 166
Mountain ≐ D 30 154
Mountainair E 5 176
Mountain Ash F 3 72
Mountain City E 3 162
Mountain Grove D 2 170
Mountain Home, Ar., U.S. D 2 170
Mountain Home, Id., U.S. D 6 178
Mountain Lake D 7 174
Mountain Nile ≐ F 3 202
Mountain Point I 29 154
Mountain View C 1 182
Mountain Zebra National Park ♦ G 6 206
Mount Airy E 3 162
Mount Aspiring National Park ♦ F 2 146
Mount Ayliff F 8 206
Mount Barker N 4 140
Mount Barney National Park ♦ B 9 144
Mount Beauty F 6 144
Mount Brydges B 3 162
Mount Buffalo National Park ♦ F 6 144
Mount Carleton Provincial Park ♦ g 13 163a
Mount Carmel F 2 164
Mount Carroll D 4 166
Mount Clemens B 2 162
Mount Cook E 3 146
Mount Cook National Park ♦ E 3 146
Mount Doreen G 11 140
Mount Edgecumbe C 4 156
Mount Edziza Provincial Park ♦ C 6 156
Mount Elgon National Park ♦ B 5 204
Mount Field National Park ♦ j 12 145a
Mount Fletcher F 8 206
Mount Forest F 3 160
Mount Gambier F 3 144
Mount Garnet D 7 142
Mount Gilead C 2 162
Mount Holly G 4 164
Mount Holly Springs F 1 164
Mount Hope M 2 142
Mount Isa F 4 142
Mount Jacinto State Park ♦ G 7 182
Mount Jackson D 4 162
Mount Kaputar National Park ♦ C 8 144
Mount Kenya National Park ♦ H 4 202
Mount Kisco E 5 164
Mount Lebanon C 3 162
Mount Magnet K 4 140
Mount Maunganui B 6 146
Mount McKinley National Park see Denali National Park ♦ E 19 154
Mountmellick C 4 75
Mount Moorosi F 7 206
Mount Morgan G 10 142
Mount Morris B 5 162
Mount Oeta National Park ♦ C 5 106
Mount Olive G 4 170
Mount Olympos National Park ♦ B 5 106
Mount Orab D 2 162
Mount Pleasant, Austl. E 2 144
Mount Pleasant, Ia., U.S. B 3 170
Mount Pleasant, Mi., U.S. B 1 162
Mount Pleasant, S.C., U.S. C 5 168
Mount Pleasant, Tn., U.S. E 5 170
Mount Pleasant, Tx., U.S. F 1 170
Mount Pleasant, Ut., U.S. C 3 176
Mount Pulaski B 4 170
Mount Rainier National Park ♦ B 3 178
Mount Remarkable National Park ♦ D 1 144
Mount Revelstoke National Park ♦ F 12 156
Mount Robson Provincial Park ♦ E 12 156
Mount Rogers National Recreation Area ♦ E 3 162
Mount Roskill B 5 146
Mount Rushmore National Memorial ♦ D 3 174
Mount Saint Helens National Volcanic Monument ♦ B 3 178
Mount Savage D 4 162
Mount's Bay c G 1 72
Mount Somers E 3 146
Mount Sterling D 2 162
Mount Stewart G 6 206
Mount Union C 5 162
Mount Vernon, Al., U.S. G 5 170
Mount Vernon, Il., U.S. C 4 170
Mount Vernon, Mo., U.S. D 1 170
Mount Vernon, Oh., U.S. C 2 162
Mount Vernon, Wa., U.S. A 2 178
Mount Wellington B 5 146
Mount William National Park ♦ i 12 145a
Moura, Braz. D 6 190
Moura, Port. F 3 86
Mouraya C 9 200
Mourdi, Dépression du •[7] B 9 200
Mourindi F 7 200
Mourne Mountains ∧∧ B 5 75
Mouscron D 2 69
Moussa 'Ali ∧ E 5 202
Moussoro C 8 200
Moutier C 5 82
Moûtiers E 4 82
Moutong E 8 134
Mouzarak C 8 200
Movenda B 3 204
Moville D 6 174
Moxico □[3] E 3 204
Moya o 19 207d
Moyahua G 8 184
Moyale B 6 204
Moyen Atlas ∧∧ C 4 198
Moyen-Chari □[3] D 8 200
Moyen-Ogooué □[3] F 7 200
Moyeuvre-Grande C 3 100
Moyie G 14 156
Moyo G 3 202
Moyo, Pulau I G 7 134
Moyobamba E 3 190
Možajsk B 10 110
Mozambique □[1] J 11 196
Mozambique Channel ʯ J 12 196
Mozdok H 14 110
Možga H 20 108
Mozia ⊥ G 2 94
Mpaka D 9 206
Mpama ≐ C 2 204
Mpé C 1 204
Mphahlele C 8 206
Mpigi G 3 202
Mpika E 5 204
Mpraeso D 4 200
Mpumalanga □[3] D 8 206
Mqanduli F 8 206
Mrągowo B 11 96
M'Ramani o 19 207d
Mrijo D 6 204
Mrkopalj C 3 104
Msagali D 6 204
M'Saken B 7 198
Mscislaŭ B 7 110
Msciž E 14 66
M'Sila B 5 198
Msoro E 5 204
Mtakataka E 5 204
Mtama E 6 204
Mtamvuna ≐ F 9 206
Mtubatuba E 10 206
Mtwara E 7 204
Mtwara □[3] E 6 204
Mu ≐ C 2 132
Muacandala D 2 204
Mualama F 6 204
Muanda D 1 204
Muang Hay D 5 132
Muang Khammouan F 7 132
Muang Không G 7 132
Muang Khôngxédôn G 7 132
Muang Pakxan E 6 132
Muang Sing D 5 132
Muang Vangviang E 5 132
Muang Xaignabouri I 5 130
Muar M 6 132
Muar ≐ M 6 132
Muarabinuangeun k 17 135b
Muarasiberut F 3 134
Muaratewe F 6 134
Mubende G 3 202
Mubi C 7 200
Muccan G 5 140
Muchinga Mountains ∧∧ E 5 204
Muchuan D 6 130
Muckadilla I 9 142
Mučkas D 18 108
Mücke B 6 100
Muconda E 3 204
Mucope F 1 204
Mucur C 6 118
Mucuri ≐ G 10 190
Muda ≐ K 5 132
Mudan ≐ C 17 128
Mudanjiang D 17 128
Mudanya B 8 106
Mud Creek ≐ G 1 170
Muddus Nationalpark ♦ C 9 64
Muddy ≐ D 1 176
Mudgee D 7 144
Mudjatik ≐ C 18 156
Mudon F 3 132
Mudug □[3] F 6 202
Mudurnu B 9 106
Muenster D 5 172
Muerto, Mar ◎ J 12 184
Muezerskij D 10 108
Mufulira E 4 204
Muggia D 9 92
Mugi H 5 126
Mu Gia, Deo)(J 7 130
Muğla D 8 106
Muğla □[3] D 8 106
Mugron E 3 80
Muḥammad Qawl C 4 202
Mühlacker D 5 100
Mühldorf am Inn D 9 100
Mühlhausen E 7 98
Muhlig-Hofmann Mountains ∧∧ D 9 208
Mühlviertel ✦[1] B 6 102
Muhola E 12 64
Muhutwe C 5 204
Muiderslot ⊥ B 4 69
Muir Woods National Monument ♦ C 1 182
Muiskraal G 4 206
Mujimbeji E 3 204
Mujnak H 21 110
Mukacheve A 7 104
Mukah E 6 134
Mukāwir ⊥ F 5 120
Mukdahan F 7 132
Mukhayyam al-Baq'ah E 5 120
Mukinbudin L 5 140
Mukomwenzo D 4 204
Mukoshima-rettō II K 9 126
Mukry C 10 116
Mukulushi ≐ E 3 204
Mukumbura F 5 204
Mula F 3 88
Mulan D 16 128
Mulanje F 6 204
Mulberry F 3 168
Mulchatna ≐ F 16 154
Mulchén E 1 195
Mul'da C 25 108
Mulde ≐ E 9 98
Muldraugh D 5 170
Muleshoe C 2 172
Mulhacén ∧ G 1 88
Mulhall B 5 172
Mülheim an der Ruhr E 3 98
Mulhouse C 5 82
Muli E 5 130
Muling, China D 18 128
Muling, China D 18 128
Muling ≐ D 19 128
Mull, Island of I D 3 74
Mullengudgery C 6 144
Mullet Peninsula >[1] B 1 75
Mullett Lake ◎ C 6 166
Mullewa K 3 140
Müllheim E 4 100
Mullingar C 4 75
Mullumbimby B 9 144
Mulongo D 4 204
Multai E 3 122
Multān C 2 122
Mulvane G 6 174
Muma B 3 204
Mumbué E 2 204
Mumcular D 7 106
Mumra G 15 110
Mun ≐ G 7 132
Muna G 15 184
Muna ≐ C 15 114
Muna, Pulau I F 8 134
Munajly F 19 110
Muncar I 22 135b
Münchberg B 8 100
Müncheberg D 11 98
München (Munich) D 8 100
Münchenstein C 5 82
Muncho Lake Provincial Park ♦ B 9 156
Munch'ŏn-ŭp E 1 126
Muncie B 6 170
Muncy E 2 164
Munda D 7 136
Mundaring L 4 140
Münden E 6 98
Mundrabilla L 9 140
Munenga D 1 204
Munfordville D 6 170
Mungar Junction H 11 142
Munger D 5 122
Mungia A 2 88
Mungindi B 7 144
Mungo E 2 204
Mungo National Park ♦ D 4 144
Munhango E 2 204
Munhango ≐ E 2 204
Munich see München D 8 100
Munising B 5 166
Munkfors C 6 66
Munku-Sardyk, gora ∧ B 4 124
Münsingen, Ger. D 6 100
Münsingen, Switz. D 5 82
Munson F 15 156
Munster, Ger. D 6 98
Münster, Ger. E 4 98
Munster, Fr. B 5 82
Münster □[6] D 4 98
Munster □[9] D 2 75
Münsterland ✦[1] E 4 98
Muntok F 5 134
Muonio C 11 64
Mupfure ≐ F 4 204
Muping H 13 128
Muqaddam, Wādī ≐ D 3 202
Muqaṭṭa' E 4 202
Muqayshiṭ I J 15 118
Muqdisho (Mogadishu) G 6 202
Mur (Mura) ≐ D 7 102
Mura (Mur) ≐ D 8 102
Muradiye C 10 118
Murai Reservoir ◎[1] i 14 134a
Murakami E 7 126
Muramvya C 4 204
Murat ≐ C 9 118
Muratlı B 7 106
Murau C 6 102
Murayama E 8 126
Murça C 3 86
Murchison B 9 206
Murchison ≐ J 3 140
Murchison Falls see Kholombidzo Falls ⌊, Mwi. F 5 204
Murchison Falls see Kabalega Falls ⌊, Ug. G 3 202
Murchison Falls National Park ♦ G 3 202
Murcia G 3 88
Murcia □[3] G 3 88
Murdo D 4 174
Mureș □[3] B 8 104
Mureș (Maros) ≐ B 6 104
Muret E 5 80
Murfreesboro, Ar., U.S. E 2 170
Murfreesboro, Tn., U.S. E 5 170
Murgab see Murghob B 2 122
Murgab ≐ C 9 116
Murgeni B 10 104
Murghob B 2 122
Muri D 7 200
Muria, Gunung ∧ k 20 135b
Muriaé D 9 194
Muri-bei Bern D 5 82
Muriedas A 7 86
Muriege D 3 204
Muriel Lake ◎ D 16 156
Müritz ◎ C 9 98
Muriwai C 6 146
Murmansk B 10 108
Murmanskaja oblast' □[6] C 11 108
Murmino B 12 110
Murnau E 8 100
Muro de Alcoy F 4 88
Muro Lucano E 5 90
Murom I 15 108
Muroran C 8 126
Muroto H 4 126
Murovani Kurylivtsi A 9 104
Murphys B 3 182
Murray, Ky., U.S. D 4 170
Murray, Ut., U.S. E 8 178
Murray ≐, Austl. E 2 144
Murray ≐, B.C., Can. D 11 156
Murray, Lake ◎ N 12 124
Murray Bridge E 2 144
Murraysburg G 6 206
Murray-Sunset National Park ♦ E 3 144
Murrébuè E 7 204
Murrhardt D 6 100
Murrumbidgee ≐ E 4 144
Murrupula F 6 204
Murska Sobota D 8 102
Murtle Lake ◎ E 12 156
Murtosa D 2 86
Murua Island I A 11 138
Murud F 2 122
Murud, Gunong ∧ E 7 134
Murupara C 6 146
Murwāra E 4 122
Murwillumbah B 9 144
Murzuq D 7 198
Murzūq, Idhān ✦[2] E 7 198
Mürzzuschlag C 7 102
Muş C 9 118
Muş □[3] C 9 118
Musa B 2 204
Mūsa Khel Bāzār C 1 122
Musala ∧ D 7 104
Musandam >[1] I 17 118
Musan-ŭp E 17 128
Musay'īd J 14 118
Muscat see Masqaṭ F 8 116
Muscatine B 3 170
Muscle Shoals E 5 170
Mushenge C 3 204
Mushie F 8 200
Mushin D 5 200
Mūsi ≐, India F 3 122
Musi ≐, Indon. F 4 134
Musicians Seamounts ✧[3] D 14 58
Muskeg Lake Indian Reserve ✦[4] E 18 156
Muskegon D 5 166
Muskegon ≐ D 6 166
Muskegon Heights D 5 166
Muskingum ≐ D 3 162
Muskogee E 1 170
Muskwa ≐ B 10 156
Muslimbāgh C 1 122
Musoma C 5 204
Musquodoboit Harbour F 12 160
Musselkanaal B 6 69
Musselshell ≐ B 10 178
Mussidan C 4 80
Mussomeli G 4 90
Mustafakemalpaşa B 8 106
Mustafa Kemal Paşa ≐ C 8 106
Mustang Draw ≐ D 3 172
Mustla C 12 66
Mustvee C 13 66
Muswellbrook D 8 144
Mûṭ, Egypt J 3 118
Mut, Tur. D 5 118
Mutanda G 5 204
Mutarara F 5 204
Mutare F 5 204
Mutsamudu o 19 207d
Mutsu D 8 126
Mutsu-wan c D 8 126

⌊ Waterfall ʯ Strait c Bay, Gulf ◎ Lake ≋ Swamp ⍓ Ice Feature ≐ Other Hydrographic Feature ✧ Submarine Feature □ Political Unit ◗ Cultural Institution ⊥ Historical Site ♦ Recreational Site ⊠ Airport ■ Military Installation ✦ Miscellaneous

269

Name	Map Ref.	Page

Symbols in the index entries represent the broad categories identified in the key at the right.
Symbols with superior numbers (⚹1) identify subcategories (see complete key on page 242).

∧ Mountain   ⚹ Mountains   )(Pass   V Valley   ≃ Plain   ↣ Cape   I Island   II Islands   ⊥ Other Topographic Feature   ≃ River   ᚐ Canal

New Zealand — Oceanside

Name	Map Ref.	Page
New Zealand □[1]	H 9	136
Neyrīz	H 16	118
Neyshābūr	D 18	118
Neyyāttinkara	H 3	122
Nezahualcóyotl, Presa ⊜[1]	I 13	184
Nez Perce Indian Reservation ◆[4]	B 5	178
Nez Perce National Historical Park ♦	C 5	178
Ngadirojo	I 20	135b
Ngadza	D 9	200
Ngali	C 2	204
Ngami, Lake ⊜	G 3	204
Ngamiland □[3]	F 3	204
Ngangla Ringco ⊜	C 4	122
Nganglong Kangri ∧∧	C 4	122
Nganjuk	k 20	135b
Ngaoundéré	D 7	200
Ngaputaw	F 2	132
Ngaruawahia	B 5	146
Ngathainggyaung	F 2	132
Ngauruhoe, Mount ∧[1]	C 5	146
Ngeaur I	D 10	134
Ngeruktabel I	D 10	134
Ng'iro, Ewaso ≃, Kenya	G 4	202
Ngiro, Ewaso ≃, Kenya	C 6	204
Ngoangoa ≃	F 2	202
Ngoboli	G 3	202
Ngoko ≃	B 2	204
Ngom ≃	B 2	130
Ngomba	D 5	204
Ngongotaha	C 6	146
Ngorengore	H 4	202
Ngoring Hu ⊜	F 3	124
Ngorongoro Crater ⍊[6]	C 5	204
Ngoulémakong	E 7	200
Ngounié □[3]	F 7	200
Ngounié ≃	F 7	200
Ngouri	C 8	200
Ngourti	B 7	200
Ngozi	C 4	204
Ngqeleni	F 8	206
Ngŭ ≃	D 3	130
Nguigmi	C 7	200
Nguiu	B 11	140
Ngulu I[1]	D 11	134
Ngum ≃	E 6	132
Ngurore	D 7	200
Nguru	C 7	200
Ngwerere	F 4	204
Nhabe ≃	G 3	204
Nhacoongo	C 11	206
Nhamundá ≃	D 7	190
N'harea	E 2	204
Nha Trang	H 9	132
Nhill	F 3	144
Nhlangano	D 9	206
Nhoma	F 3	204
Niagara Falls, N.Y., U.S.	B 4	162
Niagara Falls, On., Can.	G 4	160
Niagara Falls ⌞	B 4	162
Niah	E 6	134
Niakaramandougou	D 3	200
Niamey	C 5	200
Niamey □[3]	C 5	200
Niamtougou	D 5	200
Nianfourando	D 2	200
Niangara	B 4	204
Niangay, Lac ⊜	B 4	200
Niangoloko	C 3	200
Nia-Nia	B 4	204
Nianzishan	C 14	128
Niari □[3]	C 1	204
Niari ≃	C 1	204
Nias, Pulau I	N 3	132
Niassa □[3]	E 6	204
Nibe	B 2	68
Nica ≃	H 25	108
Nicaragua □[1]	E 3	186
Nicaragua, Lago de ⊜	F 3	186
Nicastro	F 6	94
Nice	G 5	82
Nichelino	E 3	92
Nichinan	I 3	126
Nicholas Channel ʯ	C 4	186
Nicholasville	D 6	170
Nicholl's Town	G 6	168
Nicholson	E 3	164
Nicholson ≃	D 4	142
Nickel Centre	E 3	160
Nicobar Islands II	H 6	122
Nicola	F 11	156
Nicolet	E 7	160
Nicosia, Cyp.	E 5	118
Nicosia, Italy	G 4	94
Nicotera	F 5	94
Nicoya, Golfo de ⊂	F 3	186
Nida	E 10	66
Nidda	B 5	100
Nidwalden □[3]	C 4	92
Nidzica	B 11	96
Niebüll	B 5	98
Niederbayern □[6]	D 9	100
Niederbronn-les-Bains	D 4	100
Niedere Tauern ∧∧	C 6	102
Niederkassel	F 3	98
Niederlausitz □[9]	E 11	98
Niederösterreich □[3]	A 4	104
Niedersachsen □[3]	D 5	98
Niederwiesa	F 9	98
Niekerkshoop	E 5	206
Niellim	D 8	200
Niemba	D 4	204
Nienburg, Ger.	E 8	98
Nienburg, Ger.	D 6	98
Niepołomice	C 11	96
Niesky	E 11	98
Nieuport see Nieuwpoort	C 1	69
Nieuw Amsterdam	B 8	190
Nieuwefontein	E 3	206
Nieuwegein	B 4	69
Nieuw Nickerie	B 7	190
Nieuwpoort	C 1	69
Nièvre □[3]	E 5	76
Niga	C 3	200
Niğde	D 6	118
Niğde □[3]	C 6	118
Nigel	D 8	206
Niger □[1]	G 8	196
Niger ≃	G 8	196
Niger Delta ≚[2]	E 6	200
Nigeria □[1]	H 8	196
Nighthawk	G 12	156
Nigríta	B 5	106
Nihommatsu	F 8	126
Nihuil, Embalse del ⊜[1]	D 3	195
Niigata	F 7	126
Niigata □[3]	F 7	126
Niihama	H 4	126
Niihau I	i 8	181a
Niitsu	F 7	126
Níjar	H 2	88
Nijkerk	B 4	69
Nijlen	C 3	69
Nijmegen	C 4	69
Nijverdal	B 5	69
Nikel'	B 8	108
Nikiski	F 19	154
Nikkō	F 7	126
Nikkō-kokuritsu-kōen ♦	F 8	126
Nikolaevka, Russia	F 15	110
Nikolaevka, Russia	F 11	110
Nikolaevo	C 14	66
Nikolaevsk	E 14	110
Nikolai	E 17	154
Nikolo-Berëzovka	H 20	108
Nikol'sk, Russia	J 16	108
Nikol'sk, Russia	G 16	108
Nikolski	J 10	154
Nikol'skoe	G 16	108
Nikopol'	F 8	110
Niksar	B 7	118
Nikšić	D 5	104
Nikumaroro I[1]	D 10	136
Nila, Pulau I	G 9	134
Nile ≃	B 3	202
Nile Delta ≚[2]	G 4	118
Niles, Mi., U.S.	B 5	170
Niles, Oh., U.S.	C 3	162
Nilsiä	E 13	64
Nīmach	E 2	122
Nimba, Mount (Nimba, Mont) ∧	D 3	200
Nimbāhera	E 2	122
Nîmes	G 2	82
Nimule	G 3	202
Nimule National Park ♦	G 3	202
Nīnawá □[3]	E 10	118
Nīnawá (Nineveh) ⊥	D 10	118
Nine Degree Channel ʯ	H 2	122
Ninette	G 9	158
Ninetyeast Ridge ✦[3]	H 7	58
Ninety Mile Beach ⍊[2]	G 6	144
Nineveh see Nīnawá ⊥	D 10	118
Ninfa ⊥	H 8	92
Ning'an	D 17	128
Ningari	C 4	200
Ningbo	D 15	130
Ningcheng	F 12	128
Ningde	E 14	130
Ningdu	E 12	130
Ningguo	C 14	130
Ninghai	D 15	130
Ninghua	E 13	130
Ningming	G 8	130
Ningnan	E 6	130
Ningqiang	B 8	130
Ningshan	B 9	130
Ningxia □[3]	H 5	128
Ningxiang	D 11	130
Ningyuan	F 10	130
Ninh Binh	D 8	132
Ninigo Group II	M 12	124
Ninohe	D 8	126
Ninove	D 2	69
Niny	G 13	110
Niobrara ≃	D 5	174
Nioki	C 2	204
Niokolo Koba, Parc National du ♦	C 2	200
Niono	C 3	200
Nioro	B 3	200
Nioro du Rip	C 1	200
Niort	B 3	80
Niou	C 4	200
Nipāni	F 2	122
Nipawin	E 20	156
Nipigon	G 14	158
Nipigon, Lake ⊜[1]	G 14	158
Nipissing, Lake ⊜	E 3	160
Nippers Harbour	D 16	160
Niquero	D 5	186
Nirmal	F 3	122
Niš	D 6	104
Niscemi	G 4	94
Nisporeni	B 10	104
Nisutlin ≃	F 28	154
Nītaure	D 12	66
Niterói	E 9	194
Nitra	B 10	102
Nitro	D 3	162
Niuafo'ou I	E 10	136
Niue □[2]	E 11	136
Niulakita I	D 9	136
Niulan ≃	E 6	130
Niut, Gunung ∧	N 9	132
Niutao I	D 9	136
Niuzhuang	F 14	128
Nivelles	D 3	69
Nivernais □[9]	E 10	78
Niverville	G 10	158
Nizāmābād	F 3	122
Nižegorodskaja oblast' □[6]	H 16	108
Nizhyn	D 7	110
Nizip	D 7	118
Nízke Tatry, Narodny Park ♦	D 10	96
Nižnee Kujto, ozero ⊜	D 9	108
Nižnee Romanovo	G 28	108
Nižnekamsk	I 20	108
Nižnekamskoe vodohranilišče ⊜[1]	H 19	110
Nižnelemskij	D 21	108
Nižneudinsk	B 3	124
Nižnevartovsk	F 31	108
Nižnie Sergi	H 23	108
Nižnij Novgorod (Gorky)	H 16	108
Nižnij Odes	E 21	108
Nižnij Tagil	H 23	108
Nižnij Ufalej	I 23	108
Nižnjaja Salda	G 24	108
Nižnjaja Tunguska ≃	C 11	114
Nižnjaja Tura	G 23	108
Nizwá	F 8	116
Nizza Monferrato	E 4	92
Nizzana	H 2	120
Njah	E 26	108
Njalinskoe	F 28	108
Njandoma	F 14	108
Njansimvol'	E 24	108
Njasviž	J 13	64
Njazidja I	J 12	196
Njombe	D 5	204
Njombe ≃	D 5	204
Njučpas	F 19	108
Njuk, ozero ⊜	D 9	108
Njurba	C 14	114
Njurunda	A 8	66
Nkambe	D 7	200
Nkandla	E 9	206
Nkawkaw	D 4	200
Nkhata Bay	E 5	204
Nkhotakota	E 5	204
Nkomi, Lagune ⊜	F 6	200
Nkomo	B 9	206
Nkongsamba	D 6	200
Nkoto	C 2	204
Nkwalini	E 9	206
Nmai ≃	F 4	130
Nnewi	D 6	200
Noarlunga	E 2	144
Noatak ≃	C 13	154
Nobeoka	H 3	126
Nobili	C 4	200
Noblesville	B 6	170
Noboribetsu	C 8	126
Noce ≃	C 6	92
Nocera Inferiore	D 4	94
Nocera Superiore	D 4	94
Nocona	D 5	172
Noel	D 1	170
Nogales, Az., U.S.	G 3	176
Nogales, Mex.	B 4	184
Nogara	D 7	92
Nōgata	H 3	126
Nogent-le-Rotrou	D 7	78
Nogent-sur-Oise	C 9	78
Noginsk	I 13	108
Nogoa ≃	H 8	142
Nogoyá	C 8	195
Nógrád □[3]	B 5	104
Nohfelden	C 4	100
Noia	B 2	86
Noicattaro	C 7	94
Noirmoutier, Île de I	F 4	78
Nokha Mandi	D 2	122
Nokia	B 11	66
Nokomis	F 19	156
Nokomis Lake ⊜	C 20	156
Nokou	C 7	200
Nola, C.A.R.	E 8	200
Nola, Italy	D 4	94
Nolinsk	H 18	108
Nome	D 12	154
Nomtsas	C 2	206
Nonacho Lake ⊜	D 11	150
Nonburg	D 19	108
Nondweni	E 9	206
Nong'an	D 15	128
Nong Han	F 6	132
Nong Khai	F 6	132
Nongoma	D 9	206
Nonoava	D 6	184
Nonouti I[1]	D 9	136
Nonthaburi	H 5	132
Nontron	C 4	80
Nonvianuk Lake ⊜	G 16	154
Noonamah	C 11	140
Noondil, Lake ⊜	K 5	140
Noord-Brabant □[3]	C 4	69
Noord-Holland □[3]	B 3	69
Noordoewer	E 2	206
Noordoostpolder ◆[1]	B 4	69
Noordwijk-Binnen	B 3	69
Noorvik	C 14	154
Nootka Island I	G 8	156
Nopiming Provincial Park ♦	F 11	158
Nora	C 7	66
Nora ⊥	m 10	94a
Norberg	B 7	66
Norchia ⊥	G 7	92
Norcia	G 9	92
Nord □[3], Cam.	D 7	200
Nord □[3], Fr.	B 10	78
Nord, Canal du ≅	B 10	78
Nordaustlandet I	B 5	114
Nordegg	E 13	156
Norden	C 4	98
Nordenham	C 5	98
Norderney	C 4	98
Norderstedt	C 7	98
Nordfjord ⊂	B 2	66
Nordfold	C 7	64
Nordfriesland □[9]	B 5	98
Nordhausen	E 7	98
Nordhorn	D 3	98
Nordjylland □[3]	A 2	68
Nordkapp see North Cape ›	A 12	64
Nord-Kivu □[3]	C 4	204
Nordland □[3]	C 7	64
Nördlingen	D 7	100
Nordmaling	E 9	64
Nordostrundingen ›	A 18	148
Nord-Ostsee-Kanal (Kiel Canal) ≅	A 5	96
Nord-Ouest □[3]	D 7	200
Nordrhein-Westfalen □[3]	C 4	96
Nordstemmen	D 6	98
Nord-Trøndelag □[3]	D 6	64
Nordvik	B 14	114
Nore	B 4	66
Norfolk, Ne., U.S.	D 6	174
Norfolk, Va., U.S.	E 5	162
Norfolk □[6], Eng., U.K.	E 7	72
Norfolk □[6], Ma., U.S.	D 7	164
Norfolk Broads ◆[1]	E 8	72
Norfolk Island □[2]	F 8	136
Norfork Lake ⊜[1]	D 2	170
Noril'sk	C 11	114
Normal	B 4	170
Normal ◆[8]	E 5	170
Norman	C 5	172
Norman ≃	E 6	142
Norman Bay	B 16	160
Normanby	C 5	146
Normanby Island I	N 14	124
Normand, Bocage ◆[1]	D 6	78
Normandie (Normandy) □[9]	G 7	70
Normandie, Collines de ∧∧[2]	D 6	78
Normandy see Normandie □[9]	G 7	70
Normanton	D 5	142
Norrahammar	D 6	66
Norra Kvarken (Merenkurkku) ʯ	E 10	64
Norrbotten □[3]	C 9	64
Nørresundby	A 2	68
Norris Arm	D 16	160
Norristown	F 3	164
Norrköping	C 7	66
Norrsundet	B 8	66
Norrtälje	C 9	66
Norseman	M 6	140
Norsjö	D 9	64
Norte, Cabo ›	m 16	193a
Norte, Serra do ∧∧[1]	F 7	190
Norte de Santander □[3]	F 6	186
North	C 4	168
North, Cape ›, N.S., Can.	E 13	160
North, Cape ›, S. Geor.	p 21	193c
North Adams	D 5	164
Northallerton	C 5	72
Northam, Austl.	L 4	140
Northam, Eng., U.K.	F 2	72
North America ⍊[1]	E 10	148
North American Basin ✦[1]	D 6	60
Northampton, Austl.	K 3	140
Northampton, Eng., U.K.	E 6	72
Northampton, Ma., U.S.	D 6	164
Northampton, Pa., U.S.	F 3	164
Northampton □[6]	F 3	164
Northamptonshire □[6]	E 6	72
North Andaman I	G 6	122
North Anson	A 9	162
North Atlanta	C 2	168
North Attleboro	E 7	164
North Ayrshire □[6]	B 2	72
North Battleford	E 17	156
North Bay	E 4	160
North Bend	D 1	178
North Berwick	A 4	72
North Branch	C 2	166
North Caicos I	C 6	186
North Canadian ≃	C 5	172
North Cape ›, Nor.	A 12	64
North Cape ›, N.Z.	A 4	146
North Caribou Lake ⊜	E 13	158
North Carolina □[3]	D 12	152
North Cascades National Park ♦	A 3	178
North Channel ʯ, On., Can.	H 17	158
North Channel ʯ, U.K.	D 5	70
North Charleston	C 5	168
North Chicago	D 5	166
North Collins	B 4	162
North Creek	C 5	164
North Dakota □[3]	B 7	152
North Downs ∧∧[2]	F 7	72
North Eagle Butte	C 4	174
North East	D 5	162
North-East □[3]	G 4	204
Northeast Cape	E 10	154
North Eastern □[3]	G 4	202
North East Lincolnshire □[6]	D 6	72
Northeast Providence Channel ʯ	G 6	168
Northeim	E 7	98
Northern □[3], Mwi.	E 5	204
Northern □[3], S. Afr.	C 8	206
Northern □[3], Zam.	E 5	204
Northern Cape □[3]	F 4	206
Northern Cheyenne Indian Reservation ◆[4]	C 10	178
Northern Cook Islands II	E 11	136
Northern Division □[3]	m 14	147c
Northern Donets (Sivers'kyi Donets') ≃	E 10	110
Northern Dvina ≃	E 16	108
Northern Indian Lake ⊜	C 10	158
Northern Ireland □[8]	B 5	75
Northern Mariana Islands □[1]	I 13	124
Northern Sporades II	C 6	106
Northern Territory □[3]	D 7	138
Northfield, Mn., U.S.	C 2	166
Northfield, Vt., U.S.	B 6	164
North Flinders Range ∧∧	C 2	144
North Foreland ›	F 8	72
North Fork ≃	D 2	170
North Fort Myers	F 3	168
North Frisian Islands II	D 1	68
Northglenn	F 2	174
North Haven	E 6	164
North Hero	B 5	164
North Hero Island I	B 5	164
North Highlands	B 2	182
North Horr	G 4	202
North Island I	C 5	146
North Kingsville	C 3	162
North Knife Lake ⊜	B 10	158
North Lakhimpur	D 6	122
North Lanarkshire □[6]	B 3	72
Northland □[3]	A 4	146
North Land II	B 12	114
North Las Vegas	D 1	176
North La Veta Pass)(	G 2	174
North Lincolnshire □[6]	D 6	72
North Little Rock	E 2	170
North Llano ≃	E 4	172
North Loup	E 5	174
North Loup ≃	E 5	174
North Luangwa National Park ♦	E 5	204
North Macmillan ≃	E 28	154
North Magnetic Pole ◆	B 9	148
North Manitou Island I	C 5	166
North Miami	G 4	168
North Milk ≃	A 7	178
North Moose Lake ⊜[1]	D 8	158
North Myrtle Beach	C 5	168
North Nahanni ≃	E 32	154
North Platte	E 4	174
North Platte ≃	C 7	152
North Pole ◆	D 13	61
Northport, Al., U.S.	F 5	170
Northport, Wa., U.S.	A 5	178
North Portal	G 7	158
North Providence	E 7	164
North Raccoon ≃	D 7	174
North Rim	D 2	176
North River	B 15	160
North Saskatchewan ≃	E 18	156
North Sea ⫪[2]	D 8	62
North Shore City	B 5	146
North Siberian Lowland ≚	B 13	114
North Spirit Lake ⊜	E 12	158
North Stradbroke Island I	A 9	144
North Sunderland	B 5	72
North Sydney	E 13	160
North Taranaki Bight ⊂	C 5	146
North Tunica	E 3	170
North Tyneside □[6]	B 5	72
North Uist I	C 1	74
Northumberland □[6], Eng., U.K.	B 4	72
Northumberland □[6], Pa., U.S.	F 2	164
Northumberland National Park ♦	B 4	72
Northumberland Strait ʯ	E 12	160
North Vancouver	G 10	156
North Wabasca Lake ⊜	C 15	156
North Walsham	E 8	72
Northway	E 23	154
North-West □[3]	D 6	206
North West Cape ›	G 2	140
North-Western □[3]	E 4	204
North-West Frontier □[3]	B 2	122
Northwest Highlands ∧∧	C 4	74
Northwest Pacific Basin ✦[1]	D 12	58
Northwest Providence Channel ʯ	F 5	168
North West Somerset □[6]	F 4	72
Northwest Territories □[3]	C 12	150
Northwich	D 4	72
North York	G 4	160
North York Moors National Park ♦	C 6	72
North Yorkshire □[6]	C 5	72
North Zulch	E 5	172
Norton, Eng., U.K.	C 6	72
Norton, Ks., U.S.	F 5	174
Norton, N.B., Can.	F 11	160
Norton Bay ⊂	D 13	154
Norton Shores	D 5	166
Norton Sound ʯ	E 12	154
Nortorf	B 6	98
Norvegia, Cape ›	D 7	208
Norwalk, Ct., U.S.	E 5	164
Norwalk, Ia., U.S.	B 2	170
Norwalk, Oh., U.S.	C 2	162
Norway	B 8	164
Norway □[1]	C 9	62
Norway Bay ⊂	B 12	150
Norway House	D 10	158
Norwegian Basin ✦[1]	B 23	61
Norwegian Sea ⫪[2]	D 4	64
Norwich, Ct., U.S.	E 6	164
Norwich, Eng., U.K.	E 8	72
Norwich, N.Y., U.S.	D 3	164
Norwood, Ma., U.S.	D 7	164
Norwood, N.C., U.S.	B 4	168
Norwood, Oh., U.S.	C 6	170
Norwood, On., Can.	A 4	162
Noshaq ∧	B 2	122
Noshiro	D 7	126
Nosovo	D 13	66
Nossebro	C 6	66
Nossen	E 10	98
Nossob ≃	D 4	206
Nosy-Varika	I 9	205a
Noteć ≃	B 8	96
Notikewin	C 13	156
Nótion Aiyaíon □[3]	D 7	106
Noto	H 5	94
Noto, Golfo di ⊂	H 5	94
Noto, Val di ◆[1]	G 4	94
Noto Antica ⊥	H 5	94
Noto-hantō ›[1]	F 6	126
Notozero, ozero ⊜	C 10	108
Notre-Dame, Monts ∧∧	D 10	160
Notre Dame Bay ⊂	D 16	160
Notre-Dame-du-Haut ◗[1]	C 4	82
Notre-Dame-du-Nord	B 9	166
Nottaway ≃	C 4	160
Nottingham	E 5	72
Nottingham Island I	D 17	150
Nottinghamshire □[6]	D 6	72
Nottoway	E 4	162
Notukeu Creek ≃	G 18	156
Notwane ≃	B 7	206
Nouâdhibou	E 1	198
Nouakchott	F 1	198
Nouméa	D 14	138
Nouna	C 4	200
Noupoort	F 6	206
Nouveau-Québec, Cratère du ⍊[6]	D 18	150
Nouvelle	D 10	160
Nouvelle-Calédonie (New Caledonia) I	D 14	138
Nouzonville	C 11	78
Nova Andradina	E 4	194
Novabad	B 1	122
Novacella ◗[1]	D 3	102
Nova Esperança	E 4	194
Nova Freixo see Cuamba	E 6	204
Nova Friburgo	E 9	194
Nova Gradiška	C 4	104
Nova Iguaçu	E 9	194
Novaja Kazanka	E 16	110
Novaja Ljalja	G 23	108
Novaja Sibir', ostrov I	B 17	114
Novaja Zemlja II	B 8	114
Nova Kakhovka	F 8	110
Nova Lima	D 9	194
Nova Lisboa see Huambo	E 2	204
Nova Lusitânia	F 5	204
Nova Odesa	F 7	110
Nová Paka	C 8	96
Novara	D 4	92
Novara □[6]	D 4	92
Nova Scotia □[3]	H 20	150
Novato	B 1	182
Nova Ushytsya	A 9	104
Nova Varoš	D 5	104
Nova Venécia	C 10	194
Novaya Sibir Island see Novaja Sibir', ostrov I	B 17	114
Nova Zagora	D 9	104
Nové Hrady	D 11	100
Novelda	F 4	88
Novellara	E 6	92
Nové Město nad Váhom	B 9	102
Nové Zámky	B 10	102
Novgorod	G 9	108
Novgorodskaja oblast' □[6]	G 10	108
Novhorod-Sivers'kyy	J 10	108
Novi Bečej	C 6	104
Novi Beograd	C 6	104
Novi di Modena	C 3	90
Novigrad	C 2	104
Novi Ligure	E 4	92
Novi Pazar, Bul.	D 9	104
Novi Pazar, Yugo.	D 6	104
Novi Sad	C 5	104
Novo, Lago ⊜	C 8	190
Novoaleksandrovka	K 28	108
Novoaleksandrovsk	G 12	110
Novoalekseevka	J 26	108
Novoanninskij	D 13	110
Novo Aripuanã	E 6	190
Novočerkassk	F 11	110
Novocimljanskaja	E 13	110
Novodvinsk	D 14	108
Novoe	G 28	108
Novo Hamburgo	A 12	195
Novo Horizonte	D 6	194
Novohrad-Volyns'kyy	D 5	110
Novoiljinskij	G 21	108
Novokazalinsk (Zangaqazaly)	A 9	116
Novokujbyševsk	C 16	110
Novokurovka	B 20	128
Novokuzneck	D 11	114
Novolazarevskaja ◗[3]	C 10	208
Novo Mesto	E 7	102
Novomoskovsk, Russia	I 13	108
Novomoskovs'k, Ukr.	E 9	110
Novonikolaevskij	D 13	110
Novooleksiyivka	F 9	110
Novoorsk	D 21	110
Novopetrovo	H 28	108
Novopskov	E 11	110
Novorossijsk	G 10	110
Novorybinka	K 29	108
Novošahtinsk	F 11	110
Novosergievka	C 18	110
Novosibirsk	D 11	114
Novosibirskie ostrova see New Siberian Islands II	B 17	114
Novosibirskoe vodohranilišče ⊜[1]	D 11	114
Novosil's'ke	C 10	104
Novostroevo	E 10	66
Novotroick	D 20	110
Novouzensk	D 16	110
Novovjatsk	G 18	108
Novovolyns'k	D 4	110
Novovoronežskij	D 11	110
Novozybkov	J 9	108
Novska	E 8	102
Nový Bohumín	D 10	96
Nový Bor	B 11	100
Novyj Bor	C 19	108
Nový Jičín	A 9	102
Novyj Oskol	D 10	110
Novyj Port	C 30	108
Novyj Uzen' (Zhangaözen)	H 18	110
Novyy Buh	F 8	110
Nowa Dęba	C 11	96
Nowa Ruda	C 9	96
Nowa Sól	C 8	96
Nowbarān	E 13	118
Nowe Miasto nad Pilicą	C 11	96
Nowe Warpno	B 8	96
Nowingi	E 4	144
Nowitna ≃	D 18	154
Nowogród	B 11	96
Nowra	E 8	144
Nowshera	C 2	122
Nowy Dwór Gdański	A 10	96
Nowy Dwór Mazowiecki	B 11	96
Nowy Sącz	D 11	96
Nowy Sącz □[3]	D 11	96
Nowy Targ	D 10	96
Noxen	E 2	164
Noyant	E 7	78
Noyon	C 9	78
Nqamakwe	G 7	206
Nsa	C 2	204
Nsanje	F 6	204
Nsawam	D 4	200
Nsoko	D 9	206
Nsukka	D 6	200
Ntem ≃	E 7	200
Ntomba, Lac ⊜	C 2	204
N'Tsaoueni	n 18	207d
Ntui	E 7	200
Ntusi	G 3	202
Ntwetwe Pan ≚	G 4	204
Nubian Desert ◆[2]	C 4	202
Ñuble ≃	E 2	195
Nucet	B 7	104
Nueces ≃	F 4	172
Nueltin Lake ⊜	E 12	150
Nueva, Isla I	K 6	192
Nueva-Andalucía	H 5	86
Nueva Ciudad Guerrero	G 4	172
Nueva Esparta □[3]	F 8	186
Nueva Gerona	C 4	186
Nueva Imperial	F 1	195
Nueva Italia de Ruiz	H 8	184
Nueva Rosita	C 9	184
Nueve, Canal Numero ≅	G 8	192
Nueve de Julio	D 7	195
Nuevitas	C 5	186
Nuevo, Golfo ⊂	H 7	192
Nuevo Casas Grandes	B 6	184
Nuevo Laredo	D 9	184
Nuevo León □[3]	E 10	184
Nuevo Progreso	H 13	184
Nugaal □[3]	F 6	202
Nui I[1]	D 9	136
Nuia	C 12	66
Nujiang	C 3	130
Nuku'alofa	F 10	136
Nukufetau I[1]	D 9	136
Nukunau I	D 9	136
Nukunonu I	D 10	136
Nukus	H 21	110
Nules	E 4	88
Nullagine	G 6	140
Nullarbor National Park ♦	L 10	140
Nullarbor Plain ≚	L 10	140
Numan	D 7	200
Numancia ⊥	C 2	88
Numata	F 7	126
Numazu	G 7	126
Nümbrecht	F 4	98
Numfoor, Pulau I	F 10	134
Numurkah	F 5	144
Nun ≃	E 6	200
Nunapitchuk	F 13	154
Nunawading	F 5	144
Nundah	A 9	144
Nuneaton	E 5	72
Nuñez, Cape ›	q 21	193c
Nungarin	L 5	140
Nungesser Lake ⊜	F 11	158
Nunivak Island I	F 11	154
Nunjiang	B 15	128
Nunjikompita	L 2	142
Nunspeet	B 4	69
Nuomin ≃	B 14	128
Nuoro	E 2	90
Nuoro □[6]	k 10	94a
Nuremberg see Nürnberg	C 8	100
Nurlat	I 19	108
Nurmes	E 14	64
Nürnberg	C 8	100
Nurri	I 10	94a
Nürtingen	D 6	100
Nusa Tenggara Barat □[3]	A 4	140
Nusa Tenggara Timur □[3]	A 6	140
Nusaybin	D 9	118
Nushagak Bay ⊂	G 15	154
Nu Shan ∧∧	E 4	130
Nushki	E 10	116
Nutauge, laguna ⊂	B 6	154
Nutrioso	F 4	176
Nu-Uis	A 1	206
Nuuk see Godthåb	D 22	150
Nuwerus	F 3	206
Nuweveldberge ∧∧	G 4	206
Nuyakuk Lake ⊜	F 15	154
Nxai Pan National Park ♦	F 3	204
Nxaunxau	F 3	204
Nyabing	M 5	140
Nyack	E 5	164
Nyahua	D 5	204
Nyahururu Falls	G 4	202
Nyainqêntanglha Shan ∧∧	C 6	122
Nyakakiri	C 5	204
Nyala	E 1	202
Nyamandhlovu	F 4	204
Nyamtumbo	E 6	204
Nyandekwa	C 5	204
Nyanding, Khawr ≃	F 3	202
Nyang ≃	D 2	130
Nyanga □[3]	F 7	200
Nyanga ≃	F 7	200
Nyangana	F 3	204
Nyanza	C 4	204
Nyanza □[3]	H 3	202
Nyasa, Lake see Malawi, Lake ⊜	E 5	204
Nyaunglebin	F 3	132
Nyazura	F 5	204
Nyborg	C 3	68
Nybro	D 7	66
Nyda	C 30	108
Nye □[6]	B 7	182
Nyeri	H 4	202
Nyika National Park ♦	E 5	204
Nyimba	E 5	204
Nyingchi	D 2	130
Nyiragongo, Volcan ∧[1]	C 4	204
Nyírbátor	B 7	104
Nyíregyháza	B 6	104
Nykøbing	D 4	68
Nykøbing Sjælland	C 4	68
Nyköping	C 8	66
Nylstroom	C 8	206
Nymboida ≃	B 9	144
Nymboida National Park ♦	B 9	144
Nymburk	B 12	100
Nynäshamn	C 8	66
Nyngan	C 6	144
Nyon	D 4	82
Nyong ≃	E 7	200
Nyons	F 3	82
Nýrsko	C 10	100
Nyš	B 12	124
Nysa	C 9	96
Nysa Łużycka (Lausitzer Neisse) ≃	E 11	98
Nytva	H 21	108
Nyumba ya Mungu Dam ◆[6]	H 4	202
Nyungwe	E 5	204
Nyunzu	D 4	204
Nyzhankovychi	D 12	96
Nyzhn'ohirs'kyy	G 9	110
Nzébéla	D 3	200
Nzérékoré	D 3	200
Nzilo, Lac ⊜[1]	E 4	204
Nzwani I	J 12	196

O

Name	Map Ref.	Page
Oahe, Lake ⊜[1]	C 4	174
Oahe Dam ◆[6]	C 4	174
Oahu I	i 9	181a
Oakbank	D 3	144
Oak Bay	G 10	156
Oakburn	F 8	158
Oakdale, Ca., U.S.	C 3	182
Oakdale, Ne., U.S.	D 5	174
Oakengates	E 4	72
Oakes	B 5	174
Oakfield	D 4	166
Oakham	E 6	72
Oak Harbor	A 2	178
Oak Hill	E 3	162
Oakhurst	E 6	172
Oak Lake ⊜	G 8	158
Oakland, Ca., U.S.	C 1	182
Oakland, Md., U.S.	D 4	162
Oakland, Me., U.S.	A 9	162
Oakland, Ne., U.S.	E 6	174
Oak Lawn, Il., U.S.	B 5	170
Oaklawn, Ks., U.S.	G 6	174
Oakohay Creek ≃	F 4	170
Oakover ≃	G 6	140
Oak Park	B 5	170
Oak Point	F 10	158
Oakridge, Or., U.S.	D 2	178
Oak Ridge, Tn., U.S.	A 2	168
Oak Ridge National Laboratory ◗[3]	B 2	168
Oakura	C 4	146
Oakville	B 4	162
Oakwood	B 6	170
Oamaru	F 3	146
Oates Coast ⍊[2]	D 24	208
Oaxaca □[3]	I 11	184
Oaxaca de Juárez	I 11	184
Ob' ≃	C 9	114
Obala	E 7	200
Oban	D 6	200
O Barco de Valdeorras	B 4	86
Obed	E 13	156
Obedjiwan, Réserve indienne ◆[4]	D 6	160
Obeliai	E 12	66
Oberá	G 3	194
Oberammergau	E 7	100
Oberbayern □[6]	D 8	100
Oberfranken □[6]	B 8	100
Obergurgl	D 3	102
Oberhausen	E 3	98
Oberkirch	D 5	100
Oberkochen	D 7	100
Oberlausitz □[9]	E 11	98
Oberlin, Ks., U.S.	F 4	174
Oberlin, Oh., U.S.	C 2	162
Obernai	B 5	82
Oberndorf am Neckar	D 5	100
Oberösterreich □[3]	B 5	102
Oberpfalz □[6]	C 9	100
Oberpleis	F 4	98
Ober-Ramstadt	C 5	100
Oberstdorf	C 2	102
Obersulm	C 6	100
Oberueckersee ⊜	C 10	98
Oberursel	B 5	100
Obervellach	D 5	102
Oberwart	C 8	102
Obi	D 6	200
Obi, Kepulauan II	F 9	134
Obi, Pulau I	F 9	134
Óbidos	D 7	190
Obihiro	C 9	126
Obilatu, Pulau I	F 9	134
Obion	D 4	170
Obion ≃	D 4	170
Obion, Middle Fork ≃	D 4	170
Oblivskaja	E 13	110
Obluče	B 18	128
Obninsk	I 12	108
Obo	A 4	204
Obock	E 5	202
Obojan'	D 9	110
Oborniki	B 9	96
Obrenovac	C 6	104
Obščij syrt ∧∧	D 17	110
Observatoire, Caye de l' I	D 12	138
Obskaja guba ⊂	C 10	114
Obuasi	D 4	200
Obudu	D 6	200
Obuhova	H 9	108
Obwalden □[3]	C 4	92
Ocala	E 3	168
Očamčira	H 12	110
Ocaña, Col.	F 6	186
Ocaña, Spain	E 7	86
Occhito, Lago di ⊜[1]	C 4	94
Occidental, Cordillera ∧∧	E 3	190
Ocean □[6]	G 4	164
Ocean City	G 4	164
Oceano	E 3	182
Ocean Park	B 1	178
Oceanside, Ca., U.S.	G 6	182
Oceanside, N.Y., U.S.	F 5	164

⌞ Waterfall ʯ Strait ⊂ Bay, Gulf ⊜ Lake ≚ Swamp ⍝ Ice Feature ⫪ Other Hydrographic Feature ✦ Submarine Feature □ Political Unit ◗ Cultural Institution ⊥ Historical Site ♦ Recreational Site ⊠ Airport ■ Military Installation ◆ Miscellaneous

Symbols in the index entries represent the broad categories identified in the key at the right. ▲ Mountain ⩗ Mountains ✕ Pass V Valley ≃ Plain ➤ Cape I Island II Islands ⊥ Other Topographic Feature ≏ River ≈ Canal
Symbols with superior numbers (⩗¹) identify subcategories (see complete key on page 242).

272

Paczków — Phon

Name | Map Ref. | Page

Paczków C 9 96
Padang F 4 134
Padang Endau M 6 132
Padangsidempuan N 4 132
Padany E 10 108
Paddle Prairie B 13 156
Paden City D 3 162
Paderborn E 5 98
Padjelanta Nationalpark ♦ C 8 64
Pádova D 7 92
Padova □6 D 7 92
Padre Island I G 5 172
Padre Island National Seashore ♦ G 5 172
Padre Paraíso B 10 194
Padrón B 2 86
Padsville E 13 66
Paducah D 4 170
Paektu-san ∧ C 1 126
Paeroa B 5 146
Paese D 8 92
Paestum ⊥ D 4 94
Páfos E 5 118
Pag C 3 104
Pagadenbaru k 18 135b
Pagadian D 8 134
Pagai Selatan, Pulau I F 4 134
Pagai Utara, Pulau I F 4 134
Pagalu see Annobón I F 6 200
Pagan I I 13 124
Page B 6 174
Pagėgiai E 10 66
Paget, Mount ∧ q 21 193c
Pagoda Peak ∧ B 5 176
Pagoda Point > G 1 132
Pagon, Bukit ∧ E 7 134
Pago Pago k 11 147b
Pagosa Springs D 5 176
Pahama B 7 206
Pahang □3 M 6 132
Pahang ≃ M 6 132
Pahoa j 11 181a
Pahraničny B 12 96
Pai ≃ I 3 130
Paide C 12 66
Paignton G 3 72
Paiguano B 2 195
Päijänne ⊜ B 12 66
Paillaco G 1 195
Paimio B 11 66
Painesdale B 4 166
Paint ≃ B 4 166
Painted Desert ✦2 E 3 176
Paint Lake ⊜ D 10 158
Paintsville E 2 162
Paisley B 2 72
Paiton k 21 135b
Pajaro ≃ D 2 182
Paje B 7 206
Pajer, gora ∧ C 26 108
Paj-Hoj ⋏2 C 9 114
Pakaraima Mountains ⋏ C 6 190
Pak Chong G 5 132
Pakeng F 3 202
Pakistan □1 E 10 116
Paklenica Nacionalni Park ♦ C 3 104
Pakokku E 6 122
Pak Phanang J 5 132
Pakrac E 9 102
Pakruojis E 11 66
Paks D 10 102
Pak Thong Chai G 5 132
Pakwash Lake ⊜ F 12 158
Pakxé G 7 132
Pala H 4 132
Palafrugell C 8 88
Palagiano D 6 94
Palagonia G 4 94
Palagruža, Otoci II D 4 104
Pala Indian Reservation ✦4 G 6 182
Palaiokhóra E 5 106
Palaiseau D 9 78
Palamós C 8 88
Palamu National Park ♦ E 4 122
Palamuse C 13 66
Palana D 18 114
Palanan Point > B 8 134
Palanga E 10 66
Palangkaraya F 6 134
Palani G 3 122
Palankarinna, Lake ⊜ B 2 144
Pālanpur E 2 122
Palapye B 7 206
Pālār ≃ G 3 122
Palas de Rei B 3 86
Palatka, Fl., U.S. E 4 168
Palatka, Russia C 18 114
Palau G 3 172
Palau □1 D 11 134
Palau Islands II D 10 134
Palaw H 4 132
Palawan I D 7 134
Pālayankottai H 3 122
Palazzolo Acreide G 4 94
Palazzo San Gervasio D 6 94
Palembang F 4 134
Palencia B 6 86
Palencia □6 B 6 86
Palenque I 14 184
Palenque ⊥ I 13 184
Palermo, Italy F 3 94
Palermo, Ur. C 10 195
Palermo □6 G 3 94
Palestine, Ar., U.S. E 3 170
Palestine, Tx., U.S. E 6 172
Palestine □9 F 4 120
Pāli D 2 122
Palidoro ✦8 H 8 92
Palisade C 4 176
Palisades D 8 178
Palisades Reservoir ⊜1 D 8 178
Pālitāna E 2 122
Palizada H 13 184
Paljavaam ≃ B 2 154
Palkino H 8 108
Palk Strait ɥ G 3 122
Pallasovka D 15 110
Palling D 8 156
Palliser, Cape > D 5 146
Palma E 7 204
Palma, Badia de c E 7 88
Palma del Río G 5 86
Palma de Mallorca E 7 88
Palma di Montechiaro G 3 94
Palmar, Lago Artificial del ⊜1 C 9 195
Palmares E 11 190
Palmas, Braz. F 9 190
Palmas, Braz. G 4 194
Palma Soriano C 6 186
Palm Bay E 4 168
Palm Beach F 4 168
Palmdale F 5 182
Palm Desert F 5 180
Palmeira F 5 194
Palmer, Ak., U.S. F 20 154
Palmer, Ma., U.S. D 6 164
Palmer, Tn., U.S. E 6 170
Palmer ⦊3 C 2 208
Palmer Land ✦1 D 2 208
Palmerston I1 E 11 136
Palmerston North D 5 146
Palmerton F 3 164
Palmi F 5 94
Palmira C 3 190
Palmitas C 9 195
Palm Springs G 7 182
Palmyra, N.Y., U.S. C 1 164
Palmyra, Pa., U.S. F 2 164
Palmyra ⊥ E 8 118
Palmyra Atoll I1 C 11 136
Palo Alto C 1 182
Palo Duro Canyon State Park ♦ C 3 172
Palomar Mountain ∧ G 7 182
Palomar Mountain State Park ♦ G 7 182
Palopo F 8 134
Palos see Palos de la Frontera G 4 86
Palos de la Frontera (Palos) G 4 86
Pålsboda C 7 66
Palu, Indon. F 7 134
Palu, Tur. C 9 118
Paluke D 3 200
Pama ≃ E 8 200
Pamanukan k 18 135b
Pambeguwa C 6 200
Pamekasan k 21 135b
Pameungpeuk k 18 135b
Pamiers E 5 80
Pamir ⋏ B 2 122
Pamlico Sound ɥ B 7 168
Pampa C 3 172
Pampa del Chañar B 3 195
Pampas ✦1 G 7 192
Pampeluna see Pamplona B 3 88
Pamplona, Col. G 6 186
Pamplona (Iruña), Spain B 3 88
Pamukkale (Hierapolis) ⊥ D 8 106
Pamukova B 9 106
Pana C 4 170
Panaca D 1 176
Panaitan, Pulau I G 5 134
Panaji F 2 122
Panamá, Braz. C 6 194
Panama, Il., U.S. C 4 170
Panamá, Pan. F 5 186
Panama □1 F 4 186
Panamá, Bahía de c F 5 186
Panama, Gulf of c G 5 186
Panama, Isthmus of ≚3 F 5 186
Panama Canal ≚ F 5 186
Panama City G 6 170
Panamint Range ⋏ D 6 182
Panamint Valley V D 6 182
Panay I C 8 134
Panay Gulf c C 8 134
Pančevo C 6 104
Panciu C 9 104
Pandan, Selat ɥ j 14 134a
Pandan Reservoir ⊜1 j 14 134a
Pandėlys D 12 66
Pandharpur F 2 122
Pāndhurna E 3 122
Pando D 10 195
Pandu D 8 200
Panevėžys E 12 66
Pāng ≃ C 4 132
Pangala C 1 204
Pangandaran k 19 135b
Pangani ≃ D 6 204
Pangi C 4 204
Pangkalanbuun F 6 134
Pangkalpinang F 5 134
Pangnirtung C 19 150
Pangutaran Group II D 8 134
Panié, Mont ∧ D 13 138
Panj (Pyandzh) ≃ C 10 116
Panjgūr E 9 116
Pankshin D 6 200
Panlong see Lo ≃ H 7 130
P'anmunjŏm-ni G 16 128
Panna E 4 122
Panna National Park ♦ E 3 122
Pannonhalma ⦊1 C 9 102
Panora E 7 174
Panorama D 4 194
Panovo G 17 108
Panshan F 14 128
Pantanal Matogrossense, Parque Nacional do ♦ B 2 194
Pantar, Pulau I G 8 134
Pantelleria, Isola di I H 1 94
Panu C 2 204
Pánuco G 11 184
Pánuco ≃ F 10 184
Panvel F 2 122
Panxian F 7 130
Paola E 5 94
Paoli C 5 170
Pápa C 9 102
Papagayo, Golfo de c F 3 186
Papago Indian Reservation ✦4 F 2 176
Papaikou j 11 181a
Papakura B 5 146
Papantla de Olarte G 11 184
Paparoa National Park ♦ E 3 146
Papatoetoe B 5 146
Papeete i 8 147a
Papenburg C 4 98
Papendrecht C 3 69
Papigochic ≃ C 5 184
Papilė D 11 66
Papineau □6 A 3 164
Papua, Gulf of c N 12 124
Papua New Guinea □1 N 13 124
Papun E 3 132
Pará □3 E 8 190
Pará ≃ C 8 194
Paracatu B 7 194
Paracatu ≃ B 8 194
Paracel Islands (Xisha Qundao) II B 6 134
Parachilna C 2 144
Paraćin D 6 104
Paradas G 5 86
Paradise, Ca., U.S. A 2 182
Paradise, Nv., U.S. D 1 176
Paradise Hill E 15 154
Paradise River B 15 160
Pāradwīp E 5 122
Paragould D 3 170
Paragua ≃ C 6 190
Paraguaçu ≃ F 11 190
Paraguaçu Paulista E 5 194
Paraguai (Paraguay) ≃ C 8 192
Paraguaná, Península de >1 A 4 190
Paraguarí F 2 194
Paraguarí □3 G 2 194
Paraguay □1 D 8 192
Paraguay (Paraguai) ≃ E 8 192
Paraíba □3 E 11 190
Paraíba do Sul ≃ H 10 190
Paraisópolis E 7 194
Parakou D 5 200
Paramaribo B 7 190
Paramirim F 10 190
Paramušir, ostrov I B 15 124
Paraná, Arg. B 7 195
Paranã, Braz. F 9 190
Paraná □3 D 9 192
Paranã ≃, Braz. F 9 190
Paraná ≃, S.A. F 7 192
Paranaguá F 6 194
Paranaguá, Baía de c F 6 194
Paranaíba C 5 194
Paranaíba ≃ C 5 194
Paranam B 8 190
Paranapanema ≃ H 8 190
Paranavaí E 4 194
Paranoá, Lago do ⊜1 A 7 194
Paraopeba C 8 194
Paraparaumu D 5 146
Parapetí ≃ G 6 190
Paraúna B 5 194
Paray-le-Monial D 2 82
Pārbati ≃ E 3 122
Pārbatipur D 5 122
Parbhani F 3 122
Parchim C 8 98
Parczew C 12 96
Pardes Hanna-Karkur E 4 120
Pardo ≃, Braz. G 11 190
Pardo ≃, Braz. H 9 190
Pardo ≃, Braz. H 8 190
Pardubice C 8 96
Parecis, Chapada dos ⋏ F 7 190
Paredes de Nava B 6 86
Parent E 6 160
Pareora F 3 146
Parepare F 7 134
Parfenevo F 15 108
Párga C 4 106
Paria, Gulf of c F 9 186
Paricutín ∧1 H 8 184
Parika B 7 190
Parikkala B 14 66
Parima, Sierra ⋏ C 6 190
Parintins D 7 190
Paris, Fr. D 9 78
Paris, Il., U.S. C 5 170
Paris, Ky., U.S. D 1 162
Paris, Tx., U.S. D 6 172
Parita, Bahía de c F 4 186
Parit Buntar L 5 132
Parkano A 11 66
Parker, Co., U.S. F 2 174
Parker, S.D., U.S. D 6 174
Parker Dam ✦6 E 1 176
Parkersburg D 3 162
Parkers Prairie B 7 174
Parkes D 7 144
Parkin E 3 170
Parkland B 2 178
Park Range ⋏ B 5 176
Park Rynie F 9 206
Parksville A 1 178
Parkville G 2 164
Parla D 7 86
Parlākimidi F 4 122
Parma, Id., U.S. D 5 178
Parma, Italy E 6 92
Parma, Oh., U.S. C 3 162
Parma □6 E 6 92
Parnaíba D 10 190
Parnaíba ≃ D 10 190
Parnassós ∧ C 5 106
Parnassos National Park ♦ C 5 106
Parnes National Park ♦ C 5 106
Pärnu C 12 66
Pärnu-Jaagupi C 12 66
Paromaj B 12 124
Paroo ≃ C 5 144
Páros D 6 106
Parow G 3 206
Parral E 2 195
Parral ≃ D 7 184
Parramatta D 8 144
Parras de la Fuente E 8 184
Parrsboro F 11 160
Parry Channel ɥ B 10 148
Parry Sound F 3 160
Parshall H 7 158
Parsnip ≃ D 10 156
Parsons, Ks., U.S. D 1 170
Parsons, Tn., U.S. E 4 170
Pärsti C 12 66
Partanna G 2 94
Parthenay B 3 80
Partille D 5 66
Partinico F 3 94
Partizansk C 4 126
Partizánske B 10 102
Paru ≃ D 8 190
Paru de Oeste ≃ C 7 190
Pǎrvomaj D 8 104
Paryčy C 6 110
Parys D 7 206
Pasadena, Ca., U.S. F 5 182
Pasadena, Tx., U.S. F 6 172
Pasaje D 3 190
Pa Sak ≃ F 5 132
Pascagoula G 4 170
Pascagoula ≃ G 4 170
Pașcani B 9 104
Pasco B 4 178
Pascoag E 7 164
Pas-de-Calais □3 B 9 78
Pasewalk C 11 98
Pāsighāt D 2 130
Pasinler B 9 118
Pasir Gudang i 15 134a
Pasir Mas K 5 132
Pasir Panjang j 14 134a
Pasirpengarayan N 5 132
Pasir Puteh, Malay. L 6 132
Pasir Puteh, Malay. i 15 134a
Paškovskij G 11 110
Pasłęk A 10 96
Pasmore ≃ C 2 144
Pasni E 9 116
Paso de Indios H 6 192
Paso del Cerro B 10 195
Paso de los Libres A 9 195
Paso de los Toros C 9 195
Paso Robles E 3 182
Passadumkeag F 6 164
Passaic F 4 164
Passaic □6 E 4 164
Passau D 10 100
Passero, Capo > H 5 94
Passo Fundo A 9 192
Passo Real, Represa do ⊜1 A 11 195
Passos D 7 194
Pastavy E 13 66
Pastaza ≃ D 3 190
Pasto C 3 190
Pastol Bay c E 13 154
Pasuruan k 21 135b
Pasvalys D 12 66
Pásztó B 5 104
Patagonia ✦1 H 6 192
Pātan E 2 122
Patchewollock E 4 144
Patchogue F 5 164
Patea C 5 146
Patensie G 6 206
Paterna E 4 88
Paternion D 5 102
Paternò G 4 94
Paterson, N.J., U.S. F 4 164
Paterson, S. Afr. G 6 206
Pathānkot C 3 122
Pathein (Bassein) F 2 132
Pathein see Bassein ≃ F 6 122
Pathfinder Reservoir ⊜1 D 10 178
Pati k 20 135b
Patiāla C 3 122
Pātkai Range ⋏ D 7 122
Patna, India E 5 122
Patna, India D 5 122
Patnos C 10 118
Pato Branco G 4 194
Patonga G 3 202
Patos E 11 190
Patos ≃ C 3 195
Patos, Lagoa dos c F 9 192
Patos de Minas C 7 194
Pátra see Pátrai C 4 106
Pátrai (Pátra) C 4 106
Patrai, Gulf of c C 4 106
Patricio Lynch, Isla I I 4 192
Patrocínio C 7 194
Pattada I 5 92
Pattani K 5 132
Pattaya H 5 132
Patterson C 2 182
Patterson, Mount ∧ D 27 154
Patti F 4 94
Pattoki C 2 122
Patuca ≃ E 3 186
Patumahoe B 5 146
Patuxent ≃ D 5 162
Patuxent River State Park ♦ G 1 164
Pátzcuaro H 9 184
Pau E 3 80
Pauini ≃ E 5 190
Paulding B 6 170
Paulhan G 1 82
Paulicéia D 4 194
Paulinzella ⊥ F 8 98
Paulistana E 10 190
Paullo E 7 82
Paulo Afonso E 11 190
Pauls Valley C 5 172
Paung F 3 132
Paungde E 2 132
Paunggyi F 3 132
Pauri C 3 122
Pauto ≃ B 4 190
Pāveh E 12 118
Pavia D 5 92
Pavia □6 D 5 92
Pavilion F 11 156
Pāvilosta D 10 66
Pavlikeni D 8 104
Pavlodar D 10 114
Pavlof Bay c I 14 154
Pavlof Volcano ∧1 I 13 154
Pavlohrad E 9 110
Pavlovka C 23 110
Pavlovo I 15 108
Pavlovsk, Russia C 15 66
Pavlovsk, Russia D 12 110
Pavlysh E 8 110
Pavullo nel Frignano E 6 92
Pawan ≃ F 6 134
Pawn ≃ E 3 132
Pawnee C 4 170
Pawnee City E 6 174
Paw Paw, Il., U.S. B 4 170
Paw Paw, W.V., U.S. D 4 162
Pawtucket E 7 164
Paxton E 4 174
Payakumbuh O 5 132
Paya Lebar i 15 134a
Payerne D 4 82
Payeti A 6 140
Payette ≃ D 5 178
Payette, North Fork ≃ C 5 178
Paynes Find K 4 140
Paysandú C 8 195
Payson, Az., U.S. E 3 176
Payson, Il., U.S. C 3 170
Pazar B 9 118
Pazarcık D 7 118
Pazardžik D 8 104
Pcič C 6 110
Peabody, Ks., U.S. A 5 172
Peabody, Ma., U.S. D 7 164
Peace ≃ B 15 156
Peace River C 13 156
Peachland G 11 156
Peach Orchard C 3 168
Peach Springs E 2 176
Peak Charles National Park ♦ M 6 140
Peak District National Park ♦ D 5 72
Peake Creek ≃ J 2 142
Peak Hill, Austl. I 5 140
Peak Hill, Austl. D 7 144
Peard Bay c A 15 154
Pea Ridge National Military Park ♦ D 1 170
Pearl F 3 170
Pearl ≃ G 3 170
Pearl Harbor c i 9 181a
Pearl River G 4 170
Pearse Island I D 6 156
Pearston G 6 206
Peary Land ✦1 A 16 148
Pebane F 6 204
Pebble Island I n 18 193b
Peć D 6 104
Pecatu I 22 135b
Pecica B 6 104
Pečora D 22 108
Pečora ≃ C 8 114
Pečorskaja guba c B 21 108
Pečorskoe more ⊤2 C 8 114
Pečory H 7 108
Pecos E 2 172
Pecos ≃ E 7 152
Pecos National Monument ♦ E 6 176
Pécs D 10 102
Pedder, Lake ⊜1 j 11 145a
Peddie G 7 206
Pedernales ≃ E 4 172
Pedernales Falls State Park ♦ E 4 172
Pedra Azul A 10 194
Pedras Salgadas C 3 86
Pedreiras D 10 190
Pedro Afonso A 9 190
Pedrógão Grande E 2 86
Pedro Juan Caballero E 3 194
Pedro Leopoldo C 8 194
Pedro Muñoz E 2 88
Peebles, Oh., U.S. D 2 162
Peebles, Scot., U.K. B 3 72
Pee Dee ≃ B 5 168
Peekskill E 5 164
Peel ≃ C 27 154
Peel Channel ≃ B 27 154
Peel Sound ɥ B 13 150
Peene ≃ B 10 98
Peerless A 11 178
Peers E 13 156
Pegasus Bay c E 4 146
Pegau E 9 98
Pegnitz C 8 100
Pego F 4 88
Pegtymel' ≃ B 3 154
Pegu see Bago F 3 132
Pegu ≃ F 3 132
Peguis Indian Reserve ✦4 F 9 158
Pehčevo E 7 104
Pehuajó D 7 195
Pehula B 11 66
Peigan Indian Reserve ✦4 G 15 156
Peikang G 15 130
Peine D 7 98
Peip'ing see Beijing G 11 128
Peipus, Lake ⊜ C 13 66
Peissenberg E 8 100
Peiting E 7 100
Peixe ≃ D 5 194
Peixian A 13 130
Peixoto, Represa de ⊜1 D 7 194
Pekalongan k 20 135b
Pekan M 6 132
Pekanbaru N 5 132
Pekin B 4 170
Peking see Beijing G 11 128
Péla D 3 200
Pelabuhanratu k 18 135b
Pelagie, Isole II I 2 94
Pelée, Montagne ∧1 s 26 187h
Pelee Island I H 2 160
Peleng, Pulau I F 8 134
Pelham F 5 170
Pelhřimov C 12 100
Pelican H 27 154
Pelican Lake ⊜, Mb., Can. E 8 158
Pelican Lake ⊜, Sk., Can. D 7 158
Pelican Narrows D 20 156
Pelister Nacionalni Park ♦ E 6 104
Pella B 2 170
Pélla ⊥ B 5 106
Pell City F 5 170
Pellegrini, Lago ⊜ F 4 195
Pellston C 6 166
Pelly ≃ E 26 154
Pelly Crossing E 26 154
Pelly Mountains ⋏ F 28 154
Peloponnesus >1 D 5 106
Pelopónnisos □3 D 5 106
Pelotas B 11 195
Pelotas ≃ A 9 192
Pel'vož C 27 108
Pelym G 25 108
Pemadumcook Lake ⊜ h 12 163a
Pemalang k 19 135b
Pematang O 5 132
Pematangsiantar M 4 132
Pemba E 7 204
Pemba I D 6 204
Pemba Channel ɥ D 6 204
Pemba North □3 H 5 202
Pemba South □3 I 5 202
Pemberton N 4 140
Pembina ≃, Ab., Can. E 14 156
Pembina ≃, N.A. A 5 174
Pembroke, Me., U.S. A 10 162
Pembroke, On., Can. F 5 160
Pembroke, Va., U.S. E 3 162
Pembroke, Wales, U.K. F 2 72
Pembroke Pines F 4 168
Pembrokeshire □6 F 1 72
Pembrokeshire Coast National Park ♦ E 1 72
Pembuang ≃ F 6 134
Pemigewasset ≃ C 7 164
Penafiel C 2 86
Pena-Lunanga C 4 204
Penápolis D 5 194
Peñaranda de Bracamonte D 5 86
Peñarroya-Pueblonuevo F 5 86
Penarth F 3 72
Penas, Golfo de c I 5 192
Pench National Park ♦ E 3 122
Penco E 1 195
Pender Bay c E 7 140
Pendjari ≃ C 5 200
Pendjari, Parc National de la ♦ C 5 200
Pendleton, In., U.S. B 6 170
Pendleton, Or., U.S. C 4 178
Pend Oreille ≃ A 5 178
Pend Oreille, Lake ⊜ A 5 178
Pendžikent B 1 122
Penebel I 22 135b
Penedono C 3 86
Penetanguishene F 3 160
Penfield C 4 162
Penganga ≃ F 3 122
Penglai H 13 128
Pengshui D 9 130
Pengxi C 7 130
Pengxian C 6 130
Pengze D 13 130
Penha G 6 194
Penibética, Cordillera ⋏ D 4 84
Peniche E 1 86
Penicuik B 3 72
Penida, Nusa I I 22 135b
Peninsula State Park ♦ C 5 166
Penne B 3 94
Penne-d'Agenais D 4 80
Penneru ≃ G 3 122
Penn Hills C 4 162
Pennines ⋏ C 4 72
Penns Grove G 3 164
Pennsville G 3 164
Pennsylvania □3 C 12 152
Penn Yan D 1 164
Pennyrile Forest State Resort Park ♦ D 5 170
Peno H 10 108
Penobscot ≃ h 12 163a
Peñoles H 1 172
Penong K 1 142
Penonomé F 4 186
Penrhyn I1 D 12 136
Penrith, Austl. D 8 144
Penrith, Eng., U.K. C 4 72
Pensacola G 5 170
Pensacola Mountains ⋏ E 4 208
Pentecost Island see Pentecôte I E 8 136
Pentecôte I E 8 136
Penticton G 12 156
Penticton Indian Reserve ✦4 G 12 156
Pentland Firth ɥ B 5 74
Penukonda G 3 122
Penza C 14 110
Penzance G 1 72
Penzberg E 8 100
Penzenskaja oblast' □6 C 14 110
Penžinskij hrebet ⋏ C 19 114
Peoria, Az., U.S. F 2 176
Peoria, Il., U.S. B 4 170
Peotone B 5 170
Pepel D 2 200
Peqin B 3 106
Pequot Lakes B 1 166
Perabumulih F 4 134
Perak □3 L 5 132
Perak ≃ L 5 132
Perak, Kuala c L 5 132
Peralillo D 2 195
Perämeri (Bottenviken) c D 11 64
Perchtoldsdorf B 8 102
Percival Lakes ⊜ G 8 140
Perdido ≃ G 5 170
Perdido, Monte ∧ B 5 88
Perdue E 18 156
Peregrebnoe E 26 108
Perehins'ke A 8 104
Perehonivka A 11 104
Pereira C 3 190
Pereira Barreto D 5 194
Perelesinskij D 12 110
Peremyšl' I 11 108
Pereslavl'-Zalesskij H 13 108
Pereyaslav-Khmel'nyts'kyy E 7 110
Perg B 6 102
Pergamino C 7 195
Pergamum ⊥ C 7 106
Pergola F 8 92
Péribonka ≃ D 8 160
Péribonka, Lac ⊜ C 8 160
Peridot F 3 176
Périgord □9 C 4 80
Périgueux C 4 80
Perijá, Sierra de ⋏ A 4 190
Perim I E 5 202
Periprava C 10 104
Perito Moreno I 5 192
Perkins B 5 172
Perlas, Archipiélago de las II F 5 186
Perlas, Laguna de c E 3 186
Perleberg C 8 98
Perlis □3 K 5 132
Perm' G 22 108
Permas G 16 108
Përmet B 4 106
Permskaja oblast' □6 G 23 108
Pernambuco □3 E 11 190
Pernatty Lagoon ⊜ C 1 144
Pernik D 7 104
Péronne C 9 78
Perosa Argentina E 3 92
Perote H 11 184
Perpignan F 6 80
Perrin D 4 172
Perrine G 4 168
Perris G 6 182
Perry, Ga., U.S. C 3 168
Perry, Ia., U.S. E 7 174
Perry, Mi., U.S. B 1 162
Perry □6 F 1 164
Perry Lake ⊜1 C 1 170
Perrysburg C 2 162
Perry's Victory and International Peace Memorial ⊥ C 2 162
Perryton B 3 172
Perryville D 3 170
Peršamajski F 12 66
Persepolis see Takht-e Jamshīd ⊥ G 15 118
Pershotravens'k D 5 110
Perstorp H 6 64
Pertek C 8 118
Perth, Austl. L 3 140
Perth, On., Can. F 5 160
Perth, Scot., U.K. D 5 74
Perth Amboy F 4 164
Perthshire and Kinross □6 D 5 74
Pertuis G 3 82
Peru, Il., U.S. B 4 170
Peru, In., U.S. B 5 170
Peru □1 E 7 190
Perućačko jezero ⊜1 D 5 104
Peru-Chile Trench ✣1 I 21 58
Perugia F 8 92
Perugia □6 G 8 92
Peruíbe F 7 194
Perušić C 3 104
Péruwelz D 2 69
Pervomajsk B 13 110
Pervomajskij, Russia J 21 108
Pervomajskij, Russia I 24 108
Pervomays'k A 11 104
Pervomays'kyy E 9 110
Pervoural'sk H 23 108
Pesaro F 8 92
Pesaro e Urbino □6 F 8 92
Pescadores II G 14 130
Pesčanoe E 11 108
Pescantina E 2 102
Pescara B 4 94
Pescara □6 B 3 94
Pescara ≃ B 4 94
Pescia F 6 92
Pescina B 3 94
Pesek, Pulau I j 14 134a
Peshāwar C 2 122
Peshkopi B 4 106
Peshtigo C 5 166
Peso da Régua C 3 86
Pesquería ≃ H 4 172
Pessac D 3 80
Pest □3 B 5 104
Peštera D 8 104
Pestovo G 11 108
Pestravka C 16 110
Petah Tiqwa E 3 120
Petaluma B 1 182
Pétange E 4 69
Petare F 8 186
Petatlán I 9 184
Petauke E 5 204
Petawawa F 5 160
Petegem D 2 69
Petén Itzá, Lago ⊜ I 14 184
Petenwell Lake ⊜1 C 3 166
Peterborough, Austl. D 2 144
Peterborough, Eng., U.K. E 6 72
Peterborough, N.H., U.S. D 7 164
Peterborough, On., Can. F 4 160
Peterhead C 7 74
Peter I Island I C 36 208
Peterlee C 5 72
Petermann Aboriginal Land ✦4 I 10 140
Peter Pond Lake ⊜ C 4 158
Peter Pond Lake Indian Reserve ✦4 C 16 156
Petersberg B 6 100
Petersburg, Ak., U.S. H 28 154
Petersburg, In., U.S. C 5 170
Petersburg, Va., U.S. E 5 162
Petersburg, W.V., U.S. D 4 162
Petersfield G 6 72
Petershagen, Ger. D 5 98
Petershagen, Ger. D 10 98
Petilia Policastro E 6 94
Pétion-Ville D 6 186
Petit-Bourg n 21 187e
Petite Rivière Noire, Piton de la ∧ q 21 207e
Petit-Loango F 6 200
Petit Mécatina (Little Mecatina) ≃ B 13 160
Petitot ≃ A 10 156
Petit Saint-Bernard, Col du)(E 4 82
Petitsikapau Lake ⊜ A 10 160
Petlalcingo H 11 184
Peto G 15 184
Petone D 5 146
Petoskey C 6 166
Petra see Al-Batrā' ⊥ I 4 120
Petra Velikogo, zaliv c C 3 126
Petre, Point > G 5 160
Petrer F 4 88
Petrič E 7 104
Petrified Forest National Park ♦ E 4 176
Petrila C 7 104
Petrinja E 8 102
Petrivka B 11 104
Petrodvorec G 8 108
Petrograd see Sankt-Peterburg F 9 108
Petrolia D 7 166
Petrolina E 10 190
Petropavl see Petropavlovsk I 28 108
Petropavlovka A 5 128
Petropavlovsk (Petropavl) I 28 108
Petropavlovsk-Kamčatskij B 15 124
Petrópolis E 9 194
Petroșani C 7 104
Petrovsk C 14 110
Petrovskij H 13 108
Petrov Val D 14 110
Petrozavodsk F 11 108
Petrusdal B 2 206
Petrus Steyn D 8 206
Pettus F 5 172
Petuhovo I 27 108
Peuerbach B 5 102
Peuetsagoe, Gunung ∧1 L 3 132
Peykjahlið m 22 64a
Peza ≃ D 18 108
Pézenas G 1 82
Pezinok B 9 102
Pfarrkirchen D 9 100
Pfastatt B 3 92
Pfinztal C 5 100
Pflersch see Fleres D 3 102
Pfolz D 2 206
Pforzheim D 5 100
Pfronten E 6 96
Pfullendorf E 6 100
Pfullingen D 6 100
Pfungstadt C 5 100
Pha-an F 3 132
Phaephane A 6 206
Phala B 7 206
Phalaborwa B 9 206
Phalodi D 2 122
Phan E 4 132
Phanom Thuan G 4 132
Phan Rang I 9 132
Phan Si Pan ∧ C 6 132
Phan Thiet I 9 132
Pharr G 4 172
Phato J 4 132
Phatthalung K 5 132
Phayao E 4 132
Phelps Lake ⊜ B 6 168
Phenix City F 6 170
Phetchabun F 5 132
Phetchabun Range ⋏ F 5 132
Phetchaburi H 4 132
Phichit F 5 132
Philadelphia, Ms., U.S. F 4 170
Philadelphia, Pa., U.S. G 3 164
Philadelphia, Tn., U.S. B 2 168
Philadelphia □6 F 3 164
Philae ⊥ C 3 202
Philippeville see Skikda, Alg. B 6 198
Philippeville, Bel. D 3 69
Philippi D 3 162
Philippi, Lake ⊜ H 4 142
Philippine Basin ✣1 E 10 58
Philippines □1 C 8 134
Philippine Sea ⊤2 I 9 124
Philippine Trench ✣1 F 10 58
Philippopolis see Plovdiv D 8 104
Philippsburg A 6 82
Philipsburg B 7 178
Philipstown F 6 206
Phillip Island I G 5 144
Phillips B 8 164
Phillipsburg, Ks., U.S. F 5 174
Phillipsburg, N.J., U.S. F 3 164
Philo C 4 170
Philpots Island I B 17 150
Phimai G 6 132
Phitsanulok F 4 132
Phnom Penh see Phnum Pénh I 7 132
Phnum Pénh (Phnom Penh) I 7 132
Phoenix, Az., U.S. F 2 176
Phoenix, N.Y., U.S. C 2 164
Phoenix Islands II D 10 136
Phon G 6 132

⌞ Waterfall ɥ Strait c Bay, Gulf ⊜ Lake ≋ Swamp ⍓ Ice Feature ⊤ Other Hydrographic Feature ✣ Submarine Feature □ Political Unit ⦊ Cultural Institution ⊥ Historical Site ♦ Recreational Site ⊠ Airport ■ Military Installation ✦ Miscellaneous

Phôngsali — Preto

Name — Map Ref. Page

Phôngsali D 6 132
Phon Phisai F 6 132
Phrae E 5 132
Phra Nakhon Si Ayutthaya G 5 132
Phuket K 4 132
Phuket, Ko I J 4 132
Phu Ly D 7 132
Phum Duang ≃ J 4 132
Phumĭ Béng H 7 132
Phumĭ Chhuk I 7 132
Phumĭ Kâmpóng Trâbâk H 7 132
Phuoc Long I 8 132
Phu Pan National Park ♦ F 6 132
Phu Quoc, Dao I J 6 132
Phu Tho D 7 132
Piacenza D 5 92
Piacenza □[6] E 5 92
Pialba H 11 142
Pianella B 4 94
Piatra-Neamț B 9 104
Piauí □[3] E 10 190
Piave ≃ D 8 92
Piawaning L 4 140
Piaxtla ≃ E 6 184
Piazza Armerina G 4 94
Pic ≃ G 15 158
Picacho F 3 176
Picardie (Picardy) □[9] G 9 70
Picardy see Picardie □[9] G 9 70
Picayune G 4 170
Pichanal D 7 192
Pichilemu D 1 195
Pichucalco I 13 184
Pickens B 3 168
Pickering, Eng., U.K. C 6 72
Pickering, On., Can. B 4 162
Pickstown D 5 174
Pico ∧ h 11 200a
Pico I E 5 196
Pico de Orizaba, Parque Nacional ♦ H 11 184
Pico de Orizaba, Volcán ∧[1] H 11 184
Picos E 10 190
Picquigny C 9 78
Picton, N.Z. D 4 146
Picton, On., Can. C 1 164
Pictou F 12 160
Pictured Rocks National Lakeshore ♦ B 5 166
Picuris Indian Reservation ◆[4] D 6 176
Pidurutalagala ∧ H 4 122
Piedicroce i 9 83a
Piedimonte Matese E 5 90
Piedmont B 3 168
Piedra ≃ D 5 176
Piedra del Águila, Embalse ⊜[1] G 3 195
Piedrahita D 5 86
Piedras Negras C 9 184
Piedras Negras ⊥ I 14 184
Piedra Sola C 9 195
Pieksämäki E 13 64
Pielavesi E 13 64
Pielinen ⊜ E 15 64
Pieljekaise Nationalpark ♦ C 8 64
Piemonte □[3] D 3 92
Pienaarsrivier C 8 206
Pieniński Park Narodowy ♦ D 11 96
Pieńsk E 12 98
Pierce D 6 174
Pierce City D 1 170
Pierce Lake ⊜ D 12 158
Pierre C 4 174
Pierson E 4 168
Piešt'any B 9 102
Pietarsaari E 11 64
Pietermaritzburg E 9 206
Pietersburg B 8 206
Pietraperzia G 4 94
Pietrasanta F 6 92
Piet Retief D 9 206
Pieve di Cadore C 8 92
Pigeon Forge B 3 168
Pigeon Lake ⊜ E 15 156
Pigna F 3 92
Pigs, Bay of ⊂ C 4 186
Pigüé E 6 195
Pihlajavesi ⊜ B 14 66
Pihtipudas E 12 64
Pijijiapan J 13 184
Pikalëvo G 11 108
Pikangikum Lake ⊜ F 12 158
Pike □[6] E 3 164
Pikes Peak ∧ F 2 174
Pikesville G 2 164
Piketberg G 3 206
Pikeville E 6 170
Pikou G 14 128
Pikounda B 2 204
Piła B 9 96
Piła □[3] B 9 96
Pilanesberg Game Reserve ♦ C 7 206
Pilar G 1 194
Pilas G 4 86
Pilbara ◆[1] H 5 140
Pilcomayo ≃ D 7 192
Pilibgwe B 7 206
Pīlībhīt D 3 122
Pilica ≃ C 11 96
Pillsbury State Park ♦ C 6 164
Pilot Knob D 3 170
Pilot Point H 15 154
Pilot Station F 13 154
Pilottown H 4 170
Pilsen see Plzeň C 10 100
Piltene D 10 66
Pilu ≃ D 3 132
Pim ≃ F 30 108
Pimentel E 2 190
Pina de Ebro C 4 88
Pinang see George Town L 4 132
Pinang, Pulau I L 4 132
Pınarbaşı C 7 118
Pinar del Río C 3 186
Pınarhisar B 7 106
Pinatubo, Mount ∧[1] B 8 134
Pincher Creek G 15 156
Pinckneyville C 4 170
Pińczów C 11 96
Pindaré ≃ D 9 190
Píndhos Óros (Pindus Mountains) ⩓ B 9 198
Pindos Range National park ♦ C 4 106
Pinduši E 11 108
Pindus Mountains see Píndhos Óros ⩓ B 9 198
Pine ≃ C 11 156
Pine Barrens ◆[1] G 4 164
Pine Bluff E 3 170
Pine Bush E 4 164
Pine City C 2 166
Pine Creek C 11 140
Pine Creek ≃ B 5 180
Pine Creek Indian Reserve ◆[4] E 8 158
Pineda de Mar C 7 88
Pinega D 15 108
Pinega ≃ D 15 108
Pine Grove F 2 164
Pine Hill G 8 142
Pine Hills E 4 168
Pinehouse Lake ⊜ D 5 158
Pinehurst C 5 178
Pine Island I F 3 168
Pine Island Bay ⊂ D 34 208
Pinellas Park F 3 168
Pine Mountain ⩓ E 2 162
Pine Pass)(D 10 156
Pine Point A 14 156
Pine Ridge D 3 174
Pine Ridge Indian Reservation ◆[4] D 3 174
Pine River F 8 158
Pinerolo E 3 92
Pines, Isle of see Juventud, Isla de la I C 4 186
Pines, Lake O' The ⊜[1] F 1 170
Pinetown E 9 206
Pineville, Ky., U.S. E 2 162
Pineville, La., U.S. G 2 170
Piney Woods F 4 170
Ping ≃ F 4 132
Pingba E 8 130
Pingding H 9 128
Pingdingshan B 11 130
Pingdu H 12 128
Pingelly M 4 140
Pinghe G 6 130
Pinghu C 15 130
Pingjiang D 11 130
Pingle F 10 130
Pingliang I 6 128
Pingluo G 6 128
Pingnan E 14 130
Pingquan F 12 128
Pingshan G 10 128
Pingshi B 11 130
Pingtan F 14 130
P'ingtung G 15 130
Pingxiang, China E 11 130
Pingxiang, China G 8 130
Pingyang E 15 130
Pingyao H 9 128
Pingyi I 11 128
Pingyin H 11 128
Pingyuan F 12 130
Pinheiro D 9 190
Pinheiros C 10 194
Pinhel D 3 86
Piniós ≃ C 5 106
Pinjug F 17 108
Pinnacles ♦ L 3 140
Pinnacles National Monument ♦ D 2 182
Pinnaroo E 3 144
Pinneberg C 6 98
Pinoso F 3 88
Pinos Puente G 7 86
Pinrang F 7 134
Pins, Île des I D 14 138
Pinsent's Arm B 16 160
Pinsk J 12 64
Pinta, Isla I i 13 190a
Pintada Arroyo ≃ C 1 172
Pin Valley National Park ♦ C 3 122
Pioche D 1 176
Piombino G 6 92
Pioneer L 6 140
Pioner, ostrov I B 12 114
Pionerskij E 10 66
Pionki C 11 96
Piorini, Lago ⊜ D 6 190
Piotrków □[3] C 10 96
Piotrków Trybunalski C 10 96
Piove di Sacco D 8 92
Pipe Spring National Monument ♦ D 2 176
Pipestem Creek ≃ B 5 174
Pipestem State Park ♦ E 3 162
Pipestone D 6 174
Pipestone ≃ E 13 158
Pipestone Creek ≃ G 8 158
Pipestone National Monument ♦ C 6 174
Pipi ≃ D 9 200
Pipinas G 8 192
Piqua C 1 162
Piquiri ≃ D 9 192
Pira D 5 200
Piracanjuba B 6 194
Piracanjuba ≃ B 6 194
Piracicaba E 7 194
Piracicaba ≃ E 7 194
Piraeus see Piraiévs D 5 106
Piraí do Sul F 6 194
Piraiévs (Piraeus) D 5 106
Piraju E 6 194
Pirajuí D 6 194
Piranhas B 4 194
Pīrān Shahr D 11 118
Pirapora B 8 194
Piraputanga D 3 194
Pirassununga D 7 194
Pirdop D 8 104
Pires do Rio B 6 194
Pírgos D 4 106
Pirin, Parki Narodowe ♦ E 7 104
Piripiri D 10 190
Pirmasens C 4 100
Pirna F 10 98
Pirot D 7 104
Pīr Panjāl Range ⩓ C 2 122
Piru F 9 134
Pisa F 6 92
Pisa □[6] F 6 92
Pisa, Certosa di ◗[1] F 6 92
Pisagua C 5 192
Piscataway F 4 164
Pișchia C 6 104
Pisco F 3 190
Písek C 11 100
Pishan B 3 122
Pishchana A 10 104
Pishchanka A 10 104
Piskivka D 6 110
Pismo Beach E 3 182
Pišnur H 17 108
Pisogne D 6 92
Pissos D 3 80
Pisticci D 6 94
Pistoia F 6 92
Pistoia □[6] F 6 92
Pisuerga ≃ C 6 86
Pit ≃ E 3 178
Pita C 2 200
Pitaga B 11 160
Pitalito C 3 190
Pitanga F 5 194
Pitangueiras D 6 194
Pitcairn □[2] H 17 58
Piteå D 10 64
Piteälven ≃ D 9 64
Pitești C 8 104
Pithara L 4 140
Pithiviers D 9 78
Pitkas Point E 13 154
Pitkjaranta F 9 108
Pitlochry C 6 70
Pitman G 3 164
Pitrufquén F 1 195
Pitseng Ha E 8 206
Pitt Island I J 30 154
Pittsboro B 5 168
Pittsburg, Ca., U.S. B 2 182
Pittsburg, Ks., U.S. D 1 170
Pittsburgh C 3 162
Pittsfield, Il., U.S. C 3 170
Pittsfield, Ma., U.S. D 5 164
Pittsfield, N.H., U.S. C 7 164
Pittston E 3 164
Pittsworth A 8 144
Pium F 9 190
Piura E 2 190
Pivdennyy Buh (Boug méridional) (Bug Méridional) (Bug Meridionale) (Südlic ≃ E 6 110
Pixian C 6 130
Pixley E 4 182
Pizzighettone D 5 92
Pjakupur ≃ E 31 108
Pjal'ma E 11 108
Pjaozero, ozero ⊜ C 9 108
Pjaršai E 13 66
Pjasina ≃ B 12 114
Pjasino, ozero ⊜ C 11 114
Pjatigorsk G 13 110
Pjatnickoe D 10 110
Pjažieva Sel'ga F 11 108
Placentia Bay ⊂ E 16 160
Placer □[6] A 3 182
Placerville B 3 182
Placetas C 5 186
Plainfield, N.J., U.S. F 4 164
Plainfield, Wi., U.S. C 4 166
Plains C 2 168
Plainview C 3 172
Plainville, Ct., U.S. E 6 164
Plainville, In., U.S. C 5 170
Plainwell D 6 166
Plakhtiyivka B 10 104
Plaksino A 7 110
Planada C 3 182
Planeta Rica F 5 186
Plano D 5 172
Plant City E 3 168
Plaquemine G 3 170
Plasencia D 4 86
Plast I 24 108
Plaster Rock E 10 160
Plasy C 10 100
Plata, Río de la ⊂[1] G 8 192
Plateaux □[3] C 1 204
Platen, Kapp > A 5 114
Platinum G 13 154
Plato F 6 186
Platte ≃ E 6 174
Platte Center E 6 174
Platteville, Co., U.S. E 2 174
Platteville, Wi., U.S. D 3 166
Plattsburg F 7 174
Plattsburgh B 5 164
Plau C 9 98
Plauen B 9 100
Pļaviņas D 12 66
Plavsk J 12 108
Playgreen Lake ⊜ E 10 158
Play Ku G 9 132
Plaza A 4 174
Plaza Huincul F 3 195
Pleasant Grove B 3 176
Pleasant Hill C 3 170
Pleasanton, Ca., U.S. C 2 182
Pleasanton, Tx., U.S. F 4 172
Pleasantville G 4 164
Pleaux C 6 80
Pleiku see Play Ku G 9 132
Plenty, Bay of ⊂ B 6 146
Plentywood A 2 174
Pleseck E 14 108
Plessisville E 7 160
Pleszew C 9 96
Pleternica E 9 102
Plétipi, Lac ⊜ C 8 160
Plettenberg E 4 98
Plettenberg Bay H 5 206
Pleven D 8 104
Pleyben D 3 78
Plitvička Jezera Nacionalni Park ♦ C 3 104
Pljevlja D 5 104
Płock B 10 96
Płock □[3] B 10 96
Ploești see Ploiești C 9 104
Plogastel-Saint-Germain E 2 78
Ploiești C 9 104
Plombières-les-Bains C 4 82
Plön B 7 98
Plonge, Lac la ⊜ D 18 156
Płońsk B 11 96
Płoty B 8 96
Ploudalmézeau D 2 78
Plouha D 4 78
Plovdiv D 8 104
Plovdiv □[3] D 8 104
Plumas □[6] A 3 182
Plumas-Eureka State Park ♦ A 3 182
Plummer B 5 178
Plumridge Lakes ⊜ K 8 140
Plungė E 10 66
Plutarco Elías Calles, Presa ⊜[1] C 4 184
Pluvigner E 4 78
Plymouth, Eng., U.K. G 2 72
Plymouth, Il., U.S. B 3 170
Plymouth, Ma., U.S. E 8 164
Plymouth, Monts. D 9 186
Plymouth, N.C., U.S. B 6 168
Plymouth, N.H., U.S. C 7 164
Plymouth, Pa., U.S. C 6 162
Plymouth □[6] E 8 164
Plymouth Rock ⊥ E 8 164
Plympton G 2 72
Plymstock G 2 72
Plzeň C 10 100
Pniewy B 9 96
Pô C 4 200
Po ≃ D 7 92
Pobeda, gora ∧ C 17 114
Pobeda, Mount see Pobeda, gora ∧ C 17 114
Pobedy, Peak ∧ A 4 122
Pobra de Trives B 3 86
Pocahontas C 4 170
Pocatello D 7 178
Počep J 10 108
Pöchlarn B 7 102
Pocono Mountains ⩓[2] E 3 164
Poços de Caldas D 7 194
Poddębice C 10 96
Poddore H 9 108
Poděbrady B 12 100
Podensac D 3 80
Podgorica D 5 104
Podlasie ◆[1] B 12 96
Podlesnoe D 15 110
Podol'sk I 12 108
Podor B 1 200
Podosinovec F 17 108
Podporože F 11 108
Podravina ◆[1] E 10 102
Podujevo D 6 104
Poelela, Lagoa ⊜ C 11 206
Poggibonsi F 7 92
Pogoanele C 9 104
Pogradec B 4 106
Pograničnyj B 3 126
Pogromni Volcano ∧[1] I 12 154
Pogruznaja I 19 108
P'ohang I 17 128
Pohjois-Karjala □[3] E 15 64
Pohlheim B 5 100
Pohnpei I C 7 136
Pohořelice A 8 102
Pohvistnevo J 19 108
Pöide C 11 66
Poinsett, Cape > C 20 208
Point Arena C 2 180
Point Au Fer Island I H 3 170
Pointe a la Hache H 4 170
Pointe-à-Pitre n 21 187e
Point Edward G 2 160
Pointe-Noire C 1 204
Point Fortin q 23 187f
Point Lake ⊜ C 10 150
Point Pelee National Park ♦ C 2 162
Point Pleasant, N.J., U.S. F 4 164
Point Pleasant, W.V., U.S. D 2 162
Point Reyes National Seashore ♦ B 1 182
Point Salvation Aboriginal Reserve ◆[4] K 8 140
Point Sapin E 11 160
Poisson Blanc, Lac du ⊜[1] F 6 160
Poissy D 8 78
Poitiers B 4 80
Poitou □[9] B 3 80
Pojoaque Valley E 5 176
Pokaran D 2 122
Pokharā D 4 122
Poko B 4 204
Pokrovs'ke E 9 110
Pokrovskoe J 12 108
Polack E 14 66
Pola de Laviana A 5 86
Pola de Lena A 5 86
Pola de Siero A 5 86
Poland □[1] E 11 62
Polanów A 9 96
Polar Bear Provincial Park ♦ D 16 158
Polatlı C 5 118
Połczyn-Zdrój B 8 96
Pol-e Khomrī B 1 122
Pol-e Safīd D 15 118
Polesine ◆[1] E 7 92
Poleski Park Narodowy ♦ C 12 96
Polessk E 10 66
Polesye ◆[1] D 5 110
Polevskoj H 23 108
Polgár B 6 104
Policastro, Golfo di ⊂ E 5 94
Police B 8 96
Polička A 8 102
Polignano a Mare C 7 94
Políkastron B 5 106
Polillo Islands II C 8 134
Pólis E 5 118
Polistena F 6 94
Poljarnyj B 10 108
Polk C 4 162
Pollāchi G 3 122
Pöllau C 7 102
Pollença E 7 88
Polmont A 3 72
Polnovat E 26 108
Polo A 4 170
Polohy F 10 110
Polom G 19 108
Polovinnoe B 23 110
Polski Trămbeš D 8 104
Poltava E 9 110
Poltava □[6] E 9 110
Põltsamaa C 13 66
Poluj ≃ D 28 108
Põlva C 13 66
Polynesia II D 12 136
Pomarance F 6 92
Pomarkku B 11 66
Pomene B 11 206
Pomerania □[9] B 8 96
Pomeranian Bay ⊂ B 11 98
Pomeroy, Oh., U.S. D 2 162
Pomeroy, S. Afr. E 9 206
Pomichna E 7 110
Pomona, Ca., U.S. F 6 182
Pomona, Nmb. D 1 206
Pomona Park E 4 168
Pomorskij proliv ʊ B 19 108
Pomozdino E 21 108
Pompano Beach F 4 168
Pompei ⊥ D 4 94
Pompéia E 5 194
Pompey B 4 82
Pomposa, Abbazia di ◗[1] E 8 92
Pompton Lakes F 4 164
Ponca City B 5 172
Ponce j 15 187b
Poncha Pass)(C 5 176
Ponchatoula G 3 170
Ponderay G 13 156
Pondicherry G 3 122
Pondicherry □[3] G 4 122
Pond Inlet B 17 150
Ponferrada B 4 86
Pongo ≃ F 2 202
Pongolapoortdam (Jozini Dam) ⊜[1] D 9 206
Pong-Tamale D 4 200
Poniatowa C 11 96
Ponnaiyār ≃ G 3 122
Ponoj ≃ C 13 108
Ponoka E 15 156
Ponomarëvka C 19 110
Ponorogo k 20 135b
Ponsacco F 6 92
Pont-à-Celles B 11 78
Ponta Delgada h 12 198a
Ponta Grossa F 5 194
Pontalina B 6 194
Pont-à-Mousson B 3 82
Pontão E 2 86
Ponta Porã E 3 194
Pontardawe F 3 72
Pontarlier D 4 82
Pontassieve F 7 92
Pont-Audemer C 7 78
Pont-Aven E 3 78
Pont Canavese D 3 92
Pontchartrain, Lake ⊜ G 3 170
Pontchâteau E 4 78
Pont-d'Ain D 3 82
Pont-de-Vaux D 2 82
Pontecagnano D 4 94
Ponte-Caldelas B 2 86
Pontecorvo E 4 90
Ponte de Lima C 2 86
Pontedera F 6 92
Ponte do Púngoè F 5 204
Pontefract D 5 72
Ponte nell'Alpi C 8 92
Ponte Nova D 9 194
Pontevedra B 2 86
Pontevedra □[6] B 2 86
Ponte Vedra Beach D 4 168
Pontevico D 6 92
Pontiac, Il., U.S. B 4 170
Pontiac, Mi., U.S. B 2 162
Pontiac □[6] A 2 164
Pontianak F 5 134
Pontivy D 4 78
Pont-l'Évêque C 7 78
Pontoise C 8 78
Pontremoli E 5 92
Pontresina C 5 92
Ponts C 6 88
Pont-Sainte-Maxence C 9 78
Pont-Scorff E 3 78
Pontypool F 3 72
Pontypridd F 3 72
Poochera L 2 142
Pool □[3] C 1 204
Poole G 4 72
Pooler C 4 168
Poona see Pune F 2 122
Poopó, Lago ⊜ G 5 190
Poor Man Indian Reserve ◆[4] F 19 156
Poortjie F 5 206
Popasna E 11 110
Popayán C 3 190
Poperinge D 1 69
Popil Lake ⊜ D 3 144
Popiltah Lake ⊜ D 3 144
Popinci D 8 104
Poplar B 3 166
Poplar ≃ E 10 158
Poplar, West Fork ≃ A 11 178
Poplar Bluff D 3 170
Popocatépetl, Volcán ∧[1] H 10 184
Popoh I 20 135b
Popokabaka D 2 204
Popoli B 3 94
Popondetta N 13 124
Popovka F 13 108
Popovo D 9 104
Poprad D 11 96
Popricani B 9 104
Pŏptong-ŭp G 16 128
Poquoson E 5 162
Porangatu F 9 190
Porbandar E 1 122
Porcher Island I E 6 156
Porcia D 8 92
Porcuna G 6 86
Porcupine ≃ C 23 154
Porcupine Mountains State Park ♦ B 3 166
Pordenone D 8 92
Pordenone □[6] C 8 92
Pordim D 8 104
Porecatu E 5 194
Poreckoe I 16 108
Porhov H 8 108
Pori B 10 66
Porirua D 5 146
Porjaguba C 10 108
Porlamar F 9 186
Pormpuraaw Aboriginal Land ◆[4] C 5 142
Pornic E 4 78
Poronajsk C 12 124
Póros C 4 106
Poroshkove A 7 104
Porrentruy C 5 82
Porretta Terme E 6 92
Porsangen ⊂ A 12 64
Porsgrunn C 4 66
Porsuk ≃ C 9 106
Portachuelo G 6 190
Port Adelaide E 2 144
Portadown B 5 75
Portage D 6 166
Portage la Prairie F 9 158
Portageville D 4 170
Portal A 3 174
Port Alberni G 9 156
Portalegre E 3 86
Portalegre □[3] E 3 86
Port Alfred G 7 206
Port Allegany E 9 166
Port Alsworth F 17 154
Port Angeles A 2 178
Port Antonio h 13 186a
Port Arthur, Austl. j 12 145a
Port Arthur, Tx., U.S. H 2 170
Port Askaig E 2 74
Port Augusta D 1 144
Port-au-Prince D 6 186
Porta Westfalica D 5 98
Port Barre G 3 170
Port Blair G 6 122
Port Blandford D 16 160
Port Byron E 3 166
Port Canning E 5 122
Port-Cartier D 10 160
Port Chalmers F 3 146
Port Charlotte F 3 168
Port Chester C 7 162
Port Clements E 5 156
Port Clinton C 2 162
Port Colborne B 4 162
Port-Cros, Parc National de ♦ G 4 82
Port-de-Bouc G 2 82
Port Dickson M 5 132
Port Dover B 3 162
Port Edward D 6 156
Porteirinha A 9 194
Portel D 8 190
Port Elgin F 11 160
Port Elizabeth G 6 206
Port-en-Bessin C 6 78
Porter E 6 172
Porter Lake ⊜ C 18 156
Porterville, Ca., U.S. D 4 182
Porterville, Ms., U.S. F 4 170
Port Essington D 7 156
Port Fairy G 4 144
Port Fouâd ◆[8] A 3 202
Port-Francqui see Ilebo C 3 204
Port Gamble B 2 178
Port-Gentil F 6 200
Port Gibson G 3 170
Port Glasgow B 2 72
Port-Harcourt E 6 200
Port Hawkesbury F 13 160
Porthcawl F 3 72
Port Hedland G 5 140
Port Henry B 5 164
Port Hope Simpson B 15 160
Port Hueneme F 4 182
Port Huron B 2 162
Portimão G 2 86
Port Jervis E 4 164
Port-Katon F 11 110
Port Kembla E 8 144
Port Lairge see Waterford D 4 75
Portland, Austl. G 3 144
Portland, Me., U.S. B 8 162
Portland, N.D., U.S. B 6 174
Portland, Or., U.S. C 2 178
Portland, Tx., U.S. G 5 172
Portland, Bill of > G 4 72
Portland Bay ⊂ G 3 144
Portland Bight ⊂ i 12 186a
Portland Canal ⊂ I 30 154
Portland Point > i 12 186a
Portlaoise C 4 75
Port Leyden C 3 164
Port Lincoln M 2 142
Port Loko D 2 200
Port-Louis, Guad. n 21 187e
Port Louis, Mrts. q 21 207e
Port MacDonnell G 3 144
Port Macquarie C 9 144
Portmahomack C 6 70
Portmarnock C 5 75
Port McNeill F 8 156
Port Morant i 13 186a
Portmore i 13 186a
Port Moresby N 13 124
Port Neches H 1 170
Port Neill M 3 142
Portneuf ≃ D 7 178
Port Neville F 8 156
Port Norris G 3 164
Porto (Oporto) C 2 86
Porto □[3] C 2 86
Porto Alegre, Braz. B 12 195
Porto Alegre, S. Tom./P. F 6 200
Portobelo F 4 186
Pôrto de Mós E 2 86
Porto de Moz D 8 190
Porto Empedocle G 3 94
Porto Esperidião G 7 190
Portoferraio G 6 92
Porto Ferreira D 7 194
Port of Spain q 23 187f
Portogruaro D 8 92
Porto Inglês h 11 200a
Portola A 3 182
Portomaggiore E 7 92
Porto Murtinho H 7 190
Porto Nacional F 9 190
Porto-Novo D 5 200
Port Orange E 4 168
Porto Recanati A 3 94
Porto San Giorgio A 3 94
Porto Sant'Elpidio A 3 94
Porto Seguro B 11 194
Porto Tolle E 8 92
Porto Torres I 4 92
Porto União G 5 194
Porto-Vecchio j 9 83a
Porto Velho E 6 190
Portoviejo D 2 190
Port Phillip Bay ⊂ G 5 144
Port Pirie D 1 144
Port Renfrew G 9 156
Port Richey E 3 168
Port Royal, Jam. i 13 186a
Port Royal, Pa., U.S. C 5 162
Portrush A 5 75
Port Said (Bûr Saʿîd) G 5 118
Port-Saint-Louis-du-Rhône G 2 82
Port Saint Lucie F 4 168
Port-Saint-Servan C 15 160
Port Sanilac B 2 162
Portsea G 5 144
Port Shepstone F 9 206
Portsmouth, Eng., U.K. G 5 72
Portsmouth, N.H., U.S. C 8 164
Portsmouth, Oh., U.S. D 2 162
Portsmouth, Va., U.S. E 5 162
Port Stanley G 3 160
Portstewart A 5 75
Port Sudan D 4 202
Port Talbot F 3 72
Port Taufîq ◆[8] H 5 118
Porttipahdan tekojärvi ⊜[1] B 12 64
Port Townsend A 2 178
Portugal □[1] G 6 62
Portugalete A 7 86
Portuguesa □[3] F 7 186
Portuguesa ≃ F 7 186
Portumna C 3 75
Port-Vendres F 7 80
Port Vila E 8 136
Port-Vladimir B 10 108
Port Wakefield G 18 154
Port Washington D 5 166
Porus h 12 186a
Porvenir J 5 192
Porvoo B 12 66
Posada I 5 92
Posadas, Arg. G 2 194
Posadas, Spain G 5 86
Pošehon'e G 13 108
Poset C 3 126
Posio C 14 64
Poso F 8 134
Poso, Danau ⊜ F 8 134
Posse F 9 190
Possession Bay ⊂ p 21 193c
Possession Island I D 1 206
Possidhonia ⊥ D 5 106
Pössneck F 8 98
Possum Kingdom Lake ⊜[1] D 4 172
Post D 3 172
Postmasburg E 5 206
Postojna E 6 102
Potawatomi Indian Reservation ◆[4] F 6 174
Potchefstroom D 7 206
Poteau E 1 170
Potenza D 5 94
Potenza □[6] D 5 94
Potfontein F 6 206
Potgietersrus C 8 206
Potholes Reservoir ⊜[1] B 4 178
Poti H 12 110
Potiskum C 7 200
Potomac ≃ D 5 162
Potomac, South Branch ≃ D 4 162
Potomac Heights H 1 164
Potosí G 5 190
Potrerillos E 6 192
Potrero del Llano F 1 172
Potsdam, Ger. D 10 98
Potsdam, N.Y., U.S. B 3 164
Potters Bar F 6 72
Potterville D 6 166
Pottstown F 3 164
Pottsville F 2 164
Pouancé E 5 78
Poughkeepsie E 5 164
Poulan D 3 168
Pouso Alegre E 8 194
Pouss C 7 200
Poŭthĭsăt H 6 132
Poŭthĭsăt ≃ H 6 132
Považská Bystrica A 10 102
Poverennyj F 13 110
Póvoa de Varzim C 2 86
Povorino D 13 110
Povorsk D 4 110
Povungnituk D 17 150
Poway H 6 182
Powder ≃ B 6 152
Powder, South Fork ≃ D 10 178
Powderly D 5 170
Powell, Lake ⊜[1] D 3 176
Powellhurst C 2 178
Powell River G 9 156
Powers Lake A 3 174
Powhatan Point D 3 162
Powys □[6] E 3 72
Poxoréu A 3 194
Poyang Hu ⊜ D 13 130
Poyan Reservoir ⊜[1] i 14 134a
Poynette D 4 166
Požarevac C 6 104
Poza Rica de Hidalgo G 11 184
Pozdeevka A 17 128
Požega E 9 102
Poznań B 9 96
Poznań □[3] B 9 96
Pozo Alcón G 2 88
Pozoblanco F 6 86
Pozo-Cañada F 3 88
Pozuelo de Alarcón D 7 86
Pozuelos F 8 186
Pozzallo H 4 94
Pozzuoli D 4 94
Prabuty B 10 96
Prachuap Khiri Khan I 4 132
Prades F 6 80
Prado del Rey H 5 86
Præstø C 5 68
Praglia, Monastero di ◗[1] D 7 92
Prague see Praha, Czech Rep. B 11 100
Prague, Ne., U.S. E 6 174
Praha (Prague) B 11 100
Praha □[3] B 11 100
Prahova □[3] C 8 104
Praia i 11 200a
Prainha Nova E 6 190
Prairie F 7 142
Prairie ≃ E 6 166
Prairie City C 4 178
Prairie du Chien D 3 166
Prairies, Lake of the ⊜[1] F 8 158
Prairie View E 6 172
Prairie Village F 7 174
Pran Buri H 4 132
Prānhita ≃ F 4 122
Praslin I J 7 112
Prata C 6 194
Prato F 7 92
Prato □[6] E 7 92
Pratola Peligna B 3 94
Pratt G 5 174
Pratteln C 5 82
Pravdinsk E 10 66
Prečistoe I 9 108
Predazzo C 7 92
Predești C 7 104
Preeceville F 7 158
Pré-en-Pail D 6 78
Preetz B 7 98
Pregolja ≃ E 10 66
Preila E 10 66
Preissac, Lac ⊜ D 4 160
Prekomurje ◆[1] D 8 102
Prelate F 17 156
Premià de Mar C 7 88
Premnitz D 9 98
Premont G 4 172
Prentiss G 4 170
Prenzlau C 10 98
Preobraženie C 4 126
Preparis North Channel ʊ G 2 132
Preparis South Channel ʊ G 1 132
Přerov A 9 102
Prescott, Ar., U.S. F 2 170
Prescott, Az., U.S. E 2 176
Prescott, On., Can. F 6 160
Prescott and Russell □[6] A 3 164
Prescott Island I B 13 150
Presho D 4 174
Presidencia Roca E 8 192
Presidencia Roque Sáenz Peña E 7 192
Presidente Eduardo Frei ◗[3] L 8 192
Presidente Epitácio D 4 194
Presidente Hayes □[3] E 2 194
Presidente Prudente E 5 194
Presidente Venceslau D 4 194
Presidio F 1 172
Presidio ≃ F 6 184
Presnovka I 27 108
Prešov D 11 96
Prespa, Lake ⊜ E 6 104
Presque Isle g 12 163a
Prestatyn D 3 72
Prestea D 4 200
Preston, Eng., U.K. D 4 72
Preston, Ks., U.S. B 4 172
Prestonsburg E 2 162
Prestwick B 2 72
Preto ≃, Braz. F 10 190
Preto ≃, Braz. G 9 190

Symbols in the index entries represent the broad categories identified in the key at the right. Symbols with superior numbers (⩓[1]) identify subcategories (see complete key on page 242).

∧ Mountain ⩓ Mountains)(Pass ∨ Valley ⩦ Plain > Cape I Island II Islands ⊥ Other Topographic Feature ≃ River ≡ Canal

Name	Map Ref.	Page

ㄴ Waterfall   ⋃ Strait   c Bay, Gulf   ◎ Lake   ≈ Swamp   Ice Feature   ➤ Other Hydrographic Feature   ⟂ Submarine Feature   □ Political Unit   ᗡ Cultural Institution   ⟂ Historical Site   ♦ Recreational Site   ⊕ Airport   ■ Military Installation   ➡ Miscellaneous

275

Name	Ref.	Page
Reda	A 10	96
Red Bank	F 4	164
Red Banks	E 4	170
Redberry Lake ◎	E 18	156
Red Bluff	B 2	180
Red Bluff Reservoir ◎¹	E 2	172
Redbridge □⁶	F 7	72
Redcar	C 5	72
Redcar and Cleveland □⁶	C 6	72
Redcliff	F 4	204
Redcliffe	I 11	142
Redcliffe, Mount ∧	K 6	140
Red Cliff Indian Reservation ⬧⁴	B 3	166
Red Cliffs	E 4	144
Red Deer	E 5	72
Red Deer ≃, Can.	F 16	156
Red Deer ≃, Can.	E 8	158
Red Deer Lake ◎	E 8	158
Reddersburg	E 7	206
Redding	B 2	180
Redditch	E 5	72
Red Earth Creek	C 14	156
Redfield	E 7	174
Redhead	q 24	187f
Red Indian Lake ◎	D 15	160
Redlake, Mn., U.S.	B 7	174
Red Lake, On., Can.	F 12	158
Red Lake	F 12	158
Red Lake Indian Reservation ⬧⁴	A 7	174
Redlands	F 6	182
Red Lodge	C 9	178
Redmond, Ut., U.S.	C 3	176
Redmond, Wa., U.S.	B 2	178
Redon	E 4	78
Redondela	F 2	86
Redondo Beach	G 5	182
Redoubt Volcano ∧¹	F 18	154
Red Pass	E 12	156
Red Pheasant Indian Reserve ⬧⁴	E 4	158
Red River (Hong, Song) (Yuan)	C 7	132
Red Rock	C 7	178
Red Rock Canyon State Park ⬧	G 1	172
Redruth	C 1	72
Red Sea =²	A 4	202
Red Sea Hills ⬧	D 4	202
Redstone	E 10	156
Redstone	E 32	154
Red Sucker ≃	D 12	158
Red Sucker Lake ◎	D 11	158
Red Volta (Nazinon) ≃	C 4	200
Redwater	E 15	156
Red Wing	C 2	166
Redwood City	C 1	182
Redwood Falls	C 7	174
Redwood National Park ⬧	E 1	178
Redwood Valley	C 2	180
Ree, Lough ◎	C 3	75
Reed Lake ◎	D 9	158
Reedley	D 4	182
Reedsburg	D 3	166
Reefton	E 3	146
Reelfoot Lake ◎	D 4	170
Rees	E 3	98
Reese	B 5	180
Refuge Cove	F 9	156
Refugio	F 5	172
Regalbuto	G 4	94
Regen	B 5	102
Regen ≃	C 9	100
Regensburg	C 9	100
Regenstauf	C 9	100
Reggâne	D 4	198
Reggio di Calabria	F 6	94
Reggio di Calabria □⁶	F 6	94
Reggio nell'Emilia	E 6	92
Reggio nell'Emilia □⁶	E 6	92
Reghin	B 8	104
Regina	F 6	158
Región Metropolitana □³	C 2	195
Registro	F 6	194
Regozero	D 9	108
Rehau	C 6	96
Rehoboth	B 2	206
Rehovot	F 3	120
Reichenbach	B 9	100
Reid	L 10	140
Reidsville	A 5	168
Reigate	F 6	72
Reims	C 10	78
Reinach	C 5	82
Reinbek	C 7	98
Reindeer Lake ◎	C 7	158
Reindeer Station	B 27	154
Reinfeld	C 7	98
Reinga, Cape ⤳	A 4	146
Reinosa	B 6	86
Reistersville	G 2	164
Reivilo	D 6	206
Rejowiec Fabryczny	C 12	96
Reken	B 4	100
Reliance	D 11	150
Rellingen	E 2	68
Remagen	B 4	100
Remanso	E 10	190
Rembang	k 20	135b
Remchi	E 5	84
Remer	D 7	174
Remington	B 5	170
Remiremont	B 4	82
Remscheid	E 4	98
Remsen	D 7	174
Renata	G 12	156
Rencontre East	E 16	160
Rendova I	A 12	138
Rendsburg	B 6	98
Renens	D 4	82
Renews-Cappahayden	E 17	160
Renfrew	F 5	160
Renfrew □⁶	A 2	164
Renfrewshire □⁶	B 2	72
Rengat	k 21	135b
Rengel	j 16	135b
Rengo	D 2	195
Renhua	F 11	130
Renhuai	F 11	130
Reni	C 10	104
Renick	D 3	162
Renko	B 12	66
Renmark	E 3	144
Renmin	C 15	128
Rennell I	B 13	138
Rennes	D 5	78
Renningen	D 5	100
Reno ≃	E 6	92
Reno	E 7	92
Rensjön	B 9	64
Rensselaer	B 5	170
Rensselaer, N.Y., U.S.	D 5	164
Rensselaer □⁶	D 5	164
Rentería	A 3	88
Renton	B 2	178
Renville	C 7	174
Renwick	D 8	174
Reo	G 8	134
Repolovo	F 28	108
Reposaari	B 10	66
Republic, Mo., U.S.	D 2	170
Republic, Wa., U.S.	A 4	178
Republican ≃	F 6	174
Republican, North Fork ≃	E 3	174
Republican, South Fork ≃	F 4	174
Repulse Bay	C 15	150
Requena	E 3	88
Réquista	D 6	80
Reserve	G 3	170
Resina see Ercolano	D 4	94
Resistencia	E 8	192
Reşiţa	C 6	104
Resolute	B 14	150
Resolution see Kaujuitoq	B 14	150
Resolution Island I	D 19	150
Restigouche ≃	E 10	160
Retanosa	C 10	195
Retezat, Parcul National ⬧	C 7	104
Retford	D 6	72
Rethel	C 11	78
Réthimnon	E 6	106
Retie	E 2	98
Reunion □²	L 7	112
Reus	C 6	88
Reuterstadt Stavenhagen	C 9	98
Reutlingen	D 6	100
Revda	B 11	108
Revelstoke	F 12	156
Revelstoke, Lake ◎¹	E 12	156
Reventazón	E 2	190
Reviga	C 9	104
Revilla del Campo	B 7	86
Revillagigedo, Islas II	H 3	184
Revillagigedo Island I	I 29	154
Revin	C 11	78
Revúca	E 4	122
Rewa	E 4	122
Rewari	D 8	178
Rexburg	F 5	186
Rey, Isla del I	F 5	186
Rey, Laguna del ◎	D 8	184
Reyes, Point ⤳	B 1	182
Reyhanlı	D 7	118
Reykjanes ⤳¹	n 19	64a
Reykjanes Ridge ⬧³	C 8	60
Reykjavík	m 19	64a
Reyno	D 3	170
Reynosa	D 10	184
Rezā'īyeh see Orūmīyeh	D 11	118
Rezé	E 5	78
Rēzekne	D 13	66
Rezina	B 10	104
Rezovo	D 10	104
Rezzato	D 6	92
Rhaetian Alps ⬧	C 5	92
Rhame	B 3	174
Rheda-Wiedenbrück	E 5	98
Rhede	C 5	69
Rheden	B 4	69
Rheinau	D 4	100
Rheinberg	E 3	98
Rheine	D 4	98
Rheinfelden	E 4	100
Rheinhessen-Pfalz □⁶	C 9	98
Rheinland-Pfalz □³	B 4	100
Rheinsberg	C 9	98
Rheinstetten	D 5	100
Rhenen	C 4	69
Rhine ≃	F 9	62
Rhinebeck	C 4	164
Rhinelander	C 4	166
Rhinns Point ⤳	E 2	74
Rhino Camp	G 3	202
Rhir, Cap ⤳	C 2	198
Rho	D 5	92
Rhode Island □³	C 13	152
Rhode Island I	E 7	164
Rhode Island Sound ☋	E 7	164
Rhodes see Ródhos	E 8	106
Rhodes Matopos National Park ⬧	G 4	204
Rhodes Nyanga National Park ⬧	F 5	204
Rhodes' Tomb ⬧	G 4	204
Rhodope Mountains ⬧	E 8	104
Rhön ⬧	B 6	100
Rhondda	F 3	72
Rhondda Cynon Taff □⁶	F 3	72
Rhône □³	E 2	82
Rhône (Rotten) ≃	F 2	82
Rhône au Rhin, Canal du ≖	C 6	198
Rhourde-el-Baguel	C 6	198
Rhyl	D 3	72
Riachão	A 9	190
Rianápolis	A 6	194
Riaño	A 6	86
Riau, Kepulauan II	N 7	132
Ribadavia	B 2	86
Ribe	C 1	68
Ribe □³	C 1	68
Ribeira Grande	h 10	200a
Ribeirão Preto	D 7	194
Ribera	G 3	94
Riberalta	F 5	190
Ribnica	E 6	102
Ribnitz-Damgarten	B 6	184
Ricardo Flores Magón	B 6	184
Riccarton	A 4	146
Riccione	E 6	92
Rice	D 5	172
Riceville	B 2	168
Richards	E 6	172
Richards Bay ⊂	E 9	206
Richardson	D 5	172
Richardson	B 16	156
Richardson Mountains ⬧	C 26	154
Richard Toll	B 1	200
Richelieu	H 6	78
Richey	H 6	178
Richfield, Mn., U.S.	F 2	166
Richfield, Pa., U.S.	F 8	164
Richfield Springs	D 6	164
Richland, Mt., U.S.	G 18	156
Richland, Tx., U.S.	G 5	172
Richland, Wa., U.S.	B 4	178
Richlands	B 3	162
Richmond, Austl.	F 6	142
Richmond, Austl.	D 8	144
Richmond, Austl.	j 12	145a
Richmond, B.C., Can.	G 10	156
Richmond, Ca., U.S.	C 1	182
Richmond, Eng., U.K.	C 5	72
Richmond, In., U.S.	C 6	170
Richmond, Ky., U.S.	C 5	170
Richmond, Me., U.S.	A 9	162
Richmond, N.Z.	E 3	146
Richmond, P.Q., Can.	F 7	160
Richmond, S. Afr.	F 5	206
Richmond, Ut., U.S.	E 8	178
Richmond, Va., U.S.	B 6	168
Richmond, Vt., U.S.	B 6	164
Richmond Hill	G 4	160
Richmondville	D 4	164
Rich Square	A 6	168
Richtersveld National Park ⬧	E 2	206
Richwood	C 2	162
Ricketts Glen State Park ⬧	E 2	164
Ricobayo, Embalse de ◎¹	C 4	86
Ridā'	E 8	126
Ridgecrest	E 6	182
Ridgeland, Ms., U.S.	F 3	170
Ridgeland, S.C., U.S.	C 4	168
Ridgetown	G 3	160
Ridgeway	E 7	174
Ridgway	C 4	162
Riding Mountain National Park ⬧	F 8	158
Riebeek-Oos	G 7	206
Riegersburg, Schloss ⊥	C 7	102
Riemst	E 2	98
Riesa	E 10	98
Riesco, Isla I	J 5	192
Riesi	G 4	94
Rietavas	E 10	66
Rietberg	E 5	98
Rietbron	G 5	206
Rietfontein	C 7	206
Rieti	G 8	92
Rif ⬧	C 4	198
Rift Valley □³	G 4	202
Rift Valley V	I 10	196
Rift Valley National Park ⬧	F 4	202
Rīga	D 11	66
Riga, Gulf of ◎	D 11	66
Riggins	C 5	178
Rig-Rig	C 7	200
Riguldi	C 11	66
Riihimäki	B 12	66
Riiser-Larsen Peninsula ⤳¹	C 12	208
Rijeka	E 6	102
Rijen	C 3	69
Rijssen	B 5	69
Rijswijk	B 3	69
Riksgränsen	B 9	64
Rikuzen-takata	E 8	126
Rila	E 2	82
Rilski manastir ⬧¹	D 7	104
Rima ≃	C 6	200
Rimatara I	F 12	136
Rimavská Sobota	D 10	96
Rimbo	C 9	66
Rimi	E 6	200
Rimini	E 6	92
Rimini □⁶	E 6	92
Rimouski	D 9	160
Rinca, Pulau I	G 7	134
Rincon	F 5	176
Rinconada	D 6	192
Rincón del Bonete, Lago Artificial de ◎¹	F 8	192
Rincón de Romos	B 8	184
Rincon Indian Reservation ⬧⁴	G 7	182
Rindown Castle ⊥	C 3	75
Ringaskiddy	E 3	75
Ringe	C 3	68
Ringerike	B 5	66
Ringgold	E 6	170
Ringkøbing	B 1	68
Ringkøbing □³	B 1	68
Ringsted, Den.	C 4	68
Ringsted, Ia., U.S.	D 7	174
Ringvassøya I	B 9	64
Rinjani, Gunung ∧	G 7	134
Rinteln	D 8	98
Riobamba	D 3	190
Rio Branco	C 6	190
Rio Bravo, Mex.	F 3	172
Rio Bravo, Mex.	E 10	184
Rio Bravo, Parque Internacional del ⬧	D 3	194
Rio Brilhante	D 1	194
Rio Bueno	G 1	195
Rio Ceballos	B 5	195
Rio Claro, Braz.	C 6	194
Rio Claro, Trin.	q 23	187f
Rio Colorado	F 5	195
Rio Cuarto	C 5	195
Rio de Janeiro	E 9	194
Rio de Janeiro □³	H 10	190
Rio do Sul	G 6	194
Rio Gallegos	J 6	192
Rio Grande, Arg.	J 6	192
Rio Grande, Braz.	B 12	195
Rio Grande, Mex.	f 8	184
Rio Grande, P.R.	E 16	187b
Rio Grande do Norte □³	E 11	190
Rio Grande do Sul □³	E 9	192
Riohacha	A 3	190
Rioja	C 2	190
Rio Lagartos	G 15	184
Rio Largo	E 11	190
Riom	C 7	80
Rio Mayo	I 5	192
Rio Mulatos	G 5	190
Rio Muni ⤳	E 7	200
Rio Muni □⁹	E 7	200
Rio Negro	D 5	192
Rio Negro, Pantanal do ≃	H 6	192
Riópar	F 2	88
Rio Pardo	A 11	195
Rio Rancho	F 5	176
Rio Segundo	B 5	195
Rio Tercero	C 5	195
Rio Tinto	E 11	190
Rio Verde, Braz.	B 5	194
Rioverde, Mex.	C 3	164
Rio Verde de Mato Grosso	C 3	194
Rio Vista	C 3	182
Riozinho ⬧	D 5	190
Ripatransone	A 3	94
Ripley, Eng., U.K.	C 5	72
Ripley, Oh., U.S.	D 2	162
Ripley, Tn., U.S.	E 4	170
Ripoll	B 7	88
Ripon, Ca., U.S.	C 2	182
Ripon, Eng., U.K.	C 5	72
Ripon, P.Q., Can.	F 6	160
Risca	F 3	72
Riscle	E 3	80
Rishā', Wādī ar- ≃	J 11	118
Rishiri-Rebun-Sarobetsu-kokuritsu-kōen ⬧	B 8	126
Rishiri-suidō ☋	B 8	126
Rishiri-tō I	B 8	126
Rishiri-zan ∧¹	B 8	126
Rishon LeẔiyyon	F 3	120
Rising Star	D 4	172
Risingsun	C 2	162
Risør	C 4	66
Risti	C 12	66
Ritchie	E 6	206
Ritterhude	C 5	98
Ritzville	B 4	178
Rivadavia, Arg.	B 3	195
Rivadavia, Arg.	D 6	195
Rivadavia, Chile	A 2	195
Riva del Garda	E 5	82
Rivarolo Canavese	F 3	186
Rivas	E 5	82
Rive-de-Gier	E 2	82
Rivera, Arg.	E 6	195
Rivera, Ur.	B 10	195
River Cess	D 3	200
Riverdale	D 4	182
River Falls	C 2	166
Rivergaro	E 5	92
Riverhead	F 6	164
Riverina ⬧¹	E 5	144
River Road	C 2	178
Rivers	F 8	158
Riverside	H 4	206
Riverside, Ca., U.S.	G 6	182
Riverside, Tx., U.S.	E 6	172
Riverside, Wa., U.S.	A 4	178
Riverside □⁶	G 7	182
Riverton, Austl.	E 2	144
Riverton, Wy., U.S.	D 9	178
Riverton Heights	B 2	178
Rivesaltes	F 6	80
Riviera ⬧⁸	E 6	180
Riviera Beach	F 6	168
Rivière-à-Claude	D 11	160
Rivière-à-Tonnerre	C 11	160
Rivière-du-Loup	E 9	160
Rivière du Rempart	p 21	207e
Rivière-Pentecôte	D 10	160
Rivne	D 5	110
Rivne □⁶	K 13	64
Rivoli	D 3	92
Riyadh see Ar-Riyāḍ	J 12	118
Rize	B 9	118
Rize □³	B 9	118
Rizhao	I 12	128
Rjazan'	I 13	108
Rjazanskaja oblast' □⁶	I 13	108
Rjažsk	J 14	108
Rjukan	C 4	66
Rkîz, Lac ◎	F 1	198
Roa	B 5	66
Roachdale	C 5	170
Roadford Reservoir ◎¹	G 2	72
Road Town	D 8	186
Roan Mountain	A 3	168
Roanne	D 2	82
Roanoke, In., U.S.	B 6	170
Roanoke, Va., U.S.	B 5	162
Roanoke (Staunton) ≃	A 6	168
Roanoke Rapids	A 6	168
Roaring River State Park ⬧	D 2	170
Roatán, Isla I	D 3	186
Robâa Oued Yahia	G 2	90
Robât Karīm	E 14	118
Robben Island I	G 3	206
Robbers Cave State Park ⬧	E 11	170
Robbinsville	B 3	168
Robe, Austl.	F 2	144
Robe ≃, Eth.	F 4	202
Röbel	C 9	98
Robert H. Treman State Park ⬧	C 9	164
Robert Louis Stevenson's Tomb ⊥	j 11	147b
Robert's Arm	D 16	160
Roberts Mountain ∧¹	F 11	154
Robertson, Lac ◎	C 14	160
Roberts Port	D 2	200
Roberval	D 7	160
Róbinson Crusoe, Isla I	H 7	188
Robinsons	D 14	160
Robinvale	E 4	144
Robledo	F 2	88
Robore, Mount ∧	A 12	156
Robstown	G 5	172
Roca, Cabo da ⤳	F 1	86
Roca Partida, Isla I	H 3	184
Rocas, Atol das II	D 12	190
Roccadaspide	D 5	94
Roccastrada	F 7	92
Rocha	D 10	195
Rochdale	D 4	72
Rochdale □⁶	D 4	69
Rochechouart	G 6	78
Rochefort, Bel.	D 4	69
Rochefort, Fr.	C 2	80
Rochelle, Ga., U.S.	D 3	168
Rochelle, Il., U.S.	B 4	166
Roche-Percée	G 7	158
Rochepot, Château de la ⊥	F 11	78
Rochester, Austl.	F 5	144
Rochester, Eng., U.K.	F 7	72
Rochester, Mn., U.S.	G 2	166
Rochester, N.H., U.S.	C 8	164
Rochester, N.Y., U.S.	B 4	164
Rochlitz	E 9	98
Rock ≃	D 5	62
Rockall I	D 5	62
Rockdale	D 4	172
Rockdale □⁶	D 4	69
Rockenhausen	E 4	100
Rockford, Mi., U.S.	D 6	166
Rockford, Oh., U.S.	B 1	162
Rockglen	G 19	156
Rockhampton	G 10	142
Rock Hill	G 10	168
Rockingham, Austl.	M 3	140
Rockingham, N.C., U.S.	B 7	168
Rockingham Bay ⊂	E 8	142
Rock Island	A 3	166
Rocklake	A 5	174
Rockland, Ma., U.S.	B 6	164
Rockland, On., Can.	F 2	160
Rockland □⁶	F 6	164
Rocklin	B 2	182
Rockport, Ma., U.S.	D 8	164
Rock Port, Mo., U.S.	B 1	170
Rockport, Tx., U.S.	G 5	172
Rock River	B 6	176
Rock Springs	E 9	178
Rockstone	B 7	190
Rockton	D 4	166
Rock Valley	D 6	174
Rockville, In., U.S.	C 5	170
Rockville, Md., U.S.	G 1	164
Rockwell	D 2	166
Rockwood	h 12	163a
Rocky	A 9	172
Rocky Boy's Indian Reservation ⬧⁴	A 9	178
Rocky Cape National Park ⬧	i 11	145a
Rockyford	F 15	156
Rocky Gully	N 4	140
Rocky Lake ◎	D 8	158
Rocky Lane	B 13	156
Rocky Mount	B 6	168
Rocky Mountain House	E 14	156
Rocky Mountain National Park ⬧	E 5	176
Rocky Mountains ⬧	E 8	148
Rocky Mountain Trench ⬧	D 10	156
Rocky Point ⤳	B 3	75
Rodalben	A 5	82
Rødby	D 4	68
Roddickton	C 15	160
Rodeo	E 7	156
Roderick Island I	E 7	156
Rodewisch	B 9	100
Rodez	D 6	80
Rodgau	B 5	100
Ródhos	D 8	106
Ródhos (Rhodes) I	E 8	106
Rodi Garganico	C 5	94
Roding	D 1	178
Rodman	H 2	186
Rodniki	H 14	108
Roebourne	G 4	140
Roebuck Bay ⊂	F 6	140
Roermond	C 4	69
Roeselare	D 2	69
Roes Welcome Sound ☋	D 15	150
Roff	C 5	172
Rogagua, Laguna ◎	F 5	190
Rogaguado, Laguna ◎	F 5	190
Rogaland □³	C 3	66
Rogaška Slatina	D 7	102
Rogers, Ar., U.S.	D 1	170
Rogers, Tx., U.S.	E 5	172
Rogers, Mount ∧	A 3	162
Rogers Lake ◎	F 6	180
Rogers Pass)(	F 13	156
Rogersville	A 3	168
Roggwein, Cabo ⤳	m 16	193a
Roggiano Gravina	E 6	94
Rogliano	E 6	94
Rogue ≃	D 1	178
Rogue River	D 2	178
Rohnert Park	B 1	182
Rohtak	D 3	122
Roi Et	E 4	132
Roi Georges, Îles du II	E 13	136
Roja	D 7	195
Rojas	D 7	195
Rojo, Cabo ⤳	k 14	187b
Rokan ≃	N 5	132
Rokeby National Park ⬧	B 6	142
Rokiškis	E 12	66
Rokycany	C 10	100
Roland	D 2	166
Rolândia	E 5	194
Røldal	C 3	66
Roll	F 2	176
Rolla, Ks., U.S.	G 4	174
Rolla, Mo., U.S.	D 3	170
Rolle	D 4	82
Rolleston	H 9	142
Rollingstone	E 8	142
Rolvsøya I	A 11	64
Roma, Austl.	I 9	142
Roma □³	H 8	92
Roma (Rome), Italy	H 8	92
Romagna □⁹	E 8	92
Roman ≃	B 9	104
Romang, Pulau I	G 9	134
Romania □¹	F 12	62
Roman-Kosh, hora ∧	G 9	110
Romano, Cape ⤳	G 4	168
Romano, Cayo I	D 5	186
Romanovka	D 13	110
Romanovo	G 24	108
Romanshorn	C 7	82
Romans-sur-Isère	E 3	82
Rome see Roma, Italy	H 8	92
Rome, Ga., U.S.	E 6	170
Rome, Ms., U.S.	F 3	170
Rome, N.Y., U.S.	C 3	164
Romilly-sur-Seine	D 10	78
Romny	D 4	110
Romodanovo	I 16	108
Romorantin-Lanthenay	E 8	78
Romsey	G 5	72
Røn	B 4	66
Ron, Mui ⤳	E 8	132
Rona I	A 3	74
Ronas Hill ∧²	G 9	74a
Roncador, Serra do ∧¹	B 5	194
Ronceverte	A 4	168
Ronchi dei Legionari	E 8	102
Ronchin	B 10	78
Ronda	H 5	86
Rondane Nasjonalpark ⬧	B 5	66
Rønde	B 3	68
Rondeau Provincial Park ⬧	D 8	166
Rondônia □³	F 6	190
Rondonópolis	C 3	194
Ronge, Lac la ◎	H 19	156
Rong'an	F 9	130
Rongchang	H 11	130
Ronge, Lac la ◎	H 19	156
Rongelap I¹	G 8	136
Rongjiang	F 9	130
Rongkop	i 20	135b
Rongshui	F 9	130
Rongxian, China	G 10	130
Rongxian, China	D 10	130
Rønne	I f	68a
Ronneby	D 7	68
Ronne Entrance ☋	D 8	208
Ronne Ice Shelf ⊠	D 2	208
Ronse	D 2	69
Ronuro ≃	B 2	194
Roodhouse	D 6	170
Rooidam	C 4	206
Rooiwal	D 7	206
Roorkee	D 3	122
Roosendaal	C 3	69
Rovaniemi	C 12	64
Rovato	D 6	92
Roveretto	D 7	92
Rovigo	D 7	92
Rovigo □⁶	D 7	92
Rovinj	C 2	104
Rovnoe	D 15	110
Rovubo ≃	C 5	204
Rovuma see Ruvuma ≃	E 7	204
Rowan Lake ◎	A 8	174
Rowena	B 7	144
Rowley Island I	C 17	150
Roxas	B 6	134
Roxboro	A 5	168
Roxburgh	F 2	146
Roxen ◎	C 7	66
Roxie	G 3	170
Roy	C 6	176
Royal Bay ⊂	q 22	193c
Royale, Isle I	A 4	166
Royal Gorge V	A 1	172
Royal Leamington Spa	E 5	72
Royal National Park ⬧	E 8	206
Royal Oak	B 2	162
Royalton	C 1	166
Royal Tunbridge Wells	F 7	72
Royan	C 2	80
Royston, Eng., U.K.	E 6	72
Royston, Ga., U.S.	B 3	168
Rozdil'na	B 11	104
Rozivka	F 10	110
Rožňava	D 11	96
Rožnov pod Radhoštěm	A 10	102
Roztoczański Park Narodowy ⬧	C 12	96
Roztoky	B 11	100
Rozzano	D 4	92
Rrëshen	B 3	106
Ru ≃	B 12	130
Ruacana Falls (Ruacaná, Quedas do) ◡	F 1	204
Ruaha National Park ⬧	B 5	204
Ruapehu, Mount ∧¹	C 5	146
Ruatahuna	C 6	146
Rubbestadneset	C 2	66
Rubcovsk	D 11	114
Rubi	B 4	204
Rubi ≃	E 8	202
Rubicone ≃	E 8	92
Rubizhne	E 11	110
Rubondo Island National Park ⬧	H 3	202
Rucava	D 10	66
Rucheng	F 11	130
Rudall River National Park ⬧	H 7	140
Rūdbār	D 13	118
Rüdersdorf	D 10	98
Rūdiškes	E 12	66
Rudnaja Pristan'	B 5	126
Rudnik	C 12	96
Rudnyj	C 23	112
Rudnytsya	A 10	104
Rudolf, Lake ◎	D 5	104
Rudolf, Lake ◎	G 4	202
Rudolstadt	E 3	78
Rudong	B 15	130
Rūdsar	E 8	104
Rue	B 8	78
Rufā' ah	E 3	202
Ruffieux	D 6	82
Rufiji ≃	B 7	204
Rufino	C 3	178
Rufus	C 3	178
Rugao	B 15	130
Rugby, Eng., U.K.	E 5	72
Rugby, N.D., U.S.	A 4	174
Rugeley	E 5	72
Rügen I	B 10	98
Rugufu ≃	C 5	204
Ruhengeri	F 5	202
Ruhla	F 7	98
Ruhr ≃	E 15	130
Ru'an	E 15	130
Ruidoso	F 12	150
Ruijin	F 11	130
Ruiz	G 2	184
Ruki ≃	C 2	204
Rukwa □³	C 5	204
Rukwa, Lake ◎	D 5	204
Rule	D 4	172
Rūm I	B 1	70
Ruma	C 2	166
Rumaylah, 'Urūq ar- ≃⁸	C 6	202
Rumbek	F 2	202
Rumburk	C 8	100
Rum Cay I	D 6	186
Rumigny	C 11	78
Rummah, Wādī ar- ≃	J 10	118
Rumoi	C 8	126
Rumuruti	G 4	202
Runan	B 12	130
Runazi ≃	G 5	204
Runde ≃	D 13	66
Rundu	E 3	204
Rungwa	B 5	204
Rungwa ≃	D 5	204
Rungwe Game Reserve ⬧	D 5	204
Rungwe ∧	D 5	204
Runkel	B 5	100
Runn ◎	B 7	66
Running Water Draw ≃	E 6	172
Runnymede ⊥	F 6	72
Ruo ≃	E 7	204
Ruo'ergai	D 8	130
Ruoxi	B 6	130
Rupert	D 12	162
Rural Retreat	A 3	162
Rurrenabaque	F 5	190
Rurutu I	F 12	136
Ruse	E 8	104
Rusera	H 11	122
Rush Center	F 5	174
Rushford	A 5	164
Rushan	H 13	128
Rushden	E 6	72
Rushford	G 3	166
Rusizi ≃	C 4	204

Symbols in the index entries represent the broad categories identified in the key at the right. Symbols with superior numbers (∧¹) identify subcategories (see complete key on page 242).

∧ Mountain ⬧ Mountains)(Pass V Valley ≃ Plain ⤳ Cape I Island II Islands ⊥ Other Topographic Feature ≃ River ≖ Canal

Ruskin — San Fernando de Apure

Name | Map Ref. | Page

Ruskin F 3 168
Rusnė E 10 66
Russell, Ky., U.S. D 2 162
Russell, N.Z. A 5 146
Russell, On., Can. A 3 164
Russell Cave National Monument ♦ E 6 170
Russell Island I B 13 150
Russell Islands II A 12 138
Russell Lake ◎ C 8 158
Russellville, Al., U.S. E 5 170
Russellville, Ar., U.S. E 2 170
Rüsselsheim D 5 96
Russi E 7 92
Russia □[1] C 11 114
Russian ≃ C 2 180
Russian Mission F 14 154
Russka C 14 66
Rustajskij H 16 108
Rustavi I 14 110
Rustenburg C 7 206
Ruston F 2 170
Rute G 6 86
Ruteng G 8 134
Rutenga G 5 204
Ruthin D 3 72
Rüti C 6 82
Rutland, B.C., Can. G 12 156
Rutland, Vt., U.S. C 6 164
Rutland □[6] C 6 164
Rutledge A 3 168
Rutshuru C 4 204
Rutter E 3 160
Ruvo di Puglia C 6 94
Ruvu D 6 204
Ruvuma □[3] E 6 204
Ruvuma (Rovuma) ≃ E 7 204
Ruwenzori ⋀ B 4 204
Ruwenzori National Park ♦ H 2 202
Ruzaevka, Kaz. J 27 108
Ruzaevka, Russia I 16 108
Ružany J 12 64
Ružomberok A 11 102
Rwanda □[1] I 11 196
Ryan C 5 172
Rybachye see Ysuk-Köl A 3 122
Rybačij E 10 66
Rybačij, poluostrov >[1] A 10 108
Rybinsk G 13 108
Rybinskoe vodohranilišče ◎[1] G 12 108
Rybnik C 10 96
Rybnoe I 13 108
Rychwał B 10 96
Ryd D 7 66
Ryde G 5 72
Ryder B 4 174
Rye F 5 164
Ryegate B 9 178
Ryfoss B 4 66
Ryfylke ✦[1] C 3 66
Rygnestad C 3 66
Ryley E 15 156
Ryn A 11 96
Rypin B 10 96
Rysy ∧ A 5 104
Ryukyu Islands (Nansei-shotō) II G 9 124
Ryukyu Trench ✦[1] E 10 58
Rzeszów C 12 96
Rzeszów □[3] C 11 96
Ržev H 11 108

S

Sa B 4 200
Saale ≃ E 8 98
Saalfeld B 8 100
Saalfelden C 4 102
Saar (Sarre) ≃ C 3 100
Saarbrücken C 4 100
Saarburg C 3 100
Saaremaa I C 11 66
Saarijärvi E 12 64
Saaristomeren kansallispuisto ♦ C 10 66
Saarland □[3] C 3 100
Saarlouis C 3 100
Saatlı J 16 110
Saavedra E 6 195
Saba I D 9 186
Šabac C 5 104
Sabadell C 7 88
Sabah □[3] D 7 134
Sabana Grande j 15 187b
Sabanalarga F 6 186
Sabancuy H 14 184
Sabang E 7 134
Sabará C 9 194
Sabarei G 4 202
Sābari ≃ F 4 122
Sābarmati ≃ E 2 122
Sab'atayn, Ramlat as- •[8] D 6 202
Sabawanaag E 5 202
Şāberī, Hāmūn-e ◎ D 9 116
Sabhā D 7 198
Sabie C 9 206
Sabile D 11 66
Sabina □[9] G 8 92
Sabinal F 4 172
Sabiñánigo B 4 88
Sabinas D 9 184
Sabinas ≃, Mex. D 10 184
Sabinas ≃, Mex. D 9 184
Sabinas Hidalgo D 9 184
Sabine ≃ E 9 152
Sabine Lake ◎ H 2 170
Sabine Pass ⋃ H 2 170
Sabinov D 11 96
Sabirabad I 16 110
Sable ≃ A 9 160
Sable, Cape > G 11 160
Sable, Cape >[1] G 4 168
Sable, Île de I C 12 138
Sable Island I G 14 160
Sablé-sur-Sarthe E 6 78
Sablūkah, Ash-Shallāl as- ⌊ D 3 202
Sabon Kafi C 6 200
Sabor ≃ C 3 86
Sabrātah C 7 198
Sabrina Coast ✦[2] C 21 208
Sabugal D 3 86
Sabyā D 5 202
Sabzevār D 17 118
Sac City D 7 174
Sacedón D 2 88
Săcele C 8 104
Sachigo ≃ D 14 158
Sachigo Lake ◎ E 12 158
Sachimbo D 3 204
Sachsen □[3] D 12 100
Sachsen-Anhalt □[3] E 8 98
Sachsenburg B 2 104
Sachs Harbour B 7 150
Sacile D 8 92
Šack I 14 108
Sackets Harbor C 2 164
Sackville F 11 160
Saco C 8 164
Saco ≃ C 8 164
Sacramento, Braz. C 7 194
Sacramento, Ca., U.S. B 2 182
Sacramento □[6] B 2 182
Sacramento ≃ C 3 180
Sacramento Mountains ⋀ F 6 176
Sacramento Valley ∨ C 2 180
Sacro Monte ◗[1] E 6 82
Săcueni B 6 104
Sa'dah D 5 202
Sa Dao K 5 132
Saddleback Butte State Park ♦ F 6 182
Saddle Lake Indian Reserve ✦[4] E 16 156
Saddleworth D 5 72
Sa Dec I 7 132
Sadiola C 2 200
Sado I F 7 126
Šadrinsk H 25 108
Sädvaluspen C 8 64
Şafā, Tulūl aş- ∧[1] C 8 120
Safad see Zefat D 4 120
Safâga I 5 118
Safakulevo I 25 108
Säffle C 6 66
Safford F 4 176
Saffron Walden E 7 72
Safi C 3 198
Safonovo, Russia D 17 108
Safonovo, Russia I 10 108
Safranbolu B 5 118
Saga, China D 5 122
Saga, Japan H 3 126
Saga □[3] H 3 126
Sagaba E 3 204
Sagaing D 2 132
Sagaing □[3] E 6 122
Sagamihara G 7 126
Sagami-nada c G 7 126
Saganaga Lake ◎ A 3 166
Sāgar E 3 122
Sagavanirktok ≃ B 20 154
Saginaw B 1 162
Saginaw ≃ B 2 162
Saginaw Bay c B 2 162
Šaglyteniz, ozero ◎ I 28 108
Sagres H 2 86
Sagua de Tánamo C 6 186
Sagua la Grande C 4 186
Saguaro National Park ♦ F 3 176
Saguenay ≃ D 8 160
Saguenay, Parc de conservation du ♦ f 11 163a
Sagunt (Sagunto) E 4 88
Sagunto see Sagunt E 4 88
Sa'gya D 5 122
Sagyz ≃ E 19 110
Sahaba D 3 202
Sahagún F 6 186
Sahalin, ostrov (Sakhalin) I B 12 124
Sahalinskaja oblast' □[6] B 10 126
Sahara ✦[2] F 7 196
Sahāranpur D 3 122
Sahasinaka I 9 205a
Sahel ✦[1] G 9 196
Şahin B 7 106
Sāhīwāl C 2 122
Şahneh E 12 118
Šahovskaja H 11 108
Šahrisabz B 1 122
Šahty F 11 110
Sahuayo de José María Morelos G 8 184
Šahunja H 17 108
Šahy B 10 102
Saïda C 5 198
Saidpur D 5 122
Saigon see Ho Chi Minh City I 8 132
Saiki H 3 126
Saimaa ◎ B 14 66
Saimaa Canal ≅ B 14 66
Saín Alto F 8 184
Şā'īn Dezh D 12 118
Sainte-Adresse C 6 78
Sainte Agathe G 10 158
Sainte-Agathe-des-Monts E 6 160
St.-Agrève E 2 82
St. Albans, Eng., U.K. F 6 72
St. Albans, Vt., U.S. B 5 164
St. Albans, W.V., U.S. D 3 162
St. Albert E 15 156
St.-Alexis-des-Monts E 7 160
St.-Amand-les-Eaux B 10 78
St.-Amand-Mont-Rond F 9 78
St.-Amant-Tallende C 7 80
St.-Amour D 3 82
St.-André, Cap see Vilanandro, Tanjona > k 8 205a
St.-André-Avellin A 3 164
St. Andrews, S.C., U.S. C 4 168
St. Andrews, Scot., U.K. D 6 74
Sainte-Anne-de-Beaupré g 11 163a
Sainte-Anne-du-Lac E 6 160
St. Ann's Bay h 12 186a
St.-Anselme E 8 160
St. Ansgar D 2 166
St. Anthony C 16 160
St.-Antonin-Noble-Val D 5 80
St. Arnaud F 4 144
St.-Auban G 4 82
St. Augustin ≃ C 14 160
St. Augustine E 4 168
St.-Aulaye C 4 80
St. Austell G 2 72
St.-Avold A 4 82
St. Barbe C 15 160
St.-Béat F 4 80
St. Bees Head > C 3 72
St.-Benoît-du-Sault B 5 80
St.-Bertrand-de-Comminges ◗[1] A 5 88
St.-Brieuc D 4 78
St. Catharines G 4 160
St. Catherine, Monastery of ◗[1] B 3 202
St. Catherines Island I D 4 168
St. Catherine's Point > G 5 72
St.-Céré D 5 80
St.-Chamond E 2 82
St. Charles, Il., U.S. B 4 170
St. Charles, Mi., U.S. B 1 162
St. Charles, Mo., U.S. C 3 170
St. Christopher (Saint Kitts) I m 20 187d
St.-Ciers-sur-Gironde C 3 80
St. Clair C 3 170
St. Clair ≃ B 2 162
St. Clair, Lake ◎ B 2 162
St. Clair Shores B 2 162
St.-Claude D 3 82
St. Cloud, Fl., U.S. E 4 168
St. Cloud, Mn., U.S. C 1 166
Sainte-Croix D 4 82
St. Croix I D 8 186
St. Croix ≃, N.A. h 13 163a
St. Croix ≃, U.S. C 2 166
St. Croix Falls C 2 166
St. Croix Island National Monument ♦ h 13 163a
St. Croix National Scenic Riverway ♦ C 2 166
St. Croix State Park ♦ C 2 166
St.-Cyprien D 5 80
St.-Cyr-l'École D 8 78
St.-Cyr-sur-Loire E 7 78
St. David B 3 170
St. David's Cathedral ◗[1] F 1 72
St. David's Head > F 1 72
St.-Denis, Fr. D 9 78
St.-Denis, Reu. q 20 207e
St.-Dié B 4 82
St.-Dizier D 11 78
St.-Donat-sur-l'Herbasse E 3 82
St.-Égrève E 3 82
St. Elias, Cape > G 22 154
St. Elias, Mount ∧ F 24 154
St. Elias Mountains ⋀ F 24 154
St.-Élie C 8 190
Sainte-Énimie F 1 82
St.-Étienne E 2 82
St.-Étienne-de-Saint-Geoirs E 3 82
St.-Étienne-du-Rouvray C 8 78
St.-Étienne-en-Dévoluy F 3 82
St.-Eugène D 7 160
St.-Eustache F 6 160
St. Faith's F 9 206
St.-Félicien D 7 160
St.-Florent-sur-Cher F 9 78
St.-Floris, Parc National ♦ D 9 200
St.-Flour C 7 80
St.-Fons E 2 82
Sainte-Foy E 8 160
Sainte-Foy-de-Conques, Abbaye ◗[1] D 6 80
St. Francis ≃, N.A. g 12 163a
St. Francis ≃, U.S. D 3 170
St. Francis, Cape > H 6 206
St. Francis Bay c H 6 206
St. Francis Lake ◎[1] A 6 162
St. Francisville G 3 170
St.-François n 21 187e
St.-Gabriel D 9 160
St.-Gaudens E 4 80
St.-Gaultier B 5 80
St.-Genis-Laval E 2 82
St. George, Austl. I 9 142
St. George, N.B., Can. F 10 160
St. George, Ut., U.S. D 2 176
St. George, Cape > H 6 170
St.-Georges, Fr. Gu. C 8 190
St. George's, Gren. w 29 187j
St.-Georges, P.Q., Can. E 8 160
St. George's Bay c, Nf., Can. D 14 160
St. Georges Bay c, N.S., Can. F 13 160
St. George's Channel ⋃ E 5 70
St.-Georges-sur-Loire E 6 78
St.-Germain-en-Laye D 8 78
St.-Germain-l'Herm E 1 82
St.-Gervais-d'Auvergne B 6 80
St.-Gilles G 2 82
St.-Gilles-Croix-de-Vie F 5 78
St.-Guénolé E 2 78
St.-Guilhem-le-Désert, Église de ◗[1] G 1 82
St. Helena □[2] J 7 196
St. Helena Bay c G 2 206
St. Helens, Eng., U.K. D 4 72
St. Helens, Or., U.S. C 2 178
St. Helens □[6] D 4 72
St. Helens, Mount ∧[1] B 2 178
St. Helier k 10 73b
St.-Hippolyte C 4 82
St.-Hyacinthe F 7 160
St. Ignace C 6 166
St. Ignace Island I G 15 158
St.-Imier C 5 82
St. Ives G 1 72
St. James, Mi., U.S. C 6 166
St. James, Mo., U.S. C 3 170
St. James, N.Y., U.S. F 5 164
St. James, Cape > F 6 156
St.-Jean, Lac ◎[1] D 7 160
St.-Jean-d'Angély C 3 80
St.-Jean-de-Braye E 8 78
St.-Jean-de-Luz E 2 80
St.-Jean-de-Maurienne E 4 82
St.-Jean-de-Monts F 4 78
St.-Jean-Port-Joli g 11 163a
St.-Jean-sur-Richelieu F 7 160
St.-Jérôme F 6 160
St. Joe ≃ B 5 178
St. John F 10 160
St. John I D 8 186
St. John ≃ F 10 160
St. John, Cape > D 16 160
St. John's, Antig. f 14 187c
St. Johns, Mi., U.S. B 1 162
St. John's, Nf., Can. E 17 160
St. Johns ≃ D 4 168
St. Johnsbury B 6 164
St. Joseph, Mi., U.S. D 5 166
St. Joseph, Mo., U.S. C 1 170
St. Joseph ≃ E 5 166
St. Joseph, Lake ◎ F 13 158
St.-Joseph-de-Beauce E 8 160
St. Joseph Island I H 17 158
St.-Jovite E 6 160
St.-Junien C 4 80
St.-Just-en-Chaussée C 9 78
St. Kilda F 3 146
St. Kilda I C 3 70
St. Kitts see Saint Christopher I m 20 187d
St. Kitts and Nevis □[1] D 9 186
St.-Laurent (Saint Lawrence) ≃ D 9 160
St.-Laurent du Maroni B 8 190
St.-Laurent-et-Benon C 3 80
St. Lawrence E 16 160
St. Lawrence □[6] B 3 164
St. Lawrence (Saint-Laurent) ≃ D 9 160
St. Lawrence, Gulf of c D 13 160
St. Lawrence Island I E 9 154
St. Lawrence Islands National Park ♦ F 6 160
St. Lazare F 8 158
St.-Lô C 5 78
St.-Louis, Fr. C 5 82
St. Louis, Mi., U.S. B 1 162
St. Louis, Mo., U.S. C 3 170
St.-Louis, Reu. q 20 207e
St.-Louis, Sen. B 1 200
St.-Louis de Kent E 11 160
St. Louis Park C 2 166
St. Lucia □[1] E 9 186
St. Lucia, Lake ◎ E 9 206
St. Lucia Channel ⋃ s 27 187h
St. Lucia Game Reserve ✦[4] E 10 206
Sainte-Lucie j 9 83a
St. Magnus Bay c g 9 74a
St.-Malo D 4 78
St.-Malo, Golfe de c D 4 78
St.-Marc D 6 186
St.-Marcellin E 3 82
Sainte-Marguerite ≃ C 10 160
Sainte-Marie, Cap see Vohimena, Tanjona > m 8 205a
Sainte Marie, Nosy I k 9 205a
Sainte-Marie-aux-Mines B 5 82
St. Maries B 5 178
St.-Martin (Sint Maarten) I D 9 186
St. Martin, Lake ◎ F 16 156
St.-Martin-Boulogne B 8 78
St.-Martin-d'Hères E 3 82
St. Mary Lake ◎ A 7 178
St. Mary Peak ∧ F 2 144
St. Marys, Austl. i 13 145a
St. Mary's, Nf., Can. E 17 160
St. Marys, Oh., U.S. B 6 170
St. Marys, W.V., U.S. D 3 162
St. Marys □[6] H 2 164
St. Marys ≃, U.S. D 4 168
St. Marys ≃, U.S. B 6 170
St. Mary's, Cape > E 16 160
St. Mary's Bay c, Nf., Can. E 16 160
St. Marys Bay c, N.S., Can. F 10 160
St. Matthew Island I F 8 154
St. Matthews, Ky., U.S. C 6 170
St. Matthews, S.C., U.S. C 4 168
St.-Maur-des-Fossés D 9 78
St.-Maurice ≃ E 7 160
St.-Max B 4 82
Sainte-Maxime G 4 82
St.-Méen-le-Grand D 4 78
Sainte-Mère-Église C 5 78
St. Michaels H 2 164
St.-Michel-de-Cuxa, Abbatiale de ◗[1] B 7 88
St.-Mihiel B 3 82
St.-Nazaire E 4 78
St.-Nectaire, Église de ◗[1] C 6 80
St. Neots E 6 72
St.-Nicolas D 4 69
St.-Omer B 9 78
Saintonge □[9] C 3 80
St.-Pacôme E 9 160
St.-Pascal g 12 163a
St. Paul, Ab., Can. D 16 156
St. Paul, In., U.S. C 6 170
St. Paul, Mn., U.S. C 2 166
St. Paul, Ne., U.S. E 5 174
St. Paul (Saint-Paul) ≃ C 15 160
St.-Paul, Île I I 7 58
St.-Paulien E 1 82
St. Pauls B 5 168
St.-Paul-Trois-Châteaux F 2 82
St. Peter C 8 174
St. Peter Island I L 1 142
St. Peter Port k 10 73b
St. Peters F 13 160
St. Petersburg, Fl., U.S. F 3 168
St. Petersburg see Sankt-Peterburg, Russia F 9 108
St.-Pierre, Mart. s 26 187h
St.-Pierre, Reu. q 20 207e
St.-Pierre I E 15 160
St.-Pierre, Lac ◎ E 7 160
St. Pierre and Miquelon □[2] E 15 160
St.-Pierre-des-Corps E 7 78
St.-Pierre-le-Moûtier F 10 78
St.-Pierreville F 2 82
St.-Pol-sur-Ternoise B 9 78
St.-Pons-de-Thomères E 6 80
St.-Priest E 2 82
St.-Quentin C 10 78
St.-Raphaël G 4 82
St. Regis Falls B 4 164
St. Regis Indian Reservation ✦[4] B 4 164
St.-Romuald E 8 160
Sainte Rose du Lac F 9 158
Saintes C 3 80
St.-Savin B 4 80
Sainte-Savine D 11 78
St.-Sébastien, Cap see Anorontany, Tanjona > j 9 205a
St.-Sébastien, Morne de ∧ A 8 164
St.-Seine-l'Abbaye E 11 78
St. Simons Island D 4 168
St. Simons Island I D 4 168
Saintes-Maries-de-la-Mer G 2 82
St. Stephen C 4 168
St.-Sulpice-les-Feuilles B 5 80
Sainte-Thérèse A 7 162
St. Thomas, N.D., U.S. A 6 174
St. Thomas, On., Can. G 3 160
St. Thomas I D 8 186
St.-Tite E 7 160
St.-Tropez G 4 82
St.-Valery-en-Caux C 7 78
St.-Vallier, Fr. F 11 78
St.-Vallier, Fr. E 2 82
St.-Varent F 6 78
St. Vincent □[1] E 9 186
St.-Vincent, Cap see Ankaboa, Tanjona > I 8 205a
St. Vincent, Gulf c E 2 144
St. Vincent and the Grenadines see Saint Vincent □[1] E 9 186
St. Vincent Passage ⋃ E 9 186
St.-Vith D 5 69
St.-Vivien-de-Médoc C 2 80
St. Walburg E 17 156
St.-Yvon D 11 160
Saipan I I 13 124
Saiqi E 14 130
Saitama □[3] G 7 126
Saito H 3 126
Sai Yok National Park ♦ G 4 132
Sajama, Nevado ∧ G 5 190
Šajmak' B 2 122
Sajószentpéter A 6 104
Sak ≃ F 4 206
Sakai G 4 126
Sakaiminato G 4 126
Sakākah G 9 118
Sakakawea, Lake ◎[1] B 3 174
Sakami B 5 160
Sakami ≃ B 7 160
Sakami, Lac ◎ B 5 160
Sakaraha I 8 205a
Sakarya B 9 106
Sakarya □[3] B 9 106
Sakarya ≃ B 4 118
Sakata E 7 126
Sakchu-ŭp F 15 128
Sakété D 5 200
Sakhalin see Sahalin, ostrov I B 12 124
Sakhnin D 4 120
Sakht Sar D 14 118
Şäki I 15 110
Šakiai E 11 66
Sakiet Sidi Youssef G 2 90
Sakishima-shotō II H 9 124
Sakon Nakhon F 6 132
Sakpiegu D 5 200
Sakrivier F 4 206
Sakskøbing D 4 68
Sakwaso Lake ◎ E 12 158
Saky G 8 110
Säkylä B 11 66
Sal I h 11 200a
Sal ≃ F 12 110
Šal'a, Slvk. B 9 102
Sala, Swe. C 8 66
Salaberry-de-Valleyfield F 6 160
Salacgrīva D 12 66
Sala Consilina D 5 94
Salada, Laguna ◎ A 1 184
Saladillo D 8 195
Saladillo ≃ C 6 195
Salado ≃, Arg. E 7 192
Salado ≃, Arg. G 8 192
Salado ≃, Arg. G 6 192
Salado ≃, Mex. D 10 184
Salado, Arroyo ≃ G 4 195
Salaga D 4 200
Şalāh ad-Dīn □[3] E 10 118
Salahin G 6 202
Sălaj □[3] B 7 104
Salajwe B 6 206
Salala D 3 200
Şalālah, Oman G 7 116
Salālah, Sudan C 4 202
Salamanca, Mex. G 9 184
Salamanca, N.Y., U.S. B 4 162
Salamanca, Spain D 5 86
Salamanca □[6] D 4 86
Salamat □[3] C 9 200
Salamat, Bahr ≃ D 8 200
Salamís C 5 106
Salamis ⊥ E 5 118
Salani j 11 147b
Salantai D 10 66
Salatiga k 20 135b
Salavat J 21 108
Salaverry E 3 190
Salawati I F 10 134
Sala y Gómez, Isla I G 4 188
Salcia D 8 104
Šalčininkai E 12 66
Saldaña B 6 86
Saldanha Bay c G 2 206
Saldus D 11 66
Sale, Austl. G 6 144
Sale, Eng., U.K. D 4 72
Salé, Mor. C 3 198
Salebabu, Pulau I E 9 134
Sale Creek E 6 170
Salehard C 26 108
Salem, Ia., U.S. E 3 166
Salem, Il., U.S. C 4 170
Salem, India G 3 122
Salem, Ky., U.S. D 4 170
Salem, Ma., U.S. D 8 164
Salem, N.H., U.S. D 7 164
Salem, N.J., U.S. G 3 164
Salem, Oh., U.S. C 3 162
Salem, Or., U.S. C 2 178
Salem, S.D., U.S. D 6 174
Salem, Va., U.S. E 3 162
Salem □[6] G 3 164
Salemi G 2 94
Sälen B 6 66
Salentina, Penisola >[1] E 6 90
Salerno D 4 94
Salerno □[6] D 5 94
Salerno, Golfo di c D 4 94
Salford D 4 72
Šalgačova E 13 108
Salgótarján A 5 104
Salgueiro E 11 190
Sali D 4 198
Salihli C 8 106
Salihorsk J 13 64
Salim E 2 202
Salīmah, Wāḥat ⊤[4] C 2 202
Salimani n 18 207d
Salina, Ks., U.S. F 6 174
Salina, Ut., U.S. C 3 176
Salina Cruz I 12 184
Salinas, Braz. B 9 194
Salinas, Ca., U.S. D 2 182
Salinas, Ec. D 2 190
Salinas ≃, Ca., U.S. D 2 182
Salinas ≃, N.A. I 14 184
Salinas, Pampa de las ≚ B 4 195
Salinas Pueblo Missions National Monument ♦ E 5 176
Saline F 2 170
Saline ≃ F 3 170
Salisbury, Austl. E 2 144
Salisbury, Eng., U.K. F 5 72
Salisbury, Md., U.S. H 3 164
Salisbury, Mo., U.S. C 2 170
Salisbury, N.C., U.S. B 4 168
Salisbury see Harare, Zimb. F 5 204
Salisbury Cathedral ◗[1] F 5 72
Salisbury Island I D 17 150
Salisbury Plain ≚ F 5 72
Šalja H 23 108
Şalkar, ozero ◎ D 17 110
Šalkar-Ega-Kara, ozero ◎ D 22 110
Şalkhad E 7 120
Sallanches E 4 82
Sallent C 6 88
Sallisaw E 1 170
Salluit D 17 150
Salmās C 11 118
Salmi F 9 108
Salmon C 6 178
Salmon ≃, Id., U.S. C 5 178
Salmon ≃, N.B., Can. E 11 160
Salmon, Middle Fork ≃ C 6 178
Salmon Arm F 12 156
Salmon Falls Creek ≃ D 6 178
Salmon River Mountains ⋀ C 6 178
Salmyš ≃ C 19 110
Salo, C.A.R. E 8 200
Salo, Fin. B 11 66
Salò, Italy C 3 90
Salobreña H 7 86
Salomon Islands II J 9 112
Salon-de-Provence G 3 82
Salonga, Parc National de la ♦ C 3 204
Salonica see Thessaloníki B 5 106
Salonika, Gulf of see Thermaïkós Kólpos c B 9 198
Salonta B 6 104
Saloum ≃ C 1 200
Sal'sk F 12 110
Salt ≃ F 2 176
Salta D 6 192
Salta □[3] D 7 192
Saltaim, ozero ◎ H 29 108
Saltash G 2 72
Salt Basin ◎ G 6 176
Saltcoats, Scot., U.K. E 4 74
Saltcoats, Sk., Can. F 7 158
Salt Fork State Park ♦ C 3 162
Saltillo E 9 184
Salt Lake City B 3 176
Salto, Arg. D 7 195
Salto, Ur. B 9 195
Salto, Lago del ◎[1] G 8 92
Salto da Divisa A 10 194
Salto del Guairá E 3 194
Salto Grande, Embalse de ◎[1] B 8 195
Salton Sea ◎ F 6 180
Salton Sea State Recreation Area ♦ F 6 180
Salto Santiago, Represa de ◎[1] F 4 194
Salt River Indian Reservation ✦[4] F 3 176
Saluda E 5 162
Saluda ≃ B 4 168
Salûm, Gulf of c A 2 202
Sālūr F 4 122
Saluzzo E 3 92
Salvador F 11 190
Salvador, Lake ◎ H 3 170
Salvage D 17 160
Salvatierra G 9 184
Salviac D 5 80
Salwa Bay (Salwā, Dawhat as-) c J 13 118
Salween ≃ F 16 116
Salyan J 16 110
Salyersville E 2 162
Salzburg C 5 102
Salzburg □[3] C 5 102
Salzgitter D 7 98
Salzkammergut ✦[1] C 5 102
Salzkotten E 5 98
Salzwedel D 8 98
Sam A. Baker State Park ♦ D 3 170
Samā'il F 8 116
Samalga Pass ⋃ J 10 154
Samālūt H 4 118
Samandağı D 6 118
Samandıra B 8 106
Samane C 6 206
Samangān B 1 122
Samar I C 9 134
Samara C 17 110
Samara ≃, Russia C 18 110
Samara ≃, Ukr. E 9 110
Samarai O 14 124
Samaria □[9] E 4 120
Samaria Gorge ∨ E 5 106
Samarinda F 7 134
Samarka B 4 126
Samarkand (Samarqand) B 1 122
Samarkand □[6] B 1 122
Sāmarrā' E 10 118
Samarskaja oblast' □[6] C 17 110
Samarskoe F 11 110
Samaúna E 7 190
Samba Caju D 2 204
Sambalpur E 4 122
Sambas N 9 132
Sambava j 10 205a
Sāmbhar Lake ◎ D 3 122
Sambiase F 6 94
Sambir E 3 110
Sambo E 2 204
Samborombón, Bahía c D 9 195
Sambungo D 3 204
Samch'ŏk H 17 128
Samer B 8 78
Samfya E 4 204
Samho-dong E 1 126
Sami C 4 106
Şämkir I 15 110
Şamlı C 7 106
Samoa Islands II E 10 136
Samobor C 7 102
Samofalovka E 13 110
Samokov D 7 104
Sámos I D 7 106
Samosir, Pulau I M 4 132
Samothrace see Samothráki I B 6 106
Samothráki B 6 106
Samothráki (Samothrace) I B 6 106
Sampang k 21 135b
Sampit F 6 134
Sampwe D 4 204
Sam Rayburn Reservoir ◎[1] G 1 170
Sam Son E 7 132
Samson Indian Reserve ✦[4] E 15 156
Samsun B 6 118
Samsun □[3] B 6 118
Samsun Körfezi c B 7 118
Samtredia H 13 110
Samui, Ko I J 5 132
Samut Prakan H 5 132
San C 3 200
San (Xan) ≃ H 8 132
Şan'ā' D 5 202
Sanaag □[3] E 6 202
Sanaga ≃ E 7 200
San Agustin, Cape > D 9 134
San Ambrosio, Isla I G 7 188
Sanana, Pulau I F 9 134
Sanandaj E 12 118
San Andreas B 3 182
San Andrés E 4 186
San Andrés, Isla de I A 2 190
San Andrés Tuxtla H 12 184
San Andrés y Providencia □[3] E 4 186
San Angelo E 3 172
San Antonio, Chile C 1 195
San Antonio, Tx., U.S. F 4 172
San Antonio, Ur. B 9 195
San Antonio, Cabo >[1] E 9 195
San Antonio, Cabo de > C 3 186
San Antonio, Mount ∧ F 6 182
San Antonio Abad see Sant Antoni de Portmany E 6 88
San Antonio Bay c F 5 172
San Antonio de Padua, Mission ◗[1] D 2 182
San Antonio Mountain ∧ D 5 176
San Antonio Oeste G 5 195
Sanāwad E 3 122
San Bartolomeo in Galdo C 5 94
San Benedetto del Tronto B 3 94
San Benedetto Po D 6 92
San Benedicto, Isla I H 4 184
San Benito, Guat. D 2 186
San Benito, Tx., U.S. G 5 172
San Benito □[6] D 2 182
San Benito ≃ D 2 182
San Bernardino F 6 182
San Bernardino □[6] F 7 182
San Bernardino Mountains ⋀ F 7 182
San Bernardo C 2 195
San Blas D 5 184
San Blas, Cape > H 6 170
San Bonifacio D 7 92
San Borja F 5 190
San Buenaventura D 9 184
San Cándido C 8 92
San Carlos, Ca., U.S. C 1 182
San Carlos, Chile E 2 195
San Carlos, Falk. Is. n 18 193b
San Carlos, Mex. C 9 184
San Carlos, Mex. E 10 184
San Carlos, Phil. C 8 134
San Carlos, Ur. D 10 195
San Carlos, Ven. F 7 186
San Carlos ≃, C.R. F 3 186
San Carlos ≃, Ven. B 5 190
San Carlos de Bariloche H 5 192
San Carlos de Bolívar E 7 195
San Carlos del Zulia F 7 186
San Carlos de Río Negro C 5 190
San Carlos Indian Reservation ✦[4] F 3 176
San Casciano in Val di Pesa F 7 92
San Cataldo G 3 94
Sancerre E 9 78
Sanchahe D 16 128
San Ciro de Acosta G 10 184
San Clemente, Ca., U.S. G 6 182
San Clemente, Spain E 2 88
San Clemente Island I H 5 182
Sancoins F 9 78
San Cristóbal, Arg. B 7 195
San Cristóbal, Ven. G 6 186
San Cristobal I B 13 138
San Cristóbal, Isla I j 14 190a
San Cristóbal, Volcán ∧[1] E 3 186
San Cristóbal de la Laguna i 14 85b
San Cristóbal de las Casas I 13 184
Sancti Spíritus C 4 186
Sancy, Puy de ∧ C 6 80
Sand C 3 66
Sand ≃, S. Afr. B 9 206
Sand ≃, S. Afr. F 7 206
Sanda Island I B 1 72
Sandakan D 7 134
Sandane B 3 66
Sandaozhen C 15 128
Sandared A 5 68
Sandbach D 4 72
Sande C 5 98
Sandefjord C 5 66
Sandersdorf E 8 98
Sanderson E 2 172
Sandfly Lake ◎ D 18 156
Sandhamn C 9 66
Sandia F 5 190
Sandia Indian Reservation ✦[4] E 5 176
San Diego H 6 182
San Diego □[6] G 7 182
San Diego, Cabo > J 6 192
San Diego Bay c H 6 182
Sandıklı C 9 106
Sand Lake ◎ F 11 158
Sandnes C 2 66
Sandoa D 3 204
Sandomierz C 11 96
San Donà di Piave D 8 92
San Donato Milanese D 5 92
Sandoway E 2 132
Sandown G 5 72
Sandringham E 7 72
Sandringham House ⊥ E 7 72
Sandrücken C 2 206
Sand Springs, Ok., U.S. B 5 172
Sand Springs, Tx., U.S. D 3 172
Sandston A 6 168
Sandu Ao c E 14 130
Sandusky, Mi., U.S. B 2 162
Sandusky, Oh., U.S. C 2 162
Sandvika C 5 66
Sandviken B 8 66
Sandwell □[6] E 4 72
Sandwich E 8 164
Sandwich Bay c, Nf., Can. B 14 160
Sandwich Bay c, Nmb. B 1 206
Sandy E 7 178
Sandy Bay Indian Reserve ✦[4] F 9 158
Sandy Cape > H 11 142
Sandy Hook G 4 170
Sandy Hook >[2] F 5 164
Sandykop D 2 206
Sandy Lake ◎ E 12 158
Sandy Springs C 2 168
Sandžak ✦[1] D 5 104
San Felipe, Chile C 2 195
San Felipe, Mex. G 9 184
San Felipe, Mex. B 2 184
San Felipe, Ven. F 7 186
San Felipe Indian Reservation ✦[4] E 5 176
San Félix, Isla I G 6 188
San Fernando, Ca., U.S. F 5 182
San Fernando, Chile D 2 195
San Fernando, Phil. B 8 134
San Fernando, Phil. B 8 134
San Fernando, Spain H 4 86
San Fernando, Trin. q 23 187f
San Fernando de Apure G 8 186

⌊ Waterfall ⋃ Strait c Bay, Gulf ◎ Lake ≚ Swamp ⊓ Ice Feature ⊤ Other Hydrographic Feature ✦ Submarine Feature □ Political Unit ◗ Cultural Institution ⊥ Historical Site ♦ Recreational Site ⊠ Airport ■ Military Installation ✦ Miscellaneous

Symbols in the index entries represent the broad categories identified in the key at the right. Symbols with superior numbers (▲¹) identify subcategories (see complete key on page 242).

▲ Mountain   ▲ Mountains   )(Pass   V Valley   ≃ Plain   ▸ Cape   I Island   II Islands   ● Other Topographic Feature   ≃ River   ≃ Canal

Searsport — Sinsheim

Name | Map Ref. | Page

Searsport A 9 162
Seaside D 2 182
Seaside Park G 4 164
Seattle B 2 178
Šebalino D 11 114
Sebanga N 5 132
Sebastián Vizcaíno, Bahía ⊂ C 2 184
Sebastopol F 4 144
Šebeka B 7 174
Šebekino D 10 110
Sebeş C 7 104
Sebes Körös (Crişul Repede) ≃ B 6 104
Sebewaing B 2 162
Şebinkarahisar B 7 118
Sebnitz F 11 98
Sebree D 5 170
Seckau ▶[1] C 6 102
Seclin B 9 78
Sečovce D 11 96
Security C 6 176
Seda, China B 5 130
Seda, Lith. D 11 66
Sedalia C 2 170
Sedan C 11 78
Sedano B 7 86
Sedayu k 21 135b
Seddonville D 3 146
Sederot G 3 120
Sedgwick B 5 172
Sedlčany C 11 100
Šedok G 12 110
Sedom (Sodom) ⊥ G 4 120
Sedriano D 4 92
Šedtim C 22 108
Šeduva E 11 66
Seefeld in Tirol C 3 102
Seehausen D 8 98
Seeheim D 2 206
Seeheim-Jugenheim C 5 100
Seeis B 2 206
Seekaskootch Indian Reserve ◆[4] E 17 156
Seekoei ≃ F 6 206
Seelow D 11 98
Seelze D 6 98
Seesen E 7 98
Seevetal C 6 98
Seewinkel ◆[1] C 8 102
Sefar ⊥ E 6 198
Sefare B 7 206
Seferihisar C 7 106
Sefid ≃ D 13 118
Sefrou C 4 198
Sefton □[6] D 3 72
Sefton, Mount ∧ E 3 146
Segamat M 6 132
Şegarcea C 7 104
Segen ≃ F 4 202
Segesta ⊥ G 2 94
Segeža E 10 108
Segorbe E 4 88
Ségou C 3 200
Ségou □[3] C 3 200
Šegovary E 15 108
Segovia D 6 86
Segovia □[6] C 6 86
Segozero, ozero ⊜ E 11 108
Segre ≃ G 4 80
Seguam Pass ʊ k 45 155a
Séguédine A 7 200
Séguéla D 3 200
Séguénéga C 4 200
Seguin F 5 172
Segura E 3 86
Segura ≃ F 4 88
Sehlabathebe E 8 206
Sehlabathebe National Park ♦ E 8 206
Sehnde D 6 98
Seia D 3 86
Seiche ≃ E 5 78
Seiches-sur-le-Loir E 6 78
Seilhac C 5 80
Seinäjoki E 11 64
Seine ≃, Fr. C 7 78
Seine ≃, On., Can. G 13 158
Seine, Baie de la ⊂ C 6 78
Seine-et-Marne □[3] D 10 78
Seine-Maritime □[3] C 7 78
Seine-Saint-Denis □[3] D 9 78
Seitovka F 16 110
Seitsemisen kansallispuisto ♦ B 11 66
Sejm ≃ D 8 110
Seki D 8 106
Sekoma C 5 206
Sekondi E 4 200
Šeksna G 13 108
Šelagskij, mys ⟩ B 20 114
Selangor □[3] M 5 132
Selaön I C 8 66
Selargius I 10 94a
Selaru, Pulau I G 10 134
Selatan, Tanjung ⟩ F 6 134
Selawik C 14 154
Selawik Lake ⊜ C 14 154
Selayar, Pulau I G 8 134
Selb B 9 100
Selby D 5 72
Selbyville H 3 164
Sel'co J 10 108
Selçuk D 7 106
Seldovia G 18 154
Selebi-Phikwe B 7 206
Selemadeg I 22 135b
Selemdža ≃ B 10 124
Selenge □[3] B 6 128
Selenge (Selenga) ≃ B 5 128
Selenicë B 3 106
Selennjah ≃ C 16 114
Sélestat B 5 82
Seletar ≃ i 15 134a
Seletar Reservoir ⊜[1] i 14 134a
Seleznëvo F 8 108
Selezni I 9 108
Sélibabi F 2 198
Seliger, ozero ⊜ H 10 108
Seligman D 2 170
Selinsgrove F 2 164
Selinunte ⊥ G 2 94
Seližarovo H 10 108
Selje E 2 64
Selkirk, Mb., Can. F 10 158
Selkirk, Scot., U.K. B 4 72
Selkirk Mountains ⋏ A 5 178
Šelkovskaja H 15 110
Sellersburg C 6 170
Sells G 3 176
Selma, Al., U.S. F 5 170
Selma, Ca., U.S. D 4 182
Selmer E 4 170
Selous Game Reserve ◆[4] D 6 204
Seltz B 6 82
Selu, Pulau I G 10 134
Selvagens, Ilhas II C 1 198
Selvas ◆[3] E 5 190
Selway ≃ B 6 178
Selwyn F 5 142
Selwyn Lake ⊜ A 19 156
Selwyn Mountains ⋏ E 28 154
Selwyn Range ⋏ F 5 142
Seman ≃ B 3 106
Semarang k 20 135b
Sematan N 9 132
Semau, Pulau I H 8 134
Sembawang i 14 134a
Şemdinli D 11 118
Semenanjung Malaysia □[9] L 5 132
Semenivka C 8 110
Semenov H 16 108
Semeru, Gunung ∧ I 21 135b
Semey see Semipalatinsk D 11 114
Semiluki D 11 110
Semily B 12 100
Seminoe Reservoir ⊜[1] D 10 178
Seminole C 5 172
Seminole, Lake ⊜[1] D 2 168
Seminole Draw ≃ D 2 172
Semipalatinsk D 11 114
Semliki ≃ B 4 204
Semnān E 15 118
Semnān □[3] E 16 118
Šemonaiha D 11 114
Semporna E 7 134
Semypolky D 7 110
Sên ≃ G 7 132
Senaki H 13 110
Sena Madureira E 5 190
Senanayake Samudra ⊜[1] H 4 122
Senanga F 3 204
Sendai, Japan E 8 126
Sendai, Japan I 3 126
Senden, Ger. E 4 98
Senden, Ger. D 7 100
Sendhwa E 2 122
Sêndo C 2 130
Seneca, Ks., U.S. F 6 174
Seneca, Mo., U.S. D 1 170
Seneca □[6] D 2 164
Seneca ≃ C 2 164
Seneca Falls D 2 164
Seneca Lake ⊜ D 1 164
Senegal □[1] G 6 196
Sénégal ≃ G 6 196
Senftenberg E 11 98
Senga Hill D 5 204
Sengilej I 18 108
Senhor do Bonfim F 10 190
Senica B 9 102
Senigallia F 9 92
Senirkent C 9 106
Senj C 3 104
Senja I B 8 64
Šenkursk E 15 108
Senlis C 9 78
Senmonorom H 8 132
Senneterre D 5 160
Sennori I 4 92
Sênou C 3 200
Senqu (Orange) ≃ F 7 206
Sens D 10 78
Senta C 6 104
Sentosa I j 14 134a
Sentrum C 7 206
Seoni E 3 122
Sepik ≃ M 12 124
Sępopol A 11 96
Sept-Îles C 10 160
Sept-Îles, Réserve indienne ◆[4] C 10 160
Sepúlveda C 7 86
Sequeros D 4 86
Sequoia National Park ♦ D 5 182
Šerabad B 1 122
Serafimovič E 13 110
Seraing D 4 69
Seram (Ceram) I F 9 134
Serang k 18 135b
Serangoon i 15 134a
Serangoon ≃ i 15 134a
Serangoon Harbour ⊂ i 15 134a
Serasan, Selat ʊ M 9 132
Seraya, Pulau I j 14 134a
Serbia see Srbija □[3] D 6 104
Serdobsk C 14 110
Sered' B 9 102
Sereda I 11 108
Seredejskij I 11 108
Serëdka C 13 66
Şereflikoçhisar C 5 118
Seregno D 5 92
Seremban M 5 132
Serengeti National Park ♦ C 6 204
Serengeti Plain ≚ C 5 204
Serenje E 5 204
Sergač I 16 108
Sergeevka, Kaz. J 27 108
Sergeevka, Russia B 3 126
Sergeja Kirova, ostrova II B 12 114
Sergiev Posad H 12 108
Sergipe □[3] F 11 190
Sergozero, ozero ⊜ C 12 108
Seria E 6 134
Serian N 10 132
Sericho G 4 202
Sérigny ≃ A 9 160
Serik D 9 106
Šerkaly E 26 108
Šerlovaja Gora A 11 128
Sermata, Pulau I G 9 134
Sernur H 18 108
Serov G 24 108
Serowe B 7 206
Serpentine Lakes ⊜ K 10 140
Serpents Mouth ʊ r 23 187f
Serpneve B 10 104
Serpuhov I 12 108
Serra D 10 194
Serracapriola C 5 94
Serra da Canastra, Parque Nacional da ♦ C 7 194
Serra do Navio C 8 190
Sérrai B 5 106
Serra San Bruno F 6 94
Serra Talhada E 11 190
Serravalle Scrivia E 4 92
Serres F 3 82
Serrezuela B 5 195
Serrières E 2 82
Serrinha F 11 190
Sertã E 2 86
Sertãozinho D 6 194
Serua, Pulau I G 10 134
Serui F 11 134
Serule A 7 206
Sérvia B 4 106
Sêrxü B 3 130
Sesayap ≃ E 7 134
Sese A 7 206
Sese Islands II B 3 202
Sesheke F 3 204
Sesimbra F 1 86
Sessa E 3 204
Sestao A 7 86
Sesto Calende E 6 82
Sesto Fiorentino F 7 92
Sesto San Giovanni D 5 92
Sestri Levante E 5 92
Sestu I 10 94a
Setabeng C 5 206
Sète G 1 82
Sete Lagoas C 8 194
Sétif B 6 198
Seto-naikai ᵻ[2] G 4 126
Seton Portage F 10 156
Settat C 3 198
Setté Cama F 6 200
Sette-Daban, hrebet ⋏ C 16 114
Settimo Torinese D 3 92
Setting Lake ⊜ D 9 158
Setúbal F 2 86
Setúbal □[3] F 2 86
Setúbal, Baía de ⊂ F 1 86
Seul, Lac ⊜ F 12 158
Sevan I 14 110
Sevan, Lake ⊜ I 14 110
Sévaré C 4 200
Sevastopol' G 8 110
Ševčenko see Aktau H 17 110
Sevenoaks F 7 72
Seventy Mile House F 11 156
Severn D 5 206
Severn ≃, On., Can. D 15 158
Severn ≃, U.K. E 4 72
Severnaja Osetija □[3] H 14 110
Severnaja Sos'va (Severnaya Sos'va) ≃ E 26 108
Severna Park G 2 164
Severnaya Sos'va see Severnaja Sos'va ≃ E 26 108
Severn Bridge ◆[5] F 4 72
Severn Lake ⊜ D 13 158
Severnye uvaly ⋏[2] G 19 108
Severnyj C 26 108
Severnyj Kommunar G 20 108
Severočeský □[3] B 10 100
Severodvinsk D 13 108
Severo-Enisejskij C 12 114
Severo-Kazahstan □[3] I 28 108
Severomoravský □[3] D 9 96
Severomorsk B 10 108
Severoural'sk F 24 108
Sevier ≃ C 2 176
Sevier, East Fork ≃ D 2 176
Sevier Desert ◆[2] C 2 176
Sevier Lake ⊜ C 2 176
Sevierville B 3 168
Sevilla (Seville) G 5 86
Sevilla □[6] G 5 86
Seville see Sevilla G 5 86
Sevlievo D 8 104
Sevsk J 11 108
Seward, Ak., U.S. F 20 154
Seward, Ne., U.S. E 6 174
Seward Glacier ⊓ F 24 154
Seward Peninsula ⟩[1] D 12 154
Seweweekspoort G 4 206
Sexsmith D 12 156
Sextín ≃ D 7 184
Seychelles □[1] J 7 112
Seychellois, Morne ∧ I 16 207c
Seydişehir D 4 118
Seyðisfjörður m 23 64a
Seyhan ≃ D 6 118
Seymour, Austl. F 5 144
Seymour, Ct., U.S. E 5 164
Seymour, In., U.S. C 5 170
Seymour, Mo., U.S. D 2 170
Seyne F 4 82
Seynod E 4 82
Sežana E 5 102
Sézanne D 10 78
Šežim E 23 108
Sezze H 9 92
Sfântu Gheorghe C 8 104
Sfântu Gheorghe, Braţul ≃ C 10 104
Sfax C 7 198
's-Gravenhage (The Hague) B 3 69
Sha ≃ E 13 130
Shaanxi □[3] I 7 128
Shaba □[3] D 4 204
Shabeellaha Dhexe □[3] G 6 202
Shabeellaha Hoose □[3] G 5 202
Shabeelle (Shebelē Wenz) ≃ G 5 202
Shabunda C 4 204
Shache B 3 122
Shackleton Ice Shelf ⊓ C 19 208
Shackleton Range ⋏ E 6 208
Shādegān G 13 118
Shady Grove D 3 168
Shafter D 4 182
Shaftesbury F 4 72
Shagamu D 5 200
Shageluk E 15 154
Shag Rocks II[1] J 11 192
Shāhābād, India C 3 122
Shāhābād, India F 3 122
Shah Alam M 5 132
Shāhdādkot D 1 122
Shahdol E 4 122
Shahe H 10 128
Shāhjahānpur D 3 122
Shāhpura D 3 122
Shahr-e Bābak G 16 118
Shahr-e Kord F 14 118
Shāhrūd see Emāmshahr D 16 118
Shāhrūd ≃ D 14 118
Shahryār E 14 118
Shaighālu C 1 122
Shājāpur E 3 122
Shakaskraal E 9 206
Shaker Heights C 3 162
Shaki D 5 200
Shaktoolik D 14 154
Shala Hāyk' ⊜ F 4 202
Shalalth F 10 156
Shallotte B 5 168
Shām, Jabal ash- ∧ F 8 116
Sham, Mount see Shām, Jabal ash- ∧ F 8 116
Shambe National Park ♦ F 2 202
Shambuanda D 2 204
Shamokin F 2 164
Shamrock E 3 168
Shamva F 5 204
Shan □[3] D 4 132
Shandan G 3 128
Shandatgyi E 2 132
Shandī D 3 202
Shandian ≃ E 10 128
Shandong □[3] H 12 128
Shandong Bandao ⟩[1] H 13 128
Shand uul ∧ E 5 128
Shangani ≃ F 4 204
Shangbahe C 12 130
Shangcheng C 12 130
Shangdu F 9 128
Shanghai C 15 130
Shanghai □[3] C 15 130
Shanghe H 11 128
Shangjin B 10 130
Shangqiu, China A 12 130
Shangqiu, China A 12 130
Shangrao D 13 130
Shangshui B 12 130
Shangsi G 8 130
Shangxian B 9 130
Shangying D 16 128
Shangzhi D 16 128
Shanhaiguan F 12 128
Shanhetun D 16 128
Shankou H 9 130
Shannon, Ga., U.S. E 6 170
Shannon, Il., U.S. D 4 166
Shannon ≃ D 2 75
Shannon Lake ⊜ B 8 158
Shantou G 13 130
Shanwei G 12 130
Shanxi □[3] H 9 128
Shanxian I 10 128
Shanyang B 9 130
Shanyin G 9 128
Shaoguan F 11 130
Shaowu E 13 130
Shaoxing C 15 130
Shaoyang E 10 130
Shaqrā', Sau. Ar. J 11 118
Shaqrā', Yemen E 6 202
Shara, gora ∧ H 13 110
Share D 5 200
Sharga B 3 128
Sharhulsan D 5 128
Shark Bay ⊂ I 2 140
Sharktooth Mountain ∧ B 8 156
Sharm ash-Shaykh see Sharm El Sheikh H 6 118
Sharm El Sheikh H 6 118
Sharon, N.D., U.S. B 6 174
Sharon, Pa., U.S. C 3 162
Sharpe Lake ⊜ D 12 158
Shasha F 7 202
Shashe ≃ G 4 204
Shashemenē F 4 202
Shashi C 11 130
Shasta, Mount ∧[1] E 2 178
Shasta Lake ⊜[1] E 2 178
Shatawī E 3 202
Shāṭi', Wādī ash- ≃ D 8 198
Shatt al-Arab ≃ G 12 118
Shattuck B 4 172
Shaunavon G 17 156
Shawinigan E 7 160
Shawnee, Ks., U.S. C 1 170
Shawnee, Oh., U.S. D 2 162
Shawnee, Ok., U.S. C 5 172
Shawneetown D 4 170
Shawville A 2 164
Shaxian E 13 130
Shayang C 11 130
Shay Gap G 6 140
Shaykh 'Uthmān E 6 202
Shazihe B 8 130
Shchors D 7 110
Shebelē Wenz (Shabeelle) ≃ F 5 202
Sheberghān C 10 116
Sheboygan D 5 166
Sheboygan Falls D 5 166
Shechem ⊥ E 4 120
Sheenjek ≃ C 23 154
Sheepmoor D 9 206
's-Heerenberg E 3 98
Sheerness F 7 72
Shefar'am D 4 120
Sheffield D 5 72
Sheffield □[6] D 5 72
Shehong C 7 130
Shekhūpura C 2 122
Shelagyote Peak ∧ I 31 154
Shelburn C 5 170
Shelburne G 11 160
Shelburne Bay ⊂ A 6 142
Shelby, Ia., U.S. E 7 174
Shelby, Mi., U.S. D 5 166
Shelby, N.C., U.S. B 4 168
Shelby, Oh., U.S. C 2 162
Shelbyville, Il., U.S. C 4 170
Shelbyville, In., U.S. C 6 170
Shelbyville, Tn., U.S. E 5 170
Shelbyville, Lake ⊜[1] C 4 170
Sheldon D 7 174
Shelekhov Gulf ⊂ D 18 114
Shelikof Strait ʊ H 17 154
Shellen C 7 200
Shelley D 7 178
Shellharbour E 8 144
Shell Lake C 2 166
Shell Rock ≃ D 2 166
Shelton, Ct., U.S. E 5 164
Shelton, Wa., U.S. B 2 178
Shenandoah, Pa., U.S. F 2 164
Shenandoah, Va., U.S. D 4 162
Shenandoah ≃ D 5 162
Shenandoah, South Fork ≃ D 4 162
Shenandoah National Park ♦ D 4 162
Shenchi G 8 128
Shenge D 2 200
Shengxian D 15 130
Shengze C 15 130
Shenmu G 8 128
Shenqiu B 12 130
Shenxian H 10 128
Shenyang F 14 128
Shenzhen G 12 130
Sheopur D 3 122
Shepetivka D 5 110
Shepherd G 1 170
Shepparton F 5 144
Sheppey, Isle of I F 7 72
Shepton Mallet F 4 72
Sheqi B 11 130
Sherard, Cape ⟩ B 16 150
Sherborne G 4 72
Sherbrooke, N.S., Can. F 13 160
Sherbrooke, P.Q., Can. F 8 160
Sherbrooke □[6] A 7 164
Sherburne D 3 164
Sheridan, Or., U.S. C 2 178
Sheridan, Wy., U.S. C 10 178
Sheringa L 2 142
Sherman, Ms., U.S. E 4 170
Sherman, Tx., U.S. D 5 172
Sherman Mills h 12 163a
Sherridon D 8 158
Shertallai H 3 122
's-Hertogenbosch C 4 69
Sherwood, Ar., U.S. E 2 170
Sherwood, Oh., U.S. B 6 170
Sherwood Forest ◆[3] D 5 72
Sherwood Park E 15 156
Shetland Islands □[6] g 9 74a
Shetland Islands II g 9 74a
Shewa □[3] F 4 202
Shexian D 14 130
Sheyang B 15 130
Sheyenne B 5 174
Sheyenne ≃ B 6 174
Shibadu D 10 130
Shibām D 6 202
Shibata F 7 126
Shibetsu B 9 126
Shibīn El-Kôm G 4 118
Shibogama Lake ⊜ E 14 158
Shicheng E 13 130
Shidai C 13 130
Shiga □[3] G 6 126
Shigezhuang G 11 128
Shigu E 4 130
Shiguaigou F 8 128
Shiikh F 6 202
Shijiazhuang H 10 128
Shikārpur D 1 122
Shikoku I H 4 126
Shikoku-sanchi ⋏ H 4 126
Shikotsu-ko ⊜ C 8 126
Shikotsu-Tōya-kokuritsu-kōen ♦ C 8 126
Shiliguri D 5 122
Shillelagh D 5 75
Shillong D 6 122
Shiloh D 1 162
Shiloh see Saylūn, Khirbat ⊥ E 4 120
Shiloh National Military Park ♦ E 4 170
Shilong, China G 11 130
Shilong, China B 9 132
Shimada G 7 126
Shimane □[3] G 4 126
Shimbiris ∧ E 6 202
Shimen D 10 130
Shimian D 6 130
Shimla C 3 122
Shimoda G 7 126
Shimodate F 7 126
Shimoga G 3 122
Shimonoseki G 3 126
Shinano ≃ F 7 126
Shināş J 17 118
Shīndand D 9 116
Shingbwiyang A 3 132
Shingū H 6 126
Shingwidzi B 9 206
Shinjō E 8 126
Shinkolobwe E 4 204
Shinyanga C 5 204
Shinyanga □[3] C 5 204
Shiocton C 4 166
Shiogama E 8 126
Shiono-misaki ⟩ H 5 126
Shiping, China D 8 130
Shiping, China G 6 130
Shipley D 5 72
Shippensburg C 5 162
Ship Rock ∧ D 4 176
Shiquan B 9 130
Shirakawa F 8 126
Shiranuka C 10 126
Shīrāz H 15 118
Shire ≃ F 6 204
Shire of Aurukun Aboriginal Land ◆[4] B 5 142
Shiretoko-kokuritsu-kōen ♦ B 10 126
Shiretoko-misaki ⟩ B 10 126
Shīrvān D 17 118
Shishaldin Volcano ∧[1] I 12 154
Shishi F 14 130
Shishmaref Inlet ⊂ C 11 154
Shishou D 11 130
Shitang F 10 130
Shivpuri D 3 122
Shivta, Ḫorvot (Subeita) ⊥ H 3 120
Shiwan H 7 128
Shixian C 2 126
Shiyan B 10 130
Shizunai C 9 126
Shizuoka G 7 126
Shizuoka □[3] G 7 126
Shkodra see Üsküdar A 3 106
Shoal Harbour D 17 160
Shoalhaven ≃ E 8 144
Shoals C 5 170
Shoalwater Bay ⊂ G 10 142
Shorewood D 5 166
Shoshone D 6 178
Shoshone ≃ C 9 178
Shoshone, South Fork ≃ C 9 178
Shoshone Mountains ⋏ B 6 182
Shoshone Peak ∧ C 7 182
Shoshone Range ⋏ B 5 180
Shoshoni D 9 178
Shostka D 8 110
Shouguang H 12 128
Shouning E 14 130
Shouxian B 13 130
Shouyang H 9 128
Shpola E 7 110
Shpykiv A 10 104
Shreveport F 2 170
Shrewsbury, Eng., U.K. E 4 72
Shrewsbury, Ma., U.S. D 7 164
Shri Dūngargarh D 2 122
Shropshire □[6] E 4 72
Shū see Šu B 11 116
Shū see Ču ≃, Asia B 11 116
Shu ≃, China I 12 128
Shuajingsi C 6 130
Shuangbai F 5 130
Shuangcheng D 16 128
Shuangfeng E 11 130
Shuanggetun B 17 128
Shuanggou, China A 13 130
Shuanggou, China B 11 130
Shuangliao E 14 128
Shuangpai F 10 130
Shuangyashan C 18 128
Shubrâ El-Kheima G 4 118
Shubuta G 4 170
Shucheng C 13 130
Shuibatang D 8 130
Shuiji E 14 130
Shuitou F 14 130
Shuiye H 9 128
Shujāābād D 2 122
Shuksan, Mount ∧ A 3 178
Shulan D 16 128
Shule ≃ A 7 122
Shullsburg D 3 166
Shunchang E 13 130
Shunde G 11 130
Shuqayyiqah, Nafūd ⊥[8] J 10 118
Shūr ≃, Iran G 17 118
Shūr ≃, Iran E 13 118
Shūr ≃, Iran D 17 118
Shurugwi F 5 204
Shūsh (Susa) F 13 118
Shūshtar F 13 118
Shuswap Lake ⊜ F 12 156
Shuyang A 14 130
Shwebo C 2 132
Shwegyin F 3 132
Shweli (Longchuan) ≃ G 3 130
Shyghanaq see Čiganak A 11 116
Shymkent see Šymkent A 1 122
Shyok ≃ D 12 116
Siāh Kūh, Kavīr-e ≚ F 15 118
Siālkot C 2 122
Sianów A 9 96
Siapa ≃ C 5 190
Siargao Island I D 9 134
Siasconset E 9 164
Šiaškotan, ostrov I C 14 124
Siau, Pulau I E 9 134
Šiauliai E 11 66
Sibaj C 21 110
Sibayi, Lake ⊜ D 10 206
Sibbo B 12 66
Šibenik D 3 104
Siberia ◆[1], Russia D 30 108
Siberia (Sibir') ◆[1], Russia C 12 114
Siberut, Pulau I F 3 134
Sibi D 1 122
Sibircevo B 4 126
Sibiti C 1 204
Sibiti ≃ C 5 204
Sibiu C 7 104
Sibiu □[3] C 8 104
Sibley, Ia., U.S. D 7 174
Sibley, Ms., U.S. G 3 170
Sibolga N 4 132
Sibsāgar D 6 122
Sibu E 6 134
Sibut D 8 200
Sibutu Island I E 7 134
Sibuyan Island I C 8 134
Sibuyan Sea ᵻ[2] C 8 134
Siccus ≃ C 2 144
Sichifulo ≃ F 4 204
Sichuan □[3] C 5 130
Sicié, Cap ⟩ G 3 82
Sicilia □[3] G 4 94
Sicilia see Sicily I G 3 94
Sicily (Sicilia) I G 3 94
Sicily, Strait of ʊ G 4 90
Sicuani F 4 190
Šid C 5 104
Sīdamo □[3] G 4 202
Sidareja k 19 135b
Siddhapur E 2 122
Siderno F 6 94
Sidheros, Ákra ⟩ E 7 106
Sidhi E 4 122
Sidi Akacha H 6 88
Sidi Ali D 6 84
Sīdī Barrānī A 2 202
Sidi bel Abbès B 4 198
Sidi bel Abbès □[3] E 5 84
Sidi-Bennour C 3 198
Sidi-Ifni D 2 198
Sidi-Kacem C 3 198
Sidi Okba C 6 198
Sidi-Smaïl C 3 198
Sidley, Mount ∧ D 32 208
Sidmouth G 3 72
Sidnaw B 4 166
Sidney, B.C., Can. G 10 156
Sidney, Ia., U.S. B 1 170
Sidney, N.Y., U.S. D 3 164
Sidney, Oh., U.S. C 1 162
Sidney Lanier, Lake ⊜[1] B 3 168
Sidobre ◆[1] A 7 88
Sidon see Şaydā, Leb. B 4 120
Sidon, Ms., U.S. F 3 170
Sidrolândia D 3 194
Siedlce B 12 96
Siedlce □[3] B 12 96
Siegburg F 4 98
Siegen F 5 98
Siemianowice Śląskie C 10 96
Siemiatycze B 12 96
Siĕmréab H 6 132
Siena F 7 92
Siena □[6] F 7 92
Sieradz C 10 96
Sieradz □[3] C 10 96
Sieraków B 9 96
Sierpc B 10 96
Sierra □[6] A 3 182
Sierra Blanca G 6 176
Sierra Leone □[1] H 6 196
Sierra Nevada see Nevada, Sierra ⋏ D 4 180
Sierra Nevada, Parque Nacional ♦ F 7 186
Sierra San Pedro Mártir, Parque Nacional ♦ G 6 180
Sierras Bayas E 7 195
Sierra Vista G 3 176
Sierre D 5 82
Sifangtai C 16 128
Sifié D 3 200
Sig, Alg. E 5 84
Sig, Russia D 11 108
Sigatoka n 13 147c
Sighetu Marmaţiei B 7 104
Sighişoara B 8 104
Sigli L 2 132
Siglufjördur I 21 64a
Sigmaringen D 6 100
Signa F 7 92
Signalberg D 2 206
Signy ▶[3] L 10 192
Siguatepeque E 3 186
Sigüenza C 2 88
Siguiri C 3 200
Sigulda D 12 66
Sigurd C 3 176
Sihanoukville see Kâmpóng Saôm I 6 132
Šihany C 15 110
Sihorā E 4 122
Sihote-Alin' ⋏ C 11 124
Sihui G 11 130
Siilinjärvi E 13 64
Siirt D 9 118
Siirt □[3] D 10 118
Sikanni Chief ≃ C 10 156
Sikao K 4 132
Sīkar D 3 122
Sikasso C 3 200
Sikasso □[3] C 3 200
Sikeston D 4 170
Sikiá B 5 106
Sikiang see Xi ≃ G 11 130
Siking see Xi'an A 9 130
Sikión ⊥ C 5 106
Sikkim □[3] D 5 122
Siklós ⊥ E 10 102
Sikosi F 3 204
Šikotan, ostrov (Shikotan-tō) I D 13 124
Sil ≃ B 3 86
Silacayoapan I 10 184
Šilalė E 11 66
Silandro C 6 92
Silao G 9 184
Silba C 3 104
Silchar E 6 122
Şile B 8 106
Siler City B 5 168
Silesia □[9] C 10 96
Siletiteniz, ozero ⊜ D 10 114
Silgadhī D 4 122
Siliana G 2 90
Siliana □[3] G 2 90
Silifke D 5 118
Siling Co ⊜ C 5 122
Silistra C 9 104
Silivri B 8 106
Siljan ⊜ B 7 66
Šilka B 7 124
Šilka ≃ B 7 124
Silkeborg B 2 68
Sillamäe C 13 66
Sillem Island I B 18 150
Silli C 4 200
Sillian F 9 100
Šilovo I 14 108
Silsbee G 1 170
Silsby Lake ⊜ D 11 158
Šilutė E 10 66
Silvacane, Abbaye de ▶[1] G 3 82
Silvan C 9 118
Silvassa E 2 122
Silver D 3 172
Silver City, N.C., U.S. B 5 168
Silver City, N.M., U.S. F 4 176
Silver Creek G 4 170
Silver Creek ≃ E 3 176
Silverdalen D 7 66
Silver Lake, Ks., U.S. F 7 174
Silver Lake, Mn., U.S. C 7 174
Silver Spring G 1 164
Silverthrone Mountain ∧[1] F 8 156
Silverton D 5 176
Silvi B 4 94
Silvies ≃ D 4 178
Sim I 22 108
Šimanovsk B 9 124
Simao G 5 130
Simav C 8 106
Simav ≃ C 8 106
Simbach am Inn D 10 100
Simba Sirori C 5 204
Simbo C 5 204
Simcoe G 3 160
Simcoe, Lake ⊜ F 4 160
Simen National Park ♦ E 4 202
Simeonovgrad E 9 104
Simeria C 7 104
Simeulue, Pulau I M 3 132
Simferopol' G 9 110
Simiri C 5 200
Simi Valley F 5 182
Simiyu ≃ C 5 204
Şimleu Silvaniei B 7 104
Šimnas E 11 66
Simojärvi ⊜ C 13 64
Simonhouse Lake ⊜ D 8 158
Simon's Town H 3 206
Simoom Sound F 8 156
Simpang N 6 132
Simpang-kiri ≃ M 3 132
Simplon D 2 206
Simplon Pass)(D 5 82
Simpson Desert ◆[2] H 3 142
Simpson Desert National Park ♦ H 4 142
Simpson Lake ⊜ B 31 154
Šimsk G 9 108
Simušir, ostrov I C 14 124
Sinabang M 3 132
Sinabung, Gunung ∧[1] M 3 132
Sina Dhaqa F 6 202
Sinai, Mount ∧ H 6 118
Sinaia C 8 104
Sinai Peninsula ⟩[1] H 5 118
Sinaloa □[3] E 6 184
Sinaloa ≃ D 6 184
Sinalunga F 7 92
Sinan E 9 130
Sināwin C 7 198
Sincelejo F 6 186
Sinch'ang-ŭp D 2 126
Sin-ch'on G 15 128
Sinclair C 2 206
Sinclair, Lake ⊜[1] C 3 168
Sind □[3] D 1 122
Sind ≃ D 3 122
Sindal A 3 68
Sindangbarang k 18 135b
Sindari D 2 122
Sindelfingen D 6 100
Sindi C 12 66
Sindri E 5 122
Sine ≃ C 1 200
Sinendé C 5 200
Sinezërki J 11 108
Sinfra D 3 200
Singako D 8 200
Singapore N 6 132
Singapore □[1] N 7 132
Singapore ≃ j 14 134a
Singapore, Strait of ʊ N 7 132
Singapore Strait ʊ j 15 134a
Singaraja I 22 135b
Sing Buri G 5 132
Singen E 5 100
Singida C 5 204
Singida □[3] D 5 204
Singkang F 8 134
Singkawang N 9 132
Singkep, Pulau I, Indon. F 4 134
Singkep, Pulau I, Indon. F 4 134
Singkil M 3 132
Singleton D 8 144
Sinj D 4 104
Sinjah E 3 202
Sinjai G 7 134
Sinjaja ≃ D 14 66
Sinjār D 9 118
Sinkan B 3 132
Sinkāt D 4 202
Sinnai I 10 94a
Sinnamary B 8 190
Sinnersdorf E 3 98
Sinnes C 3 66
Sinntal B 6 100
Sinnūris H 4 118
Sinop A 6 118
Sinop □[3] B 6 118
Sinp'o D 1 126
Sinsheim C 5 100

⌞ Waterfall ʊ Strait ⊂ Bay, Gulf ⊜ Lake ≡ Swamp ⊓ Ice Feature ᵻ Other Hydrographic Feature ◆ Submarine Feature □ Political Unit ▶ Cultural Institution ⊥ Historical Site ♦ Recreational Site ✈ Airport ■ Military Installation ◆ Miscellaneous

Symbols in the index entries represent the broad categories identified in the key at the right. Symbols with superior numbers (∧¹) identify subcategories (see complete key on page 242).

∧ Mountain   ∧ Mountains   ⋊ Pass   V Valley   ≃ Plain   ≻ Cape   I Island   II Islands   ⊥ Other Topographic Feature   ≃ River   ≋ Canal

Name	Map Ref. Page

⌐ Waterfall   ﹤ Strait   c Bay, Gulf   ☺ Lake   ﹦ Swamp   ⧊ Ice Feature   ﹥ Other Hydrographic Feature   ▸ Submarine Feature   □ Political Unit   ╪ Cultural Institution   ⊥ Historical Site   ♦ Recreational Site   ✈ Airport   ■ Military Installation   ▸ Miscellaneous

Name	Map Ref.	Page

Tinkisso — Tweed

Name	Map Ref.	Page
Tinkisso ≃	C 2	200
Tínos	D 6	106
Tinsukia	D 7	122
Tintaldra	E 7	144
Tintina	E 7	192
Tintioulen	C 3	200
Ti-n-Zaouâtene	A 5	200
Tioga	E 1	164
Tioga □[6], N.Y., U.S.	D 2	164
Tioga □[6], Pa., U.S.	E 1	164
Tioman, Pulau I	M 7	132
Tione di Trento	C 6	92
Tionesta	C 4	162
Tiou	C 4	200
Tipasa	H 7	88
Tipasa □[3]	H 7	88
Tipitapa	E 3	186
Tippecanoe ≃	B 5	170
Tipperary	D 3	75
Tipperary □[3]	D 4	75
Tipton	D 4	182
Tipton, Mount ∧	E 1	176
Tip Top Mountain ∧	G 16	158
Tīra	E 3	120
Tīrān, Maḍīq ꓤ	I 6	118
Tirana		
see Tiranë	B 3	106
Tiranë (Tirana)	B 3	106
Tirano	C 6	92
Tiraspol	B 10	104
Tirau	B 5	146
Tire	C 7	106
Tirebolu	B 8	118
Tiree I	D 2	74
Tires ◆[1]	E 2	198
Tirich Mīr ∧	B 2	122
Tiris Zemmour □[3]	E 3	198
Tírnavos	C 5	106
Tirol □[3]	C 3	102
Tirreno, Mare		
see Tyrrhenian Sea ⚲[2]	E 3	90
Tirschenreuth	C 9	100
Tirso ≃	F 2	90
Tirua	F 1	195
Tiruchchirāppalli	G 3	122
Tiruliai	E 11	66
Tirunelveli	H 3	122
Tirupati	G 3	122
Tiruppur	G 3	122
Tirūr	G 3	122
Tiruvannāmalai	G 3	122
Tirūvottiyūr	G 4	122
Tisdale	E 19	156
Tiskilwa	B 4	170
Tissa	D 7	200
Tīsta ≃	D 5	122
Tisza ≃	B 6	104
Tiszafüred	B 6	104
Tiszaújváros	B 6	104
Titaf	D 4	198
Titel	C 6	104
Titicaca, Lake ⊜	G 5	190
Titilāgarh	E 4	122
Titisee-Neustadt	E 5	100
Titovo Velenje	D 7	102
Tittling	D 10	100
Titu	C 8	104
Titusville, Fl., U.S.	E 4	168
Titusville, Pa., U.S.	C 4	162
Tivaouane	B 1	200
Tiverton	G 3	72
Tivoli	H 8	92
Tivoli ♠	C 5	68
Tizimín	G 15	184
Tizi-Ouzou	B 5	198
Tiznit	D 3	198
Tjukalinsk	I 29	108
Tjumen'	H 26	108
Tjumenskaja oblast' □[6]	E 30	108
Tjung ≃	C 14	114
Tjup	A 3	122
Tjuva-Guba	B 16	64
Tkvarčeli	H 12	110
Tlalnepantla	H 9	184
Tlaltenango de Sánchez Román	G 8	184
Tlapeng	B 4	206
Tlaquepaque	G 8	184
Tlaxcala □[3]	H 10	184
Tlaxcala de Xicohténcatl	H 10	184
Tlhakgameng	D 6	206
Tmīsān	D 7	198
Tnâot ≃	I 7	132
Toahayana	D 5	184
Toamasina	k 9	205a
Toamasina □[3]	k 9	205a
Toano	E 6	92
Toano Range ⋀	B 1	176
Toast	E 3	162
Toba, China	C 3	130
Toba, Japan	G 6	126
Toba, Danau ⊜	M 4	132
Tobacco Plains Indian Reserve ◆[4]	A 6	178
Tobago I	p 24	187f
Tobarra	F 3	88
Tobelo	E 9	134
Tobermorey	G 4	142
Tobermory	F 3	160
Tobin Lake ⊜	G 8	140
Tobin Lake ⊜[1]	E 7	158
Tobique ≃	g 13	163a
Tobol ≃	H 27	108
Tobol'sk	G 27	108
Tobor	C 1	200
Tobruk		
see Ţubruq	A 1	202
Tobyhanna	E 3	164
Tobyš ≃	D 19	108
Tocantínia	A 9	190
Tocantinópolis	A 9	190
Tocantins □[3]	F 9	190
Tocantins ≃	D 9	190
Tochigi □[3]	F 7	126
Töcksfors	C 5	66
Toco	D 6	192
Toconao	D 6	192
Tocopilla	D 5	192
Tocumwal	E 5	144
Tocuyo ≃	F 7	186
Todi	G 8	92
Todos Santos	F 4	184
Todos Santos, Bahía de ⊂	B 1	184
Tofield	E 15	156
Töfsingdalens Nationalpark ♠	A 5	66
Tofte	C 5	66
Togano, Monte ∧	C 4	92
Togbo	D 8	200
Togdheer □[3]	F 6	202
Togiak Bay ⊂	G 14	154
Togian, Kepulauan II	F 8	134
Togo □[1]	H 8	196
Togtoh	F 8	128
Togwotee Pass)(	D 8	178
Tohopekaliga, Lake ⊜	E 4	168
Tohta	E 18	108
Toijala	B 11	66
Toiyabe Range ⋀	B 6	182
Tok	E 23	154
Tokachi ≃	C 9	126
Tokachi-dake ∧[1]	C 9	126
Tōkamachi	F 7	126
Tokara-kaikyō ꓤ	I 2	126
Tokat	B 7	118
Tokat □[3]	B 7	118
Tokelau □[2]	D 10	136
Toklat ≃	D 20	154
Tokmak, Kyrg.	A 3	122
Tokmak, Ukr.	F 9	110
Tokomaru Bay	C 7	146
Tokoroa	C 5	146
Toktogul	A 2	122
Tokuno-shima I	K 2	126
Tokushima	G 5	126
Tokushima □[3]	H 5	126
Tokuyama	G 3	126
Tōkyō	G 7	126
Tōkyō □[3]	G 7	126
Tōkyō-daigaku-uchūkūkan-kenkyūsho ▶[3]	I 3	126
Tôlañaro	m 9	205a
Toledo, Braz.	F 4	194
Toledo, Oh., U.S.	C 2	162
Toledo, Or., U.S.	C 2	178
Toledo, Spain	E 6	86
Toledo □[6]	C 3	84
Toledo, Montes de ⋀	E 6	86
Toledo Bend Reservoir ⊜[1]	G 2	170
Tolentino	F 9	92
Tolga	C 5	198
Toliara	I 8	205a
Toliara □[3]	I 8	205a
Toljatti	J 18	108
Tolland □[6]	E 6	164
Tollarp	E 6	66
Tolmačovo	G 8	108
Tolmezzo	C 9	92
Tolmin	D 5	102
Tolna □[3]	D 10	102
Tolosa	A 2	88
Tolovana ≃	D 20	154
Tolstoj, mys ›	D 18	114
Toltén	F 1	195
Toltén ≃	F 1	195
Toluca, Nevado de ∧[1]	H 10	184
Toluca de Lerdo	H 9	184
Tolybaj	D 22	110
Tom' ≃	D 11	114
Tomah	C 3	166
Tomakomai	C 8	126
Tomanivi ∧	m 14	147c
Tomar	E 2	86
Tomashpil'	A 10	104
Tomasine ≃	B 10	166
Tomaszów Lubelski	C 12	96
Tomaszów Mazowiecki	C 10	96
Tombadonkéa	C 1	200
Tombador, Serra do ⋀[1]	F 7	190
Tombigbee ≃	F 5	170
Tombouctou (Timbuktu)	B 4	200
Tombouctou □[3]	E 4	198
Tombstone	G 3	176
Tombstone Mountain ∧	D 25	154
Tomé, Chile	E 1	195
Tome, Moz.	B 11	206
Tomelloso	E 1	88
Tomerong	E 8	144
Tomichi Creek ≃	C 5	176
Tomini	E 8	134
Tomini, Teluk ⊂	F 8	134
Tomislavgrad	D 4	104
Tommot	D 15	114
Tomo ≃	B 5	190
Tompkins	F 17	156
Tompkins □[6]	D 2	164
Tom Price, Mount ∧	H 4	140
Tomsk	D 11	114
Tomskaja oblast' □[6]	G 32	108
Toms River	G 4	164
Tona	C 7	88
Tonalá	I 13	184
Tonasket	A 4	178
Tonawanda	D 9	166
Tonbridge	F 7	72
Tondano	E 8	134
Tønder	D 1	68
Tondi	H 3	122
Tondidji	C 2	200
Tondi Kiwindi	C 5	200
Tone ≃	G 8	126
Tonekābon	D 14	118
Tonež	D 5	110
Tonga	F 3	202
Tonga □[1]	E 10	136
Tongaat	E 9	206
Tonga Islands II	E 10	136
Tong'an	F 13	130
Tongariro, Mount ∧[1]	C 5	146
Tongariro National Park ♠	C 5	146
Tongatapu I	F 10	136
Tongatapu Group II	F 10	136
Tonga Trench ✦[1]	H 14	58
Tongbai	B 11	130
Tongbei	C 16	128
Tongcheng	C 13	130
T'ongch'ŏn-ŭp	E 1	126
Tongchuan	I 7	128
Tongde	I 3	128
Tongeren	D 4	69
Tongguan, China	D 11	130
Tongguan, China	A 10	130
Tonghai	F 6	130
Tonghe	C 17	128
Tonghua	F 15	128
Tongjiang, China	C 19	128
Tongjiang, China	C 8	130
Tongjosŏn-man ⊂	G 16	128
Tongken ≃	C 16	128
Tongliang	D 7	130
Tongliao	E 13	128
Tongling	C 13	130
Tonglu	D 14	130
Tongnae	G 2	126
Tongnan	C 7	130
Tongobory	I 8	205a
Tongoy	B 2	195
Tongren	E 9	130
Tongsa Dzong	D 6	122
Tongtian ≃	C 7	122
Tongue	B 4	74
Tongue ≃	B 2	174
Tongwei	I 5	128
Tongxin	H 5	128
Tongxu	A 12	130
Tongyu	D 14	128
Tongzi	D 8	130
Tonica	B 4	170
Tonk	D 3	122
Tonkawa	B 5	172
Tonkin □[9]	D 7	132
Tonkin, Gulf of ⊂	I 8	130
Tonkwa	C 3	132
Tônlé Sab, Bœng ⊜	H 6	132
Tonle Sap		
see Tônlé Sab, Bœng ⊜	H 6	132
Tonneins	D 4	80
Tonnerre	E 10	78
Tonopah	B 6	182
Tonota	A 7	206
Tønsberg	C 5	66
Tonstad	C 3	66
Tonto Creek ≃	E 3	176
Tonto National Monument ♠	F 3	176
Tonya	B 8	118
Tooele	E 7	178
Toora-Hem	B 3	124
Toowoomba	A 8	144
Tooxin	E 7	202
Topeka	C 1	170
Topia	E 6	184
Topko, gora ∧	D 16	114
Topol'čany	B 10	102
Topoli	B 4	204
Topolog	C 10	104
Topolovgrad	D 9	104
Topozero, ozero ⊜	D 9	108
Top Springs	E 11	140
Tor	F 3	202
Torawitan, Tanjung ›	E 8	134
Torbalı	C 7	106
Torbat-e Ḩeydarīyeh	C 8	116
Torbat-e Jām	C 9	116
Torbay		
see Torquay	G 3	72
Torch ≃	E 7	158
Tordera	C 7	88
Tordesillas	C 6	86
Töreboda	C 7	66
Torekov	D 6	66
Torelló	B 7	88
Torez	E 11	110
Torfaen □[6]	F 3	72
Torgau	E 9	98
Torgelow	C 11	98
Torhamn	D 7	66
Torhout	C 2	69
Torino (Turin)	D 3	92
Torino □[6]	D 3	92
Tori-shima I	I 8	126
Torit	B 5	204
Tormes ≃	C 4	86
Tormosin	E 13	110
Torneälven (Tornionjoki) ≃	C 11	64
Tornesch	C 6	98
Torneträsk ⊜	B 9	64
Tornillo	G 5	176
Tornionjoki (Torneälven) ≃	C 11	64
Toro	C 5	86
Torodi	C 5	200
Törökszentmiklós	B 6	104
Toronto, On., Can.	G 4	160
Toronto, S.D., U.S.	C 6	174
Toropec	H 9	108
Tororo	G 3	202
Torpa ⊥	D 6	66
Torpo	B 4	66
Torquay (Torbay)	G 3	72
Torrance	G 5	182
Torrão	F 2	86
Torre Annunziata	D 4	94
Torreblanca	D 5	88
Torre del Campo	G 7	86
Torre del Greco	D 4	94
Torredonjimeno	G 6	86
Torrejoncillo	E 4	86
Torrejón de Ardoz	D 7	86
Torrelavega	A 6	86
Torremaggiore	E 5	90
Torremolinos	H 6	86
Torrens, Lake ⊜	C 1	144
Torrent, Arg.	A 9	195
Torrent (Torrente), Spain	E 4	88
Torrente		
see Torrent	E 4	88
Torreón	E 8	184
Torre Pellice	F 5	82
Torreperojil	F 7	86
Torres Martinez Indian Reservation ◆[4]	F 5	180
Torres Strait ꓤ	A 9	138
Torres Vedras	E 1	86
Torrevella	G 4	88
Torrijos	E 6	86
Torrington, Ct., U.S.	E 5	164
Torrington, Wy., U.S.	D 2	174
Torroella de Montgrí	F 7	80
Torsås	D 7	66
Torsburgen ⊥	D 9	66
Torshälla	C 8	66
Tórshavn	p 26	64b
Tortolì	F 2	90
Tortona	E 4	92
Tortosa	D 5	88
Tortue, Île de la I	C 6	186
Toruń	B 10	96
Toruń □[3]	B 10	96
Torup	D 6	66
Toržok	H 11	108
Torzym	B 8	96
Tosa	H 4	126
Tosa-shimizu	H 4	126
Toscana □[3]	F 7	92
Toscolano	D 6	92
Toshkent		
see Tashkent	A 1	122
Tosi	A 5	140
Tosno	G 9	108
Tosontsengel	B 2	128
Tostado	A 7	195
Tõstamaa	C 11	66
Tosu	H 3	126
Tosya	B 6	118
Totana	G 3	88
Tôtes	C 7	78
Tot'ma	F 15	108
Totnes	G 3	72
Tottenham	A 4	162
Totton	G 5	72
Tottori	G 5	126
Tottori □[3]	G 4	126
Touba	D 3	200
Toubkal, Jebel ∧	C 3	198
Toubori	C 7	200
Touboro	D 7	200
Touchwood Lake ⊜	D 11	158
Toudao ≃	E 16	128
Tougan	C 4	200
Touggourt	C 6	198
Tougouri	C 4	200
Tougué	C 2	200
Toul	B 3	82
Toulépleu	D 3	200
Touliu	G 15	130
Toulnustouc ≃	C 10	160
Toulon	G 3	82
Toulouse	E 5	80
Toumodi	D 3	200
Tounfafi	B 6	200
Toungoo	E 3	132
Touraine □[9]	E 7	78
Tourane		
see Da Nang	F 9	132
Tourcoing	B 9	78
Tournai	D 2	69
Tournon	E 2	82
Tournus	D 2	82
Tours	E 7	78
Toussidé, Pic ∧[1]	A 8	200
Toutle ≃	B 2	178
Touws ≃	G 4	206
Touwsrivier	G 4	206
Töv □[3]	C 6	128
Tovarkovskij	J 13	108
Tovste	A 8	104
Tovuz	I 14	110
Towada	D 8	126
Towada-Hachimantai-kokuritsu-kōen ♠	D 8	126
Towada-ko ⊜	D 8	126
Towanda, Ks., U.S.	B 5	172
Towanda, Pa., U.S.	E 2	164
Towcester	E 6	72
Tower City	B 6	174
Towerhill Creek ≃	F 7	142
Towner	G 8	158
Townsend	B 8	178
Townshend Island I	G 10	142
Townsville	E 8	142
Towson	G 2	164
Towuti, Danau ⊜	F 8	134
Toxkan ≃	A 3	122
Toyah Creek ≃	E 2	172
Toyama	F 6	126
Toyama □[3]	F 6	126
Toyama-wan ⊂	F 6	126
Toyohashi	G 6	126
Toyokawa	G 6	126
Toyooka	G 5	126
Toyota	G 6	126
Tozeur	C 6	198
Tpig	I 15	110
Traben-Trarbach	C 3	100
Trabzon	B 8	118
Trabzon □[3]	B 8	118
Tracy, Ca., U.S.	C 2	182
Tracy, Mn., U.S.	C 7	174
Tracy, P.Q., Can.	F 7	160
Tradate	D 4	92
Trade Lake ⊜	D 20	156
Trælleborg ⊥	C 4	68
Trafalgar	G 6	144
Trafalgar, Cabo ›	H 4	86
Trafford □[6]	D 4	72
Traíd	D 3	88
Traiguén	F 1	195
Trail	G 13	156
Trail of Tears State Park ♠	D 4	170
Traiskirchen	C 8	102
Trakai	E 12	66
Tralee (Trá Lí)	D 2	75
Trá Lí		
see Tralee	D 2	75
Trammel	A 3	168
Tramperos Creek (Punta de Agua Creek) ≃	B 2	172
Tramping Lake ⊜	E 17	156
Trăn	D 7	104
Tranås	C 7	66
Trancoso	D 3	86
Tranemo	D 6	66
Trang	K 4	132
Trangan, Pulau I	G 10	134
Trani	C 6	94
Tranqueras	B 9	195
Transantarctic Mountains ⋀	D 25	208
Transylvania □[9]	B 7	104
Trapalcó, Salinas de ≡	F 4	195
Trapani	F 2	94
Trapani □[6]	G 2	94
Trap Pond State Park ♠	H 3	164
Traralgon	G 6	144
Trarza □[3]	F 1	198
Trârza ◆[1]	F 1	198
Trasacco	E 4	90
Trasimeno, Lago ⊜	F 7	92
Träslövsläge	D 6	66
Trás-os-Montes □[9]	C 3	86
Trasvase Tajo Segura, Canal de ≡	F 3	88
Trat	H 6	132
Tratzberg, Schloss ⊥	C 3	102
Traun	B 6	102
Traunreut	B 8	92
Traunstein	E 9	100
Travellers Lake ⊜	D 4	144
Traverse City	C 6	166
Tra Vinh	J 8	132
Travnik	C 4	104
Trbovlje	D 7	102
Třebechovice pod Orebem	C 9	96
Trébevic, Nacionalni Park ♠	C 5	104
Třebíč	A 7	102
Trebisacce	E 6	94
Trebišov	D 11	96
Třeboň	C 11	100
Trebujena	H 4	86
Trecate	E 6	82
Tredici Archi, Ponte ◆[5]	C 4	94
Treinta y Tres	C 10	195
Trélazé	A 3	80
Trelew	H 6	192
Trelleborg	E 6	66
Tremblant, Mont ∧	E 6	160
Tremont	F 2	164
Tremp	B 5	88
Trempealeau	C 3	166
Trenčín	B 10	102
Trenggalek	I 20	135b
Trenque Lauquen	D 6	195
Trent		
see Trento	C 7	92
Trent ≃, Eng., U.K.	D 6	72
Trent ≃, On., Can.	F 5	160
Trente et Un Milles, Lac des ⊜	E 5	160
Trentino-Alto Adige □[3]	C 7	92
Trento	C 7	92
Trento □[6]	D 7	92
Trentola-Ducenta	D 3	94
Trenton, Ky., U.S.	D 5	170
Trenton, N.C., U.S.	B 6	168
Trenton, N.J., U.S.	F 4	164
Trenton, On., Can.	F 5	160
Trenton, Tn., U.S.	E 4	170
Trepuzzi	D 8	94
Tres Árboles	C 9	195
Tres Arroyos	F 7	195
Tres Esquinas	C 3	190
Três Lagoas	D 4	194
Três Marias	C 8	194
Tres Marías, Islas II	G 6	184
Três Marias, Represa de ⊜[1]	C 8	194
Três Passos	G 3	194
Tres Picos, Cerro ∧	F 7	195
Três Pontas	D 8	194
Tres Puntas, Cabo ›	I 6	192
Três Rios	E 9	194
Tres Zapotes ⊥	H 12	184
Tretten	B 5	66
Treuchtlingen	D 7	100
Treuenbrietzen	D 9	98
Treviglio	D 5	92
Treviso	D 8	92
Treviso □[6]	D 8	92
Trevorton	C 5	162
Trezzo sull'Adda	E 7	82
Trhové Sviny	D 11	100
Triánda	D 8	106
Triberg	D 5	100
Tribune	F 4	174
Tricarico	E 5	90
Tricase	E 8	94
Tricesimo	C 9	92
Trichūr	G 3	122
Trieben	C 6	102
Trier	C 3	100
Trier □[6]	C 3	100
Triest		
see Trieste	D 9	92
Trieste	D 9	92
Trieste □[6]	D 9	92
Trieste, Gulf of ⊂	E 5	102
Triggiano	C 6	94
Triglav ∧	D 5	102
Triglavski narodni park ♠	D 5	102
Trigueros	G 4	86
Tríkala	C 4	106
Trikhonís, Límni ⊜	C 4	106
Tríkomon	E 5	118
Trikora, Puncak ∧	F 11	134
Trim	C 5	75
Trincheras	B 4	184
Trincomalee	H 4	122
Trindade	B 6	194
Trindade I	G 12	188
Trinidad, Bol.	F 6	190
Trinidad, Co., U.S.	G 2	174
Trinidad, Ur.	C 9	195
Trinidad I	q 24	187f
Trinidad and Tobago □[1]	F 9	186
Trinitapoli	C 5	94
Trinity	E 6	172
Trinity ≃, Ca., U.S.	E 2	178
Trinity ≃, Tx., U.S.	E 6	172
Trinity, West Fork ≃	D 5	172
Trinity Bay ⊂, Nf., Can.	D 17	160
Trinity Bay ⊂, Tx., U.S.	H 1	170
Trinity Mountains ⋀	E 2	178
Trinity Site ⊥	F 5	176
Trino	D 4	92
Trion	E 6	170
Tripa ≃	L 3	132
Tripoli		
see Ţarābulus	C 7	198
Trípolis	D 5	106
Tripolis ⊥	D 8	106
Tripolitania □[9]	C 7	198
Tripura □[3]	E 6	122
Tristan da Cunha Group II	I 10	60
Trivandrum	H 3	122
Trivento	C 4	94
Trnava	B 9	102
Troia	C 5	94
Troick	I 24	108
Troickij	D 13	110
Troickoe	G 23	108
Troicko-Pečorsk	E 22	108
Troïlus, Lac ⊜	C 6	160
Troina	G 4	94
Troisdorf	F 4	98
Trois Fourches, Cap des ›	B 4	198
Trois-Pistoles	D 9	160
Trois-Rivières	E 7	160
Trojan	D 8	104
Trollhättan	C 6	66
Troms □[3]	B 9	64
Tromsø	B 9	64
Trona	E 6	182
Tronador, Monte ∧	H 5	192
Trondheim	E 4	64
Trondheimsfjorden ⊂	E 5	64
Troodos	E 5	118
Trooilapspan	E 4	206
Troon	B 2	72
Trophy Mountain ∧[1]	F 12	156
Tropical, Costa ≐[2]	H 1	88
Troškūnai	E 12	66
Trosna	J 11	108
Trossingen	D 5	100
Trostyanets', Ukr.	A 10	104
Trostyanets', Ukr.	D 9	110
Trout	G 2	170
Trout ≃	A 12	156
Trout Creek	B 6	178
Trout Lake	A 11	156
Trout Lake ⊜, N.T., Can.	A 11	156
Trout Lake ⊜, On., Can.	F 12	158
Trouville-sur-Mer	C 6	78
Trowbridge	F 4	72
Troy, Al., U.S.	G 5	170
Troy, Ks., U.S.	C 1	170
Troy, Mt., U.S.	A 5	178
Troy, N.H., U.S.	D 6	164
Troy, N.Y., U.S.	D 5	164
Troy, Oh., U.S.	C 1	162
Troy, Pa., U.S.	E 2	164
Troy		
see Truva ⊥	C 7	106
Troyes	D 10	78
Troyits'ke	B 11	104
Trstená	D 10	96
Truax	A 2	174
Trubč'evsk	J 10	108
Truckee ≃	A 4	182
Trudfront	G 15	110
Trujillo, Hond.	E 3	186
Trujillo, Peru	E 3	190
Trujillo, Spain	E 5	86
Trujillo, Ven.	B 4	190
Trujillo □[3]	F 7	186
Trujillo Alto	j 15	187b
Truman	D 7	174
Trumansburg	D 2	164
Trumbull	E 5	164
Trumbull, Mount ∧	D 2	176
Truro, Austl.	E 2	144
Truro, Eng., U.K.	G 1	72
Truro, N.S., Can.	F 12	160
Truskavets'	E 3	110
Truth or Consequences	F 5	176
Trutnov	C 8	96
Truva (Troy) (Ilium) ⊥	C 7	106
Tryon	B 3	168
Trysilelva (Klarälven) ≃	B 6	66
Trzcianka	B 9	96
Trzciel	B 8	96
Trzebież	B 8	96
Trzebnica	C 9	96
Tržič	D 6	102
Tsagaandörvölj	D 7	128
Tsaidam Basin ≡[1]	B 6	122
Tsangano	F 5	204
Tsaratanana	k 9	205a
Tsau	G 3	204
Tsavo	H 4	202
Tsavo East National Park ♠	H 4	202
Tsavo West National Park ♠	H 4	202
Tsawisis	D 3	206
Tsekanyani	F 4	204
Tselinograd		
see Akmola	D 10	114
Tseoge	C 5	206
Tsesane	B 6	206
Tsetserleg	C 3	128
Tsévié	D 5	200
Tshabong	D 5	206
Tshane	C 4	206
Tshangalele, Lac ⊜[1]	E 4	204
Tshela	C 1	204
Tshesebe	A 7	206
Tshikapa	D 3	204
Tshikapa		
see Chicapa ≃	D 3	204
Tshikuwi	B 8	206
Tshilenge	D 3	204
Tshimbulu	D 3	204
Tshoa	D 1	204
Tsholotsho	F 4	204
Tshuapa ≃	C 3	204
Tshukudu	B 5	206
Tshumbe (Chiumbe) ≃	E 3	204
Tsiafajavona ∧[1]	k 9	205a
Tsianaloka	k 8	205a
Tsimpsean Indian Reserve ◆[4]	D 6	156
Tsingoni	o 19	207d
Tsiombe	m 9	205a
Tsiribihina ≃	k 8	205a
Tsitsihar		
see Qiqihar	C 15	128
Tsitsikamma National Park ♠	H 5	206
Tsolo	F 8	206
Tsu	G 6	126
Tsubame	F 7	126
Tsuchiura	F 8	126
Tsugaru-kaikyō ꓤ	D 8	126
Tsu Lake ⊜	A 16	156
Tsumeb	F 2	204
Tsumkwe	F 3	204
Tsuruga	G 6	126
Tsuruoka	E 7	126
Tsushima II	G 2	126
Tsuyama	G 5	126
Tswatago	C 8	206
Tuakau	B 5	146
Tual	G 10	134
Tuamarina	D 4	146
Tuamotu, Îles II	E 13	136
Tuapse	G 11	110
Tuas	j 13	134a
Tuatapere	G 1	146
Tuban	k 21	135b
Tubarão	E 10	192
Ṭūbās	E 4	120
Tübingen	D 6	100
Tübingen □[6]	D 6	100
Ţubruq (Tobruk)	A 1	202
Tubuai I	F 13	136
Tuchów	D 11	96
Tuckahoe State Park ♠	H 3	164
Tuckerman	E 3	170
Tucson	F 3	176
Tucumán □[3]	E 6	192
Tucumcari	C 2	172
Tucupita	F 9	186
Tucuruí	D 9	190
Tucuruí, Represa de ⊜[1]	D 9	190
Tuczna	C 12	96
Tudela	B 3	88
Tudela de Duero	C 6	86
Tudmur	E 8	118
Tugela	E 9	206
Tugela ≃	E 9	206
Tugela Falls ⌊	E 8	206
Tug Fork ≃	E 2	162
Tuggerah Lake ⊂	D 8	144
Tuguegarao City	B 8	134
Tugulym	H 26	108
Tugur	B 11	124
Tui	B 2	86
Tujmazy	I 20	108
Tukangbesi, Kepulauan II	G 8	134
Tūkrah	C 9	198
Tukums	D 11	66
Tukuyu	D 5	204
Tula	I 12	108
Tulaghi	A 13	138
Tulancingo	G 10	184
Tulangbawang ≃	F 5	134
Tulare	D 4	182
Tulare □[6]	D 5	182
Tulare Lake Bed ◆[1]	D 4	182
Tularosa Valley ≡[1]	F 5	176
Tulcán	C 3	190
Tulcea	C 10	104
Tulcea □[3]	C 10	104
Tul'chyn	A 10	104
Tulemalu Lake ⊜	D 13	150
Tule River Indian Reservation ◆[4]	D 5	182
Tuli	A 8	206
Tulik Volcano ∧[1]	J 10	154
Tulita	D 32	154
Ṭūlkarm	E 4	120
Tullahoma	E 5	170
Tullamore	C 4	75
Tulle	C 5	80
Tullins	E 3	82
Tulln	B 8	102
Tullow	D 5	75
Tully	D 7	142
Tulsa	B 6	172
Tulsequah	B 4	156
Tul'skaja oblast' □[6]	J 12	108
Tuluá	C 3	190
Tulum	G 16	184
Tulum ⊥	G 16	184
Tulun	B 4	124
Tulungagung	I 20	135b
Tuma ≃	E 3	186
Tumacacori National Monument ♠	G 3	176
Tumaco	C 3	190
Tuman-gang (Tumen) ≃	C 3	126
Tumanovo	I 11	108
Tumba	C 8	66
Tumbes	D 2	190
Tumblong	E 7	144
Tumen	E 17	128
Tumen (Tuman-gang) ≃	C 3	126
Tumenzi	H 4	128
Tumeremo	G 9	186
Tumkūr	G 3	122
Tumoteqi	F 8	128
Tumuc-Humac Mountains ⋀	C 8	190
Tumut	E 7	144
Tumwater	B 2	178
Tunago Lake ⊜	C 31	154
Tunapuna	q 23	187f
Tunbridge Wells		
see Royal Tunbridge Wells	F 7	72
Tunceli	C 8	118
Tunceli □[3]	C 8	118
Tunchang	I 9	130
Tunduru	E 6	204
Tundža ≃	D 8	104
Tunga ≃	G 3	122
Tungabhadra ≃	F 3	122
Tungaru	E 3	202
Tungshih	F 15	130
Tuni	F 4	122
Tunica	E 3	170
Tunis	B 6	198
Tunis, Golfe de ⊂	B 7	198
Tunisia □[1]	E 8	196
Tunja	B 4	190
Tunkhannock	E 2	164
Tunliu	H 9	128
Tunnelton	D 4	162
Tunnsjøen ⊜	D 6	64
Tununak	F 12	154
Tunuyán	C 3	195
Tunuyán ≃	F 6	192
Tunxi	D 14	130
Tuo ≃	D 7	130
Tuokusidawan Ling ∧	B 5	122
Tuolumne □[6]	B 4	182
Tuolumne ≃	C 3	182
Tupã	D 5	194
Tupaciguara	C 6	194
Tupanciretã	A 10	195
Tupelo	E 4	170
Tupelo National Battlefield ♠	E 4	170
Tupiza	H 5	190
Tupper	D 11	156
Tupungato, Cerro ∧	F 6	192
Tuquan	D 13	128
Tura ≃	D 9	114
Turakina	D 5	146
Turbat	E 9	116
Turbo	F 5	186
Turda	B 7	104
Turek	B 10	96
Turfan Depression ≐[7]	A 5	122
Turgaj □[3]	J 27	108
Turgaj (Turgay) ≃	A 9	116
Turgajskoe plato ⋀[1]	D 23	110
Turgojak	B 22	110
Turgutlu	C 7	106
Turhal	B 7	118
Türi, Est.	C 12	66
Turi, Italy	D 7	94
Túria ≃	E 4	88
Turin		
see Torino	D 3	92
Turinsk	G 25	108
Turinskaja Sloboda	H 26	108
Turka	A 7	104
Turkey □[1]	H 14	62
Turkey Run State Park ♠	C 5	170
Turki	C 13	110
Türkmenbashy (Krasnovodsk)	B 15	118
Turkmenistan □[1]	C 8	116
Turkmenskij zaliv ⊂	J 18	110
Turks and Caicos Islands □[2]	C 7	186
Turks Island Passage ꓤ	C 7	186
Turks Islands II	C 7	186
Turku (Åbo)	B 11	66
Turku ja Pori □[3]	B 11	66
Turkwel ≃	G 4	202
Turlock	C 3	182
Turnagain ≃	B 8	156
Turnagain Arm ⊂	F 20	154
Turneffe Islands II	I 16	184
Turner	G 17	156
Turnhout	C 3	69
Türnitz	C 7	102
Turnor Lake ⊜	C 4	158
Turnov	B 12	100
Turnu Măgurele	D 8	104
Turon	G 5	174
Turquino, Pico ∧	D 5	186
Turritano ◆[1]	I 4	92
Tursunzade	B 1	122
Turtle Lake	B 4	174
Turtle Lake ⊜	E 17	156
Turtle Mountain Indian Reservation ◆[4]	A 4	174
Turtle Mountain Provincial Park ♠	A 4	174
Turuhan ≃	C 11	114
Turvo ≃	D 6	194
Turzovka	A 10	102
Tuscaloosa	F 5	170
Tuscania	G 7	92
Tuskegee	F 6	170
Tuszyn	C 10	96
Tutaev	H 13	108
Tuticorin	H 3	122
Tutin	D 6	104
Tutrakan	C 9	104
Tuttle	H 9	158
Tuttle Creek Lake ⊜[1]	F 6	174
Tuttlingen	E 5	100
Tutuila I	E 10	136
Tutupaca, Volcán ∧[1]	G 4	190
Tutzing	C 3	102
Tuul ≃	C 5	128
Tuusniemi	E 14	64
Tuva □[3]	B 2	124
Tuvalu □[1]	D 9	136
Tuwayq, Jabal ⋀	C 6	202
Tuxpan	F 7	184
Tuxpan de Rodríguez Cano	G 11	184
Tuxtepec	H 11	184
Tuxtla Gutiérrez	I 13	184
Tüy ≃, Mong.	D 3	128
Tuy ≃, Ven.	F 8	186
Tuyen Hoa	F 8	132
Tuyen Quang	D 7	132
Tuy Hoa	H 9	132
Tūysarkān	E 13	118
Tuz	E 11	118
Tuz Gölü ⊜	C 5	118
Tuzigoot National Monument ♠	E 2	176
Tuzla	C 5	104
Tuzluca	B 10	118
Tvărdica	D 8	104
Tvedestrand	C 4	66
Tver'	H 11	108
Tverskaja oblast' □[6]	H 11	108
Twardogóra	C 9	96
Tweed	B 1	164

⌊ Waterfall ꓤ Strait ⊂ Bay, Gulf ⊜ Lake ≡ Swamp ⍓ Ice Feature ⚲ Other Hydrographic Feature ✦ Submarine Feature □ Political Unit ▶ Cultural Institution ⊥ Historical Site ♠ Recreational Site ⊠ Airport ■ Military Installation ◆ Miscellaneous

Name | Map Ref. | Page

Symbols in the index entries represent the broad categories identified in the key at the right. Symbols with superior numbers (⋀¹) identify subcategories (see complete key on page 242).

⋀ Mountain ⋀ Mountains ⋃ Pass ⋁ Valley ⊡ Plain ⊁ Cape I Island II Islands ⊥ Other Topographic Feature ≃ River ⋈ Canal

284

∟ Waterfall ⋃ Strait c Bay, Gulf ⊘ Lake ≃ Swamp ≋ Ice Feature ≂ Other Hydrographic Feature ✦ Submarine Feature □ Political Unit ⊙ Cultural Institution ⊥ Historical Site ◆ Recreational Site ⊠ Airport ■ Military Installation ● Miscellaneous

Name	Map Ref.	Page

Symbols in the index entries represent the broad categories identified in the key at the right. Symbols with superior numbers (↗1) identify subcategories (see complete key on page 242).

∧ Mountain ↗ Mountains)(Pass V Valley ≡ Plain > Cape I Island II Islands ⊥ Other Topographic Feature ≈ River ≡ Canal

Xiaogan — Żywiec

Name	Map Ref.	Page
Xiaogan	C 11	130
Xiao Hinggan Ling ⩚	B 9	124
Xiaojin	C 6	130
Xiaolongtan	C 6	132
Xiaotanghe	C 1	126
Xiaoxian	A 13	130
Xiapu	E 15	130
Xiaxian	I 8	128
Xiaxiangcheng	D 4	130
Xichang	E 6	130
Xichong	C 7	130
Xifeng	E 8	130
Xigazê	D 5	122
Xihan ≃	B 7	130
Xihe	A 7	130
Xiheying	G 10	128
Xihua	B 12	130
Xiji	H 5	128
Xiliao ≃	D 13	128
Xilókastron	C 5	106
Ximakou	C 11	130
Ximalin	F 10	128
Xin ≃	D 13	130
Xin Barag Youqi	B 11	128
Xin Barag Zuoqi	B 11	128
Xincai	B 12	130
Xinchang	D 15	130
Xincheng	G 10	128
Xinfeng	F 12	130
Xing'an	F 10	130
Xingcheng	F 13	128
Xingguo	E 12	130
Xinghe	F 9	128
Xinghua	B 14	130
Xinglong	I 5	128
Xingren	F 7	130
Xingtai	H 10	128
Xingtang	G 10	128
Xingu ≃	D 8	190
Xingxian	G 8	128
Xingyi	F 7	130
Xinhua	E 10	130
Xining	H 3	128
Xinji	H 10	128
Xinjiang	I 8	128
Xinjiang □[3]	A 5	122
Xinjin, China	G 13	128
Xinjin, China	C 6	130
Xinkai ≃	E 14	128
Xinli	B 1	126
Xinlitun	E 14	128
Xinmin	E 14	128
Xinning	A 10	132
Xinping	F 5	130
Xintian	F 11	130
Xinwen	I 11	128
Xinxian, China	G 9	128
Xinxian, China	C 12	130
Xinxiang	I 9	128
Xinyang	B 12	130
Xinye	B 11	130
Xinyi	A 14	130
Xinyu	E 12	130
Xinzha	G 5	130
Xiongjiachang	A 7	132
Xiongyuecheng	F 13	128
Xiping, China	D 14	130
Xiping, China	B 12	130
Xique-Xique	F 10	190
Xırdalan	I 16	110
Xisha Qundao see Paracel Islands II	B 6	134
Xishui	C 12	130
Xiu ≃	D 12	130
Xi Ujimqin Qi	D 11	128
Xiushui	D 12	130
Xiuyan	F 14	128
Xiva	E 4	88
Xixian	B 12	130
Xixiang	B 8	130
Xiyang	H 9	128
Xizang (Tibet) □[3]	C 5	122
Xizi	F 12	128
Xochicalco ⊥	H 10	184
Xu ≃	E 13	130
Xuancheng	C 14	130
Xuan'en	D 9	130
Xuanhan	C 8	130
Xuanhua	F 10	128
Xuanwei	E 7	130
Xuchang	A 11	130
Xuddur	G 5	202
Xun ≃, China	B 16	128
Xun ≃, China	G 10	130
Xunhua	I 4	128
Xunle	F 9	130
Xunwu	F 12	130
Xupu	E 10	130
Xúquer see Júcar ≃	E 4	88
Xuwen	H 10	130
Xuyi	B 14	130
Xuyong	D 7	130
Xuzhou	A 13	130

Y

Name	Map Ref.	Page
Yaan	D 6	130
Ya'bad	E 4	120
Yabluniv	A 8	104
Yabuli	D 17	128
Yachi ≃	E 8	130
Yacuiba	H 6	190
Yādgīr	F 3	122
Yadkin ≃	B 4	168
Yadong	D 5	122
Yafran	C 7	198
Yageg	G 5	202
Yagoua	C 7	200
Yagradagzê Shan ∧	B 6	122
Yaguarón (Jaguarão) ≃	C 11	195
Yahyalı	C 6	118
Yaita	F 7	126
Yaizu	G 7	126
Yajiang	C 5	130
Yakeshi	B 13	128
Yakima	B 3	178
Yakima ≃	B 3	178
Yakima Indian Reservation ➔[4]	B 3	178
Yako	C 4	200
Yakoma	B 3	204
Yakumo	C 8	126
Yaku-shima I	I 3	126
Yakutat Bay ⊂	G 24	154
Yala, Ghana	C 4	200
Yala, Thai.	K 5	132
Yalahau, Laguna de ⊂	G 16	184
Yalata Aboriginal Land ➔[4]	L 11	140
Yale	B 2	162
Yalgoo	K 4	140
Yali	F 8	130
Yalinga	D 9	200
Yallingup Caves ♦	M 3	140
Yalobusha ≃	F 3	170
Yaloká	D 8	200
Yalong ≃	E 5	130
Yalova	B 8	106
Yalpuh, ozero ⊜	C 10	104
Yalta	G 9	110
Yalu	B 13	128
Yalu (Amnok-kang) ≃, Asia	D 1	126
Yalu ≃, China	C 14	128
Yalvaç	C 9	106
Yamagata	E 8	126
Yamagata □[3]	E 8	126
Yamaguchi	G 3	126
Yamaguchi □[3]	G 3	126
Yamal Peninsula ≻[1]	B 10	114
Yamanashi □[3]	G 7	126
Yamasaki	G 5	126
Yambéring	C 2	200
Yambio	G 2	202
Yamdena, Pulau I	G 10	134
Yame	H 3	126
Yamenying	E 14	128
Yamethin	D 3	132
Yamma Yamma, Lake ⊜	I 5	142
Yamoussoukro	D 3	200
Yampa ≃	B 4	176
Yampil', Ukr.	A 10	104
Yampil', Ukr.	D 8	110
Yamuna ≃	D 4	122
Yamzho Yumco ⊜	D 6	122
Yan ≃	H 7	128
Yan'an	H 7	128
Yanbian	A 5	132
Yanbu' al-Bahr	C 4	202
Yanceyville	A 5	168
Yanchang	H 8	128
Yancheng	B 15	130
Yanchep National Park ♦	L 3	140
Yanchi	H 6	128
Yanco	E 6	144
Yandama Creek ≃	B 3	144
Yandeyarra Aboriginal Reserve ➔[4]	G 5	140
Yandoon	F 2	132
Yangambi	B 3	204
Yangcheng	I 9	128
Yangchun	G 10	130
Yanggang-do □[3]	F 16	128
Yanggao	F 9	128
Yangiyul'	A 1	122
Yangjiang	H 10	130
Yangliuqing	G 11	128
Yangon (Rangoon)	F 2	132
Yangon □[3]	F 3	132
Yangonde	C 3	204
Yangpingguan	B 7	130
Yangquan	H 9	128
Yangshan	F 11	130
Yangshuo	F 10	130
Yangtze (Chang) ≃	B 14	130
Yangxian	B 8	130
Yangxin	D 12	130
Yangyuan	F 10	128
Yangzhou	B 14	130
Yanhe	D 9	130
Yanji, China	E 17	128
Yanji, China	E 17	128
Yankton	D 6	174
Yankton Indian Reservation ➔[4]	D 5	174
Yanqi	A 5	122
Yanqing	F 10	128
Yanrey	H 3	140
Yanshou	D 17	128
Yantabulla	B 5	144
Yantai	H 13	128
Yanting	C 7	130
Yanu	A 10	138
Yanzhou	I 11	128
Yao	C 8	200
Yaojie	H 4	128
Yaoundé	E 7	200
Yaoxian	A 9	130
Yap I	D 11	134
Yapacaní	G 6	190
Yapen, Pulau I	F 11	134
Yaqui ≃	C 5	184
Yaracuy □[3]	F 7	186
Yarbasan	C 8	106
Yardımcı Burnu ≻	D 9	106
Yardville	F 4	164
Yarí ≃	C 4	190
Yarīm	E 5	202
Yarkand see Shache	B 3	122
Yarkant see Shache	B 3	122
Yarkant ≃	A 4	122
Yarloop	M 3	140
Yarlung see Brahmaputra ≃	E 6	122
Yarmouth see Great Yarmouth, Eng., U.K.	E 8	72
Yarmouth, Me., U.S.	B 8	162
Yarmouth, N.S., Can.	G 10	160
Yarmūk, Nahr al- (HaYarmuk) ≃	D 5	120
Yarraman	I 11	142
Yarrawonga	F 5	144
Yarra Yarra Lakes ⊜	K 3	140
Yarumal	B 3	190
Yasa-Lokwa	D 2	204
Yashi	C 6	200
Yasinya	A 8	104
Yask	C 7	200
Yasothon	G 6	132
Yass	E 7	144
Yāsūj	G 14	118
Yatağan	D 8	106
Yates □[6]	D 1	164
Yathkyed Lake ⊜	D 13	150
Yating	F 8	130
Yatsushiro	H 3	126
Yauco	j 15	187b
Yautepec	H 10	184
Yavarí (Javari) ≃	D 4	190
Yavatmāl	E 3	122
Yavne	F 3	120
Yavoriv	D 12	96
Yaw ≃	E 6	122
Yawatahama	H 4	126
Yaxchilan ⊥	I 14	184
Yazd	G 16	118
Yazd □[3]	F 16	118
Yazoo ≃	F 3	170
Yazoo City	F 3	170
Ybbs an der Donau	B 6	102
Yding Skovhøj ∧[2]	C 2	68
Ye	G 3	132
Yebawgyi	E 2	132
Yebyu	G 4	132
Yecheng	B 3	122
Yech'ŏn	F 2	126
Yecla	F 3	88
Yedashe	E 3	132
Yedi Göller Milli Parkı ♦	B 9	106
Yeghegnadzor, Arm.	J 14	110
Yeghegnadzor, Arm.	C 11	118
Yegros	G 2	194
Yehud	E 3	120
Yei	G 3	202
Yei ≃	F 3	202
Yeji, China	C 12	130
Yeji, Ghana	D 4	200
Yela Island I	B 11	138
Yelarbon	B 8	144
Yélimané	B 2	200
Yellowdine	L 5	140
Yellowhead Pass ⋈	E 12	156
Yellowknife	D 10	150
Yellow River (Huang He) ⊜	D 17	116
Yellow Sea ⫪[2]	E 8	124
Yellowstone ≃	B 7	152
Yellowstone Falls ⌊	C 8	178
Yellowstone Lake ⊜	C 8	178
Yellowstone National Park ♦	C 8	178
Yellowtail Dam ➔[6]	C 9	178
Yellville	D 2	170
Yelwa	C 5	200
Yemen □[1]	G 6	116
Yen	E 7	200
Yenagoa	D 6	200
Yenakiyeve	E 11	110
Yenangyaung	D 2	132
Yen Bai	D 7	132
Yendi	D 4	200
Yengisar	B 3	122
Yengo National Park ♦	D 8	144
Yéni	C 5	200
Yenişehir	B 8	106
Yenshuichen	G 15	130
Yentna ≃	E 19	154
Yeo Lake ⊜	J 8	140
Yeovil	G 4	72
Yepes	E 7	86
Yeppoon	G 10	142
Yerbent	J 21	110
Yerevan	I 14	110
Yerington	B 4	182
Yerköy	C 6	118
Yermasóyia	E 5	118
Yerolimín	D 5	106
Yerupaja, Nevado ∧	F 3	190
Yerushalayim □[3]	F 3	120
Yeşilhisar	C 6	118
Yeşilyurt	C 8	118
Yeste	F 2	88
Yetti ➔[1]	D 3	198
Ye-u	C 2	132
Yeu, Île d' I	F 4	78
Yevlax	I 15	110
Yevpatoriya	G 8	110
Yexian, China	H 12	128
Yexian, China	B 11	130
Yi ≃, China	I 12	128
Yi ≃, China	A 11	130
Yi ≃, Ur.	C 9	195
Yi'an	C 15	128
Yibin	D 7	130
Yichang	C 10	130
Yicheng	C 10	130
Yichuan, China	H 7	128
Yichuan, China	A 11	130
Yichun, China	C 17	128
Yichun, China	E 12	130
Yidie	H 8	128
Yidu, China	H 12	128
Yidu, China	C 10	130
Yifeng	D 12	130
Yilan	C 17	128
Yıldızeli	C 7	118
Yiliang, China	E 7	130
Yiliang, China	F 6	130
Yimen	F 5	130
Yimianpo	D 17	128
Yinchuan	G 6	128
Yindarlgooda, Lake ⊜	L 7	140
Yindi	B 4	204
Ying ≃	B 12	130
Yingcheng	C 11	130
Yingchengzi	D 15	128
Yingde	F 11	130
Yinggehai	I 9	130
Yingkou, China	F 14	128
Yingkou, China	F 13	128
Yingshan	C 8	130
Yingshang	B 12	130
Yingshouyingzi	F 11	128
Yingtan	D 13	130
Yining	B 13	116
Yiningarra Aboriginal Land ➔[4]	G 10	140
Yinjiang	E 9	130
Yinnyein	F 3	132
Yio Chu Kang	i 15	134a
Yi'ong	C 2	130
Yi'ong ≃	C 2	130
Yirga 'Alem	F 4	202
Yirwa	F 2	202
Yishan	F 9	130
Yishui	I 12	128
Yishun	i 15	134a
Yisuhe	E 11	130
Yíthion	D 5	106
Yitong	E 15	128
Yitulihe	B 8	124
Yiwu	D 14	130
Yixian	F 13	128
Yiyang, China	D 11	130
Yiyang, China	D 13	130
Yiyang, China	A 11	130
Yiyuan	H 12	128
Yizhang	F 11	130
Yizikong	F 7	130
Yli-Kitka ⊜	C 13	64
Ylöjärvi	B 11	66
Yoakum	F 5	172
Yogyakarta	k 20	135b
Yoho National Park ♦	F 13	156
Yokadouma	E 7	200
Yokkaichi	G 6	126
Yoko	D 7	200
Yokohama	G 7	126
Yokosuka	G 7	126
Yokote	E 8	126
Yola	D 7	200
Yolo □[6]	B 2	182
Yolombo	C 3	204
Yolöten	C 9	116
Yom ≃	E 5	132
Yomou	D 3	200
Yonago	G 4	126
Yonezawa	F 8	126
Yong'an	E 13	130
Yongcheng	B 12	130
Yŏngch'ŏn	G 2	126
Yongch'ŏn-dong	D 2	126
Yongchuan	D 7	130
Yongdeng	H 4	128
Yongding	F 13	130
Yŏngdŏk	H 17	128
Yongfeng	E 12	130
Yŏngil-man ⊂	H 17	128
Yŏngju	H 17	128
Yongkang	D 14	130
Yongnian	H 10	128
Yongning	G 9	130
Yongping	F 4	130
Yongshan	D 6	130
Yongsheng	E 5	130
Yongshou	A 8	130
Yŏngwŏl	F 2	126
Yongwŏn-ni	D 2	126
Yongxing	E 11	130
Yongxiu	D 12	130
Yongzhou	E 10	130
Yonkers	F 5	164
Yonne □[3]	E 10	78
Yonne ≃	D 10	78
Yoontoy	H 5	202
Yopal	B 4	190
York, Eng., U.K.	D 5	72
York, N.D., U.S.	A 5	174
York, Ne., U.S.	E 6	174
York, Pa., U.S.	G 2	164
York □[6], Eng., U.K.	D 5	72
York □[6], Me., U.S.	C 8	164
York □[6], Pa., U.S.	G 2	164
York ≃	E 5	162
York, Cape ≻	A 6	142
York, Kap ≻	B 13	148
Yorke Peninsula ≻[1]	E 1	144
Yorketown	E 1	144
York Factory	C 12	158
York Minster ◗[1]	D 5	72
Yorkshire Dales National Park ♦	C 4	72
York Sound ⋓	D 8	140
Yorkton	F 7	158
Yorktown	E 5	162
Yorkville	C 3	164
Yoro, Hond.	E 3	186
Yoro, Mali	C 4	200
Yoron-jima I	K 2	126
Yosemite National Park ♦	C 4	182
Yos Sudarso, Pulau I	G 11	134
Yŏsu	I 16	128
Yōtei-zan ∧[1]	C 8	126
You ≃, China	G 8	130
You ≃, China	D 9	130
Youghal	E 4	75
Young, Austl.	E 7	144
Young, Az., U.S.	E 3	176
Youngstown, Fl., U.S.	G 6	170
Youngstown, Oh., U.S.	C 3	162
Youngsville	A 5	168
Yountville	B 1	182
Youxian	E 11	130
Youyang	D 9	130
Youyi	C 18	128
Youyi Feng (Kuytun, Mount) ∧	C 1	124
Yozgat	C 6	118
Yozgat □[3]	C 6	118
Ypsilanti	B 2	162
Yreka	E 2	178
Yssingeaux	E 2	82
Ystad	E 6	66
Yu ≃	G 9	130
Yuam ≃	F 4	132
Yuan (Hong, Song) (Red River) ≃, Asia	C 7	132
Yuan ≃, China	E 12	130
Yuan ≃, China	D 10	130
Yuanling	D 10	130
Yuanmou	F 5	130
Yuanyang	I 9	128
Yuba □[6]	A 2	182
Yuba City	A 2	182
Yūbari	C 8	126
Yubdo	F 4	202
Yucaipa	E 5	180
Yucatán □[3]	G 15	184
Yucatan Channel ⋓	C 3	186
Yucatan Peninsula ≻[1]	H 15	184
Yucca Valley	F 7	182
Yucheng	H 11	128
Yuci	H 9	128
Yudu	E 12	130
Yuechi	C 8	130
Yuendumu	H 11	140
Yuendumu Aboriginal Land ➔[4]	H 11	140
Yueqing	D 15	130
Yueyang	D 11	130
Yugan	D 13	130
Yugoslavia □[1]	G 12	62
Yukon	C 5	172
Yukon ≃	E 12	154
Yukon Territory □[3]	D 6	150
Yuli, Nig.	D 7	200
Yüli, Tai.	G 15	130
Yulin, China	G 7	128
Yulin, China	G 9	130
Yuma, Az., U.S.	F 1	176
Yuma, Co., U.S.	E 3	174
Yumbi	C 2	204
Yumen	B 7	122
Yun ≃	C 11	130
Yuna ≃	D 7	186
Yunan	G 10	130
Yuncheng, China	I 10	128
Yuncheng, China	I 8	128
Yunkanjini Aboriginal Land ➔[4]	H 11	140
Yunlong	F 4	130
Yunnan □[3]	F 5	130
Yunta	D 2	144
Yunxian	B 10	130
Yunxiao	F 13	130
Yunyang	C 9	130
Yuqing	E 8	130
Yuraygir National Park ♦	B 9	144
Yurimaguas	E 3	190
Yurok Indian Reservation ➔[4]	E 2	178
Yurungkax ≃	B 4	122
Yûsef, Bahr ⫪	H 4	118
Yushan	D 14	130
Yü Shan ∧	G 15	130
Yushu, China	D 16	128
Yushu, China	B 3	130
Yushutai	E 14	128
Yuste, Monasterio de ◗[1]	D 5	86
Yutian	B 4	122
Yutz	A 4	82
Yuxi	F 6	130
Yuxian, China	G 9	128
Yuxian, China	G 10	128
Yuxian, China	A 11	130
Yuyao	C 15	130
Yuzawa	E 8	126
Yvelines □[3]	D 8	78
Yverdon-les-Bains	D 4	82
Yvetot	C 7	78
Ywathagyi	C 2	132

Z

Name	Map Ref.	Page
Za ≃	B 2	130
Zaanstad	B 3	69
Zabalac'	F 12	66
Zabīd	E 5	202
Ząbkowice Śląskie	C 9	96
Zabłudów	B 12	96
Zābol	D 9	116
Zabolotiv	E 4	110
Zabrze	C 10	96
Zacapa	J 15	184
Zacapu	H 9	184
Zacatecas	F 8	184
Zacatecas □[3]	F 8	184
Zaculeu ⊥	J 14	184
Zadar	C 5	90
Zafra	F 4	86
Żagań	C 8	96
Žagare	D 11	66
Zagazig	G 4	118
Zaghouan	G 3	90
Zaghouan □[3]	G 3	90
Zagora	C 3	198
Zagórów	B 9	96
Zagreb	E 7	102
Zagros Mountains ⩚	F 13	118
Žagubica	C 6	104
Za'gya ≃	C 5	122
Zaharovo	I 13	108
Zahīrābād	F 3	122
Zaḥlah	B 5	120
Záhony	A 7	104
Zahrebetnoe	B 12	108
Zainsk	I 20	108
Zaire □[1]	I 10	196
Zaire □[3]	D 1	204
Zaječar	D 7	104
Zajsan (Zayzan)	A 13	116
Zakamensk	A 4	128
Zakarpattya □[6]	A 7	104
Zakhidnyy Buh (Bug) (Buh) ≃	C 12	96
Zakho	D 10	118
Zákinthos	D 4	106
Zákinthos I	D 4	106
Zaklików	C 11	96
Zakopane	D 10	96
Zakouma, Parc National de ♦	C 8	200
Zakroczym	B 11	96
Zala □[3]	B 4	104
Zalaegerszeg	D 8	102
Zalalövő	D 8	102
Zalamea de la Serena	F 5	86
Zalantun	C 14	128
Zalaszentgrót	D 8	102
Zalău	B 7	104
Zalese	E 10	66
Zalingei	E 1	202
Zalishchyky	A 8	104
Zalṭan	C 7	198
Zaltbommel	C 4	69
Žaltyr, ozero ⊜	F 17	110
Žaludok	F 12	66
Zamantı ≃	D 6	118
Zambeze see Zambezi ≃	F 6	204
Zambezi	E 3	204
Zambezi (Zambeze) ≃	F 6	204
Zambézia □[3]	F 6	204
Zambia □[1]	J 10	196
Zamboanga	D 8	134
Zamboanga Peninsula ≻[1]	D 8	134
Zambrów	B 12	96
Žambyl	A 2	122
Žambyl □[3]	A 2	122
Zamch	C 12	96
Zamfara ≃	C 6	200
Zamora	C 5	86
Zamora □[6]	C 4	86
Zamora de Hidalgo	H 8	184
Zamość	C 12	96
Zamość □[3]	C 12	96
Zana ⊥	B 6	198
Zanaga	C 1	204
Zandvoort	B 3	69
Zanesville	D 3	162
Zangaqazaly see Novokazalinsk	A 9	116
Zangasso	C 3	200
Zanjān	D 13	118
Zanjān □[3]	D 13	118
Zantiébougou	C 3	200
Zanzibar	D 6	204
Zanzibar I	D 6	204
Zanzibar Channel ⋓	D 6	204
Zaostrove	F 9	108
Zaozërnyj	D 12	114
Zaozhuang	I 11	128
Zapadnaja Dvina	H 10	108
Zapadna Morava ≃	D 6	104
Zapadno-Kazahstan □[3]	E 17	110
Zapadnyj Sajan ⩚	B 2	124
Západočeský □[3]	C 10	100
Západoslovenský □[3]	B 9	102
Zapala	F 2	195
Zapata	G 4	172
Zapole	C 14	66
Zapoljarnyj	B 9	108
Zapopan	G 8	184
Zaporizhzhya	F 9	110
Zaporizhzhya □[6]	F 9	110
Zapovednoe	E 10	66
Zaqatala	I 15	110
Zara	C 7	118
Zarāf, Baḥr az- ≃	F 3	202
Zaragoza, Mex.	F 3	172
Zaragoza (Saragossa), Spain	C 4	88
Zaragoza □[6]	C 4	88
Zarajsk	I 13	108
Zarand	G 17	118
Zaranj	D 9	116
Zarasai	E 13	66
Zárate	D 8	195
Zarautz	A 2	88
Zard Kūh ∧	F 13	118
Zargān	H 15	118
Zarghūn Shahr	C 1	122
Zaria	C 6	200
Zarichne	K 13	64
Žarkovskij	I 10	108
Žarma (Zharma)	A 13	116
Zărnești	C 8	104
Zarqā', Raqabat az- ≃	F 2	202
Zarrīneh ≃	D 11	118
Zarrīn Shahr	F 14	118
Żary	C 8	96
Zarzis	C 7	198
Zasa	D 12	66
Zašeek	C 9	108
Zāskār Mountains ⩚	C 3	122
Zaslaụe	E 13	66
Zasulle	F 13	66
Žatec	B 10	100
Zatobol'sk	C 23	110
Zauel	G 5	202
Zavallya	A 11	104
Zave	F 4	204
Zavidovići	C 5	104
Zavitinsk	A 17	128
Zavodoukovsk	H 27	108
Zavodovski Island I	J 12	188
Zavolžsk	H 14	108
Zawiercie	C 10	96
Zâwyet Shammâs	A 2	202
Zāyandeh ≃	F 14	118
Zaysan, Köli see Zaysan, ozero ⊜	A 13	116
Zaysan, ozero (Zaysan Köli) ⊜	A 13	116
Zayü ≃	D 3	130
Zazafotsy	I 9	205a
Zbiroh	C 10	100
Zbraslav	C 11	100
Žďár nad Sazavou	A 7	102
Zdolbuniv	D 4	110
Zduńska Wola	C 10	96
Zealandia	F 18	156
Zeballos	G 8	156
Zebulon	B 5	168
Zeebrugge	C 2	69
Zeehan	i 11	145a
Zeeland □[3]	C 2	69
Zeerust	C 7	206
Zefat	D 4	120
Zehdenick	D 10	98
Zeil, Mount ∧	H 12	140
Zeist	B 4	69
Zeitz	E 9	98
Zeja	B 9	124
Zeja ≃	D 15	114
Zejskoe vodohranilišče ⊜[1]	B 9	124
Zela ≃	B 9	124
Zele	A 10	78
Żelechów	C 11	96
Zelenec	E 21	108
Zelenoborskij	C 10	108
Zelenodol'sk	I 18	108
Zelenogorsk	B 14	66
Zelenogradsk	B 2	110
Zelenokumsk	G 13	110
Železnodorožnyj, Russia	E 19	108
Železnodorožnyj, Uzb.	H 21	110
Železnogorsk	J 11	108
Zelina	E 8	102
Zella-Mehlis	B 7	100
Zell am See	C 4	102
Zelów	C 10	96
Zelzate	C 2	69
Zemaitijos nacionalnis parkas ♦	D 10	66
Zémio	A 3	204
Zemmour ➔[1]	E 2	198
Zemun	C 6	104
Zenica	C 4	104
Zephyrhills	E 3	168
Zerayshan ≃	C 10	116
Zerbst	E 9	98
Žerdevka	D 12	110
Zergenta	F 14	110
Żerków	B 9	96
Zernograd	F 12	110
Zerqan	B 4	106
Žešart	E 18	108
Zetel	C 4	98
Žetykol', ozero ⊜	D 22	110
Zeulenroda	B 8	100
Zeuthen	D 10	98
Zeven	C 6	98
Zevenaar	C 5	69
Zevenbergen	C 3	69
Zevenwouden ➔[1]	B 5	69
Zeytinbağı	B 8	106
Zêzere ≃	E 2	86
Žezkazagan	A 10	116
Zgierz	C 10	96
Zgorzelec	C 8	96
Zhag'yab	C 4	130
Zhambyl see Žambyl	A 2	122
Zhangjiakou	F 10	128
Zhangping	F 13	130
Zhangpu	F 13	130
Zhangqiu	H 11	128
Zhangwu	E 14	128
Zhangye	G 3	128
Zhangzhou	F 13	130
Zhanjiang	H 10	130
Zhanyu	D 14	128
Zhao'an	G 13	130
Zhaodong	C 15	128
Zhaojue	D 6	130
Zhaoping	G 10	130
Zhaoqing	G 11	130
Zhaoxing	C 18	128
Zhaoyuan	D 15	128
Zhashkiv	E 6	110
Zhecheng	A 12	130
Zhejiang □[3]	D 15	130
Zhelin	C 15	130
Zheng'an	D 8	130
Zhengding	G 10	128
Zhengfeng	F 7	130
Zhenghe	E 14	130
Zhenglan Qi	E 10	128
Zhengxiangbai Qi	E 10	128
Zhengyang	B 12	130
Zhengzhou	A 11	130
Zhenjiang	B 14	130
Zhenlai	D 14	128
Zhenning	E 7	130
Zhenping	B 11	130
Zhenxiong	E 7	130
Zhenyuan	E 8	130
Zherong	E 14	130
Zhijiang	E 9	130
Zhijin	A 7	132
Zhmerynka	E 5	110
Zhob	C 1	122
Zhob ≃	D 10	116
Zhongcun	B 10	130
Zhonghe	E 6	130
Zhongjiang	C 7	130
Zhongning	H 5	128
Zhongshan, China	G 11	130
Zhongshan, China	F 10	130
Zhongshan ◗[3]	C 16	208
Zhongwei	H 5	128
Zhongxian	C 8	130
Zhongxiang	C 11	130
Zhongyaozhan	A 15	128
Zhoucun	H 11	128
Zhouning	E 14	130
Zhouqu	B 6	130
Zhoushan Dao I	C 16	130
Zhoushan Qundao II	C 16	130
Zhouzhi	A 8	130
Zhovti Vody	E 8	110
Zhovtneve, Ukr.	F 8	110
Zhovtneve, Ukr.	E 9	110
Zhuanghe	G 14	128
Zhuanglang	I 5	128
Zhucheng	H 12	128
Zhuhe	D 11	130
Zhuji	D 15	130
Zhujiang Kou ⊂[1]	G 11	130
Zhujiesi	B 3	130
Zhumadian	B 11	130
Zhuolu	F 10	128
Zhuozhou	G 10	128
Zhuozi	F 9	128
Zhushan	B 10	130
Zhuzhou	E 11	130
Zhytomyr	D 6	110
Zhytomyr □[6]	D 6	110
Zi ≃, China	H 12	128
Zi ≃, China	E 10	130
Zi ≃, China	B 2	130
Zia Indian Reservation ➔[4]	E 5	176
Ziārat	C 1	122
Žiar nad Hronom	B 10	102
Zibo	H 12	128
Zichang	H 7	128
Zielona Góra	C 8	96
Zielona Góra □[3]	C 8	96
Zierikzee	C 2	69
Zifta	G 4	118
Žigansk	C 15	114
Zigong	D 7	130
Ziguéy	C 8	200
Ziguinchor	C 1	200
Žigulevsk	J 18	108
Zihuatanejo	I 9	184
Zijin	G 12	130
Zilair	C 20	110
Zile	B 6	118
Žilga	A 1	122
Žilina	A 10	102
Žilino	E 10	66
Zillah	D 8	198
Zilwaukee	B 2	162
Zima	B 4	124
Zimba	F 4	204
Zimbabwe □[1]	J 10	196
Zimbabwe Ruins ⊥	G 5	204
Zimi	D 2	200
Zimnicea	D 8	104
Zimovniki	F 13	110
Zinave, Parque National de ♦	A 10	206
Zinder	C 6	200
Zinder □[3]	C 7	200
Zinga Mulike	D 6	204
Ziniaré	C 4	200
Zin'kiv	D 9	110
Zinnowitz	B 10	98
Zion	D 5	166
Zion National Park ♦	D 2	176
Zionz Lake ⊜	F 13	158
Zirgan	C 19	110
Zirndorf	C 7	100
Žirovnice	C 12	100
Zisterzienserabtei ◗[1]	C 5	100
Zitong	C 7	130
Zittau	F 11	98
Zitundo	D 10	206
Ziwa Magharibi □[3]	C 5	204
Ziway Hāyk' ⊜	F 4	202
Ziya ≃	G 11	128
Ziyang	C 7	130
Zizhong	D 7	130
Zizhou	H 7	128
Žižica	H 9	108
Zlarin	D 3	104
Zlatá Koruna ◗[1]	D 11	100
Zlaté Moravce	B 10	102
Zlatoust	I 23	108
Zlín	A 9	102
Zlīṭan	C 7	198
Złoczew	C 10	96
Złotoryja	C 8	96
Złotów	B 9	96
Żmigród	C 9	96
Zmiinyi, ostriv see Serpilor, Insula I	C 11	104
Znamensk	E 10	66
Znam'yanka	E 8	110
Znob-Novhorods'ke	C 8	110
Znojmo	B 8	102
Žodzina	E 14	66
Zoétélé	E 7	200
Zoetermeer	B 3	69
Zofingen	C 5	82
Zogno	D 5	92
Zohreh ≃	G 13	118
Zolfo Springs	F 4	168
Zollikofen	C 5	82
Zollikon	C 6	82
Zolochiv, Ukr.	D 10	110
Zolochiv, Ukr.	E 4	110
Zolotarëvka	C 14	110
Zolote	E 11	110
Zolotkovo	I 14	108
Zolotuhino	C 9	110
Zomba	F 6	204
Zongo	B 2	204
Zonguldak	B 9	106
Zonguldak □[3]	B 5	118
Zonhoven	D 4	69
Zörbig	E 9	98
Zorita	E 5	86
Zorra, Arroyo de la ≃	F 3	172
Zossen	D 10	98
Zottegem	D 2	69
Zouérat	E 2	198
Zourma	C 4	200
Zouxian	I 11	128
Zrenjanin	C 6	104
Zruč nad Sázavou	C 12	100
Zschopau	F 9	98
Zubova Poljana	I 15	108
Zudáñez	G 6	190
Zuénoula	D 3	200
Zuera	C 4	88
Zuevka	G 19	108
Zug	C 6	82
Zug □[3]	C 6	82
Zugdidi	H 12	110
Zugspitze ∧	E 8	100
Zuid-Beveland ➔[1]	C 2	69
Zuid-Holland □[3]	C 3	69
Zújar ≃	F 5	86
Žukovka	C 8	110
Zula	D 4	202
Zulia □[3]	F 6	186
Zulia ≃	F 6	186
Zülpich	F 3	98
Zumaia	A 2	88
Zumbrota	C 2	166
Zundert	C 3	69
Zune	F 6	204
Zungwini	D 9	206
Zunhua	F 11	128
Zuni Indian Reservation ➔[4]	E 4	176
Zunyi	E 8	130
Zuoxiunulemiao	B 10	128
Zuoyun	F 9	128
Zupar ➔[1]	G 7	116
Zurich, On., Can.	G 3	160
Zürich, Switz.	C 6	82
Zürich □[3]	C 6	82
Zurich, Lake ⊜	C 6	82
Zürichsee see Zurich, Lake ⊜	C 6	82
Zutphen	B 5	69
Žužemberk	E 6	102
Zvenyhorodka	E 7	110
Zverinogolovskoe	I 26	108
Zvishavane	G 5	204
Zvolen	B 11	102
Zwedru	D 3	200
Zweibrücken	C 4	100
Zwenkau	E 9	98
Zwettl	B 7	102
Zwevegem	D 2	69
Zwevezele	C 2	69
Zwickau	F 9	98
Zwiesel	C 10	100
Zwijndrecht	C 3	69
Zwolle, La., U.S.	G 2	170
Zwolle, Neth.	B 5	69
Żyrardów	B 11	96
Zyrjanovsk	E 11	114
Zyrjanovskij	H 24	108
Żywiec	D 10	96

⌊ Waterfall ⋓ Strait ⊂ Bay, Gulf ⊜ Lake ⩸ Swamp ⩓ Ice Feature ⫪ Other Hydrographic Feature ✢ Submarine Feature □ Political Unit ◗ Cultural Institution ⊥ Historical Site ♦ Recreational Site ⊠ Airport ■ Military Installation ➔ Miscellaneous

ACKNOWLEDGMENTS

The Story of the Earth

The editors would like to thank the following artists for their contributions to this book:

Eugene Fleury: pp. 10–11 *top left*, 12–13 *top left*, 14–15 *left*, 20–21 *top left*, 26–27 *top right*, 32–33 *top right*, 38–39 *bottom right*, 44–45 *right*, 47–48 *left*

Pavel Kostal: pp. 6–7, 8–9 *left & right*, 10–11 *bottom left & right*, 12–13 *center right*, 16–17 *center left & right*, 18 *bottom left*, 42–43 *bottom left*

Sharon McCausland: pp. 22–23 *left & right*, 24–25 *bottom left*, 26–27 *left & right*, 30–31 *center left & right*, 34–35 *center left & right*, 36–37 *bottom left & center right*, 38–39 *left & bottom right*, 40–41 *left & right*, 42–43 *center left & right*

Lee Peters: pp. 14–15 *bottom right*, 36–37 *bottom right*, 38–39 *left & bottom right*

Malcolm McGregor: pp. 28–29 *all*, 32–33

James G. Robins: pp. 12–13 *right*, 46–47 *bottom left*

Leslie Smith: pp. 16–17 *top & bottom right*, 46–47 *right*, 50–51 *left & right*

Ed Stuart: pp. 8–9 *top right*, 12–13 *right*, 19, 20–21 *bottom left & right*, 24–25 *center left*, 30–31 *top right*, 34–35 *bottom right*, 42–43 *bottom right*, 48–49 *right*

Andrew Thompson: pp. 34–35 *top right*, 36–37 *bottom right*, 44–45 *left*, 46–47 *left*

Hali Verrider: pp. 24–25 *bottom right*

The projection used for the illustrated maps on pages 19, 37, 39, 46, and 48 is © Bartholomew.
Reproduced by permission of Harper Collins Cartographic, Glasgow, Scotland.

The editors would like to thank the following photographic libraries for permission to reproduce their material:

Abbreviations:

EPL Environmental Picture Library

OSF Oxford Scientific Films

FLPA Frank Lane Picture Agency

SPL Science Photo Library

GSF Geoscience Features

RHPL Robert Harding Picture Library

NHPA Natural History Photographic Agency

1 SPL/NASA; 2–3 (*l–r*) SPL/NASA; SPL/NASA; SPL/NASA; 4–5 (*l–r*) SPL/NASA; FLPA/David Hosking; Images; Zefa/Bauer; 6–7 SPL/Hallas; 6 SPL/Baum; 7 *top* SPL/HST; 7 *bottom left* SPL/NRAO; 7 *bottom right* SPL/NRAO; 8 SPL/JISAS-Lockheed; 9 *top left* SPL/NASA; 9 *top center* SPL/NASA; 9 *top right* SPL/NASA; 9 *bottom left* Image Select; 9 *bottom right* (sequence) Weaver & Smith/Space Telescope Institute/NASA; 10–11 Image Select/Ann Ronan; 11 SPL/ESA/PLI; 12–13 Zefa; 12 *left* RHPL; 12 *center* RHPL/Tony Waltham; 12 *right* Zefa/T. Stewart; 12 *bottom left* Images; 12 *bottom right* OSF/Ake Lindau/Okapia; 13 *top* Zefa; 13 *left* Spectrum/D. & J. Heaton; 13 *right* Zefa/Kurt Goebel; 14 *top* Rex Features/ Butler/Bauer; 14 *center* SPL/Parker; 14 *bottom* GSF; 15 montage sequence: (*top row l–r*) GSF; Zefa; (*middle row l–r*) Images; Images; Images; (*bottom row l–r*) FLPA/F. Polking; Images; FLPA/Mark Newman; 15 *bottom right* FLPA/USDA; 16 *center left* SPL/Alfred Pasieka; 16 *center right* FLPA/Roger Tidman; box: (*top row l–r*) SPL/Alfred Pasieka; SPL/Vaughan Fleming; SPL/George Bernard; (*middle row l–r*) SPL/J.C. Revy; SPL/Roberto de Gugliemo; Natural History Museum; (*bottom row*) *left* SPL/Alfred Pasieka; SPL/Vaughan Fleming; Natural History Museum; 17 *top left* Zefa; 17 *top right* FLPA/C. Mullen; 17 *center left* SPL/James Stevenson; 17 *center right* SPL/George Bernard; 18 SPL/NASA; 18 *right* (inset) RHPL/Liaison; 20–21 Images; 21 SPL/Los Alamos National Laboratory; 22–23 *clockwise from top left* OSF/Kathie Atkinson; OSF/David Fleetham; FLPA/Earthviews; FLPA/David Fleetham/Silvestris; Zefa; NHPA/Norbert Wu; OSF/Norbert Wu; NHPA/Agence Nature; NHPA/Agence Nature; FLPA/D. P. Wilson; 23 cluster (*top*): SPL/Biophoto Associates; SPL/Jan Hinsch; 24–25 Images; 25 *top* FLPA/Wilmshurst; 25 *bottom* OSF/Kay; 26 *top left* Images; 26 *top center* Images; 26 *top right* Images; 26 *bottom* Telegraph/Sims; 26–27 Impact/Black; 27 *top right* Zefa; 27 *bottom left* Zefa/APL; 27 *bottom right* RHPL/Cavanaugh; 28 *top* RHPL/Craven; 28 *bottom* OSF/Brando; 29 *top* The Hutchison Library/Hughes; 29 *top right* OSF/Jim Holmes; 29 *center left* Rex Features/Wallace; 30–31 Tony Stone/Bushue; 30 *top* FLPA/Wisniewski; 30 *bottom* Alaska Stock; 31 *top* OSF/Allan; 31 *bottom* OSF/Allan; 32–33 *bottom* Images; 32 *center* GSF; 32 *right* GSF; 33 *top right* RHPL/Fred Klus; 33 *center left* RHPL/Paolo Koch; 33 *center* FLPA/ W. Wisniewski; 33 *center right* OSF/Tom Ulrich; 34 Images; 35 Zefa/Mehlig; 36–37 Zefa/Floris; 36 *top* FLPA/Newman; 36 *center* FLPA/Delport; 36 *bottom* Zefa; 37 *top* OSF/Turner; 37 *bottom* FLPA/Hosking; 38–39 SPL/Dr. Morley Read; 38 *bottom left* OSF/Richard Packwood; 38 *center* Images; 38 *top right* Still Pictures; 39 Still Pictures; 40 *top* Images; 40 *left center* FLPA/Hosking; 40 *center* FLPA/Hosking; 40 *right center* OSF/Henry; 40 *bottom* GSF; 41 *top* FLPA/Mullen; 41 *center* FLPA/Silvestris; 41 *bottom* RHPL/Photri; 42 *bottom left* RHPL; 42 *center* Images; 42–43 Images; 43 *top* Rex Features/Beghin; 43 *center* OSF/Reinhard/Okapia; 43 *center right* OSF/Packwood; 43 *bottom* Images; 44 SPL; 45 (*clockwise from left*): RHPL/Wheeler; Rex Features; Images; Rex Features/Cavali/SIPA; 46–47 Zefa; 46 *top* Zefa; 46 *bottom* RHPL; 47 *top* EPL; 47 *center* Zefa/Fleumer; 47 *right* RHPL/Woolfitt; 48 Tony Stone/Cunningham; 50–51 SPL/John Mead; 50 *top left* Telegraph/Roger Antrobus; 50 *center left* RHPL/Dave Jacobs; 50 *center right* The Hutchison Library/Robert Francis; 50 *bottom right* SPL/Roger Ressmeyer; 51 *center top* RHPL/Dave Jacobs; 51 *center left* Panos Pictures/Alain Le Garsmeur; 51 *bottom left* Panos Pictures/Martin Flitman; 51 *bottom center* The Hutchison Library; 51 *bottom right* Panos Pictures/Sean Sprague; 52–53 RHPL/Bildagentur Schuster/Layda; 52 *left* RHPL; 52 *center* SPL/World View; 52 *right* Images; 53 *top left* The Hutchison Library/Bernard Régent; 53 *top right* Tony Stone/Robin Smith; 53 *left* The Hutchison Library; 53 *right* Collections/Brian Shuel.

Nations of the World

Flag images supplied courtesy of The Flag Institute, Chester, England.

All cartography supplied by Eugene Fleury.

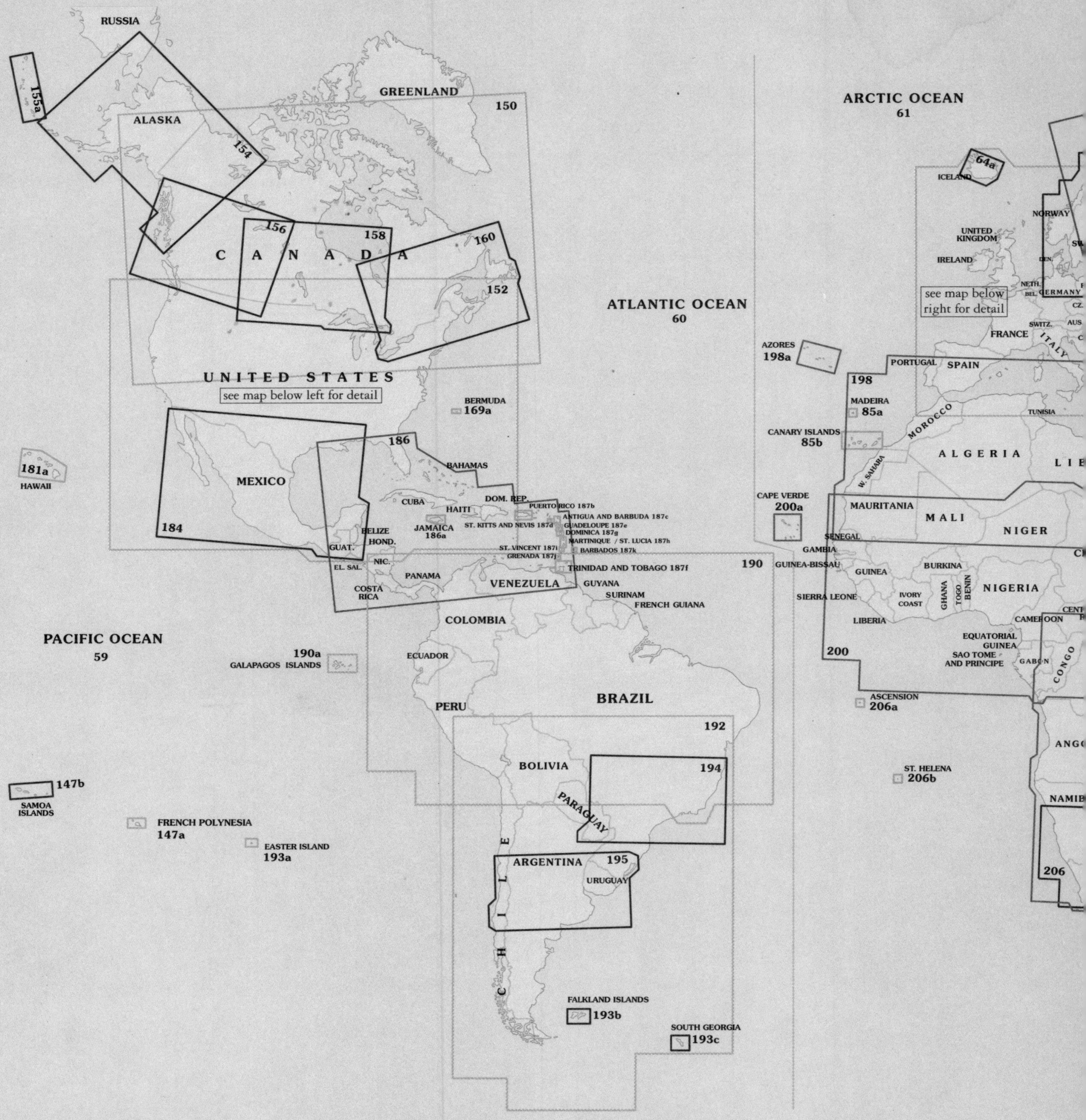

RUSSIA

155a

ALASKA

154

156

158

160

C A N A D A

GREENLAND

150

152

ARCTIC OCEAN
61

ICELAND

64a

NORWAY

UNITED
KINGDOM

IRELAND

DEN.

NETH.
BEL. GERMANY

CZ.

SWITZ. AUS.

FRANCE

ITALY

see map below
right for detail

ATLANTIC OCEAN
60

AZORES
198a

198

PORTUGAL   SPAIN

MADEIRA
85a

TUNISIA

MOROCCO

UNITED STATES
see map below left for detail

BERMUDA
169a

186

BAHAMAS

181a

HAWAII

MEXICO

184

CUBA

HAITI

DOM. REP.
PUERTO RICO 187b

ANTIGUA AND BARBUDA 187c
GUADELOUPE 187e
DOMINICA 187g
MARTINIQUE / ST. LUCIA 187h
BARBADOS 187k

JAMAICA
186a

ST. KITTS AND NEVIS 187d

ST. VINCENT 187i
GRENADA 187j

BELIZE
HOND.

GUAT.

NIC.

EL. SAL.

COSTA
RICA

PANAMA

VENEZUELA

TRINIDAD AND TOBAGO 187l

190

GUYANA

SURINAM

FRENCH GUIANA

COLOMBIA

ECUADOR

PERU

BRAZIL

192

BOLIVIA

194

CANARY ISLANDS
85b

W. SAHARA

ALGERIA

LIB

CAPE VERDE
200a

MAURITANIA

MALI

NIGER

SENEGAL

GAMBIA

GUINEA-BISSAU

GUINEA

BURKINA

SIERRA LEONE

IVORY
COAST

GHANA
TOGO
BENIN

NIGERIA

LIBERIA

CAMEROON

EQUATORIAL
GUINEA

SAO TOME
AND PRINCIPE

GABON

CONGO

CENT
R

200

ASCENSION
206a

ST. HELENA
206b

PACIFIC OCEAN
59

190a

GALAPAGOS ISLANDS

147b

SAMOA
ISLANDS

FRENCH POLYNESIA
147a

EASTER ISLAND
193a

PARAGUAY

C H I L E

ARGENTINA

195

URUGUAY

FALKLAND ISLANDS
193b

SOUTH GEORGIA
193c

ANGO

NAMIB

206

map scale

1:3,000,000

1:1,750,000

104   page reference

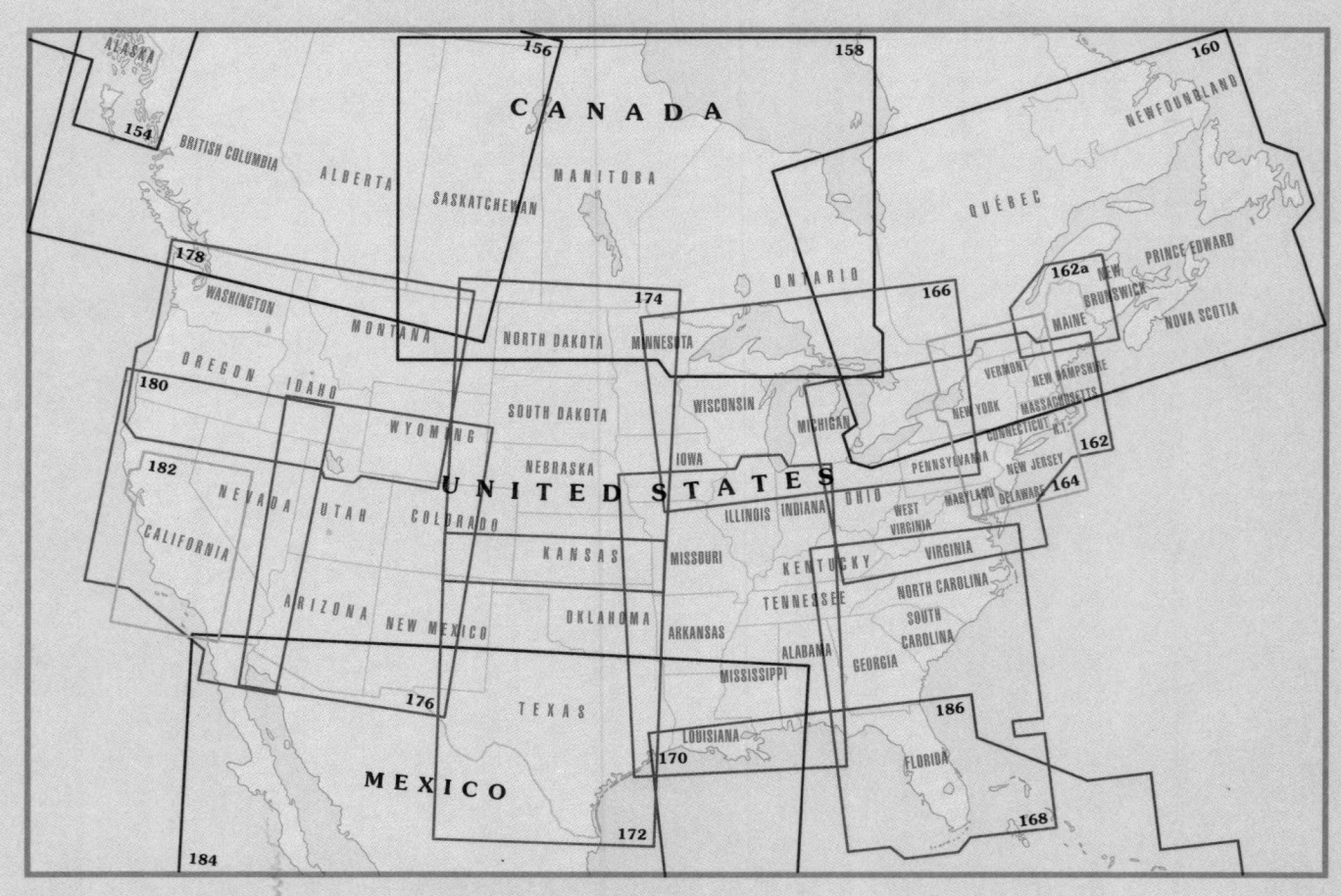

ALASKA

156

158

160

154

BRITISH COLUMBIA

C A N A D A

NEWFOUNDLAND

ALBERTA

SASKATCHEWAN

MANITOBA

QUÉBEC

178

ONTARIO

166

162a NEW
BRUNSWICK

PRINCE EDWARD

174

WASHINGTON

MONTANA

NORTH DAKOTA

MINNESOTA

MAINE

NOVA SCOTIA

OREGON

IDAHO

180

SOUTH DAKOTA

WISCONSIN

MICHIGAN

VERMONT

NEW HAMPSHIRE

WYOMING

NEW YORK

MASSACHUSETTS

182

NEBRASKA

IOWA

CONNECTICUT

NEVADA

UTAH

COLORADO

ILLINOIS

INDIANA

OHIO

PENNSYLVANIA

NEW JERSEY

162

CALIFORNIA

U N I T E D   S T A T E S

WEST
VIRGINIA

MARYLAND

DELAWARE

164

KANSAS

MISSOURI

KENTUCKY

VIRGINIA

ARIZONA

NEW MEXICO

OKLAHOMA

ARKANSAS

TENNESSEE

NORTH CAROLINA

176

T E X A S

MISSISSIPPI

ALABAMA

GEORGIA

SOUTH
CAROLINA

170

LOUISIANA

FLORIDA

186

M E X I C O

184

172

168